Lecture Notes in Computer Science 10052

Commenced Publication in 1973
Founding and Former Series Editors:
Gerhard Goos, Juris Hartmanis, and Jan van Leeuwen

More information about this series at http://www.springer.com/series/7410

Sara Foresti · Giuseppe Persiano (Eds.)

Cryptology and Network Security

15th International Conference, CANS 2016
Milan, Italy, November 14–16, 2016
Proceedings

 Springer

Editors
Sara Foresti
Università degli Studi di Milano
Crema
Italy

Giuseppe Persiano
Università degli Studi di Salerno
Fisciano
Italy

ISSN 0302-9743   ISSN 1611-3349 (electronic)
Lecture Notes in Computer Science
ISBN 978-3-319-48964-3   ISBN 978-3-319-48965-0 (eBook)
DOI 10.1007/978-3-319-48965-0

Library of Congress Control Number: 2016955512

LNCS Sublibrary: SL4 – Security and Cryptology

Printed on acid-free paper

This Springer imprint is published by Springer Nature
The registered company is Springer International Publishing AG
The registered company address is: Gewerbestrasse 11, 6330 Cham, Switzerland

Preface

These proceedings contain the papers selected for presentation at the 15th International Conference on Cryptology and Network Security (CANS 2016), held in Milan, Italy, on November 14–16, 2016. The conference was held in cooperation with the International Association of Cryptologic Research and focuses on technical aspects of cryptology and of data, network, and computer security. These proceedings contain 30 full papers (with an acceptance rate of 25.86 %) and 18 short papers selected by the Program Committee from 116 submissions. The proceedings also contain an extended abstract for the 8 posters presented at the conference.

The many high-quality submissions made it easy to build a strong program but also required rejecting good papers. Each submission was judged by at least three reviewers and the whole selection process included about six weeks of reading and discussion in the Program Committee.

The credit for the success of an event like CANS 2016 belongs to a number of people, who devoted their time and energy to put together the conference and who deserve acknowledgment. There is a long list of people who volunteered their time and energy to organize the conference, and who deserve special thanks. We would like to thank all the members of the Program Committee and all the external reviewers, for all their hard work in evaluating all the papers during the summer. We are grateful to CANS Steering Committee for their support. Thanks to Giovanni Livraga, for taking care of publicity and chairing local organization. We are very grateful to the local organizers for their support in the conference organization and logistics. We would like to thank the keynote speakers for accepting our invitation to deliver a talk at the conference.

Special thanks are due to the Università degli Studi di Milano for its support and for hosting the event, and to the Italian Association for Information Processing (AICA) for support in the secretarial and registration process.

Last but certainly not least, our thanks go to all the authors who submitted papers and posters and to all the conference's attendees. We hope you find the program of CANS 2016 interesting, stimulating, and inspiring for your future research.

November 2016

Sara Foresti
Pino Persiano
Pierangela Samarati

Organization

General Chair

Pierangela Samarati   Università degli Studi di Milano, Italy

Program Chairs

Sara Foresti   Università degli Studi di Milano, Italy
Giuseppe Persiano   Università degli Studi di Salerno, Italy

Poster Chairs

Sara Foresti   Università degli Studi di Milano, Italy
Giuseppe Persiano   Università degli Studi di Salerno, Italy
Pierangela Samarati   Università degli Studi di Milano, Italy

Publicity Chair

Giovanni Livraga   Università degli Studi di Milano, Italy

Local Arrangements Chair

Giovanni Livraga   Università degli Studi di Milano, Italy

Steering Committee

Yvo Desmedt (Chair)   The University of Texas at Dallas, USA
Juan A. Garay   Yahoo! Labs, USA
Amir Herzberg   Bar Ilan University, Israel
Yi Mu   University of Wollongong, Australia
David Pointcheval   ·   CNRS and ENS Paris, France
Huaxiong Wang   Nanyang Technological University, Singapore

Program Committee

Lejla Batina   Radboud University, The Netherlands
Carlo Blundo   Università degli Studi di Salerno, Italy
Henry Carter   Villanova University, USA
Nishanth Chandran   Microsoft Research, India
Yingying Chen   Stevens Institute of Technology, USA

Sherman S.M. Chow	Chinese University of Hong Kong, Hong Kong
Ricardo Dahab	IC-UNICAMP, Brazil
Sabrina De Capitani di Vimercati	Università degli Studi di Milano, Italy
Angelo De Caro	IBM Research, Zurich, Switzerland
Yvo Desmedt	The University of Texas at Dallas, USA
Nelly Fazio	City University of New York, USA
Georg Fuchsbauer	Ecole Normale Supérieure, France
Rosario Gennaro	City University of New York, USA
Amir Herzberg	Bar Ilan University, Israel
Vincenzo Iovino	University of Luxembourg, Luxembourg
Rob Johnson	Stony Brook University, USA
Florian Kerschbaum	SAP, Germany
Aggelos Kiayias	University of Athens, Greece
Albert Levi	Sabanci University, Turkey
Ming Li	University of Arizona, USA
Dongdai Lin	Chinese Academy of Sciences, China
Peng Liu	The Pennsylvania State University, USA
Javier Lopez	University of Malaga, Spain
Steve Lu	Stealth Software Technologies Inc., USA
Atsuko Miyaji	Osaka University/JAIST, Japan
Evagelos Markatos	University of Crete, Greece
Refik Molva	Eurecom, France
Yi Mu	University of Wollongong, Australia
Gregory Neven	IBM Research, Zurich, Switzerland
Antonio Nicolosi	Stevens Institute of Technology, USA
Svetla Nikova	KU Leuven, Belgium
Emmanuela Orsini	University of Bristol, UK
Panos Papadimitratos	KTH, Stockholm, Sweden
Stefano Paraboschi	Università di Bergamo, Italy
Gerardo Pelosi	Politecnico di Milano, Italy
Benny Pinkas	Bar Ilan University, Israel
Pierangela Samarati	Università degli Studi di Milano, Italy
Nitesh Saxena	University of Alabama at Birmingham, USA
Andreas Schaad	Huawei Research, Germany
Dominique Schroeder	Saarland University, Germany
Peter Schwabe	Radboud University, The Netherlands
Willy Susilo	University of Wollongong, Australia
Katsuyuki Takashima	Mitsubishi Electric, Japan
Qiang Tang	University of Luxembourg, Luxembourg
Meng Yu	University of Texas at San Antonio, USA
Huaxiong Wang	Nanyang Technological University, Singapore

External Reviewers

Hamza Abusalah
Zakir Akram
Duygu Karaoğlan Altop
S. Abhishek Anand
Diego Aranha
Tomer Ashur
Seiko Arita
Arash Atashpendar
Pol Van Aubel
Monir Azraoui
Saikrishna
   Badrinarayanan
Amos Beimel
Daniel Bernau
Jonas Boehler
Carl Bootland
Raphael Bost
Christina Boura
Florian Bourse
Alexandre Braga
Luigi Catuogno
Rongmao Chen
Michele Ciampi
Guo Chun
Mario Cornejo
Joan Daemen
Christophe Doche
Kaoutar Elkhiyaoui
Keita Emura
Martianus
   Frederic Ezerman
Nils Fleischhacker
Atsushi Fujioka
Yuichi Futa
Marios Georgiou
Esha Ghosh
Rishab Goyal
Le Guan
Xue Haiyang
Jin Han
Wenhui Hu

Yupeng Jiang
Süleyman Kardaş
Aniket Kate
Akinori Kawachi
Anselme Kemgne Tueno
Mathias Kohler
Anna Krasnova
Ashutosh Kumar
Jianchang Lai
Russell W.F. Lai
Obbattu Sai
   Lakshmi Bhavana
Hyung Tae Lee
Iraklis Leontiadis
Hemi Leibowitz
Bin Liu
Meicheng Liu
Naiwei Liu
Yunwen Liu
Zhen Liu
Jose M. Lopez
Isis Lovecruft
Atul Luykx
Chang Lv
Jack P.K. Ma
Mohammad Mamun
Pedro Maat Massolino
Peihan Miao
Christoph Michel
Shigeo Mitsunari
Eduardo Morais
Toru Nakanishi
Luiz Navarro
Ajaya Neupane
Khoa Nguyen
Hod Bin Noon
Maciej Obremski
Kazumasa Omote
Adam O'Neill
Melek Önen
Stjepan Picek

Fabio Piva
Elizabeth Quaglia
Srinivasan Raghuraman
Manuel Reinert
Oscar Reparaz
Vincent Rijmen
Ruben Rios
Adeline Roux-Langlois
Vipin Singh Sehrawat
Sruthi Sekar
Babins Shrestha
Maliheh Shirvanian
Roee Shlomo
Prakash Shrestha
Luisa Siniscalchi
William Skeith
Maciej Skórski
Akshayaram Srinivasan
Raymond K.H. Tai
Sri Aravinda
   Krishnan Thyagarajan
Chenyang Tu
Miguel Urquidi
Cédric Van Rompay
Dimitrios Vasilopoulos
Gabriele Viglianisi
Xiao Wang
Xiuhua Wang
Yongge Wang
Harry W.H. Wong
Brecht Wyseur
Tran Phuong Viet Xuan
Bohan Yang
Eunjung Yoon
Libo Zhang
Miaomiao Zhang
Shiwei Zhang
Tao Zhang
Yongjun Zhao
Jingyuan Zhao
Jincheng Zhuang

Contents

System Security

Functional and Homomorphic Encryption

Information Theoretic Security

Malware and Attacks

MultiParty Computation and Functional Encryption

Network Security, Privacy, and Authentication

Posters

Cryptanalysis of Symmetric Key

Linear Regression Attack with F-test: A New SCARE Technique for Secret Block Ciphers

Si Gao[1,2], Hua Chen[1(✉)], Wenling Wu[1], Limin Fan[1], Jingyi Feng[1,2], and Xiangliang Ma[1,2]

[1] Trusted Computing and Information Assurance Laboratory, Institute of Software, Chinese Academy of Sciences, Beijing 100190, People's Republic of China
{gaosi,chenhua,wwl,fanlimin,fengjingyi,maxiangliang}@tca.iscas.ac.cn
[2] University of Chinese Academy of Sciences, Beijing 100049, People's Republic of China

Abstract. The past ten years have seen tremendous progress in the uptake of side channel analysis in various applications. Among them, Side Channel Analysis for Reverse Engineering (SCARE) is an especially fruitful area. Taking the side channel leakage into account, SCARE efficiently recovers secret ciphers in a non-destructive and non-intrusive manner. Unfortunately, most previous works focus on customizing SCARE for a certain type of ciphers or implementations. In this paper, we ask whether the attacker can loosen these restrictions and reverse secret block ciphers in a more general manner. To this end, we propose a SCARE based on Linear Regression Attack (LRA), which simultaneously detects and analyzes the power leakages of the secret encryption process. Compared with the previous SCAREs, our approach uses less *a priori* knowledge, covers more block cipher instances in a completely non-profiled manner. Moreover, we further present a complete SCARE flow with realistic power measurements of an unprotected software implementation. From traces that can barely recognize the encryption rounds, our experiments demonstrate how the underlying cipher can be recovered step-by-step. Although our approach still has some limitations, we believe it can serve as an alternative tool for reverse engineering in the future.

Keywords: Linear Regression Attack · SCARE · F-test

1 Introduction

Over the past decades, Side Channel Attacks (SCA) posed a major threat for many cryptographic implementations. As a powerful tool, SCA also shows great potential in many non-key-recovery applications, including Side Channel Analysis for Reverse Engineering (SCARE). In general, reversing a secret cipher through cryptanalysis is quite difficult. With side channel leakage, things become much easier. Successful SCAREs have been proposed for many block

© Springer International Publishing AG 2016
S. Foresti and G. Persiano (Eds.): CANS 2016, LNCS 10052, pp. 3–18, 2016.
DOI: 10.1007/978-3-319-48965-0_1

ciphers, including DES-like ciphers [1–3], AES-like ciphers [4] and general SPN ciphers [5].

Despite the tremendous progress in the literature, getting SCARE out of the lab is not an easy task. Most previous SCARE techniques, explicitly stated or not, have a few limitations on their target ciphers or implementations. Guilley et al.'s Sbox recovery is the only SCARE that has been verified with realistic measurements [3]. As their attack implicitly assumes the diffusion layer is a known bit-permutation, it only applies to DES-like ciphers. Other attacks rely on theoretical simulations [4,6,7] or measurement-aided simulations [5], which makes it hard to predict their actual performances in practice. In addition, most attacks rely on "collision-detection" technique, which suggests the attacker has to find the leakages of the same Sbox computation (preferably in the first round) to build templates. This requirement imposes further restrictions on the target cipher as well as implementation.

Our Contribution. In this paper, we aim to extend the previous SCARE techniques with Linear Regression Attack (LRA) [8]. Compared with other power analyses, the advantage of LRA lies in its flexibility in the regression model. With the full basis, LRA detects any relevant power leakage, just like NICV [9]. Meanwhile, LRA can also perform regressions with different models, verifying various conjectures about the secret cipher. It is well known that the commonly used evaluation measure in LRA—coefficient of determination (R^2)— increases with the number of regressors [10]. In this paper, we suggest using F-test to fairly compare different models and reveal some inherent cryptographic operations. In SCARE, such attack further recovers the secret linear components, as well as the inputs of the Sboxes. Compared with the previous SCAREs, our approach has three advantages: first, it works in a general framework which covers many common structures (SPN, Feistel, generalized Feistel, etc.). Second, our attack takes less *a priori* knowledge about the target cipher or its implementation. In our attack, the attacker does not have to know things like the size of the Sboxes, the accurate location of each Sbox computation on the trace or the order of the permutation computation in advance. Last but not least, our approach is completely non-profiled. This means our attack works even if all the Sboxes in the encryption process are completely different, whereas all previous collision-based SCAREs fail due to lack of valid templates. We have verified our attack with power leakages from an unprotected software implementation of DES. Our experiments present the complete SCARE flow in details, demonstrating how our LRA-based SCARE helps to determine the secret cipher step-by-step.

2   Preliminaries

2.1   Previous SCARE Techniques

So far, most SCARE studies focus on block ciphers. As modern block ciphers usually contain non-linear (confusion) layers and linear (diffusion) layers, in the following, we discuss these two cases separately.

Sbox Recovery. Confusion layers often consist of several small components, called Substitution Boxes (Sboxes). For Sbox recovery, two types of SCAREs exist:

- **Collision-based SCARE** [4–6]. As a prevalent tool in SCARE [4–6], collision attack exploits the similarity between the leakages from sequential computations of the same Sbox. Although marked as a non-profiled attack, collision attacks share exactly the same routine as *Template Attack* (TA) [11]. The only difference lies in the profiling stage, where collision attacks use other sequentially-implemented Sbox computations as the profiling trace set [12]. Since the leakages of the exact same Sbox computation are not always available, this "online profiling" stage imposes restrictions on the implementations as well as the target ciphers. For instance, if the target cipher is DES, the attacker cannot build templates with the first round's Sboxes, due to the secret expansion transformation E. As DES uses 8 different Sboxes, finding collision within the first round [5] is also impossible. Besides, collision attacks usually requires the accurate points of interest to build effective templates. Without any *a priori* knowledge, finding the accurate points of interest is not an easy task in practice. As a result, none of the previous collision-based SCAREs validated their attack with realistic experiments.
- **Guilley et al.'s Sbox Recovery** [3]. In 2010. Guilley et al. proposed an Sbox recovery technique based on 1 bit CPA. As a nominal distinguisher, 1-bit CPA does not require *a priori* knowledge about the leakage model or the accurate points of interest. To our knowledge, this is the only SCARE that verified with realistic hardware implementations (DPAContest v1). However, in order to focus on one single output bit, the authors use an "output mask". Technically speaking, this means the attacker needs to find which bit in the right register should store the guessed bit, as well as the last value of this register (according to the Hamming Distance (HD) model). In other words, these masks implicitly assume the attacker already know the diffusion layer is a bit-permutation and the underlying cipher uses Feistel structure.

Linear Component Recovery. To our knowledge, Daudigny et al. 's DES recovery is the only SCARE devoted to the diffusion layer. Unfortunately, their work relies heavily on the specific implementation [1]. Specifically, in the permutation recovery, the authors assume the corresponding state is computed from the most to the least significant bit, and use the time order of all bits as the permutation table. If the implementation uses any other order, their SCARE fails. Other attacks recover linear components from the Sboxes' power consumption. In collision-based SCAREs, the linear part is treated as a secret matrix, which can be determined from a lot of collision equations [5]. In this case, recovering the linear components shares the same preconditions, as long as the unknown linear part does not hinder the Sbox recovery.

2.2 Linear Regression Attack

In 2005, Schindler et al. proposed the Stochastic Attack [13] as an efficient alternative for Template Attack [11]. With coefficient of determination (R^2),

Doget et al. further developed a non-profiled key-recovery attack [8]. In some papers [8,14], this extension is noted as "Linear Regression Attack" (LRA).

A typical LRA works as follows: if the attacker wishes to recover a secret key byte k, he can measure the power consumptions of some key-related operations in the encryption process. Denote the n-bit intermediate state as x, the data-dependent power leakage can be written as $L(x)$, where L stands for the leakage function. Since the encryption algorithm is given, with any key guess $\hat{k}$, the attacker can compute the corresponding intermediate state $x_{\hat{k}}$. As the leakage $L(x)$ only relates to the correct intermediate state x_k, comparing $L(x)$ with all $x_{\hat{k}}$ gives a clue for the correct key. Specifically, the attacker chooses a t-length regression basis $G_{\mathbf{b}} = \left(x^{b_1}, x^{b_2}, ..., x^{b_t} \right)^{\top}$, where $b_i \in F_{2^n}$ and $x^u = \prod_{i=1}^{n} x_i^{u_i}$ (x_i is the i-th bit of x and u_i is the i-th bit of u). With N times measurements l and a key guess $\hat{k}$, the leakage function can be estimated as $\hat{L}(x_{\hat{k}}) = \beta_0 + \beta_1 x_{\hat{k}}^{b_1} + \beta_2 x_{\hat{k}}^{b_2} + ... + \beta_t x_{\hat{k}}^{b_t}$, where

$$A_{\hat{k}} = \begin{pmatrix} x_{\hat{k}}^{b_1}(1) & \cdots & x_{\hat{k}}^{b_t}(1) \\ \vdots & \ddots & \vdots \\ x_{\hat{k}}^{b_1}(N) & \cdots & x_{\hat{k}}^{b_t}(N) \end{pmatrix}$$

$$\beta_{\hat{k}} = \left(A_{\hat{k}}^{\top} A_{\hat{k}} \right)^{-1} A_{\hat{k}}^{\top} (l(1), ..., l(N))^{\top}$$

$l(i)$ is the i-th measurement and $x(i)$ is the corresponding intermediate state. If the attacker uses a valid assumption about $L(x)$ (i.e. chooses a valid $G_{\mathbf{b}}$), only the correct key guess gives a valid regression. Thus, the attacker can use the coefficient of determination (R^2) as a distinguisher [8]

$$R_{\hat{k}}^2 = 1 - \frac{\sum_{i=1}^{N} \left(l_{(i)} - \hat{L}_{\hat{k}} \left(x(i) \right) \right)^2}{\sum_{i=1}^{N} \left(l_{(i)} - \bar{l} \right)^2}$$

$$k = \arg\max_{\hat{k}} \left(R_{\hat{k}}^2 \right) .$$

Theoretically speaking, R^2 provides a measure of how well the observed outcomes are replicated by the model, as the proportion of total variation of outcomes explained by the model [10]. Since the regression with the wrong intermediate state cannot effectively explain the variance, key guesses with higher R^2 are more likely to be correct.

3 LRA with F-test: A Useful Tool

Although LRA is a powerful key-recovery attack, directly applying it in SCARE gives poor results. Unlike SCA, SCARE usually needs to compare different models. Unfortunately, R^2 is not suitable for this task. In this section, we perform F-test to compare LRA results from different regression models. Although not explicitly stated, Whitnall's stepwise regression uses the same technique [14]. In this section, we take one step further and discuss how F-test can help us in the field of reverse engineering.

3.1 Motivation

In regression, R^2 is a statistical measure of how well the regression approximates the real data points. However, R^2 alone cannot be used as a meaningful comparison of models with different numbers of independent variables. As a matter of fact, R^2 spuriously increases when extra explanatory variables are added to the model. In this case, it is hard to tell whether the new model is more effective than the old one. This problem seldom affects LRA in a key-recovery scenario: in most block ciphers, the secret key only affects the value of the explanatory variables. Since all the key guesses share the same regression model, the highest R^2 indicates the best regression. In SCARE, the story is completely different: as SCARE's target involves the regression model itself, using LRA in SCARE will inevitably face the problem of comparing different regression models.

3.2 F-test with Nested Model

A well-known solution for this problem would be introducing F-test between two models [15]. In statistics, two models are "nested" if one model (the full model M_2) contains all the terms of the other (the restricted model M_1), and at least one additional term. To determine whether the restricted model is adequate, we can test the following hypothesis

H_0: *the restricted model is adequate*
H_1: *the full model is better*
with F statistic

$$\frac{RSS_1 - RSS_2}{RSS_2} \frac{N - p_2 + 1}{p_2 - p_1} \sim F(p_2 - p_1, N - p_2 + 1)$$

where p_1 (p_2) stands for the number of explanatory variables in M_1 (M_2), RSS_1 (RSS_2) represents the residual sum of squares, and N is the number of measurements. Following the notations in Sect. 2, the residual sum of squares (RSS) is defined as

$$RSS_j = \sum_i \left(l(i) - \hat{L}_j(x(i)) \right)^2$$

The null hypothesis is rejected if this statistic is greater than the critical value of the F-distribution for some desired false-rejection probability α.

3.3 Applications in SCARE

In SCAREs, LRA with F-test can help us verify various conjectures. For instance, considering the case where we wish to decide whether a regression model can explain the variance of the power measurements. Given a false-rejection probability α, F-test determines whether the regression is valid, considering both the sample size N and the number of explanatory variables. Specifically, let M_0 denote the model that contains only the constant term (*the restricted model*), while M_1 is the tested regression model (*the full model*). If the F-test above rejects H_0 with high confidence, the power measurements are somehow related to the model M_1. This test helps us distinguish whether the resultant R^2 represents a valid regression or the consequence of random noises. In the following, this test is denoted as the **ValidTest**.

Another interesting application is to separate parallel signals from signals that actually "mix" together in the cryptographic computations. Suppose we have some intermediate state x and the corresponding power leakage l, and wish to determine whether l comes from x itself or some cryptographic computations of x. Throughout this paper, we assume the majority of the power leakage follows the weighted Hamming Weight model, where $L(x) = \beta_0 + \beta_1 x_1 + ... + \beta_n x_n$. Take the two-bit $x = \{x_0, x_1\}$ as a toy example, following the weighted Hamming Weight model, the power leakage can be written as $L(x) = \beta_0 + \beta_1 x_0 + \beta_2 x_1$. If some cryptographic computations (e.g. XOR) occur, the expression of $L(x)$ also contains $\beta_3 x_0 x_1$. Thus, the following hypothesis test applies:

H_0: M_0 *with regression basis* $\{1, x_0, x_1\}$ *is adequate*
H_1: M_1 *with regression basis* $\{1, x_0, x_1, x_0 x_1\}$ *is better*

If the F-test accepts H_0 with high confidence, we can conclude that x_0 and x_1 are simply parallel implemented. Otherwise, it suggests there might be some cryptographic operations performed with both x_0 and x_1. Similarly, for a d-bit group $\{x_1, x_2, ..., x_d\}$, if we wish to test whether the i-th bit of x (x_i) mixes with other bits, we can use the following hypothesis test:

H_0: M_0 *with regression basis* $G_0 = \{x^u | u \in \mathbb{F}_{2^d} \wedge u_i = 0\} \cup \{x_i\}$ *is adequate*
H_1: M_1 *with regression basis* $G_1 = \{x^u | u \in \mathbb{F}_{2^d}\}$ *is better*

As this test aims to prune irrelevant bits, in the following sections, we denote this test as the **PruningTest**.

4 A Realistic LRA-Based SCARE

This section further explains how our LRA with F-test helps to reveal the secret cryptographic components. For this purpose, we chose an unprotected software implementation of DES as our target. The power consumptions were measured with a LeCroy WaveRunner 610Zi oscilloscope at a sampling rate of 20 MSa/s. The entire trace set contains 20 000 traces, with 80 000 samples covering the first 3 rounds. As the power consumption of unprotected software implementation can be easily exploited, in our experiments, we only use the first 2 000 traces. Throughout this section, we assume the attacker does not know the underlying cipher (DES) or the specific implementation.

4.1 Generalized Structure of the Target Cipher

In order to formally define a general flow for SCARE, we start our discussion by proposing a generalized structure that covers most common block ciphers. Many previous SCAREs assume their target ciphers use either the Substitution-Permutation Network (SPN) or the standard Feistel structure. Although those choices are quite popular, with LRA, we can do better.

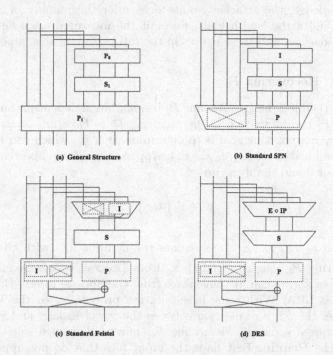

Fig. 1. Structure overview

In Fig. 1(a), P_0 and P_1 represent linear operations, while S stands for the non-linear operation. It is not hard to see that the standard SPN (Fig. 1(b)) and Feistel structure (Fig. 1(c)) can be regarded as special cases of this generalized scheme. Many other schemes, including the generalized Feistel structure, can also be expressed by the generalized structure in Fig. 1(a) similarly. It is worth mentioning that in a few cases, Fig. 1(a) may not correspond to a full encryption round: if the round function uses more than one confusion layers, it should be expressed as multiple rounds in Fig. 1(a). As we can see in Fig. 1(d), our target cipher DES fits this scheme perfectly.

Secret key in SCARE. In most SCAREs, the secret key is simply regarded as a part of the secret cipher. Specifically, if the secret key k is added before an Sbox S, SCARE can only recover an equivalent Sbox S' where $S'(x) = S(x \oplus k)$. Similar equivalence holds if k is added to other positions. In the following, we simply ignore the secret key and recover it as a part of the secret Sboxes.

4.2   Preparation

Before any reverse engineering, the attacker firstly observes the measured traces and tries to learn some basic facts about the secret encryption procedure. In our experiments, the attacker can easily identify three repetitive patterns on the trace, which correspond to the first three encryption rounds. However, locating each cryptographic operation on the trace is much harder. Indeed, without any *a priori* knowledge, the attacker cannot even infer the number of Sbox with confidence. Due to the length limit, we omit the measured trace figures here: interested reader can find these figures in the full version of this paper.

4.3   Step 1: Recovering P_0

Let n denote the block length. Assume P_0 has m_0 bits independent outputs, the operation of P_0 can be written as $(y_1, y_2, ..., y_{m_0})^\top = P_0(x_1, x_2, ..., x_n)^\top$, where P_0 is a binary matrix. Our goal is to determine each y_q, which can be written as a linear combination of $\{x_1, x_2, ..., x_n\}$. Apparently, we can also remove all x_i with coefficient 0 and simply write

$$y_q = \bigoplus_j \left(x_{q_j}\right)$$

where $\mathbf{x}_q = \left\{x_{q_1}, x_{q_2}, ..., x_{q_d}\right\}$ represents the d input bits with coefficient 1. Thus, recovering P_0 equals to finding $\mathbf{x}_q$ from $\{x_1, x_2, ..., x_n\}$. Given an input bit group guess $\tilde{\mathbf{x}}_q$, we can fit the leakage from the Sboxes' input (P_0's output) with full basis LRA. With some false-rejection probability α, the **ValidTest** shows whether there is a connection between the power leakage and $\tilde{\mathbf{x}}_q$. If there is, $\tilde{\mathbf{x}}_q$ can express some y_q. Meanwhile, $\tilde{\mathbf{x}}_q$ may still involve some irrelevant input bits. The **PruningTest** finds the input bits that do not appear in the expression of y_q. If both tests reject H_0, we can conclude that $\tilde{\mathbf{x}}_q$ is the exact relevant input for some y_q. The detailed procedure is presented in Algorithm 1. Noted the LRA in the **ValidTest** uses the constant basis $G_0 = \{1\}$ and the full basis $G_1 = \left\{\tilde{\mathbf{x}}_q^u | u \in \mathbb{F}_{2^d}\right\}$, while the LRA in the i-th **PruningTest** uses $G_2 = \left\{\tilde{\mathbf{x}}_q^u | u \in \mathbb{F}_{2^d} \wedge u_i = 0\right\} \cup \{x_{q_i}\}$ and the full basis $G_1 = \left\{\tilde{\mathbf{x}}_q^u | u \in \mathbb{F}_{2^d}\right\}$.

Theoretically, Algorithm 1 only succeeds when the target state y_q is related to every single bit in $\tilde{\mathbf{x}}_q$. According to our discussion above, XORing all bits in $\tilde{\mathbf{x}}_q$ together gives us a candidate for y_q. Thus, the attacker can perform one last **ValidTest** with this candidate bit: if this bit does lead to a valid regression, we have found some y_q. This test blocks out many undesirable cases, such as non-linear leakages or $\tilde{\mathbf{x}}_q$ expresses more than one y_q.

With Algorithm 1 identifying the correct input bits, all output bits can be found by simply enumerating all possible input guesses $\tilde{\mathbf{x}}_q$. Considering the implementation cost, designers tend to choose a lightweight matrix as the diffusion layer. Thus, the size of the correlated bit group (d) is more likely to be a small number. To this end, the enumeration starts with the smaller group guesses (smaller d) and moves towards the larger ones (larger d). As m_0 cannot

Algorithm 1. LRA based SCARE test

1: **procedure** SCARETEST($\tilde{\mathbf{x}}_q$)	
2: $[pr_1, R^2]$=ValidTest($\tilde{\mathbf{x}}_q$)	▷ Test whether $\tilde{\mathbf{x}}_q$ can explain the power variance
3: **if** $pr_1 > 1 - \alpha$ **then**	
4: **for** $i = 1$ to d **do**	
5: $pr_2[i]$=PruningTest($i,\tilde{\mathbf{x}}_q$)	▷ Test if x_{q_i} is relevant
6: **if** $pr_2[i] < 1 - \alpha$ **then**	
7: **return** "Error 2"	▷ $\tilde{\mathbf{x}}_q$ contains irrelevant bit x_{q_i}
8: **return** $\min(pr_2[1..d])R^2$	
9: **else**	
10: **return** "Error 1"	▷ $\tilde{\mathbf{x}}_q$ cannot explain the power variance

be efficiently determined in advance, the attacker must abort the enumeration whenever he believes he has found enough y_q. Assuming y_q contains at most d bits of x, the enumerations above takes C_n^d times LRA to find P_0. For $d \geqslant 8$, this approach becomes too expensive.

Optimization. Clearly, Algorithm 1 returns two types of errors: with Error 2, it suggests that $\tilde{\mathbf{x}}_q$ contains an irrelevant bit x_{q_i}. Otherwise, $\tilde{\mathbf{x}}_q$ cannot form a valid regression. As the first case limits the expression of y_q to a smaller range, we can build a more efficient version of this attack. Suppose we choose a d_g-bit group guess where $d_g > d$, Algorithm 1 verifies whether it causes a valid regression with the **ValidTest**. If it does, as the **PruningTest** gives clues about which bit is irrelevant, finding the exact input should be easy. In this case, we wish to find the minimal d_g-bit groups that covers all possible d-bit groups. This problem equals to finding the covering set of a hypergraph. According to Rödl's conclusion [16], as $n \to \infty$,

$$M(n, d_g, d) \to \frac{C_n^d}{C_{d_g}^d}$$

Thus, if the attacker estimates the expressions of all y_q contain at most d input bits, enumerating all d_g group guesses above gives all y_q. Dan Gordon's web site provides some known covering sets [17]. Note that this trick should only be applied when d is large, as the covering problem of a hypergraph is quite complicated itself. For clarity, we present the pseudo-code of this optimization in Algorithm 2.

Experiments. Considering P_0 is the first cryptographic operation in Fig. 1(a), in our experiments, we have tested our attack with the first half of the first round's trace. With $\alpha = 0.01\%$, only 32 bits pass our **ValidTest**. Since P_0's output involves half of the plaintext bits, an experienced attacker may guess that P_0 is a bit permutation. Table 1 lists our P_0's recovery with various numbers of traces. According to the IP transformation in DES, our P_0's recovery gives 100 % accurate result with 2000 traces. With 500 traces, our recovery gives one Type II error ("false negative"), which means one of P_0's output bit is filtered out.

Algorithm 2. Linear Component Recovery: the optimized approach

---

Require: n-bit input list $\mathbf{x} = \{x_1, x_2, ..., x_n\}$, guessed length d and a parameter $d_g > d$

1: **procedure** LINEARRECOVERY
2:     List=ϕ
3:     **for** each d_g-bit group $\tilde{\mathbf{x}}_q \subset \mathbf{x}$ in the covering set **do**
4:         result=SCARETEST($\tilde{\mathbf{x}}_q$)   ▷ Test if $\tilde{\mathbf{x}}_q$ is the expression of some y_i
5:         **if** result= "Error 1" **then**
6:             **continue**
7:         **else**
8:             Remove the extra bits using the **PruningTest**
9:             candidate=$\underset{j}{\oplus}\left(x_{q_j}\right)$
10:            **if** candidate passes SCARETEST **then**   ▷ Make sure $\underset{j}{\oplus}\left(x_{q_j}\right)$ is valid
11:                List=List $\cup$ $\tilde{\mathbf{x}}_q$ ▷ Add candidate as a output bit
12:     **return** List

Interestingly, our recovery did not report any Type I error ("false positive"), which means there was no incorrect bit in the recovered P_0's output.

Table 1. Recovering P_0 in the first round

α	Number of traces	Recovered bits	Correct bits	Type I error	Type II error
0.01 %	500	31	31	0	1
0.01 %	2000	32	32	0	0

Since the power measurements do not contain any information about the bit order of P_0, here we can only retrieve P_0 up to its bit-permutation equivalent. This sets stage for our next step.

4.4   Step 2: Recovering S_1

As mentioned before, after the first step, we do not have the inputs of each Sbox. In order to further recover the secret Sboxes, we have to find the actual input of each Sbox first. We can perform a similar attack to obtain the Sboxes' inputs. The only difference lies in our leakage choice: here we choose the leakage of the Sboxes' outputs instead. Typically, if an Sbox is cryptographically strong, LRA should not predict its output, unless the guessed input group $\tilde{\mathbf{x}}_q$ contains all of its input. To this end, the attack procedure is exactly the same as Step 1, except for the last "XOR test". Although the trivial enumeration works for most popular Sbox sizes, it is worth mentioning there is a trick that can significantly speed up this process.

Property 1. Let $y = S(x)$ denote the Sbox computation and $l(x)$ denote the corresponding power leakage. Suppose the $l(x)$ follows the weighted Hamming Weight model of y, as the sample size $N \to \infty$, LRA with full basis of x satisfies

$$\lim_{N \to \infty} R_f^2 = \frac{1}{1 + \frac{1}{SNR}}$$

where SNR is the Signal-to-Noise Ratio. For most commonly used S, if one bit x_i is removed from the regression basis, LRA with the partial basis of x satisfies

$$\lim_{N \to \infty} R_p^2 \approx \frac{1}{2} \frac{1}{1 + \frac{1}{SNR}}$$

Proof sketch. Without loss of generality, we first limit the output of $S(x)$ to 1 bit. In this case, the leakage can be written as $l(x) = \beta_1 S(x) + \beta_0 + \mathbf{n}$, where $\mathbf{n}$ represents the independent Gaussian noise with mean 0 and variance σ^2. It is not hard to see that

$$\lim_{N \to \infty} R_f^2 = 1 - \frac{\sigma^2}{SNR\sigma^2 + \sigma^2} = \frac{1}{1 + \frac{1}{SNR}}$$

Let $x' = \{x_1, x_2, ..., x_n\} \setminus \{x_i\}$, any $S(x)$ can be written as $S_0(x')(1 - x_i) + S_1(x')x_i$. If the target Sbox is cryptographic strong, without too much bias, we can assume $S_0(x')$ and $S_1(x')$ are nearly independent from one another[1]. Since LRA with x' combines the point of $x|x_i = 0$ and $x|x_i = 1$, according to the Least Square Regression, the resultant point $l(x') \approx 0.5\beta_1(S_0(x') + S_1(x'))$. Thus,

$$\lim_{N \to \infty} R_p^2 \approx 1 - \frac{\frac{1}{2}\beta_1{}^2 \sum_{x'}(S_0(x') - S_1(x'))^2 + N\sigma^2}{N(\frac{1}{4}\beta_1{}^2 + \sigma^2)} = \frac{1}{2} \frac{1}{1 + \frac{1}{SNR}}$$

As the output bits of an Sbox should be independent from one another, such proof sketch can easily extend to the multi-bit case.   □

Optimization. This property suggests if a whole Sbox's R^2 is high enough, part of its input has a smaller, yet still significant R^2. Suppose an Sbox involves s input bits, most of its partial inputs (proper subsets) have a larger R^2 than other irrelevant guesses. To this end, we can add some constraints in the enumeration, especially for $s - 1$ and $s - 2$-bit groups. For instance, if the **ValidTest** and **PruningTest** of a whole Sbox use significance level $\alpha = 0.01\,\%$, we can loosen the restriction on the partial inputs with lower significance levels. In our experiments, the significance level α is set to $\{1\,\%, 0.1\,\%, 0.01\,\%\}$ for input length $\{s - 2, s - 1, s\}$, respectively. Such constraints efficiently filter out many unnecessary guesses, improves the overall performance significantly. For clarity, we present the pseudo-code of this optimization in Algorithm 3.

---

[1] If x_i only appears in the linear terms or does not appear at all, the R^2 above might be biased. However, considering the other output bits, the overall bias should be small. For a cryptographic strong Sbox, x_i should appears in the non-linear terms in at least one output bit.

Algorithm 3. Sbox Recovery: the optimized approach

Require: n-bit input list $\mathbf{x} = \{x_1, x_2, ..., x_n\}$, guessed length s
1: **procedure** SBOXRECOVERY
2:     List=all possible groups with length $s - 3$
3:     **for** $s' = s - 2$ to s **do**
4:         **for** each $s' - 1$ bit group $\tilde{\mathbf{x}}_q \in$ List **do**
5:             Remove $\tilde{\mathbf{x}}_q$ from List
6:             Add a new bit into $\tilde{\mathbf{x}}_q$ ▷ Generate new input groups with length s'
7:             result=SCARETEST($\tilde{\mathbf{x}}_q$) with significance level $c[s']$
8:             **if** result $\neq$ "Error" **then**
9:                 List=List $\cup$ $\tilde{\mathbf{x}}_q$ ▷ Add all possible subsets with length s'
10:     **for** each s-bit group $\tilde{\mathbf{x}}_q \in$ List **do**   ▷ Test the left groups in List
11:         SuperSet=all $s + 1$ bit supersets of $\tilde{\mathbf{x}}_q$
12:         **if** a superset passes SCARETEST **then**   ▷ $\tilde{\mathbf{x}}_q$ is a proper subset
13:             Remove $\tilde{\mathbf{x}}_q$ from List
14:     **return** List

Determine the size of the Sbox. If the size of the Sbox (s) is not given in advance, the attacker needs to find it through a few trail-and-error procedures. Specifically, let s' denote the size of the guessed input group $\tilde{\mathbf{x}}_q$. If $s' > s$, the **PruningTest** tells us there are irrelevant bits in $\tilde{\mathbf{x}}_q$. On the other hand, if $s' < s$, according to *Property* 1, $\tilde{\mathbf{x}}_q$ should be a valid group with lower significance level. To make sure $\tilde{\mathbf{x}}_q$ is a proper subset, we can test all the supersets of $\tilde{\mathbf{x}}_q$ with size $s' + 1$. If one superset is also a valid group with higher significance level, we know for sure that $\tilde{\mathbf{x}}_q$ is a proper subset of the Sbox's input and $s' < s$.

Experiments. One major advantage of our approach, is that it does not require the actual points of interest. In theory, as our analysis only considers the power consumption of each Sbox's output, our Sbox recovery should only uses the power leakages of the Sbox's output. However, considering our **PruningTest** removes the valid regressions caused by "parallel effect", the power consumption of the Sboxes' inputs (or P_0's output) should be automatically discarded. For this reason, in our experiments, our test runs 100 times with all samples points in the first round. Since we do not know the order of P_0's output, each attempt uses a random order and returns a list of corresponding input bits. Table 2 demonstrates all the correct Sbox input groups with their success rates, as well as the incorrect group that our attack returned. With 2000 traces, our LRA-based SCARE always returns the correct Sbox input with 100 % accuracy, except for S_5. The left 5 cases returned a result list containing only 7 correct Sbox inputs. This is caused by our constraints on the enumeration procedure: with certain orders of P_0's output, our constraints may filter out the correct partial input group of S_5. If the attacker uses only 500 traces, as our discussion in Sect. 4.3, one of the output bit of P_0 is missing. As a consequence, our attack in this section cannot find the corresponding Sbox inputs (S_5). Meanwhile, with such limited trace set, our attack also returns some incorrect groups.

Table 2. Recovering the input of S

No	Success rate (N=500)	Success rate (N=2000)
S_0	100/100	100/100
S_1	100/100	100/100
S_2	90/100	100/100
S_3	100/100	100/100
S_4	65/100	100/100
S_5	0/100	95/100
S_6	86/100	100/100
S_7	30/100	100/100
Incorrect Group	17	0

Unlike the linear case, for Sboxes, we cannot determine the actual expression through the input bits. As our attack already finds each Sbox's input, the attacker can pick several points of interest using NICV (with the recovered Sbox inputs, rather than the plaintexts). Since both the Sbox inputs and the accurate points of interest are already recovered, collision attacks can further recover this Sbox. The details of the collision attacks are out of the scope of this paper. Interested readers can find this part in Rivain et al.'s paper [5].

4.5 Step 3: Recovering P_1

As a linear transformation, P_1's recovery follows exactly the same routine as P_0. The input bits include the n-bit plaintext as well as all the output bits of S. Our target leakage comes from the Sboxes' input (or P_0's output) in the second round. In our experiments, our test directly runs through all the sample points in the second round. With $\alpha = 0.01\,\%$ and $N = 2000$, our attack returns a list of 32 valid 2-bit candidates, whose XOR forms one of P_1's output bit. As we can see in Table 3, smaller trace set increases both Type I errors and Type II errors.

Table 3. Recovering P_1 with different numbers of traces

α	Number of traces	Candidates bits	Correct bits	Type I error	Type II error
0.01 %	500	36	31	5	1
0.01 %	2000	32	32	0	0

4.6 The Complete Attack

Although presented step by step, we would like to stress that this attack still needs manual intervention. Considering the enormous space of all possible secret block ciphers, the information that power traces provides is not enough to determine all the details. As a result, all SCAREs require some empirical intervention, whether by guessing the structure or guessing the input size of certain components (e.g. Sboxes). Our attack here is no exception: in both Step 1 and Step 3, the attacker needs to decide whether he has find all the output bits. Noted this does not suggest our attack is inferior to the previous SCAREs: most previous works directly assume the attacker already knows those parameters (e.g. the cryptographic structure, the size of the Sbox, the output size of the permutation, etc.). Indeed, most SCAs today still requires some manual interventions in the preparation stage, whether by identifying the encryption rounds or removing some outlier traces. We believe our SCARE should be regarded as a handy tool for experienced attackers, rather than an automatic attack. In addition, we did not bother to cover all possible block ciphers with our SCARE. Considering the enormous space of all possible secret block ciphers, we believe it make more sense to focus on the most common designs: arbitrary algorithms with exotic features usually require *ad-hoc* solutions, which is out of the scope of this paper.

5   Discussion

In the last section, we propose a general LRA-based SCARE and verify it with realistic power leakages. Specifically, our analysis uses a quite general structure, which covers most common block ciphers. Unlike the collision attacks [5], the 8 different Sboxes and the Expansion E in DES do not hinder our SCARE. In addition, in our analysis, the attacker does not have to accurately locate each Sbox on the leakage trace.

Leakage model. The major limitation of our approach, is that it only works with linear leakage in theory. This is indeed an inherent drawback: in LRA, the secret recovery relies on the fact that the attacker can decide whether the corresponding regression function looks like the correct leakage function. If the leakage function contains non-linear terms, the attacker cannot decide whether the non-linear terms come from the leakage function or the cryptographic operation. Collision attacks do not face this problem, since they use an "online profiling" stage to characterize the leakage function [5]. This is actually an inevitable trade-off: without any assumption on the leakage function, non-profiled SCA cannot successfully attack any bijective cryptographic operation [14]. Nonetheless, our LRA-based SCARE still works when the leakage function can be approximated as a linear function. As LRA with linear basis always gives good regression, adding non-linear terms cannot provide a significant better regression.

The significance level α. The significance level α plays an important role in our LRA-based SCARE. α helps to decide whether increment of R^2 should be regarded as the consequence of a better regression model or negligible noise. In our paper, we simply choose a common significance level ($\alpha = 0.01\%$) in the hypothesis testing. This α works well in our experiments in Sect. 4. For other implementations, $\alpha = 0.01\%$ may not always be a good choice. As α depends on the specific leakage features, the attacker may have to test several common values and estimate which recovery is more likely to be correct.

Parallel or Hardware Implementations. Theoretically, as our **PruningTest** automatically removes the "parallel effect", our LRA-based SCARE should also work for parallel implementations. However, in our experience, LRA-based SCARE can learn some information from parallel implementations, although the result is far from satisfying. Indeed, most previous SCAREs explicitly assume the underlying implementation is sequential. In addition, it might be interesting to ask whether our attack can be extended to hardware implementations, with the Hamming Distance (HD) model. The problem of the HD model is, it involves the state of the last round. For SCARE, learning the last state means the attacker has to learn the specific implementation code as well as the underlying data-path. Considering the context of SCARE, we believe it makes more sense to avoid such assumption: however, if the last state is already given, our attack works exactly the same way.

6   Conclusion

Despite various SCARE techniques in literature, recovering a secret cipher in practice, is not an easy task. In fact, most previous SCAREs have some limitations on their target ciphers or implementations. In this paper, we propose a new SCARE technique based on Linear Regression Attack (LRA). Specifically, in order to fairly compare different regression models, we perform F-test against the regression results. LRA with F-test helps us successfully recover linear components as well as the Sboxes' inputs, without much *a priori* knowledge about the underlying cipher or its implementation. Compared with the previous SCAREs, our approach uses less *a priori* knowledge, covers more block cipher instances in a completely non-profiled manner. We have verified our attack with real-life measurements from an unprotected software implementation of DES. Experiments confirm that our attack works well with realistic measurements, extracting valuable information for experienced attackers. Although our approach still has some limitations, we believe it can serve as an alternative tool for reverse engineering in the future.

Acknowledgements. We would like to thank the anonymous reviewers for providing valuable comments. This work is supported by the National Basic Research Program of China (No.2013CB338002) and National Natural Science Foundation of China (No. 61272476, 61672509 and 61232009).

References

1. Daudigny, R., Ledig, H., Muller, F., Valette, F.: SCARE of the DES. In: Ioannidis, J., Keromytis, A., Yung, M. (eds.) ACNS 2005. LNCS, vol. 3531, pp. 393–406. Springer, Heidelberg (2005). doi:10.1007/11496137_27

2. Réal, D., Dubois, V., Guilloux, A.-M., Valette, F., Drissi, M.: SCARE of an unknown hardware Feistel implementation. In: Grimaud, G., Standaert, F.-X. (eds.) CARDIS 2008. LNCS, vol. 5189, pp. 218–227. Springer, Heidelberg (2008). doi:10.1007/978-3-540-85893-5_16

3. Guilley, S., Sauvage, L., Micolod, J., Réal, D., Valette, F.: Defeating any secret cryptography with SCARE attacks. In: Abdalla, M., Barreto, P.S.L.M. (eds.) LAT-INCRYPT 2010. LNCS, vol. 6212, pp. 273–293. Springer, Heidelberg (2010). doi:10.1007/978-3-642-14712-8_17

4. Clavier, C., Isorez, Q., Wurcker, A.: Complete SCARE of AES-Like block ciphers by chosen plaintext collision power analysis. In: Paul, G., Vaudenay, S. (eds.) INDOCRYPT 2013. LNCS, vol. 8250, pp. 116–135. Springer, Heidelberg (2013). doi:10.1007/978-3-319-03515-4_8

5. Rivain, M., Roche, T.: SCARE of secret ciphers with SPN structures. In: Sako, K., Sarkar, P. (eds.) ASIACRYPT 2013. LNCS, vol. 8269, pp. 526–544. Springer, Heidelberg (2013). doi:10.1007/978-3-642-42033-7_27

6. Clavier, C.: An improved SCARE cryptanalysis against a secret A3/A8 GSM algorithm. In: McDaniel, P., Gupta, S.K. (eds.) ICISS 2007. LNCS, vol. 4812, pp. 143–155. Springer, Heidelberg (2007). doi:10.1007/978-3-540-77086-2_11

7. Novak, R.: Side-channel attack on substitution blocks. In: Zhou, J., Yung, M., Han, Y. (eds.) ACNS 2003. LNCS, vol. 2846, pp. 307–318. Springer, Heidelberg (2003). doi:10.1007/978-3-540-45203-4_24

8. Doget, J., Prouff, E., Rivain, M., Standaert, F.X.: Univariate side channel attacks and leakage modeling. J. Crypt. Eng. $\mathbf{1}$(2), 123–144 (2011)

9. Bhasin, S., Danger, J.L., Guilley, S., Najm, Z.: NICV: normalized inter-class variance for detection of side-channel leakage. In: 2014 International Symposium on Electromagnetic Compatibility, Tokyo (EMC 2014/Tokyo), pp. 310–313 (2014)

10. Wiki: Coefficient of determination. http://en.wikipedia.org/wiki/Coefficient_of_determination

11. Chari, S., Rao, J.R., Rohatgi, P.: Template attacks. In: Kaliski, B.S., Koç, K., Paar, C. (eds.) CHES 2002. LNCS, vol. 2523, pp. 13–28. Springer, Heidelberg (2003). doi:10.1007/3-540-36400-5_3

12. Gérard, B., Standaert, F.X.: Unified and optimized linear collision attacks and their application in a non-profiled setting: extended version. J. Crypt. Eng. $\mathbf{3}$(1), 45–58 (2013)

13. Schindler, W., Lemke, K., Paar, C.: A stochastic model for differential side channel cryptanalysis. In: Rao, J.R., Sunar, B. (eds.) CHES 2005. LNCS, vol. 3659, pp. 30–46. Springer, Heidelberg (2005). doi:10.1007/11545262_3

14. Whitnall, C., Oswald, E., Standaert, F.-X.: The myth of generic DPA…and the magic of learning. In: Benaloh, J. (ed.) CT-RSA 2014. LNCS, vol. 8366, pp. 183–205. Springer, Heidelberg (2014). doi:10.1007/978-3-319-04852-9_10

15. Allen, M.P.: Understanding Regression Analysis. Springer Science & Business Media, New York (1997)

16. Frankl, P., Rödl, V.: Near perfect coverings in graphs and hypergraphs. Eur. J. Comb. $\mathbf{6}$(4), 317–326 (1985)

17. Gordon, D.: La Jolla Covering Repository. https://www.ccrwest.org/cover.html

Compact Representation for Division Property

Yosuke Todo[1,2(✉)] and Masakatu Morii[2]

[1] NTT Secure Platform Laboratories, Tokyo, Japan
todo.yosuke@lab.ntt.co.jp
[2] Kobe University, Kobe, Japan

Abstract. The division property, which is a new method to find integral characteristics, was proposed at Eurocrypt 2015. Thereafter, some applications and improvements have been proposed. The bit-based division property is also one of such improvements, and the accurate integral characteristic of SIMON32 is theoretically proved. In this paper, we propose the compact representation for the bit-based division property. The disadvantage of the bit-based division property is that it cannot be applied to block ciphers whose block length is over 32 because of high time and memory complexity. The compact representation partially solves this problem, and we apply this technique to 64-bit block cipher PRESENT to illustrate our method. We can accurately evaluate the propagation characteristic of the bit-based division property thanks to the compact representation. As a result, we find 9-round integral characteristics, and the characteristic is improved by two rounds than previous best characteristic. Moreover, we attack 12-round PRESENT-80 and 13-round PRESENT-128 by using this new characteristic.

Keywords: Integral cryptanalysis · Division property · Compact representation · PRESENT

1 Introduction

The concept of an integral cryptanalysis was first introduced as the dedicated attack against block cipher SQUARE [4], and Knudsen and Wagner then formalized the dedicated attack as the integral attack [6]. The integral cryptanalysis is applied to many ciphers, and this is nowadays one of the most powerful cryptanalyses [6,8,16,17]. The integral cryptanalysis mainly consists of two parts: a search for integral characteristics and key recovery. The propagation of the integral property [6] and the degree estimation[1] [5,7] have been used as well-known methods to find integral characteristics.

At Eurocrypt 2015, the division property, which is a novel technique to find integral characteristics, was proposed [12]. This technique is the generalization of the integral property that can also exploit the algebraic degree at the same time. After the proposal, the new understanding of the division property and new applications have been proposed [2,10,11,14,18].

---

[1] This method is often called the higher-order differential attack [5,7].

© Springer International Publishing AG 2016
S. Foresti and G. Persiano (Eds.): CANS 2016, LNCS 10052, pp. 19–35, 2016.
DOI: 10.1007/978-3-319-48965-0_2

At FSE 2016, the bit-based division property, which is a new variant of the division property, was proposed [14][2]. To analyze n-bit block ciphers with m ℓ-bit S-boxes, the conventional division property decomposes n-bit value into m ℓ-bit values, and the division property $\mathcal{D}_{\mathbb{K}}^{\ell^m}$ is used. For convenience, we call this-type division property an integer-based division property. On the other hand, the bit-based division property decomposes n-bit value into n 1-bit values, i.e., $\mathcal{D}_{\mathbb{K}}^{1^n}$ is used. The bit-based division property can find more accurate integral characteristics than the integer-based division property. Actually, the bit-based division property proves the 15-round integral characteristic of SIMON32, and it is tight [14].

Our Contribution. In this paper, we propose a *compact representation* for the bit-based division property against S-box-based ciphers. A disadvantage of the bit-based division property is that it requires about 2^n time and memory complexity to evaluate n-bit block ciphers. Therefore, the application is limited to block ciphers with small block length like SIMON32 in [14]. Moreover, at CRYPTO 2016, Boura and Canteaut introduced the parity set, which is the so-called bit-based division property for an S-box [2], but the application is also limited to the low-data distinguisher for a few rounds of PRESENT [1]. The compact representation partially solves this problem, and we can get high-data distinguishers by reducing time and memory complexity. To demonstrate the advantage of the compact representation, we apply our new technique to PRESENT. As a result, we find new 9-round integral characteristics. Since the previous best characteristic is 7-round one [15], our new characteristic is improved by two rounds. Moreover, we attack 12-round PRESENT-80 and 13-round PRESENT-128 by using the new integral characteristic. Zhang et al. discussed the security of PRESENT against the integral attack in [19] and attacked 10-round PRESENT-80 and 11-round PRESENT-128 by using the match-through-the-S-box (MTTS) technique. Therefore, our new attack is also improved by two rounds.

2   Preliminaries

2.1   Notations

We make the distinction between the addition of $\mathbb{F}_2^n$ and addition of $\mathbb{Z}$, and we use $\oplus$ and $+$ as the addition of $\mathbb{F}_2^n$ and addition of $\mathbb{Z}$, respectively. For any $a \in \mathbb{F}_2^n$, the ith element is expressed in $a[i]$, and the Hamming weight $w(a)$ is calculated as $w(a) = \sum_{i=1}^{n} a[i]$. For any $\boldsymbol{a} \in (\mathbb{F}_2^{n_1} \times \mathbb{F}_2^{n_2} \times \cdots \times \mathbb{F}_2^{n_m})$, the vectorial Hamming weight of $\boldsymbol{a}$ is defined as $W(\boldsymbol{a}) = (w(a_1), w(a_2), \ldots, w(a_m)) \in \mathbb{Z}^m$. Moreover, for any $\boldsymbol{k} \in \mathbb{Z}^m$ and $\boldsymbol{k'} \in \mathbb{Z}^m$, we define $\boldsymbol{k} \succeq \boldsymbol{k'}$ if $k_i \geq k_i'$ for all i ($1 \leq i \leq m$). Otherwise, $\boldsymbol{k} \not\succeq \boldsymbol{k'}$. Let $\mathbb{K}$ be the set of $\boldsymbol{k}$, and $|\mathbb{K}|$ denotes the number of elements in $\mathbb{K}$.

---

[2]   In [14], they proposed two variants of the bit-based division property: the conventional bit-based division property and the bit-based division property using three subsets. In this paper, we focus on the conventional bit-based division property.

2.2 Integral Attack

The integral attack was first introduced by Daemen et al. to evaluate the security of SQUARE [4], and then it was formalized by Knudsen and Wagner [6]. Attackers first prepare N chosen plaintexts and encrypt them R rounds. If the XOR of all encrypted texts becomes 0, we say that the cipher has an R-round integral characteristic with N chosen plaintexts. Finally, we analyze the entire cipher by using the integral characteristic. There are two classical approaches to find integral characteristics. The first one is the propagation of the integral property [6] and another is based on the degree estimation [5,7].

2.3 Division Property

The division property proposed in [12] is a new method to find integral characteristics. This section briefly shows the definition and propagation rules. Please refer to [12] in detail.

Bit Product Function. The division property of a multiset is evaluated by using the bit product function defined as follows. Let $\pi_u : \mathbb{F}_2^n \to \mathbb{F}_2$ be a bit product function for any $u \in \mathbb{F}_2^n$. Let $x \in \mathbb{F}_2^n$ be the input and $\pi_u(x)$ be the AND of $x[i]$ satisfying $u[i] = 1$, i.e., it is defined as

$$\pi_u(x) := \prod_{i=1}^{n} x[i]^{u[i]}.$$

Notice that $x[i]^1 = x[i]$ and $x[i]^0 = 1$. Let $\pi_u : (\mathbb{F}_2^{n_1} \times \mathbb{F}_2^{n_2} \times \cdots \times \mathbb{F}_2^{n_m}) \to \mathbb{F}_2$ be a bit product function for any $u \in (\mathbb{F}_2^{n_1} \times \mathbb{F}_2^{n_2} \times \cdots \times \mathbb{F}_2^{n_m})$. Let $x \in (\mathbb{F}_2^{n_1} \times \mathbb{F}_2^{n_2} \times \cdots \times \mathbb{F}_2^{n_m})$ be the input and $\pi_u(x)$ be defined as

$$\pi_u(x) := \prod_{i=1}^{m} \pi_{u_i}(x_i).$$

The bit product function also appears in the Algebraic Normal Form (ANF) of a Boolean function. The ANF of a Boolean function f is represented as

$$f(x) = \bigoplus_{u \in \mathbb{F}_2^n} a_u^f \left(\prod_{i=1}^{n} x[i]^{u[i]} \right) = \bigoplus_{u \in \mathbb{F}_2^n} a_u^f \pi_u(x),$$

where $a_u^f \in \mathbb{F}_2$ is a constant value depending on f and u.

Definition of Division Property.

Definition 1 (Division Property [12]). *Let $\mathbb{X}$ be a multiset whose elements take a value of $(\mathbb{F}_2^{n_1} \times \mathbb{F}_2^{n_2} \times \cdots \times \mathbb{F}_2^{n_m})$. When the multiset $\mathbb{X}$ has the division* *property* $\mathcal{D}_{\mathbb{K}}^{n_1,n_2,\ldots,n_m}$, *where* $\mathbb{K}$ *denotes a set of* m-*dimensional vectors whose* i*th element takes a value between* 0 *and* n_i, *it fulfills the following conditions:*

$$\bigoplus_{\boldsymbol{x}\in X} \pi_{\boldsymbol{u}}(\boldsymbol{x}) = \begin{cases} unknown & if\ there\ are\ \boldsymbol{k} \in \mathbb{K}\ s.t.\ W(\boldsymbol{u}) \succeq \boldsymbol{k}, \\ 0 & otherwise. \end{cases}$$

See [12] to better understand the concept in detail, and [10] and [11] help readers understand the division property. In this paper, the division property for $(\mathbb{F}_2^n)^m$ is referred to as $\mathcal{D}_{\mathbb{K}}^{n^m}$ for the simplicity[3]. If there are $\boldsymbol{k} \in \mathbb{K}$ and $\boldsymbol{k}' \in \mathbb{K}$ satisfying $\boldsymbol{k} \succeq \boldsymbol{k}'$ in the division property $\mathcal{D}_{\mathbb{K}}^{n_1,n_2,\ldots,n_m}$, $\boldsymbol{k}$ can be removed from $\mathbb{K}$ because the vector $\boldsymbol{k}$ is redundant.

Some propagation rules for the division property are proven in [12], and the rules are summarized in [11]. We omit the description of the propagation rules in this paper because it is not always necessary to understand this paper.

2.4   Bit-Based Division Property

The bit-based division property was introduced in [14]. They showed two bit-based division properties: the conventional bit-based division property and the bit-based division property using three subsets. In this paper, we only focus on the conventional bit-based division property. To analyze n-bit block ciphers, the conventional division property uses $\mathcal{D}_{\mathbb{K}}^{\ell_1,\ell_2,\ldots,\ell_m}$, where ℓ_i and m are chosen by attackers in the range of $n = \sum_{i=1}^{m} \ell_i$. This paper focuses on the conventional bit-based division property, i.e., $\mathcal{D}_{\mathbb{K}}^{1^n}$. Note that it is not against the definition of the conventional division property.

Propagation Characteristic for S-Box. Let us consider the propagation characteristic of the bit-based division property for an S-box. Similar observation was shown by Boura and Canteaut in [2], and they introduced a new concept called the parity set as follows.

Definition 2 (Parity Set). *Let* $\mathbb{X}$ *be a set whose elements take a value of* $\mathbb{F}_2^n$. *Its parity set is defined as*

$$\mathcal{U}(\mathbb{X}) = \left\{ u \in \mathbb{F}_2^n \mid \bigoplus_{x\in\mathbb{X}} \pi_u(x) = 1 \right\}.$$

Assuming $\mathbb{X}$ has the division property $\mathcal{D}_k^n$,

$$\mathcal{U}(\mathbb{X}) \subseteq \{u \in \mathbb{F}_2^n : w(u) \geq k\}.$$

Let $\mathbb{X}$ and $S(\mathbb{X})$ denote the input set and output set of the S-box, respectively. Then, the parity set of $S(\mathbb{X})$ fulfills

$$\mathcal{U}(S(\mathbb{X})) \subseteq \cup_{u\in\mathcal{U}(\mathbb{X})} V_s(u),$$

Table 1. Sets $V_S(u)$ for all $u \in \mathbb{F}_2^4$ for the PRESENT S-box. All four-bit values are represented in hexadecimal notation. The rightmost bit of the word corresponds to the least significant bit.

	$V_S(u)$															
	0x0	0x1	0x2	0x4	0x8	0x3	0x5	0x9	0x6	0xA	0xC	0x7	0xB	0xD	0xE	0xF
$u = $ 0x0	x			x	x						x					
$u = $ 0x1		x		x		x					x					
$u = $ 0x2			x	x					x		x					
$u = $ 0x4		x		x			x				x					
$u = $ 0x8		x	x	x	x	x					x					
$u = $ 0x3			x			x	x	x	x	x	x		x			
$u = $ 0x5							x	x			x					
$u = $ 0x9			x		x	x			x	x				x		
$u = $ 0x6		x			x		x	x	x	x						
$u = $ 0xA			x	x			x	x		x		x	x	x	x	x
$u = $ 0xC			x		x		x				x					
$u = $ 0x7			x		x	x	x	x						x	x	
$u = $ 0xB			x	x	x	x			x	x	x	x		x		x
$u = $ 0xD			x	x	x		x			x		x			x	
$u = $ 0xE					x							x	x	x	x	x
$u = $ 0xF																x

where

$$V_s(u) = \{v \in \mathbb{F}_2^n \mid \text{ANF of } (\pi_v \circ S) \text{ contains } \pi_u(x)\}.$$

The definition of the parity set trivially derives the following proposition.

Proposition 1. *Let $\mathbb{X}$ be a multiset whose elements take a value of $\mathbb{F}_2^n$. When the multiset $\mathbb{X}$ has the bit-based division property $\mathcal{D}_{\mathbb{K}}^{1^n}$, the parity set of $\mathbb{X}$ fulfills*

$$\mathcal{U}(\mathbb{X}) \subseteq \{u \in \mathbb{F}_2^n : \text{there are } k \in \mathbb{K} \text{ satisfying } u \succeq k\}.$$

Moreover, assuming $\mathcal{U}(\mathbb{X}) \subseteq \mathbb{K}'$, the set $\mathbb{X}$ has the bit-based division property $\mathcal{D}_{\mathbb{K}'}^{1^n}$.

Proposition 1 shows that the bit-based division property of $S(\mathbb{X})$ can be evaluated from that of $\mathbb{X}$ via the parity set.

Case of PRESENT S-Box. As an example, let us consider the case of the PRESENT S-box. Let (x_4, x_3, x_2, x_1) and (y_4, y_3, y_2, y_1) be the input and output

---

[3]   In [12], the division property was referred to as $\mathcal{D}_{\mathbb{K}}^{n,m}$.

Table 2. Propagation of the bit-based division property for PRESENT S-box. Vectors on $\mathbb{F}_2^4$ are represented an hexadecimal notation.

k of input $\mathcal{D}_k^{1^4}$	$\mathbb{K}$ of output $\mathcal{D}_{\mathbb{K}}^{1^4}$	k of input $\mathcal{D}_k^{1^4}$	$\mathbb{K}$ of output $\mathcal{D}_{\mathbb{K}}^{1^4}$
0x0	{0x0}	0x8	{0x1, 0x2, 0x4, 0x8}
0x1	{0x1, 0x2, 0x4, 0x8}	0x9	{0x2, 0x4, 0x8}
0x2	{0x1, 0x2, 0x4, 0x8}	0xA	{0x2, 0x4, 0x8}
0x3	{0x2, 0x4, 0x8}	0xB	{0x2, 0x4, 0x8}
0x4	{0x1, 0x2, 0x4, 0x8}	0xC	{0x2, 0x4, 0x8}
0x5	{0x2, 0x4, 0x8}	0xD	{0x2, 0x4, 0x8}
0x6	{0x1, 0x2, 0x8}	0xE	{0x5, 0xB, 0xE}
0x7	{0x2, 0x8}	0xF	{0xF}

of the S-box, respectively, and the algebraic normal form of the PRESENT S-box is described as

$$y_4 = x_1x_2x_3 + x_1x_2x_4 + x_1x_3x_4 + x_2x_3 + x_1 + x_2 + x_4 + 1,$$
$$y_3 = x_1x_2x_4 + x_1x_3x_4 + x_1x_2 + x_1x_4 + x_2x_4 + x_3 + x_4 + 1,$$
$$y_2 = x_1x_2x_3 + x_1x_2x_4 + x_1x_3x_4 + x_2x_4 + x_3x_4 + x_2 + x_4,$$
$$y_1 = x_2x_3 + x_1 + x_3 + x_4.$$

Table 1 shows sets of $V_S(u)$ for all $u \in \mathbb{F}_2^4$ for the PRESENT S-box. Assuming that $\mathbb{X}$ fulfills $\mathcal{D}_k^{1^4}$, let $\mathcal{D}_{\mathbb{K}'}^{1^4}$ be the bit-based division property of $S(\mathbb{X})$ and $\mathbb{K}'$ is

$$\mathbb{K}' = \cup_{u \in \mathcal{U}(\mathbb{X})} V_s(u), \quad \mathcal{U}(\mathbb{X}) \subseteq \{u \in \mathbb{F}_2^n : u \succeq k\}$$

from Proposition 1. We compute $\mathbb{K}'$ for any $k \in \mathbb{F}_2^4$ and then remove redundant vectors. Table 2 shows the propagation characteristic of the bit-based division property for the PRESENT S-box.

3 Compact Representation for Division Property

3.1 Motivation

We can find more accurate integral characteristics by using the bit-based division property than the integer-based division property. However, this evaluation requires about 2^n time and memory complexity for n-bit block ciphers. Therefore, the bit-based division property is applied to small block-length ciphers like SIMON32 in [14]. Moreover, the application of the parity set is limited to the low-data distinguisher for a few rounds of PRESENT [2]. It is an open problem to apply the bit-based division property to high-data distinguishers for non small block-length cipher.

3.2   General Idea

The compact representation for the bit-based division property partially solves this problem. We focus on the fact that different division properties cause the same division property through an S-box. Then, we regard the different properties as the same property, and it helps us to evaluate the propagation characteristic efficiently.

Compact Representation for PRESENT S-box. The focus is that there are some input division properties whose output division property is the same. For example, the output division property from $\mathcal{D}^{1^4}_{\{0x1\}}$ is $\mathcal{D}^{1^4}_{\{0x1,0x2,0x4,0x8\}}$, which is the same as that from $\mathcal{D}^{1^4}_{\{0x2\}}$. In the compact representation, we regard their input properties as the same input property. Table 3 shows the compact representation for PRESENT S-box. While sixteen values are used to represent the bit-based division property, only seven values $\{\bar{0}, \bar{1}, \bar{3}, \bar{6}, \bar{7}, \bar{E}, \bar{F}\}$ are used in the compact representation. For simplicity, let $\mathbb{S}_c$ be

$$\mathbb{S}_c = \{\bar{0}, \bar{1}, \bar{3}, \bar{6}, \bar{7}, \bar{E}, \bar{F}\}.$$

Table 3. Compact representation for PRESENT S-box.

Compact	Real property	Output property	Redundant
$\bar{0}$	$\{0x0\}$	$\{0x0\}$	$\bar{0}, \bar{1}, \bar{3}, \bar{6}, \bar{7}, \bar{E}, \bar{F}$
$\bar{1}$	$\{0x1, 0x2, 0x4, 0x8\}$	$\{0x1, 0x2, 0x4, 0x8\}$	$\bar{1}, \bar{3}, \bar{6}, \bar{7}, \bar{E}, \bar{F}$
$\bar{3}$	$\{0x3, 0x5, 0x9, 0xA, 0xB, 0xC, 0xD\}$	$\{0x2, 0x4, 0x8\}$	$\bar{3}, \bar{7}, \bar{E}, \bar{F}$
$\bar{6}$	$\{0x6\}$	$\{0x1, 0x2, 0x8\}$	$\bar{6}, \bar{7}, \bar{E}, \bar{F}$
$\bar{7}$	$\{0x7\}$	$\{0x2, 0x8\}$	$\bar{7}, \bar{F}$
$\bar{E}$	$\{0xE\}$	$\{0x5, 0xB, 0xE\}$	$\bar{E}, \bar{F}$
$\bar{F}$	$\{0xF\}$	$\{0xF\}$	$\bar{F}$

Note that we have to check the original vectors when we remove redundant vectors. Assuming that the division property is $\mathcal{D}_{\{\bar{3},\bar{6},\bar{E}\}}$, each original vectors are represented as

$$\bar{3} \to \{0x3, 0x5, 0x9, 0xA, 0xB, 0xC, 0xD\}, \quad \bar{6} \to \{0x6\}, \quad \bar{E} \to \{0xE\}.$$

Therefore, $\bar{E}$ is redundant because $0xE \succeq 0xA$. On the other hand, there is not a vector $\boldsymbol{k}$ satisfying $0x6 \succeq \boldsymbol{k}$ in $\boldsymbol{k} \in \{0x3, 0x5, 0x9, 0xA, 0xB, 0xC, 0xD\}$. As a result, after remove redundant vectors, the division property becomes $\mathcal{D}_{\{\bar{3},\bar{6}\}}$. The right-end column in Table 3 shows redundant vectors by the compact representation.

3.3 Toy Cipher Using PRESENT S-box

We apply the compact representation to the input division property of S-boxes, and the propagated output division property is not represented by the compact representation. We need to carefully apply the compact representation to the output division property, which depends on the structure of a target cipher. For simplicity, let us consider a key-alternating cipher underlying PRESENT S-box, where the block length is 4 bits, and Fig. 1 shows the 2-round cipher. Let p and c be the plaintext and ciphertext, and x_i and y_i denote the input and output of the ith S-box, respectively. Note that the division property does not change for constant addition. Then, our aim is to evaluate the division property of c, and it is enough to manage only the compact representation of the division property in x_2. Our next aim is to evaluate the compact representation in x_2. Then, it is enough to manage only the compact representation in x_1 and the following propagation characteristic is applied.

$$\{\bar{0}\} \to \{0\text{x}0\} \to \{\bar{0}\},$$
$$\{\bar{1}\} \to \{0\text{x}1, 0\text{x}2, 0\text{x}4, 0\text{x}8\} \to \{\bar{1}\},$$
$$\{\bar{3}\} \to \{0\text{x}2, 0\text{x}4, 0\text{x}8\} \to \{\bar{1}\},$$
$$\{\bar{6}\} \to \{0\text{x}1, 0\text{x}2, 0\text{x}8\} \to \{\bar{1}\},$$
$$\{\bar{7}\} \to \{0\text{x}2, 0\text{x}8\} \to \{\bar{1}\},$$
$$\{\bar{\text{E}}\} \to \{0\text{x}5, 0\text{x}B, 0\text{x}E\} \to \{\bar{3}, (\bar{\text{E}})\},$$
$$\{\bar{\text{F}}\} \to \{0\text{x}F\} \to \{\bar{\text{F}}\}.$$

Note that the property $\bar{\text{E}}$ derives $\bar{3}$ and $\bar{\text{E}}$, but $\bar{\text{E}}$ is redundant.

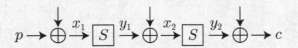

$$p \to \oplus \xrightarrow{x_1} \boxed{S} \xrightarrow{y_1} \oplus \xrightarrow{x_2} \boxed{S} \xrightarrow{y_2} \oplus \to c$$

Fig. 1. Key-alternating cipher underlying PRESENT S-box.

Example 1. Assuming the division property of p is $\{\bar{\text{E}}\}$, the division property of x_1 is also $\{\bar{\text{E}}\}$ because the division property is independent of the constant XORing. Applying the first S-box, the division property of y_1 is $\{\bar{3}, \bar{\text{E}}\}$, and $\bar{\text{E}}$ is redundant. Since the division property is independent of the constant XORing, the division property of x_2 is $\{\bar{3}\}$. Applying the second S-box, the bit-based division property of y_2 is $\mathcal{D}^{1^4}_{\{0\text{x}2, 0\text{x}4, 0\text{x}8\}}$, and the bit-based division property of c is also $\mathcal{D}^{1^4}_{\{0\text{x}2, 0\text{x}4, 0\text{x}8\}}$. Therefore, the least significant bit of c is balanced.

3.4 Core Function of PRESENT

PRESENT does not have simple key-alternating structure like Fig. 1. There is a bit permutation in the diffusion part of the round function, and we can decompose the round function of PRESENT into four subfunctions. Figure 2 shows the

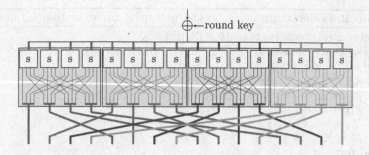

Fig. 2. Equivalent circuit of round function of PRESENT.

Algorithm 1. Generate propagation characteristic table for the sub function

1: **procedure** evalSubFunction($k \in (\mathbb{S}_c)^4$)
2:     $\mathbb{K}_i$ is the set of the propagated division property from k_i through the S-box.
3:     $\mathbb{K}'$ is an empty set.
4:     **for all** $(x, y, z, w) \in (\mathbb{K}_4 \times \mathbb{K}_3 \times \mathbb{K}_2 \times \mathbb{K}_1)$ **do**
5:         $k'_4 \Leftarrow \text{compact}(x_4 \| y_4 \| z_4 \| w_4)$
6:         $k'_3 \Leftarrow \text{compact}(x_3 \| y_3 \| z_3 \| w_3)$
7:         $k'_2 \Leftarrow \text{compact}(x_2 \| y_2 \| z_2 \| w_2)$
8:         $k'_1 \Leftarrow \text{compact}(x_1 \| y_1 \| z_1 \| w_1)$
9:         $\mathbb{K}' = \mathbb{K}' \cup \{k'\}$
10:     **end for**
11:     remove redundant vectors from $\mathbb{K}'$
12:     **return** $\mathbb{K}'$
13: **end procedure**

equivalent circuit of the round function of PRESENT. The input and output of every sub function are four four-bit values, and the position of each four-bit value then moves. Since this equivalent circuit does not have bit-oriented permutation except the interior of sub functions, we first generate the propagation characteristic table of sub functions under the compact representation. Then, we evaluate the propagation characteristic of round functions from the table under the compact representation.

Propagation Characteristic for Sub Function. Let $k = (k_4, k_3, k_2, k_1) \in (\mathbb{S}_c)^4$ be the input division property of the sub function. Then, the output division property $\mathbb{K}$ is the set whose elements are vectors in $(\mathbb{S}_c)^4$. Algorithm 1 shows the algorithm to generate the propagation characteristic table under the compact representation for the sub function. Here, compact is a function that converts from the bit-based division property to the compact representation.

Example 2 (Propagation characteristic from $(\bar{3}, \bar{6}, \bar{7}, \bar{F})$). The output bit-based division property of each S-box is evaluated from the corresponding compact representation as

---

Algorithm 2. Generate propagation characteristic table for the sub function

---

1: **procedure** evalRoundFunction($k \in (\mathbb{S}_c)^{16}$)
2:      $\mathbb{K}_i \Leftarrow$ evalSubFunction($[k_{4*i+4}, k_{4*i+3}, k_{4*i+2}, k_{4*i+1}]$)
3:      **for all** $(x, y, z, w) \in (\mathbb{K}_4 \times \mathbb{K}_3 \times \mathbb{K}_2 \times \mathbb{K}_1)$ **do**
4:          $k'_{16} = x_4, k'_{12} = x_3, k'_8 = x_2, k'_4 = x_1$
5:          $k'_{15} = y_4, k'_{11} = y_3, k'_7 = y_2, k'_3 = y_1$
6:          $k'_{14} = z_4, k'_{10} = z_3, k'_6 = z_2, k'_2 = z_1$
7:          $k'_{13} = w_4, k'_9 = w_3, k'_5 = w_2, k'_1 = w_1$
8:          $\mathbb{K}' = \mathbb{K}' \cup \{k'\}$
9:      **end for**
10:      remove redundant vectors from $\mathbb{K}'$
11:      **return** $\mathbb{K}'$
12: **end procedure**

$$\bar{3} \to \{0x2, 0x4, 0x8\}, \quad \bar{6} \to \{0x1, 0x2, 0x8\}, \quad \bar{7} \to \{0x2, 0x8\}, \quad \bar{F} \to \{0xF\}.$$

Then, let $\mathcal{D}_{\mathbb{K}'}^{1^4}$ be the output bit-based division property, and $\mathbb{K}'$ is represented as $18(= 3 \times 3 \times 2 \times 1)$ vectors

$$(0x11B5), (0x3195), (0x11F1), (0x31D1), (0x51B1), (0x7191),$$
$$(0x1935), (0x3915), (0x1971), (0x3951), (0x5931), (0x7911),$$
$$(0x9135), (0xB115), (0x9171), (0xB151), (0xD131), (0xF111).$$

Then, the compact representation of 18 vectors is

$$(\bar{1}\bar{1}\bar{3}\bar{3}), (\bar{3}\bar{1}\bar{3}\bar{3}), (\bar{1}\bar{1}\bar{F}\bar{1}), (\bar{3}\bar{1}\bar{3}\bar{1}), (\bar{3}\bar{1}\bar{3}\bar{1}), (\bar{7}\bar{1}\bar{3}\bar{1}), (\bar{1}\bar{3}\bar{3}\bar{3}), (\bar{3}\bar{3}\bar{1}\bar{3}), (\bar{1}\bar{3}\bar{7}\bar{1}),$$
$$(\bar{3}\bar{3}\bar{3}\bar{1}), (\bar{3}\bar{3}\bar{3}\bar{1}), (\bar{7}\bar{3}\bar{1}\bar{1}), (\bar{3}\bar{1}\bar{3}\bar{3}), (\bar{3}\bar{1}\bar{1}\bar{3}), (\bar{3}\bar{1}\bar{7}\bar{1}), (\bar{3}\bar{1}\bar{3}\bar{1}), (\bar{3}\bar{1}\bar{3}\bar{1}), (\bar{F}\bar{1}\bar{1}\bar{1}).$$

After remove redundant vectors, the output division property is represented as

$$(\bar{1}\bar{1}\bar{3}\bar{3}), (\bar{1}\bar{1}\bar{F}\bar{1}), (\bar{3}\bar{1}\bar{3}\bar{1}), (\bar{1}\bar{3}\bar{7}\bar{1}), (\bar{7}\bar{3}\bar{1}\bar{1}), (\bar{3}\bar{1}\bar{1}\bar{3}), (\bar{F}\bar{1}\bar{1}\bar{1})$$

by the compact representation.

4   Improved Integral Attack on PRESENT

4.1   New Algorithm to Find Integral Characteristics

We show a new algorithm to find integral characteristics of PRESENT by using the compact representation of the division property. Note that the given integral characteristic is the same as that given by the accurate propagation characteristic of the bit-based division property.

The input of the algorithm is the bit-based division property of the plaintext set. The algorithm first converts from this bit-based division property to the corresponding compact representation. In every round function, the algorithm evaluates the propagation characteristic for four sub functions independently and the relocation of 16 four-bit values. Algorithm 2 shows the algorithm to evaluate the propagation characteristic for round functions. This evaluation is repeated until there is no integral characteristic in the output of the round function.

7-Round Integral Characteristic Revisited. We first revisit the 16th order integral characteristic [15], where the lsb in the output of the 7-round PRESENT is balanced when the least sixteen bits are active and the others are constant. The bit-based division property of the plaintext set is $\mathcal{D}^{1^{64}}_{\text{0x00000000000000FF}}$, and the compact representation is

$$\bar{0}\bar{0}\bar{0}\bar{0}\bar{0}\dot{\bar{0}}\bar{0}\bar{0}\bar{0}\bar{0}\bar{0}\bar{0}\bar{0}\text{FF}.$$

Ciphertexts encrypted one round have the following compact representation

$$\bar{0}\bar{0}\bar{0}\text{F}\bar{0}\bar{0}\bar{0}\text{F}\bar{0}\bar{0}\bar{0}\text{F}\bar{0}\bar{0}\bar{0}\bar{\text{F}}.$$

Moreover, ciphertexts encrypted two rounds have the following compact representation

$$\bar{1}\bar{1}\bar{1}\bar{1}\bar{1}\bar{1}\bar{1}\bar{1}\bar{1}\bar{1}\bar{1}\bar{1}\bar{1}\bar{1}\bar{1}\bar{1}.$$

Table 4 shows the propagation characteristic, where we perfectly remove redundant vectors. After six rounds, we get 70 elements in the compact representation. We finally apply additional one-round function, and the propagated bit-based division property does not include 0x0000000000000001. Therefore, the lsb in the output of the 7-round PRESENT is balanced.

Table 4. Propagation from $\mathcal{D}^{1^{64}}_{\text{0x00000000000000FF}}$

#rounds	0	1	2	3	4	5	6	7[a]
$|\mathbb{K}|$		1	1	1	707281	349316	1450	70	63

[a]We do not use the compact representation in the final round.

New 9-Round Integral Characteristic. We next search for integral characteristics exploiting more number of active bits. Let us recall Table 3. Then, the propagated characteristic from $\bar{\text{E}}$ is $\{\text{0x5}, \text{0xB}, \text{0xE}\}$, and the output bit-based division property is most far from *unknown property* except for $\bar{\text{F}}$.

Table 5. Propagation from $\mathcal{D}^{1^{64}}_{\text{0xFFFFFFFFFFFFFFF0}}$

#rounds	0	1	2	3	4	5	6	7	8	9[a]
$|\mathbb{K}|$		1	1	81	8277	136421	2497368	343121	1393	70	63

[a]We do not use the compact representation in the final round.

We prepare the plaintext set that the least significant four bits are passive and the others are active, and the compact representation is

$$\bar{\text{F}}\bar{\text{F}}\bar{\text{F}}\bar{\text{F}}\bar{\text{F}}\bar{\text{F}}\bar{\text{F}}\bar{\text{F}}\bar{\text{F}}\bar{\text{F}}\bar{\text{F}}\bar{\text{F}}\bar{\text{F}}\bar{\text{F}}\bar{\text{F}}\bar{0}.$$

Table 6. Propagation from $\mathcal{D}_{\text{0xFFFFFFFFFFFFFFFE}}^{1^{64}}$

#rounds	0	1	2	3	4	5	6	7	8	9^a
$|\mathbb{K}|$		1	1	15	174	1053	96251	444174	19749	188	376

^{a}We do not use the compact representation in the final round.

Ciphertexts encrypted one round have the following compact representation

$$\text{FFF}\overline{\text{E}}\text{FFFFFFFFF}\overline{\text{E}}\text{FFFF}, \text{FFFFFFF}\overline{\text{E}}\text{FFFFFFFF}, \text{FFFFFFFFFFF}\overline{\text{E}}\text{FFFF}, \text{FFFFFFFFFFFFFFF}\overline{\text{E}}.$$

Moreover, the compact representation of ciphertexts encrypted two rounds consists of 81 elements, where all representations are represented by only $\overline{\text{E}}$ and $\overline{\text{F}}$. After eight rounds, we get 70 elements in the compact representation. We finally apply additional one-round function, and the propagated bit-based division property does not include 0x0000000000000001. Therefore, the lsb in the output of the 9-round PRESENT is balanced. Table 5 shows the propagation characteristic, where we perfectly remove redundant vectors.

The number of rounds that integral characteristics cover is clearly maximized when the number of active bits is 63. Therefore, we moreover search for integral characteristics exploiting 2^{63} chosen plaintexts. Then, we prepare the plaintext set that the least significant bit is passive and the others are active, and the compact representation is

$$\overline{\text{FFFFFFFFFFFFFFFE}}.$$

Ciphertexts encrypted one round have the following compact representation

$$\overline{\text{FFF}}\text{E}\overline{\text{FFFFFFFFF}}\text{F}\overline{\text{FFFF}}, \overline{\text{FFFFFFF}}\text{E}\overline{\text{FFFFFFFF}}, \overline{\text{FFFFFFFFFFFFFFF}}\text{E}.$$

Moreover, the compact representation of ciphertexts encrypted two rounds consists of 15 elements, where all compact representations are represented by only $\overline{\text{E}}$ and $\overline{\text{F}}$. After eight rounds, we get 188 elements in the compact representation. We finally apply additional one-round function, and the integral property is

$$\text{0xEEE0EEE0EEE0EEE0},$$

where E means that the 1st bit is balanced, and 0 means that all bits are balanced, i.e., 28 bits are balanced. Table 6 shows the propagation characteristic, where we perfectly remove redundant vectors.

4.2   Key Recovery with MTTS Technique and FFT Key Recovery

We attack 12-round PRESENT-80 and 13-round PRESENT-128 by using new 9-round integral characteristics. Our attack uses the match-through-the-S-box (MTTS) technique [19] and FFT key recovery [13]. We briefly explain their previous techniques.

Match-through-the-S-box (MTTS) Technique [19]. The MTTS technique was proposed by Zhang et al., and it is the extension of the meet-in-the-middle technique [9]. Let $x = (x_4, x_3, x_2, x_1)$ and $y = (y_4, y_3, y_2, y_1)$ be the input and output of the PRESENT S-box. Assuming that x_1 is balanced over a chosen plaintext set Λ, the aim is to recover round keys such that $\bigoplus_\Lambda x_1 = 0$. Then, $x_1 = y_4 y_2 \oplus y_3 \oplus y_1 \oplus 1$ from the ANF of S^{-1}, and $\bigoplus_\Lambda y_4 y_2 = \bigoplus_\Lambda y_3 \oplus y_1$ because $\bigoplus_\Lambda x_1 = 0$. Therefore, we independently evaluate the XOR of $y_4 y_2$ and that of $y_3 \oplus y_1$, and we then search for round keys that two XORs take the same value. In [19], Zhang et al. attacked 10-round PRESENT-80 and 11-round PRESENT-128 by using the MTTS technique.

Fast Fourier Transform (FFT) Key Recovery Technique [13]. The FFT key recovery was proposed by Todo and Aoki, and it was originally used for the linear cryptanalysis in [3]. We now evaluate the XOR

$$\bigoplus_\Lambda f_{k_1}(c \oplus k_2),$$

where f_{k_1} is a Boolean function depending on a round key k_1. Moreover, κ_1 and κ_2 are bit lengths of k_1 and k_2, respectively. Then, we can evaluate XORs over all (k_1, k_2) with $3\kappa_2 2^{\kappa_1 + \kappa_2}$ time complexity. Note that the time complexity does not depend on the number of chosen plaintexts. Therefore, we can easily evaluate the time complexity by only counting the bit length of involved round keys.

Integral Attack Against 12-Round PRESENT-80. Let X^i be the input of the $(i + 1)$th round function, and Y^i is computed as $Y^i = X^i \oplus K^i$, where K^i denotes the round key. Moreover, $X^i[j]$, $Y^i[j]$, and $K^i[j]$ denote the jth bit of X^i, Y^i, and K^i from the right hand, respectively. Here, X^0 is plaintexts, and Y^i is ciphertexts in i-round PRESENT. Figure 3 shows the 3-round key recovery for PRESENT.

In the first step, we choose 2^{60}-plaintext sets (denoted by Λ) and get corresponding ciphertexts after 12-round encryption. We store frequencies of two 32-bit values

$$Y_E = (Y^{12}[0], Y^{12}[2], \ldots, Y^{12}[62]) \quad Y_O = (Y^{12}[1], Y^{12}[3], \ldots, Y^{12}[63])$$

into voting tables.

In the second step, we compute the XOR of $(X^{10}[16] \times X^{10}[48])$ from Y_E by guessing involved round keys. The XOR is computed as

$$\bigoplus_\Lambda (X^{10}[16] \times X^{10}[48]) = f_{K^{10}[16,48], K^{11}[0,8,\ldots,56]}(Y_E \oplus K_E^{12}),$$

where $K_E^{12} = (K^{12}[0], K^{12}[2], \ldots, K^{12}[62])$. The FFT key recovery can evaluate the XOR with the time complexity $3 \times 32 \times 2^{2+8+32} = 3 \times 2^{47}$. Note that this time

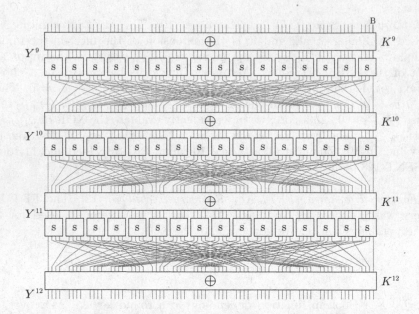

Fig. 3. 3-Round key recovery for PRESENT.

complexity is negligible because we already use 2^{60} time complexity to prepare chosen plaintexts.

In the third step, we compute the XOR of $(X^{10}[0] \oplus X^{10}[32])$ from Y_O by guessing involved round keys. The XOR is computed as

$$\bigoplus_\Lambda (X^{10}[0] \oplus X^{10}[32]) = f'_{K^{11}[4,12,\dots,60]}(Y_O \oplus K_O^{12}).$$

where $K_O^{12} = (K^{12}[1], K^{12}[3], \dots, K^{12}[63])$. Note that we do not need to guess $K^{10}[0]$ and $K^{10}[32]$ because they relate to $\bigoplus_\Lambda (X^{10}[0] \oplus X^{10}[32])$ linearly. Then, the XOR is evaluated with the time complexity $3 \times 32 \times 2^{8+32} = 3 \times 2^{45}$, and it is also negligible.

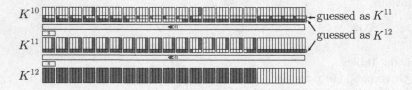

Fig. 4. Involved round keys of PRESENT-80.

In the fourth step, we search for round keys satisfying

$$\bigoplus_\Lambda (X^{10}[16]X^{10}[48]) = \bigoplus_\Lambda (X^{10}[0] \oplus X^{10}[32]).$$

Since involved round keys are 42 bits and 40 bits, the total is over 80 bits. However, from the key scheduling algorithm, the total bit length of involved round keys reduces to 68 bits (see Fig. 4). Therefore, by repeating this procedure N times, we can reduce the key space to 2^{68-N}.

Finally, we exhaustively search remaining keys, and the time complexity is 2^{80-N}. Therefore, the data complexity is $N \times 2^{60}$, and the time complexity is $(N \times 2^{60} + 2^{80-N})$ for $N \in \{1, 2, \ldots, 16\}$.

Integral Attack Against 13-Round PRESENT-128. We attack 13-round PRESENT-128 by using the similar strategy as the 12-round attack. We do not write the procedure in detail because of the page limitation.

Fig. 5. Involved round keys of PRESENT-128.

As a result, the FFT key recovery can evaluate the XOR of $(X^{10}[16] \times X^{10}[48])$ with the time complexity $3 \times 64 \times 2^{2+8+32+64} = 3 \times 2^{112}$. Moreover, the FFT key recovery can evaluate the XOR of $(X^{10}[0] \oplus X^{10}[32])$ with the time complexity $3 \times 64 \times 2^{8+32+64} = 3 \times 2^{110}$. While involved round keys are 112 bits and 110 bits, the total bit length of involved round keys reduces to 126 bits because of the key scheduling algorithm (see Fig. 5). Therefore, by repeating the procedure N times, we can reduce the key space to 2^{126-N}. Finally, we exhaustively search remaining keys. The time complexity is 2^{128-N}, and it is the dominant complexity. Therefore, the data complexity is $N \times 2^{60}$, and the time complexity is 2^{128-N} for $N \in \{1, 2, \ldots, 16\}$.

5 Conclusion

We proposed the compact representation for the bit-based division property in this paper. It is difficult to apply the bit-based division property to block ciphers whose block length is over 32 because of high time and memory complexity. The compact representation partially solves this problem. To demonstrate the advantage of our method, we applied this technique to 64-bit block cipher PRESENT. As a result, we attacked 12-round PRESENT-80 and 13-round PRESENT-128 by using new 9-round integral characteristic, and they are improved by two rounds than the previous best integral attacks.

References

1. Bogdanov, A., Knudsen, L.R., Leander, G., Paar, C., Poschmann, A., Robshaw, M.J.B., Seurin, Y., Vikkelsoe, C.: PRESENT: an ultra-lightweight block cipher. In: Paillier, P., Verbauwhede, I. (eds.) CHES 2007. LNCS, vol. 4727, pp. 450–466. Springer, Heidelberg (2007). doi:10.1007/978-3-540-74735-2_31
2. Boura, C., Canteaut, A.: Another view of the division property (2016). (Accepted to CRYPTO2016). https://eprint.iacr.org/2016/554
3. Collard, B., Standaert, F.-X., Quisquater, J.-J.: Improving the time complexity of Matsui's linear cryptanalysis. In: Nam, K.-H., Rhee, G. (eds.) ICISC 2007. LNCS, vol. 4817, pp. 77–88. Springer, Heidelberg (2007). doi:10.1007/978-3-540-76788-6_7
4. Daemen, J., Knudsen, L., Rijmen, V.: The block cipher Square. In: Biham, E. (ed.) FSE 1997. LNCS, vol. 1267, pp. 149–165. Springer, Heidelberg (1997). doi:10.1007/BFb0052343
5. Knudsen, L.R.: Truncated and higher order differentials. In: Preneel, B. (ed.) FSE 1994. LNCS, vol. 1008, pp. 196–211. Springer, Heidelberg (1995). doi:10.1007/3-540-60590-8_16
6. Knudsen, L., Wagner, D.: Integral cryptanalysis. In: Daemen, J., Rijmen, V. (eds.) FSE 2002. LNCS, vol. 2365, pp. 112–127. Springer, Heidelberg (2002). doi:10.1007/3-540-45661-9_9
7. Lai, X.: Higher order derivatives and differential cryptanalysis. In: Blahut, R.E., Costello, D.J., Maurer, U., Mittelholzer, T. (eds.) Communications and Cryptography. The Springer International Series in Engineering and Computer Science, vol. 276, pp. 227–233. Springer, Heidelberg (1994)
8. Li, Y., Wu, W., Zhang, L.: Improved integral attacks on reduced-round CLEFIA block cipher. In: Jung, S., Yung, M. (eds.) WISA 2011. LNCS, vol. 7115, pp. 28–39. Springer, Heidelberg (2012). doi:10.1007/978-3-642-27890-7_3
9. Sasaki, Y., Wang, L.: Meet-in-the-middle technique for integral attacks against feistel ciphers. In: Knudsen, L.R., Wu, H. (eds.) SAC 2012. LNCS, vol. 7707, pp. 234–251. Springer, Heidelberg (2013). doi:10.1007/978-3-642-35999-6_16
10. Sun, B., Hai, X., Zhang, W., Cheng, L., Yang, Z.: New observation on division property. IACR Cryptology ePrint Archive 2015, 459 (2015). http://eprint.iacr.org/2015/459
11. Todo, Y.: Integral cryptanalysis on full MISTY1. In: Gennaro, R., Robshaw, M. (eds.) CRYPTO 2015. LNCS, vol. 9215, pp. 413–432. Springer, Heidelberg (2015). doi:10.1007/978-3-662-47989-6_20
12. Todo, Y.: Structural evaluation by generalized integral property. In: Oswald, E., Fischlin, M. (eds.) EUROCRYPT 2015. LNCS, vol. 9056, pp. 287–314. Springer, Heidelberg (2015). doi:10.1007/978-3-662-46800-5_12
13. Todo, Y., Aoki, K.: FFT key recovery for integral attack. In: Gritzalis, D., Kiayias, A., Askoxylakis, I. (eds.) CANS 2014. LNCS, vol. 8813, pp. 64–81. Springer, Heidelberg (2014). doi:10.1007/978-3-319-12280-9_5
14. Todo, Y., Morii, M.: Bit-based division property and application to Simon family. IACR Cryptology ePrint Archive 2016, 285 (2016). (Accepted to FSE2016). https://eprint.iacr.org/2016/285
15. Wu, S., Wang, M.: Integral attacks on reduced-round PRESENT. In: Qing, S., Zhou, J., Liu, D. (eds.) ICICS 2013. LNCS, vol. 8233, pp. 331–345. Springer, Heidelberg (2013). doi:10.1007/978-3-319-02726-5_24
16. Yeom, Y., Park, S., Kim, I.: On the security of CAMELLIA against the square attack. In: Daemen, J., Rijmen, V. (eds.) FSE 2002. LNCS, vol. 2365, pp. 89–99. Springer, Heidelberg (2002). doi:10.1007/3-540-45661-9_7

17. Z'aba, M.R., Raddum, H., Henricksen, M., Dawson, E.: Bit-pattern based integral attack. In: Nyberg, K. (ed.) FSE 2008. LNCS, vol. 5086, pp. 363–381. Springer, Heidelberg (2008). doi:10.1007/978-3-540-71039-4_23
18. Zhang, H., Wu, W.: Structural evaluation for generalized feistel structures and applications to LBlock and TWINE. In: Biryukov, A., Goyal, V. (eds.) INDOCRYPT 2015. LNCS, vol. 9462, pp. 218–237. Springer, Heidelberg (2015). doi:10.1007/978-3-319-26617-6_12
19. Zhang, H., Wu, W., Wang, Y.: Integral attack against bit-oriented block ciphers. In: Kwon, S., Yun, A. (eds.) ICISC 2015. LNCS, vol. 9558, pp. 102–118. Springer, Heidelberg (2016). doi:10.1007/978-3-319-30840-1_7

An Automatic Cryptanalysis of Transposition Ciphers Using Compression

Noor R. Al-Kazaz$^{(\boxtimes)}$, Sean A. Irvine, and William J. Teahan

School of Computer Science, Bangor University,
Dean Street, Bangor, Gwynedd LL57 1UT, UK
{elp486,w.j.teahan}@bangor.ac.uk, sairvin@gmail.com
http://www.bangor.ac.uk/cs

Abstract. Automatically recognising valid decryptions as a result of ciphertext only cryptanalysis of simple ciphers is not an easy issue and still considered as a taxing problem. In this paper, we present a new universal compression-based approach to the automatic cryptanalysis of transposition ciphers. In particular, we show how a Prediction by Partial Matching (PPM) compression model, a scheme that performs well at many language modelling tasks, can be used to automatically recognise the valid decrypt with a 100 % success rate. We also show how it significantly outperforms another compression scheme, Gzip. In this paper, we propose a full mechanism for the automatic cryptanalysis of transposition ciphers which also automatically adds spaces to decrypted texts, again using a compression-based approach, in order to achieve readability.

Keywords: Cryptanalysis · Transposition ciphers · Plaintext recognition · Compression · PPM · Word segmentation

1 Introduction

Text compression is the method of deleting redundant information in some text in order to reduce space that is needed to store it, thereby minimising the time which is also needed to transmit this information without losing any information from the original text. Practically, there are two major ways of constructing text compression models: dictionary and statistical approaches [1]. Prediction by Partial Matching (or PPM) is a finite-context statistical based approach while Gzip is an example of a dictionary based approach (which uses the Lempel-Ziv algorithm [9]). PPM models perform well on English text compared to other models and they emulate human predictive ability [25].

There are variety of approaches and algorithms used for cryptanalysis. Using compression schemes as one way to tackle the plaintext recognition problem is still a relatively new approach with few publications. In essence, we investigate how to devise better solutions to the plaintext recognition problem by using transposition ciphers as a test bed. In this paper, we propose a novel compression-based approach for the automatic cryptanalysis of transposition ciphers with

© Springer International Publishing AG 2016
S. Foresti and G. Persiano (Eds.): CANS 2016, LNCS 10052, pp. 36–52, 2016.
DOI: 10.1007/978-3-319-48965-0_3

no need for any human intervention. Furthermore, we propose further methods also based on using compression to automatically insert spaces back into the decrypted texts in order to achieve readability (as we perform our experiments on English alphabetic characters).

The paper is organised as follows. The next section gives a brief description of most of the previous research into the cryptanalysis of transposition ciphers. Section 3 motivates the use of our compression-based approach as a method of tackling the plaintext recognition problem and reviews the calculations of the codelength metric used by our method which is based on the PPM and Gzip compression schemes. Transposition ciphers are described in Sect. 4. The full description of our method and the pseudo-code is illustrated in Sect. 5. Our experimental results are discussed in Sect. 6.

2   Previous Work

Various cryptanalysis methods have been used to break transposition ciphers, starting with traditional attacks such as exhaustive search and anagramming, and then leading to genetic algorithm based methods. Anagramming is a well-known traditional cryptanalysis method. It is the method of repositioning disarranged letters into their correct and original positions [10,20,22]. Although, the traditional attacks are more successful and easy to implement, but automating these types of attack is not an easy issue. It requires an experienced and trained cryptanalyst. Mathematical techniques have been used in these attacks but the main role tends to be on the human expert. The final decision is made by the human cryptanalyst with regards to which algorithm is used in attack.

Many researchers have been interested in developing and automating cryptanalysis against transposition ciphers. One of the earliest papers was published by Matthews in 1993 [17]. He presented an attack on transposition ciphers using a genetic algorithm known as GENALYST. The fitness function was based on the frequency of the common English digrams and trigrams that appear in the deciphered text. This attack was only successful at key size of 7, with no successes at key length of 9 and 11. It achieved average success rates of 2–4 %.

Clark [5] published three algorithms that used simulated annealing, genetic algorithm and tabu search in the cryptanalysis of transposition ciphers. The fitness function used also depended on the frequencies of digrams and trigrams. By using a genetic algorithm, the success rates of block sizes of 4 and 6 ranged from 5 to 91 %. Tabu search was faster than the other algorithms while simulated annealing was the slowest but with a high performance of solving ciphertexts especially with large periods. It was able to correctly recover 26 of the key elements, for a transposition cryptosystem of period 30 [4]. Dimovsk and Gligoroski [8] came to similar conclusions presented in Clark's publication. The fitness function that was used in their paper was based on bigrams statistics due to the expensive task of calculating trigrams statistics.

Toemeh and Arumugam [26] used a genetic algorithm to break transposition ciphers. They used a slightly modified list of the most common bigram and trigrams than were used in Clark paper. Three additional trigrams EEE, AND and ING were included with the Clark table. They concluded that when the ciphertext size is larger, the number of breakable keys increases.

In 2003, a genetic algorithm was presented by Grundlingh and Van Vuuren [12], which resulted in a 6–7 % success rate. The fitness function they used in their research was based on the discrepancies between the expected number of occurrences of a digram in a natural language text (per N characters), and the observed count of this digram in a ciphertext of length N. For this attack, no convergence of fitness function values had been found. They concluded that genetic algorithmic attacks were not effective against columnar transposition ciphers since this cipher is more robust than substitution ciphers. This attack was only successful at a key size of 7.

A permutation-based genetic algorithm was used by Bergmann, Scheidler and Jacob [2]. Two fitness functions were used in this research. The first function was based on calculating the redundancy of the decrypted text, then comparing it to the expected redundancy of the same sized English text and the same sized random text. The second function was based on the use of known text appearing in a message. Hamming Distance was used to check the presence of this supplied piece of known text in the decrypted text at a predetermined position. A transposition cipher with a key size of up to 12 and 500 characters in length was able to be deciphered correctly using this algorithm.

Giddy and Safavi-Naini [11] used a simulated annealing approach. The algorithm was not able to decrypt the cipher correctly, if the length of this ciphertext was short (100 characters or less). They noted that this is the supposed behaviour of all cryptanalysis schemes. Ciphertexts that have dummy characters added to them were decrypted poorly as well. The cost function here was based in terms of bigram frequencies.

As mentioned above, many of the research methods applied genetic algorithms to the automatic cryptanalysis of transposition ciphers. They used different key lengths ranging from 2 to 30 with different ciphertext lengths. None of these algorithms were able to correctly recover all the plaintext and achieve full success. In fact, Delman [7] concluded that the genetic algorithm-based approach did not deserve further effort. He stated that further investigation in traditional cryptanalysis techniques was warranted rather than for genetic algorithms.

Two heuristics were adopted by Russell, Clark and Stepeny [19]. They used the Ant Colony System algorithm which used a dictionary to recognise the plaintext, and bigrams to indicate adjacent columns. This attack was able to decipher shorter cryptograms (300 characters) by a factor of about a half compared to other previous meta-heuristic methods. Chen and Rosenthal [3] used a Markov chain Monte Carlo method to break transposition ciphers. Bigram statistics was used as a base to calculate the score function. This method presented a good performance with key length 20 and 2000 characters ciphertext. Wulandari, Rismawan and Saadah [27] presented another attack against transposition ciphers by using a differential evolution algorithm. The fitness function was based on bigram and trigram statistics. This algorithm was able to decrypt the ciphertext correctly, with key lengths up to 9; with key length equal to 10, it was able to find half of the correct answers.

Irvine [15] has been the only researcher to date to have used a compression algorithm to break a cipher system—in this case, substitution ciphers. He used a compression algorithm (PPM model) combined with simulated annealing approach to perform an automated cryptanalysis of substitution ciphers. He was able to achieve a success rate of 83 %. However, a similar approach has yet to have been applied to other ciphers systems, including transposition ciphers.

In this paper, we will propose a novel compression-based approach for the automatic recognition of the plaintext of transposition ciphers with a 100 % success rate. We will use different key lengths (ranging from 2 to 12) and different ciphertext lengths, even very short messages with only 12 characters while the shortest messages used in the previous research was not less than 100 characters. In our paper, we will present both a method for automatically decrypting transposition ciphertexts and then automatically achieving readability subsequently. This will automatically insert spaces into the decrypted text, while most of the previous works did not address or refer to this fundamental aspect of the cryptanalysis.

3   Compression as a Cryptanalysis Method

The ciphertext only attack (cryptanalysis) of simple ciphers is not a trivial issue as evidenced by the wide range of literature in the previous section. It heavily depends on the source language and its statistical features. Particularly in ciphertext only attack, it is difficult to recognise the right decrypt quickly. Many of the published cryptanalysis techniques can not run without human intervention, or they assume that at least the plaintext is known, in order to be able to detect the proper decryption quickly.

Having a computer model that is able to predict and model natural language as well as a human is critical for cryptology [24]. Teahan showed that PPM compression models had the ability to predict text with performance levels close to expert humans [25]. The basic idea of our approach depends on using the PPM model as a method for computing the compression 'codelength' of each possible permutation which is a measure of the information [15] contained in each. Permutations with shorter codelengths help to reveal better decrypts. We show how to use this to easily and automatically recognise the true decrypt in a ciphertext only attack against transposition ciphers. In this paper, we also try another compression method, Gzip, as a basis for calculating the codelength metric in order to determine which is the most effective compression method to use to recognise the valid decryptions, but with significantly less success compared to the PPM-based method.

3.1   PPM Compression Code Length Metric

Prediction by Partial Matching, or PPM, is a finite-context statistical based approach. This technique was first described in 1984 by Cleary and Witten [6]. The major concept of this modelling is dependent on using previous symbols (called the context of order k, where k represents the number of prior symbols) to predict the next or upcoming symbol. The number of symbols used in the context defines the maximum order of the context model.

For each context model, prediction probabilities can be calculated from the observation of all symbols or characters that have succeeded every length-k subsequence, as well as from the frequencies of occurrence for each character. A different predicted probability distribution is gained from each model; as a result, the probabilities of each character or symbol that has followed the previous k characters (the previous time) are used to estimate the next character. PPM models have been shown to be very effective at compressing English and have comparable performance to human experts' predictive ability [25].

Several PPM variations have been devised depending on the methods that have been suggested for computing the probabilities of each symbol. PPMD is one of these variants first developed by Howard [13]. Experiments show that in most cases, PPMD performs better than the other variants PPMA, PPMB and PPMC. It is similar to PPMC with the exception that the probability estimation of a new symbol or character is different. The treatment of the new symbols becomes more consistent [14] through adding $\frac{1}{2}$ to the count of the new symbol and to the escape count as well:

$$ e = \frac{t}{2n} \quad \text{and} \quad p(s) = \frac{2c(s) - 1}{2n} $$

where e denotes the escape probability, $p(s)$ is the probability of symbol s, $c(s)$ is the number of times that the symbol s followed the context, n denotes the number of tokens that have followed and t refers to the number of types. For example, if a specific context has occurred three times previously, with three symbols a, b and c following it one time, then, the probability of each one of them is equal to $\frac{1}{6}$ and escape symbol probability is $\frac{3}{6}$.

The essential idea of our approach depends on using a PPMD compression model to compute codelength values of each possible permutation. From a compression point of view, the 'codelength' of a permutation for a cryptogram is simply the absolute ratio of the cryptogram length (in bits) when compressed to the cryptogram length in characters. In particular, the smaller the codelength, the more likely the cryptogram is close to the language source. By using this metric for assessing the quality of the solution, it can be used for finding valid decryptions automatically.

One of the most important steps in our implementation is the step of priming the compression models using a large set of English training data. This step allow us to overcome the problem of using an uninitialised compression scheme, where at the beginning of a message there is not enough and sufficient data to effectively compress the texts.

3.2 Calculating Codelengths Using the Gzip Compression Method

Gzip or GNU zip is one of the most important compression utilities. It is one of the most common lossless compression method on the Unix operating system and on the Internet. It was written by Jean- Loup Gailly and Mark Adler. The Gzip compression scheme is a dictionary based approach (using Lempel-Ziv algorithm [9]) whereas PPM is a statistical context based approach.

The fundamental reason of experimenting with another compression method (Gzip) in our approach is to determine which is the most effective method, when applying to the problem of plaintext recognition using a compression-based approach.

In our paper, we will calculate the codelength values for the Gzip compression scheme by using a relative entropy technique. As a result, we do not need to re-implement the Gzip compression scheme itself, we can simply use "off-the-shelf" software. We calculate the codelength value using the relative entropy method using the equation $h_t = h_{T+t} - h_T$ where T is some large training data, h represents the file size after it has been compressed, and t represents the testing text. Simply, the basic idea of this method is to calculate the difference (in size) between the compressed training text with the testing text added to it compared to the size of the compressed training text by itself.

We also tested our relative entropy method using another well-known compression scheme, Bzip2. This is another lossless compression scheme that uses a block sorting algorithm. However, due to the algorithm's nature, some of the relative entropy calculations ended up being negative, so these could not be used.

4   Transposition Ciphers

In cryptography, a transposition cipher is a method of encryption by which the content of a message is concealed by rearranging groups of letters, therefore resulting in a permutation. The concept of transposition is an essential one and has been used in the design of modern ciphersystems [23]. Originally, the message was written out into a matrix in row-order and then read out by column-order [15]. The technique can be expanded to d dimensions, by dividing a message into blocks or groups of fixed size d (called the period) and perform a permutation over these blocks. This permutation represents the key. The size of the key is the same as the length of the block. Generally, if $f : Z_d \rightarrow Z_d$ is a permutation over Z_d, $Z_d = \{1, ..., d\}$, then according to f, blocks of fixed length (d characters) are encrypted by applying a permutation to the characters [18,21]. For example, if $d = 4$ and the plaintext $x = 1234$ then the encrypted message (ciphertext) f might have the permutation: $f(x)$: 4213. Here, the first character in the original message is moved to the third position, the third character in the block to the fourth position, and the fourth character to the first position. Thus the original message cryptographydemo is encrypted as:

Position: 1234 1234 1234 1234
Plaintext: cryp togr aphy demo
Ciphertext: prcy rotg ypah oedm

This ciphertext is divided into blocks of four letters and in order to hide the key size (period), a stream of characters is transmitted continuously. In the case of a short block at the end, it would be encrypted by moving the letters to their relative permutation positions with dummy letters added or just left blank.

In general, transposition ciphers are considered much harder to crack than other basic cryptosystems such as simple substitution ciphers. Many statistical tools have been developed aiding automated cryptanalysis of substitution ciphers while the automatic cryptanalysis of transposition ciphers has proven more difficult. Generally, cryptanalysis of transpositions is quite interventionist in that it requires some knowledge of the probable contents of the encrypted text to give an idea into the rearrangement order that has been used [17].

5 Our Method

In this section, we will give a full description of the new approach for the automatic cryptanalysis of transposition ciphertext. The basic idea of our approach depends on using a compression model as a method of computing the 'codelength' of each possible permutation. This compression model and the codelenghth metric represent the assessment function that can be relied on it to automatically rank alternative permutations and recover correct messages. In our method, the PPMD and Gzip compression methods are used in the experiment.

Our new approach consists of two essential phases. The main idea of the first phase (Phase I) depends on trying to break a ciphertext automatically using a transposition of specified size by exhaustively computing all possible transpositions. The second phase (Phase II) focuses on inserting spaces automatically (segmenting words) into the decrypted message which is outputted from the first phase in order to achieve readability (since we remove spaces from the ciphertext at the beginning of Phase I, as is traditional).

The pseudo-code for our method is presented in Figs. 1, 2 and 3. At the beginning of the first phase (Phase I), we remove all the spaces from the encrypted message as presented in line 3 in Fig. 1. The approach at this stage uses text comprising just 26 alphabetic English characters). The text is divided into blocks with a specified size according to the period (key size) of transposition (see line 6 in Fig. 1). Then, all possible transpositions are generated, and the compression codelength recomputed at each stage (see line 7 to 10 in the next figure). PPM and Gzip are used as the means for computing the codelength. As we start to get permutations with smaller codelength values, this means we are closer to finding the correct message. In other words, the hope is that the cryptogram that has the smallest codelength value will represent the valid decrypted message.

As the output of the previous phase are texts without any spaces, the second phase focuses on inserting spaces into the input text automatically 'segmenting words', in order to achieve readability. We have investigated two alternative ways of doing this. In the first method, Phase II-A, according to the decrypted message permutation which is outputted from the previous phase, all further possibilities are explored where a space is inserted after each character. Underperforming possibilities which have bad colelength values are pruned from the priority queue and only the best performing possibilities are returned at the end (see Fig. 2).

```
1- READ ciphertext
2- SET maximum-period of transposition to a specified size
3- REMOVE spaces from the ciphertext
4- FOR each period
5-     IF ciphertext length divided by period equal to 0 THEN
6-          DIVIDE the ciphertext into blocks according to the period
7-          FOR each possible permutation
8-               CALCULATE codelength value using PPM compression
                 model or Gzip
9-               STORE a permutation that have smaller codelength
                 value in priority queue
10-         ENDFOR
11-    ENDIF
12- ENDFOR
13- RETURN priority queue
```

Fig. 1. Pseudo-code for main decryption phase, Phase I

In the second method, Phase II-B, the Viterbi algorithm is used to search for the best probable segmentation sequences (see Fig. 3). Compression schemes are used as a base of measuring codelengths and automatically detecting correct solutions in both these two alternatives (Phase II-A and Phase II-B). The pseudo code of the two approaches are shown in Figs. 2 and 3.

In our method, we have used two variants of the PPMD model, one without update exclusions [24] and the standard PPMD. This was done to investigate

```
1- SET priority queue Q1 to have the decrypted message from the priority
   queue from Phase I
2- REPEAT
3-     SET Q2 to empty
4-     FOR each message in the priority queue Q1
5-          CREATE new message with a single space addad
6-          INSERT modified message into Q2
7-          CALCULATE codelength value for the new message using PPM
            compression model or Gzip method
8-          STORE new message that have a smaller codelength value
            than those in the priority queue Q2
9-     ENDFOR
10-    IF there is any improvement in the codelength value THEN
11-         REPLACE Q1 with Q2
12- UNTIL there is no improvement in the value of the codelength
13- RETURN front of priority queue Q1
```

Fig. 2. Pseudo-code for Phase II-A

```
1- READ message from the priority queue from Phase I
2- USE Viterbi algorithm to search for the best probable segmentation
   sequences
3- RETURN Decrypted message which have best segmentations that present
   the best encoding sequence
```

Fig. 3. Pseudo-code for Phase II-B

which is the most effective model when applied to the problem of the automatic cryptanalysis of transposition ciphers.

In order to clarify and organize our experiments and results, we divide our different experiments into different variants with a specified label as shown in the Table 1.

Table 1. Variants used in our experiments

Variants	Phase I	Phase II-A	Phase II-B
Variant A	PPMD with no update exclusions	PPMD with no update exclusions	
Variant B	PPMD with no update exclusions		PPMD with no update exclusions
Variant C	PPMD	PPMD	
Variant D	PPMD		PPMD
Variant G	Gzip	Gzip	

According to Table 1, the first variant is called Variant A. In this variant, PPMD without update exclusions is used to calculate the compression code-length values. This is used for the main deception phase—Phase I and for Phase II-A as well. All cryptograms can be solved using an order-4 model. In the second variant Variant B, PPMD4 without update exclusions is used in both phases Phase I and in Phase II-B. The Viterbi algorithm is used in the second phase.

A different version of the PPMD compression model is used in the third variant, which is named "Variant C". The standard PPMD4 (with update exclusion) is used as the method for calculating the codelength values for both phases (Phase I and Phase II-A). Variant D uses the standard order-4 PPMD, as well in the calculation of the codelength values. For the second phase, Phase II-B, this compression model is also used as a basis for segmenting the words.

For variant G, we examine the effectiveness of another type of compression method which is the Gzip compression system. The Gzip algorithm is used in the main decryption phase and for the second phase "Phase II-A", as the basis for computing the codelength metric.

6   Experimental Results

In our method, the order-4 PPMD models were trained on nineteen novels and the Brown corpus using 26 and 27 character (including space) English text. After this training operation, these models remain static during cryptanalysis. In our experiments, we use a corpus of 90 cryptograms with different lengths form different resources as testing texts. The lengths of the ciphertexts that have been examined in our experiments are ranging from 12 letters to over 600 letters. Table 2 presents a sample of decryption.

Table 2. Output sample for the different phases for the ciphertext 'prcy rotg ypah oedm'. (Compression codelengths are listed in bits with the lowest 5 results presented for Phase-II-A.)

Phase I	Phase II-A	Phase II-B
53.73 cryptographydemo	42.85 cryptography demo	Cryptography demo
	50.94 cryptographyde mo	
	59.41 cryptographyd emo	
	59.68 cryptograph ydemo	
	67.64 c ryptographydemo	

A random key is generated to encipher the original text (plaintext) for each run. After that, the attack is performed on the ciphertext. Different key sizes (period or permutation size) and different ciphertexts with different lengths have been experimented in our method. The results of the first phase Phase I by using the PPM method showed that all the valid decryptions were recognised and all the ciphertexts were able to be decrypted successfully with no errors. In our method, and with different variants, except Variant G, we achieve a success rate of 100 %. We have used different key size (block sizes) from two to twelve. We experimented with 90 different standard ciphertexts with different lengths (including very short) with different key sizes and all can be solved correctly. In contrast, by using the Gzip algorithm in the last variant (G), we achieved a success rate of 94 % as result of Phase I.

For each variant, we have performed two types of experiments (except for Variant G). Since in Phase I we deal with texts without any spaces included, our first experiment is done by using PPMD models after being trained on 26 English characters (instead of 27) as the basis of calculating codelengths. In the other experiment, PPMD compression models trained on 27 character English texts were used. The output result from these two experiments is the same achieving a 100 % success rate.

The second phase focused on inserting spaces automatically into the decrypted message that is outputted from the first phase. We used the Levenshtein distance as a metric of measuring differences between the plaintext and the decrypted text with spaces. Levenshtein distance metric is a commonly used string metric for counting the differences between two strings (such as insertions, deletions or substitution) [16]. In our approach, in almost all cases the correct (readable) solution was found. The next table (Table 3) provides example output (with spaces) produced by the different variants.

Table 3. Example of solved cryptograms with spaces by different variants.

Variants	Number of errors	Decrypted message (with spaces)
Variant A	2	an excuse is worse and more terrible than
		a **lief or** an excuse is a lie guarded
Variant B	0	an excuse is worse and more terrible than
		a lie for an excuse is a lie guarded
Variant C	3	an**e**xcuse is worse and more terrible than
		a **lief or** an excuse is a lie guarded
Variant D	1	an**e**xcuse is worse and more terrible than
		a lie for an excuse is a lie guarded
Variant G	14	an**e**xcuse**i**s**w**orse and**m**ore**t**errible
		than**alieforan**excuse**i**s**a**lie**g**uarded

For variant A, Fig. 4 shows the number of errors for each testing text as a result of the second phase. Clearly, we can see that most of the space insertion errors are less than two. The results show that 50 % of texts have correctly inserted spaces with no errors, and more than 45 % of the cryptograms are solved with three errors or less. The errors that occurred in some of the solved cryptograms were minor ones, all involving spaces only. There are just three examples that showed either 6 or 7 errors, the main reason being that each of these examples had unusual words on particular topics not occurring in the training data.

Variant B produces less errors than other variants. The results show that 59 % of the decrypted texts have correctly added spaces with no errors. Furthermore, over 36 % of the examples are spaced with just two or one errors, and about 4 % with three errors. Just two examples had six errors and all of these are shown in Fig. 5.

Variant C produces slightly worse results, with just 46 % of examples having successfully inserted spaces without any errors with about 45 % are spaced with three errors or less. In addition, nine of the solved cryptograms have four errors or more. Figure 6 shows the results of variant C. On the other hand, variant D presents very good results, it produces similar results to variant B but with a few minor differences.

Figure 7 presents the number of errors for variant G as a result of phase two. Clearly the number of errors for each solved cryptogram is much higher, in this case with most of the space insertion errors being greater than 15. Moreover,

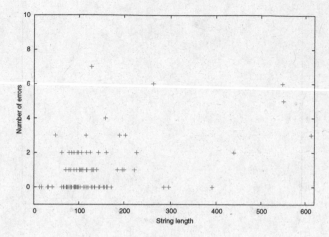

Fig. 4. Errors produced from variant A

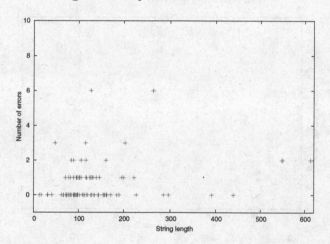

Fig. 5. Errors produced from variant B

none of the examples produced no errors and there is just five decrypted texts that were spaced with less than 10 errors.

Table 4 presents results concerning the average number of space insertion errors for the 90 texts we experimented with for each of the variants. It is clear that variant B produces the best results although other variants produce good results as well. What is interesting is that the PPM method without update exclusions which usually does slightly worse at the task of compression, does better here at decryption.

The last column in the table presents the number of average errors for variant G. The results show that the Gzip algorithm is not a good way for finding the right solutions with a high average number of errors.

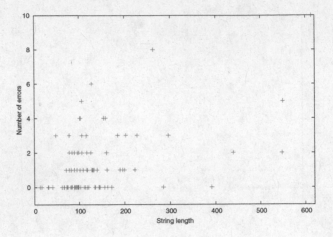

Fig. 6. Errors produced from variant C

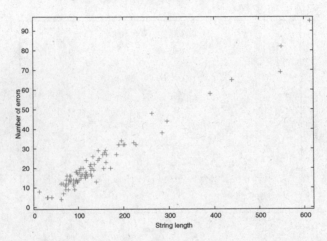

Fig. 7. Errors produced from variant G

In order to investigate further the accuracy of our spaces insertion algorithms in segmenting the 90 decrypted texts, we used three further metrics: recall rate, precision rate and error rate. Recall is calculated by dividing the number of correctly segmented words (using a compression model) by the total number of words in our original 90 testing texts. The error rate metric is calculated by dividing the number of incorrectly segmented words by the total number of words in the testing texts. Precision is calculated by dividing the number of correctly segmented words by the total number of words which are correctly and incorrectly segmented.

According to Table 5, it is clear that the first four variants, which are based on PPMD compression models, achieve quit high recall rates, which indicates

Table 4. Average number of errors for the phase two variants.

Variants	A	B	C	D	G
Average errors	1.02	0.69	1.30	0.81	21.62

Table 5. Recall, precision and error rates for the different variants on segmenting words.

Variants	Recall rate %	Precision rate %	Error rate %
Variant A	95.08	95.08	4.92
Variant B	96.30	96.38	3.70
Variant C	93.91	94.34	6.09
Variant D	95.71	95.91	4.29
Variant G	3.96	16.11	96.04

high accuracy of segmenting the 90 decrypted texts. All the errors generated, which are quite low, are those on unusual words not found in the training texts.

The average elapsed time that is required to find the valid decryptions of the transposition ciphertexts with different lengths for different key size is presented in Table 6. This table shows the average execution time for decrypting three ciphertexts of different lengths, for both the main decryption and spaces insertion phases combined (labelled as 'Both' in the table) and just for the main decryption phase (Phase I). The time which is needed to insert spaces automatically into the decrypted text (the second phase) is based on the execution of Phase II-A (slightly additional time is needed when using Phase II-B). The average execution time in seconds for each ciphertext is calculated by running the program ten times and then calculating the average.

In summary, the results showed that we are able to achieve 100 % success rate as a result of the first phase (Phase I) either by using standard PPMD or PPMD with-no update exclusions models. We manage to recognise all the plaintexts and solve all the cryptograms in this phase without any errors. We have used different block sizes (periods) ranging from two to twelve.

Table 6. Average required time to automatically cryptanalysis ciphertexts with different lengths for different keys size.

Ciphertext length (letter)	Key size											
	Time (in seconds)											
	5		6		7		8		9		10	
	Both	Phase I	Both	Phase I	Both	Phase I	Both	Phase I	Both	Phase I	Both	Phase I
40	0.72	0.68	0.73	0.69	0.77	0.75	0.97	0.93	2.40	2.38	12.07	12.06
150	1.12	0.7	1.14	0.73	1.20	0.80	1.77	1.35	13.75	10.06	48.07	47.07
300	3.39	0.71	3.62	0.75	3.71	0.87	4.86	1.97	23.01	20.41	95.32	92.41

In the second phase, we add spaces to these texts to improve readability by using two methods. The first method is a slightly faster new method based on a priority queue while the second method uses Viterbi algorithm to segment words. Our results show that almost all decrypted texts are segmented correctly. The maximum average number of errors (due to space insertions in incorrect places), when using PPMD compression models, is just slightly over one (for Variant C). This variant depends on the standard PPMD compression model as a basis for calculating the codelength values in Phase II-A. The results showed that by using the Viterbi algorithm (Phase II-B), we can gain slightly better results than the other method (Phase II-A), but it needs slightly more execution time. Variant B showed the best results. This variant depends on using a PPMD without update exclusions model using the Viterbi method as the basis for segmenting words.

7   Conclusions

We have introduced another use of the compression-based approach for cryptanalysis. A novel universal automatic cryptanalysis method for transposition ciphers and plaintext recognition method have been described in this paper. Experimental results have shown a 100 % success rate at automatically recognising the true decryptions for a range of different length ciphertexts and using different key sizes. This effective algorithm completely eliminates any need for human intervention. The basic idea of our approach depends on using a compression scheme as a base of calculating the 'codelength' metric, which is an accurate way of measuring information in the text. In this paper, we provided pseudo-code for two main phases: automatically decrypting ciphertexts and then automatically achieving readability using compression models to automatically insert spaces into the decrypted texts, as we performed our experiments on ciphertext in alphabetic English characters, while most previous works did not address this essential problem.

Two compression schemes have been investigated in our paper which are Predication by Partial Matching (PPM) and Gzip. The experimental results showed that PPM notably outperforms the other compression scheme Gzip. We also found that both PPMD variants were able to recognise all the valid decryptions. Concerning automatically adding spaces (word segmentation) afterwards, PPMD without update exclusions performs slightly better than the standard PPMD method (with update exclusions). The algorithm was able to achieve 100 % success rate using the PPM compression model on different amounts of ciphertext ranging from 12 to 625 characters, and with different key lengths ranging from 2 to 12. Larger key sizes and longer ciphertext length can be used, but of course it will require longer execution times to perform the decryptions.

Acknowledgments. The authors would like to thank the Iraqi Ministry of Higher Education and Scientific Research (MOHESR)-Baghdad University-College of science for women for supporting (sponsoring) this work.

References

1. Bell, T.C., Cleary, J.G., Witten, I.H.: Text Compression. Prentice-Hall, Upper Saddle River (1990)
2. Bergmann, K.P., Scheidler, R., Jacob, C.: Cryptanalysis using genetic algorithms. In: Proceedings of the 10th Annual Conference on Genetic and Evolutionary Computation, pp. 1099–1100. ACM, July 2008
3. Chen, J., Rosenthal, J.S.: Decrypting classical cipher text using Markov chain Monte Carlo. Stat. Comput. **22**(2), 397–413 (2012)
4. Clark, A.J.: Optimisation heuristics for cryptology. Ph.D. thesis, Queensland University of Technology (1998)
5. Clark, A.J.: Modern optimisation algorithms for cryptanalysis. In: Proceedings of the 1994 Second Australian and New Zealand Conference on Intelligent Information Systems, pp. 258–262. IEEE, December 1994
6. Cleary, J., Witten, I.: Data compression using adaptive coding and partial string matching. IEEE Trans. Commun. **32**(4), 396–402 (1984)
7. Delman, B.: Genetic algorithms in cryptography (2004)
8. Dimovski, A., Gligoroski, D.: Attacks on the transposition ciphers using optimization heuristics. In: International Scientific Conference on Information, Communication and Energy Systems and Technologies, ICEST, October 2003
9. Gailly, J.L.: GNU gzip (2010)
10. Gaines, H.F.: Cryptanalysis: Study a of Ciphers and Their Solutions. Dover, New York (1956)
11. Giddy, J.P., Safavi-Naini, R.: Automated cryptanalysis of transposition ciphers. Comput. J. **37**(5), 429–436 (1994)
12. Grundlingh, W., Van Vuuren, J.H.: Using genetic algorithms to break a simple cryptographic cipher. Retrieved 31 March 2003
13. Howard, P.G.: The design and analysis of efficient lossless data compression systems (1993)
14. Howard, P.G., Vitter, J.S.: Practical implementations of arithmetic coding. Department of computer science. Brown university. Providence, Rhode Island 02912, CS-91-45, July 1991
15. Irvine, S.A.: Compression and cryptology. Ph.D. thesis, University of Waikato, NZ (1997)
16. Levenshtein, V.I.: Binary codes capable of correcting deletions, insertions, and reversals. Sov. Phys. Dokl. **10**(8), 707–710 (1966)
17. Matthews, R.A.: The use of genetic algorithms in cryptanalysis. Cryptologia **17**(2), 187–201 (1993)
18. Robling, D., Dorothy, E.: Cryptography and data security (1982)
19. Russell, M.D., Clark, J.A., Stepney, S.: Making the most of two heuristics: breaking transposition ciphers with ants. In: The 2003 Congress on Evolutionary Computation, CEC 2003, vol. 4, pp. 2653–2658. IEEE, December 2003
20. Seberry, J., Pieprzyk, J.: Cryptography: An Introduction to Computer Security. Prentice Hall, Sydney (1989)
21. Shannon, C.E.: Communication theory of secrecy systems. Bell Syst. Tech. J. **28**(4), 656–715 (1949)
22. Sinkov, A.: Elementary Cryptanalysis. Mathematics Association of America, Random House (1966)
23. Stamp, M., Low, R.M.: Applied Cryptanalysis: Breaking Ciphers in the Real World. John Wiley and Sons, Hoboken (2007)

24. Teahan, W.J.: Modelling English text. Ph.D. thesis, University of Waikato, New Zealand (1998)
25. Teahan, W.J., Cleary, J.G.: The entropy of English using PPM-based models. In: Proceedings Data Compression Conference, Snowbird, Utah, pp. 53–62 (1996)
26. Toemeh, R., Arumugam, S.: Breaking Transposition Cipher with Genetic Algorithm. Electron. Electr. Eng. **7**(79) (2007)
27. Wulandari, G.S., Rismawan, W., Saadah, S.: Differential evolution for the cryptanalysis of transposition cipher. In: 2015 3rd International Conference on Information and Communication Technology (ICoICT), pp. 45–48. IEEE, May 2015

SideChannel Attacks and Implementation

Side-Channel Attacks on Threshold Implementations Using a Glitch Algebra

Serge Vaudenay[✉]

EPFL, 1015 Lausanne, Switzerland
serge.vaudenay@epfl.ch
http://lasec.epfl.ch

Abstract. Threshold implementations allow to implement circuits using secret sharing in a way to thwart side-channel attacks based on probing or power analysis. It was proven they resist to attacks based on glitches as well. In this report, we show the limitations of these results. Concretely, this approach proves security against attacks which use the average power consumption of an isolated circuit. But there is no security provided against attacks using a non-linear function of the power traces (such as the mean of squares or the majority of a threshold function), and there is no security provided for cascades of circuits, even with the power mean. We take as an example the threshold implementation of the AND function by Nikova, Rechberger, and Rijmen with 3 and 4 shares. We further consider a proposal for higher-order by Bilgin *et al.*

1 Introduction

Since the late 1990's, many side-channel attacks based on either power analysis or probing have been presented. We consider essentially two types of attacks. In Differential power attacks (DPA), the adversary collects many samples of the sum of the power used by all gates of the circuit with noise. In Probing attacks, the adversary gets a few intermediate values of the computation by probing the circuit. All measures are subject to noise and can be modeled [2]. Duc *et al.* have shown that these two attacks are essentially equivalent [4].

One devastating type of attack is based on "glitches". It takes into account that electric signals are not necessarily a classical 0/1 signal but a real function over a clock period which is non constant. For instance, the signal can be intermediate between 0 and 1, or switching several times between 0 and 1 during the clock period, or a signal with a very short switching peak, etc. The CMOS technology uses very little power. Signals switching in between clock periods use power. Essentially, only signal switches use power. So, a glitch induces an abnormal power consumption which is visible during a clock period [5].

To avoid these attacks, *masking* is a common method. Essentially, instead of running the computations based on inputs x and y to obtain a result z, we first use a secret sharing for x and y to split it into n random shares $(x_1, \ldots, x_n)$ and $(y_1, \ldots, y_n)$ and run the computation on the shares to obtain a sharing $(z_1, \ldots, z_n)$ of z. Usually, the secret sharing is the simple (n, n)-scheme in which

© Springer International Publishing AG 2016
S. Foresti and G. Persiano (Eds.): CANS 2016, LNCS 10052, pp. 55–70, 2016.
DOI: 10.1007/978-3-319-48965-0_4

$x = x_1 \oplus \cdots \oplus x_n$, $y = y_1 \oplus \cdots \oplus y_n$, and $z = z_1 \oplus \cdots \oplus z_n$. Trichina, Korkishko, and Lee [11] proposed an implementation of an AND gate with $n = 2$.

In [7], Nikova, Rechberger, and Rijmen proposed the *threshold implementation* which transforms a gate (such as an AND gate) into a circuit which resists to probing attacks with a single probe or DPA based on the average of the power consumption. One construction uses $n = 3$ and another one with $n = 4$ has the property that output shares are always balanced. In [1], Bilgin *et al.* extend this method to higher orders, to make circuits resisting to 2 probes or DPA based on a 2nd order moment of the power consumption. They propose an implementation of an AND gate with $n = 5$ but this implementation requires internal flip/flop registers, thus induce latencies, just to have a secure AND circuit. These constructions were recently consolidated in [9].

Our results. As the glitch propagation model highly depends on concrete implementations, in this paper, we consider several models for accounting glitches obtained by the XOR of two glitched signals. We do not advertise any model to be better but rather show how little influence the model has on the security results. In a first model, the "double-glitch" simply counts as twice a normal glitch. In this model, the mean power for the construction with $n = 2$ does not leak. In a second model, the double-glitch counts as a normal one. In a third model, the two glitches cancel each other and do not count. In the two latter models, the construction with $n = 2$ leaks from the mean power.

In the mentioned constructions using $n > 2$, we show that two probes leak, that some non-linear function of the power (such as the mean of squares or the majority of a threshold function) leak, and that by composing two circuits implementing two AND gates, one probe leaks.

Finally we show that in the three models, the AND construction using $n = 5$ (the one resisting 2nd order attacks) does not resist to an attack with two probes when we do not add internal flip/flop registers.

The security claims coming with these implementations from the literature are of the form "if [*conditions*] then we have security". We do not contradict any of these results. In this paper, we complement them by showing that when the conditions are not met, we clearly have insecurity. So, these conditions are not only sufficient: they are also necessary.

2   The Theory

2.1   The Glitch Algebra

Algebra is "the part of mathematics in which letters and other general symbols are used to represent numbers and quantities in formulae and equations". Herein, we propose to represent glitches as well and to do operations on glitches.

In what follows we use the following conventions: a "signal" is a function from a clock cycle $[0, \tau]$ to $\mathbf{R}$; we consider real numbers as constant signals, we consider bits as real numbers in $\{0, 1\}$; $+$ and $\times$ denote the addition and multiplication of reals; $\oplus$, $\vee$, and $\wedge$ denote the XOR, OR, and AND of signals.

A signal "represents" a bit. To avoid confusion, from now on we denote with regular letters a signal and we denote with a bar the bit it is supposed to represent. We say that a signal x has no glitch if it is constant and equal to the bit $\bar{x}$ it represents. The functions $\oplus$, $\vee$, and $\wedge$ are defined by the gates implementing these functions. We only know that they match what we know about bits: $a \oplus b = a + b \mod 2$, $a \vee b = \max(a, b)$, and $a \wedge b = ab$ when a and b have no glitch. Furthermore, we define a function glitch giving the "number of glitches" in a signal and a function power giving the power consumption of a gate. We assume that $\mathsf{glitch}(x) = 0$ if x has no glitch. The function glitch applies to a signal but the function power applies to a gate. Concretely, a gate $g = \mathsf{op}(a, b)$ with output signal c corresponds to $\mathsf{power}(g) = \mathsf{glitch}(c)p_{\mathsf{op}}$ where p_{op} is a constant. So, $\mathsf{power}(g) = 0$ if $\mathsf{op}(a, b)$ has no glitch. Actually, this is an approximation. Essentially, it is assumed that a stable signal uses very little power while a glitch induces a high power consumption, like in the CMOS technology [5]. The assumption on the influence of glitches on the power consumption may be a bit arbitrary. In the sequel, we take for granted that when y has no glitch, then $x \oplus y$ has the same glitch as x. When y has no glitch and $\bar{y} = 0$, we assume that $x \wedge y$ has no glitch either (due to the AND with 0). When y has no glitch and $\bar{y} = 1$, we assume that $x \wedge y$ has the same glitch as x. So,

$$\mathsf{glitch}(x \wedge y) = \begin{cases} 0 & \text{if } \mathsf{glitch}(y) = 0 \text{ and } \bar{y} = 0 \\ \mathsf{glitch}(x) & \text{if } \mathsf{glitch}(y) = 0 \text{ and } \bar{y} = 1 \end{cases}$$

$$\mathsf{glitch}(x \oplus y) = \mathsf{glitch}(x) \text{ if } \mathsf{glitch}(y) = 0$$

We further define $\Sigma\mathsf{power}$ as the sum of $\mathsf{power}(g)$ for all gates g in a circuit.

It is not quite clear how to define $\mathsf{glitch}(x \wedge y)$ for two glitched signals x and y in general. Even for $\mathsf{glitch}(x \oplus y)$, we may take one of the following assumptions:

$$\mathsf{glitch}(x \oplus y) = \mathsf{glitch}(x) + \mathsf{glitch}(y) \tag{1}$$
$$\mathsf{glitch}(x \oplus y) = \max(\mathsf{glitch}(x), \mathsf{glitch}(y)) \tag{2}$$
$$\mathsf{glitch}(x \oplus y) = \mathsf{glitch}(x) \oplus \mathsf{glitch}(y) \tag{3}$$

These assumptions are quite reasonable in theory. (1) accounts for glitches which cumulate, for instance because they occur at different time in a clock period. (2) assumes that a glitch can be hidden by another one. (3) comes from saying that two perfectly identical glitches should cancel each other in a XOR. However, reality is more complex and probably a mixture of these three models:

$$\mathsf{glitch}(x \oplus y) = F(\mathsf{glitch}(x), \mathsf{glitch}(y))$$

for some symmetric function F. For simplicity, we will study these simple assumptions. We will see that nearly all assumptions give the same results. Each defines some kind of "glitch algebra" on which we can do computations.

In this report, we consider two types of side-channel attacks based on glitches.

– Power analysis: the adversary can see $\Sigma\mathsf{power}$ with noise.
– Probing attack: for a gate g, the adversary can get $\mathsf{glitch}(g)$ with some noise.

Duc *et al.* have shown that these two attacks are equivalent [4].

2.2   Side-Channel Attack with Noise

In side-channel attack, we measure a quantity S in a discrete domain $\mathcal{D}$ but the measurement comes with noise so we obtain $Z = S + \mathsf{noise}$. We assume that S follows a distribution P_b^S depending on a secret bit b. We want to make a guess X for b. An algorithm taking some random input and giving X as output is a distinguisher. The Type I error is $\alpha = \Pr[X = 1|b = 0]$. The Type II error is $\beta = \Pr[X = 0|b = 1]$. The error probability is $P_e = \Pr[X \neq b] = \alpha \Pr[b = 0] + \beta \Pr[b = 1]$ so depends on the distribution of b. The advantage of the distinguisher is $\mathsf{Adv} = |\Pr[X = 1|b = 0] - \Pr[X = 1|b = 1]| = |\alpha + \beta - 1|$.

If P_b^Z denotes the obtained distribution for Z. We know that the largest advantage using one single sample Z is $\mathsf{Adv} = d(P_0^Z, P_1^Z)$ defined by the statistical distance between P_0^Z and P_1^Z.

$$d(P_0^Z, P_1^Z) = \frac{1}{2} \sum_z |\Pr[Z = z|b = 0] - \Pr[Z = z|b = 1]|$$

Theorem 1 (Precision amplification). *Given an elementary distinguisher computing X from Z, with Type I error probability $\alpha \leq \frac{1}{2}$ and Type II error probability $\beta \leq \frac{1}{2}$, for any N we can construct a distinguisher such that from i.i.d. samples $Z_1, \ldots, Z_N$ we compute X with error probability*

$$P_e' \leq e^{-N\left(\frac{1}{2} - \min(\alpha, \beta)\right)^2} \tag{4}$$

Taking $N = 2\left(\frac{1}{2} - \min(\alpha, \beta)\right)^{-2}$, we obtain $P_e' \leq e^{-2} \approx 13\,\%$.

Proof. We use the elementary distinguisher to compute the $X_1, \ldots, X_N$ corresponding to $Z_1, \ldots, Z_N$. Then, we compute $X = \mathsf{majority}(X_1, \ldots, X_N)$.

Using the Chernoff bound (Lemma 2 below), we obtain a new distinguisher with errors α_N and β_N such that $\alpha_N \leq e^{-N\left(\frac{1}{2} - \alpha\right)^2}$ and $\beta_N \leq e^{-N\left(\frac{1}{2} - \beta\right)^2}$. So, the error probability $P_e' = \alpha_N \Pr[b = 0] + \beta_N \Pr[b = 1]$ obtained by taking the majority vote decreases exponentially fast with N. As $\min(\alpha, \beta) \leq \alpha, \beta \leq \frac{1}{2}$, we obtain the result. $\qquad\square$

Lemma 2 (Chernoff [3]). *Let $X_1, X_2, \ldots, X_N$ be N independent boolean variables such that that $E(X_i) = p$ for all i. We define $X = \mathsf{majority}(X_1, \ldots, X_N)$. For all $p < \frac{1}{2}$, we have*

$$\Pr[X \neq 0] \leq e^{-N\left(\frac{1}{2} - p\right)^2}$$

For all $p > \frac{1}{2}$, we have

$$\Pr[X \neq 1] \leq e^{-N\left(\frac{1}{2} - p\right)^2}$$

In what follows, we assume that the noise is Gaussian, centered, independent from S, and that the ratio of the standard deviation of the noise and of S is a given value σ. So, noise has a variance of $\sigma^2 V(S)$. Hence,

$$\Pr[\mathsf{noise} \leq -x] = \frac{1}{2}\mathsf{erfc}\left(\frac{x}{\sqrt{2\sigma^2 V(S)}}\right)$$

Threshold distinguisher. We consider the distinguisher computing $X = 1_{Z \leq \tau}$. In the Gaussian noise model, the Type I error is

$$\alpha = \Pr[X = 1 | b = 0] = \sum_s \Pr[S = s | b = 0] \Pr[\text{noise} \leq \tau - s]$$

by symmetry of the noise distribution, the Type II error is

$$\beta = \Pr[X = 0 | b = 1] = \sum_s \Pr[S = s | b = 1] \Pr[\text{noise} \leq s - \tau]$$

By adjusting τ so that $\alpha = \beta = P_e$, we obtain that $N = 2 \left(\frac{1}{2} - P_e \right)^{-2}$ is enough to reach $P_e' \approx 13 \%$.

Case study for $S = 1 - b$ and b uniform. If $S = 1 - b$ and b is uniform, we have $V(S) = \frac{1}{4}$. We adjust $\tau = \frac{1}{2}$ and obtain $\alpha = \beta = \frac{1}{2}\text{erfc} \left(\frac{0.5}{\sigma} \sqrt{2} \right)$. We obtain from Theorem 1 that $N = 2 \left(\frac{1}{2} - \frac{1}{2}\text{erfc} \left(\frac{0.5}{\sigma} \sqrt{2} \right) \right)^{-2}$. For instance, with $\sigma = 1$, we have $P_e \approx 16 \%$ and $N = 17$. With $\sigma = 2$, we have $P_e \approx 31 \%$ and $N = 55$. We obtain that $N \sim_{\sigma \to +\infty} 4\pi\sigma^2$ using $\text{erfc}(t) = 1 - \frac{2t}{\sqrt{\pi}} + o(t)$ for $t \to 0$. So, we see that $N = \mathcal{O}(\sigma^2)$ is enough to guess b with error limited to a constant. This is a quite favorable attack as we can measure b directly.

Attack for $n = 1$. As an example, given an AND gate $z = x \wedge y$ (with no threshold protection, or equivalently $n = 1$), assuming that y is stable equal to some secret $\bar{y}$ and that $\text{glitch}(x) = 1$, we have $\text{glitch}(z) = \bar{y}$. So, an attack measuring $S = \text{glitch}(z)$ deduces $\bar{y}$ trivially. We are in the case where $S = \text{glitch}(z) = \bar{y}$ is binary and balanced. So, the above equation governs the complexity N of recovering $\bar{y}$ using no threshold implementation and noise characterized by σ.

Pushing to higher order measures. We can wonder what happens if, for some reasons, S does not leak but S^2 leaks. Then, we should look at Z^2 instead of Z. But $Z^2 = S^2 + \text{noise}'$ with $\text{noise}' = 2S\text{noise} + \text{noise}^2$. By neglecting the quadratic noise, we have $V(\text{noise}') \approx 4V(S)V(\text{noise}) = 4\sigma^2 V(S)^2$. Assuming $V(S^2) \approx V(S)^2$, we can see that the effect of moving from S to S^2 is only in doubling the value of σ. As we will see, a motivation of threshold cryptography is to prevent leaks at a lower order S to make the adversary look at higher order. This actually penalizes a bit the adversary.

3   Implementation with $n = 2$

Trichina *et al.* [11] proposed an implementation of the AND gate to compute $z = x \wedge y$ by using $n = 2$: 1. (secret sharing for x) pick $a \in_U \mathbf{Z}_2$ and compute $\tilde{x} = a \oplus x$; 2. (secret sharing for y) pick $b \in_U \mathbf{Z}_2$ and compute $\tilde{y} = b \oplus y$; 3. (secret sharing for z) pick $c \in_U \mathbf{Z}_2$; 4. compute

$$\tilde{z} = (((c \oplus (a \wedge b)) \oplus (a \wedge \tilde{y})) \oplus (b \wedge \tilde{x})) \oplus (\tilde{x} \wedge \tilde{y})$$

by respecting the order of the parentheses; 5. the output $(\tilde{z}, c)$ shares $z = c \oplus \tilde{z}$.

In [7], Nikova, Rechberger, and Rijmen observe that if the input signal x has a glitch and y is a secret input, then by analyzing the power consumption of the above gate we can easily deduce y. Indeed, assuming that an AND or XOR gate uses an abnormal power scheme proportional to the number of "glitch" on their result, the number of gates using an abnormal power scheme depends on y. So, we assume that $\mathsf{glitch}(x) = 1$ and $\mathsf{glitch}(\{a, b, c, y\}) = 0$.

We have

$$
\begin{aligned}
\mathsf{glitch}(\tilde{x}) &= 1 & \mathsf{glitch}(\tilde{x} \wedge \tilde{y}) &= \bar{\tilde{y}} = \bar{b} \oplus \bar{y} \\
\mathsf{glitch}(\tilde{y}) &= 0 & \mathsf{glitch}((c \oplus (a \wedge b) \oplus (a \wedge \tilde{y})) \oplus (b \wedge \tilde{x})) &= \bar{b} \\
\mathsf{glitch}(b \wedge \tilde{x}) &= \bar{b} &&
\end{aligned}
$$

so

$$
\mathsf{glitch}(z) = \begin{cases} \bar{b} + \bar{\tilde{y}} \text{ with Assumption (1)} \\ \bar{b} \vee \bar{\tilde{y}} \text{ with Assumption (2)} \\ \bar{y} \quad \text{ with Assumption (3)} \end{cases}
$$

$$
\Sigma\mathsf{power} = (\bar{b} + \bar{\tilde{y}})p_{\mathsf{AND}} + \left\{ \begin{array}{l} 2\bar{b} + \bar{\tilde{y}} \quad \text{ with Assumption (1)} \\ \bar{b} + \bar{b} \vee \bar{\tilde{y}} \text{ with Assumption (2)} \\ \bar{b} + \bar{y} \quad \text{ with Assumption (3)} \end{array} \right\} \cdot p_{\mathsf{XOR}}
$$

If $\bar{y} = 0$, we have $\bar{\tilde{y}} = \bar{b}$ so

$$
\Sigma\mathsf{power} = 2\bar{b}p_{\mathsf{AND}} + \left\{ \begin{array}{l} 3\bar{b} \text{ with Assumption (1)} \\ 2\bar{b} \text{ with Assumption (2)} \\ \bar{b} \ \text{ with Assumption (3)} \end{array} \right\} \cdot p_{\mathsf{XOR}}
$$

For $\bar{y} = 1$, this is $\Sigma\mathsf{power} = p_{\mathsf{AND}} + (1 + \bar{b}) \cdot p_{\mathsf{XOR}}$ for Assumptions (1, 2, 3). So,

$$
E(\Sigma\mathsf{power}|\bar{y} = 1) - E(\Sigma\mathsf{power}|\bar{y} = 0) = \left\{ \begin{array}{l} 0 \text{ with Assumption (1)} \\ \frac{1}{2} \text{ with Assumption (2)} \\ 1 \text{ with Assumption (3)} \end{array} \right\} \cdot p_{\mathsf{XOR}}
$$

It is explicitly said in [8, p. 297] that

"The power consumption caused by the glitch is related to the number of gates that *see* the glitch. It is clear [...] that the energy consumption depends on the values of [b and $\tilde{y}$]. Since the <u>mean power consumption</u> is different for $y = 0$ and $y = 1$, the power consumption leaks information on the value y."

The computation done in [8] to analyze the leakage was based on Assumption (1) as we can easily check from [8, Table 1]. So, we contradict this claim for Assumption (1): $E(\Sigma\mathsf{power})$ is independent from $\bar{y}$ in this case. However, it is true that $E(\Sigma\mathsf{power})$ leaks $\bar{y}$ for Assumptions (2) and (3). For this implementation, the choice of the "glitch algebra" gives different conclusions.

Similarly, in attacks based on probing z, we can see that $E(\mathsf{glitch}(z)) = 1$ which is independent from $\bar{y}$ in Assumption (1). For Assumption (2), we have

$E(\mathsf{glitch}(z)) = \frac{1}{2}$ which is also independent from $\bar{y}$. For Assumption (3), we have $\mathsf{glitch}(z) = \bar{y}$. In the latter case, we can see that $E(\mathsf{glitch}(z))$ leaks $\bar{y}$ so noisy samples for $\mathsf{glitch}(z)$ leak $\bar{y}$ using the amplification technique of Eq. (4).

This made [7] propose a "threshold implementation" of an AND gate using $n = 3$ or $n = 4$ shares, the above example being an example using $n = 2$ shares. They prove that, contrarily to this example, probing a single gate in the computation leaks no information on any of the input x and y, on average. They deduce that their implementations resist to the above attacks based on glitches. We will show the limitations of this result with effective attacks.

4   Implementation with $n = 3$

Assuming that (x_1, x_2, x_3) shares x, (y_1, y_2, y_3) shares y, and (z_1, z_2, z_3) shares z, Nikova, Rechberger, and Rijmen [7] propose

$$z_1 = (x_2 \wedge y_2) \oplus ((x_2 \wedge y_3) \oplus (x_3 \wedge y_2))$$
$$z_2 = (x_3 \wedge y_3) \oplus ((x_1 \wedge y_3) \oplus (x_3 \wedge y_1))$$
$$z_3 = (x_1 \wedge y_1) \oplus ((x_1 \wedge y_2) \oplus (x_2 \wedge y_1))$$

This construction satisfies the conditions from Nikova et al. [7]. We quote [7]:

"**Theorem 3.** [...] the mean power consumption of a circuit implementing realization [above] is independent of $[\bar{x}, \bar{y}]$, even in the presence of glitches or the delayed arrival of some inputs."

Although we do not contradict the independence of the mean with the input values, we show that a probing attack can leak $\bar{y}$ easily. We further show that a cascade of this construction also leaks with the mean of power consumption.

In the attacks, we will assume that none of the y_i variables have a glitch, and that they are independent from the glitches in the x_i variables.

With Assumption (1), we have

$$\mathsf{glitch}(x_i \wedge y_j) = \mathsf{glitch}(x_i)\bar{y}_j$$
$$\mathsf{glitch}((x_i \wedge y_j) \oplus (x_j \wedge y_i)) = \mathsf{glitch}(x_i)\bar{y}_j + \mathsf{glitch}(x_j)\bar{y}_i$$
$$\mathsf{glitch}(z_1) = \mathsf{glitch}(x_2)(\bar{y}_2 + \bar{y}_3) + \mathsf{glitch}(x_3)\bar{y}_2$$
$$\mathsf{glitch}(z_2) = \mathsf{glitch}(x_3)(\bar{y}_3 + \bar{y}_1) + \mathsf{glitch}(x_1)\bar{y}_3$$
$$\mathsf{glitch}(z_3) = \mathsf{glitch}(x_1)(\bar{y}_1 + \bar{y}_2) + \mathsf{glitch}(x_2)\bar{y}_1$$

so

$$\Sigma\mathsf{power} = \sum_{i,j} \mathsf{glitch}(x_i)\bar{y}_j p_{\mathsf{AND}} + \sum_i \mathsf{glitch}(x_i)(2\bar{y}_1 + 2\bar{y}_2 + 2\bar{y}_3 - \bar{y}_i)p_{\mathsf{XOR}}$$

In the glitch value of each gate, we can see that at least one variable $\bar{y}_i$ is not present (indeed, the construction was made for that). Since the $\bar{y}_i$ are uniformly distributed conditioned to $\bar{y} = \bar{y}_1 \oplus \bar{y}_2 \oplus \bar{y}_3$, no matter the value of $\bar{y}$, the two present $\bar{y}_i$ variables are uniformly distributed. So, the distribution of any glitch value is independent from $\bar{y}$. Consequently, it is the case for their mean value. Since Σpower is a linear combination of these values, due to the linearity of the mean operator, this is also the case for Σpower.

With Assumption (2), by writing $\max(\bar{y}_i, \bar{y}_j) = \bar{y}_i \vee \bar{y}_j$, we have

$$\mathsf{glitch}(x_i \wedge y_j) = \mathsf{glitch}(x_i)\bar{y}_j$$
$$\mathsf{glitch}((x_i \wedge y_j) \oplus (x_j \wedge y_i)) = \max(\mathsf{glitch}(x_i)\bar{y}_j, \mathsf{glitch}(x_j)\bar{y}_i)$$
$$\mathsf{glitch}(z_1) = \max(\mathsf{glitch}(x_2)(\bar{y}_2 \vee \bar{y}_3), \mathsf{glitch}(x_3)\bar{y}_2)$$
$$\mathsf{glitch}(z_2) = \max(\mathsf{glitch}(x_3)(\bar{y}_3 \vee \bar{y}_1), \mathsf{glitch}(x_1)\bar{y}_3)$$
$$\mathsf{glitch}(z_3) = \max(\mathsf{glitch}(x_1)(\bar{y}_1 \vee \bar{y}_2), \mathsf{glitch}(x_2)\bar{y}_1)$$

Like above, the mean value of any of these expression is independent from $\bar{y}$.

With Assumption (3), we have

$$\mathsf{glitch}(x_i \wedge y_j) = \mathsf{glitch}(x_i)\bar{y}_j$$
$$\mathsf{glitch}((x_i \wedge y_j) \oplus (x_j \wedge y_i)) = \mathsf{glitch}(x_i)\bar{y}_j \oplus \mathsf{glitch}(x_j)\bar{y}_i$$
$$\mathsf{glitch}(z_1) = \mathsf{glitch}(x_2)(\bar{y}_2 \oplus \bar{y}_3) \oplus \mathsf{glitch}(x_3)\bar{y}_2$$
$$\mathsf{glitch}(z_2) = \mathsf{glitch}(x_3)(\bar{y}_3 \oplus \bar{y}_1) \oplus \mathsf{glitch}(x_1)\bar{y}_3$$
$$\mathsf{glitch}(z_3) = \mathsf{glitch}(x_1)(\bar{y}_1 \oplus \bar{y}_2) \oplus \mathsf{glitch}(x_2)\bar{y}_1$$

so

$$\Sigma\mathsf{power} = \sum_{i,j} \mathsf{glitch}(x_i)\bar{y}_j p_{\mathsf{AND}} + \left(\sum_i \mathsf{glitch}(x_i)((\bar{y}_i \oplus \bar{y}_{i+1}) + \bar{y}_{i-1}) \right.$$
$$\left. - \sum_i \mathsf{glitch}(x_i)\mathsf{glitch}(x_{i+1})((\bar{y}_i \oplus \bar{y}_{i+1})\bar{y}_i) \right) p_{\mathsf{XOR}}$$

Like above, the mean value of any of these expression is independent from $\bar{y}$.

4.1 Power Analysis not Based on the Mean Value (All Assumptions)

We have already seen that no glitch value has a distribution which depends on $\bar{y}$. So let us focus on the distribution of Σpower. With $\mathsf{glitch}(x_1) = 1$ and $\mathsf{glitch}(x_2) = \mathsf{glitch}(x_3) = 0$, we obtain with Assumption (1) that

$$\Sigma\mathsf{power} = (\bar{y}_1 + \bar{y}_2 + \bar{y}_3)(p_{\mathsf{AND}} + 2p_{\mathsf{XOR}}) - \bar{y}_1 p_{\mathsf{XOR}}$$

With Assumption (2), our previous computations simplify to

$$\mathsf{glitch}(x_i \wedge y_j) = \begin{cases} 0 & \text{if } i \neq 1 \\ \bar{y}_j & \text{if } i = 1 \end{cases}$$

$$\mathsf{glitch}((x_2 \wedge y_3) \oplus (x_3 \wedge y_2)) = 0 \qquad \mathsf{glitch}(z_1) = 0$$
$$\mathsf{glitch}((x_3 \wedge y_1) \oplus (x_1 \wedge y_3)) = \bar{y}_3 \qquad \mathsf{glitch}(z_2) = \bar{y}_3$$
$$\mathsf{glitch}((x_1 \wedge y_2) \oplus (x_2 \wedge y_1)) = \bar{y}_2 \qquad \mathsf{glitch}(z_3) = \bar{y}_1 \vee \bar{y}_2$$

so
$$\Sigma\mathsf{power} = (\bar{y}_1 + \bar{y}_2 + \bar{y}_3)p_{\mathsf{AND}} + ((\bar{y}_1 \vee \bar{y}_2) + \bar{y}_2 + 2\bar{y}_3)p_{\mathsf{XOR}}$$

With Assumption (3), we have the same results except $\mathsf{glitch}(z_3) = \bar{y}_1 \oplus \bar{y}_2$. So

$$\Sigma\mathsf{power} = (\bar{y}_1 + \bar{y}_2 + \bar{y}_3)p_{\mathsf{AND}} + ((\bar{y}_1 \oplus \bar{y}_2) + \bar{y}_2 + 2\bar{y}_3)p_{\mathsf{XOR}}$$

We count the number of gates with a glitched output following the two assumptions. We also indicate $\Sigma\mathsf{power}$ assuming that $p_{\mathsf{AND}} = 1$ and $p_{\mathsf{XOR}} = 4$.[1] The results are on Table 1.

Table 1. Distributions for a glitch in x_1 in the threshold implementation

$\bar{y}$	$\bar{y}_1$	$\bar{y}_2$	$\bar{y}_3$	Assumption (1)			Assumption (2)			Assumption (3)		
				#AND	#XOR	Σpower	#AND	#XOR	Σpower	#AND	#XOR	Σpower
0	0	0	0	0	0	0	0	0	0	0	0	0
0	0	1	1	2	4	18	2	4	18	2	4	18
0	1	0	1	2	3	14	2	3	14	2	3	14
0	1	1	0	2	3	14	2	2	10	2	1	6
mean				1.5	2.5	11.5	1.5	2.25	10.5	1.5	2	9.5
variance				0.75	2.25	46.75	0.75	2.1875	44.75	0.75	2.5	48.75
1	0	0	1	1	2	9	1	2	9	1	2	9
1	0	1	0	1	2	9	1	2	9	1	2	9
1	1	0	0	1	1	5	1	1	5	1	1	5
1	1	1	1	3	5	23	3	4	19	3	3	15
mean				1.5	2.5	11.5	1.5	2.25	10.5	1.5	2	9.5
variance				0.75	2.25	46.75	0.75	1.1875	26.75	0.75	0.5	4.75
stat. dist.				1	1	1	1	0.5	1	1	0.5	1

Clearly, the distributions of $\Sigma\mathsf{power}|\bar{y} = 0$ and $\Sigma\mathsf{power}|\bar{y} = 1$ are very different. For instance, the parity of #AND is always equal to $\bar{y}$. The supports of the distributions $\#\mathsf{XOR}|\bar{y} = 0$ and $\#\mathsf{XOR}|\bar{y} = 1$ are disjoint with Assumption (1). So, we can distinguish them with one sample with advantage 1. With Assumptions (2) or (3), the statistical distance of the distributions $\#\mathsf{XOR}|\bar{y} = 0$ and $\#\mathsf{XOR}|\bar{y} = 1$ is $\frac{1}{2}$. So, a trivial statistic with a couple of samples would recover $\bar{y}$ assuming no noise.

We consider several types of distinguishers base on measuring #XOR. As the impact of the glitched XORs on $\Sigma\mathsf{power}$ is bigger, we can assume we measure it this way. We could also consider other side channel attacks which can separate the XORs from and ANDs.

---

[1] We took $p_{\mathsf{XOR}} = 4p_{\mathsf{AND}}$ as an example, which justifies by assuming that we use 4 NAND gates to make a XOR gate. But this must only be taken as an example. Note that an AND requires two NAND gates but the second one which is used as a NOT gate can often cancel with subsequent gates.

Best Distinguisher. With Assumption (1) and #XOR, the best distinguisher returns 0 if #XOR $\in \{0,3,4\}$ and it returns 1 if #XOR $\in \{1,2,5\}$. A statistical distance of 1 means that we can guess $\bar{y}$ with an error probability 0. A statistical distance of 0.5 means that we can guess $\bar{y}$ with an error probability $\frac{1}{4}$.

In practice, measuring #XOR may give a noisy value making it hard to implement this distinguisher. I.e., 0 and 1 may be too close to be distinguishable, as well as 2 and 3, and 4 and 5.

Threshold Distinguisher. We consider the distinguisher giving $1_{\#\text{XOR}+\text{noise}\leq\tau}$, i.e. 1 if #XOR (rather its noisy value from a side channel) is below a given threshold τ. Assuming that noise follows an independent normal distribution with mean 0 (w.l.o.g. by adjusting τ) and variance $\sigma^2 V(\#\text{XOR})$, we have

$$\Pr[\text{noise} \leq -x] = \frac{1}{2}\text{erfc}\left(\frac{x}{\sqrt{2\sigma^2 V(\#\text{XOR})}}\right)$$

so the Type I error in guessing $\bar{y}$ is

$$\alpha = \frac{1}{2}\sum_i \text{erfc}\left(\frac{i-\tau}{\sqrt{2\sigma^2 V(\#\text{XOR})}}\right)\Pr[\#\text{XOR}=i|\bar{y}=0]$$

The Type II error is

$$\beta = 1 - \frac{1}{2}\sum_i \text{erfc}\left(\frac{i-\tau}{\sqrt{2\sigma^2 V(\#\text{XOR})}}\right)\Pr[\#\text{XOR}=i|\bar{y}=1]$$

For Assumption (1), we have $V(\#\text{XOR}) = \frac{9}{4}$ and

$$\alpha = \frac{1}{2}\sum_{i=0}^{5}\text{erfc}\left(\frac{i-\tau}{\frac{3\sigma}{2}\sqrt{2}}\right)\Pr[\#\text{XOR}=i|\bar{y}=0]$$

$$= \frac{1}{8}\left(\text{erfc}\left(\frac{-\tau}{\frac{3\sigma}{2}\sqrt{2}}\right) + 2\text{erfc}\left(\frac{3-\tau}{\frac{3\sigma}{2}\sqrt{2}}\right) + \text{erfc}\left(\frac{4-\tau}{\frac{3\sigma}{2}\sqrt{2}}\right)\right)$$

For $\tau = 2.5$, using $\text{erfc}(-x) = 2 - \text{erfc}(x)$, we obtain

$$\alpha = \frac{1}{4} + \frac{1}{8}\left(-\text{erfc}\left(\frac{2.5}{\frac{3\sigma}{2}\sqrt{2}}\right) + 2\text{erfc}\left(\frac{0.5}{\frac{3\sigma}{2}\sqrt{2}}\right) + \text{erfc}\left(\frac{1.5}{\frac{3\sigma}{2}\sqrt{2}}\right)\right)$$

Similarly, we have $\beta = \alpha$. So, we have $P_e = \alpha = \beta$ and

$$P_e = \frac{1}{4} + \frac{1}{8}\left(-\text{erfc}\left(\frac{2.5}{\frac{3\sigma}{2}\sqrt{2}}\right) + \text{erfc}\left(\frac{1.5}{\frac{3\sigma}{2}\sqrt{2}}\right) + 2\text{erfc}\left(\frac{0.5}{\frac{3\sigma}{2}\sqrt{2}}\right)\right) = \frac{1}{2} - \Omega(\sigma^{-3})$$

As σ goes from 0 to infinity, P_e grows from $\frac{1}{4}$ to $\frac{1}{2}$. For instance, for $\sigma = \frac{1}{2}$, we have $P_e \approx 38\%$. For $\sigma = 1$, we have $P_e \approx 46\%$. For $\sigma = 2$, we have $P_e \approx 49.35\%$.

So, even with a big noise, we can recover $\bar{y}$ with an interesting advantage with only one sample.

Of course, we can amplify this advantage by using several samples. Since we have $\alpha = \beta = P_e$, by using (4) we obtain a new error probability of $P'_e = e^{-2} \approx 13\%$ with $N = 2\left(\frac{1}{2} - P_e\right)^{-2} = \mathcal{O}(\sigma^6)$. We obtain the following table:

σ:	0.5	1	1.5	2	2.5	3	3.5	4
N:	143	1 417	9 979	46 765	163 627	465 879	1 141 284	2 495 478

So, measuring the number of XORs (a number between 0 and 5) with a big noise of standard deviation twice what we want to measure still allows to deduce $\bar{y}$ with less than 50 000 samples with Assumption (1).

Moment Distinguisher. Instead of computing the average of Σpower, we compute the moment $E((\Sigma\text{power})^d)$ of order d, just like in Moradi [6,10].

With Assumption (1), we have

$$E(\Sigma\text{power}|y = 0) = E(\Sigma\text{power}|y = 1) = \frac{3}{2}p_{\text{AND}} + \frac{5}{2}p_{\text{XOR}}$$

$$V(\Sigma\text{power}|y = 0) = V(\Sigma\text{power}|y = 1) = \frac{3}{4}p_{\text{AND}}^2 + \frac{5}{2}p_{\text{AND}}p_{\text{XOR}} + \frac{9}{4}p_{\text{XOR}}^2$$

but the moments of order $d = 3$ differ. So $(\Sigma\text{power})^3$ leaks $\bar{y}$.

With Assumption (2), we have

$$E(\Sigma\text{power}|y = 0) = E(\Sigma\text{power}|y = 1) = \frac{3}{2}p_{\text{AND}} + \frac{9}{4}p_{\text{XOR}}$$

$$V(\Sigma\text{power}|y = 0) = \frac{3}{4}p_{\text{AND}}^2 + \frac{9}{4}p_{\text{AND}}p_{\text{XOR}} + \frac{35}{16}p_{\text{XOR}}^2$$

$$V(\Sigma\text{power}|y = 1) = \frac{3}{4}p_{\text{AND}}^2 + \frac{7}{4}p_{\text{AND}}p_{\text{XOR}} + \frac{19}{16}p_{\text{XOR}}^2$$

$$V(\Sigma\text{power}|y = 0) - V(\Sigma\text{power}|y = 1) = \frac{1}{2}p_{\text{AND}}p_{\text{XOR}} + p_{\text{XOR}}^2$$

With Assumption (3), we have

$$V(\Sigma\text{power}|y = 0) = \frac{3}{4}p_{\text{AND}}^2 + 2p_{\text{AND}}p_{\text{XOR}} + \frac{5}{2}p_{\text{XOR}}^2$$

$$V(\Sigma\text{power}|y = 1) = \frac{3}{4}p_{\text{AND}}^2 + \frac{1}{2}p_{\text{AND}}p_{\text{XOR}} + \frac{1}{2}p_{\text{XOR}}^2$$

$$V(\Sigma\text{power}|y = 0) - V(\Sigma\text{power}|y = 1) = \frac{3}{2}p_{\text{AND}}p_{\text{XOR}} + 2p_{\text{XOR}}^2$$

Clearly, the mean of $(\Sigma\text{power})^2$ (i.e., $d = 2$) leaks $\bar{y}$ with Assumptions (2) and (3). For Assumption (1), the same holds with $(\Sigma\text{power})^3$.

If $E(\Sigma\text{power})$ is known and we measure $Z = S + \text{noise}$ with $S = \Sigma\text{power} - E(\Sigma\text{power})$ and a centered Gaussian noise of variance $\sigma^2 V(\Sigma\text{power})$, we can compute $Z' = S^2 + \text{noise}'$ with $\text{noise}' = 2S\text{noise} + \text{noise}^2 - \sigma^2 V(\Sigma\text{power})$. So, it is as if we measured S^2 with noise noise'. The variance of noise' is roughly $4\sigma^2 V(S^2)$, so the attack works as if we just doubled σ. For instance, our previous computation shows that by doubling σ we roughly multiply N by 50. With this approach, threshold implementation penalizes the precision of the measurement.

4.2 Probing Attack with Two Probes Based on the Mean Value (All Assumptions)

We can further see what probing can yield.

With Assumptions (1, 3), we have $\text{glitch}(z_2) = \bar{y}_3$ and $\text{glitch}(z_3) = \bar{y}_1 \oplus \bar{y}_2$. So, probing both z_2 and z_3 is enough to recover $\bar{y}$.

With Assumption (2), this leaks $(\bar{y}_3, \bar{y}_1 \vee \bar{y}_2)$. For $\bar{y} = 0$, the distribution of this couple is $\Pr[(0,0)] = \frac{1}{4}$, $\Pr[(0,1)] = \frac{1}{4}$, $\Pr[(1,1)] = \frac{1}{2}$. For $\bar{y} = 1$, the distribution of this couple is $\Pr[(0,1)] = \frac{1}{2}$, $\Pr[(1,0)] = \frac{1}{4}$, $\Pr[(1,1)] = \frac{1}{4}$. So, the statistical distance is $\frac{1}{2}$ and the probability of error for guessing $\bar{y}$ is $\frac{1}{4}$.

As an example, with Assumption (1) we compute $S = \text{glitch}(z_2) + \text{glitch}(z_3) - \text{glitch}(z_2)\text{glitch}(z_3)$. Assuming that both $\text{glitch}(z_2)$ and $\text{glitch}(z_3)$ are subject to some noise with same parameter σ, the value we obtain for S is similar to a noisy value with the parameter σ multiplied by a constant factor less than 3. In our table, this results in a complexity N multiplied by a factor 300.

We recall that [7] claims no security when probing two values.

4.3 Power Analysis and Probing Attack on Two ANDs Based on the Mean Value (Assumptions (2) or (3))

We use two consecutive threshold AND gates to compute the AND between z and another shared bit u to obtain $v = x \wedge y \wedge u$. We assume no glitch on the y and u variables. We assume that only x_1 has a glitch. We have

$$z_1 = (x_2 \wedge y_2) \oplus ((x_2 \wedge y_3) \oplus (x_3 \wedge y_2)) \quad v_1 = (z_2 \wedge u_2) \oplus ((z_2 \wedge u_3) \oplus (z_3 \wedge u_2))$$
$$z_2 = (x_3 \wedge y_3) \oplus ((x_1 \wedge y_3) \oplus (x_3 \wedge y_1)) \quad v_2 = (z_3 \wedge u_3) \oplus ((z_1 \wedge u_3) \oplus (z_3 \wedge u_1))$$
$$z_3 = (x_1 \wedge y_1) \oplus ((x_1 \wedge y_2) \oplus (x_2 \wedge y_1)) \quad v_3 = (z_1 \wedge u_1) \oplus ((z_1 \wedge u_2) \oplus (z_2 \wedge u_1))$$

With Assumption (1), the linearity of the equations make sure that the expected value of the glitch variables are independent from $\bar{y}$.

Now, under Assumption (2), we have

$$\text{glitch}(z_1) = 0 \qquad \text{glitch}(v_1) = \max(\text{glitch}(z_2)(\bar{u}_2 \vee \bar{u}_3), \text{glitch}(z_3)\bar{u}_2)$$
$$\text{glitch}(z_2) = \bar{y}_3 \qquad \qquad\quad = \max(\bar{y}_3(\bar{u}_2 \vee \bar{u}_3), (\bar{y}_1 \vee \bar{y}_2)\bar{u}_2)$$
$$\text{glitch}(z_3) = \bar{y}_1 \vee \bar{y}_2$$

so we can now try to probe v_1. We have the 3 following cases:

- $\bar{u}_2 = \bar{u}_3 = 0$ (probability $\frac{1}{4}$): we have $v_1 = 0$, no glitch and nothing leaks.

- $\bar{u}_2 = 0$ and $\bar{u}_3 = 1$ (probability $\frac{1}{4}$): v_1 has a glitch if and only if $\bar{y}_3 = 1$.
- $\bar{u}_2 = 1$ (probability $\frac{1}{2}$): v_1 has a glitch when $\bar{y}_1 \vee \bar{y}_2 \vee \bar{y}_3 = 1$. For $\bar{y} = 1$, there is always a glitch. For $\bar{y} = 0$, there is a glitch with probability $\frac{3}{4}$.

So, if $\bar{y} = 0$, we observe a glitch in v_1 with probability $\frac{1}{4} \times 0 + \frac{1}{4} \times \frac{1}{2} + \frac{1}{2} \times \frac{3}{4} = \frac{1}{2}$. If $\bar{y} = 1$, the probability becomes $\frac{1}{4} \times 0 + \frac{1}{4} \times \frac{1}{2} + \frac{1}{2} \times 1 = \frac{5}{8}$. Hence, the mean value reveals $\bar{y}$. A single sample gives an error probability of $\frac{7}{17}$.

Now, under Assumption (3), we have

$$\begin{aligned} \mathsf{glitch}(z_1) &= 0 & \mathsf{glitch}(z_3) &= \bar{y}_1 \oplus \bar{y}_2 \\ \mathsf{glitch}(z_2) &= \bar{y}_3 & \mathsf{glitch}(v_1) &= \bar{y}_3(\bar{u}_2 \oplus \bar{u}_3) \oplus (\bar{y}_1 \oplus \bar{y}_2)\bar{u}_2 \end{aligned}$$

so we can try to probe v_1 again. With probability $\frac{1}{4}$, we have $\bar{u}_2 \oplus \bar{u}_3 = \bar{u}_2 = 1$ so $\mathsf{glitch}(v_1) = \bar{y}$. Otherwise, $\mathsf{glitch}(v_1)$ is uniformly distributed. So, for $\bar{y} = 0$, $E(\mathsf{glitch}(v_1)) = \frac{3}{8}$ and for $\bar{y} = 1$, $E(\mathsf{glitch}(v_1)) = \frac{5}{8}$. Again, $\bar{y}$ leaks from the mean value. A single sample gives an error probability of $\frac{3}{8}$.

The attack with noisy values is hardly more complicated than for $n = 1$.

Note that [7] does not claim any security on the composition of two AND gates. But this attacks clearly shows the limitation of this approach.

5   Implementation with $n = 4$

Assuming that (x_1, x_2, x_3, x_4) shares x, (y_1, y_2, y_3, y_4) shares y, and (z_1, z_2, z_3, z_4) shares z, Nikova, Rechberger, and Rijmen [7] propose

$$\begin{aligned} z_1 &= ((x_3 \oplus x_4) \wedge (y_2 \oplus y_3)) \oplus y_2 \oplus y_3 \oplus y_4 \oplus x_2 \oplus x_3 \oplus x_4 \\ z_2 &= ((x_1 \oplus x_3) \wedge (y_1 \oplus y_4)) \oplus y_1 \oplus y_3 \oplus y_4 \oplus x_1 \oplus x_3 \oplus x_4 \\ z_3 &= ((x_2 \oplus x_4) \wedge (y_1 \oplus y_4)) \oplus y_2 \oplus x_2 \\ z_4 &= ((x_1 \oplus x_2) \wedge (y_2 \oplus y_3)) \oplus y_1 \oplus x_1 \end{aligned}$$

It was proposed as an improvement to the $n = 3$ scheme as it makes all z_i shares balanced. This property is called *uniformity* in [8]. It was used to address composition. So, we look again at the composition of two AND circuits.

Again, we assume $\mathsf{glitch}(x_1) = 1$, $\mathsf{glitch}(x_2) = \mathsf{glitch}(x_3) = \mathsf{glitch}(x_4) = \mathsf{glitch}(y_i) = 0$ for $i = 1, \ldots, 4$ and $\mathsf{glitch}(x_1) = 1$. So, $\mathsf{glitch}(z_1) = 0$, $\mathsf{glitch}(z_2) = (\bar{y}_1 \oplus \bar{y}_4) + 1$, $\mathsf{glitch}(z_3) = 0$, and $\mathsf{glitch}(z_4) = (\bar{y}_2 \oplus \bar{y}_3) + 1$ with Assumption (1).

We compute $v = z \wedge u = (x \wedge y) \wedge u$ using the threshold implementation with

$$\begin{aligned} v_1 &= ((z_3 \oplus z_4) \wedge (u_2 \oplus u_3)) \oplus u_2 \oplus u_3 \oplus u_4 \oplus z_2 \oplus z_3 \oplus z_4 \\ v_2 &= ((z_1 \oplus z_3) \wedge (u_1 \oplus u_4)) \oplus u_1 \oplus u_3 \oplus u_4 \oplus z_1 \oplus z_3 \oplus z_4 \\ v_3 &= ((z_2 \oplus z_4) \wedge (u_1 \oplus u_4)) \oplus u_2 \oplus z_2 \\ v_4 &= ((z_1 \oplus z_2) \wedge (u_2 \oplus u_3)) \oplus u_1 \oplus z_1 \end{aligned}$$

So, we have

$$\mathsf{glitch}(v_1) = (\bar{y}_2 \oplus \bar{y}_3 + 1)(\bar{u}_2 \oplus \bar{u}_3) + (\bar{y}_1 \oplus \bar{y}_4) + (\bar{y}_2 \oplus \bar{y}_3) + 2$$
$$\mathsf{glitch}(v_2) = \bar{y}_2 \oplus \bar{y}_3 + 1$$
$$\mathsf{glitch}(v_3) = ((\bar{y}_1 \oplus \bar{y}_4) + (\bar{y}_2 \oplus \bar{y}_3) + 2)(\bar{u}_1 \oplus \bar{u}_4) + \bar{y}_1 \oplus \bar{y}_4 + 1$$
$$\mathsf{glitch}(v_4) = ((\bar{y}_1 \oplus \bar{y}_4) + 1)(\bar{u}_2 \oplus \bar{u}_3)$$

Hence, we can just probe v_1 and see if it has a glitch. With probability $\frac{1}{2}$, we have $\bar{u}_2 = \bar{u}_3$ so $\mathsf{glitch}(v_1) = 2(\bar{y}_2 \oplus \bar{y}_3) + (\bar{y}_1 \oplus \bar{y}_4) + 3$. In other cases, we have $\mathsf{glitch}(v_1) = (\bar{y}_1 \oplus \bar{y}_4) + (\bar{y}_2 \oplus \bar{y}_3) + 2$ which is uniformly distributed. So, by repeating enough times, the majority of $\mathsf{glitch}(v_1)$ is $\bar{y}$ with high probability.

The attack with noisy values is hardly more complicated than for $n = 1$.

Computations with Assumptions (2) or (3) are similar.

Note that [7] does not claim any security on the composition of two AND gates. However, the $n = 4$ implementation was made to produce a balanced sharing of the output to address composability through pipelining, meaning by adding a layer of registers between the circuits we want to compose. Here, we consider the composition of two AND gates without pipelining. Indeed, we certainly do not want to add registers in between two single gates! But our attacks shows that the entire layer of circuit that we want to compose through pipelining must be analyzed as a whole, since single gates clearly do not compose well.

6 Higher-Order Threshold Implementation with $n = 5$

In [1], Bilgin *et al.* propose an example of higher-order threshold implementation. Equation (1) in [1] implements $\bar{y} = 1 \oplus \bar{a} \oplus \bar{b}\bar{c}$. To obtain the implementation of an AND gate, we just remove the 1 and the a terms and obtain

$$
\begin{aligned}
y_1 &= (b_2 \wedge c_2) \oplus (b_1 \wedge c_2) \oplus (b_2 \wedge c_1) & y_6 &= (b_2 \wedge c_4) \oplus (b_4 \wedge c_2) \\
y_2 &= (b_3 \wedge c_3) \oplus (b_1 \wedge c_3) \oplus (b_3 \wedge c_1) & y_7 &= (b_5 \wedge c_5) \oplus (b_2 \wedge c_5) \oplus (b_5 \wedge c_2) \\
y_3 &= (b_4 \wedge c_4) \oplus (b_1 \wedge c_4) \oplus (b_4 \wedge c_1) & y_8 &= (b_3 \wedge c_4) \oplus (b_4 \wedge c_3) \\
y_4 &= (b_1 \wedge c_1) \oplus (b_1 \wedge c_5) \oplus (b_5 \wedge c_1) & y_9 &= (b_3 \wedge c_5) \oplus (b_5 \wedge c_3) \\
y_5 &= (b_2 \wedge c_3) \oplus (b_3 \wedge c_2) & y_{10} &= (b_4 \wedge c_5) \oplus (b_5 \wedge c_4)
\end{aligned}
$$

Then, Eq. (2) in [1] decreases the number of shares to 5 by

$$
\begin{aligned}
z_1 &= (b_2 \wedge c_2) \oplus (b_1 \wedge c_2) \oplus (b_2 \wedge c_1) & z_5 &= (b_2 \wedge c_3) \oplus (b_3 \wedge c_2) \oplus (b_2 \wedge c_4) \oplus \\
z_2 &= (b_3 \wedge c_3) \oplus (b_1 \wedge c_3) \oplus (b_3 \wedge c_1) & &= (b_4 \wedge c_2) \oplus (b_5 \wedge c_5) \oplus (b_2 \wedge c_5) \oplus \\
z_3 &= (b_4 \wedge c_4) \oplus (b_1 \wedge c_4) \oplus (b_4 \wedge c_1) & &= (b_5 \wedge c_2) \oplus (b_3 \wedge c_4) \oplus (b_4 \wedge c_3) \oplus \\
z_4 &= (b_1 \wedge c_1) \oplus (b_1 \wedge c_5) \oplus (b_5 \wedge c_1) & &\quad (b_3 \wedge c_5) \oplus (b_5 \wedge c_3) \oplus (b_4 \wedge c_5) \oplus \\
& & &\quad (b_5 \wedge c_4)
\end{aligned}
$$

This 2nd order implementation is supposed to resist to probing attacks with two probes. Normally, the transform of $(y_1, \ldots, y_{10})$ to $(z_1, \ldots, z_5)$ by $z_i = y_i$ for $i < 5$ and $z_5 = y_5 \oplus \cdots \oplus y_{10}$ must be done with intermediate registers to avoid the propagation of glitches. We wonder what happens without these registers.

Let consider an attack probing z_4 and z_5. If there is a glitch in b_5 and no other input share, we have $\mathsf{glitch}(z_4) = \bar{c}_1$ and

Table 2. Distribution of $(\text{glitch}(z_4), \text{glitch}(z_5))$ for a glitch in b_5 in the 2nd order threshold implementation

$\bar{c}\,\bar{c}_1\bar{c}_2\bar{c}_3\bar{c}_4\bar{c}_5$	A. (1)	A. (2)	A. (3)	$\bar{c}\,\bar{c}_1\bar{c}_2\bar{c}_3\bar{c}_4\bar{c}_5$	A. (1)	A. (2)	A. (3)
0 0 0 0 0 0	$(0,0)$	$(0,0)$	$(0,0)$	1 0 0 0 0 1	$(0,1)$	$(0,1)$	$(0,1)$
0 0 0 0 1 1	$(0,2)$	$(0,1)$	$(0,0)$	1 0 0 0 1 0	$(0,1)$	$(0,1)$	$(0,1)$
0 0 0 1 0 1	$(0,2)$	$(0,1)$	$(0,0)$	1 0 0 1 0 0	$(0,1)$	$(0,1)$	$(0,1)$
0 0 1 0 0 1	$(0,2)$	$(0,1)$	$(0,0)$	1 0 1 0 0 0	$(0,1)$	$(0,1)$	$(0,1)$
0 0 0 1 1 0	$(0,2)$	$(0,1)$	$(0,0)$	1 0 0 1 1 1	$(0,3)$	$(0,1)$	$(0,1)$
0 0 1 0 1 0	$(0,2)$	$(0,1)$	$(0,0)$	1 0 1 0 1 1	$(0,3)$	$(0,1)$	$(0,1)$
0 0 1 1 0 0	$(0,2)$	$(0,1)$	$(0,0)$	1 0 1 1 0 1	$(0,3)$	$(0,1)$	$(0,1)$
0 0 1 1 1 1	$(0,4)$	$(0,1)$	$(0,0)$	1 0 1 1 1 0	$(0,3)$	$(0,1)$	$(0,1)$
0 1 0 0 0 1	$(1,1)$	$(1,1)$	$(1,1)$	1 1 0 0 0 0	$(1,0)$	$(1,0)$	$(1,0)$
0 1 0 0 1 0	$(1,1)$	$(1,1)$	$(1,1)$	1 1 0 0 1 1	$(1,2)$	$(1,1)$	$(1,0)$
0 1 0 1 0 0	$(1,1)$	$(1,1)$	$(1,1)$	1 1 0 1 0 1	$(1,2)$	$(1,1)$	$(1,0)$
0 1 1 0 0 0	$(1,1)$	$(1,1)$	$(1,1)$	1 1 1 0 0 1	$(1,2)$	$(1,1)$	$(1,0)$
0 1 0 1 1 1	$(1,3)$	$(1,1)$	$(1,1)$	1 1 0 1 1 0	$(1,2)$	$(1,1)$	$(1,0)$
0 1 1 0 1 1	$(1,3)$	$(1,1)$	$(1,1)$	1 1 1 0 1 0	$(1,2)$	$(1,1)$	$(1,0)$
0 1 1 1 0 1	$(1,3)$	$(1,1)$	$(1,1)$	1 1 1 1 0 0	$(1,2)$	$(1,1)$	$(1,0)$
0 1 1 1 1 0	$(1,3)$	$(1,1)$	$(1,1)$	1 1 1 1 1 1	$(1,4)$	$(1,1)$	$(1,0)$
mean	$(\frac{1}{2},2)$	$(\frac{1}{2},\frac{15}{16})$	$(\frac{1}{2},\frac{1}{2})$	mean	$(\frac{1}{2},2)$	$(\frac{1}{2},\frac{15}{16})$	$(\frac{1}{2},\frac{1}{2})$
variance	$(\frac{1}{4},1)$	$(\frac{1}{2},\frac{15}{256})$	$(\frac{1}{2},\frac{1}{4})$	variance	$(\frac{1}{4},1)$	$(\frac{1}{2},\frac{15}{256})$	$(\frac{1}{2},\frac{1}{4})$

$$\text{glitch}(z_5) = \text{glitch}((b_5 \wedge c_2) \oplus (b_5 \wedge c_3) \oplus (b_5 \wedge c_4) \oplus (b_5 \wedge c_5))$$

With Assumption (1), this is $\text{glitch}(z_5) = \bar{c}_2 + \bar{c}_3 + \bar{c}_4 + \bar{c}_5$. With Assumption (2), this is $\text{glitch}(z_5) = \max(\bar{c}_2, \bar{c}_3, \bar{c}_4, \bar{c}_5)$. With Assumption (3), this is $\text{glitch}(z_5) = \bar{c}_2 \oplus \bar{c}_3 \oplus \bar{c}_4 \oplus \bar{c}_5$. So, we obtain the distributions for $(\text{glitch}(z_4), \text{glitch}(z_5))$ which is on Table 2. As we can see, the mean and the variance do not leak (as intended). However, the distributions are quite far apart.

Indeed, for Assumption (3), we have $\bar{c} = \text{glitch}(z_4) \oplus \text{glitch}(z_5)$ so it is clear that $\bar{c}$ leaks. For Assumption (1), we have $\bar{c} = \text{glitch}(z_4) \oplus (\text{glitch}(z_5) \bmod 2)$ so it is clear that $\bar{c}$ leaks as well. For Assumption (2), the distributions are

Distribution	$(0,0)$	$(0,1)$	$(1,0)$	$(1,1)$
$(\text{glitch}(z_4), \text{glitch}(z_5))\vert\bar{c} = 0$	1/16	7/16	0/16	8/16
$(\text{glitch}(z_4), \text{glitch}(z_5))\vert\bar{c} = 1$	0/16	8/16	1/16	7/16

so the statistical distance is $\frac{1}{8}$. This means that from a single value we can deduce $\bar{c}$ with an error probability of $P_e = \frac{1}{2} - \frac{1}{16}$. Of course, this amplifies like in (4) using more samples. Hence, two probes leak quite a lot. So, we clearly see that avoiding the extra registers needed to avoid the number of shares to inflate makes the implementation from [1] insecure.

7   Conclusion

We have shown that the threshold implementations are quite weak against many simple attacks: distinguishers based on non-linear functions on the power traces (as simple as a threshold function or a power function), multiple probes, and linear distinguishers for a cascade of circuits. Although they do not contradict the results by their authors, these attacks show severe limitations on this approach.

We have seen that compared to the attack on the AND gate with no protection, the threshold implementation proposals only have the effect to amplify the noise of the side-channel attack by a constant factor. Therefore, we believe that there is no satisfactory protection for attacks based on glitches.

References

1. Bilgin, B., Gierlichs, B., Nikova, S., Nikov, V., Rijmen, V.: Higher-order threshold implementations. In: Sarkar, P., Iwata, T. (eds.) ASIACRYPT 2014. LNCS, vol. 8874, pp. 326–343. Springer, Heidelberg (2014). doi:10.1007/978-3-662-45608-8_18
2. Chari, S., Jutla, C.S., Rao, J.R., Rohatgi, P.: Towards sound approaches to counteract power-analysis attacks. In: Wiener, M. (ed.) CRYPTO 1999. LNCS, vol. 1666, pp. 398–412. Springer, Heidelberg (1999). doi:10.1007/3-540-48405-1_26
3. Chernoff, H.: A measure of asymptotic efficiency for tests of a hypothesis based on the sum of observations. Ann. Math. Stat. 23(4), 493–507 (1952)
4. Duc, A., Dziembowski, S., Faust, S.: Unifying leakage models: from probing attacks to noisy leakage. In: Nguyen, P.Q., Oswald, E. (eds.) EUROCRYPT 2014. LNCS, vol. 8441, pp. 423–440. Springer, Heidelberg (2014). doi:10.1007/978-3-642-55220-5_24
5. Mangard, S., Popp, T., Gammel, B.M.: Side-channel leakage of masked CMOS gates. In: Menezes, A. (ed.) CT-RSA 2005. LNCS, vol. 3376, pp. 351–365. Springer, Heidelberg (2005). doi:10.1007/978-3-540-30574-3_24
6. Moradi, A.: Statistical tools flavor side-channel collision attacks. In: Pointcheval, D., Johansson, T. (eds.) EUROCRYPT 2012. LNCS, vol. 7237, pp. 428–445. Springer, Heidelberg (2012). doi:10.1007/978-3-642-29011-4_26
7. Nikova, S., Rechberger, C., Rijmen, V.: Threshold implementations against side-channel attacks and glitches. In: Ning, P., Qing, S., Li, N. (eds.) ICICS 2006. LNCS, vol. 4307, pp. 529–545. Springer, Heidelberg (2006). doi:10.1007/11935308_38
8. Nikova, S., Rijmen, V., Schläffer, M.: Secure hardware implementation of nonlinear functions in the presence of glitches. J. Cryptology 24, 292–321 (2011)
9. Reparaz, O., Bilgin, B., Nikova, S., Gierlichs, B., Verbauwhede, I.: Consolidating masking schemes. In: Gennaro, R., Robshaw, M. (eds.) CRYPTO 2015. LNCS, vol. 9215, pp. 764–783. Springer, Heidelberg (2015). doi:10.1007/978-3-662-47989-6_37
10. Standaert, F.-X., Veyrat-Charvillon, N., Oswald, E., Gierlichs, B., Medwed, M., Kasper, M., Mangard, S.: The world is not enough: another look on second-order DPA. In: Abe, M. (ed.) ASIACRYPT 2010. LNCS, vol. 6477, pp. 112–129. Springer, Heidelberg (2010). doi:10.1007/978-3-642-17373-8_7
11. Trichina, E., Korkishko, T., Lee, K.H.: Small size, low power, side channel-immune AES coprocessor: design and synthesis results. In: Dobbertin, H., Rijmen, V., Sowa, A. (eds.) AES 2004. LNCS, vol. 3373, pp. 113–127. Springer, Heidelberg (2005). doi:10.1007/11506447_10

Diversity Within the Rijndael Design Principles for Resistance to Differential Power Analysis

Merrielle Spain[1]([✉]) and Mayank Varia[2]

[1] MIT Lincoln Laboratory, Lexington, USA
merrielle.spain@ll.mit.edu
[2] Boston University, Boston, USA
varia@bu.edu

Abstract. The winner of the Advanced Encryption Standard (AES) competition, Rijndael, strongly resists mathematical cryptanalysis. However, side channel attacks such as differential power analysis and template attacks break many AES implementations.

We propose a cheap and effective countermeasure that exploits the diversity of algorithms consistent with Rijndael's general design philosophy. The secrecy of the algorithm settings acts as a second key that the adversary must learn to mount popular side channel attacks. Furthermore, because they satisfy Rijndael's security arguments, these algorithms resist cryptanalytic attacks.

Concretely, we design a 72-bit space of SubBytes variants and a 36-bit space of ShiftRows variants. We investigate the mathematical strength provided by these variants, generate them in SageMath, and study their impact on differential power analysis and template attacks against field-programmable gate arrays (FPGAs) by analyzing power traces from the DPA Contest v2 public dataset.

Keywords: Side channel attack · Side channel countermeasure · Guessing entropy · Differential power analysis · Template attack · Hamming weight · Advanced Encryption Standard · Rijndael · FPGA

1 Introduction

Differential power analysis (DPA) [1] and template attacks [2] can quickly break secure, correctly implemented cryptographic algorithms [3]. They harness information leaked by the physical implementation of a cryptosystem—outside the scope of cryptographic models, provable security claims, and mathematical cryptanalysis. Researchers have proposed countermeasures to side channel

This work is sponsored by the Office of Naval Research under Air Force Contract FA8721-05-C-002. Opinions, interpretations, conclusions and recommendations are those of the authors and are not necessarily endorsed by the United States Government.

M. Varia—Research performed while consulting at MIT Lincoln Laboratory.

© Springer International Publishing AG 2016
S. Foresti and G. Persiano (Eds.): CANS 2016, LNCS 10052, pp. 71–87, 2016.
DOI: 10.1007/978-3-319-48965-0_5

attacks ranging from isolating the device to masking the signal [4,5]. However, these approaches have drawbacks, especially for lightweight and mobile security.

We leverage work from the Advanced Encryption Standard (AES) [6] process to argue cryptanalytic security, while deriving side channel resilience from diversity available within the design principles of the winner Rijndael. NIST's burdensome competition only certified a single algorithm for standardization, even though Rijndael's security arguments cover a range of settings.

We explore the space of Rijndael variants that stay within these security arguments to maintain optimal cryptanalytic security. These "tunable knobs" increase resistance to DPA and template attacks by introducing a second source of entropy. Additionally, as with Clavier et al. [7], our method complements masking and shuffling techniques.

1.1 Prior Work

Barkan and Biham explored *dual ciphers* of AES [8], which are variant ciphers whose plaintexts, ciphertexts, and keys can be mapped to those of AES via invertible transformations. Initial works showed 240 duals of AES that arise from the choice of 30 irreducible polynomials of degree 8 in $GF(2)[x]$ and 8 choices of the primitive root of this polynomial. Rostovtsev and Shemyakina [9] further propose that each of the 16 SubBytes operations could be different.

Kerckhoffs's principle notwithstanding, one might hope that choosing a random variant on the fly could obfuscate the AES circuitry. Indeed, several works have designed and implemented modular FPGAs that can choose on the fly between the 240 duals, either for performance reasons [10] or in hope of improving security [11]. However, Moradi and Mischke [12] demonstrated that a single, reconfigurable chip implementing the AES duals (without LUTs) is insecure because power side channels can leak the variant choice. Moreover, even while subsequent works have discovered up to 61,200 AES duals [13,14], the space of duals remains small enough to brute force.

To overcome this limitation, other prior work seeks to design a large corpus of variants based on Rijndael, without connecting mathematical security to that of the standard. Jing et al. [15] initiate this line of research by proposing variations of SubBytes and MixColumns; these results have since been superceded by other works. Jing et al. [16] extensively analyze the space of SubBytes variants possible through the use of different affine transformations. Several works propose varying the 4 row shift offsets in the ShiftRows operation [7,16]. Finally, a few works find alternate MixColumns matrices with higher multiplicative order [17,18].

1.2 Our Contributions

This paper proposes a moving target defense against a side channel attacker. We contribute the first work that simultaneously:

1. Generates variants that maintain both the design and mathematical strength of AES.
2. Leverages the variation in round function components for improved resistance to differential power analysis (DPA) and template attacks.

By contrast, prior work either abandons the structure of AES, weakens its cryptanalytic strength, or fails to justify improved side channel resistance. Jing et al. claim that variation increases strength against attacks, but fail to specify any attacks [16]. Furthermore, they allow fixed points in SubBytes, which reduces cryptanalytic strength. They also fail to identify redundancy between components or quantify the security provided.

Section 2 describes the structure of our Rijndael variants and calculates the number of unique variants. Section 3 determines the implementation cost of our scheme. Section 4 demonstrates that our variants retain the design principles necessary to argue for its resistance to common cryptanalytic attacks; we also provide open-source SageMath code that automatically produces variants and tests them against cryptanalytic metrics (https://github.com/mit-ll/Diversity-Within-Rijndael). Section 5 argues that our variants' diversity impedes DPA and template attacks; we augment these claims with analysis of the DPA Contest v2 dataset [3].

1.3   Envisioned Usage

As side channel resistance depends on usage, this work focuses on Rijndael variants implemented on field-programmable gate arrays (FPGAs). More concretely, we envision each FPGA being hardcoded with a single variant.[1] This technique is simpler and more performant (in runtime and chip size) than prior work [11,12,16] that envisioned a single FPGA that can change variants on the fly.

We stress the compatibility of this approach with Kerckhoffs's principle. Our approach treats pieces of the round structure internals as a second component of the key. While a particular variant is fixed at compilation time, this choice can be altered by reprogramming the device or obtaining a new one.

In some scenarios, altering an algorithm costs more than altering a key; in those cases, key evolution [20] could make a better side-channel deterrent. Our techniques suit an environment where: Varying the algorithm costs no more than varying the key. Continuous rekeying costs too much, in computation or communication, or insufficient robustness can harm the availability of communication. A block cipher must remain robust against side channel attacks for a long time.

One such scenario involves military communication devices that require high availability, are difficult to adjust in the field, and are reconfigured easily back at home.

---

[1] For instance, one can modify Manteena's implementation of AES in VHDL [19, Appendix D] to produce different, static mappings of byte values in SubBytes, mappings of byte locations in ShiftRows, and matrix constants in MixColumns.

2   The Design of Our Rijndael Variants

AES [6] operates on a 16-byte state organized into a 4×4 matrix of bytes. It performs several rounds that comprise four algorithms: SubBytes, ShiftRows, MixColumns, and AddRoundKey. The round function satisfies the two primary concepts for designing ciphers from Claude Shannon: confusion and diffusion [21]. Confusion states that the effects should be key-dependent and hard to predict. In AES, AddRoundKey provides key-dependence and SubBytes provides non-linearity. Diffusion states that a minor change in the input should disperse to many output locations. In AES, MixColumns provides local diffusion within a column and ShiftRows spreads the diffusion globally. The synergy between AES components produces strength beyond Shannon's original vision: its *wide trail strategy* [22] permits strong claims of AES' resistance to differential and linear cryptanalytic attacks.

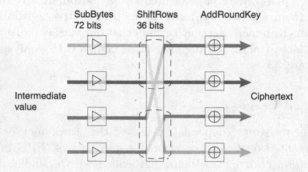

Fig. 1. Schema of last round of AES, simplified to four bytes in two columns. SubBytes and AddRoundKey act on each byte independently, and ShiftRows disperses bytes to different columns (dashed regions) without altering values.

Figure 1 shows a simplified last round of AES along with our theoretical estimates of the variety possible within components. First, we describe the four round function operations in AES and our variants of these operations. Second, we calculate how the entropies of our variations combine.

2.1   SubBytes

In AES, SubBytes is a fixed nonlinear permutation that independently replaces each byte of the input with a different value. It provides limited confusion at low cost. Concretely, SubBytes concatenates three steps:

1. Inversion $f_p(x) = x^{-1}$ over the finite field $\mathrm{GF}(256) = GF(2)[x]/(p(x))$, where $p(x) = x^8 + x^4 + x^3 + x + 1$.

2. Linear transformation $g(\boldsymbol{x}) = A\boldsymbol{x}$ over the vector space $\mathrm{GF}(2)^8$.
3. Addition[2] of a constant $h(\boldsymbol{x}) = \boldsymbol{x} + \boldsymbol{b}$ in $\mathrm{GF}(2)^8$.

AES' security relies on three properties of SubBytes. First, the function has high algebraic complexity when viewed in a single mathematical space [23]. Second, SubBytes must be *highly nonlinear*: possessing low linear biases and difference propagations. Third, SubBytes cannot have any fixed or anti-fixed points.

Our variations follow Jing et al.'s procedure to preserve the first two properties [16]. In the inversion step, we choose the modulus p from any of the 30 irreducible polynomials of degree 8 over $\mathrm{GF}(2)$.[3] In the linear transformation, we pick an invertible matrix A (i.e., having linearly independent rows) from the $\prod_{i=0}^{7}(256 - 2^i) \approx 1.16 \times 2^{62}$ such choices.

Unlike Jing et al. [16], our variations also preserve the third property by restricting $\boldsymbol{b} \in \mathrm{GF}(2)^8$ to choices that avoid any (anti-)fixed points in the completed SubBytes permutation. We approximate the fraction of choices that meet this constraint by replacing f and g with a truly random function R. In this case, $\mathrm{Pr}_R[R(\boldsymbol{x}) + \boldsymbol{b}$ has no (anti-)fixed points$] = (254/256)^{256} \approx 0.134$. Our empirical analysis with 50 million randomly-sampled choices shows that the fraction of valid $\boldsymbol{b}$ is 0.135, close to our theoretical estimate. Hence, there are slightly more than 5 bits of entropy in the choice of the constant $\boldsymbol{b}$.

Finally, we observe that the three steps contribute independent sources of entropy. That is, for all pairs of inverse functions f_p and $f_{p'}$, linear transformations g and g', and constant addition steps h and h', $h \circ g \circ f_p \neq h' \circ g' \circ f_{p'}$ unless the pairs are identical. This statement follows by rearranging the above inequality to $(h' \circ g')^{-1} \circ h \circ g \neq f_{p'} \circ (f_p)^{-1}$ and empirically verifying that the right side is nonaffine for $p \neq p'$ whereas the left side is affine.

In total, our design yields more than 2^{72} variants of SubBytes.[4] We will show in Sect. 4 that the variants retain Rijndael's resistance toward mathematical cryptanalysis.

2.2   ShiftRows

AES' ShiftRows operation transposes the 16 bytes of state by shifting each row of the state matrix cyclically to the left by a fixed number of bytes. ShiftRows contributes to the wide trail strategy due to its *diffusion optimality*: it maps the 4 bytes within each column of the round state to 4 different

---

[2] Our variants perform XOR, just as AES does. By contrast, Rijmen and Oswald [13] create variants that preserve AES' original SubBytes functionality, at the cost of replacing XOR with a (slower and leakier) table lookup.

[3] It is also possible to choose the primitive root of the polynomial used to represent elements of GF(256) [9]. This yields 3 bits of entropy independent of the affine transformation. However, SageMath encapsulates its choice of primitive root, so our work skips this extra flexibility.

[4] We remark that Jing et al.'s calculation of this value [16] is inaccurate by a multiplicative factor of 7. Coincidentally, this 1/7 error closely matches the omitted 13.5 % throughput of SubBytes lacking fixed points.

columns [22, Definition 9.4.1]. We describe three, increasingly large, families of ShiftRows variants that maintain diffusion optimality.

Cyclic preserving. Permutations in this family maintain AES SubBytes' *cyclic* nature. Previously considered [7,16], these variants choose different cyclic offsets for each row of ShiftRows. This family contains $4! = 24$ variants.

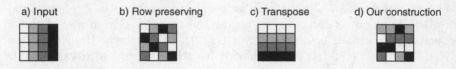

Fig. 2. Depiction of the action of ShiftRows. The input (a) is colored by column, and two outputs are displayed for transpositions that are row preserving (b) and not (d).

Row preserving. A higher entropy variation breaks the cyclic property of ShiftRows, but keeps each byte in its original row. The first row has $4!$ permutations. In the second row, there are 3 choices for the location of the white block consistent with diffusion optimality, and 3 locations for the block of the color above the white block (black, in the case of Fig. 2b). Let E denote the event that this block is placed directly under the white block of row 1, as is the case in Fig. 2b. In the third row, there are 2 locations for the white block. Afterward, there exist 2 choices to complete the ShiftRows variant if event E occurred and 1 choice otherwise. In total, this procedure yields $4! \cdot 3 \cdot (1 \cdot 4 + 2 \cdot 2) = 576 = (4!)^2$ variants.

Our construction. We stress the irrelevance of row preservation to diffusion optimality. We propose a $(4!)^8$ family of diffusion-optimal byte transpositions that we construct in three steps.

1. Transpose the 4×4 input matrix to satisfy diffusion optimality (Fig. 2c).
2. Independently shuffle the entries within each row (Fig. 2c).
3. Independently shuffle the entries within each column (Fig. 2d).

This construction independently chooses 8 permutations: 4 on the rows in Step 2 and 4 on the columns in Step 3. All choices are distinct and maintain diffusion optimality. Hence, our construction yields $(4!)^8 \approx 1.60 \times 2^{36}$ variants.

2.3   MixColumns

AES' MixColumns operation separately multiplies the 4 bytes in each column of the state by a fixed, invertible, circulant 4×4 matrix over the field GF(256) (using the same representation as described in AES' SubBytes). Specifically, the matrix in AES uses the following coefficients in the first column: $c_0 = 02$, $c_1 = 01$, $c_2 = 01$, and $c_3 = 03$. The last round of AES omits MixColumns.

The need for the MixColumns matrix to have differential and linear branch numbers of 5 governs the choice of the constants. Grosek and Zajac [18] determined the satisfactory choices: For the matrix to be invertible, $\sum c_i \neq 0$. To follow the wide trail strategy, $c_i \neq 0$, $c_i \neq c_{i+2}$, $c_i c_{i+1} \neq c_{i+2} c_{i+3}$, and $c_i^2 \neq c_{i+1} c_{i-1}$ for all i, considering indices mod 4. Most settings satisfy these constraints, so around 32 bits of entropy exist in the design of MixColumns.

2.4 AddRoundKey

AES XORs each state byte with a round key byte, itself a fixed function of the AES key. This operation concludes each round, and an extra AddRoundKey precedes the first round. The key schedule's design provides three important security properties: round-dependent constants break symmetry to prevent slide attacks, SubBytes provides confusion to thwart related-key attacks, and a diffusive structure resists partial-key attacks [22]. Furthermore, the simplicity of AddRoundKey's XOR operation facilitates the wide trail strategy arguments that decompose the cryptanalytic strength of AES to a function of the strength of its parts. Hence, our variants keep AddRoundKey's structure *intact* in order to retain the security properties of AES.

We note that SubBytes' usage inside key expansion induces a tradeoff. If we use the standard AES SubBytes inside the key schedule, then our variants require larger chip area to store two different SubBytes permutations. On the other hand, using our SubBytes variant inside the key expansion reduces key agility; the expanded key must be recomputed whenever the SubBytes variant changes. In this work, we choose to maintain AES' AddRoundKey entirely. Hence, updating the key would be identical to AES.

2.5 Total Entropy Provided by Our Variants

Determining the total entropy of our variants requires measuring redundancy between components. The variations of SubBytes and ShiftRows are independent by design: one function changes byte values and the other changes byte positions. Hence, we sum the entropies of SubBytes and ShiftRows to arrive at a total of more than 2^{108} variants.

Although we described variations of MixColumns, we exclude them from our design for two reasons. First, care must be taken to avoid dependences on the previous variants: for instance, applying a scalar multiplication or cyclic rotation to the MixColumns matrix is redundant with the variations to SubBytes and ShiftRows, respectively [16]. Second, varying MixColumns fails to affect many side channel attacks because the final round omits MixColumns.

Similarly, it may appear tempting to vary the round constants in AddRound-Key. However, changing the round constants fails to introduce new entropy over variations of SubBytes' modulus p, SubBytes' affine transformation A and b, and MixColumns' circulant matrix entries c_0 through c_3 [8].

3   Implementation Cost

This section recaps our changes to argue that the cost of implementing a variant in an FPGA roughly equals AES in energy expended and chip area consumed. We highlight our envisioned usage (as detailed in Sect. 1.3) where each FPGA implements a *single* variant; by contrast, the FPGAs designed in prior work could switch between variants at higher cost [11,12,16].

First, our SubBytes variants differ from the AES SubBytes. Nevertheless, as 256-bit mappings, they can be implemented via lookup tables (LUTs), with size independent of the values. Additionally, because our SubBytes variants also perform a mathematical inversion in GF(256) (albeit with a different field representation), we can employ Paar and Rosner's efficient inversion of GF(256) in FPGAs [24]; this technique shrinks LUTs in exchange for a few arithmetic operations. For maximal resistance to side channel attacks (cf. Sect. 5), we recommend designing an FPGA to compute all 16 SubBytes operations in a single round concurrently.

Second, our ShiftRows variants cost roughly equal to AES' ShiftRows on FPGAs, 8-bit microcontrollers, 32-bit software, and ASICs; we simply modify the mapping between input and output bytes. Existing implementations on these platforms do not require ShiftRows to be cyclic or row-preserving. For example, OpenSSL's AES implementation [25] is *column-oriented*, with the 32-bit integers s0 through s3 denoting the four columns of AES:

```
t0 = Te0[s0 >> 24] ^ Te1[(s1 >> 16) & 0xff] ^ Te2[(s2 >> 8) & 0xff] ^ Te3[s3 & 0xff] ^ rk[4];
```

The corresponding code for a variant would reference each column once (as required by diffusion optimality), and perform the same right-shifts, bitwise-ands, and table lookups. Only the order of these operations would change (i.e., which input column is shifted by which amount and fed into which table), yielding identical runtime.

Third, our MixColumns matches that of AES. In principle, this may incur some cost because the AES MixColumns performs finite field multiplication with a different representation of GF(256) than our SubBytes variant. Hence, if we wanted to compute SubBytes and MixColumns mathematically, we could need two multiplication routines. We are saved from this expense by following the common practice of computing MixColumns using LUTs instead.

Fourth, our AddRoundKey matches that of AES. This incurs a cost because key expansion uses the AES SubBytes. Hence, an FPGA for our variant needs additional chip size to implement two SubBytes routines. Nevertheless, the energy expended during encryption is independent of this change. Moreover, we could reduce the impact on chip size by using a small but slow implementation of the AES SubBytes since key expansion occurs less frequently than encryption and decryption [26].

4   Cryptanalytic Attacks

Because we chose our round function components to be consistent with the design of AES, our variants retain much of AES' strength against cryptanalysis.

First, our Rijndael variants retain maximal resistance against differential and linear cryptanalysis. Analytically, this can be shown by measuring the maximal linear bias and maximal difference probability of the 30 inversion polynomials f_p and observing that these values are invariant under affine transformations [27]. Empirically, we tested the maximal linear bias and maximal difference probability of 3 million SubBytes variants (of 2^{72}) using SageMath [28]. For comparison, we did the same for 3 million uniformly random permutations (of 2^{1684}). Figure 3 shows histograms in both settings; it demonstrates that the SubBytes variants exhibit optimal linear bias (16) and difference propagation (4), a vanishingly rare occurrence for random permutations. Intuitively, our variants are "as far from linear as possible," just like AES. Additionally, ShiftRows remains diffusion optimal and MixColumns remains unchanged. As a result, the wide trail strategy's analysis [22, Theorem 9.4.1] still yields a minimum weight of 150 for any four-round differential trail and a maximum correlation contribution of 2^{-75} for any four-round linear trail.

In more detail, our SageMath software produces new constants compatible with the Rijndael design philosophy and embeds them in the algorithm. To generate SubBytes in SageMath, we randomly select an irreducible modulus polynomial and an invertible affine transformation. We check each result for fixed and anti-fixed points. Empirically, we find that 13.5 % of our SubBytes variants lacked (anti-)fixed points; we restrict our attention to these SubBytes. Additionally, we generate random diffusion-optimal ShiftRows transpositions following the method described in Sect. 2.2.

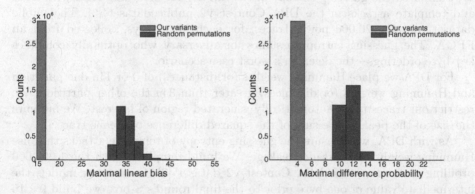

Fig. 3. Our approach preserves the cryptanalytic properties of AES SubBytes. Left: Our approach generates SubBytes variants (green) with the optimal maximal linear bias of 16, in contrast, random permutations (blue) achieve poor values. Right: Our SubBytes variants (green) attain the optimal maximal difference probability of 4, while random permutations (blue) yield worse values. We tested 3 million of each type. (Color figure online)

Second, our Rijndael variants slightly improve resistance to impossible differential and saturation (also called square or structural) attacks. Impossible differentials are tuples of byte positions with the following property: if a pair of inputs match except for one byte position, then after several AES rounds the outputs mismatch in all byte positions. These attacks show promise on reduced-round variants of AES [29]. Crucially, a one-to-one mapping exists from an impossible differential on AES to one on our variants, with the choice of ShiftRows merely altering its byte position and the choice of SubBytes having no effect. Hence, our variants and AES are equally susceptible to impossible differential attacks. Moreover, the uncertainty provided by ShiftRows' entropy increases the attack difficulty with our variants. By a similar argument, our variants also withstand saturation attacks [30] equivalently to AES.

5   Side Channel Attacks

Side channel attacks harness unintentional leakage (e.g., changes in timing, acoustics, power) from the physical implementation of a cipher to infer secret keys. This section focuses on the importance of SubBytes and ShiftRows toward two prominent power-based side channel attacks: differential power analysis (DPA) and template attacks. These attacks require knowledge of SubBytes to calculate intermediate values. An attack with Hamming distance leakage requires ShiftRows, unlike one with Hamming weight leakage. Conversely, DPA and template attacks ignore MixColumns.

5.1   Side Channel Methods

We computed the guessing entropy of the full key for attacking AES with DPA and template attacks in the DPA Contest v2 public dataset [3]. The public dataset contains 20,000 power traces, for each of 32 keys, collected from an FPGA. The guessing entropy assumes an adversary who optimally combines key byte orderings—the defender's worst case scenario.

For DPA we place Hamming weights (or distances) of 0 or 1 in one partition and Hamming weights (or distances) greater than 3 in the other partition. We restrict our traces to an automatically generated region of interest. We measure the size of the peak as the sum of the squared difference of means trace.

As with DPA, we measure the guessing entropy of template attacks that use Hamming weight and distance leakage. We build templates with the 1,000,000 profiling traces from the DPA Contest v2 dataset [3]. Our attack models the intermediate value of one byte prior to the final round's S-box: we build 9×16 templates, one for each Hamming weight (or distance) of each byte's intermediate value. We restrict our traces to the same region of interest. We project the traces onto the 10 principal components and calculate the log-likelihood with the pooled covariance matrix [31].

Using the same templates (with 100 principal components) we explore whether an adversary can determine the Hamming weight profile of a SubBytes variant (motivated in Sect. 5.4). We split traces into sets based on ciphertext XOR key and evaluate the probability of observing a set of traces given the nine Hamming weight templates. Then, we calculate how the likelihoods reduce the attacker's uncertainty about the SubBytes variant.

5.2 Side Channel Results

To verify the effect of performing an attack with correct and incorrect SubBytes, we compute the guessing entropy of the full key for attacking AES with DPA and template attacks, up to the full 20,000 traces per key. Figure 4 (left) shows the guessing entropy as a function of the number of traces. The standard attacks fail when assuming an incorrect SubBytes variant.

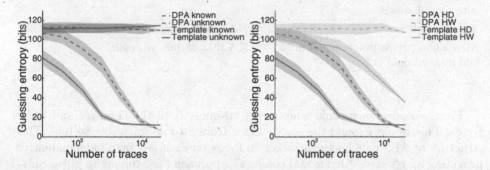

Fig. 4. We measure the full guessing entropy remaining after side channel attacks as a function of attack dataset size, given optimal combination of key bytes' values. We compare two attack types: DPA (dashed lines) and template attacks (solid lines) ± standard deviation (shaded regions). Left: Impact of employing incorrect SubBytes. This models Hamming distance leakage from a field-programmable gate array. We find that otherwise successful attacks (blue lines) will fail when employing the wrong SubBytes variant (red lines). Right: Impact of unknown ShiftRows forcing attacker from Hamming distance (HD) to Hamming weight (HW). We find that attacks based on Hamming distance leakage of an intermediate value (blue lines) outperform those based on Hamming weight leakage (yellow lines) for both attack types. (Color figure online)

To show the effect of moving from Hamming distance to Hamming weight to compensate for incorrect ShiftRows, we compute the guessing entropy for attacking AES with DPA and template attacks. Figure 4 (right) shows the guessing entropy as a function of the number of traces. For both attacks, Hamming weight performs much worse than Hamming distance on these FPGA data.

5.3 SubBytes Discussion

Diversity in SubBytes forces the side channel attacker into unattractive options listed in Table 1. DPA takes a "guess and check" approach: the adversary guesses a key byte value, deduces an intermediate value on the other side of SubBytes (see Fig. 1), calculates the physical leakage induced by such a value, and checks the traces for matching leakage. Here, we catalog how an adversary might mount a DPA attack with an unknown SubBytes.

Table 1. Impact of SubBytes variants on DPA and template attacks.

Attack	Impact
Guess both a key byte and SubBytes	Expands search space from 8 to 80 bits
Attack with SubBytes unknown [32]	Profiles both key and SubBytes
Reverse engineer SubBytes with side channels [7,33]	Expected to fail on hardware [7,33]
Reverse engineer SubBytes' HW profile with side channels	Depends on noise level of device
Attack mask reuse	NA for concurrent execution of bytes [12]
Attack concurrent processing of mask and masked data [12]	NA if mask not processed

First, an adversary could adapt DPA to guess both the key byte and Sub-Bytes. This would expand the search space from 8 to an infeasible 80 bits. The structure of AES enables the attacker to focus on each key byte independently, providing an effective "divide and conquer" approach [34]. Having to guess Sub-Bytes and a key byte simultaneously renders the "divide" ineffective.

Second, an attacker could apply similarity analysis [32] to target key bytes directly without knowledge of SubBytes. However, similarity analysis requires operations that depend on few unknown bits. Adapting this to simultaneously attack SubBytes would lead to the same "divide and conquer" loss.

Third, an attacker could physically inspect a device to discover SubBytes. The defender would take a systems approach, including hardware protection such as placing SubBytes in an encrypted FPGA bitstream. As a result, physically observing SubBytes is equivalent to attacking key storage.

Fourth, an attacker could attempt to reverse engineer SubBytes itself using side channels. This type of attack is called Side-Channel Analysis for Reverse Engineering (SCARE). The first work in this direction depended on the attacked S-box being a compressive function [35], unlike SubBytes. More recent work assumes that collisions in SubBytes output can be retrieved perfectly [7] to adapt SCARE to AES variants. Other work has incorporated templates to address imperfect collision detection [33]. Both evaluate on simulations, saying that because these attacks rely on sequential SubBytes computations they are more appropriate for software. Clavier et al. state "our attack should not be feasible on an hardware AES implementation" [7].

Moradi and Mischke apply a correlation collision attack to AES dual ciphers [12]. The four factors that affect the robustness of their scheme are mask reuse, concurrent processing of mask and masked data, zero value, and unbalance. We argue that none of these factors substantively impact our variants. First, it is possible to implement AES duals such that SubBytes leakages cannot be separated, preventing a mask reuse attack [12]. Second, concurrent processing of the mask and masked data and multiplicative masking of zero arise because Moradi and Mischke designed a single FPGA that switches between duals; our approach avoids both problems by providing a LUT. Finally, we tested unbalance empirically. Our variants exclude (anti-)fixed points, so the distribution of output values (over the choice of SubBytes variant) for a given input value should ideally be uniform over 254 entries (i.e., possess 7.99 bits of entropy). We tested 1 million SubBytes variants and observed distributions close to this ideal bound: the maximum entropy loss resulting from unbalance (other than fixed point exclusion) was 0.0002 bits, and the maximum statistical distance between the ideal and observed distributions was 0.01. Hence, our variants are free from dual ciphers' unbalance problem. We investigate reverse engineering SubBytes from FPGA traces next.

5.4   Template Attack to Discover SubBytes

When making the standard assumption that traces can be modeled as multivariate Gaussian, template attacks provide "the strongest form of side channel attack possible in an information theoretic sense" [2]. Unknown plaintext template attacks [36] measure Hamming weights of intermediate values to reduce uncertainty about the key. In this section, we also measure Hamming weights, but to reverse engineer an unknown SubBytes variant instead.

Table 2. Entropy of S^{-1} and ℓ on a single input value, before and after a template attack on SubBytes. Experiment attacked AES SubBytes in DPA Contest v2 data, and averaged over 16 bytes.

Entropy metric	Entropy before template attack	Entropy after template attack	Information gained (bits)
$H(S^{-1})$	8	7.986	3.537
$H_\infty(S^{-1})$	8	7.237	—
$H(\ell)$	2.544	2.526	4.78

Section 5.1 describes our methods. We execute a final round[5] Hamming weight template attack with a twist: the attacker knows the AES key and thus the value of $x = \mathsf{ct}_b \oplus \mathsf{key}_b$ for all bytes b. Hence, instead of predicting the key, the attacker predicts the intermediate value $S^{-1}(x)$ or its Hamming weight $\ell(x) = \mathsf{HW}(S^{-1}(x))$.

Table 2 displays the Shannon entropy and min-entropy in S^{-1} (or ℓ) for a single value of x under the uniform (or binomial) distribution before and after a template attack. Additionally, Table 2 extrapolates the total information that a template attack reveals about SubBytes as the reduction in entropy (i.e., uncertainty) remaining in S^{-1} or ℓ.

Concretely, we estimate that a template attack reveals at most $(8 - 7.986) \times 256 = 3.537$ bits of information about SubBytes. Hence, even with restricting

---

[5] This analysis generalizes to plaintext attacks.

SubBytes to our variants, more than 68 bits of uncertainty remain. Similarly, we estimate that a template attack reveals no more than $(2.544-2.526) \times 256 = 4.78$ bits of information about the Hamming weight profile of SubBytes.

These estimates depend on three simplifying heuristics. First, we assume that the entropy of each of the 256 inputs to S^{-1} or ℓ contributes independently to the overall entropy of the function; in reality, the permutation constraint makes this false, but how to exploit this remains unclear. Second, although the DPA Contest v2 dataset only includes power traces of the AES SubBytes, we assume that these data are representative of the leakage of our variants due to their structural similarity. Third, our metrics postulate that all 16 bytes of state provide similar information under a template attack.

Given the small amount of information revealed about SubBytes and its Hamming weight profile, we found the template attack to discover SubBytes ineffective on FPGA data.

5.5 ShiftRows Discussion

As Fig. 1 shows, ShiftRows changes the physical location of bytes while leaving their values unchanged. Calculating Hamming distance (the number of changed bits) requires knowledge of the physical location of a byte. However, Hamming weight (the number of ones in a value) disregards location.

Table 3. Impact of ShiftRows variants on DPA and template attacks.

Attack	Impact
Guess ShiftRows in adapted DPA attack	Extra 2^6–2^{36} computational effort
Use HW or other leakage mode	Loses stronger HD leakage mode

We randomly selected a diffusion optimal permutation for ShiftRows. This makes the attacker choose between the two possible attacks in Table 3. The first approach guesses ShiftRows for a Hamming distance attack, either partially or fully. If an attacker can distinguish a correct guess of ShiftRows from an incorrect one, a divide and conquer approach adds a minimum of 6 bits to the guessing entropy; in the attacker's worst case, a brute force attack adds 36 bits. The second approach applies Hamming weight, but Fig. 4 (right) shows that the Hamming distance often harnesses leakage better.

6 Conclusion

This research aimed to overcome standard side channel attacks by finding a large pool of Rijndael variants from which to select. While these variants differ from AES, they maintain its mathematical security while counterbalancing side channel attacks. DPA and template attacks (with a feasible number of templates) require knowledge of SubBytes; we described how to generate 2^{72} variants of SubBytes that maintain AES' cryptanalytic properties. These attacks require knowledge of ShiftRows to employ a Hamming distance leakage mode; we describe how to generate 2^{36} variants of ShiftRows that maintain AES' cryptanalytic properties. As these variants follow the mathematical structure of Rijndael, this approach can be implemented mathematically on embedded devices, as well as with lookup tables.

The large variety in the round functions renders the divide and conquer approach of DPA and template attacks infeasible. After losing access to information needed to mount a successful attack, the attacker must attempt to reverse engineer the round function. Based on our experiments with a novel template attack to recover the lost information, we found insufficient signal-to-noise to reverse engineer SubBytes from FPGA traces. Indeed, previous work considers Side-Channel Analysis for Reverse Engineering (SCARE) of SubBytes ineffective against hardware implementations [7, 33]. Also, our variants are balanced, reducing the effectiveness of a correlation collision attack [12].

Our SageMath software generates variants of AES by changing the round function (https://github.com/mit-ll/Diversity-Within-Rijndael). As well as random SubBytes and ShiftRows, the software can choose a MixColumns consistent with the wide trail strategy requirements. This code includes functions to generate variants of AES, test correctness, and test cryptanalytic properties.

Our approach complements masking and shuffling [7]. We believe that our round functions can be implemented securely in hardware; demonstrating this remains future work.

Acknowledgments. We gratefully acknowledge the support of Sukarno Mertoguno in the Office of Naval Research. The second author also acknowledges NSF grant 1414119. Additionally, we thank our colleagues Rob Cunningham and Ben Fuller for their valuable guidance and support.

References

1. Kocher, P., Jaffe, J., Jun, B.: Differential power analysis. In: Wiener, M. (ed.) CRYPTO 1999. LNCS, vol. 1666, pp. 388–397. Springer, Heidelberg (1999). doi:10. 1007/3-540-48405-1_25

2. Chari, S., Rao, J.R., Rohatgi, P.: Template attacks. In: Kaliski, B.S., Koç, K., Paar, C. (eds.) CHES 2002. LNCS, vol. 2523, pp. 13–28. Springer, Heidelberg (2003). doi:10.1007/3-540-36400-5_3

3. DPA Contest v2. http://www.dpacontest.org/v2/. Accessed 12 September 2014

4. Weingart, S.H.: Physical security devices for computer subsystems: a survey of attacks and defenses. In: Koç, Ç.K., Paar, C. (eds.) CHES 2000. LNCS, vol. 1965, pp. 302–317. Springer, Heidelberg (2000). doi:10.1007/3-540-44499-8_24

5. Akkar, M.-L., Giraud, C.: An implementation of DES and AES, secure against some attacks. In: Koç, Ç.K., Naccache, D., Paar, C. (eds.) CHES 2001. LNCS, vol. 2162, pp. 309–318. Springer, Heidelberg (2001). doi:10.1007/3-540-44709-1_26

6. National Institute of Standards and Technology: Federal Information Processing Standards Publication 197: Announcing the Advanced Encryption Standard, November 2001

7. Clavier, C., Isorez, Q., Wurcker, A.: Complete SCARE of AES-like block ciphers by chosen plaintext collision power analysis. In: Paul, G., Vaudenay, S. (eds.) INDOCRYPT 2013. LNCS, vol. 8250, pp. 116–135. Springer, Heidelberg (2013). doi:10.1007/978-3-319-03515-4_8

8. Barkan, E., Biham, E.: In how many ways can you write Rijndael? In: Zheng, Y. (ed.) ASIACRYPT 2002. LNCS, vol. 2501, pp. 160–175. Springer, Heidelberg (2002). doi:10.1007/3-540-36178-2_10

9. Rostovtsev, A., Shemyakina, O.: AES side channel attack protection using random isomorphisms. Cryptology ePrint Archive, Report 2005/087 (2005)

10. Wu, S.-Y., Lu, S.-C., Laih, C.S.: Design of AES based on dual cipher and composite field. In: Okamoto, T. (ed.) CT-RSA 2004. LNCS, vol. 2964, pp. 25–38. Springer, Heidelberg (2004). doi:10.1007/978-3-540-24660-2_3

11. Ghellar, F., Lubaszewski, M.S.: A novel AES cryptographic core highly resistant to differential power analysis attacks. In: Symposium on Integrated Circuits and System Design (2008)

12. Moradi, A., Mischke, O.: Comprehensive evaluation of AES dual ciphers as a side-channel countermeasure. In: Qing, S., Zhou, J., Liu, D. (eds.) ICICS 2013. LNCS, vol. 8233, pp. 245–258. Springer, Heidelberg (2013). doi:10.1007/978-3-319-02726-5_18

13. Rijmen, V., Oswald, E.: Representations and Rijndael descriptions. In: Advanced Encryption Standard (2004)

14. Karroumi, M.: Protecting white-box AES with dual ciphers. In: Rhee, K.-H., Nyang, D.H. (eds.) ICISC 2010. LNCS, vol. 6829, pp. 278–291. Springer, Heidelberg (2011). doi:10.1007/978-3-642-24209-0_19

15. Jing, M.H., Hsu, C., Truong, T.K., Chen, Y.H., Chang, Y.: The diversity study of AES on FPGA application. In: Field-Programmable Technology (2002)

16. Jing, M.H., Chen, Z.H., Chen, J.H., Chen, Y.H.: Reconfigurable system for high-speed and diversified AES using FPGA. Microprocess. Microsyst. **31**, 94–102 (2007)

17. Grosek, O., Siska, J.: Semigroup of matrices over GF2^s and its relation to AES. Comput. Artif. Intell. 22, 417–426 (2003)

18. Grosek, O., Zajac, P.: Searching for a different AES-class MixColumns operation. In: WSEAS International Conference on Applied Computer Science (2006)

19. Manteena, R.: A VHDL Implemetation of the Advanced Encryption Standard-Rijndael Algorithm. Ph.D. thesis, University of South Florida (2004)

20. Dziembowski, S., Kazana, T., Wichs, D.: Key-evolution schemes resilient to space-bounded leakage. In: Rogaway, P. (ed.) CRYPTO 2011. LNCS, vol. 6841, pp. 335–353. Springer, Heidelberg (2011). doi:10.1007/978-3-642-22792-9_19

21. Shannon, C.E.: Communication theory of secrecy systems. Bell Syst. Tech. J. **28**, 656–715 (1949)

22. Daemen, J., Rijmen, V.: The Design of Rijndael. Springer, New York (2002)

23. Murphy, S., Robshaw, M.J.B.: Essential algebraic structure within the AES. In: Yung, M. (ed.) CRYPTO 2002. LNCS, vol. 2442, pp. 1–16. Springer, Heidelberg (2002). doi:10.1007/3-540-45708-9_1

24. Paar, C., Rosner, M.: Comparison of arithmetic architectures for Reed-Solomon decoders in reconfigurable hardware. In: Field-Programmable Custom Computing Machines (FCCM) (1997)

25. OpenSSL: Optimised ANSI C code for the Rijndael cipher (now AES). https://github.com/openssl/openssl/blob/master/crypto/aes/aes_core.c. Accessed 3 April 2016

26. Rouvroy, G., Standaert, F., Quisquater, J., Legat, J.: Compact and efficient encryption/decryption module for FPGA implementation of the AES Rijndael very well suited for small embedded applications. In: International Conference on Information Technology: Coding and Computing (2004)

27. Cusick, T.W., Stanica, P.: Cryptographic Boolean Functions and Applications. Academic Press, San Diego (2009)

28. Stein, W., et al.: Sage Mathematics Software (Version 6.2). The Sage Development Team (2015). http://www.sagemath.org

29. Biham, E., Keller, N.: Cryptanalysis of reduced variants of Rijndael. In: 3rd AES Conference (2000)

30. Piret, G., Quisquater, J.J.: Impossible differential and square attacks: cryptanalytic link and application to Skipjack (2001)

31. Choudary, O., Kuhn, M.G.: Efficient template attacks. IACR Cryptology ePrint Archive (2013)

32. Dichtl, M.: A new method of black box power analysis and a fast algorithm for optimal key search. J. Cryptographic Eng. 1, 255–264 (2011)

33. Rivain, M., Roche, T.: SCARE of secret ciphers with SPN structures. In: Sako, K., Sarkar, P. (eds.) ASIACRYPT 2013. LNCS, vol. 8269, pp. 526–544. Springer, Heidelberg (2013). doi:10.1007/978-3-642-42033-7_27

34. Veyrat-Charvillon, N., Gérard, B., Renauld, M., Standaert, F.-X.: An optimal key enumeration algorithm and its application to side-channel attacks. In: Knudsen, L.R., Wu, H. (eds.) SAC 2012. LNCS, vol. 7707, pp. 390–406. Springer, Heidelberg (2013). doi:10.1007/978-3-642-35999-6_25

35. Novak, R.: Side-channel attack on substitution blocks. In: Zhou, J., Yung, M., Han, Y. (eds.) ACNS 2003. LNCS, vol. 2846, pp. 307–318. Springer, Heidelberg (2003). doi:10.1007/978-3-540-45203-4_24

36. Hanley, N., Tunstall, M., Marnane, W.P.: Unknown plaintext template attacks. In: Youm, H.Y., Yung, M. (eds.) WISA 2009. LNCS, vol. 5932, pp. 148–162. Springer, Heidelberg (2009). doi:10.1007/978-3-642-10838-9_12

NEON-SIDH: Efficient Implementation of Supersingular Isogeny Diffie-Hellman Key Exchange Protocol on ARM

Brian Koziel[1]([⊠]), Amir Jalali[2], Reza Azarderakhsh[3], David Jao[4], and Mehran Mozaffari-Kermani[5]

[1] Texas Instruments, Wylie, USA
kozielbrian@gmail.com
[2] CE Department, RIT, Rochester, USA
amirjalali65@gmail.com
[3] CEECS Department and I-SENSE FAU, Boca Raton, USA
razarderakhsh@fau.edu
[4] C&O Department, University of Waterloo, Waterloo, Canada
djao@uwaterloo.ca
[5] EME Department, RIT, Rochester, USA
mmkeme@rit.edu

Abstract. We investigate the efficiency of implementing the Jao and De Feo isogeny-based post-quantum key exchange protocol (from PQCrypto 2011) on ARM-powered embedded platforms. In this work we propose new primes to speed up constant-time finite field arithmetic and perform isogenies quickly. Montgomery multiplication and reduction are employed to produce a speedup of 3 over the GNU Multiprecision Library. We analyze the recent projective isogeny formulas presented in Costello et al. (Crypto 2016) and conclude that affine isogeny formulas are much faster in ARM devices. We provide fast affine SIDH libraries over 512, 768, and 1024-bit primes. We provide timing results for emerging embedded ARM platforms using the ARMv7A architecture for the 85-, 128-, and 170-bit quantum security levels. Our assembly-optimized arithmetic cuts the computation time for the protocol by 50 % in comparison to our portable C implementation and performs approximately 3 times faster than the only other ARMv7 results found in the literature. The goal of this paper is to show that isogeny-based cryptosystems can be implemented further and be used as an alternative to classical cryptosystems on embedded devices.

Keywords: Elliptic curve cryptography · Post-quantum cryptography · Isogeny-based cryptosystems · ARM embedded processors · Finite-field arithmetic · Assembly implementation

1 Introduction

Post-quantum cryptography (PQC) refers to research on cryptographic primitives (usually public-key cryptosystems) that are not efficiently breakable using

© Springer International Publishing AG 2016
S. Foresti and G. Persiano (Eds.): CANS 2016, LNCS 10052, pp. 88–103, 2016.
DOI: 10.1007/978-3-319-48965-0_6

quantum computers. Most notably, Shor's algorithm [1] can be efficiently implemented on a quantum computer to break standard Elliptic Curve Cryptography (ECC) and RSA cryptosystems. There are some alternatives secure against quantum computing threats, such as the McEliece cryptosystem, lattice-based cryptosystems, code-based cryptosystems, multivariate public key cryptography, and others. Recent work such as [2–4] demonstrates efficient implementations of such quantum-safe cryptosystems on embedded systems. None of these works consider an approach based on quantum-resistant elliptic curve cryptosystems. Hence, they introduce and implement new cryptosystems with different security metrics and performance characteristics.

To avoid quantum computing attacks, Jao and De Feo [5] proposed an elliptic curve based alternative to Elliptic Curve Diffie-Hellman (ECDH) which is not susceptible to Shor's attack, namely the Supersingular Isogeny Diffie-Hellman (SIDH) key exchange protocol. Isogeny computations constitute an algebraic map between elliptic curves, which appear to be resistant to quantum attacks. Thus, this system improves upon traditional ECC and represents a strong candidate for quantum-resistant cryptography. Faster isogeny constructions would speed up such cryptosystems, increase the viability of existing proposals, and make new designs feasible. Existing results on the implementation of isogeny-based key exchange include De Feo et al. [5,6] and Costello et al. [7]. However, implementations on emerging embedded devices have not been fully investigated. It is expected that mobile devices, such as smartphones, tablets, and emerging embedded systems, will become more widespread in the coming years for increasingly sensitive applications. In this work, we investigate the applicability of advances in theoretical quantum-resistant algorithms on real-world applications by providing several efficient implementations on emerging embedded systems. Our goal is to improve the performance of isogeny-based cryptosystems to the point where deployment is practical.

In a recent announcement at PQC 2016 [8], NIST announced a preliminary plan to start the gradual transition to quantum-resistant protocols. As such, there is a tremendous need to discover and implement new proposed methods that are resistant to both classical computers and quantum computers. NIST will evaluate these PQC schemes based on security, speed, size, and tunable parameters. Isogeny-based cryptography provides a suitable replacement for standard ECC or RSA protocols because it provides small key sizes, provides forward secrecy, and has a Diffie-Hellman-like key exchange available. Furthermore, key compression schemes have been proposed in [7,9] to aid in the storage and transmission of ephemeral keys. Lastly, isogeny-based cryptography utilizes standard ECC point multiplication schemes, allowing for re-use of existing ECC libraries and even hybrid schemes that simultaneously use ECC and isogenies to provide quantum resistance, such as the hybrid scheme proposed in [7].

Our contributions:

- We provide efficient libraries[1] for the key exchange protocol presented in [5] using highly optimized C and ASM.
- We present fast and secure prime candidates for 85-bit, 128-bit, and 170-bit quantum security levels.
- We provide hand-optimized finite field arithmetic computations over various ARM-powered processors to produce constant-time arithmetic that is 3 times as fast as GMP.
- We analyze the effectiveness of projective [7] and affine [6] isogeny computation schemes.
- We provide implementation results for embedded devices running Cortex-A8 and Cortex-A15. For the latter, an entire quantum-resistant key exchange with 85-bit quantum security operates in approximately a tenth of a second. Further, our Cortex-A15 assembly optimized results are 3 times faster than [10], the fastest results available in the literature.

2   SIDH Protocol

This serves as a quick introduction to the Supersingular Isogeny Diffie-Hellman key exchange. For a full mathematical background of the protocol, we point the reader to the original works proposing it in [5,6] or [11] for a complete look at elliptic curve theory.

2.1   Key Exchange Protocol Based on Isogenies

Two parties, Alice and Bob, want to exchange a secret key over an insecure channel in the presence of malicious third-parties. They agree on a smooth isogeny prime p of the form $\ell_A^a \ell_B^b \cdot f \pm 1$ where ℓ_A and ℓ_B are small primes, a and b are positive integers, and f is a small cofactor to make the number prime. They define a supersingular elliptic curve, $E_0(\mathbb{F}_q)$ where $q = p^2$. Lastly, they agree on four points on the curve that form two independent bases. Over a starting supersingular curve E_0, these are a basis $\{P_A, Q_A\}$ and $\{P_B, Q_B\}$ which generate $E_0[\ell_A^{e_A}]$ and $E_0[\ell_B^{e_B}]$, respectively, such that $\langle P_A, Q_A \rangle = E_0[\ell_A^{e_A}]$ and $\langle P_B, Q_B \rangle = E_0[\ell_B^{e_B}]$.

As first noted in [12], consider a graph of all supersingular elliptic curves of a fixed isogeny graph under $\mathbb{F}_{p^2}$. In this graph, the vertices represent each isomorphism class of supersingular elliptic curves and the edges represent the degree-ℓ isogenies of a particular isomorphism class. Essentially, each party takes seemingly random walks in the graph of supersingular isogenies of degree ℓ_A^a and ℓ_B^b to both arrive at supersingular elliptic curves with the same isomorphism class and j-invariant, similar to a Diffie-Hellman key exchange. In a graph of supersingular isogenies, the infeasibility to discover a path that connects two particular vertices provides security for this protocol.

---

[1] Code is available at https://github.com/kozielbrian/NEON-SIDH_ARMv7.

Alice chooses two private keys $m_A, n_A \in \mathbb{Z}/\ell_A^a\mathbb{Z}$ with the stipulation that both are not divisible by ℓ_A^a. On the other side, Bob chooses two private keys $m_B, n_B \in \mathbb{Z}/\ell_B^b\mathbb{Z}$, where both private keys are not divisible by ℓ_B^b. From there, the key exchange protocol can be broken down into two rounds of the following:

1. Compute $R = \langle[m]P + [n]Q\rangle$ for points P, Q.
2. Compute the isogeny $\phi : E \rightarrow E/\langle R\rangle$ for a supersingular curve E.
3. Compute the images $\phi(P)$ and $\phi(Q)$ for the basis of the opposite party for the first round.

The key exchange protocol proceeds as follows. Alice performs the double point multiplication with her private keys to obtain a kernel, $R_A = \langle[m_A]P + [n_A]Q\rangle$ and computes an isogeny $\phi_A : E_0 \rightarrow E_A = E_0/\langle[m_A]P + [n_A]Q\rangle$. She performs the large degree isogeny efficiently by performing many small isogenies of degree ℓ_A. She then computes the projection $\{\phi_A(P_B), \phi_A(Q_B)\} \subset E_A$ of the basis $\{P_B, Q_B\}$ for $E_0[\ell_B^b]$ under her secret isogeny ϕ_A, which can be done efficiently by pushing the points P_B and Q_B through each isogeny of degree ℓ_A. Over a public channel, she sends these points and curve E_A to Bob. Likewise, Bob performs his own double-point multiplication and computes his isogeny over the supersingular curve E with $\phi_B : E_0 \rightarrow E_B = E_0/\langle[m_B]P + [n_B]Q\rangle$. He also computes his projection $\{\phi_B(P_A), \phi_B(Q_A)\} \subset E_B$ of the basis $\{P_A, Q_A\}$ for $E_0[\ell_A^a]$ under his secret isogeny ϕ_B and sends these points and curve E_B to Alice. For the second round, Alice performs the double point multiplication to find a second kernel, $R_{AB} = \langle[m_A]\phi_B(P_A) + [n_A]\phi_B(Q_A)\rangle$, to compute a second isogeny $\phi'_A : E_B \rightarrow E_{AB} = E_B/\langle[m_A]\phi_B(P_A) + [n_A]\phi_B(Q_A)\rangle$. Bob also performs a double point multiplication and computes a second isogeny $\phi'_B : E_A \rightarrow E_{BA} = E_A/\langle[m_B]\phi_A(P_B) + [n_B]\phi_A(Q_B)\rangle$. Alice and Bob now have isogenous curves and can use the common j-invariant as a shared secret key.

$$
\begin{aligned}
E_{AB} &= \phi'_B(\phi_A(E_0)) = \phi'_A(\phi_B(E_0)) \\
&= E_0/\{[m_A]P_A + [n_A]Q_A, [m_B]P_B + [n_B]Q_B\}, \\
j(E_{AB}) &\equiv j(E_{BA}).
\end{aligned}
$$

2.2 Protocol Optimizations

Many optimizations have been proposed in [6,7] for computing isogenies. To begin with, all arithmetic is performed on Montgomery curves [13] as they have been shown to have fast scalar point multiplication and fast isogeny formulas. We refer to the Explicit Formulas Database (EFD) [14] for the fastest operation counts on elliptic curves. The Kummer representation for Montgomery curves provides extremely fast curve arithmetic by performing operations on the curve's Kummer line [13]. Points are represented as $(X : Z)$, where $x = X/Z$. Under this scheme, there is no difference between points P and $-P$. The EFD provides explicit formulas for differential addition and point doubling. Note that P and $-P$ generate the same subgroup of points on the elliptic curve, so isogenies can be evaluated correctly on the Kummer line. Lastly, the optimal path to compute large-degree isogenies involves finding an optimal strategy of point multiplications and isogeny evaluations. The general trend has been to use isogeny graphs of base 2 and 3, since fast isogenies between Montgomery curves and fast scalar point multiplications can be performed over these isogeny graphs.

Our implementation style closely follows the methods of [6]. We use a 3-point Montgomery differential ladder (also presented in [6]) for a constant set of operations for double point multiplcations and their "affine" isogeny formulas for computing and evaluating large degree isogenies. We note that [6] does not scale the Z-coordinates of the inputs to the ladder to 1. This would decrease the cost of a 3-point step by 2 multiplications per step. An alternative approach to the double-point multiplication is to utilize a uniform double-point multiplication algorithm, such as those proposed in [15] or [16]. Costello et al. [7] recently proposed "projective" isogeny formulas that represent the curve coefficients of a Montgomery curve in projective space (i.e. a numerator and denominator), so that isogeny calculations do not need inversion until the very end of a round of a key exchange. We also note that [7] proposes sending isogenies evaluated over the points P, Q, and PQ in Kummer coordinates to the other party in the first round and that isogenies of degree 4 have been shown to be faster than isogenies of degree 2.

3   Proposed Choice of SIDH-Friendly Primes

The primes used in the key exchange protocol are the foundation of the underlying arithmetic. Since supersingular curves are used, it is necessary to generate primes to allow the curve to have smooth order so that the isogenies can be computed quickly. For this purpose, smooth isogeny primes of the form $p = \ell_A^a \ell_B^b \cdot f \pm 1$ are selected. Within that group of primes, [6,7] specifically chose isogeny-based cryptosystem parameters of $\ell_A = 2$ and $\ell_B = 3$. These isogeny graph bases provides efficient formulas for isogenies of degree 2 and 3, as shown in [6,7].

Smooth isogeny primes do not feature the distinct shape of a Mersenne prime (e.g. $2^{521} - 1$) or pseudo-Mersenne prime, but the choice of $\ell_A = 2$ does provide for several optimizations to finite-field arithmetic, covered in more detail in Sect. 4.

The security of the underlying isogeny-based cryptosystem is directly related to the relative magnitude of ℓ_A^a and ℓ_B^b, or rather $\min(\ell_A^a, \ell_B^b)$. Whichever isogeny graph is spanned by the smaller prime power is easier to attack. Therefore, a prime should be chosen where these prime powers are approximately equal. As demonstrated in [6], the classical security of the prime is approximately its size in bits divided by 4 and quantum security of a prime is approximately its size in bits divided by 6. Based on this security assessment, the SIDH protocol over a 512-bit, 768-bit, and 1024-bit prime feature approximately 85, 128, and 170 bits of quantum security, respectively.

3.1   Proposed Prime Search

We searched for primes by setting balanced isogeny orders ℓ_A^a and ℓ_B^b for $\ell_A = 2$ and $\ell_B = 3$ and searching for factors f that produce a prime ± 1. However, using

+1 in the form of the prime produces a prime where $-1 \bmod p$ is a quadratic residue, which is not optimal for performing arithmetic in the extension field $\mathbb{F}_{p^2}$. Therefore, we primarily investigated only primes of the form $p = 2^a 3^b \cdot f - 1$. Our primes were found by using a Sage script that changes f to find such primes. We did not search for primes with an f value greater than 100. The primes that we discovered were compared and selected based on the following parameters:

- **Security**: The relative security of SIDH over a prime is based on $\min(\ell_A^a, \ell_B^b)$. Therefore, the prime should have balanced isogeny graphs and a small f term.
- **Size**: These primes are designed to be used in ARM processors, some that are limited in memory. These primes should feature a size slightly less than a power of 2 to allow for some speed optimizations such as lazy reduction and carry cancelling, while still featuring a high quantum security.
- **Speed**: These primes efficiently use space to reduce the number of operations per field arithmetic, but also have nice properties for the field arithmetic. Notably, all primes of the form $p = 2^a \ell_B^b \cdot f - 1$ will have the Montgomery friendly property [17] because the least significant half of the prime will have all bits set to '1'.

Table 1 contains a list of strong prime candidates for 512, 768, and 1024-bit SIDH implementations. Each of these primes feature approximately balanced isogeny graphs. Each prime requires the least number of total bits for a quantum security level. We provide a prime with the f term to be 1 for each security level, but that is not a requirement.

Table 1. Proposed smooth isogeny primes

Security level	Prime size (bits)	$p = \ell_A^a \ell_B^b \cdot f \pm 1$	$\min(\ell_A^a, \ell_B^b)$	Classical security	Quantum security
p_{512}	499	$2^{251} 3^{155} 5 - 1$	3^{155}	123	82
	503	$2^{250} 3^{159} - 1$	2^{250}	125	83
	510	$2^{252} 3^{159} 37 - 1$	2^{252}	126	84
p_{768}	751	$2^{372} 3^{239} - 1$	2^{372}	186	124
	758	$2^{378} 3^{237} 17 - 1$	3^{237}	188	125
	766	$2^{382} 3^{238} 79 - 1$	3^{238}	189	126
p_{1024}	980	$2^{493} 3^{307} - 1$	3^{307}	243	162
	1004	$2^{499} 3^{315} 49 - 1$	2^{499}	249	166
	1008	$2^{501} 3^{316} 41 - 1$	3^{316}	250	167
	1019	$2^{508} 3^{319} 35 - 1$	3^{319}	253	168

We provide several primes within each security level to give tunable parameters for an SIDH implementation. Costello et al. [7] propose using the prime $2^{372} 3^{239} - 1$ for a 768-bit implementation. This prime is actually 751 bits, allowing for 17 bits of freedom for speed optimizations in systems using 32 or 64-bit words. However, as Table 1 shows, the prime $2^{378}3^{237}17 - 1$ is a 758-bit prime that gives 1 more bit of quantum security and still has 10 bits of freedom to allow for speed optimizations. We find it useful to have several strong primes to work with, which could allow for a variety of speed techniques.

For our design, we chose to implement over the primes:

$$p_{512} = 2^{250}3^{159} - 1$$
$$p_{768} = 2^{372}3^{239} - 1$$
$$p_{1024} = 2^{501}3^{316}41 - 1$$

4   Proposed Finite-Field Arithmetic

For any cryptosystem featuring large finite-fields, the finite-field arithmetic lies at the heart of the computations. This work is no exception. The critical operations are finite-field addition, squaring, multiplication, and inversion. The abundance of these operations throughout the entire key exchange protocol calls for numerous optimizations to the arithmetic, even at the assembly level. This work targets the ARMv7-A architectures. All operations are done in the Montgomery domain [18] to take advantage of the extremely fast Montgomery reduction for the primes above.

All arithmetic below is for $\mathbb{F}_p$. Since supersingular curves can be defined over $\mathbb{F}_{p^2}$, a reduction modulus must be defined to simplify the multiplication between elements of $\mathbb{F}_{p^2}$. With the prime choice of $p = 2^a \ell_B^b \cdot f - 1$, -1 is never a quadratic residue of the prime and $x^2 + 1$ can be used as a modulus for the extension field. We utilized reduced arithmetic in $\mathbb{F}_{p^2}$ based on fast arithmetic in $\mathbb{F}_p$.

4.1   Field Addition

Finite-field addition performs $A + B = C$, where $A, B, C \in \mathbb{F}_p$. Essentially, this just means that there is a regular addition of elements A and B to produce a third element C. If $C \geq p$, then $C = C - p$. For ARMv7, this can be efficiently done by using the *ldmia* and *stmia* instructions, which load and store multiple registers at a time, incrementing the address each time. The operands are loaded into multiple registers and added with the carry bit. If the resulting value is larger than the prime for a field, then a subsequent subtraction by the prime occurs. For a constant-time implementation, the conditional flags are used to alter a mask that is applied to the prime as the subtraction occurs. In the case that the value is not larger than the prime, the masked prime becomes 0. Finite-field subtraction is nearly identical to addition, but subtraction with borrow is used and if the borrow flag is set at the end of the subtraction, then the prime is added to the resulting value.

4.2   Field Multiplication and Squaring

Finite-field multiplication performs $A \times B = C$, where $A, B, C \in \mathbb{F}_p$. This equates to a regular multiplication of A and B to produce a third element C. However,

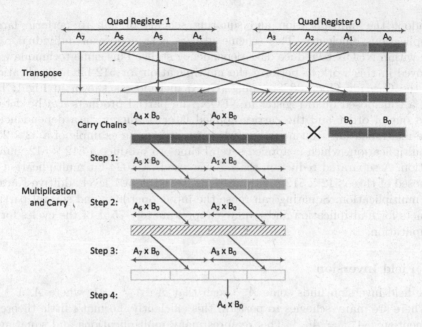

Fig. 1. Finite-field Multiplication using NEON

if elements A and B are both m-bits, then the result, C, is $2m$-bits. A reduction must be made so that the result is still within the field. Montgomery multiplication and reduction [18] was chosen because of its fast reduction method. Introduced in [7], smooth isogeny primes of the form $2^a \ell^b f - 1$ feature a fast reduction based on simplifying the Montgomery reduction formula [18]:

$$ c = (a + (aM' \bmod R)p)/R = (a - aM' \bmod R)/R + ((p+1)(aM' \bmod R)) $$

where $R = 2^m$ is slightly larger than the size of the prime (e.g. $R = 2^{512}$ for p_{512}), a is a result of a multiplication and less than $2m$ bits long, $M' = -p^{-1} \bmod R$, and $c = a \bmod p$. In this equation, $p + 1$ has many least-signficant limbs of '0', since approximately half of the least-significant limbs of p are all '1'. Thus, many partial products can be avoided for reduction over this scheme. An alternative to the above scheme is to leave the Montgomery reduction in its standard form, but perform the first several partial products as subtractions since $0xFF \times A = A \times 2^8 - A$ and the least significant limbs are all '1'.

The typical scheme for Montgomery multiplication is to use $M' = -p^{-1} \bmod 2^w$, where w is the word size. We note that the form of the prime $2^a \ell^b f - 1$ guarantees that $M' = 1$ as long as $2^a > 2^{64}$, for our ARMv7 implementation. This reduces the complexity of Montgomery reduction from $k^2 + k$ to k^2 single-precision multiplication operations, where k is the number of words of an element within the field that must be multiplied.

We utilize the ARM-NEON vector unit to perform the multiplications because it can hold many more registers and parallelize the multiplications.

We adopt the multiplication and squaring scheme of [19] to perform large multiplications efficiently. This scheme utilizes a transpose of individual registers within NEON to reduce data dependency stalls. This same technique was employed in this work to perform the multiplication for 512-bit multiplication with the Cascade Operand Scanning (COS) method, as shown in Fig. 1. By using a transposed quad register in NEON, the partial products can be determined out of order and the carries applied later, reducing data dependencies in the multiplication sequence. Figure 1 demonstrates an example of a 32×256 bit multiplication, which is applied several times to produce a 512×512 multiplication. A separated reduction scheme was used. A 1024-bit multiplication is composed of three 512×512 multiplications, based on a 1 level additive Karatsuba multiplication. Squaring can reuse the input operands and several partial products for multiplication and requires approximately 75 % of the cycles for a multiplication.

4.3 Field Inversion

Finite-field inversion finds some A^{-1} such that $A \cdot A^{-1} = 1$, where $A, A^{-1} \in \mathbb{F}_p$. There are many schemes to perform this efficiently. Fermat's little theorem exponentiates $A^{-1} = A^{p-2}$. This requires many multiplications and squarings, but is a constant set of operations. The Extended Euclidean Algorithm (EEA) has a significantly lower time complexity of $O(\log^2 n)$ compared to $O(\log^3 n)$ for Fermat's little theorem. EEA uses a greatest common divisor algorithm to compute the modular inverse of elements a and b with respect to each other, $ax + by = \gcd(a, b)$. Based on the analysis presented in Sect. 5, the EEA was chosen because it made affine SIDH much faster than projective SIDH. The GMP library already employs a highly optimized version of EEA for various architectures. EEA performs an inversion quickly, but does leak some information about the value being inverted from the timing information. Therefore, to take advantage of this fast inversion and provide some protections against simple power analysis and timing attacks, a random value was multiplied to the element before and after the inversion, effectively obscuring what value was initially being inverted. This requires two extra multiplications, but the additional defense against timing and simple power analysis attacks is necessary for a secure key exchange protocol.

5   Affine or Projective Isogenies

Here, we analyze the complexity of utilizing the new "projective" isogeny formulas presented by Costello et al. in [7] to the "affine" isogeny formulas presented by De Feo et al. in [6]. Notably, the projective formulas allow for constant-time inversion implementations without greatly increasing the total time of the protocol. However, in terms of non-constant inversion, we will show that the affine isogeny formulas are still much faster for ARMv7 devices. For cost comparison between these formulas, let I, M, and S refer to inversion, multiplication, and squaring in $\mathbb{F}_p$, respectively. A tilde above the letter indicates that the operation is in $\mathbb{F}_{p^2}$.

Table 2. Comparison of I/M ratios for various computer architectures based on GMP library

Architecture	Device	I/M ratio		
		p_{512}	p_{768}	p_{1024}
ARMv7 Cortex-A8	Beagle Board Black	7.0	6.4	6.1
ARMv7 Cortex-A15	Jetson TK1	7.1	6.1	5.9
ARMv8 Cortex-A53	Linaro HiKey	8.2	7.3	6.5
Haswell x86-64	i7-4790k	14.9	14.7	13.8

Table 3. Affine isogeny formulas vs. projective isogenies formulas

Computation	Affine cost [6]	Projective cost [7]
Point Mult-by-3	$7\tilde{M} + 4\tilde{S}$	$8\tilde{M} + 5\tilde{S}$
Iso-3 Computation	$1\tilde{I} + 5\tilde{M} + 1\tilde{S}$	$3\tilde{M} + 3\tilde{S}$
Iso-3 Evaluation	$4\tilde{M} + 2\tilde{S}$	$6\tilde{M} + 2\tilde{S}$
Point Mult-by-4	$6\tilde{M} + \tilde{S}$	$8\tilde{M} + 4\tilde{S}$
Iso-4 Computation	$1\tilde{I} + 3\tilde{M}$	$5\tilde{S}$
Iso-4 Evaluation	$6\tilde{M} + 4\tilde{S}$	$9\tilde{M} + 1\tilde{S}$

We introduce the idea of the inversion/multiplication ratio, or for SIDH over $\mathbb{F}_{p^2}$, $\tilde{I}/\tilde{M}$, as a metric to compare the relative cost of inversion and multiplication and decide between the effectiveness of affine or projective formulas. This inversion/multiplication ratio is dependent on the size of elements in $\mathbb{F}_p$, the processor, as well as the inversion used. For a constant-time inversion using Fermat's little theorem, the ratio is most likely several hundred since it requires several hundred multiplications and squarings for the inversion exponentiation. However, for non-constant time inversion, such as EEA or Kaliski's almost inverse [20], the ratio is much smaller. Table 2 compares the I/M ratio for different computer architectures over the GNU Multiprecision Library (GMP). We note that with optimized multiplication, this ratio would generally be higher, but it gives an idea of the relative difference between I/M ratios for ARM architectures and x86 architectures. As Table 2 shows, the I/M ratio for a PC is much greater than ARM architectures, by a factor of 2. This shows that ARM implementations benefit much more from using affine isogeny computations.

In Table 3, we compare the relative computational costs of affine isogeny formulas presented in [6] and projective isogeny formulas presented in [7] over isogenies of degree 3 and 4. Point multiplications by ℓ are over Kummer coordinates with affine or projective curve coefficients. Isogeny computations compute the map between two points and isogeny evaluations push a point through the mapping, both of these are of degree ℓ. Affine isogeny computations cost more than their projective counterpart because certain calculations are performed that are reused across each affine isogeny evaluation.

Table 4. Relative costs of computing large-degree isogenies based on affine vs. projective isogeny formulas

Prime	#3P	#3eval	#3comp	LargeIso3Cost	#4P	#4eval	#4comp	LargeIso4Cost
Affine Isogeny Computations								
p_{512}	496	698	159	$159\tilde{I} + 9417\tilde{M}$	457	410	124	$124\tilde{I} + 6966\tilde{M}$
p_{768}	780	1176	239	$239\tilde{I} + 15163\tilde{M}$	771	638	185	$185\tilde{I} + 11215\tilde{M}$
p_{1024}	1123	1568	316	$316\tilde{I} + 21005\tilde{M}$	1061	942	250	$250\tilde{I} + 15974\tilde{M}$
Projective Isogeny Computations								
p_{512}	500	691	159	$11525\tilde{M}$	423	441	124	$9182\tilde{M}$
p_{768}	811	1124	239	$18623\tilde{M}$	638	771	185	$14865\tilde{M}$
p_{1024}	1129	1558	316	$25792\tilde{M}$	981	1013	250	$21076\tilde{M}$

From this table, we created optimal strategies for traversing the large-degree isogeny graphs. The affine and projective optimal strategy differed because the ratio of point multiplication over isogeny evaluation differed. Similar to the method proposed by [6] and also implemented in [7], we created an optimal strategy to traverse the graph. We based the cost of traversing the graph with the relationship $\tilde{S} = 0.66\tilde{M}$, since there are 2 multiplications in $\mathbb{F}_p$ for $\tilde{S}$ and 3 multiplications in $\mathbb{F}_p$ for $\tilde{M}$. We performed this experiment for our selected primes in the 512-bit, 768-bit, and 1024-bit categories, shown in Table 4. In Table 4, we count the total number of point multiplications by ℓ as $\#\ell P$, the total number of ℓ−isogeny evaluations as $\#\ell$eval, and the total number of ℓ−isogeny computations as $\#\ell$comp. From the cost of these operations in affine or projective coordinates, shown in Table 3, we calculated the total cost of the large-degree isogeny in terms of multiplications and inversions in $\mathbb{F}_{p^2}$ under LargeIsoℓCost.

We note that the difference in performance is also much greater for the first round of the SIDH protocol, as the other party's basis points are pushed through the isogeny mapping. This includes 3 additional isogeny evaluations per isogeny computation, as P, Q, and $P - Q$ are pushed through the isogeny. In Table 5, we compare the break-even points for when the cost of affine and projective isogenies are the same. If the ratio is smaller than the break-even point, then the large-degree isogeny computation is faster with affine isogeny formulas. Alice operates over degree 4 isogenies and Bob operates over degree 3 isogenies. We utilize $\tilde{I} = I + 3.33\tilde{M}$ to get the break-even points for operations in $\mathbb{F}_p$ since we used a Karatsuba-based inversion. Thus, $I/M = 3(\tilde{I}/\tilde{M} - 3.33)$. As an example, the break-even point for Alice's round 1 isogeny is $I = 53M$ at the 512-bit level. Thus, even with conservative estimates for the cost of using projective coordinates, affine coordinates trump projective coordinates for small I/M ratios.

Table 5. Comparison of break-even inversion/multiplication ratios for large-degree isogenies at different security levels. When the inversion over multiplication ratio is at the break-even point, affine isogenies require approximately the same cost as projective isogenies. Ratios smaller than these numbers are faster with affine formulas.

Prime	Alice round 1 Iso	Bob round 1 Iso	Alice round 2 Iso	Bob round 2 Iso
p_{512}	$\tilde{I} = 20.87\tilde{M}$	$\tilde{I} = 19.26\tilde{M}$	$\tilde{I} = 17.87\tilde{M}$	$\tilde{I} = 13.26\tilde{M}$
p_{768}	$\tilde{I} = 22.73\tilde{M}$	$\tilde{I} = 20.48\tilde{M}$	$\tilde{I} = 19.73\tilde{M}$	$\tilde{I} = 14.48\tilde{M}$
p_{1024}	$\tilde{I} = 23.41\tilde{M}$	$\tilde{I} = 21.15\tilde{M}$	$\tilde{I} = 20.41\tilde{M}$	$\tilde{I} = 15.15\tilde{M}$
p_{512}	$I = 52.62M$	$I = 47.78M$	$I = 43.62M$	$I = 29.78M$
p_{768}	$I = 58.20M$	$I = 51.44M$	$I = 49.20M$	$I = 33.46M$
p_{1024}	$I = 60.23M$	$I = 53.46M$	$I = 51.23M$	$I = 35.46M$

6 Implementation Results and Discussion

In this section, we review the ARM architectures that were used as testing platforms, how we optimized the assembly code around them, and present our results.

6.1 ARM Architectures

As the name Advanced RISC Machines implies, ARM implements architectures that feature simple instruction execution. The architectures have evolved over the years, but this work will focus on the ARMv7-A. The ARMv7-A family employs a 32-bit architecture that uses 16 general-purpose registers, although registers 13, 14, and 15 are reserved for the stack pointer, link register, and program counter, respectively. ARM-NEON is a Single-Instruction Multiple-Data (SIMD) engine that provides vector instructions for the ARMv7 architecture. ARMv7's NEON features 32 registers that are 64-bits wide or alternatively viewed as 16 registers that are 128-bits wide. NEON provides nice speedups over standard register approaches by taking advantage of data paralellism in the large register sizes. This comes in handy primarily in multiplication, squaring, and reduction.

We benchmarked the following boards running these ARM architectures:

- A BeagleBoard Black running a single ARMv7 Cortex-A8 processor operating at 1.0 GHz.
- A Jetson TK1 running 4 ARMv7 Cortex-A15 cores operating at 2.3 GHz.

6.2 Testing Methodology

The key exchange was written in the standard C language. We used GMP version 6.1.0. The code was compiled using the standard operating system and development environment on the given device. A parameters file defining the agreed upon curve, basis points, and strategies for the key exchange was generated externally using Sage. The strictly C code with GMP is fairly portable and can be used with primes of any size, as long as it is provided with a valid parameters file. There are separate versions which include the 512-bit and 1024-bit assembly optimizations that only work with primes up to these sizes. The protocols are identical in both the C and ASM implementations. The primes that were used can be found in Table 3.

6.3   Results and Comparison

The results for this experiment are presented in Tables 6 and 7 for the Beagle-Board Black and Jetson TK1, respectively. This provides the timings, in clock cycles, of individual finite field operations in $\mathbb{F}_p$ and $\mathbb{F}_{p^2}$ as well as the total computation time of each party for the protocol. The expected time to run this protocol is roughly Alice or Bob's computation time and some transmission cost.

The Beagle Board Black achieved a speedup of 2.27 over the 512-bit primes and a speedup of 2.00 over 1024-bit primes when using our hand-optimized assembly code over our generic C code. The Jetson TK1 achieved a speedup of 1.94 for 512-bit primes and a speedup of 1.59 for 1024-bit primes when using the assembly code. These speedups came as a result of the optimized finite field arithmetic over $\mathbb{F}_p$. Addition is generally a fraction of the cost. Multiplication and squaring are almost twice as fast with the ASM. The most significant improvement is reduction around 3-3.5 times as fast with the ASM. Addition in $\mathbb{F}_{p^2}$ is approximately 5–7 times faster with assembly because the intermediate elements were guaranteed to be in the field, only requiring a subtraction with a mask as a modulus. With the assembly optimizations, the Beagle Board Black performs one party's computations in approximately 0.223 s and 1.65 s over 85-bit and 170-bit quantum security, respectively. The Jetson TK1 performs one party's computations in approximately 0.066 s and 0.491 s over 85-bit and 170-bit quantum security, respectively.

Table 6. Timing results of key exchange on Beagle Board Black ARMv7 device for different security levels

Beagle Board Black (ARM v7) Cortex-A8 at 1.0 GHz using C										
Field size	$\mathbb{F}_p$ [cc]					$\mathbb{F}_{p^2}$ [cc]				Key Exch. [cc × 10³]	
	A	S	M	mod	I	$\tilde{A}$	$\tilde{S}$	$\tilde{M}$	$\tilde{I}$	Alice	Bob
p_{512}	115	1866	2295	3429	40100	1241	12229	14896	72400	483,968	514,786
p_{768}	142	3652	4779	6325	71500	1404	23167	28459	135400	1,406,381	1,525,215
p_{1024}	168	5925	8202	10150	111900	1558	38046	46891	211400	3,135,526	3,367,448
Beagle Board Black (ARM v7) Cortex-A8 at 1.0 GHz using ASM and NEON										
Field size	$\mathbb{F}_p$ [cc]					$\mathbb{F}_{p^2}$ [cc]				Key Exch. [cc × 10³]	
	A	S	M	mod	I	$\tilde{A}$	$\tilde{S}$	$\tilde{M}$	$\tilde{I}$	Alice	Bob
p_{512}	70	718	953	962	40100	279	4445	6736	52756	216,503	229,206
p_{1024}	120	2714	3723	3956	111900	375	15714	23682	150795	1,597,504	1,708,383

Table 7. Timing results of key exchange on NVIDIA Jetson TK-1 ARMv7 device for different security levels

Jetson TK-1 Board (ARM v7) Cortex-A15 at 2.3 GHz using C										
Field size	$\mathbb{F}_p$ [cc]				$\mathbb{F}_{p^2}$ [cc]				Key Exch. [cc × 10^3]	
	A	S	M	mod	I	$\tilde{A}$	$\tilde{S}$	$\tilde{M}$	$\tilde{I}$	Alice	Bob
p_{512}	83	926	1152	2271	24302	877	7256	8776	42481	285,026	302,332
p_{768}	99	1679	2403	4024	39100	982	13467	16216	73922	783,303	848,461
p_{1024}	117	2955	4144	6053	59800	1122	21558	26286	115437	1,728,183	1,851,782
Jetson TK-1 Board (ARM v7) Cortex-A15 at 2.3 GHz using ASM and NEON										
Field size	$\mathbb{F}_p$ [cc]				$\mathbb{F}_{p^2}$ [cc]				Key Exch. [cc × 10^3]	
	A	S	M	mod	I	$\tilde{A}$	$\tilde{S}$	$\tilde{M}$	$\tilde{I}$	Alice	Bob
p_{512}	39	516	640	732	24302	158	3025	4579	34049	148,003	154,657
p_{1024}	73	1856	2464	2961	59800	273	11273	17007	97594	1,118,644	1,140,626

Our implementation follows the algorithms and formulas of the affine key exchange protocol given in [6]. Our implementation also includes side-channel resistance. Our finite-field arithmetic is constant-time, except for inversion which applies extra multiplications for protection, and we utilize a constant set of operations that deal with the secret keys. Lastly, our C implementation is portable because it only requires a C compiler and the GNU library.

The only other portable implementations of SIDH for ARMv7 are [7,10]. Of these, [7] only operates with projective isogeny formulas over the 751-bit prime, $2^{372}3^{239}-1$, and uses a generic, constant-time, implementation with Montgomery reduction. [10] uses the same affine formulas as our implementation, but uses primes that are not as efficient. Table 8 contains a comparison of these implementations for ARM Cortex-A15. We note that the assembly optimizations are not applied for our 768-bit version. Similarly, [7] has generic arithmetic with Montgomery reduction. Our assembly optimized implementation is approximately 3 times faster than the implementation in [10] and the portable C implementation is about 5 times faster than the projective isogeny implementation in [7].

Table 8. Comparison of affine and projective isogeny implementations on ARM Cortex-A15 embedded processors. Our work and [7] was done on a Jetson TK1 and [10] was performed on an Arndale ARM Cortex-A15.

Work	Lang	Field size [bits]	PQ Sec. [bits]	Iso. Eq	Timings [cc × 10^6]				
					Alice R1	Bob R1	Alice R2	Bob R2	Total
Costello et al. [7][1]	C	751	124	Proj.	1,794	2,120	1,665	2,001	7,580
Azarderakhsh et al. [10]	C	521	85	Affine	N/A	N/A	N/A	N/A	1,069
	C	771	128		N/A	N/A	N/A	N/A	3,009
	C	1035	170		N/A	N/A	N/A	N/A	6,477
This work	ASM	503	83	Affine	83	87	66	68	302
	C	751	124		437	474	346	375	1,632
	ASM	1008	167		603	657	516	484	2,259

1. Targeted x86-64 architectures, but is portable on ARM. All arithmetic is in generic C.

Moreover, [10] does not consider side-channel attacks, but [7] is a constant-time implementation, which is inherently protected against simple power analysis and timing attacks.

There are several other popular post-quantum cryptosystems that have been implemented in the literature. The ones that consider embedded system have typically used FPGA's or 8-bit microcontrollers, such as the lattice-based system in [2], code-based system in [4], or McEllice system in [3]. The comparison with any of these works is difficult because the algorithms are extremely different and the implementations did not use ARM-powered embedded devices.

7   Conclusion

In this paper, we proved that isogeny-based key exchanges can be implemented efficiently on emerging ARM embedded devices and represent a new alternative to classical cryptosystems. Both efficient primes and the impact of projective isogeny formulas were investigated. Without transmission overhead, a party can compute their side of the key exchange in fractions of a second. We hope that the initial investigation of this protocol on embedded devices will inspire other researchers to continue looking into isogeny-based implementations as a strong candidate for NIST's call for post-quantum resistant cryptosystems. As a future work, we plan to investigate redundant arithmetic schemes with NEON and apply our assembly optimizations to the projective isogeny formulas for a constant-time implementation. We note that robust and high-performance implementations provide critical support for industry adoption of isogeny-based cryptosystems.

Acknowledgment. The authors would like to thank the reviewers for their constructive comments. This material is based upon work supported by the National Science Foundation under grant No. CNS-1464118 awarded to Reza Azarderakhsh.

References

1. Shor, P.W.: Algorithms for quantum computation: discrete logarithms and factoring. In: 35th Annual Symposium on Foundations of Computer Science (FOCS 1994), pp. 124–134 (1994)
2. Güneysu, T., Lyubashevsky, V., Pöppelmann, T.: Practical lattice-based cryptography: a signature scheme for embedded systems. In: Prouff, E., Schaumont, P. (eds.) CHES 2012. LNCS, vol. 7428, pp. 530–547. Springer, Heidelberg (2012). doi:10.1007/978-3-642-33027-8_31
3. Heyse, S.: Implementation of Mceliece based on quasi-dyadic goppa codes for embedded devices. In: Yang, B.-Y. (ed.) PQCrypto 2011. LNCS, vol. 7071, pp. 143–162. Springer, Heidelberg (2011). doi:10.1007/978-3-642-25405-5_10
4. Heyse, S., Maurich, I., Güneysu, T.: Smaller keys for code-based cryptography: QC-MDPC McEliece implementations on embedded devices. In: Bertoni, G., Coron, J.-S. (eds.) CHES 2013. LNCS, vol. 8086, pp. 273–292. Springer, Heidelberg (2013). doi:10.1007/978-3-642-40349-1_16

5. Jao, D., Feo, L.: Towards quantum-resistant cryptosystems from supersingular elliptic curve isogenies. In: Yang, B.-Y. (ed.) PQCrypto 2011. LNCS, vol. 7071, pp. 19–34. Springer, Heidelberg (2011). doi:10.1007/978-3-642-25405-5_2
6. De Feo, L., Jao, D., Plut, J.: Towards quantum-resistant cryptosystems from supersingular elliptic curve isogenies. J. Math. Cryptology **8**(3), 209–247 (2014)
7. Costello, C., Longa, P., Naehrig, M.: Efficient algorithms for supersingular isogeny Diffie-Hellman. In: Robshaw, M., Katz, J. (eds.) CRYPTO 2016. LNCS, vol. 9814, pp. 572–601. Springer, Heidelberg (2016). doi:10.1007/978-3-662-53018-4_21
8. Chen, L., Jordan, S.: Report on post-quantum cryptography, NIST IR 8105 (2016)
9. Azarderakhsh, R., Jao, D., Kalach, K., Koziel, B., Leonardi, C.: Key compression for isogeny-based cryptosystems. In: Proceedings of the 3rd ACM International Workshop on ASIA Public-Key Cryptography, AsiaPKC 2016, pp. 1–10. ACM, New York (2016)
10. Azarderakhsh, R., Fishbein, D., Jao, D.: Efficient implementations of a quantum-resistant key-exchange protocol on embedded systems. Technical report, University of Waterloo (2014)
11. Silverman, J.H.: The Arithmetic of Elliptic Curves. GTM, vol. 106. Springer, New York (1992)
12. Mestre, J.F.: La méthode des graphes. Exemples et applications. In: Proceedings of the International Conference on Class Numbers and Fundamental Units of Algebraic Number Fields (Katata, 1986), pp. 217–242. Nagoya Univ., Nagoya (1986)
13. Montgomery, P.: Speeding the pollard and elliptic curve methods of factorization. Math. Comput. **48**, 243–264 (1987)
14. Bernstein, D.J., Lange, T.: Explicit-formulas database (2007). http://www.hyperelliptic.org/EFD/
15. Bernstein, D.J.: Differential addition chains. Technical report (2006). http://cr.yp.to/ecdh/diffchain-20060219.pdf
16. Azarderakhsh, R., Karabina, K.: A new double point multiplication algorithm and its application to binary elliptic curves with endomorphisms. IEEE Trans. Comput. **63**(10), 2614–2619 (2014)
17. Gueron, S., Krasnov, V.: Fast prime field elliptic-curve cryptography with 256-bit primes. J. Cryptograph. Eng. **5**(2), 141–151 (2014)
18. Montgomery, P.L.: Modular multiplication without trial division. Math. Comput. **44**(170), 519–521 (1985)
19. Seo, H., Liu, Z., Grobschadl, J., Kim, H.: Efficient arithmetic on ARM-NEON and its application for high-speed RSA implementation. Cryptology ePrint Archive, Report 2015/465 (2015)
20. Kaliski, B.S.: The montgomery inverse and its applications. IEEE Trans. Comput. **44**(8), 1064–1065 (1995)

Lattice-Based Cryptography

Server-Aided Revocable Identity-Based Encryption from Lattices

Khoa Nguyen[✉], Huaxiong Wang, and Juanyang Zhang[✉]

Division of Mathematical Sciences, School of Physical and Mathematical Sciences,
Nanyang Technological University, Singapore, Singapore
{khoantt,hxwang,zh0078ng}@ntu.edu.sg

Abstract. Server-aided revocable identity-based encryption (SR-IBE), recently proposed by Qin et al. at ESORICS 2015, offers significant advantages over previous user revocation mechanisms in the scope of IBE. In this new system model, almost all the workloads on users are delegated to an untrusted server, and users can compute decryption keys at any time period without having to communicate with either the key generation center or the server.

In this paper, inspired by Qin et al.'s work, we design the first SR-IBE scheme from lattice assumptions. Our scheme is more efficient than existing constructions of lattice-based revocable IBE. We prove that the scheme is selectively secure in the standard model, based on the hardness of the Learning with Errors problem. At the heart of our design is a "double encryption" mechanism that enables smooth interactions between the message sender and the server, as well as between the server and the recipient, while ensuring the confidentiality of messages.

1 Introduction

Identity-based encryption (IBE), envisaged by Shamir [33] in 1984, allows to use arbitrary strings representing users' identities (e.g., email addresses) as public keys, and thus, greatly simplifies the burden of key management in traditional public-key infrastructure (PKI). In an IBE scheme, there is a trusted authority, called the Key Generation Center (KGC), who is in charge of generating a private key corresponding to each identity and sending it to the user through a secret channel. Such private key enables the user to recover messages encrypted under his identity. Shamir's ideas triggered an exciting search for provably secure IBE systems, but the first realizations only appeared in 2001, when Boneh and Franklin [7] and Cocks [12] presented constructions based on pairings and on the quadratic residual problem, respectively. The third class of IBE, pioneered by Gentry et al. [15] in 2008, is based on lattice assumptions.

As for many multi-user cryptosystems, an efficient revocation mechanism is necessary and imperative in the IBE setting. If some identities have been revoked due to certain reasons (e.g., the user misbehaves or his private key is stolen), the mechanism should ensure that: (i) the revoked identities no longer possess the decryption capability; (ii) the workloads of the KGC and the non-revoked users in

© Springer International Publishing AG 2016
S. Foresti and G. Persiano (Eds.): CANS 2016, LNCS 10052, pp. 107–123, 2016.
DOI: 10.1007/978-3-319-48965-0_7

updating the system are "small". Designing an IBE scheme supported by efficient revocation turned out to be a challenging problem. A naïve solution, suggested by Boneh and Franklin in their seminal work [7], requires users to periodically renew their private keys by communicating with the KGC per time epoch, via a secure channel. This solution, while yielding a straightforward revocation method (i.e., revoked identities are not given new keys), is too impractical to be used for large-scale system, as the workload of the KGC grows linearly in the number of users N. Later on, Boldyreva, Goyal and Kumar (BGK) [5] formally defined the notion of revocable identity-based encryption (RIBE), and employed the tree-based revocation techniques from [26] to construct the first scalable RIBE in which the KGC's workload is only logarithmic in N. In the BGK model, however, the non-revoked users have to communicate with the KGC regularly to receive the update keys. Although this key updating process can be done through a public channel, it is somewhat inconvenient and bandwidth-consuming.

To improve the situation, Qin et al. [29] recently proposed server-aided revocable identity-based encryption (SR-IBE) - a new revocation approach in which almost all workloads on users are outsourced to a server, and users can compute decryption keys at any time period without having to communicate with either the KGC or the server. Moreover, the server can be untrusted (in the sense that it does not possess any secret information) and should just perform correct computations. More specifically, an SR-IBE scheme functions as follows. When setting up the system, the KGC issues a long-term private key to each user. The update keys are sent only to the server (via a public channel) rather than to all users. The ciphertexts also go through the server who transforms them to "partially decrypted ciphertexts" which are forwarded to the intended recipients. The latter then can recover the messages using decryption keys derived from their long-term keys. This is particularly well-suited for applications such as secure email systems, where email addresses represent users' identities and the (untrusted) email server performs most of the computations. In [29], apart from introducing this new model, Qin et al. also described a pairing-based instantiation of SR-IBE.

In this work, inspired by the advantages and potentials of SR-IBE, we put it into the world of lattice-based cryptography, and design the first SR-IBE scheme from lattice assumptions.

RELATED WORKS. The subset cover framework, originally proposed by Naor, Naor and Lotspiech (NNL) [26] in the context of broadcast encryption, is arguably the most well-known revocation technique for multi-user systems. It uses a binary tree, each leaf of which is designated to each user. Non-revoked users are partitioned into disjoint subsets, and are assigned keys according to the Complete Subtree (CS) method or the Subset Difference (SD) method. This framework was first considered in the IBE setting by Boldyreva et al. [5]. Subsequently, several pairing-based RIBE schemes [17,23,32] were proposed, providing various improvements. Among them, the work by Seo and Emura [32] suggested a strong security notion for RIBE, that takes into account the threat of decryption key exposure attacks. The NNL framework also found applications in the context of revocable group signatures [20,21].

The study of IBE with outsourced revocation was initiated by Li et al. [18], who introduced a method to outsource the key update workload of the trusted KGC to a semi-trusted KGC. Indeed, revocation mechanisms with an online semi-trusted third party (called mediator) had appeared in earlier works [6, 13,22]. However, all these approaches are vulnerable against collusion attacks between revoked users and the semi-trusted KGC or the mediator.

Lattice-based cryptography has been an exciting research area since the seminal works of Regev [30] and Gentry et al. [15]. Lattices not only allow to build powerful primitives (e.g., [14,16]) that have no feasible instantiations in conventional number-theoretic cryptography, but they also provide several advantages over the latter, such as conjectured resistance against quantum adversaries and faster arithmetic operations. In the scope of lattice-based IBE and hierarchical IBE (HIBE), numerous schemes have been introduced, in the random oracle model [2,15] and the standard model [1,9,35,36]. Chen et at. [10] employed Agrawal et al.'s IBE [1] and the CS method to construct the first revocable IBE from lattices, which satisfies selective security in the standard model. The second scheme, proposed by Cheng and Zhang [11], achieves adaptive security, via the SD method. Both of these works follow the BGK model [5].

OUR RESULTS AND TECHNIQUES. We introduce the first construction of lattice-based SR-IBE. We inherit the main efficiency advantage of Qin et al.'s model over the BGK model for RIBE: the system users do not have to communicate with any party to get update keys, as they are capable of computing decryption keys for any time period on their own. As for previous lattice-based RIBE schemes [10,11], our proposal works with one-bit messages, but multi-bit variants can be achieved with small overhead, using standard techniques [1,15]. The public parameters and the ciphertexts produced by the scheme have bit-sizes comparable to those of [10,11]. The long-term private key of each user has size constant in the number of all users N, but to enable the delegation of decryption keys, it has to be a trapdoor matrix with relatively large size. The full efficiency comparison among the schemes from [10,11] and ours is given in Table 1.

As a high level, our design approach is similar to the pairing-based instantiation by Qin et al., in the sense that we also employ an RIBE scheme [10] and a two-level HIBE scheme [1] as the building blocks. In our setting, the server simultaneously plays two roles: it is the decryptor in the RIBE block (i.e., it

Table 1. Comparison among known lattice-based revocable IBE schemes. Here, λ is the security parameter, N is the maximum number of users, r is the number of revoked users. For the scheme from [11], the number ϵ is a small constant such that $\epsilon < 1/2$. The notation "-" means that such an item does not exist in the corresponding scheme.

		Public Params. Size	Token Size	Private Key Size	Update Key Size	Ciphertext Size	Model
[10]		$\tilde{O}(\lambda^2)$	-	$O(\log N) \cdot \tilde{O}(\lambda)$	$r \log \dfrac{N}{r} \cdot \tilde{O}(\lambda)$	$\tilde{O}(\lambda)$	Selective
[11]		$\tilde{O}(\lambda^{2+\epsilon})$	-	$O(\log^2 N) \cdot \tilde{O}(\lambda)$	$(2r-1) \cdot \tilde{O}(\lambda)$	$\tilde{O}(\lambda^{1+\epsilon})$	Adaptive
Ours	Server	$\tilde{O}(\lambda^2)$	$O(\log N) \cdot \tilde{O}(\lambda)$	-	$r \log \dfrac{N}{r} \cdot \tilde{O}(\lambda)$	$\tilde{O}(\lambda)$	Selective
	User	-	-	$\tilde{O}(\lambda^2)$	-	$\tilde{O}(\lambda)$	

receives ciphertexts from senders and performs the decryption mechanism of RIBE - which is called "partial decryption" here), and at the same time, it is the sender in the HIBE block. The users (i.e., the message recipients), on the other hand, only work with the HIBE block. Their identities are placed at the first level of the hierarchy, while the time periods are put at the second level. This enables the user with private key for id to delegate a decryption key for an ordered pair of the form (id, t).

However, looking into the details, it is not straightforward to make the two building blocks operate together. Qin et al. address this problem by using a key splitting technique which currently seems not available in the lattice setting. Instead, we adapt a double encryption mechanism, recently employed by Libert et al. [19] in the context of lattice-based group signatures with message-dependent opening [31], which works as follows. The sender encrypts the message under the HIBE to obtain an initial ciphertext of the form $(\mathbf{c}_2, c_0)$, where c_0 is an element of $\mathbb{Z}_q$ (for some $q > 2$) and is the ciphertext component carrying the message information. Next, he encrypts the binary representation of c_0, i.e., vector $\mathrm{bin}(c_0) \in \{0,1\}^{\lceil \log q \rceil}$, under the RIBE to obtain $(\mathbf{c}_1, \hat{\mathbf{c}}_0)$. The final ciphertext is then set as $(\mathbf{c}_1, \mathbf{c}_2, \hat{\mathbf{c}}_0)$ and is sent to the server. The latter will invert the second step of the encryption mechanism to get back to the initial ciphertext $(\mathbf{c}_2, c_0)$. Receiving $(\mathbf{c}_2, c_0)$ from the server, the user should be able to recover the message.

The security of our SR-IBE scheme relies on that of the two lattice-based building blocks, i.e., Agrawal et al.'s HIBE [1] and Chen et al.'s RIBE. Both of them are selectively secure in the standard model, assuming the hardness of the Learning with Errors (LWE) problem - so is our scheme.

ORGANIZATION. The rest of this paper is organized as follows. Section 2 provides definitions of SR-IBE and some background on lattice-based cryptography. Our construction of lattice-based SR-IBE and its analysis are presented in Sects. 3 and 4, respectively. We summarize our results and discuss open problems in Sect. 5.

2   Background and Definitions

NOTATIONS. The acronym PPT stands for "probabilistic polynomial-time". We say that a function $d : \mathbb{N} \to \mathbb{R}$ is negligible, if for sufficient large $\lambda \in \mathbb{N}$, $|d(\lambda)|$ is smaller than the reciprocal of any polynomial in λ. The statistical distance of two random variables X and Y over a discrete domain Ω is defined as $\Delta(X;Y) \triangleq \frac{1}{2} \sum_{s \in \Omega} |\Pr[X = s] - \Pr[Y = s]|$. If $X(\lambda)$ and $Y(\lambda)$ are ensembles of random variables, we say that X and Y are statistically close if $d(\lambda) \triangleq \Delta(X(\lambda); Y(\lambda))$ is a negligible function of λ. For a distribution χ, we often write $x \hookleftarrow \chi$ to indicate that we sample x from χ. For a finite set Ω, the notation $x \xleftarrow{\$} \Omega$ means that x is chosen uniformly at random from Ω.

We use bold upper-case letters (e.g., $\mathbf{A}, \mathbf{B}$) to denote matrices and use bold lower-case letters (e.g., $\mathbf{x}, \mathbf{y}$) to denote column vectors. For two matrices $\mathbf{A} \in \mathbb{Z}^{n \times m}$ and $\mathbf{B} \in \mathbb{Z}^{n \times m_1}$, $[\mathbf{A}|\mathbf{B}] \in \mathbb{Z}^{n \times (m+m_1)}$ is the concatenation of the columns of $\mathbf{A}$ and $\mathbf{B}$. For a vector $\mathbf{x} \in \mathbb{Z}^n$, $||\mathbf{x}||$ denotes the Euclidean norm of $\mathbf{x}$. We use $\widetilde{\mathbf{A}}$ to denote the Gram-Schmidt orthogonalization of matrix $\mathbf{A}$, and $\|\mathbf{A}\|$ to denote the Euclidean norm of the longest column in $\mathbf{A}$. If n is a positive integer, $[n]$ denotes the set $\{1, .., n\}$. For $c \in \mathbb{R}$, let $\lfloor c \rceil = \lceil c - 1/2 \rceil$ denote the integer closest to c.

2.1 Server-Aided Revocable Identity-Based Encryption

We first recall the definition and security model of SR-IBE, put forward by Qin et al. [29]. A server-aided revocable identity-based encryption (SR-IBE) scheme involves 4 parties: KGC, sender, recipient, and server. Algorithms among the parties are as follows:

Sys(1^λ) is run by the KGC. It takes as input a security parameter λ and outputs the system parameters params.

Setup(params) is run by the KGC. It takes as input the system parameters params and outputs public parameters pp, a master secret key msk, a revocation list RL (initially empty), and a state st. We assume that pp is an implicit input of all other algorithms.

Token(msk, id, st) is run by the KGC. It takes as input the master secret key msk, an identity id, and state st. It outputs a token τ_{id} and an updated state st. The token τ_{id} is sent to the server through a public channel.

UpdKG(msk, t, RL, st) is run by the KGC. It takes as input the master secret key msk, a time t, the current revocation list RL, and state st. It outputs an update key uk_t, which is sent to the server through a public channel.

TranKG(τ_{id}, uk_t) is run by the server. It takes as input a token τ_{id} and an update key uk_t, and outputs a transformation key $tk_{id, t}$.

PrivKG(msk, id) is run by the KGC. It takes as input the master key msk and an identity id, and outputs a private key sk_{id}, which is sent to the recipient through a *secret* channel.

DecKG(sk_{id}, t) is run by the recipient. It takes as input the private key sk_{id} and a time t. It outputs a decryption key $dk_{id, t}$.

Enc(id, t, M) is run by the sender. It takes as input the recipient's identity id, a time t, and a message M. It outputs a ciphertext $ct_{id, t}$, which is sent to the server.

Transform$(ct_{id,t}, tk_{id,t})$ is run by the sever. It takes as input a ciphertext $ct_{id, t}$, and a transformation key $tk_{id,t}$. It outputs a partially decrypted ciphertext $ct'_{id,t}$, which is sent to the recipient through a public channel.

Dec$(ct_{id,t}, dk_{id,t})$ is run by the recipient. On input a partially decrypted ciphertext $ct'_{id,t}$ and a decryption key $dk_{id,t}$, this algorithm outputs a message M or a symbol $\perp$.

Revoke(id, t, RL, st) is run by the KGC. It takes as input an identity id to be revoked, a revocation time t, the current revocation list RL, and a state st. It outputs an updated revocation list RL.

The correctness requirement for an SR-IBE scheme states that: For any $\lambda \in \mathbb{N}$, all possible state st, and any revocation list RL, if id is not revoked on a time t, and if all parties follow the prescribed algorithms, then $\mathbf{Dec}(ct_{id,t}, dk_{id,t}) = M$.

Qin et al. [29] defined semantic security against adaptive-identity chosen plaintext attacks for SR-IBE. Here, we will consider selective-identity security - a weaker security notion suggested by Boldyreva et al. [5], in which the adversary announces the challenge identity id* and time t* before the execution of algorithm **Setup**.

Definition 1 (SR-sID-CPA Security). *Let $\mathcal{O}$ be the set of the following oracles:*

1. **Token**$(\cdot)$: *On input an identity* id, *return* τ_{id} *by running* **Token**(msk, id, st).
2. **UpdKG**$(\cdot)$: *On input a time* t, *return* uk_t *by running* **UpdKG**(msk, t, RL, st).
3. **PrivKG**$(\cdot)$: *On input an identity* id, *return* sk_{id} *by running* **PrivKG** (msk, id).
4. **DecKG**$(\cdot, \cdot)$: *On input an identity* id *and a time* t, *return* $dk_{id,t}$ *by running* **DecKG**$(sk_{id, t})$, *where* sk_{id} *is from* **PrivKG**(msk, id).
5. **Revoke**$(\cdot, \cdot)$: *On input an identity* id *and a time* t, *update* RL *by running* **Revoke**(id, t, RL, st).

An SR-IBE scheme is SR-sID-CPA secure if any PPT adversary $\mathcal{A}$ has negligible advantage in the following experiment:

$$\boxed{\mathsf{Exp}_{\mathcal{A}}^{SR\text{-}sID\text{-}CPA}(\lambda)}$$

$$\text{params} \leftarrow \mathbf{Sys}(1^{\lambda}); \; \text{id}^*, \text{t}^* \leftarrow \mathcal{A}$$
$$(\text{pp, msk, st, RL}) \leftarrow \mathbf{Setup}(\text{params})$$
$$M_0, M_1 \leftarrow \mathcal{A}^{\mathcal{O}}(\text{pp})$$
$$r \xleftarrow{\$} \{0, 1\}; \; \text{ct}_{\text{id}^*, \text{t}^*} \leftarrow \mathbf{Enc}(\text{id}^*, \text{t}^*, M_r)$$
$$r' \leftarrow \mathcal{A}^{\mathcal{O}}(\text{ct}_{\text{id}^*, \text{t}^*}); \; Return \; 1 \; if \; r' = r \; and \; 0 \; otherwise.$$

Beyond the conditions that M_0, M_1 belong to the message space $\mathcal{M}$ and they have the same length, the following restrictions are made:

1. **UpdKG**$(\cdot)$ *and* **Revoke**$(\cdot, \cdot)$ *can only be queried on time that is greater than or equal to the time of all previous queries.*
2. **Revoke**$(\cdot, \cdot)$ *can not be queried on time* t *if* **UpdKG**$(\cdot)$ *has already been queried on time* t.
3. *If* **PrivKG**$(\cdot)$ *was queried on the challenge identity* id*, *then* **Rovoke**$(\cdot, \cdot)$ *must be queried on* (id*, t) *for some* $t \leq t^*$.
4. *If* id* *is non-revoked at time* t*, *then* **DecKG**$(\cdot, \cdot)$ *can not be queried on* (id*, t*).

The advantage of $\mathcal{A}$ in the experiment is defined as:

$$\mathsf{Adv}_{\mathcal{A}}^{SR\text{-}sID\text{-}CPA}(\lambda) = \left| \Pr\left[\mathsf{Exp}_{\mathcal{A}}^{SR\text{-}sID\text{-}CPA}(\lambda) = 1 \right] - \frac{1}{2} \right|.$$

2.2 Background on Lattices

Let n, m, and $q \geq 2$ be integers. For matrix $\mathbf{A} \in \mathbb{Z}_q^{n \times m}$, define the m-dimensional lattice:

$$\Lambda_q^\perp(\mathbf{A}) = \left\{ \mathbf{x} \in \mathbb{Z}^m : \ \mathbf{A} \cdot \mathbf{x} = \mathbf{0} \bmod q \right\} \subseteq \mathbb{Z}^m.$$

For any $\mathbf{u}$ in the image of $\mathbf{A}$, define the coset $\Lambda_q^\mathbf{u}(\mathbf{A}) = \left\{ \mathbf{x} \in \mathbb{Z}^m : \ \mathbf{A} \cdot \mathbf{x} = \mathbf{u} \bmod q \right\}$.

Trapdoors for Lattices. A fundamental tool of lattice-based cryptography is an algorithm that generates a matrix $\mathbf{A} \in \mathbb{Z}_q^{n \times m}$ that is statistically close to uniform, together with a short trapdoor basis for the associated lattice $\Lambda_q^\perp(\mathbf{A})$.

Lemma 1 ([3,4,25]). *Let $n \geq 1, q \geq 2$ and $m \geq 2n \log q$ be integers. Then, there exists a PPT algorithm $\mathsf{TrapGen}(n, q, m)$ that outputs a pair $(\mathbf{A}, \mathbf{T_A})$ such that $\mathbf{A}$ is statistically close to uniform over $\mathbb{Z}_q^{n \times m}$ and $\mathbf{T_A} \in \mathbb{Z}_q^{m \times m}$ is a basis for $\Lambda_q^\perp(\mathbf{A})$ satisfying $\|\widetilde{\mathbf{T_A}}\| \leq O(\sqrt{n \log q})$ and $\|\mathbf{T_A}\| \leq O(n \log q)$.*

Meanwhile, there exist matrices with particular structures, that admit easy-to-compute short bases. Micciancio and Peikert [25] consider such a matrix $\mathbf{G}$, which they call *primitive matrix*.

Lemma 2 ([25,28]). *Let $q \geq 2, n \geq 1$ be integers and let $k = \lceil \log q \rceil$. Let $\mathbf{g} = (1, 2, \cdots, 2^{k-1}) \in \mathbb{Z}^k$ and $\mathbf{G} = \mathbf{I}_n \otimes \mathbf{g}$. Then the lattice $\Lambda_q^\perp(\mathbf{G})$ has a known basis $\mathbf{T_G} \in \mathbb{Z}^{nk \times nk}$ with $\|\widetilde{\mathbf{T_G}}\| \leq \sqrt{5}$ and $\|\mathbf{T_G}\| \leq \max\{\sqrt{5}, \sqrt{k}\}$.*

We also define $\mathsf{bin} : \mathbb{Z}_q \to \{0,1\}^k$ as the function mapping w to its binary decomposition $\mathsf{bin}(w)$. Note that, for all $w \in \mathbb{Z}_q$, we have $\mathbf{g} \cdot \mathsf{bin}(w) = w$.

Discrete Gaussians over Lattices. Let Λ be a lattice in $\mathbb{Z}^m$. For any vector $\mathbf{c} \in \mathbb{R}^m$ and any parameter $s \in \mathbb{R}_{>0}$, define $\rho_{s,\mathbf{c}}(\mathbf{x}) = \exp(-\pi \frac{\|\mathbf{x} - \mathbf{c}\|^2}{s^2})$ and $\rho_{s,\mathbf{c}}(\Lambda) = \sum_{\mathbf{x} \in \Lambda} \rho_{s,\mathbf{c}}(\mathbf{x})$. The *discrete Gaussian distribution* over Λ with center $\mathbf{c}$ and parameter s is $\mathcal{D}_{\Lambda,s,\mathbf{c}}(\mathbf{y}) = \frac{\rho_{s,\mathbf{c}}(\mathbf{y})}{\rho_{s,\mathbf{c}}(\Lambda)}$, for $\forall \mathbf{y} \in \Lambda$. If $\mathbf{c} = \mathbf{0}$, we conveniently use ρ_s and $\mathcal{D}_{\Lambda,s}$.

Sampling Algorithms. It was shown in [1,9,15] that, given a lattice $\Lambda_q^\perp(\mathbf{A})$ equipped with a short basis, one can efficiently sample short pre-images, as well as delegate an equally short basis for a super-lattice. We will employ algorithms $\mathsf{SamplePre}$, $\mathsf{SampleBasisLeft}$ and $\mathsf{SampleLeft}$ from those works, defined below.

$\mathsf{SamplePre}(\mathbf{A}, \mathbf{T_A}, \mathbf{u}, s)$: On input a full-rank matrix $\mathbf{A} \in \mathbb{Z}_q^{n \times m}$, a trapdoor $\mathbf{T_A}$ of $\Lambda_q^\perp(\mathbf{A})$, a vector $\mathbf{u} \in \mathbb{Z}_q^n$, and a Gaussian parameter $s \geq \|\widetilde{\mathbf{T_A}}\| \cdot \omega(\sqrt{\log m})$, it outputs a vector $\mathbf{e} \in \mathbb{Z}^m$ sampled from a distribution statistically close to $\mathcal{D}_{\Lambda_q^\mathbf{u}(\mathbf{A}),s}$.

SampleBasisLeft $(\mathbf{A}, \mathbf{M}, \mathbf{T_A}, s)$: On input a full-rank matrix $\mathbf{A} \in \mathbb{Z}_q^{n \times m}$, a matrix $\mathbf{M} \in \mathbb{Z}_q^{n \times m_1}$, a trapdoor $\mathbf{T_A}$ of $\Lambda_q^\perp(\mathbf{A})$ and a Gaussian parameter $s \geq \|\widetilde{\mathbf{T_A}}\| \cdot \omega(\sqrt{\log(m + m_1)})$, it outputs a basis $\mathbf{T_F}$ of $\Lambda_q^\perp(\mathbf{F})$, where $\mathbf{F} = [\mathbf{A} \,|\, \mathbf{M}] \in \mathbb{Z}_q^{n \times (m + m_1)}$, while preserving the Gram-Schmidt norm of the basis (i.e., such that $\|\widetilde{\mathbf{T_F}}\| = \|\widetilde{\mathbf{T_A}}\|$).

SampleLeft $(\mathbf{A}, \mathbf{M}, \mathbf{T_A}, \mathbf{U}, s)$: On input a full-rank matrix $\mathbf{A} \in \mathbb{Z}_q^{n \times m}$, a matrix $\mathbf{M} \in \mathbb{Z}_q^{n \times m_1}$, a trapdoor $\mathbf{T_A}$ of $\Lambda_q^\perp(\mathbf{A})$, a matrix $\mathbf{U} = [\mathbf{u}_1 | \dots | \mathbf{u}_k] \in \mathbb{Z}_q^{n \times k}$, and a Gaussian parameter $s \geq \|\widetilde{\mathbf{T_A}}\| \cdot \omega(\sqrt{\log(m + m_1)})$, it outputs a matrix $\mathbf{E} = [\mathbf{e}_1 | \dots | \mathbf{e}_k] \in \mathbb{Z}^{(m + m_1) \times k}$, where for each $j = 1, \dots, k$, the column $\mathbf{e}_j$ is sampled from a distribution statistically close to $\mathcal{D}_{\Lambda_q^{\mathbf{u}_j}(\mathbf{F}), s}$. Here we also define $\mathbf{F} = [\mathbf{A} \,|\, \mathbf{M}] \in \mathbb{Z}_q^{n \times (m + m_1)}$.

2.3   The LWE Problem and Its Hardness Assumption

The Learning With Errors (LWE) problem, first introduced by Regev [30], plays the central role in lattice-based cryptography.

Definition 2 (LWE). *Let $n, m \geq 1, q \geq 2$, and let χ be a probability distribution on $\mathbb{Z}$. For $\mathbf{s} \in \mathbb{Z}_q^n$, let $\mathbf{A}_{\mathbf{s}, \chi}$ be the distribution obtained by sampling $\mathbf{a} \xleftarrow{\$} \mathbb{Z}_q^n$ and $e \hookleftarrow \chi$, and outputting the pair $(\mathbf{a}, \mathbf{a}^\top \mathbf{s} + e) \in \mathbb{Z}_q^n \times \mathbb{Z}_q$. The (n, q, χ)-LWE problem asks to distinguish m samples chosen according to $\mathbf{A}_{\mathbf{s}, \chi}$ (for $\mathbf{s} \xleftarrow{\$} \mathbb{Z}_q^n$) and m samples chosen according to the uniform distribution over $\mathbb{Z}_q^n \times \mathbb{Z}_q$.*

If q is a prime power, $B \geq \sqrt{n} \cdot \omega(\log n)$, $\gamma = O(nq/B)$, then there exists an efficient sampleable B-bounded distribution χ (i.e., χ outputs samples with norm at most B with overwhelming probability) such that (n, q, χ)-LWE is as least as hard as worst-case lattice problem SIVP$_\gamma$ (see [24,25,27,30]).

Since its introduction in 2005, the LWE problem has been used in hundreds of lattice-based cryptographic constructions. In the following, we will recall 2 such schemes, which are the building blocks of our SR-IBE in Sect. 3.

2.4   The Agrawal-Boneh-Boyen (H)IBE Scheme

In [1], Agrawal, Boneh, and Boyen (ABB) constructed a lattice-based IBE which is proven secure in the standard model, and then extended to the hierarchical setting. In their system, the KGC possesses a short basis $\mathbf{T_B}$ for a public lattice $\Lambda_q^\perp(\mathbf{B})$, generated via algorithm TrapGen. Each identity in the hierarchy is associated with a super-lattice of $\Lambda_q^\perp(\mathbf{B})$, a short basis of which can be delegated from $\mathbf{T_B}$ using algorithm SampleBasisLeft. Given such a trapdoor basis, each identity can run algorithm SamplePre to compute a short vector that allows to decrypt ciphertexts generated via a variant of the Dual-Regev cryptosystem [15].

Let n, m, q, s be the scheme parameters and let χ be the LWE error distribution. The scheme makes use of an efficient encoding function $\mathsf{H} : \mathbb{Z}_q^n \to \mathbb{Z}_q^{n \times n}$, that is full-rank differences (FRD). Namely, for all distinct $\mathbf{u}, \mathbf{w} \in \mathbb{Z}_q^n$, the difference $H(\mathbf{u}) - H(\mathbf{w})$ is a full-rank matrix in $\mathbb{Z}_q^{n \times n}$. In this work, we will employ the two-level variant of the ABB HIBE.

Setup$_{\mathsf{HIBE}}$: Generate $(\mathbf{B}, \mathbf{T_B}) \leftarrow \mathsf{TrapGen}(n, q, m)$. Pick $\mathbf{v} \xleftarrow{\$} \mathbb{Z}_q^n$ and $\mathbf{B}_1, \mathbf{B}_2 \xleftarrow{\$} \mathbb{Z}_q^{n \times m}$. Output $\mathsf{pp}_{\mathsf{HIBE}} = (\mathbf{B}, \mathbf{B}_1, \mathbf{B}_2, \mathbf{v})$ and $\mathsf{msk}_{\mathsf{HIBE}} = \mathbf{T_B}$.

Extract$_{\mathsf{HIBE}}$: For an identity $\mathsf{id} \in \mathbb{Z}_q^n$ at depth 1, output the private key $\mathsf{sk}_{\mathsf{id}}$ by running $\mathsf{SampleBasisLeft}(\mathbf{B}, \mathbf{B}_1 + H(\mathsf{id})\mathbf{G}, \mathbf{T_B}, s)$.

Derive$_{\mathsf{HIBE}}$: For an identity $\mathsf{id} = (\mathsf{id}', \mathsf{id}'') \in \mathbb{Z}_q^n \times \mathbb{Z}_q^n$ at depth 2, let $\mathsf{sk}_{\mathsf{id}'}$ be the private key of id' and $\mathbf{B}_{\mathsf{id}'} = [\mathbf{B}|\mathbf{B}_1 + H(\mathsf{id}')\mathbf{G}] \in \mathbb{Z}_q^{n \times 2m}$. Output $\mathsf{sk}_{\mathsf{id}}$ by running $\mathsf{SampleBasisLeft}(\mathbf{B}_{\mathsf{id}'}, \mathbf{B}_2 + H(\mathsf{id}'')\mathbf{G}, \mathsf{sk}_{\mathsf{id}'}, s)$.

Enc$_{\mathsf{HIBE}}$: To encrypt a message bit $b \in \{0, 1\}$ under an identity $\mathsf{id} = (\mathsf{id}', \mathsf{id}'') \in \mathbb{Z}_q^n \times \mathbb{Z}_q^n$ at depth 2, let $\mathbf{B}_{\mathsf{id}} = [\mathbf{B}|\mathbf{B}_1 + H(\mathsf{id}')\mathbf{G}|\mathbf{B}_2 + H(\mathsf{id}'')\mathbf{G}] \in \mathbb{Z}_q^{n \times 3m}$. Choose $\mathbf{s} \xleftarrow{\$} \mathbb{Z}_q^n$, $\mathbf{x} \hookleftarrow \chi^m$, $y \hookleftarrow \chi$ and $\S_1, \S_2 \xleftarrow{\$} \{-1, 1\}^{m \times m}$. Set $\mathbf{c}_1 = \mathbf{B}_{\mathsf{id}}^\top \mathbf{s} + [\mathbf{x}|\S_1^\top \mathbf{x}|\S_2^\top \mathbf{x}]^\top \in \mathbb{Z}_q^{3m}$ and $c_0 = \mathbf{v}^\top \mathbf{s} + y + b \cdot \lfloor \frac{q}{2} \rfloor \in \mathbb{Z}_q$. Output $\mathsf{ct}_{\mathsf{id}} = (\mathbf{c}_1, c_0) \in \mathbb{Z}_q^{3m} \times \mathbb{Z}_q$.

Dec$_{\mathsf{HIBE}}$: Sample $\mathbf{e}_{\mathsf{id}} \leftarrow \mathsf{SamplePre}(\mathbf{B}_{\mathsf{id}}, \mathsf{sk}_{\mathsf{id}}, \mathbf{v}, s)$. Compute $d = c_0 - \mathbf{e}_{\mathsf{id}}^\top \mathbf{c}_1 \in \mathbb{Z}_q$ and output $\lfloor \frac{2}{q} d \rceil \in \{0, 1\}$.

Agrawal, Boneh and Boyen showed that their scheme satisfies the notion of indistinguishability of ciphertexts under a selective-identity chosen-plaintext attack (IND-sID-CPA), proposed by Canetti et al. [8]. We restate their result in Theorem 1.

Theorem 1. (Excerpted from [1]). *The ABB HIBE scheme is IND-sID-CPA secure, provided that the (n, q, χ)-LWE assumption holds.*

2.5 Chen et al.'s RIBE Scheme

In [10], Chen et al. proposed the first RIBE scheme from lattice assumptions. Their revocation mechanism relies on the Complete Subtree (CS) method of Naor et al. [26], which was first adapted into the context of RIBE by Boldyreva et al. [5]. We will briefly recall this method.

The CS method makes use of the node selection algorithm KUNode. In the algorithm, we use the following notation: If θ is a non-leaf node, then θ_ℓ and θ_r denote the left and right child of θ, respectively. $\mathsf{Path}(\theta)$ denotes the set of nodes on the path from θ to root. Each identity id is randomly assigned to a leaf node ν_{id} and $(\nu_{\mathsf{id}}, \mathsf{t}) \in \mathsf{RL}$ if id is revoked at time t. KUNode algorithm takes as input a binary tree BT, revocation list RL and time t, and outputs a set of nodes Y. The description of KUNode is given below and an example is illustrated in Fig. 1.

> KUNode(BT, RL, t)
>
> $X, Y \leftarrow \emptyset$
>
> $\forall (\theta_i, \mathsf{t}_i) \in \mathsf{RL}$, if $\mathsf{t}_i \leq \mathsf{t}$, then add $\mathsf{Path}(\theta_i)$ to X
>
> $\forall \theta \in X$, if $\theta_\ell \notin X$, then add θ_ℓ to Y; if $\theta_r \notin X$, then add θ_r to Y
>
> Return Y

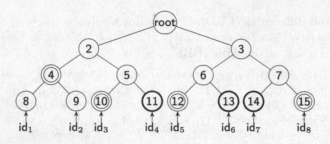

Fig. 1. Assuming that id_4, id_6 and id_7 have been revoked at time t, then $\{\theta_{11}, \theta_{13}, \theta_{14}\}$ are nodes in RL. We can get KUNode(BT, RL, t) $\rightarrow \{\theta_4, \theta_{10}, \theta_{12}, \theta_{15}\}$. For identity id_2 assigned to node θ_9, Path(θ_9) = (root = $\theta_1, \theta_2, \theta_4, \theta_9$) and has an intersection with KUNode(BT, RL, t) at node θ_4. For the revoked identity id_6 at node θ_{13}, Path(θ_{13}) does not contain any nodes in KUNode(BT, RL, t).

Chen et al.'s RIBE scheme employs two instances of the ABB IBE scheme to deal with user's identity and time, respectively. To link identity to time for each tree node, the syndrome $\mathbf{u} \in \mathbb{Z}_q^n$, which is part of the public parameter, is split into two random vectors $\mathbf{u}_1, \mathbf{u}_2$ for each node. We adopt a variant of Chen et al.'s RIBE scheme, described below, to encrypt k-bit messages instead of one-bit messages.

Setup$_{\mathsf{RIBE}}$: Generate $(\mathbf{A}, \mathbf{T_A}) \leftarrow \mathsf{TrapGen}(n, q, m)$. Pick $\mathbf{A}_1, \mathbf{A}_2 \overset{\$}{\leftarrow} \mathbb{Z}_q^{n \times m}$ and $\mathbf{U} \overset{\$}{\leftarrow} \mathbb{Z}_q^{n \times k}$. Initialize the revocation list RL = $\emptyset$ and let st := BT where BT is a binary tree. Output RL, st, pp$_{\mathsf{RIBE}}$ = $(\mathbf{A}, \mathbf{A}_1, \mathbf{A}_2, \mathbf{U})$ and msk$_{\mathsf{RIBE}}$ = $\mathbf{T_A}$.

PrivKG$_{\mathsf{RIBE}}$: Randomly issue an identity id $\in \mathbb{Z}_q^n$ to an unassigned leaf node ν_{id} in BT. For each $\theta \in \mathsf{Path}(\nu_{\mathsf{id}})$, if $\mathbf{U}_{1,\theta}, \mathbf{U}_{21,\theta}$ are undefined, then pick $\mathbf{U}_{1,\theta} \overset{\$}{\leftarrow} \mathbb{Z}_q^{n \times k}$ and set $\mathbf{U}_{2,\theta} = \mathbf{U} - \mathbf{U}_{1,\theta}$. Return sk$_{\mathsf{id}}$ = $(\theta, \mathbf{E}_{1,\theta})_{\theta \in \mathsf{Path}(\nu_{\mathsf{id}})}$ where $\mathbf{E}_{1,\theta} \leftarrow \mathsf{SampleLeft}(\mathbf{A}, \mathbf{A}_1 + \mathsf{H}(\mathsf{id})\mathbf{G}, \mathbf{T_A}, \mathbf{U}_{1,\theta}, s)$.

UpdKG$_{\mathsf{RIBE}}$: For $\theta \in \mathsf{KUNodes}(\mathsf{BT}, \mathsf{RL}, \mathsf{t})$, retrieve $\mathbf{U}_{2,\theta}$. Output uk$_\mathsf{t}$ = $(\theta, \mathbf{E}_{2,\theta})_{\theta \in \mathsf{KUNodes}(\mathsf{BT}, \mathsf{RL}, \mathsf{t})}$ where $\mathbf{E}_{2,\theta} \leftarrow \mathsf{SampleLeft}(\mathbf{A}, \mathbf{A}_2 + \mathsf{H}(\mathsf{t})\mathbf{G}, \mathbf{T_A}, \mathbf{U}_{2,\theta}, s)$.

Enc$_{\mathsf{RIBE}}$and Dec$_{\mathsf{RIBE}}$ are similar as in the ABB HIBE scheme. When encrypting a k-bit message, one obtains a ciphertext of the form ct$_{\mathsf{id,t}}$ = $(\mathbf{c}_1', \mathbf{c}_0') \in \mathbb{Z}_q^{3m} \times \mathbb{Z}_q^k$. A non-revoked identity id at time t can obtain the pair $(\mathbf{E}_{1,\theta}, \mathbf{E}_{2,\theta})$ at the intersection node $\theta \in \mathsf{Path}(\nu_{\mathsf{id}}) \cap \mathsf{KUNodes}(\mathsf{BT}, \mathsf{RL}, \mathsf{t})$, which satisfies $[\mathbf{A}|\mathbf{A}_1 + \mathsf{H}(\mathsf{id})\mathbf{G}] \cdot \mathbf{E}_{1,\theta} + [\mathbf{A}|\mathbf{A}_2 + \mathsf{H}(\mathsf{t})\mathbf{G}] \cdot \mathbf{E}_{2,\theta} = \mathbf{U}$, and which allows him to perform decryption.

Revoke$_{\mathsf{RIBE}}$: Add (id, t) to RL for all nodes associated with id and return RL.

In [10], Chen et al. proved that the one-bit version of their scheme satisfies the IND-sRID-CPA security notion defined in [5], assuming the hardness of the LWE problem. The security proof can be easily adapted to handle the multi-bit case, based on the techniques from [1,15]. We thus have the following theorem.

Theorem 2 (Adapted from [10]). *The RIBE scheme described above is IND-sRID-CPA secure, provided that the (n, q, χ)-LWE assumption holds.*

3   Our Lattice-Based SR-IBE Scheme

Our SR-IBE scheme is a combination of the ABB HIBE and Chen et al.'s RIBE schemes via a double encryption technique. The KGC, holding master secret keys for both schemes, issues HIBE private keys to users, and gives tokens consisting of RIBE private keys to the server. At each time period, the KGC sends RIBE update keys to the server. The encryption algorithm is a two-step procedure:

1. Encrypt the message M under the HIBE, with respect to an ordered pair $(\mathsf{id}, \mathsf{t})$, to obtain an initial ciphertext of the form $(\mathbf{c}_2, c_0) \in \mathbb{Z}_q^{3m} \times \mathbb{Z}_q$.
2. Encrypt the binary representation $\mathsf{bin}(c_0) \in \{0, 1\}^k$ of c_0, where $k = \lceil \log q \rceil$, under the RIBE, with respect to id and t, to obtain $(\mathbf{c}_1, \hat{\mathbf{c}}_0) \in \mathbb{Z}_q^{3m} \times \mathbb{Z}_q^k$. The final ciphertext is defined as $\mathsf{ct}_{\mathsf{id},\mathsf{t}} = (\mathbf{c}_1, \mathbf{c}_2, \hat{\mathbf{c}}_0) \in \mathbb{Z}_q^{3m} \times \mathbb{Z}_q^{3m} \times \mathbb{Z}_q^k$.

If id is not revoked at time t, then the server can partially decrypt $\mathsf{ct}_{\mathsf{id},\,\mathsf{t}}$, using a transformation key which is essentially the RIBE decryption key. Note that the "partially decrypted ciphertext" is nothing but the initial ciphertext $(\mathbf{c}_2, c_0)$. Receiving $(\mathbf{c}_2, c_0)$ from the server, the user decrypts it using a decryption key delegated from his long-term private key.

In the following, we will formally describe the scheme.

Sys(1^λ): On input security parameter λ, the KGC works as follows:

1. Set $n = O(\lambda)$, and choose $N = poly(\lambda)$ as the maximal number of users that the system will support.
2. Let $q = \widetilde{O}(n^4)$ be a prime power, and set $k = \lceil \log q \rceil, m = 2nk$. Note that parameters n, q, k specify vector $\mathbf{g}$, function $\mathsf{bin}(\cdot)$ and primitive matrix $\mathbf{G}$ (see Sect. 2.2).
3. Choose a Gaussian parameter $s = \widetilde{O}(\sqrt{m})$.
4. Set $B = \widetilde{O}(\sqrt{n})$ and let χ be a B-bounded distribution.
5. Select an FRD map $\mathsf{H} : \mathbb{Z}_q^n \to \mathbb{Z}_q^{n \times n}$ (see Sect. 2.4).
6. Let the identity space be $\mathcal{I} = \mathbb{Z}_q^n$, the time space be $\mathcal{T} \subset \mathbb{Z}_q^n$ and the message space be $\mathcal{M} = \{0, 1\}$.
7. Output $\mathsf{params} = (n, N, q, k, m, s, B, \chi, \mathsf{H}, \mathcal{I}, \mathcal{T}, \mathcal{M})$.

Setup(params): On input system parameters params, the KGC works as follows:

1. Use algorithm $\mathsf{TrapGen}(n, q, m)$ to get two independent pairs $(\mathbf{A}, \mathbf{T_A})$ and $(\mathbf{B}, \mathbf{T_B})$.
2. Select $\mathbf{U} \overset{\$}{\leftarrow} \mathbb{Z}_q^{n \times k}, \mathbf{v} \overset{\$}{\leftarrow} \mathbb{Z}_q^n$ and $\mathbf{A}_1, \mathbf{A}_2, \mathbf{B}_1, \mathbf{B}_2 \overset{\$}{\leftarrow} \mathbb{Z}_q^{n \times m}$.
3. Initialize the revocation list $\mathsf{RL} = \emptyset$. Obtain a binary tree BT with at least N leaf nodes and set the state $\mathsf{st} = \mathsf{BT}$.
4. Set $\mathsf{pp} = (\mathbf{A}, \mathbf{A}_1, \mathbf{A}_2, \mathbf{U}, \mathbf{B}, \mathbf{B}_1, \mathbf{B}_2, \mathbf{v})$ and $\mathsf{msk} = (\mathbf{T_A}, \mathbf{T_B})$.
5. Output $(\mathsf{pp}, \mathsf{msk}, \mathsf{RL}, \mathsf{st})$.

Token(msk, id, st): On input the master secret key msk, an identity $\mathsf{id} \in \mathcal{I}$ and state st, the KGC works as follows:

1. Randomly choose an unassigned leaf node ν_{id} in BT and assign it to id.

2. For each $\theta \in \mathsf{Path}(\nu_{\mathsf{id}})$, if $\mathbf{U}_{1,\theta}, \mathbf{U}_{2,\theta}$ are undefined, then pick $\mathbf{U}_{1,\theta} \xleftarrow{\$} \mathbb{Z}_q^{n \times k}$, set $\mathbf{U}_{2,\theta} = \mathbf{U} - \mathbf{U}_{1,\theta}$ and store the pair $(\mathbf{U}_{1,\theta}, \mathbf{U}_{12,\theta})$ in node θ. Sample $\mathbf{E}_{1,\theta} \leftarrow \mathsf{SampleLeft}\,(\mathbf{A}, \mathbf{A}_1 + \mathsf{H}(\mathsf{id})\mathbf{G}, \mathbf{T_A}, \mathbf{U}_{1,\theta}, s)$. Let $\mathbf{A}_{\mathsf{id}} = [\mathbf{A}|\mathbf{A}_1 + \mathsf{H}(\mathsf{id})\mathbf{G}] \in \mathbb{Z}_q^{n \times 2m}$. Note that $\mathbf{E}_{1,\theta} \in \mathbb{Z}^{2m \times k}$ and $\mathbf{A}_{\mathsf{id}} \cdot \mathbf{E}_{1,\theta} = \mathbf{U}_{1,\theta}$.
3. Output the updated state st and $\tau_{\mathsf{id}} = (\theta, \mathbf{E}_{1,\theta})_{\theta \in \mathsf{Path}(\nu_{\mathsf{id}})}$.

UpdKG$(\mathsf{msk}, \mathsf{t}, \mathsf{st}, \mathsf{RL})$: On input the master secret key msk, a time $\mathsf{t} \in \mathcal{T}$, state st and the revocation list RL, the KGC works as follows:

1. For each $\theta \in \mathsf{KUNodes}(\mathsf{BT}, \mathsf{RL}, \mathsf{t})$, retrieve $\mathbf{U}_{2,\theta}$ (pre-defined by algorithm **Token**), and sample $\mathbf{E}_{2,\theta} \leftarrow \mathsf{SampleLeft}\,(\mathbf{A}, \mathbf{A}_2 + \mathsf{H}(\mathsf{t})\mathbf{G}, \mathbf{T_A}, \mathbf{U}_{2,\theta}, s)$. Let $\mathbf{A}_\mathsf{t} = [\mathbf{A}|\mathbf{A}_2 + \mathsf{H}(\mathsf{t})\mathbf{G}] \in \mathbb{Z}_q^{n \times 2m}$. Note that we have $\mathbf{E}_{2,\theta} \in \mathbb{Z}^{2m \times k}$ and $\mathbf{A}_\mathsf{t} \cdot \mathbf{E}_{2,\theta} = \mathbf{U}_{2,\theta}$.
2. Output $\mathsf{uk}_\mathsf{t} = (\theta, \mathbf{E}_{2,\theta})_{\theta \in \mathsf{KUNodes}(\mathsf{BT}, \mathsf{RL}, \mathsf{t})}$.

TranKG$(\tau_{\mathsf{id}}, \mathsf{uk}_\mathsf{t})$: On input a token $\tau_{\mathsf{id}} = (\theta, \mathbf{E}_{1,\theta})_{\theta \in I}$ and an update key $\mathsf{uk}_\mathsf{t} = (\theta, \mathbf{E}_{2,\theta})_{\theta \in J}$ for some set of nodes I, J, the server works as follows:

1. If $I \cap J = \emptyset$, output $\perp$.
2. Otherwise, choose $\theta \in I \cap J$ and output $\mathsf{tk}_{\mathsf{id},\mathsf{t}} = (\mathbf{E}_{1,\theta}, \mathbf{E}_{2,\theta})$. Note that $\mathbf{A}_{\mathsf{id}} \cdot \mathbf{E}_{1,\theta} + \mathbf{A}_\mathsf{t} \cdot \mathbf{E}_{2,\theta} = \mathbf{U}$.

PrivKG$(\mathsf{msk}, \mathsf{id})$: On input the master secret key msk and an identity $\mathsf{id} \in \mathcal{I}$, the KGC works as follows:

1. Sample $\mathbf{T}_{\mathsf{id}} \leftarrow \mathsf{SampleBasisLeft}\,(\mathbf{B}, \mathbf{B}_1 + \mathsf{H}(\mathsf{id})\mathbf{G}, \mathbf{T_B}, s)$.
2. Output $\mathsf{sk}_{\mathsf{id}} = \mathbf{T}_{\mathsf{id}} \in \mathbb{Z}^{2m \times 2m}$.

DecKG$(\mathsf{sk}_{\mathsf{id}}, \mathsf{t})$: On input a private key $\mathsf{sk}_{\mathsf{id}} = \mathbf{T}_{\mathsf{id}}$ and a time $\mathsf{t} \in \mathcal{T}$, the recipient works as follows:

1. Sample $\mathbf{e}_{\mathsf{id},\mathsf{t}} \leftarrow \mathsf{SampleLeft}\,(\mathbf{B}_{\mathsf{id}}, \mathbf{B}_2 + \mathsf{H}(\mathsf{t})\mathbf{G}, \mathbf{T}_{\mathsf{id}}, \mathbf{v}, s)$ where let $\mathbf{B}_{\mathsf{id}} = [\mathbf{B}|\mathbf{B}_1 + \mathsf{H}(\mathsf{id})\mathbf{G}] \in \mathbb{Z}_q^{n \times 2m}$.
2. Output $\mathsf{dk}_{\mathsf{id},\mathsf{t}} = \mathbf{e}_{\mathsf{id},\mathsf{t}} \in \mathbb{Z}^{3m}$.

Enc$(\mathsf{id}, \mathsf{t}, b)$: On input an identity $\mathsf{id} \in \mathcal{I}$, a time $\mathsf{t} \in \mathcal{T}$ and a message $M \in \mathcal{M}$, the sender works as follows:

1. Set $\mathbf{A}_{\mathsf{id},\mathsf{t}} = [\mathbf{A}|\mathbf{A}_1 + \mathsf{H}(\mathsf{id})\mathbf{G}|\mathbf{A}_2 + \mathsf{H}(\mathsf{t})\mathbf{G}] \in \mathbb{Z}_q^{n \times 3m}$ and $\mathbf{B}_{\mathsf{id},\mathsf{t}} = [\mathbf{B}|\mathbf{B}_1 + \mathsf{H}(\mathsf{id})\mathbf{G}|\mathbf{B}_2 + \mathsf{H}(\mathsf{t})\mathbf{G}] \in \mathbb{Z}_q^{n \times 3m}$.
2. Sample $\mathbf{s}, \mathbf{s}' \xleftarrow{\$} \mathbb{Z}_q^n$, $\mathbf{x}, \mathbf{x}' \hookleftarrow \chi^m$, $\mathbf{y} \hookleftarrow \chi^k$, and $y' \hookleftarrow \chi$.
3. Choose $\mathbf{R}_1, \mathbf{R}_2, \S_1, \S_2 \xleftarrow{\$} \{-1, 1\}^{m \times m}$.
4. Set $\mathbf{c}_1 = \mathbf{A}_{\mathsf{id},\mathsf{t}}^\top \mathbf{s} + \begin{bmatrix} \mathbf{x} \\ \mathbf{R}_1^\top \mathbf{x} \\ \mathbf{R}_2^\top \mathbf{x} \end{bmatrix} \in \mathbb{Z}_q^{3m}$ and $\mathbf{c}_2 = \mathbf{B}_{\mathsf{id},\mathsf{t}}^\top \mathbf{s}' + \begin{bmatrix} \mathbf{x}' \\ \S_1^\top \mathbf{x}' \\ \S_2^\top \mathbf{x}' \end{bmatrix} \in \mathbb{Z}_q^{3m}$.
5. Compute $c_0 = \mathbf{v}^\top \mathbf{s}' + y' + M \cdot \lfloor \frac{q}{2} \rfloor \in \mathbb{Z}_q$, and then set $\hat{\mathbf{c}}_0 = \mathbf{U}^\top \mathbf{s} + \mathbf{y} + \mathsf{bin}(c_0) \cdot \lfloor \frac{q}{2} \rfloor \in \mathbb{Z}_q^k$. (Recall that $\mathsf{bin}(c_0)$ is the binary decomposition of c_0.)
6. Output $\mathsf{ct}_{\mathsf{id},\mathsf{t}} = (\mathbf{c}_1, \mathbf{c}_2, \hat{\mathbf{c}}_0) \in \mathbb{Z}_q^{3m} \times \mathbb{Z}_q^{3m} \times \mathbb{Z}_q^k$.

Transform$(\mathsf{ct}_{\mathsf{id},\mathsf{t}}, \mathsf{tk}_{\mathsf{id},\mathsf{t}})$: On input a ciphertext $\mathsf{ct}_{\mathsf{id},\mathsf{t}} = (\mathbf{c}_1, \mathbf{c}_2, \hat{\mathbf{c}}_0)$ and a transformation key $\mathsf{tk}_{\mathsf{id},\mathsf{t}} = (\mathbf{E}_1, \mathbf{E}_2)$, the server works as follows:

1. Parse $\mathbf{c}_1 = \begin{bmatrix} \mathbf{c}_{1,0} \\ \mathbf{c}_{1,1} \\ \mathbf{c}_{1,2} \end{bmatrix}$ where $\mathbf{c}_{1,i} \in \mathbb{Z}_q^m$, for $i = 0, 1, 2$. Compute $\mathbf{w} = \hat{\mathbf{c}}_0 -$
$\mathbf{E}_1^\top \begin{bmatrix} \mathbf{c}_{1,0} \\ \mathbf{c}_{1,1} \end{bmatrix} - \mathbf{E}_2^\top \begin{bmatrix} \mathbf{c}_{1,0} \\ \mathbf{c}_{1,2} \end{bmatrix} \in \mathbb{Z}_q^k$.

2. Compute $\hat{c}'_0 = \mathbf{g} \cdot \lfloor \frac{2}{q} \mathbf{w} \rceil \in \mathbb{Z}_q$. (Recall that $\mathbf{g} = (1, 2, \cdots, 2^{k-1}) \in \mathbb{Z}^k$.)
3. Output $\mathsf{ct}'_{\mathsf{id},\mathsf{t}} = (\mathbf{c}_2, \hat{c}'_0) \in \mathbb{Z}_q^{3m} \times \mathbb{Z}_q$.

$\mathbf{Dec}(\mathsf{ct}'_{\mathsf{id},\mathsf{t}}, \mathsf{dk}_{\mathsf{id},\mathsf{t}})$: On input a partially decrypted ciphertext $\mathsf{ct}'_{\mathsf{id},\mathsf{t}} = (\mathbf{c}_2, \hat{c}'_0)$ and a decryption key $\mathsf{dk}_{\mathsf{id},\mathsf{t}} - \mathbf{e}_{\mathsf{id},\mathsf{t}}$, the recipient works as follows:
1. Compute $w' = \hat{c}'_0 - \mathbf{e}^\top_{\mathsf{id},\mathsf{t}} \mathbf{c}_2 \in \mathbb{Z}_q$.
2. Output $\lfloor \frac{2}{q} w' \rceil \in \{0, 1\}$.

$\mathbf{Revoke}(\mathsf{id}, \mathsf{t}, \mathsf{RL}, \mathsf{st})$: On input an identity id, a time t, the revocation list RL and state $\mathsf{st} = \mathsf{BT}$, the KGC adds $(\mathsf{id}, \mathsf{t})$ to RL for all nodes associated with identity id and returns RL.

4   Analysis

We now analyze the efficiency, correctness and security of our SR-IBE scheme.
Efficiency. The efficiency aspect of our SR-IBE scheme is as follows:

- The bit-size of the public parameters pp is $(6nm + nk + n) \log q = \widetilde{O}(\lambda^2)$.
- The private key $\mathsf{sk}_{\mathsf{id}}$ is a trapdoor matrix of bit-size $\widetilde{O}(\lambda^2)$.
- The bit-size of the token τ_{id} is $O(\log N) \cdot \widetilde{O}(\lambda)$.
- The update key uk_{t} has bit-size $O\left(r \log \frac{N}{r}\right) \cdot \widetilde{O}(\lambda)$.
- The ciphertext $\mathsf{ct}_{\mathsf{id},\mathsf{t}}$ has bit-size $(6m + k) \log q = \widetilde{O}(\lambda)$.
- The partially decrypted ciphertext $\mathsf{ct}'_{\mathsf{id},\mathsf{t}}$ has bit-size $(3m + 1) \log q = \widetilde{O}(\lambda)$.

Correctness. When the scheme is operated as specified, if recipient id is non-revoked at time t, then $\mathsf{tk}_{\mathsf{id},\mathsf{t}} = (\mathbf{E}_1, \mathbf{E}_2)$ satisfies that $\mathbf{A}_{\mathsf{id}} \cdot \mathbf{E}_1 + \mathbf{A}_\mathsf{t} \cdot \mathbf{E}_2 = \mathbf{U}$. During the **Transform** algorithm performed by the server, one has:

$$
\begin{aligned}
\mathbf{w} &= \hat{\mathbf{c}}_0 - \mathbf{E}_1^\top \begin{bmatrix} \mathbf{c}_{1,0} \\ \mathbf{c}_{1,1} \end{bmatrix} - \mathbf{E}_2^\top \begin{bmatrix} \mathbf{c}_{1,0} \\ \mathbf{c}_{1,2} \end{bmatrix} \\
&= \mathbf{U}^\top \mathbf{s} + \mathbf{y} + \mathsf{bin}(c_0) \cdot \lfloor \tfrac{q}{2} \rfloor - \mathbf{E}_1^\top \left(\mathbf{A}_{\mathsf{id}}^\top \mathbf{s} + \begin{bmatrix} \mathbf{x} \\ \mathbf{R}_1^\top \mathbf{x} \end{bmatrix} \right) - \mathbf{E}_2^\top \left(\mathbf{A}_\mathsf{t}^\top \mathbf{s} + \begin{bmatrix} \mathbf{x} \\ \mathbf{R}_2^\top \mathbf{x} \end{bmatrix} \right) \\
&= \mathsf{bin}(c_0) \cdot \lfloor \tfrac{q}{2} \rfloor + \underbrace{\mathbf{y} - \mathbf{E}_1^\top \begin{bmatrix} \mathbf{x} \\ \mathbf{R}_1^\top \mathbf{x} \end{bmatrix} - \mathbf{E}_2^\top \begin{bmatrix} \mathbf{x} \\ \mathbf{R}_2^\top \mathbf{x} \end{bmatrix}}_{\text{error}}.
\end{aligned}
$$

Note that if the error term above is bounded by $q/5$, i.e., $\|\mathsf{error}\|_\infty < q/5$, then in Step 2 of the **Transform** algorithm, one has that $\lfloor \frac{2}{q} \mathbf{w} \rceil = \mathsf{bin}(c_0)$ which implies $\hat{c}'_0 = \mathbf{g} \cdot \lfloor \frac{2}{q} \mathbf{w} \rceil = c_0$. Then, in the **Dec** algorithm run by the recipient, one has:

$$
\begin{aligned}
w' = \hat{c}'_0 - \mathbf{e}_{\mathsf{id},\mathsf{t}}^\top \mathbf{c}_2 &= \mathbf{v}^\top \mathbf{s}' + y' + M \cdot \lfloor \tfrac{q}{2} \rfloor - \mathbf{e}_{\mathsf{id},\mathsf{t}}^\top \left(\mathbf{B}_{\mathsf{id},\mathsf{t}}^\top \mathbf{s}' + \begin{bmatrix} \mathbf{x}' \\ \mathbf{S}_1^\top \mathbf{x}' \\ \mathbf{S}_2^\top \mathbf{x}' \end{bmatrix} \right) \\
&= M \cdot \lfloor \tfrac{q}{2} \rfloor + \underbrace{y' - \mathbf{e}_{\mathsf{id},\mathsf{t}}^\top \begin{bmatrix} \mathbf{x}' \\ \mathbf{S}_1^\top \mathbf{x}' \\ \mathbf{S}_2^\top \mathbf{x}' \end{bmatrix}}_{\text{error}'}.
\end{aligned}
$$

Similarly, if the error term is less than $q/5$, i.e., $|\text{error}'| < q/5$, then the recipient should be able to recover the plaintext. As in [1,10], the two error terms above are both bounded by $sm^2 B \cdot \omega(\log n) = \widetilde{O}(n^3)$, which is much smaller than $q/5$, as we set $q = \widetilde{O}(n^4)$. This implies the correctness of our scheme.

Security. The selective security of our scheme is stated in the following theorem.

Theorem 3. *The SR-IBE scheme described in Sect. 3 is SR-sID-CPA secure, provided that the (n, q, χ)-LWE assumption holds.*

In the proof of Theorem 3, we demonstrate that if there is a PPT adversary $\mathcal{A}$ succeeding in breaking the SR-sID-CPA security of our SR-IBE scheme, then we can use it to construct a PPT algorithm $\mathcal{S}$ breaking either the IND-sRID-CPA security of Chen et al.'s RIBE scheme or the IND-sID-CPA security of the ABB HIBE scheme. The theorem then follows from the facts that the two building blocks are both secure under the (n, q, χ)-LWE assumption (see Theorems 1 and 2). The details of the proof are given in the full version.

5 Conclusion and Open Problems

We present the first server-aided RIBE from lattice assumptions. In comparison with previous lattice-based realizations [10,11] of RIBE, our scheme has a noticeable advantage in terms of computation and communication costs on the user side. The scheme only satisfies the weak notion of selective security. Nevertheless, adaptive security in the standard model can possibly be achieved (at the cost of efficiency) by replacing the two building blocks by adaptively-secure lattice-based constructions, e.g., the RIBE from [11] and the HIBE schemes from [34,36]. One limitation of the scheme is the large size of user's long-term secret key: while being independent of the number of users, it is quadratic in the security parameter λ. Reducing this key size (e.g., making it linear in λ) is left as an open question.

Another question that we left unsolved is how to construct a lattice-based scheme secure against decryption key exposure attacks considered by Seo and Emura [32]. Existing pairing-based RIBE schemes satisfying this strong notion all employ a randomization technique in the decryption key generation procedure, that seems hard to adapt into the lattice setting. Finally, it is worth investigating whether our design approach (i.e., using a double encryption mechanism with an RIBE and an HIBE that have suitable plaintext/ciphertext spaces) would yield a generic construction for SR-IBE.

Acknowledgements. We thank Baodong Qin, Sanjay Bhattacherjee, and the anonymous reviewers for helpful discussions and comments. The research was supported by the "Singapore Ministry of Education under Research Grant MOE2013-T2-1-041". Huaxiong Wang was also supported by NTU under Tier 1 grant RG143/14.

References

1. Agrawal, S., Boneh, D., Boyen, X.: Efficient lattice (H)IBE in the standard model. In: Gilbert, H. (ed.) EUROCRYPT 2010. LNCS, vol. 6110, pp. 553–572. Springer, Heidelberg (2010). doi:10.1007/978-3-642-13190-5_28
2. Agrawal, S., Boneh, D., Boyen, X.: Lattice basis delegation in fixed dimension and shorter-ciphertext hierarchical IBE. In: Rabin, T. (ed.) CRYPTO 2010. LNCS, vol. 6223, pp. 98–115. Springer, Heidelberg (2010). doi:10.1007/978-3-642-14623-7_6
3. Ajtai, M.: Generating hard instances of the short basis problem. In: Wiedermann, J., Emde Boas, P., Nielsen, M. (eds.) ICALP 1999. LNCS, vol. 1644, pp. 1–9. Springer, Heidelberg (1999). doi:10.1007/3-540-48523-6_1
4. Alwen, J., Peikert, C.: Generating shorter bases for hard random lattices. Theor. Comput. Syst. **48**(3), 535–553 (2011)
5. Boldyreva, A., Goyal, V., Kumar, V.: Identity-based encryption with efficient revocation. In: CCS 2008, pp. 417–426. ACM (2008)
6. Boneh, D., Ding, X., Tsudik, G., Wong, C.: A method for fast revocation of public key certificates and security capabilities. In: 10th USENIX Security Symposium, pp. 297–310. USENIX (2001)
7. Boneh, D., Franklin, M.: Identity-based encryption from the Weil pairing. In: Kilian, J. (ed.) CRYPTO 2001. LNCS, vol. 2139, pp. 213–229. Springer, Heidelberg (2001). doi:10.1007/3-540-44647-8_13
8. Canetti, R., Halevi, S., Katz, J.: A forward-secure public-key encryption scheme. In: Biham, E. (ed.) EUROCRYPT 2003. LNCS, vol. 2656, pp. 255–271. Springer, Heidelberg (2003). doi:10.1007/3-540-39200-9_16
9. Cash, D., Hofheinz, D., Kiltz, E., Peikert, C.: Bonsai trees, or how to delegate a lattice basis. In: Gilbert, H. (ed.) EUROCRYPT 2010. LNCS, vol. 6110, pp. 523–552. Springer, Heidelberg (2010). doi:10.1007/978-3-642-13190-5_27
10. Chen, J., Lim, H.W., Ling, S., Wang, H., Nguyen, K.: Revocable Identity-Based Encryption from Lattices. In: Susilo, W., Mu, Y., Seberry, J. (eds.) ACISP 2012. LNCS, vol. 7372, pp. 390–403. Springer, Heidelberg (2012). doi:10.1007/978-3-642-31448-3_29
11. Cheng, S., Zhang, J.: Adaptive-ID secure revocable identity-based encryption from lattices via subset difference method. In: Lopez, J., Wu, Y. (eds.) ISPEC 2015. LNCS, vol. 9065, pp. 283–297. Springer, Heidelberg (2015). doi:10.1007/978-3-319-17533-1_20
12. Cocks, C.: An identity based encryption scheme based on quadratic residues. In: Honary, B. (ed.) Cryptography and Coding 2001. LNCS, vol. 2260, pp. 360–363. Springer, Heidelberg (2001). doi:10.1007/3-540-45325-3_32
13. Ding, X., Tsudik, G.: Simple identity-based cryptography with mediated RSA. In: Joye, M. (ed.) CT-RSA 2003. LNCS, vol. 2612, pp. 193–210. Springer, Heidelberg (2003). doi:10.1007/3-540-36563-X_13
14. Gentry, C.: Fully homomorphic encryption using ideal lattices. In: STOC 2009, pp. 169–178. ACM (2009)
15. Gentry, C., Peikert, C., Vaikuntanathan, V.: Trapdoors for hard lattices and new cryptographic constructions. In: STOC 2008, pp. 197–206. ACM (2008)
16. Gorbunov, S., Vaikuntanathan, V., Wee, H.: Predicate encryption for circuits from LWE. In: Gennaro, R., Robshaw, M. (eds.) CRYPTO 2015. LNCS, vol. 9216, pp. 503–523. Springer, Heidelberg (2015). doi:10.1007/978-3-662-48000-7_25
17. Lee, K., Lee, D.H., Park, J.H.: Efficient revocable identity-based encryption via subset sifference methods. Cryptology ePrint Archive, Report 2014/132 (2014). http://eprint.iacr.org/2014/132

18. Li, J., Li, J., Chen, X., Jia, C., Lou, W.: Identity-based encryption with outsourced revocation in cloud computing. IEEE Trans. Comput. **64**(2), 425–437 (2015)
19. Libert, B., Mouhartem, F., Nguyen, K.: A lattice-based group signature scheme with message-dependent opening. In: Manulis, M., Sadeghi, A.-R., Schneider, S. (eds.) ACNS 2016. LNCS, vol. 9696, pp. 137–155. Springer, Heidelberg (2016). doi:10.1007/978-3-319-39555-5_8
20. Libert, B., Peters, T., Yung, M.: Group signatures with almost-for-free revocation. In: Safavi-Naini, R., Canetti, R. (eds.) CRYPTO 2012. LNCS, vol. 7417, pp. 571–589. Springer, Heidelberg (2012). doi:10.1007/978-3-642-32009-5_34
21. Libert, B., Peters, T., Yung, M.: Scalable group signatures with revocation. In: Pointcheval, D., Johansson, T. (eds.) EUROCRYPT 2012. LNCS, vol. 7237, pp. 609–627. Springer, Heidelberg (2012). doi:10.1007/978-3-642-29011-4_36
22. Libert, B., Quisquater, J.: Efficient revocation and threshold pairing based cryptosystems. In: ACM Symposium on Principles of Distributed Computing, PODC 2003, pp. 163–171. ACM (2003)
23. Libert, B., Vergnaud, D.: Adaptive-ID secure revocable identity-based encryption. In: Fischlin, M. (ed.) CT-RSA 2009. LNCS, vol. 5473, pp. 1–15. Springer, Heidelberg (2009). doi:10.1007/978-3-642-00862-7_1
24. Micciancio, D., Mol, P.: Pseudorandom knapsacks and the sample complexity of LWE search-to-decision reductions. In: Rogaway, P. (ed.) CRYPTO 2011. LNCS, vol. 6841, pp. 465–484. Springer, Heidelberg (2011). doi:10.1007/978-3-642-22792-9_26
25. Micciancio, D., Peikert, C.: Trapdoors for lattices: simpler, tighter, faster, smaller. In: Pointcheval, D., Johansson, T. (eds.) EUROCRYPT 2012. LNCS, vol. 7237, pp. 700–718. Springer, Heidelberg (2012). doi:10.1007/978-3-642-29011-4_41
26. Naor, D., Naor, M., Lotspiech, J.: Revocation and tracing schemes for stateless receivers. In: Kilian, J. (ed.) CRYPTO 2001. LNCS, vol. 2139, pp. 41–62. Springer, Heidelberg (2001). doi:10.1007/3-540-44647-8_3
27. Peikert, C.: Public-key cryptosystems from the worst-case shortest vector problem: extended abstract. In: STOC 2009, pp. 333–342. ACM (2009)
28. Peikert, C.: A decade of lattice cryptography. Found. Trends Theor. Comput. Sci. **10**(4), 283–424 (2016)
29. Qin, B., Deng, R.H., Li, Y., Liu, S.: Server-aided revocable identity-based encryption. In: Pernul, G., Ryan, P.Y.A., Weippl, E. (eds.) ESORICS 2015. LNCS, vol. 9326, pp. 286–304. Springer, Heidelberg (2015). doi:10.1007/978-3-319-24174-6_15
30. Regev, O.: On lattices, learning with errors, random linear codes, and cryptography. In: STOC 2005, pp. 84–93. ACM (2005)
31. Sakai, Y., Emura, K., Hanaoka, G., Kawai, Y., Matsuda, T., Omote, K.: Group signatures with message-dependent opening. In: Abdalla, M., Lange, T. (eds.) Pairing 2012. LNCS, vol. 7708, pp. 270–294. Springer, Heidelberg (2013). doi:10.1007/978-3-642-36334-4_18
32. Seo, J.H., Emura, K.: Revocable identity-based encryption revisited: security model and construction. In: Kurosawa, K., Hanaoka, G. (eds.) PKC 2013. LNCS, vol. 7778, pp. 216–234. Springer, Heidelberg (2013). doi:10.1007/978-3-642-36362-7_14
33. Shamir, A.: Identity-based cryptosystems and signature schemes. In: Blakley, G.R., Chaum, D. (eds.) CRYPTO 1984. LNCS, vol. 196, pp. 47–53. Springer, Heidelberg (1985). doi:10.1007/3-540-39568-7_5
34. Singh, K., Rangan, C.P., Banerjee, A.K.: Adaptively secure efficient lattice (H)IBE in standard model with short public parameters. In: Bogdanov, A., Sanadhya, S. (eds.) SPACE 2012. LNCS, vol. 7644, pp. 153–172. Springer, Heidelberg (2012)

35. Yamada, S.: Adaptively secure identity-based encryption from lattices with asymptotically shorter public parameters. In: Fischlin, M., Coron, J.-S. (eds.) EURO-CRYPT 2016. LNCS, vol. 9666, pp. 32–62. Springer, Heidelberg (2016). doi:10.1007/978-3-662-49896-5_2

36. Zhang, J., Chen, Y., Zhang, Z.: Programmable hash functions from lattices: short signatures and IBEs with small key sizes. In: Robshaw, M., Katz, J. (eds.) CRYPTO 2016. LNCS, vol. 9816, pp. 303–332. Springer, Heidelberg (2016). doi:10.1007/978-3-662-53015-3_11

Speeding up the Number Theoretic Transform for Faster Ideal Lattice-Based Cryptography

Patrick Longa$^{(\boxtimes)}$ and Michael Naehrig

Microsoft Research, Redmond, USA
{plonga,mnaehrig}@microsoft.com

Abstract. The Number Theoretic Transform (NTT) provides efficient algorithms for cyclic and nega-cyclic convolutions, which have many applications in computer arithmetic, e.g., for multiplying large integers and large degree polynomials. It is commonly used in cryptographic schemes that are based on the hardness of the Ring Learning With Errors (R-LWE) problem to efficiently implement modular polynomial multiplication.

We present a new modular reduction technique that is tailored for the special moduli required by the NTT. Based on this reduction, we speed up the NTT and propose faster, multi-purpose algorithms. We present two implementations of these algorithms: a portable C implementation and a high-speed implementation using assembly with AVX2 instructions. To demonstrate the improved efficiency in an application example, we benchmarked the algorithms in the context of the R-LWE key exchange protocol that has recently been proposed by Alkim, Ducas, Pöppelmann and Schwabe. In this case, our C and assembly implementations compute the full key exchange 1.44 and 1.21 times faster, respectively. These results are achieved with full protection against timing attacks.

Keywords: Post-quantum cryptography · Number Theoretic Transform (NTT) · Ring Learning With Errors (R-LWE) · Fast modular reduction · Efficient implementation

1 Introduction

Fast Fourier Transform (FFT) algorithms to compute the Discrete Fourier Transform (DFT) have countless applications ranging from digital signal processing to the fast multiplication of large integers. The cyclic convolution of two integer sequences of length n can be computed by applying an FFT algorithm to both, then multiplying the resulting DFT sequences of length n coefficient-wise and transforming the result back via an inverse FFT. This operation corresponds to the product of the corresponding polynomials modulo $X^n - 1$, and for large n, a computation via FFTs as above was suggested to be used in the ring-based encryption scheme NTRUEncrypt in [15].

© Springer International Publishing AG 2016
S. Foresti and G. Persiano (Eds.): CANS 2016, LNCS 10052, pp. 124–139, 2016.
DOI: 10.1007/978-3-319-48965-0_8

When the sequence (or polynomial) coefficients are specialized to come from a finite field, the DFT is called the Number Theoretic Transform (NTT) [8] and can be computed with FFT algorithms that work over this specific finite field. Polynomial multiplication over a finite field is one of the fundamental operations required in cryptographic schemes based on the Ring Learning With Errors (R-LWE) problem, and the NTT has shown to be a powerful tool that enables this operation to be computed in quasi-polynomial complexity.

R-LWE-Based Cryptography. Since its introduction by Regev [28], the Learning With Errors (LWE) problem has been used as the foundation for many new lattice-based constructions with a variety of cryptographic functionalities. It is currently believed to be sufficiently hard, even for attackers running a large scale quantum computer. Hence cryptographic schemes with security based on the hardness of the LWE problem are promising candidates for post-quantum (or quantum-safe) cryptography.

The Ring LWE (R-LWE) problem, introduced by Lyubashevsky, Peikert and Regev [20], is a special instance of the LWE problem that is essentially obtained by adding a ring structure to the underlying lattice. R-LWE-based schemes have been proposed for public-key encryption [20,24,31], digital signatures [11,19], and key exchange [2,5,10,24,32]. Furthermore, the most efficient proposals for (fully) homomorphic encryption are also based on R-LWE, e.g., [6].

The advantage of R-LWE over LWE is a significant increase in efficiency. When working with vectors of dimension n, it allows a factor n space reduction and the possibility of using FFT algorithms to compute polynomial products instead of matrix-vector or matrix-matrix operations; this leads to an improvement from roughly n^2 base ring multiplications to roughly $n \log n$ such multiplications.

One particularly efficient parameter instantiation in the context of R-LWE is such that the dimension n is a power of 2 and polynomial products are taken modulo the $2n$-th cyclotomic polynomial $X^n + 1$ with coefficients modulo a prime q. Here, the polynomial product corresponds to a nega-cyclic convolution of the coefficient sequences. In this setting, the NTT is usually computed with a special type of FFT algorithm that can be used efficiently when q is a prime that satisfies the congruence condition $q \equiv 1 \bmod 2n$ (cf. [21, Sect. 2.1]), which in turn means that the underlying finite field contains primitive $2n$-th roots of unity. Many state-of-the-art instantiations of R-LWE-based cryptography choose n and q as above in order to harness the efficiency of the NTT; for example, the BLISS signature implementations (I-IV) set $n = 512$ and $q = 12289$ [11] and the fastest R-LWE-based key exchange implementation to date sets $n = 1024$ and $q = 12289$ [2].

Our Contributions. We present a new modular reduction algorithm for the special moduli that are required to invoke the NTT. While this new routine can be used to replace existing modular reduction algorithms and give standalone performance improvements, we further show that calling it inside a modified

NTT algorithm can give rise to additional speedups. We illustrate these improvements by providing and benchmarking both our portable C and AVX2 assembly implementations (see Sect. 5 for complete details). Our software is publicly available as part of the LatticeCrypto library [18].

Given the ubiquity of the NTT in (both the existing and foreseeable) high-speed instantiations of R-LWE-based primitives, we emphasize that an improved NTT simultaneously improves a large portion of all lattice-based cryptographic proposals. While our algorithm will give a solid speedup to signature schemes like Lyubashevsky's [19] and BLISS [11], it will give a more drastic overall improvement in common encryption and key exchange schemes. In these scenarios, there are different ways of removing the need for obtaining high-precision samples from a Gaussian distribution [22], for example, the number of R-LWE samples per secret can be bounded, or one can use the Kullback-Leibler or Renyi divergences [3]. Subsequently, the cost of sampling the error distribution decreases dramatically, and the NTT becomes the bottleneck of the overall computation.

To highlight the practical benefits of the new approach in an example of a cryptographic protocol, we implemented the recent key exchange instantiation due to Alkim, Ducas, Pöppelmann and Schwabe [2], and show that the overall key exchange is approximately 1.44 times faster (portable C implementation) and 1.21 times faster (AVX2 assembly implementation) using our improved NTT.

Beyond the faster modular reduction itself, the specific improvements over the approach in [2] that have led to this speedup are as follows:

- The new modular reduction algorithm allows coefficients to grow up to 32 bits in size, which eliminates the need for modular reductions after any addition during the NTT. As a consequence, reductions are only carried out after multiplications.
- The new modular reduction is very flexible and enables efficient implementations using either integer arithmetic or floating point arithmetic. Since it minimizes the use of multiplications, using the higher throughput of floating point instructions on the latest Intel processors does not have as big an impact as for more multiplication-heavy methods like Montgomery reduction. Hence, the method is especially attractive for implementations with a focus on simplicity, particularly in plain C.
- Related to the previous point, our implementation uses signed integer arithmetic in the NTT. This allows for signed integers to represent error polynomials and secret keys, which saves conversions from negative to positive integers (e.g., this reduces the number of additions during error sampling and before modular reductions in the NTT).
- We show how to merge the scaling by n^{-1} with our conversion from redundant to standard integer representation at the end of the inverse NTT. In addition, by pulling this conversion into the last stage of the inverse NTT, we eliminate $n/2$ multiplications and reductions, all at the cost of precomputing only two integers.

Organization. Section 2 gives the background on R-LWE and the NTT. Section 3 contains our two main contributions: the improved modular reduction and NTT algorithms. Section 4 revises the details in the R-LWE key exchange scheme from [2], which is used as a case study to give a practical instance where our improved NTT gives rise to faster cryptography. Finally, Sect. 5 provides a performance analysis and benchmarks.

2   Preliminaries

This section provides details about the ring structure in the R-LWE setting, the NTT, and the FFT algorithm to compute the NTT and its inverse. The original proposal of R-LWE [20] restricts to cyclotomic rings, i.e. rings generated over the integers by primitive roots of unity. We immediately focus on 2-power cyclotomic rings as this is the most commonly used case and seems to provide the most efficient arithmetic.

2.1   The Ring Learning with Errors (R-LWE) Setting

Let $N = 2^d$, $d > 1$ be a power of two and let $n = \varphi(N) = 2^{d-1} = N/2$. Then the N-th cyclotomic polynomial is given by $\Phi_N(X) = X^n + 1$. Let R be the ring of cyclotomic integers, i.e. $R = \mathbb{Z}[X]/(\Phi_N(X)) = \mathbb{Z}[X]/(X^n + 1)$. Any element $a \in R$ can be written as $a = \sum_{i=0}^{n-1} a_i X^i$, $a_i \in \mathbb{Z}$. Furthermore, let $q \in \mathbb{Z}$ be a positive integer modulus such that $q \equiv 1 \pmod{N}$. The quotient ring $R/(q)$ is isomorphic to $R_q = \mathbb{Z}_q[X]/(X^n + 1)$ and for any $a \in R_q$, we write $a = \sum_{i=0}^{n-1} a_i X^i$, $a_i \in \mathbb{Z}_q$. We use the same symbol a to also denote both the coefficient vector $a = (a_0, a_1, \ldots, a_{n-1}) \in \mathbb{Z}_q^n$ and the sequence $a = (a[0], a[1], \ldots, a[n-1]) \in \mathbb{Z}_q^n$.

2.2   The Number Theoretic Transform (NTT)

The NTT is a specialized version of the discrete Fourier transform, in which the coefficient ring is taken to be a finite field (or ring) containing the right roots of unity. It can be viewed as an exact version of the complex DFT, avoiding round-off errors for exact convolutions of integer sequences. While Gauss apparently used similar techniques already in [12], laying the ground work for modern FFT algorithms to compute the DFT and therefore the NTT is usually attributed to Cooley and Tukey's seminal paper [8].

Notation and Background. With parameters as above, i.e. n being a power of 2 and q a prime with $q \equiv 1 \pmod{2n}$, let $a = (a[0], \ldots, a[n-1]) \in \mathbb{Z}_q^n$, and let ω be a primitive n-th root of unity in $\mathbb{Z}_q$, which means that $\omega^n \equiv 1 \pmod{q}$. The forward transformation $\tilde{a} = \text{NTT}(a)$ is defined as $\tilde{a}[i] = \sum_{j=0}^{n-1} a[j]\omega^{ij} \bmod q$ for $i = 0, 1, \ldots, n-1$. The inverse transformation is given by $b = \text{INTT}(\tilde{a})$, where $b[i] = n^{-1} \sum_{j=0}^{n-1} \tilde{a}[j] \omega^{-ij} \bmod q$ for $i = 0, 1, ..., n-1$, and we have $\mathrm{INTT}(\mathrm{NTT}(a)) = a$.

As mentioned above, the NTT can be used directly to perform the main operation in R-LWE-based cryptography, that is, polynomial multiplication in $R_q = \mathbb{Z}_q[X]/(X^n + 1)$. However, since applying the NTT transform as described above provides a cyclic convolution, computing $c = a \cdot b \bmod (X^n + 1)$ with two polynomials a and b would require applying the NTT of length $2n$ and thus n zeros to be appended to each input; this effectively doubles the length of the inputs and also requires the computation of an explicit reduction modulo $X^n + 1$. To avoid these issues, one can exploit the *negative wrapped convolution* [21]: let ψ be a primitive $2n$-th root of unity in $\mathbb{Z}_q$ such that $\psi^2 = \omega$, and let $a = (a[0], ..., a[n-1])$, $b = (b[0], ..., b[n-1]) \in \mathbb{Z}_q^n$ be two vectors. Also, define $\hat{a} = (a[0], \psi a[1]..., \psi^{n-1} a[n-1])$ and $\hat{b} = (b[0], \psi b[1]..., \psi^{n-1} b[n-1])$. The negative wrapped convolution of a and b is defined as $c = (1, \psi^{-1}, \psi^{-2}, ..., \psi^{-(n-1)}) \circ \mathrm{INTT}(\mathrm{NTT}(\hat{a}) \circ \mathrm{NTT}(\hat{b}))$, where $\circ$ denotes component-wise multiplication. This operation satisfies $c = a \cdot b$ in R_q.

Previous Optimizations. Some additional optimizations are available to the NTT-based polynomial multiplication. Previous works explain how to merge multiplications by the powers of ω with the powers of ψ and ψ^{-1} inside the NTT. Consequently, important savings can be achieved by precomputing and storing in memory the values related to these parameters. In particular, Roy et al. [29] showed how to merge the powers of ψ with the powers of ω in the forward transformation. This merging did not pose any difficulty in the case of the well-known *decimation-in-time* NTT, which is based on the Cooley-Tukey butterfly [8] that was used in the first implementations of R-LWE-based schemes. Similarly, Pöppelmann et al. [26] showed how to merge the powers of ψ^{-1} with the powers of ω in the inverse transformation. In this case, however, it was necessary to switch from a decimation-in-time NTT to a *decimation-in-frequency* NTT [13], which is based on the Gentleman-Sande (GS) butterfly. In this work we exploit the combination of both transformations for optimal performance.

Other optimizations focus on the NTT's butterfly computation. Relevant examples are the use of precomputed quotients, as exploited in Shoup's butterfly algorithm [30], and the use of redundant representations that enable the elimination of several conditional modular corrections, as shown by Harvey [14]. In particular, Harvey showed how to apply the latter technique on Shoup's butterfly and on a butterfly variant based on Montgomery arithmetic. In Sect. 5, we compare our improved NTT algorithms with the approaches by Melchor et al. [1] and Alkim et al. [2], both of which adopted and specialized Harvey's butterfly algorithms.

Several works in the literature (e.g., [2, 17, 25, 29]) have applied a relatively expensive reordering or bit-reversal step before or after the NTT computation. This is due to the restrictive nature of certain forward and inverse algorithms that only accept inputs in standard ordering and produce results in bit-reversed ordering. However, Chu and George [7] showed how to also derive forward and inverse FFT algorithms working for the reversed case, i.e., accepting inputs in bit-reversed ordering and producing outputs in standard ordering. Accordingly, [26] adapted and suitably combined the algorithms in the context of NTTs in order to eliminate the need of the bit-reversal step.

From hereon, we denote by $\texttt{NTT} := \texttt{NTT}_{CT,\Psi_{rev}}$ an algorithm that computes the forward transformation based on the Cooley-Tukey butterfly that absorbs the powers of ψ in bit-reversed ordering. This function receives the inputs in standard ordering and produces a result in bit-reversed ordering. Similarly, we denote by $\texttt{INTT} := \texttt{INTT}_{GS,\Psi_{rev}^{-1}}$ an algorithm computing the inverse transformation based on the Gentleman-Sande butterfly that absorbs the powers of ψ^{-1} in the bit-reversed ordering. This function receives the inputs in bit-reversed ordering and produces an output in standard ordering. Following Pöppelmann et al. [26], the combination of these two functions eliminates any need for a bit-reversal step. Optimized algorithms for the forward and inverse NTT are presented in Algorithms 1 and 2, respectively. These algorithms are based on the ones detailed in [26, Appendix A.1]. Note that we have applied a few modifications and corrected some typos.

Pöppelmann et al. [26] avoid the final scaling by n^{-1} during the inverse NTT by shifting the computation to a polynomial transformation that is (in their target application of BLISS signatures) assumedly performed offline. In general, however, that assumption does not necessarily hold; for example, in [2], all of the polynomials to be multiplied are generated *fresh* per key exchange connection. Accordingly, Algorithm 2 includes scaling by n^{-1}.

Algorithm 1. Function NTT based on the Cooley-Tukey (CT) butterfly.

Input: A vector $a = (a[0], a[1], ..., a[n-1]) \in \mathbb{Z}_q^n$ in standard ordering, where q is a prime such that $q \equiv 1 \bmod 2n$ and n is a power of two, and a precomputed table $\Psi_{rev} \in \mathbb{Z}_q^n$ storing powers of ψ in bit-reversed order.
Output: $a \leftarrow \texttt{NTT}(a)$ in bit-reversed ordering.

1: $t = n$
2: **for** $(m = 1; \; m < n; \; m = 2m)$ **do**
3:     $t = t/2$
4:     **for** $(i = 0; \; i < m; \; i{+}{+})$ **do**
5:         $j_1 = 2 \cdot i \cdot t$
6:         $j_2 = j_1 + t - 1$
7:         $S = \Psi_{rev}[m + i]$
8:         **for** $(j = j_1; \; j \le j_2; \; j{+}{+})$ **do**
9:             $U = a[j]$
10:            $V = a[j + t] \cdot S$
11:            $a[j] = U + V \bmod q$
12:            $a[j + t] = U - V \bmod q$
13: **return** a

Algorithm 2. Function INTT based on the Gentleman-Sande (GS) butterfly.

Input: A vector $a = (a[0], a[1], ..., a[n-1]) \in \mathbb{Z}_q^n$ in bit-reversed ordering, where q is a prime such that $q \equiv 1 \bmod 2n$ and n is a power of two, and a precomputed table $\Psi_{rev}^{-1} \in \mathbb{Z}_q^n$ storing powers of ψ^{-1} in bit-reversed order.

Output: $a \leftarrow \text{INTT}(a)$ in standard ordering.

```
1:  t = 1
2:  for (m = n; m > 1; m = m/2) do
3:      j₁ = 0
4:      h = m/2
5:      for (i = 0; i < h; i++) do
6:          j₂ = j₁ + t − 1
7:          S = Ψ⁻¹_rev[h + i]
8:          for (j = j₁; j ≤ j₂; j++) do
9:              U = a[j]
10:             V = a[j + t]
11:             a[j] = U + V mod q
12:             a[j + t] = (U − V) · S mod q
13:         j₁ = j₁ + 2t
14:     t = 2t
15: for (j = 0; j < n; j++) do
16:     a[j] = a[j] · n⁻¹ mod q
17: return a
```

3   Modular Reduction and Speeding up the NTT

Most FFT algorithms to compute the NTT over a finite field or ring need certain roots of unity. In the specific setting discussed in the previous section, one needs primitive $2n$-th roots of unity to exist[1] modulo q, which imposes a congruence condition on q, namely $q \equiv 1 \pmod{2n}$. The parameters for R-LWE-based cryptosystems tend to have relatively large dimension n and relatively small moduli q, which means that moduli satisfying the congruence have the form $q = k \cdot 2^m + 1$, where $2n \mid 2^m$ and $k \geq 3$ is a very small integer.

Modular Reduction. In this section, we introduce a new modular reduction method for moduli of this special shape. We note that it works similarly for any modulus of the form $k \cdot 2^m \pm l$, where k and l are small positive integers such that $k \geq 3$ and $l \geq 1$. However, for ease of exposition and to focus on the case most relevant in the context of the NTT, we only treat the case $q = k \cdot 2^m + 1$. When k is odd and $2^m > k$, these numbers are known as Proth numbers [27], and a general algorithm for reduction modulo such integers is discussed in [9, Section 9.2.3].

Let $0 \leq a, b < q$ be two integers modulo q and let $C = a \cdot b$ be their integer product. Then $0 \leq C < q^2 = k^2 2^{2m} + k 2^{m+1} + 1$. The goal is to reduce C modulo

---

[1] For an algorithm that does not require such roots, but has the disadvantage of needing to pad the inputs to double length to compute nega-cyclic convolutions, see Nussbaumers algorithm ([23] and [16, Exercise 4.6.4.59]).

q using the special shape of q, namely using the fact that $k2^m \equiv -1 \pmod{q}$. Write $C = C_0 + 2^m C_1$, where $0 \le C_0 < 2^m$. Then $0 \le C_1 = (C - C_0)/2^m < k^2 2^m + 2k + 1/2^m = kq + k + 1/2^m$. We have that $kC \equiv kC_0 - C_1 \pmod{q}$, and given the above bounds for C_0 and C_1, it follows that the integer $kC_0 - C_1$ has absolute value bounded by $|kC_0 - C_1| < (k + 1/2^m)q$. As k is a small integer, the value $kC_0 - C_1$ can be brought into the range $[0, q)$ by adding or subtracting a small multiple of q. The maximal value for C is $(q - 1)^2 = k^2 2^{2m}$, in which case $C_0 = 0$ and $C_1 = k^2 2^m = k(q-1)$, meaning that $(k - 1)q$ must be added to $kC_0 - C_1$ to fully reduce the result. In our application to the NTT, however, we do not intend to perform this final reduction into $[0, q)$ throughout the computation, but rather only at the very end of the algorithm. We are therefore content with the output of the function K-RED defined as follows:

> **function** K-RED(C)
> $C_0 \leftarrow C \bmod 2^m$
> $C_1 \leftarrow C/2^m$
> **return** $kC_0 - C_1$

The function K-RED can take any integer C as input. It then returns an integer D such that $D \equiv kC \pmod{q}$ and $|D| < q + |C|/2^m$. Although this function alone does not properly reduce the value C modulo q, we still call it a reduction because it brings D close to the desired range; note that for $|C| > (2^m/(2^m-1))q$, we have $|D| < |$K-RED$(C)|$, i.e. it reduces the size of C. As a specific example, take $q = 12289 = 3 \cdot 2^{12} + 1$. Then $k = 3$ and K-RED returns $3C_0 - C_1 \equiv 3C \pmod{q}$ using the equivalence $3 \cdot 2^{12} \equiv -1 \pmod{q}$.

In the context of a specific, longer computation, and depending on the parameter n and the target platform, we note that additional reductions might need to be applied to a limited number of intermediate values, for which overflow may occur. In this case, as an optimization, two successive reductions can be merged as follows. Let the input operand C be decomposed as $C = C_0 + C_1 \cdot 2^m + C_2 2^{2m}$ with $0 \le C_0, C_1 < 2^m$. Then we can reduce C via the following function K-RED-2x.

> **function** K-RED-2x(C)
> $C_0 \leftarrow C \bmod 2^m$
> $C_1 \leftarrow C/2^m \bmod 2^m$
> $C_2 \leftarrow C/2^{2m}$
> **return** $k^2 C_0 - kC_1 + C_2$

Speeding up the NTT. In the context of the NTT algorithm, we use a redundant representation of integers modulo q by allowing them to grow up to 32 bits and, when necessary, apply the reduction function K-RED to reduce the sizes of coefficients. We keep track of the factors of k that are implicitly multiplied to the result by an invocation of K-RED. For the sake of illustration, consider Algorithm 1. The main idea is to apply the function K-RED only after multiplications, i.e., one reduction per iteration in the inner loop, letting intermediate coefficient values grow such that the final coefficient values become congruent to $K \cdot a[\cdot] \bmod q$ for a fixed factor K. This factor can then be used at the end of the NTT-based polynomial multiplication to correct the result to the desired value. Next, we specify the details of the method for $n \in \{256, 512, 1024\}$ for the prime $q = 12289$. We limit the analysis to platforms with native 32 (or higher)-bit multipliers, but note that the presented algorithms can be easily modified to cover other settings.

The case $q = 12289$. The modified NTT algorithms using K-RED and K-RED-2x are shown in Algorithm 3 and Algorithm 4 for the modulus $q = 12289$, which in practice is used with $n = 512$ (for BLISS signatures [11]) or 1024 (for key exchange [2]). In Steps 7 of Algorithm 3 and Step 7 of Algorithm 4, we are using the precomputed values scaled by k^{-1}, i.e. we use precomputed tables $\Psi_{rev,k^{-1}}[\cdot] = k^{-1} \cdot \Psi_{rev}[\cdot]$ and $\Psi_{rev,k^{-1}}^{-1}[\cdot] = k^{-1} \cdot \Psi_{rev}^{-1}[\cdot]$. We denote these modified algorithms by $\mathtt{NTT}^K := \mathtt{NTT}^K_{CT, \psi_{rev,k^{-1}}}$ and $\mathtt{INTT}^K := \mathtt{INTT}^K_{GS, \Psi_{rev,k^{-1}}^{-1}}$, respectively.

Algorithm 3. Modified function $\mathtt{NTT}^K$ using K-RED and K-RED-2x for reduction modulo $q = 12289$ (32 or 64-bit platform).

Input: A vector $a = (a[0], a[1], ..., a[n-1]) \in \mathbb{Z}_q^n$ in standard ordering, where $n \in \{256, 512, 1024\}$, and a precomputed table $\Psi_{rev,k^{-1}} \in \mathbb{Z}_q^n$ of scaled powers of ψ in bit-reversed order.

Output: $a \leftarrow \mathtt{NTT}^K(a)$ in bit-reversed ordering.

```
 1: t = n
 2: for (m = 1; m < n; m = 2m) do
 3:     t = t/2
 4:     for (i = 0; i < m; i++) do
 5:         j₁ = 2 · i · t
 6:         j₂ = j₁ + t - 1
 7:         S = Ψ_{rev,k⁻¹}[m + i]
 8:         for (j = j₁; j ≤ j₂; j++) do
 9:             U = a[j]
10:             V = a[j + t] · S
11:             if m = 128 then
12:                 U = K-RED(U)
13:                 V = K-RED-2x(V)
14:             else
15:                 V = K-RED(V)
16:             a[j] = U + V
17:             a[j + t] = U - V
18: return a
```

Given two input vectors a and b, let $c = \mathtt{INTT}(\mathtt{NTT}(a) \circ \mathtt{NTT}(b))$ be computed using Algorithms 1 and 2. It is easy to see that the resulting coefficients after applying Algorithms 3 and 4, i.e., after computing $\mathtt{INTT}^K(\mathtt{NTT}^K(a) \circ \mathtt{NTT}^K(b))$, are congruent to $K \cdot c[\cdot]$ modulo q for a certain fixed integer $K = k^s$ and an integer s. Note that by scaling the precomputed twiddle factors by $k^{-1} \mod q$, we can limit the growth of the power of k introduced by the reduction steps.

Algorithm 4. Modified function INTT^K using K-RED and K-RED-2x for reduction modulo $q = 12289$ (32 or 64-bit platform).

Input: A vector $a = (a[0], a[1], ..., a[n-1]) \in \mathbb{Z}_q^n$ in bit-reversed ordering, where $n \in \{256, 512, 1024\}$, a precomputed table $\Psi_{rev,k-1}^{-1} \in \mathbb{Z}_q^n$ of scaled powers of ψ^{-1} in bit-reversed order, and constants $n_K^{-1} = n^{-1} \cdot k^{-11}$, $\Psi_K^{-1} = n^{-1} \cdot k^{-10} \cdot \Psi_{rev,k-1}^{-1}[1] \in \mathbb{Z}_q$, where $k = 3$.
Output: $a \leftarrow \text{INTT}^K(a)$ in standard ordering.

1: $t = 1$
2: **for** $(m = n; \; m > 2; \; m = m/2)$ **do**
3:     $j_1 = 0$
4:     $h = m/2$
5:     **for** $(i = 0; \; i < h; \; i{+}{+})$ **do**
6:         $j_2 = j_1 + t - 1$
7:         $S = \Psi_{rev,k-1}^{-1}[h + i]$
8:         **for** $(j = j_1; \; j \le j_2; \; j{+}{+})$ **do**
9:             $U = a[j]$
10:             $V = a[j + t]$
11:             $a[j] = U + V$
12:             $a[j + t] = (U - V) \cdot S$
13:             **if** $m = 32$ **then**
14:                 $a[j] = \text{K-RED}(a[j])$
15:                 $a[j + t] = \text{K-RED-2x}(a[j + t])$
16:             **else**
17:                 $a[j + t] = \text{K-RED}(a[j + t])$
18:         $j_1 = j_1 + 2t$
19:     $t = 2t$
20: **for** $(j = 0; \; j < t; \; j{+}{+})$ **do**
21:     $U = a[j]$
22:     $V = a[j + t]$
23:     $a[j] = \text{K-RED}((U + V) \cdot n_K^{-1})$
24:     $a[j + t] = \text{K-RED}((U - V) \cdot \Psi_K^{-1})$
25: **return** a

For example in Line 7 of Algorithm 3 the value S carries a factor k^{-1} which then cancels with the factor k introduced by K-RED in Step 15. Only additional reductions such as those in Steps 12 and 13 increase the power of k in the final result.

At the end of the computation, the final results can be converted back to the standard representation by multiplying with the inverse of the factor K. Moreover, this conversion can be obtained for free if the computation is merged with the scaling by n^{-1} during the inverse transformation, that is, if scaling is performed by multiplying the resulting vector with the value $n^{-1} \cdot K^{-1}$. However, we can do even better: by merging the second entry of the table $\Psi_{rev,k-1}$ with the fixed value $n^{-1} \cdot K^{-1}$, we eliminate an additional $n/2$ multiplications and modular reductions. This is shown in Steps 21–24 of Algorithm 4.

4   Case Study: R-LWE Key Exchange

This section explains how we apply our new modular reduction and the improved NTT algorithms, together with a simplified message encoding, to the key exchange implementation that was proposed by Alkim, Ducas, Pöppelmann and Schwabe in [2]; the protocol is depicted in Fig. 1. Accordingly, from hereon we fix $n = 1024$ and $q = 12289$ and the error distribution is defined to be the centered binomial distribution ψ_{12}, from which one samples by computing $\sum_{i=1}^{16}(b_i - b_i')$, where the $b_i, b_i' \in \{0, 1\}$ are uniform independent bits. The functions HelpRec and Rec are modified instantiations of Peikert's reconciliation functions [24, Sect. 3] that essentially turn approximate key agreement into *exact* key agreement – see [2]. The function SHAKE-128 is the extended output function (XOF) based on Keccak [4], which is also used to derive the 256-bit shared secret key in both Alice and Bob's final steps. Following [2], the random value a is generated directly in the NTT domain.

Public parameters	
$n = 1024$, $q = 12289$, error distribution ψ_{12}	
Alice (server)	**Bob (client)**
$seed \xleftarrow{\$} \{0,1\}^{256}$	
$a \leftarrow$ SHAKE-128($seed$)	
$s, e \xleftarrow{\$} \psi_{12}^n$	$s', e', e'' \xleftarrow{\$} \psi_{12}^n$
$b \leftarrow as + e \quad \xrightarrow{\ m_A = (b, seed)\ }$	$a \leftarrow$ SHAKE-128($seed$)
	$u \leftarrow as' + e'$
	$v \leftarrow bs' + e''$
$v' \leftarrow us \quad \xleftarrow{\ m_B = (u, r)\ }$	$r \xleftarrow{\$}$ HelpRec(v)
$\nu \leftarrow$ Rec(v', r)	$\nu \leftarrow$ Rec(v, r)
$\mu \leftarrow$ SHA3-256(ν)	$\mu \leftarrow$ SHA3-256(ν)

Fig. 1. The key exchange instantiation from [2].

Viewing Fig. 1, we identify the following NTT-based computations:

Alice	Bob
$b \leftarrow a \circ \mathrm{NTT}(s) + \mathrm{NTT}(e)$	$u \leftarrow a \circ \mathrm{NTT}(s') + \mathrm{NTT}(e')$
$v' \leftarrow \mathrm{INTT}\left(u \circ \mathrm{NTT}(s)\right)$	$v \leftarrow \mathrm{INTT}\left(b \circ \mathrm{NTT}(s') + \mathrm{NTT}(e'')\right)$

The sequence of NTT and INTT operations above are used to determine the value of K that results from our target parameters; note that $q = 3 \cdot 2^{12} + 1$ and thus $k = 3$. For determining K, Alice's and Bob's NTT/INTT computations can be seen as *two* polynomial operations: (1) the first operation begins with the computation of b on Alice's side, who then transmits it in the NTT domain to Bob for computing v and giving the result back in the standard domain; and similarly (2) the second operation consists of the computation of u on Bob's side followed by the computation of v' on Alice's side.

We first point out that if we include two extra reductions at stage $m = 128$ and $m = 32$ of the NTT and INTT algorithms, respectively, then intermediate values never grow beyond 32 bits during a full NTT or INTT computation (see steps 11–13 of Algorithm 3 and steps 13–15 of Algorithm 4). Following Sect. 3, the factor k introduced by every invocation of K-RED is canceled out by the corresponding multiplication with an entry from the $\Psi_{\mathrm{rev},k^{-1}}$ and $\Psi_{\mathrm{rev},k^{-1}}^{-1}$ tables. Hence, only the extra reductions above introduce a factor k to the intermediate results of the NTT and INTT.

Secondly, we point out that after performing component-wise multiplications of polynomials in the NTT domain, the individual factors get compounded. The results after these multiplications require two additional reductions and a conditional subtraction per coefficient to fully reduce them modulo q (this is required to avoid overflows and, when applicable, to transmit messages and derive shared keys in fully reduced form). It is important to keep track of these factors and to (i) ensure that they are balanced (i.e., the same) before, e.g., adding two summands that are the result of different NTT operations, and (ii) ensure that they are corrected at the end of the computation. Careful analysis of the above sequence of NTT operations reveals that the final factor is $K = k^{10} = 3^{10}$ for the two full polynomial operations mentioned before.

Message Encoding and Decoding. Internally, polynomials are encoded as 1024-element little-endian arrays, where each element or coefficient is represented either by a 32-bit signed integer (for secret keys and error polynomials) or a 32-bit unsigned integer (for everything else). Each coefficient that is part of a message is fully reduced modulo q before transmission and therefore only uses a fraction of the integer size (i.e., 14 bits). We simply encode messages in little endian format as a concatenation of these 1024 14-bit coefficients (for b and u; see Fig. 1) immediately followed by the 256-bit *seed* in Alice's message and the 1024 2-bit array r in Bob's message. Accordingly, m_A and m_B consist of 1824 and 2048 bytes, respectively.

5   Implementation Results

In this section, we present implementation results showcasing the performance of the new NTT algorithms and, in particular, benchmark them in the context of the Ring-LWE key exchange by Alkim et al. [2].

5.1   Performance Benchmarks

To ease the comparison with the state-of-the-art NTT implementation, we followed [2] and implemented *two* versions of the proposed NTT algorithms [18]:

a portable and compact implementation written in the C language, and a high-speed implementation written in x64 assembly and exploiting AVX2 instructions. For the AVX2 implementation we decided to use vector integer instructions, which are easier to work with and, according to our theoretical analysis, are expected to provide similar performance to a version using vector floating-point instructions.

The benchmarking results of our implementations are shown at the top of Table 1. These results were obtained by running the implementations on a 3.4 GHz Intel Core i7-4770 Haswell processor with TurboBoost disabled. For compilation we used gcc v4.9.2 for the C implementation and clang v3.8.0 for the AVX2 implementation.

As one can see, for the C version, the new forward and inverse NTT implementations are 1.84 and 1.88 times faster than the corresponding implementations from Alkim et al. [2]. In contrast, for the AVX2 version, the new algorithms appear to be slightly slower. However, this direct comparison does not account for the additional benefits of our technique that are not observable at the NTT level. This includes the efficient use of signed arithmetic and the elimination of costly conversion routines required by the Montgomery arithmetic (as used in [2]) that are performed outside of the NTT. As we show below, our algorithms perform significantly better in practice when all this additional overhead is considered in the cost.

Table 1. Benchmarking results (in terms of 10^3 cycles) of our C and AVX2 implementations of the NTT and the key-exchange instantiation proposed by Alkim et al. [2] on a 3.4 GHz Intel Core i7-4770 Haswell processor with TurboBoost disabled. Results are compared with Alkim et al.'s implementation results. At the bottom of the table, we show the total cost of a key-exchange, including Alice's and Bob's computations.

	C implementation		AVX2 implementation	
	ADPS [2]	This work	ADPS [2]	This work
NTT	55.4	30.1	8.4	9.1
INTT	59.9	31.8	9.5	9.7
Generating a	43.6	39.5	36.9	37.8
Error sampling	32.7	31.4	5.9	4.8
`HelpRec`	14.6	12.9	3.4	2.4
`Rec`	10.1	7.2	2.8	1.2
Key gen (server)	259.0	**170.9**	89.1	**70.4**
Key gen + shared key (client)	385.1	**287.6**	111.2	**95.2**
Shared key (server)	86.3	**48.8**	19.4	**15.7**
Total (key exchange)	730.4	**507.3**	219.7	**181.3**

To illustrate the *overall* performance benefits of the new reduction and NTT algorithms, we implemented the full key-exchange instantiation proposed by Alkim et al. [2]. To ease the comparison, we reuse the same implementations of ChaCha20 and SHAKE-128 used in Alkim et al.'s software for the seed expansion during the generation of a and for the polynomial error sampling, respectively.

Our results for the key exchange are summarized in Table 1. The C and AVX2 implementations are roughly 1.44x and 1.21x faster, respectively, than the corresponding C and AVX2 implementations by Alkim et al. These improvements are mostly due to the new NTT algorithms which exhibit a faster reduction and avoid the costly conversions that are required when working with Montgomery arithmetic. The new reduction also motivates the use of signed arithmetic, which makes computations more efficient because corrections from negative to positive values are not required in several of the key exchange routines. In particular, the effect of using signed arithmetic can be observed in the performance improvement for the generation of a, HelpRec and Rec. We remark that these performance improvements are obtained with significantly simpler integer arithmetic.

A different Ring-LWE based key-exchange implementation has been recently reported by Aguilar-Melchor et al. [1]. Direct comparisons with this work are especially difficult because they use different parameters and the most recent version of their implementation appears not to be protected against timing and cache attacks. As a point of reference, we mention that [1, Table 2] reports that their NTT implementation using $n = 512$ and a 30-bit modulus runs in $13\,K$ cycles on a $2.9\,GHz$ Intel Haswell machine (scaled from $4.5\,\mu s$). This is more than 1.4x slower than our NTT using $n = 1024$ and a 14-bit modulus.

6 Conclusion

We describe a new modular reduction technique and improved FFT algorithms to compute the NTT. The improved NTT algorithms were applied to a recent key exchange proposal and showed significant improvements in performance using both a plain C implementation and a vectorized implementation that does not require floating-point arithmetic.

Although both the modular reduction and the improved NTT were motivated by (and are somewhat tailored towards) applications in R-LWE cryptography that use power-of-2 cyclotomic fields, our improvements should be of independent interest and might be applicable to other scenarios. Our method offers flexibility for implementations with different design goals without sacrificing performance.

Likewise, we expect that the new algorithms offer similar performance improvements on platforms such as microcontrollers and ARM processors. We leave this as future work, as well as the evaluation of the proposed NTT algorithms in the implementation and optimization of R-LWE signature schemes such as BLISS.

References

1. Aguilar-Melchor, C., Barrier, J., Guelton, S., Guinet, A., Killijian, M.-O., Lepoint, T.: NFLlib: NTT-based fast lattice library. In: Sako, K. (ed.) CT-RSA 2016. LNCS, vol. 9610, pp. 341–356. Springer, Heidelberg (2016). doi:10.1007/978-3-319-29485-8_20
2. Alkim, E., Ducas, L., Pöppelmann, T., Schwabe, P.: Post-quantum key exchange - a new hope. In: Holz, T., Savage, S. (eds.) 25th USENIX Security Symposium, USENIX Security 16, Austin, TX, USA, pp. 327–343. USENIX Association, 10–12 August 2016
3. Bai, S., Langlois, A., Lepoint, T., Stehlé, D., Steinfeld, R.: Improved security proofs in lattice-based cryptography: using the Rényi divergence rather than the statistical distance. In: Iwata, T., Cheon, J.H. (eds.) ASIACRYPT 2015. LNCS, vol. 9452, pp. 3–24. Springer, Heidelberg (2015). doi:10.1007/978-3-662-48797-6_1
4. Bertoni, G., Daemen, J., Peeters, M., Van Assche, G.: Keccak. In: Johansson, T., Nguyen, P.Q. (eds.) EUROCRYPT 2013. LNCS, vol. 7881, pp. 313–314. Springer, Heidelberg (2013). doi:10.1007/978-3-642-38348-9_19
5. Bos, J.W., Costello, C., Naehrig, M., Stebila, D.: Post-quantum key exchange for the TLS protocol from the ring learning with errors problem. In: 2015 IEEE Symposium on Security and Privacy, SP 2015, pp. 553–570. IEEE Computer Society (2015)
6. Brakerski, Z., Gentry, C., Vaikuntanathan, V.: (Leveled) fully homomorphic encryption without bootstrapping. TOCT **6**(3), 13:1–13:36 (2014)
7. Chu, E., George, A.: Inside the FFT Black Box Serial and Parallel Fast Fourier Transform Algorithms. CRC Press, Boca Raton (2000)
8. Cooley, J.W., Tukey, J.W.: An algorithm for the machine calculation of complex fourier series. Math. Comput. **19**(90), 297–301 (1965)
9. Crandall, R., Pomerance, C.: Prime Numbers: A Computational Perspective. Springer, Heidelberg (2005)
10. Ding, J., Xie, X., Lin, X.: A simple provably secure key exchange scheme based on the learning with errors problem. Cryptology ePrint Archive, Report 2012/688 (2012). http://eprint.iacr.org/2012/688
11. Ducas, L., Durmus, A., Lepoint, T., Lyubashevsky, V.: Lattice signatures and bimodal Gaussians. In: Canetti, R., Garay, J.A. (eds.) CRYPTO 2013. LNCS, vol. 8042, pp. 40–56. Springer, Heidelberg (2013). doi:10.1007/978-3-642-40041-4_3
12. Gauss, C.F.: Nachlass, theoria interpolationis methodo nova tractata. In: Carl Friedrich Gauss Werke, Band 3, pp. 265–330 (1866)
13. Gentleman, W.M., Sande, G.: Fast, fourier transforms: for fun and profit. In: Fall Joint Computer Conference, AFIPS 1966, pp. 563–578, ACM, New York (1966)
14. Harvey, D.: Faster arithmetic for number-theoretic transforms. J. Symb. Comput. **60**, 113–119 (2014)
15. Hoffstein, J., Pipher, J., Silverman, J.H.: NTRU: a ring-based public key cryptosystem. In: Buhler, J.P. (ed.) ANTS 1998. LNCS, vol. 1423, pp. 267–288. Springer, Heidelberg (1998). doi:10.1007/BFb0054868
16. Knuth, D.E.: Seminumerical algorithms. In: Lai, V.S., Mahapatra, R.K. (eds.) The Art of Computer Programming, 3rd edn. Addison-Wesley, Reading (1997)
17. Liu, Z., Seo, H., Roy, S.S., Großschädl, J., Kim, H., Verbauwhede, I.: Efficient ring-LWE encryption on 8-Bit AVR processors. In: Güneysu, T., Handschuh, H. (eds.) CHES 2015. LNCS, vol. 9293, pp. 663–682. Springer, Heidelberg (2015). doi:10.1007/978-3-662-48324-4_33

18. Longa, P., Naehrig, M.: LatticeCrypto (2016). https://www.microsoft.com/en-us/research/project/lattice-cryptography-library/

19. Lyubashevsky, V.: Lattice signatures without trapdoors. In: Pointcheval, D., Johansson, T. (eds.) EUROCRYPT 2012. LNCS, vol. 7237, pp. 738–755. Springer, Heidelberg (2012). doi:10.1007/978-3-642-29011-4_43

20. Lyubashevsky, V., Peikert, C., Regev, O.: On ideal lattices and learning with errors over rings. In: Gilbert, H. (ed.) EUROCRYPT 2010. LNCS, vol. 6110, pp. 1–23. Springer, Heidelberg (2010). doi:10.1007/978-3-642-13190-5_1

21. Lyubashevsky, V., Micciancio, D., Peikert, C., Rosen, A.: SWIFFT: a modest proposal for FFT hashing. In: Nyberg, K. (ed.) FSE 2008. LNCS, vol. 5086, pp. 54–72. Springer, Heidelberg (2008). doi:10.1007/978-3-540-71039-4_4

22. Micciancio, D., Peikert, C.: Hardness of SIS and LWE with small parameters. In: Canetti, R., Garay, J.A. (eds.) CRYPTO 2013. LNCS, vol. 8042, pp. 21–39. Springer, Heidelberg (2013). doi:10.1007/978-3-642-40041-4_2

23. Nussbaumer, H.J.: Fast polynomial transform algorithms for digital convolution. IEEE Trans. Acoust. Speech Sig. Process. **28**(2), 205–215 (1980)

24. Peikert, C.: Lattice cryptography for the internet. In: Mosca, M. (ed.) PQCrypto 2014. LNCS, vol. 8772, pp. 197–219. Springer, Heidelberg (2014). doi:10.1007/978-3-319-11659-4_12

25. Pöppelmann, T., Güneysu, T.: Towards practical lattice-based public-key encryption on reconfigurable hardware. In: Lange, T., Lauter, K., Lisoněk, P. (eds.) SAC 2013. LNCS, vol. 8282, pp. 68–85. Springer, Heidelberg (2014). doi:10.1007/978-3-662-43414-7_4

26. Pöppelmann, T., Oder, T., Güneysu, T.: High-performance ideal lattice-based cryptography on 8-bit ATXmega microcontrollers. In: Lauter, K., Rodríguez-Henríquez, F. (eds.) LATINCRYPT 2015. LNCS, vol. 9230, pp. 346–365. Springer, Heidelberg (2015). doi:10.1007/978-3-319-22174-8_19

27. Proth, F.: Théorèmes sur les nombres premiers. Comptes Rendus des Séances de l'Académie des Sciences, Paris **87**, 926 (1878)

28. Regev, O.: On lattices, learning with errors, random linear codes, and cryptography. In: Proceedings of the 37th Annual ACM Symposium on Theory of Computing, pp. 84–93 (2005)

29. Roy, S.S., Vercauteren, F., Mentens, N., Chen, D.D., Verbauwhede, I.: Compact ring-LWE cryptoprocessor. In: Batina, L., Robshaw, M. (eds.) CHES 2014. LNCS, vol. 8731, pp. 371–391. Springer, Heidelberg (2014). doi:10.1007/978-3-662-44709-3_21

30. Shoup, V.: Number Theory Library (NTL), 1996–2016. http://www.shoup.net/ntl

31. Stehlé, D., Steinfeld, R.: Making NTRU as secure as worst-case problems over ideal lattices. In: Paterson, K.G. (ed.) EUROCRYPT 2011. LNCS, vol. 6632, pp. 27–47. Springer, Heidelberg (2011). doi:10.1007/978-3-642-20465-4_4

32. Zhang, J., Zhang, Z., Ding, J., Snook, M., Dagdelen, Ö.: Authenticated key exchange from ideal lattices. In: Oswald, E., Fischlin, M. (eds.) EUROCRYPT 2015. LNCS, vol. 9057, pp. 719–751. Springer, Heidelberg (2015). doi:10.1007/978-3-662-46803-6_24

An Efficient Lattice-Based Multisignature Scheme with Applications to Bitcoins

Rachid El Bansarkhani[✉] and Jan Sturm

Technische Universität Darmstadt, Darmstadt, Germany
elbansarkhani@cdc.informatik.tu-darmstadt.de, jansturm92@googlemail.com

Abstract. Multisignature schemes constitute important primitives when it comes to save the storage and bandwidth costs in presence of multiple signers. Such constructions are extensively used in financial applications such as Bitcoins, where more than one key is required in order to authorize Bitcoin transactions. However, many of the current state-of-the-art multisignature schemes are based on the RSA or discrete-log assumptions, which may become insecure in the future, for example due to the possibility of quantum attacks. In this paper we propose a new multisignature scheme that is built on top of the intractability of lattice problems that remain hard to solve even in presence of powerful quantum computers. The size of a multisignature is quasi optimal and our scheme can also easily be transformed into a more general aggregate signature scheme. Finally, we give an efficient implementation of the scheme which testifies its practicality and competitive capacity.

Keywords: Multisignature scheme · Lattice-based crypto · Post-quantum

1 Introduction

The security notion of most cryptographic applications changes in the presence of quantum computers. In the breakthrough work [22] in 1994, Shor pointed out that cryptographic schemes with security based on the hardness of number theoretic assumptions can efficiently be attacked by means of quantum computers. Since then, many efforts have been spent on the search for alternatives in order to face this challenge. Lattice-based cryptography is a promising candidate that has the potential to meet the security needs of future business and private applications. As opposed to the discrete log problem and factoring, lattice problems are conjectured to withstand quantum attacks. Moreover, its unique security property to provide worst-case hardness of average-case instances represents a major cornerstone in cryptography in general as there exist no other hardness assumptions with the same security guarantees. In the last couples of years, a number of efficient cryptosystems emerged that base the security on the hardness of well-studied lattice problems. Unlike classical constructions such as RSA, there exists up to date no subexponential time attack on lattice problems,

© Springer International Publishing AG 2016
S. Foresti and G. Persiano (Eds.): CANS 2016, LNCS 10052, pp. 140–155, 2016.
DOI: 10.1007/978-3-319-48965-0_9

that are relevant for practice. All known attacks run in exponential time and thus provide a solid argument for a transition to lattice-based cryptosystems.

In a multisignature (MS) scheme n parties with public keys $pk_1, ..., pk_n$ agree to collectively construct a multisignature on a message m of choice such that the size of the multisignature is considerably smaller than the size of trivially bundled signatures while certifying that m has indeed been signed under the public keys $pk_1, ..., pk_n$ simultaneously. Such constructions have a great magnitude of applications and are utilized whenever storage and bandwidth costs are subject of minimizations. For instance, wireless sensor networks are characterized by constrained resources inherently asking for mechanisms that optimize the amount of traffic and the memory consumption. Many different multisignature schemes have been proposed in the past years. They are mainly based on classical assumptions such as RSA or the discrete-log problem. In [7] a lattice-based sequential aggregate signature scheme has been proposed, which can trivially be transformed into a sequential multisignature scheme, where the signers sequentially sign the same message. However, there is no multisignature scheme as such, to our knowledge, that is based on hardness assumptions that withstand quantum attacks. In order to allow for a smooth transition into a world surrounded by large scale quantum computers, it is desperately needed to realize such primitives due to its importance for financial applications such as Bitcoins.

Related Works. The concept of multisignature schemes was first introduced in [11]. Since then many works have been proposed, however failing to provide a security proof or even an appropriate adversary model. As a result, the constructions introduced in [13,16] were completely broken. In fact, only the works of Okamoto et al. [20] and Micali et al. [18] meet these requirements for the first time and present different security models. Nevertheless, the security notion of [18] is considered to be even stronger, since [20] does not consider attacks in the key generation phase (e.g. rogue-key attacks). On the other hand, for the scheme in [18] to be applied the set of signers has to be known beforehand. Following these works, Bolydreva et al. [6] give a new construction of a multisignature scheme employing the Gap-Diffie-Hellman problem as the underlying hardness assumption. In the work [15], Lu et al. remove the need for a random oracle and propose a multisignature scheme based on bilinear pairings. In 2006 Bellare and Neven propose a new multisignature scheme in the plain public key model [5]. This scheme gets rid of the drawbacks arising in other schemes such as the proof of knowledge for the secret key needed in [18]. The only requirement is that each signer has a certified public key, that is generated individually by each user. However, it is an interactive protocol, where the users have to collaborate prior to outputting a multisignature. But there exist also sophisticated concepts such as identity based multisignature schemes, which make the resulting schemes even more compact [2,4] in terms of memory consumption as the public keys are derived from a public and short identity.

Contribution. In this paper we propose the first lattice-based multisignature scheme that is provably secure in the random oracle model. We also show that it can easily be transformed into a lattice-based aggregate signature scheme. Our construction is built on top of the signature scheme due to Güneysu et al. [8,9] which represents a key component. In fact, we modify the corresponding scheme to an interactive multisignature scheme that is simple in terms of operations. As a result, we obtain a highly efficient scheme that is optimized both in terms of performance and multisignature size. In particular, the size of the multisignature is essentially as large as a single one (see Fig. 5) while providing security guarantees, that indeed each user signed the message, based on the hardness to solve certain lattice problems. We further discuss how our scheme can be utilized within the scope of Bitcoin/Blockchain transactions. Finally, we give an thorough implementation and several optimizations, thus moving the scheme towards practicality.

Organization. This paper is structured as follows. In Sect. 2 we start with some background notations of our work. In Sect. 3 we introduce our lattice-based multisignature scheme together with a proof of security. Section 4 contains a detailed description of our implementation and optimizations. In Sect. 5 we present the experimental results and an analysis.

2   Preliminaries

2.1   Notation

We will use the polynomial rings $\mathcal{R} = \mathbb{Z}[x]/\langle f(x) \rangle$ and $\mathcal{R}^q = \mathbb{Z}_q[x]/\langle f(x) \rangle$ for a polynomial $f(x)$ that is monic and irreducible over $\mathbb{Z}$. For any positive integer k, we denote by $\mathcal{R}^q_k$ the set of polynomials in $\mathcal{R}^q$ with coefficients in the range $[-k, k]$. For the ring-LWE problem we consider the cyclotomic polynomials, such as $f(x) = x^n + 1$ for n being a power of 2. The m-th cyclotomic polynomial with integer coefficients is the polynomial of degree $n = \phi(m)$ whose roots are the primitive m-th roots of unity. We denote ring elements by boldface lower case letters e.g. $\mathbf{p}$. By D^n_{32} we denote the set of polynomials of degree at most $n - 1$ with 32 coefficients ± 1 and zero coefficients else. Other required ingredients will be introduced in the respective sections.

Definition 1 ($\mathbf{DCK}_{q,n}$ problem, [9]). *We define the $\mathbf{DCK}_{q,n}$ problem (Decisional Compact Knapsack problem) to be the problem of distinguishing between the uniform distribution over $\mathcal{R}^q \times \mathcal{R}^q$ and the distribution $(\mathbf{a}, \mathbf{as}_1 + \mathbf{s}_2)$ where $\mathbf{a}$ is uniformly random in $\mathcal{R}^q$ and $\mathbf{s}_i$ are uniformly random in $\mathcal{R}^q_1$.*

3   Multisignature Scheme

In the following section we present the first lattice-based multisignature scheme that is provably secure in the random oracle model. At the core of our security proof we make use of the Forking Lemma [5], which allows us to derive a solution to a Ring-SIS instance. As a key component we deploy the efficient signature scheme due to Güneysu et al. in order to instantiate the scheme. But we also note, that other variants (e.g. [17]) are also possible requiring a slight modification in the security proof. One may also want to base the scheme on standard lattice problems or module representations of larger rank [12] allowing to hedge against future weaknesses of currently applied representations.

We start with a description of a formal model for multisignature schemes and the associated algorithms. A multisignature scheme consists of 3 algorithms $\mathcal{M} = (\mathsf{MKeyGen}, \mathsf{MSign}, \mathsf{MVerify})$. Let $S = \{S_1, \ldots, S_N\}$ be the set of N users agreeing to collectively sign a message M.

- $\mathsf{MKeyGen}(1^n)$: On input 1^n with security parameter n the probabilistic algorithm outputs for each signer a secret key and verification key $(\mathsf{sk}_i, \mathsf{pk}_i)$.

- $\mathsf{MSign}(L, M)$: On input a message M and any subgroup of signers $L = \{S_{i_1}, \ldots, S_{i_k}\}$ with indices $I = \{i_1, \ldots, i_k\}$ the algorithm outputs a multisignature σ_L, the set of signers L collaborating to construct σ_L and the message M.

- $\mathsf{MVerify}(\sigma_L, M, \mathbf{T})$: On input a multisignature or aggregate signature σ_L, a set of signers L, a message M, and the set of verification keys T associated to the signers in L the deterministic algorithm outputs $\mathbf{1}$, if the multisignature is valid and all signers indeed signed the message, otherwise $\mathbf{0}$.

We note that our interactive MS scheme can be turned into an ordinary aggregate signature scheme. This can be realized when replacing the message M by the tuple of messages $M_1||\mathsf{id}_1, \ldots, M_N||\mathsf{id}_N$ each for a different signer. In Definition 2 we define the notion of optimality in the context of multisignature schemes, which is typically not achieved by existing schemes.

Definition 2 (Optimal MS-Schemes, [10]). *In an optimal multisignature scheme the optimal size of a multisignature is identical to that of a single signature and the verification time is (almost) identical to that of a single signature.*

3.1 Our Construction

In the following section we give a detailed description of our construction and subsequently present a security proof in an appropriate security model.

Key Generation. At the start of the algorithm, all signers agree on a uniform random polynomial $\mathbf{a} \in \mathcal{R}^q$, which is attained, for instance, by interaction, generated by a trusted source or from a seed. The secret keys sk_i of each signer S_i are random polynomials $(\mathbf{s}_i^{(1)}, \mathbf{s}_i^{(2)}) \xleftarrow{\$} \mathcal{R}_d^q \times \mathcal{R}_d^q$, where d is a very small parameter (such as $d \in \{2, ..., 6\}$ for $n = 512$ and $d = 1$ for $n = 1024$), and the public key $\mathbf{T}_i = \mathbf{a} \cdot \mathbf{s}_i^{(1)} + \mathbf{s}_i^{(2)}$ is derived by use of the secret keys and $\mathbf{a}$. Larger values of d increase the security against key recovery attacks at the expense of a slower signing engine. For instance, if $d = 1$ and $q = 8383489$ we just obtain the parameter sets of the standard signature scheme from [8].

Multisignature Generation. For the security proof, we require two crypto-graphic hash functions $H_0 : \mathcal{R}^q \to \mathcal{R}^q$ and $H_1 : \{0,1\}^* \to D_{32}^n$ modeled as random oracles (RO). Every signer proceeds as follows in order to obtain a mul-tisignature on a message M: Similar to the basic signature scheme [8], each signer i samples $\mathbf{y}_i^{(1)}$ and $\mathbf{y}_i^{(2)}$ from $\mathcal{R}_k^q$. The parameter k controls the trade-off between the security and the runtime of our scheme. Subsequently, each signer computes $\mathbf{r}_i = a\mathbf{y}_i^{(1)} + \mathbf{y}_i^{(2)}$ and queries H_0 on input $\mathbf{r}_i$ outputting $\mathbf{t}_i = H_0(\mathbf{r}_i)$. This step is crucial for the security proof in order to program the RO. The par-ties then broadcast $\mathbf{t}_i$ to the other cosigners, who in turn wait for the reception of all $\mathbf{t}_j$ for $1 \leq j \leq N$ before broadcasting the corresponding input values $\mathbf{r}_j$. As a result, each signer is able to check the validity of $\mathbf{r}_j$ using $\mathbf{t}_j$ and computes $\mathbf{r} = \sum_{j=1}^N \mathbf{r}_j, \bmod\, q$ as one part of the multisignature. Subsequently, $H_1(\mathbf{T}_i, \mathbf{r}, \mathbf{T}, M)$ is queried with $\mathbf{T} = \{\mathbf{T}_1, \ldots, \mathbf{T}_N\}$ in order to obtain $\mathbf{c}_i$ of signer i. The following two protocol steps 9 and 10 essentially correspond to the sign-ing steps 3 and 4 of [8] with the minor modification that the whole protocol is restarted, if one signature fails the validity checks. The probability of not restarting the protocol is given by

$$\mathrm{Prob}[\mathbf{success}] = \left(1 - \frac{d \cdot 64}{2k+1}\right)^{2Nn} \Leftrightarrow k(E,N,n) = \left\lfloor \frac{1}{2} \cdot \left(\frac{d \cdot 64}{1 - \sqrt[2Nn]{1/E}} - 1\right) \right\rfloor \quad (1)$$

yielding $E = 1/\mathrm{Prob}[\mathbf{success}]$ expected number of trials. If all restrictions are satisfied the signature parts $\mathbf{z}_i$ will be shared among the cosigners and the mul-tisignature $(\mathbf{z}, \mathbf{r})$ is output, where $\mathbf{z} = \sum_{i=1}^N \mathbf{z}_i$.

We also highlight at this point that the signing engine can further be opti-mized by outputting $(\mathbf{z}, \{\mathbf{c}_i\}_{i=1}^N)$ rather than $(\mathbf{z}, \mathbf{r})$ in case the bit size of $\mathbf{r}$ is larger than the size of $\{\mathbf{c}_i\}_{i=1}^N$. This happens to occur whenever the inequality $N \cdot 160 < n \log q$ holds, since $\mathbf{c}_i$ consisting of at most 32 non-zero coefficients can be recovered from 160 bits ([8]). From the verifier's point of view, we can choose both representations, since $\mathbf{r}$ can be recovered from $\{\mathbf{c}_i\}_{i=1}^N$ and vice versa.

Multisignature Verification. The verification engine computes all $\mathbf{c}_i \leftarrow H_1(\mathbf{T}_i, \mathbf{r}, \mathbf{T}, M)$ and checks that the conditions $\mathbf{z}^{(1)}, \mathbf{z}^{(2)} \in \mathcal{R}_{N \cdot (k - d \cdot 32)}^q$ and $\mathbf{a} \cdot \mathbf{z}^{(1)} + \mathbf{z}^{(2)} = \mathbf{r} + \sum_{i=1}^N \mathbf{T}_i \mathbf{c}_i$ are satisfied. If these validity checks are successful, the algorithm outputs $\mathbf{1}$, else $\mathbf{0}$.

This scheme can also be built on top of the scheme presented in [17]. However, it has to be taken care of how to program the random oracle.

3.2   Security

Our security model is inspired by [5]. In particular, we show that forging a multisignature is as hard as solving a hard lattice problem assuming the existence of at least one honest signer in this group. We therefore allow the forger to control the private keys of all participants except for one honest signer (Fig. 1).

MKeyGen	MSign
Signing key $sk_i = \mathbf{S}_i$ with $\mathbf{S}_i = (\mathbf{s}_i^{(1)}, \mathbf{s}_i^{(2)}) \overset{\$}{\leftarrow} \mathcal{R}_d^q \times \mathcal{R}_d^q$ Verification key $vk_i = (\mathbf{a}, \mathbf{T}_i)$ $\quad \mathbf{a} \overset{\$}{\leftarrow} \mathcal{R}^q,$ $\quad \mathbf{T}_i \leftarrow \mathbf{a} \cdot \mathbf{s}_i^{(1)} + \mathbf{s}_i^{(2)}$ Output key pair (sk_i, vk_i)	Signer i $\qquad\qquad\qquad$ Cosigners 1: $\mathbf{Y}_i = \left(\mathbf{y}_i^{(1)}, \mathbf{y}_i^{(2)}\right) \overset{\$}{\leftarrow} \mathcal{R}_k^q \times \mathcal{R}_k^q \quad 1 \le j \le N, j \ne i$ 2: $\mathbf{r}_i \leftarrow \mathbf{a}\mathbf{y}_i^{(1)} + \mathbf{y}_i^{(2)}$ 3: $\mathbf{t}_i \leftarrow H_0(\mathbf{r}_i)$ 4: $\xrightarrow{\mathbf{t}_i}$ broadcast $\quad \xleftarrow{\mathbf{t}_j}$ broadcast 5: $\xrightarrow{\mathbf{r}_i}$ broadcast $\quad \xleftarrow{\mathbf{r}_j}$ broadcast

MVerify	
$\mathbf{c}_i \leftarrow H_1(\mathbf{T}_i, \mathbf{r}, \mathbf{T}, m)$ Accept iff $\mathbf{z} \in \mathcal{R}_{N \cdot (k-d \cdot 32)}^q \times \mathcal{R}_{N \cdot (k-d \cdot 32)}^q$ and $\mathbf{a} \cdot \mathbf{z}^{(1)} + \mathbf{z}^{(2)} = \mathbf{r} + \sum_{i=1}^{N} \mathbf{T}_i \mathbf{c}_i$	6: Check $\mathbf{t}_j \overset{?}{=} H_0(\mathbf{r}_j)$ for all $i \ne j$ 7: $\mathbf{r} \leftarrow \sum_{j=1}^{N} \mathbf{r}_j \bmod q$ 8: $\mathbf{c}_i \leftarrow H_1(\mathbf{T}_i, \mathbf{r}, \mathbf{T}, M)$ 9: $\mathbf{z}_i = (\mathbf{z}_i^{(1)}, \mathbf{z}_i^{(2)}) \leftarrow \mathbf{S}_i \mathbf{c}_i + \mathbf{Y}_i$ 10: if $\mathbf{z}_i \notin \mathcal{R}_{k-d \cdot 32}^q \times \mathcal{R}_{k-d \cdot 32}^q$ restart protocol 11: $\xrightarrow{\mathbf{z}_i}$ broadcast $\quad \xleftarrow{\mathbf{z}_j}$ broadcast 12: $\mathbf{z} \leftarrow \sum_{j=1}^{N} \mathbf{z}_j$ 13: Output $(\mathbf{z}, \mathbf{r})$

Fig. 1. Multisignature scheme

We consider the notion of adaptive chosen-message attacks, where $\mathcal{A}$ is allowed to make arbitrary many multisignature queries to the honest signer on messages of its choice. The advantage $\mathsf{AdvMSign}_{\mathcal{A}}^*$ of $\mathcal{A}$ is the success probability in the following experiment.

Experiment. $\mathrm{Exp}_{\mathcal{A}, SAS}^{MS-SU-CMA}(n)$
$(\mathbf{S}, \mathbf{T}) \longleftarrow \mathsf{KeyGen}(1^n),$
where $\mathbf{T} = \{\mathbf{T}_1, \dots, \mathbf{T}_N\}$ and $\mathbf{S} = \{\mathbf{S}_1, \dots, \mathbf{S}_N\}$
$(\mathbf{z}^*, \mathbf{r}^*) \longleftarrow \mathcal{A}^{\mathsf{OMSign}(\mathbf{S}^*, *, *)}(\mathbf{T}, \mathbf{S} \backslash \mathbf{S}^*, M)$
Let $\mathbf{T}^*$ be the challenge public key in $\mathbf{T}$ and
M be the message.
Let $\Sigma = ((\mathbf{T}, M_l), (\mathbf{z}_l, \mathbf{r}_l))_{l=1}^{Q_{MS}}$ be query-response tuples generated in
interaction with $\mathsf{OMSign}(\mathbf{S}^*, *, *)$
Return 1 if $\mathsf{MVerify}(\mathbf{z}^*, \mathbf{r}^*, \mathbf{T}, M) = \mathsf{valid}$
$\quad$ and $((\mathbf{T}, M), (\mathbf{z}^*, \mathbf{r}^*)) \notin \Sigma$

Following this experiment, the adversary is allowed to query the signing oracle OMSign on messages of its choice and he is also given random oracle access. He obtains as input all public keys, the secret keys of all parties other than the honest user and a message M of choice to be signed by all parties. Eventually, he outputs a forgery $(\mathbf{z}^*, \mathbf{r}^*)$ for a message M under public keys $\mathbf{T}$ containing the challenge public key $\mathbf{T}^*$. The adversary is said to be successful in this experiment, if he efficiently provides a valid multisignature with non-negligible advantage.

Definition 3 (MS-SU-CMA). *Let $\mathbf{T}^*$ be the challenge public key of the honest signer and $\mathbf{T} = \{\mathbf{T}_1, \ldots, \mathbf{T}_N\}$ the set of public keys in a multisignature scheme (MS). The MS is said to be strongly unforgeable under adaptive chosen message attacks (SU-CMA) if for all PPT algorithms $\mathcal{A}$, there exists a negl. function $\epsilon(n)$ s.t.*

$$\mathsf{AdvMSign}_{\mathcal{A}}^{SU-CMA}(n) = \mathrm{Prob}[(\mathbf{z}, \mathbf{r}, M) \leftarrow \mathcal{A} \mid \mathsf{MVerify}(\mathbf{z}, \mathbf{r}, \mathbf{T}, M) = \mathsf{valid}] \leq \epsilon(n).$$

Theorem 1 contains our main security statement of this section.

Theorem 1. *Suppose there exists a polynomial-time forger $\mathcal{F}$, who makes at most h queries to H, initiates at most s signing protocols with the honest signer involving at most N_{max} public keys and succeeds in providing a forgery with probability δ. Then, there exists an algorithm $\mathcal{A}$ with the same time complexity as $\mathcal{F}$ that for a given $\mathbf{A} = (\mathbf{a}, 1) \overset{\$}{\leftarrow} \mathcal{R}^{q^n} \times \{1\}$ (in fact any $\mathbf{A} = (\mathbf{a}, \mathbf{v})$ with invertible $\mathbf{v}$) finds non-zero $\mathbf{u}_1, \mathbf{u}_2 \in \mathbb{Z}_q^n$ with probability of at least*

$$\left(\frac{1}{2} - 2^{-100}\right) \cdot \left(\delta - \frac{2(h+s+1)^2}{g}\right) \cdot \left(\frac{\delta - 2(h+s+1)^2/g}{t} - \frac{1}{|D_{H_1}|}\right) \approx \frac{\delta^2}{2(h+s)}$$

for $g = \min\{|D_{H_0}|, |D_{H_1}|\}$ such that $\|\mathbf{u}_i\|_\infty \leq 2N_{\mathsf{max}}(k-d\cdot 32)$ and $\mathbf{au}_1 + \mathbf{u}_2 = \mathbf{0}$.

Proof. Let $D_{H_0} = \mathbb{Z}_q^n$ and $D_{H_1} = \{\mathbf{c} \ : \ \mathbf{c} \in \{-1, 0, 1\}^\kappa, \|\mathbf{c}\| \leq \kappa\}$ denote the ranges of the random oracles H_0 and H_1. The core idea of the security model is to let the forger $\mathcal{F}$ control the private keys of all but at least one honest signer. Thus, the forger is allowed to select the verification keys $\mathbf{T}_i = \mathbf{AS}_i$ of the fake signers by choosing the private keys $\mathbf{S}_i$. Given the forger $\mathcal{F}$ consider the algorithm $\mathcal{A}$, which behaves as follows. On input parameters ϕ, ψ corresponding to the random coins of the forger $\mathcal{F}$ and the honest signer, random oracle responses $\mathbf{h}_1, \ldots, \mathbf{h}_t$, target verification keys $\mathbf{A} = (\mathbf{a}, 1) \in \mathcal{R}^{q^n} \times \{1\}$ and $\mathbf{T}^* = \mathbf{AS}^*$, where $\mathbf{S}^* = (\mathbf{s}^{(1)}, \mathbf{s}^{(2)})$ with $\mathbf{s}^{(1)}, \mathbf{s}^{(2)} \in \{-d, \ldots, 0, \ldots, d\}^n$ denotes the secret key of the honest signer, the algorithm $\mathcal{A}$ runs the forger $\mathcal{F}$, who makes at most $t = h + s$ calls to the random oracle H during the attack. The random oracle is programmed either by calling it directly or when requesting to see a signature. At the beginning of the algorithm, $\mathcal{A}$ initializes 2 counters ctr_1 and ctr_2 and 3 associative lists $B_0[\cdot]$, $B_1[\cdot]$ and $B_2[\cdot]$, where $B_2[\cdot]$ is used to identify the different public keys by unique indices $1 \leq i \leq h + N_{max} \cdot s$. List B_2 is initially filled with $B_2[\mathbf{T}^*] \leftarrow 0$, meaning that the public key of the honest signer is always identified with the index 0. The algorithm responds to random oracle queries $H_0(\mathbf{r}_j)$ by selecting a random value $\mathbf{b}_i \overset{\$}{\leftarrow} \mathbb{Z}_p^n$ and setting $B_0[\mathbf{r}_j] = \mathbf{b}_i$, if it has yet not been defined, and outputs $B_0[\mathbf{r}_j]$. In case $H_1(\cdot)$ is called on input values $\mathbf{T}_i, \mathbf{Q}$, $\mathcal{A}$ checks the content of $B_2[\mathbf{T}_i]$. If $B_2[\mathbf{T}_i]$ is not defined, it increases ctr_1 and sets $B_2[\mathbf{T}_i] = ctr_1$. If $\mathbf{Q}$ parses as $\mathbf{r}, \mathbf{T}, M$, it furthermore ensures that $B_2[\mathbf{T}_j]$ is defined for all $\mathbf{T}_j \in \mathbf{T}$ and $1 \leq j \leq N$. Let $j = B_2[\mathbf{T}_i]$ be the unique index of $\mathbf{T}_i$. In case $B_1[i, \mathbf{Q}]$ has not yet been set, the algorithm selects random values for all $B_1[l, \mathbf{Q}]$, where $1 \leq l \leq h + N_{max} \cdot s$, and finally sets $B_0[0, \mathbf{Q}] = \mathbf{h}_{ctr_1}$. Whenever $\mathcal{F}$ requests from the honest signer a signature on a message M and verification keys $\mathbf{T}$, the algorithm proceeds as follows. If $\mathbf{T}^* \notin \mathbf{T}$, output $\perp$, else parse $\mathbf{T}$ as $\{\mathbf{T}_1 = \mathbf{T}^*, \mathbf{T}_2, \ldots, \mathbf{T}_N\}$. Then, it ensures that all entries $B_2[\mathbf{T}_j]$ are defined for $2 \leq j \leq N$ and increments the counter ctr_1. Subsequently, it sets $\mathbf{c}_1 \leftarrow \mathbf{h}_{ctr_1}$, randomly picks $\mathbf{z}_1 \in \mathcal{R}^q_{k-d\cdot 32} \times \mathcal{R}^q_{k-d\cdot 32}$, computes $\mathbf{r}_1 = \mathbf{A}\mathbf{z}_1 - \mathbf{T}_1\mathbf{c}_1$ and transmits $\mathbf{t}_0 = H_0(\mathbf{r}_1)$ to the other cosigners simulated by $\mathcal{F}$. Simultaneously, $\mathcal{A}$ looks up in the list B_0 for input vectors $\mathbf{r}_i$ such that $\mathbf{t}_i = B_0[\mathbf{r}_i]$, where $\mathbf{t}_i$ are receivings from the cosigners $2 \leq i \leq N$. In case a vector $\mathbf{r}_i$ corresponding to $\mathbf{t}_i$ cannot be found, $\mathcal{A}$ sets the flag $alert \leftarrow true$ and sends $\mathbf{r}_1$ to all cosigners. If B_0 contains more than one value for any $\mathbf{t}_i$, the event bad_1 occured and $\mathcal{A}$ stops the protocol returning $\perp$. In the other case, $\mathcal{A}$ computes $\mathbf{r} = \sum_{i=1}^{N} \mathbf{r}_i$ and subsequently checks whether $B_1[0, \mathbf{Q}]$ is defined for $\mathbf{Q}$ parsed as $\mathbf{r}, \mathbf{T}, M$. If $B_1[0, \mathbf{Q}]$ is already set, bad_2 occured and $\mathcal{A}$ aborts with output $\perp$. Otherwise it samples $B_1[0, \mathbf{Q}] \leftarrow \mathbf{c}_1$ and $B_1[l, \mathbf{Q}] \overset{\$}{\leftarrow} D_{H_0}$ for $1 \leq l \leq h + N \cdot s$. Finally it broadcasts $\mathbf{r}_1$, while receiving $\mathbf{r}_i$ from the other participants. $\mathcal{A}$ stops the protocol returning $\perp$ if there exists a vector $\mathbf{r}_i$ such that $H_0(\mathbf{r}_i) \neq \mathbf{t}_i$ or in case $H_0(\mathbf{r}_i) = \mathbf{t}_i$ for all $1 \leq i \leq N$ and $alert = true$. In the latter case the event bad_3 occured. Otherwise, it broadcasts $\mathbf{z}_1$ to the participants while receiving $\mathbf{z}_i$ from the cosigners. Finally, $\mathcal{A}$ computes $\mathbf{z} = \sum_{i=1}^{N} \mathbf{z}_i \mod p$ and outputs $(\mathbf{r}, \mathbf{z})$ as the multisignature. Once the forger $\mathcal{F}$ finishes the execution it eventually outputs a valid forgery $(\mathbf{r}, \mathbf{z})$ together with a list of public keys $\mathbf{T}$ and a message M with probability $\delta' = \delta - \sum_{i=0}^{3} P[bad_i]$. Therefore, we have $\|\mathbf{z}\|_\infty \leq N \cdot (k - d \cdot 32)$ and $\mathbf{A}\mathbf{z} - \sum_{i=1}^{N} \mathbf{T}_i\mathbf{c}_i = \mathbf{r}$ with probability δ, where $\mathbf{c}_i = H(\mathbf{T}_i, \mathbf{r}, \mathbf{T}, M)$.

If the random oracle H_1 has not been queried before, the probability of correctly selecting all vectors $\mathbf{c}_i$ such that $\mathbf{c}_i = H_1(\mathbf{T}_i, \mathbf{r}, \mathbf{T}, M)$ is $1/|D_{H_1}|^l$. Once calling H_1 during the signing step leads to the assignment of all $B_1[i, \mathbf{r}, \mathbf{T}, M]$ for $1 \leq i \leq h + N_{max}s$. Thus, the success probability of $\mathcal{F}$ to provide a valid signature with $\mathbf{c}^* = \mathbf{h}_j$ and $\mathbf{c}_i = H_1(\mathbf{T}_i, \mathbf{r}, \mathbf{T}, M)$ for $1 \leq i \leq N$ and $1 \leq j \leq t$ is at least $\delta - N/|D_{H_1}|$. Assuming this, let $1 \leq J \leq t$ be the index such that $B_1[0, \mathbf{r}, \mathbf{T}, M] = \mathbf{h}_J$. We first record the tuple $(\mathbf{r}, \mathbf{z}, \mathbf{h}_J)$ and by the forking lemma we obtain another tuple $(\mathbf{r}', \mathbf{z}', \mathbf{h}'_J)$ with probability of at least

$$(\delta' - N/|D_{H_1}|) \cdot \left(\frac{\delta' - N/|D_{H_1}|}{t} - \frac{1}{|D_{H_1}|} \right)$$

In both runs the same message M and set of keys $\mathbf{T}$ is used. This is due since the environments of $\mathcal{F}$ provided by $\mathcal{A}$ are identical up to the first call of $H_1(\mathbf{T}_i, \mathbf{r}, \mathbf{T}, M)$ or $H_1(\mathbf{T}_i, \mathbf{r}', \mathbf{T}', M')$, which leads to the assignments

$B_1[0, \mathbf{r}, \mathbf{T}, M] = \mathbf{h}_J$ and $B_1[0, \mathbf{r}', \mathbf{T}', M'] = \mathbf{h}'_J$. As a result, we must have $M' = M, \mathbf{r}' = \mathbf{r}$ and $\mathbf{T}' = \mathbf{T}$ because up to this point the same random tape, values $\mathbf{h}_1, \ldots, \mathbf{h}_{J-1}$ and random oracle responses have been used. Thus, let N^* be the number of occurrences of $\mathbf{T}^*$ in $\mathbf{T}$. Furthermore, prior to the assignment $B_1[0, \mathbf{r}, \mathbf{T}, M] \leftarrow \mathbf{h}_J$ all entries $B_2[\mathbf{T}_i]$ and $\mathbf{c}_i = B_1[B_2[\mathbf{T}_i], \mathbf{r}, \mathbf{T}, M]$ are initialized. Consequently, the random vectors $\mathbf{c}_i = \mathbf{c}'_i$ are also the same in both executions for $\mathbf{T}_i \neq \mathbf{T}^*$. For $\mathbf{T}^*$ we have $\mathbf{c}^* = \mathbf{h}_J$ and $\mathbf{c}'^* = \mathbf{h}'_J$ for the first and second run, where $\mathbf{h}_J \neq \mathbf{h}'_J$. Let the index set I^* contain all indices $1 \leq i \leq l$ such that $\mathbf{T}_i = \mathbf{T}^*$. From $\mathbf{Az} - \sum_{i=1}^{l} \mathbf{T}_i \mathbf{c}_i = \mathbf{r}' = \mathbf{r} = \mathbf{Az}' - \sum_{i=1}^{l} \mathbf{T}_i \mathbf{c}'_i$ it follows

$$\mathbf{A}(\mathbf{z} - \mathbf{z}' + |I^*| \cdot \mathbf{S}^*(\mathbf{c}^* - \mathbf{c}'^*)) = 0$$

Due to $\|\mathbf{z}\|_{\infty}, \|\mathbf{z}\|'_{\infty} \leq N(k - d \cdot 32)$ and $\|\mathbf{S}^* \mathbf{c}^*\|_{\infty}, \|\mathbf{S}^* \mathbf{c}'^*\|_{\infty} \leq d \cdot 32$ we have $\|\mathbf{z} - \mathbf{z}' + |N^*| \cdot \mathbf{S}^*(\mathbf{c}^* - \mathbf{c}'^*)\|_{\infty} \leq 2N(k - d \cdot 32) + 2|N^*| \cdot d \cdot 32$. Using $\mathbf{A} = (\mathbf{a}, 1)$ (or in general $\mathbf{A} = \mathbf{v}^{-1} \mathbf{A}'$ for $\mathbf{A}' = (\mathbf{a}, \mathbf{v})$ and invertible $\mathbf{v}$) and $\mathbf{S}^* = (\mathbf{s}^{(1)}, \mathbf{s}^{(2)})$ we obtain the following equivalent presentation for the equality from above

$$\mathbf{a}\left(\mathbf{z}^{(1)} - \mathbf{z}^{(1)'} + |N^*| \cdot \mathbf{s}^{(1)}(\mathbf{c}^* - \mathbf{c}')\right) + \left(\mathbf{z}^{(2)} - \mathbf{z}^{(2)'} + |N^*| \cdot \mathbf{s}^{(2)}(\mathbf{c}^* - \mathbf{c}')\right) = 0.$$

A quick view to this equation shows that we found in accordance to [8,17] two polynomials $\mathbf{b}_1$ and $\mathbf{b}_2$ with small coefficients such that $\mathbf{a} \cdot \mathbf{b}_1 + \mathbf{b}_2 = 0$. This solves Ring-SIS$_{n,2,\beta}$ for $\beta \leq 2N(k - d \cdot 32) + 2|N^*| \cdot d \cdot 32$, which is presumed to be hard. We note that the number of cosigners $N \leq N_{max}$ should not be too large. □

The following lemma provides a bound on the size of a multisignature. In practice the bound is much smaller than the assumed bound $N \cdot k$.

Lemma 1 (Hoeffding's Lemma). *Let X be any real-valued random variable with mean $E[X] = 0$ and such that $a \leq X \leq b$ almost surely. Then for all $\lambda \in \mathbb{R}$ it holds $E[e^{\lambda X}] \leq e^{\lambda^2 (b-a)^2 / 8}$.*

Lemma 2 (Signature Size). *Let $X_i \leftarrow_R [-k, \ldots, 0, \ldots, k]$ be uniform random variables for $1 \leq i \leq N$ with $E[X_i] = 0$. Define $X = \sum X_i$. Then, it holds $P[|X| \geq \sqrt{2cNk}] \leq e^{-c}$. For a vector $\mathbf{z} = \sum \mathbf{z}_i \in \mathbb{Z}^n$ with n components, the probability is given by $P[\|\mathbf{z}\|_{\infty} < \sqrt{2cNk}] \leq (1 - e^{-c})^n$.*

Lemma 2 follows from Lemma 1 by straight forward calculations.

3.3 Application Scenario: Signed Bitcoin Transactions

Multisignature schemes are applied whenever a group of signers wishes to sign the same data resulting in an aggregate signature of reduced size. Relevant financial application scenarios are Bitcoin[1] transactions, where multisignatures are

---

[1] Bitcoin is an open source project for the identically named currency on a peer-to-peer basis which was first mentioned in [19].

applied in order to validate crypto currency transactions prior to being written into the public Blockchain, which can subsequently not be changed anymore. The Blockchain technology itself is considered to be one of the most promising disruptive technologies in the financial sector due to its decentral characteristic to avoid the need of trusted parties such as banks or other intermediaries in order process transactions. Applied to the real world the economy may save a lot of time and huge amounts of money due to the ommission of intermediaries. With a signed transaction Bitcoin users can send virtual money anonymously over the network. Moreover, Bitcoin allows to make a multisignature transaction, where the signature of more than one private key is required. Usually we have an m-of-n address with n private keys for $m \leq n$.

More specifically, transferring Bitcoins from one address to another requires signatures from at least m keys (see Fig. 2). This has several advantages: On the one hand it gets very hard for an adversary to steal Bitcoins, because he needs to compromise m machines in order to mount his attack. With a 2-of-2 address, for instance, two keys could have been stored on two different machines and the attacker would have to compromise them both. On the other hand multisignature transactions can be used for redundancy in order to protect against loss. With a 2-of-3 address, for instance, a transaction can still be executed, though an arbitrary key gets lost. It can also be utilized for wallet sharing, where an address is shared by multiple members of an organization and a majority vote is required to use the funds.

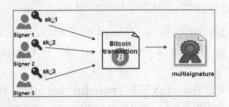

Fig. 2. Bitcoin multisignature

Our scheme from Sect. 3.1 can optimally be exploited for such purposes, especially for the case, where a user requires m private keys to successfully process financial transactions. In this case, the interactive nature of our protocol has no negative performance impact due to 2 reasons. First, in such protocols the number of private keys m required to sign transactions is rather small, i.e. $m \leq 5$. Second, the major part of the communication cost is restricted to the respective user himself without involving any other party within the P2P network such that the costs are minimal. Once the multisignature is created by the user, it is transmitted to the different P2P participants within the Bitcoin/Blockchain network. In this case, there are no additional communication costs beside of the transmission of a multisignature of reduced storage size. In fact, we show in Fig. 4 that the multisignature has essentially the size of a single signature, thus saving about 4 signatures in case we have $m = 5$ private keys involved. Obviously, the signature size can never be smaller than a single signature. Therefore, we conclude that our proposed multisignature scheme is indeed practical in such scenarios, where the performance of generating multisignatures does not represent a bottleneck. This is often the case within companies, institutions or in case of individuals.

4 Fast Polynomial Arithmetic

4.1 Polynomial Multiplication

If we neglect the time which is consumed to broadcast data, queries with a large input to the random oracle H_1 and polynomial multiplication are by far the most time-consuming operations in this scheme. Here we focus on fast polynomial multiplication. In order to achieve quasi-linear runtime in $\mathcal{O}(n \log n)$ for this operation, we use highly optimized versions of the Fast Fourier Transformation (FFT) and the Number Theoretic Transformation (NTT). The difference between those transformations is that the NTT is defined over a finite field $\mathbb{Z}/q\mathbb{Z}$ by means of a primitive n-th root of unity $\omega_n \in \mathbb{Z}/q\mathbb{Z}$, whereas the FFT has a complex representation of $\omega_n \in \mathbb{C}$.

Definition 4. (Root of Unity, [3]). ω_n *is a primitive n-th root of unity modulo q, if $\omega_n^n = 1 \pmod q$ and $\omega_n^{\frac{n}{d}} \neq 1 \pmod q$ for every divisor d of n.*

FFT and NTT Transformations. We assume that n is a power of two. The n-point $\mathrm{FFT}_\omega(a)$ of a coefficient vector $a = (a_0, ..., a_{n-1})$ to $y = (y_0, y_1, ..., y_{n-1})$ with $A(x) = \sum_{j=0}^{n-1} a_j x^j$ is defined as $y_i = A(\omega_n^i) = \sum_{j=0}^{n-1} a_j \omega_n^{ij}$ for $i = 0, 1, ..., n-1$. We basically evaluate a polynomial of degree $n-1$ at the powers of the n-th roots of unity ω_n^i. Due to the orthogonality relations between the n-th roots of unity, we can compute the inverse $\mathrm{FFT}_\omega^{-1}(y)$ by just using ω_n^{-1} instead of ω_n and dividing every resulting element by n.

The n-point $\mathrm{NTT}_\omega(a)$ with components in $\mathbb{Z}_q$ is defined analogous with additional modular reduction by q and the restriction that $q \equiv 1 \bmod 2n$. This restriction ensures the existence of a primitive $2n$-th root of unity ψ, because the order of ψ has to divide the group order. Both transformations exploit the special properties of the roots of unity such that the divide-and-conquer approach improves the computation time from $\mathcal{O}(n^2)$ to $\mathcal{O}(n \log n)$ [21].

For lattice-based cryptography it is convenient that many schemes prefer to operate in rings $\mathbb{Z}_q[x]/\langle x^n + 1 \rangle$ due to its nice properties. This allows, for instance, to apply the convolution theorem, which gives us a modular reduction by $x^n + 1$ for free. In fact, it can be applied with both FFT and NTT.

In [9] the authors proposed a highly optimized iterative NTT algorithm. While the NTT is restricted to a fixed prime q and n satisfying $q \equiv 1 \bmod 2n$, there is a need to extend this implementation to other representations in order to provide various efficiency and security trade-offs. We will now briefly review some of these optimizations and how to adapt them to a more generic and highly optimized FFT algorithm.

4.2 Optimizations

AVX. The first optimization is to use the Advanced Vector Extensions (AVX) in order to run certain basic computations in parallel. AVX is an extension of the x86 instruction set of modern Intel and AMD CPUs, i.e. Intel Sandy Bridge,

Intel Ivy Bridge or AMD Bulldozer, to perform *Single Instruction Multiple Data*
(SIMD) operations. SIMD instructions allow us to operate similar instructions
on multiple data in a single CPU cycle. In case of AVX, we have 16 256-bit wide
registers ymm, which can store any multiple of 32-bit or 64-bit floating-point
type that add up to 128 or 256 bits, as well as multiples of integer values not
exceeding 128 bits [14]. We can represent a polynomial of degree $n-1$ by an array
of n double floating-point values. By use of AVX we can operate on four of these
64-bit coefficients all at once. This implies a theoretical speedup of 4. However,
due to load- and store instructions it is not possible to exploit the complete
bandwidth. Moreover, it depends on how many operations have to be executed
between these load- and store instructions. If we consider, for instance, the simple
function that adds or subtracts two polynomials, we just get a speedup of 1.7
using AVX since there is only one single vaddpd/vsubpd instruction between the
load- and store process. There are some more operations that can be executed
in parallel, e.g. modular reduction, the NTT transformation and polynomial
multiplication, which allow for an increased speedup. We can construct two more
functions poly_equal and poly_elementof that check, if two polynomials are equal
and the coefficients of a polynomial. To this end, we require the instructions
vcmppd and the vmovmskpd.

According to Fig. 3 the vcmppd instruction fills
the respective register values with either only ones,
in case the condition is true, or only zeros, if it is
false. The condition can be specified with a certain hex-code (0x1c for NEQ, 0xe for GT or 0x1
for LT). Following this, the instruction vmovmskpd
extracts the MSB of all four values and returns an
integer bitmask of the MSBs. In case the bitmask

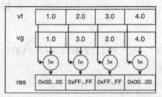

Fig. 3. vcmppd instruction

is non-zero at some point (and we assume that the coefficients are in the predefined range $[-(q-1)/2, (q-1)/2])$, the respective check fails. By means of
these two functions, we can achieve a speedup of about 3 as compared to its
serial counterpart. As shown in detail in [9, Sect. 3.2] the NTT, especially the
butterfly operations, run with AVX in parallel as well. To minimize memory
access they decide to split up the outer loop of the iterative NTT-algorithm
and merge several so-called levels together. The idea is to save store and load
instructions by holding some values in AVX registers, directly accessible for further computations.

Regarding convolutions within the NTT/FFT almost every step of the polynomial multiplication can be parallelized with AVX: We start by multiplying
the powers of ψ to the coefficient vector with some vmulpd instructions. Subsequently, we transform these vectors into the above mentioned parallel NTT circuit in order to carry out point-wise multiplication on four coefficients at once.
Finally, we apply the inverse transformation and multiply the resulting vector
with $\psi^{-i} n^{-1}$ in parallel. Realizing an implementation with different values for q
requires to apply the FFT rather than the NTT for specific representations. To
this end, we have to deal with complex numbers (complex n-th roots of unity

$\omega_n = e^{2\pi i/n}$). In particular, we represent a polynomial by two arrays of n double floating-point values. One for the real part and one for the imaginary part. Essentially, we now have to apply all the above explained operations from the NTT twice for the FFT, since the real- and imaginary part are treated separately. Only for the inverse FFT step we can avoid computations with the imaginary part, since the overall result is real. Another difference to the NTT algorithm is that we do not need modular reduction in every single butterfly operation anymore, because we are in the complex plane. Solely at the end of the polynomial multiplication we have to perform one modular reduction step after rounding all the resulting coefficients to the nearest integer. This rounding step is necessary due to the fact that we lose some precision caused by the imprecise floating point arithmetic. Furthermore, the point-wise multiplication has to be adapted to a parallel complex alternative. Let $v = a + ib$ and $w = c + id$ be two complex numbers, where the product is $v \cdot w = (ac - bd) + i(ad + bc)$. Thus we need four vmulpd, one vaddpd and one vsubpd operations to compute the poin-twise multiplication of two complex numbers. As opposed to the optimized NTT algorithm from [9], we relinquish merging several levels together since we have only 16 available ymm registers to cache data. However, we need almost twice as much registers because of the real- and imaginary part. This approach does not scale well in practice leading to less efficient allocations.

5   Performance Analysis and Benchmarks

In this section we analyze the performance of our software and report benchmarks for the signing (multisig_sign) and verification (multisig_verify) algorithm. We performed the experiments on the following machine: An Ultrabook, Intel Core i5-6200U (Skylake) at 2300 MHz and 8 GB RAM running Linux 64 Bit. All software was compiled with gcc-5.4.0 and compiler flags -Ofast -msse2avx -march=core-avx2.

5.1   Experimental Results of Our Multisignature Scheme

In Fig. 4 we report the average of 500–1000 signature generations for message sizes of 100 bytes. We also report the timings for MSign of one single signer ignoring the time, which is consumed, to broadcast data. This reflects the fact that in practice all signers run the protocol in parallel. In order to achieve 100 bits of security for $n = 1024$ we sample the coefficients of the secret polynomials from the set $\{-1, 0, 1\}$, i.e. for $d = 1$. We applied the large set of security analysis tools from [1] to estimate the security level of the scheme. We note that the NTT can only be used for moduli up to $\log(q) = 23$ bits due to the imprecise representation of q^{-1} in floating point modulo operations for larger values of q. In the following table, we provide timings (ms) and sizes (kB) for different parameter sets, where $n = 1024$ is chosen to be fixed. In particular, we provide performance results for a various number of signers N and different moduli q for a fixed number of protocol repetitions E.

	n=1024		d=1	Bit Security $\approx$ 120 [1]			
N	Modulus	E	k	log(k)	MSign	MVerify	SigSize $|\sigma|$	Multisignature Size $|\Sigma|$
10	$q = 8380417$ $\log(q) = 23$ NTT	100	142325	17.1	21.5 ms	0.2 ms	4.6 kB	$\approx$ 1 signature (out of 10)
		50	167540	17.4	11.5 ms		4.6 kB	$\approx$ 1 signature (out of 10)
		10	284635	18.1	2.3 ms		4.8 kB	$\approx$ 1 signature (out of 10)
		5	407214	18.6	1.1 ms		4.9 kB	$\approx$ 1 signature (out of 10)
5	$q = 8380417$ $\log(q) = 23$ NTT	100	71170	16.1	12.1 ms	0.1 ms	4.3 kB	$\approx$ 1 signature (out of 5)
		50	83778	16.4	6.0 ms		4.4 kB	$\approx$ 1 signature (out of 5)
		10	142325	17.1	1.3 ms		4.6 kB	$\approx$ 1 signature (out of 5)
		5	203615	17.6	0.6 ms		4.7 kB	$\approx$ 1 signature (out of 5)

Fig. 4. Timings (in ms) for signing and verification ($n = 512, d = 3$), sizes for the corresponding multisignatures and compression factors ϑ.

This term indicates according to Eq. 1 how often the protocol has to be restarted in order to obtain a valid multisignature. The compression factor for the signature size is defined as $\vartheta = 1 - \frac{|\Sigma|}{N \cdot |\sigma|}$, where $|\Sigma|$ denotes the multisignature size and $|\sigma|$ the size of a single signature.

Our experiments show that the timings for the signing procedure increase linearly with the number of signers N and the expected value E. However, it depends only quasi linear on the polynomial degree n. The respective timings for the FFT are slightly slower. We observe that the multisignature size ($|\Sigma| = 2n \cdot \log(N \cdot 2(k-32)+1) + 160N$ bits) is almost as large as a single signature and thus remains almost constant as required in an optimal multisignature scheme according to Definition 2. The compression factor ϑ increases the more signers participate. However, the verification time is not constant but linear in the number of signers N.

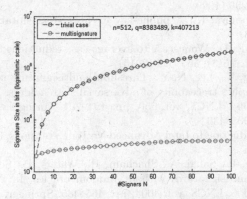

Fig. 5. Comparison of signature sizes with and without MS scheme.

References

1. Albrecht, M.R., Player, R., Scott, S.: On the concrete hardness of learning with errors. J. Math. Cryptology **9**, 169–203 (2015)
2. Bagherzandi, A., Jarecki, S.: Identity-based aggregate and multi-signature schemes based on RSA. In: Nguyen, P.Q., Pointcheval, D. (eds.) PKC 2010. LNCS, vol. 6056, pp. 480–498. Springer, Heidelberg (2010). doi:10.1007/978-3-642-13013-7_28
3. Baktir, S., Sunar, B.: Achieving efficient polynomial multiplication in Fermat fields using the fast Fourier transform. In: ACM Southeast Regional Conference Proceedings of the 44th Annual Southeast Regional Conference, pp. 549–554. ACM Press (2006)
4. Bellare, M., Neven, G.: Identity-based multi-signatures from RSA. In: Abe, M. (ed.) CT-RSA 2007. LNCS, vol. 4377, pp. 145–162. Springer, Heidelberg (2006). doi:10.1007/11967668_10
5. Bellare, M., Neven, G.: Multi-signatures in the plain public-key model and a general forking lemma. In: Juels, A., Wright, R.N., De Capitani di Vimercati, S. (eds.) ACM CCS 06 13th Conference on Computer and Communications Security, pp. 390–399. ACM Press, October/November 2006
6. Boldyreva, A.: Threshold signatures, multisignatures and blind signatures based on the Gap-Diffie-Hellman-Group signature scheme. In: Desmedt, Y.G. (ed.) PKC 2003. LNCS, vol. 2567, pp. 31–46. Springer, Heidelberg (2003). doi:10.1007/3-540-36288-6_3
7. Bansarkhani, R., Buchmann, J.: Towards lattice based aggregate signatures. In: Pointcheval, D., Vergnaud, D. (eds.) AFRICACRYPT 2014. LNCS, vol. 8469, pp. 336–355. Springer, Heidelberg (2014). doi:10.1007/978-3-319-06734-6_21
8. Güneysu, T., Lyubashevsky, V., Pöppelmann, T.: Practical lattice-based cryptography: a signature scheme for embedded systems. In: Prouff, E., Schaumont, P. (eds.) CHES 2012. LNCS, vol. 7428, pp. 530–547. Springer, Heidelberg (2012). doi:10.1007/978-3-642-33027-8_31
9. Güneysu, T., Oder, T., Pöppelmann, T., Schwabe, P.: Software speed records for lattice-based signatures. In: Gaborit, P. (ed.) PQCrypto 2013. LNCS, vol. 7932, pp. 67–82. Springer, Heidelberg (2013). doi:10.1007/978-3-642-38616-9_5
10. Harn, L.: Digital multisignature with distinguished signing authorities. Electron. Lett. **35**(4), 294–295 (1999)
11. Itakura, K., Nakamura, K.: A public-key cryptosystem suitable for digital multisignatures (1983)
12. Langlois, A., Stehlé, D.: Worst-case to average-case reductions for module lattices. Des. Codes Crypt. **75**(3), 565–599 (2015)
13. Li, C.-M., Hwang, T., Lee, N.-Y.: Threshold-multisignature schemes where suspected forgery implies traceability of adversarial shareholders. In: Santis, A. (ed.) EUROCRYPT 1994. LNCS, vol. 950, pp. 194–204. Springer, Heidelberg (1995). doi:10.1007/BFb0053435
14. Lomont, C.: Introduction to Intel Advanced Vector Extensions, June 2011. https://software.intel.com
15. Lu, S., Ostrovsky, R., Sahai, A., Shacham, H., Waters, B.: Sequential aggregate signatures and multisignatures without random oracles. In: Vaudenay, S. (ed.) EUROCRYPT 2006. LNCS, vol. 4004, pp. 465–485. Springer, Heidelberg (2006). doi:10.1007/11761679_28
16. Lysyanskaya, A.: Unique signatures and verifiable random functions from the DH-DDH separation. In: Yung, M. (ed.) CRYPTO 2002. LNCS, vol. 2442, pp. 597–612. Springer, Heidelberg (2002). doi:10.1007/3-540-45708-9_38

17. Lyubashevsky, V.: Lattice signatures without trapdoors. In: Pointcheval, D., Johansson, T. (eds.) EUROCRYPT 2012. LNCS, vol. 7237, pp. 738–755. Springer, Heidelberg (2012). doi:10.1007/978-3-642-29011-4_43

18. Micali, S., Ohta, K., Reyzin, L.: Accountable-subgroup multisignatures: extended abstract. In: ACM CCS 01: 8th Conference on Computer and Communications Security, pp. 245–254. ACM Press, November 2001

19. Nakamoto, S.: Bitcoin: a peer-to-peer electronic cash system (2008). http://fastbull.dl.sourceforge.net/project/bitcoin/Design%20Paper/bitcoin.pdf/bitcoin.pdf

20. Ohta, K., Okamoto, T.: Multi-signature scheme secure against active insider attacks. IEICE Trans. Fundam. Electron. Commun. Comput. Sci. 82(1), 21–31 (1999)

21. Roy, S.S., Vercauteren, F., Mentens, N., Chen, D.D., Verbauwhede, I.: Compact Ring-LWE cryptoprocessor. In: Batina, L., Robshaw, M. (eds.) CHES 2014. LNCS, vol. 8731, pp. 371–391. Springer, Heidelberg (2014). doi:10.1007/978-3-662-44709-3_21

22. Shor, P.W.: Polynomial-time algorithms for prime factorization and discrete logarithms on a quantum computer. SIAM J. Comput. 26(5), 1484–1509 (1997)

Virtual Private Network

Breaking PPTP VPNs via RADIUS Encryption

Matthias Horst$^{(\boxtimes)}$, Martin Grothe, Tibor Jager, and Jörg Schwenk

Horst Görtz Institute, Ruhr-University Bochum, Bochum, Germany
{matthias.horst,martin.grothe,tibor.jager,joerg.schwenk}@rub.de

Abstract. We describe an efficient *cross-protocol* attack, which enables an attacker to learn the VPN session key shared between a victim client and a VPN endpoint. The attack recovers the key which is used to encrypt and authenticate VPN traffic. It leverages a weakness of the RADIUS protocol executed between a VPN endpoint and a RADIUS server, and allows an "insider" attacker to read the VPN traffic of other users or to escalate its own privileges with significantly smaller effort than previously known attacks on MS-CHAPv2.

1 Introduction

The *Point-to-Point Tunneling* (PPTP) protocol [5] implements a confidential and authenticated virtual private network (VPN) tunnel in public computer networks like the Internet. In this work, we analyze the security of PPTP using MS-CHAPv2 in combination with a RADIUS authentication server. This is a standard setting, which is used in large-scale and enterprise networks, where RADIUS is used to centralize user management and to perform authentication for different applications. Large scale analysis of public VPN service providers shows that over 60 % of these still offer PPTP [14].

Contributions. We describe an efficient *cross-protocol* attack, which enables an attacker to learn the VPN session key shared between a victim client and a VPN endpoint. The attack recovers the key which is used to encrypt and authenticate VPN traffic, usually with the Microsoft Point-to-Point Encryption (MPPE) [9] scheme. The attack leverages a weakness of the RADIUS protocol executed between the VPN endpoint and the RADIUS server.

VPN session establishment with RADIUS authentication. In order to be able to sketch our attack, we first describe how a VPN session is established with RADIUS authentication. VPN session establishment with RADIUS involves three parties:

- The *client* which connects to the VPN endpoint. It shares a secret password with the RADIUS server. The RADIUS server is used to authenticate the client (or the user that uses this client). We assume that this password is a strong, high-entropy password, such that a dictionary attack is infeasible.

© Springer International Publishing AG 2016
S. Foresti and G. Persiano (Eds.): CANS 2016, LNCS 10052, pp. 159–175, 2016.
DOI: 10.1007/978-3-319-48965-0_10

- The *VPN endpoint* relies on the RADIUS server to authenticate users. It shares a *RADIUS secret S* with the RADIUS server. We assume that S is a cryptographically strong high-entropy key.
- The *RADIUS server* is a trusted party, which performs user authentication on behalf of the VPN endpoint, using that it shares the password with the client and the RADIUS secret S with the VPN endpoint.

Establishment of a VPN session works as follows:

1. The client initiates a PPTP session with the VPN endpoint.
2. At the beginning of the PPTP session, it authenticates itself by running the MS-CHAPv2 protocol. The VPN endpoint relays all MS-CHAPv2 messages between the client and the RADIUS server. As a result of the MS-CHAPv2 protocol, client and RADIUS server obtain a shared session key k_{MPPE} for the connection between client and VPN endpoint. Additionally, the VPN endpoint transmits a random nonce, called the *Request Authenticator* (Req_{Auth}) to the RADIUS server.
3. The RADIUS server uses the RADIUS secret S shared with the VPN endpoint to encrypt and send k_{MPPE} to the VPN endpoint. Here the so-called *RADIUS encryption* scheme Enc_{RADIUS} is used, which *essentially* computes a ciphertext $Enc_{\mathsf{RADIUS}}(k_{\mathsf{MPPE}})$ encrypting k_{MPPE} as

$$Enc_{\mathsf{RADIUS}}(k_{\mathsf{MPPE}}) = (\mathsf{Salt}, \mathrm{MD5}(S||Req_{\mathsf{Auth}}||\mathsf{Salt}) \oplus k_{\mathsf{MPPE}})$$

where Salt is a short random 11 bit Salt and Req_{Auth} is the random nonce selected in Step 2 by the VPN endpoint. (a full description of RADIUS encryption can be found in Subsect. 2.3)
4. The VPN endpoint decrypts this message. Now the client and the VPN endpoint share a session key k_{MPPE}, which can be used to encrypt VPN payload data, using the Microsoft Point-to-Point Encryption (MPPE) protocol.

A detailed description with our attack can be found in Fig. 2.

High-level attack description. Our attack is based on the following observations about RADIUS encryption as used in the setting described above.

- The "pseudorandom" value $\mathrm{MD5}(S||Req_{\mathsf{Auth}}||\mathsf{Salt})$ used to encrypt k_{MPPE} depends *deterministically* on S, Req_{Auth}, and Salt.
- The *same* value of S is used to encrypt *all* ciphertexts sent from the RADIUS server to the VPN endpoint.
- Salt has only 11 bits of entropy, therefore it is very likely that it is repeated in different ciphertexts sent from the RADIUS server to the VPN endpoint.
- The Req_{Auth} is a random nonce with high entropy (128 bits), however, it is *chosen by the VPN endpoint* and transmitted in *plain and unauthenticated* form from the VPN endpoint to the server.

Our attack leverages these observations as follows. We consider a setting with an attacker that meets the following two requirements:

- The attacker is able to monitor all data exchanged between the VPN endpoint and the RADIUS server, and it is able to inject packets.
- The attacker is an "insider", who is also able to establish VPN connections (but possibly with lower permissions than other users), whose goal is to learn the session key of *another* user.

This is a very practical setting in many applications of PPTP. We require the attacker to perform only a very small amount of computations, which could even be performed on a constrained device or a smartphone within a very short time (a few seconds). We also sketch below how the assumption of an "insider" attacker can be removed.

1. While the victim initiates a VPN connection, the attacker observes all messages exchanged between VPN endpoint and RADIUS server. In particular, it records Req_{Auth} and $Enc_{RADIUS}(k_{MPPE}) = (Salt, MD5(S||Req_{Auth}||Salt) \oplus k_{MPPE})$.

2. The attacker also initiates a VPN session *as an honest user*[1] and proceeds as follows:
   (a) The attacker runs the MS-CHAPv2 protocol to establish a shared session key k^*_{MPPE} shared with the RADIUS server.
   (b) When the VPN endpoint sends a random RADIUS Request authenticator Req^*_{Auth} to the RADIUS server, then the attacker *replaces* Req^*_{Auth} with the previously recorded value Req_{Auth} sent from the VPN endpoint.
   (c) The RADIUS server will respond to the VPN endpoint with a RADIUS encryption

   $$Enc_{RADIUS}(k^*_{MPPE}) = (Salt^*, MD5(S||Req_{Auth}||Salt^*) \oplus k^*_{MPPE})$$

   If $Salt^* = Salt$ (which happens with high probability, because the salt is a short random string of only 11 bits), then the attacker is able to use the fact that it knows k^*_{MPPE} to easily compute

   $$MD5(S||Req^*_{Auth}||Salt^*) = MD5(S||Req_{Auth}||Salt)$$

   from $Enc_{RADIUS}(k^*_{MPPE})$. This is sufficient to decrypt the session key contained in the message $Enc_{RADIUS}(k_{MPPE})$ of the victim's session.

Experimental analysis of the attack. We have implemented the attack in Python on a Ubuntu Linux machine. The target RADIUS server was the FreeRadius Server 3.0.10.

Our analysis shows that computing the session key of a victim user takes about 62 s in our setting on average.

---

[1] Recall here that in the basic setting we assume that the attacker is an "insider", which aims at learning the key k_{MPPE} of the victim in order to read the traffic or to escalate its own privileges.

Comparison to other attacks on MS-CHAPv2. It is well-known that MS-CHAPv2 is cryptographically weak, as it is based on the DES encryption scheme with 56 bit keys [13]. The previously best known attacks on MS-CHAPv2 were passive (=eavesdropping) attacks that recover the DES key, which required an exhaustive search over the key space of size 2^{56} (which is feasible on high-performance hardware, but relatively expensive) or were based on the use of low-entropy passwords [7,13].

In contrast, we show an active attack allowing to break MS-CHAPv2 authentication in PPTP with RADIUS authentication with *significantly* smaller effort of only 2^{14}, which is feasible even without access to high-performance hardware.

Extension to "outsider" attackers. Our attack assumes an "insider" attacker, but we note that it generalizes easily to "outsider" attackers as well. An outsider would first run the attack from Schneier and Mudge [13] to break MS-CHAPv2, in order to recover the secret of one user to become an "insider", and then mount our attack.

The main advantage of this approach is that the attacker has to execute the (feasible, but relatively expensive) attack of Schneier and Mudge only *once*, while without our attack technique he would have to executed it once for each victim user.

Further related work. Schneier and Mudge [13] as well as Eisinger [4] analyzed the security of MS-CHAPv2 and showed the maximum security is one full DES key space search. MPPE security was analyzed most recently by Patterson et al. [10], who exploited biases in the RC4 keystream, in order to mount plaintext recovery attacks. Downgrade attacks on PPTP were showed by Ornaghi et al. [8], which tried to force PAP or MS-CHAPv1 as authentication protocol instead of MS-CHAPv2.

2   Foundations

Our attack utilizes three different protocols, as described in Sect. 1 and therefore can be split into three different parts:

1. The first part is the setup of an PPTP channel over any PPP channel between the client and the VPN endpoint using the Link Control Protocol and Network Control Protocol. All data is transfered encapsulated in GRE packets. This is described in Subsect. 2.1.
2. The second part is the login procedure of the client at the RADIUS server. Here the data is transported again with GRE on the side between client and VPN endpoint and is then repacked into RADIUS packets and send from the VPN endpoint to the RADIUS server. This part is described in Subsect. 2.2
3. After the client is successfully logged in, he and the RADIUS server both compute a key k_{MPPE} and the RADIUS server encrypts this key using the RADIUS encryption Subsect. 2.3 and sends it to the VPN endpoint. Now that

the client and VPN endpoint both have the same key, they derive a session key from that and can start MPPE encrypted data communication. This part is described in Subsect. 2.4.

After we describe this setting in detail, we introduce an attacker that can get the key k_{MPPE}, with a few messages send to the RADIUS server under certain assumptions. We will then show, how the attacker can use the key to decrypt all messages from the secured MPPE channel. Our attack is described in Sect. 3.

2.1 PPTP

The Point-to-Point-Tunneling Protocol (PPTP) was designed to allow for clients that are not part of a network to tunnel their data trough a Point-to-Point protocol to that network to extend the original one with a virtual one. This allows to create Virtual Private Networks (VPNs). The Point-to-Point method was chosen, so that it was not necessary to have a working Ethernet connection between the networks, but phone communication or others could also be used.

PPTP uses a control channel over TCP and a second channel that is encapsulated in GRE to transfer the data.

PPP. The Point-to-Point-Protocol (PPP) was introduced in 1994 in RFC 1661 [1]. It is a layer-2 protocol to transmit arbitrary data packets over a full duplex point-to-point connection that can be established over many underlying systems.

Aside from the channel that transmits the actual data, the PPP uses two distinct protocols to agree how the channel is build: 1. Link Control Protocol (LCP) and 2. Network Control Protocol (NCP).

The LCP focuses on all management between the two parties constructing the channel, while the NCP controls how the selected payload protocol is used in the transfer later.

While the original PPP protocol was designed to allow transfer over Point-to-Point connections, the protocol was extended with Point-to-Point-over-Ethernet to also work in a Ethernet environment that is not a direct two point connection. This allows the use of all protocols based on PPP to be used over the Internet. This allows PPTP Endpoint to work directly with clients coming over the Internet and others using phone-lines with the same protocol.

PPTP. The PPP protocol itself does not offer security protection. As a result the Point-to-Point-Tunneling-Protocol (PPTP) was designed. In the beginning when PPP was only used over direct Point-to-Point connected endpoints, the security was derived from this direct connection. Now that it also possible to use the Internet as the underlying layer, these security guarantees are not valid anymore and additional security is needed. In the original PPTP specification in RFC 2637 [5], which was mainly driven by Microsoft, Ascend and a few others, were already different authentication mechanism introduced. The PPTP supports PAP, CHAP and the Microsoft version MS-CHAP. After MS-CHAP v1 was proven to be insecure, Microsoft developed v2. This standard has some security difficulties, but until today still has a complexity of 2^{56} for an attacker to get the password of a client. We will make use of this attack later. Besides the authentication Microsoft introduced the encryption Microsoft Point-to-Point Encryption (MPPE), which we describe in Subsect. 2.4.

Microsoft used PPTP as default way to construct secure VPN connections in its operating system Windows for a long time. Today still all Windows OSs have build in support for PPTP with the Microsoft authentication mechanisms MS-CHAPv1/v2. Further 60 % of publicly available VPN service providers still offer PPTP as a possible VPN mechanism [14]. Also every smartphone with Android or iOS supports PPTP by default.

GRE. The Generic Routing Encapsulation (GRE) is an older standard described in RFC 1701 [6]. It does not influence the security and will not be discussed in the paper.

2.2   MS-CHAPv2

During the setup of a PPTP connection a variety of protocols can be utilized to authenticate the users. MS-CHAPv2 is one example. It is used together with Microsoft's implementation of the Point-to-Point tunneling Protocol. In Microsoft environments PPTP is used together with Microsoft Point-to-Point Encryption algorithm (MPPE). An example protocol run is as follows. First the client requests an authenticator challenge from the server. The server then creates a 16 byte random authenticator challenge (C_S) and sends it back to the requesting client.

Next the client creates a new random 16 byte long challenge. This challenge together with the *name of the client user* and the challenge created on the server side are hashed via SHA-1 and the first 8 bytes results in the client hash (Chall$_{Hash}$). For the creation of the client response of the server challenge a key for the DES algorithm is created by hashing the user's password via the message digest algorithm 4 (MD4). The resulting hash is afterwards concatenated with 5 zero bytes. These constant 5 bytes lead to some major security issues as described by Schneier et al. [13]. The resulting bytes stored in k are then split up into 3 keys (k_1, k_2, k_3) and used for 3 different DES encryptions with Chall$_{Hash}$ as input data for every encryption. All ciphertexts are concatenated and stored as the client response in R_C. The values R_C, C_C and U_{Name} are sent back to the server. To verify the credentials of the user, the server recreates the client response. Therefore, it uses the password it stored for the corresponding user name received with the client response, as well as the Chall$_{Hash}$ recomputed by the server. It then compares its created client response with the received R_C. In case the values are equal the server continues with the authentication process. The next protocol message created by the server is the server response R_S. As a preparation the server double hashes the password of the user with the MD4 algorithm. The resulting hash value is used together with client response and a constant string value $(\mathsf{const})^2$. This hash value $(\mathcal{H}_{\mathsf{SHA1}})$ is used together with the previous created $\mathsf{Chall}_{\mathsf{Hash}}$ and the constant string value pad^3 as input for another SHA1 run. The result is named server response R_{S} and send to the client, which verifies the value. In case the verification ends successfully the mutual authentication process is also completed successfully [13,15].

Schneier et al. Attack on MS-CHAPv2. As mentioned earlier, MS-CHAPv2 can be broken by doing just one exhaustive key search of the DES key space. This is possible due to the fact that the input data $(\mathsf{Chall}_{\mathsf{Hash}})$ for all three DES encryption runs stays the same. Thus, 2^{56} encryption executions are necessary to find all three keys $(K[0\dots6]$, $K[7\dots13]$ and $K[14\dots20])$. This is accomplished by trying every $K \in Z_{2^{56}}$ as encryption key, when $\mathsf{Chall}_{\mathsf{Hash}}$ is input into the DES encryption and compare the corresponding result with Enc_1, Enc_2 and Enc_3. As soon as one key matches, it can be stored and the search continues until all three keys are found [13].

2.3 RADIUS Encryption

The RADIUS protocol defines its own encryption scheme. This scheme is mandatory for PPTP, and is used by default in software like the FreeRADIUS [11] server. The algorithm is defined in two RFCs: RFC 2865 [12], which is the default RFC for RADIUS, defines how RADIUS encrypted user passwords are send. RFC 2868 [17] defines how RADIUS is used in tunnel scenarios. Both versions only differ in the point that the RFC for the tunnel scenarios adds an additional Salt. We will focus on the tunnel version from now on, because this version is used to encrypt the MPPE key (k_{MPPE}).

The specification does not take care of key management for the RADIUS encryption. As a result the shared key has to be established manually on the VPN endpoint and the RADIUS server. If this shared key is of low-entropy, it can be computed using dictionary attacks [2]. Therefore, we assume that only high-entropy keying material is used.

Basically the RADIUS encryption is a stream cipher, with an input seed consisting of the (static) RADIUS secret and some (pseudo-)random values $(RA$ and Salt for the first block, c_i and Salt for the others) hashed using a MD5 hash function to generate the keystream. The ciphertext is then generated by computing the XOR of the keystream and the plaintext (cf. Fig. 1).

The pseudorandom values are used to prevent the keystream output of MD5 from always being identical for a single RADIUS secret. The Request Authenticator (Req_{Auth}) is chosen by the client before encrypting the data and is 16 bytes long.

The Salt is 2 bytes long. The first bit is fixed to 1, indicating that the salt was chosen by the server. This is followed by a 4 bit offset that is always incremented

---

[2] "Magic server to client constant".

[3] "Pad to make it do more than one iteration".

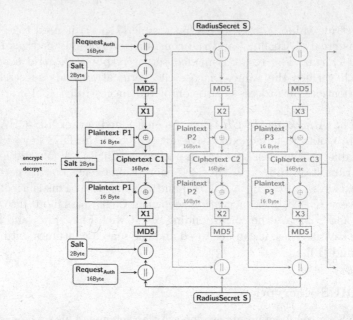

Fig. 1. RADIUS encryption and decryption

by 1. The remaining 11 bits are chosen at random. The salt is transmitted as a prefix to the encrypted data.

In the formal way the RADIUS encryption can be defined as two algorithms (Enc, Dec) with

$$c = \mathsf{Enc}(S, Req_{Auth}, p, SaO) \quad \text{and} \quad p = \mathsf{Dec}(S, Sa, Req_{Auth}, c)$$

Request Authenticator. In the RADIUS standards, there is some confusion on the term "Request Authenticator" (Req_{Auth}). In the original version of RADIUS encryption [12], the client selects Req_{Auth} and uses it as nonce and an IV for the encryption. The IV is used together with the RADIUS secret to encrypt data which should be sent to the server. The Req_{Auth} is a 16 byte value and stored in the message field named RADIUS Authenticator (RA). In case no encryption is used, Req_{Auth} is just a nonce value and not an IV in the RADIUS encryption. Thus, every RADIUS message from the client to the server contains a new value stored in the field RA.

Of course there are also RADIUS messages send from the server to the client. The server use the message field RA for authentication purposes. It creates a Message Authentication Code (MAC) called "Response Authenticator". The MAC is computed over are all encrypted message fields, except the RA field. Afterwards, the MAC ($Resp_{Auth}$) is stored in this Req_{Auth} field. As a consequence the field cannot be used to store the new IV needed for the used RADIUS encryption. Thus, the IV (Req_{Auth}) from the last message from the client to the server is used. In short, the client controls which IV is used by the server for the encryption.

Algorithm 1. Algorithm Encrypt	**Algorithm 2.** Algorithm Decrypt
Input: Key Material:	**Input:** Key Material:
RadiusSecret $S \in \{ASCII\}^{sc}$ with $1 < sc \leq 16$	RadiusSecret $S \in \{ASCII\}^{sc}$ with $1 < sc \leq 16$
$Req_{\text{Auth}} \in \{0,1\}^{128}$	Salt Sa with
Last SaltOffset SaO	SaltOffset $0 < SaO < 15$
Plaintext $p \in \{0,1\}^t$ as	SaltRandom SaR $\in \{0,1\}^{15}$
$[p_1 \in \{0,1\}^{256}, p_2, ... p_n \in \{0,1\}^{256}]$ with $n = \lceil \frac{t}{256} \rceil$	$Req_{\text{Auth}} \in \{0,1\}^{128}$
Output: Ciphertext $C \in \{0,1\}^t$ as	Ciphertext $c \in \{0,1\}^t$ as
$[c_1 \in \{0,1\}^{256}, c_2, ... c_n \in \{0,1\}^{256}]$	$[c_1 \in \{0,1\}^{256}, c_2, ... c_n \in \{0,1\}^{256}]$ with $n = \lceil \frac{t}{256} \rceil$
1: $SaO = (SaO + 1) \bmod 16$	**Output:** Plaintext $p \in \{0,1\}^t$ as
2: $SaR \xleftarrow{\$} \{0,1\}^{15}$	$[p_1 \in \{0,1\}^{256}, p_2, ... p_n \in \{0,1\}^{256}]$
3: $Sa = 1\|SaO\|SaR$	1: $r = MD5(S\|Req_{\text{Auth}}\|Sa)$
4: $r = MD5(S\|Req_{\text{Auth}}\|Sa)$	2: **for** $i = 1; i < n; i + +$ **do**
5: **for** $i = 1; i < n; i + +$ **do**	3: $p_i = c_i \oplus r$
6: $c_i = p_i \oplus r$	4: $r = MD5(S\|c_i)$
7: $r = MD5(S\|c_i)$	5: **end for**
8: **end for**	6: **return** p as $[p_1, p_2, ..., p_n]$
9: **return** Sa, c as $[c_1, c_2, ..., c_n]$	

The RADIUS RFC [12] defines that the RAs should not be used twice with the same RADIUS secret, but this is not checked by the server. This behavior allows a successful attack against PPTP.

2.4 MPPE

For the PPTP protocol an additional encryption protocol is needed in order to encrypt the user data. Because PPTP itself does not offer such an encryption, Microsoft presented the Microsoft Point-to-Point Encryption protocol (MPPE) [9]. MPPE offers 3 different lengths for the key: 40, 56 and 128 bits. We assume that the strongest option with 128 bits is used, because the other options were designed to fulfill other regulations like export limitations.

MPPE was designed for the use case of PPTP. As a result the protocol expects an open PPTP channel and that a key was derived there. The encryption is done by using the standard RC4 algorithm. MPPE only defines how the keys and the data are fitted to be used in the RC4 encryption algorithm.

MPPE offers the functionality to exchange the key while transmitting data and to synchronize keys again if the synchronization is lost at some point. This allows MPPE to change the keys after a set schedule. The keys only depend on older keys. If the first key is compromised, all others could be computed by an attacker. Thus, there is no real key freshness. In this paper we will focus only on the first key for a session.

Key Derivation. MPPE utilizes the keys derived by other protocols for its own key derivation. This is then used in the RC4 algorithm. The protocols from which MPPE can derive keys are MS-CHAPv1, MS-CHAPv2 and TLS as specified in RFC 3079 [16].

For MS-CHAPv2 it works as follows: the key is split in two halves, one for sending data from the client to the VPN endpoint called "Send-Key" and one for the other way around called "Recv-Key". This is done by hashing the MS-CHAP key together with different magic constants. The Send-Key is computed as follows:

$$\text{Send-Key} = \mathcal{H}_{\text{SHA1}}(Key\|pad\|const\_send\|pad)$$

and the Recv-Key the same way with another constant. These keys are used as the starting point for the session keys that are used for the encryption. The actual keys used for the encryption are called session keys, and the first is derived only from the Send-Key and Recv-Key, while the following also use the last session key. Here again as hashing function only SHA1 is used. The key is derived as follows:

$$\text{Session-Send-Key} = \mathcal{H}_{\text{SHA1}}(\text{Send-Key}\|Pad\|\text{Send-Key}\|Pad)$$

In consecutive runs the second Send-Key in the formula would be exchanged with the last Session-Send-Key. When the keys are switched is depending on the configuration of the VPN endpoint. It allows for sessions that run over a long period of time to change the keys in between, without having to do a full restart.

Format of Key Fields in RADIUS. Microsoft extended the RADIUS format with vendor specific attributes in order to be able to transport keys in encrypted form. This was necessary, because no fields for these purposes were available before. Thus, Microsoft introduced the field *MS-MPPE-RECV-KEY* and *MS-MPPE-SEND-KEY* to transmit the keys in both directions for MPPE.

Today these fields are reused to transport keys for other protocols that do not have any connection to the MPPE protocol. One of the best known protocol that use these field are the EAP protocols like EAP-(T)TLS that use this field to transmit the PMK.

3   Attack

For our attack we will first describe the scenario and its requirements. Further we will show that this scenario is quite common and can even be relaxed if our attack is mixed with other attacks later. Then we will introduce our known-plaintext attack against RADIUS that allows us to learn about the key material that is used for a key stream of a stream cipher. Then we will show that this attack which is not specific for the PPTP VPN scenario can be used to mount an chosen-ciphertext attack against the VPN which drastically reduces the complexity of known attacks against it. Finally we show our real life test results of this attack against the well used RADIUS implementation FreeRADIUS.

3.1   Scenario

Our attack works in every scenario, in which the attacker can wiretap and inject packets to the local network of the VPN endpoint and RADIUS server. An example of such a scenario is a university. In general students have access to the network via wireless LAN. Due to the high amount of consumer devices (e.g. smartphones, tablets, notebooks) there is a demand for wireless access, therefore universities have many access points installed. In general these access points are not protected well physically and can simply be exchanged against another arbitrary device by an attacker. This way a MitM attack is easy to mount. Many universities also use RADIUS to manage the authentication process of the users. In addition, universities often provide PPTP VPN services so students can access university servers from abroad (e.g. ERASMUS), Internet cafes or from home. A further requirement are valid MS-CHAPv2 credentials for the VPN.

So we will, from this point on say that the attacker fulfills the following requirements:

1. The attacker can act as a MitM between an VPN device and the RADIUS Server
2. The network offers PPTP with MS-CHAPv2 (also other internal protocols like MS-CHAPv1 would also work, but they are already broken)
3. The attacker has valid credentials for the network

Getting valid MS-CHAPv2 credentials is as easy as applying for an arbitrary study in the university scenario. But this assumption can also easily be fulfilled for other company networks, for which one could not just register. Here the attack presented by Schneier et al. [13], described in Sect. 2.2, can be executed to brute-force the credentials of an arbitrary user from any wiretapped PPTP connection. Note, that breaking the weakest credentials of some user is enough for our attack. Afterwards, these credentials can be used to run our attack against every other user using the PPTP VPN of the closed network.

3.2   Known-Plaintext Attack on RADIUS Encryption

In this section we will introduce our attack to get the key material that is sent encrypted with the RADIUS encryption. We will use a known plaintext attack on the RADIUS encryption that allows us to recover the first 16 bytes of the key material of a target ciphertext. We have already shown that PPTP only allows keys with the length of 40, 56 or 128 bits, so this always gets the attacker the complete key in the final attack in the next chapter.

Overview Known-Plaintext Attack on RADIUS to partially decrypt MPPE. The problem of the RADIUS encryption is that the Req_{Auth} is used as an initialization vector IV for the encryption but is not chosen by the RADIUS server who performs the encryption, but by the client. This allows for a simple and fast attack on the RADIUS encryption that has the following features:

1. To decrypt a value that is encrypted with the RADIUS encryption one only needs the output $X1$ of the MD5 hash function (cf. Fig. 1). This value is the key stream that is used to be xored with the plaintext.
2. This MD5 result depends on the 3 inputs: RADIUS secret, the Req_{Auth} and the Salt. While the secret only changes if manually reconfigured, it can be assumed to be constant. To prevent an easy known-plaintext attack a Req_{Auth} is chosen with a length of 128 bits, so that it is statistically unlikely that one RA is chosen twice in a measurable amount of time.

3. The Salt is only part of the encryption if the tunneled RADIUS mode is used. This is done to add an easy way to check for the correct order by adding the 4 bit salt counter. In addition, the salt differs in the first bit if send from the client to the server or the other direction, so that a message encrypted in one direction cannot be injected in traffic in the opposite direction.

The attack is using the fact that the Req_{Auth} was designed to be chosen by the party, which use the RADIUS encryption to encrypt messages. This is not true in case the message originates from the server. Then the field RA is used in another way namely to store the Response Authenticator. As described in section Sect. 2.3, the server utilizes the last received Req_{Auth} as IV for the encryption instead of choosing it on its own. This is the point the attack applies. In RADIUS the messages from the client to the server are not integrity protected (just from server to client), so that an attacker could easily exchange this Req_{Auth} and force two of the three input values for the MD5 to be the same.

Now only the Salt remains changing, which based on its structure, is not a big problem. The first bit is always 1 if the message is from the server and the next 4 bits are a counter that increases by 1 per use in the encryption. But the tunneled encryption is used twice in the RADIUS message, so that it is the same every 8 protocol runs. Only the remaining 11 bits are random meaning an attacker can get every 8 protocol runs a chance with probability of 2^{-11} to get the same key stream. This allows for an efficient known-plaintext attack against the tunneled version of the RADIUS encryption. In principal, the attack works also for the non-tunneled version from RFC 2865 [12], but here in practice the Req_{Auth} is always chosen by the sender and not the responding party.

3.3   Chosen-Ciphertext Attack on PPTP

Chosen RA Attack on RADIUS Encryption. The attack to get the key-stream for MPPE k_{MPPE} uses the known-plaintext attack idea outlined in Subsect. 3.2 to get the Req_{Auth} and combines it with the PPTP scenario.

As described previously the client and VPN endpoint need a shared key to establish a connection secured by MPPE. But only the client and RADIUS server share any common keys. The VPN endpoint and the RADIUS server share the RADIUS secret S. So the idea is for the VPN endpoint to just relay the MS-CHAPv2 login messages from the client to the RADIUS server and if the login is successful, to get key material from the RADIUS server. The client can compute the same key material from the MS-CHAPv2 protocol results (cf. Subsect. 2.2).

The key material k_{MPPE} is transferred in the RADIUS packet from the RADIUS server to the VPN endpoint. It is transferred in the MS-MPPE-RECV-KEY and MS-MPPE-SEND-KEY attribute fields in the RADIUS message. Because there was no attribute designed to transport keys encrypted, Microsoft created this one that is nowadays used also for other protocols, even if they are not using MPPE at all.

The MS-MPPE fields contains 18 changing bytes, while the rest defines the field as MS-MPPE. RADIUS allows for vendor specific fields and this is one of them, so it has to be clearly defined, because it is not part of the original RFC.

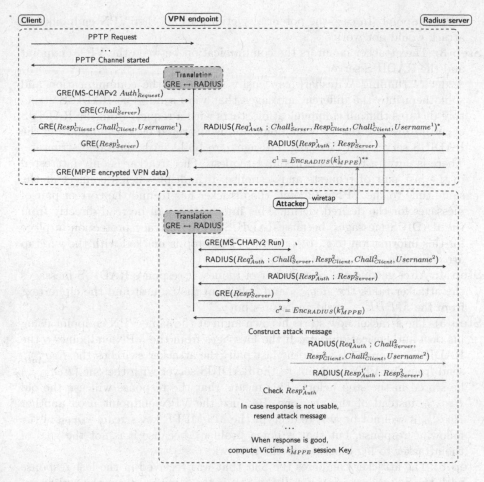

Fig. 2. Attack protocol flow

The 18 bytes contain: 2 bytes Salt and 16 bytes encrypted key. If not the strong version of MPPE, which uses 128 bits keys is used, then the key is even smaller. This means 16 bytes are encrypted using the RADIUS tunnel Encryption Enc_{RADIUS}, while the two bytes Salt are sent in clear. The values can be seen in Fig. 2 where the ciphertext C^1 is the encrypted first 16 bytes. The RADIUS encryption would allow to send more blocks for longer keys, as it is used for example in EAP-TTLS but here only one block is used. The attack is shown in Fig. 2 and is divided into the following 7 steps:

Step 1: The attacker needs to get himself in the position that he has MitM capabilities on the designated connection between VPN endpoint and RADIUS server.

Step 2: After the attacker is set, he has to wait for the victim user to start a PPTP session and login with MS-CHAPv2 to the VPN through a wiretapped

VPN endpoint. In case the potential victim uses another VPN endpoint the attack would not work.

Step 3: The attacker monitors the communication between the VPN endpoint and the RADIUS server.

A device running Wireshark can easily collect all the communication and split them into the different messages that were send. The RADIUS structure dictates that all communication starts with a request from the RADIUS client in this case the VPN endpoint and is answered by a response from the RADIUS server. All following messages are build with the same structure. There is never a response without a request. The attacker is only interested in the last pair of requests and response. If multiple clients connect at the same time to the VPN endpoint, the attacker has to find the correct pair of messages for the desired victim. This information can be read directly from the RADIUS messages, because RADIUS has no privacy protection in place for this information (e.g., $Username$). This step is marked with the wiretap arrows in Fig. 2

Step 4: After getting the correct pair of request / response RADIUS messages the attacker takes the Req_{Auth} and Salt from the request and the ciphertext from the $MPPE_{Key}$ field and stores both.

Step 5: The attacker now starts his own login at the same VPN endpoint using his own authentication data. If the messages from the VPN endpoint to the RADIUS server reach again the last pair, the attacker switches the Req^2_{Auth} send from the VPN endpoint to the RADIUS server with the one (Req^1_{Auth}) he stored in the step before. This means that the response will use the old Req_{Auth} instead of the new one. Because the VPN endpoint used another Req_{Auth} it will not be able to decrypt the MS-MPPE key stream k_{MPPE} in the following response, but that is not a problem, because it is not the goal of the attacker to log himself into the network.

Step 6: The attacker compares the Salt that was received in the last response with the Salt stored in step 4. If the Salt is the same he stores the ciphertext again and this time also the plaintext. The attacker has access to the plaintext, because he acts also as a client in the MS-CHAPv2 run and can compute the MPPE-Key k_{MPPE} from internal key material. If the Salt is not the same, the attacker goes back to step 5 and starts there again. The Salt is only 2 bytes (16 bit) long which would offer 65k possible Salts, but the Salt is restricted in different ways (cf. Sect. 2). The first bit is always set to 1, because the message is sent from the server. This protects the encryption from using the client as decryption oracle, but limits the possible Salts. Bits 2 to 5 are used to store the offset. Every time the Salt is used for encryption, the offset is incremented by 1. Due to the fact that two encryptions are done per response from the server ($MS\text{-}MPPE\text{-}RECV\text{-}KEY$ and $MS\text{-}MPPE\text{-}SEND\text{-}KEY$), the offset repeats after 8 request and not after 16. As a result the attacker only needs to check every 8th response from the server for the correct Salt. Only the remaining 11 bits are chosen at random, so that after 2048 tries with the same offset the attacker should have found the same random Salt values. On Average an attacker would need 8 * 1024 = 8192 tries.

The Salt was included into the RADIUS encryption to prevent reuse of the RA, but it will show it does not help enough, because the 2048 tries could be done in a short time.

Step 7: The attacker now takes the plaintext and ciphertext he has collected in the last step and computes the XOR of the first 16 bytes of the plaintext called p1 and of the ciphertext called c1 (cf. Fig. 1). We will call this intermediate value X1. This value X1 is now the same as in the stored communication of the victim and in the stored communication of the attacker. This results from the identical Req_{Auth} and Salt. The RADIUS Secret S always stays the same, so that now all input for the MD5 Algorithm is identical, which leads to identical output. The attacker now can XOR the value X1 with the first block of the victims C^1. The result are the first 16 plaintext bytes, which is the MPPE-Key k_{MPPE} of the victim.

3.4 Practical Evaluation

Setup. The setup consists of four different Virtualbox machines, one acting as the client, one as the VPN endpoint, one as the RADIUS server and the last machine performing the attack. As the operating system *Ubuntu Linux 15.04* with Kernel *3.19.0-39-generic* was used. The client had *pptp-linux 1.7-2.7* installed for the pptp client. The VPN endpoint used *pppd 2.4.6* as PPTP server and the *FreeRadius Client 1.1.7* for the connection to the RADIUS server. The attack was tested against FreeRADIUS. We used the version 3.0.10 in the default configuration, without any further modifications. The host machine was equipped with an Intel Core i5-6600K @ 3.5 GHz and 16 Gbyte of DDR4 memory.

Results. The attack was run for 432 times on the attack machine (see. Sect. 3.4). The evaluation showed that for these 432 attack runs the average time was 62 s and it took on average 18847 protocol runs until the Salt was correct. The theoretical average is $2^{14} = 16384$. This shows that the random salts generated by the RADIUS server are chosen as random as roughly expected. For this test we ran 8,1 Million protocol runs in total. Our cross protocol attack thus reduced the complexity by 2^{42} compared to the attack of Schneier et al. [13] and Marlinspike [7]. Still today brute-forcing DES keys on an FPGA cluster takes an average of 7 h (25,200 s) and hardware costs of around $140,000 [3]. This means, our attack speeds up the time for the decryption process by factor of 124, compared to the traditional brute-force approach and is achievable on standard computer hardware, which cost around $700 US (reduction by factor 200).

4 Conclusion

In the paper we showed two novel attacks. A known-plaintext attack on RADIUS encryption and a chosen-ciphertext attack on PPTP VPN. We describe how both of these attacks can be combined in a cross protocol attack to decrypt PPTP VPN sessions. Analyzes of public VPN services providers showed that PPTP is used by 60 % of them [14]. Further, all Windows and Linux operating systems currently support PPTP VPNs. For our attacks we give a description of PPTP VPN and how they are used together with MS-CHAPv2 and RADIUS server. Based on the description we show how an attacker can use our cross protocol attack to decrypt PPTP VPN sessions in a realistic scenario in one minute. In contrast to previous published attacks [7,13], we reduced the computational complexity by factor 2^{42}. The decryption of a PPTP VPN session is now achievable with just 2^{14} protocol runs. Our attacks do not need special hardware and run on every modern device, from standard computers down to smartphones. Further, the attack needs on average 62 s, leading to a time reduction by the factor of 124, compared to the brute-force of the complete DES key space, which also required special cracking hardware [3].

We saw with this attack that even after 18 years a protocol is in the wild improvements for attacks can be found, by taking a look on cross protocol usage. At first we tried to drive the attack on EAP-(T)TLS implementations [2], but realized during the testing, that an additional MAC over the whole message is computed preventing our attack.

In the RFC 2868 [17], which specified the used RADIUS attributes, multiple protocols are defined, we analyzed only PPTP. Similar attacks may be possible on other protocols like L2TP, depending on the used key derivation function and are worth looking at in future research.

References

1. The Point-to-Point protocol (PPP). RFC 1661, IETF, July 1994
2. Aboba, B.D., Calhoun, P.: RADIUS (remote authentication dial in user service) support for extensible authentication protocol (EAP). RFC 3579, IETF, September 2003
3. Amy, V.: The state of the art in key cracking (2016). https://www.voltage.com/breach/the-state-of-the-art-in-key-cracking/
4. Eisinger, J.: Exploiting known security holes in microsoft's PPTP authentication extensions (MS-CHAPv2). University of Freiburg [cit. 27 May 2008], Dostupné (2001)
5. Hamzeh, K., Pall, G., Verthein, W., Taarud, J., Little, W., Zorn, G.: Point-to-Point tunneling protocol. RFC 2637, IETF, July 1999
6. Hanks, S., Li, T., Farinacci, D., Traina, P.: Generic routing encapsulation (GRE). RFC 1701, IETF, October 1994
7. Marlinspike, M.M., Hulton, D., Ray, M.: Defeating PPTP VPNs and WPA2 enterprise with MS-CHAPv2. Defcon, July 2012
8. Ornaghi, A., Valleri, M.: Man in the middle attacks demos. Blackhat 19 (2003)
9. Pall, G., Zorn, G.: Microsoft Point-To-Point encryption (MPPE) protocol. RFC 3078, IETF, March 2001
10. Paterson, K.G., Poettering, B., Schuldt, J.C.N.: Big bias hunting in amazonia: large-scale computation and exploitation of RC4 biases (invited paper). In: Sarkar, P., Iwata, T. (eds.) ASIACRYPT 2014. LNCS, vol. 8873, pp. 398–419. Springer, Heidelberg (2014). doi:10.1007/978-3-662-45611-8_21
11. Project, F.S.: Freeradius server. http://freeradius.org

12. Rigney, C., Willens, S., Rubens, A., Simpson, W.: Remote authentication dial in user service (RADIUS). RFC 2865, IETF, June 2000
13. Schneier, B., Mudge, P.: Cryptanalysis of microsoft's point-to-point tunneling protocol (PPTP), pp. 132–141. In: CCS (1998)
14. Site, T.O.P.: Detailed VPN comparison chart. https://thatoneprivacysite.net/vpn-comparison-chart/
15. Zorn, G.: Microsoft PPP CHAP extensions, version 2. RFC 2759, IETF, January 2000
16. Zorn, G.: Deriving keys for use with microsoft Point-to-Point encryption (MPPE). RFC 3079, IETF, March 2001
17. Zorn, G., Leifer, D., Rubens, A., Shriver, J., Holdrege, M., Goyret, I.: RADIUS attributes for tunnel protocol support. RFC 2868, IETF, June 2000

LEAP: A Next-Generation Client VPN and Encrypted Email Provider

Elijah Sparrow[1], Harry Halpin[2]([✉]), Kali Kaneko[1], and Ruben Pollan[1]

[1] LEAP Encryption Access Project, PO Box 442, Seattle, WA 98194, USA
{elijah,kali,meskio}@leap.se
[2] INRIA, 2 Simone Iff, 75012 Paris, France
harry.halpin@inria.fr

Abstract. As demonstrated by the revelations of Edward Snowden on the extent of pervasive surveillance, one pressing danger is in the vast predominance of unencrypted messages, due to the influence of the centralizing silos such as Microsoft, Facebook, and Google. We present the threat model and architectural design of the LEAP platform and client applications, which currently provisions opportunistic email encryption combined with a VPN tunnel and cross-device synchronization.

Keywords: Encryption · Email · VPN

1 Introduction

Why in the era of mass surveillance is encrypted email still nearly impossible? Take for example the case of the journalist Glenn Greenwald, who could not properly set-up encrypted email when Edward Snowden contacted him to leak the NSA secrets. This lack of progress in over three decades in securing emails is precisely what allows both content and meta-data analysis of email by agencies such as the NSA to be pervasive and nearly inescapable. Well-understood technologies such as OpenPGP-based email encryption are not used by the vast majority of people for reasons that have been understood for nearly a decade and a half [7]. While there has been considerable progress in the deployment of increased use of TLS and even IP-address level anonymity via the Tor project [1], most people rely on insecure and centralized silos for email. There are few working solutions for encrypted and privacy-preserving email. While Tor provides the best solution for IP-level anonymity, this purpose is defeated when users rely on centralized email systems, where the danger of their communication being intercepted via disclosures by the service provider are considerable [1]. For example, many users simply use Tor to 'anonymize' their access to email services such as Gmail that can simply hand over their data, or even systems such as *riseup.net* that likely have all outgoing and ingoing traffic monitored even if the server itself refuses requests for user data. Although email is often sent over an encrypted network channel via TLS and upgraded from an insecure channel

© Springer International Publishing AG 2016
S. Foresti and G. Persiano (Eds.): CANS 2016, LNCS 10052, pp. 176–191, 2016.
DOI: 10.1007/978-3-319-48965-0_11

using STARTTLS, typically network traffic is not properly authenticated and even network-level encryption tends to fail during mail transfer [2].

Beyond email, Off-the-Record messaging for chat works well, but requires synchronous chat between two users,[1] while Signal is not an open standard or decentralized [6]. High-profile efforts such as Mailpile are aimed at essentially replacing the user-experience of Thunderbird and Enigmail, not at actually solving the underlying problems of key management and provisioning encrypted email.[2] Although message security rests entirely on a foundation of authenticity, since without proper validation of encryption keys a user cannot be assured of confidentiality or integrity, current systems of establishing message authenticity are so difficult to use that many users simply ignore this step. To achieve mass adoption of encrypted email, the steps of key provisioning, key validation to determine message authenticity, and managing the server-side must be done automatically so that email is encrypted opportunistically. Opportunistic email encryption also needs to include an excellent client-side user experience, particularly if there are errors that the server cannot resolve.

Our solution to this problem is called LEAP, a recursive acronym for the "LEAP Encryption Access Project." LEAP is still in development, although the core functionality of basic opportunistic encryption email is now available for beta testing.[3] The project source-code on Github is available to all.[4] LEAP infrastructure will be supported by providers such as *riseup.net*.

2 Goals and Requirements

2.1 Goal

The primary goal of LEAP is to provide easy-to-use software for *end-to-end encrypted communication* between individual users. The long-term goals are that the communication services should offer a user experience free of any 'privacy tax' on the user in the form of limited features as well as any additional cognitive load and labor compared to non-encrypted communication. It should be backwards-compatible with existing SMTP (Simple Mail Transfer Protocol) email. Thus, LEAP's primary goal is enabling the use of OpenPGP-enabled SMTP, but in a more secure and user-friendly way than commonly used today by toolsets such as Thunderbird and Enigmail. Thus in addition, we have chosen to prioritize the following secondary goals:

– *Memorable user identifiers*: Users should be able to utilize familiar and memorable user handles such as *username@domain* that are typically already used in email when identifying themselves for purposes of communication.

---

[1] http://www.cypherpunks.ca/otr/.
[2] http://mailpile.is.
[3] To try, follow instructions on http://demo.bitmask.net.
[4] https://github.com/leapcode/.

– *Resilience*: The communication system as a whole should continue to function
  even if most of the organizations and infrastructure that constitute the whole
  system have been eliminated or compromised by a malicious attacker.
– *Untrusted*: A third-party service provider should not have access to the content of a user's communication (via hosting cleartext, decryption keys, or passwords) and minimize the amount of metadata they can access to the amount
  needed to route the message.

There are many other possible goals that end-to-end encrypted communications system wish to provide. There are a number of possible goals that we are
explicitly not addressed by LEAP at this time:

– *Device protection*: If a user's client device is subject to an ongoing compromise
  while the device is powered on, then LEAP does not offers security benefits
  as the private key is stored on the device. Possible mitigations are under
  investigation.
– *Anonymity*: The LEAP system does not offer anonymous communications at
  this time as users and service providers are given stable identifiers. However,
  LEAP may be used in conjunction with IP anonymization such as Tor and
  LEAP is currently exploring the feasibility of using mix networking for anonymous messaging.

2.2   Threat Model

In our threat model, we are considering two distinct types of attackers, an *active
server attacker* that focuses on decrypting messages on the server, and a *global
passive adversary* that simply copies all messages in transit between servers
(encrypted or not). For attackers, the goal is both (1) to gain access to the
content of the encrypted messages and (2) to determine the social graph of
who is communicating to whom. For the former goal of decrypting messages,
attacking a single server with many clients makes more sense than attacking
many clients for most attackers. For this section, we will consider only the first
attacker, as the second requires advanced approaches such as mix-networking.

The active server attacker uses either technical attacks or legal means to force
a server to hand over the private keys of its users so the attacker can decrypt the
encrypted messages. To prevent this, the private key material must not reach
or remain in cleartext form on any server. It should be that an attacker cannot
decrypt the encrypted message by compromising the server or placing the server
under compulsion. An example would be Lavabit, which had a single point of failure in the form of the system administrator himself: Ladar Levinson had access
to the key material for all his users, defeating the purpose of having end-to-end
encrypted email.[5] Strangely enough, other services such as Protonmail[6] seem to
be repeating this flawed model for encrypted messaging. Lastly, this is trivially

---

[5] https://www.thoughtcrime.org/blog/lavabit-critique/.
[6] https://protonmail.ch.

true (as shown by the NSA Prism programme) for centralized messaging services such as GMail that do not store the content of messages encrypted. Server seizures are a threat in the USA that legally resist backdoors, such as recent seizures against a Mixminion anonymous re-mailer on *riseup.net*.[7] In terms of the second *global passive attacker* who is aiming at collecting metadata, most systems today offer no protection. Given the difficulty of defending against this attacker, our current system does not currently aim provide metadata anonymity from their perspective. That being said, LEAP aims not reveal the social graph of a user via techniques for key validation such as the OpenPGP keyservers that display the 'web of trust' of users to the public.

2.3   Requirements

When a system claims to offer security for a user's communication data, typically the focus is on confidentiality and integrity. Although confidentiality and integrity are certainly preconditions for any secure system, in order to achieve high usability a public-key communication system should additionally focus on these requirements:

- *High data availability*: Users expect to be able to access their data across multiple devices with little delay and have the data backed up to redundant cloud storage.
- *Automatic public key authenticity*: If key authentication is difficult, then there is low effective confidentiality for any user who might be subject to an active attack. Since existing systems of public key authentication for messages are either very difficult for users or require a central authority, the confidentiality of existing messaging system is often low in practice.

The LEAP architecture is designed around a federated model, like traditional SMTP-based email or XMPP, where each user registers an account with a service provider (that consists of one or more servers) of their choice and runs their own client on a local device to connect to the provider in order to retrieve encrypted e-mail. Both distributed (peer-to-peer) and centralized architectures were considered, but both fell short of our requirements. A detailed analysis of our approach in comparison to others such as is maintained online.[8] In contrast to LEAP's design, competing encrypted e-mail services rely on centralized key escrows or a web-browser that are vulnerable to an active server attacker. On a high level, LEAP's requirements are met in the following manner:

- *High data availability*: A user's message data is client encrypted and synchronized with redundant federated cloud servers and with a user's other devices. Their data quickly downloaded when needed and so not lost if a user's device is destroyed.

---

[7] http://www.infosecisland.com/blogview/21186-FBI-Overreaches-with-May-First-Riseup-Server-Seizure.html.
[8] https://leap.se/en/docs/tech/secure-email.

- *Automatic key authenticity*: With the assistance of a network of federated servers containing the latest public key information of their users, the user's client intelligently manages public keys automatically by following a series of rules that embody best practices and so validate public keys to the greatest extent possible. As the public key information of LEAP-enabled users is kept redundantly by a number of different servers, the client can audit the validation of a key without relying on a single trusted server.
- *Unmappability*: As much metadata is possible is stored so that the provider has no access to this information. Key validation is done via Nicknym (as described in Sect. 3.4) as to not reveal the social graph of users to unnecessary third-parties, unlike OpenPGP's 'web of trust' keyservers. In future work, LEAP will extend this to the metadata of messages in transit (including size and timing information), by incorporating mix networking into the delivery of messages and a CONIKS-style architecture for key validation [4].

2.4   General Design

The design of LEAP tackles each of the requirements for high data availability, automatic key authenticity, and unmappability. The primary new contribution of LEAP is tackling the problem of high data availability while defending against active server attackers: How can we keep the key material from being inaccessible to the server and at the same time having the keys and data available for synchronization across devices?

The problem can be broken down into a number of distinct components: Server-side infrastructure, usable client software, and the fundamental protocols needed to communicate between the server and the client. What is necessary is to have the client and server actively work together in order to encrypt the message, as to prevent the situation where private key materials stored only on the server are only defended by weak defenses such as passwords. Simply storing the private key on a single device of the user, as done by most encrypted mail programs, is not enough as users need to access their email through multiple devices and keep the state of their inbox synchronized. Thus the main problem facing such a system is safely getting the correct keys onto users' devices, a problem known as *key synchronization*. This becomes an even more important problem if best practices such as frequent key rotation are to be employed.

LEAP solves the problem of key synchronization through the installation of a multi-purpose LEAP client application called Bitmask, that appears to the user mainly as an OpenVPN client.[9] However, there is more to Bitmask than just a VPN. Inside of the Bitmask client are the routines for generating, validating, and discovering keys as well as synchronizing keys and related material (such as the status of messages being "read" across multiple devices). The LEAP client appears to be a VPN as many users likely would install a VPN (but not special 'key manager' software) and the VPN provides additional security benefits by creating an authenticated and encrypted channel for all traffic between the LEAP client and server.

---

[9] http://openvpn.net/.

When a user installs a LEAP client, the LEAP client asks the user for a username and master passphrase, and to select a LEAP-enabled provider. A 'recovery code' is made for the device (currently a 22 digit code) that is used to derive a device key. The first time that an user authenticates a new device against that LEAP-enabled provider after installing a LEAP client, the keymanager on the LEAP client will attempt to perform a Soledad synchronization (Soledad is described in Sect. 3.2). If the user has created a new account and so no valid keypair is found, the LEAP client will generate a public-private OpenPGP keypair on the user's device. After such generation is completed, the keypair will be symmetrically encrypted with a key derived from the master passphrase and the wrapped key will be uploaded to the remote Soledad replica in the server, in order to let the user add new devices and synchronize them with Soledad. For incoming email, messages are received by the service provider's MX servers, encrypted to the current user's public key, and stored in the user's database in an incoming message queue. The LEAP client then fetches the incoming message queue as part of a periodic Soledad synchronization, decrypting each message and saving it in the user's inbox, stored in the local Soledad database. The mail module exposes the stored messages through a local IMAP server, so that the messages can be accessed using any standard MUA.

Since email is distributed to the client and stored via the Soledad API, any changes to the mailbox will eventually be synchronized to all devices. The mutable parts of the messages and the attachments are kept in separate documents, so that the sync overhead is kept low. Soledad allows for selective synchronization so that header documents can be synchronized first, leaving the ability to download attachments on the background or under demand, which will be specially interesting for mobile.

For outgoing email, the LEAP client runs a thin SMTP proxy on the user's device, bound to *localhost*, and the mail user agent (MUA)[10] is configured to bind outgoing SMTP to *localhost*. When this SMTP proxy receives an email from the MUA, it issues queries to a local keymanager (Nicknym agent) for the user's private key and public keys of all recipients. The message is then signed, and encrypted to each recipient. If a recipient's key is missing, email goes out in cleartext (unless user has configured the LEAP client to send only encrypted email). Finally, the message is relayed to provider's SMTP relay. The LEAP approach outlined is similar to the approach taken by Garfinkle [3] and Symantec,[11] although these systems do not include key discovery, key validation, encryption of incoming messages, secure storage, or synchronization of email among devices.

3   The LEAP Architecture

In detail, the LEAP federated architecture consists of three-components: (1) a server-side platform automation system; (2) an easy-to-use client application;

---

[10] Such as Thunderbird, Evolution, or Outlook.
[11] http://www.symantec.com/desktop-email-encryption.

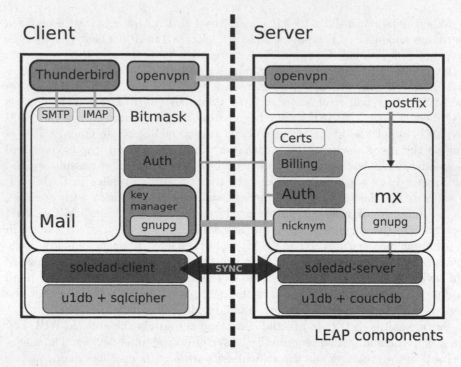

Fig. 1. Components of LEAP Email Architecture

and (3) new protocols such as Soledad and Nicknym that allow the user to place minimal trust in the provider, as well as well-known and standardized protocols such as IMAP. These components are illustrated in Diagram 1.[12] The cryptographic details are also subject to change (in particular, migrating from large RSA keys to Curve 25519 when possible) and are maintained online.[13]

The LEAP platform offers a set of automation tools to allow an organization to deploy and manage a complete infrastructure for providing user communication services in the servers controlled by them. The LEAP client is an application that runs on the user's local device and is tightly bound to the server components of the LEAP platform. The client is cross-platform, auto-configuring, and auto-updating, with the initial configuration and updates verified via The Update Framework[14] in order to prevent a compromised server from forcing new key material or accessing the existing client key material via a compromised update.

---

[12] Note that parts of Sect. 3 are modified versions of material available on the LEAP wiki at http://leap.se/en/docs.

[13] https://bitmask.net/en/features/cryptography.

[14] http://theupdateframework.com/.

3.1   LEAP Platform

The "provider instance" is a self-contained encapsulation of everything about an organization's server infrastructure (except for actual user data). The LEAP platform consists of a command line tool and a set of complementary puppet recipes allow an organization to easily operate one or more clusters of servers to provision LEAP-enabled services. With the LEAP command line tool, a system administrator can rapidly deploy a large number of servers, each automatically configured with the proper daemons, firewall, encrypted tunnels, and certificates.

LEAP Data Storage. One design goal of the LEAP platform is for a service provider to act as an 'untrusted cloud' where data are encrypted by the client before being sent to the server, and we push as much of the communication logic to the client as possible. There are a few cases where the server must have knowledge about a user's information, such as when resolving email aliases or when processing support requests. Every user has a personal database for storing client encrypted documents, like email and chat messages. In the current implementation, data storage is handled by CouchDB although this may be changed in future versions.

The unencrypted information stored on the server needed to resolve email, including the database for routing incoming and outgoing email, is similar to any traditional email provider, with the one exception that user accounts don't have traditional passwords. Mail is received via a Soledad synchronization session (detailed in Sect. 3.2) and authenticated using Secure Remote Password (SRP), a standardized password-authenticated key agreement (PAKE) mechanism that can be strengthened via device keys.[15] Mail is sent using SMTP with standard SASL (Simple Authentication and Security Layer) authentication using client certificates.[16] In detail, the unencrypted database of user information maintained by the service provider includes:

- *username*: The login name for the user. This is not necessarily the user portion of 'user@domain.'
- *SRP verifier*: Akin to a hashed password, but used in SRP 'zero-knowledge' dual pass mutual authentication between client and server.
- *uuid*: Random internal identifier for internal usage.
- *identities*: One or more 'user@domain' identities, with corresponding public keys and separate authentication credentials for SMTP (stored as a finger-print to an x.509 client certificate). Each identity has its own authentication credentials so that the email headers show that the user authenticated with the SMTP server using their identity username, not their real username. Each identity includes delivery information, either to a uuid or to a third party email address that messages should be forwarded to. One or more devices are tied to an identity.

---

[15] https://tools.ietf.org/html/rfc2945.
[16] https://tools.ietf.org/html/rfc4422.

For email delivery, the receiving MX (Mail exchanger record) servers do not have access to the entire database. They only have read-only access to 'identities.' This allows the implementation of the Nicknym protocol (described in Sect. 3.4) for resolving pseudonyms. Additionally, there are several non-encrypted databases containing the minimal information needed to connect user accounts to optional support tickets and even billing details. The LEAP platform includes a web application for user and administrator access to these non-encrypted databases, although future research will hopefully be able to minimize if not eliminate this information.

3.2   Soledad

Soledad ("Synchronization Of Locally Encrypted Data Among Devices") is responsible for client-encrypting user data, keeping the data synchronized with the copy on the server and on all the other devices of each user, and for providing local applications with a simple API for document storage, indexing, and search that is akin to CouchDB and related document-centric NoSQL databases. The document that is saved and synchronized with Soledad can be any structured JSON document, with binary attachments. Soledad is implemented on the LEAP client to store email messages, the user's public and private OpenPGP keys, and a contact database of validated public keys. Soledad is based on U1DB, but modified to support the encryption of both the local database replica and every document before it is synchronized with the server.[17] Local database encryption is provided by a block-encrypted SQLite database[18] via SQLcipher.[19] Documents synchronized with the server are individually block encrypted using a key produced via an HMAC of the unique document id and a long storage secret. In order to prevent the server from sending forged or old documents, each document record stored on the server includes an additional client-computed MAC derived from the document id, the document revision number, and the encrypted content. The server time-stamps each update of the database, so that Soledad's MAC and HMAC keys used to encrypt the client database can only send the server new databases. Each time the LEAP client is online (both after re-connecting with the LEAP platform and after each pre-set time interval), the client re-synchronizes the messages and key material.

In addition to synchronizing public-private key materials and a contact list of validated keys, Soledad is used to encrypt and synchronize email. This has the benefit of not storing sensitive metadata on the server and allowing for searchable locally-encrypted database of messages on the client side. For efficiency, a single email is stored in several different documents (for example, for headers, for attachments, and for the nested MIME structures). While in transit between

---

[17] https://one.ubuntu.com/developer/data/u1db/.
[18] https://sqlite.org/.
[19] http://sqlcipher.net/.

LEAP-enabled SMTP servers and the LEAP client, there are three different forms of encryption that a single message is subject to:

1. Encrypted by sender, or on arrival by recipient's service provider using OpenPGP.
2. Decrypted from and re-encrypted in an SQLcipher database using AES block encryption.
3. Individually re-encrypted for storage on a service provider that supports the LEAP platform using block encryption with a nonce.

3.3   LEAP Client

The *LEAP client* (also known as Bitmask[20]) is a cross-platform application that runs on a user's own device and is responsible for all encryption of user data. It currently includes the following components: *Bitmask VPN*, *Soledad* (multi-device user data synchronization), *Key Manager* (Nicknym agent and contact database), and *email proxy* (opportunistic email encryption). The client must be installed in the user's device before they can access any LEAP services (except for user support via the web application). Written in Python (with QT, Twisted, OpenVPN, SQLcipher), the LEAP client currently runs on Linux and Android, with Windows and Mac being under development.[21] When a user installs a LEAP client, a *first-run* wizard walks the user through the simple process of authenticating or registering a new account with the LEAP provider of their choice, using the Secure Remote Password (SRP) protocol so that a cleartext copy of the password never reaches the server. The SRP encoded password can also be strengthened by wrapping it with a device key and so stored multiple times, once per device key. The password's strength is assessed via *zxcvbn*.[22] Note that when a user authenticates with the client, via a username and password, these credentials as provided are used to both authenticate with the service provider (via SRP) and also to unlock locally encrypted secrets (via Soledad).

One threat would be that an active server attacker would compel a LEAP-enabled server to push a malicious update to the clients to compromise their keys. This threat applies equally to any browser or plug-in based approach, and in fact to the installation of *any* software. LEAP employs mitigation strategies to prevent this attack. When distributed through the self-contained bundles, the client has auto-updating capabilities, using The Update Framework (TUF) to update LEAP code and other library dependencies as needed using the same Thandy library as deployed by Tor [5].[23] Unlike other update systems, TUF updates are controlled by a timestamp file that is signed each day. This ensures that the client will not miss an important update and cannot be pushed an old or compromised update by an attacker. Updates to the LEAP client via TUF

---

[20] https://bitmask.net/.
[21] The Android version tends to lag behind development compared to the Linux version due to the design having to be re-coded in Java.
[22] https://github.com/dropbox/zxcvbn.
[23] https://gitweb.torproject.org/thandy.git.

require signatures from multiple keys, held by LEAP developers in different jurisdictions. Lastly, LEAP has started work on a system of reproducible builds, which is working in an automated fashion for Android and in the future should apply to all other platforms.[24]

VPN. The goal with LEAP's VPN service is to provide an automatic, always on, trouble-free way to encrypt a user's network traffic. The VPN service encrypts all of a user's traffic and works hard to prevent data leakage from DNS, IPv6, and other common client misconfigurations that are not tackled by OpenVPN via a strict egress firewall. Currently OpenVPN is used for the transport. OpenVPN was selected because it is fast, open source, and cross-platform. In the future, LEAP plans to add support for Tor as an alternate transport. We believe LEAP is the only VPN that autoconfigures and auto-restarts when connectivity is lost. When started, the LEAP client discovers the LEAP-enabled service provider's proxy gateways, fetches a short-lived X.509 client certificate from the provider if necessary, and probes the network to attempt to connect. If there are problems connecting, the LEAP VPN client will try different protocol and port combinations to bypass common ISP firewall settings since VPN access is typically blocked crudely by simple port and protocol rules rather than deep packet inspection. In terms of deep packet inspection, obfsproxy[25] integration is under development to hide the VPN connection to an observer. By default, the LEAP client will auto-connect the VPN service the next time a user starts the computer if the encrypted proxy was switched on when the user the client quit or the machine was shutdown. If network connectivity is lost while the proxy is active, the LEAP client will automatically attempt to reconnect when the network is again available. A firewall is also activated before launching the VPN service, providing a fail-close mechanism that limits the unprotected access to the network in case of client malfunction or crashes. Due to its stringent security requirements, the LEAP VPN does not work when the user is behind a captive network portal.

3.4 Nicknym Key Management

One of the main features of the LEAP system is to provide strong authentication of public keys in a way that is easy for users. To do this, LEAP relies on a protocol called Nicknym in the form of *username@domain* (similar to an email address). Nicknym maps user nicknames to public keys. With Nicknym, the user is able to think solely in terms of nicknames, while still being able to communicate with a high degree of security (confidentiality, integrity, and authenticity). Another goal of Nicknym is to, unlike the OpenPGP 'Web of Trust' mechanism, not reveal the social graph of the user to the public.[26]

---

[24] See work by Debian on reproducible builds that LEAP is applying to its code: https://wiki.debian.org/ReproducibleBuilds.

[25] https://www.torproject.org/projects/obfsproxy.html.en.

[26] Details at https://leap.se/nicknym.

Although various new key validation infrastructure schemes have been recently proposed, most of the new opportunistic encrypted email projects have proposed starting with some sort of "Trust On First Use," (TOFU) but the term itself is undefined. LEAP specifies generic rules for automatic key management that can form a basis for defining a version of TOFU and to transition from TOFU to more advanced forms of key validation. In particular, the rules try to define when a user agent should use one public key over another. This section is written from the point of view of Alice, a user who wants to send an encrypted email to Bob, although she does not yet have his public key.

LEAP assumes the goal is to automate the process of binding an email address to a public key. Alice knows Bob's email address, but not his public key and either Alice might be initiating contact with Bob or he might be initiating contact with her. Likewise, Bob might use an email provider that facilitates key discovery and/or validation in some way, or he might not. Unless otherwise specified, *key* in this text always means *public key*. A *key directory* is an online service that stores public keys and allows clients to search for keys by address or fingerprint. A key directory does not make any assertions regarding the validity of an address and key binding. A *key validation level* is the level of confidence the key manager has that it has the right key for a particular address, where *key registration* is when a key manager assigns a validation level, being somewhat analogous to adding a key to a user's keyring. A *key endorser* is an organization such as a LEAP provider that makes assertions regarding the binding of *username@domain* address to public key, typically by signing public keys. When supported, all such endorsement signatures must apply only to the uid corresponding to the address being endorsed. *Binding information* is evidence that the key manager uses to make an educated guess regarding what key to associate with what email address. This information could come from the headers in an email, a DNS lookup, a key endorser, and so on. A *verified key transition* is a process where a key owner generates a new public/private key pair and signs the new key with a prior key. An *endorsement key* is the public/private key pair that a service provider or third party endorser uses to sign user keys. Currently, LEAP implements these rules when encountering new keys or finding keys from other providers.

LEAP Key Manager Rules.

1. First contact: When a new key is first discovered for a particular address, the key's the highest validation level is registered.
2. Regular refresh: All keys are regularly refreshed to check for modified expirations, or new subkeys, or new keys signed by old keys.
   (a) This refresh should happens via an anonymizing mechanism (currently Tor) in order to prevent targeted attacks on particular servers.
   (b) The key should not be revoked before the expiration date of the key, unless it can be proved that there is a new version of the key or the key has been compromised.

3. Key replacement: A registered key must be replaced by a new key in one of the following situations, and only these situations:
   (a) Verified key transitions (when the new key is signed by the previously registered key for same address).
   (b) If the user manually verifies the fingerprint of the new key (using an out-of-band authenticated channel).
   (c) If the registered key is expired or revoked and the new key is of equal or higher validation level.
   (d) If the registered key has never been successfully used and the new key has a higher validation level.
   (e) If the registered key has no expiration date.

Previously registered keys must be retained by the key manager for the purpose of signature authentication. However, these old keys are never used for sending messages. A public key for Bob is considered successfully used by Alice if and only if Alice has sent a message encrypted to the key and received an authenticated response.

Validation Levels. A number of validation levels are described, from lowest to highest validation level.

Weak chain: Bob's key is obtained by Alice from a non-auditable source via a weak chain. The chain of custody for 'binding information' is broken as at some point the binding information was transmitted over a connection that was not authenticated.

Provider trust: Alice obtains binding information for Bob's key from Bob's service provider via a non-auditable source over a strong chain. By strong chain, we mean that every connection in the chain used to determine the 'binding information' from Bob's provider to Alice is done over an authenticated channel. To subvert this 'provider-trust' validation, an attacker must compromise Bob's service provider or a certificate authority (or parent zones when using DNSSEC), so this level of validation places a high degree of trust on service providers and CAs.

Provider endorsement: Alice is able to ask Bob's service provider for the key bound to Bob's email address and Bob is able to audit these endorsements. Rather than simple transport level authenticity, these endorsements are time stamped signatures of Bob's key for a particular email address. These signatures are made using the provider's 'endorsement key.' Alice must obtained and register the provider's endorsement key with validation level at 'provider-trust' or higher. An auditable endorsing provider must follow certain rules:

– The keys a service provider endorses must be regularly audited by its users. Alice has no idea if Bob's key manager has actually audited Bob's provider, but Alice can know if the provider is written in such a way that the same client libraries that allow for submitting keys to a provider allow auditing of these keys. Otherwise, it is considered to be the same as 'provider-trust' validation.

– Neither Alice nor Bob should contact Bob's service provider directly. Provider endorsements should be queried through an anonymizing transport like Tor [1]. Without this, it is easy for provider to prevent Bob from auditing its endorsements, and the validation level is the same as 'provider-trust.'

Note that with provider endorsement, a service provider may summarily publish bogus keys for a user. Even if a user's key manager detects this, the damage may already be done. However, if a provider is suspected of being caught 'cheating,' the evidence should be submitted to a third-party endorser (ideally with an audit log) so that can Bob (and other providers) can query the third-party, as should happen during third-party endorsement and provider consensus. Regardless, a provider endorsement is a higher level of validation than 'provider trust' because there is a good chance that the provider would get caught if they issue bogus keys, raising the cost for doing so.

Third-party endorsement: Alice asks a third-party key endorsing service for binding information, using either an email address of key fingerprint as the search term. This could involve asking a key endorser directly, via a proxy, or asking a key directory that includes endorsement information from a key endorser. A third-party key endorser must follow certain rules:

– The third-party key endorser must be regularly audited by the key manager of users. If there are conflicts, the key should be reduced to 'provider trust' validation until the conflict is resolved.
– The key endorser must either require verified key transitions or require that old keys expire before a new key is endorsed for an existing email address. This is to give a key manager time to prevent the user's service provider from obtaining endorsements for bogus keys. If a key endorsement system is not written in this way, Alice's key manager must consider it to have the same level of validation as 'provider-endorsement.'
– Key endorsers should provide information about key endorsements to key owners to the user through an authenticated channel not controlled by the provider (such as Tor) so the user can detect possible 'cheating' by their own provider.

Third-party consensus: This is the same as third-party endorsement, but Alice's user agent has queried a quorum of third party endorsers and all their endorsements for a particular user address agree.

Auditing: This works similar to third-party endorsement, but with better ability to audit key endorsements. With historical auditing, a key endorser must publish an append-only log of all their endorsements. Independent agents can watch these logs to ensure new entries are always appended to old entries. The benefit of this approach is that an endorser is not able to temporarily endorse and publish a bogus key and then remove this key before Alice's key manager is able to check what key has been endorsed. The endorser could try to publish an entire bogus log in order to endorse a bogus key, but this is very likely to be eventually detected. As with other endorsement models, the endorsement key must be bootstrapped using a validation level of provider trust or higher.

Fingerprint Verification: Alice has manually confirmed the validity of the key by inspecting the full fingerprint or by using a short authentication string with a limited time frame. For established endorsers like LEAP providers, this authenticated key has to be then hard-coded as known by the software.

As currently written, Nicknym relies on an approach based on network perspectives as enabled by Tor (i.e. retrieving the key from multiple network locations given by Tor exit nodes) to detect endorser equivocation, which allows for the possibility that the endorser could publish a bogus key for a short period of time in order to evade detection although eventually a discrepancy would be detected by other key endorsers (via third-party consensus) and the history of endorsed keys via a CONIKS-style approach would also detect this attack [4]. Any endorser equivocation should be widely reported and proven via audit logs so that the users of a malicious endorser can detect the attack. To mitigate the problem of stolen keys (either by a malicious or compromised provider or a third-party adversary), LEAP is working on a system where a user can contact their service provider (revealing their identity) and prove their identity via a one-time passphrase generated at installation of the LEAP client on a device in order to revoke verified key transitions.

4   Current State and Future Work

As of September 2016, the current LEAP architecture provides a VPN service and end-to-end encrypted e-mail service available via *bitmask.net*. The LEAP platform, Soledad, Nicknym, and the basic Key Manager are currently complete. However, there is still ongoing work on greater scalability and reliability for the LEAP platform's encrypted data-storage. On the side of the LEAP client, LEAP is pursuing greater compatibility with existing IMAP clients, improved usability, and better network probing for the VPN. In co-operation with Thoughtworks, we are working on a custom user-interface called Pixelated[27] to be bundled with LEAP client for users looking for alternatives to existing e-mail clients. Immediate goals also include porting LEAP from Android and Unix-based environments (Linux and MacOS) to iOS and Windows environments. Work is ongoing to improve the key validation rules (including key verification revocation) and support validation with multiple network perspectives. In terms of research, LEAP plans to add both Tor and mix-networking for messaging in transit both in between LEAP providers and clients to prevent metadata collection by passive global attackers, support for CONIKS for key validation [4], the use of the Signal protocol or simplified variant between LEAP-enabled providers as a higher-security alternative to SMTP with perfect forward secrecy [6], increased security for key material on the server and back-ups for stolen key material using

---

[27] The source code for Pixelated is available here: https://github.com/pixelated-project/.

threshold password authenticated key exchange (TPAKE) and secret sharing (TPASS), two-factor authentication for users to strengthen passwords for user authentication, and deploying reproducible builds. In the future, LEAP may expand its basic federated infrastructure to also provide hosting for other end-to-end encrypted and traffic-analysis resistant services needed by users, such as chat and voice-over-IP.

At this moment, email providers such as *riseup.net* provide centralized email providers to tens of thousands of highly sensitive users such as activists that are likely targets of surveillance. Likewise, many ordinary users and organizations want to migrate from centralized silos that are easily compromised by programs such as PRISM. Therefore, it is critical that technical solutions be provided that work today with existing heavily-used protocols such as SMTP to combat surveillance. The LEAP solution, by providing an integrated client and server that stores all SMTP email encrypted without having the server have access to the keys and that automates key management for the user, presents the first open architecture for enabling widespread open federated end-to-end encryption for email.

Acknowledgements. The authors are supported by NEXTLEAP (EU H2020 ref: 688722) and the Open Technology Fund.

References

1. Dingledine, R., Mathewson, N., Syverson, P.: Tor: the second-generation onion router. In: Proceedings of the 13th USENIX Security Symposium, p. 2 (2004)
2. Foster, I.D., Larson, J., Masich, M., Snoeren, A.C., Savage, S., Levchenko, K.: Security by any other name: on the effectiveness of provider based email security. In: Proceedings of the 22nd ACM SIGSAC Conference on Computer and Communications Security, pp. 450–464. ACM (2015)
3. Garfinkel, S.L.: Enabling email confidentiality through the use of opportunistic encryption. In: Proceedings of the 2003 Annual National Conference on Digital Government Research, dg.o '03, pp. 1–4. Digital Government Society of North America (2003)
4. Melara, M.S., Blankstein, A., Bonneau, J., Felten, E.W., Freedman, M.J., Coniks: Bringing key transparency to end users. In: 24th USENIX Security Symposium (USENIX Security 15), pp. 383–398 (2015)
5. Samuel, J., Mathewson, N., Cappos, J., Dingledine, R.: Survivable key compromise in software update systems. In Proceedings of the 17th ACM Conference on Computer and Communications Security, CCS 2010, pp. 61–72. ACM, New York (2010)
6. Unger, N., Dechand, S., Bonneau, J., Fahl, S., Perl, H., Goldberg, I., Smith, M.: Sok: Secure messaging. In: 2015 IEEE Symposium on Security and Privacy, pp. 232–249. IEEE (2015)
7. Whitten, A., Tygar, J.D.: Why Johnny can't encrypt: a usability evaluation of pgp. 5.0. In: Proceedings of the 8th Conference on USENIX Security Symposium, vol. 8, SSYM'99, pp. 14. USENIX Association, Berkeley (1999)

Implementation State of HSTS and HPKP
in Both Browsers and Servers

Sergio de los Santos[✉], Carmen Torrano, Yaiza Rubio, and Félix Brezo

Telefonica Digital, Ronda de la Comunicación,
s/n (Distrito Telefónica), Madrid, Spain
labs@11paths.com
http://www.elevenpaths.com

Abstract. HSTS and HPKP are relatively recent protocols aimed to enforce HTTPS connections and allow certificate pinning over HTTP. The combination of these protocols improves and strengthens HTTPS security in general, adding an additional layer of trust and verification, as well as ensuring as far as possible that the connection is always secure. However, the adoption and implementation of any protocol that is not yet completely settled, usually involves the possibility of introducing new weaknesses, opportunities or attack scenarios. Even when these protocols are implemented, bad practices prevent them from actually providing the additional security they are expected to provide. In this document, we have studied the quantity and the quality of the implementation both in servers and in most popular browsers and discovered some possible attack scenarios.

Keywords: Certificates · HPKP · HSTS · Web browsing · Privacy

1 Introduction

HTTPS and SSL/TLS were created to provide confidentiality and integrity to web browsing. However, they have also suffered serious security problems regarding conceptualization, implementation and structure. At the conceptualization and implementation level, some well-known failures are BEAST [1], POODLE [2], CRIME [3] or Heartbleed [4].

Despite being designed to ensure confidentiality, integrity and authentication, there have also been cases of MiTM attacks on TLS. In 2014 several researchers presented client impersonation attacks against TLS renegotiations, wireless networks, challenge-response protocols, and channel-bound cookies [5]. In 2015 Jia et al. [6] presented cache-poisoning attacks on different browsers. In addition, there are other attacks that have been known for years such as SSL Strip techniques [7]. In late 2010, the Firesheep extension [8] showed how sensitive information, in particular cookies, could be easily obtained from websites if all HTTP content was not encrypted throughout the whole browsing experience, not only during the login process.

© Springer International Publishing AG 2016
S. Foresti and G. Persiano (Eds.): CANS 2016, LNCS 10052, pp. 192–207, 2016.
DOI: 10.1007/978-3-319-48965-0_12

Moreover, one of the main problems with TLS and HTTPS is the impersonation of intermediate authorities in a certificate chain. In this regard, in the recent years several incidents have called attention to the prevention of this issue. Some of those significant incidents are Comodo security breach [9], Diginotar [9], TurkTrust [11], the case of the French government [10], the Indian Controller of Certifying Authorities (India CCA) [11], etc.

The coexistence of HTTPS (TLS over HTTP) for the transfer of sensitive information leaves some room for unsafe areas even on those platforms that enforce HTTPS and do care about redirecting traffic to protected sites. With the use of HSTS a server can notify the browser that it wants to be always accessed by its secure version, thus preventing user errors, lapses or redirection tricks. The HPKP protocol is created in the context of certificate pinning to allow the servers to send their own certificate (in a hashed format called "pins") to the browsers via HTTP, so browsers may remember them and detect MiTM scenarios.

Beyond explaining some of its specifications, this document addresses the implementation details of these protocols and their characteristics depending on their acceptance level, both at server and web browsing (client) levels. The remaining sections of this document are structured as follows: Sect. 2 defines the background of HSTS and HPKP and related work. Sections 3 and 4 are an introductory study for these protocols. Section 5 discusses their implementation at server level. Section 6 describes some implementation weaknesses in client level and finally, Sect. 7 includes the conclusions drawn from this study.

2   Background

The HSTS and HPKP protocols have been presented as solutions to provide additional security to the "traditional" HTTPS protocol. The following is a review of several of these alternatives aimed to provide additional security for the TLS system in general, and the HTTPS system in particular.

One of the oldest and most notable solutions is DNS-based Authentication of Named Entities (DANE) [12]. DANE is partly based on the infrastructure of DNS Security Extensions (DNSSEC), used for securing the DNS protocol. DANE is still modestly accepted. It leverages the DNSSEC infrastructure to store and sign keys/certificates that will be used in TLS. Thus, domain names are linked to cryptographic keys (certificates).

Another proposal is Trust Assertions for Certificate Keys (TACK) [13]. In their draft from 2013, Moxie Marlinspike and T. Perrie suggested an extension for the TLS protocol itself to allow the registration of the certificate chain.

Certificate Transparency is a proposal promoted by Google to create a centralized certificate log that is verifiable by anyone, and to which only information can be added. The idea is that all issued certificates are public and added to this log (transparency model) so users or browsers can evaluate whether the are fraudulent or not.

However, none of the initiatives have been massively adopted. Certificate Transparency [15] is the one that, thanks to Google's impetus and the support from certification authorities, may become the most widely adopted standard, although for now it has been only implemented in Chrome in an experimental mode.

With regard to browsers, Firefox has a wide variety of extensions that improve HTTPS and TLS security in general, like Certificate Patrol [14] and Convergence [16] among others. Some of them implement a security protocol in the background that could be applied to other browsers. But the use of extensions and the initiatives behind them have not driven HTTPS' securitization, nor have they solved fundamental problems, as they have not been massively welcomed or adopted (a requirement for many of them to work properly).

It seems that HSTS and HPKP, thanks to a slow but steady adoption, together with their easy implementation, can become the true best improvement standard of HTTPS security. But they also suffer problems and attacks, as we will show in this document. One of the main contributions of this paper is presenting an attack over the Firefox implementation that makes possible to deactivate the use of these protocols for certain domains. Deactivating these protocols implies that the domain will not be accessed through HTTPS or that modifications on the certificate chain will go undetected, leaving the communication unprotected.

2.1   Related Work

In relation to the work presented in this document, there are several studies analyzing the level (but usually not the quality) of implementation of the HSTS and HPKP protocols in different environments. Among them, the studies by Garron et al. [21] and by Kranch and Bonneau [22] are noteworthy, although [21] focuses on HSTS and Alexa domains and both papers only on the server side.

With regard to attacks and weaknesses against protocols, we should also mention the work of Jose Selvi [23]. In 2014, the author presented a tool, Delorean, which takes advantage of weaknesses in the implementation of the NTP protocol to move the system time back or forward with a man in the middle attack and invalidating HSTS making its maximum validity date expire.

At the Toorcon conference in the summer of 2015 [17], a formula was presented that allows us to know, by measuring the time of connection to known servers, if an attacker has visited or not a specific website that uses HSTS. In addition, a method was presented to use one of HPKPs options (report-uri) as a permanent user tracking system. When such idea was presented, no browsers were implementing this option described in the RFC.

As far as we know, not many attacks against the implementation of the HPKP and HSTS protocols in browsers have been described to date (except [34]), nor even a well documented description about how these protocols are implemented in different browsers has been provided.

3   HSTS Specifications

In November 2012, the Internet Engineering Task Force (IETF) [24] published the RFC 6797 [18], which contains the details on the HTTP Strict Transport Security protocol (HSTS). The HTTP Strict Transport Security protocol (HSTS) can turn HTTP requests into HTTPS from the browser itself. If a server decides to send HSTS headers to a browser, any subsequent visit to the domain from that browser is automatically and transparently converted to HTTPS from the browser, avoiding unsafe requests from the starting point of the connection itself. The application of the HSTS protocol is transparent to the user, i.e., browsers themselves are responsible for redirecting and remembering for how long domains should be visited via HTTPS if they have notified via HSTS. The domain transmits HSTS information to the browser with the Strict-Transport-Security header. This header provides three more fields:

- max-age (mandatory): The expiration time. In practice, the browser remembers for this long (in seconds) that connections should always be made via HTTPS, and thus it makes the necessary changes in the browser bar. After this time it deletes the entry and (if not preloaded) reconnects via HTTP.
- includeSubdomains (optional): This field states that the current configuration will also affect subdomains of the domain sending it.
- preload (optional): If the server intends to be always used via HTTPS, it can include this option in the header indicating that it has been added to the permanent lists preloaded to the browser.

4   HPKP Specifications

The draft RFC related to the HTTP Public Key Pinning protocol (HPKP) was dated February 2014. Its final version is in RFC 7469 [19], of April 2015. The idea behind the certificate pinning is to be able to detect when a chain of trust has been modified. In order to do so, a digital certificate present in a certificate chain needs to be unequivocally associated, usually in the browser, with a specific domain. Thus, a domain A, e.g. www.google.com, will be linked to a specific certificate/certification authority B. If for any reason a different certification authority B' (which depends on a trusted root certification authority) tries to issue a certificate associated with domain A, an alarm is launched. In general, any modification of the certification chain is suspected of a possible alteration.

The pinning can be performed from the client's side or with the assistance of the server, as it is the case of the HPKP solution. This HTTP Public Key Pinning protocol (HPKP) defines a new HTTP header (Public-Key-Pins) in which the domain sends information to the browser on its certificates and pinning policy.

This header allows various directives:

- pin-sha256 (mandatory): It contains the Subject Public Key Information field (SPKI) base64 coded SHA-256 hash of the digital certificate that the server wants to pin. Although the maximum number of appearances of this directive is not defined, the RFC states that at least the hashes from two certificates should be offered. At least one of them must be in the certificate chain offered by the server, unlike the other one, which will be considered as a backup.

- max-age (mandatory): This is the number of seconds, from the current date, for which the browser must store the certificate information provided in the previous field. Its "right" value depends on the exchange rate policy for server certificates. From this point forward, the browser will refresh the information provided by the server with the new provided pins in the event that they have been modified.
- includeSubdomains (optional): This field states that the set configuration will also affect subdomains.
- report-uri (optional): If an error occurs during verification, a POST request is sent to the URI specified in this field. This URI provides information on the domains provided by the server, and which were the ones expected by the browser.

4.1   General Security Considerations

In this section, we will highlight the most interesting known problems related to implementation prevented in their RFCs.

HSTS: Regarding HSTS, some dangers may arise from the misuse of includeSubdomains. Using this directive is always recommended in order to protect any subdomain, that might be created in the future. This is not always possible, as some subdomains may not have the TLS service properly configured. In these situations, if an attacker is able to register a different subdomain over which they have control, domain cookies (associated with the whole main domain) could be obtained in plaintext by the attacker, since they are also issued under such subdomain that they control in plaintext and not protected by HSTS.

The RFC recommends that servers should not send HSTS headers over HTTP connections and browsers should ignore them, a practice that all browsers follow.

Like many of the suggested solutions, HSTS has, by definition, a weakness in the moment of first contact with the domain. This weakness is called Trust On First Use, and it is based on the fact that the protocol must trust the first connection used, and it remembers it as a reference in future dialogues between those involved. This first use is the time when, in the event the network is compromised and a man in the middle attack has taken place, the information sent in the headers can be deleted or modified and can deceive the browser. This situation repeats itself periodically whenever the max-age sent by the server expires.

In practice, the usual situation is that the first time a browser connects via HTTP to a domain that prefers to be visited by HTTPS, a redirect at HTTP protocol level takes place, telling the browser where the real resource that it wants to access to is. It is usually in this response to such redirect where the

HSTS headers are sent to the browser if it is enabled on the server. From the moment that these headers are received, the unsafe redirect is not required during the time specified in the max-age field, and it will be the browser that will turn by itself to HTTPS, even if the user tries to visit HTTP. However, the moment when the first redirect takes place (or when max-age expires) still represents a window of opportunity for a potential attacker. To mitigate this weakness, browsers provide extra protection in the form of preloaded HSTS sites. The embedded list is public and shared by multiple browsers.

A reasonable value in max-age is recommended, not too short since every time it expires, the connection may be negotiated again in a HTTP context and a new opportunity window opens up.

HPKP: A misuse of includeSubdomains in HPKP could cause for certain subdomains to be left unprotected or denied, depending on the pins used. With respect to backup pins, the use of requests of still undeveloped certificates is recommended to prevent their theft or loss and minimize costs.

It should be noted that backup pins may be used as a tracking method on some sites. A server might offer unique backup pins associated with each user, and as long as it offers other valid pin, this would not affect the navigation process. This unique backup pin would be stored in the users browser. Any subsequent comparison on the server would univocally tell that user apart.

5   Implementation at Web Server Level

Although both the HSTS and HPKP protocols were accepted as RFC in 2012 and 2015 respectively, their use is not yet widespread, neither at browser level nor at server level. This section studies to which extent (and how) these protocols are implemented to this day on web servers.

Although there are other studies from the point of view of HSTS and HPKP's implementation, such as the study by Garron et al. [21] and the one by Crunch and Bonneau [22], these are usually based on the analysis of the most popular domains in the Alexa ranking. In this case, we have complemented it and compared it with some other domains not regarding popularity (using Shodan as of November 2015 to find domains that implement them, searching between over 82 million domains using HTTP and 46 million using HTTPS), plus analyzing the quality of the implementation focusing on the possible mistakes when using features and directives in these protocols. For analyzing data in Shodan, we have searched for the headers and assume HTTPS port is 443 and HTTP is used in 80 and 8080 ports.

For analyzing the one million most popular domains by Alexa as of March 2016, we have connected to the domain referenced in the list (and its www subdomain) via HTTPS and HTTP. We have in this way obtained 707008 headers that have been used in the analysis.

Table 1 shows not only a low global implementation, but a substantial number of servers that uses HPKP and HSTS over insecure HTTP. Many of them

Table 1. Comparing global and Alexa's most popular domains using HSTS y HPKP and its directives under HTTP and HTTPS

Security protocol	Connection protocol	Global (Shodan)	Alexa
HSTS	HTTP	91860 (0.11 %)	1692 (0.23 %)
	includeSubdomains	52.57 %	36.17 %
	preload	0.86 %	9.81 %
	HTTPS	400516 (0.87 %)	45808 (6.48 %)
	includeSubdomains	50.03 %	26.11 %
	preload	6,93 %	12.22 %
HPKP	HTTP	636 $(7.72 * 10^{-4}\%)$	7 (0.001 %)
	includeSubdomains	73.26 %	100 %
	report-uri	13.89 %	0.00 %
	HTTPS	4477 (0.01 %)	617 (0.09 %)
	includeSubdomains	81.38 %	43.43 %
	report-uri	37.50 %	13,61 %

may redirect later to a real HTTPS connection with the same (and now effective) headers, but in the case of a browser not ignoring these headers or lack of redirection, this would allow an attacker not just to manipulate the information, but stablishing some kind of "wrong memory" into the client visiting it. The collateral damage to this could go, in practice, from a denial of service in the client (that would be unable to get to the web because it would not honor HPKP protocol and browsers would refuse to connect); up to a more sophisticated phishing attack in which the victim could not tell a fraudulent certificate.

The directive report-uri is surprisingly adopted, despite that (as of March 2016) Chrome is the only browser implementing this directive and only from September 2015. If we take into account that this directive will have no effect in any other browser, it turns out to be even more interesting the percentage of webs using report-uri over HTTP connections (13,89 %), something completely discouraged (and useless) since the goal of HPKP is comparing certificates stored against the current certificate chain, and HTTP does not provide this chain. Besides, among the Alexa domains using report-uri, 7 of them (a 8,3 %) use the same domain for reporting a problem, something totally discouraged.

We show some other relevant data about the values in the headers, related with those 707008 headers taken from Alexa's million most popular domains and its www subdomains. The Table 2 shows the most usual values for max-age in HSTS and HPKP and the percentage of web sites using them.

From Table 2 we may conclude that the most popular value is 31536000 seconds (a year) for HSTS and 5184000 (60 days) for HPKP. This is a much more conservative value in opposite to HSTS, which seems logical since in the case of stolen certificates, compromised or server changes, a chance of blocking access is taken.

Table 2. Percentage of sites using different values for max-age in HSTS and HPKP.

HSTS max-age	Percentage of sites	HPKP max-age	Percentage of sites
31536000	21956 (46,12 %)	5184000	204 (32,58 %)
15552000	6336 (13,31 %)	2592000	142 (22,68 %)
63072000	4528 (9,51 %)	31536000	58 (9,26 %)
15768000	4255 (8,92 %)	604800	37 (5,91 %)
0	1876 (3,94 %)	15768000	34 (5,43 %)
43200	1697 (3,56 %)	86400	24 (3,83 %)
(Others)	6955 (14,61 %)	(Others)	123 (19,64 %)

Table 3 shows, from the 707008 headers taken, the number of domains using a certain number of pins. Despite the recommended values are using between 3 and 4 pins, some domains use from just one pin (violating the RFC) up to 17, which seems to be an irregularity that reduces the efficiency. Almost a 27 % of the most popular webs using HPKP use 0 or 1 pins, which is useless from the browser standpoint since it will ignore it.

Table 3. Domains using different number of HPKP pins.

0	1	2	3	4	5	6	7	8
5 (0,7 %)	167 (26,6 %)	302 (48,2 %)	73 (11,6 %)	52 (8,3 %)	11 (1,7 %)	7 (1.1 %)	1 (0.1 %)	0
9	10	11	12	13	14	15	16	17
0	2 (0.3 %)	0	2 (0.3 %)	0	0	2 (0.3 %)	0	2 (0.3 %)

6   Study and Analysis of Implementation Weaknesses

Beyond the errors described, adoption level, and security recommendations, we have prepared a lab environment and studied different situations in which it is possible to remove, or at least reduce, the security of these protocols under certain circumstances. The problems, weaknesses or failures described may come both from the implementation of the browser, and from the administration of the protocol carried out by the domain administrator.

6.1   Orphaned Domains

The implementation of HSTS and HPKP must evaluate whether the security coverage offered by each protocol should apply to all subdomains of the main domain, or to each domain and subdomain individually. This is achieved with the use of includeSubdomains. It is also very common for administrators to redirect visits to web subdomains when accessed through the main domain. For example, it is quite usual to observe that domain.com redirects to www.domain.com through an HTTP 301 response.

A misguided combination of the redirect and a misuse of includeSubdomains can lead to the appearance of what we have called orphaned domains. Usually, this problem will affect just the main domain, which in turn will not be under HSTS or HPKP protection. Two conditions must apply for this situation to take place:

– A domain visited under HTTP or HTTPS redirects to a subdomain under HTTPS. In this contact, no HSTS or HPKP headers are offered.
– After the redirect, the header provides HSTS or HPKP protection.

Whether the subdomain to which it has been redirected uses includeSubdomains or not, the original domain will be unprotected (orphan). The browser will remember www.domain.com as a domain protected by HSTS or HPKP, but not domain.com, which, if not explicitly visited by HTTPS from the browser, will again and again suffer the redirect process under the unsecure HTTP.

Regarding this, we consider that the includeSubdomains directive is not clearly enough stated in the RFC. As we have already seen, given a domain www.domain.com that issues HSTS or HPKP headers with includeSubdomains, browser implementation does not protect the main domain example.com, but only protects that same domain and subdomains associated (for example a.www.example.com, b. www.example.com... but never ftp.example.com).

For example, a request is done to https://example.com, which redirects to https://www.example.com with a *Location* header. This first request does not contain the HSTS or HPKP headers, but they are only found when visiting the subdomain https://www.example.com. We will see that, from the browser standpoint, only www.example.com is protected, while any visit to http://example.com from the browser will still be redirected through an unsafe channel that can be exploited by an attacker to hijack the connection. If the same content is served from the main domain (example.com/content.html) and from the subdomain (www.example.com/content.html), the overall effect is that the headers will not offer effective protection to the user.

During our experiments, we have found that this problem is more common than might be expected, even for popular domains. Popular affected domains include the following: outlook.com, hotmail.com, facebook.com, youtube.com, microsoft.com, python.org, quora.com, openssl.org, freebsd.org, ccn-cert.cni.es, icloud.org, confianzaonline.es, instagram.com, f-secure.com, yammer.com... From our investigation, a significant 5,33 % of domains using HSTS from Alexa's most popular ones, may create orphaned domains if they are not "preloaded" sites.

6.2   Implementation of Protocols in Firefox

This section describes the most relevant aspects with regard to the implementation of these protocols in Firefox (which seems identical on Android, Mac, Linux and Windows). Firefox supports HSTS from version 4, introduced in 2010 [27], and HPKP from version 32, dated 2014 [28]. This section describes some of the implementation details as well as the weaknesses that may arise from them.

Storage: Although introduced in 2010, since 2012, Firefox stores information about these protocols in the SiteSecurityServiceState.txt text file, which is located in the user profile associated with the browser. The argument used in development forums of the application [29] for keeping this information in a simple text file was that these headers were rarely used in their origins, so it was not necessary to add complexity to their management.

This file is a tab-separated plaintext file with no official documentation and with the following structure:

- The first column is the domain, along with the type of header received (HSTS or HPKP) after the ":" character.
- The second column is a value known as score. It is initialized at 0 the first time a domain is visited and is incremented by one (and only by one, regardless of the days that have passed between visits) for each subsequent day that the website is visited, taking as a reference the current system date and time in contrast to the value stored in the third column. In short and for all practical purposes, the score represents how many different days that specific domain has been visited since stored for the first time. This value will increase even if the certificate is not validated, which we consider an implementation error, as the updating of values should be conditional on the TLS or SSL handshake being correct, and on the verification that the stored parameters are valid. It can also be operated if the system date has been altered. For example, if the current system date is artificially modified or increased, a visit on the same day to domains protected by HSTS or HPKP will increase the score for that domains by one. Again for all practical purposes, the score is related to the user's browsing habits. If the max-age has not expired, the most visited domains will be those with a higher score.
- The third column corresponds to the number of days from January 1, 1970 (Epoch) to the system date for the last request or visit. This value is always updated with each request. When there is a new request, Firefox calculates the number of days from Epoch to the current date. If it increases with respect to the stored data, the value of this column is updated and the score is increased as well. Thus, the score is only updated when the number of days from Epoch to the current date exceeds the number of days from Epoch to the date of the last visit, that is, when at least one day has passed since the last visit to the domain.
- The fourth column stores several fields separated by ",":
  - The first one corresponds to mozilla:pkix:time. This is the expiration time of the header (max-age) in extended Epoch (in milliseconds since January 1, 1970).
  - The second one stores the SecurityPropertyState field, which can have three different values, depending on whether the property is disabled (SecurityPropertyUnset, 0), enabled (SecurityPropertySet, (1) or is being overwritten (SecurityPropertyKnockout, (2) [30]. This information is for browsers internal use and is not documented.
  - The third one is the flag indicating whether subdomains will be affected by this header (if includeSubdomains has been established or not).

- In the event that the header refers to HPKP, there will be a fourth field in which the array of pins received will be included in a concatenated way. Pins will be spaced between them with the character "=".

In ElevenPaths Labs we have developed a plugin called PinPatrol to ease the access to this information so that users can check which data their browsers are holding regarding HPKP and HSTS. The plugin is freely available from the Mozilla official repository [31].

Retention Policy: The storage policy in SiteSecurityServiceState.txt has an interesting peculiarity. The Firefox file only holds the first 1024 sites visited with these headers. In the event that this limit is exceeded, the least visited entry will be deleted, i.e., the one with the lower score. If there is more than one entry with minimum score, an indeterminate one from those with the minimum value will be deleted. In fact, the entry that is first found (the one that appears higher in SiteSecurityServiceState.txt) is the one deleted, but these are not fixed positions, as domains are reordered with an internal browser's criteria. This situation in which all positions of the table have been used, is defined by the browser's developers as bad or unwanted. It should be noted that the browser saves 1024 entries for HPKP and HSTS headers, implying that a domain that uses both protocols, occupies two entries. Therefore, if a webpage is able to inject strategically more than 1024 HSTS or HPKP entries into the browser from a single webpage connection to a server using different subdomains, this pool of 1024 slots stack will quickly fill up in Firefox. Recall that when the same domain is visited at least 24 h later than the last visit, the "score" is incremented by 1. Then, if the attacker gets the "score" associated to these domains to be higher than 0 (what is possible by repeating this attack in 24 h separated moments), the final effect is that only a free slot (with "score" 0) will be available in the file of the browser for storing new domains and it will be continously replaced, making HSTS and HPKP practically disabled. The chances that a new domain, expired or low valued max-age, cannot be stored by the browser are high. Even more, domains with a very low "score" value may be replaced from the table by other new domains visited, making the whole system ineffective.

We have successfully set up an environment able to easily reproduce this undesired scenario, implementing for the first time this kind of attack, that it is persistent as long as the preferences of the browser are not deleted, as the effect of the attack remains working. Additionally, the attack can be accelerated and be concluded in only a few seconds visiting a website with a simple JavaScript (for instance) code and does not need to be performed in a compromised network.

On the other hand, according to the RFC 7469, at least one of the pins sent via web must match the visited certificate validation chain. If pins are correct, they are validated and stored. With respect to the pins validation policy, there are several situations in which Firefox does not store them:

- When the root certificate has been entered by the user in the browsers list of trusted certificates. The main reason is to enable certificate installation

when antivirus solutions or proxies installed in corporate environments need to inspect the TLS traffic.
- When the server sends more than one kilobyte of pins (about 22), whether they are different or not.
- When they are not in double quotes.
- When they do not meet the proper format. However, it accepts pins without the final character =, which will be stored in a concatenated way, provided that there is a valid one in the set.

In Firefox, if a domain with the right pins stored accesses internally a domain whose pins do not correspond with those stored (an inner HPKP fail occurs), the browser will not load that domain... but neither will warn the user that the reason is a potential MiTM attack. This is an implementation weakness that should be noted. The problem with the lack of an explicit warning is that an attack might go unnoticed and be considered as a network error. In this case, the way to proceed should be the same one as when unsafe resources are accessed within a site that is accessed by TLS. In these cases, the browser launches a warning to alert the user of the problem.

6.3   Implementation of Protocols in Chrome

The Google Chrome browser and other browsers that belong to that same family (including Chromium and Opera) support, both in desktop and in mobile environments, HSTS and HPKP protocols from versions 38 [32] and 4 [33], respectively. The report-uri directive in HPKP is only supported on Chrome from version 46.

Storage: Chrome stores the headers of these protocols in memory, but it quickly dumps results in the TransportSecurity file, in the local profile of the user for Chrome. Chromes strategy is to store a Json with the structure shown in next paragraph. Unlike Firefox, a hash of the domain is stored in order to keep some confidentiality. In theory, it is not possible to know the domain if only the hash is possessed.

```
{4dDOnhqrwjFImpcYPTTXDOuiw4vxPiWsiO5eWK+Dw5o=: {
"dynamic_spki_hashes": [
  "sha256/dDwJ9ZN1FXKMtMNttLS+kGiZLsCbCZ/SnqWl7ruaFKk=",
],
"dynamic_spki_hashes_expiry": 1448348962.746452,
"expiry": 1474700962.746436, "mode": "force-https",
"pkp_include_subdomains": false, "pkp_observed": 1443164962.746452,
"sts_include_subdomains": false, "sts_observed": 1443164962.746442}
```

Each field in the file represents the following:

- The dynamic_spki_hashes field comprises a list of hashes corresponding to the domains (SPKI).

- The expiry field represents the date of expiry of the HSTS or HPKP header.
- The mode field has the force-https literal as a value, which indicates that the behavior expected from that domain is forcing access via HTTPS.
- The dynamic_spki_hashes_expiry field is the date when SPKIs expire.
- Pkp_include_subdomains can be true or false, depending on whether the policies defined in HPKP need to be applicable to all subdomains of the domain.
- Pkp_observed shows the moment when the pins have been observed, i.e., when a site has been visited.
- Sts_include_subdomains can have store true or false values, depending on whether the policy defined in HSTS is applicable to all subdomains of the affected domain.
- Sts_observed is the time when the pins have been observed, i.e., when a site with this header has been visited.

In addition to this file, Chrome has its own interface, available through the browser, that allows to check the status of domains. It is available in chrome://net-internals/hsts#hsts. This interface uses the internal file, in addition to the information preloaded in the browser, and allows to check, set and delete domains.

Retention Policy: Chrome does not have a removal policy for domains excess. The browser remembers the data indefinitely as long as the browser history is not deleted. This opens the door to a possible attack, where a webpage may send different subdomains HSTS and HPKP headers very frequently and with an abnormally high number of pins. TransportSecurity will grow up will grow up in space (up to several hundred of megabytes in a few minutes) and the browser will start to work erratically when trying to open it or even causing it not to work at all until the whole history is manually deleted and all information lost. We have successfully set up an environment able to easily reproduce this undesired scenario implementing for the first time this kind of attack.

Validation Policy: In Chrome, as stated in the RFC, at least one of the HPKP pins sent through the web must match the visited certificate validation chain. Chrome's peculiarity is that it stores any number of pins received form the server (unlike Firefox), whether or not they are different from each other, there being no theoretical limit. In practice, it will accept as many pins as the HTTP header can store and the browser can read. This makes the aforementioned possible denial of service attack easier.

Unlike Firefox, Chrome stores the pins if the root certificate has been entered by the user in the list of trusted certificates of the operating system. Chrome stores pins even if they are sent between single quotes in the header.

Just like Firefox, Chrome lacks of an explicit warning when an inner HPKP error occurs, so an attack might go unnoticed and be considered as a network error. Under Android 4.0 versions, Chrome does not even store HPKP pins. Although the presence of this operative system is residual (about 2 % during

2016) it is worth noting this users are not protected. This problem has not been mentioned explicitly in either Chrome or Android official site before.

6.4   Implementation of Protocols in Internet Explorer (and Edge)

The Edge browser or its immediately earlier version, Internet Explorer, only support HSTS from Internet Explorer 11 on Windows 7 and 8.1. They still do not support HPKP. As far as we know, there is no technical documentation (official or unofficial) on how this system works in the browser or stores the information. From the point of view of forensic investigations, to date and to our knowledge, there are no independent studies published or tools to facilitate the study or analysis of Internet Explorer's behavior with regard to the HSTS protocol. In Fig. 1 we show one of the tables for Internet Explorer where this data is stored, which has not been reversed so far.

HstsEntry_5 [Table ID = 58, 7 Columns]						
EntryId	MinimizedRDomainHash	MinimizedRDomainLength	IncludeSubdomains	Expires	LastTimeUsed	RDomain
3926	9120546676738812763	15	0	22/07/2016 8:20:53	18/03/2016 8:20:53	
3925	4882444638216186715	11	0	15/09/2016 8:20:52	18/03/2016 8:20:52	
3929	2375066247904815963	13	0	18/03/2017 9:36:36	18/03/2016 9:36:36	
3930	6430462819344509787	10	05/05/1829 23:50:03	18/03/2017 9:36:38	18/03/2016 9:36:38	
3931	6430462819344509787	10	0	18/03/2017 9:36:51	18/03/2016 9:36:51	
3927	8733428533329849179	21	0	18/03/2017 15:36:30	18/03/2016 9:36:30	
3928	8733428533329849179	21	0	18/03/2017 15:36:30	18/03/2016 9:36:30	
3924	6309426421137861467	11	0	1373390016508192 47	18/03/2016 8:00:46	
9	6703755249848609627	10	05/05/1829 23:50:03	9223372036854775807	9223372036854775807	
10	4506072807924493147	15	05/05/1829 23:50:03	9223372036854775807	9223372036854775807	
11	6919771534091545435	7	05/05/1829 23:50:03	9223372036854775807	9223372036854775807	
12	4587362928086412123	7	05/05/1829 23:50:03	9223372036854775807	9223372036854775807	
13	5877742408575413082	21	05/05/1829 23:50:03	9223372036854775807	9223372036854775807	

Fig. 1. Edge database storing HSTS values.

Basically, the function or API that manages HSTS in Windows is located in the WININET.DLL library, and it is called HttpIsHostHstsEnabled, for which there appears to be no official documentation. We understand that knowing the system in depth would require extensive reverse engineering and forensic work, which is beyond the scope of this report. In recent versions of Internet Explorer (and even Edge), Microsoft uses a type of proprietary database called Extensible Storage Engine (ESE) to store HSTS data among many others. The base file with the bulk of information is usually hosted in WebCacheV01.dat file under the user profile, in WebCache folder. A low level study of the system HSTS's actual capabilities is beyond the scope of this report and requires in-depth study.

7   Conclusions

Although the HSTS and HPKP protocols are intended to provide an additional layer of security to HTTPS communications, their implementation is not widespread. At server level, many of the network's most relevant domains do not even implement them. Moreover, among the minority of domains that do use them, there has been a significant number of implementation errors, even a disregard of the recommendations of their respective RFCs. This situation shows both low level adoption and, somehow, some misunderstanding about how to take full advantage of the protocols.

About the client side, browsers do not have a standard way to implement described RFCs. The way they handle these protocols is undocumented and, in the case of Firefox, even dangerous under certain circumstances that may cause a false sense of security as we have proven in our labs. In the case of Chrome, a malicious user may cause a denial of service, aside some weaknesses (previously undescribed) in both that gives us the idea that there is still much more to standardize and work to be done in them. Edge (formerly Internet Explorer) does not even implement HPKP yet.

We conclude that implementation, either in server or client side, is not mature enough yet as to prevent potential attack scenarios associated with denial of service, full domain protection, RFC right implementation or even fulfilling what the protocols are intended to achieve in the first place.

Some recommendations for administrators implementing the protocols in the server side are keeping a good understanding of how protocol works and how it is implemented; have a robust plan and planning for actually pinning and for key rotation or potential problems; and being cautious with max-age values and pins actually pinned. For users using the browsers, we would suggest using some additional pinning system in the terms of plugins aforementioned, for example, and checking their browser's HSTS and HPKP data regularly.

References

1. Rizzo, J., Duong, T.: BEAST. Ekoparty (2011)
2. Mller, B., Duong, T., Kotowicz, K.: This POODLE bites: exploiting the SSL 3.0 fallback (2014). https://www.openssl.org/~bodo/ssl-poodle.pdf. REPASAR
3. Rizzo, J., Duong, T.: The CRIME Attack. Ekoparty (2012)
4. Codenomicon: The Heartbleed Bug. Ekoparty (2014)
5. Bhargavan, K., Delignat-Lavaud, A., Fournet, C., Pironti, A., Strub, P.: Triple handshakes and cookie cutters: breaking and fixing authentication over TLS. In: IEEE Symposium on Security and Privacy (2014)
6. Jia, Y., Chen, Y., Dong, X., Saxena, P., Mao, J., Liang, Z.: Man-in-the-browser-cache: persisting HTTPS attacks via browser cache poisoning. Comput. Secur. **55**, 62–80 (2015)
7. Marlinspike, M.: New Tricks for Defeating SSL in Practice. BlackHat (2009). http://www.thoughtcrime.org/software/sslstrip/
8. Paul, I.: Firefox Add-on Firesheep Brings Hacking to the Masses. PCWorld (2010)
9. Mandalia, R.: Security Breach in CA Networks - Comodo, DigiNotar, GlobalSign. ISC^2 Blog (2012). http://blog.isc2.org/isc2_blog/2012/04/test.html
10. Langley, A.: Further improving digital certificate security. Google Security Blog (2013). https://security.googleblog.com/2013/12/further-improving-digital-certificate.html

11. Langley, A.: Maintaining digital certificate security. Google Security Blog (2014). https://security.googleblog.com/2014/07/maintaining-digital-certificate-security.html
12. Hoffman, P.: The DNS-Based Authentication of Named Entities (DANE). Transport Layer Security (TLS) Protocol: TLSA. https://www.rfc-editor.org/rfc/rfc6698.txt
13. Marlinspike, M., Perrin, T.: Tacks. http://tack.io/draft.html
14. Loesch, C.: Certificate Patrol. https://addons.mozilla.org/es/firefox/addon/certificate-patrol/
15. Wendlandt, D., Andersen, D., Perrig, A.: Perspectives: Improving SSH-style Host Authentication with Multi-Path Probing (2008). http://static.usenix.org/event/usenix08/tech/full_papers/wendlandt/wendlandt_html/
16. Marlinspike, M.: Convergence (2011). http://convergence.io/
17. Yan: Weird New Tricks for Browser Fingerprinting (2015). https://zyan.scripts.mit.edu/presentations/toorcon2015.pdf
18. Internet Engineering Task Force (IETF): HTTP Strict Transport Security (HSTS). RFC 6797(2012). https://tools.ietf.org/html/rfc6797
19. Internet Engineering Task Force (IETF): Public Key Pinning Extension for HTTP. RFC 7469(2015). https://tools.ietf.org/html/rfc7469
20. Internet Engineering Task Force (IETF): Certificate Transparency (2013). https://tools.ietf.org/html/rfc6962
21. Garron, L., Bortz, A., Boneh, D.: The State of HSTS Deployment: A Survey and Common Pitfalls (2014)
22. Kranch, M., Bonneau, J.: Upgrading HTTPS in mid-air: an empirical study of strict transport security and key pinning. In: Network and Distributed System Security Symposium (NDSS) (2015)
23. Selvi, J.: Bypassing HTTP Strict Transport Security. BlackHat Europe (2014)
24. IETF: IETF. https://www.ietf.org/
25. Shodan: Shodan. http://www.shodan.io
26. Alexa internet Inc: Alexa. http://www.alexa.com/
27. Deveria, A.: Can I use Strict Transport Security? (2016). http://caniuse.com/#feat=stricttransportsecurity
28. Monica: Firefox 32 supports Public Key Pinning (2014). http://monica-at-mozilla.blogspot.de/2014/08/firefox-32-supports-public-key-pinning.html
29. Bugzilla: Bugzilla@Mozilla (2014). https://bugzilla.mozilla.org/show_bug.cgi?id=775370
30. Mozilla: Mozilla Code (2014). https://dxr.mozilla.org/comm-central/source/mozilla/security/manager/ssl/nsSiteSecurityService.h
31. ElevenPaths: PinPatro. https://addons.mozilla.org/es/firefox/addon/pinpatrol/
32. Deveria, A.: Can I Use Public Key Pinning (2015). http://caniuse.com/#feat=publickeypinning
33. Deveria, A.: Can I use HSTS? (2015). http://caniuse.com/#search=HSTS
34. Nishimura, M.: Appended period to hostnames can bypass HPKP and HSTS protections. https://www.mozilla.org/en-US/security/advisories/mfsa2015-13/

Signatures and Hash

Signer-Anonymous Designated-Verifier Redactable Signatures for Cloud-Based Data Sharing

David Derler[1(✉)], Stephan Krenn[2], and Daniel Slamanig[1]

[1] IAIK, Graz University of Technology, Graz, Austria
{david.derler,daniel.slamanig}@tugraz.at
[2] AIT Austrian Institute of Technology GmbH, Vienna, Austria
stephan.krenn@ait.ac.at

Abstract. Redactable signature schemes allow to black out predefined parts of a signed message without affecting the validity of the signature, and are therefore an important building block in privacy-enhancing cryptography. However, a second look shows, that for many practical applications, they cannot be used in their vanilla form. On the one hand, already the identity of the signer may often reveal sensitive information to the receiver of a redacted message; on the other hand, if data leaks or is sold, everyone getting hold of (redacted versions of) a signed message will be convinced of its authenticity.

We overcome these issues by providing a definitional framework and practically efficient instantiations of so called *signer-anonymous designated-verifier redactable signatures* (AD-RS). As a byproduct we also obtain the first *group redactable signatures*, which may be of independent interest. AD-RS are motivated by a real world use-case in the field of health care and complement existing health information sharing platforms with additional important privacy features. Moreover, our results are not limited to the proposed application, but can also be directly applied to various other contexts such as notary authorities or e-government services.

1 Introduction

Digitalization of data and processes as well as the use of promising IT-trends such as cloud computing is prevalent, steadily increasing and meanwhile outreaches even sensitive fields such as the health care sector.[1] Given the sensitivity of the involved data and the high demands in data correctness and quality, the health care domain is a prime example for the beneficial application of cryptographic

---

The full version of this paper is available in the IACR Cryptology ePrint Archive. All authors have been supported by EU H2020 project PRISMACLOUD, grant agreement n°644962. S. Krenn has additionally been supported by EU H2020 project CREDENTIAL, grant agreement n°653454.

[1] See e.g., http://www.healthcaredive.com/news/407746/.

© Springer International Publishing AG 2016
S. Foresti and G. Persiano (Eds.): CANS 2016, LNCS 10052, pp. 211–227, 2016.
DOI: 10.1007/978-3-319-48965-0_13

means such as encryption and digital signatures. This work is dedicated to the development of a cryptographically enhanced solution for a real world hospital, which is currently planning to complement its existing information sharing system for electronic patient data with additional privacy features. The overall idea of the system is to grant patients access to all their medical records via a cloud-based platform. The patients are then able to use this as a central hub to distribute their documents to different stakeholders, e.g., to request reimbursement by the insurance, or to forward (parts of) the documents to the family doctor for further treatment. While means for access control and data confidentiality are already in place, the system should be complemented by strong authenticity guarantees. At the same time a high degree of privacy should be maintained, i.e., by allowing the patients, on a fine-granular basis, to decide which parts of which document should be visible to which party. For instance, the family doctor might *not* need to learn the precise costs of a treatment; similarly a medical research laboratory should *not* learn the patients' identities.

From a research point of view, one motivation behind this work is to show how rather complex real world scenarios with conflicting interests and strong security and privacy requirements can be elegantly and securely realized by means of rigorous cryptographic design and analysis. More importantly, we can indeed come up with provably secure and practical solutions being well suited for real world use. Now, we discuss the motivation for our design.

Redactable Signatures. A trivial solution for the above problem would be to let the hospital cloud create a fresh signature on the information to be revealed every time the user wishes to forward authentic subsets of a document to other parties. However, this is not satisfactory as it would require strong trust assumptions into the cloud: one could not efficiently guarantee that the signed data has not been altered over time by the cloud or by a malicious intruder. It is therefore preferable to use *redactable signatures* (RS). These are signature schemes that allow to black out (redact) predefined parts of a signed message while preserving the validity of the signature, thereby guaranteeing the authenticity of the redacted message. That is, it is not necessary to let the cloud attest the authenticity of the forwarded data, as the signature on the redacted document can be extracted from the doctor's signature on the original document without requiring the doctor's secret signing key or further interaction with the doctor.

Designated Verifiers. Unfortunately, using redactable signatures in their vanilla form in our scenario would lead to severe privacy problems, i.e., everyone getting hold of a signed document would be convinced of its authenticity. In such a case, for instance, an employer who gets hold of a signed health record of an employee, might reliably learn the employee's disease, who, in further consequence, might get dismissed. What is therefore needed is a *designated verifier* for each redacted version of a document. That is, when redacting a document, the patient should be able to define the intended receiver. Then, while everybody can check the validity of a leaked document, *only* the designated verifier is convinced about its authenticity. This can be achieved by constructing the schemes in a way that the designated verifier can fake indistinguishable signatures on its own. Moreover, the public verifiability property might as well be a motivation for designated verifiers to not leak/sell documents, as this reduces the circle of possible suspects to the data owner and the designated verifier.

Group Signatures. Another problem of RS is that they only support a single signer. However, a hospital potentially employing hundreds of doctors will not use a single signing key that is shared by all its employees. By doing so, the identity of the signing doctor could not be revealed in case of a dispute, e.g., after a malpractice. However, using different keys for different doctors poses a privacy risk again. For instance, if the document was signed using an oncologist's key, one could infer sensitive information about the disease—even though the diagnosis was blacked out. What is therefore needed are features known from *group signatures*, where towards the verifier the doctor's identity remains hidden within the set of doctors in the hospital, while re-identification is still possible by a dedicated entity.

Contribution. The properties we need for our scenario are contributed by three distinct cryptographic concepts and what we actually need can be considered as a *signer-anonymous designated-verifier redactable signature scheme.* However, while a lot of existing work studies the different concepts in isolation, there is no work which aims at combining them in a way to profit from a combination of their individual properties. Trying to obtain this by simply combining them in an ad-hoc fashion, however, is dangerous. It is well known that the ad-hoc combination of cryptographic primitives to larger systems is often problematic (as subtle issues often remain hidden when omitting formal analysis) and security breaches resulting from such approaches are often seen in practice. Unlike following such an ad-hoc approach, we follow a rigorous approach and formally model what is required by the use-case, introduce a comprehensive security model and propose two (semi-)black-box constructions that are provably secure within our model. While such a (semi-)black-box construction is naturally interesting from a theoretical point of view, our second construction is also entirely practical and thus also well suited to be used within the planned system. Finally, as a contribution which may be of independent interest, we also obtain the first *group redactable signatures* as a byproduct of our definitional framework.

Technical Overview. Our constructions provably achieve the desired functionality by means of a two-tier signature approach: a message is signed using a freshly generated RS key pair where the corresponding public key of this "one-time RS" is certified using a group signature. For the designated verifier feature, we follow two different approaches. Firstly, we follow the naïve approach and use a disjunctive non-interactive proof of knowledge which either demonstrates knowledge of a valid RS signature on the message, *or* it demonstrates knowledge of a valid signature of the designated verifier on the same message. While this approach is very generic, its efficiency largely depends on the complexity to prove knowledge of an RS signature. To this end, we exploit key-homomorphic signatures, which we introduce and which seem to be of independent interest. In particular, we use the observation that a large class of RS can easily be turned into RS admitting the required key-homomorphism, to obtain a practical construction. More precisely, besides conventional group signatures and conventional redactable signatures, our approach only requires to prove a single statement demonstrating knowledge of the relation between two RS keys *or* demonstrating knowledge of the designated verifier's secret key. For instance, in the discrete logarithm setting when instantiating this proof using Fiat-Shamir transformed [15] Σ-protocols, they are highly efficient as they only require two group exponentiations.

Related Work. Redactable signature schemes have been independently introduced in [18,27]. Although such schemes suffer from the aforementioned problems, we can use them as an important building block. In particular, we will rely on the general framework for such signatures as presented in [13]. Besides that, redactable signatures with an unlinkability property have been introduced in [9,21].[2] Unfortunately, apart from lacking practical efficiency, even unlinkable redactable signatures are not useful to achieve the desired designated verifier functionality. There is a large body of work on signatures with designated verifiers, which are discussed subsequently. However, none of the approaches considers selective disclosure via redaction or a group signing feature.

In designated verifier (DV) signatures (or proofs) [17], a signature produced by a signer can only be validated by a single user who is designated by the signer during the signing process (cf. [19] for a refined security model). Designation can only be performed by the signer and verification requires the designated verifier's secret. Thus, this concept is not directly applicable to our setting. In [17] also the by now well known "*OR trick*" was introduced as a DV construction paradigm.

Undeniable signatures [11] are signatures that can not be verified without the signer's cooperation and the signer can either prove that a signature is valid or invalid. This is not suitable for us as this is an interactive process.

Designated confirmer signatures [10] introduce a third entity besides the signer and the verifier called designated confirmer. This party, given a signature, has the ability to privately verify it as well as to convince anyone of its validity or invalidity. Additionally, the designated confirmer can convert a designated confirmer signature into an ordinary signature that is then publicly verifiable. This is not suitable for our scenario, as it is exactly the opposite of what we require, i.e., here the signature for the confirmer is not publicly verifiable, but the confirmer can always output publicly verifiable versions of this signature.

Another concept, which is closer to the designation functionality that we require, are universal designated verifier (UDV) signatures introduced in [26]. They are similar to designated verifier signatures, but universal in the sense that any party who is given a publicly verifiable signature from the signer can designate the signature to any designated verifier by using the verifiers public key. Then, the designated verifier can verify that the message was signed by the signer, but is unable to convince anyone else of this fact. Like with ordinary DV signatures, UDV signatures also require the designated verifier's secret key for verification. There are some generic results for UDV signatures. In [29] it was shown how to convert various pairing-based signature schemes into UDV

---

[2] Similar to the related concept of unlinkable sanitizable signatures [7,8,16].

signatures. In [25] it was shown how to convert a large class of signature schemes into UDV signatures. Some ideas in our second construction are conceptually related to this generic approach. However, as we only require to prove relations among public keys, our approach is more tailored to efficiency.

2   Preliminaries

We denote algorithms by sans-serif letters, e.g., A, B. All algorithms are assumed to return a special symbol $\perp$ on error. By $y \leftarrow A(x)$, we denote that y is assigned the output of the potentially probabilistic algorithm A on input x and fresh random coins. Similarly, $y \xleftarrow{R} S$ means that y was sampled uniformly at random from a set S. We let $[n] := \{1, \ldots, n\}$. We write $\Pr[\Omega : \mathcal{E}]$ to denote the probability of an event $\mathcal{E}$ over the probability space Ω. We use $\mathcal{C}$ to denote challengers of security experiments, and $\mathcal{C}_\kappa$ to make the security parameter explicit.

A function $\varepsilon(\cdot) : \mathbb{N} \to \mathbb{R}_{\geq 0}$ is called negligible, iff it vanishes faster than every inverse polynomial, i.e., $\forall\, k : \exists\, n_k : \forall\, n > n_k : \varepsilon(n) < n^{-k}$.

Followingly, we recap required cryptographic building blocks. Due to space constraints we omit formal definitions for well known primitives such as a digital signature scheme $\Sigma = (\mathsf{KeyGen}, \mathsf{Sign}, \mathsf{Verify})$ and a (non-interactive) proof system $\Pi = (\mathsf{Setup}, \mathsf{Proof}, \mathsf{Verify})$ here, and present them in the extended version.

Redactable Signatures. Below, we recall the generalized model for redactable signatures from [13], which builds up on [6]. As done in [13], we do not make the structure of the message explicit. That is, we assume that the message m to be signed is some arbitrarily structured data. We use ADM to denote a data structure encoding the admissible redactions of some message m and we use MOD to denote a data structure containing modification instructions for some message. We use $\mathring{m} \overset{\text{ADM}}{\preceq} m$ to denote that a message $\mathring{m}$ is derivable from a message m under ADM and $\mathring{m} \overset{\text{MOD}}{\longleftarrow} m$ to denote that $\mathring{m}$ is obtained by applying MOD to m. Likewise, we use $\mathring{\text{ADM}} \overset{\text{MOD}}{\longleftarrow} \text{ADM}$ to denote the derivation of $\mathring{\text{ADM}}$ from ADM with respect to MOD. We use $\text{ADM} \preceq m$ to denote that ADM matches m, and $\text{MOD} \preceq \text{ADM}$ to denote that MOD matches ADM.

Definition 1. *An* RS *is a tuple* $(\mathsf{KeyGen}, \mathsf{Sign}, \mathsf{Verify}, \mathsf{Redact})$ *of PPT algorithms, which are defined as follows:*

$\mathsf{KeyGen}(1^\kappa)$: *Takes a security parameter κ as input and outputs a keypair* $(\mathsf{sk}, \mathsf{pk})$.

$\mathsf{Sign}(\mathsf{sk}, m, \text{ADM})$: *Takes a secret key* sk, *a message* m *and admissible modifications* ADM *as input, and outputs a message-signature pair* (m, σ) *together with some auxiliary redaction information* RED.[3]

$\mathsf{Verify}(\mathsf{pk}, m, \sigma)$: *Takes a public key* pk, *a message* m, *and a signature σ as input, and outputs a bit b.*

$\mathsf{Redact}(\mathsf{pk}, m, \sigma, \text{MOD}, \text{RED})$: *Takes a public key* pk, *a message* m, *a valid signature σ, modification instructions* MOD, *and auxiliary redaction information* RED *as input. It returns a redacted message-signature pair* $(\mathring{m}, \mathring{\sigma})$ *and an updated auxiliary redaction information* $\mathring{\text{RED}}$.

---

[3] As it is common for RS, we assume that ADM can always be recovered from (m, σ).

While we omit correctness, we recall the remaining RS security definitions below.

Definition 2 (Unforgeability). *An* RS *is unforgeable, if for all PPT adversaries* $\mathcal{A}$ *there exists a negligible function* $\varepsilon(\cdot)$ *such that*

$$\Pr\left[\begin{matrix} (\mathsf{sk},\mathsf{pk}) \leftarrow \mathsf{KeyGen}(1^\kappa), \\ (\mathsf{m}^*,\sigma^*) \leftarrow \mathcal{A}^{\mathsf{Sign}(\mathsf{sk},\cdot,\cdot)}(\mathsf{pk}) \end{matrix} : \begin{matrix} \mathsf{Verify}(\mathsf{pk},\mathsf{m}^*,\sigma^*) = 1 \wedge \\ \nexists\ (\mathsf{m},\mathsf{ADM}) \in \mathcal{Q}^{\mathsf{Sign}} : \mathsf{m}^* \overset{\mathsf{ADM}}{\preceq} \mathsf{m} \end{matrix}\right] \leq \varepsilon(\kappa),$$

where the environment keeps track of the queries to the signing oracle via $\mathcal{Q}^{\mathsf{Sign}}$.

Definition 3 (Privacy). *An* RS *is private, if for all PPT adversaries* $\mathcal{A}$ *there exists a negligible function* $\varepsilon(\cdot)$ *such that*

$$\Pr\left[\begin{matrix} (\mathsf{sk},\mathsf{pk}) \leftarrow \mathsf{KeyGen}(1^\kappa),\ b \overset{R}{\leftarrow} \{0,1\}, \\ \mathcal{O} \leftarrow \{\mathsf{Sign}(\mathsf{sk},\cdot,\cdot), \mathsf{LoRRedact}(\mathsf{sk},\mathsf{pk},\cdot,\cdot,b)\}, \\ b^* \leftarrow \mathcal{A}^{\mathcal{O}}(\mathsf{pk}) \end{matrix} : b = b^*\right] \leq 1/2 + \varepsilon(\kappa),$$

where LoRRedact *is defined as follows:*

   LoRRedact$(\mathsf{sk},\mathsf{pk},(\mathsf{m}_0,\mathsf{ADM}_0,\mathsf{MOD}_0),(\mathsf{m}_1,\mathsf{ADM}_1,\mathsf{MOD}_1),b)$:
   1: *Compute* $((\mathsf{m}_c,\sigma_c),\mathsf{RED}_c) \leftarrow \mathsf{Sign}(\mathsf{sk},\mathsf{m}_c,\mathsf{ADM}_c)$ *for* $c \in \{0,1\}$.
   2: *Let* $((\mathring{\mathsf{m}}_c,\mathring{\sigma}_c),\mathsf{R\mathring{E}D}_c) \leftarrow \mathsf{Redact}(\mathsf{pk},\sigma_c,\mathsf{m}_c,\mathsf{MOD}_c,\mathsf{RED}_c)$ *for* $c \in \{0,1\}$.
   3: *If* $\mathring{\mathsf{m}}_0 \neq \mathring{\mathsf{m}}_1 \vee \mathsf{A\mathring{D}M}_0 \neq \mathsf{A\mathring{D}M}_1$, *return* $\perp$.
   4: *Return* $(\mathring{\mathsf{m}}_b,\mathring{\sigma}_b)$.

Here, the admissible modifications $\mathsf{A\mathring{D}M}_0$ *and* $\mathsf{A\mathring{D}M}_1$ *corresponding to the redacted messages are implicitly defined by (and recoverable from) the tuples* $(\mathring{\mathsf{m}}_0,\mathring{\sigma}_0)$ *and* $(\mathring{\mathsf{m}}_1,\mathring{\sigma}_1)$ *and the oracle returns* $\perp$ *if any of the algorithms returns* $\perp$.

We call an RS *secure*, if it is correct, unforgeable, and private.

Group Signatures. Subsequently, we recall the established model for static group signatures from [3]. Again, we slightly adapt the notation to ours.

Definition 4. *A group signature scheme* GS *is a tuple* (KeyGen, Sign, Verify, Open) *of PPT algorithms which are defined as follows:*

KeyGen$(1^\kappa, n)$: *Takes a security parameter* κ *and the group size* n *as input. It generates and outputs a group verification key* gpk, *a group opening key* gok, *as well as a list of group signing keys* $\mathsf{gsk} = \{\mathsf{gsk}_i\}_{i \in [n]}$.

Sign$(\mathsf{gsk}_i, \mathsf{m})$: *Takes a group signing key* gsk_i *and a message* m *as input and outputs a signature* σ.

Verify$(\mathsf{gpk}, \mathsf{m}, \sigma)$: *Takes a group verification key* gpk, *a message* m *and a signature* σ *as input, and outputs a bit* b.

Open$(\mathsf{gok}, \mathsf{m}, \sigma)$: *Takes a group opening key* gok, *a message* m *and a signature* σ *as input, and outputs an identity* i.

The GS security properties are formally defined as follows (we omit correctness).

Definition 5 (Anonymity). *A* GS *is anonymous, if for all PPT adversaries* $\mathcal{A}$ *there exists a negligible function* $\varepsilon(\cdot)$ *such that*

$$\Pr\left[\begin{array}{l}(\mathsf{gpk}, \mathsf{gok}, \mathsf{gsk}) \leftarrow \mathsf{KeyGen}(1^\kappa, n), \\ b \xleftarrow{R} \{0,1\}, \ \mathcal{O} \leftarrow \{\mathsf{Open}(\mathsf{gok}, \cdot, \cdot)\}, \\ (i_0^*, i_1^*, \mathsf{m}^*, \mathsf{st}) \leftarrow \mathcal{A}^{\mathcal{O}}(\mathsf{gpk}, \mathsf{gsk}), \\ \sigma \leftarrow \mathsf{Sign}(\mathsf{gsk}_{i_b^*}, \mathsf{m}^*), \ b^* \leftarrow \mathcal{A}^{\mathcal{O}}(\sigma, \mathsf{st})\end{array} : \begin{array}{c} b = b^* \ \wedge \\ (\mathsf{m}^*, \sigma) \notin \mathcal{Q}_2^{\mathsf{Open}}\end{array}\right] \leq \varepsilon(\kappa),$$

where $\mathcal{A}$ *runs in two stages and* $\mathcal{Q}_2^{\mathsf{Open}}$ *records the* Open *queries in stage two.*

Definition 6 (Traceability). *A* GS *is traceable, if for all PPT adversaries* $\mathcal{A}$ *there exists a negligible function* $\varepsilon(\cdot)$ *such that*

$$\Pr\left[\begin{array}{l}(\mathsf{gpk}, \mathsf{gok}, \mathsf{gsk}) \leftarrow \mathsf{KeyGen}(1^\kappa, n), \\ \mathcal{O} \leftarrow \{\mathsf{Sig}(\cdot, \cdot), \mathsf{Key}(\cdot)\}, \\ (\mathsf{m}^*, \sigma^*) \leftarrow \mathcal{A}^{\mathcal{O}}(\mathsf{gpk}, \mathsf{gok}), \\ i \leftarrow \mathsf{Open}(\mathsf{gok}, \mathsf{m}^*, \sigma^*)\end{array} : \begin{array}{c} \mathsf{Verify}(\mathsf{gpk}, \mathsf{m}^*, \sigma^*) = 1 \ \wedge \\ (i = \bot \ \vee \ (i \notin \mathcal{Q}^{\mathsf{Key}} \ \wedge \\ (i, \mathsf{m}^*) \notin \mathcal{Q}^{\mathsf{Sig}}))\end{array}\right] \leq \varepsilon(\kappa),$$

where $\mathsf{Sig}(i, \mathsf{m})$ *returns* $\mathsf{Sign}(\mathsf{gsk}_i, \mathsf{m})$, $\mathsf{Key}(i)$ *returns* gsk_i, *and* $\mathcal{Q}^{\mathsf{Sig}}$ *and* $\mathcal{Q}^{\mathsf{Key}}$ *record the queries to the signing and key oracle respectively.*

We call a GS *secure*, if it is correct, anonymous and traceable.

3   Security Model

Now we formally define signer-anonymous designated-verifier redactable signature schemes (AD-RS). To obtain the most general result, we follow [13] and do not make the structure of the messages to be signed explicit. Inspired by [20], we view signatures output by Sign as being of the form $\sigma = (\underline{\sigma}, \overline{\sigma})$. That is, signatures are composed of a public signature component $\underline{\sigma}$ and a private signature component $\overline{\sigma}$, where $\underline{\sigma}$ may also be empty. For the sake of simple presentation we model our system for static groups, since an extension to dynamic groups [4] is straight forward.

Definition 7 (AD-RS). *An* AD-RS *is a tuple* (Setup, DVGen, Sign, GVerify, Open, Redact, Verify, Sim) *of PPT algorithms, which are defined as follows.*

Setup($1^\kappa, n$): *Takes a security parameter* κ *and the group size* n *as input. It generates and outputs a group public key* gpk, *a group opening key* gok, *and a list of group signing keys* $\mathsf{gsk} = \{\mathsf{gsk}_i\}_{i \in [n]}$.

DVGen(1^κ): *Takes a security parameter* κ *as input and outputs a designated verifier key pair* $(\mathsf{vsk}_j, \mathsf{vpk}_j)$.

Sign($\mathsf{gsk}_i, \mathsf{m}, \mathsf{ADM}$): *Takes a group signing key* gsk_i, *a message* m, *and admissible modifications* ADM *as input, and outputs a signature* σ.

GVerify($\mathsf{gpk}, \mathsf{m}, \sigma$): *Takes a group public key* gpk, *a message* m, *and a signature* σ *as input, and outputs a bit* b.

Open(gok, m, σ): *Takes a group opening key* gok, *a message* m, *and a valid signature* σ *as input, and outputs an identity* i.

Redact(gpk, vpk$_j$, m, σ, MOD): *Takes a group public key* gpk, *a designated-verifier public key* vpk$_j$, *a message* m, *a valid signature* σ, *and modification instructions* MOD *as input, and returns a designated-verifier message-signature pair* ($\overset{\circ}{m}$, ρ).

Verify(gpk, vpk$_j$, m, ρ): *Takes a group public key* gpk, *a designated-verifier public key* vpk$_j$, *a message* m, *and a designated-verifier signature* ρ. *It returns a bit* b.

Sim(gpk, vsk$_j$, m, ADM, MOD, $\underline{\sigma}$): *Takes a group public key* gpk, *a designated-verifier secret key* vsk$_j$, *a message* m, *admissible modifications* ADM, *modification instructions* MOD, *and a valid public signature component* $\underline{\sigma}$ *as input and outputs a designated-verifier message signature pair* ($\overset{\circ}{m}$, ρ).

Oracles. We base our security notions on the following oracles and assume that (gpk, gok, gsk) generated in the experiments are implicitly available to them. The environment stores a list DVK of designated-verifier key pairs, and a set of public signature components SIG. Each list entry and each set is initially set to $\perp$.

Key(i): This oracle returns gsk$_i$.

DVGen(j): If DVK[j] $\neq \perp$ this oracle returns $\perp$. Otherwise, it runs (vsk$_j$, vpk$_j$) $\leftarrow$ DVGen(1^κ), sets DVK[j] $\leftarrow$ (vsk$_j$, vpk$_j$), and returns vpk$_j$.

DVKey(j): This oracle returns vsk$_j$.

Sig(i, m, ADM): This oracle runs $\sigma = (\underline{\sigma}, \overline{\sigma}) \leftarrow$ Sign(gsk$_i$, m, ADM), sets SIG $\leftarrow$ SIG $\cup \{\underline{\sigma}\}$ and returns σ.

Open(m, σ): This oracle runs $i \leftarrow$ Open(gok, m, σ) and returns i.

Sim(j, m, ADM, MOD, $\underline{\sigma}$): If $\underline{\sigma} \notin$ SIG, this oracle returns $\perp$. Otherwise, it runs ($\overset{\circ}{m}$, ρ) $\leftarrow$ Sim(gpk, vsk$_j$, m, ADM, MOD, $\underline{\sigma}$) and returns ($\overset{\circ}{m}$, ρ).

RoS(b, j, m, ADM, MOD, σ): If $b = 0$, this oracle runs ($\overset{\circ}{m}$, ρ) $\leftarrow$ Redact(gpk, vpk$_j$, m, σ, MOD) and returns ($\overset{\circ}{m}$, ρ). Otherwise, it uses the Sim oracle to obtain ($\overset{\circ}{m}$, ρ) $\leftarrow$ Sim(j, m, ADM, MOD, $\underline{\sigma}$) and returns ($\overset{\circ}{m}$, ρ).

Ch(i, j, (m$_0$, ADM$_0$, MOD$_0$), (m$_1$, ADM$_1$, MOD$_1$), b): This oracle runs $\sigma_c \leftarrow$ Sign(gsk$_i$, m$_c$, ADM$_c$), ($\overset{\circ}{m}_c$, ρ_c) $\leftarrow$ Redact(vpk$_j$, m$_c$, σ_c, MOD$_c$), for $c \in \{0, 1\}$. If $\overset{\circ}{m}_0 \neq \overset{\circ}{m}_1 \vee$ A$\overset{\circ}{D}$M$_0 \neq$ A$\overset{\circ}{D}$M$_1$, it returns $\perp$ and ($\overset{\circ}{m}_b$, $\underline{\sigma}_b$, ρ_b) otherwise.[4]

The environment stores the oracle queries in lists. In analogy to the oracle labels, we use $\mathcal{Q}^{\mathsf{Key}}$, $\mathcal{Q}^{\mathsf{DVGen}}$, $\mathcal{Q}^{\mathsf{DVKey}}$, $\mathcal{Q}^{\mathsf{Sig}}$, $\mathcal{Q}^{\mathsf{Open}}$, $\mathcal{Q}^{\mathsf{Sim}}$, $\mathcal{Q}^{\mathsf{RoS}}$, and $\mathcal{Q}^{\mathsf{Ch}}$ to denote them.

Security Notions. We require AD-RS to be correct, group unforgeable, designated-verifier unforgeable, simulatable, signer anonymous, and private.

Correctness guarantees that all honestly computed signatures verify correctly.

Formally, we require that for all $\kappa \in \mathbb{N}$, for all $n \in \mathbb{N}$, for all (gpk, gok, gsk) $\leftarrow$ Setup(1^κ, n), for all (vsk$_j$, vpk$_j$) $\leftarrow$ DVGen(1^κ), for all (vsk$_\ell$, vpk$_\ell$) $\leftarrow$ DVGen(1^κ), for all (m, ADM, MOD) where MOD $\preceq$ ADM $\wedge$ ADM $\preceq$ m, for all (m', ADM', MOD') where MOD' $\preceq$ ADM' $\wedge$ ADM' $\preceq$ m' for all $i \in [n]$, for all $\sigma = (\underline{\sigma}, \overline{\sigma}) \leftarrow$ Sign(gsk$_i$, m, ADM), for all $u \leftarrow$ Open(gok, m, σ), for all ($\overset{\circ}{m}$, ρ) $\leftarrow$ Redact(gpk, vpk$_j$, m, σ, MOD), for all

---

[4] Here A$\overset{\circ}{D}$M$_0$ and A$\overset{\circ}{D}$M$_1$ are derived from ADM$_0$ and ADM$_1$ with respect to MOD$_0$ and MOD$_1$.

$(\mathring{\mathsf{m}}', \rho') \leftarrow \mathsf{Sim}(\mathsf{gpk}, \mathsf{vsk}_\ell, \mathsf{m}', \mathrm{ADM}', \mathrm{MOD}', \underline{\sigma})$, it holds with overwhelming probability that $\mathsf{GVerify}(\mathsf{gpk}, \mathsf{m}, \sigma) = 1 \ \wedge \ i = u \ \wedge \ \mathsf{Verify}(\mathsf{gpk}, \mathsf{vpk}_j, \mathring{\mathsf{m}}, \rho) = 1 \ \wedge \ \mathsf{Verify}$ $(\mathsf{gpk}, \mathsf{vpk}_\ell, \mathring{\mathsf{m}}', \rho') = 1$ and that $\mathring{\mathsf{m}} \xleftarrow{\text{MOD}} \mathsf{m} \ \wedge \ \mathring{\mathsf{m}}' \xleftarrow{\text{MOD}'} \mathsf{m}'$.

Group unforgeability captures the intuition that the only way of obtaining valid signatures on messages is by applying "allowed" modifications to messages which were initially signed by a group member. Moreover, this property guarantees that every valid signature can be linked to the original signer by some authority.

Technically, the definition captures the traceability property of group signatures while simultaneously taking the malleability of RS into account.

Definition 8. *An* AD-RS *is group unforgeable, if for all PPT adversaries $\mathcal{A}$ there is a negligible function $\varepsilon(\cdot)$ such that*

$$\Pr \begin{bmatrix} (\mathsf{gpk}, \mathsf{gok}, \mathsf{gsk}) \leftarrow \mathsf{Setup}(1^\kappa, n), \\ \mathcal{O} \leftarrow \{\mathsf{Sig}(\cdot, \cdot, \cdot), \mathsf{Key}(\cdot)\}, \\ (\mathsf{m}^\star, \sigma^\star) \leftarrow \mathcal{A}^\mathcal{O}(\mathsf{gpk}, \mathsf{gok}), \\ u \leftarrow \mathsf{Open}(\mathsf{gok}, \mathsf{m}^\star, \sigma^\star) \end{bmatrix} : \begin{matrix} \mathsf{GVerify}(\mathsf{gpk}, \mathsf{m}^\star, \sigma^\star) = 1 \ \wedge \\ (u = \bot \ \vee \ (u \notin \mathcal{Q}^{\mathsf{Key}} \ \wedge \\ \nexists (u, \mathsf{m}, \mathrm{ADM}) \in \mathcal{Q}^{\mathsf{Sig}} : \mathsf{m}^\star \overset{\text{ADM}}{\preceq} \mathsf{m})) \end{matrix} \end{bmatrix} \leq \varepsilon(\kappa).$$

Designated-verifier unforgeability models the requirement that a designated-verifier signature can only be obtained in two ways: either by correctly redacting a signature (which can be done by everybody having access to the latter), or by having access to the secret key of the designated verifier. The former option would be chosen whenever a signature is to be legitimately forwarded to a receiver, while the latter enables the designated verifier to fake signatures.

Together with the previous definition, designated-verifier unforgeability guarantees that no adversary can come up with a designated-verifier signature for a foreign public key: by Definition 8 it is infeasible to forge a signature—and Definition 9 states that the only way of generating a designated-verifier signature for somebody else is to know a valid signature to start from.

Definition 9. *An* AD-RS *is designated-verifier unforgeable, if there exists a PPT opener $\mathsf{O} = (O_1, O_2)$ such that for every PPT adversary $\mathcal{A}$ there is a negligible function $\varepsilon_1(\cdot)$ such that*

$$\left| \begin{matrix} \Pr\left[(\mathsf{gpk}, \mathsf{gok}, \mathsf{gsk}) \leftarrow \mathsf{Setup}(1^\kappa, n) : \mathcal{A}(\mathsf{gpk}, \mathsf{gok}, \mathsf{gsk}) = 1\right] \ - \\ \Pr\left[(\mathsf{gpk}, \mathsf{gok}, \mathsf{gsk}, \tau) \leftarrow O_1(1^\kappa, n) : \mathcal{A}(\mathsf{gpk}, \mathsf{gok}, \mathsf{gsk}) = 1\right] \end{matrix} \right| \leq \varepsilon_1(\kappa),$$

and for every PPT adversary $\mathcal{A}$ there is a negligible function $\varepsilon_2(\cdot)$ such that

$$\Pr \begin{bmatrix} (\mathsf{gpk}, \mathsf{gok}, \mathsf{gsk}, \tau) \leftarrow O_1(1^\kappa, n), \\ \mathcal{O} \leftarrow \{\mathsf{Sig}(\cdot, \cdot, \cdot), \mathsf{Key}(\cdot), \\ \mathsf{DVGen}(\cdot), \mathsf{DVKey}(\cdot), \\ \mathsf{Sim}(\cdot, \cdot, \cdot, \cdot, \cdot)\}, \\ (\mathsf{m}^\star, \rho^\star, v^\star) \leftarrow \mathcal{A}^\mathcal{O}(\mathsf{gpk}, \mathsf{gok}), \\ u \leftarrow O_2(\tau, \mathsf{DVK}, \mathsf{m}^\star, \rho^\star, v^\star) \end{bmatrix} : \begin{matrix} \mathsf{Verify}(\mathsf{gpk}, \mathsf{vpk}_{v^\star}, \mathsf{m}^\star, \rho^\star) = 1 \ \wedge \\ v^\star \notin \mathcal{Q}^{\mathsf{DVKey}} \ \wedge \\ \wedge \ (u = \bot \ \vee \ (u \notin \mathcal{Q}^{\mathsf{Key}} \ \wedge \\ \nexists (u, \mathsf{m}, \mathrm{ADM}) \in \mathcal{Q}^{\mathsf{Sig}} : \mathsf{m}^\star \overset{\text{ADM}}{\preceq} \mathsf{m})) \ \wedge \\ \nexists (v^\star, \mathsf{m}, \mathrm{ADM}, \cdot, \cdot) \in \mathcal{Q}^{\mathsf{Sim}} : \mathsf{m}^\star \overset{\text{ADM}}{\preceq} \mathsf{m}) \end{matrix} \end{bmatrix} \leq \varepsilon_2(\kappa).$$

In our definition, we assume a simple key registration for designated verifiers to ensure that all designated-verifier key pairs have been honestly created and thus an adversary is not able to mount rogue key attacks. In practice, this requirement can often be alleviated by introducing an option to check the honest generation of the keys (cf. [23]), which we omit for simplicity.

Simulatability captures that designated verifiers can simulate signatures on arbitrary messages which are indistinguishable from honestly computed signatures.

Definition 10. *An* AD-RS *satisfies the simulatability property, if for all PPT adversaries $\mathcal{A}$ there is a negligible function $\varepsilon(\cdot)$ such that it holds that*

$$\Pr\left[\begin{array}{l} (\mathsf{gpk}, \mathsf{gok}, \mathsf{gsk}) \leftarrow \mathsf{Setup}(1^\kappa, n),\ b \xleftarrow{R} \{0,1\}, \\ \mathcal{O} \leftarrow \{\mathsf{DVGen}(\cdot), \mathsf{DVKey}(\cdot)\}, \\ ((\mathsf{m}_0, \mathsf{ADM}_0, \mathsf{MOD}_0), (\mathsf{m}_1, \mathsf{ADM}_1), \\ i^*, j^*, \mathsf{st}) \leftarrow \mathcal{A}^{\mathcal{O}}(\mathsf{gpk}, \mathsf{gok}, \mathsf{gsk}), \\ \sigma = (\underline{\sigma}, \overline{\sigma}) \leftarrow \mathsf{Sign}(\mathsf{gsk}_{i^*}, \mathsf{m}_b, \mathsf{ADM}_b), \\ (\mathring{\mathsf{m}}_0, \rho) \leftarrow \mathsf{RoS}(b, j^*, \mathsf{m}_0, \mathsf{ADM}_0, \mathsf{MOD}_0, \sigma), \\ b^* \leftarrow \mathcal{A}^{\mathcal{O}}(\underline{\sigma}, \mathring{\mathsf{m}}_0, \rho, \mathsf{st}) \end{array} : \begin{array}{c} b = b^* \wedge \\ \mathsf{ADM}_0 \preceq \mathsf{m}_0 \wedge \\ \mathsf{ADM}_1 \preceq \mathsf{m}_1 \end{array}\right] \leq 1/2 + \epsilon(\kappa).$$

As mentioned earlier, we assume that signatures consist of a private and a public component (the latter being denoted by $\underline{\sigma}$). To eliminate potential privacy issues associated with a public $\underline{\sigma}$, we also give $\underline{\sigma}$ as input to the simulator and the adversary, and require that the adversary cannot tell real and faked signatures apart *even when knowing $\underline{\sigma}$*. This way, our definitional framework guarantees that these parts do not contain any sensitive information.

In a realization of the system, the public parts of all signatures issued by the hospital would be made publicly available (without further meta-information).

Signer anonymity requires that only the opening authority can determine the identity of a signer.

Definition 11. *An* AD-RS *is signer anonymous, if for all PPT adversaries $\mathcal{A}$ there is a negligible function $\varepsilon(\cdot)$ such that*

$$\Pr\left[\begin{array}{l} (\mathsf{gpk}, \mathsf{gok}, \mathsf{gsk}) \leftarrow \mathsf{Setup}(1^\kappa, n), \\ b \xleftarrow{R} \{0,1\}, \mathcal{O} \leftarrow \{\mathsf{Open}(\cdot, \cdot)\}, \\ (i_0^*, i_1^*, \mathsf{m}^*, \mathsf{ADM}^*, \mathsf{st}) \leftarrow \mathcal{A}^{\mathcal{O}}(\mathsf{gpk}, \mathsf{gsk}), \\ \sigma \leftarrow \mathsf{Sign}(\mathsf{gsk}_{i_b^*}, \mathsf{m}^*, \mathsf{ADM}^*), \\ b^* \leftarrow \mathcal{A}^{\mathcal{O}}(\sigma, \mathsf{st}) \end{array} : \begin{array}{c} b = b^* \wedge \\ \nexists (\mathsf{m}, (\underline{\sigma}, \cdot)) \in \mathcal{Q}_2^{\mathsf{Open}} : \\ \mathsf{m} \stackrel{\mathsf{ADM}}{\preceq} \mathsf{m}^* \end{array}\right] \leq 1/2 + \varepsilon(\kappa),$$

and $\mathcal{A}$ runs in two stages and $\mathcal{Q}_2^{\mathsf{Open}}$ records queries to oracle Open *in stage two.*

The definition guarantees that—no matter how many signatures already have been opened—the signers' identities for all other signatures remain secret. The formulation is, up to the last clause of the winning condition, similar to the anonymity definition of group signature schemes (cf. Definition 5). We, however, need to adapt the last clause because Definition 5 requires signatures to be non-malleable. In contrast, our signatures are malleable by definition. However, we can still require parts of the signature, and in particular the public part, to be non-malleable. By doing so, we can achieve a strong notion that resembles anonymity in the sense of group signatures whenever honestly generated signatures have different public components with overwhelming probability. This is in particular the case for our instantiations provided in the next sections.

Privacy guarantees that a redacted designated-verifier signature does not leak anything about the blacked-out parts of the original message.

Definition 12. *An* AD-RS *is private, if for all PPT adversaries $\mathcal{A}$ there is a negligible function $\varepsilon(\cdot)$ such that*

$$\Pr\left[\begin{array}{l}(\mathsf{gpk},\mathsf{gok},\mathsf{gsk}) \leftarrow \mathsf{Setup}(1^{\kappa}, n),\ \ b \xleftarrow{R} \{0,1\},\\ \mathcal{O} \leftarrow \{\mathsf{Sig}(\cdot,\cdot,\cdot),\mathsf{Ch}(\cdot,\cdot,\cdot,\cdot,b)\},\\ b^{*} \leftarrow \mathcal{A}^{\mathcal{O}}(\mathsf{gpk},\mathsf{gok},\mathsf{gsk})\end{array} : b = b^{*}\right] \leq 1/2 + \varepsilon(\kappa).$$

We call an AD-RS *secure*, if it is correct, group unforgeable, designated-verifier unforgeable, simulatable, signer anonymous, and private.

Group Redactable Signatures. When omitting the DV-related notions and oracles, one directly obtains a definition of group redactable signatures, which may also be useful for applications that require revocable signer-anonymity.

4   A Generic Construction

Now we present a simple generic construction which can be built by combining any GS, any RS, and any Π that admits proofs of knowledge in a black-box way. In Scheme 1 we present our construction which follows the intuition given in the introduction. We use Π to prove knowledge of a witness for the following **NP** relation R required by the verification of designated-verifier signatures.

$$((\mathsf{m},\mathsf{pk},\mathsf{vpk}_j),\ (\sigma_{\mathsf{R}},\sigma_{\mathsf{V}})) \in R \iff$$
$$\mathsf{RS.Verify}(\mathsf{pk},\mathsf{m},\sigma_{\mathsf{R}}) = 1 \ \lor \ \Sigma.\mathsf{Verify}(\ vpk_j,\mathsf{m},\sigma_{\mathsf{V}}) = 1.$$

The rationale behind choosing R in this way is that this yields the most general result. That is, no further assumptions on RS or Σ are required.

Theorem 1 (proven in the extended version). *If* GS, RS, *and* Σ *are secure and* Π *is witness indistinguishable and admits proofs of knowledge, then Scheme 1 is secure.*

For an instantiation of our construction we can use standard GS and standard RS, where multiple practically efficient instantiations exist. Thus, the time required for signature creation/verification is mainly determined by the cost of the proof of knowledge of the RS signature σ_{R}. We, however, want to emphasize that—depending on the concrete RS—this proof can usually be instantiated by means of relatively cheap Σ-protocols. Ultimately, as we will show below, we can replace this proof with a much cheaper proof by exploiting properties of the used RS.

$\mathsf{Setup}(1^\kappa, n)$: Run $(\mathsf{gpk}, \mathsf{gok}, \mathsf{gsk}) \leftarrow \mathsf{GS.KeyGen}(1^\kappa, n)$, $\mathsf{crs} \leftarrow \Pi.\mathsf{Setup}(1^\kappa)$, set $\mathsf{gpk}' \leftarrow (\mathsf{gpk}, \mathsf{crs})$ and return $(\mathsf{gpk}', \mathsf{gok}, \mathsf{gsk})$.

$\mathsf{DVGen}(1^\kappa)$: Run $(\mathsf{vsk}_j, \mathsf{vpk}_j) \leftarrow \Sigma.\mathsf{KeyGen}(1^\kappa)$ and return $(\mathsf{vsk}_j, \mathsf{vpk}_j)$.

$\mathsf{Sign}(\mathsf{gsk}_i, \mathsf{m}, \mathsf{ADM})$: Run $(\mathsf{sk}, \mathsf{pk}) \leftarrow \mathsf{RS.KeyGen}(1^\kappa)$ and return $\sigma = (\underline{\sigma}, \overline{\sigma}) \leftarrow ((\mathsf{pk}, \sigma_\mathsf{G}),$ $(\sigma_\mathsf{R}, \mathsf{RED}))$, with

$$\sigma_\mathsf{G} \leftarrow \mathsf{GS.Sign}(\mathsf{gsk}_i, \mathsf{pk}), \text{ and } ((\mathsf{m}, \sigma_\mathsf{R}), \mathsf{RED}) \leftarrow \mathsf{RS.Sign}(\mathsf{sk}, \mathsf{m}, \mathsf{ADM}).$$

$\mathsf{GVerify}(\mathsf{gpk}, \mathsf{m}, \sigma)$: Parse σ as $((\mathsf{pk}, \sigma_\mathsf{G}), (\sigma_\mathsf{R}, \cdot))$ and return 1 if the following holds and 0 otherwise:

$$\mathsf{GS.Verify}(\mathsf{gpk}, \mathsf{pk}, \sigma_\mathsf{G}) = 1 \quad \wedge \quad \mathsf{RS.Verify}(\mathsf{pk}, \mathsf{m}, \sigma_\mathsf{R}) = 1.$$

$\mathsf{Open}(\mathsf{gok}, \mathsf{m}, \sigma)$: Parse σ as $((\mathsf{pk}, \sigma_\mathsf{G}), \overline{\sigma})$ and return $\mathsf{GS.Open}(\mathsf{gok}, \mathsf{pk}, \sigma_\mathsf{G})$.

$\mathsf{Redact}(\mathsf{gpk}, \mathsf{vpk}_j, \mathsf{m}, \sigma, \mathsf{MOD})$: Parse σ as $((\mathsf{pk}, \sigma_\mathsf{G}), (\sigma_\mathsf{R}, \mathsf{RED}))$ and return $(\mathring{\mathsf{m}}, \rho)$, where

$$((\mathring{\mathsf{m}}, \mathring{\sigma}_\mathsf{R}), \cdot) \leftarrow \mathsf{RS.Redact}(\mathsf{pk}, \mathsf{m}, \sigma_\mathsf{R}, \mathsf{MOD}, \mathsf{RED}),$$
$$\pi \leftarrow \Pi.\mathsf{Proof}(\mathsf{crs}, (\mathring{\mathsf{m}}, \mathsf{pk}, \mathsf{vpk}_j), (\mathring{\sigma}_\mathsf{R}, \bot)), \text{ and }$$
$$\rho \leftarrow ((\mathsf{pk}, \sigma_\mathsf{G}), \pi).$$

$\mathsf{Verify}(\mathsf{gpk}, \mathsf{vpk}_j, \mathsf{m}, \rho)$: Parse ρ as $((\mathsf{pk}, \sigma_\mathsf{G}), \pi)$ and return 1 if the following holds, and 0 otherwise:

$$\mathsf{GS.Verify}(\mathsf{gpk}, \mathsf{pk}, \sigma_\mathsf{G}) = 1 \quad \wedge \quad \Pi.\mathsf{Verify}(\mathsf{crs}, (\mathsf{m}, \mathsf{pk}, \mathsf{vpk}_j), \pi) = 1.$$

$\mathsf{Sim}(\mathsf{gpk}, \mathsf{vsk}_j, \mathsf{m}, \mathsf{ADM}, \mathsf{MOD}, \underline{\sigma})$: If $\mathsf{MOD} \preceq \mathsf{ADM} \wedge \mathsf{ADM} \preceq \mathsf{m}$, parse $\underline{\sigma}$ as $(\mathsf{pk}, \sigma_\mathsf{G})$, run $\mathring{\mathsf{m}} \xleftarrow{\mathsf{MOD}} \mathsf{m}$, and return $(\mathring{\mathsf{m}}, \rho)$, where

$$\sigma_\mathsf{V} \leftarrow \Sigma.\mathsf{Sign}(\mathsf{vsk}_j, \mathring{\mathsf{m}}),$$
$$\pi \leftarrow \Pi.\mathsf{Proof}(\mathsf{crs}, (\mathring{\mathsf{m}}, \mathsf{pk}, \mathsf{vpk}_j), (\bot, \sigma_\mathsf{V})), \text{ and }$$
$$\rho \leftarrow (\underline{\sigma}, \pi).$$

Otherwise, return $\bot$.

Scheme 1. Black-Box AD-RS

5 Boosting Efficiency via Key-Homomorphisms

In [13] it is shown that RS can be generically constructed from any EUF-CMA secure signature scheme and indistinguishable accumulators [12]. In our setting it is most reasonable to consider messages as an (ordered) sequence of message blocks. A straight forward solution would thus be to build upon [13, Scheme 2], which is tailored to signing ordered sequences of messages $\mathsf{m} = (m_1, \ldots, m_n)$. Unfortunately, this construction aims to conceal the number of message blocks in the original message, and the positions of the redactions. This can be dangerous in our setting, since it might allow to completely change the document semantics. Besides that, it inherently requires a more complex construction.

To this end, we pursue a different direction and require another message representation: we make the position i of the message blocks m_i in the message explicit and represent messages as sets $\mathsf{m} = \{1\|m_1, \ldots, n\|m_n\}$. Besides solving the aforementioned issues, it also allows us to build upon the (simpler) RS paradigm for sets [13, Scheme 1]. This paradigm subsumes the essence of many existing RSs and works as follows. Secret keys, public keys, and signatures are split into two parts each. One corresponds to the signature scheme Σ, and one corresponds to the accumulator Λ. Then, Λ is used to encode the message, whereas Σ is used to sign the encoded message. Consequently, we can look at RS key pairs and signatures as being of the form $(\mathsf{sk}, \mathsf{pk}) = ((\mathsf{sk}_\Sigma, \mathsf{sk}_\Lambda, \mathsf{pk}_\Lambda), (\mathsf{pk}_\Sigma, \mathsf{pk}_\Lambda))$ and $\sigma_R = (\sigma_\Sigma, \sigma_\Lambda)$ where the indexes denote their respective types. We emphasize that for accumulators it holds by definition that sk_Λ is an optional trapdoor which may enable more efficient computations, but all algorithms also run without sk_Λ and the output distribution of the algorithms does not depend on whether the algorithms are executed with or without sk_Λ [12,13]. We require this property to be able to create designated verifier signatures (cf. Sim) and use $(\mathsf{sk}_\Sigma, \bot, \mathsf{pk}_\Lambda)$ to denote an RS secret key without sk_Λ.

RS following this paradigm only require Σ (besides correctness) to be EUF-CMA secure. We observe that additional constraints on Σ—and in particular the key-homomorphism as we define it below—does not influence RS security, while it enables us to design the relation R such that it admits very efficient proofs.

Key-Homomorphic Signatures. Informally, we require signature schemes where, for a given public key and a valid signature under that key, one can adapt the public key and the signature so that the resulting signature is valid with respect to the initial message under the new public key. Moreover, adapted signatures need to be identically distributed as fresh signatures under the secret key corresponding to the adapted public key.

Key-malleability in the sense of adapting given signatures to other signatures under related keys has so far mainly been studied in context of related-key attacks (RKAs) [2], where one aims to rule out such constructions. Signatures with re-randomizable keys which allow to consistently update secret and public keys, but without considering adaption of existing signatures, have recently been introduced and studied in [16]. As we are not aware of any constructive use of and definitions for the functionality we require, we define key-homomorphic signatures inspired by key-homomorphic symmetric encryption (cf. [1]).

Let $\Sigma = (\mathsf{KeyGen}, \mathsf{Sign}, \mathsf{Verify})$ be an EUF-CMA secure signature scheme where the secret and public keys live in groups $(\mathbb{H}, +)$ and $(\mathbb{G}, \cdot)$, respectively. Inspired by the definition for encryption schemes in [28], we define the following.

Definition 13 (Secret-Key to Public-Key Homomorphism). *A signature scheme Σ provides a secret-key to public-key homomorphism, if there exists an efficiently computable map $\mu : \mathbb{H} \to \mathbb{G}$ such that for all $\mathsf{sk}, \mathsf{sk}' \in \mathbb{H}$ it holds that $\mu(\mathsf{sk} + \mathsf{sk}') = \mu(\mathsf{sk}) \cdot \mu(\mathsf{sk}')$, and for all $(\mathsf{sk}, \mathsf{pk})$ output by KeyGen, it holds that $\mathsf{pk} = \mu(\mathsf{sk})$.*

Now, we define key-homomorphic signatures, where we focus on the class of functions Φ^+ representing linear shifts. We stress that Φ^+ is a finite set of functions, all with the same domain and range, and, in our case depends on the public key of the signature scheme (which is not made explicit). Moreover, Φ^+ admits an efficient membership test and its functions are efficiently computable.

Definition 14 (Φ^+-Key-Homomorphic Signatures). *A signature scheme is called Φ^+-key-homomorphic, if it provides a secret-key to public-key homomorphism and an additional PPT algorithm* Adapt, *defined as:*

Adapt(pk, m, σ, Δ): *Takes a public key* pk, *a message* m, *a signature* σ, *and a function $\Delta \in \Phi^+$ as input, and outputs a public key* pk$'$ *and a signature* σ',

where for all $\Delta \in \Phi^+$, all (sk, pk) $\leftarrow$ KeyGen(1^κ), *all messages* m, *all* $\sigma \leftarrow$ Sign(sk, m), *all* (pk$'$, σ') $\leftarrow$ Adapt(pk, m, σ, Δ) *it holds that* Verify(pk$'$, m, σ') = 1 *and* pk$'$ = Δ(pk).

For simplicity we sometimes identify a function $\Delta \in \Phi^+$ with its "shift amount" $\Delta \in \mathbb{H}$. To model that freshly generated signatures look identical as adapted signatures on the same message, we introduce the following additional property.

Definition 15 (Adaptability of Signatures). *A Φ^+-key-homomorphic signature scheme provides adaptability of signatures, if for every $\kappa \in \mathbb{N}$, and every message* m, *it holds that* Adapt(pk, m, Sign(sk, m), Δ) *and* (pk $\cdot$ $\mu(\Delta)$, Sign(sk $+$ Δ, m)) *as well as* (sk, pk) *and* (sk$'$, $\mu(\text{sk}')$) *are identically distributed, where* (sk, pk) $\leftarrow$ KeyGen(1^κ), sk$'$ $\overset{R}{\leftarrow}$ $\mathbb{H}$, *and* $\Delta \overset{R}{\leftarrow} \Phi^+$.

For an in-depth treatment and examples of key-homomorphic signatures, we refer the reader to a more recent work [14]. The important bottom-line here is that there are various efficient schemes that satisfy Definition 15. For instance, Schnorr signatures [24], BLS signatures [5], the recent scheme by Pointcheval and Sanders [22] or Waters signatures [30].

Φ^+-Key-Homomorphic Redactable Signature Schemes. When instantiating the RS construction paradigm from [13] (as outlined above) with a Φ^+-key-homomorphic signature scheme, the key homomorphism of the signature scheme straight-forwardly carries over to the RS and we can define Adapt as follows.

Adapt(pk, m, σ, Δ): Parse pk as (pk$_\Sigma$, pk$_\Lambda$) and σ as (σ_Σ, σ_Λ), run (pk$'_\Sigma$, σ'_Σ) $\leftarrow$ Adapt(pk$_\Sigma$, Λ(m), σ_Σ, Δ) and return (pk$'$, σ') $\leftarrow$ ((pk$'_\Sigma$, pk$_\Lambda$), (σ'_Σ, σ_Λ)).

This allows us to concisely present our construction in Scheme 2. The **NP** relation, which needs to be satisfied by valid designated-verifier signatures is as follows.

$$((\text{pk}, \text{vpk}_j), (\text{sk}, \text{vsk}_j)) \in R \iff \text{pk} = \mu(\text{sk}) \lor \Sigma.\text{VKey}(\text{vsk}_j, \text{vpk}_j) = 1.$$

In the discrete logarithm setting such a proof requires an OR-Schnorr proof of two discrete logs, i.e., only requires *two group exponentiations*.

Theorem 2 (proven in the extended version). *If* GS *is secure,* RS *is an adaptable* RS *following [13, Scheme 1], Σ is secure, and Π is witness indistinguishable and admits proofs of knowledge, then Scheme 2 is also secure.*

$\mathsf{Redact}(\mathsf{gpk}, \mathsf{vpk}_j, \mathsf{m}, \sigma, \mathsf{MOD})$: Parse σ as $((\mathsf{pk}, \sigma_G), (\sigma_R, \mathsf{RED}))$ and return $(\mathring{\mathsf{m}}, \rho)$, where

$\quad\quad \mathsf{sk}' \xleftarrow{R} \mathbb{H}, \; \mathsf{pk}' \leftarrow \mu(\mathsf{sk}'), \; (\mathsf{pk}_R, \sigma'_R) \leftarrow \mathsf{Adapt}(\mathsf{pk}, \mathsf{m}, \sigma_R, \mathsf{sk}'),$

$\quad\quad ((\mathring{\mathsf{m}}, \mathring{\sigma}'_R), \cdot) \leftarrow \mathsf{RS}.\mathsf{Redact}(\mathsf{pk}_R, \mathsf{m}, \sigma'_R, \mathsf{MOD}, \mathsf{RED}),$

$\quad\quad \pi \leftarrow \Pi.\mathsf{Proot}(\mathsf{crs}, (\mathsf{pk}', \mathsf{vpk}_j), (\mathsf{sk}', \bot)), \text{ and } \rho \leftarrow ((\mathsf{pk}, \sigma_G), \mathsf{pk}', \mathring{\sigma}'_R, \pi)$

$\mathsf{Verify}(\mathsf{gpk}, \mathsf{vpk}_j, \mathsf{m}, \rho)$: Parse ρ as $((\mathsf{pk}, \sigma_G), \mathsf{pk}', \mathring{\sigma}'_R, \pi)$, let $\mathsf{pk} = (\mathsf{pk}_\Sigma, \mathsf{pk}_\Lambda)$, compute $\mathsf{pk}_R \leftarrow (\mathsf{pk}_\Sigma \cdot \mathsf{pk}', \mathsf{pk}_\Lambda)$ and return 1 if the following holds, and 0 otherwise:

$\quad\quad \mathsf{GS}.\mathsf{Verify}(\mathsf{gpk}, \mathsf{pk}, \sigma_G) = 1 \quad \wedge \quad \Pi.\mathsf{Verify}(\mathsf{crs}, (\mathsf{pk}', \mathsf{vpk}_j), \pi) = 1$

$\quad\quad\quad\quad\quad \wedge \quad \mathsf{RS}.\mathsf{Verify}(\mathsf{pk}_R, \mathsf{m}, \mathring{\sigma}'_R) = 1.$

$\mathsf{Sim}(\mathsf{gpk}, \mathsf{vsk}_j, \mathsf{m}, \mathsf{ADM}, \mathsf{MOD}, \underline{\sigma})$: If $\mathsf{MOD} \preceq \mathsf{ADM} \; \wedge \; \mathsf{ADM} \preceq \mathsf{m}$, parse $\underline{\sigma}$ as $((\mathsf{pk}_\Sigma, \mathsf{pk}_\Lambda), \sigma_G)$ and return $(\mathring{\mathsf{m}}, \rho)$, where

$\quad\quad \mathsf{sk}_R^\Sigma \xleftarrow{R} \mathbb{H}, \; \mathsf{pk}_R^\Sigma \leftarrow \mu(\mathsf{sk}_R^\Sigma), \; \mathsf{pk}' \leftarrow \mathsf{pk}_\Sigma^{-1} \cdot \mathsf{pk}_R^\Sigma,$

$\quad\quad ((\mathsf{m}, \sigma'_R), \mathsf{RED}) \leftarrow \mathsf{RS}.\mathsf{Sign}((\mathsf{sk}_R^\Sigma, \bot, \mathsf{pk}_\Lambda), \mathsf{m}, \mathsf{ADM}),$

$\quad\quad ((\mathring{\mathsf{m}}, \mathring{\sigma}'_R), \cdot) \leftarrow \mathsf{RS}.\mathsf{Redact}((\mathsf{pk}_R^\Sigma, \mathsf{pk}_\Lambda), \mathsf{m}, \sigma'_R, \mathsf{MOD}, \mathsf{RED}),$

$\quad\quad \pi \leftarrow \Pi.\mathsf{Proof}(\mathsf{crs}, (\mathsf{pk}', \mathsf{vpk}_j), (\bot, \mathsf{vsk}_j)), \text{ and } \rho \leftarrow (\underline{\sigma}, \mathsf{pk}', \mathring{\sigma}'_R, \pi).$

Scheme 2. Semi-Black-Box AD-RS where Setup, DVGen, Sign, GVerify, and Open are as in Scheme 1.

6   Conclusion

We introduce the notion of signer-anonymous designated-verifier redactable signatures, extending redactable signatures in their vanilla form in several important directions. These additional features are motivated by a real world use-case in the health care field, demonstrating its practical relevance. Besides rigorously modelling this primitive, we provide two instantiations. While both are interesting from a theoretical point of view, the latter is also interesting in practice. In particular, due to using key-homomorphic signatures as we introduce them in this paper, we obtain a simple and practically efficient solution (a performance analysis confirming the practical efficiency is provided in the extended version).

References

1. Applebaum, B., Harnik, D., Ishai, Y.: Semantic security under related-key attacks and applications. In: ICS (2011)
2. Bellare, M., Cash, D., Miller, R.: Cryptography secure against related-key attacks and tampering. In: Lee, D.H., Wang, X. (eds.) ASIACRYPT 2011. LNCS, vol. 7073, pp. 486–503. Springer, Heidelberg (2011). doi:10.1007/978-3-642-25385-0_26
3. Bellare, M., Micciancio, D., Warinschi, B.: Foundations of group signatures: formal definitions, simplified requirements, and a construction based on general assumptions. In: Biham, E. (ed.) EUROCRYPT 2003. LNCS, vol. 2656, pp. 614–629. Springer, Heidelberg (2003). doi:10.1007/3-540-39200-9_38
4. Bellare, M., Shi, H., Zhang, C.: Foundations of group signatures: the case of dynamic groups. In: Menezes, A. (ed.) CT-RSA 2005. LNCS, vol. 3376, pp. 136–153. Springer, Heidelberg (2005). doi:10.1007/978-3-540-30574-3_11

5. Boneh, D., Lynn, B., Shacham, H.: Short signatures from the weil pairing. J. Cryptology **17**(4), 297–319 (2004)
6. Brzuska, C., et al.: Redactable signatures for tree-structured data: definitions and constructions. In: Zhou, J., Yung, M. (eds.) ACNS 2010. LNCS, vol. 6123, pp. 87–104. Springer, Heidelberg (2010). doi:10.1007/978-3-642-13708-2_6
7. Brzuska, C., Fischlin, M., Lehmann, A., Schröder, D.: Unlinkability of sanitizable signatures. In: Nguyen, P.Q., Pointcheval, D. (eds.) PKC 2010. LNCS, vol. 6056, pp. 444–461. Springer, Heidelberg (2010). doi:10.1007/978-3-642-13013-7_26
8. Brzuska, C., Pöhls, H.C., Samelin, K.: Efficient and perfectly unlinkable sanitizable signatures without group signatures. In: Katsikas, S., Agudo, I. (eds.) EuroPKI 2013. LNCS, vol. 8341, pp. 12–30. Springer, Heidelberg (2014). doi:10.1007/978-3-642-53997-8_2
9. Camenisch, J., Dubovitskaya, M., Haralambiev, K., Kohlweiss, M.: Composable and modular anonymous credentials: definitions and practical constructions. In: Iwata, T., Cheon, J.H. (eds.) ASIACRYPT 2015. LNCS, vol. 9453, pp. 262–288. Springer, Heidelberg (2015). doi:10.1007/978-3-662-48800-3_11
10. Chaum, D.: Designated confirmer signatures. In: Santis, A. (ed.) EUROCRYPT 1994. LNCS, vol. 950, pp. 86–91. Springer, Heidelberg (1995). doi:10.1007/BFb0053427
11. Chaum, D., Antwerpen, H.: Undeniable signatures. In: Brassard, G. (ed.) CRYPTO 1989. LNCS, vol. 435, pp. 212–216. Springer, Heidelberg (1990). doi:10.1007/0-387-34805-0_20
12. Derler, D., Hanser, C., Slamanig, D.: Revisiting cryptographic accumulators, additional properties and relations to other primitives. In: Nyberg, K. (ed.) CT-RSA 2015. LNCS, vol. 9048, pp. 127–144. Springer, Heidelberg (2015). doi:10.1007/978-3-319-16715-2_7
13. Derler, D., Pöhls, H.C., Samelin, K., Slamanig, D.: A general framework for redactable signatures and new constructions. In: Kwon, S., Yun, A. (eds.) ICISC 2015. LNCS, vol. 9558, pp. 3–19. Springer, Heidelberg (2016). doi:10.1007/978-3-319-30840-1_1
14. Derler, D., Slamanig, D.: Key-homomorphic signatures and applications to multiparty signatures. IACR Cryptology ePrint Archive 2016, 792 (2016)
15. Fiat, A., Shamir, A.: How to prove yourself: practical solutions to identification and signature problems. In: Odlyzko, A.M. (ed.) CRYPTO 1986. LNCS, vol. 263, pp. 186–194. Springer, Heidelberg (1987). doi:10.1007/3-540-47721-7_12
16. Fleischhacker, N., Krupp, J., Malavolta, G., Schneider, J., Schröder, D., Simkin, M.: Efficient unlinkable sanitizable signatures from signatures with rerandomizable keys. In: Cheng, C.-M., Chung, K.-M., Persiano, G., Yang, B.-Y. (eds.) PKC 2016. LNCS, vol. 9614, pp. 301–330. Springer, Heidelberg (2016). doi:10.1007/978-3-662-49384-7_12
17. Jakobsson, M., Sako, K., Impagliazzo, R.: Designated verifier proofs and their applications. In: Maurer, U. (ed.) EUROCRYPT 1996. LNCS, vol. 1070, pp. 143–154. Springer, Heidelberg (1996). doi:10.1007/3-540-68339-9_13
18. Johnson, R., Molnar, D., Song, D., Wagner, D.: Homomorphic signature schemes. In: Preneel, B. (ed.) CT-RSA 2002. LNCS, vol. 2271, pp. 244–262. Springer, Heidelberg (2002). doi:10.1007/3-540-45760-7_17
19. Lipmaa, H., Wang, G., Bao, F.: Designated verifier signature schemes: attacks, new security notions and a new construction. In: Caires, L., Italiano, G.F., Monteiro, L., Palamidessi, C., Yung, M. (eds.) ICALP 2005. LNCS, vol. 3580, pp. 459–471. Springer, Heidelberg (2005). doi:10.1007/11523468_38

20. Monnerat, J., Pasini, S., Vaudenay, S.: Efficient deniable authentication for signatures. In: Abdalla, M., Pointcheval, D., Fouque, P.-A., Vergnaud, D. (eds.) ACNS 2009. LNCS, vol. 5536, pp. 272–291. Springer, Heidelberg (2009). doi:10.1007/978-3-642-01957-9_17
21. Pöhls, H.C., Samelin, K.: Accountable redactable signatures. In: ARES (2015)
22. Pointcheval, D., Sanders, O.: Short randomizable signatures. In: Sako, K. (ed.) CT-RSA 2016. LNCS, vol. 9610, pp. 111–126. Springer, Heidelberg (2016). doi:10.1007/978-3-319-29485-8_7
23. Ristenpart, T., Yilek, S.: The power of proofs-of-possession: securing multi-party signatures against rogue-key attacks. In: Naor, M. (ed.) EUROCRYPT 2007. LNCS, vol. 4515, pp. 228–245. Springer, Heidelberg (2007). doi:10.1007/978-3-540-72540-4_13
24. Schnorr, C.: Efficient signature generation by smart cards. J. Cryptology 4(3), 161–174 (1991)
25. Shahandashti, S.F., Safavi-Naini, R.: Construction of universal designated-verifier signatures and identity-based signatures from standard signatures. In: Cramer, R. (ed.) PKC 2008. LNCS, vol. 4939, pp. 121–140. Springer, Heidelberg (2008). doi:10.1007/978-3-540-78440-1_8
26. Steinfeld, R., Bull, L., Wang, H., Pieprzyk, J.: Universal designated-verifier signatures. In: Laih, C.-S. (ed.) ASIACRYPT 2003. LNCS, vol. 2894, pp. 523–542. Springer, Heidelberg (2003). doi:10.1007/978-3-540-40061-5_33
27. Steinfeld, R., Bull, L., Zheng, Y.: Content extraction signatures. In: Kim, K. (ed.) ICISC 2001. LNCS, vol. 2288, pp. 285–304. Springer, Heidelberg (2002). doi:10.1007/3-540-45861-1_22
28. Tessaro, S., Wilson, D.A.: Bounded-collusion identity-based encryption from semantically-secure public-key encryption: generic constructions with short ciphertexts. In: Krawczyk, H. (ed.) PKC 2014. LNCS, vol. 8383, pp. 257–274. Springer, Heidelberg (2014). doi:10.1007/978-3-642-54631-0_15
29. Vergnaud, D.: New extensions of pairing-based signatures into universal designated verifier signatures. In: Bugliesi, M., Preneel, B., Sassone, V., Wegener, I. (eds.) ICALP 2006. LNCS, vol. 4052, pp. 58–69. Springer, Heidelberg (2006). doi:10.1007/11787006_6
30. Waters, B.: Efficient identity-based encryption without random oracles. In: Cramer, R. (ed.) EUROCRYPT 2005. LNCS, vol. 3494, pp. 114–127. Springer, Heidelberg (2005). doi:10.1007/11426639_7

Group Signature with Deniability:
How to Disavow a Signature

Ai Ishida[1,2]([⊠]), Keita Emura[3], Goichiro Hanaoka[2], Yusuke Sakai[2],
and Keisuke Tanaka[1,4]

[1] Tokyo Institute of Technology, Tokyo, Japan
`ishida0@is.titech.ac.jp`
[2] AIST, Tokyo, Japan
[3] NICT, Tokyo, Japan
[4] JST CREST, Tokyo, Japan

Abstract. Group signatures are a class of digital signatures with
enhanced privacy. By using this type of signature, a user can sign a message on behalf of a specific group without revealing his identity, but in
the case of a dispute, an authority can expose the identity of the signer.
However, it is not always the case that we need to know the specific
identity of the signature. In this paper, we propose the notion of *deniable
group signature*, where the authority can issue a proof showing that the
specified user is NOT the signer of the signature, without revealing the
actual signer. We point out that existing efficient non-interactive zero-
knowledge proof systems cannot be straightforwardly applied to prove
such a statement. We circumvent this problem by giving a fairly practical construction through extending the Groth group signature scheme
(ASIACRYPT 2007). In particular, a denial proof in our scheme consists
of 96 group elements, which is about twice the size of a signature in the
Groth scheme. The proposed scheme is provably secure under the same
assumptions as those of the Groth scheme.

Keywords: Group signature · Deniability · Non-interactive zero-
knowledge proof · Bilinear map

1 Introduction

Background and Motivation. Anonymity is often required in various applications in which the users' personal information or privacy should be protected,
and a *group signature* scheme is one of the most popular cryptographic tools for
obtaining anonymity. By using a group signature, a user can generate digital
evidence (i.e., signature) which proves that he/she is a member of a specified

Y. Sakai—This author is supported by a JSPS Fellowship for Young Scientists.

K. Tanaka—A part of this work was supported by a grant of I-System Co. Ltd., NTT
Secure Platform Laboratories, Nomura Research Institute, Input Output Hongkong,
and MEXT/JSPS KAKENHI 16H01705.

© Springer International Publishing AG 2016
S. Foresti and G. Persiano (Eds.): CANS 2016, LNCS 10052, pp. 228–244, 2016.
DOI: 10.1007/978-3-319-48965-0_14

group without revealing his/her identity. Furthermore, if needed, an authority can extract the "embedded" identity from the above-mentioned signature and generate another digital evidence (i.e., opening proof) of this opening result. Therefore, in normal situations, users can anonymously prove their membership, and in the case of incidents (e.g., crimes), the identity of the actual signer can be revealed. Such a property seems quite useful for protecting the users' anonymity and tracing malicious users simultaneously. However, for some situations, this property is insufficient.

For example, assume that the police needs to know whether a suspect was in a specific building at the time of a crime, and the entrance and exit control for the building is managed using a group signature. A naive way to check this is to ask the authority (i.e., the manager of the building) to just reveal the signer identities of *all* signatures that were used for the authentication within that specified time period. This is what can be done by a standard group signature. Obviously, this results in a serious violation of the privacy of the innocent users who have entered the building in that time period.

One may think that traceable signature [16] can be employed for solving this problem. That is, one can check whether the suspect was in the building by using the token of the suspect. However, if the suspect was not in the building and this suspect is innocent, serious privacy violation of the suspect happens since the token can also be used for any signature generated at another time than that of the crime.

To avoid this situation, it is further required that the group signature scheme provides a functionality for generating yet another kind of digital evidence, which *only* proves that, for a given signature and identity of a suspect, the signer of the signature is NOT the suspect.

Our Contribution. In this paper, we describe the construction of a group signature that provides the above-mentioned functionality. In particular, we propose the notion of a *deniable group signature*, a method for designing it, and a concrete instantiation. In addition to *all* the functionalities of a standard group signature, a deniable group signature provides another functionality that the authority (i.e., opener) can generate a *denial proof* that proves non-ownership of a signature. In other words, in a deniable group signature, for a given signature and an identity of a user, the authority can generate a proof of the fact that the actual signer is NOT that particular user (if this is the case).

We first discuss the possibility of generically constructing such a group signature by extending the Bellare-Shi-Zhang technique [3] and clarify the main difficulty for designing practical instantiations. In particular, we point out that it is not straightforward to apply the Groth-Sahai proofs [14] for generating denial proofs. The problem here is to find a way to prove that a user j is not the actual signer i, i.e., $i \neq j$, but such kind of language is not covered with the Groth-Sahai proof. We overcome this problem and show a concrete deniable group signature scheme based on the (modified) Groth group signature [13,28] together with a dedicated technique for overcoming the above-mentioned difficulty.

The proposed scheme is provably secure in the standard model under the decisional linear (DLIN) assumption, q-strong Diffie-Hellman (q-SDH) assumption, q-U assumption, universal one-wayness of hash functions, and strong unforgeability of one-time signatures. The denial proof in the proposed scheme consists of nine commitments, four pairing product equations, and five multi-scalar multiplication equations. The total size is 96 group elements and is about twice the size of a group signature in the Groth scheme.

Related Work. Komano, Ohta, Shimbo, and Kawamura [19] pointed out that *"the ring signature scheme allows the signer to shift the blame to entities (victims) because of its anonymity,"* and proposed a deniable ring signature, where a verifier and a user run interactive confirm/disavow protocols and the user can insist that "I am the actual signer" (confirm) or "I am NOT the actual signer" (disavow). Komano et al.'s scheme is secure in the random oracle model, and later, Zeng et al. [30] proposed an improved scheme which is provably secure in the standard model. In deniable ring signatures, the *user* can claim that he is not the signer of the signature, while in the case of deniable group signatures, the *opener* can generate the proof of non-ownership of the signature. That is, in deniable group signatures, if all users except for a user collude, his anonymity is still guaranteed unless the opener is not corrupted by them, unlike in the case of deniable ring signatures.

As group signatures with additional functionality, group signatures with message-dependent opening (GS-MDO) [27] were considered in order to restrict the authority of the opener. In GS-MDO, the opener can open group signatures on specific signed messages, as decided by another authority called the admitter. In particular, an automated parking garage scenario was considered as an application of GS-MDO. In this case, a customer generates a group signature on the date he/she enters a garage, and if there is an accident (e.g., a person is murdered) in the garage, the opener opens all the signatures for the date of the accident to determine the customers present in the garage at the time of the accident. Again, if multiple customers enter the garage on the same date, then the false accusation problem occurs.

Abe et al. [1] considered non-snatching and undeniability in the traceable signature context, where no one (but the actual signer) can claim to be the signer of a signature, and no actual signer can deny being the signer of his signatures, respectively. Abe et al.'s traceable signature scheme, in addition to the opening and user tracing, allows the signer to claim non-ownership of a signature (as in the case of deniable ring signatures [19,30]) while in the case of deniable group signatures, the opener can generate the proof for non-ownership of a signature. That is, as we discussed about deniable ring signatures, a user's anonymity is not guaranteed if all users except for the user collude.

Lyuu and Wu [24] considered group undeniable signatures where a verifier and a group manager run an interactive protocol that can prove the validity/invalidity of signatures without compromising anonymity. To the contrary, deniable group signatures support the non-interactive verification.

Brickell et al. [8] proposed direct anonymous attestations (DAA), which can be seen as group signatures without the opening functionality. They introduced a tag, called basename, which enables to link signatures produced by the same user with the same basename. After that, Desmoulins et al. [10] introduced DAA with dependent basename opening (DAA-DBO), which is the extension of DAA. In these primitives, even if the user can simply use a different basename for each time to sign a message, he can only prove that he generated the signature by producing a new signature on the same message with the same basename. That is, he cannot prove that he did not generate the signature.

Recently, Blazy et al. [5] proposed group signatures with verifiable controllable linkability (VCL-GS), where a dedicated linking authority (LA) can determine whether two given signatures stem from the same signer without being able to identify the signer(s). Compared to group signatures with controllable linkability, VCL-GS does not require trusted LAs.

2   Preliminaries

In this section, we give definitions of building blocks of the modified Groth and our schemes and the decisional linear assumption which is used in the security proof of our scheme.

Bilinear Map. Bilinear groups are groups G and G_T with prime order p that have an efficiently computable bilinear map $e : G \times G \to G_T$. Let $\mathcal{G}(1^k)$ be a probabilistic polynomial time algorithm which outputs a group parameter $gk = (p, G, G_T, e, g)$ where k is a security parameter, p is the order of G and G_T, g is a generator of G, and e is a non-degenerate bilinear map $e : G \times G \to G_T$, i.e. $\forall a, b \in \mathbb{Z}, e(g^a, g^b) = e(g, g)^{ab}$ and $e(g, g) \neq 1$.

The Decisional Linear Assumption (DLIN Assumption). The decisional linear assumption was introduced [7]. The decisional linear assumption holds for $\mathcal{G}$, when it is hard to distinguish for randomly chosen group elements and exponents (f, g, h, f^r, g^s, h^t) whether $t = r + s$ or t is random.

Universal One-way Hash Function. A function family $\text{HashGen}(1^k)$ takes as input a security parameter k and outputs a function $\mathcal{H}$. The function $\mathcal{H}$ is said to be universal one-way when $\Pr[(x, s) \leftarrow \mathcal{A}(1^k); \mathcal{H} \leftarrow \text{HashGen}(1^k); x' \leftarrow \mathcal{A}(\mathcal{H}, s) : \mathcal{H}(x) = \mathcal{H}(x') \wedge x \neq x']$ is negligible for any polynomial time algorithm $\mathcal{A}$.

Strong One-time Signature. A signature scheme consists of three algorithms $(\text{KeyGen}, \text{Sign}, \text{Ver})$, which satisfy the following correctness condition: For any security parameter $k \in \mathbb{N}$, any message $m \in \{0, 1\}^*$, the condition $\text{Ver}_{vk}(m, \text{Sign}_{sk}(m)) = 1$ holds, where vk and sk are output by KeyGen as $(vk, sk) \leftarrow \text{KeyGen}(1^k)$. In this paper, we use a one-time signature scheme: a scheme secure against an adversary who mounts a single chosen message attack. The one-time signature is said to be strong, if the adversary cannot even create a different signature on the chosen message he already got signed. See [12] for a formal definition.

Non-interactive Proof. For a relation $R \in \{0,1\}^* \times \{0,1\}^*$ defining $L = \{x \mid (x,w) \in R \text{ for some } w\}$, a non-interactive proof system consists of three algorithms $(\mathsf{K}, \mathsf{P}, \mathsf{V})$ which satisfy the following correctness and soundness.

- Correctness: For any security parameter $k \in \mathbb{N}$, any common reference string $crs \leftarrow \mathsf{K}(1^k)$, and any pair $(x,w) \in R$, it holds $\mathsf{V}(crs, x, \mathsf{P}(crs, x, w)) = 1$.
- Soundness: For any security parameter $k \in \mathbb{N}$, any probabilistic polynomial time algorithm $\mathcal{A}$, the probability $\Pr[crs \leftarrow \mathsf{K}(1^k); (x,\pi) \leftarrow \mathcal{A}(crs) : \mathsf{V}(crs, x, \pi) = 1 \wedge x \notin L]$ is negligible.

Groth and Sahai introduced a framework for very efficient non-interactive proof for the satisfiability of relations in bilinear groups, including pairing product equations [14]. The proof system consists of algorithms $(\mathsf{K}_{\mathrm{NI}}, \mathsf{P}, \mathsf{V}, \mathsf{X})$. The algorithm $\mathsf{K}_{\mathrm{NI}}(gk)$ takes a group parameter gk as input and outputs (crs, xk) where crs is a common reference string and xk is an extraction key which can extract a witness from a proof. The algorithm $\mathsf{P}(crs, x, w)$ takes crs, an equation description x, and its witness w as input and outputs a proof π. This proof can be verified by running $\mathsf{V}(crs, x, \pi)$. The algorithm $\mathsf{X}_{xk}(crs, x, \pi)$ extracts a witness w from the proof π.

There are two types of the Groth-Sahai proof systems, $(\mathsf{K}_{\mathrm{NI}}, \mathsf{P}_{\mathrm{NIWI}}, \mathsf{V}_{\mathrm{NIWI}}, \mathsf{X}_{\mathrm{NIWI}})$ provides witness-indistinguishability and $(\mathsf{K}_{\mathrm{NI}}, \mathsf{P}_{\mathrm{NIZK}}, \mathsf{V}_{\mathrm{NIZK}}, \mathsf{X}_{\mathrm{NIZK}})$ provides zero-knowledge. The two types of proof can share a single common reference string. (Thus, multiple systems can use a common K_{NI}.) There exists a simulator that outputs a simulated common reference string crs and a trapdoor key tk. These simulated common reference strings are computationally indistinguishable from the common reference strings produced by K under the DLIN assumption. We say a proof system is perfect witness-indistinguishable, if, on a simulated common reference string, the proof π does not reveal anything about which witness was used by the prover when creating the proof. We say a proof system is perfect zero-knowledge, if there exists a simulator that produces a simulated proof and the simulated proof is perfectly indistinguishable from the proof which is produced by using a witness and a simulated common reference string.

In the Groth-Sahai proof system, to prove that committed variables satisfy a set of relations, the prover computes one commitment per variable and one proof element per relation. The non-interactive zero-knowledge (NIZK) proofs are available for pairing product equations, which are relations of the type $\prod_{i=1}^n e(\mathcal{A}_i, \mathcal{X}_i) \cdot \prod_{i=1}^n \prod_{j=1}^n e(\mathcal{X}_i, \mathcal{X}_j)^{a_{ij}} = t_T$ with $t_T = 1$ for variables $\mathcal{X}_1, \ldots, \mathcal{X}_n \in G$ and constants $\mathcal{A}_1, \ldots, \mathcal{A}_n \in G, a_{ij}$, for $i, j \in \{1, \ldots n\}$. Even if $t_T \neq 1$, still we can construct NIZK proofs if t_T can be decomposed to known base group elements $\tilde{g}, \hat{g} \in G$ such that $t_T = e(\tilde{g}, \hat{g})$. NIZK proofs also can be constructed for multi-scalar multiplication equations, which are of the form $\prod_{i=1}^m \mathcal{A}_i^{y_i} \cdot \prod_{j=1}^n \mathcal{X}_j^{b_j} \cdot \prod_{i=1}^m \prod_{j=1}^n \mathcal{X}_j^{y_i \gamma_{ij}} = T$ for variables $\mathcal{X}_1, \ldots, \mathcal{X}_n \in G, y_1, \ldots, y_m \in \mathbb{Z}_p$ and constants $T, \mathcal{A}_1, \ldots, \mathcal{A}_m \in G, b_1, \ldots, b_m \in \mathbb{Z}_p$, and $\gamma_{ij} \in G$, for $i \in \{1, \ldots, m\}$ and $j \in \{1, \ldots, n\}$. Here, we note that though the Groth-Sahai NIZK proof is efficient, it has a limitation of language. Especially, inequality statements (e.g., $a \neq b$) are not covered by the languages which can be proved by the Groth-Sahai NIZK proof. Also, as mentioned above, if a witness is a target group element, it needs to be decomposed into base group elements to apply the Groth-Sahai proof. However, it is hard because of the pairing inversion problem [11].

Kiltz' Tag-based Encryption. We will use Kiltz' construction of tag-based encryption [18], which is explained below. Let $gk = (p, G, G_T, e, g)$ be a group description. The key generation algorithm $G(1^k)$ chooses random integers $\zeta, \eta \leftarrow \mathbb{Z}_p$ and random elements $K, L \leftarrow G$, and sets the public key $pk = (F, H, K, L)$ where $F = g^\zeta$ and $H = g^\eta$ and the decryption key $dk = (\zeta, \eta)$. The encryption algorithm $E_{pk}(t, m)$ outputs $y = (y_1, y_2, y_3, y_4, y_5) = (F^r, H^s, mg^{r+s}, (g^t K)^r, (g^t L)^s)$ where m is a plaintext, t is a tag, and r, s are randomness. The validity of the ciphertext is publicly verifiable by checking the two equations $e(F, y_4) = e(y_1, g^t K)$ and $e(H, y_5) = e(y_2, g^t L)$. Here, let $\mathsf{ValidCiphertext}_{pk}(t, y)$ be an algorithm verifying the validity of a ciphertext. The decryption algorithm $D_{dk}(t, y)$ outputs $m = y_3/(y_1^{-\zeta} y_2^{-\eta})$ if the above two equations hold, otherwise outputs $\perp$. This tag-based encryption is secure against selective-tag weak chosen ciphertext attack under the DLIN assumption [18]. In the modified Groth scheme and our scheme, we use the same F, H as in the common reference string of non-interactive proofs.

3 Deniable Group Signatures

In this section, we give the definition of deniable group signature which is a natural extension of the Bellare-Shi-Zhang (BSZ) model [3]. More precisely, we base our definition on the Sakai et al. model [28], which slightly modifies the BSZ model by introducing opening soundness.

3.1 Modification to the BSZ Model

For the ease of understanding (particularly for readers familiar with the standard group signature), we first highlight the differences between our definition and the BSZ model and then, provide the formal comprehensive definitions.

In deniable group signatures, we require that for the signature Σ of a message m and a user j, the opener can establish a proof that the open result is not j. Hence in addition to the standard functionality of group signature, we add *new algorithms*, namely DOpen and DJudge, to the Sakai et al. model. The opener produces this denial proof by using the DOpen algorithm and validity of the proof can be judged by the DJudge algorithm.

Due to the addition of the two algorithms, we also need to change the security definitions. Since we allow the opener to produce the new type of opening, namely denial opening, we need to ensure that such openings do not compromise the anonymity of group signatures. In a deniable group signature scheme, the denial proofs will provide the adversary with additional information which potentially could improve his abilities to attack the scheme. Thus, we allow the adversary to obtain denial proofs for any group signatures of his/her choice, as the BSZ definition allows him/her to obtain opening proofs of any signature. Furthermore, it is natural to expect that a denial proof for a signature Σ with respect to a user j does not leak any information beyond the fact that Σ is not generated by j. To capture this intuition, we allow the adversary in the anonymity game to obtain denial proofs *for the challenge*.

3.2 Formal Definition

We give the formal definition of deniable group signatures. First, we define the syntax of deniable group signature. We stress that the algorithms except DOpen and DJudge are exactly the same as those of the Sakai et al. model.

Definition 1 (Deniable Group Signature). *A deniable group signature scheme $\mathcal{D}\text{-}\mathcal{GS}$ consists of the algorithms* (GKg, UKg, Join/Iss, GSig, GVf, Open, Judge, DOpen, DJudge):

GKg: *The group key generation algorithm takes as input a security parameter* 1^k *($k \in \mathbb{N}$), and returns a group public key gpk, an issuer key ik, and an opening key ok.*

UKg: *The user key generation algorithm, which is run by a user i, takes as input* 1^k *and gpk, and returns a public and private key pair* (upk_i, usk_i).

Join/Iss: *The pair of (interactive) algorithms are run by a user and the issuer, and takes as input gpk, upk_i, and usk_i from user i and gpk, upk_i, and ik from the issuer, respectively. If successful, the issuer stores the registration information of user i in* reg[i] *and the user obtains the corresponding secret signing key gsk_i. We denote* reg $= \{$reg[i]$\}_i$.

GSig: *The group signing algorithm takes as input gpk, gsk_i and a message m, and returns a group signature Σ.*

GVf: *The verification algorithm takes as input gpk, Σ, and m, and returns either 1 (indicating that Σ is a valid group signature), or 0.*

Open: *The opening algorithm takes as input gpk, ok, m, Σ, and* reg, *and returns* (i, τ_O), *where i is a user identity, and τ_O is a proof that user i computed Σ.*

Judge: *The judgement algorithm takes as input gpk, i, upk_i, m, Σ, and τ_O, and returns 1 (indicating that Σ is produced by user i), or 0.*

DOpen: *The denial opening algorithm takes as input gpk, j, ok, m, Σ, and* reg, *and returns $\tau_{D(j)}$, where j is a user identity, and $\tau_{D(j)}$ is a proof that user j did not compute Σ.*

DJudge: *The denial judgement algorithm takes as input gpk, j, upk_j, m, Σ, and $\tau_{D(j)}$, and returns 1 (indicating that Σ is not produced by user j), or 0.*

Here, we note that $\mathsf{Judge}(gpk, i, upk_i, m, \Sigma, \tau_O) = 0$ does not imply that the signature Σ is not generated by the user i. For example, if the proof τ_O is not generated honestly, the Judge algorithm outputs 0. Similarly, $\mathsf{DJudge}(gpk, j, upk_j, m, \Sigma, \tau_{D(j)}) = 0$ does not imply that the signature Σ is generated by the user j. For example, if the proof $\tau_{D(j)}$ is not generated honestly, the DJudge algorithm outputs 0.

The model in [3] introduces four requirements for a group signature, namely, correctness, anonymity, non-frameability, and traceability. Furthermore, opening soundness is introduced by [28]. In this paper, we provide the definitions of correctness, anonymity, non-frameability, traceability, and opening soundness for a deniable group signature. The security model is extended from the dynamic group signature defined by Sakai et al. [28] and therefore, is almost the same *except for anonymity*. We define the security of anonymity in the following. However, due to the page limitation, the formal definitions of the other notions are given in the full version of this paper [15].

Anonymity. We first define several oracles used in anonymity game. We newly introduce the DOpen oracle in addition to Sakai et al.'s definition.

CrptU: This corrupt-user oracle allows $\mathcal{A}$ to add corrupt users. On input an identity i and upk, this oracle sets $upk_i \leftarrow upk$ and adds i to CU.

SndToU: This send-to-user oracle takes as input a user identity i, at first sets up a user public and private key pair $(upk_i, usk_i) \leftarrow \mathsf{UKg}(1^k, gpk)$ and adds i to HU. Then the oracle interacts with $\mathcal{A}$ who corrupts the issuer by running $\mathsf{Join}(gpk, upk_i, usk_i)$.

Ch: This challenge oracle takes as input a bit b, two identities i_0, i_1, and m, and returns $\Sigma^* \leftarrow \mathsf{GSig}(gpk, gsk_{i_b}, m)$ if both $i_0 \in \mathsf{HU}$ and $i_1 \in \mathsf{HU}$. If not, the oracle returns $\bot$. The oracle stores (m, Σ^*) in GSet, and stores i_0 and i_1 in ISet.

Open: This opening oracle takes as input m and Σ, and returns $(i, \tau_O) \leftarrow \mathsf{Open}(gpk, ok, m, \Sigma, \mathsf{reg})$ if $(m, \Sigma) \notin \mathsf{GSet}$ and $\bot$ otherwise.

DOpen: This deniable opening oracle takes as input a user identity j, m and Σ, and returns $\tau_{D(j)} \leftarrow \mathsf{DOpen}(gpk, j, ok, m, \Sigma, \mathsf{reg})$ if $(m, \Sigma) \notin \mathsf{GSet} \lor j \notin \mathsf{ISet}$ and $\bot$ otherwise.

USK: This user secret keys oracle takes as input $i \in \mathsf{HU}$, and returns the secret keys usk_i and gsk_i.

WReg: This write-registration-table oracle takes as input i and a value ρ, and modifies the contents of reg by setting $\mathsf{reg}[i] \leftarrow \rho$.

Now, we give the definition of anonymity. In the following, we first describe the difference between the anonymity of group signatures and the anonymity of deniable group signatures. The anonymity of group signatures [28] is required so that an adversary, who can corrupt the issuer and malicious users cannot extract any user information from group signatures of honest users in the case when the adversary is able to access the Open oracle. In the anonymity of deniable group signatures, the adversary can also access the DOpen oracle. As mentioned above, the adversary can even query the challenge signature to the DOpen oracle except for querying the challenge users i_0 and i_1. Then, anonymity is guaranteed even if denial proofs for all users except i_0 and i_1 are provided for the challenge group signature.[1]

---

[1] Recall that we exclude the case that an adversary requests a denial proof of either i_0 or i_1 for the challenge signature, since this trivially breaks the anonymity. (See the definition of DOpen oracle above.).

Definition 2 (Anonymity). *For an adversary $\mathcal{A}$, we define the experiment* $\mathrm{Exp}_{\mathsf{D\text{-}GS},\mathcal{A}}^{anon}(k)$ *as follows.*

$\mathrm{Exp}_{\mathsf{D\text{-}GS},\mathcal{A}}^{anon}(k):$

   $b \leftarrow \{0,1\}$

   $(gpk, ik, ok) \leftarrow \mathsf{GKg}(1^k);\ \mathsf{CU} \leftarrow \emptyset;\ \mathsf{HU} \leftarrow \emptyset;\ \mathsf{GSet} \leftarrow \emptyset;\ \mathsf{ISet} \leftarrow \emptyset$

   $b' \leftarrow \mathcal{A}^{\mathsf{CrptU}(\cdot,\cdot),\mathsf{SndToU}(\cdot),\mathsf{WReg}(\cdot,\cdot),\mathsf{USK}(\cdot),\mathsf{Open}(\cdot,\cdot),\mathsf{DOpen}(\cdot,\cdot,\cdot),\mathsf{Ch}(b,\cdot,\cdot,\cdot)}(gpk, ik)$

   Return 1 if $b' = b$, otherwise return 0

A deniable group signature scheme is said to be anonymous if the advantage $\mathrm{Adv}_{\mathsf{D\text{-}GS},\mathcal{A}}^{anon} := |\Pr[\mathrm{Exp}_{\mathsf{D\text{-}GS},\mathcal{A}}^{anon}(k) = 1] - \frac{1}{2}|$ *is negligible for any PPT adversary $\mathcal{A}$.*

4   The Proposed Deniable Group Signature Scheme

Here, we show that a deniable group signature can be constructed by applying this technique to the generic construction of a (standard) group signature presented by Bellare, Shi, and Zhang (BSZ) [3]. Then, we explain the difficulty of instantiating an efficient scheme even when a generic construction of a deniable group signature is given, and present our deniable group signature scheme, which is fairly efficient. Lastly, we discuss the size of the denial proofs of the proposed scheme.

4.1   Generic Construction and Its Limitation

Here, we give a generic construction of deniable group signature which is an extension of the BSZ construction [3]. In the BSZ construction, each user i has a key pair (vk_i, sk_i) of a signature scheme. The issuer also has a key pair (vk_s, sk_s) of a signature scheme and the opener has a key pair (pk_e, sk_e) of a public key encryption scheme. To issue a signing key to a user i, the issuer signs the message (i, vk_i) using his key sk_s and sends the signature $cert_i$ to the user i. A signer i can produce a signature s on a message m under vk_i. To make this verifiable without losing anonymity, the user makes an encryption C of $(i, vk_i, cert_i, s)$ using pk_e and also makes an NIZK proof π which proves that $cert_i$ is a valid certificate on (i, vk_i), i.e., $\mathsf{Vrfy}_{vk_s}((i, vk_i), cert_i) = 1$, s is a valid signature on m, and the ciphertext C is correctly generated. The opener can identity i by decrypting C using sk_e. Then, the opener produces an NIZK proof τ which proves that C decrypts to $(i, vk_i, cert_i, s)$ under sk_e.

We can add deniability to the BSZ construction as follows. The opener produces an NIZK proof τ' where C decrypts to $(i, vk_i, cert_i, s)$ under sk_e and $cert_i$ is NOT a valid certificate on (j, vk_j), i.e., $\mathsf{Vrfy}_{vk_s}((j, vk_j), cert_i) \neq 1$. Though this denial proof can be constructed by using general NIZK proofs [6], it is quite inefficient. The next attempt is to add deniability to an efficient group signature scheme (e.g., the modified Groth scheme [28][2]) by using an efficient NIZK proof (e.g., the Groth-Sahai proofs [14]). Unfortunately, this type of language (i.e., inequality statement) is not compatible with the Groth-Sahai proofs, especially the Groth-Sahai NIZK proof.

4.2   The Proposed Scheme

We will now present the proposed scheme. In the case of a deniable group signature, the opener needs to issue a denial proof, which proves that the user j is not the actual signer without revealing user i itself. Here, we review the technique for proving an inequality statement $i \neq j$ introduced by, e.g., [29] as follows: The technique is that to prove $a \neq b$, the prover picks $\ell \in \mathbb{Z}_p$ randomly and sets $c := (a/b)^\ell$ and the verifier checks $c \neq 1$ and the knowledge of ℓ. We note that this technique for proving inequality cannot be straightforwardly applied to the modified Groth scheme (See **Remark** in Sect. 4.2 for details).

We give our proposed scheme in Fig. 1. The proposed scheme is an extension of the modified Groth scheme [28], which has opening soundness added to the Groth scheme [13]. The modified Groth scheme uses a universal one-way hash function $\mathcal{H} : \{0,1\}^* \rightarrow \mathbb{Z}_p$, the Groth-Sahai proof systems $(\mathsf{K_{NI}}, \mathsf{P_{NIWI}}, \mathsf{V_{NIWI}}, \mathsf{X_{NIWI}})$ and $(\mathsf{K_{NI}}, \mathsf{P_{NIZK}}, \mathsf{V_{NIZK}}, \mathsf{X_{NIZK}})$, and a strong one-time signature $(\mathsf{KeyGen}, \mathsf{Sign}, \mathsf{Ver})$ as building blocks. Note that in the modified Groth scheme, we use a common $\mathsf{K_{NI}}$ for both systems and $\mathsf{X_{NIZK}}$ is not used.

First, we will explain the GSig and Open algorithms of the modified Groth scheme. In the GSig algorithm, a signer constructs two Groth-Sahai proofs. The first proof π, constructed via $\mathsf{P_{NIWI}}$ shows the knowledge of a signature σ, a verification key v, and a part b of a certificate (a,b) that satisfies $e(a, hv)e(f,b) = T \wedge e(\sigma, vg^{\mathcal{H}(vk_{\mathrm{sots}})}) = e(g,g)$. The first part a can be revealed in the group signature. The second proof ψ, constructed via $\mathsf{P_{NIZK}}$ demonstrates that the plaintext of y is the same as the witness σ used in π. That is, for a commitment $c = (c_1, c_2, c_3) = (F^{rc}U^t, H^{sc}V^t, g^{rc+sc}W^t\sigma)$ contained in π, there exists (r,s,t) such that $(c_1 y_1^{-1}, c_2 y_2^{-1}, c_3 y_3^{-1}) = (F^r U^t, H^s V^t, g^{r+s}W^t)$. In the Open algorithm, the opener reveals $\tau_F = y_1^{1/d_F} = g^r$ and $\tau_H = y_2^{1/d_H} = g^s$ as a part of an opening proof. If a third party, given τ_F and τ_H wants to check the correspondence between the ciphertext (y_1, y_2, y_3) and the plaintext σ, he/she checks whether $e(F, \tau_F) = e(y_1, g)$, $e(H, \tau_H) = e(y_2, g)$, $\sigma \tau_F \tau_H = y_3$, and $e(\sigma, v_i g^{\mathcal{H}(vk_{\mathrm{sots}})}) = e(g,g)$ hold or not.

We note that a simple modification, where the opener makes an NIZK proof for $e(\sigma, v_j g^{\mathcal{H}(vk_{\mathrm{sots}})}) \neq e(g,g)$, does not work because of the limitation of languages of the "zero-knowledge version" of the Groth-Sahai proof (See **Remark** in Sect. 4.2 for details). To break the barrier, all witnesses need to be base group

---

[2] Libert, Peters, and Yung (LPY) [23] proposed a short dynamic group signature scheme in the standard model under simple assumptions. Since the scheme is secure in the sense of the Kiayias-Yung model [17] and the model does not require that the opener produces the opening proof, we cannot directly employ our technique to the LPY scheme. Therefore, we leave it as a future work.

elements. Therefore, to prove $i \neq j$, we define the inequality to be proved on the base group G such that $v_i \neq v_j$ where $v_i, v_j \in G$. That is, the opener takes random $\ell \leftarrow \mathbb{Z}_p$ and set $c = \tau_\ell \cdot (\tau'_\ell)^{-1}$ where $\tau_\ell = v_i^\ell$ and $\tau'_\ell = v_j^\ell$. The proof ϕ, constructed via $\mathsf{P}_{\mathrm{NIZK}}$, shows the knowledge of the opening proof $(i, (\sigma, \tau_F, \tau_H))$, v_i, τ_ℓ, and τ'_ℓ which satisfy

$$e(F, \tau_F) = e(y_1, g) \ \wedge \ e(H, \tau_H) = e(y_2, g) \wedge \ \sigma \tau_F \tau_H = y_3$$
$$\wedge \ e(\sigma, v_i g^{\mathcal{H}(vk_{\mathrm{sots}})}) = e(g, g) \wedge \ e(v_i, \tau'_\ell) = e(v_j, \tau_\ell) \ \wedge \ c = \tau_\ell \cdot (\tau'_\ell)^{-1}.$$

The first four equations demonstrate that i is the actual signer of Σ and the fifth equation demonstrates that the discrete logarithm of τ_ℓ and that of τ'_ℓ are the same. In the DJudge algorithm, one checks the NIZK proof and whether $c \neq 1$.

Performance Evaluation. Since the proposed scheme is exactly the same as the modified Groth scheme [13], except for the algorithms for generating and verifying denial proofs, the efficiency of the other algorithms is identical to that of the modified Groth scheme. Hence, we estimate the size of the denial proof.

We modify the equations above to produce a zero-knowledge proof as follows. The first equation $e(F, \tau_F) = e(y_1, g)$ is changed to two equations $e(F, \tau_F) \cdot e(y'_1, g^{-1}) = 1 \ \wedge \ y'_1 \cdot y_1^{-1} = 1$ where y'_1 is a new witness. In the same way, $e(H, \tau_H) = e(y_2, g)$ is changed to $e(H, \tau_H) \cdot e(y'_2, g^{-1}) = 1 \ \wedge \ y'_2 \cdot y_2^{-1} = 1$ where y'_2 is a witness. Moreover, $e(\sigma, v_i g^{\mathcal{H}(vk_{\mathrm{sots}})}) = e(g, g)$ is changed to $e(\sigma, v_i g^{\mathcal{H}(vk_{\mathrm{sots}})}) \cdot e(g', g^{-1}) = 1 \ \wedge \ g' \cdot g^{-1} = 1$ where g' is a witness.

Therefore, this denial proof consists of 6 commitments and 3 new commitments, which consist of 3 group elements each, and 4 pairing product equations, which consist of 9 group elements but a linear equation consisting of 3 group elements, and 5 multi-scalar multiplication equations, which consist of 9 group elements each. The denial proof consists of 96 group elements in total.

Next, we analyze the adequacy of the size of the denial proof. In our scheme, the opener proves that "a signer is a member of the group," and "the signer does not generate a group signature without revealing the signer itself." The first part of denial proof can be regarded as a group signature, and the second part of denial proof can be regarded as the revocation functionality, which proves that a signer is not revoked without revealing the signer itself. Since revocable group signature schemes, e.g., [2,21,22,25], require approximately 50–100 group elements in addition to the membership proof part, it seems reasonable that denial proof requires 96 group elements in total.

Remark. In the modified Groth scheme, we can confirm that the user i is an actual signer by checking the equation $e(\sigma, v_i g^{\mathcal{H}(vk_{\mathrm{sots}})}) = e(g, g)$. Now, the statement that we want to prove is $e(\sigma, v_j g^{\mathcal{H}(vk_{\mathrm{sots}})}) \neq e(g, g)$. From these, it is natural to think that when $\{e(\sigma, v_i g^{\mathcal{H}(vk_{\mathrm{sots}})}) / e(\sigma, v_j g^{\mathcal{H}(vk_{\mathrm{sots}})})\}^\ell = c$, where i is the actual signer, a user j is not the signer and ℓ is a randomness, we check whether $c \neq 1$. However, the Groth-Sahai proof [14] has a limitation related to languages. If we provide an NIZK proof for the equation $\{e(\sigma, v_i g^{\mathcal{H}(vk_{\mathrm{sots}})}) / e(\sigma, v_j g^{\mathcal{H}(vk_{\mathrm{sots}})})\}^\ell = c$ in the Groth-Sahai proof, we need to

$\mathsf{GKg}(1^k)$:
$gk = (p, G, G_T, e, g) \leftarrow \mathcal{G}(1^k)$
$\mathcal{H} \leftarrow \mathsf{HashGen}(1^k)$
$f, h, z \leftarrow G$
$T \leftarrow e(f, z)$
$(crs, xk) \leftarrow \mathsf{K_{NI}}(gk)$
$(F, H, U, V, W, U', V', W') \leftarrow crs$
$K, L \leftarrow G$
$pk \leftarrow (F, H, K, L)$
Return (gpk, ik, ok)
$\quad \leftarrow ((gk, \mathcal{H}, f, h, T, crs, pk), z, xk)$

Join/Iss(User i:gpk; Issuer:gpk, ik):
Run the coin-flipping protocol
$\quad$ The user obtains $v_i = g^{x_i}$ and x_i
$\quad$ and the issuer obtains v_i
$\quad$ (Repeat until $v_i \neq \mathsf{reg}[j]$ for all j)
Issuer:
$\quad r \leftarrow \mathbb{Z}_p$
$\quad (a_i, b_i) \leftarrow (f^{-r}, (v_i h)^r z)$
$\quad$ set $\mathsf{reg}[i] \leftarrow v_i$
$\quad$ send (a_i, b_i) to the user
User:
$\quad$ If $e(a_i, hv_i)e(f, b_i) = T$
$\quad$ set $gsk_i \leftarrow (x_i, a_i, b_i)$

GSig(gpk, gsk_i, m):
$(vk_{\mathrm{sots}}, sk_{\mathrm{sots}}) \leftarrow \mathsf{KeyGen_{sots}}(1^k)$
$\quad$ (Repeat until $\mathcal{H}(vk_{\mathrm{sots}}) \neq -x_i$)
$\rho \leftarrow \mathbb{Z}_p; a \leftarrow a_i f^{-\rho}; b \leftarrow b_i (hv_i)^\rho$
$\sigma \leftarrow g^{1/(x_i + \mathcal{H}(vk_{\mathrm{sots}}))}$
$\pi \leftarrow \mathsf{P_{NIWI}}(crs, (gpk, a, \mathcal{H}(vk_{\mathrm{sots}})),$
$\qquad\qquad\qquad\qquad (b, v_i, \sigma))$
$y \leftarrow \mathsf{E}_{pk}(\mathcal{H}(vk_{\mathrm{sots}}), \sigma)$
$\psi \leftarrow \mathsf{P_{NIZK}}(crs, (gpk, y, \pi), (r, s, t))$
$\sigma_{\mathrm{sots}} \leftarrow \mathsf{Sign}_{sk_{\mathrm{sots}}}(vk_{\mathrm{sots}}, m, a, \pi, y, \psi)$
Return $\Sigma = (vk_{\mathrm{sots}}, a, \pi, y, \psi, \sigma_{\mathrm{sots}})$

GVf$(gpk, \mathsf{reg}, m, \Sigma)$:
Return 1 if the following holds:
$1 = \mathsf{Ver}_{vk_{\mathrm{sots}}}((vk_{\mathrm{sots}}, m, a, \pi, y, \psi), \sigma_{\mathrm{sots}})$
$1 = \mathsf{V_{NIWI}}(crs, (gpk, a, \mathcal{H}(vk_{\mathrm{sots}})), \pi)$
$1 = \mathsf{V_{NIZK}}(crs, (gpk, y, \pi), \psi)$
$1 = \mathsf{ValidCiphertext}_{pk}(\mathcal{H}(vk_{\mathrm{sots}}), y)$
$\mathsf{reg}[i] \neq \mathsf{reg}[j]$ for all $i \neq j$
else return 0

Open$(gpk, ok, \mathsf{reg}, m, \Sigma)$:
If GVf$(gpk, \mathsf{reg}, m, \Sigma) = 0$, return $(0, \perp)$
$(b, v, \sigma) \leftarrow \mathsf{X}_{xk}(crs, (gpk, a, \mathcal{H}(vk_{\mathrm{sots}})), \pi)$
$(d_F, d_H) \leftarrow xk$
$(y_1, y_2, \ldots, y_5) \leftarrow y$
$\tau_F \leftarrow y_1^{1/d_F}, \tau_H \leftarrow y_2^{1/d_H}$
Return $(i, (\sigma, \tau_F, \tau_H))$
$\quad$ if there is i so $v = \mathsf{reg}[i]$,
else $(0, \perp)$

Judge$(gpk, i, \mathsf{reg}, m, \Sigma, (\sigma, \tau_F, \tau_H))$:
$v_i \leftarrow \mathsf{reg}[i]$
Return 1 if the following hold:
$\quad$ GVf$(gpk, \mathsf{reg}, m, \Sigma) = 1$
$\quad i \neq 0, e(\sigma, v_i g^{\mathcal{H}(vk_{\mathrm{sots}})}) = e(g, g)$
$\quad e(F, \tau_F) = e(y_1, g), e(H, \tau_H) = e(y_2, g)$
$\quad \sigma\tau_F\tau_H = y_3$
else return 0

DOpen$(gpk, j, ok, \mathsf{reg}, m, \Sigma)$:
$(i, (\sigma, \tau_F, \tau_H)) \leftarrow \mathsf{Open}(gpk, ok, \mathsf{reg}, m, \Sigma)$
If $(i, (\sigma, \tau_F, \tau_H)) = (0, \perp)$, return $\perp$
$\ell \leftarrow \mathbb{Z}_p; \tau_\ell \leftarrow v_i^\ell; \tau'_\ell \leftarrow v_j^\ell$
$c \leftarrow \tau_\ell \cdot (\tau'_\ell)^{-1}$
$\phi \leftarrow \mathsf{P_{NIZK}}(crs, (gpk, y, v_j, c),$
$\qquad\qquad\qquad (\sigma, \tau_F, \tau_H, v_i, \tau_\ell, \tau'_\ell))$
Return (ϕ, c)

DJudge$(gpk, j, \mathsf{reg}, m, \Sigma, (\phi, c))$:
Return 1 if the following hold:
$\quad$ GVf$(gpk, \mathsf{reg}, m, \Sigma) = 1$
$\quad 1 = \mathsf{V_{NIZK}}(crs, (gpk, y, v_j, c), \phi)$
$\quad c \neq 1$
else return 0

Fig. 1. The Proposed Deniable Group Signature Scheme

find $\tilde{g}, \hat{g} \in G$ such that $c = e(\tilde{g}, \hat{g})$. However, this is the pairing inversion problem [11], which is believed to be hard. In contrast, in the proposed scheme, all witnesses are base group elements in our construction. Therefore, we can avoid the pairing inversion problem since all target group elements are decomposed into known base group elements.

Blazy et al. [4] proposed a new NIZK proof of non-membership based on the Groth-Sahai proof. However, for the same reason, the NIZK proof is not directly applicable to prove deniability in the modified Groth scheme. Nguyen [26] proposed a revocable group signature scheme by employing accumulators, where a user specific value is accumulated to a constant-size value and a user whose value is accumulated can prove that the value is accumulated without revealing the value. Since Li et al. [20] and Damgård et al. [9] extended this membership proofs to non-membership proofs where a user can prove that the value is not accumulated without revealing the value, this technique might be applied to realize the deniability. However, as in the Nguyen group signature scheme, a signer is required to compute an updated accumulated value and this cost depends on the number of (revoked) users, and therefore this solution does not yield an efficient construction.

5   Security Analysis

In the proof of anonymity, an adversary is allowed to issue DOpen queries even for the challenge group signature. Since the opening query for the challenge group signature is not allowed in the anonymity game of the modified Groth scheme, we cannot use the challenger of the modified Groth scheme. That is, the simulator needs to respond DOpen queries for the challenge group signature without knowing its opening result. The detail is given in Theorem 1. Except for from Game 7 to Game 8, translations between games are almost same as those of the modified Groth scheme [28].

Due to space limitation, we will give the proofs of other security requirements, correctness, non-frameability, traceability, and opening soundness in the full version of this paper [15]. In the proofs of these security requirements, we can directly break the modified Groth scheme by using an adversary who breaks our scheme if the wining conditions are independent of deniability. In the deniability-related parts, we can also give a proof in a similar way by assuming the security of building blocks.

Theorem 1. *The proposed group signature scheme satisfies anonymity if the DLIN assumption holds in G, the one-time signature scheme is strong existential unforgeable, and the hash function is universal one-way.*

Proof. Let $\mathcal{A}_{anon}$ be an adversary that has the advantage ϵ in the anonymity game. Now, we gradually modify the game played by $\mathcal{A}_{anon}$. In the following S_i denotes the event that $\mathcal{A}_{anon}$ successfully guesses the bit $b = b'$ interacting with the environment of Game i.

Game 0. Game 0 is identical to the game in the definition of anonymity. In this game, we have $\Pr[S_0] = \frac{1}{2} + \epsilon$.

Game 1. We modify the behavior of the Open oracle and the DOpen oracle as follows. If they receive a valid group signature which reuses the verification key vk^*_{sots} of the challenge signature Σ^*, the game aborts. By the strong existential unforgeability of one-time signature scheme, this modification does not change the success probability of $\mathcal{A}_{anon}$ with more than negligible amount, that is, we have that $|\Pr[S_0] - \Pr[S_1]|$ is negligible.

Game 2. We further modify the Open oracle and the DOpen oracle to abort when a queried group signature contains vk_{sots} where $\mathcal{H}(vk_{\text{sots}}) = \mathcal{H}(vk^*_{\text{sots}})$. By the universal one-wayness of the hash function, this modification does not change the success probability of $\mathcal{A}_{anon}$ with more than negligible amount, that is, we have that $|\Pr[S_1] - \Pr[S_2]|$ is also negligible.

Game 3. Now, we modify the way to generate the public key for the tag-based encryption. We set $K = g^\kappa, L = g^\lambda$ and store κ, λ. This modification does not vary the behavior of the adversary $\mathcal{A}_{anon}$, that is, $\Pr[S_2] = \Pr[S_3]$.

Game 4. We then modify how the Open oracle and the DOpen oracle obtain a signer identity i. Until Game 3, when the Open oracle and the DOpen oracle receive a query, they first extract a witness (b, v, σ) from the proof π by using the extraction key xk and search for i such that $\text{reg}[i] = v$. However, in Game 4, the Open oracle and the DOpen oracle search for i such that $e(\sigma, v_i g^{\mathcal{H}(vk_{\text{sots}})}) = e(g, g)$ going through reg. This verification equation uniquely defines v_i given σ and $\mathcal{H}(vk_{\text{sots}})$. Furthermore, since the soundness of π guarantees that σ is a valid signature on $\mathcal{H}(vk_{\text{sots}})$ under the extracted v, v_i identified in above equation must be identical to v. Hence, $\Pr[S_3] = \Pr[S_4]$.

Game 5. In Game 5, we modify how the Open oracle and the DOpen oracle obtain the signature σ. When the oracles receive a valid group signature, they use κ and λ to decrypt the ciphertext of the tag-based encryption and extract σ instead of extracting from the proof of knowledge π. By the validity check of the ciphertext of the tag-based encryption and the soundness of the NIZK proof ψ, this gives the same signature σ which we obtain when running the extractor on the NIWI proof of knowledge. Hence, $\Pr[S_4] = \Pr[S_5]$.

Game 6. Now, we change how we produce (τ_F, τ_H), which is a part of an opening proof. Instead of using xk, the Open oracle and the DOpen oracle use κ and λ to compute (τ_F, τ_H) as $\tau_F = (y_4/y_1^\kappa)^{1/\mathcal{H}(vk_{\text{sots}})}, \tau_H = (y_5/y_2^\lambda)^{1/\mathcal{H}(vk_{\text{sots}})}$, and $\sigma = y_3/\tau_F\tau_H$. The response of the Open oracle and the DOpen oracle in Game 6 are exactly the same as those in Game 5. Hence, $\Pr[S_5] = \Pr[S_6]$.

Game 7. In Game 6, the Open oracle and the DOpen oracle no longer need the extraction key xk. We therefore now switch to using a simulated common reference string crs that provides perfect witness-indistinguishability and perfect zero-knowledge. Since a simulated common reference string and a real common reference string are computationally indistinguishable under the DLIN assumption, the success probability of the adversary $\mathcal{A}_{anon}$ will not change by more than a negligible amount, hence we have that $|\Pr[S_6] - \Pr[S_7]|$ is negligible. Furthermore, proofs ψ and ϕ are simulated with a trapdoor.

Game 8. Finally, we change the component y_3 in the challenge to a random element. As shown in [28], this will not introduce more than a negligible change in the success probability of the adversary $\mathcal{A}_{anon}$ assuming the DLIN assumption holds. However, one point is different from the proof of the modified Groth scheme. In the anonymity game of deniable group signature, the adversary can query even the challenge signature to the DOpen oracle except for the challenge users. Therefore, a denial proof $\phi \leftarrow \mathsf{P}_{\mathrm{NIZK}}(crs, (gpk, y, v_j, c), (\sigma, \tau_F, \tau_H, v_i, \tau_\ell, \tau'_\ell))$ needs to be generated even though the witnesses $(\sigma, \tau_F, \tau_H, v_i, \tau_\ell, \tau'_\ell)$ are not known. Since a denial proof in the proposed scheme is a NIZK proof, the simulator can produce a simulated proof. More precisely, when the simulator receives a denial open query (m, Σ, j), the simulator verifies the signature first and, if it is not valid, he returns $\perp$. In the case that the signature is valid, he generates a simulated proof ϕ from the trapdoor and random c from G, and outputs (ϕ, c). The randomness c has the same distribution as $(v_i/v_j)^\ell$ where ℓ is random in $\mathbb{Z}_p$, hence $|\Pr[S_7] - \Pr[S_8]|$ is negligible.

In Game 8, we can conclude that $\Pr[S_8] = \frac{1}{2}$, because the view of the adversary is independent from the challenge bit b. First of all, the oracles behaves independently of b. Also, the challenge $(vk^*_{\mathrm{sots}}, a, \pi, y, \psi, \sigma^*_{\mathrm{sots}})$ contains no information of bit b. Indeed, vk^*_{sots} is independently generated, a is re-randomized and uniformly random, the perfectly witness-indistinguishable proof π is distributed independently from the witness, and y is a random encryption. The proof ψ does not contain the information of b since the proof is computed from y and π by using the zero-knowledge trapdoor. Moreover, since σ^*_{sots} is a signature of $(vk^*_{\mathrm{sots}}, m, a, \pi, y, \psi)$, it is independently of bit b.   □

References

1. Abe, M., Chow, S.S.M., Haralambiev, K., Ohkubo, M.: Double-trapdoor anonymous tags for traceable signatures.. In: Lopez, J., Tsudik, G. (eds.) ACNS 2011. LNCS, vol. 6715, pp. 183–200. Springer, Heidelberg (2011). doi:10.1007/978-3-642-21554-4_11
2. Attrapadung, N., Emura, K., Hanaoka, G., Sakai, Y.: A Revocable Group Signature Scheme from Identity-Based Revocation Techniques: Achieving Constant-Size Revocation List. In: Boureanu, I., Owesarski, P., Vaudenay, S. (eds.) ACNS 2014. LNCS, vol. 8479, pp. 419–437. Springer, Heidelberg (2014). doi:10.1007/978-3-319-07536-5_25
3. Bellare, M., Shi, H., Zhang, C.: Foundations of Group Signatures: The Case of Dynamic Groups. In: Menezes, A. (ed.) CT-RSA 2005. LNCS, vol. 3376, pp. 136–153. Springer, Heidelberg (2005). doi:10.1007/978-3-540-30574-3_11
4. Blazy, O., Chevalier, C., Vergnaud, D.: Non-interactive zero-knowledge proofs of non-membership. In: Nyberg, K. (ed.) CT-RSA 2015. LNCS, vol. 9048, pp. 145–164. Springer, Heidelberg (2015). doi:10.1007/978-3-319-16715-2_8
5. Blazy, O., Derler, D., Slamanig, D., Spreitzer, R.: Non-interactive plaintext (In-)Equality proofs and group signatures with verifiable controllable linkability. In: Sako, K. (ed.) CT-RSA 2016. LNCS, vol. 9610, pp. 127–143. Springer, Heidelberg (2016). doi:10.1007/978-3-319-29485-8_8

6. Blum, M., Feldman, P., Micali, S.: Non-interactive zero-knowledge and its applications. In: STOC, pp. 103–112 (1988)
7. Boneh, D., Boyen, X., Shacham, H.: Short group signatures. In: Franklin, M. (ed.) CRYPTO 2004. LNCS, vol. 3152, pp. 41–55. Springer, Heidelberg (2004). doi:10.1007/978-3-540-28628-8_3
8. Brickell, E.F., Camenisch, J., Chen, L.: Direct anonymous attestation. In: ACM-CCS, pp. 132–145 (2004)
9. Damgård, I., Triandopoulos, N.: Supporting non-membership proofs with bilinear-map accumulators. IACR Cryptology ePrint Archive 2008, 538 (2008)
10. Desmoulins, N., Lescuyer, R., Sanders, O., Traoré, J.: Direct anonymous attestations with dependent basename opening. In: Gritzalis, D., Kiayias, A., Askoxylakis, I. (eds.) CANS 2014. LNCS, vol. 8813, pp. 206–221. Springer, Heidelberg (2014). doi:10.1007/978-3-319-12280-9_14
11. Galbraith, S.D., Hess, F., Vercauteren, F.: Aspects of pairing inversion. IEEE Trans. Inf. Theor. **54**(12), 5719–5728 (2008)
12. Goldwasser, S., Micali, S., Rivest, R.L.: A digital signature scheme secure against adaptive chosen-message attacks. SIAM J. Comput. **17**(2), 281–308 (1988)
13. Groth, J.: Fully anonymous group signatures without random oracles. In: Kurosawa, K. (ed.) ASIACRYPT 2007. LNCS, vol. 4833, pp. 164–180. Springer, Heidelberg (2007). doi:10.1007/978-3-540-76900-2_10
14. Groth, J., Sahai, A.: Efficient non-interactive proof systems for bilinear groups. In: Smart, N. (ed.) EUROCRYPT 2008. LNCS, vol. 4965, pp. 415–432. Springer, Heidelberg (2008). doi:10.1007/978-3-540-78967-3_24
15. Ishida, A., Emura, K., Hanaoka, G., Sakai, Y., Tanaka, K.: Group signature with deniability: how to disavow a signature. IACR Cryptology ePrint Archive 2015, 43 (2015)
16. Kiayias, A., Tsiounis, Y., Yung, M.: Traceable signatures. In: Cachin, C., Camenisch, J.L. (eds.) EUROCRYPT 2004. LNCS, vol. 3027, pp. 571–589. Springer, Heidelberg (2004). doi:10.1007/978-3-540-24676-3_34
17. Kiayias, A., Yung, M.: Secure scalable group signature with dynamic joins and separable authorities. IJSN **1**(1/2), 24–45 (2006)
18. Kiltz, E.: Chosen-ciphertext security from tag-based encryption. In: Halevi, S., Rabin, T. (eds.) TCC 2006. LNCS, vol. 3876, pp. 581–600. Springer, Heidelberg (2006). doi:10.1007/11681878_30
19. Komano, Y., Ohta, K., Shimbo, A., Kawamura, S.: Toward the Fair Anonymous Signatures: Deniable Ring Signatures. In: Pointcheval, D. (ed.) CT-RSA 2006. LNCS, vol. 3860, pp. 174–191. Springer, Heidelberg (2006). doi:10.1007/11605805_12
20. Li, J., Li, N., Xue, R.: Universal accumulators with efficient nonmembership proofs. In: Katz, J., Yung, M. (eds.) ACNS 2007. LNCS, vol. 4521, pp. 253–269. Springer, Heidelberg (2007). doi:10.1007/978-3-540-72738-5_17
21. Libert, B., Peters, T., Yung, M.: Group signatures with almost-for-free revocation. In: Safavi-Naini, R., Canetti, R. (eds.) CRYPTO 2012. LNCS, vol. 7417, pp. 571–589. Springer, Heidelberg (2012). doi:10.1007/978-3-642-32009-5_34
22. Libert, B., Peters, T., Yung, M.: Scalable group signatures with revocation. In: Pointcheval, D., Johansson, T. (eds.) EUROCRYPT 2012. LNCS, vol. 7237, pp. 609–627. Springer, Heidelberg (2012). doi:10.1007/978-3-642-29011-4_36
23. Libert, B., Peters, T., Yung, M.: Short group signatures via structure-preserving signatures: standard model security from simple assumptions. In: Gennaro, R., Robshaw, M. (eds.) CRYPTO 2015. LNCS, vol. 9216, pp. 296–316. Springer, Heidelberg (2015). doi:10.1007/978-3-662-48000-7_15

24. Lyuu, Y.-D., Wu, M.-L.: Convertible group undeniable signatures. In: Lee, P.J., Lim, C.H. (eds.) ICISC 2002. LNCS, vol. 2587, pp. 48–61. Springer, Heidelberg (2003). doi:10.1007/3-540-36552-4_4

25. Nakanishi, T., Funabiki, N.: Revocable group signatures with compact revocation list using accumulators. In: Lee, H.-S., Han, D.-G. (eds.) ICISC 2013. LNCS, vol. 8565, pp. 435–451. Springer, Heidelberg (2014). doi:10.1007/978-3-319-12160-4_26

26. Nguyen, L.: Accumulators from bilinear pairings and applications. In: Menezes, A. (ed.) CT-RSA 2005. LNCS, vol. 3376, pp. 275–292. Springer, Heidelberg (2005). doi:10.1007/978-3-540-30574-3_19

27. Sakai, Y., Emura, K., Hanaoka, G., Kawai, Y., Matsuda, T., Omote, K.: Group signatures with message-dependent opening. In: Abdalla, M., Lange, T. (eds.) Pairing 2012. LNCS, vol. 7708, pp. 270–294. Springer, Heidelberg (2013). doi:10.1007/978-3-642-36334-4_18

28. Sakai, Y., Schuldt, J.C.N., Emura, K., Hanaoka, G., Ohta, K.: On the Security of Dynamic Group Signatures: Preventing Signature Hijacking. In: Fischlin, M., Buchmann, J., Manulis, M. (eds.) PKC 2012. LNCS, vol. 7293, pp. 715–732. Springer, Heidelberg (2012). doi:10.1007/978-3-642-30057-8_42

29. Schuldt, J.C.N., Matsuura, K.: Efficient convertible undeniable signatures with delegatable verification. IEICE Trans. 94(A(1)), 71–83 (2011)

30. Zeng, S., Jiang, S.: A new framework for conditionally anonymous ring signature. Comput. J. 57(4), 567–578 (2014)

Sandwich Construction for Keyed Sponges: Independence Between Capacity and Online Queries

Yusuke Naito[⊠]

Mitsubishi Electric Corporation, Kanagawa, Japan
Naito.Yusuke@ce.MitsubishiElectric.co.jp

Abstract. We study the pseudo-random function (PRF) security of keyed sponges that use a sponge function with extendable outputs in a black-box way. "Capacity" is a parameter of a keyed sponge that usually defines a dominant term in the PRF-bound. The previous works have improved the capacity term in the PRF-bound of the "prefix" keyed sponge, where the key is prepended to an input message, and then the resultant value is inputted into the sponge function. A tight bound for the capacity term was given by Naito and Yasuda (FSE 2016): $(qQ + q^2)/2^c$ where c is the capacity, q is the number of online queries and Q is the number of offline queries. Thus the following question is naturally arisen: *can we construct a keyed sponge with beyond the $(q^2 + qQ)/2^c$ bound security?*

In this paper, we consider the "sandwich" keyed sponge, where the key is both prepended and appended to an input message, and then the resultant value is inputted into the sponge function. We prove that the capacity term becomes $rQ/2^c$ for the rate r, which is usually $r \ll q$ and $r \ll Q$. Therefore, by the sandwich construction, the dependence between the capacity term and the number of online queries can be removed.

Keywords: PRF · Keyed sponge · Sandwich construction · Game playing · Coefficient H technique · Stirling's approximation

1 Introduction

The sponge construction by Bertoni *et al.* [5] is a state-of-the-art permutation-based mode of operation for keyless functions. Since the SHA-3 competition [20], it has attracted a great deal of public attention. The sponge construction was firstly adopted to the SHA-3 functions (a.k.a. Keccak) [4,19]. After that, it has been adopted to numerous cryptographic functions e.g., [3,6–8]. One of the reason why the sponge construction has been widely used was that it has the capability of extendable output, namely, it can produce variable length outputs. Indeed, the sponge construction is used to design a number of cryptographic functions. We call such functions "sponge functions."

- The SHA-3 functions have, in addition to hash functions, two sort of extendable output functions (XOFs): SHAKE128 and SHAKE256 [19]. As mentioned in FIPS202 [19], these sponge functions can be used as key derivation functions.

© Springer International Publishing AG 2016
S. Foresti and G. Persiano (Eds.): CANS 2016, LNCS 10052, pp. 245–261, 2016.
DOI: 10.1007/978-3-319-48965-0_15

- A number of lightweight hash functions e.g., [2,9,13] use the sponge construction with extendable outputs. Usually, hash functions are used as the components of message authentication codes and PRFs (Pseudo-Random Functions).

In order to securely use these sponge functions in the keyed settings, we need to confirm the PRF-security of keyed sponges that use a sponge function with extendable outputs in a black-box way.

Sponge Construction with Extendable Outputs. The sponge construction consists of a sequential application of a permutation on an internal state of b bits. This internal state is partitioned into an r-bit part and a c-bit part with $b = r+c$. Here r is called rate, c is called capacity, the first r-bit part is called outer part, and the remaining c-bit part is called inner part. The internal state is updated, by xor-ing the current message block of r bits with the outer part of the previous internal state and then inputting the xor-ed result into the next permutation call. After absorbing message blocks, an (r-bit) output block is generated, by squeezing the outer part of the current internal state and then inputting the internal state into the next permutation. This procedure is executed until an output with a desired length is obtained. In the indifferentiability framework of Maurer et al. [15], Bertoni et al. [5] proved that the sponge construction is secure up to the $O(2^{c/2})$ birthday-type bound regarding the capacity, assuming the underlying permutation is a random permutation. Therefore, sponge functions such as SHAKE128, SHAKE256 and the lightweight hash functions are usually designed so that $c > 0$. This paper deals with sponge functions with $c > 0$.

Prefix Keyed Sponge. Bertoni et al. suggested (e.g., [5]) that a keyed sponge should simply occur by appending the key to the prefixes of messages, where the output is defined as $H(K\|M)$ for a sponge function H, a message M and a (padded) secret key K. We call the keyed sponge "prefix keyed sponge." The security of the prefix keyed sponge has been evaluated in the sense of PRF-security in the random permutation model, where a distinguisher has oracle access to the prefix keyed sponge (in the real world) or a random function (in the ideal world), and a random permutation. Security parameters of keyed sponges include the state size b, the capacity c, the rate r, and the key size k. Especially, the capacity yields a dominant term in a security bound.

The PRF-security of the prefix keyed sponge can be derived from the indifferentiability of the sponge construction [5]. Roughly, the dominant term has the form $(\ell q + Q)^2/2^c$ against a distinguisher with parameters q, Q, and ℓ: the number of online queries (queries to prefix keyed sponge/random function), the number of offline queries (queries to random permutation), and the maximum number of permutation calls by an online query, respectively. However, the indifferentiability-based PRF-bound is rather loose, and the actual PRF-security of the prefix keyed sponge should be much higher, as first noticed by Bertoni et al. [6].

Andreeva *et al.* [1] successfully removed the term $Q^2/2^c$ and obtained a PRF-bound which was basically $((\ell q)^2 + \mu Q)/2^c$. Here, μ is an adversarial parameter called "multiplicity" and lies somewhere between $2\ell q/2^r$ and $2\ell q$. Gaži *et al.* [12] succeeded in giving a tight PRF-bound but their result supports only single-block outputs. Recently, Naito and Yasuda [18] provided a tight PRF-bound of the prefix keyed sponge with extendable outputs which is basically $(q^2 + qQ)/2^c$.

Motivation. The previous works attained the tight result on the capacity term of the PRF-security of the prefix keyed sponge. Thus it is natural to move on to find another type of keyed sponge with beyond the $(q^2 + qQ)/2^c$ bound security.

Mouha *et al.* proposed a sponge-based MAC algorithm Chaskey [17] with beyond the $(q^2 + qQ)/2^c$ bound security. However, this mode of operation supports only single block outputs and cannot use a sponge function in a black-box way.[1] This immediately raises the question: *can we construct a keyed sponge with beyond the $(q^2 + qQ)/2^c$ bound security that uses a sponge function with extendable outputs in a black-box way?*

Our Result. In this paper, we consider the sandwich construction [22,23], where a secret key is prepend an appended to an input message and then the resultant value is inputted into the sponge function. Namely, the output is defined as $H(K\|M\|K)$ for a sponge function H, a message M and a (padded) secret key K. We call the construction "sandwich keyed sponge." Regarding the PRF-security of the sandwich keyed sponge, the indifferentiable security of the sponge construction offers the capacity term in the PRF-bound: $(\ell q + Q)^2/2^c$ against a distinguisher with parameters q, Q, and ℓ.

We thus improve the PRF-bound where the capacity term is $rQ/2^c$. Consequently, by using the sandwich construction for keyed sponges, beyond the $(q^2 + qQ)/2^c$ bound security can be achieved. In Table 1, the PRF-bounds for the prefix keyed sponge and the sandwich keyed sponge are summarized, where for simplicity, the k-terms (k is the key size) are omitted, and we assume that

Table 1. Comparison of PRF-bounds for keyed sponges. For simplicity, k-terms (key size term) are omitted from these PRF-bounds and we assume that $r \leq q \leq Q$.

Prefix keyed sponge	Sandwich keyed sponge
$O\left(\dfrac{(\ell q + Q)^2}{2^c}\right)$ [5] (Indifferentiability)	$O\left(\dfrac{(\ell q + Q)^2}{2^c}\right)$ [5] (Indifferentiability)
$O\left(\dfrac{(\ell q)^2 + \mu Q}{2^c}\right)$ [1]	$O\left(\dfrac{rQ}{2^c} + \left(\dfrac{\ell q Q}{2^b}\right)^{1/2} + \dfrac{(\ell q)^2}{2^b}\right)$ **[Ours]**
$O\left(\dfrac{q^2 + qQ}{2^c} + \left(\dfrac{\ell q Q}{2^b}\right)^{1/2} + \dfrac{(\ell q)^2}{2^b}\right)$ [18]	

---

[1] In Chaskey, $c = 0$, the initial value is replaced with the key, and the permutation at the last block is sandwiched with the key.

$r \ll q \leq \ell q \leq Q$. Here we compare our bound with Naito-Yasuda's tight bound of the prefix keyed sponge [18].

- We first consider SHAKE128 and SHAKE256 whose parameters are $(b, c) = (1600, 128)$ and $(b, c) = (1600, 256)$, respectively. In this case, it may safely be assumed that b-terms are negligible compared with the capacity terms. The PRF-bound of the prefix keyed sponge becomes a constant if $qQ = O(2^c)$, whereas the PRF-bound of the sandwich keyed sponge becomes a constant if $rQ = O(2^c)$. Therefore, the sandwich keyed sponge achieves a higher level of security than the prefix keyed sponge.
- We next consider sponge-based lightweight hash functions e.g., [2,9,13], which have $b/2 < c < b$. The PRF-bound of the prefix keyed sponge becomes a constant if $qQ = O(2^c)$ or $\ell qQ = O(2^b)$, and our bound of the sandwich keyed sponge becomes a constant if $rQ = O(2^c)$ or $\ell qQ = O(2^b)$. Therefore, if $2^c < 2^b/\ell$ ($\ell < 2^r$), then qQ affects the security of the prefix keyed sponge, and thus the sandwich keyed sponge has a higher level of security than the prefix keyed sponge. On the other hand, if $2^c \geq 2^b/\ell$ ($\ell \geq 2^r$), then the sandwich keyed sponge is as secure as the prefix keyed sponge.

Note that compared with the prefix keyed sponge, the sandwich keyed sponge requires additional permutation invocations to absorb the key appended to messages. However, as mentioned above, the sandwich keyed sponge achieves a higher level of security than the prefix keyed sponge.

Regarding the security proof, we take a similar approach to Naito-Yasuda's proof for the prefix keyed sponge [18]. The proof makes use of the game-playing technique, introducing just one intermediate game between the real and ideal worlds. This transition between the games heavily relies on the coefficient H technique of Patarin [21]. In this proof, we need to consider "bad" events in which a distinguisher may distinguish between the real and ideal worlds. The bad events come from collisions for b-bit internal state values, since in the real world the collisions may occur whereas in the ideal world the collisions never occur due to a monolithic random function. Regarding the prefix keyed sponge, a distinguisher can control the outer part by message blocks and thus the collision probability largely depends on the inner part. On the other hand, regarding the sandwich keyed sponge, no distinguisher can control the outer part, since the outer part are hidden by a secret key appended to messages. The appended key weakens the dependence between the collisions and the capacity, and thereby, the sandwich construction achieves beyond the $(q^2 + qQ)/2^c$ bound security.

More Related Works. Several works considered keyed sponge constructions with the aim of improving the efficiency. Chang et al. [10] introduced an inner keyed sponge, where the initial value of the inner part in the sponge function is replaced with a key. Bertoni et al. [7] introduced a donkey sponge, which is the prefix keyed sponge with the capacity size $c = 0$. Several works improved the PRF-security of the inner keyed sponge and the donkey sponge e.g., [1,12,16,18]. Note that these keyed sponges cannot use a sponge function in a black-box way.

2 Preliminaries

Notations. Let $\{0,1\}^*$ be the set of all bit strings, for an integer $b \geq 0$, $\{0,1\}^b$ the set of b-bit strings, 0^b the bit string of b-bit zeroes, and λ an empty string. For integers $0 \leq i \leq b$ and a bit string $X \in \{0,1\}^b$, let $\mathsf{msb}_i(X)$ be the most significant i-bit string of X. For a bit string X, $Y \leftarrow X$ means that X is assigned to Y. For a finite set $\mathcal{X}$ and a integer $l \geq 1$, $X_1, \ldots, X_l \xleftarrow{\$} \mathcal{X}$ means that l elements are independently and randomly drawn from $\mathcal{X}$, and are assigned to $X_1, \ldots, X_l$, respectively. For a set $\mathcal{X}$, let $\mathsf{Perm}(\mathcal{X})$ be the set of all permutations: $\mathcal{X} \rightarrow \mathcal{X}$. For sets $\mathcal{X}$ and $\mathcal{Y}$, let $\mathsf{Func}(\mathcal{X}, \mathcal{Y})$ be the set of all functions: $\mathcal{X} \rightarrow \mathcal{Y}$. For sets $\mathcal{X}$ and $\mathcal{Y}$, $\mathcal{X} \leftarrow \mathcal{Y}$ means that $\mathcal{Y}$ is assigned to $\mathcal{X}$, and $\mathcal{X} \xleftarrow{\cup} \mathcal{Y}$ means $\mathcal{X} \leftarrow \mathcal{X} \cup \mathcal{Y}$. For a bit string X and a set $\mathcal{X}$, let $|X|$ and $|\mathcal{X}|$ be the bit length of X and the number of elements in $\mathcal{X}$, respectively. For a bit string X and an integer r, let $|X|_r := \lceil |X|/r \rceil$ be the length of X in r-bit blocks.

PRF-Security. For integers $\tau, k \geq 1$, let $\mathcal{F}_K^{\mathcal{P}} : \{0,1\}^* \rightarrow \{0,1\}^\tau$ be a keyed function using a permutation $\mathcal{P}$ and having a key $K \in \{0,1\}^k$. Although we deal with keyed sponges that produce variable length outputs, for simplicity, we fix the output length τ to the maximum length in outputs. Note that outputs whose lengths are less than τ bit can be obtained by truncation. The PRF-security of the keyed function is defined in terms of indistinguishability between the real and ideal worlds. The security proof will be done in the ideal model, regarding the underlying permutation as a random permutation $\mathcal{P} \xleftarrow{\$} \mathsf{Perm}(\{0,1\}^b)$. We denote by $\mathcal{P}^{-1}$ its inverse. Through this paper, a distinguisher is denoted by $\mathbf{D}$ and is a computationally unbounded algorithm. It is given query access to one or more oracles. Its complexity is solely measured by the number of queries made to its oracles. In the real world, $\mathbf{D}$ has query access to $\mathcal{F}_K^{\mathcal{P}}$, $\mathcal{P}$, and $\mathcal{P}^{-1}$ for a key $K \xleftarrow{\$} \{0,1\}^k$ and $\mathcal{P} \xleftarrow{\$} \mathsf{Perm}(\{0,1\}^b)$. In the ideal world, $\mathbf{D}$ has query access to a random function $\mathcal{R}$, $\mathcal{P}$, and $\mathcal{P}^{-1}$, for $\mathcal{R} \xleftarrow{\$} \mathsf{Func}(\{0,1\}^*, \{0,1\}^\tau)$ and $\mathcal{P} \xleftarrow{\$} \mathsf{Perm}(\{0,1\}^b)$. After interacting with oracles $\mathcal{O}$, it outputs $y \in \{0,1\}$ whose event is denoted by $\mathbf{D}^{\mathcal{O}} \Rightarrow y$. We define the advantage function as

$$\mathbf{Adv}_{\mathcal{F}}^{\mathsf{prf}}(\mathbf{D}) = \Pr[\mathbf{D}^{\mathcal{F}_K^{\mathcal{P}}, \mathcal{P}, \mathcal{P}^{-1}} \Rightarrow 1] - \Pr[\mathbf{D}^{\mathcal{R}, \mathcal{P}, \mathcal{P}^{-1}} \Rightarrow 1].$$

We call queries to $\mathcal{F}_K^{\mathcal{P}}/\mathcal{R}$ "online queries" and queries to $(\mathcal{P}, \mathcal{P}^{-1})$ "offline queries." Though this paper, without loss of generality, we assume that $\mathbf{D}$ is deterministic and makes no repeated query, which includes offline queries such that once $\mathbf{D}$ obtains the offline query-response pair (X, Y) such that $Y = \mathcal{P}(X)$, it does not make a query X to $\mathcal{P}$ nor Y to $\mathcal{P}^{-1}$.

3 Sandwich Keyed Sponge and the Security

3.1 The Construction of Sandwich Keyed Sponge

▶ **Sponge Function.** For an integer $b > 0$, let $\mathcal{P} \in \mathsf{Perm}(\{0,1\}^b)$ denotes the permutation used in the sponge function, and $\mathsf{Sponge}^{\mathcal{P}}$ denotes the sponge function. Let $r > 0, c \geq 0$ and $\ell_{\mathrm{out}} > 0$ be integers with $b = r + c$. r is the bit length called rate. c is the bit length called capacity. ℓ_{out} is the output length of $\mathtt{Sponge}^{\mathcal{P}}$ in r-bit blocks.

For an input $M \in \{0, 1\}^*$, the output $\mathtt{Sponge}^{\mathcal{P}}(M) = Z$ is defined as follows. Firstly, a bit string $\mathsf{pad}(|M|)$ is appended to M such that the bit length of $m\|\mathsf{pad}(|M|)$ becomes a multiple of r, e.g., $M\|\mathsf{pad}(|M|) = M\|1\|0^*\|1$, which means that 1, the minimum number of zeros and 1 are appended to M so that the bit length becomes a multiple of r. Secondly, $M\|\mathsf{pad}(|M|)$ is partitioned into r-bit blocks $M_1, \ldots, M_n$. Thirdly, b-bit internal state S is updated as: $S \leftarrow 0^b$; for $i = 1, \ldots n - 1$ do $S \leftarrow \mathcal{P}(S \oplus M_i\|0^c)$. Finally, the $\ell_{\mathrm{out}} \times r$-bit string Z is defined as $Z \leftarrow \lambda; S \leftarrow S \oplus M_n$; for $i = 1, \ldots \ell_{\mathrm{out}}$ do $S \leftarrow \mathcal{P}(S); Z \leftarrow Z\|\mathsf{msb}_r(S)$.

▶ **Sandwich Keyed Sponge.** For an integer $k > 0$, let $K \in \{0, 1\}^k$ be a secret key. $\mathtt{SwSponge}_K^{\mathcal{P}}$ denotes the sandwich keyed sponge function using $\mathtt{Sponge}^{\mathcal{P}}$ and having the key K. Then for a message $M \in \{0, 1\}^*$, the $(\ell_{\mathrm{out}} \times r)$-bit output $\mathtt{SwSponge}_K^{\mathcal{P}}(M)$ is defined as $\mathtt{SwSponge}_K^{\mathcal{P}}(M) = \mathtt{Sponge}^{\mathcal{P}}(K\|0^*\|M\|10^*\|K)$. Here, $K\|0^*$ is the prefix key, where the minimum number of zeros are appended to K so that the bit length becomes a multiple of r; $M\|10^*$ is the padded message, where 1 and the minimum number of zeros are appended to M so that the bit length becomes a multiple of r.

The concrete procedure is given in the following. Let $pad := \mathsf{pad}(|K\|0^*\|M\|10^*\|K|)$ be the padding bit string in $\mathtt{Sponge}^{\mathcal{P}}$. Let $\kappa_{\mathsf{pf}} = |K\|0^*|/r$ be the r-bit block length of the prefix key $K\|0^*$, and $\kappa_{\mathsf{sf}} = |K\|pad|/r$ the r-bit block length of the suffix key $K\|pad$. The output $\mathtt{SwSponge}_K^{\mathcal{P}}(M) = Z$ is defined as follows.

1. Partition $K\|0^*$ into r-bit blocks $K_1^*, \ldots, K_{\kappa_{\mathsf{pf}}}^*$; $W_0 \leftarrow 0^b$
2. For $i = 1, \ldots, \kappa_{\mathsf{pf}}$ do $U_i \leftarrow W_{i-1} \oplus (K_i^*\|0^c)$; $W_i \leftarrow \mathcal{P}(U_i)$

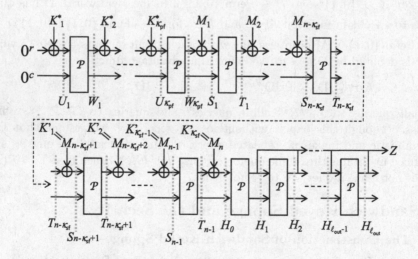

Fig. 1. Sandwich keyed sponge construction

3. Partition $M\|10^*\|K\|pad$ into r-bit blocks $M_1, \ldots, M_n$; $T_0 \leftarrow W_{\kappa_{pf}}$
4. For $i = 1, \ldots, n-1$ do $S_i \leftarrow T_{i-1} \oplus (M_i\|0^c)$; $T_i \leftarrow \mathcal{P}(S_i)$
5. $H_0 \leftarrow T_{n-1} \oplus (M_n\|0^c)$; $Z \leftarrow \lambda$
6. For $i = 1, \ldots, \ell_{out}$ do $H_i \leftarrow \mathcal{P}(H_{i-1})$; $Z \leftarrow Z\|\mathsf{msb}_r(H_i)$
7. Return Z

The Fig. 1 shows the above procedure, where $K\|pad = K_1'\|K_2'\|\cdots\|K_{\kappa_{sf}}'$ with $|K_i| = r$ $(i = 1, \ldots, \kappa_{sf})$, and $K\|pad = M_{n-\kappa_{sf}+1}\|M_{n-\kappa_{sf}+2}\|\cdots\|M_n$. Note that our proof uses the above notations.

3.2   The PRF-Security of Sandwich Keyed Sponge

We assume that $r \times \ell_{out}$ is the maximum output length in bits, i.e., the maximum length in r-bit blocks is ℓ_{out}. Let ℓ_{in} be the maximum number of n, i.e., $n \leq \ell_{in}$, and $\ell = \ell_{in} + \ell_{out}$. Let q be the number of online queries, and Q the number of offline queries. Then the PRF-bound of the sandwich keyed sponge is given in the following, and the proof is given in the next section.

Theorem 1. *For any distinguisher $\mathbf{D}$, we have*

$$\mathbf{Adv}_{\mathsf{SwSponge}}^{\mathrm{prf}}(\mathbf{D}) \leq \frac{2r(Q + \kappa_{pf})}{2^c} + \left(\frac{44\ell q(Q + \kappa_{pf})}{2^b}\right)^{1/2} + \frac{6\ell^2 q^2}{2^b} + \lambda(Q) + \frac{q}{2^k},$$

where $\lambda(Q) = \frac{Q}{2^k}$ if $k \leq r$; $\lambda(Q) = \frac{1}{2^b} + \frac{Q}{2^{\left(\frac{1}{2} - \frac{\log_2(3b)}{2r} - \frac{1}{r}\right)k}}$ otherwise.

4   Proof of Theorem 1

We give the PRF-bound of the sandwich keyed sponge via three games. We denote these by Game 1, Game 2, and Game 3. For $i \in \{1, 2, 3\}$, we denote by G_i the set of oracles $(L_i, \mathcal{P}, \mathcal{P}^{-1})$ to which $\mathbf{D}$ has query access in Game i. In each game, $\mathcal{P}$ is independently drawn as $\mathcal{P} \xleftarrow{\$} \mathrm{Perm}(\{0, 1\}^b)$. Let $L_1 := \mathsf{SwSponge}_K^{\mathcal{P}}$ and $L_3 := \mathcal{R}$. We will define L_2 in the Subsect. 4.1. Then we have

$$\mathbf{Adv}_{\mathsf{SwSponge}}^{\mathrm{prf}}(\mathbf{D}) = \sum_{i=1}^{2} \left(\Pr[\mathbf{D}^{G_i} \Rightarrow 1] - \Pr[\mathbf{D}^{G_{i+1}} \Rightarrow 1]\right). \tag{1}$$

Hereafter, for $i \in \{1, 2\}$ we upper bound $\Pr[\mathbf{D}^{G_i} \Rightarrow 1] - \Pr[\mathbf{D}^{G_{i+1}} \Rightarrow 1]$.

In this proof, for $\beta \in \{1, \ldots, Q\}$, we denote the β-th offline query to $\mathcal{P}$ (resp., $\mathcal{P}^{-1}$) by X^β (resp., Y^β) and the response by Y^β (resp., X^β), where $Y^\beta = \mathcal{P}(X^\beta)$ (resp., $X^\beta = \mathcal{P}^{-1}(Y^\beta)$). For $\alpha \in \{1, \ldots, q\}$, we denote the α-th online query by M^α and the response by Z^α, where $Z^\alpha = L_i(M^\alpha)$ $(i \in \{1, 2, 3\})$. For $i \in \{1, 2, 3\}$, we also use the superscript symbol for internal values in L_i, e.g., for $\alpha \in \{1, \ldots, q\}$, $S_1^\alpha, T_1^\alpha, n^\alpha$ etc.

4.1 Upper Bound of $\Pr[\mathbf{D}^{G_1} \Rightarrow 1] - \Pr[\mathbf{D}^{G_2} \Rightarrow 1]$

We start by defining L_2. Let $\mathcal{F}_1, \ldots, \mathcal{F}_{\ell_{\mathrm{in}}-1}, \mathcal{G}_1, \ldots, \mathcal{G}_{\ell_{\mathrm{out}}} \xleftarrow{\$} \mathsf{Func}(\{0,1\}^b, \{0,1\}^b)$ be random functions, and let $K \xleftarrow{\$} \{0,1\}^k$ be a secret key. Random functions $\mathcal{F}_1, \ldots, \mathcal{F}_{\ell_{\mathrm{in}}-1}$ are used to absorb message blocks and the suffix key, and random functions $\mathcal{G}_1, \ldots, \mathcal{G}_{\ell_{\mathrm{out}}}$ are used to squeeze output blocks. For an online query $M \in \{0,1\}^*$, the response $L_2(M) = Z$ is defined as follows.

1. Partition $K\|0^*$ into r-bit blocks $K_1^*, K_2^*, \ldots, K_{\kappa_{\mathrm{pf}}}^*$; $W_0 \leftarrow 0^b$
2. For $i = 1, \ldots, \kappa_{\mathrm{pf}}$ do $U_i \leftarrow W_{i-1} \oplus (K_i^*\|0^c)$; $W_i \leftarrow \mathcal{P}(U_i)$
3. Partition $M\|10^*\|K\|pad$ into r-bit blocks $M_1, \ldots, M_n$; $T_0 \leftarrow W_{\kappa_{\mathrm{pf}}}$
4. For $i = 1, \ldots, n-1$ do $S_i \leftarrow T_{i-1} \oplus (M_i\|0^c)$; $T_i \leftarrow \mathcal{F}_i(S_i)$
5. $H_0 \leftarrow T_{n-1} \oplus (M_n\|0^c)$; $Z \leftarrow \lambda$
6. For $i = 1, \ldots, \ell_{\mathrm{out}}$ do $H_i \leftarrow \mathcal{G}_i(H_{i-1})$; $Z \leftarrow Z\|\mathsf{msb}_r(H_i)$
7. Return Z

Hereafter, we call the block with input S_i (defined at the step 4) "i-th input block," and the block with output H_i (defined at the step 6) "i-th output block."

Transcript

Since $\mathbf{D}$ is deterministic, its output is determined by the transcript, which is a list of values obtained by its queries. Let T_1 be the transcript in Game 1 obtained by sampling $K \xleftarrow{\$} \{0,1\}^k$ and $\mathcal{P} \xleftarrow{\$} \mathsf{Perm}(\{0,1\}^b)$. Let T_2 be the transcript in Game 2 obtained by sampling $K \xleftarrow{\$} \{0,1\}^k$, $\mathcal{P} \xleftarrow{\$} \mathsf{Perm}(\{0,1\}^b)$ and $\mathcal{F}_1, \ldots, \mathcal{F}_{\ell_{\mathrm{in}}-1}, \mathcal{G}_1, \ldots, \mathcal{G}_{\ell_{\mathrm{out}}} \xleftarrow{\$} \mathsf{Func}(\{0,1\}^b, \{0,1\}^b)$. We call a transcript τ valid if an interaction with their oracles could render this transcript, namely, $\Pr[\mathsf{T}_i = \tau] > 0$ for $i \in \{1,2\}$. Then $\Pr[\mathbf{D}^{G_1} \Rightarrow 1] - \Pr[\mathbf{D}^{G_2} \Rightarrow 1]$ is upper bounded by the statistical distance of transcripts, i.e.,

$$\Pr[\mathbf{D}^{G_1} \Rightarrow 1] - \Pr[\mathbf{D}^{G_2} \Rightarrow 1] \le \mathsf{SD}(\mathsf{T}_1, \mathsf{T}_2) = \frac{1}{2}\sum_\tau |\Pr[\mathsf{T}_1 = \tau] - \Pr[\mathsf{T}_2 = \tau]|,$$

where the sum is over all valid transcripts.

Regarding $\mathbf{D}$'s transcript, it obtains the following sets of query-response pairs by its queries: $\tau_L = \{(M^1, Z^1), \ldots, (M^q, Z^q)\}$ the set of query-response pairs defined by online queries; $\tau_{\mathcal{P}} = \{(X^1, Y^1), \ldots, (X^Q, Y^Q)\}$ the set of query-response pairs defined by offline queries. In addition, we define the following sets.

- For $i = 1, \ldots, \ell_{\mathrm{in}} - 1$, let $\tau_i^{\mathrm{in}} := \bigcup_{\alpha=1}^q \{(S_i^\alpha, T_i^\alpha)\}$ be the set of input-output pairs at the i-th input block. Note that if (S_i^α, T_i^α) is not defined, i.e., $n^\alpha \le i$, then $\{(S_i^\alpha, T_i^\alpha)\} := \emptyset$.
- For $i = 1, \ldots, \ell_{\mathrm{out}}$, let $\tau_i^{\mathrm{out}} := \bigcup_{\alpha=1}^q \{(H_{i-1}^\alpha, H_i^\alpha)\}$ be the set of input-output pairs at the i-th output block.
- Let $\tau_K := \{(U_1, W_1), \ldots, (U_{\kappa_{\mathrm{pf}}}, W_{\kappa_{\mathrm{pf}}})\}$ be the set of input-output pairs obtained by the prefix key $K\|0^*$.

Let $\tau^{\text{in}} := \bigcup_{i=1}^{\ell_{\text{in}}-1} \tau_i^{\text{in}}$, and $\tau^{\text{out}} := \bigcup_{i=1}^{\ell_{\text{out}}} \tau_i^{\text{out}}$. This proof permits $\mathbf{D}$ to obtain these sets and the secret key K after $\mathbf{D}$'s interaction but before it outputs a result. Thus $\mathbf{D}$'s transcript is summarized as $\tau = (\tau_L, \tau_P, \tau^{\text{in}}, \tau^{\text{out}}, \tau_K, K)$.

Coefficient H Technique

We upper bound $\Pr[\mathbf{D}^{G_1} \Rightarrow 1] - \Pr[\mathbf{D}^{G_2} \Rightarrow 1]$ by using the coefficient H technique [11,21]. In this technique, firstly, we need to partition valid transcripts into good transcripts $\mathcal{T}_{\text{good}}$ and bad transcripts $\mathcal{T}_{\text{bad}}$. Then we can upper bound the difference by the following lemma, and the proof is given in e.g., [11].

Lemma 1 (Coefficient H Technique). *Let* $0 \leq \varepsilon \leq 1$ *be such that for all* $\tau \in \mathcal{T}_{\text{good}}$, $\frac{\Pr[\mathsf{T}_1=\tau]}{\Pr[\mathsf{T}_2=\tau]} \geq 1-\varepsilon$. *Then,* $\Pr[\mathbf{D}^{G_1} \Rightarrow 1] - \Pr[\mathbf{D}^{G_2} \Rightarrow 1] \leq \varepsilon + \Pr[\mathsf{T}_2 \in \mathcal{T}_{\text{bad}}]$.

Hereafter, we first define good and bad transcripts. We then upper bound ε and $\Pr[\mathsf{T}_2 \in \mathcal{T}_{\text{bad}}]$. Finally, we obtain the upper bound of $\Pr[\mathbf{D}^{G_1} \Rightarrow 1] - \Pr[\mathbf{D}^{G_2} \Rightarrow 1]$ by putting these upper bounds to the lemma.

Good and Bad Transcripts

In order to define good and bad transcripts, we need to recall the modification from Game 1 and Game 2, where the underlying primitive definition b-bit outputs W_i, T_i and H_i is modified. In Game 1, outputs W_i, T_i and H_i in L_1 are defined by using $\mathcal{P}$. On the other hand, in Game 2, outputs W_i, T_i and H_i in L_2 are defined by using $\mathcal{P}$, $\mathcal{F}_i$ and $\mathcal{G}_i$, respectively. Namely, in Game 2, (1) T_i and H_i are independently defined, and (2) T_i and H_i are defined independently of offline queries (X_i, Y_i) and W_i-values. In addition, (3) T_i and T_j with $i \neq j$ are also independently defined, and the same is true for H_i and H_j with $i \neq j$. Therefore, if Game 1 and Game 2 are indistinguishable, then these independences for (1), (2) and (3) should also hold in Game 1. Thus we consider conditions $\mathsf{hit}_{\text{sx,ty}}$, $\mathsf{hit}_{\text{hx,hy}}$, $\mathsf{hit}_{\text{sh,th}}$, $\mathsf{hit}_{\text{ss,tt}}$ and hit_{hh}, which define good and bad transcripts. $\mathsf{hit}_{\text{sh,th}}$ comes from the independence for (1), $\mathsf{hit}_{\text{sx,ty}}$ and $\mathsf{hit}_{\text{hx,hy}}$ come from the independence for (2), $\mathsf{hit}_{\text{ss,tt}}$ and hit_{hh} come from the independence for (3). In addition, by the PRP-PRF switch from Game 1 to Game 2, we need to consider a condition with respect to output collisions of random functions, denoted by coll. These definitions are given in the following.

- $\mathsf{hit}_{\text{sx,ty}} \Leftrightarrow \exists (S,T) \in \tau^{\text{in}}, (X,Y) \in \tau_P \cup \tau_K$ s.t. $S = X \vee T = Y$
- $\mathsf{hit}_{\text{hx,hy}} \Leftrightarrow \exists (H,H') \in \tau^{\text{out}}, (X,Y) \in \tau_P \cup \tau_K$ s.t. $H = X \vee H' = Y$
- $\mathsf{hit}_{\text{sh,th}} \Leftrightarrow \exists (S,T) \in \tau^{\text{in}}, (H,H') \in \tau^{\text{out}}$ s.t. $S = H \vee T = H'$
- $\mathsf{hit}_{\text{ss,tt}} \Leftrightarrow \exists i,j \in \{1,\dots,\ell_{\text{in}} - 1\}$ with $i \neq j$ s.t. $\exists (S_i,T_i) \in \tau_i^{\text{in}}, (S_j,T_j) \in \tau_j^{\text{in}}$ s.t. $S_i = S_j \vee T_i = T_j$
- $\mathsf{hit}_{\text{hh}} \Leftrightarrow \exists i,j \in \{1,\dots,\ell_{\text{out}}\}$ with $i \neq j$ s.t. $\exists (H_{i-1},H_i) \in \tau_i^{\text{out}}, (H_{j-1},H_j) \in \tau_j^{\text{out}}$ s.t. $H_{i-1} = H_{j-1} \vee H_i = H_j$
- $\mathsf{coll} \Leftrightarrow \exists (S,T), (S',T') \in \tau^{\text{in}} \cup \tau^{\text{out}}$ s.t. $S \neq S' \wedge T = T'$.

We define $\mathcal{T}_{\text{bad}}$ by the set of transcripts which satisfy one of the above conditions, and $\mathcal{T}_{\text{bad}}$ by the set of transcript which do not satisfy any of the above conditions.

Upper Bound of $\Pr[\mathsf{T}_2 \in \mathcal{T}_{\mathsf{bad}}]$

First we note that $\Pr[\mathsf{T}_2 \in \mathcal{T}_{\mathsf{bad}}] = \Pr[\mathsf{hit}_{\mathsf{sx,ty}} \vee \mathsf{hit}_{\mathsf{hx,hy}} \vee \mathsf{hit}_{\mathsf{sh,th}} \vee \mathsf{hit}_{\mathsf{ss,tt}} \vee \mathsf{hit}_{\mathsf{hh}} \vee \mathsf{coll}]$, where these conditions are considered within Game 2. In this evaluation, we use the randomness of internal values S_i, T_i and H_i, where $S_1 = W_{\kappa_{\mathsf{pf}}} \oplus (M_1 \| 0^c)$ where $W_{\kappa_{\mathsf{pf}}}$ is defined by $\mathcal{P}$, and other values are defined by random functions. In order for $W_{\kappa_{\mathsf{pf}}}$ to become a (almost) b-bit random value, we use the condition: $\mathsf{hit}_{\mathsf{ux,wy}} \Leftrightarrow \exists (U_{\kappa_{\mathsf{pf}}}, W_{\kappa_{\mathsf{pf}}}) \in \tau_{\mathcal{P}}$, meaning $\mathbf{D}$ obtains the pair $(U_{\kappa_{\mathsf{pf}}}, W_{\kappa_{\mathsf{pf}}})$ by some offline query. Under the condition $\neg \mathsf{hit}_{\mathsf{ux,wy}}$, $\mathbf{D}$ does not know $W_{\kappa_{\mathsf{pf}}}$, and thereby it can be seen as a (almost) b-bit random value. By basic probability theory, we have

$$\Pr[\mathsf{T}_2 \in \mathcal{T}_{\mathsf{bad}}] \leq \Pr[\mathsf{hit}_{\mathsf{ux,wy}}] + \Pr[\mathsf{hit}_{\mathsf{sx,ty}} \wedge \neg \mathsf{hit}_{\mathsf{ux,wy}}] + \Pr[\mathsf{hit}_{\mathsf{hx,hy}}]$$
$$+ \Pr[\mathsf{hit}_{\mathsf{sh,th}} \wedge \neg \mathsf{hit}_{\mathsf{ux,wy}}] + \Pr[\mathsf{hit}_{\mathsf{ss,tt}}] + \Pr[\mathsf{hit}_{\mathsf{hh}}] + \Pr[\mathsf{coll}]. \quad (2)$$

Hereafter, we evaluate these probabilities. Without loss of generality, we assume that $(U_1, W_1), \ldots, (U_{\kappa_{\mathsf{pf}}}, W_{\kappa_{\mathsf{pf}}})$ are defined in τ_K before $\mathbf{D}$'s interaction.

▶ **Upper Bound of** $\Pr[\mathsf{hit}_{\mathsf{ux,wy}}]$. The same condition appears at the security proofs of the prefix keyed sponge function in [1,12,18], where the following upper bound was given: $\Pr[\mathsf{Hit}_{\mathsf{ux,wy}}] \leq \lambda(Q) + \frac{2\kappa_{\mathsf{pf}}Q}{2^b}$. We use the upper bound.

▶ **Upper Bound of** $\Pr[\mathsf{hit}_{\mathsf{sx,ty}} \wedge \neg \mathsf{hit}_{\mathsf{ux,wy}}]$. Due to lack of space, we give only an intuition of deriving the upper bound. The condition $\mathsf{hit}_{\mathsf{sx,ty}}$ considers a collision between τ^{in} and $\tau_{\mathcal{P}} \cup \tau_K$, where $\tau^{\mathsf{in}} = \tau_1^{\mathsf{in}} \cup \left(\bigcup_{i=2}^{\ell_{\mathsf{in}}-1} \tau_i^{\mathsf{in}} \right)$. In order to upper bound $\Pr[\mathsf{hit}_{\mathsf{sx,ty}} \wedge \neg \mathsf{hit}_{\mathsf{ux,wy}}]$, the randomness of elements in τ^{in} is used.

- For $\forall (S, T) \in \tau_1^{\mathsf{in}}$, the output element T is defined as $T \xleftarrow{\$} \{0,1\}^b$ by a random function, and the input element S is of the form $S = W_{\kappa_{\mathsf{pf}}} \oplus M_1 \| 0^c$. By $\neg \mathsf{hit}_{\mathsf{ux,wy}}$, $W_{\kappa_{\mathsf{pf}}}$ is randomly drawn from at least $2^b - \kappa_{\mathsf{pf}}$ values of b bits.
- All elements in $\bigcup_{i=2}^{\ell_{\mathsf{in}}-1} \tau_i^{\mathsf{in}}$, which are defined by random functions, can be seen as b-bit random values.

Since $|\tau_1^{\mathsf{in}}| \leq q$, $|\bigcup_{i=2}^{\ell_{\mathsf{in}}-1} \tau_i^{\mathsf{in}}| \leq (\ell - 2)q$, $|\tau_{\mathcal{P}} \cup \tau_K| \leq Q + \kappa_{\mathsf{pf}}$, we have

$$\Pr[\mathsf{hit}_{\mathsf{sx,ty}} \wedge \neg \mathsf{hit}_{\mathsf{ux,wy}}] \leq \frac{q(Q + \kappa_{\mathsf{pf}})}{2^b - \kappa_{\mathsf{pf}}} + \frac{q(Q + \kappa_{\mathsf{pf}})}{2^b} + 2 \times \frac{(\ell - 2)q(Q + \kappa_{\mathsf{pf}})}{2^b}$$
$$\leq \frac{2\ell q(Q + \kappa_{\mathsf{pf}})}{2^b}, \text{ assuming } \kappa_{\mathsf{pf}} \leq 2^{b-1}.$$

▶ **Upper Bound of** $\Pr[\mathsf{hit}_{\mathsf{hx,hy}}]$. The condition $\mathsf{hit}_{\mathsf{hx,hy}}$ considers a collision between τ^{out} and $\tau_{\mathcal{P}} \cup \tau_K$, where $\tau^{\mathsf{out}} = \bigcup_{i=1}^{\ell_{\mathsf{in}}-1} \tau_i^{\mathsf{in}}$. Similar to the evaluation of $\Pr[\mathsf{hit}_{\mathsf{sx,ty}}]$, in order to upper bound $\Pr[\mathsf{hit}_{\mathsf{hx,hy}}]$, the randomness of elements in τ^{out} is used. However, we need to care the fact that $\mathbf{D}$ can obtain the rate values of these elements from the corresponding outputs of L_2. This implies that the randomness of the rate values cannot be used in this evaluation. In order to reduce the influence of this fact, we use the analysis based on a multi-collision on the rate values, which have been used in many security proofs of sponge-based functions e.g., [1, 14, 18].

Let $\mathcal{H} := \bigcup_{\alpha=1}^{q} \{H_1^{\alpha}, \ldots, H_{\ell_{out}}^{\alpha}\}$ be the set of outputs defined by $\mathcal{G}_1, \ldots, \mathcal{G}_{\ell_{out}}$. Note that $\mathcal{H}_{out}$ does not include $H_0^1, \ldots, H_0^q$. Then we define a condition for a multi-collision in rate values of $\mathcal{H}_{out}$.

$$\mathsf{mcoll} \Leftrightarrow \exists H^{(1)}, \ldots, H^{(\rho)} \in \mathcal{H} \text{ s.t. } \mathsf{msb}_r(H^{(1)}) = \cdots = \mathsf{msb}_r(H^{(\rho)})$$

where ρ is a free parameter which will be defined later. Then we have

$$\Pr[\mathsf{hit}_{\mathsf{hx,hy}}] \leq \Pr[\mathsf{mcoll}] + \Pr[\mathsf{hit}_{\mathsf{hx,hy}} \wedge \neg \mathsf{mcoll}].$$

Firstly, we upper bound $\Pr[\mathsf{mcoll}]$. Fix $H \in \{0,1\}^r$ and $H^{(1)}, \ldots, H^{(\rho)} \in \mathcal{H}$. Since $H^{(1)}, \ldots, H^{(\rho)} \xleftarrow{\$} \{0,1\}^b$, the probability that $H = \mathsf{msb}_r(H^{(1)}) = \cdots = \mathsf{msb}_r(H^{(\rho)})$ holds is $\leq (\frac{1}{2^r})^{\rho}$. Since $|\mathcal{H}_{out}| \leq \ell q$, we have $\Pr[\mathsf{mcoll}] \leq 2^r \times \binom{\ell q}{\rho} \times (\frac{1}{2^r})^{\rho} \leq 2^r \times (\frac{e\ell q}{\rho 2^r})^{\rho}$, using Stirling's approximation $(x! \geq (x/e)^x$ for any x, where $e = 2.71828\cdots$ is Napier's constant).

Secondly, we upper bound $\Pr[\mathsf{hit}_{\mathsf{hx,hy}} \wedge \neg \mathsf{mcoll}]$. The strategy of deriving the upper bound is simple but we need to deal with several types of values for H_i, which yields many cases. Due to lack of space, we give only an intuition of deriving the upper bound.

- For a collision between $\tau_P \cup \tau_K$ and elements $\{H_0^1, H_0^2, \ldots, H_0^q\}$ in τ^{out}, $H_0^1, H_0^2, \ldots, H_0^q$ are defined by random functions and thus can be seen as b-bit random values. Thus the collision probability is $\leq q \times (Q + \kappa_{pf}) \times 1/2^b$.
- For a collision between $\tau_P \cup \tau_K$ and other elements $\{H_1^1, \ldots, H_1^q, H_2^1, \ldots\}$ in τ^{out}, we use the condition $\neg \mathsf{mcoll}$. Although $\mathbf{D}$ can obtain the rate values of $\{H_1^1, \ldots, H_1^q, H_2^1, \ldots\}$ from outputs of L_2, by $\neg \mathsf{mcoll}$, for each element E in $\tau_P \cup \tau_K$, the number of elements in $\{H_1^1, \ldots, H_1^q, H_2^1, \ldots\}$ whose rate value equal to $\mathsf{msb}_r(E)$ is at most ρ. Since the capacity values of $\{H_1^1, \ldots, H_1^q, H_2^1, \ldots\}$ are randomly drawn from $\{0,1\}^c$ by random functions, the probability that one of the ρ values collides with E is $\leq \rho/2^c$. Thus the collision probability is $\leq 2(Q + \kappa_{pf}) \times \rho/2^c$.

Thus, we have $\Pr[\mathsf{hit}_{\mathsf{hx,hy}} \wedge \neg \mathsf{mcoll}] \leq q(Q + \kappa_{pf})/2^b + 2\rho(Q + \kappa_{pf})/2^c$.

Finally, we have $\Pr[\mathsf{hit}_{\mathsf{hx,hy}}] \leq \frac{q(Q+\kappa_{pf})}{2^b} + \frac{2\rho(Q+\kappa_{pf})}{2^c} + 2^r \times \left(\frac{e\ell q}{\rho 2^r}\right)^{\rho}$, and putting $\rho = \max\left\{r, \left(\frac{2^c e\ell q}{2^r(Q+\kappa_{pf})}\right)^{1/2}\right\}$ gives

$$\Pr[\mathsf{hit}_{\mathsf{hx,hy}}] \leq \frac{q(Q+\kappa_{pf})}{2^b} + \frac{2r(Q+\kappa_{pf})}{2^c} + 2 \times \left(\frac{e\ell q(Q+\kappa_{pf})}{2^b}\right)^{1/2}$$

$$+ 2^r \times \left(\frac{e\ell q}{\left(\frac{2^c e\ell q}{2^r(Q+\kappa_{pf})}\right)^{1/2} 2^r}\right)^{r}$$

$$\leq \frac{q(Q+\kappa_{pf})}{2^b} + \frac{2r(Q+\kappa_{pf})}{2^c} + \left(\frac{44\ell q(Q+\kappa_{pf})}{2^b}\right)^{1/2}.$$

β-th query

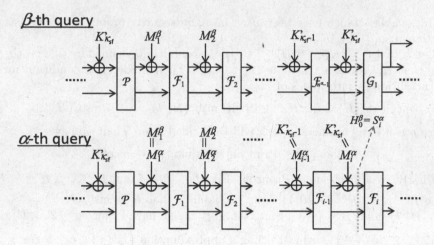

Fig. 2. $\mathsf{hit}_{sh}^{(0)} \wedge (i = n^\beta) \wedge (\mathsf{msb}_{r \cdot d^\beta}(M^\alpha) = M^\beta \| 10^* \| K \| pad^\beta)$

▶ **Upper Bound of** $\Pr[\mathsf{hit}_{sh,th} \wedge \neg \mathsf{hit}_{ux,wy}]$. This evaluation makes use of the existence of the suffix key that avoids the attack using the iterated structure of L_2: for two message block sequences $M_1^\alpha, M_2^\alpha, \ldots, M_{n^\alpha}^\alpha$ and $M_1^\beta, M_2^\beta, \ldots, M_{n^\beta}^\beta$, if the message blocks are the same up to the i-th block, namely, $M_1^\alpha = M_1^\beta, \ldots, M_i^\alpha = M_i^\beta$, then input-output pairs of the underlying random functions are the same up to the i-th block. By this property, $\mathsf{hit}_{sh,th}$ may be satisfied. Concretely, this property may yield the collision $S_i^\alpha = H_0^\beta$ as shown in Fig. 2. However, **D** needs to make a query including the suffix key, and thereby this attack can be avoided without a negligible probability. The detail analysis is given in the following, where this case is considered in the sub condition $\mathsf{hit}_{sh}^{(0)}$ of $\mathsf{hit}_{sh,th}$ defined bellow.

We split the condition $\mathsf{hit}_{sh,th}$ into the following three conditions with respect to the collisions $S = H, T = H$ and the block numbers of H.

- $\mathsf{hit}_{sh}^{(0)} \Leftrightarrow \exists \alpha, \beta \in \{1, \ldots, q\}, i \in \{1, \ldots, n^\alpha - 1\}$ s.t. $S_i^\alpha = H_0^\beta$
- $\mathsf{hit}_{sh}^{(1)} \Leftrightarrow \exists \alpha, \beta \in \{1, \ldots, q\}, i \in \{1, \ldots, n^\alpha - 1\}, j \in \{1, \ldots, \ell_{out} - 1\}$ s.t. $S_i^\alpha = H_j^\beta$
- $\mathsf{hit}_{th} \Leftrightarrow \exists \alpha, \beta \in \{1, \ldots, q\}, i \in \{1, \ldots, n^\alpha - 1\}, j \in \{1, \ldots, \ell_{out}\}$ s.t. $T_i^\alpha = H_j^\beta$

Since $\mathsf{hit}_{sh,th} = \mathsf{hit}_{sh}^{(0)} \vee \mathsf{hit}_{sh}^{(1)} \vee \mathsf{hit}_{th}$, we have

$$\Pr[\mathsf{hit}_{sh,th} \wedge \neg \mathsf{hit}_{ux,wy}] \leq \Pr[\mathsf{hit}_{sh}^{(0)} \wedge \neg \mathsf{hit}_{ux,wy}] + \Pr[\mathsf{hit}_{sh}^{(1)} \wedge \neg \mathsf{hit}_{ux,wy}] + \Pr[\mathsf{hit}_{th}].$$

Firstly, we upper bound $\Pr[\mathsf{hit}_{sh}^{(0)} \wedge \neg \mathsf{hit}_{ux,wy}]$. We assume that $\mathsf{hit}_{ux,wy}$ is not satisfied, and then evaluate the probability that $\mathsf{hit}_{sh}^{(0)}$ is satisfied. We divide $\mathsf{hit}_{sh}^{(0)}$ into the following three cases. Note that in this condition, $n^\alpha > n^\beta$ holds.

- $\mathsf{hit}_{sh}^{(0)} \wedge (i = n^\beta) \wedge (\mathsf{msb}_{r \cdot n^\beta}(M^\alpha) = M^\beta \| 10^* \| K \| pad^\beta)$: The equation $i = n^\beta$ ensures that the block numbers of S_i^α and H_0^β are the same, and $\mathsf{msb}_{r \cdot n^\beta}(M^\alpha) =$

$M^\beta \| 10^* \| K \| pad^\beta$ ensures that for each block up to the i-th block, the inputs by the α-th and β-th online queries are the same (See also the Fig. 2). Thus, if this case occurs, then $\mathbf{D}$ makes an online query including the secret key K. Since $K \xleftarrow{\$} \{0,1\}^k$, the probability that this case occurs is $\leq q/2^k$.

- $\mathsf{hit}_{\mathsf{sh}}^{(0)} \wedge (i = n^\beta) \wedge (\mathsf{msb}_{r \cdot n^\beta}(M^\alpha) \neq M^\beta \| 10^* \| K \| pad^\beta)$: By the condition $\mathsf{msb}_{r \cdot n^\beta}(M^\alpha) \neq M^\beta \| 10^* \| K \| pad^\beta$, there exists $j \in \{1, \dots, n^\beta - 1\}$ such that $S_j^\alpha \neq S_j^\beta$ and $S_{j+1}^\alpha = S_{j+1}^\beta$, where $S_{n^\beta}^\beta := H_0^\beta$. Note that for $\gamma \in \{\alpha, \beta\}$ $S_{j+1}^\gamma = T_j^\gamma \oplus M_{j+1}^\gamma \| 0^c$. By $S_j^\alpha \neq S_j^\beta$, $T_j^\alpha, T_j^\beta \xleftarrow{\$} \{0,1\}^b$. Thus, fixing α, β, the probability that for some j, $S_j^\alpha \neq S_j^\beta \wedge S_{j+1}^\alpha = S_{j+1}^\beta$ holds is $\leq \ell \times 1/2^b$. Therefore, the probability that this case holds is $\leq \binom{q}{2} \times \ell/2^b \leq 0.5\ell q^2/2^b$.

- $\mathsf{hit}_{\mathsf{sh}}^{(0)} \wedge (i \neq n^\beta) \wedge (i = 1)$: Note that $S_1^\alpha = W_{\kappa_{\mathsf{pf}}} \oplus M_1^\alpha \| 0^c$, and by $\neg \mathsf{hit}_{\mathsf{ux,wy}}$, $W_{\kappa_{\mathsf{pf}}}$ is randomly drawn from at least $2^b - (Q + \kappa_{\mathsf{pf}})$ values of b bits. Thus, fixing α, β, the probability that $S_1^\alpha = H_0^\beta$ holds is $\leq 1/(2^b - (Q + \kappa_{\mathsf{pf}})) \leq 2/2^b$, assuming $Q + \kappa_{\mathsf{pf}} \leq 2^{b-1}$. Therefore, the probability that this case holds is $\leq q \times q \times 2/2^b = 2q^2/2^b$.

- $\mathsf{hit}_{\mathsf{sh}}^{(0)} \wedge (i \neq n^\beta) \wedge (i \neq 1)$: Note that $S_i^\alpha = T_{i-1}^\alpha \oplus M_i^\alpha \| 0^c$ and $H_0^\beta = T_{n^\beta-1}^\beta \oplus M_{n^\beta}^\beta \| 0^c$. By $i \neq n^\beta$, $T_{i-1}^\alpha, T_{n^\beta-1}^\beta \xleftarrow{\$} \{0,1\}^b$, and thereby, the probability that $S_i^\alpha = H_0^\beta$ holds is $\leq 1/2^b$. Thus the probability that this case holds is $\leq (\ell - 2)q \times q \times 1/2^b = (\ell - 2)q^2/2^b$.

Thus, we have $\Pr[\mathsf{hit}_{\mathsf{sh}}^{(0)}] \leq q/2^k + 1.5\ell q^2/2^b$.

Secondly, we upper bound $\Pr[\mathsf{hit}_{\mathsf{sh}}^{(1)} \wedge \neg \mathsf{hit}_{\mathsf{ux,wy}}]$. Note that $S_i^\alpha = T_{i-1}^\alpha \oplus M_i^\alpha \| 0^c$ where $T_0^\alpha := W_{\kappa_{\mathsf{pf}}}$. By $\neg \mathsf{hit}_{\mathsf{ux,wy}}$, $W_{\kappa_{\mathsf{pf}}}$ is randomly drawn from at least $2^b - (Q + \kappa_{\mathsf{pf}})$ values of b bits, and $T_{i-1}^\alpha \xleftarrow{\$} \{0,1\}^b$ for $i \neq 1$. We thus have $\Pr[\mathsf{hit}_{\mathsf{sh}}^{(1)}] \leq q \times \ell_{\mathsf{out}} q \times 1/(2^b - (Q + \kappa_{\mathsf{pf}})) + (\ell_{\mathsf{in}} - 2)q \times \ell_{\mathsf{out}} q/2^b \leq \ell^2 q^2/2^b$, assuming that $Q + \kappa_{\mathsf{pf}} \leq 2^{b-1}$.

Thirdly, we upper bound $\Pr[\mathsf{hit}_{\mathsf{th}}]$. Since $T_i^\alpha, H_j^\beta \xleftarrow{\$} \{0,1\}^b$, we have $\Pr[\mathsf{hit}_{\mathsf{th}}] \leq \ell_{\mathsf{in}} q \times \ell_{\mathsf{out}} q \times 1/2^b \leq \ell^2 q^2/2^b$.

Finally, we have $\Pr[\mathsf{hit}_{\mathsf{sh,th}}] \leq \frac{q}{2^k} + \frac{3.5\ell^2 q^2}{2^b}$.

▶ **Upper Bound of** $\Pr[\mathsf{hit}_{\mathsf{ss,tt}}]$. Note that $\mathsf{hit}_{\mathsf{ss,tt}} \Leftrightarrow \exists \alpha, \beta \in \{1, \dots, q\}, i \in \{1, \dots, n^\alpha - 1\}, j \in \{1, \dots, n^\beta - 1\}$ with $i \neq j$ s.t. $S_i^\alpha = S_j^\beta \vee T_i^\alpha = T_j^\beta$. Without loss of generality, we assume that $j \neq 1$. Regarding the equation $S_i^\alpha = S_j^\beta$, $S_i^\alpha = T_{i-1}^\alpha \oplus M_i^\alpha \| 0^c$ and $S_j^\beta = T_{j-1}^\beta \oplus M_i^\beta \| 0^c$, where $T_0^\alpha := W_{\kappa_{\mathsf{pf}}}$. By $i \neq j$, T_{i-1}^α and T_{j-1}^β are independently drawn, and $T_{j-1}^\beta \xleftarrow{\$} \{0,1\}^b$. Thus, the probability that for some α, β, i, j, $S_i^\alpha = S_j^\beta$ holds is $\leq q^2 \times \binom{\ell}{2} \times 1/2^b = 0.5\ell^2 q^2/2^b$. Regarding the equation $T_i^\alpha = T_j^\beta$, by $i \neq j$, T_i^α and T_j^β are independently drawn, and $T_j^\beta \xleftarrow{\$} \{0,1\}^b$. Hence, the probability that for some α, β, i, j, $T_i^\alpha = T_j^\beta$ holds is $\leq 0.5\ell^2 q^2/2^b$. Finally, we have $\Pr[\mathsf{hit}_{\mathsf{ss,tt}}] \leq \frac{\ell^2 q^2}{2^b}$.

▶ **Upper Bound of** $\Pr[\mathsf{hit_{hh}}]$. Note that $\mathsf{hit_{hh}} \Leftrightarrow \exists \alpha, \beta \in \{1, \ldots, q\}$ s.t. ($\exists i, j \in \{0, \ldots, \ell_{out}\}$ with $i \neq j$ s.t. $H_i^{\alpha} = H_j^{\beta}$). Since for $\gamma \in \{\alpha, \beta\}$, $H_i^{\gamma} \xleftarrow{\$} \{0,1\}^b$ for $i \neq 0$, and $H_0^{\gamma} := T_{n^{\gamma}-1}^{\gamma} \oplus M_{n^{\gamma}} \| 0^c$ where $T_{n^{\gamma}-1}^{\gamma} \xleftarrow{\$} \{0,1\}^b$, we have $\Pr[\mathsf{hit_{hh}}] \leq \binom{(\ell_{out}+1)q}{2} \times \frac{1}{2^b} \leq \frac{\ell q}{2^b} \leq \frac{0.5\ell^2 q^2}{2^b}$.

▶ **Upper Bound of** $\Pr[\mathsf{coll}]$. By the birthday analysis, $\Pr[\mathsf{coll}] \leq \frac{0.5(\ell q)^2}{2^b}$.

■ **Upper Bound of** $\Pr[\mathsf{T}_2 \in \mathcal{T}_{bad}]$. Putting the above upper bounds into (2) gives

$$\Pr[\mathsf{T}_2 \in \mathcal{T}_{bad}] \leq \frac{2r(Q + \kappa_{pf})}{2^c} + \left(\frac{44\ell q(Q + \kappa_{pf})}{2^b}\right)^{1/2} + \frac{5.5\ell^2 q^2}{2^b} + \lambda(Q) + \frac{q}{2^k}.$$

Upper Bound of ε

Let $\tau \in \mathcal{T}_{good}$ be a good transcript. For $i = 1, 2$, let all_i be the set of all oracles in Game i, and let $\mathsf{comp}_i(\tau)$ be the set of oracles compatible with τ in Game i. Then $\Pr[\mathsf{T}_1 = \tau] = \frac{|\mathsf{comp}_1(\tau)|}{|\mathsf{all}_1|}$ and $\Pr[\mathsf{T}_2 = \tau] = \frac{|\mathsf{comp}_2(\tau)|}{|\mathsf{all}_2|}$.

Firstly, we evaluate $|\mathsf{all}_1|$. Since $K \in \{0,1\}^k$ and $\mathcal{P} \in \mathsf{Perm}(\{0,1\}^b)$, we have $|\mathsf{all}_1| = 2^k \cdot 2^b!$.

Secondly, we evaluate $|\mathsf{all}_2|$. Since $K \in \{0,1\}^k$, $\mathcal{P} \in \mathsf{Perm}(\{0,1\}^b)$, and $\mathcal{F}_1, \ldots, \mathcal{F}_{\ell_{in}-1}, \mathcal{G}_1, \ldots, \mathcal{G}_{\ell_{out}} \in \mathsf{Func}(\{0,1\}^b, \{0,1\}^b)$ we have $|\mathsf{all}_2| = 2^k \cdot (2^b!) \cdot ((2^b)^{2^b})^{\ell_{in}+\ell_{out}-1}$.

Thirdly, we evaluate $|\mathsf{comp}_1(\tau)|$. For $i \in \{1, \ldots, \ell_{in}-1\}$, let γ_i^{in} be the number of pairs in τ_i^{in}. For $i \in \{1, \ldots, \ell_{out}\}$, let γ_i^{out} be the number of pairs in τ_i^{out}. Let $\gamma_{\mathcal{P}}$ be the number of pairs in $\tau_{\mathcal{P}} \cup \tau_K$. Let $\gamma^{in} = \sum_{i=1}^{\ell_{in}-1} \gamma_i^{in}$ and $\gamma^{out} = \sum_{i=1}^{\ell_{out}} \gamma_i^{out}$. Let $\gamma = \gamma^{in} + \gamma^{out} + \gamma_{\mathcal{P}}$. Note that $\tau_1^{in}, \ldots, \tau_{\ell_{in}-1}^{in}, \tau_1^{out}, \ldots, \tau_{\ell_{out}}^{out}$, and $\tau_{\mathcal{P}} \cup \tau_K$ are defined so that these sets do not overlap each other. Moreover, K is uniquely determined. Hence we have $|\mathsf{comp}_1(\tau)| = (2^b - \gamma)!$

Finally we evaluate $|\mathsf{comp}_2(\tau)|$. $\gamma_1^{in}, \ldots, \gamma_{\ell_{in}-1}^{in}, \gamma_1^{out}, \ldots, \gamma_{\ell_{out}}^{out}, \gamma^{in}, \gamma^{out}, \gamma_{\mathcal{P}}$ and γ are analogously defined. Note that K is uniquely determined. We thus have $|\mathsf{comp}_2(\tau)| = (2^b - \gamma_{\mathcal{P}})! \cdot \prod_{i=1}^{\ell_{in}-1}(2^b)^{2^b-\gamma_i^{in}} \cdot \prod_{i=1}^{\ell_{out}}(2^b)^{2^b-\gamma_i^{out}} = (2^b - \gamma_{\mathcal{P}})! \cdot (2^b)^{(\ell_{in}+\ell_{out}-1)2^b-\gamma+\gamma_{\mathcal{P}}}$.

Hence we have

$$\frac{\Pr[\mathsf{T}_1 = \tau]}{\Pr[\mathsf{T}_2 = \tau]} \geq \frac{(2^b - \gamma)!}{2^k \cdot 2^b!} \cdot \frac{2^k \cdot (2^b!) \cdot (2^b)^{(\ell_{in}+\ell_{out}-1)2^b}}{(2^b - \gamma_{\mathcal{P}})! \cdot (2^b)^{(\ell_{in}+\ell_{out}-1)2^b-\gamma+\gamma_{\mathcal{P}}}} \geq 1.$$

We thus have $\varepsilon = 0$.

Upper Bound of $\Pr[\mathsf{D}^{G_1} \Rightarrow 1] - \Pr[\mathsf{D}^{G_2} \Rightarrow 1]$

By Lemma 1, we have $\Pr[G_1] - \Pr[G_2]$

$$\leq \frac{2r(Q + \kappa_{pf})}{2^c} + \left(\frac{44\ell q(Q + \kappa_{pf})}{2^b}\right)^{1/2} + \frac{5.5\ell^2 q^2}{2^b} + \lambda(Q) + \frac{q}{2^k}. \tag{3}$$

4.2 Upper Bound of $\Pr[\mathbf{D}^{G_2} \Rightarrow 1] - \Pr[\mathbf{D}^{G_3} \Rightarrow 1]$

Note that L_3 is a random function $\mathcal{R}$. We show the following lemma.

Lemma 2. L_2 and $\mathcal{R}$ are indistinguishable unless the following events occur in Game 2.

$$\mathsf{coll_h} \Leftrightarrow \exists \alpha, \beta \in \{1, \dots, q\} \text{ with } \alpha \neq \beta \text{ and } \exists i \in \{0, \dots, \ell_{\mathsf{out}} - 1\} \text{ s.t. } H_i^\alpha = H_i^\beta.$$

Proof. If $\mathsf{coll_h}$ does not hold then for any online query to L_2 the response is freshly and randomly drawn from $\{0,1\}^{\ell_{\mathsf{out}} \times r}$. Hence, L_2 and $\mathcal{R}$ are indistinguishable. $\square$

By the above lemma, $\Pr[\mathbf{D}^{G_2} \Rightarrow 1 | \neg \mathsf{coll_h}] = \Pr[\mathbf{D}^{G_3} \Rightarrow 1]$ holds. Hence, we have

$$\Pr[\mathbf{D}^{G_2} \Rightarrow 1] - \Pr[\mathbf{D}^{G_3} \Rightarrow 1] \leq \Pr[\mathsf{coll_h}].$$

The upper bound is given in the following. Due to lack of space, we omit the detail for the evaluation of $\Pr[\mathsf{coll_h}]$. The upper bound can be obtained by using the birthday analysis for the random functions in L_2.

$$\Pr[\mathbf{D}^{G_2} \Rightarrow 1] - \Pr[\mathbf{D}^{G_3} \Rightarrow 1] \leq \Pr[\mathsf{coll_h}] \leq \frac{0.5 \ell q^2}{2^b}. \tag{4}$$

4.3 Upper Bound of the Advantage

Putting (3) and (4) into (1) gives

$$\mathbf{Adv}^{\mathsf{prf}}_{\mathsf{SwSponge}}(\mathbf{D}) \leq \frac{2r(Q + \kappa_{\mathsf{pf}})}{2^c} + \left(\frac{44 \ell q(Q + \kappa_{\mathsf{pf}})}{2^b} \right)^{1/2} + \frac{6 \ell^2 q^2}{2^b} + \lambda(Q) + \frac{q}{2^k}.$$

References

1. Andreeva, E., Daemen, J., Mennink, B., Van Assche, G.: Security of keyed sponge constructions using a modular proof approach. In: Leander, G. (ed.) FSE 2015. LNCS, vol. 9054, pp. 364–384. Springer, Heidelberg (2015). doi:10.1007/978-3-662-48116-5_18

2. Aumasson, J.-P., Henzen, L., Meier, W., Naya-Plasencia, M.: QUARK: a lightweight hash. In: Mangard, S., Standaert, F.-X. (eds.) CHES 2010. LNCS, vol. 6225, pp. 1–15. Springer, Heidelberg (2010). doi:10.1007/978-3-642-15031-9_1

3. Bertoni, G., Daemen, J., Peeters, M., Assche, G.: Duplexing the sponge: single-pass authenticated encryption and other applications. In: Miri, A., Vaudenay, S. (eds.) SAC 2011. LNCS, vol. 7118, pp. 320–337. Springer, Heidelberg (2012). doi:10.1007/978-3-642-28496-0_19

4. Bertoni, G., Daemen, J., Peeters, M., Assche, G.: Keccak. In: Johansson, T., Nguyen, P.Q. (eds.) EUROCRYPT 2013. LNCS, vol. 7881, pp. 313–314. Springer, Heidelberg (2013). doi:10.1007/978-3-642-38348-9_19

5. Bertoni, G., Daemen, J., Peeters, M., Assche, G.: On the indifferentiability of the sponge construction. In: Smart, N. (ed.) EUROCRYPT 2008. LNCS, vol. 4965, pp. 181–197. Springer, Heidelberg (2008). doi:10.1007/978-3-540-78967-3_11

6. Bertoni, G., Daemen, J., Peeters, M., Assche, G.V.: On the security of the keyed sponge construction. In: Symmetric Key Encryption Workshop (SKEW), February 2011

7. Bertoni, G., Daemen, J., Peeters, M., Assche, G.V.: Permutation-based encryption, authentication and authenticated encryption. In: Directions in Authenticated Ciphers (2012)

8. Bertoni, G., Daemen, J., Peeters, M., Assche, G.: Sponge-based pseudo-random number generators. In: Mangard, S., Standaert, F.-X. (eds.) CHES 2010. LNCS, vol. 6225, pp. 33–47. Springer, Heidelberg (2010). doi:10.1007/978-3-642-15031-9_3

9. Bogdanov, A., Knežević, M., Leander, G., Toz, D., Varıcı, K., Verbauwhede, I.: SPONGENT: a lightweight hash function. In: Preneel, B., Takagi, T. (eds.) CHES 2011. LNCS, vol. 6917, pp. 312–325. Springer, Heidelberg (2011). doi:10.1007/978-3-642-23951-9_21

10. Chang, D., Dworkin, M., Hong, S., Kelsey, J., Nandi, M.: A keyed sponge construction with pseudorandomness in the standard model. In: NIST SHA-3 2012 Workshop (2012)

11. Chen, S., Steinberger, J.: Tight security bounds for key-alternating ciphers. In: Nguyen, P.Q., Oswald, E. (eds.) EUROCRYPT 2014. LNCS, vol. 8441, pp. 327–350. Springer, Heidelberg (2014). doi:10.1007/978-3-642-55220-5_19

12. Gaži, P., Pietrzak, K., Tessaro, S.: The exact PRF security of truncation: tight bounds for keyed sponges and truncated CBC. In: Gennaro, R., Robshaw, M. (eds.) CRYPTO 2015. LNCS, vol. 9215, pp. 368–387. Springer, Heidelberg (2015). doi:10.1007/978-3-662-47989-6_18

13. Guo, J., Peyrin, T., Poschmann, A.: The PHOTON family of lightweight hash functions. In: Rogaway, P. (ed.) CRYPTO 2011. LNCS, vol. 6841, pp. 222–239. Springer, Heidelberg (2011). doi:10.1007/978-3-642-22792-9_13

14. Jovanovic, P., Luykx, A., Mennink, B.: Beyond $2^{c/2}$ security in sponge-based authenticated encryption modes. In: Sarkar, P., Iwata, T. (eds.) ASIACRYPT 2014. LNCS, vol. 8873, pp. 85–104. Springer, Heidelberg (2014). doi:10.1007/978-3-662-45611-8_5

15. Maurer, U., Renner, R., Holenstein, C.: Indifferentiability, impossibility results on reductions, and applications to the random oracle methodology. In: Naor, M. (ed.) TCC 2004. LNCS, vol. 2951, pp. 21–39. Springer, Heidelberg (2004). doi:10.1007/978-3-540-24638-1_2

16. Mennink, B., Reyhanitabar, R., Vizár, D.: Security of full-state keyed sponge and duplex: applications to authenticated encryption. In: Iwata, T., Cheon, J.H. (eds.) ASIACRYPT 2015. LNCS, vol. 9453, pp. 465–489. Springer, Heidelberg (2015). doi:10.1007/978-3-662-48800-3_19

17. Mouha, N., Mennink, B., Herrewege, A., Watanabe, D., Preneel, B., Verbauwhede, I.: Chaskey: an efficient MAC algorithm for 32-bit microcontrollers. In: Joux, A., Youssef, A. (eds.) SAC 2014. LNCS, vol. 8781, pp. 306–323. Springer, Heidelberg (2014). doi:10.1007/978-3-319-13051-4_19

18. Naito, Y., Yasuda, K.: New bounds for keyed sponges with extendable output: independence between capacity and message length. In: Peyrin, T. (ed.) FSE 2016. LNCS, vol. 9783, pp. 3–22. Springer, Heidelberg (2016). doi:10.1007/978-3-662-52993-5_1

19. NIST: SHA-3 standard: permutation-based hash and extendable-output functions. In: FIPS PUB 202 (2015)

20. NIST: Announcing request for candidate algorithm nominations for a new cryptographic hash algorithm (SHA-3) family. Federal Regist. **27**(212), 62212–62220 (2007)

21. Patarin, J.: The "Coefficients H" technique. In: Avanzi, R.M., Keliher, L., Sica, F. (eds.) SAC 2008. LNCS, vol. 5381, pp. 328–345. Springer, Heidelberg (2009). doi:10.1007/978-3-642-04159-4_21

22. Tsudik, G.: Message authentication with one-way hash functions. In: INFOCOM, pp. 2055–2059

23. Yasuda, K.: "Sandwich" is indeed secure: how to authenticate a message with just one hashing. In: Pieprzyk, J., Ghodosi, H., Dawson, E. (eds.) ACISP 2007. LNCS, vol. 4586, pp. 355–369. Springer, Heidelberg (2007). doi:10.1007/978-3-540-73458-1_26

MultiParty Computation

Secure Error-Tolerant Graph Matching Protocols

Kalikinkar Mandal[1(✉)], Basel Alomair[2], and Radha Poovendran[1]

[1] Network Security Lab, Department of Electrical Engineering,
University of Washington, Seattle, WA 98195, USA
{kmandal,rp3}@uw.edu
[2] National Center for Cybersecurity Technologies, King Abdulaziz City
for Science and Technology (KACST), Riyadh, Saudi Arabia
alomair@uw.edu

Abstract. We consider a setting where there are two parties, each party holds a private graph and they wish to jointly compute the structural dissimilarity between two graphs without revealing any information about their private input graph. Graph edit distance (GED) is a widely accepted metric for measuring the dissimilarity of graphs. It measures the minimum cost for transforming one graph into the other graph by applying graph edit operations. In this paper we present a framework for securely computing approximated GED and as an example, present a protocol based on threshold additive homomorphic encryption scheme. We develop several new sub-protocols such as private maximum computation and optimal assignment protocols to construct the main protocol. We show that our protocols are secure against semi-honest adversaries. The asymptotic complexity of the protocol is $O(n^5 \ell \log^*(\ell))$ where ℓ is the bit length of ring elements and n is the number of nodes in the graph.

Keywords: Secure two-party computation · Graph edit distance · Privacy · Graph algorithms

1 Introduction

Graph matching is a task of assessing the structural similarity of graphs. There are two types of graph matching, namely *exact matching* and *error-tolerant matching* (also known as inexact matching) [1, 26, 29]. The exact graph matching aims to determine, whether two graphs – a source graph and a target graph – are identical. The later one aims to find a distortion or dissimilarity between two graphs. Graph edit distance is a metric that measures the structural dissimilarity between two graphs. The graph edit distance is quantified as the minimum costs of edit operations required to transform the source graph into the target graph. We consider an attribute graph consisting of a set of nodes, a set of edges and labels assigned to nodes and edges. Examples of such graphs are social network graphs and fingerprint graphs [20, 24]. A standard set of graph edit operations on an attribute graph includes insertion, and deletion and substitution

© Springer International Publishing AG 2016
S. Foresti and G. Persiano (Eds.): CANS 2016, LNCS 10052, pp. 265–283, 2016.
DOI: 10.1007/978-3-319-48965-0_16

of edges and nodes and substitution of vertex and edge labels. Unfortunately, there is no polynomial time algorithm for computing the exact graph edit distance between two graphs. However, several algorithms have been developed for computing approximated or suboptimal graph edit distance in polynomial time [1,9,24,26,29]. A common strategy used for computing the GED is to find an optimal assignment between each node of one graph to each node of the other graph with minimum cost. The optimal assignment is computed by solving an assignment problem with a cost matrix derived using the structure of the graphs and the costs of graph edit operations. Graph edit distance has many applications in social network graph computation, pattern recognition and biometrics such as in fingerprint identification systems [20,24].

Our Contributions. In this paper, for the first time, we consider secure two-party graph edit distance computation where each party has a private graph and they wish to jointly compute an approximated graph edit distance between two private graphs, without leaking any information about their input graph. A private graph is meant by the structure of the graph represented by an adjacency matrix, node labels and edge labels are private, only the number of nodes is public. First, we propose a general framework for securely computing approximated graph edit distance, which consists of securely computing the entries of the cost matrix from the private input graphs, securely solving the assignment problem and securely processing an optional phase to obtain the graph edit distance. Then, as an example, we develop a protocol for securely computing an approximated graph edit distance, determining the error-tolerant graph matching, based on the algorithm by Riesen and Bunke [26]. Our protocol construction relies on threshold additive homomorphic encryption scheme [13] instantiated by the threshold Paillier encryption scheme [25]. The reason for choosing homomorphic encryption in the construction is to design efficient protocols by exploiting the structures of the GED algorithms. To construct the main protocol, we develop several sub-protocols such as a private maximum computation protocol and an optimal assignment protocol based on the Hungarian algorithm. We prove the security of the protocol in the semi-honest model. The difference between the workloads of the parties is negligible. The asymptotic complexity for the proposed protocol is $O(n^5(\ell \log^*(\ell)))$, where ℓ is the bit length of ring elements and n is the maximum among the numbers of nodes in two graphs.

2   Related Work

Secure Two-party Computation. Secure two-party computation is a powerful tool that enables two parties to jointly compute a function on their private inputs without revealing any information about the inputs except the output of the function. Works on secure two-party computation began with the seminal work of Yao [28] that showed that any function can be securely evaluated in the presence of semi-honest adversaries by first generating a garbled circuit computing that function and then sending it to the other party. Then the other party can obtain the output by evaluating the garbled circuit using a 1-out-of-2 Oblivious Transfer (OT) protocol. A series of work on secure two-party computation have been done under different security settings and on optimization of garbled circuits [4,15,17], to name a few and a number of tools and compilers such as Fairplay [19] and TASTY [14] have been developed for secure computation.

Secure Processing of Graph Algorithms. Graph algorithms have a wide variety of use in many secure applications. Recently secure and data oblivious graph algorithms have been studied in [2,5,6]. Aly et al. [2] proposed secure data-oblivious algorithms for shortest path and maximum flow algorithms. In [6], Blanton et al. proposed secure data-oblivious algorithms for breadth-first search, single-source single-destination shortest path, minimum spanning tree, and maximum flow problems. In [5], Blanton and Saraph proposed secure data-oblivious algorithms for finding maximum matching size in a bipartite graph. In our work, as a sub-task, we need to find a perfect matching for computing the optimal cost in a complete weighted bipartite graph.

Secure Edit Distance Computation. An edit distance measures the dissimilarity (similarity) between two strings. In [3], Atallah et al. proposed a privacy-preserving protocol for computing an edit distance between two strings based on an additive homomorphic encryption scheme. Jha et al. [16] presented privacy-preserving protocols for computing edit distance between two strings. The protocols are constructed using oblivious transfer and Yao's garbled circuits method. Later on, Huang et al. [15] developed a faster protocol for edit distance computation with the garbled circuit approach. Recently, Cheon et al. [7] proposed a privacy-preserving scheme for computing edit distance for encrypted strings. Their protocol is based on a somewhat homomorphic encryption scheme.

3 Preliminaries

In our construction, we use the threshold Paillier encryption scheme (TPS) $\mathsf{TPS} = (\pi_{\mathrm{DistKeyGen}}, \pi_{\mathrm{DistSk}}, \mathrm{Enc}, \pi_{\mathrm{DistDec}})$ in the two-party setting, due to Hazay el al. [13] where $\pi_{\mathrm{DistKeyGen}}$ is the protocol for distributively generating a RSA modulus $N = pq$, π_{DistSk} is the protocol for distributed generation of shared private key and π_{DistDec} is the protocol for the distributed Paillier decryption of shared private key. The encryption algorithm Enc is defined as follows. For a plaintext message m with randomness $r \in_R \mathbb{Z}_N$ the ciphertext is computed as $c = \mathrm{Enc}(m, r) = r^N (N + 1)^m \bmod N^2$. where $N = pq$ and p and q are two large primes of equal length. Assume that the bit length of N is ℓ. The Paillier encryption scheme has (1) additive homomorphic property: $E(m_1 + m_2) = \mathrm{Enc}(m_1) \cdot \mathrm{Enc}(m_2)$ and $\mathrm{Enc}(km_1) = \mathrm{Enc}(m_1)^k$ and (2) rerandomizing property meaning for a ciphertext c, without knowing the private key, another ciphertext $c' = \mathsf{Rand}(pk, \mathrm{Enc}(m; r), r') = r'^N r^N (N+1)^m = (rr')^N (N+1)^m$ can be created. For the details about other protocols, the reader is referred to [13].

The computation of the GED involves operations on negative numbers as well. We represent the negative numbers in modular arithmetic in the encryption as $[\lceil \frac{N}{2} \rceil, N - 1] \equiv [-\lfloor \frac{N}{2} \rfloor, -1]$. The positive numbers lie in the range $[0, \lfloor \frac{N}{2} \rfloor]$ and the negative numbers lie in the range $[\lceil \frac{N}{2} \rceil, N - 1]$.

4   Problem Formulation

We consider an undirected attribute graph $G = (V, E, l_G, \zeta_G)$ where V is a finite set of vertices, E is the set of edges, and l_G is the vertex labeling function and ζ_G is the edge labeling function. Assume that the graph G does not contain any multi-edges and self-loops. Let $G_1 = (V_1, E_1, l_{G_1}, \zeta_{G_1})$ be a source graph and $G_2 = (V_2, E_2, l_{G_2}, \zeta_{G_2})$ be a target graph. The graph edit distance [1,26] between G_1 and G_2 is defined by $f_{GED}(G_1, G_2) = \min_{(eo_1, \ldots, eo_k) \in \Gamma(G_1, G_2)} \sum_{i=1}^{k} c(eo_i)$ where $\Gamma(G_1, G_2)$ is the set of all edit paths that transform G_1 into G_2 and $c(eo_i)$ denotes the cost for the edit operation eo_i. The reader is referred to Appendix B for the details about graph edit operations.

In this work we consider a setting where there are two parties P_1 and P_2, P_1 has a private graph G_1 and P_2 has another private graph G_2. The parties wish to compute an approximated graph edit distance $f_{GED}(G_1, G_2)$ between G_1 and G_2 without leaking anything about their input graph, where f_{GED} is a function running in polynomial time computing an approximated graph edit distance between G_1 and G_2. At the end of the execution of the protocol, each party P_i should learn nothing about other party's input graph G_{3-i}, beyond the edit distance value $f_{GED}(G_1, G_2)$, $i = 1, 2$. A private graph is meant by node and edge labels and the structure of the graph represented by an adjacency matrix are private, only the number of nodes in the graph is public.

Adversary model. We define the security of the protocol for the GED computation against *honest-but-curious* or *semi-honest* adversaries where a party compromised by an adversary follows the prescribed actions of the protocol and aims to learn some unintended information from the execution of the protocol. Let $\mathcal{A}$ be a probabilistic polynomial time adversary that can corrupt at most one party at the beginning of the execution of the protocol. The adversary $\mathcal{A}$ sends all input messages of the corrupted party during the execution of the protocol and receives messages from the honest party. The honest party follows the instruction of the protocol.

Let $\mathcal{A}$ corrupts the party P_i. We denote the view of P_i in the real execution of the protocol Π by $\mathsf{VIEW}_{P_i}^{\Pi}(1^\lambda, G_1, G_2) = \{G_i, R_i, m_1, m_2, \cdots, m_T\}$, $i = 1$ or 2, where G_i is P_i's private input graph, $m_1, m_2, \cdots, m_T$ are the messages received from P_{3-i} and R_i is P_i's random tape used during the execution of the protocol.

Definition 1. *Let $f_{GED}(G_1, G_2)$ be the functionality computing an approximated graph edit distance. We say that a two-party protocol Π securely evaluates $f_{GED}(G_1, G_2)$ in the presence of semi-honest adversaries if there exists a PPT simulator $\mathcal{S} = (\mathcal{S}_{P_1}, \mathcal{S}_{P_2})$ such that for all G_1 and G_2, it holds that*

$$\{\mathcal{S}_{P_i}(1^\lambda, G_i, f_{GED}(G_1, G_2))\} \stackrel{c}{\approx} \{VIEW_{P_i}^{\Pi}(1^\lambda, G_1, G_2)\}$$

where $\stackrel{c}{\approx}$ denotes the computational indistinguishably of two distribution ensembles.

5   Description of Proposed GED Protocols

This section presents a framework for the two-party graph edit distance computation based on the assignment problem. As an example, we present a protocol for the graph edit distance computation and prove its security in the semi-honest model.

5.1   A Framework for Two-Party GED Computation

Figure 1 provides the process of an approximated GED computation. At a high level, the graph edit distance computation consists of three phases, namely the construction of the cost matrix, solving the optimal assignment problem with the cost matrix and further processing (optional processing) using the results from the assignment problem and inputs graphs to improve the approximated GED. The cost matrix construction phase takes graph inputs from the parties and computes the entries of the matrix in terms of the costs of graph edit operations. Solving the assignment problem does not take any graph inputs from parties. Based on the approximation factor of the approximated GED, the optional processing is performed. The general structure of the protocols for two-party graph edit distance computation consists of secure two-party evaluations of the cost matrix construction, the optimal assignment problem and optional processing. At the end of secure processing of each phase, we ensure that there is no leakage of information from the output, except the final output that will be known to both parties.

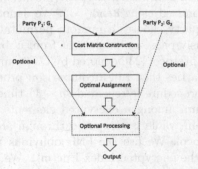

Fig. 1. A block diagram for two-party graph edit distance computation

In the current paper, we perform the secure evaluation of graph edit distance, following the above framework, using the threshold Paillier additive homomorphic encryption scheme. The private key of the encryption scheme is shared between two parties. First, the parties construct an encrypted cost matrix using the input graphs and then they run the optimal assignment protocol on the encrypted cost matrix. The encrypted outputs from the optimal assignment protocol along with the input graphs if needed are used in the optional processing phase to obtain the graph edit distance. In Sect. 5.3, we present an approximated graph edit distance computation protocol.

5.2 Sub-protocols

Secure equality testing and comparison protocols have been extensively studied in the literature under different two-party computation settings, e.g., in [8,11,18,27]. We present a variant of encrypted equality test protocol, denoted by π_{EQ} in the Appendix. We use the greater-than protocol of Toft [27] with the modification that we replace the equality test protocol by π_{EQ}. In this section we present two sub-protocols **Private Maximum Computation** protocol and **Optimal Assignment** protocol that are necessary for the main protocols for graph edit distance. As our protocol construction uses an equality check, comparison, oblivious transfer and oblivious polynomial evaluation protocol, we denote the functionalities by $\mathcal{F}_{EQ}$, $\mathcal{F}_{CMP}$ $\mathcal{F}_{OT}$, and $\mathcal{F}_{OPE}$ and corresponding protocols by π_{EQ}, π_{CMP}, π_{OT} and π_{OPE}, respectively.

Private Maximum Computation Protocol. Let P_1 and P_2 hold a vector of encrypted numbers $\mathbf{c} = (c_1, c_2, ..., c_n)$ with $c_i = \text{Enc}(x_i)$ for the plaintext vector $\mathbf{x} = (x_1, x_2, ..., x_n)$. Let x_{mi} be the maximum value in $\mathbf{x}$ for index mi, $1 \leq mi \leq n$. The private maximum computation (PMC) protocol is to jointly compute the encrypted maximum value $\text{Enc}(x_{mi})$ and the encrypted index $\text{Enc}(mi)$ from $\mathbf{c}$ without revealing x_{mi} and mi.

We develop a two-party protocol for private maximum computation. The basic idea behind the construction of the PMC protocol is that one party shuffles the order of the elements of $\mathbf{c}$ through a secret permutation π_1 and after shuffling, each element is re-randomized using $\text{Rand}(\cdot, \cdot,)$. We denote the resultant vector by $\mathbf{c}'$. Next, the other party chooses a random permutation π_2 and using this permutation, it obliviously picks up an element from $\mathbf{c}'$ by running a 1-out-of-n oblivious transfer (OT) protocol [23], denoted by OT_1^n, and then randomizes the chosen element. Both parties then run a comparison protocol to determine the maximum value. This procedure is repeated $(n-1)$ times for $\pi_2(i), 2 \leq i \leq n$ to compute the maximum among n encrypted elements. The encrypted index $\text{Enc}(mi)$ for the maximum value is computed through an oblivious polynomial evaluation (OPE) protocol. We use the FNP oblivious polynomial evaluation protocol [10] to obtain the encrypted index $\text{Enc}(mi)$. We describe the details of the protocol in Fig. 2.

Complexity. We evaluate the communication and computation overhead of the π_{PMC} protocol, which is composed of π_{CMP}, an OT_1^n protocol and an OPE protocol. Since the round complexity of π_{CMP} is $O(\log(\ell) \log^*(\ell))$, the total communication complexity for π_{CMP} is $(n \log(\ell) \log^*(\ell))$. The communication overhead

---

Protocol: Private MAX Computation π_{PMC}

Input: A ciphertext vector $\mathbf{c} = (c_1, c_2, ..., c_n)$ of $\mathbf{x} = (x_1, x_2, ..., x_n)$ where $c_i = \mathsf{Enc}(x_i), 1 \leq i \leq n$.

Output: Encryption of the maximum value $\mathsf{Enc}(x_{\mathsf{mi}})$ and its encrypted position $\mathsf{Enc}(\mathsf{mi})$.

1. P_1 chooses a random permutation π_1 on $\{1, 2, ..., n\}$ and computes $(c_{\pi_1(1)}, c_{\pi_1(2)}, ..., c_{\pi_1(n)})$. It then randomizes this vector and obtains $\mathbf{c}' = (c_1', c_2', ..., c_n')$ where $c_i' = \mathsf{Rand}(pk, c_{\pi_1(i)}, r_i), 1 \leq i \leq n$ where r_i is a random number.

2. P_2 chooses a random and secret permutation π_2 on $\{1, 2, ..., n\}$. It then runs an OT_1^n protocol with inputs $\mathbf{c}'$ from P_1 and $\pi_2(1)$ from P_2. Let $c_{\pi_2(1)}'$ be the output of the OT protocol. P_2 randomizes $c_{\pi_2(1)}'$ as $c_1'' = \mathsf{Rand}(pk, c_{\pi_2(1)}', r_1')$ and sends c_1'' to P_1.

3. Both parties set $c_{Index} \leftarrow c_1''$. P_2 assigns $Index \leftarrow \pi_2(1)$.

4. For each $t \in [2, n]$, P_1 and P_2 performs the following steps:
   (a) P_2 chooses $\pi_2(t)$.
   (b) P_1 and P_2 run the OT_1^n protocol with inputs $\mathbf{c}'$ from P_1 and $\pi_2(t)$ from P_2 Let $c_{\pi_2(t)}'$ be the output of the OT protocol received by P_2.
   (c) P_2 randomizes $c_{\pi_2(t)}'$ as $c_t'' = \mathsf{Rand}(pk, c_{\pi_2(1)}', r_t')$ and sends c_t'' to P_1.
   (d) P_1 and P_2 run the comparison protocol π_{CMP} with inputs c_t'' and c_{Index} and let $\mathsf{Enc}(b_{t-1})$ be the output. They run the threshold decryption protocol $\mathsf{DistDec}(\mathsf{Enc}(b_{t-1}))$. If $b_{t-1} = 1$, both parties update $c_{Index} \leftarrow c_t''$ and P_2 updates $Index \leftarrow \pi_2(t)$.

5. P_1 computes the polynomial representation of π_1^{-1} using the Lagrange interpolation with coefficients in $\mathbb{Z}_n$ and let $Q_{\pi_1^{-1}}(x) = \sum_{j=0}^{n-1} Q_j x^j$ be the polynomial of degree at most $(n-1)$.

6. P_1 and P_2 run the FNP OPE protocol with inputs $Q_{\pi^{-1}}(x)$ from P_1 and $Index$ from P_2 to compute the encrypted index $\mathsf{Enc}(\mathsf{mi})$ where $\mathsf{mi} = Q_{\pi_1^{-1}}(Index)$.
   (a) P_1 encrypts the coefficients of $Q_{\pi_1^{-1}}(x)$ as $(\mathsf{Enc}(Q_0), \mathsf{Enc}(Q_1), \cdots, \mathsf{Enc}(Q_{n-1}))$ and sends it to P_2.
   (b) P_2 computes $\mathsf{Enc}(Q_{\pi_1^{-1}}(Index)) = \prod_{j=0}^{n-1}(\mathsf{Enc}(Q_1))^{Index^j}$ and sends $\mathsf{Enc}(Q_{\pi_1^{-1}}(Index))$ to P_1.

Fig. 2. Protocol for private maximum computation

for OT_1^n is $O(n)$. Therefore the overall communication complexity for π_{PMC} is $O(n^2 + n\ell \log(\ell) \log^*(\ell))$. It is easy to see that the computation complexity of the protocol is also $O(n^2 + n\ell \log(\ell) \log^*(\ell))$.

Theorem 1. *The protocol π_{PMC} securely computes the encrypted maximum value and its encrypted maximum index, in the presence of semi-honest adversaries.*

Proof. The proof follows from the semantic security of the Paillier encryption scheme. The details of the proof can be found in the full paper [21].

Optimal Assignment (OA) Protocol. The assignment problem is one of the fundamental optimization problems. Given two sets $X = \{u_1, u_2, \cdots, u_n\}$ and $Y = \{v_1, v_2, \cdots, v_n\}$ and a cost matrix $W = (w_{ij})_{n \times n}$ where w_{ij} is the cost of assigning u_i to v_j, the assignment problem is to find a permutation ρ on $[1, n]$ that maximizes $\sum_{i=1}^{n} w_{i\rho(i)}$. We denote an assignment problem instance and its solution by $(\rho, \sum_{i=1}^{n} w_{i\rho(i)}) \leftarrow \mathsf{AssignProb}(X, Y, W)$, which can be solved by the Hungarian algorithm with time complexity $O(n^3)$ [22]. The assignment problem can also be viewed as the problem of finding a perfect bipartite matching in a
- complete weighted bipartite graph $G = (V, E, W)$ with $V = X \cup Y, X \cap Y = \phi$ where the cost matrix W is the weight matrix consisting of weights of the edges. In this paper, we consider the perfect bipartite matching variant of the Hungarian algorithm. An optimal assignment ρ that minimizes $\sum_{i=1}^{n} w_{i\rho(i)}$ can be obtained from this by making the entries of the cost matrix W negative.

Given an encrypted cost matrix $W = (\mathsf{Enc}(w_{ij}))_{n \times n}$ for $\mathsf{AssignProb}(\mathsf{X, Y,}$ W), we develop a two-party protocol for the assignment protocol based on the Hungarian algorithm for computing $\mathsf{Enc}(\sum_{i=1}^{n} w_{i\rho(i)})$ for an optimal assignment ρ. In the secure two-party computation protocol, we resolve the following challenges (a) securely computing and updating the labeling of nodes in X and Y; (b) hiding the edges in the perfect matching set as it eventually determines the optimal assignment ρ; and (c) securely computing augmenting paths and updating the matching set. Since the order of node and/or edge operations during the execution of the algorithm leaks information about the assignment, we prevent this by encrypting the matching set $\mathcal{M}$ and shuffling the order of nodes while keeping the assignment problem invariant. We make the following observation about the assignment problem when it solved using the Hungarian algorithm.

Observation 1. *Let* $(\rho, \sum_{i=1}^{n} w_{i\rho(i)}) \leftarrow \mathsf{AssignProb}(X, Y, W)$ *be an assignment problem as described above. Let* π *be a permutation on* $[1, n]$. *Define* $X^\pi = \{u_{\pi(1)}, \cdots, u_{\pi(n)}\}$ *and* $Y^\pi = \{v_{\pi(1)}, \cdots, v_{\pi(n)}\}$ *and* $W^\pi = (w_{\pi(i)\pi(j)})_{n \times n}$. *If the assignment problems* (X, Y, W) *has an optimal value* $\sum_{i=1}^{n} w_{i\rho(i)}$ *with assignment mapping* ρ, *then the assignment problem* $\mathsf{AssignProb}(X^\pi, Y^\pi, W^\pi)$ *has the same optimal value with assignment mapping* $\rho_1 = \pi \circ \rho \circ \pi^{-1}$.

Our main idea for constructing the OA protocol is to choose a secret permutation π shared between two parties and transform the problem $\mathsf{AssignProb}(X, Y, W)$ into $\mathsf{AssignProb}(X^\pi, Y^\pi, W^\pi)$ and then securely execute the steps of the bipartite matching algorithm on the encrypted cost matrix. The party P_1 chooses a secret permutation π_1 and P_2 chooses another secret permutation π_2. Then they jointly construct the encrypted cost matrix $W^\pi = (\mathsf{Enc}(w_{\pi(i)\pi(j)}))$ where $\pi = \pi_2 \circ \pi_1$. We compute the initial labelings of nodes in X using the private maximum computation protocol π_{PMC}. We encrypt node identities $u_i \in X$ and $v_j \in Y$ of the bipartite graph and their labels, denoted by $\mathsf{lbl}_X(u)$ for $u \in X$ and $\mathsf{lbl}_Y(v)$ for $v \in Y$ and construct 2-tuple sequences as $(\mathsf{Enc}(u_i), \mathsf{Enc}(\mathsf{lbl}_X(u_i))), 1 \leq i \leq n$ for both X and Y. We use the same permutation π to hide the order of each sequence of 2-tuple encrypted values component-wise for both X and Y. Denoting $\mathcal{M} = \{(\mathsf{Enc}(u), \mathsf{Enc}(v)) : u \in X, v \in Y\}$ by the matching set containing encrypted edges, $\{\mathsf{Enc}(u) : u \in X\}$

the set all encrypted tail node ids in $\mathcal{M}$ by $\mathcal{M} \star X$ and $\{\text{Enc}(v) : v \in Y\}$ the set all encrypted head node ids in $\mathcal{M}$ by $\mathcal{M} \star Y$. The initial matching is found by using the π_{EQ} and π_{DistDec} protocol. An encrypted equality graph EQ^{lbl} represented by an encrypted adjacency matrix is constructed from encrypted labels for X and Y and encrypted cost matrix W using the π_{EQ} protocol. The perfect matching is found by extending the matching set by finding an encrypted augmenting path. An encrypted augmenting path is found by executing the breadth-first-search (BFS) algorithm on the encrypted equality graph EQ^{lbl} where the source and target vertices are free vertices in X and Y. We adopt a variant of Blanton et al.'s BFS algorithm [6] in our setting where the secret key for the decryption algorithm is shared between two parties and we denote this protocol by π_{BFS}. We don't provide the technical details due to space limit. For an encrypted equality graph $\mathcal{P} := \text{Enc}(t_0) - \text{Enc}(t_1) - \text{Enc}(t_2) - \cdots - \text{Enc}(t_k)$ of length $k - 1$, the set of encrypted edges are given by $\mathcal{P}_{edge} = \{(\text{Enc}(t_0), \text{Enc}(t_1)), (\text{Enc}(t_2), \text{Enc}(t_1)), \cdots, (\text{Enc}(t_{k-1}), \text{Enc}(t_k))\}$. After finding $\mathcal{P}_{edge}$, the matching set is updated as $M \leftarrow M \Delta \mathcal{P}_{edge}$ where Δ is the symmetric difference set operation. We use two dummy counters of length n for keeping track of encrypted free nodes of X and Y. For computing the GED, we only need the maximum value $\sum_{i=1}^{n} w_{i\rho(i)}$. Thus the protocol outputs only $\sum_{i=1}^{n} w_{i\rho(i)}$. Figure 3 presents the details of our secure protocol for the assignment problem.

Complexity. From π_{OA}, it can be seen that the time complexity for finding the initial matching (Step 1 to Step 7) is $O(n^3 + n^2\ell \log(\ell) \log^*(\ell))$. If the initial matching is not a perfect matching, the computational complexity for terminating the protocol is $O(n^5\ell \log^*(\ell) + n^4\ell \log(\ell) \log^*(\ell)) = O(n^5\ell \log^*(\ell))$. An insecure version of the Hungarian algorithm runs in $O(n^3)$ steps. The overhead of the protocol due to security is $(n^2\ell \log^*(\ell))$.

Theorem 2. *The protocol π_{OA} securely computes the encrypted optimal value in the presence of semi-honest adversaries.*

Proof. We prove the security of the protocol in the hybrid model. In the protocol, one party receives messages from the other party and also from the trusted third party computing a functionality. The simulator also needs to simulate the outputs for the trusted third party functionalities. We construct two different simulators for the view of the adversary.

When P_1 is corrupted. Let $\mathcal{A}$ be the adversary controlling the party P_1. $\mathcal{S}_1$ chooses $2n$ uniformly random tapes $\mathbf{r}_0 = \{(r_i^0, r_i^1)\}_{i=1}^n$ from $\mathbb{Z}_N$ and computes the encrypted 2-tuple vector LBL^Y. It emulates the outputs $\text{Enc}(\text{lbl}_X(u_i))$ and $\text{Enc}(d_i), 1 \leq i \leq n$ for the trusted third party functionality $\mathcal{F}_{\text{PMC}}$ on ith row W_i. $\mathcal{S}_1$ chooses n random tapes $\mathbf{r}_1 = \{r_i^2\}_{i=1}^n$ uniformly at random for P_1 and computes the encryptions of $i, 1 \leq i \leq n$. $\mathcal{S}_1$ picks a permutation π_1 and $(6n + n^2)$ random tapes $\mathbf{r}_2 = \{\{(r_i^3, r_i^4, r_i^5, r_i^6, r_i^7, r_i^8)\}_{i=1}^n, (r_{ij}^0)_{n \times n}\}$ uniformly at random for P_1 and computes $LBL^{X\pi_1}, LBL^{Y\pi_1}, D^{\pi_1}$ and W^{π_1} and

Protocol: Optimal Assignment based on the Hungarian algorithm π_{OA}

Input: The cost matrix $\text{Enc}(W) = (\text{Enc}(w_{ij}))_{n \times n}$ $w_{ij} = cost(u_i, v_j)$.

Output: Optimal assignment value $\text{Enc}(\sum_{i=1}^{n} w_{i\rho(i)})$.

1. P_1 computes $(\text{Enc}(\text{lbl}_Y(v_1) : 1 \leq i \leq n)$ with $\text{lbl}_Y(v_i) = 0, v_i \in Y$ and $(\text{Enc}(i) : 1 \leq i \leq n)$ and constructs $LBL^Y = \Big((\text{Enc}(\text{lbl}_Y(v_i)), \text{Enc}(i)) : 1 \leq i \leq n\Big)$ and sends it to P_2.

2. $\mathcal{L} \leftarrow \phi; \mathcal{VP} \leftarrow \phi; \mathcal{M} \leftarrow \phi;$

3. For each $u_i \in X$, P_1 and P_2 run π_{PMC} with input ith row $W_i = (w_{i1}, w_{i2}, ..., w_{in})$ and obtain output $\text{Enc}(\text{lbl}_X(u_i))$ and $\text{Enc}(d_i)$ where $\text{lbl}_X(u_i) = w_{id_i} = \max_{v_j \in Y}\{w_{ij}\}, u_i \in X$ and $1 \leq d_i \leq n$.

   (a) Construct $LBL^X = \Big((\text{Enc}(\text{lbl}_X(u_i)), \text{Enc}(i)) : 1 \leq i \leq n\Big)$.

   (b) Construct $D = ((\text{Enc}(i), \text{Enc}(d_i)) : 1 \leq i \leq n)$.

   (c) Update $\mathcal{L} \leftarrow \mathcal{L} \cup \{(\text{Enc}(\text{lbl}_X(u_i)), \text{Enc}(\text{lbl}_Y(v_i)))\}$.

4. P_1 chooses a random perm π_1 and computes the following and sends all to P_2

   (a) $LBL^{Y\pi_1} := \Big((\text{Enc}(\text{lbl}_Y(v_{\pi_1(j)})), \text{Enc}(\pi_1(j))) : 1 \leq j \leq n\Big), LBL^{X\pi_1} := \Big((\text{Enc}(\text{lbl}_X(u_{\pi_1(j)})), \text{Enc}(\pi_1(j))) : 1 \leq j \leq n\Big)$

   (b) $D^{\pi_1} := ((\text{Enc}(\pi_1(j)), \text{Enc}(d_{\pi_1(j)})) : 1 \leq j \leq n)$

   (c) $W^{\pi_1} = (\text{Enc}(w_{\pi_1(i)\pi_1(j)}))_{n \times n}$

   (d) Rerandomize each encrypted value above

5. P_2 chooses a random perm π_2 and computes the following and sends all to P_1

   (a) $LBL^{Y\pi_2 \circ \pi_1} := \Big((\text{Enc}(\text{lbl}_Y(v_{\pi_2 \circ \pi_1(j)})), \text{Enc}(\pi_2 \circ \pi_1(j))) : 1 \leq j \leq n\Big),$

   (b) $LBL^{X\pi_2 \circ \pi_1} := \Big((\text{Enc}(\text{lbl}_X(u_{\pi_2 \circ \pi_1(j)})), \text{Enc}(\pi_2 \circ \pi_1(j))) : 1 \leq j \leq n\Big)$

   (c) $D^{\pi_2 \circ \pi_1} := ((\text{Enc}(\pi_2 \circ \pi_1(j)), \text{Enc}(d_{\pi_2 \circ \pi_1(j)})) : 1 \leq j \leq n)$

   (d) $W^{\pi_2 \circ \pi_1} = (\text{Enc}(w_{\pi_2 \circ \pi_1(i)\pi_2 \circ \pi_1(j)}))_{n \times n}$

   (e) Rerandomize each encrypted value above. Set $\pi = \pi_2 \circ \pi_1$.

6. For each $(\text{Enc}(\pi(i)), \text{Enc}(d_{\pi(i)})) \in D^{\pi}$, $i = 1, ..., n$, P_1 and P_2 run π_{EQ} protocol with inputs $\text{Enc}(d_{\pi(i)})$ and $\text{Enc}(d_{\pi(j)})$ and obtain $\text{Enc}(b_{ij}), b_{ij} \in \{0, 1\}$ for $j = 1, ..., i-1$. Compute $R = \prod_{j=1}^{i-1} \text{Enc}(b_{ij})$. P_1 and P_2 run π_{EQ} protocol with inputs R and $\text{Enc}(0)$ and obtain $\text{Enc}(b_i)$ as output. P_1 and P_2 then jointly decrypt $\text{Enc}(b_i)$. If $b_i = 1$, perform $\mathcal{M} \leftarrow \mathcal{M} \cup \{(\text{Enc}(\pi(i)), \text{Enc}(d_{\pi(i)}))\}$.

7. If $|\mathcal{M}| = n$, **return** the encrypted optimal value is $\text{Enc}(\sum_{i=1}^{n} \text{lbl}_X(u_{\pi(i)}) + \sum_{i=1}^{n} \text{lbl}_Y(v_{\pi(i)})) = \prod_{i=1}^{n} \text{Enc}(\text{lbl}_X(u_{\pi(i)})) \prod_{i=1}^{n} \text{Enc}(\text{lbl}_Y(v_{\pi(i)}))$. Else, P_1 and P_2 execute the following steps.

8. P_1 and P_2 construct a matrix $EQ^{\text{lbl}} = (\text{Enc}(e_{ij}))_{n \times n}$ by running the π_{EQ} protocol with inputs $\text{Enc}(\text{lbl}_X(u_{\pi(i)}) + \text{lbl}_Y(v_{\pi(j)}))$ and $\text{Enc}(w_{\pi(i)\pi(j)})$ where $\text{Enc}(e_{ij})$ is the output $1 \leq i, j \leq n$ and $e_{ij} \in \{0, 1\}$.

9. Initialize $S \leftarrow \phi$ and $T \leftarrow \phi$.

10. P_1 and P_2 find $\text{Enc}(u_{\pi(i)})$ such that $\text{Enc}(u_{\pi(i)}) \notin \mathcal{M} \star X$, then $S \leftarrow S \cup \{\text{Enc}(u_{\pi(i)})\}$.

11. P_1 and P_2 compute $N_{\text{lbl}}(S)$ for each $\text{Enc}(u_{\pi(i)}) \in S$ as

    (a) For row $EQ_i^{\text{lbl}} = (\text{Enc}(e_{i1}), \text{Enc}(e_{i2}), \cdots, \text{Enc}(e_{in}))$ of EQ^{lbl}, compute $Z_i = (\text{Enc}(e_{i1} \cdot v_1), \text{Enc}(e_{i2} \cdot v_2), \cdots, \text{Enc}(e_{in} \cdot v_n))$ from EQ_i^{lbl} where $\text{Enc}(e_{ik} \cdot k) = \text{Enc}(e_{ik})^k$.

    (b) Run π_{SR} protocol with input $Z_i = (\text{Enc}(e_{i1} \cdot v_1), \text{Enc}(e_{i2} \cdot v_2), \cdots, \text{Enc}(e_{in} \cdot v_n))$ and obtain the output $Z_i' = (z_1, z_2, \cdots, z_n)$

    (c) Run π_{EQ} with inputs z_j and $\text{Enc}(0)$ and obtain the output $\text{Enc}(b_j)$. Run DistDec on input $\text{Enc}(b_i)$ and obtain b_j for $1 \leq j \leq n$. If $b_j = 0$, perform $N_{\text{lbl}}(S) \leftarrow N_{\text{lbl}}(S) \cup \{\text{Enc}(v_j)\}$.

Fig. 3. Secure optimal assignment protocol based on the Hungarian algorithm

---

Protocol: Optimal Assignment π_{OA} (Cont.)

12. P_1 and P_2 check the equality of sets $N_{1bl}(S)$ and T running π_{EQ} and $\pi_{DistDec}$ protocols.

13. If $N_{1bl}(S) = T$
   (a) P_1 and P_2 compute $T = ((LBL_1^{V_\pi} \star Y) - T)$ from sets $LBL^{Y_\pi} \star Y$ and T by running π_{EQ} and $\pi_{DistDec}$ protocols.
   (b) For each $\text{Enc}(u_{\pi(i)}) \in S$ and $\text{Enc}(v_j) \in \bar{T}$, P_1 and P_2 compute $\text{Enc}(lbl_{ij}) = \text{Enc}(\text{lbl}_X(u_{\pi(i)}) + \text{lbl}_Y(v_j) - w_{\pi(i)\pi(j)})$.
   (c) P_1 and P_2 compute $\text{Enc}(\delta_{1bl}) = \min\{\text{Enc}(lbl_{ij}) : \text{Enc}(i) \in S, \text{Enc}(j) \in T\}$ using the π_{PMC} protocol.
   (d) P_1 and P_2 update the label lbl as

$$\text{Enc}(\text{lbl}_X(u)) = \text{Enc}(\text{lbl}_X(u)) \cdot \text{Enc}(\delta_{1bl})^{-1} \qquad \text{if } E(u) \in S$$
$$\text{Enc}(\text{lbl}_Y(v)) = \text{Enc}(\text{lbl}_Y(v)) \cdot \text{Enc}(\delta_{1bl}) \qquad \text{if } E(v) \in T$$

14. If $N_{1bl}(S) \neq T$
   (a) P_1 and P_2 choose $\text{Enc}(v_j) \in N_{1bl}(S) - T$.
   (b) If $\text{Enc}(v_j) \notin \mathcal{M} \star Y$, find an augmenting path $\mathcal{P} := \text{Enc}(u_k) - \text{Enc}(v_j)$ by running the π_{BFS} protocol with inputs EQ^{1bl} and $\text{Enc}(v_j)$.
   (c) Update $\mathcal{M} \leftarrow \mathcal{M} \Delta \mathcal{P}_{edge}$. Goto Step 7.
   (d) If $\text{Enc}(v_j) \in \mathcal{M} \star Y$ and $(\text{Enc}(u_{\pi(\ell)}), \text{Enc}(v_j)) \in \mathcal{M}$, extend alternating tree $S \leftarrow S \cup \{\text{Enc}(u_{pi(\ell)})\}$ and $T \leftarrow T \cup \{\text{Enc}(v_j)\}$. Goto Step 11.

Fig. 3. (*continued*)

rerandomizes each encrypted value. $\mathcal{S}_1$ chooses π_2 and $(6n + n^2)$ random tapes $\mathbf{r}_3 = \{\{(r_i^3, r_i^4, r_i^5, r_i^6, r_i^7, r_i^8)\}_{i=1}^n, (r_{ij}^1)_{n \times n}\}$ uniformly at random and computes $LBL^{X_{\pi_2 \circ \pi_1}}$, $LBL^{Y_{\pi_2 \circ \pi_1}}$, $D^{\pi_2 \circ \pi_1}$ and $W^{\pi_2 \circ \pi_1}$ and rerandomizes each encrypted value using $\mathbf{r}_3$. In Step 5, for each $\text{Enc}(d_{\pi(i)}), 1 \leq i \leq n$, the simulator generates b_{ij} at random and computes $\text{Enc}(b_{ij})$ for $\mathcal{F}_{EQ}$ with inputs $\text{Enc}(d_{\pi(i)})$ and $\text{Enc}(d_{\pi(j)}), 1 \leq j \leq i - 1$ and obtains $\mathbf{b}_1 = (b_1, b_2, \cdots, b_n)$. $\mathcal{S}_1$ computes R from $\mathbf{b}_1$. $\mathcal{S}_1$ computes $\mathcal{M}$. In Steps 10 – 14, $\mathcal{S}_1$ simulates the output of the functionalities $\mathcal{F}_{EQ}$, $\mathcal{F}_{DistDec}$, $\mathcal{F}_{PMC}$ and $\mathcal{F}_{BFS}$ while ensuring the loop terminates in $O(n^3)$ steps. The outputs at ℓ-th iteration for Steps 10 – 14 are $\mathbf{b}_3^\ell = (b_1, b_2, \cdots, b_n)$ (Step 10); $\mathbf{z}^\ell = (z_1, z_2, \cdots, z_n)$ and $\mathbf{b}_4^\ell = (b_1, b_2, \cdots, b_n)$ (Step 11); $\mathbf{b}_5^\ell = (b_1, b_2, \cdots, b_{|T| \cdot |N_{1bl}(S)|})$ (Step 12); $\mathbf{b}_6^\ell = (b_1, b_2, \cdots, b_t), t \leq n$, (Step 13); $\mathbf{b}_7^\ell = (b_1, b_2, \cdots, b_t), t \leq n$, $\mathcal{P}_{sim}^\ell = \text{Enc}(u) - \text{Enc}(v)$ (simulated augmenting path), $\mathbf{b}_8^\ell = (b_1, b_2, \cdots, b_{|\mathcal{M}| \cdot |\mathcal{P}_{edge}|})$ and $\mathbf{b}_9^\ell = (b_1, b_2, \cdots, b_t), t \leq n$ (Step 14). Define $\mathbf{B}^\ell = (\mathbf{b}_3^\ell, \mathbf{z}^\ell, \mathbf{b}_5^\ell, \mathbf{b}_6^\ell, \mathbf{b}_7^\ell, \mathcal{P}_{sim}^\ell, \mathbf{b}_8^\ell, \mathbf{b}_9^\ell)$. The output of $\mathcal{S}_1$ is $\mathcal{S}_1(1^\lambda, n, X, Y, W) = (\mathbf{r}_1, \pi_1, \ \mathbf{r}_2, LBL^{X_{\pi_2 \circ \pi_1}}, LBL^{Y_{\pi_2 \circ \pi_1}}, D^{\pi_2 \circ \pi_1}, W^{\pi_2 \circ \pi_1}, EQ^{1bl}, \mathbf{b}_1, \mathbf{b}_2, \{\mathbf{B}^\ell\})$. The distributions for $LBL^{X_{\pi_2 \circ \pi_1}}, LBL^{Y_{\pi_2 \circ \pi_1}}, D^{\pi_2 \circ \pi_1}$ and $\mathbf{B}^\ell$ in the real and ideal executions are identically distributed since the random tapes for $\mathbf{r}_1$ and $\mathbf{r}_2$ were chosen uniformly at random, the Paillier encryption scheme is semantically secure and the permutation π_2 for the honest party in the real execution of the protocol is unknown to $\mathcal{S}_1$.

When P_2 is corrupted. Let the adversary $\mathcal{A}$ controlling the party P_2. The construction of the simulator is similar to that of $\mathcal{S}_1$, except Step 1. We don't

provide the details of the simulator $\mathcal{S}_2$. The view of $\mathcal{A}$ output by $\mathcal{S}_2$ is
$\mathcal{S}_2(1^\lambda, n, X, Y, W) = (\mathbf{r}_3, \pi_2, LBL^{X_{\pi_1}}, LBL^{Y_{\pi_1}}, D^{\pi_1}, W^{\pi_1}, EQ^{1\text{b}1}, \mathbf{b}_1, \mathbf{b}_2, \{\mathbf{B}^\ell\})$.
Applying the similar argument, the views for the adversary in the real and ideal
execution of the protocol are identically distributed.

As the protocols π_{EQ}, π_{PMC}, π_{SR}, π_{DistDec} and π_{BFS} are secure, applying the
composition theorem, π_{OA} is secure in the hybrid model against semi-honest
adversaries and hence π_{OA} is secure in the real execution of the protocol.   □

5.3   The Main Protocol for Graph Edit Distance

In this section we present a secure realization of the approximated GED computation by Riesen and Bunke [26], based on bipartite graph. We consider the two-
party computation in the semi-honest model. We consider a setting where there
are two parties P_1 and P_2, each party has a private graph $G_i = (V_i, E_i, l_{G_i}, \zeta_{G_i})$
with $n_i = |V_i| \geq 3$ and $n = n_1 + n_2$. For simplicity, we consider the cost matrix
W that includes only the costs of node edit operations[1]. The parties start the
protocol execution by computing a cost matrix. We start by explaining how the
parties jointly construct the cost matrix.

Encrypted Cost Matrix Construction. We assume that each party secretly
defines the costs for the graph edit operations deletion, insertion and substitution
of nodes and/or edges. The edit operation costs for nodes are defined as follows.
Let $l_{G_1}(u_i) = \alpha_i \in \mathbb{Z}_N$ be the node labeling function of G_1 and $l_{G_2}(v_j) = \beta_j \in \mathbb{Z}_N$ be the node labeling function of G_2. The party P_1 chooses the edit costs of
node insertion and deletion operations as $c(u_i \to \epsilon) = c(\epsilon \to u_i) = C_1 \in \mathbb{Z}_N$.
Similarly, the party P_2 decides the costs of insertion and deletion operations for
nodes as $c(\epsilon \to v_j) = c(v_j \to \epsilon) = C_2 \in \mathbb{Z}_N$. The cost of the node substitution
operation is defined as $w_{ij} = c(u_i \to v_j) = \min\{(c(u_i \to \epsilon) + c(\epsilon \to v_j)), c'(u_i \to v_j)\} = \min\{(C_1 + C_2), |\alpha_i - \beta_j|\}$ where $c'(u_i \to v_j) = |\alpha_i - \beta_j|$, $\alpha_i, \beta_j \in \mathbb{Z}_N$.
This definition of the cost function can be found in [24]. Each entry of the cost
matrix is computed by running a joint protocol.

We now explain how to construct the encrypted cost matrix $W = (\text{Enc}(w_{ij}))_{n \times n}$. For insertion and deletion operations, the party P_i encrypts its
cost $\text{Enc}(C_i)$ and sends it to the other party. For the substitution cost, the
parties exchange respective encrypted costs of insertion and deletion operations and encrypted node labels. Let the parties P_1 and P_2 have encryptions
$\text{Enc}(d_1)$ and $\text{Enc}(d_2)$ of numbers d_1 and d_2, respectively and they would like
to compute $\text{Enc}(|d_1 - d_2|)$ where $|d_1 - d_2|$ is the absolute difference between
d_1 and d_2. The absolute difference between d_1 and d_2 can be computed as
$|d_1 - d_2| = (d_1 - d_2) + b(d_2 - d_1) = (1 - b)d_1 + (b - 1)d_2$ where $b = 0$, $d_1 < d_2$;
otherwise, $b = 1$. We use this relation to compute encrypted absolute difference

---

[1] Several constructions of cost matrix can be found in [9,26] for the improvement of
the approximation of the actual GED. However, the two-party computation of GED
remains same, except the cost matrix construction.

between two encrypted numbers. We provide the details of the protocol in Fig. 6 in Appendix A.

Description of the Protocol. We are now ready to describe the protocol. The parties P_1 and P_2 initiate the protocol by generating the public key and the shares of the private key for the threshold Paillier encryption scheme using $\pi_{\text{DistKeyGen}}$ and π_{DistSk}, respectively. Each party encrypts its node labels for the construction of the encrypted cost matrix. The computation of GED consists of two main phases. First, the parties construct the encrypted cost matrix $\text{Enc}(W) = (\text{Enc}(w_{ij}))_{n \times n}$ using the function defined above and then solve the assignment problem with input as the encrypted cost matrix $\text{Enc}(W)$ to find an optimal of the nodes of the graphs. The parties use the distributed decryption protocol DistDec to obtain the graph edit distance $f_{GED}(G_1, G_2) = (\sum_{i=1}^{n} w_{id_i})$. Figure 4 presents the details of the approximated GED computation protocol.

Protocol: Protocol Π_{GED}
Input: Graph $G_1 = (V_1, E_1, l_{G_1})$ from P_1 and $G_2 = (V_2, E_2, l_{G_2})$ from P_2.
Output: Approximated graph edit distance $d = f_{GED}(G_1, G_2)$ or $\perp$.

1. P_1 and P_2 run the distributed key generation protocol $\pi_{\text{DistKeyGen}}$, followed by the distributed shared secret key generation protocol π_{DistSk}.
2. P_1 encrypts the cost for node insertion and deletion $\text{Enc}(C_1)$ and $\{\text{Enc}(\alpha_i) : u_i \in V_1\}$.
3. P_2 encrypts the cost for node insertion and deletion $\text{Enc}(C_2)$ and $\{\text{Enc}(\beta_j) : v_j \in V_2\}$.
4. For each $u_i \in V_1$ and $v_j \in V_2$, P_1 and P_2 run π_{Sub} with inputs $\text{Enc}(C_1)$ and $\text{Enc}(\alpha_i)$ from P_1 and inputs $\text{Enc}(C_2)$ and $\text{Enc}(\beta_j)$ from P_2 and obtain the output $\text{Enc}(w_{ij})$.
5. P_1 and P_2 make all the entries of $E(W)$ negative, i.e., $W' = (\text{Enc}(w'_{ij}))_{n \times n} = (\text{Enc}(w_{ij})^{-1})_{n \times n}$ where $w'_{ij} = -w_{ij}$.
6. Run the optimal assignment protocol π_{OA} with input $\text{Enc}(W')$ and obtain the output the encrypted the minimum cost $\text{Enc}(\sum_{i=1}^{n} w'_{id_i})$.
7. P_1 and P_2 jointly run the distributed decryption protocol π_{DistDec} on $\text{Enc}(\sum_{i=1}^{n} w'_{id_i})^{-1}$ and obtain the approximated graph edit distance $d = (\sum_{i=1}^{n} w_{id_i})$.

Fig. 4. Protocol for computing an approximated graph edit distance based on bipartite graph

Complexity of Π_{GED}. For computing encrypted node labels, each party performs $O(n)$ operations. The computation complexity for constructing the encrypted cost matrix is $O(n^2)$. The parties run the optimal assignment protocol on the encrypted matrix. The computational complexity and the communication complexity of the graph edit distance protocol Π_{GED} is atmost $O(n^5 \ell \log^*(\ell))$.

The complexity of the protocol is dominated by that of the optimal assignment protocol. In the protocol execution, the parties do almost an equal amount of computation.

Theorem 3. *Assuming the threshold Paillier encryption scheme is secure, the protocol Π_{GED} is secure in the presence of the semi-honest adversaries.*

Proof. The protocol Π_{GED} sequentially invokes the protocols for distributed key generation $\pi_{DistKeyGen}$ and π_{DistSk}, the cost matrix construction π_{Sub} and the optimal assignment π_{OA}, and the distributed decryption $\pi_{DistDec}$ for the approximated GDE. The protocols $\pi_{DistKeyGen}$, π_{DistSk} and $\pi_{DistDec}$ are secure according to [13]. The construction of π_{Sub} based on π_{CMP}. The security of the π_{Sub} protocol relies on that of π_{CMP}, which is proven secure in [27]. Theorem 2 guarantees the parties securely solves the assignment problem. According to the sequential composition theorem [12], Π_{GED} is secure against semi-honest adversaries in the real execution of the protocol.   □

6   Conclusions

In this paper we considered secure two-party computation of graph edit distance measuring the dissimilarity between two graphs where each party has a private graph and they wish to jointly compute graph edit distance of two private graphs. We proposed a framework for the graph edit distance computation and, as an example, developed a protocol for computing of graph edit distance. To construct main protocols for graph edit distance, we developed sub-protocols such as private maximum computation and optimal assignment protocol based on the Hungarian algorithm. The asymptotic complexities of both protocols are $O(n^5(\ell \log^*(\ell)))$. Our protocol is secure against semi-honest adversaries and has applications in two-party social network graph computations for measuring structural similarity and fingerprint identifications.

Acknowledgement. This work was supported by ONR grant N00014-14-1-0029 and a grant from the King Abdulaziz City for Science and Technology (KACST). The authors would like to thank Seny Kamara for conducting several discussions during the initial phase of this work. The authors also thank the anonymous reviewers of CANS 2016 for bringing the references [3,16] into our attention and for their helpful comments.

A   Description of Sub-protocols

A.1   Encrypted Equality Test Protocol and Comparison Protocol

Given encryptions $\text{Enc}(y_1)$ and $\text{Enc}(y_2)$ of y_1 and y_2, respectively, where y_1 and y_2 are of ℓ-bit numbers in $\mathbb{Z}_N$. In our setting, the secure equality testing protocol outputs the encrypted value $\text{Enc}(b)$ where $b = 0$ if $y_1 \neq y_2$ and $b = 1$ if $y_1 = y_2$, without revealing y_1, y_2 and b where y_1 and y_2 are of ℓ bits. Our equality testing protocol is based on the idea of plaintext-space reduction introduced in [11], which can also be found in [18]. The setting of the equality check is different from the one proposed in [11]. In our case, the private key is shared between the parties, but in [11], one party holds the private key and the other party holds the encrypted numbers. We describe a secure encrypted equality test protocol based on plaintext-space reduction in Fig. 5. We use the greater-than protocol of Toft [27] with the modification that we replace the equality test protocol by π_{EQ}. We denote this protocol by π_{CMP} which takes inputs $\mathrm{Enc}(x)$ and $\mathrm{Enc}(y)$ and

---

Protocol: Equality Test π_{EQ}
Input: Two encrypted numbers $\mathrm{Enc}(y_1)$ and $\mathrm{Enc}(y_2)$.
Output: $\mathrm{Enc}(b)$ where $b = 0$ if $y_1 \neq y_2$ and $b = 1$ if $y_1 = y_2$.

1. Denote $y = y_1 - y_2$. P_1 and P_2 perform the operation: $\mathrm{Enc}(y) = \frac{\mathrm{Enc}(y_1)}{\mathrm{Enc}(y_2)}$.
2. P_1 generates a random number A^1 and represents it in binary as $A^1 = A^1_{\ell-1}A^1_{\ell-2}...A^1_0$ and computes $c_1 \leftarrow \mathrm{Enc}(y + A^1)$ and $C^1_i \leftarrow \mathrm{Enc}(A^1_i), 0 \leq i \leq n-1$ and send $\{c_1, C^1_i, 0 \leq i \leq \ell-1\}$ to P_2.
3. P_2 generates a random number A^2 and represents it in binary as $A^2 = A^2_{\ell-1}A^2_{\ell-2}...A^2_0$ and computes $c_2 \leftarrow \mathrm{Enc}(y + A^1 + A^2)$ and computes $C^2_i \leftarrow \mathrm{Enc}(A^2_i), 0 \leq i \leq n-1$ and send $\{c_2, C^2_i, 0 \leq i \leq \ell-1\}$ to P_1.
4. P_1 and P_2 run π_{DistDec} to decrypt c_2 to obtain x where $x = y + A^1 + A^2 = y + A$ and $A = A^1 + A^2$.
5. P_1 and P_2 compute ciphertexts $\mathrm{Enc}(A_i)$ with $A = A_{\ell-1}...A_0$ using $C^1_i, C^2_i, 0 \leq i \leq \ell-1$ and additive circuits of two integers as follows. P_1 and P_2 computes $\mathrm{Enc}(s_0)$ with $s_0 = 0$. For $i = 0$ to $\ell-1$, P_1 and P_2 execute the following steps and for each encryption operation parties re-randomize the ciphertext:
   (a) P_1 computes $\mathrm{Enc}(A^1_i s_i) = \mathrm{Enc}(s_i)^{A^1_i}$ and $\mathrm{Enc}(2A^1_i s_i) = \mathrm{Enc}(s_i)^{2A^1_i}$ from $\mathrm{Enc}(s_i)$ and send these two to P_2.
   (b) P_2 computes $\mathrm{Enc}(A^2_i s_i) = \mathrm{Enc}(s_i)^{A^2_i}$ and $\mathrm{Enc}(2A^2_i s_i) = \mathrm{Enc}(s_i)^{2A^2_i}$ from $\mathrm{Enc}(s_i)$ and send these two to P_1.
   (c) Using $\mathrm{Enc}(2A^2_i s_i)$, P_1 computes $\mathrm{Enc}(2A^2_i A^1_i s_i) = \mathrm{Enc}(2A^2_i s_i)^{A^1_i}$ and using $\mathrm{Enc}(A^1_i s_i)$, P_2 computes $\mathrm{Enc}(2A^1_i A^2_i s_i) = \mathrm{Enc}(A^1_i s_i)^{A^2_i}$.
   (d) P_1 computes $\mathrm{Enc}(s_{i+1}) = (C^2_i)^{A^1_i} \cdot \mathrm{Enc}(A^1_i s_i) \cdot \mathrm{Enc}(A^2_i s_i) = \mathrm{Enc}(A^1_i A^2_i + A^1_i s_i + A^2_i s_i)$.
   (e) P_2 computes $\mathrm{Enc}(s_{i+1}) = (C^1_i)^{A^2_i} \cdot \mathrm{Enc}(A^1_i s_i) \cdot \mathrm{Enc}(A^2_i s_i) = \mathrm{Enc}(A^1_i A^2_i + A^1_i s_i + A^2_i s_i)$.
6. P_1 and P_2 independently perform the following steps:
   (a) Compute $\mathrm{Enc}(A_i) = \frac{\mathrm{Enc}(A^1_i) \cdot \mathrm{Enc}(A^2_i) \cdot \mathrm{Enc}(s_i) \cdot \mathrm{Enc}_{pk}(4s_i A^1_i A^2_i)}{\mathrm{Enc}(2A^1_i s_i) \cdot \mathrm{Enc}(2A^2_i s_i)}$.
   (b) Compute $\mathrm{Enc}(Z_i) = \frac{\mathrm{Enc}(A_i) \cdot \mathrm{Enc}(x_i)}{\mathrm{Enc}(2x_i A_i)}$ using $\mathrm{Enc}(A_i)$ and x_i where $Z_i = x_i \oplus A_i = x_i + A_i - 2x_i A_i$.
   (c) Compute $\mathrm{Enc}(Z)$ as $\mathrm{Enc}(Z) = \prod_{i=0}^{\ell-1} \mathrm{Enc}(Z_i)$ where $Z = \sum_{i=0}^{\ell-1} Z_i$.
7. Set $\mathrm{Enc}(y) \leftarrow \mathrm{Enc}(Z)$, P_1 and P_2 execute Step 2 to Step 6 $\log^*(\ell)$ times.
8. P_1 and P_2 compute $\mathrm{Enc}(1 - Z)$. Output $\mathrm{Enc}(1 - Z)$.

Fig. 5. Protocol for equality of encrypted numbers using Paillier threshold encryption

outputs $\text{Enc}(b)$ where $b = 1$ iff $x \geq y$ and $b = 0$, otherwise. Its round complexity is $O(\log(\ell))$ and computation complexity is $O(\ell \log(\ell) \log^*(\ell))$.

A.2   Substitution Cost Protocol

Figure 6 presents the protocol for computing the substitution cost for constructing the cost matrix. The proof of the security of the protocols can be found in the full paper.

B   Graph Edit Operations and Cost Matrix

A standard set of graph edit operations are node *insertion* ($\epsilon \to u$), *deletion* ($u \to \epsilon$) and *substitution* ($u \to v$) and edge *insertion* ($\epsilon \to e$), *deletion* ($e \to \epsilon$) and *substitution* ($e_1 \to e_2$) and substitution of node and edge labels where ϵ denotes empty nodes or edges. The edge edit operations can be defined in terms of the node edit operations as follows. Let $e_1 = (u_1, u_2) \in E_1$ and $e_2 = (v_1, v_2) \in E_2$ where $u_1, u_2 \in V_1 \cup \{\epsilon\}$ and $v_1, v_2 \in V_2 \cup \{\epsilon\}$. An edge substitution operation between e_1 and e_2, denoted by $e_1 \to e_2$, is defined as the node substitution operations $u_1 \to v_1$ and $u_2 \to v_2$. If there is no edge e_1 in E_1 and $e_2 \in E_2$, then the edge insertion in G_1, denoted by $(\epsilon \to e_2)$ is defined by $\epsilon \to v_1$ and $\epsilon \to v_2$. Similarly, if there is an edge $e_1 \in E_1$ and no edge e_2 in E_2, then the edge deletion, denoted by $(e_1 \to \epsilon)$ is defined by $u_1 \to \epsilon$ and $v_2 \to \epsilon$.

The cost matrix is constructed by considering substitution costs of vertices and the costs of vertex insertions and deletions. The structure of the edit cost

---

Protocol: Substitution Cost π_{Sub}
Input: P_1's inputs $\text{Enc}(C_1)$ and $\text{Enc}(\alpha_i)$; P_2's inputs $\text{Enc}(C_2)$ and $\text{Enc}(\beta_j)$;
Output: $\text{Enc}(w_{ij})$ with $w_{ij} = c(u_i \to v_j) = \min\{(c(u_i \to \epsilon) + c(\epsilon \to v_j)), |\alpha_i - \beta_j|\}$.

1. P_1 computes $\text{Enc}(C_1)$ and $\text{Enc}(\alpha_i)$ and sends these to P_2.
2. P_2 computes $\text{Enc}(C_2)$ and $\text{Enc}(\beta_j)$ and sends these to P_1.
3. P_1 and P_2 compute $\text{Enc}(C_1 + C_2) = \text{Enc}(c(u_i \to \epsilon) + c(\epsilon \to v_j))$ by multiplying $\text{Enc}(C_1)$ and $\text{Enc}(C_2)$.
4. P_1 and P_2 run π_{CMP} with inputs $\text{Enc}(\alpha_i)$ and $\text{Enc}(\beta_j)$ and obtain $\text{Enc}(b)$.
5. P_1 first computes $\text{Enc}(1 - b)$ from $\text{Enc}(b)$ and then computes $\text{Enc}((1 - b)\alpha_i)$ and sends $\text{Enc}((1 - b)\alpha_i)$ to P_2.
6. P_2 first computes $\text{Enc}(b - 1)$ from $\text{Enc}(b)$ and then computes $\text{Enc}((b - 1)\beta_j)$ and sends $\text{Enc}((b - 1)\beta_j)$ to P_1.
7. Both parties compute $\text{Enc}(|\alpha_i - \beta_j|) = \text{Enc}((1 - b)\alpha_i) \cdot \text{Enc}((b - 1)\beta_j)$.
8. P_1 and P_2 run π_{CMP} with inputs $\text{Enc}(C_1 + C_2)$ and $\text{Enc}(|\alpha_i - \beta_j|)$ and obtain $\text{Enc}(b')$. If $b' = 0$, output $\text{Enc}(w_{ij}) = \text{Enc}(C_1 + C_2))$, otherwise output $\text{Enc}(|\alpha_i - \beta_j|)$.

Fig. 6. Protocol for computing node substitution cost $c(u_i \to v_j)$

matrix $W = (w_{ij})_{(n+m)\times(n+m)}$ has the following form [26]:

$$C = \begin{bmatrix} w_{11} & w_{12} & \cdots & w_{1m} & w_{1\epsilon} & \infty & \cdots & \infty \\ \vdots & \vdots & \vdots & \vdots & \vdots & \vdots & \vdots & \vdots \\ w_{n1} & w_{n2} & \cdots & w_{nm} & \infty & \infty & \cdots & w_{n\epsilon} \\ \infty & w_{\epsilon 2} & \cdots & \infty & 0 & 0 & \cdots & 0 \\ \vdots & \vdots & \vdots & \vdots & \vdots & \vdots & \vdots & \vdots \\ \infty & \infty & \cdots & w_{\epsilon m} & 0 & 0 & \cdots & 0 \end{bmatrix} = \begin{bmatrix} W_1 & W_2 \\ W_3 & W_4 \end{bmatrix}$$

where the submatrix W_1 is corresponding to the cost assignment of nodes ($i \rightarrow j$), W_2 and W_3 are corresponding to the cost assignment of node deletion ($i \rightarrow \epsilon$) and insertion ($\epsilon \rightarrow i$) of nodes. The insertion and deletion of edges are not taken care of in the cost matrix. However, it is not hard to incorporate the edge substitution cost into the matrix entries. We omit the details here.

References

1. Aggarwal, C.C., Wang, H.: Managing and Mining Graph Data. Springer, US (2010)
2. Aly, A., Cuvelier, E., Mawet, S., Pereira, O., Vyve, M.: Securely solving simple combinatorial graph problems. In: Sadeghi, A.-R. (ed.) FC 2013. LNCS, vol. 7859, pp. 239–257. Springer, Heidelberg (2013). doi:10.1007/978-3-642-39884-1_21
3. Atallah, M.J., Kerschbaum, F., Wenliang, D.: Secure and private sequence comparisons. In: Proceedings of the 2003 ACM Workshop on Privacy in the Electronic Society, WPES 2003, pp. 39–44. ACM, New York (2003)
4. Bellare, M., Hoang, V.T., Rogaway, P.: Foundations of garbled circuits. In: Proceedings of the 2012 ACM Conference on Computer and Communications Security, CCS 2012, pp. 784–796. ACM, New York (2012)
5. Blanton, M., Saraph, S.: Oblivious maximum bipartite matching size algorithm with applications to secure fingerprint identification. In: Pernul, G., Ryan, P.Y.A., Weippl, E. (eds.) ESORICS 2015. LNCS, vol. 9326, pp. 384–406. Springer, Heidelberg (2015). doi:10.1007/978-3-319-24174-6_20
6. Blanton, M., Steele, A., Alisagari, M.: Data-oblivious graph algorithms for secure computation and outsourcing. In: Proceedings of the 8th ACM SIGSAC Symposium on Information, Computer and Communications Security, ASIA CCS 2013, pp. 207–218. ACM, New York (2013)
7. Cheon, J.H., Kim, M., Lauter, K.: Homomorphic computation of edit distance. In: Brenner, M., Christin, N., Johnson, B., Rohloff, K. (eds.) FC 2015. LNCS, vol. 8976, pp. 194–212. Springer, Heidelberg (2015). doi:10.1007/978-3-662-48051-9_15
8. Damgård, I., Fitzi, M., Kiltz, E., Nielsen, J.B., Toft, T.: Unconditionally secure constant-rounds multi-party computation for equality, comparison, bits and exponentiation. In: Halevi, S., Rabin, T. (eds.) TCC 2006. LNCS, vol. 3876, pp. 285–304. Springer, Heidelberg (2006). doi:10.1007/11681878_15
9. Fankhauser, S., Riesen, K., Bunke, H.: Speeding up graph edit distance computation through fast bipartite matching. In: Jiang, X., Ferrer, M., Torsello, A. (eds.) GbRPR 2011. LNCS, vol. 6658, pp. 102–111. Springer, Heidelberg (2011). doi:10.1007/978-3-642-20844-7_11

10. Freedman, M.J., Nissim, K., Pinkas, B.: Efficient private matching and set inter-
    section. In: Cachin, C., Camenisch, J.L. (eds.) EUROCRYPT 2004. LNCS, vol.
    3027, pp. 1–19. Springer, Heidelberg (2004). doi:10.1007/978-3-540-24676-3_1
11. Gentry, C., Halevi, S., Jutla, C.S., Raykova, M.: Private database access with he-
    over-oram architecture. IACR Cryptology ePrint Archive **2014**, 345 (2014)
12. Goldreich, O.: Foundations of Cryptography Volume II Basic Applications, vol. II.
    Cambridge University Press, New York (2004)
13. Hazay, C., Mikkelsen, G.L., Rabin, T., Toft, T.: Efficient RSA key generation
    and threshold paillier in the two-party setting. In: Dunkelman, O. (ed.) CT-RSA
    2012. LNCS, vol. 7178, pp. 313–331. Springer, Heidelberg (2012). doi:10.1007/
    978-3-642-27954-6_20
14. Henecka, W., Stefan, K., Sadeghi, A.-R., Schneider, T., Wehrenberg, I.: Tasty: tool
    for automating secure two-party computations. In: Proceedings of the 17th ACM
    Conference on Computer and Communications Security, CCS 2010, pp. 451–462.
    ACM, New York (2010)
15. Huang, Y., Evans, D., Katz, J., Malka, L.: Faster secure two-party computation
    using garbled circuits. In: Proceedings of the 20th USENIX Conference on Security,
    SEC 2011, pp. 35–35. USENIX Association, Berkeley (2011)
16. Jha, S., Kruger, L., Shmatikov, V.: Towards practical privacy for genomic compu-
    tation. In: Proceedings of the 2008 IEEE Symposium on Security and Privacy, SP
    2008, pp. 216–230. IEEE Computer Society, Washington, DC (2008)
17. Lindell, Y., Pinkas, B.: An efficient protocol for secure two-party computa-
    tion in the presence of malicious adversaries. In: Naor, M. (ed.) EUROCRYPT
    2007. LNCS, vol. 4515, pp. 52–78. Springer, Heidelberg (2007). doi:10.1007/
    978-3-540-72540-4_4
18. Lipmaa, H., Toft, T.: Secure equality and greater-than tests with sublinear online
    complexity. In: Proceedings of the Automata, Languages, and Programming - 40th
    International Colloquium, ICALP 2013, Part II, Riga, Latvia, 8–12 July 2013, pp.
    645–656 (2013)
19. Malkhi, D., Nisan, N., Pinkas, B., Sella, Y.: Fairplay–a secure two-party com-
    putation system. In: Proceedings of the 13th Conference on USENIX Security
    Symposium, SSYM 2004, vol. 13, p. 20. USENIX Association, Berkeley (2004)
20. Maltoni, D., Maio, D., Jain, A.K., Prabhakar, S.: Handbook of Fingerprint Recog-
    nition, 2nd edn. Springer Publishing Company, London (2009)
21. Mandal, K., Alomair, B., Poovendran, R.: Secure error-tolerant graph matching
    protocols. Cryptology ePrint Archive, Report 2016/908 (2016). http://eprint.iacr.
    org/
22. Munkres, J.: Algorithms for the assignment and transportation problems. J. Soc.
    Ind. Appl. Math. **5**(1), 32–38 (1957)
23. Naor, M., Pinkas, B.: Efficient oblivious transfer protocols. In: Proceedings of the
    Twelfth Annual ACM-SIAM Symposium on Discrete Algorithms, SODA 2001, pp.
    448–457. Society for Industrial and Applied Mathematics, Philadelphia (2001)
24. Neuhaus, M., Bunke, H.: A graph matching based approach to fingerprint clas-
    sification using directional variance. In: Kanade, T., Jain, A., Ratha, N.K. (eds.)
    AVBPA 2005. LNCS, vol. 3546, pp. 191–200. Springer, Heidelberg (2005). doi:10.
    1007/11527923_20
25. Paillier, P.: Public-key cryptosystems based on composite degree residuosity
    classes. In: Stern, J. (ed.) EUROCRYPT 1999. LNCS, vol. 1592, pp. 223–238.
    Springer, Heidelberg (1999). doi:10.1007/3-540-48910-X_16
26. Riesen, K., Bunke, H.: Approximate graph edit distance computation by means of
    bipartite graph matching. Image Vision Comput. **27**(7), 950–959 (2009)

27. Toft, T.: Sub-linear, secure comparison with two non-colluding parties. In: Catalano, D., Fazio, N., Gennaro, R., Nicolosi, A. (eds.) PKC 2011. LNCS, vol. 6571, pp. 174–191. Springer, Heidelberg (2011). doi:10.1007/978-3-642-19379-8_11
28. Yao, A.C.-C: How to generate and exchange secrets. In: Proceedings of the 27th Annual Symposium on Foundations of Computer Science, SFCS 1986, pp. 162–167. IEEE Computer Society, Washington, DC (1986)
29. Zeng, Z., Tung, A.K.H., Wang, J., Feng, J., Zhou, L.: Comparing stars: on approximating graph edit distance. Proc. VLDB Endow. 2(1), 25–36 (2009)

Efficient Verifiable Computation of XOR for Biometric Authentication

Aysajan Abidin[1]([✉]), Abdelrahaman Aly[1], Enrique Argones Rúa[1],
and Aikaterini Mitrokotsa[2]

[1] ESAT/COSIC, KU Leuven and iMinds, Leuven, Belgium
{Aysajan.Abidin,Abdelrahaman.Aly,Enrique.ArgonesRua}@esat.kuleuven.be
[2] Chalmers University of Technology, Gothenburg, Sweden
aikmitr@chalmers.se

Abstract. This work addresses the security and privacy issues in remote biometric authentication by proposing an efficient mechanism to verify the correctness of the outsourced computation in such protocols. In particular, we propose an efficient verifiable computation of XOR-ing encrypted messages using an XOR linear message authentication code (MAC) and we employ the proposed scheme to build a biometric authentication protocol. The proposed authentication protocol is both secure and privacy-preserving against *malicious* (as opposed to *honest-but-curious*) adversaries. Specifically, the use of the verifiable computation scheme together with an homomorphic encryption protects the privacy of biometric templates against malicious adversaries. Furthermore, in order to achieve unlinkability of authentication attempts, while keeping a low communication overhead, we show how to apply Oblivious RAM and biohashing to our protocol. We also provide a proof of security for the proposed solution. Our simulation results show that the proposed authentication protocol is efficient.

Keywords: Verifiable computation · Universal hash functions · Homomorphic encryption · Biometric authentication · Template privacy and security

1 Introduction

Following the rapid growth of mobile and cloud computing, outsourcing computations to the cloud has increasingly become more attractive. Many practical applications, however, require not only the privacy of the sensitive data in such computations, but also the verifiability of correctness of the outsourced computations. There has been a wealth of work on verifiable computations in recent years, see, e.g., [1–3] and the references therein. One type of outsourced computation, in biometric authentication with distributed entities, is the computation over encrypted bitstrings (e.g., encrypted biometric templates) to obtain the XOR of two bitstrings (e.g., the XOR of the fresh and reference biometric templates). Consider, for instance, the following biometric authentication protocol

© Springer International Publishing AG 2016
S. Foresti and G. Persiano (Eds.): CANS 2016, LNCS 10052, pp. 284–298, 2016.
DOI: 10.1007/978-3-319-48965-0_17

consisting of three entities, namely, a set $\mathcal{C}$ of clients $\mathcal{C}_i$, for $i = 1, \cdots, N$, one for each user $\mathcal{U}_i$, a cloud server $\mathcal{CS}$ with a database $\mathcal{DB}$, and an authentication server $\mathcal{SP}$. Each client $\mathcal{C}_i$ has a sensor that extracts biometric templates from its owner's biometrics (e.g., fingerprints). The cloud server $\mathcal{CS}$ stores the reference biometric templates and performs calculations. The authentication server $\mathcal{SP}$ takes the final decision depending on whether there is a match between the fresh and the reference biometric templates. This is a reasonable model adopted in many research papers (cf. Related Work) and the industry (e.g., [4]) considering the fast rise of cloud computing and storage services, and also the widespread use of smartphones with embedded biometric sensors. However, the privacy of biometric features must be seriously taken into account in such architectures, since its disclosure may lead to breaches in security and traceability of users among services, besides the inherent private information disclosure.

Let us consider a simple example of a biometric authentication protocol using an homomorphic encryption scheme. Let $\mathsf{HE} = (\mathsf{KeyGen}, \mathsf{Enc}, \mathsf{Dec})$ be a hypothetical homomorphic encryption (HE) scheme and f a function such that $f\big(\mathsf{Enc}(m), \mathsf{Enc}(m')\big) = \mathsf{Enc}(m \oplus m')$, for m, m' in the domain of Enc, where $\oplus$ is the XOR operation. Suppose that the encryption/decryption keys pk/sk are generated by the authentication server $\mathcal{SP}$ and pk is distributed to $\mathcal{CS}$ and all $\mathcal{C}_i$. Then, the protocol works as follows. During the *enrollment phase*, the client $\mathcal{C}_i$ provides an encrypted reference biometric template $\mathsf{Enc}(b_i)$, along with the user ID_i for storage in the database $\mathcal{DB}$ on the $\mathcal{CS}$ side. During the *authentication phase*, the client $\mathcal{C}_i$ provides an encrypted fresh biometric template $\mathsf{Enc}(b_i')$ and a claimed user ID_i to $\mathcal{CS}$, which then retrieves $\mathsf{Enc}(b_i)$ corresponding to ID_i from its database, computes $\mathsf{ct}_{b_i \oplus b_i'} = f\big(\mathsf{Enc}(b_i), \mathsf{Enc}(b_i')\big) = \mathsf{Enc}\big(b_i \oplus b_i'\big)$ and sends $\mathsf{ct}_{b_i \oplus b_i'}$ to $\mathcal{SP}$. Finally, $\mathcal{SP}$ decrypts $\mathsf{ct}_{b_i \oplus b_i'}$ and checks if the Hamming weight $\mathsf{HW}(b_i \oplus b_i) \leq \tau$, where τ is a predefined authentication threshold. If $\mathsf{HW}(b_i \oplus b_i) \leq \tau$, then the user is granted access; otherwise, he/she is rejected. Note that $\mathsf{HW}(b_i \oplus b_i')$ is equal to the Hamming distance $\mathsf{HD}(b_i, b_i')$.

At a first glance, the protocol may seem secure against a malicious $\mathcal{CS}$, with respect to both the fresh and the stored template privacy. However, this only holds under the assumption that $\mathcal{CS}$ honestly performs the intended calculation, since there is no mechanism in place to prevent or detect cheating. By computing a function, g, different than what the protocol specifies (or the intended function f but on different inputs than the legitimate ones), and using $\mathcal{SP}$ as an oracle, $\mathcal{CS}$ can learn information about either the stored reference biometric template b_i or the fresh biometric template b_i'. As an example $\mathcal{CS}$ could compute $g(\mathsf{Enc}(b_i), \mathsf{Enc}(v))$, where v is a chosen vector by $\mathcal{CS}$, and subsequently send the result to $\mathcal{SP}$, which outputs $\mathsf{Out}_{\mathcal{SP}}$. By mounting a variant of the *hill climbing attack* [5], performing multiple repeated attempts, each time carefully choosing v, the stored template b_i can be retrieved. Such attacks against several protocols proposed in [6–8] are presented in [9–11]. Therefore, in similar applications it is important to verify the correctness of the outsourced computation, namely, the computation of XORing encrypted bitstrings. Moreover, verifiable computation of XOR is what we need in order to mitigate such an attack by a malicious

$\mathcal{CS}$ on the above presented protocol. Here, we propose an efficient scheme for verifying the correctness of the outsourced XOR computation and apply it to biometric authentication. To our knowledge, the employment of verifiable computation in privacy-preserving biometric authentication has not been studied before, although the infeasibility of (fully) homomorphic encryption alone for privacy-preserving cloud computing is already known [12].

Contributions. In this work, we propose an efficient verifiable computation of XORing encrypted messages using an XOR linear message authentication code (MAC) and we build a biometric authentication protocol that is secure and privacy-preserving in the *malicious* (as opposed to the *honest-but-curious*) adversary model. In the proposed protocol, the use of homomorphic encryption (HE) and the XOR linear MAC scheme protects the privacy of biometric templates against the malicious cloud, while the secret identity to an index map provides anonymity. However, the authentication protocol does not hide access patterns from the cloud. This could be avoided using Private Information Retrieval, but at the expense of a large communication overhead. Hence we further propose an extension of the protocol using oblivious RAM (ORAM). Since $b_i \oplus b_i'$ is revealed to $\mathcal{SP}$ in the proposed protocol, we also discuss how to make it robust against leakage of information regarding the user's biometric characteristics by employing biohashing techniques.

Related Work. Privacy-preserving biometric authentication has attracted considerable attention over the last decade. Multiple protocols for privacy-preserving biometric authentication are based on secure multi-party computation techniques including oblivious transfer [13] and homomorphic encryption [14,15], as well as on private information retrieval [16,17]. Bringer *et al.* [8] proposed a distributed biometric authentication protocol using the Goldwasser-Micali cryptosystem [15] to protect the privacy of the biometric templates against *honest-but-curious* (or *passive*) adversaries. Nevertheless, some attacks on this protocol were reported in [5,11,18]. In [11], the authors have also improved upon the Bringer *et al.* protocol to achieve security against malicious but non-colluding adversaries. Simoens *et al.* [5] also presented a framework for analysing the security and privacy-preserving properties of biometric authentication protocols. In particular, they showed how biometric authentication protocols designed to be secure against *honest-but-curious* adversaries can be broken in the presence of *malicious* insider adversaries. They described several attacks against protocols proposed in [8,18,19]. There are also other protocols for privacy-preserving biometric authentication that are based on additive HE [14,20] such as [21] for face recognition and its subsequent improvement in [22], as well as the protocol in [23]. Yasuda *et al.* proposed two biometric authentication protocols using somewhat HEs based on ideal lattices [6] and ring learning with errors [7], and the security of these protocols is scrutinised in [9,10]. In most of these schemes, biometric templates are extracted as bitstrings and the similarity of two biometric templates is measured by computing the Hamming distance between them. For this reason, in [24] the authors have proposed protocols for secure Hamming distance computation based on oblivious transfer. These have potential applications in privacy-preserving biometric authentication. Recently Bringer *et al.* [25] generalised their results for secure computation of other distances such as the Euclidean and the normalised Hamming distance. Oblivious transfer was also used in SCiFi [26].

Outline. The rest of the paper is organised as follows. Section 2 introduces the necessary background. Section 3 presents our adversary model. In Sect. 4, we present our protocol for biometric authentication employing the scheme for verifiable computation of XOR. Section 5 shows how ORAM can be applied to our protocol. Finally, Sect. 6 concludes the paper.

2 Preliminaries

Homomorphic Encryption. For our purposes, the employed HE scheme must be such that given $\mathsf{Enc}(m)$ and $\mathsf{Enc}(m')$, it is possible to homomorphically compute $\mathsf{Enc}(\mathsf{Dist}(m, m'))$, where Dist is a distance metric. We require the HE scheme to have semantic security against chosen plaintext attacks. Consider the following game played between a probabilistic polynomial time (PPT) adversary and a challenger:

$$
\begin{aligned}
&\mathsf{Exp}_{\mathsf{HE},\mathcal{A}}^{\mathsf{IND\text{-}CPA}}(\lambda): \\
&\quad (\mathsf{pk},\mathsf{sk}), \leftarrow \mathsf{KeyGen}(\lambda); \qquad (m_0, m_1), \; m_0 \neq m_1 \leftarrow \mathcal{A}(\lambda, \mathsf{pk}); \\
&\quad \beta \xleftarrow{R} \{0,1\}; \qquad c \leftarrow \mathsf{Enc}(m_\beta, \mathsf{pk}); \qquad \beta' \leftarrow \mathcal{A}(m_0, m_1, c, \mathsf{pk}); \\
&\quad \text{Return 1 if } \beta' = \beta, \; 0 \text{ otherwise}
\end{aligned}
$$

and define the adversary's advantage in this game as $\mathsf{Adv}_{\mathsf{HE},\mathcal{A}}^{\mathsf{IND\text{-}CPA}}(\lambda) = \left| 2 \Pr \left\{ \mathsf{Exp}_{\mathsf{HE},\mathcal{A}}^{\mathsf{IND\text{-}CPA}}(\lambda) = 1 \right\} - 1 \right|$.

Definition 1. *We say that HE is IND-CPA-secure if all PPT adversaries have a negligible advantage in the above game:* $\mathsf{Adv}_{\mathsf{HE},\mathcal{A}}^{\mathsf{IND\text{-}CPA}}(\lambda) \leq \mathsf{negl}(\lambda)$.

Definition 2. *A function* $\mathsf{negl} : \mathbb{N} \mapsto [0, 1]$ *is called negligible if for all positive polynomials* poly *and sufficiently large* $\lambda \in \mathbb{N}$: $\mathsf{negl}(\lambda) < 1/\mathsf{poly}(\lambda)$.

Message Authentication Codes. A message authentication code (MAC) consists of $(\mathsf{KeyGen}, \mathsf{TAG}, \mathsf{VRFY})$ (associated with a key space, a message space and a tag space). KeyGen, a key generation algorithm, takes a security parameter λ as input and outputs a key k (i.e., $\mathsf{k} \leftarrow \mathsf{KeyGen}(\lambda)$). TAG, a tag generation algorithm, takes a message m and a key k as input, and outputs a tag (i.e., $t \leftarrow \mathsf{TAG}(m, \mathsf{k})$). VRFY, a verification algorithm, takes a message m, a tag t and a key k as input, and outputs a decision $\mathsf{Out}_{\mathsf{MAC}}$ (i.e., $\mathsf{Out}_{\mathsf{MAC}} \leftarrow \mathsf{VRFY}(m, t, \mathsf{k})$), which is 1 if the message-tag pair (m, t) is valid, and 0 otherwise.

A typical construction of a MAC is via the use of Universal$_2$ (U_2) hash functions, see [27–29] for more on U_2 hash functions. There are constructions of U_2 hash functions that are $\oplus$-linear [30], from which one can construct an $\oplus$-linear MAC scheme. Note that a MAC scheme is called $\oplus$-linear if $\mathsf{TAG}(m_1 \oplus m_2, \mathsf{k}) = \mathsf{TAG}(m_1, \mathsf{k}) \oplus \mathsf{TAG}(m_2, \mathsf{k})$.

Definition 3. *A MAC is called (Q_T, Q_V, t, ϵ)-secure (or simply ϵ-secure) if no PPT adversary $\mathcal{A}$ running in time at most t cannot generate a valid message-tag pair, even after making Q_T tag generation queries to TAG and Q_V verification queries to VRFY, except with probability ϵ.*

Privacy-Preserving Biometric Authentication. A privacy-preserving biometric authentication (PPBA) protocol comprises:

– Setup: In this step, a trusted party runs the key generation algorithm KeyGen for the employed cryptographic primitives (e.g., homomorphic encryption) using a security parameter λ as input: $(\mathsf{pk}, \mathsf{sk}) \leftarrow \mathsf{KeyGen}(\lambda)$. The keys are distributed to the relevant parties.
– Enroll: This process collects the encrypted reference biometric template $\mathsf{Enc}(b_i)$ and stores it along with additional user information such as the user's identity ID_i in the database $\mathcal{DB}$, i.e., $\mathcal{DB} \leftarrow \mathsf{Enroll}\big(\mathsf{Enc}(b_i), \mathsf{ID}_i\big)$.
– Authen: This process takes an encrypted fresh biometric template $\mathsf{Enc}(b_i')$ and a claimed identity ID_i, and involves actions from the protocol actors. This can be abstracted as $\mathsf{Out}_{\mathcal{SP}} \leftarrow \mathsf{Authen}(\mathsf{Enc}(b_i'), \mathsf{ID}_i)$.

The PPBA protocol is *correct* if the following definition is satisfied.

Definition 4 (Correctness). *We say that a privacy-preserving biometric authentication protocol PPBA is correct if, for all enrolled user identities ID_i with the corresponding reference biometric templates b_i, and for all fresh biometric templates b_i', $\mathsf{Authen}(\mathsf{Enc}(b_i'), \mathsf{ID}_i)$ results in a successful authentication of the user with ID_i if and only if $\mathsf{Dist}(b_i, b_i') \leq \tau$.*

We define the security of PPBA against a malicious adversary $\mathcal{A}$ as follows. Consider the following game:

$\mathsf{Exp}_{\mathsf{PPBA}, \mathcal{A}}^{\mathsf{Priv}}(\lambda)$:
   $(\mathsf{pk}, \mathsf{sk}) \leftarrow \mathsf{KeyGen}(\lambda);\quad \mathcal{DB} \leftarrow \mathsf{Enroll}(\mathsf{ID}_i, \mathsf{Enc}(b_i));\quad b_{i_0}', b_{i_1}', b_{i_0}' \neq b_{i_1}' \leftarrow \mathcal{A}(\mathsf{ID}_i, \lambda, \mathsf{pk});$
   $\beta \xleftarrow{R} \{0, 1\};\quad \mathsf{Out} \leftarrow \mathsf{Authen}(\mathsf{ID}_i, \mathsf{Enc}(b_{i_\beta}'));\quad \beta' \leftarrow \mathcal{A}(\mathsf{ID}_i, \lambda, \mathsf{pk}, b_{i_0}', b_{i_1}', \mathsf{Enc}(b_{i_\beta}'), \mathcal{DB}, \mathsf{Out});$
   Return 1 if $\beta' = \beta$, 0 otherwise
---

and define the adversary's advantage in this game as $Adv_{\mathsf{PPBA}, \mathcal{A}}^{\mathsf{Priv}}(\lambda) = \big|2 \Pr\{\mathsf{Exp}_{\mathsf{PPBA}, \mathcal{A}}^{\mathsf{Priv}}(\lambda) = 1\} - 1\big|$.

Definition 5 (Security and privacy). *We say that PPBA is secure if, for all PPT adversaries $\mathcal{A}$, $Adv_{\mathsf{PPBA}, \mathcal{A}}^{\mathsf{Priv}}(\lambda) \leq \mathsf{negl}(\lambda)$.*

We assume that the adversary is given an oracle access to Authen and is allowed to query it polynomially many times, e.g., $\mathsf{poly}(\lambda)$ times, where λ may depend on the false acceptance rate. The adversary is also given $\mathsf{Enc}(b_{i_\beta}')$. If the adversary cannot distinguish whether it is $(\mathsf{ID}_i, b_{i_0}')$ or $(\mathsf{ID}_i, b_{i_1}')$ that is being used by Authen, then we say that the protocol *preserves privacy* of the biometric templates.

3   Adversary Model

In this paper, we focus on *malicious* as opposed to *honest-but-curious*, adversaries and we consider a distributed setting, namely, each user $\mathcal{U}_i$ has his/her own client $\mathcal{C}_i$, a cloud computing server $\mathcal{CS}$ with its own database, and an authentication server $\mathcal{SP}$. The client $\mathcal{C}_i$ (e.g., a smartphone owned by the user $\mathcal{U}_i$) has a biometric sensor that extracts biometric templates from the user. By requiring that each user $\mathcal{U}_i$ has a client $\mathcal{C}_i$, potential damages can be minimised in case the client $\mathcal{C}_i$ is stolen or lost. We assume that each user trusts his/her own client device only to the extent that the biometric sensor and the extracted biometric template are only accessible by the authorised apps on the user device. This is the minimal reasonable assumption given the fact that most people nowadays have a smartphone with an embedded biometric sensor, and without such a trust, users *cannot* use their devices to remotely access services. This assumption has also to be made in any type of authentication using client devices, e.g., password- or token-based remote access. This assumption does not rule out the case where an adversary is using several clients $\mathcal{C}_i$, in collusion with the cloud server, to impersonate a user that is not the owner of compromised clients. However, we do note that if a client $\mathcal{C}_i$ is compromised, say, infected by malware, then the reference biometric template of the owner $\mathcal{U}_i$ can be recovered using the fresh biometric template provided by $\mathcal{U}_i$ by hill climbing attacks [31].

The authentication server $\mathcal{SP}$ handles the keys for the employed encryption scheme and is responsible for making the authentication decision based on the underlying matching process used. We also consider the authentication server $\mathcal{SP}$ as a trusted key managing entity which keeps the secret keys secure and performs its task honestly. However, we do not trust any biometric template to $\mathcal{SP}$. The malicious party that we want to have a full protection against is the cloud server $\mathcal{CS}$. In our case the cloud has a database that stores the encrypted reference biometric templates. Additionally, $\mathcal{CS}$ performs computations on the encrypted fresh and reference biometric templates. The results of the computation will allow the authentication server to make its decision. We consider a malicious cloud server as a PPT adversary. We do not consider denial-of-service type of attacks, which are easy to mount by $\mathcal{CS}$, since it can always send a wrong response which would with high probability result in a false rejection.

Regarding communication among the protocol actors, we assume that the communication channel between the protocol entities is secure in order to avoid replay attacks. This can be achieved by using TLS or IPsec. We also only consider the case of a single client for each user, a single cloud server, and a single authentication server.

4   The Scheme and the Protocol

The main idea behind the verifiable computation of XOR is that the client stores homomorphically encrypted message-tag pairs (e.g., $\mathsf{Enc}(m)$, $\mathsf{Enc}(t)$, where $t = \mathsf{TAG}(m, \mathsf{k})$) in the cloud server. When the client provides a new homomorphically encrypted message-tag pair (e.g., $\mathsf{Enc}(m')$, $\mathsf{Enc}(t')$, where $t' = \mathsf{TAG}(m', \mathsf{k})$), the cloud server computes the designated function on the encrypted messages and tags separately (e.g., $\mathsf{ct}_{m \oplus m'} = f(\mathsf{Enc}(m), \mathsf{Enc}(m'))$ and $\mathsf{ct}_{t \oplus t'} = f(\mathsf{Enc}(t), \mathsf{Enc}(t'))$), and returns the results to the client. The client decrypts the results and checks if the tag is valid (i.e., $m \oplus m' \leftarrow \mathsf{Dec}(\mathsf{ct}_{m \oplus m'})$, $t \oplus t' \leftarrow \mathsf{Dec}(\mathsf{ct}_{t \oplus t'})$, and $\mathsf{VRFY}(m \oplus m', t \oplus t', \mathsf{k})$). If the MAC verification is successful, then the client can be sure (up to the security of the MAC scheme) that the cloud server has performed the correct computation.

Below, we apply this simple method to build a privacy-preserving biometric authentication protocol. In the description, HE is an encryption scheme which allows the computation of XOR of encrypted messages, i.e., $f(\mathsf{Enc}(m), \mathsf{Enc}(m')) = \mathsf{Enc}(m \oplus m')$, and MAC is an XOR linear MAC. The enrollment procedure Enroll involves the following interactions:

- $\mathcal{SP}$ generates $(\mathsf{pk}, \mathsf{sk}) \leftarrow \mathsf{HE.KeyGen}(\lambda)$ using a security parameter λ.
- The user $\mathcal{U}_i$ is asked to provide a user identity ID_i (e.g., a username or a pseudonym, etc.) by his/her client $\mathcal{C}_i$, which sends his ID_i as part of an enrollment request to $\mathcal{SP}$.
- $\mathcal{SP}$ maps ID_i to an index i (i.e., $i \leftarrow \mathsf{ID}_i$) using a secret process known only to itself. It then generates a key for the MAC using the security parameter λ and ID_i: $\mathsf{k}_i \leftarrow \mathsf{MAC.KeyGen}(\lambda, \mathsf{ID}_i)$. The tuple $(i, \mathsf{pk}, \mathsf{k}_i)$ is sent to $\mathcal{C}_i$, and pk to $\mathcal{CS}$ (the latter is only done once).
- After receiving $(i, \mathsf{pk}, \mathsf{k}_i)$, $\mathcal{C}_i$ first obtains the reference biometric template b_i from the user $\mathcal{U}_i$, computes $t_i = \mathsf{TAG}(b_i, \mathsf{k}_i)$, and encrypts the reference biometric template and the tag to obtain $\mathsf{Enc}(b_i)$ and $\mathsf{Enc}(t_i)$, respectively. $\mathcal{C}_i$ then provides $(i, \mathsf{Enc}(b_i), \mathsf{Enc}(t_i))$ to the database $\mathcal{DB}$ on the cloud server side for storage.
- $\mathcal{C}_i$ and $\mathcal{SP}$ store (i, k_i) locally.

It is important for security that the user enrollment is performed in a secure and controlled environment.

The authentication Authen involves the following interactions:

- The user $\mathcal{U}_i$ initiates the authentication process by providing his/her identity ID_i and a fresh biometric template b_i' to $\mathcal{C}_i$, which then computes $t_i' = \mathsf{TAG}(b_i', \mathsf{k}_i)$.
- $\mathcal{C}_i$ sends ID_i as part of an authentication request to $\mathcal{SP}$, and obtains pk from $\mathcal{SP}$.
- $\mathcal{C}_i$ computes $\mathsf{Enc}(b_i')$ and $\mathsf{Enc}(t_i')$, and sends $(i, \mathsf{Enc}(b_i'), \mathsf{Enc}(t_i'))$ to $\mathcal{CS}$.
- $\mathcal{CS}$ retrieves $(\mathsf{Enc}(b_i), \mathsf{Enc}(t_i))$ corresp. to i from $\mathcal{DB}$ and computes $\mathsf{ct}_{b_i \oplus b_i'} = f(\mathsf{Enc}(b_i), \mathsf{Enc}(b_i')) = \mathsf{Enc}(b_i \oplus b_i')$ and $\mathsf{ct}_{t_i \oplus t_i'} = f(\mathsf{Enc}(t_i), \mathsf{Enc}(t_i')) = \mathsf{Enc}(t_i \oplus t_i')$, and sends $(\mathsf{ct}_{b_i \oplus b_i}, \mathsf{ct}_{t_i \oplus t_i'}, i')$ to $\mathcal{SP}$.
- $\mathcal{SP}$ extracts i from ID_i and checks if the extracted i and the index i' received from $\mathcal{CS}$ are equal. If $i \neq i'$, $\mathcal{SP}$ outputs $\perp$. Otherwise, $\mathcal{SP}$ retrieves the locally stored k_i corresponding to i, decrypts $\mathsf{ct}_{b_i \oplus b_i'}$ and $\mathsf{ct}_{t_i \oplus t_i'}$ to obtain $b_i \oplus b_i'$ and

---

$t_i \oplus t'_i$, respectively. If $\mathsf{VRFY}(b_i \oplus b'_i, t_i \oplus t'_i, \mathsf{k}_i) == 0$, it outputs $\bot$. Otherwise, it checks if the Hamming weight $\mathsf{HW}(b_i \oplus b'_i) \leq \tau$. If this is the case, $\mathcal{SP}$ authenticates the user $\mathcal{U}_i$; otherwise, it outputs $\bot$.

From now on, we denote this protocol by PPBA-HE-MAC. It is straightforward to see that PPBA-HE-MAC is correct, since a legitimate user with his/her own legitimate device can always successfully authenticate himself/herself as long as the fresh biometric template matches the reference biometric template.

Security and Privacy Analysis. Intuitively, PPBA-HE-MAC is secure as long as the employed HE scheme is IND-CPA-secure (cf. Definition 1) and the MAC scheme is ϵ-secure (cf. Definition 3). In any biometric template recovery attack that makes use of the side channel information (i.e., $\mathsf{Out}_{\mathcal{SP}}$), $\mathcal{CS}$ needs to be able to submit to $\mathcal{SP}$ a $\mathsf{ct}_{b_i \oplus b'_i}$ and $\mathsf{ct}_{t_i \oplus t'_i}$ that encrypt a valid message-tag pair. The ϵ-security of the employed MAC scheme does not allow this to happen. Furthermore, if $\mathsf{Out}_{\mathcal{SP}} == \bot$, $\mathcal{CS}$ does not know whether it is due to the MAC verification failure or the mismatch between the fresh and the reference biometric template. Hence, the protocol is secure against the malicious $\mathcal{CS}$. The following summarises the security of our protocol, and the proof is given in Appendix-6.

Theorem 1 (Security and privacy) . *The protocol PPBA-HE-MAC is secure and privacy-preserving against the malicious $\mathcal{CS}$ according to our Definition 5, if the employed HE is IND-CPA-secure and MAC ϵ-secure.*

Simulation. PPBA-HE-MAC is efficient because both the MAC scheme and the HE scheme can be implemented efficiently. The efficiency of the $\oplus$-linear MAC scheme in our case depends on the efficiency of the employed U_2 hash functions. One suitable family of U_2 hash functions for our instantiation is the construction by Krawczyk [30], which exploits a Linear Feedback Shift Register to allow efficient hardware implementations. This construction is also efficient on software. We refer the curious reader to [32] for more on the software performance of U_2 hash functions.

Note that our utilisation of a lightweight MAC scheme for verifying the correctness of the outsourced computation contrasts nicely with the existing verifiable computation schemes. More precisely, efficiency is the main issue with the existing verifiable computation schemes since they are very heavy computationally and have a large overhead [33]. On the other hand, our approach using a MAC scheme is very efficient regarding computation cost.

Regarding the HE scheme, we demonstrate its efficiency by simulating the Goldwasser-Micali encryption scheme [15] for various security levels and biometric template lengths. The Goldwasser-Micali encryption scheme supports homomorphic evaluation of the XOR operation, and their primitives are the most heavy ones in our construction.

The simulations were performed on a Intel®Core™2 Duo CPU E8400 @ 3.00 GHz x2 64 bit CentOS Linux 7 computer. The simulation software, written in C++, linked the NTL v9.4.0 (Number Theory Library [34]), GNU Multiple Precision Arithmetic Library v6.0.0 [35], for efficient multiprecision arithmetics support. The security level and the corresponding size of the prime factors are chosen according to the ECRYPT II recommendations and the length of the biometric binary templates is chosen following Daugman [36] and SCiFI [26].. The simulation setup and results are shown in Table 1, the source code can be provided upon request via anonymous channels.

Table 1. Simulation setup and results for the Goldwasser-Micali scheme.

Security level in bits	Size of prime factors in bits	Binary biometric template length	Mean template encoding time [s]	Mean template decoding time [s]
80	1248	900	$9.22 \cdot 10^{-3}$	$2.06 \cdot 10^{-1}$
		2048	$2.09 \cdot 10^{-2}$	$4.69 \cdot 10^{-1}$
128	3248	900	$3.79 \cdot 10^{-2}$	$6.51 \cdot 10^{-1}$
		2048	$8.60 \cdot 10^{-2}$	1.48

We remark that since our aim is to show the feasibility of the HE scheme, the implementation is not optimised. Also, the simulations are run on single core, even though the Goldwasser-Micali encryption and decryption procedures can be done in parallel, since it is a bitwise encryption scheme. Therefore, the simulation results show that the HE scheme required for our instantiation is not only feasible, but also efficient.

5   Protocol Extensions

Oblivious RAM (ORAM) for Hiding Access Patterns. Our protocol can be easily extended to protect the access pattern of the client C_i towards the cloud server CS. However, existing methods such as Private Information Retrieval (PIR) come at an elevated communication overhead. To reduce such costs, we suggest the use of ORAM instead, as a more suitable mechanism, and its use, as presented by this work, would not alter the underlying security properties of the main protocol. ORAM allows a client to hide the entry as well as the access pattern from the server at a significantly reduced communication vs PIR. Moreover, ORAM security is derived from the indistinguishability of any two access patterns $A(y)$ and $A(y')$, for any two respective queries y and y'. The concept was initially presented by Goldreich and Ostrovsky [37] in 1996. Since then, the field has seen the introduction of various protocols with improved mechanisms and primitives, e.g., [38]. These advances on protocol efficiency have motivated the apparition of new applications such as, biometric identification [39]. Typically, ORAMs are designed and used to solve the problem of DB outsourcing [40]. This model would require the user to execute various ORAM primitives so that the remote database is correctly shuffled. To alleviate this processing task, and to make our protocol user agnostic, we propose to use a Secure Multiparty Computation (MPC) scheme. MPC schemes have been suggested in combination with ORAM constructions in recent works (e.g., [41]). Under this extended protocol, every time a new user data (e.g., $\mathsf{Enc}(b_i)$ and $\mathsf{Enc}(t_i)$) is added to the ORAM $\mathcal{DB}$. The index i is used to store the data mapping in a separate ORAM. The following are the additional parties, operations and the protocol extension:

- $\mathcal{MPC}$ **Agent:** MPC mechanisms provide security against semi-honest or malicious adversaries and in various coalitions, including computational security against dishonest majorities e.g., [42]. An $\mathcal{MPC}$ agent, composed by different distrustful players (computational parties) with competing interests can be added to our scheme. These computational parties can be as many as needed, to give the users confidence on the scheme and could be allocated by any combination of the scheme participants. This agent has to store, in shared form, an ORAM containing the mapping of the template database using i.
- **MAP**(i): It returns the mapping of the template based on the shared index i from the user. The mapping corresponds to the position to be queried on the remote ORAM $\mathcal{DB}$ template.
- **Sh**(i): It is used to represent the secure secret sharing of the index i.
- **Enrollment:** The enrollment procedure is the same as described in Sect. 4. However, at the end of the scheme, the client $\mathcal{C}_i$ provides $(\mathsf{Sh}(i), \mathsf{Enc}(b_i), \mathsf{Enc}(t_i))$ to the $\mathcal{MPC}$ agent, who then stores i on its local mapping ORAM and appends $\mathsf{Enc}(b_i), \mathsf{Enc}(t_i)$ to the $\top$ position of the physical $\mathcal{DB}$ of the cloud ORAM.
- **Authentication:** Similarly to the Enrollment, the authentication procedure follows the same steps that are described at Sect. 4. In the same spirit as before, once the client $\mathcal{C}_i$ has computed $(\mathsf{Enc}(b_i'), \mathsf{Enc}(t_i'))$, it is sent to the $\mathcal{MPC}$ agent instead, together with the stored index i in shared form. Then, the agent uses i to extract the template and grants access to the cloud storage, so that the original process can continue. To avoid revealing i to the $\mathcal{CS}$, the $\mathcal{MPC}$ agent sends the index directly towards the $\mathcal{SP}$ as i'.

These protocol extensions are oriented towards a task distribution. Hence, they do not have an impact on the security properties of the authentication scheme. It is worth noticing, however, that the security with respect to the access pattern will depend solely on the underlying ORAM and MPC protocols used by any implementation.

Biohashing for Avoiding Linkability of Error Patterns. The error pattern $b_i \oplus b_i'$ is disclosed to $\mathcal{SP}$ at the end of the authentication phase, as shown in Sect. 4. This can disclose some information about the binary biometric templates. For instance, the reliability of each bit can be different among different users, so the error patterns can be used for tracking users. In the ideal case, all the error patterns should be equiprobable for all the users. In this case, disclosing the error patterns would not provide any advantage to $\mathcal{SP}$. However, this is difficult to achieve in practice.

A practical solution to this problem is to use biohashing techniques [43]. The usual approach for obtaining binary templates b_i from biometric features f_i is by using a user-independent binarization transformation $b_i = B(f_i)$. Biohashing consists of using a user-specific random transformation $b_i = B_i(f_i)$ instead. The specific design of these transformations ensures a minimum distortion in the distances in the transformed domain with respect to the distances in the original domain, thus keeping the discrimination ability of the biometrics unaffected. And the dependency between the error patterns and the user-specific binary templates' reliability is avoided, since changing B_i leads to an independent error pattern.

The incorporation of biohashing into our system is straightforward. The user-specific random transformation B_i is generated during the enrollment phase in the user client C_i, where it is stored and used to obtain the enrollment binary template $b_i = B_i(f_i)$. During the authentication phase, this transformation is used by C_i to obtain $b'_i = B_i(f'_i)$. When the user enrolls again, a new random transformation would be generated, thus avoiding linkability between the previous and the new error patterns.

6   Conclusions

We proposed an efficient scheme for verifiable computation of XORing encrypted messages, and successfully applied it to the scenario of distributed biometric authentication, where the storage of the encrypted biometric templates and part of the computations are outsourced to a cloud server. The security and privacy of the proposed scheme has been proved in a challenging and reasonable malicious internal adversarial scenario, as opposed to the more usual and less realistic honest-but-curious scenario. Additionally, ORAM is employed instead of prevalent PIR schemes to reduce the communication overhead while keeping the access pattern hidden from the cloud. Moreover, Biohashing techniques are proposed to avoid the disclosure of linkable error patterns. The efficiency of the proposed scheme has been assessed by simulating the most computationally costly parts of the proposed scheme, i.e. the homomorphic encryption primitives, showing the feasibility and efficiency of the proposed solution.

Acknowledgments. This work was funded by the European Commission through the FP7 project "EKSISTENZ," with grant number: 607049. This work was also partially supported by the FP7-STREP project "BEAT: Biometric Evaluation and Testing", grant number: 284989 and the VR project PRECIS.

A   Proof of Theorem 1

Proof. Let Π be the PPBA-HE-MAC protocol. The security of Π against a malicious adversary $\mathcal{A}$ (i.e., $\mathcal{CS}$) is defined via the following game.

$$\mathsf{Exp}^{\mathsf{Priv}}_{\Pi,\mathcal{A}}(\lambda, \mathsf{ID}_i):$$
　　$(\mathsf{pk}, \mathsf{sk})$, k_i, $\mathsf{MAC}.\mathcal{K} \leftarrow \mathsf{KeyGen}(\lambda, \mathsf{ID}_i)$;　　$\mathcal{DB} \leftarrow \mathsf{Enroll}(\mathsf{ID}_i, \mathsf{Enc}(b_i), \mathsf{k}_i)$
　　(b'_{i_0}, b'_{i_1}), $b'_{i_0} \neq b'_{i_1} \leftarrow \mathcal{A}(\mathsf{ID}_i, \lambda, \mathsf{pk}, \mathsf{MAC}.\mathcal{K})$;
　　$\beta \xleftarrow{R} \{0,1\}$;　　$t'_{i_\beta} \leftarrow \mathsf{TAG}(b'_{i_\beta}, \mathsf{k}_i)$;　　$\mathsf{Out} \leftarrow \mathsf{Authen}(\mathsf{ID}_i, \mathsf{Enc}(b'_{i_\beta}), \mathsf{Enc}(t'_{i_\beta}))$;
　　$\beta' \leftarrow \mathcal{A}(\mathsf{ID}_i, \lambda, \mathsf{pk}, b'_{i_0}, b'_{i_1}, \mathsf{Enc}(t'_{i_\beta}), \mathsf{Enc}(t'_{i_\beta}), \mathcal{DB}, \mathsf{Out})$;
Return 1 if $\beta' = \beta$, 0 otherwise

where $\mathsf{MAC}.\mathcal{K}$ is the key space for the employed MAC. The adversary's advantage is defined as $\mathsf{Adv}^{\mathsf{Priv}}_{\Pi,\mathcal{A}} = \left| 2\Pr\{\mathsf{Exp}^{\mathsf{Priv}}_{\Pi,\mathcal{A}}(\lambda, \mathsf{ID}_i) = 1\} - 1 \right|$. If the advantage is $\leq \mathsf{negl}(\lambda)$, we say that Π is secure (and preserves the privacy of biometric templates) against $\mathcal{A}$.

The details of $\mathsf{Authen}(\mathsf{ID}_i, \mathsf{Enc}(b'_{i_\beta}), \mathsf{Enc}(t'_{i_\beta}))$ are given below.

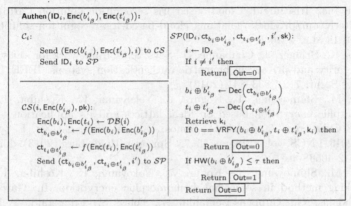

The proof is based on the following two hybrid games.

game 0: This is the original game. Let S_0 be the event that $\beta' = \beta$.

game 1: This is the same as **game** 0, except that now $\mathcal{CS}$ always performs the correct computation. Let S_1 be the event that $\beta' = \beta$ in **game** 1.

Since providing a different index i' than the correct one i always results in $\perp$ output, it does not help the adversary (i.e., the cloud) to win any of the games. So we assume that $\mathcal{CS}$ always provides the correct index i.

Claim 1: $|\Pr\{S_0\} - \Pr\{S_1\}|$ is negligible. This follows from the ϵ-security of the MAC scheme. Precisely, the difference between the two games is that in **game** 0, $\mathsf{VRFY}(b_i \oplus b'_{i_\beta}, t_i \oplus t'_{i_\beta}, \mathsf{k}_i) == 0$ if $\mathcal{CS}$ does not perform the computation correctly, except for probability ϵ, while in **game** 1, that does not happen as it performs the computation correctly. So the difference between the winning probabilities in **game** 0 and **game** 1 is negligible.

Claim 2: The adversary has negligible advantage in **game** 1, i.e., $|2\Pr\{S_1\} - 1| \leq \mathsf{negl}(\lambda)$. This follows from the IND-CPA-security of the employed HE scheme. Since otherwise, we can use the adversary $\mathcal{A}$ as a blackbox to construct another PPT adversary $\mathcal{A}'$ that can win the IND-CPA game against the HE scheme with non-negligible probability in a straightforward fashion. More precisely, the adversary $\mathcal{A}'$ can use the challenge ciphertext in the IND-CPA game to simulate the Π for $\mathcal{A}$, and use $\mathcal{A}$'s guess to win the IND-CPA game against the HE scheme. Hence, combining the two claims, we have that $\mathsf{Adv}^{\mathsf{Priv}}_{\Pi,\mathcal{A}}$ is negligible.

References

1. Costello, C., Fournet, C., Howell, J., Kohlweiss, M., Kreuter, B., Naehrig, M., Parno, B., Zahur, S.: Geppetto: Versatile verifiable computation. In: IEEE S&P. IEEE, pp. 253–270 (2015)
2. Gennaro, R., Gentry, C., Parno, B.: Non-interactive verifiable computing: outsourcing computation to untrusted workers. In: Rabin, T. (ed.) CRYPTO 2010. LNCS, vol. 6223, pp. 465–482. Springer, Heidelberg (2010). doi:10.1007/978-3-642-14623-7_25
3. Zhang, L.F., Safavi-Naini, R.: Batch verifiable computation of outsourced functions. In: Designs, Codes and Cryptography, pp. 1–23 (2015)
4. IIriTech. Inc.: Irisecureid: Cloud-based iris recognition solution (2016). http://www.iritech.com/products/solutions/cloud-based-iris-recognition-solution-0. Accessed 18 May 2016
5. Simoens, K., Bringer, J., Chabanne, H., Seys, S.: A framework for analyzing template security and privacy in biometric authentication systems. IEEE Trans. Inf. Forensics Secur. 7(2), 833–841 (2012)
6. Yasuda, M., Shimoyama, T., Kogure, J., Yokoyama, K., Koshiba, T.: Packed homomorphic encryption based on ideal lattices and its application to biometrics. In: Cuzzocrea, A., Kittl, C., Simos, D.E., Weippl, E., Xu, L. (eds.) CD-ARES 2013. LNCS, vol. 8128, pp. 55–74. Springer, Heidelberg (2013). doi:10.1007/978-3-642-40588-4_5
7. Yasuda, M., Shimoyama, T., Kogure, J., Yokoyama, K., Koshiba, T.: Practical packing method in somewhat homomorphic encryption. In: Garcia-Alfaro, J., Lioudakis, G., Cuppens-Boulahia, N., Foley, S., Fitzgerald, W.M. (eds.) DPM/SETOP -2013. LNCS, vol. 8247, pp. 34–50. Springer, Heidelberg (2014). doi:10.1007/978-3-642-54568-9_3
8. Bringer, J., Chabanne, H., Izabachène, M., Pointcheval, D., Tang, Q., Zimmer, S.: An application of the Goldwasser-Micali cryptosystem to biometric authentication. In: Pieprzyk, J., Ghodosi, H., Dawson, E. (eds.) ACISP 2007. LNCS, vol. 4586, pp. 96–106. Springer, Heidelberg (2007). doi:10.1007/978-3-540-73458-1_8
9. Abidin, A., Mitrokotsa, A.: Security aspects of privacy-preserving biometric authentication based on ideal lattices and ring-lwe. In: Proceedings of the IEEE Workshop on Information Forensics and Security, pp. 1653–1658 (2014)
10. Abidin, A., Pagnin, E., Mitrokotsa, A.: Attacks on privacy-preserving biometric authentication. In: Proceedings of the 19th Nordic Conference on Secure IT Systems (NordSec 2014), pp. 293–294. Tromso, Norway (2014)
11. Abidin, A., Matsuura, K., Mitrokotsa, A.: Security of a privacy-preserving biometric authentication protocol revisited. In: Gritzalis, D., Kiayias, A., Askoxylakis, I. (eds.) CANS 2014. LNCS, vol. 8813, pp. 290–304. Springer, Heidelberg (2014). doi:10.1007/978-3-319-12280-9_19
12. Van Dijk, M., Juels, A.: On the impossibility of cryptography alone for privacy-preserving cloud computing. In: Proceedings of the 5th USENIX Conference on Hot Topics in Security, HotSec 2010, pp. 1–8. USENIX Association (2010)
13. Yao, A.C.C.: How to generate and exchange secrets. In: 27th Annual Symposium on Foundations of Computer Science, pp. 162–167. IEEE (1986)
14. Paillier, P.: Public-key cryptosystems based on composite degree residuosity classes. In: Stern, J. (ed.) EUROCRYPT 1999. LNCS, vol. 1592, pp. 223–238. Springer, Heidelberg (1999). doi:10.1007/3-540-48910-X_16

15. Goldwasser, S., Micali, S.: Probabilistic encryption & how to play mental poker keeping secret all partial information. In: Proceedings of the Fourteenth Annual ACM Symposium on Theory of Computing, STOC 1982, pp. 365–377. ACM (1982)

16. Chor, B., Kushilevitz, E., Goldreich, O., Sudan, M.: Private information retrieval. J. ACM **45**(6), 965–981 (1998)

17. Ostrovsky, R., Skeith, W.E.: A survey of single-database private information retrieval: techniques and applications. In: Okamoto, T., Wang, X. (eds.) PKC 2007. LNCS, vol. 4450, pp. 393–411. Springer, Heidelberg (2007). doi:10.1007/978-3-540-71677-8_26

18. Barbosa, M., Brouard, T., Cauchie, S., Sousa, S.M.: Secure biometric authentication with improved accuracy. In: Mu, Y., Susilo, W., Seberry, J. (eds.) ACISP 2008. LNCS, vol. 5107, pp. 21–36. Springer, Heidelberg (2008). doi:10.1007/978-3-540-70500-0_3

19. Stoianov, A.: Security issues of biometric encryption. In: Proceedings of the 2009 IEEE Toronto International Conference on Science and Technology for Humanity (TIC- STH), pp. 34–39, September 2009

20. Damgård, I., Geisler, M., Krøigaard, M.: Efficient and secure comparison for on-line auctions. In: Pieprzyk, J., Ghodosi, H., Dawson, E. (eds.) ACISP 2007. LNCS, vol. 4586, pp. 416–430. Springer, Heidelberg (2007). doi:10.1007/978-3-540-73458-1_30

21. Erkin, Z., Franz, M., Guajardo, J., Katzenbeisser, S., Lagendijk, I., Toft, T.: Privacy-preserving face recognitiond. In: Goldberg, I., Atallah, M.J. (eds.) PETS 2009. LNCS, vol. 5672, pp. 235–253. Springer, Heidelberg (2009). doi:10.1007/978-3-642-03168-7_14

22. Sadeghi, A.-R., Schneider, T., Wehrenberg, I.: Efficient privacy-preserving face recognition. In: Lee, D., Hong, S. (eds.) ICISC 2009. LNCS, vol. 5984, pp. 229–244. Springer, Heidelberg (2010). doi:10.1007/978-3-642-14423-3_16

23. Huang, Y., Malka, L., Evans, D., Katz, J.: Efficient privacy-preserving biometric identification. In: NDSS (2011)

24. Bringer, J., Chabanne, H., Patey, A.: SHADE: secure hamming distance computation from oblivious transfer. In: Financial Cryptography Workshops, pp. 164–176 (2013)

25. Bringer, J., Chabanne, H., Favre, M., Patey, A., Schneider, T., Zohner, M.: GSHADE: faster privacy-preserving distance computation and biometric identification. In: Proceedings of the 2nd ACM Workshop on Information Hiding and Multimedia Security, pp. 187–198. ACM (2014)

26. Osadchy, M., Pinkas, B., Jarrous, A., Moskovich, B.: SCiFI - a system for secure face identification. In: IEEE S&P 2010, pp. 239–254, May 2010

27. Carter, L., Wegman, M.N.: Universal classes of hash functions. J. Comput. Syst. Sci. **18**, 143–154 (1979)

28. Stinson, D.R.: Universal hashing and authentication codes. In: Feigenbaum, J. (ed.) CRYPTO 1991. LNCS, vol. 576, pp. 74–85. Springer, Heidelberg (1992). doi:10.1007/3-540-46766-1_5

29. Abidin, A., Larsson, J.Å.: New universal hash functions. In: Armknecht, F., Lucks, S. (eds.) WEWoRC 2011. LNCS, vol. 7242, pp. 99–108. Springer, Heidelberg (2012). doi:10.1007/978-3-642-34159-5_7

30. Krawczyk, H.: LFSR-based hashing and authentication. In: Desmedt, Y.G. (ed.) CRYPTO 1994. LNCS, vol. 839, pp. 129–139. Springer, Heidelberg (1994). doi:10.1007/3-540-48658-5_15

31. Pagnin, E., Dimitrakakis, C., Abidin, A., Mitrokotsa, A.: On the leakage of information in biometric authentication. In: Meier, W., Mukhopadhyay, D. (eds.) INDOCRYPT 2014. LNCS, vol. 8885, pp. 265–280. Springer, Heidelberg (2014). doi:10.1007/978-3-319-13039-2_16

32. Nevelsteen, W., Preneel, B.: Software performance of universal hash functions. In: Stern, J. (ed.) EUROCRYPT 1999. LNCS, vol. 1592, pp. 24–41. Springer, Heidelberg (1999). doi:10.1007/3-540-48910-X_3

33. Walfish, M., Blumberg, A.J.: Verifying computations without reexecuting them. Commun. ACM **58**(2), 74–84 (2015)

34. Shoup, V.: NTL: A library for doing number theory (2016). http://www.shoup.net/ntl/. Accessed 26 Feb 2016

35. GMP: The GNU Multiple Precision Arithmetic Library (2016). https://gmplib.org/. Accessed 26 Feb 2016

36. Daugman, J.: How iris recognition works. In: ICIP (1), pp. 33–36 (2002)

37. Goldreich, O., Ostrovsky, R.: Software protection and simulation on oblivious rams. J. ACM **43**(3), 431–473 (1996)

38. Faber, S., Jarecki, S., Kentros, S., Wei, B.: Three-party ORAM for secure computation. In: Iwata, T., Cheon, J.H. (eds.) ASIACRYPT 2015. LNCS, vol. 9452, pp. 360–385. Springer, Heidelberg (2015). doi:10.1007/978-3-662-48797-6_16

39. Bringer, J., Chabanne, H., Patey, A.: Practical identification with encrypted biometric data using oblivious RAM. In: ICB 2013, pp. 1–8 (2013)

40. Karvelas, N., Peter, A., Katzenbeisser, S., Tews, E., Hamacher, K.: Privacy-preserving whole genome sequence processing through proxy-aided ORAM. In: WPES 2014, pp. 1–10. ACM (2014)

41. Keller, M., Scholl, P.: Efficient, oblivious data structures for MPC. In: Sarkar, P., Iwata, T. (eds.) ASIACRYPT 2014. LNCS, vol. 8874, pp. 506–525. Springer, Heidelberg (2014). doi:10.1007/978-3-662-45608-8_27

42. Damgård, I., Pastro, V., Smart, N., Zakarias, S.: Multiparty computation from somewhat homomorphic encryption. In: Safavi-Naini, R., Canetti, R. (eds.) CRYPTO 2012. LNCS, vol. 7417, pp. 643–662. Springer, Heidelberg (2012). doi:10.1007/978-3-642-32009-5_38

43. Teoh, A.B.J., Yuang, C.T.: Cancelable biometrics realization with multispace random projections. IEEE Trans. Syst. Man Cybern. Part B (Cybern.) **37**(5), 1096–1106 (2007)

Verifiable Message-Locked Encryption

Sébastien Canard[1], Fabien Laguillaumie[2], and Marie Paindavoine[1,2(✉)]

[1] Orange Labs, Applied Crypto Group, Caen, France
{sebastien.canard,marie.paindavoine}@orange.com
[2] LIP (U.Lyon, CNRS, ENS Lyon, INRIA, UCBL),
Université Claude Bernard Lyon 1, Villeurbanne, France
{fabien.laguillaumie,marie.paindavoine}@ens-lyon.fr

Abstract. One of today's main challenge related to cloud storage is to maintain the functionalities and the efficiency of customers' and service providers' usual environments, while protecting the confidentiality of sensitive data. Deduplication is one of those functionalities: it enables cloud storage providers to save a lot of memory by storing only once a file uploaded several times. But classical encryption blocks deduplication. One needs to use a "message-locked encryption" (MLE), which allows the detection of duplicates and the storage of only one encrypted file on the server, which can be decrypted by any owner of the file. However, in most existing scheme, a user can bypass this deduplication protocol. In this article, we provide servers verifiability for MLE schemes: the servers can verify that the ciphertexts are well-formed. This property that we formally define forces a customer to prove that she complied to the deduplication protocol, thus preventing her to deviate from *the prescribed functionality* of MLE. We call it *deduplication consistency*. To achieve this deduplication consistency, we provide (i) a generic transformation that applies to any MLE scheme and (ii) an ElGamal-based deduplication-consistent MLE, which is secure in the random oracle model.

1 Introduction

Cloud computing is often promoted towards companies as a way to reduce their costs while increasing accessibility and flexibility. It is common sense to have one large computing infrastructure that companies would share instead of replicating smaller ones. This saves money and is an eco-friendlier way to distribute resources. But cloud platforms are neither cheap nor eco-friendly. The larger amount of data these platforms host, the more expensive they become. Impact on the environment grows as well. One way to address this issue is to delete identical files stored by different users. This method, called *deduplication*, is widely used by cloud providers. However, some of the cloud storage users may want to encrypt their data, distrusting honest-but-curious providers. If they use a classical encryption scheme, deduplication is not possible anymore: two encryptions of the same plaintext under different keys yield indistinguishable ciphertexts. A new kind of encryption is needed, under which it is possible to determine whether two different ciphertexts are *locked* to the same message or not.

© Springer International Publishing AG 2016
S. Foresti and G. Persiano (Eds.): CANS 2016, LNCS 10052, pp. 299–315, 2016.
DOI: 10.1007/978-3-319-48965-0_18

Previous Work. The work on the *message-locked encryption* model has been initiated by Douceur et al. [8] with their *convergent encryption* (CE) scheme. The main idea is very simple: everyone that encrypts the same message m will obtain the *same* ciphertext c. The convergent encryption protocol CE given in [8] uses a hash function H (which is modelled as a random oracle for the security proof) and a deterministic symmetric encryption scheme SE: it sets the encryption and decryption key as $K = H(M)$, where M is the message to be encrypted, and the ciphertext C is computed as SE.Encrypt(M, K). The ciphertext is concatenated to a tag $\tau = H(C)$ which allows the server to easily detect duplicates. When the server receives a new ciphertext, it discards the file if the tag equals one already in its database. Following this protocol, several schemes have been given, focussing mainly on improving efficiency e.g. [7,10,18].

However, in [4], the authors point out the lack of a formal security investigation of this emerging model. They formally introduce the concept of *message-locked encryption* (MLE) and provide a complete security analysis. In particular, they show that a secure MLE does not need to be deterministic to achieve its goal. It is sufficient (and more general) to provide an equality testing procedure that publicly checks if two ciphertexts encrypt the same plaintext, as shown in [1]. The interactive case has recently been studied in [3].

Security. As other kinds of "searchable encryption", MLE stands at the boundary of deterministic and probabilistic encryption worlds. As such, it cannot provide the standard notions of semantic security. Likewise, security can only be achieved for unpredictable data. If one can guess a possible message, one can encrypt it and then easily test ciphertexts for equality. In previous works the following privacy properties (PRV for short) were defined. The first one is PRV\$-CDA [4] that states that the semantic security should hold when messages are unpredictable (having high min-entropy), even for an adversary being able to choose the distribution where the messages are drawn (hence the notion of CDA, for Chosen Distribution Attack). In this experiment, the adversary has to distinguish a ciphertext according to a distribution of its choice from a random bit sequence. The second one is PRV-CDA2 [1] that adds the parameter dependence setting, for which the security should hold even for messages that depend on the public parameters. They are then given to the adversary who chooses a distribution. Abadi et al. [1] have also slightly modified the security experiment, compared to [4], introducing a real-or-random oracle that gives to the encryption algorithm either a set of (unpredictable) messages drawn from the adversary's chosen distribution, or a true randomly chosen set of (unpredictable) messages. The adversary has to distinguish between both cases. Additionally to these indistinguishability-type properties, the authors in [4] introduce the natural requirement of *tag consistency*, whose goal is to make it impossible to undetectably replace a message by a fake one. It states that if two tags are equal, then the underlying messages should be equal.

Our contributions. In this article, we investigate the converse: if two messages are equal, does the server always perform deduplication? Strangely enough, in almost all previous CE and MLE schemes [3,4,8], it is straightforward for a user to avoid the deduplication process altogether. The main feature for which those schemes were introduced is not achieved. In those schemes, the server does not actually verify that the key has actually been computed as required.

In this context, we have three contributions in this paper. First, we formalize this new security requirement, namely *deduplication consistency*, second we provide a generic transformation of a non-deduplication consistent MLE scheme into a deduplication consistent one and third we give a ElGamal-based construction.

In order to achieve verifiability in MLE, we introduce a new notion of *deduplication consistency*. It states that an equality test run on two valid ciphertexts with the same underlying plaintext will output 1 with overwhelming probability. Verifiability is a classical notion to prevent denial-of-service attacks, but this can be also useful in many scenarios. A court could oblige a cloud service provider to delete *all* copies of a given file, for example a newspaper article (right-to-be-forgotten) or a media file (for copyright infringement). If users are able to escape the deduplication process, the cloud service provider would not be able to prove that he complied to the court decision. A different scenario could be a collaborative database. Some attributes need to have a unique value in each row. If two users want to upload the same information, then the database would want to enforce deduplication.

A natural way to provide the verifiability of a ciphertext in a scheme of e.g. [8], is to provide a NIZK proof that the key $K = H(M)$ is correctly computed from the message M, and the ciphertext $C = \mathsf{SE.Encrypt}(M, K)$ is also consistent w.r.t. the same message M and key K. Based on this, we propose a generic construction to turn any MLE scheme into a deduplication consistent scheme.

To instantiate this generic scheme, we rely on an ElGamal-based construction. Indeed, another important issue in cloud storage is efficiency, as people usually expect instant uploading and responses from the cloud storage provider. Moreover, the ciphertexts' expansion should be carefully controlled, as the deduplication main goal is to save space storage. As such, neither generic non-interactive zero-knowledge proof (NIZK) used in [1] nor fully homomorphic encryption used in [3] could be considered as acceptable solutions. Combining an ElGamal encryption with an algebraic hash function makes possible to use efficient NIZK over discrete logarithm relation sets [16] to prove that these computations are all consistent one with each other. Our construction is the first one that provably achieves deduplication consistency. As this is a strong security requirement, our scheme is far less efficient than convergent-like solutions, but it is still more efficient than those of Abadi et al. [1] or those of Bellare and Keelveedhi [3] whose goal is also to strengthen security.

Organization of the paper. The paper is now organized as follows. In the next section, we provide some background that will be useful all along the paper. In Sect. 3, we give the security model for message-locked encryption. Section 4 introduces our new notion of deduplication consistency and the generic construction and Sect. 5 describes the ElGamal-based construction. Finally, in Sect. 6, we provide the security proofs and discuss efficiency.

2 Preliminaries

2.1 Bilinear Groups

Our construction relies on pairings, so we recall the definition of *bilinear groups* that are a set of three groups $\mathbb{G}_1, \mathbb{G}_2, \mathbb{G}_T$ of prime order p together with a bilinear map $e : \mathbb{G}_1 \times \mathbb{G}_2 \to \mathbb{G}_T$ such that (i) for all $X_1 \in \mathbb{G}_1, X_2 \in \mathbb{G}_2$ and $a, b \in \mathbb{Z}_p$, $e(X_1^a, X_2^b) = e(X_1, X_2)^{ab}$, (ii) for $X_1 \neq 1_{\mathbb{G}_1}$ and $X_2 \neq 1_{\mathbb{G}_2}$, $e(X_1, X_2) \neq 1_{\mathbb{G}_T}$, and (iii) e is efficiently computable. We use *type 3* pairings for which there are no efficiently computable homomorphisms between $\mathbb{G}_1$ and $\mathbb{G}_2$.

2.2 Computational Assumptions

Our construction security relies on the following computational assumptions.

Assumption 1 (blinded-DDH (bl-DDH)). Given $(t_1, t_1^u, g_1, g_1^r, g_1^z) \in \mathbb{G}_1^5$ and $(t_2, t_2^{u \cdot k}) \in \mathbb{G}_2^2$ for random $(u, r, k) \in (\mathbb{Z}_p^*)^3$, it is hard to decide whether $z = r \cdot k$ or z is a random element from $\mathbb{Z}_p^*$. We define $\mathsf{Adv}_{\mathcal{A}}^{\mathsf{bl\text{-}DDH}}(\lambda)$ as the advantage of a polynomial-time adversary $\mathcal{A}$ against bl-DDH.

In the security proof of our scheme, we use the following generalization of the bl-DDH assumption. We stress that $(1, 1)$-bl-DDH is the bl-DDH assumption.

Assumption 2 ((T, ℓ)-blinded-DDH ((T, ℓ)-bl-DDH)). Let T and ℓ be two integers. Let $\left[u_h, \{r_{i,h}\}_{i=1}^{\ell}, k_h \right]_{h=1}^{T}$ be random in $(\mathbb{Z}_p^*)^{T(\ell+2)}$. Given $(t_1, g_1, \ldots, g_\ell)$ in $\mathbb{G}_1^{\ell+1}$, t_2 in $\mathbb{G}_2$, $\left[t_1^{u_h}, \{g_i^{r_{h,i}}\}_{i=1}^{\ell}, \{g_i^{z_{h,i}}\}_{i=1}^{\ell} \right]_{h=1}^{T} \in \mathbb{G}_1^{T(2\ell+1)}$ and $\left[t_2^{u_h \cdot k_h} \right]_{h=1}^{T} \in \mathbb{G}_2^T$, for all $h = 1, \ldots, T$ and for all $i = 1, \ldots, \ell$, it is hard to decide whether $z_{h,i} = r_{h,i} \cdot k_h$ or z is a random element from $\mathbb{Z}_p^*$. We define $\mathsf{Adv}_{\mathcal{A}}^{(T,\ell)\text{-}\mathsf{bl\text{-}DDH}}(\lambda)$ as the advantage of a polynomial-time adversary $\mathcal{A}$ against (T, ℓ)-bl-DDH.

To assert the strength of our hypothesis, we prove the following reduction to the tripartite decisional Diffie-Hellman assumption [5].

Theorem 1. *The blinded-DDH assumption is polynomially reducible to the tripartite Diffie-Hellman assumption. The (T, ℓ)-blinded-DDH assumption is polynomially reducible to the blinded-DDH assumption.*

2.3 Commitment Schemes

A commitment scheme aims at masking a secret while allowing a later revelation.

Generic Description. Formally, those schemes are made up with three algorithms, namely the Setup which on input a security parameter λ outputs the public parameters pp, the Commit which on input pp and a message M outputs a commit C and a witness r, and the Open which on input a commit C, a message M and a witness r outputs 1 if C is a commitment of M for the witness r, and 0 otherwise. A commitment scheme Γ is considered to be cryptographically secure if it verifies both the *hiding* and the *binding* properties. We focus on the latter as it is the one that matters the most in our constructions and proofs.

The commitment binding experiment $\mathsf{Exp}^{\mathsf{binding}}_{\Gamma,\mathcal{A}}(\lambda)$ starts by executing the Setup to obtain pp. On input pp, the adversary $\mathcal{A}$ outputs a commitment C, and two pairs (M, r) and (M', r'). The experiment outputs 1 iff $\mathsf{Open}(C, M, r) = \mathsf{Open}(C, M', r') = 1$. We say that the commitment scheme Γ is binding if for all polynomial time adversaries $\mathcal{A}$ the following advantage is negligible for all λ:
$\mathsf{Adv}^{\mathsf{binding}}_{\Gamma,\mathcal{A}}(\lambda) = \Pr\left(\mathsf{Exp}^{\mathsf{binding}}_{\Gamma,\mathcal{A}}(\lambda) = 1\right)$.

The Pedersen Commitment. Let $\mathbb{G}$ be a group of prime order p and let g and h be generators of $\mathbb{G}$. The Pedersen Commitment [13] allows a prover to commit on a secret value $m \in \mathbb{Z}_p$. During the Commit execution, one computes $C = g^m h^r$ with $r \in \mathbb{Z}_p$ picked uniformly at random to the verifier. The Open algorithm is straightforward. This commitment scheme is perfectly hiding and is computationally binding under the discrete logarithm assumption.

2.4 Non-Interactive Zero-Knowledge (NIZK) Proofs

We use NIZK proofs of membership in NP languages to achieve the notion of deduplication consistency that we introduced.

Generic Description. Let Π be a proof system in NP languages for a NP-relation rel. Such a system is given by two probabilistic polynomial-time machines $\mathcal{P}$ and $\mathcal{V}$ such that (i) for all $(y, w) \in \mathsf{rel}$ (that is $\mathsf{rel}(y, w) = \mathsf{true}$), $\mathcal{P}$ takes as input (y, w) and $\mathcal{V}$ takes as input y and (ii) at the end of the protocol between $\mathcal{P}$ and $\mathcal{V}$, $\mathcal{V}$ outputs a bit d of acceptance ($d = 1$) or rejection ($d = 0$). We require the following properties: (i) *Completeness* for all $(y, w) \in \mathsf{rel}$, $\mathcal{V}$ returns 1 with probability 1; and (ii) *Soundness*: for all $y \in \{0, 1\}^*$, if $\mathcal{V}$ returns 1, then it exists w such that $(y, w) \in \mathsf{rel}$ with overwhelming probability.

We also need this proof system to be *zero-knowledge*. This means that a distinguisher $\mathcal{D}$ cannot distinguish between the proofs produced by a real prover or the ones produced by a simulator. We denote $\mathsf{Adv}^{\mathsf{zk}}_{\Pi,\mathcal{D}}(\lambda)$ the advantage of an adversary $\mathcal{A}$ in this distinguishing game, and we say that a non-interactive proof system $(\mathcal{P}, \mathcal{V})$ is (statistically) zero-knowledge if there exists a polynomial time simulator sim such that for any polynomial time distinguisher $\mathcal{D}$, the function $\mathsf{Adv}^{\mathsf{zk}}_{\Pi,\mathcal{D}}(\lambda)$ is negligible.

Double Discrete Logarithms Proofs. For our ElGamal-based scheme, the NIZK proofs we use are conjunctions of classical discrete logarithm relations [16]. They are made non-interactive thanks to the Fiat-Shamir transform [9], proven to be secure in the random oracle model [14]. The main time-consuming part is a double logarithm NIZK proof (with a statistical zero-knowledge property, as shown in [17]), where the statement has the form: $\mathsf{NIZK}\left(s : V_1 = h^{x^s} \wedge V_2 = y^s\right)$, where $h, y \in \mathbb{Z}_p$ and $x \in \mathbb{Z}_p^*$ are public, while $s \in \mathbb{Z}_p^*$ is secret.

2.5   Hashing Block Sources

Message-locked encryption, like deterministic encryption, can only protect messages that are hard to guess. To model this fact, Bellare et al. propose in [2] a definition of privacy, which states that no information about multiple dependent messages is leaked from their encryptions. Though unpredictable, the adversary $\mathcal{A}$ can choose the distribution over the messages, allowing them to be correlated. In order to avoid brute force attacks, the distribution of messages should guarantee a minimal entropy of the messages. The *min-entropy* of a random variable X is defined as $H_\infty(X) = -\log(\max_x(\Pr[X = x]))$. A random variable X such that $H_\infty(X) \geq \mu$ is a μ-source. A (T, μ)-source is a random variable $\mathbf{X} = (X_1, \ldots, X_T)$ where each X_i is a μ-source. A (T, μ)-block source is a random variable $\mathbf{X} = (X_1, \ldots, X_T)$ where each $X_i|_{X_1=x_1,\ldots,X_{i-1}=x_{i-1}}$ is a μ-source.

One of the crucial point in our construction of MLE is the hashing of such block sources. The Leftover Hash Lemma [12] is a classic tool for extracting random-looking strings from an uncertain source of entropy. Precise and tight results from [6] will help us to prove the privacy of our MLE when the keys are derived from messages produced from a block source. The following theorem from [6] states that if H is a 2-universal hash function applied to some elements of a block source $(X_1, \ldots, X_T)$, the distribution $(H, H(X_1), \ldots, H(X_T))$ is close to the uniform distribution. Let us recall that a family $\mathcal{H}$ of hash functions mapping $\{0,1\}^n$ to $\{0,1\}^\ell$ is said to be 2-*universal* if for all distinct x and y, the probability that $H(x) = H(y)$ equals $\frac{1}{2^\ell}$, when H is drawn at random.

Theorem 2. *[6, Theorem 3.5] Let $H : \{1, \ldots, 2^n\} \to \{1, \ldots, 2^m\}$ be a random hash function from a 2-universal family $\mathcal{H}$. Let $\mathbf{X} = (X_1, \ldots, X_T)$ be a (T, μ)-block source over $\{1, \ldots, 2^n\}^T$. For every $\varepsilon > 0$ such that $\mu > m + \log(T) + 2\log(1/\varepsilon)$, the hashed sequence $(H, \mathbf{Y}) = (H, H(X_1), \ldots, H(X_T))$ is ε-close to uniform in $\mathcal{H} \times \{1, \ldots, 2^m\}^T$.*

3   Message-Locked Encryption: Definition and Security

There are two different definitions for message-locked encryption (MLE) in the literature. The first one is due to Bellare, Keelveedhi and Ristenpart [4] and the second one from Abadi, Boneh, Mironov, Raghunathan and Segev [1]. Our definition, as well as the security model, is based on the ones from [1]. This definition is more general than Bellare et al.'s, but makes the notion of tag less present. In [4], the tag generation is performed only from the ciphertext, and the tag correctness ensures that one message encrypted by two different users will have the same tag, so that a server will be able to remove one of the ciphertexts. Abadi et al.'s definition of MLE (denoted MLE2) introduces a validity test to check the validity of ciphertext, and an equality test to deduplicate redundant files. This allows to handle randomized tags instead of deterministic. Even though there is no tag generation anymore, the security notion of tag consistency is kept, and we will sometimes informally call "tags" the parts of the ciphertext that are involved in the equality test.

3.1 Syntactic Definition

A Message-Locked Encryption (MLE) scheme is defined by the six following algorithms (PPGen, KD, Enc, Dec, EQ, Valid) operating over the plaintext space $\mathcal{M}$, ciphertext space $\mathcal{C}$ and keyspace $\mathcal{K}$, with λ as a security parameter.

- The parameter generation algorithm PPGen takes as input 1^λ and returns the public parameters $pp \leftarrow PPGen(1^\lambda)$.
- The key derivation function KD takes as input the public parameters pp, a message M, and outputs a message-derived key $k_M \leftarrow KD(pp, M)$.
- The encryption algorithm Enc takes as input pp, a message-derived key k_M, and a message M. It outputs a ciphertext $c \leftarrow Enc(pp, k_M, M)$.
- The decryption algorithm Dec takes as input pp, a secret key k_M, a ciphertext c and outputs either a message M or $\bot$: $\{M, \bot\} \leftarrow Dec(pp, k_M, c)$.
- The equality algorithm EQ takes as input public parameters pp, and two ciphertexts c_1 and c_2 and outputs 1 if both ciphertexts are generated from the same underlying message, and 0 otherwise: $\{0, 1\} \leftarrow EQ(pp, c_1, c_2)$.
- The validity-test algorithm Valid takes as input public parameters pp and a ciphertext c and outputs 1 if the ciphertext c is a valid ciphertext, and 0 otherwise: $\{0, 1\} \leftarrow Valid(pp, c)$.

A message-locked encryption is said to be *correct* if for all $\lambda \in \mathbb{N}$, all $pp \leftarrow PPGen(1^\lambda)$, all message $M \in \mathcal{M}$ and all $c \leftarrow Enc(pp, KD(pp, M), M)$,

(i) $M = Dec(pp, KD(pp, M), c)$ and $Valid(pp, c) = 1$, and
(ii) $EQ(pp, Enc(pp, KD(pp, M), M; \omega), Enc(pp, KD(pp, M), M; \omega')) = 1$.

This last property is equivalent to tag correctness in [4] (and we explicitly wrote the randomness ω and ω' to recall that encryption is probabilistic). To avoid trivial solutions, we recall that keys kept for decryption must be shorter than the message. As mentioned in [4], there must exist constants $c, d < 1$ such that the function that on input $\lambda \in \mathbb{N}$ returns $\max_{pp,M}(\Pr[|KD(pp, M)| > d|M|^c])$ is negligible, where $pp \in PPGen(1^\lambda)$ and $M \in \mathcal{M}$.

3.2 Privacy

The main security requirement for message-locked encryption is privacy of unpredictable messages. No MLE scheme can provide indistinguishability for predictable messages (drawn for a polynomial-size space), because of the equality testing procedure EQ. Our privacy notion is a combination of those existent. We rely on a PRV-CDA2-like requirement [1], however, like in [4], our scheme does not achieve the privacy property when the message distribution chosen by the adversary depends on the public parameters. Therefore, we call our privacy property PRV-piCDA, for *Privacy under parameter independent Chosen Distribution Attack*. It captures privacy of messages that are unpredictable but independent of the public parameters. Let us first define the real-or-random encryption oracle.

Definition 1 (Real-or-Random encryption oracle). *The real-or-random encryption oracle takes as input pairs* $(\mathsf{mode}, \mathbb{M})$ *with* $\mathsf{mode} \in \{\mathsf{real}, \mathsf{rand}\}$, *and* $\mathbb{M}$ *a polynomial size circuit representing a joint distribution over* T *messages from* $\mathcal{M}$. *If* $\mathsf{mode} = \mathsf{real}$ *then the oracle samples* $(M_1, \ldots, M_T) \leftarrow \mathbb{M}$ *and if* $\mathsf{mode} = \mathsf{rand}$ *then the oracle samples* T *uniform and independent messages from* $\mathcal{M}$. *Then the oracle outputs a ciphertexts vector* $\mathbf{C} = (c_1, \ldots, c_T)$ *such that, for each* i *the oracle computes* $k_{M_i} = \mathsf{KD}(\mathsf{pp}, M_i)$ *and* $c_i = \mathsf{Enc}(\mathsf{pp}, k_{M_i}, M_i)$.

Following [15], we consider adversaries whose restriction on their queries is that they are samplable by a polynomial-size circuit in the random oracle model.

Definition 2 (q-query polynomial-sampling complexity adversary). *We consider* (T, μ)-*block source. Let* $\mathcal{A}(1^\lambda)$ *be a probabilistic polynomial-time algorithm that is given an oracle access to* $\mathsf{RoR}(\mathsf{mode}, \mathsf{pp}, \cdot)$ *for some* $\mathsf{mode} \in \{\mathsf{real}, \mathsf{rand}\}$. *Then,* $\mathcal{A}$ *is a* q-*query* (T, μ)-*source adversary if, for each of* $\mathcal{A}$'s RoR-*queries* $\mathbb{M}$, *it holds that* $\mathbb{M}$ *is a* (T, μ)-*block source that is samplable by a polynomial-size circuit that uses at most* q *queries to the random oracle.*

Informally, PRV-piCDA security notion requires that encryptions of random messages should be indistinguishable from encryptions of messages drawn from a (T, μ)-block source.

Definition 3 (PRV-piCDA Security). *An MLE scheme* Π *is* (T, μ)-*block source* PRV-piCDA *secure if, for any probabilistic polynomial-time* (T, μ)-*block source adversary* $\mathcal{A} = (\mathcal{A}_0, \mathcal{A}_1)$, *there exists a negligible function* $\nu(\lambda)$ *such that:*

$$\mathsf{Adv}_{\Pi, \mathcal{A}}^{\mathsf{PRV-piCDA}}(\lambda) = \left| Pr\left[\mathbf{Exp}_{\Pi, A}^{\mathsf{real}} = 1 \right] - Pr\left[\mathbf{Exp}_{\Pi, A}^{\mathsf{rand}} = 1 \right] \right| \leq \nu(\lambda),$$

where the game $\mathbf{Exp}_{\Pi, \mathcal{A}}^{mode}(\lambda)$ *is defined Fig. 1.*

Experiment $\mathbf{Exp}_{\Pi, \mathcal{A}}^{TC}(\lambda)$

$\mathsf{pp} \leftarrow \mathsf{PPGen}(1^\lambda);$
$(M_0, c_1) \leftarrow \mathcal{A}(1^\lambda, \mathsf{pp});$
If $\mathsf{Valid}(\mathsf{pp}, c_1) = 0$ or $M_0 = \bot$ return 0;
$k_M \leftarrow \mathsf{KD}(\mathsf{pp}, M_0);$
$c_0 \leftarrow \mathsf{Enc}(\mathsf{pp}, k_M, M_0);$
$M_1 \leftarrow \mathsf{Dec}(\mathsf{pp}, k_M, c_1);$
If $(\mathsf{EQ}(\mathsf{pp}, c_0, c_1) = 1) \wedge (M_0 \neq M_1) \wedge (M_1 \neq \bot)$
return 1;
Else return 0.

Experiment $\mathbf{Exp}_{\Pi, \mathcal{A}}^{mode}(\lambda)$

$\mathbb{M} \leftarrow \mathcal{A}_0(1^\lambda);$
$\mathsf{pp} \leftarrow \mathsf{PPGen}(1^\lambda);$
$b \leftarrow \mathcal{A}_1^{\mathsf{RoR}(\mathsf{mode}, \mathbb{M})}(1^\lambda, \mathsf{pp})$
Return b.

Fig. 1. PRV-piCDA Game: $\mathbf{Exp}_{\Pi, \mathcal{A}}^{mode}(\lambda)$

Fig. 2. Tag Consistency Game : $\mathbf{Exp}_{\Pi, \mathcal{A}}^{TC}(\lambda)$

As stated in [1, Theorem 4.6], the case where $\mathcal{A}$ can query the RoR oracle multiple times is equivalent to the case where $\mathcal{A}$ can query this oracle just once.

3.3   Tag Consistency

Tag consistency is a major requirement of any MLE scheme. It ensures that the server will not discard a file if it doesn't have another file encrypting the same plaintext. We use the game defined by Abadl et al. in [1].

Definition 4 (Tag consistency). *An MLE scheme Π is* tag consistent *if for any probabilistic polynomial-time $\mathcal{A}$, there exists a negligible function $\nu(\lambda)$ such that:*

$$\mathsf{Adv}^{TC}_{\Pi,\mathcal{A}}(\lambda) = Pr\left[\mathbf{Exp}^{TC}_{\Pi,\mathcal{A}} = 1\right] \leq \nu(\lambda),$$

where the random experiment $\mathbf{Exp}^{TC}_{\Pi,\mathcal{A}}(\lambda)$ is described in Fig. 2.

4   Deduplication Consistency

In precedent works, the main security requirement, besides privacy, was tag consistency, meaning that if the equality test $\mathsf{EQ}(c_1, c_2)$ outputs 1 on two ciphertexts, then the underlying plaintexts are the same. As sketched in the introduction, we tackle here the converse case: if two ciphertexts c_1 and c_2 are meant to encrypt the same message, we require that $\mathsf{EQ}(c_1, c_2)$ outputs 1 with overwhelming probability. To capture such a security issue, we introduce in the following a new security notion for message-locked encryption, called *deduplication consistency*. This notion ensures that a MLE scheme *provably* provides deduplication.

4.1   Overview

The main point of deduplication consistency is to make a MLE scheme *verifiable*. In fact, if a server makes use of an MLE scheme for which it cannot be convinced that deduplication is actually enforced, he will loose the benefit he has expected from deduplication. In most existing schemes indeed (see below), only users are responsible for a smooth deduplication process. Then these schemes can easily be "deviate[d] from [their] prescribed functionality"[1].

In addition to save space storage, verifiable deduplication is a functionality that can have an interest of its own. Today, a really hot topic is the right-to-be-forgotten. An important question related to this topic is how a server can prove that he really deleted some given files. The problem is even more difficult if the files are encrypted on the server: the right to privacy of a user cannot prevail over the right to privacy of other users. It can happen however that a court asks a cloud service provider to remove a defamatory newspaper article or video from its storage space. Then the server's manager could encrypt this specific file with a verifiable MLE scheme and match it against the other files in the server. If the equality test returns one, deleting the corresponding file will be sufficient to prove that no user can now access to this file, as no user can bypass the deduplication procedure.

---

[1] Oded Goldreich, The Foundations of Cryptography, Preface.

4.2   Formal Definition

We define the deduplication experiment $\mathbf{Exp}_{\Pi,\mathcal{A}}^{DC}(1^\lambda)$ described on Fig. 3.

Definition 5 (Deduplication consistency). *An MLE scheme Π is deduplication consistent if for any probabilistic polynomial-time $\mathcal{A}$, there exists a negligible function $\nu(\lambda)$ such that:*

$$\mathsf{Adv}_{\Pi,\mathcal{A}}^{DC}(\lambda) = Pr\left[\mathbf{Exp}_{\Pi,\mathcal{A}}^{DC} = 1\right] \le \nu(\lambda),$$

where the random experiment $\mathbf{Exp}_{\Pi,\mathcal{A}}^{DC}(1^\lambda)$ is described in Fig. 3.

Experiment $\mathbf{Exp}_{\Pi,\mathcal{A}}^{DC}(\lambda)$

$\mathsf{pp} \leftarrow \mathsf{PPGen}(1^\lambda)$;
$(M, c_0, c_1) \leftarrow \mathcal{A}(1^\lambda, \mathsf{pp})$;
If $(\mathsf{Valid}(\mathsf{pp}, c_0) = 0) \vee (\mathsf{Valid}(\mathsf{pp}, c_1) = 0)$ then return 0;
If $\mathsf{EQ}(\mathsf{pp}, c_0, c_1) = 1$ then return 0;
$k_M \leftarrow \mathsf{KD}(\mathsf{pp}, M)$;
$M_0 \leftarrow \mathsf{Dec}(\mathsf{pp}, k_M, c_0)$; $M_1 \leftarrow \mathsf{Dec}(\mathsf{pp}, k_M, c_1)$;
If $M \ne M_0 \vee M \ne M_1$ then return 0;
Return 1;

Fig. 3. Deduplication Security Game : $\mathbf{Exp}_{\Pi,\mathcal{A}}^{DC}(\lambda)$

As for previous schemes, none of them formalizes this notion. Moreover, it is obvious that the different solutions given by Bellare et al. [4] do not achieve deduplication consistency. We have the intuition that the randomized scheme proposed by Abadi et al. [1] is deduplication consistent due to the presence of the NIZK, but a formal proof remains an open problem.

4.3   A Generic Construction

We first describe a generic construction permitting to transform any private and tag consistent MLE scheme Λ into a MLE scheme Λ' additionally achieving the deduplication consistency.

Our construction. For this purpose, we need a secure commitment scheme Γ and a NIZK proof system Π (see Sect. 2). Our scheme is described as follows.

- PPGen. This step executes (i) Λ.PPGen which outputs Λ.pp, (ii) Γ.Setup which gives Γ.pp and (iii) the generation of a reference string R for the NIZK proof. Then, Λ'.pp $= (\Lambda$.pp$, \Gamma$.pp$, R)$.
- KD. On input Λ'.pp and a message M, this algorithm simply corresponds to the execution of Λ.KD, which outputs $k_M = \Lambda$.KD$(\Lambda$.pp$, M)$.

– Enc. There are three steps during the encryption algorithm. At first, we execute the $\Lambda.\mathsf{Enc}(\Lambda.\mathsf{pp}, k_M, M)$ which outputs c. Then, we compute a commitment on M, as $(C, r) = \Gamma.\mathsf{Commit}(\Gamma.\mathsf{pp}, M)$. Finally, we provide the following NIZK proof:

$$\pi = \mathsf{NIZK}\Big(M, r : c = \Lambda.\mathsf{Enc}(\Lambda.\mathsf{pp}, \Lambda.\mathsf{KD}(\Lambda.\mathsf{pp}, M), M)$$
$$\wedge (C, r) = \Gamma.\mathsf{Commit}(\Gamma.\mathsf{pp}, M) \Big)$$

and the output ciphertext is $c' = (c, C, \pi)$.
– Valid. On input $c' = (c, C, \pi)$, this algorithm executes $\Lambda.\mathsf{Valid}(\Lambda.\mathsf{pp}, c)$ and verifies that the NIZK π is correct.
– Dec. On input $c' = (c, C, \pi)$ and k_M, this algorithm first executes Valid, and, if it returned 1, it executes $\Lambda.\mathsf{Dec}(\Lambda.\mathsf{pp}, k_M, c)$ to obtain M.
– EQ. On input $c_1' = (c_1, C_1, \pi_1)$ and $c_2' = (c_2, C_2, \pi_2)$, this algorithm first executes Valid on both ciphertexts, and then, if both returned 1, it executes $\Lambda.\mathsf{EQ}(\Lambda.\mathsf{pp}, c_1, c_2)$.

Security. Regarding the security of the above construction, it verifies the privacy and the tag consistency properties. This is mainly due to the fact that the addition of the commitment and the NIZK proof does not affect the security proofs related to both privacy and tag consistency, for obvious reasons.

More precisely, regarding the privacy property, the NIZK proof can be simulated during the experiment (by the real-or-random oracle), using the zero-knowledge property. We have a slight loss in security, corresponding to the advantage of the adversary against the hiding property of the used commitment scheme Γ. Regarding the tag consistency property, this is similarly obvious.

The deduplication consistency is given by the following theorem.

Theorem 3. *The scheme Λ' given above is deduplication-consistent, assuming that Λ is tag consistent, Γ is binding, and π is a sound zero-knowledge proof.*

Proof. Our aim in this proof is to reduce the deduplication consistency of our construction to the binding property of the commitment scheme. We consider the commitment binding experiment given in Sect. 2 and play the role of an adversary $\mathcal{A}$ against it. $\mathcal{A}$ has the parameters $\Gamma.\mathsf{pp}$ of the scheme Γ. His aim is to output a commitment C and two pairs (M, r) and (M', r') such that $\mathsf{Open}(C, M, r) = \mathsf{Open}(C, M', r') = 1$. We assume that $\mathcal{A}$ has access to an adversary $\mathcal{B}$ which has a non-negligible advantage against the deduplication consistency experiment of our scheme.

Parameter generation. We first generate the parameter of the MLE system, executing $\Lambda.\mathsf{PPGen}$, generating a reference string R for the NIZK proof, and adding the commitment parameter $\Gamma.\mathsf{pp}$ obtained above. We then give $(\Lambda.\mathsf{pp}, \Gamma.\mathsf{pp}, R)$ to the adversary $\mathcal{B}$.

Adversary's answer. At any time of the experiment, using its advantage against deduplication consistency, $\mathcal{B}$ outputs (M, c_0', c_1'), with $c_0' = (c_0, C_0, \pi_0)$ and

$c_1' = (c_1, C_1, \pi_1)$, such that all the conditions related to the deduplication consistency experiment are verified. In particular, we have $\Lambda'.\mathsf{Valid}(\mathsf{pp}, c_0') = 1$, $\Lambda'.\mathsf{Valid}(\mathsf{pp}, c_1') = 1$ and $\Lambda.\mathsf{EQ}(\mathsf{pp}, c_0, c_1) = 0$.

Answer to the commitment challenge. Using the soundness property of the NIZK, $\mathcal{A}$ is then able to extract, from π_0 and π_1, the underlying secret messages M_0' and M_1', related to c_0 and c_1 respectively. As we have $\Lambda.\mathsf{EQ}(\mathsf{pp}, c_0, c_1) = 0$, and since Λ is tag consistent, we necessarily have $M_0' \neq M_1'$.

As $\mathcal{B}$ is successful in the DC experiment, and using c_0 and c_1 respectively, $\mathcal{A}$ computes $k_M = \Lambda.\mathsf{KD}(\mathsf{pp}, M)$, and then $M_0 = \Lambda.\mathsf{Dec}(\mathsf{pp}, k_M, c_0)$ and $M_1 = \Lambda.\mathsf{Dec}(\mathsf{pp}, k_M, c_1)$, with $M = M_0 = M_1$.

It means that it exists $i \in \{0, 1\}$ such that $M_i \neq M_i'$. As both ciphertexts are valid, for both M_i and M_i', there is a sound zero-knowledge proof provided by $\mathcal{B}$ from which $\mathcal{A}$ is able to extract the corresponding witnesses r_i and r_i'. $\mathcal{A}$ sends $C_i, (M_i, r_i), (M_i', r_i')$ to the binding challenger. It is a winning output for the binding experiment of Γ, with an advantage at least equal to the one of $\mathcal{B}$ against deduplication consistency, which concludes the proof.

5   A Concrete Message Locked Encryption with Deduplication Consistency

In this section, we describe our construction of a deduplication consistent MLE. Compared to the fully randomized message-locked encryption from [1], the main difference is that the secret key is derived from the message using a hash function which has algebraic properties. Thus, we avoid generic NIZK [11], gaining efficiency. More precisely, the message M is cut into small blocks $(m_1 \| \dots \| m_\ell)$ of ρ bits, and the key is computed as $k_M = \prod_{i=1}^{\ell} a_i^{m_i} \mod p$ for publicly known a_i's. By using Theorem 2, we prove that if the messages come from a source with high enough min-entropy, the key k_M is indistinguishable from a uniform key.

These blocks m_i are chosen small enough to be efficiently decrypted, as we encrypt them using the ElGamal encryption with messages in the exponent, and the key k_M: $T_{1,i} = g_i^{r_i}$ and $T_{2,i} = h^{m_i} \cdot g_i^{r_i \cdot k_M}$. In order to achieve DC, those equations should be included in the NIZK proof.

It remains to create a suitable tag, which is done by using the same technique as in [1]. More precisely, we provide a pair $(\tau_1 = t_1^u, \tau_2 = t_2^{u \cdot k_M})$, which will make it possible to detect a duplication using a pairing computation. We add the following relations to the NIZK proof: $\tau_1 = t_1^u$ and $e(\tau_1, t_2)^{k_M} = e(t_1, \tau_2)$.

We finally provide a Pedersen commitment C of the m_i's using a generator x of $\mathbb{Z}_p$ and a random s: $C = \prod_{i=1}^{\ell} a_i^{m_i} \cdot x^s = k_M \cdot x^s \mod p$.

The main point regarding our NIZK is that we need to prove that the secret k_M (as an exponent for the groups $\mathbb{G}_1$ and $\mathbb{G}_T$) involved in the tag, the commitment and the ciphertexts is the same secret k_M as the one (as an element of the group $\mathbb{Z}_p^*$ of order p) computed from the message. Regarding the tag and the ElGamal ciphertext equations, the key k_M is seen as an exponent, and we can thus use standard and efficient ZK proofs *à la* Schnorr [16], making them non-interactive using the Fiat-Shamir heuristic [9].

The correctness of the commitment is easily proven. It remains to make the link between the message and the key. Equation $e(\tau_1, t_2)^{k_M} = e(t_1, \tau_2)$ can be rewritten as: $e(\tau_1, t_2)^C = e(t_1, \tau_2)^{x^s}$. Proving that this last equation is true involves the use of a double discrete logarithm. We use the techniques from [17] described in Sect. 2, which alter the efficiency of our construction.

Description

In this section, we formally describe our verifiable message-locked encryption Λ.

- PPGen. Let λ be the security parameter, and ℓ, ρ be integers. The parameter generation consists in generating a bilinear environment $(p, \mathbb{G}_1, \mathbb{G}_2, \mathbb{G}_T, e)$ where p is a λ-bit prime, $\mathbb{G}_1$, $\mathbb{G}_2$ and $\mathbb{G}_T$ are three multiplicative groups of same order p and $e : \mathbb{G}_1 \times \mathbb{G}_2 \longrightarrow \mathbb{G}_T$ is a bilinear asymmetric pairing. Let $t_1, \{g_i\}_{i=1,\ldots,\ell}, h$ be generators of $\mathbb{G}_1$ and t_2 be a generator of $\mathbb{G}_2$. We finally need $\ell + 1$ public elements $x, a_1, \ldots, a_\ell$ that generates $\mathbb{Z}_p^*$.
  $\mathsf{pp} = \{p, \mathbb{G}_1, \mathbb{G}_2, \mathbb{G}_T, e, t_1, \{g_i\}_{i=1,\ldots,\ell}, h, t_2, x, \{a_i\}_{i=1,\ldots,\ell}\}$.
- KD. On input public parameters pp and a message $M = (m_1\|\ldots\|m_\ell)$ divided into ℓ blocks of ρ bits, it computes the key $k_M = \prod_{i=1}^{\ell} a_i^{m_i} \mod p$.
- Enc. On input public parameters pp, a message $M = (m_1\|\ldots\|m_\ell)$ and a key k_M, the ciphertext is computed as follows:
  1. uniformly pick $u \in \mathbb{Z}_p^*$, compute $\tau = (\tau_1, \tau_2) = (t_1^u, t_2^{u \cdot k_M})$;
  2. uniformly pick $s \in \mathbb{Z}_p^*$ and compute a Pedersen commitment over the m_i's: $C = k_M \cdot x^s = \prod_{i=1}^{\ell} a_i^{m_i} \cdot x^s \mod p$;
  3. for all $1 \leq i \leq \ell$, pick uniform and independent $r_i \in \mathbb{Z}_p^*$ and compute $T_{1,i} = g_i^{r_i}$ and $T_{2,i} = h^{m_i} \cdot g_i^{r_i \cdot k_M}$;
  4. compute the following non-interactive zero knowledge proof

$$\pi = \mathsf{NIZK}\Big(u, \{r_i\}_{i=1,\ldots,\ell}, M, k_M, s : \tau_1 = t_1^u \wedge e(\tau_1, t_2)^{k_M} = e(t_1, \tau_2)$$

$$\wedge\, T_{1,1} = g_1^r \wedge \cdots \wedge T_{1,\ell} = g_\ell^r \wedge T_{2,1} = T_{1,1}^{k_M} g^{m_1} \wedge \cdots \wedge T_{2,\ell} = T_{1,l}^{k_M} g^{m_\ell}$$

$$\wedge\, C = \prod_{i=1}^{\ell} a_i^{m_i} \cdot x^s \wedge e(\tau_1, t_2)^C = e(t_1, \tau_2)^{x^s}\Big).$$

Finally output $c = (\tau, \{T_{1,i}, T_{2,i}\}_{i=1,\ldots,\ell}, C, \pi)$.
- Valid. On input a ciphertext $c = (\tau, \{T_{1,i}, T_{2,i}\}_i, C, \pi)$, this algorithm outputs 1 iff π is correct.
- Dec. On input pp, a key k_M and a valid ciphertext c, the procedure is:
  1. for all $i \in \{1, \ldots, \ell\}$ compute $h^{m_i} = T_{2,i}/T_{1,i}^{k_M}$ as in a standard ElGamal decryption procedure;
  2. for all $i \in \{1, \ldots, \ell\}$, retrieve the m_i with a discrete logarithm computation (this step is made possible by the choice of a small ρ);
  3. output $M = (m_1\|\ldots\|m_\ell)$.

– EQ. On input pp and two valid ciphertexts $c = (\tau, \{T_{1,i}, T_{2,i}\}_i, C, \pi)$ and $\tilde{c} = (\tilde{\tau}, \{\tilde{T}_{1,i}, \tilde{T}_{2,i}\}, \tilde{C}, \tilde{\pi})$, parse τ as $\tau_1 = t_1^u$ and $\tau_2 = t_2^{u \cdot k}$ and $\tilde{\tau}$ as $\tilde{\tau}_1 = t_1^{\tilde{u}}$ and $\tilde{\tau}_2 = t_2^{\tilde{u} \cdot k}$. This algorithm outputs 1 iff $e(\tau_1, \tilde{\tau}_2) = e(\tilde{\tau}_1, \tau_2)$.

Correctness. Correctness is directly derived from the correctness of the ElGamal encryption scheme and properties of bilinear maps.

6 Security and Efficiency Arguments

6.1 Privacy

Theorem 4. *Let ε and μ be two non-zero positive reals, p a prime number and T, ℓ be integers such that $\mu > \log p + \log(T) + 2\log(1/\varepsilon)$. Our scheme Λ is PRV-piCDA secure for (T, μ)-block sources under the (T, ℓ)-bl-DDH assumption in the random oracle model.*

Sketch of Proof. As the inner product $\langle \cdot, \cdot \rangle : \left(\mathbb{Z}_p^\ell\right)^T \to \mathbb{Z}_p$ is a 2-universal hash function, we can apply Theorem 2: the keys extracted from the adversarially chosen (T, μ)-block source random variable $\mathbf{M} = (M_1, \ldots, M_T)$, will be indistinguishable from uniform. More precisely, if $\mu \geq \log(p) + \log(T) + 2\log(1/\varepsilon)$, the distribution of the keys is at distance ε from the uniform distribution in $\mathbb{Z}_p^\ell \times \mathbb{Z}_p^T$.

We construct a simulator $\mathcal{S}$ of the real-or-random encryption oracle against which q_H-query (T, μ)-block source polynomial-sampling complexity adversary $\mathcal{A}$ for the PRV-piCDA game has advantage exactly $\frac{1}{2}$, using a sequence of games.

Game G_0. This is the original game. We consider an adversary $\mathcal{A}$ able to break the PRV-piCDA security. In this game, $\mathcal{A}$ chooses a distribution $\mathbb{M}$ of the messages. She then queries the real-or-random oracle. Only after the query to this oracle, the public parameters of the scheme are generated.

The adversary $\mathcal{A}$ has access to a vector of T ciphertexts and she must return the value b' (real or random), matching how the plaintexts were generated by the real-or-random oracle. Let S_i be the event that $b = b'$ in game G_i. We have:

$$\mathsf{Adv}_{\Lambda, \mathcal{A}}^{\mathsf{PRV-piCDA}}(\lambda) = \left| \Pr\left[\mathbf{Exp}_{\Lambda, \mathcal{A}}^{\mathsf{real}} = 1\right] - \Pr\left[\mathbf{Exp}_{\Lambda, \mathcal{A}}^{\mathsf{rand}} = 1\right] \right| = 2\left|\Pr(S_0) - \frac{1}{2}\right|.$$

Game G_1. In this game, $\mathcal{S}$ simulates the T non-interactive zero-knowledge proofs, using the random oracle, rather than computing them. The advantage of $\mathcal{A}$ against the zero-knowledge property of the NIZK proof is bounded by $\mathsf{Adv}_{\Pi, \mathcal{A}}^{\mathsf{zk}}(\lambda)$. Moreover, this simulation is computationally indistinguishable for $\mathcal{A}$ if there is no collision in the requests of the hash oracle. Let q_H the number of queries $\mathcal{A}$ makes to the random hash oracle.

$$|\Pr(S_0) - \Pr(S_1)| \leq \frac{q_H}{2^{\rho \ell T} p^{T(2+\ell)}} + \mathsf{Adv}_{\Pi, \mathcal{A}}^{\mathsf{zk}}(\lambda).$$

Game G_2. We address the key generation. Instead of computing the keys with the KD procedure, S draws keys uniformly from $\mathbb{Z}_p$. From now on, the encryption key does not depend on the messages. From Theorem 2, $(k_{M_1}, \ldots, k_{M_T})$ is at distance ε from the uniform distribution in $\mathbb{Z}_p^T$, independently on how the messages were generated: $|\Pr(S_1) - \Pr(S_2)| \leq \varepsilon$.

Game G_3. With those simulated keys, the view of the adversary is exactly a (T, ℓ)-bl-DDH instance. Let $\mathcal{B}$ be an adversary against (T, ℓ)-bl-DDH, then for all $\mathcal{B}$, we have: $|\Pr(S_2) - \Pr(S_3)| \leq \mathsf{Adv}_{\mathcal{B}}^{(T,\ell)\text{-bl-DDH}}(\lambda)$.

Game G_4. In this game, S behaves as the real-or-random oracle, computing a Pedersen commitment over the m_i's. Thus we have $\Pr(S_3) = \Pr(S_4)$.

Moreover, $\mathcal{A}$'s advantage for breaking the indistinguishability of the Pedersen commitment is exactly $\frac{1}{2}$, as it is perfectly hiding. Then we have:

$$\left|\Pr(S_0) - \frac{1}{2}\right| \leq \mathsf{Adv}_{\Pi,\mathcal{A}}^{\mathsf{zk}}(\lambda) + \frac{q_H}{2^{\rho\ell T} p^{T(2+\ell)}} + \varepsilon + \mathsf{Adv}_{\mathcal{B}}^{(T,\ell)\text{-bl-DDH}}(\lambda),$$

and the probability for $\mathcal{A}$ to win the PRV-piCDA game is negligible. $\qquad\square$

6.2 Tag Consistency and Deduplication Consistency

Theorem 5. *Our scheme Λ is tag consistent as that the key derivation function is collision-free (the inner product is a 2-universal hash-function).*

The proof derives from the EQ procedure : the bilinearity property of the pairing implies that if two ciphertexts are considered duplicate, then the keys used to generate them must be equal. Which means that $\mathcal{A}$ is able to find collisions for the key-derivation function with non-negligible probability.

Theorem 6. *As a Pedersen commitment is computationally binding, our scheme Λ is deduplication-consistent in the random oracle model.*

As our construction is an instantiation of the generic construction given Sect. 4, the proof of this theorem directly follows from the proof of Theorem 3.

6.3 Efficiency

As [1,3], we improve upon security of convergent encryption, resulting in a loss in efficiency. We are however obviously more efficient than [1] as it uses generic NIZK (for a hash function represented as a circuit) and than [3] as it uses several times a fully homomorphic encryption. But a complete comparison is difficult as the three schemes achieve completely different security properties.

The most time and space consuming steps of our construction are the NIZK proof computation (especially the double logarithm), and the decryption which requires ℓ small discrete logarithm computation.

Acknowledgment. This work is supported by the European Union SUPERCLOUD Project (H2020 Research and Innovation Program grant 643964 and Swiss Secretariat for Education Research and Innovation contract 15.0091) and by ERC Starting Grant ERC-2013-StG-335086-LATTAC. The authors want to thank Benoit Libert, Olivier Sanders, Jacques Traoré and Damien Vergnaud for helpful discussions.

References

1. Abadi, M., Boneh, D., Mironov, I., Raghunathan, A., Segev, G.: Message-locked encryption for lock-dependent messages. In: Canetti, R., Garay, J.A. (eds.) CRYPTO 2013. LNCS, vol. 8042, pp. 374–391. Springer, Heidelberg (2013). doi:10. 1007/978-3-642-40041-4_21
2. Bellare, M., Boldyreva, A., O'Neill, A.: Deterministic and efficiently searchable encryption. In: Menezes, A. (ed.) CRYPTO 2007. LNCS, vol. 4622, pp. 535–552. Springer, Heidelberg (2007). doi:10.1007/978-3-540-74143-5_30
3. Bellare, M., Keelveedhi, S.: Interactive message-locked encryption and secure deduplication. In: Katz, J. (ed.) PKC 2015. LNCS, vol. 9020, pp. 516–538. Springer, Heidelberg (2015). doi:10.1007/978-3-662-46447-2_23
4. Bellare, M., Keelveedhi, S., Ristenpart, T.: Message-locked encryption and secure deduplication. In: Johansson, T., Nguyen, P.Q. (eds.) EUROCRYPT 2013. LNCS, vol. 7881, pp. 296–312. Springer, Heidelberg (2013). doi:10.1007/ 978-3-642-38348-9_18
5. Boneh, D., Sahai, A., Waters, B.: Fully collusion resistant traitor tracing with short ciphertexts and private keys. In: Vaudenay, S. (ed.) EUROCRYPT 2006. LNCS, vol. 4004, pp. 573–592. Springer, Heidelberg (2006). doi:10.1007/11761679_34
6. Chung, K.-M., Vadhan, S.: Tight bounds for hashing block sources. In: Goel, A., Jansen, K., Rolim, J.D.P., Rubinfeld, R. (eds.) APPROX/RANDOM - 2008. LNCS, vol. 5171, pp. 357–370. Springer, Heidelberg (2008). doi:10.1007/ 978-3-540-85363-3_29
7. Cox, L.P., Murray, C.D., Noble, B.D.: Pastiche: making backup cheap and easy. In: Proceedings of the 5th Symposium on Operating Systems Design and implementation, OSDI 2002, pp. 285–298. ACM (2002)
8. Douceur, J.R., Adya, A., Bolosky, W.J., Simon, D., Theimer, M.: Reclaiming space from duplicate files in a serverless distributed file system. In: ICDCS, pp. 617–624 (2002)
9. Fiat, A., Shamir, A.: How to prove yourself: practical solutions to identification and signature problems. In: Odlyzko, A.M. (ed.) CRYPTO 1986. LNCS, vol. 263, pp. 186–194. Springer, Heidelberg (1987). doi:10.1007/3-540-47721-7_12
10. The Flud backup system. http://flud.org
11. Groth, J.: Short non-interactive zero-knowledge proofs. In: Abe, M. (ed.) ASIACRYPT 2010. LNCS, vol. 6477, pp. 341–358. Springer, Heidelberg (2010). doi:10. 1007/978-3-642-17373-8_20
12. Impagliazzo, R., Levin, L.A., Luby, M.: Pseudo-random generation from one-way functions. In: Proceedings of the Twenty-first Annual ACM Symposium on Theory of Computing, STOC 1989, pp. 12–24. ACM (1989)
13. Pedersen, T.P.: Non-interactive and information-theoretic secure verifiable secret sharing. In: Feigenbaum, J. (ed.) CRYPTO 1991. LNCS, vol. 576, pp. 129–140. Springer, Heidelberg (1992). doi:10.1007/3-540-46766-1_9
14. Pointcheval, D., Stern, J.: Security arguments for digital signatures and blind signatures. J. Crypt. **13**(3), 361–396 (2000)

15. Raghunathan, A., Segev, G., Vadhan, S.: Deterministic public-key encryption for adaptively chosen plaintext distributions. In: Johansson, T., Nguyen, P.Q. (eds.) EUROCRYPT 2013. LNCS, vol. 7881, pp. 93–110. Springer, Heidelberg (2013). doi:10.1007/978-3-642-38348-9_6

16. Schnorr, C.P.: Efficient identification and signatures for smart cards. In: Brassard, G. (ed.) CRYPTO 1989. LNCS, vol. 435, pp. 239–252. Springer, Heidelberg (1990). doi:10.1007/0-387-34805-0_22

17. Stadler, M.: Publicly verifiable secret sharing. In: Maurer, U. (ed.) EUROCRYPT 1996. LNCS, vol. 1070, pp. 190–199. Springer, Heidelberg (1996). doi:10.1007/3-540-68339-9_17

18. Wilcox-O'Hearn, Z., Warner, B.: Tahoe: the least-authority filesystem. In: 4th ACM Workshop StorageSS 2008, pp. 21–26. ACM (2008)

Symmetric Cryptography and Authentication

Security of Online AE Schemes in RUP Setting

Jian Zhang[1,2] and Wenling Wu[1(⊠)]

[1] Institute of Software, Chinese Academy of Sciences, Beijing 100190, China
{zhangjian,wwl}@tca.iscas.ac.cn
[2] State Key Laboratory of Cryptology, Beijing 100190, China

Abstract. Authenticated encryption (AE) combines privacy with data integrity, and in the process of decryption, the plaintext is always kept until successful verification. But in applications with insufficient memory or with realtime requirement, release of unverified plaintext is unavoidable. Furthermore most of present online AE schemes claim to keep the unverified plaintext, leading to online encryption but offline decryption, which seems unreasonable for online applications. Thus, security of the releasing unverified plaintext (RUP) setting, especially for online AE scheme need to be taken seriously. The notion of plaintext awareness (PA) together with IND-CPA have been formalized to achieve privacy in RUP setting by Andreeva et al. in 2014. But notion of PA is too strong and conflicts to online property, namely no online AE scheme can be PA secure according to their results, leading PA to lose its practical significance. In this paper, we define a similar security notion OPA and combine OPA with OPRP-CPA (IND-CPA) to achieve privacy of online AE scheme in RUP setting, which solves the conflicts between PA and online property. And we analysis the relation between OPA and some other notions. Then we study OPA security of existing online AE schemes, and show OPA insecurity of Stream Structure and structures with the property of "*controll ciphertext to jump between two plaintexts*" (CCJP), which are adopted by most of schemes in the ongoing CAESAR competition. At last, combining the property CCJP with the simple tag-producing process, we look upon the INT-RUP insecurity of existing schemes from new different angle.

Keywords: Online authenticated encryption · Releasing unverified plaintext · Plaintext extractor · INT-RUP · CAESAR competition

1 Introduction

The design and analysis of authenticated encryption (AE) have recently attracted a great deal of scholarly attention in cryptography, mostly driven by the NIST-funded CAESAR competition for authenticated encryption [1]. The decryption process of conventional AE schemes consists of two phases: decryption and verification, and the temporary plaintext has to be kept up to successful verification. But in many practical applications, releasing unverified plaintext (RUP) before verification can not be unavoidable at times. For example, when

© Springer International Publishing AG 2016
S. Foresti and G. Persiano (Eds.): CANS 2016, LNCS 10052, pp. 319–334, 2016.
DOI: 10.1007/978-3-319-48965-0_19

AE scheme is implemented on resource-constrained devices like smart cards, sensors, RFIDs, it is almost impossible to store entire temporary plaintext because of the limited buffer. Another situation is the real-time requirement for online applications, which may not be met if plaintext is released after verification. Most of the present online AE schemes require to store the plaintext before verification, leading to online encryption but offline decryption which seems quite unreasonable. Even beyond these settings, if a scheme is secure in RUP setting, it can increase efficiency of certain applications. For instance, to prevent release of unverified plaintext on the devices with insecure memory [24], the two-pass Encrypt-then-MAC composition can be used: a first pass to verify the Tag, and second to decrypt the ciphertext. However, a single pass AE scheme which is secure against the release of unverified plaintext can increase the efficiency.

Related Work: In Asiacrypt 2014, Andreeva et al. [4] formalized the security of AE scheme in RUP setting. They defined the security notion of PA (PA1 and PA2), and proposed to use PA1 along with IND-CPA to achieve privacy of the scheme. An AE scheme is PA1 if there exists a plaintext extractor which can successfully fool the adversary by simulating the decryption oracle. It becomes infeasible to distinguish between answers from the real decryption oracle and from the plaintext extractor for the adversary, then the release of unverified plaintext becomes harmless. The feature of security notion PA1 is to describe the security of decryption separately from encryption in RUP setting. To achieve integrity of ciphertext, they used INT-CTXT in RUP setting, called INT-RUP. And they also showed INT-RUP insecurity of schemes like OCB [22] and COPA [5].

In FSE2014, Abed et al. [2] used the notion of OPRP-CCA which borrowed from online ciphers [6] to achieve the privacy of online AE schemes in RUP setting. An AE scheme is OPRP-CCA if the adversary can not distinguish between the world with real encryption oracle and decryption oracle and the world with random online permutation and its inverse permutation. This notion is just applicable to online schemes, and weaker than PA1, which accepts privacy up to repetition and privacy up to longest common prefix.

In 2015, Chakrakraborti et al. [11] considered the INT-RUP security of the blockcipher based AE schemes. They first gave an INT-RUP attack on iFeed, an AE scheme submitted to the CAESAR competition, and then generalized the attack to any feedback mode of AE schemes. Using samilar ways, they also provided generic INT-RUP attack on the "rate-1" blockcipher based AE schemes, and concluded that no "rate-1" affine domain AE scheme can be INT-RUP secure.

Problems of Security Notions in RUP Setting: In the security setting of PA1, E called plaintext extractor tries to fool the adversary with access just to encryption query histories, and the adversary is allowed to use the response of decryption oracle as the query to encryption oracle without any other restrictions, which is always prohibited in conventional AE security settings. Both two lead to a trivial distinguishing attack on most of the present AE schemes (Proposition 1 in [4]). For the encryption scheme $\Pi = (\mathcal{E}_K, \mathcal{D}_K)$, if $\mathcal{E}_K$ is bijective, then for arbitrary IV and ciphertext C, there exists $\mathcal{E}_K(IV, \mathcal{D}_K(IV, C)) = C$.

Knowing this, the adversary can easily distinguish between the real decryption oracle $\mathcal{D}_K$ and the plaintext extractor E just by one decryption query and one encryption query. Then it is concluded that AE schemes with bijective encryption can not be PA1 secure. At this point, we can find that PA1 is a quite strong security notion, and there are only several schemes can achieve PA1 security, such as SIV [23], BTM [18], HBS [19]. Those PA1 secure schemes are almost all two-pass and thus offline, which conflicts to one of the original goals to achieve online property in RUP setting. Thus we can find the strong notion PA1 that conflicts to online property lose most of its practical significance.

OPRP-CCA is a security notion for online schemes, and weaker than PA. It is defined based on the "online cipher" and "online permutation", where IV is default to be reused and leakage of common prefix is acceptable. But in some applications, the leakage of common prefix may bring about disasters, such as the the SPSS attack [16] proposed recently. Thus OPRP-CCA may be not enough to describe the privacy in RUP setting when IV is not allowed to be reused. Furthermore, we consider it more helpful for comprehensive understanding of the privacy to define the security of encryption and decryption separately.

Our Contribution: Finding appropriate balances between security and practical constraints is an impactful and active research endeavor where the goal is not necessarily to achieve some strong notion of security but to have the "best possible" security under given practical constraints [6]. Thus, in this paper, we define a more practical security notion called OPA for online schemes in RUP setting described in Fig. 1. A set H which is used to keep the query histories is appended to the right world. Each time when the plaintext extractor receive a decryption query, it first checks the set H to see if the query or the prefix with the same IV has ever been queried, and return a plaintext with known prefix to fool the adversary by mimicking the decryption algorithm. We use both OPRP-CPA (IND-CPA) and OPA to achieve privacy and also INT-RUP to achieve integrity. We also study the relations between OPA and some other related security notions, and then analyze the OPA security of some existing AE schemes. The results are concluded in Table 1, we find that some structures adopted by many AE schemes are not OPA secure, and some well designed schemes which are not PA1 secure can achieve OPA security, like POET [2], ELmD [12] and McOE-G [14]. At last, we explain the INT-RUP insecurity of some AE schemes from a new angle.

2 Preliminaries

Notations. The length of a string $x \in \{0,1\}^*$ is denoted by $|x|$, and for any two strings $x, y \in \{0,1\}^*$ we use $x||y$ and xy interchangeably to denote the concatenation of x and y. For integers $n, l, d \geq 1$, $D_n^d = (\{0,1\}^n)^d$ denotes the set of all strings whose length is d blocks of n bits, and $D_n^* = \bigcup_{d \geq 0} D_n^d$. Note that D_n^0 only contains the empty string ϵ. If $P \in D_n^d$, we can write $P = (p_1, p_2, \cdots, p_d)$ with $p_i \in D_n^1$, and we use $(P)_l$, $(l \leq d)$ to denote the truncation of the first l

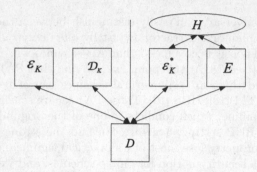

Fig. 1. The security model of OPA, where D is the adversary. The set H is used to keep the query histories with $H = \{(IV, P, C)\}$. Left: real world with encryption oracle $\mathcal{E}_K$ and decryption oracle $\mathcal{D}_K$. Right: simulated world with encryption oracle $\mathcal{E}_K^*$ and plaintext extractor E. E and $\mathcal{E}_K^*$ always give responses according to the set H.

blocks of P, namely $(P)_l = (p_0, \cdots, p_{l-1})$. For $P, R \in D_n^*$, say, $P \in D_n^p$ and $R \in D_n^r$, define the *length of the longest common prefix* of P and R as

$$\text{LLCP}_n(P, R) = \max\{i | p_1 = r_1, \cdots, p_i = r_i\}$$

Let H a non-empty set of strings in D_n^*, then define the *length of longest common prefix* of a string and a set $\text{LLCP}_n(H, P)$ as $\max_{R \in H} \text{LLCP}_n(R, P)$.

For a multiset $H = A \times B \times C$, where $A, B, C \subseteq \{0, 1\}^*$, we use $H|_A = \{a | \exists (b, c) : (a, b, c) \in H\}$ to denote *restriction on a set*. And for a fixed string $a_0 \in A$, we denote $H^{a_0} = \{(b, c) | (a_0, b, c) \in H\}$ to denote *fix on a set*.

We use \$ to denote the random strings, and $\$^{|P|}$ means the random string with the same number of blocks as message P.

Adversaries and Advantages. An adversary is a Turing machine to make a distinguish by interacting with oracles from two worlds, real world and simulated world. Let $\mathbb{D}$ be some class of computationally bounded adversaries, and for convenience, we use the notation

$$\underset{D}{Dis}(f; g) := \max_{D \in \mathbb{D}} |Pr[D^f = 1] - Pr[D^g = 1]|$$

to denote the upperbound of the distinguishing advantages over all adversaries to distinguish oracles f and g of two worlds, where D^O indicates the value output by D after interacting with oracle O. The probabilities are defined over the random coins used by the oracles and the random coins of the adversary. And $\underset{D}{Dis}(f_1, f_2; g_1, g_2)$ denotes to distinguish the world with oracles f_1, f_2 and the world with oracles g_1, g_2.

2.1 Authenticated Encryption (AE) Scheme

A conventional AE scheme is a tuple of two functions, encryption algorithm $\mathcal{E}$ and decryption algorithm $\mathcal{D}$, where $\mathcal{D}$ contains two process: decryption and verification. While under RUP environment, it becomes more reasonable to disconnect the decryption algorithm from the verification algorithm, because the decryption algorithm always releases the plaintext even if the verification process fails. Then the new AE scheme is a triplet $\Pi = (\mathcal{E}, \mathcal{D}, \mathcal{V})$ with algorithms of encryption $\mathcal{E}$, decryption $\mathcal{D}$, and verification $\mathcal{V}$. An AE scheme is also associated with some parameter sets, for instance, IV space $\mathcal{IV}$, associated data space $\mathcal{A}$, message space $\mathcal{M}$, key space $\mathcal{K}$, ciphertext space $\mathcal{C}$, and tag space $\mathcal{T}$. In this paper we omit the associated data for convenience, and we just consider the nonce IV and arbitrary IV schemes, where the IV value is not allowed to be reused in nonce IV scheme, and is arbitrary in the other case. Moreover, we consider the message space $\mathcal{M}$ is subspace of D_n^*, indicating the messages are all in blocks of n bits, which is a reasonable assumption because the fractional messages can be easily padded by proper means.

Then encryption algorithm $\mathcal{E}$ takes $IV \in \mathcal{IV}$, $K \in \mathcal{K}$, $M \in \mathcal{M}$ as inputs and outputs a tagged ciphertext $(C, T) \in \mathcal{C} \times \mathcal{T}$. Decryption algorithm $\mathcal{D}$ and verification algorithm $\mathcal{V}$ take $IV \in \mathcal{IV}$, $K \in \mathcal{K}$, $(C, T) \in \mathcal{C} \times \mathcal{T}$ as inputs and $\mathcal{D}$ outputs $M \in \mathcal{M}$ even if verification fails, $\mathcal{V}$ outputs $\perp$ (reject) or $\top$ (accept). More formally,

$$\mathcal{E}_K(IV, M) \to (C, T), \quad \mathcal{D}_K(IV, C, T) \to M, \quad \mathcal{V}_K(IV, C, T) \to \perp/\top$$

As in the conventional setting, the *correctness condition* of an AE scheme indicates that $\forall K \in \mathcal{K}, \forall IV \in \mathcal{IV}$ and $\forall M \in \mathcal{M}$, $\mathcal{D}_K(IV, \mathcal{E}_K(IV, M)) = M$ and $\mathcal{V}_K(IV, \mathcal{E}_K(IV, M)) = \top$.

2.2 Security Definitions Under RUP Environment

We borrow the security notion OPRP-CPA and OPRP-CCA from Bellare et al. [6] for online schemes. And we will describe some related security notions in new syntax. Let $\Pi = (\mathcal{E}, \mathcal{D})$ denote an encryption scheme, and P denote a random online permutation.

Definition 1 (IND-CPA Advantage). *Let D be a computationally bounded adversary with access to the encryption oracle. Then the IND-CPA advantage of D relative to Π is given by*

$$\mathrm{CPA}_\Pi(D) := \underset{D}{Dis}(\mathcal{E}_K; \$),$$

where $K \xleftarrow{R} \mathcal{K}$, the probability is defined over the key K, the random coins of D, and the random coins of E.

Definition 2 (OPRP-CPA Advantage). *Let D be a computationally bounded adversary with access to the encryption oracle and P be a random online permutation. Then the OPRP-CPA advantage of D associated to Π is given by*

$$OPRP\text{-}CPA_\Pi(D) := \underset{D}{Dis}(\mathcal{E}_k; P),$$

where $K \xleftarrow{R} \mathcal{K}$, the probability is defined over the key K and the random coins of D.

For an encryption scheme to be OPRP-CPA secure, the above advantage should be negligible for any adversary D. And it is well known that the OPRP-CPA secure scheme can always achieve the IND-CPA security when IV is not allowed to be reused. However, the same IV can be used many times in decryption queries, leading to that the IND-CCA security can never be achieved for online schemes. Then we will not consider the IND-CCA security in this paper.

Definition 3 (PA1 Advantage). *Let D be a computationally bounded adversary with access to the encryption oracle and decryption oracle in real world or simulated world. Let E be an algorithm with access to the history of encryption queries, called PA1 extractor. The PA1 advantage of D associate to Π and E is given by*

$$\mathrm{PA1}_{\Pi}^{E}(D) := \underset{D}{Dis}(\mathcal{E}_K, \mathcal{D}_K; \mathcal{E}_K, E),$$

Where $K \xleftarrow{R} \mathcal{K}$, the probability is defined over the key K, the random coins of D, and the random coins of E.

For an encryption scheme to achieve PA1 security, the above advantage should be negligible for any adversary D. From the discussion in Sect. 1.2, we know PA1 is a strong security notion. Andreeva et al. [4] also defines a stronger notion PA2 in which E even has no access to the encryption query histories.

Definition 4 (OPRP-CCA Advantage). *If Π is an online scheme, and P is a random online permutation. Let D be a computationally bounded adversary with access to the encryption oracle and decryption oracle in two worlds. The OPRP-CCA advantage of D associated to Π is given by*

$$OPRP\text{-}CCA_{\Pi} := \underset{D}{Dis}(\mathcal{E}_K, \mathcal{D}_K; P, P^{-1}),$$

Where $K \xleftarrow{R} \mathcal{K}$, the probability is defined over the key K and the random coins of D.

For an encryption scheme to be OPRP-CCA secure, the above advantage should be neligible for any adversary D. The notion OPRP-CCA is weaker than PA1, with privacy up to longest common prefix. It describes the security of encryption and decryption process at the same time and IV is default to be reused in encryption process.

Conventional integrity requirement of AE scheme can be achieve by INT-CTXT, where the adversary can make encryption queries and decryption queries, but the decryption oracle always returns $\bot$. While under RUP environment, the ability to observe the unverified plaintexts is given to the adversary, and the integrity requirement should be modified.

Definition 5 (Integrity under RUP Environment (INT-RUP)). *Let D be a computationally bounded adversary with access to oracles $\mathcal{E}_K$, $\mathcal{D}_K$, and $\mathcal{V}_K$. Then the INT-RUP advantage of D associate to Π is given by*

$$INT\text{-}RUP_{\Pi} := Pr[D^{\mathcal{E}_K, \mathcal{D}_K, \mathcal{V}_K} \neq \bot]$$

Where $K \xleftarrow{R} \mathcal{K}$, *the probability is defined over the key* K *and the random coins of* D.

3 New Security Notion and Relations

In this section, we will first give the definition of E and $\mathcal{E}_K^*$ in detail, and then study the relations between OPA and some other security notions.

The setting of OPA still adopts the framework of plaintext extractor similar to PA1 with the feature of achieving security of decryption process separately from encryption process. As described in Fig. 1, the adversary D tries to distinguish the real world from simulated world, while E tries to mimic the decryption oracle $\mathcal{D}_K$ to fool the adversary. Some significant differences are introduced in the setting of OPA for online AE schemes. A set $H = (IV, P_i, C_i)$ is appended to the simulated world to keep the query histories. Each time when E receives a query (IV_0, C), it tries to mimic the decryption oracle by returning a plaintext P. Let $H^{IV_0} = \{(P_i, C_i)|(IV_0, P_i, C_i) \in H\}$, if IV_0 together with prefix of C have been found in H and $LLCP_n(H^{IV_0}|_C, C) = l$, P must satisfy

$$LLCP_n(P_j, P) = l$$

where $(P_j, C_j) \in H^{IV_0}$ and $LLCP_n(C_j, C)$ equals l.

When the encryption oracle $\mathcal{E}_K^*$ in the simulated world receives a query (IV_0, P), it behaves as follows,

1. Computes $C' = \mathcal{E}_K(IV_0, P)$
2. Checks if IV_0 together with prefix of P exist in H or not
3. If not, $C = C'$
4. Otherwise, if $LLCP_n(H^{IV_0}|_P, P) = l$, find $(P_j, C_j) \in H^{IV_0}$, s.t. $LLCP_n(P_j, P) == l$. Replace prefix of C' with $(C_j)_l$ to get C.
5. $H = H \cup (IV_0, P, C)$ and returns C.

Here we should pay more attentions to the difference of $\mathcal{E}_K^*$ and $\mathcal{E}_K$ when the adversary uses the (prefix of) output of decryption oracle to make encryption queries. One example is that the adversary ask a query $\mathcal{E}(IV, \mathcal{D}(IV, C))$, the response is always C no matter the encryption and decryption oracle is from real world or from simulated world, then the attack in Sect. 1.2 can not work under notion of OPA.

Let $\Pi = (\mathcal{E}, \mathcal{D})$ denote an encryption scheme, the advantage of OPA security is defined as follows,

Definition 6 (OPA Advantage). *Let* D *be a computationally bounded adversary with access to the encryption oracle and decryption oracle in two worlds, the plaintext extractor* E *is an algorithm with access to the history of queries made by* D. *The encryption algorithm* $\mathcal{E}_K^*$ *and* E *are defined as above. Then the OPA advantage of* D *associated to* Π *and* E *is given by*

$$\mathrm{OPA}_{\Pi}^E(D) := \underset{D}{Dis}(\mathcal{E}_K, \mathcal{D}_K; \mathcal{E}_K^*, E),$$

Where $K \xleftarrow{R} \mathcal{K}$, and the probability is defined over the key K, the random coins of D, and the random coins of E.

The encryption oracle in the simulated world is denoted by $\mathcal{E}_K^*$ because its output may be different from $\mathcal{E}_K$ when the query or the prefix has been found in the set H. The adversary D tries to distinguish the two worlds while E tries to simulate the decryption oracle $\mathcal{D}_K$ to fool the adversary.

The security notion of OPA is defined dedicatedly for online AE schemes. Thus there is no explicit relation between PA1 and OPA, but we have the following theorem.

Theorem 1 (OPRP-CPA +OPA $\Leftrightarrow$ OPRP-CCA). *Let Π be an encryption scheme. Then Π is OPRP-CCA secure if and only if it is OPA secure and OPRP-CPA secure.*

Proof. Let D be a computationally bounded adversary, and P be the random online permutation. Firstly, we show

$$\text{OPRP-CPA} + \text{OPA} \Rightarrow \text{OPRP-CCA},$$

By the triangle inequality,

$$\text{OPRP-CCA}_\Pi = \underset{D}{Dis}(\mathcal{E}_K, \mathcal{D}_K; P, P^{-1})$$

$$\leq \underset{D}{Dis}(\mathcal{E}_K, \mathcal{D}_K; \mathcal{E}_K^*, P^{-1}) + \underset{D}{Dis}(\mathcal{E}_K^*, P^{-1}; P, P^{-1})$$

From the definition of OPA extractor E, we can easily construct E associated to Π using the random online permutation P^{-1}. When E receives queries, it forwards them to P^{-1}, and uses the outputs of P^{-1} as the responses. Hence,

$$\underset{D}{Dis}(\mathcal{E}_K, \mathcal{D}_K; \mathcal{E}_K^*, P^{-1}) = \underset{D}{Dis}(\mathcal{E}_K, \mathcal{D}_K; \mathcal{E}_K^*, E),$$

The first term is just the $\text{OPA}_\Pi^E(D)$.

Furthermore, the random online permutation P or P^{-1} is independent of $\mathcal{E}_K$, then there exists a adversary D_1, such that

$$\underset{D}{Dis}(\mathcal{E}_K^*, P^{-1}; P, P^{-1}) \leq \underset{D_1}{Dis}(\mathcal{E}_K, P),$$

where D_1 can be viewed as an OPRP-CPA adversary, and

$$\underset{D_1}{Dis}(\mathcal{E}_K, P) = \text{OPRP-CPA}_\Pi(D_1).$$

We define D_1 as follows. It runs D, and directly forwards D's encryption oracle queries to its own oracles. The adversary D_1 responds to D's decryption query (IV_0, C_0) just like P^{-1}. Namely, if IV_0 together with prefix of C_0 have been found in query histories, it responds using the plaintext with corresponding prefix, otherwise, it responds using random strings. Therefore, the game to distinguish the world with oracles $\mathcal{E}_K^*, P^{-1}$ and the world with P, P^{-1} can be perfectly simulated by D_1.

Then, we get

$$\text{OPRP-CCA}_\Pi(D) \leq \text{OPA}_\Pi^E(D) + \text{OPRP-CPA}_\Pi(D_1).$$

In the opposite direction, it is easy to know that OPRP-CCA security implies OPRP-CPA security. To show the equivalence, we just need to prove

$$\text{OPRP-CCA} \Rightarrow \text{OPA},$$

Let D be a computationally bounded adversary, and E the OPA extractor associated to Π. We construct E using inverse of an online permutation, denoted by P^{-1}. Then, by triangle inequality,

$$\begin{aligned}
\text{OPA}_\Pi^E &= \underset{D}{Dis}(\mathcal{E}_K, \mathcal{D}_K; \mathcal{E}_K^*, P^{-1}) \\
&\leq \underset{D}{Dis}(\mathcal{E}_K, \mathcal{D}_K; P, P^{-1}) + \underset{D}{Dis}(P, P^{-1}; \mathcal{E}_K^*, P^{-1})
\end{aligned}$$

The first term is just $\text{OPRP-CCA}_\Pi(D)$. Because $\mathcal{E}_K$ is independent of P and P^{-1}, we define the adversary D' and have

$$\underset{D}{Dis}(P, P^{-1}; \mathcal{E}_K^*, P^{-1}) \leq \text{OPRP-CPA}_\Pi(D'),$$

where D' is the OPRP-CPA adversary. Therefore,

$$\text{OPA}_\Pi^E(D) \leq \text{OPRP-CCA}_\Pi(D) + \text{OPRP-CPA}_\Pi(D').$$

Then, we get the equivalence between OPRP-CCA and OPRP-CPA+OPA and we can easily deduce separations between OPRP-CPA and OPA. Considering the SPSS attack, and that OPRP-CPA scheme can achieve IND-CPA security if IV is not allowed to be reused, we use IND-CPA+OPA to achieve the privacy of the encryption scheme in RUP setting if the IV is not allowed to be reused, otherwise we use OPRP-CPA together with OPA to achieve the privacy.

4   Security Analysis of Existing Schemes

We have already known most of the existing AE schemes, including OCB [22], SpongeWrap [8], CCM [25], GCM [20], COPA [5], and so on, can not achieve PA1 security, because the encryption process is a bijective function [11]. In this section, we will study the security of existing AE schemes under the weaker security notion OPA. Note that the proof of all the propositions and claims can be found in the full version of the paper [27].

Among the existing AE schemes, some may have similar structures. One example is that many schemes first produce keystreams by iteration of the encryption function, and then the ciphertext is generated by XOR of the plaintext and the keystream, which is similar to the process of stream cipher. We call this structure *Stream Structure*.

Definition 7 (Stream Structure). *Let* $\Pi = (\mathcal{E}_K, \mathcal{D}_K)$ *be an encryption scheme. If the ciphertext is produced by xor of the plaintext and the keystream, where the keystream is generated by iterations of the encryption function, we call Π is in Stream Structure.*

The great advantage of this structure is its inverse-free property in the decryption process. It means the decryption algorithm will not invoke the inverse of the primitives which can save the hardware cost and improve efficiency. A great deal of schemes adopt the Stream Structure, such as GCM, SpongeWrap, and all the dedicated AE schemes, here "dedicated" just mean the scheme is not block cipher based, like ALE [10], AEGIS [26], ASCON [13] and so on. It is well known that the reuse of IV for the schemes with Stream Structure is insecure because of leaking xor difference of the first block pair that differs between the two messages. And similarly, we can deduce the schemes in Stream Structure can not achieve OPA security and OPRP-CPA security at the same time.

Proposition 1. *If a scheme $\Pi = (\mathcal{E}_K, \mathcal{D}_K)$ is in Stream Structure, then there exists an adversary D such that for all extractor E, there exists an adversary D_1 and*

$$1 - OPRP\text{-}CPA_\Pi(D_1) \le OPA_\Pi^E(D),$$

where D makes one encryption query and one decryption query, and D_1 is as efficient as D plus one query to E.

We have observed some other structures used frequently also can not be both OPA and OPRP-CPA secure. Before describing them, we first define an interesting property as follows.

Definition 8 (CCJP). *Let Π be an encryption scheme, N be an arbitrary IV value, and $C_0 = (C_0^0, C_1^0, \cdots, C_{l-1}^0)$, $C_1 = (C_0^1, C_1^1, \cdots, C_{l-1}^1)$ be two ciphertexts under N. The corresponding plaintext are $M_0 = (M_0^0, M_1^0, \cdots, M_{l-1}^0)$, $M_1 = (M_0^1, M_1^1, \cdots, M_{l-1}^1)$. If $\forall \delta = (\delta_0, \delta_1, \cdots, \delta_{l-1}), \delta_i \in \{0,1\}$, we can find a ciphertext $C^\delta = f(C_0, C_1) = (C_0', C_1', \cdots, C_{l-1}')$ to make corresponding plaintext $M^\delta = (M_0^{\delta_0}, \cdots, M_{n-1}^{\delta_{n-1}})$, where f is a function. Then we call this property **controll ciphertext to jump between two plaintexts (CCJP)**.*

If an encryption scheme Π has CCJP property, we can easily see that it can not achieve OPA security and OPRP-CPA security at the same time.

Proposition 2. *If an encryption scheme $\Pi = (\mathcal{E}_K, \mathcal{D}_K)$ has CCJP property, then there exists an adversary D such that for all extractors E, there exists an adversary D_1 and*

$$1 - OPRP\text{-}CPA_\Pi(D_1) \le OPA_\Pi^E(D),$$

where D makes one encryption query and two decryption queries, and D_1 is as efficient as D plus one query to E.

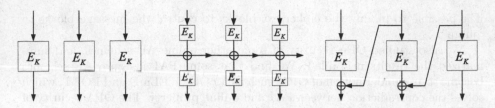

Fig. 2. Structures which are OPA insecure. Left: ECB structrue. Middle: Simplified EME structure. Right: PFB structure.

The parallelism is a attractive property of an AE scheme, always accompanied with incremental property, both contribute to the excellent performance of the scheme. Full parallelism require that each message block is processed independently, then all the message blocks can be handled at the same time. To achieve full parallelism, many schemes adopt ECB structure (Fig. 2 left) such as OCB. Some other schemes adopt a similar EME (Encrypt-Mix-Encrypt) structure [15] with partial parallelism but stronger security. But the linear layer of EME can be simplified like COPA to achieve full parallelism in decryption process (Fig. 2 middle). We can find these two structures both have the CCJP property and can not achieve OPA security according to Proposition 2. The scheme ELmD [12] adopts the similar structure but with a linear transform ρ, which makes the scheme not really achieve full parallelism, and ELmD has no CCJP property. Then, we conclude,

Claim. The OPRP-CPA secure schemes in ECB structure and in simplified EME structure with full parallelism can not achieve OPA security.

It seems like that the full parallelism conflicts to the OPA security because of CCJP property, which makes us consider some other schemes that claimed to achieve full parallelism, and also find the OPA insecurity. The scheme iFeed and CPFB are both the CAESAR candidates, and are claimed to achieve full parallelism. In2015, Chakrabori et al. [11] give a INT-RUP attack on these two schemes, and we find the property they exploited to attack is just the CCJP property. The two schemes both adopt the structure based on PFB (plaintext feedback) mod (Fig. 2 right) with some modifications. The feedback plaintexts have been truncated in CPFB and masked by secret message in iFeed. Then, we have

Claim. The OPRP-CPA secure schemes in PFB structure can not achieve OPA security.

In this section, we mainly proved OPA insecurity of AE schemes in some conventional structures. And we described an interesting flaw property CCJP for an AE scheme. But it may not be an easy work to find out whether the scheme has the CCJP property, and there is no uniform ways. However, we require the value of δ in the definition of CCJP property to be arbitrary, then we just propose to study the two consecutive block cipher calls, and consider if it possible to modify the ciphertext blocks to control the message blocks to "jump".

We also studied OPA security of some other online AE schemes, and summarized the results in Table 1. We find that some PA1 insecure AE schemes become secure under notion of OPA, such as McOE-G, ELmD and POET, which solves the contradiction between PA1 and online property. The OPA security of POET can be deduced from the OPRP-CCA security given by the designers. And we studied the OPA security of McOE-G and ELmD, and gave the proof for ELmD in Appendix A. We also find that nearly no nonce IV scheme can achieve OPA security. The reason may be the IV are allowed to be reused in decryption process, namely the adversary can use the same IV to query decryption oracle many times, or use the same IV as the one in some encryption query, both two may lead to attacks on nonce IV schemes. Then there comes a puzzle if the arbitrary IV scheme must be OPA secure intuitively. The answer is of course "no" which can be testified by insecurity of COPA.

Table 1. Summary of OPA security of existing online AE schemes.

IV Reuse	Schemes	OPA	PA1	Remark
×	OCB [22], CBA [17]	×	×	ECB, CCJP
✓	COPA [5]	×	×	EME, CCJP
×	GCM [20], PAEQ [9]	×	×	CTR, Stream Structure
×	Spongewrap	×	×	Stream Structure
×	Dedicated AE	×	×	Stream Structure
×	CPFB [21], iFeed [28]	×	×	PFB, CCJP
✓	POET [2]	✓	×	OPRP-CCA [2]
✓	McOE-G [14], ELmD [12]	✓	×	[27]
✓	APE [3]	✓	✓	backward decryption

5 Security of Verification

INT-RUP clearly implies INT-CTXT, and the opposite is not necessarily true, which is proven in [4]. Chakrabori et al. [11] have studied the INT-RUP security of blockcipher based AE schemes. They gave an INT-RUP attack on iFeed and CPFB and then generalized the attack and drew a significant conclusion that *no "rate-1" block-cipher based affine AE construction can be INT-RUP secure*. Their results concern the no. of block-cipher calls required to have a secure AE scheme, and their methods to prove may be not so easy to understand. Here, in this paper, we look upon the INT-RUP insecurity of the schemes uniformly from new different angle. Namely, the reason resulting in INT-RUP insecurity of all schemes found by [4,11] may be the same from our angle.

If the encryption process of the AE scheme has CCJP property, and the tag-producing process is simple, then we can find an INT-RUP attack. Here "simple" means input of the function to generate the tag is mainly subject to linear combinations of all message blocks, and the checksum is the most common "simple" ways to produce the tag.

Proposition 3. *For an AE scheme, encryption process with CCJP property, together with the "simple" tag-producing process, will lead to an INT-RUP attack.*

The proof of this proposition is trivial. We just take an INT-RUP attack on COPA as an example to testify the proposition, although Andreeva et al. [4] have ever claimed the INT-RUP insecurity of COPA.

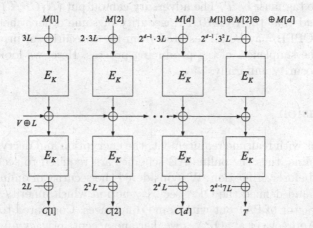

Fig. 3. Structure of COPA. V is generated from associated data and $L = E_K(0)$.

The AE scheme COPA (Fig. 3) adopts the simplified EME structure which we have proved the CCJP property and the input to generate the tag is the XOR of the message blocks. Then we will exploit the property to give an INT-RUP attack.

Firstly, the adversary queries $\mathcal{E}_K(N, M) = (N, C, T)$), where $M = ((M_0, M_1), \cdots, (M_{2l-2}, M_{2l-1}))$ consists $2l$ blocks of n bits, and $2l \geq n$. Let $C = ((C_0, C_1), \cdots, (C_{2l-2}, C_{2l-1}))$, and $Z = M_1 \oplus M_2 \oplus \cdots \oplus M_{2l-1}$.

Now, the adversary chooses $C^0 = ((C_0^0, C_1), \cdots, (C_{2l-2}^0, C_{2l-1}))$, and $C^1 = ((C_0^1, C_1), \cdots, (C_{2l-2}^1, C_{2l-1}))$, and makes queries (N, C^0, T^0) and (N, C^1, T^1) to the decryption oracle $\mathcal{D}_K$ with arbitrary T_0, T_1, and gets the corresponding unverified plaintexts $M^0 = ((M_0^0, M_1^0), \cdots, (M_{2l-2}^0, M_{2l-1}^0))$ and $M^1 = ((M_0^1, M_1^1), \cdots, (M_{2l-2}^1, M_{2l-1}^1))$. Fixing the second element in each ciphertext pair can ensure the state after process message pairs is equal, then to make a success forgery, the adversary only need to find a $\delta = (\delta_0, \cdots, \delta_{l-1})$ where $\delta_i \in \{0, 1\}$ such that

$$Z = \oplus_{i=0}^{l-1}(((M_i^0 \oplus M_{i+1}^0) \cdot \delta_i) \oplus ((M_i^1 \oplus M_{i+1}^1) \cdot (\delta_i \oplus 1))),$$

where $\delta_i = 1$ corresponds to selecting the pair (M_i^0, M_{i+1}^0), and $\delta_i = 1$ to selecting pair (M_i^1, M_{i+1}^1) as the ith message block pair of forged message. Because of linearity, this expression can be converted into n equations, one for every bit j,

$$Z[j] = \oplus_{i=0}^{l-1}(((M_i^0[j] \oplus M_{i+1}^0[j]) \cdot \delta_i) \oplus ((M_i^1[j] \oplus M_{i+1}^1[j]) \cdot (\delta_i \oplus 1))),$$

where $j = 0, 1, \cdots, n - 1$.

This is a linear equations system with n equations and l unknowns. Bellare et al. [7] have ever studied this system, and get the conclusion the probability that the system has a solution is at least $1 - 2^{n-l}$. Then, by Gaussian elimination, the adversary can find the solution δ. Thus because of the CCJP property, for δ, the adversary can construct the ciphertext $C^f = ((C_0^{\delta_0}, C_1), \cdots, (C_{2l-2}^{\delta_{l-1}}, C_{2l-1}))$, and knows the tag must be T. The adversary can output (N, C^f, T) as a forgery.

We can find that the INT-RUP insecurity of some other schemes, such as OCB, iFeed, CPFB may be all resulted from the insecurity of privacy in RUP setting and the simpleness of tag-producing process. Here, we look upon these INT-RUP insecurity uniformly.

6   Conclusion

In applications with realtime requirement, the encryption and decryption always need to be online, thus the online AE schemes are required to securely output the plaintext before verification. We considered the security of online schemes in RUP setting, and defined the OPA security notion which inherits the frame of plaintext extractor of PA1 but with some differences. Compared to PA1 notion proposed by Andreeva et al., OPA is weaker and accepts privacy up to repetition and privacy up to longest common prefix, which solves the conflicts between PA1 and online property. We showed relations between different notions and gave some OPA security analysis of existing schemes. Under OPA notion, some well-designed schemes which can not achieve PA1 security become secure in RUP setting, such as McOE-G, ELmD and POET.

We have noticed that the leakage of the longest common prefix have been used to give an CPSS attack by Rogaway et al. [16]. But in decryption process, the CPSS attack may make no sense. And the reuse of IV in decryption process is unavoidable even for nonce IV schemes, which results in OPA insecurity of most existing online schemes. A solution to solve this problem is to use random IV schemes or transform the existing schemes to random IV schemes by ways proposed in [4], but with some extra cost. The differences between decryption and encryption is our main consideration to use OPRP-CPA (IND-CPA) together with OPA to achieve the privacy of online AE schemes in RUP setting.

Acknowledgments. We would like to thank anonymous referees for their helpful comments and suggestions. The research presented in this paper is supported by the National Basic Research Program of China (No. 2013CB338002) and National Natural Science Foundation of China (No. 61272476, 61672509 and 61232009).

References

1. Cryptographic competitions: Caesar. http://competitions.cr.yp.to/caesar-call. html
2. Abed, F., Fluhrer, S., Forler, C., List, E., Lucks, S., McGrew, D., Wenzel, J.: Pipelineable on-line encryption. In: Cid, C., Rechberger, C. (eds.) FSE 2014. LNCS, vol. 8540, pp. 205–223. Springer, Heidelberg (2015). doi:10.1007/978-3-662-46706-0_11
3. Andreeva, E., Bilgin, B., Bogdanov, A., Luykx, A., Mennink, B., Mouha, N., Yasuda, K.: APE: authenticated permutation-based encryption for lightweight cryptography. In: Cid, C., Rechberger, C. (eds.) FSE 2014. LNCS, vol. 8540, pp. 168–186. Springer, Heidelberg (2015). doi:10.1007/978-3-662-46706-0_9
4. Andreeva, E., Bogdanov, A., Luykx, A., Mennink, B., Mouha, N., Yasuda, K.: How to securely release unverified plaintext in authenticated encryption. In: Sarkar, P., Iwata, T. (eds.) ASIACRYPT 2014. LNCS, vol. 8873, pp. 105–125. Springer, Heidelberg (2014). doi:10.1007/978-3-662-45611-8_6
5. Andreeva, E., Bogdanov, A., Luykx, A., Mennink, B., Tischhauser, E., Yasuda, K.: Parallelizable and authenticated online ciphers. In: Sako, K., Sarkar, P. (eds.) ASIACRYPT 2013, Part I. LNCS, vol. 8269, pp. 424–443. Springer, Heidelberg (2013)
6. Bellare, M., Boldyreva, A., Knudsen, L.R., Namprempre, C.: Online ciphers and the hash-CBC construction. In: Kilian, J. (ed.) CRYPTO 2001. LNCS, vol. 2139, pp. 292–309. Springer, Heidelberg (2001)
7. Bellare, M., Micciancio, D.: A new paradigm for collision-free hashing: incrementality at reduced cost. In: Fumy, W. (ed.) EUROCRYPT 1997. LNCS, vol. 1233, pp. 163–192. Springer, Heidelberg (1997)
8. Bertoni, G., Daemen, J., Peeters, M., Van Assche, G.: Duplexing the sponge: single-pass authenticated encryption and other applications. In: Miri, A., Vaudenay, S. (eds.) SAC 2011. LNCS, vol. 7118, pp. 320–337. Springer, Heidelberg (2012)
9. Biryukov, A., Khovratovich, D.: Paeq (2014). http://competitions.cr.yp.to/caesar-submissions.html
10. Bogdanov, A., Mendel, F., Regazzoni, F., Rijmen, V., Tischhauser, E.: ALE: AES-based lightweight authenticated encryption. In: Moriai, S. (ed.) FSE 2013. LNCS, vol. 8424, pp. 447–466. Springer, Heidelberg (2014). doi:10.1007/978-3-662-43933-3_23
11. Chakraborti, A., Datta, N., Nandi, M.: Int-rup analysis of block-cipher based authenticated encryption schemes (2015). https://groups.google.com/forum/forum/crypto-competitions
12. Datta, N., Nandi, M.: Elmd (2014). http://competitions.cr.yp.to/caesar-submissions.html
13. Dobraunig, C., Eichlseder, M., Mendel, F., Schlaffer, M.: Ascon (2014). http://competitions.cr.yp.to/caesar-submissions.html
14. Fleischmann, E., Forler, C., Lucks, S.: McOE: a family of almost foolproof on-line authenticated encryption schemes. In: Canteaut, A. (ed.) FSE 2012. LNCS, vol. 7549, pp. 196–215. Springer, Heidelberg (2012)
15. Halevi, S., Rogaway, P.: A parallelizable enciphering mode. In: Okamoto, T. (ed.) CT-RSA 2004. LNCS, vol. 2964, pp. 292–304. Springer, Heidelberg (2004)
16. Hoang, V.T., Reyhanitabar, R., Rogaway, P., Vizár, D.: Online authenticated-encryption and its nonce-reuse misuse-resistance. In: Gennaro, R., Robshaw, M. (eds.) CRYPTO 2015. LNCS, vol. 9215, pp. 493–517. Springer, Heidelberg (2015). doi:10.1007/978-3-662-47989-6_24

17. Hosseini, H., Khazaei, S.: Cba (2014). http://competitions.cr.yp.to/caesar-sub missions.html
18. Iwata, T., Yasuda, K.: BTM: a single-key, inverse-cipher-free mode for deterministic authenticated encryption. In: Jacobson, M.J., Rijmen, V., Safavi-Naini, R. (eds.) SAC 2009. LNCS, vol. 5867, pp. 313–330. Springer, Heidelberg (2009). doi:10.1007/978-3-642-05445-7_20
19. Iwata, T., Yasuda, K.: HBS: a single-key mode of operation for deterministic authenticated encryption. In: Dunkelman, O. (ed.) FSE 2009. LNCS, vol. 5665, pp. 394–415. Springer, Heidelberg (2009)
20. McGrew, D., Viega, J.: The galois/counter mode of operation (gcm) (2004). http://csrc.nist.gov/CryptoToolkit/modes/proposedmodes/gcm/gcm-spec.pdf
21. Montes, M., Penazzi, D.: Cpfb (2014). http://competitions.cr.yp.to/caesar-submissions.html
22. Rogaway, P., Bellare, M., Black, J.: OCB: a block-cipher mode of operation for efficient authenticated encryption. ACM Trans. Inf. Syst. Secur. (TISSEC) 6(3), 365–403 (2003)
23. Rogaway, P., Shrimpton, T.: A provable-security treatment of the key-wrap problem. In: Vaudenay, S. (ed.) EUROCRYPT 2006. LNCS, vol. 4004, pp. 373–390. Springer, Heidelberg (2006). doi:10.1007/11761679_23
24. Tsang, P.P., Smith, S.W.: Secure cryptographic precomputation with insecure memory. In: Chen, L., Mu, Y., Susilo, W. (eds.) ISPEC 2008. LNCS, vol. 4991, pp. 146–160. Springer, Heidelberg (2008). doi:10.1007/978-3-540-79104-1_11
25. Whiting, D., Ferguson, N., Housley, R.: Counter with cbc-mac (ccm). Submission to NIST Modes of Operation Process (2012)
26. Wu, H., Preneel, B.: AEGIS: a fast authenticated encryption algorithm. In: Lange, T., Lauter, K., Lisoněk, P. (eds.) SAC 2013. LNCS, vol. 8282, pp. 185–201. Springer, Heidelberg (2014). doi:10.1007/978-3-662-43414-7_10
27. Zhang, J., Wu, W.: Security of online AE schemes in RUP setting (full version) (2016). http://www.escience.cn/people/zjcrypto/index.html
28. Zhang, L., Wu, W., Sui, H., Wang, P.: ifeed (2014). http://competitions.cr.yp.to/caesar-submissions.html

An Efficient Entity Authentication Protocol with Enhanced Security and Privacy Properties

Aysajan Abidin[(✉)], Enrique Argones Rúa, and Bart Preneel

ESAT/COSIC, KU Leuven and iMinds, Leuven, Belgium
{Aysajan.Abidin,Enrique.ArgonesRua,Bart.Preneel}@esat.kuleuven.be

Abstract. User authentication based on biometrics is getting an increasing attention. However, privacy concerns for biometric data have impeded the adoption of cloud-based services for biometric authentication. This paper proposes an efficient distributed two-factor authentication protocol that is privacy-preserving even in the presence of colluding internal adversaries. One of the authentication factors in our protocol is biometrics, and the other factor can be either knowledge-based or possession-based. The actors involved in our protocol are users, user/client devices with biometric sensors, service provider, and cloud for storing protected biometric templates. Contrary to the existing biometric authentication protocols that offer security only in the *honest-but-curious* adversarial model, our protocol provides enhanced security and privacy properties in the *active* (or *malicious*) adversarial model. Specifically, our protocol offers identity privacy, unlinkability, and user data (i.e., the biometric template data and the second factor) privacy against compromised cloud storage service, and preserves the privacy of the user data even if the cloud storage service colludes with the service provider. Moreover, our protocol only employs lightweight schemes and thus is efficient. The distributed model combined with the security and privacy properties of our protocol paves the way towards a new cloud-based business model for privacy-preserving authentication.

Keywords: Biometrics · Security · Privacy · Privacy-preserving authentication

1 Introduction

As biometric authentication is becoming more popular and ubiquitous, protecting and ensuring the privacy of biometric templates is of utmost importance. Biometrics poses a serious threat to user privacy. Not only does it reveal sensitive information about users such as medical condition, race and ethnicity, but it can also be used for mass surveillance. A number of privacy-preserving authentication protocols involving biometrics have been proposed over the last decade. Most of them, however, are designed to be secure in the *honest-but-curious* (HBC) adversarial model. In this work, we go beyond the HBC model and propose an efficient privacy-preserving biometric authentication protocol

© Springer International Publishing AG 2016
S. Foresti and G. Persiano (Eds.): CANS 2016, LNCS 10052, pp. 335–349, 2016.
DOI: 10.1007/978-3-319-48965-0_20

with enhanced security and privacy properties in the *malicious* adversary model. Our protocol also utilises an additional short secret, e.g., a password, as a second factor. Privacy of users is protected from two different threats: disclosure of privacy-sensitive data (i.e., biometric templates and other secrets) and disclosure of behavioural information (i.e., user's identity when using an online service) to *malicious* internal adversaries. We employ a distributed model for the protocol participants and categorise them as the user, the client device (i.e., sensor), the service provider, and the cloud storage.

A Brief Overview of the Protocol. It consists of a set of N (≥ 1) users U, a set of N sensors S (one for each user), a service provider SP, and a cloud storage provider which we just call database DB throughout the paper. During the enrolment phase, the sensor S_i obtains from a user U_i a biometric reference template b_i, a password pw_i (for simplicity, we regard the second factor as a password, but any knowledge-based or possession-based factor could be used instead) and an identity ID_i. It then derives a random bitstring r_i of the same length as b_i from pw_i and ID_i using a key derivation function KDF [1] (i.e., $r_i \leftarrow \mathsf{KDF}(pw_i, ID_i)$), computes $b_i \oplus r_i$, and sends $(ID_i, b_i \oplus r_i)$ to the service provider SP. Since we are using a combination (i.e., XOR) of factors, this has to be taken into consideration when choosing security parameters for these factors (cf. Sect. 3.1). SP then maps the ID_i to an index i (i.e., $i \leftarrow ID_i$) using a procedure known only to itself and forwards $(i, b_i \oplus r_i)$ to the database DB for storage. SP itself stores (i, ID_i).

During the authentication phase, a user U_i authenticates himself to the service provider as follows. The sensor S_i obtains a fresh biometric template b_i', the user password pw_i and an identity ID_i from the user. S_i then generates r_i using the same procedure as in the enrolment phase, computes $b_i' \oplus r_i$, and sends $(ID_i, b_i' \oplus r_i)$ to SP. The service provider SP retrieves i corresponding to ID_i from its own storage and retrieves $b_i \oplus r_i$ from DB by employing a private information retrieval PIR scheme. This scheme allows SP to retrieve $b_i \oplus r_i$ from DB without revealing to DB the value of the retrieved information (under information-theoretic or computational security assumptions, cf. Sect. 3). SP then XORs $b_i \oplus r_i$ and $b_i' \oplus r_i$ to get $b_i \oplus b_i'$, and grants the user U_i access (or simply authenticates the user) if the Hamming weight $\mathsf{HW}(b_i \oplus b_i') \leq \tau$, where τ is a predefined authentication threshold. Note that $\mathsf{HW}(b_i \oplus b_i') = \mathsf{HD}(b_i, b_i')$, where HD is the Hamming distance.

This two-factor authentication protocol employs a combination of a private information retrieval scheme and a key derivation function to achieve strong privacy. It preserves the privacy of the biometric templates, password and password-derived key against malicious and colluding service provider and database; and also offers identity privacy and unlinkability against malicious database, due to the database anonymisation and the use of a PIR during authentication.

Applications. Cloud computing provides an interesting set of advantages, such as increased availability and flexibility, reduced risks related to data losses, and reduced costs in terms of technology infrastructure. Due to privacy concerns, however, the adoption of cloud-based services for biometric authentication has been delayed. Our new protocol enables a new secure and privacy-preserving authentication cloud service business model. Services provided by the Database actor in our protocol can be securely transferred to a cloud-based service. This cloud-based Protected Biometrics Database service can scalably provide secure and private storage and retrieval of user's authentication data to different Service Providers.

Remarks. Some design decisions in our system must be explained in more depth, to make clear that they are realistic and fully justified.

First, we choose to work with biometric binary templates instead of other alternative representations based on integers or real numbers. This is justified by the existence of many biometrics based on binary templates, e.g. iris patterns are represented by IrisCodes [2]; or where a binary representation can be derived, e.g. even behavioural biometrics such as online signatures can be represented in binary templates [3]. Furthermore, binary templates can be compared using the Hamming distance, which is very convenient for simple and well-known homomorphic encryption schemes, thus avoiding the need for a specific design of a new cryptosystem. Using other representations requires using much more complex crypto schemes, e.g. computing the Euclidean distance requires a fully homomorphic encryption or coupling additive homomorphic encryption scheme with an oblivious transfer or garbled circuits.

Second, we combine several factors. This may influence usability, since the processes for using the system in both enrollment and verification will take longer and the users will experience usability issues related to both authentication factors. However, the combination of several authentication factors, as demonstrated in this paper, minimizes the risks associated with the use of each of the authentication factors. Specifically, the security of the system is significantly increased, making attacks much more difficult to the typical adversaries, and the privacy concerns posed by the use of biometrics are minimized by using the additional authentication factor for binding the binary biometric information. The proposed solution is simple yet effective.

Related Work. Privacy-preserving biometric authentication has attracted a considerable amount of research over the last decade. Many of the existing privacy-preserving biometric authentication protocols are based on secure multi-party computation techniques including oblivious transfer [4,5] and homomorphic encryption [6,7], as well as on private information retrieval [8,9]. For example, Bringer et al. [10] proposed a protocol using the Goldwasser-Micali cryptosystem [7]. This protocol by Bringer et al. and the subsequent protocols by Barbosa et al. [11] and Stoianov [12] all use a distributed entity model. However, all of the these protocols are designed to achieve security in the HBC model, and their security is also critcized [11,13–16]. To the best of our knowledge, most (if not all) of the protocols using biometrics as single authentication factor presented in the literature are at best secure against HBC adversaries only. Recently, Abidin *et al.* [17] describe a simple attack on the Bringer *et al.* [10] protocol and proposes an improvement to achieve security against malicious but not colluding insider adversaries, utilizing additional secret keys. As in the original Bringer *et al.* protocol, Abidin *et al.* protocol also stores the reference biometric templates in the clear.

There have been other works combining biometrics with other authentication factors, such as knowledge-based (e.g., passwords) and/or possession-based (e.g., tokens). This multi-factor approach involving biometrics has been a popular approach to remote biometric authentication [18]. For example, in [19] a scheme combining biometrics with a password and a smart card was proposed by Lee *et al.*. Weaknesses of this scheme were identified subsequently in [20], where the authors also propose a flexible remote authentication scheme based on fingerprints and ElGammal cryptosystem. However, this latter scheme was vulnerable to, among others, spoofing attacks as identified by Khan and Zhang [21]. More efficient schemes were also proposed in [18, 22, 23] in the past couple of years, although some of them turned out to have security weaknesses [24]. A common feature among these schemes is that they use smart cards to store authentication information. Hence a drawback of these schemes is that if the smart card is stolen or lost, then either the security is at risk or the user can no longer authenticate himself.

Outline. After giving the necessary background material and our threat model in Sect. 2, we give a detailed presentation of our protocol, paying particular attention to the key derivation function and the private information retrieval scheme in Sect. 3. Next, we analyse its privacy and security in Sect. 4. Finally, Sect. 5 summarises the paper.

2   Background and Threat Model

This section presents the necessary background material and the security requirements for the cryptographic primitives used in our protocol.

Definition 1. *A function* negl : $\mathbb{N} \mapsto [0, 1]$ *is said to be negligible if for all positive polynomials* poly *and all sufficiently large* $\lambda \in \mathbb{N}$, *we have* negl$(\lambda) <$ $1/$poly(λ).

2.1   Security and Privacy Definitions

Definition 2. *Let* Π *be a two-factor authentication protocol. Then* Π *is secure if no probabilistic polynomial time (PPT) adversary* $\mathcal{A}$ *can successfully authenticate itself to the verifier as the legitimate user it impersonates, even when given all protocol transcripts and all inputs of the verifier and all provers (i.e., users) with the exception of at least one authentication factor of the user it tries to impersonate.*

Regarding privacy, we consider unlinkability, identity privacy and user data privacy. Let Π be as before in all of the following definitions.

Unlinkability. Intuitively, if the adversary cannot distinguish a user who is authenticating himself from a user who is not, then unlinkability holds. Therefore, we define unlinkability as follows.

Definition 3. *Suppose that any two distinct users U_{i_0} and U_{i_1}, where i_0, $i_1 \geq 1$, are given and that U_{i_β}, $\beta \in \{0,1\}$, makes an authentication attempt. Then, Π has unlinkability, if any PPT adversary $\mathcal{A}$ cannot guess β, except with a negligible advantage. Here, the adversary's advantage is defined as $\left| \Pr\{\beta = \beta'\} - 1/2 \right|$, where β' is the adversary's guess.*

Identity privacy. If the adversary cannot tell to which ID a given authentication credential belongs, then we say that the identity privacy is preserved. Formally, this is defined as follows.

Definition 4. *Suppose that any identity ID_i and two credentials $c_{i_0} = b_{i_0} \oplus r_{i_0}$ and $c_{i_1} = b_{i_1} \oplus r_{i_1}$, where i_0, $i_1 \geq 1$ and c_{i_β}, $\beta \in \{0,1\}$, belongs to ID_i, are given. Then, Π preserves the identity privacy, if any PPT adversary $\mathcal{A}$ cannot guess β, except with a negligible advantage. Here again, the adversary's advantage is defined as $\left| \Pr\{\beta = \beta'\} - 1/2 \right|$, where β' is the adversary's guess.*

User data privacy. If the adversary cannot learn anything about the sensitive user data (i.e., biometric data and the second authentication factor), then we say that the user data privacy is preserved.

Definition 5. *We say that Π preserves the privacy of the user data, i.e., the biometric templates (both fresh and reference), the password and/or the password-derived key, if no PPT adversary $\mathcal{A}$ can gain more information on the user data than what is allowed by the protocol transcripts, except with a negligible probability.*

2.2 Key Derivation Function

A key derivation function (KDF) is a (deterministic) function that can be used to derive keys for cryptographic applications using a secret input data, such as passwords. We require that the KDF satisfies the following security definition [1].

Definition 6. *A key derivation function KDF is said to be secure with respect to a source of input with sufficient min-entropy γ if no probabilistic polynomial time (PPT) attacker $\mathcal{A}$ can distinguish its output from a random output of equal length, except with a negligible probability $negl(\gamma)$.*

2.3 Private Information Retrieval

A PIR scheme allows a user to retrieve a value from a database without revealing to the database which value is retrieved. For example, using a PIR scheme a user can retrieve the i-th bit (or the i-th block) from a database of N-bits (or a database of N blocks) without revealing the value of i to the database. We require that the PIR scheme satisfies the following definition.

Definition 7. *Suppose that the database contains an N data blocks with block-length ℓ bits each, with both $N, \ell \geq 1$ (i.e., the database contains $x_1 x_2 \cdots x_N$, where the length of x_i is ℓ, for $i = 1, \cdots, N$.) And let PIR be the private information retrieval scheme employed to retrieve the i-th block from the database (i.e., $x_i \leftarrow \mathsf{PIR}(i)$). Then the database should not have any information about the value of i and x_i. If the database is assumed to be computationally unbounded, the PIR is called information-theoretic PIR; otherwise, it is called computational PIR.*

2.4 Threat Model

In the typical security analysis, adversaries are divided into two main categories: (i) *honest-but-curious* (HBC) adversaries, and (ii) *malicious* adversaries. In the HBC adversarial model, corrupted parties follow the protocol specification. However, the adversary may obtain the internal state of all corrupted parties (i.e., transcript of all received messages) and may attempt to use this information to recover sensitive data (e.g., biometric templates) that should remain private. In the malicious adversarial model, the corrupted parties may arbitrarily deviate from the protocol specification in order to break the security and privacy of the protected data. Since external adversaries cannot obtain more information than the internal ones, we consider exclusively *malicious* internal adversaries that may arbitrarily deviate from the protocol specification.

To be privacy-preserving, a biometric authentication protocol should satisfy not only the security requirement (cf. Definition 2), but also the following privacy requirements:

1. *Biometric reference privacy:* An adversary $\mathcal{A}$ should not be able to recover the stored reference biometric template (cf. Definition 5).
2. *Biometric sample privacy:* $\mathcal{A}$ should not be able to recover the fresh biometric sample (cf. Definition 5).
3. *Password privacy:* $\mathcal{A}$ should not be able to recover the password or the key derived from the password (cf. Definition 5).
4. *Identity privacy:* $\mathcal{A}$ should not be able to link a database entry to a user identity ID. Note that the protocol does not require ID to be personally identifiable information, and so this privacy requirement only concerns whether a database entry is associated to a specific user ID employed in the protocol (cf. Definition 4).
5. *Unlinkability:* $\mathcal{A}$ should not be able to link an authentication attempt to a user (cf. Definition 3).

In this paper, we only consider adversaries that attempt to violate these privacy requirements and skip denial-of-service type of attacks.

Depending on the attack scenario (i.e., depending on which protocol entity is compromised or malicious), the privacy requirements change accordingly. For instance, the service provider SP always knows which user is authenticating himself so the unlinkability and identity privacy are not relevant, although the latter can be achieved using anonymous IDs. Therefore, whenever the SP is compromised, either colluding or not colluding with the DB, we only focus on the biometric samples and the password (or password-derived key) secrecy. On the other hand, if the attacker is the database DB all of the requirements must hold.

The Sensor is trusted, i.e. it does not deviate the protocol, it does not store ID or biometric samples, and the information it handles during the enrollment and verification phases is discarded and only accessible to the legitimate application at run time; and we are not considering the case where it is compromised, e.g. infected by malicious software. We assume that each user has a client device (e.g., a smartphone) with a biometric sensor. It is quite common nowadays that people use their smartphones to do even bank transactions. This does not make the user devices trustworthy, but if the users cannot trust the devices used to log in, a secure access to their remote services cannot be accomplished.

A further assumption we make is that the communication among the protocol entities takes place over a secure channel. This means that an adversary cannot intercept or modify a message in transit. Lastly, we require that before any user authenticates himself to the service provider, the service provider authenticates itself to the client device (i.e., the sensor). This can be achieved by using secure transmission protocols, e.g. TLS or IPsec. Hence, at the conclusion of the protocol there should be a mutual entity authentication, where the service provider is authenticated first and then the user authenticates himself to the service provider. This is to preclude phishing attacks, i.e. to ensure that the user does not blindly give away his identity and authentication data to attackers. The authentication mechanism for the server and the way it is coupled to the user authentication is left outside the scope of this paper.

3   The Protocol

The protocol comprises a set S of N sensors, one for each user in a set U of N users, a service provider SP, and a database DB. Each user is assumed to have a client device (e.g., a smartphone), which has a biometric sensor.

Enrolment. The enrolment works as follows. The sensor S_i prompts the user U_i, for $i = 1, \cdots, N$, for his biometrics and password pw_i, and outputs $b_i \oplus r_i$, where b_i is a (binary) reference biometric template of bitlength ℓ extracted by the sensor from the user provided biometrics and $r_i \leftarrow \text{KDF}(pw_i, ID_i)$ is also of bitlength ℓ. Then, S_i sends $(ID_i, b_i \oplus r_i)$ to the service provider SP, that first maps the ID_i to a unique index i and locally stores (i, ID_i), and forwards $(i, b_i \oplus r_i)$ to DB for storage.

The service provider does not need to store (i, ID_i). Instead, what SP needs is a deterministic one-to-one map to map ID_i to an index i. For the sake of simplicity, however, we assume that SP locally stores the pair (i, ID_i), and that during authentication it just retrieves the index i corresponding to a received ID_i from its local storage.

User Authentication. A user U_i authenticates himself to the service provider as follows. After authenticating the service provider, the sensor S_i prompts the user for his data: fresh biometrics, password and identity. Then, the sensor extracts a fresh biometric template b_i' from the user provided biometrics, receives the user password pw_i and identity ID_i from the user U_i. Subsequently, S_i derives r_i using the key derivation function KDF with pw_i and ID_i as input, computes $b_i' \oplus r_i$, and sends $(ID_i, b_i' \oplus r_i)$ to the service provider SP. SP first obtains i corresponding to ID_i from its own local storage and retrieves $b_i \oplus r_i$ from DB by employing a private information retrieval PIR scheme (see Sect. 3.1 on PIR for details). SP then XORs $b_i \oplus r_i$ and $b_i' \oplus r_i$ to obtain $b_i \oplus b_i'$. Finally, the user is authenticated if the Hamming weight $HW(b_i \oplus b_i') \leq \tau$; rejected, otherwise.

Note that the sensors S_i, $i = 1, \cdots, N$, do not store any user information (i.e., biometric template data and/or password), thus user's data privacy is still preserved if his terminal is stolen or lost. When a user U_i presents his biometrics to the sensor S_i, it only outputs the XOR of the extracted biometric template with the derived key r_i, i.e., $b_i' \oplus r_i$ or $b_i \oplus r_i$ depending on the protocol phase, and never outputs the biometric template data or the password-derived key r_i in the clear or stores them. Also, the r_i's are generated at run time using the password pw_i and user ID_i as input to a KDF, and r_i and pw_i are erased from memory immediately after use.

To highlight the feasibility of our protocol, below we elaborate further on the KDF and the PIR scheme that can be employed in our protocol. However, since we would like to keep it as generic as possible, we leave the choice for specific KDF and PIR schemes for the users of our protocol.

3.1 KDF

In our protocol, both the reference b_i and fresh b_i' biometric templates are bound (i.e., XORed) with keys r_i generated from the second authentication factor (e.g., password) using a KDF. KDF is a useful tool in cryptography and often used in diverse applications to derive cryptographic keys from a secret input. According to PKCS # 5 [25], for a password-based KDF, it is recommended to salt the password in order to prevent dictionary attacks and to compute the hash many times to slow down the KDF process, which is also known as *key-stretching* [26]. If password is used as the second factor in our protocol, then the salt needs to be stored in the user device. We refer the interested reader to Yao *et al.* [27] for a formal treatment of password-based KDF, and to Krawczyk [1] for a more general treatment and rigorous security definitions of KDF. What is important to note when choosing a specific KDF for our protocol is that the chosen KDF must be secure according to our Definition 6.

Regarding the security requirements on the inputs to the KDF, we note that the password should have at least the same min-entropy as the one required for the output. Since only the XOR of the KDF output with the biometric template is stored, the security requirement should be referred to this combination (i.e., $r_i \oplus b_i$), whose min-entropy is greater than or equal to $\max\{H_\infty(r_i), H_\infty(b_i)\}$, where H_∞ stands for min-entropy. Therefore, as long as one of the factors provides sufficient min-entropy, the entropy requirement on the other can be relaxed if the security is our only concern. However, the min-entropy of the second authentication factor impacts privacy. The min-entropy of the second factor should be greater than or equal to the entropy of the biometric template for avoiding biometric information leakage to internal adversaries.

3.2 PIR

As mentioned briefly in Sect. 2, PIR schemes allow for the retrieval of the content of a database entry, say the i-th bit of an N-bit database, without revealing to the database which content or entry is retrieved (i.e., the value of i in the example). Chor et $al.$ [8] were the first to introduce the notion of PIR, and they studied information-theoretically secure PIRs in the case of single database or multiple non-communicating databases. Since then, there has been a substantial amount of work on PIR; we present here a quick review of the work relevant to our protocol.

Recall that we assume that there is a single database. In practice, however, one can use multiple databases (e.g., multiple cloud storage providers) storing the same information. This is more robust, because even if some databases are down, e.g., due to power outage, users can still authenticate themselves to the service provider. So, we divide our discussions on PIR into single database PIR and multiple database PIR.

Single DB PIR. Since Kushilevitz and Ostrovsky [28] proposed the first single DB PIR scheme, the field has evolved and important connections between single DB PIR and other cryptographic primitives, such as oblivious transfer and collision resistant hashing, have been identified [29]. Ostrovsky and Skeith give a nice survey on single DB PIR schemes in [29]. Here we describe a simple scheme that appeared in [10], which utilises the Goldwasser-Micali cryptosystem [7], a bit-wise encryption scheme with an homomorphic property: $\mathsf{Enc}(m)\mathsf{Enc}(m') = \mathsf{Enc}(m \oplus m')$, where m and m' are two message bits. Suppose that the SP wants to retrieve the i-th user's data item $b_i \oplus r_i$ from the DB. Also suppose that SP generates a private and public key pair $(\mathsf{sk}, \mathsf{pk})$ for the Goldwasser-Micali encryption schemes, and gives the public key pk to the database and keeps the secret key sk to itself. Assume from now on that the content of the DB is an $N \times \ell$ binary matrix A. Then, SP forms $\mathrm{PIR}(i)$ as follows: for $j = 1, \cdots, N$, $s_j = 1$, if $j = i$, 0 otherwise. It sends $\mathsf{Enc}(s) = \big(\mathsf{Enc}(s_1), \cdots, \mathsf{Enc}(s_N)\big)$ to the DB, which computes, for $n = 1, \cdots, \ell$, $C_{i,n} := \big(\prod_{j=1}^{N} \mathsf{Enc}(s_j)^{A_{j,n}}\mathsf{Enc}(0)\big) = \mathsf{Enc}\big(A_{i,n}\big) = \mathsf{Enc}\big(b_{i,n} \oplus r_{i,n}\big)$, and returns $C_i = (C_{i,1}, \cdots, C_{i,\ell})$ to SP. Note that $\mathsf{Enc}(0)$ is used to randomise the response in order to resist an attack similar to the one described by Barbosa et $al.$ [11]. Finally, SP decrypts C_i to obtain $b_i \oplus r_i$. This scheme has a communication complexity of $\mathcal{O}(Nc + \ell c)$, where c is the ciphertext length, which needs to be at least 2048 bits for 112-bit security. Furthermore, this PIR scheme is computationally secure according to our Definition 7, if the Goldwasser-Micali encryption is IND-CPA secure [10].

Multiple DB PIR. When there are k ($\geqslant 1$) copies of $(i, b_i \oplus r_i)$, for $i = 1, \cdots, N$, stored in k DBs, we can use the following information-theoretic PIR scheme in our protocol. Suppose that there are 2 DBs and that the SP wants to retrieve i entry, which is $b_i \oplus r_i$, from the DBs. Then, the PIR scheme works as follows:

- The SP prepares the queries as follows:
  - generate at random a bitstring s of length N.
  - flip the i-th bit of s; let us denote the resulting bitstring by s'.
  - send s to DB1, and s' to DB2.
- DB1 returns $t = sA \mod 2$, where s is used as a row vector, to SP.
- DB2 returns $t' = s'A \mod 2$, where s' is used as a row vector, to SP.
- Finally, SP computes $t \oplus t' = sA \oplus s'A = (s \oplus s')A = b_i \oplus r_i$. Note that $s \oplus s'$ is all 0s except at the i-th position, where it has a 1.

Obviously, this 2-DB PIR scheme has a communication complexity of $\mathcal{O}(N + \ell)$. And the computation performed by the DBs is just the XOR of the rows (of A) corresponding to the components of s (or s') that are 1. We note that this scheme, or for that matter most k-DB PIR schemes, assumes that the DBs are trusted not to collude with each other; otherwise, the DBs can learn the value of i. There are, however, also k-DB PIR schemes that remain secure even if all databases collude with each other [30]. We refer to the excellent survey by Gasarch [31] for more on multiple DB PIR.

4   Security and Privacy Analysis

We assume that the protocol setup and enrolment phases are done securely and all involved entities behaved honestly in these phases. Therefore, we focus on the authentication phase in our analysis. We distinguish the following attack scenarios from each other.

1. *Attacker = The service provider SP*: Its objective is to learn the user biometric template or the user password. It has access to $b_i' \oplus r_i$ and $b_i \oplus r_i$, and $b_i' \oplus b_i$. The identity privacy and unlinkability, however, are not relevant if SP is compromised, as it knows the user IDs.
2. *Attacker = The database DB*: Its objectives are to learn (a) user identity, (b) biometric templates, (c) passwords or password-derived keys, and (d) link different authentication attempts. It knows only $b_i \oplus r_i$, but it does not know to which user it belongs, since the database is anonymised. Also, since a secure PIR is employed during authentication, the identity privacy and unlinkability requirements are also satisfied. So all of the privacy requirements are satisfied in this case.
3. *Attacker = SP+DB*: Their objective is to learn the user biometric template or the user password. In this case, they know $b_i \oplus r_i$, $b_i' \oplus r_i$, and $b_i \oplus b_i'$, as in the case of the attacker being SP. Therefore, against the collusion between SP and DB, the biometric template (both reference and sample) privacy and the password (or the password-derived key r_i) privacy are preserved.

4. *Attacker = The sensor* S_i: we only consider the case where S_i is used by a malicious user to impersonate its legitimate owner. Since the sensor does not store any information about its legitimate user's biometrics and password, the attacker cannot learn anything or impersonate the user.

We now state the security and privacy properties of our protocol. The proofs are presented in Appendix 5.

Theorem 1. *Our proposed protocol is secure according to our Definition 2, if the employed KDF and PIR are secure according to Definitions 6 and 7, respectively, and $i \leftarrow ID_i$ procedure is known only to the SP.*

Unlinkability against malicious DB. Recall that if the adversary cannot distinguish a user who is authenticating himself from a user who is not, then unlinkability holds. Therefore, we state the unlinkability result against malicious DB as follows.

Theorem 2. *Our proposed protocol has unlinkability against malicious DB according to Definition 3, if the employed PIR is secure according to Definition 7.*

Identity privacy against malicious DB. If the DB cannot tell to which ID a database entry belongs, then we say that the identity privacy is preserved. This is summarised in the next theorem.

Theorem 3. *Our proposed protocol has identity privacy against malicious DB according to Definition 4, if the employed PIR is secure according to Definition 7 and $i \leftarrow ID_i$ procedure is known only to the SP.*

User data privacy against malicious SP+DB. Our last result relates to the privacy of user data, i.e., the fresh and reference biometric templates, password and password-derived key. Note that when we say that the password has sufficient min-entropy, the word "password" is used just as a reference to the second authentication factor which is given as an input to the KDF. The following theorem states that as long as the KDF is secure, the privacy of the user data is preserved against malicious and colluding SP and DB.

Theorem 4. *Our protocol preserves the privacy of the user data (i.e., the fresh and reference biometric templates, password and password-derived key) against malicious SP+DB according to Definition 5, if the employed KDF is secure according to Definition 6 and the password has sufficient min-entropy.*

5   Conclusions

In this paper, we proposed a two-factor privacy-preserving authentication protocol that is secure against malicious and possibly colluding adversaries. The second factor (e.g., password) adds another layer of security in that even if an attacker successfully forges a user biometrics (e.g., a fingerprint), he/she cannot impersonate the user without knowing the password. Furthermore, as our analysis shows, the privacy of the users' identities, their passwords and biometric template data is preserved even if the protocol actors are compromised. The protocol is efficient and employs a distributed model for the protocol actors and thus suitable for applications where users authenticate themselves to a service provider using their smart devices that have embedded biometric sensors and where part of the user data (i.e., the encrypted biometric reference template) are outsourced to cloud storage providers. Hence, our protocol paves the way towards a secure and privacy-preserving authentication cloud service business model. In this model, services provided by the Database in our protocol can be securely transferred to one or several cloud-based services. Such cloud storage services can provide a secure and private storage and retrieval of user's authentication data to different Service Providers.

Acknowledgements. This work was funded by the European Commission through the FP7 project "EKSISTENZ," with grant number: 607049.

A   Proofs

Proof (of Theorem 1). The proof is split into two cases. In the first case, the adversary $\mathcal{A}$ is given a valid password (e.g., $\mathcal{A}$ is given pw_i of user U_i). In the second case, $\mathcal{A}$ is given a valid biometrics, (e.g., $\mathcal{A}$ is given b_i' of user U_i). In both cases, if $\mathcal{A}$ can provide $b_i' \oplus r_i$ such that $HW(b_i \oplus b_i') \leq \tau$, then $\mathcal{A}$ succeeds in impersonating the user U_i.

Case 1: Assume that the attacker can successfully impersonate a user with a non-negligible probability. This means that $\mathcal{A}$ either (a) can forge the user biometrics and generate b_i' that matches the reference template b_i of the user U_i, or (b) knows $i \leftarrow ID_i$ so that it can collude with DB to learn b_i. However, the probability of case (a) happening is bounded by the false acceptance rate, which can be bounded to be arbitrarily small, at the price of increased false rejection rate. And case (b) requires that $\mathcal{A}$ can learn i from $PIR(i)$ or can derive i from ID_i, which contradicts both the security of the PIR scheme and the fact that $i \leftarrow ID_i$ is only known to SP. Therefore, $\mathcal{A}$ cannot impersonate a user knowing only the password.

Case 2: Assume again that the attacker can successfully impersonate a user with a non-negligible probability. As in *Case 1*, this means that $\mathcal{A}$ either can guess the password (or the password-generated key r_i) or knows $i \leftarrow ID_i$ so that it can collude with DB to learn r_i. However, while the probability of the former is negligible in $H_\infty(pw)$, the latter requires that $\mathcal{A}$ can learn i from $PIR(i)$ or knows $i \leftarrow ID_i$.

Therefore, $\mathcal{A}$ cannot successfully impersonate any user without having access to both authentication factors. Note that the use of salt prevents the adversary from practical dictionary attacks. Hence, it is important to salt the KDF, e.g. with the user ID, so that the security of the protocol in *Case 2* can be related to $H_\infty(pw)$.

Proof (of Theorem 2). Suppose that the adversary (i.e., the malicious DB) has a non-negligible advantage, i.e., $\left| \Pr\{\beta = \beta'\} - 1/2 \right| \geq \mathsf{negl}(\lambda)$, where λ is a chosen security parameter for the protocol. Then, that means DB can guess the value of β (or i_β) from $\mathsf{PIR}(i_\beta)$ with a non-negligible probability. This in turn implies that DB can break the security of the underlying PIR scheme with a non-negligible probability, which contradicts the assumption that PIR is secure according to Definition 7. □

Proof (of Theorem 3). Suppose that the adversary can distinguish $(\mathsf{ID}_{i_0}, c_{i_0})$ from $(\mathsf{ID}_{i_0}, c_{i_1})$. Then the adversary can infer from $\mathsf{PIR}(i_0)$ (and the response to the query) the value of i_0, or infer from ID_{i_0} the value of i_0. This contradicts the security assumptions on the PIR, or the secrecy assumption on the correspondence between ID_{i_0} and i_0, respectively. □

Proof (of Theorem 4). Since the adversary (i.e., malicious SP+DB) has access to $b_i \oplus r_i$, $b'_i \oplus r_i$ and $b_i \oplus b'_i$ only, for all $i \in [1, N]$, it cannot learn more than what can already be learnt from these about b_i, b'_i and r_i (or the password from which the r_i is generated), as long as the KDF is secure and the password has sufficient min-entropy. The adversary can attempt to guess the value of b_i, b'_i or r_i at random using what the information at its disposal, but in order to verify whether the guess is correct, it needs access to an oracle that can answer whether the guessed values are correct. If the KDF is secure and the second factor has sufficient min-entropy, the expected number of queries needed to finally get an affirmative answer from such oracle is exponential in the min-entropy of r_i. □

References

1. Krawczyk, H.: Cryptographic extraction and key derivation: the HKDF scheme. In: Rabin, T. (ed.) CRYPTO 2010. LNCS, vol. 6223, pp. 631–648. Springer, Heidelberg (2010)
2. Daugman, J.: The importance of being random: statistical principles of iris recognition. Pattern Recogn. **36**(2), 279–291 (2003)
3. Rua, E.A., Maiorana, E., Castro, J.L.A., Campisi, P.: Biometric template protection using universal background models: an application to online signature. IEEE Trans. Inf. Forensics Secur. **7**(1), 269–282 (2012)
4. Rabin, M.O.: How to exchange secrets with oblivious transfer. IACR Cryptology ePrint Archive 2005, 187 (2005)
5. Yáo, A.C.C.: How to generate and exchange secrets. In: 27th Annual Symposium on Foundations of Computer Science, pp. 162–167. IEEE (1986)
6. Paillier, P.: Public-key cryptosystems based on composite degree residuosity classes. In: Stern, J. (ed.) EUROCRYPT 1999. LNCS, vol. 1592, pp. 223–238. Springer, Heidelberg (1999)
7. Goldwasser, S., Micali, S.: Probabilistic encryption & how to play mental poker keeping secret all partial information. In: STOC, pp. 365–377. ACM (1982)
8. Chor, B., Kushilevitz, E., Goldreich, O., Sudan, M.: Private information retrieval. J. ACM **45**(6), 965–981 (1998)
9. Ostrovsky, R., Skeith III, W.E.: A survey of single-database private information retrieval: techniques and applications. In: Okamoto, T., Wang, X. (eds.) PKC 2007. LNCS, vol. 4450, pp. 393–411. Springer, Heidelberg (2007)

10. Bringer, J., Chabanne, H., Izabachène, M., Pointcheval, D., Tang, Q., Zimmer, S.: An application of the Goldwasser-Micali cryptosystem to biometric authentication. In: Pieprzyk, J., Ghodosi, H., Dawson, E. (eds.) ACISP 2007. LNCS, vol. 4586, pp. 96–106. Springer, Heidelberg (2007)

11. Barbosa, M., Brouard, T., Cauchie, S., de Sousa, S.M.: Secure biometric authentication with improved accuracy. In: Mu, Y., Susilo, W., Seberry, J. (eds.) ACISP 2008. LNCS, vol. 5107, pp. 21–36. Springer, Heidelberg (2008)

12. Stoianov, A.: Cryptographically secure biometrics. In: SPIE 7667, Biometric Technology for Human Identification VII, pp. 76670C-1–76670C-12 (2010)

13. Simoens, K., et al.: A framework for analyzing template security and privacy in biometric authentication systems. IEEE Trans. Inf. Forensics Secur. **7**(2), 833–841 (2012)

14. Abidin, A., Mitrokotsa, A.: Security aspects of privacy-preserving biometric authentication based on ideal lattices and ring-lwe. In: Proceedings of the IEEE Workshop on Information Forensics and Security, pp. 1653–1658 (2014)

15. Abidin, A., Pagnin, E., Mitrokotsa, A.: Attacks on privacy-preserving biometric authentication. In: Proceedings of the 19th Nordic Conference on Secure IT Systems (NordSec 2014), pp. 293–294. Tromso, Norway (2014)

16. Pagnin, E., Dimitrakakis, C., Abidin, A., Mitrokotsa, A.: On the leakage of information in biometric authentication. In: Meier, W., Mukhopadhyay, D. (eds.) INDOCRYPT 2014. LNCS, vol. 8885, pp. 265–280. Springer, Heidelberg (2014). doi:10.1007/978-3-319-13039-2_16

17. Abidin, A., Matsuura, K., Mitrokotsa, A.: Security of a privacy-preserving biometric authentication protocol revisited. In: Gritzalis, D., Kiayias, A., Askoxylakis, I. (eds.) CANS 2014. LNCS, vol. 8813, pp. 290–304. Springer, Heidelberg (2014)

18. Syta, E., Wolinsky, D., Fischer, M., Silberschatz, A., Ford, B., Gallegos-Garcia, G.: Efficient and privacy-preserving biometric authentication. Yale University Technical Report TR1469 (2012)

19. Lee, J., Ryu, S., Yoo, K.: Fingerprint-based remote user authentication scheme using smart cards. Electron. Lett. **38**(12), 554–555 (2002)

20. Lin, C.H., Lai, Y.Y.: A flexible biometrics remote user authentication scheme. Comput. Stand. Interfaces **27**(1), 19–23 (2004)

21. Khan, M.K., Zhang, J.: Improving the security of flexible biometrics remote user authentication scheme. Comput. Stand. Interfaces **29**(1), 82–85 (2007)

22. Li, C.T., Hwang, M.S.: An efficient biometrics-based remote user authentication scheme using smart cards. J. Netw. Comput. Appl. **33**(1), 1–5 (2010)

23. Li, X., Niu, J.W., Ma, J., Wang, W.D., Liu, C.L.: Cryptanalysis and improvement of a biometrics-based remote user authentication scheme using smart cards. J. Netw. Comput. Appl. **34**(1), 73–79 (2011)

24. Li, X., Niu, J., Khan, M.K., Liao, J.: An enhanced smart card based remote user password authentication scheme. J. Netw. Comput. Appl. **36**(5), 1365–1371 (2013)

25. Kaliski, B.: PKCS #5: password-based cryptography specification version 2.0. RFC 2898 (2000)

26. Kelsey, J., Schneier, B., Hall, C., Wagner, D.: Secure applications of low-entropy keys. In: Okamoto, E., Davida, G., Mambo, M. (eds.) ISW 1997. LNCS, vol. 1396, pp. 121–134. Springer, Heidelberg (1998). doi:10.1007/BFb0030415

27. Yao, F.F., Yin, Y.L.: Design and analysis of password-based key derivation functions. In: Menezes, A. (ed.) CT-RSA 2005. LNCS, vol. 3376, pp. 245–261. Springer, Heidelberg (2005)

28. Kushilevitz, E., Ostrovsky, R.: Replication is not needed: single database, computationally-private information retrieval. In: FOCS, pp. 364–373. IEEE Computer Society (1997)
29. Ostrovsky, R., Skeith III, W.E.: A survey of single-database private information retrieval: techniques and applications. In: Okamoto, T., Wang, X. (eds.) PKC 2007. LNCS, vol. 4450, pp. 393–411. Springer, Heidelberg (2007)
30. Goldberg, I.: Improving the robustness of private information retrieval. In: IEEE SP 2007, pp. 131–148. IEEE (2007)
31. Gasarch, W.: A survey on private information retrieval. Bull. EATCS **82**, 72–107 (2004)

Probabilistic Generation of Trapdoors: Reducing Information Leakage of Searchable Symmetric Encryption

Kenichiro Hayasaka[1(✉)], Yutaka Kawai[1], Yoshihiro Koseki[1], Takato Hirano[1], Kazuo Ohta[2], and Mitsugu Iwamoto[2]

[1] Mitsubishi Electric Corporation, Kamakura, Japan
Hayasaka.Kenichiro@bc.MitsubishiElectric.co.jp,
Kawai.Yutaka@da.MitsubishiElectric.co.jp,
Koseki.Yoshihiro@ak.MitsubishiElectric.co.jp,
Hirano.Takato@ay.MitsubishiElectric.co.jp
[2] University of Electro-Communications, Chofu, Japan
{kazuo.ohta,mitsugu}@uec.ac.jp

Abstract. Searchable symmetric encryption (SSE) enables a user to outsource a collection of encrypted documents in the cloud and to perform keyword searching without revealing information about the contents of the documents and queries. On the other hand, the information (called *search pattern*) whether or not the same keyword is searched in each query is always leaked in almost all previous schemes whose trapdoors are generated deterministically. Therefore, reducing the search pattern leakage is outside the scope of almost all previous works. In this paper, we tackle to the leakage problem of search pattern, and study methodology to reduce this leakage. Especially, we discuss that it might be possible to reduce the search pattern leakage in cases where a trapdoor does not match any encrypted document. We also point out that the same search pattern is leaked regardless of probabilistic or deterministic generation of trapdoors when the user searches using a keyword which has already searched and matched a certain encrypted document. Thus, we further aim to construct SSE schemes with fast "re-search" process, in addition to reducing the search pattern leakage. In order to achieve the above, we introduce a new technique "trapdoor locked encryption" which can extract a deterministic trapdoor from a probabilistic trapdoor, and then propose a new SSE scheme which can generate trapdoors probabilistically and reduce the search pattern leakage. Our scheme is constructed by applying our technique to the well-known and influential scheme SSE-2 (ACM CCS 2006) and can be proved secure in the standard model.

1 Introduction

1.1 Background

Searchable encryption of symmetric-key type is called *searchable symmetric encryption* or *SSE* and its concrete schemes have been proposed (e.g., [1–13, 15–26, 28–33]). SSE consists of *document storing process* and *keyword searching*

© Springer International Publishing AG 2016
S. Foresti and G. Persiano (Eds.): CANS 2016, LNCS 10052, pp. 350–364, 2016.
DOI: 10.1007/978-3-319-48965-0_21

process, and the processes are executed by the same user in the simple user setting. In the document storing process, the user encrypts documents and generates an *encrypted index* $\mathcal{I}$ from a secret key K, and the server stores a pair of encrypted documents (*ciphertexts* hereafter) and encrypted index $\mathcal{I}$. In the keyword searching process, the user generates an encrypted query called *trapdoor* from the secret key K and a keyword w, and the server searches on the ciphertexts that contain the keyword w by applying the trapdoor to the encrypted index $\mathcal{I}$. Finally, the server obtains a document identifier set S as a search result.

Several security models for SSE have been studied. Especially, the security model formalized by Curtmola et al. [9] covers the security of both the document storing process and the keyword searching process. Curtmola et al. carefully examined unavoidable information leaked from the document storing process and the keyword searching process of a general SSE scheme, and they formalized *acceptable leakage information* in SSE, namely history, access pattern and search pattern. Then, they defined that an SSE scheme is secure if no information except the acceptable leakage information is revealed from the processes of the scheme. Since their security framework is considered practical in current SSE literature, many previous works [1,3–5,7–12,15–26,29–33] employ this security model and its slightly modified variants.

The information (called *search pattern*) whether or not the same keyword is searched in each query is included in the acceptable leakage information, and always leaked in almost all previous schemes. Therefore, this search pattern leakage is outside the scope of almost all previous works.

1.2 Motivations

Search Pattern Hiding. Contrary to the security definition of Curtmola et al., leaking search patterns might be a serious problem in real situations. For example, an adversary might reveal hidden keywords from trapdoors by executing frequency analysis if the adversary obtains background knowledge (e.g., distribution on age or family names). In previous SSE works, search patterns are always leaked because trapdoors are generated deterministically. Of course, we can easily construct a scheme with no search pattern leakage, by using strong primitives like oblivious RAMs or fully homomorphic encryption [14,27]. However, these techniques incur high computation or communication cost. Therefore, in this paper, we aim to use only light-weight cryptographic primitives like pseudorandom function (PRF) and symmetric key encryption (SKE), and to construct a non-interactive scheme as in previous SSE works.

In addition to deterministic generation of trapdoors, SSE schemes based on hash functions or PRFs must leak search patterns when the searched keyword w is contained in documents, because of the following current methodology for constructing encrypted indexes. In many SSE schemes, each entry of an encrypted index $\mathcal{I}$ can be formed as (val, id)[1] abstractly, where val is generated from a

---

[1] In several SSE schemes like [7], *id* is encrypted.

keyword w by using hash functions or PRFs and id is an identifier of a document. In keyword searching process, the server generates val by using a trapdoor t and checks whether the encrypted index $\mathcal{I}$ contains val. If the document matches the trapdoor t (that is, the document contain the keyword w), the server can find the same val in $\mathcal{I}$. Then, if two trapdoors generated from the same keyword w, the server computes the same val from these trapdoors in the search process, and thereby the search pattern is always leaked regardless of the probabilistic or deterministic generation of trapdoors.

On the other hand, in cases where a trapdoor does not match any encrypted document (that is, the identifier set S output by the search process is empty), it might be possible to hide the search pattern. Hence, we aim to propose a new SSE scheme which can generate trapdoors probabilistically and have leakage resilience to search patterns if a trapdoor matches no encrypted documents.

Speeding Up for "Re-Search". By generating trapdoor probabilistically, we can achieve that no search pattern is leaked when a trapdoor does not match any encrypted document. However, the server has to execute the keyword searching process to an entry of the encrypted index one by one because of probabilistic trapdoor. Thus, the search time is quite slower than SSE schemes whose trapdoors are generated deterministically. In order to reduce this search cost, we will propose a new SSE scheme that provides high speed search only when the same keyword has already been searched. We call this situation "re-search". Re-search means that the user searches once again by using the same keyword which has already been matched some documents in the previous search phase.

In this paper, we achieve the above goals, *probabilistic trapdoor generation* and *fast re-search* by introducing new technique "trapdoor locked encryption technique" which is explained in the next subsection.

1.3 Key Technique: Trapdoor Locked Encryption Technique

Difficulties. In order to achieve the above purposes, in the first step, we try to randomize the trapdoors of SSE-2 [9], which is first adaptive semantic secure SSE scheme, as Table 1 (we call this scheme Tentative Scheme). In SSE-2, an entry of encrypted index is generated by $(\kappa_j = F(K, w, j), id_j)$ and a trapdoor is generated by $t = F(K, w', j)$ where F is a PRF, id_j is an identifier of j-th document D_j in the document collection in the server, respectively. The server can confirm that the trapdoor t matches the entry of encrypted index by checking $t = \kappa_j$. In Tentative scheme, the user generates $(t = F'(F(K, w', j), u), u)$ as the trapdoor where F' is a PRF and u is a randomness. The server can confirm whether the trapdoor matches or not by checking $t = F'(\kappa_j, u)$ using randomness u, which is the second component of the trapdoor.

In Tentative scheme, search patterns are hidden from the trapdoor if the keyword w does not match any stored document by using the randomness u. However, the server computation for searching is inefficient compared with SSE-2 scheme, because the keyword searching process in Table 1 is executed $m \times n$ times where m and n are the numbers of keywords and documents which are stored in the server, respectively.

Through the above discussion, in the case that trapdoors match any entry of the encrypted index, search patterns are leaked even if trapdoors are generated probabilistically. Additionally, the same search pattern is leaked regardless of the probabilistic or deterministic generation of trapdoors when the user searches for a keyword which is matched once, because the server can compute and find same val by using deterministic/probabilistic trapdoors where (val, id) is an entry of encrypted index. Thus, we have a possibility of speed-up of re-searching process by using *deterministic* trapdoors instead of probabilistic trapdoors in the case that the user searches the same keyword which matches encrypted index. From the above observation, we will set up a goal of Re-Search case as follows: we aim the speed up of re-search by using *deterministic* trapdoors when re-searching process is executed.

In order to achieve this purpose, we construct another encrypted index $\mathcal{I}'$ to further speed up search process. In re-search phase, the server searches documents by using this encrypted index $\mathcal{I}'$. In this paper, our re-search performance aims at $O(\log n')$ equal to the structured encryption scheme of Chase and Kamara [7] where n' is the number of indexes in $\mathcal{I}'$. In order to search in $O(\log n')$, $\mathcal{I}'$ should contain deterministic information for searched keywords. Hence, we adopt the following goals.

(1) In the first search phase, a trapdoor should be generated probabilistically for search pattern hiding. Additionally, the user should not give any information of keywords to the server if the trapdoor does not match any document.
(2) At the same time, to construct another encrypted index $\mathcal{I}'$, the server has to obtain deterministic information for the keyword if the trapdoor matches with some entry of the encrypted index $\mathcal{I}$ in the keyword searching process.
(3) In re-search phase, the server executes searching process by using encrypted index $\mathcal{I}'$ which consists of deterministic information for searched keywords.

The user can choose executing of searching process or re-searching process when the user generates trapdoors. In Tentative scheme, the server cannot generate deterministic encrypted index $\mathcal{I}'$. On the other hand, the search patterns are leaked to the server if the user generates deterministic trapdoor. In order to overcome this seemingly contradictory situation, we introduce a new technique *trapdoor locked encryption technique*.

Trapdoor Locked Encryption Technique. For the above purposes, the user should send deterministic information of keywords to the server and trapdoors

Table 1. SSE-2 v.s. Tentative scheme

	SSE-2 [9]	Tentative scheme
Entry of encrypted index:	$(\kappa_j = F(K, w, j), id_j)$ $\Rightarrow$	$(\kappa_j = F(K, w, j), id_j)$
Trapdoor:	$t = F(K, w', j)$ $\Rightarrow$	$(t = F'(F(K, w', j), u), u)$
Search:	$t \overset{?}{=} \kappa_j$ $\Rightarrow$	$t \overset{?}{=} F'(\kappa_j, u)$

Table 2. SSE-2 v.s. Proposed scheme

	SSE-2 [9]		Proposed scheme
Entry of $\mathcal{I}$:	$(\kappa_j = F(K, w, j), id_j)$	$\Rightarrow$	$(\kappa_j = F(K, w, j), id_j)$
Trapdoor:	$(t = F(K, w', j))$	$\Rightarrow$	$(t = \mathtt{SKE.Enc}(F(K, w', j), F(K', w')\|r), r)$
Search:	$t \overset{?}{=} \kappa_j$	$\Rightarrow$	$X\|r' = \mathtt{SKE.Dec}(\kappa_j, t)$
			$r \overset{?}{=} r'$
Entry of $\mathcal{I}'$:	not available	$\Rightarrow$	$X = F(K', w')$
Re-Search:	not available	$\Rightarrow$	$F(K', w'') \overset{?}{=} X$

(Note that w, w' and w'' are keywords which are used in the document storing process, the searching process, and the re-searching process, respectively.)

should be probabilistic value to the third parties and the server when the keyword is searched for the first time. Then, we consider that trapdoors are generated probabilistically by *encrypting* deterministic information of the keyword using a symmetric key encryption (e.g., AES-CBC or AES-CTR). However, search patterns are leaked to the server if the sever can *always* decrypt trapdoors. We need to develop the method that the server can decrypt *only* when the trapdoor matches with some entry of the encrypted index $\mathcal{I}$ by using one component of a part of the entry of encrypted index $\mathcal{I}$ as the secret key of a symmetric key encryption.

In SSE-2, an entry of encrypted index is formed as $(F(K, w, j), id_j)$. Then, in our scheme, the user generates a ciphertext by using $\kappa_j = F(K, w, j)$ as the key of symmetric key encryption. If the trapdoor matches, the server can decrypt the trapdoor (ciphertext) correctly since the server has $\kappa_j = F(K, w, j)$. On the other hand, if the trapdoor does not match, the server cannot decrypt it and cannot obtain the deterministic information since the server does not have the key $\kappa_j = F(K, w, j)$.

The overview of proposed method is as follows. The user generates $t = \mathtt{SKE.Enc}(F(K, w', j), F(K', w')\|r)$ as the trapdoor where $\mathtt{SKE.Enc}$ is a symmetric key encryption algorithm and K' is a PRF key which is different from K, $F(K', w')$ is deterministic information for re-search and r is a l-bit randomness. This trapdoor matches if the low order l bits of the decryption result is equivalent to r. We call this technique "trapdoor locked encryption technique". The construction overview is described in Table 2.

1.4 Our Contributions

- This paper presents a reasonable and useful definition which covers reducing search pattern leakage and fast re-search. First, we define the syntax of our SSE scheme (see Sect. 3). In our concept, the server can obtain deterministic information from trapdoors and update the encrypted index $\mathcal{I}'$ from the information in order to re-search quickly. After that, the user can generate a deterministic trapdoor of keywords which have been already searched, and the server can quickly re-search by using it. We define `DetTrpdr` and `QuickSearch` as a deterministic trapdoor generation algorithm and a search algorithm by using deterministic trapdoors, respectively. Additionally, we propose a security definition, adaptive semantic security, which takes into account search pattern hiding (see Sect. 3.2).

– This paper proposes the first adaptive secure and search pattern hiding SSE scheme based on SSE-2 [9] (see Sect. 4.1). Security of our scheme is proved under the existence of PRFs in the standard model (see Sect. 4.2).

1.5 Related Works

There are SSE schemes closely related to our work [15,24]. Moataz and Shikfa proposed the SSE scheme which can generate trapdoors probabilistically [24]. Their trapdoor is expressed as a vector form, and all trapdoors obtained from the same keyword can be represented as scalar multiplications of some vector. Therefore, anyone can easily check whether given trapdoors contain the same keyword. That is, their scheme cannot reduce search pattern leakage. The SSE scheme providing a quick re-searching algorithm was also proposed by Hahn and Kerschbaum [15]. Their strategy for quick re-searching is similar to ours. However, the trapdoors of their scheme are generated deterministically (i.e. their search pattern of the scheme is leaked more than that of our proposed scheme), and no trapdoor locked encryption technique is used.

2 Preliminaries

Notations. We denote the set of positive real numbers by $\mathbb{R}^+$. We say that a function $\texttt{negl} : \mathbb{N} \rightarrow \mathbb{R}^+$ is negligible if for any (positive) polynomial p, there exists $n_0 \in \mathbb{N}$ such that for all $n \geq n_0$, it holds that $\texttt{negl}(n) < 1/p(n)$. We denote by $\texttt{poly}(n)$ unspecified polynomial in n. If A is a probabilistic algorithm, $y \leftarrow A(x)$ denotes running A on input x with a uniformly-chosen random tape and assigning the output to y. $A^{\mathcal{O}}$ denotes an algorithm with oracle access to $\mathcal{O}$. We denote the empty set by $\emptyset$. For an associative array $\mathcal{I}'$, its value for a key s is denoted by $\mathcal{I}'[s]$, and $\mathcal{I}'[s] \leftarrow x$ represents assignment of x to $\mathcal{I}'[s]$. We denote by $|S|$ the cardinality for a finite set S, and the bit length for a bit string S. If S is a finite set, $s \xleftarrow{u} S$ denotes that s is uniformly chosen from S. We denote a security parameter by λ throughout this paper.

Cryptographic Primitives. We recall the definition of pseudo-random functions (PRF). A function $f : \{0,1\}^\lambda \times \{0,1\}^m \rightarrow \{0,1\}^n$ is pseudo-random if f is polynomial-time computable in λ, and for any probabilistic polynomial-time (PPT) algorithm $\mathcal{A}$, it holds that

$$|\Pr[1 \leftarrow \mathcal{A}^{f(K,\cdot)}(1^\lambda) \mid K \xleftarrow{u} \{0,1\}^\lambda] - \Pr[1 \leftarrow \mathcal{A}^{g(\cdot)}(1^\lambda) \mid g \xleftarrow{u} \mathcal{F}_{m,n}]| \leq \texttt{negl}(\lambda),$$

where $\mathcal{F}_{m,n}$ is the set of functions mapping $\{0,1\}^m$ to $\{0,1\}^n$.

We recall the definition of *pseudo-randomness against the chosen plaintext attack* (PCPA) for a symmetric-key encryption scheme $SKE = (Gen, Enc, Dec)$. Let $\mathbf{PCPA}_{\mathcal{A}, SKE}(\lambda)$ be an experiment for an adversary $\mathcal{A}$ and SKE as follows:

1. A key K is generated by $SKE.Gen(1^\lambda)$.
2. $\mathcal{A}$ is given oracle access to $SKE.Enc(K, \cdot)$.
3. $\mathcal{A}$ outputs a message m.
4. Two ciphertexts c_0 and c_1 are generated as follows: $c_0 \leftarrow SKE.Enc(K, m)$ and $c_1 \xleftarrow{u} \mathcal{C}$, where $\mathcal{C}$ denotes the set of all possible ciphertexts. A random bit $b \xleftarrow{u} \{0, 1\}$ is chosen, and c_b is given to $\mathcal{A}$.
5. $\mathcal{A}$ is given oracle access to $SKE.Enc(K, \cdot)$, and outputs a bit $b' \in \{0, 1\}$.
6. The output of the experiment is 1 if $b' = b$, 0 otherwise.

We say that SKE is PCPA-secure if for any PPT adversary $\mathcal{A}$,

$$\left| \Pr[\mathbf{PCPA}_{\mathcal{A}, SKE}(\lambda) = 1] - \frac{1}{2} \right| \leq \mathtt{negl}(\lambda),$$

where the probability is taken over the random coins of Gen and Enc.

Document Collections. Let w be a keyword, and $\Delta \subseteq \{0, 1\}^\ell$ be a set of d keywords.

Let $D \in \{0, 1\}^*$ be a document (or file), and $\mathbf{D} = (D_1, \ldots, D_n)$ be a document collection. Let $\mathbf{C} = (C_1, \ldots, C_n)$ be a ciphertext collection of $\mathbf{D}$, where C_i is a ciphertext of D_i for $1 \leq i \leq n$. We assume that the ciphertext C_i contain a unique identifier (or file name) $id_i \in \{0, 1\}^\nu$. For $\mathbf{D} = (D_1, \ldots, D_n)$, let $\mathbf{D}(w)$ be a set of identifiers of documents that contain the keyword w. That is, $\mathbf{D}(w) = \{id_{i_1}, \ldots, id_{i_n}\}$.

3   Definitions

In this section, we define our new SSE scheme which has two keyword search algorithms. One is a search algorithm for a trapdoor generated *probabilistically*. The other is a search algorithm for a trapdoor generated *deterministically*.

The former algorithm can reduce the amount of the search pattern leakage. On the other hand, the latter algorithm using deterministically-generated trapdoors can reduce computational cost of a re-searching case when the user wants to search using a keyword which has already been searched. Furthermore, index updating algorithm is also provided in order to achieve the above quick re-searching.

3.1   Syntax

We now define new SSE scheme over a Δ, $SSE = (Gen, Enc, Trpdr, Search, Dec, Update, DetTrpdr, QuickSearch)$, which consists of the following algorithms:

- $K \leftarrow \text{Gen}(1^\lambda)$: is a probabilistic algorithm which generates a secret key K, where λ is a security parameter.
- $(\mathcal{I}, \mathbf{C}, \mathcal{I}') \leftarrow \text{Enc}(K, \mathbf{D})$: is a probabilistic algorithm which outputs two encrypted indexes $\mathcal{I}$ and $\mathcal{I}'$, and a ciphertext collection $\mathbf{C} = (C_1, \ldots, C_n)$.
- $t(w) \leftarrow \text{Trpdr}(K, w)$: is a *probabilistic* algorithm which outputs a *probabilistic* trapdoor $t(w)$ for a keyword w.
- $S(w) \leftarrow \text{Search}(\mathcal{I}, t(w))$: is a deterministic algorithm which outputs an identifier set $S(w)$.
- $D \leftarrow \text{Dec}(K, C)$: is a deterministic algorithm which outputs a plaintext D of C.
- $\mathcal{I}' \leftarrow \text{Update}(\mathcal{I}', \mathcal{I}, t(w))$: is a deterministic algorithm which outputs an updated encrypted index $\mathcal{I}'$.
- $T(w) \leftarrow \text{DetTrpdr}(K, w)$: is a deterministic algorithm which outputs a deterministic trapdoor $T(w)$ for a keyword w.
- $S(w) \leftarrow \text{QuickSearch}(\mathcal{I}', T(w))$: is a deterministic algorithm which outputs an identifier set $S(w)$.

Here, the SSE scheme is correct if for all $\lambda \in \mathbb{N}$, all $w \in \Delta$, all K output by $\text{Gen}(1^\lambda)$, all $\mathbf{D}$, and $(\mathcal{I}, \mathbf{C}, \mathcal{I}')$ output by $\text{Enc}(K, \mathbf{D})$, the following conditions hold: (i) $\text{Search}(\mathcal{I}, \text{Trpdr}(K, w)) = \mathbf{D}(w)$, and $\text{Dec}(K, C_i) = D_i$ ($1 \leq i \leq n$), (ii) $\text{QuickSearch}(\mathcal{I}', \text{DetTrpdr}(K, w)) = \mathbf{D}(w)$ if $\mathbf{D}(w)$ is not empty and $\text{Update}(\mathcal{I}', \mathcal{I}, \text{Trpdr}(K, w))$ has been run at least once so far, $\text{QuickSearch}(\mathcal{I}', \text{DetTrpdr}(K, w)) = \perp$ otherwise.

3.2   Security

We define *Adaptive Semantic Security under the Chosen Keyword Attack* as follows, based on [7]. In our SSE, since there are two trapdoor generation algorithms, Trpdr or DetTrpdr, we denote a query by (w, β) where $\beta \in \{0, 1\}$ is used to switch these trapdoor generation algorithms. Namely, a probabilistic trapdoor $t(w)$ is generated for a query $(w, 0)$ by Trpdr and is to be input to Search. In contrast, a deterministic trapdoor $T(w)$ is generated for a query $(w, 1)$ by DetTrpdr and is to be input to QuickSearch. We denote a query sequence whose length is q by $\mathbf{w}_q = ((w_1, \beta_1), \ldots, (w_q, \beta_q))$, and a set of trapdoors by $\mathcal{T}$.

Definition 1. *Let* SSE *be an SSE scheme, λ be a security parameter, and $\mathcal{L}_1, \mathcal{L}_2$ be leakage functions. For PPT algorithms $\mathcal{A} = (\mathcal{A}_0, \mathcal{A}_1, \ldots, \mathcal{A}_{q+1})$ with its state $st_{\mathcal{A}}$ and $\mathcal{S} = (\mathcal{S}_0, \mathcal{S}_1, \ldots, \mathcal{S}_q)$ with its state $st_{\mathcal{S}}$ such that $q = \text{poly}(\lambda)$, define the following games $\mathbf{Real}_{SSE,\mathcal{A}}^{adpt}(\lambda)$ and $\mathbf{Sim}_{SSE,\mathcal{A},\mathcal{S}}^{adpt}(\lambda)$.*

$\mathbf{Real}_{SSE,\mathcal{A}}^{adpt}(\lambda)$:

   $K \leftarrow \text{Gen}(1^\lambda)$
   $(\mathbf{D}, st_{\mathcal{A}}) \leftarrow \mathcal{A}_0(1^\lambda)$
   $(\mathcal{I}, \mathbf{C}, \mathcal{I}') \leftarrow \text{Enc}(K, \mathbf{D})$
   $\mathcal{T} \leftarrow \emptyset$
   for $1 \leq i \leq q$,

$(w_i, \beta_i, st_\mathcal{A}) \leftarrow \mathcal{A}_i(st_\mathcal{A}, \mathcal{I}, \mathbf{C}, \mathcal{I}', \mathcal{T})$

$if \ \beta_i = 0 \ then$

$t(w_i) \leftarrow \mathtt{Trpdr}(K, w_i) \ and \ \mathcal{T} \leftarrow \mathcal{T} \cup \{t(w_i)\}$

$else$

$T(w_i) \leftarrow \mathtt{DetTrpdr}(K, w_i) \ and \ \mathcal{T} \leftarrow \mathcal{T} \cup \{T(w_i)\}$

$b \leftarrow \mathcal{A}_{q+1}(st_\mathcal{A}, \mathcal{I}, \mathbf{C}, \mathcal{I}', \mathcal{T}), \ output \ b$

$\mathbf{Sim}^{\mathrm{adpt}}_{\mathrm{SSE},\mathcal{A},\mathcal{S}}(\lambda):$

$(\mathbf{D}, st_\mathcal{A}) \leftarrow \mathcal{A}_0(1^\lambda)$

$(\mathcal{I}, \mathbf{C}, \mathcal{I}', st_\mathcal{S}) \leftarrow \mathcal{S}_0(\mathcal{L}_1(\mathbf{D}))$

$\mathcal{T} \leftarrow \emptyset$

$for \ 1 \leq i \leq q,$

$(w_i, \beta_i, st_\mathcal{A}) \leftarrow \mathcal{A}_i(st_\mathcal{A}, \mathcal{I}, \mathbf{C}, \mathcal{I}', \mathcal{T})$

$if \ \beta_i = 0 \ then$

$(t(w_i), st_\mathcal{S}) \leftarrow \mathcal{S}_i(st_\mathcal{S}, \mathcal{L}_2(\mathbf{D}, \mathbf{w}_i)) \ and \ \mathcal{T} \leftarrow \mathcal{T} \cup \{t(w_i)\}$

$else$

$(T(w_i), st_\mathcal{S}) \leftarrow \mathcal{S}_i(st_\mathcal{S}, \mathcal{L}_2(\mathbf{D}, \mathbf{w}_i)) \ and \ \mathcal{T} \leftarrow \mathcal{T} \cup \{T(w_i)\}$

$b \leftarrow \mathcal{A}_{q+1}(st_\mathcal{A}, \mathcal{I}, \mathbf{C}, \mathcal{I}', \mathcal{T}), \ output \ b$

SSE *is secure in the sense of adaptive semantic security under the chosen keyword attacks if for any PPT adversary* $\mathcal{A}$, *there exists a PPT simulator* $\mathcal{S}$ *such that*

$$|Pr[\mathbf{Real}^{\mathrm{adpt}}_{\mathrm{SSE},\mathcal{A}}(\lambda) = 1] - Pr[\mathbf{Sim}^{\mathrm{adpt}}_{\mathrm{SSE},\mathcal{A},\mathcal{S}}(\lambda) = 1]| \leq \mathtt{negl}(\lambda).$$

4   Specific Construction

In this section, we firstly give a construction of our scheme based on SSE-2 proposed by Curtmola et al. [9]. Secondly, we define three *acceptable information leakage* functions H, α and σ in our construction. Finally, we prove that our construction is adaptive semantic secure for these leakage functions.

4.1   A Construction of Our Scheme

Here, we give our construction of SSE. In this construction, F is a pseudo-random function such that $F : \{0,1\}^\lambda \times \{0,1\}^* \rightarrow \{0,1\}^\mu$, SKE $=$ (Gen, Enc, Dec) is a PCPA-secure symmetric key encryption scheme, $\mathcal{I}'$ is a associative array and $n = |\mathbf{D}|$. We denote by id_j the j-th identifier in $\mathbf{D}$.

- Gen(1^λ): Sample $K_1, K_2 \overset{u}{\leftarrow} \{0,1\}^\lambda$, generate $K_3 \leftarrow$ SKE.Gen(1^λ), and output $K = (K_1, K_2, K_3)$.
- Enc($K, \mathbf{D}$): $\mathcal{I} \leftarrow \emptyset$
    for $1 \leq i \leq |\Delta|$ do
        for $1 \leq j \leq n$ do
            if $id_j \in \mathbf{D}(w_i)$ then
                $\mathcal{I} \leftarrow \mathcal{I} \cup \{(F(K_2, w_i, j), id_j)\}$

else
$$\mathcal{I} \leftarrow \mathcal{I} \cup \{(F(K_2, w_i, n+j), id_j)\}$$
$\mathbf{C} \leftarrow \emptyset$
for $1 \le i \le n$ **do**
     $\mathbf{C} \leftarrow \mathbf{C} \cup \{\text{SKE.Enc}(K_3, D_i)\}$
Set $\mathcal{I}'$ to empty associative array
return $(\mathcal{I}, \mathbf{C}, \mathcal{I}')$
– Trpdr(K, w):
$r \xleftarrow{u} \{0, 1\}^\lambda$
for $1 \le j \le n$ **do**
     $t_j(w) \leftarrow \text{SKE.Enc}(F(K_2, w, j), F(K_1, w) \parallel r)$
return $t(w) = (t_1(w), t_2(w), \ldots, t_n(w), r)$
– Search$(\mathcal{I}, t(w))$:
$S(w) \leftarrow \emptyset$
for $1 \le i \le n$ **do**
     for $\forall(\kappa_j, id_{i_j}) \in \mathcal{I}$ **do**
          $a \leftarrow \text{SKE.Dec}(\kappa_j, t_i(w))$, and parse a as $s \parallel r'$
          if $r = r'$ **then**
               $S(w) \leftarrow S(w) \cup \{id_{i_j}\}$
return $S(w)$
– Dec(K, C): **return** $D \leftarrow \text{SKE.Dec}(K_3, C)$
– Update$(\mathcal{I}', \mathcal{I}, t(w))$:
if Search$(\mathcal{I}, t(w)) \ne \emptyset$ **then**
     retrieve s such that $r = r'$ from $t(w)$ in the same manner as Search
     $\mathcal{I}'[s] \leftarrow \text{Search}(\mathcal{I}, t(w))$
return $\mathcal{I}'$
– DetTrpdr(K, w): **return** $T(w) \leftarrow F(K_1, w)$
– QuickSearch$(\mathcal{I}', T(w))$: **return** $\mathcal{I}'[T(w)]$

4.2 Security

In this section, let us discuss *acceptable information leakage* $\mathcal{L}_1$ and $\mathcal{L}_2$ of our SSE, in order to formalize security of our SSE. First, we define the leakage functions H, α and σ that the server can obtain from $(\mathcal{I}, \mathbf{C}, \mathcal{I}', \mathcal{T})$ in our SSE. H, α and σ represent history, access pattern and search pattern, respectively as the security definition of Curtmola et al. [9]. The most important difference between our SSE and ordinary SSE is the probabilistic generation of trapdoors. By using probabilistic trapdoors, we can reduce the leakage of the search pattern σ in the case where $\mathbf{D}(w) = \emptyset$ in contrast to a ordinary SSE which always leaks the search pattern.

– If a ciphertext C_i of a document D_i is stored in the server, then the server can easily infer the bit length $|D_i|$, and thereby $|D_1|, \ldots, |D_n|$ are always leaked in SSE. Let $H(\mathbf{D}) = (|D_1|, \ldots, |D_n|)$.
– For a probabilistic trapdoor $t(w)$, the server can easily obtain the search result of $t(w)$, i.e. the set of identifiers $\mathbf{D}(w)$. On the other hand, for a deterministic

trapdoor $T(w)$, the search result will be $\mathbf{D}(w)$ or $\perp$. If $\mathbf{D}(w) \neq \emptyset$ and a probabilistic trapdoor $t(w)$ has been used at least once before searching with $T(w)$, $\mathcal{I}'$ is updated by running Update. The search result with $T(w)$ will be $\mathbf{D}(w)$ then. Otherwise, the search result of $T(w)$ is $\perp$ since updating $\mathcal{I}'$ has never occurred. Then, let $\alpha(\mathbf{D}, \mathbf{w}_k)$ be a function as follows:

$$\alpha(\mathbf{D}, \mathbf{w}_k) = \begin{cases} \mathbf{D}(w_k) & \text{if } (\beta_k = 0) \vee ((\mathbf{D}(w_k) \neq \emptyset) \wedge ((w_k, 0) \in \mathbf{w}_k)), \\ \perp & \text{otherwise.} \end{cases}$$

- As ordinary SSE whose trapdoors are generated deterministically, the server immediately infer whether the i-th query $(w_i, 1)$ and the j-th query $(w_j, 1)$ are the same or not by checking $T(w_i) = T(w_j)$. On the other hand, for probabilistic trapdoors $t(w_i)$ and $t(w_j)$, it is hard for the server to decide whether $w_i =, w_j$ from $t(w_i) = t(w_j)$. However, the server can decide it when $\mathbf{D}(w_i) \neq \emptyset$ and $\mathbf{D}(w_j) \neq \emptyset$ in our SSE, since a combination of entries that a query w matches in an encrypted index $\mathcal{I}$ is unique to w unless $\mathbf{D}(w) = \emptyset$. Furthermore, for queries $(w_i, \beta_i), (w_j, \beta_j)$ such that $(\beta_i = 0$ or $\beta_j = 0)$ and $\mathbf{D}(w_i) = \mathbf{D}(w_j) = \emptyset$, it is hard for the server to decide $w_i = w_j$ because no information which is effective to infer whether $w_i = w_j$ is disclosed. Therefore, for k queries $(w_1, \beta_1), \ldots, (w_k, \beta_k)$, the following binary matrix H_k is always leaked in our SSE. For $1 \leq i < j \leq k$, the element in the i-th row and the j-th column, $H_k[i, j]$, is defined as below:

$$H_k[i,j] = \begin{cases} 1 & \text{if } ((\beta_i = \beta_j = 1) \vee (\mathbf{D}(w_i) \neq \emptyset \vee \mathbf{D}(w_j) \neq \emptyset)) \wedge (w_i = w_j), \\ 0 & \text{if } ((\beta_i = \beta_j = 1) \vee (\mathbf{D}(w_i) \neq \emptyset \vee \mathbf{D}(w_j) \neq \emptyset)) \wedge (w_i \neq w_j), \\ \perp & \text{if } (\beta_i = 0 \vee \beta_j = 0) \wedge (\mathbf{D}(w_i) = \mathbf{D}(w_j) = \emptyset), \end{cases}$$

Let $\sigma(\mathbf{D}, \mathbf{w}_k) = (H_k, \beta_1, \ldots, \beta_k)$, where $\mathbf{w}_k = ((w_1, \beta_1), \ldots, (w_k, \beta_k))$.

We now have the following theorem for the leakage $\mathcal{L}_1(\mathbf{D}) = H(\mathbf{D})$ and $\mathcal{L}_2(\mathbf{D}, \mathbf{w}) = (\alpha(\mathbf{D}, \mathbf{w}), \sigma(\mathbf{D}, \mathbf{w}))$.

Theorem 1. *If $F : \{0,1\}^\lambda \times \{0,1\}^* \to \{0,1\}^\mu$ is a pseudo-random function and SKE is PCPA-secure symmetric key encryption scheme, our scheme is adaptive semantic secure for the above leakage $(\mathcal{L}_1, \mathcal{L}_2)$.*

Proof. We construct a PPT simulator $\mathcal{S} = (\mathcal{S}_0, \mathcal{S}_1, \ldots, \mathcal{S}_q)$ such that for any PPT-adversary $\mathcal{A} = (\mathcal{A}_0, \mathcal{A}_1, \ldots, \mathcal{A}_{q+1})$, the outputs of $\mathbf{Real}_{\text{SSE}, \mathcal{A}}^{\text{adpt}}(\lambda)$ and $\mathbf{Sim}_{\text{SSE}, \mathcal{A}, \mathcal{S}}^{\text{adpt}}(\lambda)$ are computationally indistinguishable.

Firstly, we construct $\mathcal{S} = \{\mathcal{S}_0, \mathcal{S}_1, \ldots, \mathcal{S}_q\}$ as follows.

- $\mathcal{S}_0(\mathcal{L}_1(\mathbf{D}))$: Generate $\mathcal{I}^*$, $\mathbf{C}^* = \{C_1^*, C_2^*, \ldots, C_n^*\}$ and $\mathcal{I}'^*$ from $\mathcal{L}_1(\mathbf{D}) = H(\mathbf{D})$ as follows:
  - Set $\mathcal{I}^* \leftarrow \emptyset$.
    For $1 \leq i \leq |\Delta|, 1 \leq j \leq n$:
    * Generate $\kappa_{i,j}^* \xleftarrow{u} \{0,1\}^\mu$

* Set $\mathcal{I}^* \leftarrow \mathcal{I}^* \cup \{(\kappa_{i,j}^*, id_j)\}$.
- Generate $C_i^* \xleftarrow{u} \{0,1\}^{|D_i|}$ $(1 \leq i \leq n)$, and set $\mathbf{C}^* = (C_1^*, \ldots, C_n^*)$.
- Set $\mathcal{I}'^* \leftarrow \emptyset$ and $st_S \leftarrow \mathcal{I}^*$.
- Output $(\mathcal{I}^*, \mathbf{C}^*, \mathcal{I}'^*, st_S)$.

$- \mathcal{S}_i(st_S, \mathcal{L}_2(\mathbf{D}, \mathbf{w}_i))$: Generate $t^*(w_i) = (t_1^*(w_i), \ldots, t_n^*(w_i), r_i)$ or $T^*(w)$ from $\mathcal{L}_2(\mathbf{D}, \mathbf{w}_i) = (\alpha(\mathbf{D}, \mathbf{w}_i), \sigma(\mathbf{D}, \mathbf{w}_i))$ as follows:

1. Firstly, $\mathcal{S}_i$ checks if w_j such that $w_j = w_i$ $(j < i)$ exists using $\sigma(\mathbf{D}, \mathbf{w}_i)$. Namely, $\mathcal{S}_i$ tries to find w_j such that $H_i[j,i] = 1$ ($\mathcal{S}_i$ ignores a case that $H_i[j,i] = \perp$).

2. If such w_j does not exist:
   (a) Pick $\delta_i \xleftarrow{u} \{0,1\}^\mu$.
   (b) If $\beta_i = 0$, $\mathcal{S}_i$ chooses $n_i = |\alpha(\mathbf{D}, \mathbf{w}_i)|$ entries $\{(\kappa_{i,k}^*, id_{i_k})\}_{k=1,\ldots,n_i} \subseteq \mathcal{I}^*$ for all elements $id_{i_k} \in \alpha(\mathbf{D}, \mathbf{w}_i)$, where $\kappa_{i,k}^*$ have never chosen by $\mathcal{S}_{i'}$ $(i' < i)$. $\mathcal{S}_i$ picks $r_i \xleftarrow{u} \{0,1\}^\lambda$ and sets $t_k^*(w_i) \leftarrow$ $\mathsf{SKE.Enc}(\kappa_{i,k}^*, \delta_i \| r_i)$. Additionally, $\mathcal{S}_i$ sets $t_k^*(w_i) \xleftarrow{u} \{0,1\}^{\mu+\lambda}$ for $n_i + 1 \leq k \leq n$. Finally, $\mathcal{S}_i$ outputs $t^*(w_i)$ and $st_S \leftarrow st_S \cup (i, \delta_i, \kappa_{i,1}^*, \ldots, \kappa_{i,n_i}^*)$.
   (c) If $\beta_i = 1$, $\mathcal{S}_i$ outputs $T^*(w_i) \leftarrow \delta_i$ and $st_S \leftarrow st_S \cup (i, \delta_i)$.

3. Otherwise:
   (a) In the case of $\beta_i = 0$, if (w_i, β_i) is the first query such that $\beta_i = 0$, $\kappa_{j,k}^*$ has not created in st_S yet. In such case, $\mathcal{S}_i$ chooses them from $\mathcal{I}^*$ in the same manner as the case 2-(b) above, and complements the entry by the $\kappa_{j,k}^*$. $\mathcal{S}_i$ now has the retrieved δ_j and $\kappa_{j,k}^*$ in st_S, then $\mathcal{S}_i$ picks $r_i \xleftarrow{u} \{0,1\}^\lambda$ and computes $t_k^*(w_i)$ for $1 \leq k \leq n$ as mentioned in the case 2-(b). Finally, $\mathcal{S}_i$ outputs $t^*(w_i)$ and st_S.
   (b) If $\beta_i = 1$, $\mathcal{S}_i$ outputs $T^*(w_i) \leftarrow \delta_j$ and st_S since $\mathcal{S}_i$ can retrieve it from st_S.

Let us analyze each output of $\mathcal{S}_i$ for $0 \leq i \leq q$. We denote the set of the trapdoor which is output of $\mathcal{S}_i$ by T^*. Firstly, we show that Search, Update and $\mathsf{QuickSearch}$ on $(\mathcal{I}^*, \mathbf{C}^*, \mathcal{I}', T^*)$ behave in the same way as these on $(\mathcal{I}, \mathbf{C}, \mathcal{I}', T)$ do. After that, we show that each component of $(\mathcal{I}^*, \mathbf{C}^*, T^*)$ is computationally indistinguishable from the corresponding component of $(\mathcal{I}, \mathbf{C}, T)$.

We consider queries (w_i, β_i) and (w_j, β_j) such that $j < i$. In the case of $\not\exists w_j$ such that $H_i[j,i] = 1$, namely $((\beta_j = 0 \vee \beta_i = 0) \wedge \mathbf{D}(w_j) = \mathbf{D}(w_i) = \emptyset) \vee (w_j \neq w_i)$ for $\forall j < i$, we have the following facts:

- If $\beta_i = 0$ and $\mathbf{D}(w_i) = \emptyset$: Since $\mathcal{S}_i$ sets $t_k^*(w_i) \xleftarrow{u} \{0,1\}^{\mu+\lambda}$, all $t_k^*(w_i)$ will not match any entry in $\mathcal{I}^*$ with all but negligible probability. Therefore, Search just outputs $S(w_i) = \emptyset$, and Update does nothing.
- If $\beta_i = 0$ and $\mathbf{D}(w_i) \neq \emptyset$: Since $\mathcal{S}_i$ sets $t_k^*(w_i) \leftarrow \mathsf{SKE.Enc}(\kappa_{i,k}^*, \delta_i \| r_i)$ to match the entries associated with $id_{i_k} \in \mathbf{D}(w_i)$ by choosing $\kappa_{i,k}^*$ and generating δ_i that have never appeared previously, $t^*(w_i)$ matches the entries that are distinct from the entries any past trapdoor has matched with all but negligible probability. Therefore, Search outputs $S(w_i) = \mathbf{D}(w_i)$ and Update sets the entry $\mathcal{I}'[\delta_i] \leftarrow \mathbf{D}(w_i)$.

- If $\beta_i = 1$: Since $\mathcal{S}_i$ generates $\delta_i \xleftarrow{u} \{0,1\}^\mu$ and sets $T^*(w_i) \leftarrow \delta_i$, QuickSearch outputs $\perp$ with all but negligible probability. Note that QuickSearch outputs $\perp$ even if $\mathbf{D}(w_i) \neq \emptyset$ in real side since we have $w_j \neq w_i$ for $\forall j < i$ in this case, namely Update for w_i has never run so far.

Subsequently, we consider the other case, $\exists w_j$ such that $H_i[j,i] = 1$, namely $((\beta_j = \beta_i = 1) \vee (\mathbf{D}(w_j) \neq \emptyset \vee \mathbf{D}(w_i) \neq \emptyset)) \wedge (w_j = w_i)$ for $\exists j < i$:

- If $\beta_i = 0$ and $\mathbf{D}(w_i) = \emptyset$: As is the previous case $\beta_i = 0$ and $\mathbf{D}(w_i) = \emptyset$, Search just outputs $S(w_i) = \emptyset$, and Update does nothing.
- If $\beta_i = 0$ and $\mathbf{D}(w_i) \neq \emptyset$: Since $\mathcal{S}_i$ can retrieve $\kappa^*_{j,k}$ and δ_j which are previously used from $st_\mathcal{S}$, Search and Update run in the same way as these for $t^*(w_j)$.
- If $\beta_i = 1$: Since $\mathcal{S}_i$ can retrieve δ_j from $st_\mathcal{S}$ and set $T^*(w_i) \leftarrow \delta_j$, QuickSearch run in the same way as it for $T^*(w_j)$.

We now show that $(\mathcal{I}, \mathbf{C}, \mathcal{T})$ and $(\mathcal{I}^*, \mathbf{C}^*, \mathcal{T}^*)$ are computationally indistinguishable for any PPT adversary $\mathcal{A}$.

- $\mathcal{I}$ and $\mathcal{I}^*$: Since all the elements $\kappa_{i,k}$ in $\mathcal{I}$ are outputs of PRF F and $\mathcal{A}$ does not have K_2 with all but negligible probability, any $\mathcal{A}$ cannot distinguish κ and a random string whose length is μ. Therefore, $\mathcal{I}^*$ is indistinguishable from $\mathcal{I}$.
- $\mathbf{C}$ and $\mathbf{C}^*$: Since all the elements $C_i \in \mathbf{C}$ are ciphertexts of the PCPA-secure scheme SKE and $\mathcal{A}$ does not have K_3 with all but negligible probability, any $\mathcal{A}$ cannot distinguish C_i and a random string whose length is $|D_i|$. Therefore, $\mathbf{C}^*$ is indistinguishable from $\mathbf{C}$.
- $\mathcal{T}$ and $\mathcal{T}^*$:
  - $t(w_i)$ and $t^*(w_i)$: Since all the elements $t_k(w_i)$ such that $n_i + 1 \leq k \leq n$ are ciphertexts of the PCPA-secure scheme SKE and $\mathcal{A}$ does not have $\kappa_{i,k}$ with all but negligible probability, any $\mathcal{A}$ cannot distinguish $t_k(w_i)$ and a random string whose length is $\mu + \lambda$. For all the elements $t_k(w_i)$ such that $1 \leq k \leq n_i$, $\mathcal{A}$ can obtain the δ_i and a random string r_i as its decryption result with key $\kappa_{i,k} \in \mathcal{I}$. Since δ_i are outputs of F and $\mathcal{A}$ does not have K_1 with all but negligible probability, any $\mathcal{A}$ cannot distinguish $\delta_i \| r_i$ and a random string whose length is $\mu + \lambda$. Therefore, $t^*(w_i)$ is indistinguishable from $t(w_i)$.
  - $T(w_i)$ and $T^*(w_i)$: For all the elements $T(w_i)$ are outputs of F and $\mathcal{A}$ does not have K_1 with all but negligible probability, any $\mathcal{A}$ cannot distinguish $T(w_i)$ and a random string whose length is μ. Therefore, $T^*(w_i)$ is indistinguishable from $T(w_i)$. □

5 Conclusion

In this paper, we focused on the information, search pattern, leaked from trapdoors in ordinary SSE, and pointed out that the amount of the search pattern can be reduced if a trapdoor is not matched any entry of an encrypted index.

We formalized the security definition of SSE which can generate trapdoors probabilistically. Then, we proposed the SSE scheme which can reduce computational cost in the re-searching case where the same keyword is searched again, and showed that our scheme is secure in the sense of the security definition in the standard model.

References

1. Asharov, G., Naor, M., Segev, G., Shahaf, I.: Searchable symmetric encryption: Optimal locality in linear space via two-dimensional balanced allocations. STOC **2016**, 1101–1114 (2016)
2. Boldyreva, A., Chenette, N.: Efficient fuzzy search on encrypted data. In: Cid, C., Rechberger, C. (eds.) FSE 2014. LNCS, vol. 8540, pp. 613–633. Springer, Heidelberg (2015)
3. Cash, D., Jaeger, J., Jarecki, S., Jutla, C., Krawczyk, H., Roşu, M., Steiner, M.: Dynamic searchable encryption in very-large databases: data structures and implementation. In: NDSS 2014 (2014)
4. Cash, D., Jarecki, S., Jutla, C., Krawczyk, H., Roşu, M.-C., Steiner, M.: Highly-scalable searchable symmetric encryption with support for Boolean queries. In: Canetti, R., Garay, J.A. (eds.) CRYPTO 2013, Part I. LNCS, vol. 8042, pp. 353–373. Springer, Heidelberg (2013)
5. Cash, D., Tessaro, S.: The locality of searchable symmetric encryption. In: Nguyen, P.Q., Oswald, E. (eds.) EUROCRYPT 2014. LNCS, vol. 8441, pp. 351–368. Springer, Heidelberg (2014)
6. Chang, Y.-C., Mitzenmacher, M.: Privacy preserving keyword searches on remote encrypted data. In: Ioannidis, J., Keromytis, A.D., Yung, M. (eds.) ACNS 2005. LNCS, vol. 3531, pp. 442–455. Springer, Heidelberg (2005)
7. Chase, M., Kamara, S.: Structured encryption and controlled disclosure. In: Abe, M. (ed.) ASIACRYPT 2010. LNCS, vol. 6477, pp. 577–594. Springer, Heidelberg (2010)
8. Chase, M., Shen, E.: Substring-searchable symmetric encryption. In: PETS 2015, vol. 2015(2), pp. 263–281 (2015)
9. Curtmola, R., Garay, J., Kamara, S., Ostrovsky, R.: Searchable symmetric encryption: improved definitions and efficient constructions. ACM CCS **2006**, 79–88 (2006)
10. Curtmola, R., Garay, J., Kamara, S., Ostrovsky, R.: Searchable symmetric encryption: improved definitions and efficient constructions. J. Comput. Secur. **19**(5), 895–934 (2011)
11. Dong, C., Russello, G., Dulay, N.: Shared and searchable encrypted data for untrusted servers. J. Comput. Secur. **19**(3), 367–397 (2011)
12. Faber, S., Jarecki, S., Krawczyk, H., Nguyen, Q., Rosu, M., Steiner, M.: Rich queries on encrypted data: beyond exact matches. In: Pernul, G., Ryan, P.Y.A., Weippl, E. (eds.) ESORICS 2015. LNCS, vol. 9327, pp. 123–145. Springer, Heidelberg (2015). doi:10.1007/978-3-319-24177-7_7
13. Goh, E.J.: Secure indexes. Cryptology ePrint Archive, Report 2003/216 (2003). http://eprint.iacr.org/2003/216
14. Goldreich, O., Ostrovsky, R.: Software protection and simulation on oblivious RAMs. J. ACM **43**(3), 431–473 (1996)

15. Hahn, F., Kerschbaum, F.: Searchable encryption with secure and efficient updates. ACM CCS **2014**, 310–320 (2014)
16. Kamara, S., Papamanthou, C., Roeder, T.: Dynamic searchable symmetric encryption. ACM CCS **2012**, 965–976 (2012)
17. Kamara, S., Papamanthou, C.: Parallel and dynamic searchable symmetric encryption. In: Sadeghi, A.-R. (ed.) FC 2013. LNCS, vol. 7859, pp. 258–274. Springer, Heidelberg (2013)
18. Kurosawa, K.: Garbled searchable symmetric encryption. In: Christin, N., Safavi-Naini, R. (eds.) FC 2014. LNCS, vol. 8437, pp. 232–249. Springer, Heidelberg (2014)
19. Kurosawa, K., Ohtaki, Y.: UC-secure searchable symmetric encryption. In: Keromytis, A.D. (ed.) FC 2012. LNCS, vol. 7397, pp. 285–298. Springer, Heidelberg (2012)
20. Kurosawa, K., Ohtaki, Y.: How to update documents *Verifiably* in searchable symmetric encryption. In: Abdalla, M., Nita-Rotaru, C., Dahab, R. (eds.) CANS 2013. LNCS, vol. 8257, pp. 309–328. Springer, Heidelberg (2013)
21. Kuzu, M., Islam, M.S., Kantarcioglu, M.: Efficient similarity search over encrypted data. IEEE ICDE **2012**, 1156–1167 (2012)
22. Li, J., Wang, Q., Wang, C., Cao, N., Ren, K., Lou, W.: Fuzzy keyword search over encrypted data in cloud computing. In: IEEE INFOCOM 2010 (Mini-Conference), pp. 1–5 (2010)
23. van Liesdonk, P., Sedghi, S., Doumen, J., Hartel, P., Jonker, W.: Computationally efficient searchable symmetric encryption. In: Jonker, W., Petković, M. (eds.) SDM 2010. LNCS, vol. 6358, pp. 87–100. Springer, Heidelberg (2010)
24. Moataz, T., Shikfa, A.: Boolean symmetric searchable encryption. ASIACCS **2013**, 265–276 (2013)
25. Naveed, M., Prabhakaran, M., Gunter, C.A.: Dynamic searchable encryption via blind storage. In: IEEE S&P 2014, pp. 639–654 (2014)
26. Ogata, W., Koiwa, K., Kanaoka, A., Matsuo, S.: Toward practical searchable symmetric encryption. In: Sakiyama, K., Terada, M. (eds.) IWSEC 2013. LNCS, vol. 8231, pp. 151–167. Springer, Heidelberg (2013)
27. Ostrovsky, R.: Efficient computation on oblivious rams. STOC 1990, 514–523 (1990)
28. Song, D., Wagner, D., Perrig, A.: Practical techniques for searching on encrypted data. In: IEEE S&P 2000, pp. 44–55 (2000)
29. Stefanov, E., Papamanthou, C., Shi, E.: Practical dynamic searchable encryption with small leakage. In: NDSS 2014 (2014)
30. Taketani, S., Ogata, W.: Improvement of UC secure searchable symmetric encryption scheme. In: Tanaka, K., Suga, Y. (eds.) IWSEC 2015. LNCS, vol. 9241, pp. 135–152. Springer, Heidelberg (2015)
31. Wang, C., Ren, K., Yu, S., Urs, K.M.R.: Achieving usable and privacy-assured similarity search over outsourced cloud data. IEEE INFOCOM **2012**, 451–459 (2012)
32. Yang, Y.J., Ding, X.H., Deng, R.H., Bao, F.: Multi-user private queries over encrypted databases. Intl. J. Appl. Cryptography **1**(4), 309–319 (2009)
33. Yavuz, A.A., Guajardo, J.: Dynamic searchable symmetric encryption with minimal leakage and efficient updates on commodity hardware. In: Dunkelman, O., Keliher, L. (eds.) SAC 2015. LNCS, vol. 9566, pp. 241–259. Springer, Heidelberg (2015)

System Security

AAL and Static Conflict Detection in Policy

Jean-Claude Royer[1]([☒]) and Anderson Santana De Oliveira[2]

[1] Mines Nantes, 4 rue A. Kastler, 44307 Nantes, France
Jean-Claude.Royer@mines-nantes.fr
[2] SAP Labs France, 805 Avenue du Dr Donat Font de l'Orme, 06250 Mougins,
Sophia Antipolis, France
anderson.santana.de.oliveira@sap.com

Abstract. Security and privacy requirements in ubiquitous systems
need a sophisticated policy language with features to express access
restrictions and obligations. Ubiquitous systems involve multiple actors
owning sensitive data concerning aspects such as location, discrete and
continuous time, multiple roles that can be shared among actors or evolve
over time. Policy consistency is an important problem in languages supporting these aspects. In this paper we present an abstract language
(AAL) to specify most of these security and privacy features and compare
it with XACML. We also classified the existing conflict detection mechanisms for XACML in dynamic, testing, or static detection. A thorough
analysis of these mechanisms reveals that they have several weaknesses
and they are not applicable in our context. We advocate for a classic
approach using the notion of logical consistency to detect conflicts in
AAL.

1 Introduction

Security and privacy requirements demand sophisticated policy language features to express access restrictions and obligations meaningfully. Ubiquitous
computing applications involve multiple actors often handling sensitive data (*e.g.*
Health Care data), in distributed networks. These applications deal with aspects
such as location, discrete and continuous time, where the roles of the subjects
accessing data evolve. Along the paper, we present multiple examples involving this kind of constraints. Former approaches to security and privacy policies
would hardly address the needs in diverse new scenarios brought by the internet
of things, cloud computing, and mobile devices we are already facing today.

Research has shown that it is difficult to find the balance between expressiveness and enforceability (see [1,2,16,20] to cite a few): the more expressive the
policy language is; the more room for writing inconsistent and conflicting policies is. The designers of the XACML standard adopted a straightforward option
to address conflicts. They are solved at runtime by the policy decision point
(PDP) who applies a disambiguation pattern defined in the policy (for instance,
deny-overrides, permit-overrides, first applicable, and so on). This makes it hard
to understand the behavior of the policy at design time. Moreover, the language

© Springer International Publishing AG 2016
S. Foresti and G. Persiano (Eds.): CANS 2016, LNCS 10052, pp. 367–382, 2016.
DOI: 10.1007/978-3-319-48965-0_22

has some limitations making it cumbersome to address the requirements raised by ubiquitous applications.

In this paper, we present a static conflict detection approach for the Abstract Accountability Language (AAL) for declarative policies (introduced in [3]). It is a formal language based on first-order and linear temporal logic with types and signatures. It has features allowing for expressing usage control rules, roles, delegation and obligations. Our approach also allows us to check whether policies are compliant with respect to standards or regulations provided in AAL. The major contributions we present here are: *(i)* an expressive and flexible language for addressing various privacy and security concerns, *(ii)* a thorough review of related work supporting the XACML standard on policy inconsistency and conflict resolution, and evidences of their weaknesses, *(iii)* a practical policy verification approach at design time for AAL, and experimental results with scalable performance using a state of the art theorem prover. The remainder of the paper is structured as follows. The related work section classifies the conflict detection in dynamic, testing, or static solutions. The third section is devoted to a presentation of our language with examples addressing various needs for security and privacy. Section 4 discusses the different approaches for conflict detection and illustrates their weaknesses. Section 5 advocates for the use of a SAT solver or a prover and shows its effectiveness with AAL. Finally, the conclusion summarizes our work.

2   Related Work

We comment here only recent references which are dedicated to conflict detection and the XACML standard and mainly published in the last 10 years. We roughly classify these approaches in dynamic, testing or static conflict detection. We are not interested in errors thus we focus on correct rules and policies without the indeterminate value. Furthermore, we will only focus on the conclusions: action is permitted or denied, or some obligations. Thus discarding the not applicable case. Note that in AAL these behaviours can be embedded with additional rules but it does not change the way to detect conflicts. XACML provides two structures for the rule level and the policy level. Some work captures this distinction but others do not and consider that all are sort of rules with combining algorithms. These are assumptions we will use to simplify and to more easily compare with other approaches.

Dynamic Detection. Some approaches suggest a dynamic detection, that is each request is evaluated at runtime and conflicts are detected and resolved.

XACML is a standardized XML language for attribute-based access control policies [17]. XACML specifications are collections of policies, themselves being collections of rules. A rule in XACML matches incoming access requests against conditions expressed using attributes values. A rule will produce then an access decision, among the following possible values *permit, deny, or not-applicable*, the latter is the output generated by the Policy Decision Point (PDP) when the request is not matched by any rule in the policy. On the other hand, more than one rule can apply to the same request within the same policy. Similarly, distinct policies may also overlap, producing potentially contradicting decisions. In order to solve conflicts, the XACML standard introduces *combining algorithms* for rules and polices such as: *permit-overrides*, *deny-overrides*, *first-applicable*. The standard allows for the definition of custom algorithms. The semantics of these algorithms are straightforward given their names.

The authors of [16] consider access control policies with hierarchy of concepts and define an algorithm for dynamic conflict detection. The exact rule language is not described and it is not also clear which part of XACML is covered by this analysis. [7] analyzes the principle of combining algorithm in XACML and argues that "strategy that combines all these policies into a single super policy may not work for all situations". They propose a resolution mechanism with an algorithm choosing the combining rule dynamically. The fundamental problem of this proposal is that there is no algorithm which can always guess what is the good answer in case of conflicts.

Testing Detection. In this case the method is to generate a set of requests and to test if a conflict occurs using the request evaluation process. [12] focuses on multiple-duty and conflicts in access control rules. This work generates a finite set of requests and check for their consistency. [9] focuses on anomalies detection in web policies using XACML. The technique uses two levels of partition (rules and requests) and consider the entire request space of a rule. They do not consider obligations and discrete time.

Static Detection. In the static approaches various means are used to identify conflict situations but they do not rely on a requests generation.

The work from [11] proposes a translation of XACML into formal models on which Boolean satisfiability is possible. The purpose is mainly to do general verification not static detection of conflict, but it seems straightforward to add this kind of checking. The authors identifies some limitations due to the use of the bounded SAT technique. [1] analyzes some access control models. It proposes an access control model with permission and prohibition, first-order conditions, dynamic groups, and a type system which ensures the absence of conflict. The model does allow neither obligation nor temporal logic. [20] recognizes the importance of static conflict detection and argues for a new method more efficient than logical approaches. The authors propose to reuse an algorithm from machine learning. The base language supports access control and delegation but neither temporal logic nor obligation. [22] states the "inadequacy of conflict resolution mechanism" and explains that the complexity of the mechanism comes from historical and legacy reasons. This work uses a more abstract and non technical language and a writing method based on more complex conditions to group several rules into a single one. [25] argues for a static conflict detection and identifies two kinds of conflicts: authorizations and resource conditions. The approach uses model-checking in a context with hierarchical resources. However, the proposed approach is rather limited: no obligation, no hierarchy on roles, and no linear time. [2] proposes an SMT approach to check for conflicts. The interesting thing is that it locates the pair of rules which are conflicting but it assumes that rules are only authorizations with conjunction of atoms. The approach in [5] is not directly related to XACML but it is a good example of a static conflict detection approach. The context is rather privacy and exchange information than access control but the principle can apply to access control policies. They propose a simple algorithm to detect conflicts between pairs of rules. [23] proposes a verification detection approach based on an SMT tool support. Other verification approaches are mainly Boolean based, but numeric and string theories are important in actual policies. This work focuses on subsumption (refinement or compliance), it does not explicitly consider conflict detection between rules. The authors do not tackle obligation and linear time, this should make the approach really more complex to apply. [21] exposes the critical importance of the static conflict detection and defines an algorithm for that. The main novelty is the proof of the algorithm processed thanks to the Coq prover. This work considers a subset of XACML, mainly focusing on continuous time constraints, but without obligation and temporal logic. Our language (AAL [3]) allows access control but also obligations. It is a typed language which enables hierarchies for resources, subjects, roles, actions, with continuous and discrete linear time. We advocate for a static detection approach reusing logical satisfiability.

3 Usage Control Policies in AAL

AAL, for Abstract Accountability Language, is devoted to accountability but as such it covers classic security and privacy concepts. The accountability feature is described in [3] we focus here on the security and privacy part which is called *usage expression* in AAL. From the point of view of conflict detection there is no difference between usage expression and accountability. Generally rules for access control need a subject, an object and an action. But often roles for subjects are required and also some parameters for the various attributes as well as complex conditions ("if the data is owned by Kim then KardioMon is allowed to transfer it to Croatia but only during working days and a notification will be sent to the data subject".) Thus having a flexible language is an important requirement if we do not address a specific, well-delimited domain.

We show with few examples how AAL addresses access control, privacy concerns, delegation and other features. For a more detailed presentation of the syntax and the semantics the reader can see [3]. The semantics rely on the translation into FOTL (First-Order Linear Temporal Logic) and the decision for satisfiability uses the TSPASS prover [15]. The main motivation to use a logical prover is that we are at an abstract level which is easier to link with end-users obligations. Using a model-checker forces us to define a more operational behaviour for the agents and we need a more flexible support for data and agent quantifiers.

3.1   Security and Privacy Concepts

We illustrate some security and privacy constructions and thanks to the flexibility of AAL (predicates are uninterpreted) many kinds of them can be defined. An obligation is identified with an action in this paper. Note that FOTL does not support theories for integer, real, string and so on, contrary to SMT approaches. Our prototype implementation[1] offers dedicated translation for duration, for instance, but generally the specifier has to express this kind of knowledge as a composition of predicates. There is no specific construction for confidentiality, integrity or availability, most of these features should be manually specified.

Authorizations and Obligations. The AAL language allows to express permissions and prohibitions with PERMIT and DENY keywords. A prohibition is the negation of a permission. Expression in Listing 1.1 means that for all data if Kim (a patient) is the owner, then the Hospital (an agent, for example a cloud provider) is not allowed to process the data.

Listing 1.1. A simple prohibition

```
FORALL d:Data (d.subject==Kim) => DENY Hospital.process(d)
```

Note that AAL provides conditions, data types with subtypes and also quantifiers and Boolean operators. AAL can also express obligations, that is an action to perform under some conditions as in Listing 1.2.

Listing 1.2. An obligation example

```
FORALL d:Data (d.subject==Kim) AND Hospital.process(d) => Hospital.notify[Kim]("processing")
```

Any obligation or authorization can be used in clauses, especially in conditions. In order to process an action its permission should be established, this is automatically checked by the tool.

Expressing Time. Time is an essential feature in ubiquitous systems. AAL supports full linear temporal logic with all the operators: NEXT, UNTIL, UNLESS, ALWAYS, SOMETIME and a past operator (ONLYWHEN). For instance, Listing 1.3 expresses that if Kim inputs a data to the Hospital, the Hospital will send, in the future, an acknowledgement.

Listing 1.3. A linear time example

```
ALWAYS FORALL d:Data (Kim.input[Hospital](d) =>
            SOMETIME EXISTS ack:Receipt Hospital.received[Kim](ack))
```

Linear discrete time is not always sufficient and AAL proposes a limited way to express real time constraints. Listing 1.4 means that the Hospital should delete Kim's data before two months. Using predicates expressing dates and predicate compositions the specifier can build its proper time constraints.

Listing 1.4. Data retention example

```
ALWAYS FORALL a:Data (d.subject=Kim) => Hospital.delete(d) :BEFORE 2months
```

---

[1] AccLab tool http://web.emn.fr/x-info/acclab/.

Explicit Consent and Purpose. Classic privacy statements add to access control: data subject preferences, data retention, data transfer, explicit consent, processing purpose and notification. These are all expressible in AAL. We have already seen how to express access control, privacy preferences, notifications, data retention, and usage control using the concepts of authorizations and actions. Of course we can express time evolution of these rights either with linear discrete time or real time constraints. The feature "explicit consent" means that the privacy user will explicitly give its consent for data processing (see Listing 1.5).

Listing 1.5. Explicit consent

```
FORALL d:data  (d.subject=Kim) =>
              ((NOT Hospital.process(d)) UNTIL Kim.giveConsent[Hospital](d))
```

The processing purpose can be easily captured with a set of discrete values and an additional parameter in the concerned actions or with dedicated predicates.

Data Transfer. Data transfer and location controls are easily expressed as soon as we defined geographic areas as a partition of types. The type system supports all the Boolean operators and thus making it easy to define type hierarchies. Once you declared a type in AAL the prefix "@" denotes the associated type predicate. Example 1.6 states that Hospital can transfer if and only if the target is inside a European country.

Listing 1.6. Data transfer example

```
ALWAYS FORALL d:Data target:Agent @Europe(target) => PERMIT Hospital.transfer[target](d) AND
ALWAYS FORALL d:Data target:Agent NOT @Europe(target) => DENY Hospital.transfer[target](d)
```

Note that here the natural sentence "Hospital is allowed to transfer to European countries" can be interpreted strictly as above or in a more permissive way (removing the second clause) or in a negative way (keeping only the second clause).

3.2 Advanced Concepts

With AAL we are also able to embed various security related models but also to write complex protocols.

Delegation. AAL does not provide specific feature for authority delegation but a manual translation can be done based on the following example (Listing 1.7) coming from [20] and generalized with parameters.

Listing 1.7. Delegation example in AAL

```
// the @ prefix denotes a predicate, @rights collects three permissions
FORALL a:Agent d:DBase (@rights(a, d) <=> PERMIT (a.read(d) AND a.write(d) AND a.delete(d)))
// P1: Administrator can read, write and delete database.
AND FORALL a:Administrator d:DBase @rights(a, d)
// P2: Technician can read, and write database.
AND FORALL c:Technician d:DBase PERMIT (c.read(d) AND c.write(d))
// P3: Administrator can delegate his rights to technician.
AND FORALL a:Administrator c:Technician d:DBase (a.delegate[c]() => @rights(c, d))
// P4: Action delete can only be performed by administrators.
AND FORALL a:Agent d:DBase ((PERMIT a.delete(d)) <=> @Administrator(a))
```

Many other kind of access control models can be embedded in AAL, like attributes or roles based access control. For instance, we can easily embed the PEPS language from [5] in AAL.

Complex Dependencies. AAL allows to define role sharing, dynamically evolving roles and dynamic dependencies between authorizations and obligations. In other words AAL allows the definition of protocols involving permissions and obligations. All theses things are not generally covered by simple access control rules. An example of sharing and dynamic evolution of roles appears in Listing 1.8, a person is a student until he starts a PhD and then becomes a professor.

Listing 1.8. Sharing and dynamic roles

```
FORALL p:Person ((NOT p.getPhD()) UNTIL p.startPhD()) AND // start a PhD before to get it
// a person is not a professor until he starts his PhD and then becomes a professor
FORALL p:Person ((NOT @Professor(p)) UNTIL (p.startPhD() AND (ALWAYS @Professor(p)))) AND
FORALL p:Person (@Student(p) UNTIL (p.getPhD() AND (ALWAYS NOT @Student(p))))
```

Let us mimic the following protocol: Kim can be admitted to and be discharged from the Hospital. He will get the permission to read only if he has been admitted, that is after an admission and until a discharge. Listing 1.9 expresses permissions that are depending on actions and vice-versa (without parameters to simplify).

Listing 1.9. Permission and obligation dependencies

```
(ALWAYS ((NOT (Kim.admit() AND Kim.discharge())) AND  // events exclusivity
  NOT ((PERMIT Kim.read()) AND Kim.admit()) AND NOT ((PERMIT Kim.read()) AND Kim.admit())))
AND (DENY Kim.read()) AND (ALWAYS (Kim.discharge() => NEXT Kim.admit())) AND
(ALWAYS (Kim.admit() => NEXT (Kim.discharge() OR PERMIT Kim.read()))) AND
(ALWAYS (PERMIT Kim.read() => NEXT (Kim.discharge() OR PERMIT Kim.read()))))
```

The writing of this kind of protocol is not obvious but can be assisted using an automatic generation from an automaton description. We can mix, in a dynamic setting, dependencies between roles, permissions, obligations, conditions in a uniform and unlimited way. That does not mean that these expressions are simple to understand thus requiring analysis and verification tools, preferably automatic tools.

3.3   Comparisons with XACML

We need to restrict the expressiveness of AAL to make a clear comparison to the XACML standard. In the following we only consider authorizations and obligations and single policies containing rule sets. While both languages are quite generic on resources and subjects, XACML is also generic on actions (AnyAction). This is not an important drawback since generally we have systems enabling only a finite set of actions others are eliminated by a kind of static checking. To summarize some main differences with XACML:

1. AAL defines a true negation (a permission is a negation of a prohibition, and it allows negative obligations), and explicit quantifiers.
2. AAL enables subtype hierarchy for resources, subjects, roles, actions

3. AAL provides attributes but also dynamic roles and roles sharing, XACML can manage these features by using an external component.
4. AAL supports both real time and discrete linear time and allows complex dependencies between authorizations and obligations.

The main strength of XACML is its policy enforcement. We have a first approach with the AccMon monitoring includes in the AccLab tool but this is out of the scope of this paper. Lastly, another main difference is the way to detect conflict, it is discussed in the next sections.

4   Existing Conflict Detection Mechanisms

This section discusses different ways to detect conflicts in rules in proposals related to XACML. *Conflict detection* means to check if a set of rules contains an inconsistency, each rule is supposed to be correct or consistent alone. *Conflict localization* is the activity to find precisely where is located the conflict, generally to find the pairs of rules which are conflicting. *Conflict resolution* tries to propose a solution to remove a conflict. We focus here only on conflict detection and compare most of the existing approaches to reveal their weaknesses. A more precise analysis, illustrated by examples, is needed in order to understand why the existing solutions are not sufficient enough in more complex languages.

4.1   Dynamic Detection

We summarize here the main critics to the dynamic detection of XACML which is the most representative of this tendency. The principle is to analyze, at runtime, each request and to look for conflicting results. In case of conflict a combining algorithm is used to choose one reply to the request.

Processing dynamically can add an overhead which is not small in case of many rules or policies. The presence of conflicts and the use of combining mechanisms is the second challenge quoted by [14]. The number of rules is growing with the number of agents, resources, roles, the hierarchical structure of these elements, etc. Conflicts can occur during maintenance, merging of policy sets and evolution of policy sets, but also because of rules distribution and the number of specifiers or policy administrators which are critical factors. For instance [1,7,9,12,16,22,26] comment these problems. In case of dynamic resolution the algorithm is statically chosen from a finite set of solutions. Note that this set was enlarged from XACML V2 to its current V3 but as quoted by [6,7,13,22] this is not sufficient. We can precise two additional arguments.

Most of the conflicts occurring in a set of rules are not intended, they result from various errors, great number of rules, several administration domains, etc. [22] considers that "The risk of error is by definition 50 % and can produce false positives or false negatives". But in fact the real situation is worse because it does not take into account errors. In case of a conflict, the maximum probability for the specifier to make a good choice is $(1 - q)/2$ where q is the probability of a requirement error in a rule. We do not have a precise estimation of q but it is not null, related statistics for firewalls can be found in [24]. Should we consider that a system with less than 50 % of success is a good system? What is the meaning of solving a conflict for a situation the privacy or security officer is not aware of?

The second problem has a more theoretical nature, this is a problem of completeness of the conflict resolution. Dynamic resolution with a finite set of combining algorithms is definitively limited, [13] gives some concrete examples of policy not specifiable in XACML. Scalability is an important aspect in case of several policy sets, written by different officers in a distributed setting. In this case an automatic management is needed, but it is not possible because merging several sets of rules will add new conflicts and combining algorithms are not closed by composition. The combining algorithm could implement one choice but the number of possible choices (or functions) is exponential. Thus, even if the combining algorithm language would be closed by composition, it is undecidable to automatically make the right choice.

4.2   Testing

The testing approach is based on the notion of consistency, that is any request does not lead to contradictory conclusions (or deductions). The testing approaches have two main drawbacks: an exhaustive covering is difficult or impossible to achieve and it is costly. Even an automatic generation of request tests does not solve completely these problems. If a static approach without request generation exists then it is better to use it, providing it is efficient and correct.

4.3   Static Detection

The principle of the static detection is to use an algorithm, at design time, to detect conflicts but without the drawbacks of the requests generation. One strong advantage of it compared to the combining algorithms way is that in case of merging it is an automatic approach, it does not need a combining algorithm and it does not add runtime overhead. Another critical benefit is that the conflict is immediately reported to the privacy or security officer, at design time, and resolved by him which is the only one who can reasonably find a correct solution. There are several approaches to statically detect conflicts in XACML but mainly ad-hoc approaches like [1,2,5,12,20–22,26]. They are often focusing on some specific access control or privacy aspects, for instance hierarchy of resources, data transfers, dynamic and negative roles, and so on. We will illustrate few examples and problems of these previous approaches.

Static Detection Mechanisms. To clarify our discussion we will consider a logical framework with rules. The rules syntax is an important issue and critical aspects are explicit quantifiers, obligations, negation without restrictions and specific modal operators. Some frameworks use simple rules with only conjunctions of atoms in conditions while others rely on general conditions. This makes a great difference in the ability to decide for conflicting situations. To compare more easily the different approaches we assume to faithfully translate all the examples in AAL. A rule will be a pair of logical expressions noted A => B with the implication operator and where variables are implicitly universally quantified.

Abstractly, an access control or privacy system can be viewed as a function from request to replies. Replies are usually permit or deny keywords but in a more general context it could be anything (roles, obligations, etc.). We know that partial functions are more general and more convenient than total ones. In the case of requests to an authorization system we can assume that some requests are discarded for different reasons before to be submitted to the authorization system. Without lost of generality we will consider a partial authorization process: a unary function F with a definition domain D. While a request x is a closed term defining specific input information for the function F, it is a correct request if $D(x)$ is true.

There are several possible definitions for a conflict and it is often related to a property called *consistency*. In many work we can find a definition of a conflict which essentially says that two policies or rules are consistent or without conflict when conjoined, no user can have both the permission and the prohibition to do something (or they do not have contradictory conclusions). A more general formulation is: two rules are conflicting if their conditions are conjointly satisfiable and their conclusions are contradictory (or not satisfiable). Remember that *satisfiability* is a semantic notion which means that it exists an assignment (or a model) of the variables which makes a clause true. This approach is implemented with various algorithms in [2,5,9,20–22] and allows to localize precisely the conflicting rules.

In classic logic *consistency* means that we cannot derive a formula and its negation from the formal system. It means that we cannot deduce (or prove) a contradiction or Phi AND NOT Phi. In the sequel we will show that these two notions of consistency are generally not equivalent by exhibiting some examples. Furthermore, looking for conflicting rules cannot be extended to situations where rules conclusions are complex. Logical consistency is the most general and is correct even if we have logical clauses not only A => B rules.

Non Verified Algorithms. First of all, in the examples from [1,5,20] the complete conditions are lacking to get a conflict. One such an example from [1] is described in Listing 1.10.

Listing 1.10. AAL translation of [1] example

```
FORALL e:Hospital NOT (@Doctor(e) AND @Nurse(e)) AND
FORALL p:PatientRecord d:Doctor (PERMIT (d.read(p) AND d.write(p))) AND
FORALL p:PatientRecord d:Doctor (@sameward(d, p) => PERMIT d.read(p)) AND
FORALL p:PatientRecord c:Chief  PERMIT c.read(p) AND
FORALL p:PatientRecord n:Nurse ((NOT @sameward(n, p)) => DENY n.read(p))
```

"we find an inconsistency in this access control example, which arises if there are nurses that are also chiefs". But this is not exact because it needs that "the nurse not assigned to the patient's ward" is true. Another similar example is related to Listing 1.7. We do not report all the examples here due to lack of space but we observe omissions in conditions to get a conflict, sometime due to implicit hypotheses about non empty sets or types disjunction. We think that these problems comes from the fact that the algorithms are not backed up by formal proofs of correctness.

Partial Systems. Most of the existing algorithms are looking for pair of conflicting rules. In Listing 1.11 the example is consistent and any request verifying A(x) AND B(x) will have a unique response. But, the second rule is conflicting with the first under the condition A(x) AND B(x) and it will be considered as a conflict. However, this is not a global conflict because the above condition is not satisfiable in the global system.

Listing 1.11. Conflicting pairs of rules are not necessary

```
(FORALL x:Agent (A(x) => PERMIT)) AND (FORALL x:Agent (B(x) => DENY))  AND
(FORALL x:Agent ((A(x) AND B(x)) => PERMIT)) AND (FORALL x:Agent ((A(x) AND B(x)) => DENY))
```

The above system represents a partial computation where the two last rules defined the definition domain. In this case the authorization control models only a partial function, for instance in the above example, requests not verifying A(x) AND B(x) are discarded. The conflicting pairs algorithm only enables some systems because conflicts are local to a pair of rules and the algorithm does not check it against a possible context, hence it is considered as a global conflict.

Forcing Exclusivity. Indeed this mechanism forces the rules to be mutually exclusive if they have opposite conclusions, which is often desirable and more readable. However, in case of role sharing or dynamic evolution it is difficult to achieve and even not desirable for readability (see Listing 1.8 for instance). In RBAC policy [10] considers that the separation of duty is the most important constraint and it complicates the policy management.

Boolean Equivalence. Checking the incompatibility of two rules is simple if we have atomic conclusions (like permit, deny, or role names). But it is more complicated if we allow Boolean expressions in the conclusion, for instance in case of positive and negative obligations. To have complex conclusions is not surprising if we expect to follow some composition rules like (A => B) AND (A => C) is equivalent to A => (B AND C). This kind of transformation also exists for conditions and are often bearable. But it is easy to see that looking for conflicting pairs of rules is not stable over these equivalences. This problem still decreases understandability and readability of the set of rules [22].

Extensibility. In a general context where conclusions are not strictly atomic looking for conflicting pairs does not work because it is not able to detect all the problems. To cope with complex conclusions the natural extension of the conflict checking will look for a pair of rules with unsatisfiable conclusions and satisfiable conditions. Let us consider the following propositional example in Listing 1.12. This system is globally inconsistent for any choice of the propositions A and B. Looking for a possible conflict between the first and the second or the first and the third rule, the conjunction of the conclusions are satisfiable thus there is no conflict to catch. The problem here is still that checking pairs of rules is a local algorithm which does not cope with the global context inferred by the set of rules.

Listing 1.12. Conflicting pairs of rules is not sufficient

```
(X => A) AND (X => B) AND (X => (NOT A OR NOT B)) AND
(NOT X => A) AND (NOT X => B) AND (NOT X => (NOT A OR NOT B))
```

One can remark that checking three rules can reveal the problem, but more generally a correct solution should consider the global set of rules. Implementing a derivation or proof system is a solution, but proof of correctness and termination are challenging.

Translating XACML rules (without the meta-policies) into some decidable first-order logic fragments is possible and this paves the way of correct static approaches for the conflict detection. Previous related work here is [8] which defines a first-order language for policies and with conflict detection but in a strict context without obligation. The detection mechanism relies on logical consistency. Other logical approaches use model-checker or SAT solver [11,23].

Defining an ad-hoc algorithm carries out three important challenges: proof of correctness (which is often lacking), efficiency, and faithful implementation. Extending these algorithms to cover more complex cases: dynamic roles, discrete and dense time, positive and negative obligations, complex dependencies between roles and obligations are other non obvious challenges. The next section will discuss the AAL static detection solution.

5   Conflict Detection in AAL

AAL is a language which enables implication rules with unrestricted conclusions, with obligations and temporal logic and without restriction on conditions. However, as exemplified in Sect. 3, it is not strictly restricted to rules as discussed in the previous section. The previous analysis of the detection mechanisms shows that checking for conflicting pair of rules is not a correct algorithm in such a context. Our approach is based on the idea that any request will have at most only one reply that is to rely on the notion of logical consistency. In a *complete* classic logical context consistency is equivalent to the semantic notion of satisfiability (or existence of a model). This completeness property exists for classic logic: propositional, FOL, and LTL. For FOTL with the monodic constraint, [4] has demonstrated the completeness of the temporal resolution process. There are various algorithms to check the satisfiability of propositional, LTL or FOL clauses. However, there is currently only one implemented algorithm for checking satisfiability in FOTL. The algorithm, its proof and implementation are detailed in [15]. In the sequel we sketch the conditions and the principles of this temporal resolution process. A necessary condition for the resolution mechanism is the monodic constraint. That means at most one free variable under the scope of any temporal operator. Moreover, we target decidable fragments of first-order logic (see [4] for instance). The algorithm is based on the resolution process for first-order logic which used clausal normal form and the unification process. Before to use first-order resolution the FOTL clauses are put in a divided separated normal form. Then the temporal normalized problem is transformed into a set of pure first-order clauses by adding, in the predicates, a new parameter that denotes linear time. Finally, a saturation (semi)-algorithm is used on the input problem until a contradiction is raised or there is no new clause to consider.

Thus unsatisfiability (or inconsistency checking) can detect the presence of conflicts in a general context as proposed by AAL. Our solution relies on a classic and general principle which is correct and more general than the detection of conflicting pairs of rules. This covers in a uniform way conflict in permissions, in obligations and any other kinds of conflicts. We think it is more reliable to be founded on a classic logic or model-checking approach because the underlining theories are well established, there are efficient tools and evidences that these tools are well tested.

5.1 Examples

Let us consider Listing 1.8 of the previous section and add some authorizations as described in Listing 1.13. This seems correct, however, there is a conflict as soon as we assume that there exist marks in each computation state.

Listing 1.13. A conflict with evolving and shared roles

```
(ALWAYS FORALL d:Mark x:Professor PERMIT x.read(d)) AND // professors can read marks
// students can read their marks
(ALWAYS FORALL d:Mark x:Student  @owner(x, d) => PERMIT x.read(d)) AND
// complete prohibition
(ALWAYS FORALL d:Data a:Agent ((NOT @Professor(a) OR NOT @Marks(d)) => DENY a.read(d))) AND
(ALWAYS FORALL d:Data a:Agent ((NOT @Student(a) OR NOT @owner(a, d) OR NOT @Marks(d))
        => DENY x.read(d)))
```

Considering the protocol example in Listing 1.9, we can detect a conflict with the first line in Listing 1.14. This line states a situation where a discharge has been done, and then a read but without an admit before the read action. While the second line can be proved to be a logical consequence of the protocol or in other word, it is compliant with the protocol. It means that in any state of the system after an admit we cannot admit unless a discharge action has been done.

Listing 1.14. Complex dependencies: Conflict and compliance examples

```
(SOMETIME (Kim.discharge() AND (NOT Kim.admit() UNTIL Kim.read())))     // 1
(ALWAYS (Kim.admit() => NEXT (NOT Kim.admit() UNLESS Kim.discharge()))) // 2
```

One drawback of this solution is: we can detect the conflicts but it is more difficult to precisely localize them. To localize the conflicting rules in a policy is another problem, read for example [18]. The author suggests to use clause masking to help in conflict localization and our tool implements a basic approach of this kind. The resolution needs a good support for localization and as we argue it, it should be done manually by the privacy officer (but a smart assistance is welcome). We think that more can be done here, from the point of view of efficiency and relevance of information to the privacy officer.

5.2   Performance Tests

Regarding efficiency, the theoretical resolution complexity behind TSPASS is not elementary, but despite this, the TSPASS implementation was compared with several classic LTL model-checkers and SAT solvers and [19] concludes that no one dominates or solves all instances. We describe here some time measures to show that the TSPASS tool can be used in a real context, examples are provided with our AccLab tool. We provide only TSPASS time, the translation done by AccLab has a linear time complexity. The idea is to give a rough estimation of the time performance (MacBook Pro, 2,5 GHz, 16 Go RAM, OS X 10.11.5) not to strictly compare with other benchmarks because of our language expressiveness. All the previous examples in this paper will generate until 560 clauses and the checking time in each case is less than 0.01 s.

We manually translate the two CONTINUE XACML policies[2], nearly 25 XML files containing 44 rules. The process comprises a manual translation of XACML into AAL, check it with TSPASS and fix some mismatches between the AAL and the XACML files. We have 4 concrete actions plus 1 abstract, 4 concrete role types plus 1 abstract and 23 resource types. The Table 1 reports the total number of clauses generated by TSPASS and the global time to show satisfiability. Step 1 is the original writing, step 2 is after fixing 6 reporting errors, step 3 introduces abstract actions in 2 rules, and step 4 adds some ternary predicates. We also manually translate the CONTINUE B policy which is an improved version of the previous one with similar metrics.

We have done a previous healthcare use case in [3] and express accountability, data transfer and temporal logic expressions. For instance, the compliance in the use case was a formula with more than 1200 identifiers and it can be proved valid in less than 4 s. The last example is extracted from a demonstrator done in the A4Cloud project[3]. The context is composed of 6 agent types plus 4 abstract, 6 actions, 15 concrete data types plus 2 abstract, 50 concrete location types plus 8 abstract. The WearableCo policy has 39 access control, 1 data retention and 1 data transfer clauses. The KardioMon policy has 63 access control, 1 data retention and 2 data transfer clauses. The first version of KardioMon is incorrect with a conflict and the second one is correct. Checking the consistency of KardioMonPolicy2 and WearableCoPolicy, and that KardioMonPolicy2 implies the WearableCo policy were also reported (KandW and K=>W columns in Table 1).

Table 1. CONTINUE and Wearable tests.

CONT. A	step 1	step 2	step 3	step 4	CONT. B
# clause	715	687	481	102	578
Time (s)	0.022	0.023	0.016	0.01	0.019
Wearable	WearableCoPolicy	KardioMonPolicy1	KardioMonPolicy2	KandW	K=>W
# clause	647	922	3310	4627	23967
Time (s)	0.03 s	0.04 s	0.2 s	0.35	2.8

---

[2] http://cs.brown.edu/research/plt/software/margrave/versions/01-01/examples/.
[3] http://www.a4cloud.eu/.

6   Conclusion

We propose a language to declare privacy and security concerns. This language can embed various access control models and delegation mechanisms. It overcomes some current limitations: hierarchy for roles, actions and data types. It proposes discrete linear time and dense time and it enables to write complex dependencies between actions and permissions, that is, true protocols.

Our analysis confirms that approaches performing dynamic analysis or testing are not good solutions for conflict detection in policy languages like XACML. We also analyze most of the proposals for static conflict detection and we show limits regarding partial systems and policy readability. We also consider an extension of the conflicting rules principle and show that it cannot work in a general context with complex conclusions. Our ultimate conclusion is that satisfiability checking is a general and correct mechanism for conflict detection. Furthermore, it relies on a well-founded theory and an efficient tool support which is effective for our AAL language. Future work will focus on the integration of specific models with efficient solutions, as the one from [8] and other verification.

References

1. Adi, K., Bouzida, Y., Hattak, I., Logrippo, L., Mankovskii, S.: Typing for conflict detection in access control policies. In: Babin, G., Kropf, P., Weiss, M. (eds.) E-Technologies: Innovation in an Open World. LNBIP, vol. 26, pp. 212–226. Springer, Heidelberg (2009)
2. Armando, A., Ranise, S.: Automated and efficient analysis of role-based access control with attributes. In: Cuppens-Boulahia, N., Cuppens, F., Garcia-Alfaro, J. (eds.) DBSec 2012. LNCS, vol. 7371, pp. 25–40. Springer, Heidelberg (2012)
3. Benghabrit, W., Grall, H., Royer, J.C., Sellami, M.: Abstract accountability language: translation, compliance and application. In: APSEC, pp. 214–221. IEEE Computer Society, New Delhi (2015)
4. Degtyarev, A., Fisher, M., Konev, B.: Monodic temporal resolution. ACM Trans. Comput. Logic 7(1), 108–150 (2006)
5. Delmas, R., Polacsek, T.: Formal methods for exchange policy specification. In: Salinesi, C., Norrie, M.C., Pastor, Ó. (eds.) CAiSE 2013. LNCS, vol. 7908, pp. 288–303. Springer, Heidelberg (2013)
6. Dunlop, N., Indulska, J., Raymond, K.: Methods for conflict resolution in policy-based management systems. In: Enterprise Distributed Object Computing Conference, pp. 98–111. IEEE Computer Society (2003)
7. Fatema, K., Chadwick, D.: Resolving policy conflicts - integrating policies from multiple authors. In: Iliadis, L., Papazoglou, M., Pohl, K. (eds.) CAiSE Workshops 2014. LNBIP, vol. 178, pp. 310–321. Springer, Heidelberg (2014)
8. Halpern, J.Y., Weissman, V.: Using first-order logic to reason about policies. ACM Trans. Inf. Syst. Secur. 11(4), 1–41 (2008)
9. Hu, H., Ahn, G.J., Kulkarni, K.: Discovery and resolution of anomalies in web access control policies. IEEE Trans. Dependable Sec. Comput 10(6), 341–354 (2013)

10. Huang, C., Sun, J., Wang, X., Si, Y.: Inconsistency management of role based access control policy. In: International Conference on E-Business and Information System Security (2009)
11. Hughes, G., Bultan, T.: Automated verification of access control policies using a SAT solver. Int. J. Softw. Tools Technol. Transfer 10(6), 503–520 (2008)
12. Hwang, J., Xie, T., Hu, V.C.: Detection of multiple-duty-related security leakage in access control policies. In: Secure Software Integration and Reliability Improvement, pp. 65–74. IEEE Computer Society (2009)
13. Li, N., Wang, Q., Qardaji, W.H., Bertino, E., Rao, P., Lobo, J., Lin, D.: Access control policy combining: theory meets practice. In: Carminati, B., Joshi, J. (eds.) Proceedings of SACMAT, pp. 135–144. ACM (2009)
14. Liu, A.X., Chen, F., Hwang, J., Xie, T.: Xengine: a fast and scalable XACML policy evaluation engine. In: Liu, Z., Misra, V., Shenoy, P.J. (eds.) Proceedings of SIGMETRICS, pp. 265–276. ACM (2008)
15. Ludwig, M., Hustadt, U.: Implementing a fair monodic temporal logic prover. AI Commun. 23(2–3), 69–96 (2010)
16. Mohan, A., Blough, D.M., Kurç, T.M., Post, A.R., Saltz, J.H.: Detection of conflicts and inconsistencies in taxonomy-based authorization policies. In: Wu, F.X., Zaki, M.J., Morishita, S., Pan, Y., Wong, S., Christianson, A., Hu, X. (eds.) International Conference on Bioinformatics and Biomedicine, pp. 590–594. IEEE Computer Society (2011)
17. OASIS Standard: eXtensible Access Control Markup Language (XACML) Version 3.0, 22 January 2013. http://docs.oasis-open.org/xacml/3.0/xacml-3.0-core-spec-os-en.html (2013)
18. Schuppan, V.: Towards a notion of unsatisfiable and unrealizable cores for LTL. Sci. Comput. Program. 77(7–8), 908–939 (2012)
19. Schuppan, V., Darmawan, L.: Evaluating LTL satisfiability solvers. In: Bultan, T., Hsiung, P.-A. (eds.) ATVA 2011. LNCS, vol. 6996, pp. 397–413. Springer, Heidelberg (2011)
20. Shaikh, R.A., Adi, K., Logrippo, L., Mankovski, S.: Inconsistency detection method for access control policies. In: Information Assurance and Security, pp. 204–209. IEEE Computer Society (2010)
21. St-Martin, M., Felty, A.P.: A verified algorithm for detecting conflicts in XACML access control rules. In: Avigad, J., Chlipala, A. (eds.) Proceedings of the Conference on Certified Programs and Proofs, pp. 166–175. ACM (2016)
22. Stepien, B., Matwin, S., Felty, A.P.: Strategies for reducing risks of inconsistencies in access control policies. In: Availability, Reliability, and Security, pp. 140–147. IEEE Computer Society (2010)
23. Turkmen, F., den Hartog, J., Ranise, S., Zannone, N.: Analysis of XACML policies with SMT. In: Focardi, R., Myers, A. (eds.) POST 2015. LNCS, vol. 9036, pp. 115–134. Springer, Heidelberg (2015)
24. Wool, A.: Trends in firewall configuration errors: measuring the holes in swiss cheese. IEEE Internet Comput. 14(4), 58–65 (2010)
25. Xia, X.: A conflict detection approach for XACML policies on hierarchical resources. In: Proceedings of Conference on Green Computing and Communications, pp. 755–760. IEEE Computer Society (2012)
26. Xiao, Z., Nandhakumar Kathiresshan, Y.X.: A survey of accountability in computer networks and distributed systems. Security and Communication. Networks 5(10), 1083–1085 (2012)

Component-Oriented Access Control for Deployment of Application Services in Containerized Environments

Kirill Belyaev[✉] and Indrakshi Ray

Computer Science Department, Colorado State University, Fort Collins, USA
kirill.belyaev@outlook.com, Indrakshi.Ray@colostate.edu

Abstract. With the advancements in multi-core CPU architectures, it is now possible for a server operating system (OS) such as Linux to handle a large number of concurrent application services on a single server instance. Individual service components of such services may run in different isolated environments, such as chrooted jails or application containers, and may need controlled access to system resources and the ability to collaborate and coordinate with each other in a regulated and secure manner. In an earlier work, we motivated the need for an access control framework that is based on the principle of least privilege for formulation, management, and enforcement of policies that allows controlled access to system resources and also permits controlled collaboration and coordination for service components deployed in disjoint containerized environments under a single OS instance. The current work provides a more in-depth treatment of secure inter-component communication in such environments. We show the policies needed for such communication and demonstrate how they can be enforced through a Linux Policy Machine that acts as the centralized reference monitor. The inter-component interaction occurs through the persistent layer using a tuple space abstraction. We implemented a tuple space library that provides operations on the tuple space. We present preliminary experimental results of its implementation that discuss the resource usage and performance.

Keywords: Access control · Data and application security · Denial of service protection · Distributed systems security · Security architectures

1 Introduction

The advancements in contemporary multi-core CPU architectures have greatly improved the ability of modern server operating systems (OS) such as Linux to deploy a large number of concurrent application services on a single server instance. The emergence of application containers [7], introduction of support

This work was supported by a grant from NIST under award no. 70NANB15H264, 60NANB16D249 and 60NANB16D250.

© Springer International Publishing AG 2016
S. Foresti and G. Persiano (Eds.): CANS 2016, LNCS 10052, pp. 383–399, 2016.
DOI: 10.1007/978-3-319-48965-0_23

for kernel namespaces [11] allows a set of loosely coupled service components to be executed in isolation from each other and also from the main operating system. This enables application service providers to lower their total cost of ownership by deploying large numbers of application services on a single server instance and possibly minimize horizontal scaling of applications across multiple nodes. Executing the individual service components in isolated containers has its benefits. If a single containerized application runtime is compromised by the attacker, the attack surface is limited in its scope to a single component. This theoretically limits the possibility of disrupting the entire data service. Moreover, such an approach also simplifies the management and provision of service components.

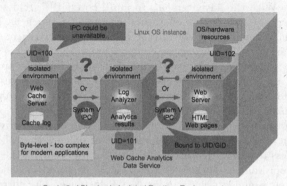

Controlled Sharing in Isolated Runtime Environments

Fig. 1. Problems of controlled sharing

In this model, the individual isolated service components may need to coordinate and collaborate to provide the service and the various service components may not have access to a common centralized database management system or a key-value store for the purpose of communication. Moreover, many services may not rely on database storage in the first place. For instance, consider a real-world service deployment scenario illustrated in Fig. 1. A Linux server has three applications, namely, *Squid Web Cache Server*, *Squid Log Analyzer*, and *HTTP Web Server*, deployed in three separate isolated environments (chrooted jail directories), each under a distinct unprivileged user identifier (UID). Combined, all three applications represent individual components of a single service – ISP web caching that caches Internet HTTP traffic of a large customer base to minimize the utilization of ISP's Internet backbone. *Squid Web Cache Server* component generates daily operational cache logs in its respective runtime environment. *Squid Log Analyzer* component needs to perform data analytics on those operational log files on a daily basis. It then creates analytical results in the form of HTML files that need to be accessible by the *HTTP Web Server* component to be available through the web browser for administrative personnel. In such a case, there is a need to access and share data objects across the applications in disjoint containerized environments. Due to isolation properties, those applications cannot write data objects to a shared storage area of the server OS such as /var directory to simplify their interaction. Usual Inter-Process Communication (IPC) primitives such as message queues, memory-mapped files and shared memory may cause unauthorized access or illegal information flow and therefore could be disabled in targeted deployments [3].

In conventional UNIX or Linux OS, applications can be deployed in isolated (containerized) environments, such as chrooted jails. Such isolated environments limit the access of the applications beyond some designated directory tree and have the potential to offer enhanced security and performance. However, no mechanism is provided for controlled communication and sharing of data objects between isolated applications across such environments. A new type of access control targeting multi-service deployments on contemporary server hardware has been recently introduced through Linux Policy Machine (LPM) [3] framework. The framework proposed such a component-oriented access control for isolated service components that controls access to OS resources, and regulates the inter-component communication under a single service. LPM is a user-space reference monitor that allows the formulation and enforcement of component-oriented policies.

The regulated communication between isolated service components relies on the access control that is based on the adaptation of generative communication paradigm introduced by Linda programming model [8] which uses the concept of tuple spaces for process communication. However, the traditional tuple spaces lack any security features and also have operational limitations [3]. Most implementations are limited to tuple space communication within a single memory address space of an application and do not offer simple ways to interact between separate component processes with independent runtime environments. Moreover, main memory based solutions could be subjected to heavy disk swapping with simultaneous transfers of large data objects. That essentially eliminates the advantages of using purely memory resident tuple spaces with hardware that has limited RAM capacity. In our current work we enhance the original paradigm and provide the initial experimental results of the developed Tuple Space Library (TSL) that relies on the persistent storage approach [5] and provides personal tuple space per service component for security reasons. The communication between applications is mediated through a Tuple Space Controller (TSC) – the component of the LPM reference monitor which is allowed limited access to an application's tuple space. The component-oriented access control allows a regulated way of coordinating and collaborating among components of a single service through tuple spaces. We also present the formal model for expressing component-oriented policies.

The rest of the paper is organized as follows. Section 2 provides the overview of component-oriented access control targeting isolated runtime environments. Section 3 describes the architecture for inter-component communication. Section 4 demonstrates the preliminary experimental results for the developed TSL library. Section 5 covers some related works. Section 6 concludes the paper.

2   Communicative Access Control

In order to address the requirements of the regulated communication between isolated service components, we introduce the notion of a *communicative policy class* that consists of a group of applications (service components) that reside in different isolated environments and need to collaborate and/or coordinate with each other in order to provide a service offering. Our notion of communicative policy class is different from the conventional notion of UNIX groups. In the conventional groups, the privileges assigned to a group are applied uniformly to all members of that group. In this case, we allow controlled sharing of private data objects among members of the communicative policy class via object replication. Such a sharing can be very fine-grained and it may be *unidirectional* – an isolated application can request a replica of data object belonging to another isolated application but not the other way around.

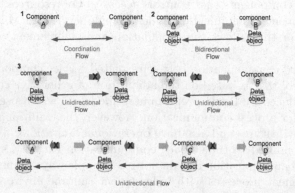

Fig. 2. Flow control of isolated service components (Color figure online)

Some applications may require *bidirectional* access requests where both applications can request replicas of respective data objects. Such types of possible information flow are depicted in Fig. 2 where green arrow denotes the granted request for a replicated data object in the direction of an arrow, while red one with a cross signifies the forbidden request. Implementing such rules may be nontrivial as isolated environments are non-traversable due to isolation properties. This necessitates proposing alternative communication constructs.

The access control policies of a communicative policy class specify how the individual applications in such a class can request a replica of mutual data objects. Only applications within the same communicative class can communicate and therefore communication across different communicative policy classes is forbidden. Such a regulation is well-suited for multiple data services hosted on a single server instance. The assignment of individual data service to a separate policy class facilitates the fine-grained specification of communication policies between various isolated service components.

The construct of communicative policy class is designed to support the following communication patterns among the applications in a single class. (i) *coordination* – often applications acting as a single service do not require direct access to mutual data objects or their replicas but rather need an exchange of messages to perform coordinated invocation or maintain collective state [3]. Coordination across mutually isolated environments is problematic. However, if applications belong to a single communicative policy class, it enables the exchange of coordination messages without reliance on usual UNIX IPC mechanisms that may be unavailable under security constrained conditions. (ii) *collaboration* – components acting as a single data service may need to access mutual data or runtime file objects to collaborate and perform joint or codependent measurements or calculations as illustrated in the description of the web caching service. Empowering an application with the ability to obtain a replica of a data object that belongs to another application in the same communicative policy class makes such collaboration possible.

Based on the described communication patterns between service components, a single communicative policy class can be classified as a *coordinative policy class* if it contains a set of coordination policies. Consequently, it can also be classified as a *collaborative policy class* if it contains a set of collaboration policies.

3   Communications Architecture

We now discuss the enforcement architecture for communicative policy class model.

3.1   IPC Constraints

In general, applications that need to communicate across machine boundaries use TCP/IP level communication primitives such as sockets. However, that is unnecessary for individual applications located on a single server instance [12]. Applications that need to communicate on a modern UNIX-like OS may use UNIX domain sockets or similar constructs. However, socket level communication is usually complex and requires the development and integration of dedicated network server functionality into an application. Modern data service components also prefer information-oriented communication at the level of objects [4]. The necessity of adequate authentication primitives to prove application identity may also be non-trivial. Moreover, as illustrated in Sect. 2, many localized applications may require to communicate across isolated environments but may not need access to the network I/O mechanisms. Thus, more privileges must be conferred to these applications just for the purpose of collaboration or coordination, which violates our principle of least privilege [3].

Reliance on kernel-space UNIX IPC primitives may also be problematic. First, such an IPC may be unavailable for security reasons in order to avoid potential malicious inter-application exchange on a single server instance that hosts a large number of isolated application services. In other words, IPC may be disabled on the level of OS kernel. Second, modern applications often require more advanced, higher-level message-oriented communication that is not offered by the legacy byte-level IPC constructs. Third, UNIX IPC is bound to UID/GID access control associations that does not provide fine-grained control at the level of individual applications. Therefore kernel-space IPC mechanisms do not offer regulated way of inter-application interaction. The usage of system-wide user-space IPC frameworks such as D-Bus [9] may also be problematic due to security reasons and absence of flexible access control mechanisms despite its ability to transport arbitrary byte strings (but not file objects) [3].

3.2   Tuple Space Paradigm

In order to address the complexities introduced in Sect. 3.1, we applied an alternative approach that can be classified as a special case of *generative communication* paradigm introduced by Linda programming model [8]. In this approach, processes communicate *indirectly* by placing tuples in a *tuple space*, from which other processes can read or remove them. Tuples do not have an address but rather are accessible by matching on content therefore being a type of content-addressable associative memory [12]. This programming model allows decoupled interaction between processes separated in time and space: communicating processes need not know each other's identity, nor have a dedicated connection established between them [15]. However, the lack of any protection mechanism in the basic model [12,15] makes the single global shared tuple space unsuitable for interaction and coordination among untrusted components. The traditional in-memory implementation of tuple space makes it unsuitable in our current work due to security issues and memory utilization overheads [3]. Another problem identified with the RAM-based tuple spaces is that it is suitable mainly for a single application with multiple threads that share the same memory address space. That makes such a construct problematic for use between independent processes [3].

We implemented a tuple space calculus that is compliant with the base model introduced in [8] but is applied on dedicated tuple spaces of individual applications instead of a global space. Our *tuple space calculus* comprises the following operations: (i) *create tuple space* operation, (ii) *delete tuple space* operation – deletes tuple space only if it is empty, (iii) *read* operation – returns the value of individual tuple without affecting the contents of a tuple space, (iv) *append* operation – adds a tuple without affecting existing tuples in a tuple space, and (v) *take* operation – returns a tuple while removing it from a tuple space. We adhere to the *immutability* property – tuples are immutable and applications can either append or remove tuples in a tuple space without changing contents of individual tuples.

An application is allowed to perform all the described operations in its tuple space while LPM is restricted to read and append operations only. Note that the take operation is the only manner in which tuples get deleted from a tuple space because the delete tuple space operation is allowed only on an empty tuple space.

Tuple space is implemented as an abstraction in the form of a filesystem directory with its calculus performed via TSL employed by the applications and the LPM. Therefore, this part of the unified framework is not transparent and the applications may need to be modified in order to utilize the tuple space communication. However, in certain cases that may not be necessary. For instance, if applications require only limited collaboration, such as periodic requests for replicas of data objects (the case for daily logs), a separate data requester application that employs TSL can handle such a task without the need to modify the existing application such as a log analyzer.

The LPM plays a mediating role in the communication between applications. The communication takes place through two types of tuples: *control tuples* and *content tuples*. Control tuples can carry messages for coordination or requests for sharing. Content tuples are the mechanism by which data gets shared across applications (service components). The LPM periodically checks for control tuples in the tuple spaces for applications registered in its database. Note, that in our calculus, at most one control tuple and one content tuple could be appended into a tuple space at any given time.

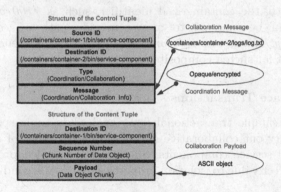

Fig. 3. Tuples structure

The structure of the tuples is shown in Fig. 3. Control tuples are placed by an application into its tuple space for the purpose of coordination or for requesting data from other applications. A control tuple has the following fields: (i) *Source ID* – indicates an absolute path of the application that acts as an application ID of the communication requester. (ii) *Destination ID* – indicates an absolute path of the application that acts as an application ID of the communication recipient. (iii) *Type* – indicates whether it is a collaborative or coordinative communication. (iv) *Message* – contains the collaborative/coordinative information. For collaboration it is the request for an absolute path of data object. Coordination message may be opaque as other entities may be oblivious of this inter-application communication. It may even be encrypted to ensure the security and privacy of inter-application coordination efforts. XML or JSON are possible formats that can be used for the representation of coordination messages. LPM merely shuttles the coordination tuples between respective applications' spaces and is not aware of their semantics. Content tuples are used for sharing data objects across applications and they have the following fields: (i) *Destination ID* – indicates the ID of recipient application that is an absolute path of an application. (ii) *Sequence Number* – indicates the sequence number of a data object chunk that is transported. ASCII objects in the form of chunks are the primary target of inter-application collaboration. (iii) *Payload* – contains the chunk of a data object. Content tuples are placed by the LPM reference monitor into corresponding tuple space of the requesting application that needs to receive content. Note that content tuples are designed for collaboration only. Coordination is performed exclusively through control tuples.

Containerized service components are often not aware of whether they are deployed in an isolated runtime environment, such as a chrooted jail or not. Therefore, tuple fields, such as Source/Destination IDs and object paths that technically require the absolute path to the object on the filesystem can be substituted with the isolated environment ID, such as a container ID. This permits the service deployment with individual components that are only aware of immediate containerized path locations or corresponding components' service identifiers. For instance, the containerized identifier, such as */100/opt/bin/service-component-2* can be mapped to a system-wide path of */opt/containers/container-100/opt/bin/service-component-2* by the LPM reference monitor with a proper support for such a composite service mapping.

3.3   Tuple Space Transactions

We provide the sample transactional flow involved in tuple space operations, necessary to carry out collaborative and coordinative types of communication between isolated service components. Since loosely coupled processes can not communicate directly due to isolation properties, the flow is conducted indirectly via the TSC.

Coordinative Transaction. Coordinative communication between two components is depicted in Fig. 4. Intrinsically, coordination is bidirectional, since both endpoints need to obtain coordinative messages. Both components need to create the corresponding tuple spaces in the isolated runtime environments. In the first phase, Component 1 delivers a message to Component 2.

- [**Step 1:**] Component 1 appends a control tuple (see the structure of tuples in Fig. 3) to its tuple space *TS 1*. This control tuple (denoted as message A) has to be subsequently delivered to Component 2;
- [**Step 2:**] TSC reads the control tuple from *TS 1*;
- [**Step 3:**] Component 1 retracts the control tuple via the take operation;
- [**Step 4:**] TSC appends the control tuple into tuple space *TS 2* of Component 2;
- [**Step 5:**] Component 2 takes the appended control tuple (message A from Component 1) from its tuple space *TS 2*.

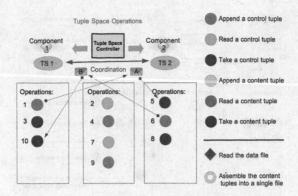

Fig. 4. Coordination through tuple spaces

In the next phase of coordinative communication, Component 2 has to deliver its coordination message to Component 1. Such a message could contain independently new coordinative information, or serve as the acknowledgement for the control tuple that has just been received. Such a decision is service-specific. However, we require that coordinative transactional flow is terminated through such a confirmative control tuple from Component 2. The steps in the second phase are described next.

- [**Step 6:**] Component 2 appends a control tuple to its tuple space *TS 2*. This control tuple (denoted as message B) has to be subsequently delivered to Component 1;
- [**Step 7:**] TSC reads the control tuple from *TS 2*;
- [**Step 8:**] Component 2 retracts the control tuple via the take operation;
- [**Step 9:**] TSC appends the control tuple into tuple space *TS 1* of Component 1;
- [**Step 10:**] Component 1 takes the appended control tuple (message B from Component 2) from its tuple space *TS 1*. This step completes the coordinative transaction.

Note, that the coordination messages could be of any type. Therefore, our communication architecture allows full transparency in inter-component exchange and does not require proprietary formats. Most common formats that could be incorporated into the message field of a control tuple is XML, JSON or text strings. Such a choice is service-dependent. Moreover, the service components could utilize the serialization libraries such as XStream [16], to represent class objects in the form of XML messages. In this case, isolated components that use our TSL library can perform complete object-based transport within a single service solely through provided tuple space communication.

Collaborative Transaction. Collaborative communication is depicted in Fig. 5. Intrinsically, collaboration is unidirectional, since the workflow is only

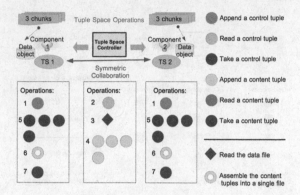

Fig. 5. Collaboration through tuple spaces

directed from a single requester to TSC and back in the form of content tuples. In contrast to a control tuple, a content tuple only has a Destination ID field, as depicted in Fig. 3. However, at the level of service logic, collaboration flow could conceptually be bidirectional. Both endpoints could obtain replicas of mutual data objects through TSC, if such a replication is explicitly permitted in the policies store of a reference monitor. Such a scenario of symmetric collaboration is depicted in Fig. 5. The steps of collaborative transaction, on the left, are shown below.

- [**Step 1:**] Component 1 appends a control tuple to its tuple space *TS 1* with indication of request for data object that is owned by Component 2;
- [**Step 2:**] TSC reads the control tuple from *TS 1*;
- [**Step 3:**] TSC reads the requested data object on the filesystem. Note, that this step is not a part of the actual transactional flow, but represents the internal operations of TSL;
- [**Step 4:**] TSC appends the replica of a data object, fragmented in three content tuples, into tuple space *TS 1*, one tuple at a time. Note, that TSC can append the next content tuple only after the current one is taken from a tuple space. The step shows four actual tuples – TSC has to append a special End of Flow (EOF) content tuple to indicate the end of data flow. Such a tuple has the Payload field set to empty string and Sequence Number field set to −1 to indicate the EOF condition;
- [**Step 5:**] Component 1 takes appended content tuples, one tuple at a time;
- [**Step 6:**] Component 1 assembles the appended content tuples into a replica of the requested data object. Note, that this step is not a part of the actual transactional flow, but represents the internal operations of TSL;
- [**Step 7:**] Component 1 takes a control tuple from its tuple space *TS 1*. This step completes the collaborative transaction.

The flow of second collaborative transaction, on the right, is identical. The communication starts with creation of a tuple space and ends with its deletion after the transactional flow completes. The complexity for both types of communication is hidden from applications. TSL provides public Application Programming Interface (API) methods without exposing internal operations of tuple space calculus.

3.4 Security Aspects

Tuple space communication addresses the confidentiality, integrity, and availability issues with respect to tuple space implementation. Only members of the same communicative policy class can coordinate and/or share data. Extra protection mechanisms are also incorporated for each application's tuple space. Each application (service component) creates its own tuple space in the directory structure of the filesystem allocated to its isolated runtime environment. Only the individual application can perform all the operations, namely, *create tuple space*, *delete tuple space*, *read*, *append*, and *take*. TSC can only perform *read* and *append* operations on the tuple space. Thus, no one other than the application itself can remove anything from its tuple space. Moreover, the confidentiality and integrity are guaranteed by virtue of isolation from other services deployed on the node. Note that, from the confidentiality standpoint a malicious application cannot request a replica of a data object that belongs to another application deployed in a separate isolated runtime environment unless it is registered in the policy database containing communicative policies classes of the LPM and has the appropriate policy records. Removing it from the associated communicative policy class will disable the collaboration with other service components [3]. Unrestricted inter-application communication is avoided through the notion of *trust* between applications that is implicit for components of a single data service. Such components should be logically placed in the same communicative policy class as indicated in Sect. 2.

Applications may misbehave and cause Denial-of-Service (DOS) attacks by exhausting system resources. Our TSL facilitates the data and control flow that prevents an application from using all the allocated filesystem space in the directory structure of the isolated environment. The implementation of append operation for collaboration ensures that such an operation writes only a single content tuple at a given time and the application has to take the tuple before a new one is written in its tuple space. Such a strategy avoids overconsumption of filesystem space, alleviates disk/filesystem access loads with large numbers of concurrent transactions, and also serves as an acknowledgement mechanism before the next chunk of the replicated data object is written.

4 Experimental Results

The initial prototype of the TSL implemented in Java SE is publicly available through the LPM's GitHub repository [2]. The specification of the machine involved in the benchmarking is depicted in Table 1. Memory utilization and time information has been obtained using JVM's internal Runtime and System packages. Due to space limitations, we do not provide the benchmarking results for coordinative transaction. Despite its implementation complexity, such a transaction involves only exchange of two control tuples and therefore does not incur any significant performance overheads in terms of CPU and RAM utilization. The actual unit test for coordination is available at: https://github.com/kirillbelyaev/tinypm/blob/LPM/src/test/java/TSLib_UnitTests_Coordination.java.

Table 1. Node specifications

Attribute	Info
CPU	Intel(R) Xeon (R) X3450 @ 2.67 GHz; Cores: 8
Disk	SATA: 3Gb/s; RPM: 10 000; Model: WDC; Sector size: 512 bytes
Filesystem	EXT4-fs; Block size: 4096 bytes; Size: 53 GB; Use: 1%
RAM	8 GB
OS	Fedora 23, Linux kernel 4.4.9–300
Java VM	OpenJDK 64-Bit Server SE 8.0_92

For collaboration, the payload of individual content tuple is set at 1 MB. Therefore, for instance, it takes 64 content tuples to replicate a 64 MB data object. Six sizes of data objects have been chosen - 64, 128, 256, 512, 1024 and 2048 MB objects respectively. Collaborative transactional flow, as discussed in Sect. 3, is performed on the EXT4 filesystem, where the requesting service component creates a tuple space in its isolated directory structure and assembles the content tuples appended by the TSC into a replica in its isolated environment outside the tuple space directory.

Replication performance for sequential collaboration is depicted in Fig. 6. The create_ObjectReplica() method in Utilities package of the TSL library is a reference method that sequentially executes the collaborative transaction conducted between TSC and the service component within a single thread of execution. We can observe that the replication time progressively doubles with an increase of the object size. On average, it takes 0.625 s to replicate a 64 MB object, 1.065 s a 128 MB object, 1.955 s a 256 MB object, 3.950 s a 512 MB object, 8.550 s a 1024 MB object and 17.505 s to replicate a 2048 MB object. Java Virtual Machine (JVM) memory utilization during sequential collaboration has been observed to be negligible. That is largely due to the usage of Java NIO library in our Utilities package that is designed to provide efficient access to the low-level I/O operations of modern operating systems. On average, memory usage is 23 MB for replication of a 64 MB object, 34 MB for a 128 MB object, 56 MB for a 256 MB object, 305 MB for a 512 MB object (an outlier, repeatedly observed with this object size that might be specific to the garbage collector for this particular JVM), 58 MB for a 1024 MB objects, and 36 MB for replication of a 2048 MB object. Note, that since the measured JVM memory utilization takes into account the processing of both TSC and requester components within a single thread of execution, the

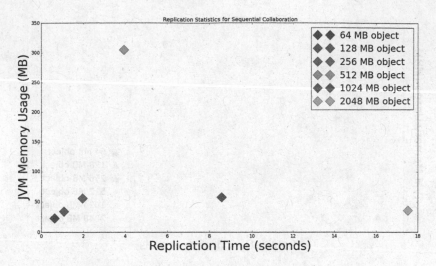

Fig. 6. Replication performance for sequential collaboration

actual JVM utilization will be roughly twice lower for two endpoints in the collaborative transaction when endpoints execute in separate JVMs. This shows the practical feasibility of our collaborative implementation even for replication of large data objects. According to obtained results, we can anticipate that TSC can handle a large number of concurrent collaborative transactions without consuming significant amounts of physical RAM. We observed partially full utilization of a single CPU core during replication of the largest data object (2048 MB). The actual unit test for sequential collaboration is available at: https://github.com/kirillbelyaev/tinypm/blob/LPM/src/test/java/TSLib_Utilities_UnitTests.java.

In real-world settings TSC and service component execute concurrently in separate threads, and in fact in different JVMs. Replication performance for concurrent collaboration is depicted in Fig. 7, where TSC and service component execute as concurrent threads in a single JVM. In such settings, TCS thread performs a short sleep in its section of TSL library after every append operation to allow the service component thread to take a content tuple from its tuple space. That results in a longer replication time compared to sequential execution depicted in Fig. 6. Due to concurrent execution, two CPU cores have been partially utilized by the JVM during concurrent collaboration. The obtained results show that replication time is sufficient for non-critical, non-real-time services where medium-size data objects need to be replicated across service components. Further decrease in replication time is possible through the usage of faster storage media, such as Solid-State Drives (SSDs) and Non-Volatile Memory (NVM) [5]. Again, we can observe that the replication time progressively doubles with an increase of the object size. On average, it takes 17.152 s to replicate a 64 MB object, 23.8 s a 128 MB object, 37.1 s a 256 MB object, 63.8 s a 512 MB object, 117.5 s a 1024 MB object and 246.505 s to replicate a 2048 MB object. In line with sequential collaboration, JVM memory utilization during concurrent

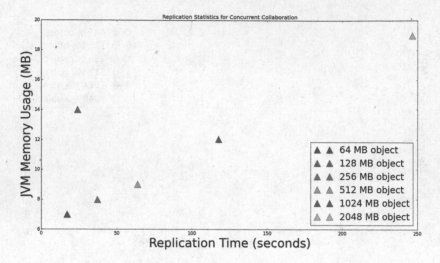

Fig. 7. Replication performance for concurrent collaboration

collaboration also has been observed to be negligible. On average, memory usage is 7 MB for replication of a 64 MB object, 14 MB for a 128 MB object, 8 MB for a 256 MB object, 9 MB for a 512 MB object, 12 MB for a 1024 MB objects, and 19 MB for replication of a 2048 MB object. In fact, the utilization is much lower then in case of sequential collaboration. Again, when executed in separate JVMs, the memory footprint for every endpoint in the transactional flow will be further diminished. Therefore, TSC memory usage during real-life operations for handling multi-component collaborative transactions is expected to be minimal. Note, that due to preliminary nature of conducted transactional benchmarks, the focus is on functionality, rather then availability. Therefore, no actual saturation of storage media has been attempted. The actual unit test for concurrent collaboration is available at: https://github.com/kirillbelyaev/tinypm/blob/LPM/src/test/java/TSLib_UnitTests_Collaboration.java.

5   Related Work

For the complete coverage of relevant research efforts, we direct the interested reader to our original work on the subject [3]. Application-defined decentralized access control (DCAC) for Linux has been recently proposed by Xu et al. [17] that allows ordinary users to perform administrative operations enabling isolation and privilege separation for applications. In DCAC applications control their privileges with a mechanism implemented and enforced by the operating system, but without centralized policy enforcement and administration. DCAC is configurable on a per-user basis only [17]. The objective of DCAC is decentralization with facilitation of data sharing between users in a multi-user environment. Our work is designed for a different deployment domain – provision of access control framework for isolated applications where access control has to be managed and enforced by the centralized user-space reference monitor at the granularity of individual applications using expressive high-level policy language without a need to modify OS kernel.

The application-level access control is emphasized in Decentralized Information Flow Control (DIFC) [13]. DIFC allows application writers to control how data flows between the pieces of an application and the outside world. As applied to privacy, DIFC allows untrusted software to compute with private data while trusted security code controls the release of that data. As applied to integrity, DIFC allows trusted code to protect untrusted software from unexpected malicious inputs. In either case, only bugs in the trusted code, which tend to be small and isolated, can lead to security violations. Current DIFC systems that run on commodity hardware can be broadly categorized into two types: language-level and operating system-level DIFC [10,14]. Language level solutions provide no guarantees against security violations on system resources, like files and sockets. Operating system solutions can mediate accesses to system resources, but are inefficient at monitoring the flow of information through fine-grained program data structures [14]. However, application code has to be modified and performance overheads are incurred on the modified binaries. Moreover the complexities of rewriting parts of the application code to use the DIFC security guarantees are not trivial and require extensive API and domain knowledge [14]. These challenges, despite the provided benefits, limits the widespread applicability of this approach. Our solution allows to divide the information flow between service components into data and control planes that are regulated through the user-space reference monitor. Therefore, no modification to OS kernel is required. The rewrite of existing applications for utilization of data flow may not be necessary, since a separate flow requesting application that leverages our TSL can handle such a task and deliver the replica of a data object to unmodified application.

In the mobile devices environment, Android Intents [6] offers message passing infrastructure for sandboxed applications; this is similar in objectives to our tuple space communication paradigm for the enforcement of regulated inter-application communication for isolated service components using our model of communicative policy classes. Under the Android security model, each application runs in its own process with a low-privilege user ID (UID), and applications can only access their own files by default. That is similar to our deployment scheme. Despite their default isolation, Android applications can optionally communicate via message passing. However, communication can become an attack vector since the Intent messages can be vulnerable to passive eavesdropping or active denial of service attacks [6]. We eliminate such a possibility in our communication architecture due to the virtue of tuple space communication that offers connectionless inter-application communication as discussed in Sect. 3. Malicious applications cannot infer on or intercept the inter-application traffic of other services deployed on the same server instance because communication is performed via isolated tuple spaces on a filesystem. Moreover, message spoofing is also precluded by our architecture since the enforcement of message passing is conducted via the centralized LPM reference monitor that regulates the delivery of messages according to its policies store.

We have adapted the original Linda model to serve the requirements of inter-component communication. As covered in Sect. 3, the original paradigm has a number of resource-oriented limitations and does not offer security guarantees. For that matter, many researchers [4,12,15,18] have conducted adaptation of the original tuple space model to fit the domain-specific requirements. The LightTS tuple space framework [1] has adapted the original operations on Linda tuple space for use in context-aware applications. LightTS offers support for aggregated content matching of tuple objects and other advanced functionality such as matches on value ranges and support for uncertain matches. Our adaptation allows coordination and collaboration between isolated service components based on content matching on a set of tuple fields. To the best of our knowledge, we offer the first persistent tuple space implementation that facilitates the regulated inter-application communication without a need for applications to share a common memory address space [3].

6   Conclusion and Future Work

In this work we implemented the communication sub-layer necessary for enforcement of inter-component access control policies expressed through the notion of communicative policy class. We have demonstrated how inter-application communication for isolated service components can take place through persistent tuple spaces. The prototype of TSL library demonstrates the feasibility of our approach. A lot of work remains to be done. A carrier-grade TSC, that is necessary for the enforcement of communicative policy class model needs to be developed for inclusion into our LPM reference monitor. Therefore, we plan to measure system utilization and performance degradation with a large number of concurrent tuple space transactions. The Parser and Persistence layers of LPM also have to be extended to support formulation and storage of policies for communicative class model.

References

1. Balzarotti, D., Costa, P., Picco, G.P.: The LighTS tuple space framework and its customization for context-aware applications. WAIS **5**(2), 215–231 (2007)
2. Belyaev, K.: Linux Policy Machine (LPM) - Managing the Application-Level OS Resource Control in the Linux Environment (2016). https://github.com/kirillbelyaev/tinypm/tree/LPM. Accessed 18 Sep 2016
3. Belyaev, K., Ray, I.: Towards access control for isolated applications. In: Proceedings of SECRYPT, pp. 171–182. SCITEPRESS (2016)
4. Cabri, G., Leonardi, L., Zambonelli, F.: XML dataspaces for mobile agent coordination. In: Proceedings of ACM SAC, pp. 181–188. ACM (2000)
5. Chen, X., Sha, E.H.-M., Zhuge, Q., Jiang, W., Chen, J., Chen, J., Xu, J.: A unified framework for designing high performance in-memory and hybrid memory file systems. JSA **68**, 51–64 (2016)

6. Chin, E., Felt, A.P., Greenwood, K., Wagner, D.: Analyzing inter-application communication in android. In: Proceedings of ACM MobiSys, pp. 239–252. ACM (2011)
7. Docker Developers. What is Docker? (2016). https://www.docker.com/what-docker/. Accessed 18 Sep 2016
8. Gelernter, D.: Generative communication in Linda. ACM TOPLAS **7**(1), 80–112 (1985)
9. Havoc Pennington Red Hat, Inc.: D-Bus Specification (2016). https://dbus.freedesktop.org/doc/dbus-specification.html. Accessed 18 Sep 2016
10. Krohn, M., Yip, A., Brodsky, M., Cliffer, N., Kaashoek, M.F., Kohler, E., Morris, R.: Information flow control for standard OS abstractions. ACM SIGOPS OSR **41**(6), 321–334 (2007)
11. Linux Programmer's Manual. Kernel Namespaces (2016). http://man7.org/linux/man-pages/man7/namespaces.7.html. Accessed 18 Sep 2016
12. Minsky, N.H., Minsky, Y.M., Ungureanu, V.: Making tuple spaces safe for heterogeneous distributed systems. In: Proceedings of ACM SAC, pp. 218–226 (2000)
13. Myers, A.C., Liskov, B.: Protecting privacy using the decentralized label model. ACM TOSEM **9**(4), 410–442 (2000)
14. Roy, I., Porter, D.E., Bond, M.D., Mckinley, K.S., Witchel, E.: Laminar: practical fine-grained decentralized information flow control. ACM SIGPLAN Not. **44**(6), 63–74 (2009)
15. Vitek, J., Bryce, C., Oriol, M.: Coordinating processes with secure spaces. Sci. Comput. Program. **46**(1), 163–193 (2003)
16. XStream Developers. XStream Serialization Library (2016). http://x-stream.github.io/. Accessed 18 Sep 2016
17. Xu, Y., Dunn, A.M., Hofmann, O.S., Lee, M.Z., Mehdi, S.A., Witchel, E.: Application-defined decentralized access control. In: Proceedings of USENIX ATC, pp. 395–408 (2014)
18. Yu, J., Buyya, R.: A novel architecture for realizing grid workflow using tuple spaces. In: Proceedings of International Workshop on Grid Computing, pp. 119–128. IEEE (2004)

Generic Access Control System for Ad Hoc MCC and Fog Computing

Bilel Zaghdoudi[1]([✉]), Hella Kaffel-Ben Ayed[2], and Wafa Harizi[3]

[1] LIPAH, Faculty of Science of Tunis, University of El Manar, Tunis, Tunisia
zaghdoudibilel@gmail.com
[2] CRISTAL Laboratory, National School of Computer Science,
University of Manouba, Manouba, Tunisia
[3] Faculty of Science of Tunis, University of El Manar, Tunis, Tunisia

Abstract. The goal of this paper is to propose an approach based on DHT toward access control for ad hoc MCC and Fog computing. We rely on Chord DHTs to create a scalable, generic and robust access control solution. We use simulations to evaluate the performances of the proposal. We focus on a set of metrics to measure the overhead of the system. We considered a variable network size, a variable responsible nodes percentage and different hash function as simulation parameter. The obtained results show acceptable overhead for relatively average networks sizes. Simulations show that all the metrics increase with the nodes number and the number of responsible nodes.

Keywords: Access control · Ad hoc mobile cloud · Fog computing · DHT

1 Introduction

The research community is interested in the use of shared, heterogeneous resources. The numerous benefits that distributed computing can provide in the field of big data, latency-sensitive applications, mobile applications, video-on-demand service and Smart Grids led to the emergence of new distributed computing paradigms such as Fog computing and ad hoc MCC.

Fog computing is a systematic, highly virtual, secure and network-integrated platform that provides computing, storage, and networking services at the edge of the network [1]. Resources and services are available and are closer to the end-user. They are located between endpoints and the traditional Cloud [3]. Fog computing is located outside the Cloud to ensure the provision of resources in a truly distributed way [10]. This helps eliminating service latency, improves QoS and removes other possible obstacles in relation with data transfer and mobile data high cost. All these characteristics make the Fog computing paradigm well positioned for big data and real time analytics. It supports mobile computing and data streaming [1].

© Springer International Publishing AG 2016
S. Foresti and G. Persiano (Eds.): CANS 2016, LNCS 10052, pp. 400–415, 2016.
DOI: 10.1007/978-3-319-48965-0_24

Ad hoc MCC is one particular scenario of Fog computing where mobile devices are used as resource providers. These devices are connected via spontaneous ad hoc networks and are evolving in the end-users local vicinity. Compared to older mobile cloud approaches such as Cloudlet [18], the ad hoc MCC presents many advantages. It is spontaneously deployed, easy to access, cost effective and does not rely on central servers or connections to infrastructure networks.

Ad hoc MCC can support various applications such as sharing GPS/Internet data, sensor data applications, crowd computing, multimedia search, image processing, language processing, social networking, and disaster recovery [15]. It is promising in various locations such as airports, stations, cafes, museums, battlefield or any environment where connectivity to cloud services is not available and where ad hoc communities can be gathered. The scenario detailed below can take advantage of a mobile cloud over ad hoc networks.

In this scenario, a massive disaster such as an earthquake or a tsunami has ravaged the land causing human loss and infrastructure destruction. Internet services providing satellite images, maps, reliefs or buildings such as Google Earth or Google maps are now useless. Since internet infrastructure is destroyed and almost landmarks like bridges, highways, and buildings are collapsed, rescue teams conducting search and rescue operations face many problems. Indeed, the absence of a clear image of the terrain and buildings harms the efficiency of the rescue effort. Thanks to ad hoc MCC, the disaster survivors and rescue teams members can share the resources of their mobile terminals interconnected over ad hoc networks. They take pictures with their smartphones or tablets cameras. These pictures can be processed and stored locally or using the resources provided by other mobile terminals. Then, users can access the shared storage spaces to discover the new face of the disaster sites.

The goal of this paper is to propose an approach toward access control in the context of ad hoc MCC and Fog computing. This paper is structured as follows: Sect. 2 is a reminder of our previous work. In Sect. 3, we present the literature review related to access control in Fog computing and P2P systems. Section 4 introduces the proposed access control model. Section 5 depicts the performance evaluation of the proposal. Finally, in Sect. 6, we conclude the paper and present ongoing works.

2 Related Works

Ad hoc MCC and fog computing rise a number of security and privacy considerations that are mostly regarding access to resources and services [17,20]. Fog computing faces various challenging security issues. In the following, we focus on access control and present preliminary approaches and studies aiming to implement access control in fog environment. In addition, from the analysis of different distributed paradigms, we observe that Fog computing has multiple similarities with P2P [12]. such as: Decentralization, heterogeneity, autonomy, support for mobility, resource sharing, large number of nodes, real-time interaction, predominance of wireless access, edge located. Consequently, we introduce, the main approaches of access control in P2P systems.

2.1   Related Works on Access Control in Fog

Due to its infancy, there are very few research works on access control in fog computing. In traditional systems, subjects are assigned with identities. During users' identification, these identities are presented to the system and then verified during authentication. After a successful authentication process, access control involves the authorization process which is to decide whether an access request should be permitted or denied. For the arbitrarily changing number of nodes in a fog area, assigning and verifying identities for every node is not possible. On one hand, not all services might be publicly available. On the other hand some services might require consumer identification. This urges the need for an access control system that can consider information describing subjects, objects and the context of operation.

In [17], the authors propose a distributed access control system using identities and attributes for authentication and authorization purposes. A deep discussion of Fog computing access control requirements is also presented, to finally conclude by suggesting the main features of a proper access control system. The first suggestion is to use an Attribute-Based Access Control (ABAC). It is an access control approach based on attributes, which can be implemented within an organization such as a fog environment. Attributes are characteristics, defined as name-value pairs, which can contain information about subjects, objects and context. Context attributes, or environmental conditions, allow ABAC implementations to be context-aware, thus making it an ideal candidate for fog applications, where context is a factor that affects the entire system behavior. The second suggestion for implementing a suitable access control model for fog is to use a reference monitor (RM). The reference monitor is constituted of the Policy Decision Point (PDP) and the Policy Enforcement Point (PEP). The PDP's role is to make the access decisions. The PEP is responsible for making access request and enforcing authorization decisions. In traditional computing environments, the reference monitor is usually implemented in a centralized way [9]. However this approach is not viable in the dynamic and highly distributed fog environment and will impose significant latency. The distributed reference monitor based on ABAC presented in [17] can overcome this issue.

Authors in [6] propose a policy-based resource access control in fog computing, to support secure collaboration and interoperability between heterogeneous resources. They demonstrated the feasibility and practicality of their approach through a proof of concept implementation of a fog computing environment based on use case scenarios. However, the work lacks in clarity since it is preliminary, and authors did not present any conclusive implementation and evaluation results of any reliability tests. The approach presented in [11] is based on trust propagation. Instead of granting access based on conventional criteria such as roles and identities, the access to resources is granted based on the trustworthiness of the user. A node may be able to grant access to users even if they are previously unknown. It can do so without requiring any intervention from the users. The trustworthiness of an unknown user may be established through trust propagation.

The literature review about access control models in fog computing shows that we are at the beginning and there is still a lot of work to be done. All the studied works tried to underline the requirements of access control and to study the applicability of existent schemes on fog computing.

2.2 Related Works on Access Control in P2P Systems

In this section, we present a set of P2P access control approaches according to three types: Discretionary access control (DAC), Certificate based and Role based access control (RBAC).

Various approaches rely on identity based access control to determine the access rules for resources in P2P systems. This kind of access control called Discretionary Access Control (DAC) is based on the user's identity and the authorizations he/she possesses [8]. DAC models are mostly used with legacy applications and have a non-negligible management overhead in the context of distributed environments.

In [22], the authors propose a DAC based approach and introduce an authorization framework as a solution for the problem of access to computational resources in a grid environment. The main goal of this framework is to help in reasoning about the behavior of resource owners and their clients. This solution is enhanced in [2] by adding XML encryption files. It is based on the user's identity and the authorizations he/she possesses. The work in [21] extends DAC models to P2P file-sharing systems. Trust is integrated by means of a reputation model that maps two dimensions into rating certificates: trust and contribution. This approach is not suitable to the decentralized nature of MANETs because it assumes that there is a node in the network that classifies users, assigns users access rights and authenticates nodes. Another scheme presented in [8], provides authorization capabilities for file sharing over pure P2P networks. The authors make use of public key certificates to store security clearances as attributes. These clearances are issued by content providers and used to classify them. The access to content is granted when the peer's security clearance is at least the same level of the content.

Other approaches propose certificate based access control models which use digital certificates, as medium for transferring access control data concerning a node. The work presented in [7] is based on this model. The authors propose an access control system for mobile P2P collaborative environments. They assume the presence of a specific peer providing authorization certification to other peers in the network. In order to be allowed to access shared files, users must present their authorization certificates to the service providers. This approach is vulnerable to Man in the middle attacks. Since the certificate does not carry any information for the authentication of the owner, an attacker can use it to gain access to shared files. Authors in [23], propose a trusted computing architecture based on an abstract layer of trustworthy hardware. Every peer has a role defined by the integration of his attributes according to his identity and his certificate. To ensure the authenticity of the certificates, the use of a Public Key Infrastructure is required.

In Role-based access control models (RBAC), users have access to objects based on their assigned roles. Roles are defined according to job functions while permissions are defined according to job authorities and responsibilities which in their turn simplify the administration and management of permissions. When using a RBAC model there is no need to configure privileges for every user of the system. This can enhance scalability for distributed architecture. Authors in [16] present a scalable role based access control approach for two different architectures. It is based on the use of Lightweight Peer Certificates. The access control decision is centralized in specific peers called super-peers. The assumption that the network is composed of two different types of nodes or superposing two networks is not suitable to P2P environment over ad-hoc networks. This may generate an overhead that affects the scalability of the system.

Access control models for P2P have shortcomings related to the requirements of Fog and ad hoc MCC access control presented in Sect. 4.1. However, it appears to be a good start in the design of a suitable access control approach as it takes into consideration the similarities of the two environments presented above.

3   Previous Work

In a previous work, we propose an architecture and a protocol supporting the deployment of ad hoc mobile MCC. This solution permits to use the resources of mobile terminals in a MANET to create a virtual cloud meeting the mobile community resources provider needs.

3.1   The Architecture

Our Cloud system is composed of two main entities: Provider nodes acting as resources provider, Customer nodes acting as cloud clients. The role of Providers is to offer services to the Customers such as tasks execution and data storage, or collecting information. We proposed a protocol for the deployment and the management of nodes in a mobile Ad hoc Cloud over MANETs named C-Protocol. As for the layered model of our architecture, we integrated the C-Protocol as a meta-layer within the TCP/IP stack under the Cloud framework layer. C-Protocol provides a set of services that allow MCC management and to abstract and simplify a part of MANET networks operation. Among its main services: On-demand Cloud deployment, Dynamic management of Provider and Customer nodes.

3.2   The Protocol

C-Protocol is composed of two main phases, the Setup phase and the dynamic nodes management. It uses a set of UDP messages exchanged between nodes. The MCC Setup phase aims at setting up an ad hoc MCC over a spontaneous MANET. Any node in the ad hoc network with resource shortage can start the Setup by broadcasting a request on the network. At the end of this phase, a cloud provider system (CPS) composed of provider nodes is created. Access lists are generated and delivered to all nodes. The dynamic networks topology and the variable capacity of devices in terms of resources result in the necessity to manage the group of Providers: new providers can join the ad hoc MCC to satisfy Customers' needs while others can leave it and similarly for customers. C-Protocol handles the arrival and the departure of Customers or Providers. To be able to do that, we implemented the following processes: Add provider process, Add Customer process, MCC member departure process.

3.3 Results

The performances of the proposed protocol is evaluated by simulation using the NS-3 simulator. Our solution presents latency issues for the dynamic management of nodes and ACL recovery and update mechanisms. In Fig. 1, we present results for adding Customer in small networks. The time required to add a Customer in a network composed of 50 nodes is equal to 8.19 s.

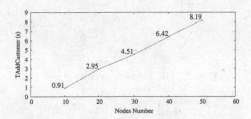

Fig. 1. Required time to add a customer

4 The Proposal

The main goal of this work is to provide a generic solution to prevent unauthorized access of malicious nodes to the Cloud Provider System or pretending to be service providers. Our Solution ensures that only nodes members of the MCC can communicate with each other. We present the mechanisms and the design of the security approach.

4.1 The Requirements

An access control model for fog computing must fulfill a set of requirements, which are derived from requirements for access control in mobile ad hoc systems, P2P networks, and other distributed paradigms sharing the same characteristics. Fog computing introduces the following requirements for access control: Decentralization, Nodes identification and classification, Context-awareness, Resource constraint, Network availability, Decision latency. These requirements present a challenge from the point of view of the security mechanisms that should be applied to provide access control.

4.2   The Proposed Mechanisms

In order to propose a solution as generic as possible with regard to mobile computing characteristics, we propose an DHT overlay based model. Figure 2 presents the architecture of the system composed of two different layers. The upper layer is the MCC architecture composed of Provider and Customer nodes. The lower layer is the overlay network created based on the Providers and Customers lists (PL, CL) provided by the C-Protocol after the Setup of the main MCC architecture.

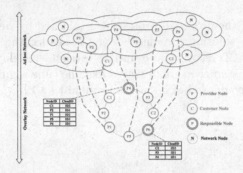

Fig. 2. The system architecture

We assume the existence of a clustering algorithm, which will select nodes to be responsible nodes from the provider nodes list based on a set of criteria. Responsible nodes are a group of nodes selected from the PL to maintain the access control data hash table and make decision about nodes requesting access to the MCC network. As we mentioned in the previous work section, two access lists, i.e. Provider list and Customer list are created by the initiator node during the Setup phase. All authorized nodes are known by the initiator. The lists are delivered to all registered nodes after the creation of the mobile cloud. The integrity of these lists are maintained by an update and a recovery mechanisms when nodes join or leave the MCC. From the simulation results of our proposal, we have shown that our solution faces latency and ACL management issues.

To solve these problems, we propose to distribute the creation and the update of access control lists. We rely on distributed hash tables (DHT) as a substitute to ACLs. DHT is a class of distributed system which partitions the key space among participating peers [4,14]. The DHT determines the peer in the system which is responsible for storing the data and retrieves the data that are stored as (key, value) pairs among a number of peers [19]. DHT are usually implemented in structured overlay networks.

We studied and compared between the most known structured overlay networks, i.e. Pastry, Tapestry, CAN and Chord [13]. From that comparison, we can conclude that Chord is designed to offer the required functionalities to implement general purpose systems while preserving maximum flexibility. It is an efficient distributed lookup system based on consistent hashing [5]. Tapestry has an advantage against Chord protocol because the algorithm knows the network topology, so queries never travel more than the network distance required to reach them. However, it does not handle node joins and failures like Chord. Like Tapestry, Pastry takes into account the network locality; it seeks to minimize the distance using a scalar proximity metric like the number of IP routing hops. However, it has a more complicated join protocol. A new node's routing table will be populated with information from nodes along the path taken by the join message. This leads to latency.

From the studied research works, theoretical analysis, simulations, and experiments confirm that Chord scales well with the number of nodes, recovers from large numbers of simultaneous node failures and joins, and answers most lookups correctly even during recovery. We believe that Chord will be a valuable component for our solution.

We propose the use of Chord to implement access lists using Chord distributed hash tables in order to authenticate nodes accessing the Fog or the ad hoc MCC. This permits to benefit of Chord advantages for the creation of a scalable, generic and robust access control solution. Figure 3.a presents the Chord DHT structure. The DHT has two primitive operations: put() is a function that puts data V into the DHT space with a key K. Get() is a function that gets the original data using a given key K. Although extremely simple, these two primitives are suitable for a great variety of applications and provide good robustness and high efficiency, especially in large-scale systems.

We will modify the Chord DHT to meet the access control needs. The new DHT called access control DHT is presented in Fig. 3.b. It is created during the creation of the overlay for each responsible node of the overlay ring. It is updated and maintained dynamically. The access control DHT consists of a two-dimensional table containing the set of pairs of nodes' identifiers and their respective role identifier (NodeID, CloudID). The node's identifier is mapped from the node's mac address and a random sequence by a hash function and it is a substitute for the key K in the original DHT. The CloudID is a unique identifier generated for each ad hoc MCC created and added to the Chord layer. In order to back up the role of each authorized node, we use the CloudID concatenated with a random sequence to identify the two possible role respectively Customer or Provider. These two unique identifiers will replace the data V in the classic structure.

Furthermore, in order to prevent the replay of sensitive messages such us requesting access to resources messages, we propose to include a nonce (unique for each message and easy to check). The nonce is calculated as defined bellow using concatenated and hashed information, which are able to guaranty the authenticity of received messages. These information are the responsible node identifier associated to the node creating the nonce and the message transmission time. In the requesting resources case, the processing of the nonce is defined as follows:

- Nonce generation: is processed by the node requesting access. The Chord layer is requested about its responsible node's identifier. This layer will replay with a message containing a NodeID which is a hash of the responsible node's MAC address and a random sequence. At the C-Protocol level, this identifier is concatenated with the message transmission time creating the nonce.
- Nonce checking: The first verification of the nonce is accomplished at the Chord layer level. A request is sent by the C-Protocol to the Chord layer to verify the relation between the MAC address of the requesting node and the NodeID received in the message. If the Chord layer responds with a message to affirm that the NodeID is the identifier of the responsible node of that MAC address. The C-Protocol verifies the transmission time to check the authenticity of the message.

Key	Value
Key1	Value1
Key2	Value2
Key3	Value3
Key4	Value4

a - Chord DHT

Node-ID	Cloud-ID
Node1-ID	CloudID1
Node2-ID	CloudID1
Node3-ID	CloudID2
Node4-ID	CloudID1

b - Access control DHT

Fig. 3. Data hash table structure

4.3   The Protocol:

We define the process through which nodes have to follow in order to access to mobile cloud resources. The process is based on the whole Chord mechanism. All the nodes member of the MCC have a replicas on the Chord ring. When added to the ring, a node gets its unique identifier which is the hash of the node's MAC address and a random sequence forming the NodeID. Every authorized node has an entry in the DHT of its responsible node composed of the NodeID and the CloudID.

- The Setup: At the end of the MCC setup, a Provider and Customer lists will be generated by the C-Protocol. These two lists store all the nodes member of the Cloud provider system and the Customer nodes authorized to access shared resources. The Chord layer uses these lists to create the overlay network. This overlay is a replicas of the Ad hoc network where the nodes are placed on the Chord ring. The first step in the setup phase is to create the ring and place the first node. Taking into consideration the selection algorithm assumption presented above, the first nodes in the PL are responsible nodes. So, an empty DHT will be created. Then, Chord will hash nodes' identifiers and place them on the ring in an ascending order. When the overlay replicas network is created with empty DHTs, the Chord layer will launch the setting of authorizing nodes.

It is about placing nodes in responsible nodes' distributed hash tables. Nodes can be added in the local DHT, also a lookup operation for responsible node can be performed and an InsertNode message is sent to add the node in a distant node's DHT.

- The Authentication: In a traditional system, each user willing to access a resource or a service, must pass through an authentication/authorization process with a centralized entity. In our system, this process is discreet. The node requesting access does not communicate directly with an authentication server. When a node receives a request to access resource, the message is passed to the Chord layer to authorize the node. The Chord layer reconstructs the NodeID and identifies the responsible node of the node requesting access. Then a message SearchRequest is sent to the responsible node to verify if the NodeID is present in its DHT. If the result is affirmative, the node's role is verified according to the CloudID coupled with its identifier. Then access is permitted and an Access-authorized message is returned to the C-Protocol. Otherwise, access is denied.
- The node management: The dynamic networks topology and the variable capacity of devices in terms of resources result in the necessity to manage the group of Providers. New providers can join the ad hoc MCC to satisfy Customers needs while other can leave it and similarly for Customers. C-Protocol handles the arrival and the departure of Customers or Providers. To ensure homogeneity between the physical ad hoc network and the overlay network. All nodes' management operations should be replicated on the ring.

5 Performance Evaluation

To evaluate the performances of our access control solution, we used a combination of the NS-3 simulator and the OpenChord API. It is an open source implementation of the Chord distributed hash table. OpenChord provides the possibility to use the Chord distributed hash table within Java applications by providing an API to store all serializable Java objects within the distributed hash table. We performed 20 runs for each simulation scenario and computed the 95 % confidence interval for all simulations results. We define the following metrics:

- TChord: This metric measures the time required for the deployment of the overlay network.
- TCloudG: This metric measures the global time required for the setting up of the mobile Cloud (C-Protocol and Chord Layer). TCloudG = TCloud + TChord where TCloud is the time required to create the CPS.
- TAccess: This metric measures the time required to authenticate a node.
- TAdd: This metric measures the time required for adding a node to the overlay network.
- TDelete: This metric measures the time required for deleting a node from the overlay network.

5.1   Simulation Model

In the following simulations, the nodes number varies between 10 and 300 nodes. The percentage of responsible nodes in the Chord ring varies between 20 % to 100 % for two scenarios (Effect of responsible nodes percentage on TChord and TAccess) and equal to 30 % in the other scenarios. SHA-1 as Chord hash function for the majority of simulated scenarios. To study the effect of changing the hash function on the selected metrics, we used MD5, SHA-1 and SHA-2 hash functions.

5.2   Evaluation of TChord

Our goal here is to have an estimation of the time required for the creation of the overlay network. Through this estimation, we will study the influence of the responsible nodes percentage on TChord.

Effect of the Responsible Nodes Percentage on TChord: In the first scenario, we simulated the deployment of 4 networks composed respectively of 10, 50, 150 and 300 nodes. We varied the percentage of responsible nodes in the ring. For the four simulated networks, Fig. 4.a shows that TChord increases with the percentage of responsible nodes. TChord is relatively low for small number of responsible nodes (up to 30 %). It is equal to 0.15 s for the 10 nodes network, 1.37 s in a network composed of 50 nodes, 7.59 s for 150 nodes and 29.51 s for 300 nodes with a percentage of responsible nodes equal to 30 %. For large percentage of responsible nodes in the network, TChord reaches the value of 82.08 s and 181.67 s respectively for 150 and 300 nodes networks. All the nodes are responsible nodes. We can consider acceptable the obtained values of TChord for the setting up of the overlay network with a percentage of responsible nodes up to 30 %.

Estimation of TChord: In order to estimate TChord and show the impact of the network size, we vary the number of nodes from 10 to 300. The percentage of responsible nodes in the network is fixed to 30 %. Figure 4.b shows that the TChord increases with the number of nodes in the network.

Effect of the Hash Function on TChord: The OpenChord API gives the user the ability to use 3 different hash functions respectively MD5, SHA-1, SHA-2. We studied the effect of changing the hash function on TChord. From the simulation results, we concluded that the lowest values of TChord are measured when using MD5 hash function while SHA-2 has the highest TChord values. The effect of the hash function is the same for all measured metrics: TChord, TAccess, TAdd and TDelete.

5.3   Evaluation of TCloudG

Our goal here is to have an estimation of the time required for setting up the mobile Cloud infrastructure and to identify the factors that influence this metric. In previous research work, we estimated and studied the time required for the CPS setup using the NS-3 simulator that we called TCloud. We considered acceptable the obtained values of TCloud for the setting up of CPS in small networks (up to 100 nodes). Also, we concluded that like TChord, TCloud increases with the number of nodes. The density of the network has an important impact on TCloud, which is not significantly affected by the nodes' speed for medium size networks. In addition, TCloud is higher when using AODV and it is not impacted by the data rate when using OLSR.

The lower curve in Fig. 5 shows the value of TCloud. It is considered as the MCC deployment time without security. The upper curve in the same figure shows the TCloudG which is the sum of the TCloud and the TChord. TCloudG inherits the properties of TCloud and TChord. It increases with nodes number and we can consider acceptable the obtained values of TCloudG for the setting up of the mobile MCC in small networks (up to 100 nodes).

5.4   Evaluation of TAccess

Effect of the Responsible Nodes Percentage on TAccess: We study here the effect of varying the responsible nodes percentage on TAccess. In this scenario, we simulated 4 networks composed respectively of 10, 50, 150 and 300 nodes while varying the responsible nodes percentage between 20 % and 100 % and measured the time required to authenticate a node. We observe in Fig. 6.a that the curves of TAccess have the same shape for each simulated network. TAccess is equal to 15.61 ms, 16.34 ms, 18.21 ms and 19.57 ms respectively for 10, 50, 150, 300 nodes networks when 30 % of the nodes are responsible nodes and it reaches the values of 17.28 ms, 18.81 ms, 21.57 ms and 24.17 ms for the same networks when all the nodes of the Chord ring are responsible nodes. We can conclude that TAccess is not significantly affected by the responsible nodes percentage for different size networks.

Estimation of TAccess: In order to show the impact of the network size on TAccess, we vary the number of nodes from 10 to 300 while the percentage of responsible nodes is fixed to 30 %. Figure 6.b shows that TAccess increases with the number of nodes. It is equal to 16.34 ms in a network composed of 50 nodes and reaches 19.57 ms when authenticating a node in a 300 nodes network.

5.5   Evaluation of TAdd and TDelete

Figure 7 shows the simulation results of respectively TAdd and TDelete. We varied the number of nodes from 10 to 300 nodes and used a responsible nodes percentage equal to 30 %. Each figure presents two curves, the lower curves show

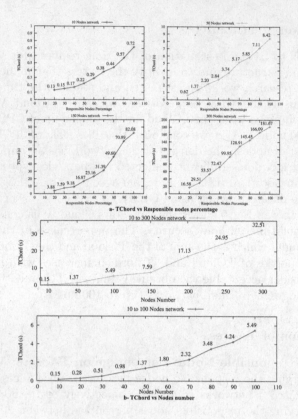

a- TChord vs Responsible nodes percentage

b- TChord vs Nodes number

Fig. 4. TChord study

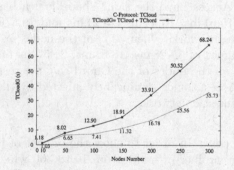

Fig. 5. TCloudG vs Nodes number

all measures of TAdd and respectively TDelete for normal node joining or leaving the Chord ring while the upper ones show the results for the responsible node join/leave operations.

In a network composed of 50 nodes, the required time to add a normal node is equal to 21.54 ms compared to responsible node TAdd equal to 26.40 ms. TAdd

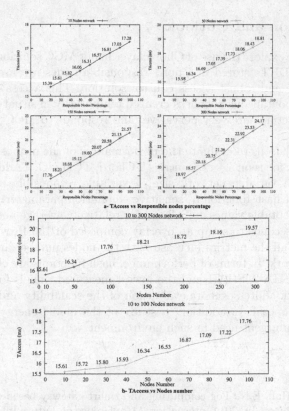

a- TAccess vs Responsible nodes percentage

b- TAccess vs Nodes number

Fig. 6. TAccess study

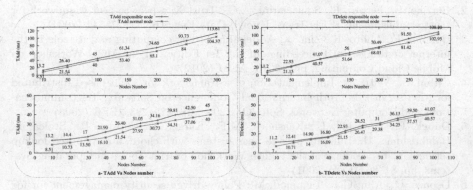

a- TAdd Vs Nodes number

b- TDelete Vs Nodes number

Fig. 7. Simulation results of TAdd and TDelete

and TDelete increase with the number of nodes. In more populated networks for example a 300 nodes network, TDelete is equal to 102.95 ms when deleting a normal node and 108.3 ms when it is a responsible node.

6   Conclusion and Outlook

In this paper, we explore the use of Chord layer in our MCC solution architecture. This layer and DHTs stored in Chord responsible nodes are used to create a scalable, generic and robust access control solution. This access control model would befit to spontaneous networks created temporarily in situations where the mobile infrastructures are very pervasive, and responds to MCC access control requirements.

We use simulations to evaluate the performances of the proposed access control solution. We focus on a set of metrics TChord, TCloudG, TAdd and TDelete. We considered a variable network size, a variable responsible nodes percentage and different hash function as sensitive simulation parameter. The obtained results show acceptable values of TChord for relatively average networks since it takes around 8 seconds to setup an overlay composed of 150 Providers. Simulations show that all the metrics increase with the nodes number and the responsible nodes network. In terms of performance, hash functions are classified in the following order SHA-2, SHA-1 and the lowest measured time is for MD5.

Ongoing work addresses more evaluation of the scalability and the overhead of the global proposal. In addition, a study of the model energy consumption appears to be an urgent need in such environment.

References

1. Aazam, M., Huh, E.N.: Fog computing and smart gateway based communication for cloud of things. In: 2014 International Conference on Future Internet of Things and Cloud (FiCloud), pp. 464–470. IEEE (2014)
2. Bertino, E., Ferrari, E., Squicciarini, A.C.: Trust-X: a peer-to-peer framework for trust establishment. IEEE Trans. Knowl. Data Eng. **16**(7), 827–842 (2004)
3. Bonomi, F., Milito, R., Zhu, J., Addepalli, S.: Fog computing and its role in the internet of things. In: Proceedings of the 1st Edition of the MCC Workshop on Mobile Cloud Computing, pp. 13–16. ACM (2012)
4. Cirani, S., Veltri, L.: Implementation of a framework for a dht-based distributed location service. In: 16th International Conference on Software, Telecommunications and Computer Networks, SoftCOM 2008, pp. 279–283. IEEE (2008)
5. Dabek, F., Brunskill, E., Kaashoek, M.F., Karger, D., Morris, R., Stoica, I., Balakrishnan, H.: Building peer-to-peer systems with chord, a distributed lookup service. In: Proceedings of the Eighth Workshop on Hot Topics in Operating Systems, pp. 81–86. IEEE (2001)
6. Dsouza, C., Ahn, G.J., Taguinod, M.: Policy-driven security management for fog computing: preliminary framework and a case study. In: 2014 IEEE 15th International Conference on Information Reuse and Integration (IRI), pp. 16–23. IEEE (2014)
7. Fenkam, P., Dustdar, S., Kirda, E., Reif, G., Gall, H.: Towards an access control system for mobile peer-to-peer collaborative environments. In: Proceedings of the Eleventh IEEE International Workshops on Enabling Technologies: Infrastructure for Collaborative Enterprises, WET ICE 2002, pp. 95–100. IEEE (2002)
8. González, E.P.: Content authentication and access control in pure peer-to-peer networks. Universidad Carlos Iii De Madrid (2008)

9. Gupta, R., Bhide, M.: A generic XACML based declarative authorization scheme for Java. In: di Vimercati, S.C., Syverson, P.F., Gollmann, D. (eds.) ESORICS 2005. LNCS, vol. 3679, pp. 44–63. Springer, Heidelberg (2005)

10. Hajibaba, M., Gorgin, S.: A review on modern distributed computing paradigms: Cloud computing, jungle computing and fog computing. CIT. J. Comput. Inf. Technol. **22**(2), 69–84 (2014)

11. Hasan, O., Pierson, J.M., Brunie, L.: Access control in ubiquitous environments based on subjectivity eliminated trust propagation. In: IEEE/IFIP International Conference on Embedded and Ubiquitous Computing, EUC 2008, vol. 2, pp. 603–609. IEEE (2008)

12. Kahanwal, D., Singh, D.T., et al.: The distributed computing paradigms: P2P, grid, cluster, cloud, and jungle. arXiv preprint arXiv:1311.3070 (2013)

13. Lua, E.K., Crowcroft, J., Pias, M., Sharma, R., Lim, S.: A survey and comparison of peer-to-peer overlay network schemes. IEEE Commun. Surv. Tutorials **7**(2), 72–93 (2005)

14. Lv, E., Duan, Z., Qi, J.J., Cao, Y., Peng, Z.: Incorporating clusters into hybrid P2P network. In: First International Conference on the Digital Society, ICDS 2007, p. 17. IEEE (2007)

15. Marinelli, E.E.: Hyrax: cloud computing on mobile devices using mapreduce. Technical report, DTIC Document (2009)

16. Park, J.S., Hwang, J.: Role-based access control for collaborative enterprise in peer-to-peer computing environments. In: Proceedings of the Eighth ACM Symposium on Access Control Models and Technologies, pp. 93–99. ACM (2003)

17. Salonikias, S., Mavridis, I., Gritzalis, D.: Access control issues in utilizing fog computing for transport infrastructure. In: Rome, E., Theocharidou, M., Wolthusen, S. (eds.) CRITIS 2015. LNCS, vol. 9578, pp. 15–26. Springer, Heidelberg (2016). doi:10.1007/978-3-319-33331-1_2

18. Satyanarayanan, M., Bahl, P., Caceres, R., Davies, N.: The case for vm-based cloudlets in mobile computing. IEEE Pervasive Comput. **8**(4), 14–23 (2009)

19. Sibakov, S.: Simulating a Mobile Peer-to-Peer Network. Ph.D. thesis. Citeseer (2009)

20. Stojmenovic, I., Wen, S.: The fog computing paradigm: scenarios and security issues. In: 2014 Federated Conference on Computer Science and Information Systems (FedCSIS), pp. 1–8. IEEE (2014)

21. Tran, H., Hitchens, M., Varadharajan, V., Watters, P.: A trust based access control framework for P2P file-sharing systems. In: Proceedings of the 38th Annual Hawaii International Conference on System Sciences, HICSS 2005, p. 302c. IEEE (2005)

22. Winslett, M., Zhang, C.C., Bonatti, P.A.: Peeraccess: a logic for distributed authorization. In: Proceedings of the 12th ACM Conference on Computer and Communications Security, pp. 168–179. ACM (2005)

23. Zhang, Y., Li, X., Huai, J., Liu, Y.: Access control in peer-to-peer collaborative systems. In: 25th IEEE International Conference on Distributed Computing Systems Workshops, pp. 835–840. IEEE (2005)

Functional and Homomorphic Encryption

SecReach: Secure Reachability Computation on Encrypted Location Check-in Data

Hanyu Quan[1,2], Boyang Wang[2], Iraklis Leontiadis[2], Ming Li[2(✉)], and Yuqing Zhang[1,3]

[1] School of Cyber Engineering, Xidian University, Xi'an, China
quanhanyu@gmail.com
[2] Department of Electrical and Computer Engineering,
The University of Arizona, Tucson, AZ, USA
{boyangwang,leontiad,lim}@email.arizona.edu
[3] University of Chinese Academy of Sciences, Beijing, China
zhangyq@ucas.ac.cn

Abstract. Reachability, which answers whether one person is reachable from another through a sequence of contacts within a period of time, is of great importance in many domains such as social behavior analysis. Recently, with the prevalence of various location-based services (LBSs), a great amount of spatiotemporal location check-in data is generated by individual GPS-equipped mobile devices and collected by LBS companies, which stimulates research on reachability queries in these location check-in datasets. Meanwhile, a growing trend is for LBS companies to use scalable and cost-effective clouds to collect, store, and analyze data, which makes it necessary to encrypt location check-in data before outsourcing due to privacy concerns. In this paper, for the first time, we propose a scheme, SecReach, to securely evaluate reachability queries on encrypted location check-in data by using somewhat homomorphic encryption (SWHE). We prove that our scheme is secure against a semi-honest cloud server. We also present a proof-of-concept implementation using the state-of-the-art SWHE library (i.e., HElib), which shows the efficiency and feasibility of our scheme.

Keywords: Reachability · Location privacy · Homomorphic encryption

1 Introduction

Reachability, which answers whether a user is reachable from another through a sequence of contacts in a period of time, is of great importance in many domains, e.g., social behavior analysis, friend recommendations, public health monitoring, to name a few. Due to the prevalence of various location-based services (LBSs), such as Google Maps, Foursquare, Yelp, etc., a great amount of location check-in data is generated by individual GPS-equipped mobile devices and collected by these LBS companies. This stimulates research on reachability analysis in these location check-in datasets [19,21]. For instance, if two people are in close

© Springer International Publishing AG 2016
S. Foresti and G. Persiano (Eds.): CANS 2016, LNCS 10052, pp. 419–434, 2016.
DOI: 10.1007/978-3-319-48965-0_25

proximity to each other, we can infer that they are socially connected or an item (e.g., an infectious virus) could spread from one to another. Base on these inferences, companies or other authorized parties such as governments are able to build customized advertising systems, identify certain targets or trace epidemic contacts.

Meanwhile, with the increase in the volume of data (for example, there are millions of new check-ins in Foursquare each day), a growing trend is for LBS companies to use scalable and cost-effective cloud services to store and analyze data. For instance, both Foursquare and Yelp use Amazon S3 (Amazon Simple Storage Service) to store their data. Moreover, advanced cloud services (such as Amazon Kinesis Firehose) allow mobile LBS applications to send data directly to cloud stores (e.g., Amazon S3) from users' mobile devices, which enables LBS companies to scale location check-in data collection on clouds. However, outsourcing location check-in data to clouds poses the privacy concerns of users. Location check-ins are sensitive because they reveal private individual information including home addresses, interests, and state of health [20]. Furthermore, the anonymity of location check-in data is difficult to achieve. A recent research work [5] shows that in a dataset, where the locations are specified hourly, four spatiotemporal points are enough to uniquely identify most of the individuals. Given the sensitivity of location information, users, who are willing to make their locations available to LBS companies, may not fully trust third party clouds. On the other hand, LBS companies also do not want to reveal individually generated location check-in data to public clouds, due to legal and commercial reasons.

To prevent clouds from learning location check-in data, the most effective way is to use end-to-end data encryption. However, the analysis of the encrypted check-in data in clouds remains to be a very challenging problem. Specifically, in this paper, we study how to evaluate reachability queries on encrypted location check-in data. Theoretically, Fully Homomorphic Encryption (FHE) [7] allows an untrusted party to compute any functions on encrypted data, however, the state-of-the-art FHEs are far from being practical [16]. Somewhat Homomorphic Encryption (SWHE), which supports additions and a few multiplications, is more efficient than FHE. Unfortunately, it cannot be directly used for evaluating reachability queries, because the limited number of multiplications is not sufficient for comparisons in reachability queries. On the other hand, some recent methods have been proposed for similar queries on encrypted location data, such as trajectory similarity [12] and kNN [6,17], in which they combine partially homomorphic encryption and secure two-party computation to implement comparisons on ciphertexts. However, this kind of method is ordinarily based on the system model of two cloud servers, which introduces extensive interactions.

In this paper, we propose a scheme for reachability queries evaluation on encrypted location check-in data. Our main contributions are as follows:

- To the best of our knowledge, this is the first work that studies reachability queries evaluation on encrypted location check-in data. We propose a method to compute 2-hop reachability using additions and a limited number of multiplications, instead of relying on comparisons which implies interactions.

With the use of SWHE and Bloom filters, the evaluation of reachability queries is non-interactive between a cloud server and a data analyzer. One of the key innovations in our scheme is a new method to determine whether an integer number is equal to a given integer k or whether it is in the range of $[0, k-1]$ in the ciphertext domain without decryption.

- We formally analyze the security of our scheme against a semi-honest server, and it is shown that our scheme does not leak any user locations, intermediate results or final reachability results to the server. We also present a proof-of-concept implementation, and experimental results show our scheme is feasible and efficient in practice.

The rest of this paper is organized as follows. Section 2 presents the problem statement and Sect. 3 introduces the preliminaries of our scheme. In Sect. 4 we describe the idea and details of our scheme. We analyze the security of our scheme in Sect. 5 and present a proof-of-concept implementation with a performance analysis in Sect. 6. Finally, Sect. 7 reviews the related work and Sect. 8 concludes the paper.

2   Problem Statement

In this paper we study the problem of evaluating reachability queries on encrypted location check-in data. In this section, we first introduce our system and adversarial model. Then, we state the data format of location check-ins and definition of reachability. Finally, we present our design objectives.

2.1   System and Adversarial Model

System Model. Our system model, as shown in Fig. 1, consists of a set of *users*, a *data owner*, a *data analyzer*, and a *cloud server*. Specifically, each user generates location check-in data on personal devices (e.g., smartphones or tablets), and uploads location check-ins to the cloud server over time. As a result, the cloud server stores and maintains a dataset containing a set of location check-ins, where each location check-in (also referred to as a *tuple*) is reported by one of the users at a certain time. Said differently, each tuple consists of three properties, including *who*, *where* and *when*. The dataset belongs to the data owner (e.g., an LBS company). The data analyzer is able to submit reachability queries to the cloud server to discover the reachability of a certain user to other users. Note that the data analyzer could also be the data owner itself. The cloud server should be able to perform the evaluation of reachability queries in a location check-in dataset, and return results to the data analyzer.

Adversarial Model. We assume users trust the data owner, but not the cloud server. Specifically, we assume the cloud server is *semi-honest* (i.e., *honest-but-curious*), which means it follows protocols correctly but may try to learn the private location of each tuple in a location check-in dataset. To be more precise, given a location check-in, the cloud server tries to figure out *where* this location check-in is reported. Due to the privacy concerns of users, each location is

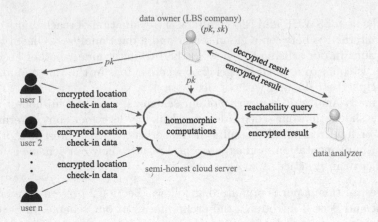

Fig. 1. The system model.

encrypted with a public key of the data owner before uploading it to the cloud. Therefore, given a reachability query, the cloud server computes it on encrypted data, and returns encrypted result back to the data analyzer. The data analyzer asks the data owner to decrypt the result. Only the data owner can decrypt the result with its secret key. We assume the data analyzer and the cloud server do not collude. Previous examples of this type of system model can also be found in recent secure medical computation applications such as [3, 26].

2.2 Location Check-in Data, Proximity and Reachability

Location Check-in Data. As discussed in [19], location check-in data is associated with both space dimension and time dimension as users move within a space over time. We define a location check-in data as a tuple $d = (u, l, t)$, where u is a user identity (i.e., who), l is the location of this user (i.e., where), and t is the time slot of generating this location check-in (i.e., when). Moreover, we leverage a square grid to index locations, as shown in Fig. 2. Specifically, a location $l = (x, y)$ is the center of a cell, and a user's location is reported as l on condition that its physical location is within this cell. Similar as square grid, other types of grids, such as hexagonal grid [15] can also be leveraged in location check-in data.

Proximity and Reachability. Given a tuple $d = (u, l, t)$, where $l = (x, y)$, we define the *proximity range* of user u as its square neighborhood including nine cells, where the center of this square is (x, y) and the size of this square can be configured by changing the cell size. This square is in fact the Moore neighborhood of the cell (x, y) with a specific range, which is frequently used in geographic information system (GIS). If another user's location is inside the proximity range of user u in the same time slot t, we say that the two users are in *direct contact*. Correspondingly, two users can be in *indirect contact* if they

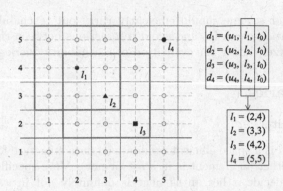

Fig. 2. An example of location check-in data generated by four users. The locations (i.e., *where*) are indexed using a grid. In this example, u_3 is reachable from u_1 through u_2 (i.e., there is a contact path $u_1 \rightarrow u_2 \rightarrow u_3$).

have a common direct-contact user. A *contact path*, which is bidirectional, exists between two users if they are in contact (either direct or indirect). A reachability query of a user u_i to another user u_j tells whether there is a contact path between them in a given time interval T (including several time slots). In other words, it is a way to decide whether one user is reachable from another user within T.

Figure 2 shows an example of location check-in data generated by four users in time slot t_0. In this example, for user u_3 and user u_1 in time interval $T = t_0$, u_3 is outside the proximity range of u_1, but it is inside the proximity range of u_2, who is in the proximity range of u_1. Thus, there is a contact path $u_1 \rightarrow u_2 \rightarrow u_3$ from u_1 to u_3, i.e., u_3 is reachable from u_1 through u_2. For user u_4 and user u_1, because u_4 is outside all the proximity ranges of the other three users, it is not reachable from any of those three users. More details about the definition of reachability can be found in [19].

2.3 Design Objectives

In this paper, we aim at designing a secure scheme to compute reachability queries under the preceding system and adversarial model. Our main design objectives include two aspects, data privacy and efficiency. Specifically,

- **Data Privacy.** The cloud server is not be able to reveal any of the locations in a location check-in dataset or the results of any reachability queries. In addition, the cloud server cannot reveal intermediate results (e.g., the proximity between users). The reason of such high level of privacy protection is that, if we leak either intermediate proximity results or final reachability results to the cloud server, the cloud server may be able to infer users' locations by encrypting locations of its choice and then conduct proximity tests with the locations in the dataset, and use triangulation attacks to learn users' locations with reasonable accuracy [11].

- **Efficiency.** Our scheme should efficiently carry out reachability queries on encrypted location check-ins and avoid interactions between the cloud server and data analyzer during the evaluation of reachability queries.

3   Preliminaries

3.1   Bloom Filters

A Bloom filter [1] is a space-efficient randomized data structure for membership testing (i.e., whether an element is in a set or not). More specifically, a Bloom filter is able to decide either an element is definitely not in a set or it is in a set with a very high probability. A (m, k)-Bloom filter $\mathsf{BF} = (b_1, \ldots, b_m)$ is essentially a binary vector of m bits, which are initially all set as 0s. There are k independent hash functions $h_1, \ldots, h_k$, where the hash values of each of those hash functions is within the range of $[1, m]$ and each value within this range maps a component index in a Bloom filter.

To add an element x to a Bloom filter BF, bits $\{b_{h_1(x)}, \ldots, b_{h_k(x)}\}$ are set as 1s. To query if an element y is in a set, we check whether $\{b_{h_1(y)}, \ldots, b_{h_k(y)}\}$ are all 1s. If not, then y is definitely not a member of the set; otherwise, y is in the set with a small false positive probability. We denote the above two algorithms as BF.add and BF.query, respectively.

3.2   Somewhat Homomorphic Encryption

Somewhat homomorphic encryption (SWHE) is a fundamental building block of fully homomorphic encryption (FHE), which can be extended to FHE by utilizing bootstrapping [7]. Compared to FHE, SWHE can only carry out a limited number of multiplications, but it is much faster than FHE [14].

A typical public-key SWHE scheme consists of five algorithms, including SWHE.KeyGen, SWHE.Enc, SWHE.Dec, SWHE.Add and SWHE.Mul. Specifically, SWHE.KeyGen(1^λ) takes as input a security parameter and outputs a pair of public and secret keys (pk, sk). $c \leftarrow$ SWHE.Enc(pk, m) and $m \leftarrow$ SWHE.Dec(sk, c) are used for encryption and decryption, respectively, where m and c are a pair of plaintext/ciphertext. In addition, SWHE.Add and SWHE.Mul are used for homomorphically additions and multiplications, respectively. More concretely, SWHE.Add(c_1, c_2) takes as input two ciphertexts c_1 and c_2 and outputs a new ciphertext c_{add}, where c_1 is the ciphertext of m_1, c_2 is the ciphertext of m_2, and c_{add} is the ciphertext of $m_1 + m_2$. Similarly, SWHE.Mul(pk, c_1, c_2) outputs c_{mul}, which is the ciphertext of $m_1 m_2$.

4   SecReach: Secure Reachability Computation

As we discussed above, given two users (u_i, u_j) and a time interval T, a reachability query answers whether there is a contact path from u_i to u_j within time interval T. In this paper, we begin with the very fundamental problem, i.e., whether u_j is reachable from u_i by a contact path with two hops, which we call it a 2-hop reachability query. This type of queries can be easily seen in practice, e.g., finding a friend of a friend in social networks [23]. In the following, for ease of presentation, we first assume all the location check-ins are reported in one time slot t_0, and the query time interval is $T = t_0$. Then we will explain how to extend our scheme to support queries with different time slots.

4.1 Our Main Idea

Assume each user generates a location check-in in time slot t_0, and there are n users in total. Given a 2-hop reachability query of (u_i, u_j) in $T = t_0$, our main idea is to evaluate whether there is at least one user, e.g., u_k, is in direct contact with both u_i and u_j. If it is, then it implies that u_j is reachable from u_i within 2 hops, and there is at least one contact path, e.g., $u_i \rightarrow u_k \rightarrow u_j$; otherwise, u_i and u_j are not 2-hop reachable.

By following this logic, our method can be broken down in two steps. First, we compute the contacts between u_i and all the n users, and represent the results as an n-bit binary vector $\mathbf{v}_i$, which is referred to as the *contact vector* of user u_i. If user u_i and u_k $(1 \leq k \leq n)$ are in direct contact, the k-th position of contact vector $\mathbf{v}_i$ is set to 1 (i.e., $\mathbf{v}_i[k] = 1$); otherwise, it is set to 0. Similarly, we can compute a contact vector $\mathbf{v}_j$ for user u_j. In the second step of our approach, we compute an inner product of $\mathbf{v}_i$ and $\mathbf{v}_j$, which is represented as $\langle \mathbf{v}_i, \mathbf{v}_j \rangle$. If this inner product is equal to or greater than 1, i.e., $\langle \mathbf{v}_i, \mathbf{v}_j \rangle \geq 1$, it indicates there is at least one user (e.g., u_k) in direct contact with both of the two users, and these two users are reachable within 2 hops. Note that, at least one same index is assigned as 1 in both of the two contact vectors $\mathbf{v}_i, \mathbf{v}_j$, e.g., $\mathbf{v}_i[k] = \mathbf{v}_j[k] = 1$.

In order to decide whether user u_i is in direct contact with a user u_k, or said differently, whether this user u_k is inside user u_i's proximity range, we describe each user's proximity as a set of locations that are close to it, and leverage a Bloom filter to represent this set. As a result, whether user u_i is in direct contact with user u_k is equivalent to say whether user u_k's location is a member of the Bloom filter of user u_i. The essential reason that we utilize membership testing other than computing and comparing distances of two locations, is because membership testing is more efficient on encrypted data. Specifically, we leverage inner product to conduct membership testing in Bloom filter, which can be efficiently computed on encrypted data using SWHE (with one homomorphic multiplication). Moreover, we present a new way to convert the result of this inner product to a binary number in ciphertext domain so as to build the contact vector described above.

4.2 The Details of Our Scheme

In the following, we describe the details of our scheme. Our scheme leverages a public-key somewhat homomorphic encryption scheme SWHE and we denote by $[\![x]\!]$ the ciphertext of x encrypted under SWHE.

Encrypt Locations on the User Side. Given a location check-in tuple $d_i = (u_i, l_i, t_0)$ generated by user u_i in time slot t_0, user u_i encrypts its location l_i as follows:

1. Enumerate and add all the locations in its proximity range to an (m, k)-Bloom filter BF using BF.add. Here we use an m-bit vector $\boldsymbol{\alpha}_i$ to represent BF and refer to it as the *proximity vector* of user u_i.
2. Create another m-bit vector $\boldsymbol{\beta}_i$, where all bits are initialized as 0s, and set the $h_j(l_i)$-th bit of $\boldsymbol{\beta}_i$ to 1, for $1 \leq j \leq k$, where h_j $(1 \leq j \leq k)$ are the k hash functions of BF. $\boldsymbol{\beta}_i$ is called the *location vector* of user u_i.
3. Encrypt $\boldsymbol{\alpha}_i$ and $\boldsymbol{\beta}_i$ using SWHE.Enc. More concretely,

$$[\![\boldsymbol{\alpha}_i]\!] \leftarrow (\mathsf{SWHE.Enc}(pk, \boldsymbol{\alpha}_i[1]), \dots, \mathsf{SWHE.Enc}(pk, \boldsymbol{\alpha}_i[m])) \tag{1}$$

$$[\![\boldsymbol{\beta}_i]\!] \leftarrow (\mathsf{SWHE.Enc}(pk, \boldsymbol{\beta}_i[1]), \dots, \mathsf{SWHE.Enc}(pk, \boldsymbol{\beta}_i[m])) \tag{2}$$

Note that the above encryptions are bit-wise, where we encrypt each bit in vector $\boldsymbol{\alpha}_i$ and $\boldsymbol{\beta}_i$ separately.

In the end, user u_i obtains an encrypted location check-in as $(u_i, [\![\boldsymbol{\alpha}_i]\!], [\![\boldsymbol{\beta}_i]\!], t_0)$, and sends it to the cloud server.

Evaluate 2-Hop Reachability on Cloud Server. Assume user u_i sends one encrypted location check-in $(u_i, [\![\boldsymbol{\alpha}_i]\!], [\![\boldsymbol{\beta}_i]\!], t_0)$, and there are n encrypted location check-ins in total from the n users. The cloud server stores these encrypted location check-ins in a data table with n rows and four columns as shown in Fig. 3. Note that the fourth column is empty before any computation.

user ID	proximity vector	location vector	contact vector
u_1	$[\![\boldsymbol{\alpha}_1]\!]$	$[\![\boldsymbol{\beta}_1]\!]$	$[\![\mathbf{v}_1]\!]$
u_2	$[\![\boldsymbol{\alpha}_2]\!]$	$[\![\boldsymbol{\beta}_2]\!]$	$[\![\mathbf{v}_2]\!]$
$\vdots$	$\vdots$	$\vdots$	$\vdots$
u_n	$[\![\boldsymbol{\alpha}_\mathrm{n}]\!]$	$[\![\boldsymbol{\beta}_\mathrm{n}]\!]$	$[\![\mathbf{v}_\mathrm{n}]\!]$

Fig. 3. The data table maintained by the cloud server, and one table per time slot.

Given a 2-hop reachability query of (u_1, u_2) in time interval $T = t_0$, the cloud server first checks whether the contact vectors $[\![\mathbf{v}_1]\!]$ and $[\![\mathbf{v}_2]\!]$ have been computed and stored in the data table. If not, it computes $[\![\mathbf{v}_1]\!]$ and/or $[\![\mathbf{v}_2]\!]$ by Algorithm 1, and stores them in the data table. Specifically, in Algorithm 1, we present a novel approach, i.e., by homomorphically evaluating a function $f(x) = (k!)^{-1} \prod_{i=0}^{k-1}(x-i)$ on an encrypted integer x to check whether x is equal to k or whether $0 \leq x \leq k - 1$, and represent the result as an encrypted binary number in order to build the contact vector. Then, with $[\![\mathbf{v}_1]\!]$ and $[\![\mathbf{v}_2]\!]$, the cloud server computes $[\![\langle \mathbf{v}_1, \mathbf{v}_2 \rangle]\!]$ using SWHE.Add and SWHE.Mul and returns it to the data analyzer. $[\![\langle \mathbf{v}_1, \mathbf{v}_2 \rangle]\!]$ is the ciphertext of the inner product of vectors $\mathbf{v}_1$ and $\mathbf{v}_2$. Note that the cloud server does not decrypt any encrypted data during this above evaluation, and all the computations are operated on encrypted data correctly based on the homomorphic properties of SWHE.

Algorithm 1. Compute contact vector $[\![\mathbf{v}_i]\!]$ of u_i by the cloud server

---

Input: $[\![\boldsymbol{\alpha}_i]\!]$ of u_i, $[\![\boldsymbol{\beta}_j]\!]$ of u_j $(1 \leq j \leq n)$
Output: The encrypted contact vector $[\![\mathbf{v}_i]\!]$ of u_i
1: **for** $j = 1$ to n **do**
2:     **if** $i == j$ **then**
3:         $[\![\mathbf{v}_i[j]]\!] \leftarrow$ SWHE.Enc$(pk, 1)$
4:         **continue**
5:     **else**
6:         $[\![x]\!] = [\![\langle \boldsymbol{\alpha}_i, \boldsymbol{\beta}_j \rangle]\!]$ // using SWHE.Add and SWHE.Mul
7:         $[\![\mathbf{v}_i[j]]\!] = [\![f(x)]\!]$ // $f(x) = (k!)^{-1} \prod_{i=0}^{k-1}(x - i)$ where $(k!)^{-1}$ is the inverse of $(k!)$ in message space of SWHE, using SWHE.Add and SWHE.Mul
8:         // Note that here SWHE.Add and SWHE.Mul should take as input $[\![(k!)^{-1}]\!]$ and $[\![1]\!], [\![2]\!], \ldots, [\![(k-1)]\!]$, which can be pre-computed using SWHE.Enc by the cloud server.
9:     **end if**
10: **end for**
11: **return** $[\![\mathbf{v}_i]\!] = ([\![\mathbf{v}_i[1]]\!], [\![\mathbf{v}_i[2]]\!], \ldots, [\![\mathbf{v}_i[n]]\!])$

Decrypt the Query Result. The data analyzer sends $[\![\langle \mathbf{v}_1, \mathbf{v}_2 \rangle]\!]$ to the data owner. And the data owner decrypts it using its secret key sk. Specifically, the data owner computes

$$\langle \mathbf{v}_1, \mathbf{v}_2 \rangle \leftarrow \text{SWHE.Dec}(sk, [\![\langle \mathbf{v}_1, \mathbf{v}_2 \rangle]\!]) \tag{3}$$

If $\langle \mathbf{v}_1, \mathbf{v}_2 \rangle$ equals 0, the data owner returns 0 to the data analyzer, which means there is no 2-hop reachability from u_1 to u_2. If $\langle \mathbf{v}_1, \mathbf{v}_2 \rangle$ is non-zero, the data owner returns 1 to the data analyzer, which means u_2 is reachable from u_1 within 2 hops. Note that the data analyzer could also be the data owner itself. In this case, the data owner simply decrypts $[\![\langle \mathbf{v}_1, \mathbf{v}_2 \rangle]\!]$ with its secret key.

Correctness. In the plaintext domain, at line 6 in Algorithm 1, it essentially evaluates whether the location l_j of user u_j is in the Bloom filter BF generated by user u_i, where BF contains all the locations in u_i's proximity range. Obviously, if it is, x, i.e., the inner product of vector $\boldsymbol{\alpha}_i$ and $\boldsymbol{\beta}_j$, is equal to k, i.e., the number of hash functions used in Bloom filters; otherwise, $0 \leq x \leq k-1$. In other words, we use the inner product $\langle \boldsymbol{\alpha}_i, \boldsymbol{\beta}_j \rangle$ instead of BF.query to decide whether location l_j is in Bloom filter BF.

At line 7, $f(x)$ represents the binary number to indicate whether x is equal to k. Specifically, if $x = k$, $f(x) = 1$; if $x \in \{0, 1, \ldots, (k-1)\}$, $f(x) = 0$. We would like to emphasize that this mapping from x to $f(x)$ is important for the subsequent computations. Note that the calculation of the inner product of $\langle \alpha_i, \beta_j \rangle$ and the mapping from x to $f(x)$ together only contains additions and a limited number of multiplications, which can be implemented with SWHE.Add and SWHE.Mul on encrypted data by the cloud server.

Therefore, if user u_i and u_j are in direct contact, then $[\![\mathbf{v}_i[j]]\!] = [\![1]\!]$; otherwise, $[\![\mathbf{v}_i[j]]\!] = [\![0]\!]$. For the 2-hop reachability from u_1 and u_2, if there is a user u_3 in direct contact with both u_1 and u_2, then both $\mathbf{v}_1[3]$ and $\mathbf{v}_2[3]$ equal 1, which implies the inner product $\langle \mathbf{v}_1, \mathbf{v}_2 \rangle$ will definitely not be zero (i.e., at least 1). Note that u_1 and u_2 could be in direct contact, in this case, w.l.o.g., u_3 could be either u_1 or u_2.

Process Reachability with Different Time Slots. Our scheme can be extended to support reachability with different time slots. More specifically, given a 2-hop reachability query of (u_1, u_2) in time interval $T = [t_x, t_y]$, which includes $y - x + 1$ time slots, i.e., $t_x, t_{x+1}, \ldots, t_y$, if there is a contact path $u_1 \rightarrow u_3 \rightarrow u_2$, the second contact $u_3 \rightarrow u_2$ should happen in a time slot that is later than the time slot of the first contact $u_1 \rightarrow u_3$ happens. More precisely, assume $u_1 \rightarrow u_3$ occurs in time slot t_i while $u_3 \rightarrow u_2$ occurs in time slot t_j, then we have $x \leq i \leq j \leq y$.

user ID	contact vector		user ID	contact vector		user ID	contact vector
u_1	$[\![\mathbf{v}_{11}]\!]$		u_1	$[\![\mathbf{v}_{21}]\!]$		u_1	$[\![\mathbf{v}_{31}]\!]$
u_2	$[\![\mathbf{v}_{12}]\!]$		u_2	$[\![\mathbf{v}_{22}]\!]$		u_2	$[\![\mathbf{v}_{32}]\!]$
$\vdots$	$\vdots$		$\vdots$	$\vdots$		$\vdots$	$\vdots$
u_n	$[\![\mathbf{v}_{1n}]\!]$		u_n	$[\![\mathbf{v}_{2n}]\!]$		u_n	$[\![\mathbf{v}_{3n}]\!]$
time slot t_1			time slot t_2			time slot t_3	

Query: whether $u_1 \rightarrow u_3 \rightarrow u_2$ in T = $[t_1, t_3]$?
Solution: $u_1 \rightarrow u_3 \rightarrow u_2$ in T = $[t_1, t_3]$ if and only if
$\langle \mathbf{v}_{11}, \mathbf{v}_{12} \rangle + \langle \mathbf{v}_{11}, \mathbf{v}_{22} \rangle + \langle \mathbf{v}_{11}, \mathbf{v}_{32} \rangle + \langle \mathbf{v}_{21}, \mathbf{v}_{22} \rangle + \langle \mathbf{v}_{21}, \mathbf{v}_{32} \rangle + \langle \mathbf{v}_{31}, \mathbf{v}_{32} \rangle \neq 0$

Fig. 4. The data tables maintained by the cloud server for 3 time slots (for the limitation of space we omit the second and third columns) and an example of reachability query about two users u_1 and u_2 within time interval $T = [t_1, t_3]$.

To evaluate this 2-hop reachability query, the cloud server should search all the possible combinations of t_i and t_j within $T = [t_x, t_y]$ to find out whether there is such a contact path $u_1 \rightarrow u_3 \rightarrow u_2$. Specifically, for each time slot, the cloud server maintains a data table as described above and returns the query results as $[\![\sum_{i=x}^{y}(\sum_{j=i}^{y}(\langle \mathbf{v}_{i1}, \mathbf{v}_{j2}\rangle))]\!]$, where $\mathbf{v}_{i1}$ is the contact vector of u_1 in time slot t_i and $\mathbf{v}_{j2}$ is the contact vector of u_2 in time slot t_j. It is easy to prove that the 2-hop reachability exists if and only if $\sum_{i=x}^{y}(\sum_{j=i}^{y}(\langle \mathbf{v}_{i1}, \mathbf{v}_{j2}\rangle)) \geq 1$. Figure 4 is an example for a query about $T = [t_1, t_3]$.

5   Security Analysis

In this section we analyze the security of our scheme against the semi-honest cloud server. Our scheme does not reveal any input locations, intermediate or final results to the semi-honest cloud, except the dataset size.

Formally, the location privacy guarantee of our scheme can be modeled under a standard CPA game for *multiple encryptions* as denoted in Theorem 11.6 [9]. A challenger $\mathcal{C}$ chooses public and secret keys of a public encryption scheme (pk, sk). An adversary $\mathcal{A}$ submits two series of messages $\{m_0^i\}_{i=1}^n, \{m_1^i\}_{i=1}^n$, and $\mathcal{C}$ chooses $b \leftarrow \{0, 1\}$ uniformly at random and sends $\mathcal{A}$ encryptions of $\{m_b^i\}_{i=1}^n$. Finally $\mathcal{A}$ outputs its guess b'. Privacy is guaranteed if $\Pr[b' = b] \leq \frac{1}{2} + \mathsf{negl}(\lambda)$, where λ is the security parameter.

Theorem 1. *If public-key somewhat homomorphic encryption scheme SWHE is CPA-secure, then it also has indistinguishable multiple encryptions.*

In our scheme, given a location check-in data (u_i, l_i, t_i), the encryption of location l_i is $([\![\boldsymbol{\alpha}_i]\!], [\![\boldsymbol{\beta}_i]\!])$, where

$$[\![\boldsymbol{\alpha}_i]\!] = (\mathsf{SWHE.Enc}(pk, \boldsymbol{\alpha}_i[1]), \ldots, \mathsf{SWHE.Enc}(pk, \boldsymbol{\alpha}_i[m])) \tag{4}$$

$$[\![\boldsymbol{\beta}_i]\!] = (\mathsf{SWHE.Enc}(pk, \boldsymbol{\beta}_i[1]), \ldots, \mathsf{SWHE.Enc}(pk, \boldsymbol{\beta}_i[m])) \tag{5}$$

In other words, the encryption of a location in our scheme consists of *multiple encryptions* under SWHE. According to Theorem 1, we can conclude that, *given a CPA-secure somewhat homomorphic encryption scheme SWHE, the encryptions of locations in our scheme are indistinguishable under chosen plaintext attack.* Proof of Theorem 1 can be found in Theorem 11.6 [9]. Also, the privacy of the intermediate results (e.g., the proximity vector $\mathbf{v}_i$) and the query results are protected under the security of the SWHE.

In the adversarial model, we assume that the data analyzer and the cloud server do not collude. Otherwise, the 2-hop reachability results are revealed and a semi-honest cloud server may be able to infer the users' locations by, for example, the triangulation attacks in [11]. But the impact of this attack should be much smaller since no direct proximity is known. Moreover, in practice, we can limit the risk of such collusion attack by letting the data owner restricting reachability queries to only authorized data analyzers.

6   Proof of Concept and Experimental Results

In this section, we present a proof-of-concept implementation of our scheme. We leverage the state-of-the-art SWHE scheme as the building block for our scheme, and examine the performance of our design over synthetic location check-ins. Specifically, we implement our scheme using HElib [8], which is a C++ library that implements the BGV SWHE scheme [2].

Parameters and Encoding of Messages. The parameters of our scheme consist of the parameters of Bloom filters and the parameters of HElib. In our scheme, each user adds nine locations to an empty Bloom filter to generate its proximity vector. We choose the number of hash functions as $k = 3$ and the length of Bloom filters as $m = 220$, such that the false positive probability of Bloom filters is around 0.001 (the probability is taken from [1]). As a result, the length of a proximity vector and a location vector is $|\alpha| = |\beta| = m = 220$.

Furthermore, given $k = 3$, our scheme needs $2k + 2 = 8$ depth of homomorphic multiplication ($k + 1$ for computing encrypted contact vector $[\![\mathbf{v}]\!]$ in Algorithm 1 and double $(k + 1)$ for computing $[\![\langle \mathbf{v}_i, \mathbf{v}_j \rangle]\!]$). Therefore, the depth of homomorphic multiplication of the SWHE should at least be eight. We set the parameters of HElib as shown in Table 1 to meet this requirement.

The underlying SWHE scheme (BGV) of HElib is based on the "ring learning with errors" (RLWE) problem, which means messages that can be encrypted with HElib are polynomials. We use *scalar encoding* to encode an integer by representing it as constant coefficient of a plaintext polynomial. Note that, if a constant coefficient increases beyond the plaintext base p', it will automatically be reduced by modulo p'. We choose $p' = 1009$, which means it can support up to one thousand users (e.g., in the worst case, if both user u_i and u_j are in contact with all the other $1000 - 1$ users in one time slot, the final result $\langle \mathbf{v}_i, \mathbf{v}_j \rangle$ will be equal to 1000, which is less than p').

Table 1. The parameters of HElib in our implementation, where p' is the plaintext base, r' is the lifting, L' is the number of levels in the modulus chain, c' is the number of columns in the key-switching matrics, w' is the hamming weight of secret key, d' is the degree of the filed extension, and k' is the security parameter.

p'	r'	L'	c'	w'	d'	k'
1009	1	16	3	64	0	80

Experimental Results. Our proof-of-concept implementation runs on a Ubuntu 14.04 virtual machine (VM) with 4 GB memory. The VM is hosted in a desktop PC with Inter(R) Core(TM) i7-4790 CPU @ 3.60 GHz and 8 GB memory. We test the running time for generating one encrypted contact vector $[\![\mathbf{v}]\!]$, and evaluate the performance of answering 2-hop reachability query of two users within one time slot (i.e., computing $[\![\langle \mathbf{v}_i, \mathbf{v}_j \rangle]\!]$). The experimental results are illustrated in Fig. 5. Even with our un-optimized implementation, a 2-hop reachability query between two users can be evaluated on encrypted location data in approximately 100 seconds for a system contains 1,000 users. Although from Fig. 5(a), computing an encrypted contact vector seems to be time-consuming,

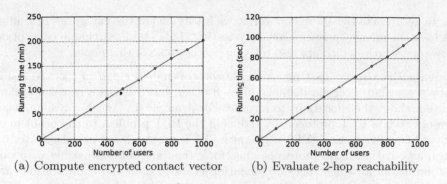

(a) Compute encrypted contact vector   (b) Evaluate 2-hop reachability

Fig. 5. The performance of our proof-of-concept implementation for one time slot

we argue that this computation is only a one time operation. In other words, if a user has been queried before, the cloud server does not have to compute it again. Moreover, our implementation can be further optimized using more efficient message encoding methods. In addition, the implementation of SWHE (and FHE) on high performance computing platforms (e.g., GPU) is itself a question of interest (and has been studied recently in, e.g., [4,10]), and the efficiency of our scheme can be significantly boosted up if we implement it with GPU. For instance, [10] implements a SWHE using GPU, which results in a speedup of 104x in homomorphic multiplication over the implementations with CPU.

7   Related Work

To the best of our knowledge, current work does not tackle the problem of computing reachability on encrypted location check-in data. The previous works most relevant to ours are [18, 27].

In [27], Yi et al. propose an optimized 2-hop labeling (which is an index of a graph), namely m-2-hop, for privacy-preserving reachability queries in a sparse graph. In their system model, there is a data owner who owns graph data and pre-computes an m-2-hop index offline. Then, the data owner encrypts the m-2-hop index and outsources it to the cloud server. A reachability query is processed on the encrypted m-2-hop index. Their solution is essentially for the reachability queries in static graph data (from which they can abstract an index first). However, in our work, we consider the reachability queries over individually generated location check-in data, which has both space and time dimension and cannot be represented as a static graph. Therefore, their work is not able to address our problem.

In [18], Shahabi et al. propose an extensible framework, PLACE, which consists of some building blocks including location proximity block, and enables privacy-preserving inference of social relationships from location check-in data. Specially, they state one of the use cases of PLACE is to analyze the reachability of two users. However, this work does not present any concrete designs.

In addition to the above two works, we briefly review two categories of studies on location privacy, private proximity testing (PPT) and searchable encryption for range search, which are also relevant to the topic of this paper.

Private Proximity Testing. A PPT protocol enables a pair of users to test if they are within a certain distance of each other, but otherwise reveal no information about their locations to anyone. For example, in [15], Narayanan et al. present several PPT protocols by reducing the PPT problem to the problem of private equality testing (PET). However, PPT protocols are essentially secure two-party computation protocols, therefore, they are not compatible with our system model in which encrypted location check-in data and computations are centralized on an untrusted cloud server.

Searchable Encryption for Range Search. Recently, a couple of searchable encryption schemes for range search, e.g., [24,25], have been proposed. In [25], Wang et al. propose two searchable encryption schemes supporting circular range search on encrypted spatial data. They improve their work to support arbitrary geometric range search in [24]. However, in these searchable encryption schemes, a database server (e.g., a cloud server) will know search results, while our scheme does not leak those information.

Our work is also relevant to another problem called privacy-preserving location data publication. The works on this problem generally leverage non-cryptography anonymization techniques, such as k-anonymity [22]. Specially, in [13], Liu et al. propose the problem of reachability preserving anonymization (RPA), and design an RPA algorithm which supports computing reachability over anonymous graph. These anonymization techniques are generally very efficient, however, the security of these schemes cannot be proven formally and the results are not accurate because they have to modify the original data to achieve anonymization. Moreover, like [27], the method in [13] is designed for static graph, which cannot be used for the spatiotemporal location check-in data generated by individual users over time.

From a technical point of view, based on Wilson's Theorem $(p-1)! \equiv -1 \pmod{p}$ with p as a prime number greater than 2, Wang et al. [26] propose a function $g(x) = -\prod_{i=1}^{p-1}(i-x) \pmod{p}$ to check whether an integer x equals 0 or whether $1 \le x \le p-1$, which is similar to the $f(x)$ in Algorithm 1 in our design. Plausibly, we can also use $g(x)$ to check whether x is equal to k by checking whether $(k-x)$ equals 0. However, to compute "mod p" on encrypted data, they use *scalar encoding* and set p as the plaintext base (recall that in *scalar encoding*, the plaintext will automatically modulo p). In other words, their method is limited to applications with small message space, otherwise it will exceed the limitation of SWHE on the number of multiplications.

8   Conclusion and Future Work

In this paper we studied the problem of reachability queries on encrypted location check-in data. Specifically, we presented a scheme, namely SecReach, to support

2-hop reachability queries, which is based on a fresh approach of combining Somewhat Homomorphic Encryption and Bloom filters. Our scheme is provably secure and our experimental results demonstrate its practicality.

As part of future work, we are going to consider indexing location check-in data with more efficient data structures to improve efficiency (for instance, splitting the location space into smaller partitions including less users). Also, we plan to extend our scheme to enable multi-hop reachability queries, in which the length of a contact path is greater than 2, and implement our extension on high performance computing platforms (e.g., GPU).

Acknowledgments. We would like to thank the anonymous reviewers for their valuable comments. This work was supported by the US NSF grant CNS-1218085, the 111 Project of China (No. B16037), the National Natural Science Foundation of China (No.61272481, No. 61572460), the National Key Research and Development Plan of China (No. 2016YFB0800703), and the China Scholarship Council.

References

1. Bloom, B.H.: Space/time trade-offs in hash coding with allowable errors. Commun. ACM **13**(7), 422–426 (1970)
2. Brakerski, Z., Gentry, C., Vaikuntanathan, V.: (leveled) fully homomorphic encryption without bootstrapping. In: Proceedings of the 3rd Innovations in Theoretical Computer Science Conference, pp. 309–325. ACM (2012)
3. Cheon, J.H., Kim, M., Lauter, K.: Homomorphic computation of edit distance. In: Brenner, M., Christin, N., Johnson, B., Rohloff, K. (eds.) FC 2015 Workshops. LNCS, vol. 8976, pp. 194–212. Springer, Heidelberg (2015)
4. Dai, W., Sunar, B.: cuHE: a homomorphic encryption accelerator library. In: Pasalic, E., Knudsen, L.R. (eds.) BalkanCryptSec 2015. LNCS, vol. 9540, pp. 169–186. Springer, Heidelberg (2016). doi:10.1007/978-3-319-29172-7_11
5. De Montjoye, Y.A., Hidalgo, C.A., Verleysen, M., Blondel, V.D.: Unique in the crowd: The privacy bounds of human mobility. Sci. Rep. **3** (2013)
6. Elmehdwi, Y., Samanthula, B.K., Jiang, W.: Secure k-nearest neighbor query over encrypted data in outsourced environments. In: 2014 IEEE 30th International Conference on Data Engineering, pp. 664–675. IEEE (2014)
7. Gentry, C.: A fully homomorphic encryption scheme. Ph.D. thesis, Stanford University (2009)
8. Halevi, S., Shoup, V.: Algorithms in HElib. In: Garay, J.A., Gennaro, R. (eds.) CRYPTO 2014, Part I. LNCS, vol. 8616, pp. 554–571. Springer, Heidelberg (2014)
9. Katz, J., Lindell, Y.: Introduction to Modern Cryptography, 2nd edn. CRC Press, Boca Raton (2014)
10. Khedr, A., Gulak, G.: Securemed: Secure medical computation using gpu-accelerated homomorphic encryption scheme. Cryptology ePrint Archive, Report 2016/445 (2016)
11. Li, M., Zhu, H., Gao, Z., Chen, S., Yu, L., Hu, S., Ren, K.: All your location are belong to us: Breaking mobile social networks for automated user location tracking. In: Proceedings of the 15th ACM International Symposium on Mobile Ad Hoc Networking and Computing, pp. 43–52. ACM (2014)

12. Liu, A., Zhengy, K., Liz, L., Liu, G., Zhao, L., Zhou, X.: Efficient secure similarity computation on encrypted trajectory data. In: 2015 IEEE 31st International Conference on Data Engineering, pp. 66–77. IEEE (2015)

13. Liu, X., Wang, B., Yang, X.: Efficiently anonymizing social networks with reachability preservation. In: Proceedings of the 22nd ACM International Conference on Information and Knowledge Management, pp. 1613–1618. ACM (2013)

14. Naehrig, M., Lauter, K., Vaikuntanathan, V.: Can homomorphic encryption be practical? In: Proceedings of the 3rd ACM workshop on Cloud computing security workshop. pp. 113–124. ACM (2011)

15. Narayanan, A., Thiagarajan, N., Lakhani, M., Hamburg, M., Boneh, D.: Location privacy via private proximity testing. In: NDSS (2011)

16. Peikert, C.: A decade of lattice cryptography. Cryptology ePrint Archive, Report 2015/939 (2015). http://eprint.iacr.org/2015/939

17. Samanthula, B.K., Elmehdwi, Y., Jiang, W.: K-nearest neighbor classification over semantically secure encrypted relational data. IEEE Trans. Knowl. Data Eng. **27**(5), 1261–1273 (2015)

18. Shahabi, C., Fan, L., Nocera, L., Xiong, L., Li, M.: Privacy-preserving inference of social relationships from location data: a vision paper. In: Proceedings of the 23rd SIGSPATIAL International Conference on Advances in Geographic Information Systems, p. 9. ACM (2015)

19. Shirani-Mehr, H., Banaei-Kashani, F., Shahabi, C.: Efficient reachability query evaluation in large spatiotemporal contact datasets. Proc. VLDB Endowment **5**(9), 848–859 (2012)

20. Shokri, R., Theodorakopoulos, G., Le Boudec, J.Y., Hubaux, J.P.: Quantifying location privacy. In: 2011 IEEE Symposium on Security and Privacy, pp. 247–262. IEEE (2011)

21. Strzheletska, E.V., Tsotras, V.J.: RICC: fast reachability query processing on large spatiotemporal datasets. In: Claramunt, C., Schneider, M., Wong, R.C.-W., Xiong, L., Loh, W.-K., Shahabi, C., Li, K.-J. (eds.) SSTD 2015. LNCS, vol. 9239, pp. 3–21. Springer, Heidelberg (2015). doi:10.1007/978-3-319-22363-6_1

22. Sweeney, L.: k-anonymity: a model for protecting privacy. Int. J. Uncert. Fuzz. Knowl.-Based Syst. **10**(05), 557–570 (2002)

23. Von Arb, M., Bader, M., Kuhn, M., Wattenhofer, R.: Veneta: serverless friend-of-friend detection in mobile social networking. In: 2008 IEEE International Conference on Wireless and Mobile Computing, Networking and Communications, pp. 184–189. IEEE (2008)

24. Wang, B., Li, M., Wang, H.: Geometric range search on encrypted spatial data. IEEE Trans. Inf. Forensics Secur. **11**(4), 704–719 (2016)

25. Wang, B., Li, M., Wang, H., Li, H.: Circular range search on encrypted spatial data. In: 2015 IEEE Conference on Communications and Network Security (CNS), pp. 182–190. IEEE (2015)

26. Wang, S., Zhang, Y., Dai, W., Lauter, K., Kim, M., Tang, Y., Xiong, H., Jiang, X.: Healer: Homomorphic computation of exact logistic regression for secure rare disease variants analysis in gwas. Bioinformatics **32**(2), 211–218 (2016)

27. Yi, P., Fan, Z., Yin, S.: Privacy-preserving reachability query services for sparse graphs. In: 2014 IEEE 30th International Conference on Data Engineering Workshops (ICDEW), pp. 32–35. IEEE (2014)

FHE Over the Integers and Modular Arithmetic Circuits

Eunkyung Kim[1] and Mehdi Tibouchi[2(✉)]

[1] Department of Mathematics, Ewha Womans University, Seoul, Republic of Korea
ekkim0410@ewhain.net
[2] NTT Secure Platform Laboratories, Tokyo, Japan
tibouchi.mehdi@lab.ntt.co.jp

Abstract. Fully homomorphic encryption (FHE) over the integers, as proposed by van Dijk et al. in 2010 and developed in a number of papers afterwards, originally supported the evaluation of Boolean circuits (i.e. mod-2 arithmetic circuits) only. It is easy to generalize the somewhat homomorphic versions of the corresponding schemes to support arithmetic operations modulo Q for any $Q > 2$; but bootstrapping those generalized variants into fully homomorphic schemes is not easy. Thus, Nuida and Kurosawa settled a significant open problem in 2015 by showing that one could in fact construct FHE over the integers with message space $\mathbb{Z}/Q\mathbb{Z}$ for any constant prime Q.

As a result of their work, we now have two different ways of homomorphically evaluating a mod-Q arithmetic circuit with an FHE scheme over the integers: one could either use their scheme with message space $\mathbb{Z}/Q\mathbb{Z}$ directly, or one could first convert the arithmetic circuit to a Boolean one, and evaluate that converted circuit using an FHE scheme with binary message space. In this paper, we compare both approaches and show that the latter is often preferable to the former.

1 Introduction

Fully homomorphic encryption. A *fully homomorphic encryption* (FHE) scheme is an encryption scheme that supports the homomorphic evaluation of arbitrary efficiently computable functions on ciphertexts. In other words, it is a usual encryption scheme (KeyGen, Encrypt, Decrypt) together with an additional algorithm Evaluate that takes as input ciphertexts $c_1, \ldots, c_n$ together with the description of a function f (and public-key information), and returns a new ciphertext c^* such that

$$\mathsf{Decrypt}(\mathsf{sk}, c^*) = f\big(\mathsf{Decrypt}(\mathsf{sk}, c_1), \ldots, \mathsf{Decrypt}(\mathsf{sk}, c_n)\big).$$

FHE is a very powerful primitive with applications to secure multiparty computation, verifiable computation outsourcing, encrypted search and more. It was already envisioned by Rivest, Adleman and Dertouzos in 1978 [RAD78], but the first construction was only proposed in 2009 in a seminal paper of Gentry [Gen09b, Gen09a]. Since then, many other FHE schemes have been proposed,

© Springer International Publishing AG 2016
S. Foresti and G. Persiano (Eds.): CANS 2016, LNCS 10052, pp. 435–450, 2016.
DOI: 10.1007/978-3-319-48965-0_26

but all constructions (of FHE scheme in a strict sense, as opposed to relaxed variants such as "leveled fully-homomorphic" schemes) essentially follow Gentry's original approach, based on a technique called *bootstrapping*.

Gentry's blue-print. That approach (the "blue-print" for homomorphic encryption) can be roughly described as follows. First, one starts from a so-called *somewhat homomorphic encryption* (SHE) scheme, in which ciphertexts contain some "noise", and can be added and multiplied together homomorphically provided that the noise (which can increase during homomorphic operations) remains small. These features make it possible to evaluate a moderately large class $\mathcal{C}$ of functions on ciphertexts (essentially "low-degree" polynomials), but not arbitrary functions.

Then, in a second step, Gentry proposes to express the decryption circuit of the SHE scheme as a function belonging to $\mathcal{C}$. This is not always possible, and when it is, it usually involves a significant amount of technical hurdles, but for the concrete schemes considered Gentry's paper and later works, it can be done. This is called *squashing*, and the resulting scheme is said to be *bootstrappable*.

Finally, one publishes an encryption c_{sk} of the secret key sk. As a result, for any ciphertext c, anyone can homomorphically evaluate the function f_c defined by $f_c(\mathsf{sk}) = \mathsf{Decrypt}(\mathsf{sk}, c)$ on c_{sk}: that function belongs to the class $\mathcal{C}$ of supported functions thanks to the squashing step. And the resulting ciphertext c^* encrypts the same plaintext as c. However, the size of its noise depends only on the fixed noise in c_{sk}, and not on the noise in c. In particular, by setting parameters appropriately, one can ensure that c^* supports at least one additional homomorphic additional and/or multiplication, regardless of how noisy c may be. Therefore, if we carry out this "ciphertext refresh" procedure after each homomorphic addition and multiplication, we obtain a scheme that supports arbitrarily many homomorphic addition and multiplication operations. In other words, the resulting scheme can evaluate all efficient polynomial functions (or equivalently, all polynomial-size arithmetic circuits on the plaintext space). When the plaintext space is a finite field of constant (or at most logarithmic) size, all efficient functions are of that form, and we obtain fully homomorphic encryption. This is called *bootstrapping*, and the "ciphertext refresh" procedure that takes a noisy ciphertext and reduces its noise by homomorphically evaluating the decryption algorithm is sometimes also called a *bootstrapping operation*.

Fully-homomorphic encryption over the integers. A comparatively simple example of Gentry's blue-print is the fully homomorphic encryption scheme over the integers, initially proposed by van Dijk et al. [DGHV10], and refined in a number of papers afterwards, including [CMNT11, CNT12, CCK+13, CLT14, CS15].

Those schemes essentially share the same basic structure. In their symmetric-key, somewhat homomorphic versions, the secret key is a prime number p, the message space is $\mathbb{Z}/2\mathbb{Z}$, and $m \in \mathbb{Z}/2\mathbb{Z}$ is encrypted as:

$$c = q \cdot p + 2r + m \qquad (1)$$

where $r \ll p$ is a small random noise value, and q is uniformly random in $[0, 2^\gamma/p)$ for ciphertext size γ. We can decrypt c using p by computing $m = (c \bmod p) \bmod 2$. Under the hardness of the Approximate GCD problem, the scheme is semantically secure, and it is also clearly somewhat homomorphic: as long as the noise remains small, the sum and the product of two ciphertexts c, c' decrypt to the sum and the product modulo 2 of the associated plaintexts. One can thus evaluate low-degree polynomials on ciphertexts.

However, the scheme is not bootstrappable as is: the decryption algorithm

$$p \mapsto (c \bmod p) \bmod 2 = (c \bmod 2) \oplus (p \cdot \lfloor c/p \rfloor) \bmod 2$$

involves a division by p, which is a function of very large when represented as a binary polynomial—provably too large, in fact, to be permitted by the somewhat homomorphic scheme. Squashing is therefore required. This is done by approximating the value $1/p$ by a sparse subset sum $\sum_i s_i \cdot y_i$, $s_i \in \{0, 1\}$, of (pseudo-)random fixed point real numbers y_i with sufficient precision to ensure that

$$\lfloor c/p \rfloor = \left\lfloor \sum_i s_i \cdot (c y_i) \right\rfloor$$

for all supported ciphertexts c. The resulting decryption algorithm is then a simple iterated addition of fixed point numbers, with only a small number of non zero terms (by the sparseness condition), and that only needs to be evaluated with enough precision to get its integral part. The resulting binary polynomial is of much lower degree than the original division, and makes it possible to choose parameters in such a way that the scheme becomes bootstrappable.

Message space and Nuida–Kurosawa FHE. As observed for example in [PAD12,CCK+13], it is easy to obtain a variant of the somewhat homomorphic scheme above that supports homomorphic operations in the message space $\mathbb{Z}/Q\mathbb{Z}$ for some other modulus $Q \neq 2$. It suffices to use ciphertexts of the form:

$$c = q \cdot p + Q \cdot r + m$$

instead of the form (1). The security argument is identical, as is the verification that the scheme supports the homomorphic evaluation of low-degree polynomials over $\mathbb{Z}/Q\mathbb{Z}$ (i.e. low-depth mod-Q arithmetic circuits).

However, obtaining *fully* homomorphic encryption based on that SHE scheme appeared to be quite hard. Indeed, to carry out squashing in the mod-Q setting, one has to represent the decryption algorithm, and in particular the large integer division of c by p, as a low-degree polynomial *over* $\mathbb{Z}/Q\mathbb{Z}$. This is a much less familiar setting than Boolean circuits, and even in small characteristic, mod-Q arithmetic circuits are known to be exponentially less powerful than Boolean circuits with respect to depth [vzGS91].

Nevertheless, in a paper presented at EUROCRYPT 2015, Nuida and Kurosawa [NK15] solved an interesting open problem by describing the first FHE over the integers with non-binary message space. Their construction supports arbitrary prime fields of constant size, and is in fact the first FHE scheme supporting homomorphic evaluation in a field of characteristic different from 2.

Of course, the Nuida–Kurosawa scheme does not really extend the scope of computations that can be carried out homomorphically using FHE schemes. One can also perform arithmetic operations modulo $\mathbb{Z}/Q\mathbb{Z}$ using an FHE scheme with binary message space. It suffices to represent an element of $\mathbb{Z}/Q\mathbb{Z}$ as the binary expansion of its integer value in $\{0, \ldots, Q-1\}$, encrypt it bit by bit, and carry out arithmetic operations on such representations by using Boolean circuits for modular addition and modular multiplication. However, the Nuida–Kurosawa scheme can be seen as an optimization: if we need to evaluate a specific arithmetic circuit, it lets us do so directly without conversion to and from mod-Q representations.

Our contributions. Since the Nuida–Kurosawa approach is an optimization, it is interesting to explore how much it gains, if at all, compared to the binary setting.

It is relatively clear that the optimization cannot be worthwhile for large values of Q. This is due to the fact that the squashed decryption circuit has a depth polynomial in Q, so the overall scheme incurs an overhead polynomial in Q (and that overhead is really intrinsic to the mod-Q setting, by the optimality results on polynomial degree given in [NK15, Sect. 3–4]). By contrast, there are Boolean circuits for addition and multiplication modulo Q of size polylogarithmic in Q, so the overhead of converting everything to the binary setting and using an FHE scheme with binary message space is at most polylogarithmic in Q.

But a more careful analysis is needed to compare the efficiency of both approaches even when Q is relatively small. This is what we propose to do in this paper. To make the playing field as level as possible, we compare the Nuida–Kurosawa scheme to itself, pitting its mod-Q version to its own binary message space version.

More precisely, let us simply compare the Nuida–Kurosawa scheme for modulus Q, denoted by NK_Q, with the scheme $\mathsf{Convert}\text{-}\mathsf{NK}_2$ that takes a mod-Q arithmetic circuit, converts it to a Boolean circuit in a straightforward way (using simple, explicit circuits for addition, multiplication and modular reduction) and evaluates it homomorphically using NK_2. Then ciphertexts in $\mathsf{Convert}\text{-}\mathsf{NK}_2$ (which are tuples of $(\log_2 Q)$ ciphertexts in NK_2) are shorter than ciphertexts in NK_Q by a factor of $\Omega(Q^6/\log Q)$. Moreover, denote by T_Q the time complexity of a single ciphertext refresh operation in NK_Q, and by T_2' the time complexity of carrying out a multiplication mod Q in $\mathsf{Convert}\text{-}\mathsf{NK}_2$ (by homomorphically evaluating the Boolean circuit for modular multiplication, with a refresh operation after each AND gate). Then we show that:

$$\frac{T_2'}{T_Q} = O\left(\frac{\log^4 Q}{Q^7}\right)$$

and the implied constant in the big-O is relatively small (about 2,000).

2 Preliminaries

In this section, we introduce the notation used throughout this paper, and review the Nuida–Kurosawa fully homomorphic encryption (NK FHE) scheme, giving a concrete description of the squashed decryption circuit, bootstrapping procedure, and parameter choice.

2.1 Notation

For a real number x, $\lfloor x \rfloor$ denotes the largest integer less than or equal to x, $\lceil x \rceil$ denotes the smallest integer greater than or equal to x, and $\lfloor x \rceil$ denotes the nearest integer to x. For an integer $n > 0$, we identify the quotient ring $\mathbb{Z}/n\mathbb{Z}$ of integers modulo n with the set $\{0, 1, 2, \cdots, n-1\}$, and define $x \bmod n$ as the unique integer $y \in [0, n)$ with $y \equiv x \pmod{n}$ and $[x]_n$ as the unique integer $z \in (-n/2, n/2]$ with $z \equiv x \pmod{n}$. We denote the set $\{1, 2, \cdots, n\}$ by $[n]$ for a positive integer n. Furthermore, for a prime Q, an integer a and an integer $b \in \mathbb{Z}/Q\mathbb{Z}$, we define $\binom{a}{b}_Q := a(a-1)\cdots(a-b+1) \cdot \mathrm{Inv}_Q(b!)$ where $\mathrm{Inv}_Q(x)$ is the unique integer $y \in [0, Q)$ with $xy \equiv 1 \pmod{Q}$. Note that $\binom{a}{b}_Q$ is congruent to the binomial coefficient $\binom{a}{b}$ modulo Q. We will use notation $\log A := \log_2 A$ the logarithm of a real number A to base 2 unless otherwise stated. We often identify an integer $m \bmod Q$ with its binary expansion $(m_{n-1}, \cdots, m_0)$ which is the binary string of the length $n = \lceil \log(Q+1) \rceil$ such that $m = \sum_{i=0}^{n-1} m_i 2^i$, and call n the size of m. For a Q-ary representation $A = (a_0.a_1, a_2, a_3, \cdots)_Q$ of a real number A, denote $(A)_L := (a_0.a_1, a_2, \cdots, a_L)_Q$ with an integer $L \geq 0$.

2.2 Nuida–Kurosawa Fully Homomorphic Encryption Scheme

Let λ be the security parameter, then we have parameters depending on λ: γ the size of ciphertexts, η the size of secret prime, and ρ the size of small error. There are more parameters L, τ, θ, κ and Θ, whose conditions will be presented later. Then NK FHE scheme with message space $\mathcal{M} = \mathbb{Z}/Q\mathbb{Z}$ is constructed as follows:

- NK. KeyGen(1^λ) $\to$ (pk, sk):
  - Choose η-bit prime p uniformly random and choose $q \leftarrow [1, 2^\gamma/p) \cap \mathbb{Z}$ such that $\gcd(q, p) = 1$, $\gcd(q, Q) = 1$ and q has no prime factors less than 2^{λ^2}. Set $N = qp$.
  - Choose $e_{\xi,0}$, $e_{\xi,1}$ for $\xi \in \{1, \cdots, \tau\}$ and e_0', e_1' by $e_{\xi,0}, e_0' \leftarrow [0, q) \cap \mathbb{Z}$, $e_{\xi,1}, e_1' \leftarrow (-2^\rho, 2^\rho) \cap \mathbb{Z}$. Let x_ξ be the unique integer in $(-N/2, N/2]$ satisfying

$$x_\xi \equiv e_{\xi,0} \pmod{q} \text{ and } x_\xi \equiv e_{\xi,1} Q \pmod{p}$$

and let x' be the unique integer in $(-N/2, N/2]$ satisfying

$$x' \equiv e_0' \pmod{q} \text{ and } x' \equiv e_1' Q + 1 \pmod{p}.$$

- Choose uniformly at random a Θ-bit vector $(s_1, \cdots, s_\Theta) \in \{0,1\}^\Theta$ with Hamming weight θ.
- Set $X_p = \lfloor Q^\kappa([p]_Q)/p \rceil$. For $i \in [\Theta]$, choose $u_i \leftarrow [0, Q^{\kappa+1}) \cap \mathbb{Z}$ in such a way that

$$\sum_{i=1}^{\Theta} s_i u_i \equiv X_p \pmod{Q^{\kappa+1}}.$$

- Choose $q_i \leftarrow [0, q_0) \cap \mathbb{Z}$ and $r_i \leftarrow (-2^\rho, 2^\rho) \cap \mathbb{Z}$, and generate $v_i \leftarrow [pq_i + Qr_i + s_i]_N$ for $i \in [\Theta]$.
- Output a public key $\mathsf{pk} = \langle N, \{x_\xi\}_{\xi \in [\tau]}, x', \{u_i\}_{i \in [\Theta]}, \{v_i\}_{i \in [\Theta]} \rangle$, and a secret key $\mathsf{sk} = (s_1, \cdots, s_\Theta)$.

- NK. Encrypt$(\mathsf{pk}, m) \to c$: Given a plaintext $m \in \mathcal{M}$, output a ciphertext c defined by

$$c := \left[mx' + \sum_{\xi \in T} x_\xi \right]_N$$

where $T \subset [\tau]$ is a uniformly random subset.
- NK. Decrypt$(\mathsf{sk}, c) \to m$: Given a ciphertext c, compute $z_i := (cu_i/Q^\kappa)_L = (z_{i;0}.z_{i;1} \cdots z_{i;L})$. Then output

$$m := c - \left\lfloor \sum_{i \in [\Theta]} s_i z_i \right\rceil \bmod Q.$$

- NK.SHE Evaluate$(\mathsf{pk}, f, \langle c_1, \cdots, c_t \rangle) \to c^*$: Given a polynomial f with integer coefficients and ciphertexts $c_1, \cdots, c_t$, output

$$c^* := [f(c_1, \cdots, c_t)]_N$$

- NK. Evaluate$(\mathsf{pk}, f, \langle c_1, \cdots, c_t \rangle) \to c^*$ is obtained using Gentry's bootstrapping technique by applying NK.SHE Evaluate to the squashed decryption circuit NK. Decrypt.

Let us briefly explain the correctness of NK scheme [NK15, Sect. 7]. For a ciphertext c, we can write as $c = \alpha(c) \cdot p + \beta(c) \cdot Q + m$ where $\alpha(c)$ and $\beta(c)$ are some integers depending on c, and $|\beta(c) \cdot Q + m|$ is smaller than p. For z_i's, which are computed in Decrypt(sk, c), we have $\left\lfloor \sum_{i=1}^{\Theta} s_i z_i \right\rceil = \alpha(c) \cdot p + \beta' \cdot Q$ for the same $\alpha(c)$, and hence we can decrypt c correctly:

$$c - \left\lfloor \sum_{i=1}^{\Theta} s_i z_i \right\rceil = \alpha(c) \cdot p + \beta(c) \cdot Q + m - (\alpha(c) \cdot p + \beta' \cdot Q) \equiv m \pmod{Q}.$$

2.3 More Remarks on NK Scheme

For NK scheme to be bootstrappable, we have to squash Decrypt – namely lower the depth of the decryption circuit – so that it is expressed as a low-degree polynomial. This is done in [DGHV10] for the case of $Q = 2$, but generalizing this for the case of $Q > 2$ was not easy. Then, in [NK15], the authors resolved the problem by constructing a mod-Q half adder and extending the decryption circuit of [DGHV10] to mod-Q message spaces.

They first constructed a polynomial $f_{carry,Q}(x,y) = \sum_{i=1}^{Q-1} \binom{x}{i}_Q \binom{y}{Q-i}_Q$ of degree Q (it is proved that the degree Q is lowest), for which one can easily check that $c = f_{carry,Q}(x,y) \bmod Q$ where $x + y = c \cdot Q + s$ for $x, y \in \mathbb{Z}/Q\mathbb{Z}$. Then given $x, y \in \mathbb{Z}/Q\mathbb{Z}$ as input, a mod-Q half adder HA_Q computes the sum $s = x + y \bmod Q$ and the carry $c = f_{carry,Q}(x,y) \bmod Q$. See Algorithm 1 below.

Algorithm 1. HA_Q, a mod-Q half adder

Input: $x, y \in \mathbb{Z}/Q\mathbb{Z}$
Output: $(c, s)_Q$ where $x + y = c \cdot Q + s$
  $s \leftarrow x + y \bmod Q$
  $c \leftarrow f_{carry,Q}(x,y) \bmod Q$
  return $(c, s)_Q$

The following lemma tells us that NK.Decrypt can be computed by polynomials of degree less than $Q^3 \lambda$.

Lemma 1 *[NK15, Theorem 4]. For any positive integer Θ and for $L = \lceil \log_Q \lambda \rceil + 2$ with λ a security parameter, there are $L + 1$ polynomials of degree $\leq Q^{L+1} \sim Q^3 \lambda$ over $\mathbb{Z}/Q\mathbb{Z}$ which compute the mod-Q sum of Θ Q-ary real numbers with L digits of precision after the Q-ary point.*

Finally, we recall the concrete choice of parameters given in [NK15, Sect. 5], where message size Q is regarded as constant.

- $\rho = \Theta(\lambda \log \log \log \lambda)$, $\eta = \Theta(\lambda^2 \log \log \lambda)$, $\gamma = \Theta(\lambda^4 \log^2 \lambda)$, and $\tau = \gamma + \lambda$
- $L = \lceil \log_Q \theta \rceil + 2$, $\kappa = \lceil (\gamma - \log(4Q - 5))/\log Q \rceil + 2$, $\Theta = \Theta((\lambda \log \lambda)^4)$, and $\theta = \lambda$.

In a nutshell, we compare the case $Q > 2$ with the case $Q = 2$, so we have to handle Q more carefully. We will study the dependence of parameters on Q in Sect. 4.1.

3 Homomorphic Evaluation of mod-Q Arithmetic Circuit Using FHE Scheme with Binary Message Space

In this section, we present a way to homomorphically perform arithmetic operations in $\mathbb{Z}/Q\mathbb{Z}$ using an FHE scheme with binary message space. For a given

FHE scheme $\Pi_2 = (\mathsf{KeyGen}_2, \mathsf{Encrypt}_2, \mathsf{Decrypt}_2, \mathsf{Evaluate}_2)$ with the message space $\mathcal{M} = \mathbb{Z}/2\mathbb{Z}$, one can construct an FHE scheme $\Pi_Q = (\mathsf{KeyGen}_Q, \mathsf{Encrypt}_Q, \mathsf{Decrypt}_Q, \mathsf{Evaluate}_Q)$ with message space $\mathcal{M} = \mathbb{Z}/Q\mathbb{Z}$ by encrypting messages bit by bit in their binary expansions ($n = \lceil \log(Q+1) \rceil$):

- $\mathsf{KeyGen}_Q(1^\lambda) \to (\mathsf{pk}, \mathsf{sk})$: Given a security parameter λ, run

$$(\mathsf{pk}, \mathsf{sk}) \leftarrow \mathsf{KeyGen}_2(1^\lambda).$$

Then output a public key pk and a secret key sk.
- $\mathsf{Encrypt}_Q(\mathsf{pk}, m) \to \boldsymbol{c}$: Given a plaintext $m \in \mathcal{M}$, write $m = (m_{n-1}, \cdots, m_0)$ as its binary expansion. Encrypt each bit m_i using

$$c_i \leftarrow \mathsf{Encrypt}_2(\mathsf{pk}, m_i).$$

Then output a ciphertext tuple $\boldsymbol{c} := (c_{n-1}, \cdots, c_0)$.
- $\mathsf{Decrypt}_Q(\mathsf{sk}, \boldsymbol{c}) \to m$: Given a ciphertext $\boldsymbol{c} = (c_{n-1}, \cdots, c_0)$, decrypt component-wise to get

$$m_i \leftarrow \mathsf{Decrypt}_2(\mathsf{sk}, c_i)$$

and output $m := \sum_{i=0}^{n-1} m_i 2^i$.

A ciphertext of the scheme Π_Q is an n-tuple of ciphertexts of the scheme Π_2, so the ciphertext size of Π_Q is $\log Q$ times that of Π_2.

3.1 $\mathsf{Evaluate}_Q$ and mod-Q Arithmetic Circuits

In what follows, we describe Boolean circuits BAdd_Q and BMult_Q to perform addition and multiplication on two n-bit integers modulo Q (these circuits are mostly chosen for their simplicity, and are far from optimal, particularly in terms of depth, but they will be sufficient for our purpose). Then, the evaluation algorithm $\mathsf{Evaluate}_Q$ of Π_Q is obtained by carrying out the homomorphic evaluation of these Boolean circuits on ciphertext tuples.

For $m, m' \in \mathbb{Z}/Q\mathbb{Z}$, BAdd_Q first adds two numbers over $\mathbb{Z}$, and reduces it mod Q. See Algorithm 2. Note that reducing $m + m'$ mod Q is done by first checking whether it is greater than or equals to Q, and subtracting Q only if it is so. Subtracting Q or nothing is sufficient for modular reduction since $0 \le m + m' < 2Q$. We denote the circuit carrying out this reduction step by Mod_Q^{n+1} (see Fig. 1).

BMult_Q circuit computes $m \cdot m' = \sum_{i=0}^{n-1} m \cdot m_i' 2^i$ by using the formular $(\cdots((m \cdot m_{n-1}' \cdot 2 + m \cdot m_{n-2}') \cdot 2 + m \cdot m_{n-3}') \cdots) \cdot 2 + m \cdot m_0'$. See Algorithm 3. Whenever the possibility that intermediate values are getting bigger than Q occurs, apply Mod_Q^{n+1} circuit to the current value.

We finish this section by counting the complexities of the two circuits BAdd_Q and BMult_Q in terms of the number of AND gates they use. This is a reasonable measure of complexity, as the homomorphic evaluation of those AND gates are

Algorithm 2. BAdd_Q, Boolean circuit for mod-Q addition

Input: $m, m' \in \mathbb{Z}/Q\mathbb{Z}$
Output: $m + m' \bmod Q$
   sum $\leftarrow m + m'$ *n bit addition* (2n AND)
   sum $\leftarrow$ sum $- 0$ or Q Mod_Q^{n+1} (7n AND)
   return sum

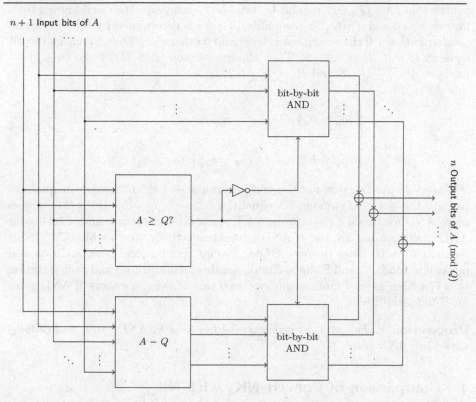

Fig. 1. $\mathsf{Mod}_\mathbf{Q}^{\mathbf{n+1}}$: For an $(n+1)$-bit input integer A with $0 \leq A < 2Q$, the circuit Mod_Q^{n+1} outputs $A \bmod Q$. The '$A \geq Q$?' part takes an $(n+1)$-bit integer A as input and returns 1 if $A \geq Q$ and 0 otherwise. 'bit-by-bit AND' part takes an n-bit string $(a_{n-1}, \cdots, a_0)$ and a bit b as inputs, and output n-bit string $(a_{n-1} \wedge b, \cdots, a_0 \wedge b)$

Algorithm 3. BMult_Q, Boolean circuit for mod-Q multiplication

---

Input: $m, m' = (m'_{n-1}, \cdots, m'_0) \in \mathbb{Z}/Q\mathbb{Z}$
Output: $m \cdot m' \bmod Q$
   prod $\leftarrow m \cdot m'_{n-1}$
   for $i = n-2, \cdots, 1, 0$ **do**
      prod $\leftarrow$ (prod $\ll 1$) $- 0$ or Q Mod_Q^{n+1} (7n AND)
      next $\leftarrow m \cdot m_i$ *n bit-by-bit AND operation* (n AND)
      prod $\leftarrow \mathsf{BAdd}_Q$(prod, next) BAdd_Q (9n AND)
   end for
   return prod

---

typically the costly operation in the underlying scheme Π_2: for example, in the Nuida–Kurosawa scheme, they correspond to a large integer modular multiplication followed by an expensive ciphertext refresh (i.e. bootstrapping) operation.

Since the usual full adder and full subtractor can be realized by using 2 AND gates, both n-bit addition and subtraction circuits are constructed using $2n$ AND gates. The circuit Mod_Q^{n+1} consists of one comparison $(A \geq Q?)$, one subtraction $(A - Q)$, and two bit-by-bit AND operations. It is well known that, for two bits b and b', the bit inequality $(b > b')$ is determined by $b \wedge \neg b'$ (where $(statement) = 1$ if the statement is true, and 0 otherwise). One can check the bit equality $(b = b')$ from $b \oplus \neg b'$. Then the comparison $(A > B)$ of two $(n + 1)$-bit integers $A = \sum_{i=0}^{n} a_i 2^i$ and $B = \sum_{i=0}^{n} b_i 2^i$ is:

$$\begin{cases} (a_n > b_n), \text{ or} \\ (a_n = b_n) \wedge (a_{n-1} > b_{n-1}), \text{ or} \\ \quad \vdots \\ (a_n = b_n) \wedge \cdots \wedge (a_1 = b_1) \wedge (a_0 > b_0). \end{cases}$$

We need $3n$ AND gates for the comparison; $n + 1$ AND for bit inequalities $(a_i > b_i)$, $n - 1$ AND among bit equalities $(a_n = b_n) \wedge \cdots \wedge (a_1 = b_1)$, and n more AND for the last parts $\wedge(a_i > b_i)$. An n bit subtraction and a bit-by-bit AND operation use $2n$ and n AND gates, respectively, and so Mod_Q^{n+1} circuit requires $7n$ AND gates in total. BAdd_Q circuit contains one n-bit addition and one call to Mod_Q^{n+1}, and BMult_Q circuit iterates about n times and each iteration uses $17n$ AND gates. Summarizing, we need the following numbers of AND gates for BAdd_Q and BMult_Q:

Proposition 1. *For an n-bit prime Q, BAdd_Q uses $9n$ AND gates, and BMult_Q uses $17n^2$ AND gates.*

4   Comparison of **Convert-NK$_2$** with **NK$_Q$**

The main goal of this paper is to understand how much of an improvement that Nuida–Kurosawa's approach to the homomorphic evaluation of modular arithmetic circuits have achieved over a more naive technique based on conversions to and from binary representations.

In this section, we quantify this improvement in concrete terms, by comparing the efficiency of two approaches that evaluate mod-Q message homomorphically, focusing on the NK scheme. For any prime Q, denote by NK_Q the NK FHE scheme with message space $\mathcal{M} = \mathbb{Z}/Q\mathbb{Z}$, and by $\mathsf{Convert\text{-}NK}_2$ the FHE scheme obtained from $\Pi_2 = \mathsf{NK}_2$ using the naive conversion method described in Sect. 3. Then we will compare the two schemes $\mathsf{Convert\text{-}NK}_2$ and NK_Q in terms of the size of ciphertexts and the time complexity of basic operations carried out during homomorphic evaluation.

As mentioned in the introduction, it is easy to see that $\mathsf{Convert\text{-}NK}_2$ will be more efficient than NK_Q for large values of Q, due to the fact that the squashed decryption circuit (and hence each ciphertext refresh operation) of NK_Q has a depth polynomial in Q, whereas the overhead incurred by using bitwise representations as in $\mathsf{Convert\text{-}NK}_2$ is at most polylogarithmic in Q. However, a more careful analysis is needed to compare the relative efficiencies of NK_Q and $\mathsf{Convert\text{-}NK}_2$ for very small Q, such as Q is $3, 5$ or 7.

4.1   Dependence of NK_Q Parameters upon Q

As we pointed out above, there are several factors making parameters depend on the message size Q. Decrypting a ciphertext is done by a circuit of degree $Q^3\lambda$ as in Lemma 1. As a result, the noise of a refreshed ciphertext is $Q^3\lambda$ times larger than that of encrypted secret key bits. To ensure the correctness, the secret prime p should be larger than that noise bound. Thus, Q affects the size η of p since the multiplicative degree of $\mathsf{Bootstrap}$ is related to the degree of $\mathsf{Decrypt}$ and hence it depends on Q. Although Q is regarded as constant in the parameter selection of [NK15], estimating how it concretely affects the parameters is necessary to compare $\mathsf{Convert\text{-}NK}_2$ with NK_Q.

In the key generation step of NK_Q, the secret key bits s_i's are encrypted as $v_i = pq_i + Qr_i + s_i$ with $|r_i| < 2^\rho$, and then we have $|Qr_i + s_i| \le Q|r_i| + 1 \le Q \cdot 2^\rho$. Note that v_i's are published as a part of the public key, and one can execute bootstrapping with input v_i's to refresh a ciphertext. Meanwhile, by Lemma 1 the decryption is done by a circuit of degree $Q^3\lambda$. Therefore, for any encryption c of a message m, the refreshed ciphertext $c^* \leftarrow \mathsf{Bootstrap}(\mathsf{pk}, c)$ will be of the form $c^* = pq^* + Qr^* + m$ with $\log|Qr^* + m| \le Q^3\lambda \cdot (\log Q + \rho) \propto Q^3$ (since $\log Q \ll \rho$). Since the size η of p should be greater than $\log|Qr^* + m|$ to prevent a decryption failure, we can conclude that η is proportional to Q^3: $\eta \propto Q^3$. Similarly the size γ of N is proportional to Q^6 as $\gamma \propto \eta^2$: $\gamma \propto Q^6$. We will use subscript notation η_Q and γ_Q to emphasize this dependence. Obviously, the number L of digits of precision depends on Q by definition, so we denote it by L_Q. Note that since $p \in [2^{\eta_Q - 1}, 2^{\eta_Q}) \cap \mathbb{Z}$ and $N \in [1, 2^{\gamma_Q}) \cap \mathbb{Z}$, p and N also rely on Q. So we also denote them by p_Q and N_Q to highlight the effect of Q.

On the other hand, there are also some parameters independent of Q. The error size ρ is chosen so that the approximate GCD problem is hard, and the number Θ of secret bits s_i is chosen so that the sparse subset sum problem is hard [NK15, Sect. 5]. These two problems remain unaffected by change of Q, so the same ρ and Θ will work for both $\mathsf{Convert\text{-}NK}_2$ and NK_Q schemes. We restate the selection of parameters of Sect. 2.3 with the effect of Q:

$$\eta_Q = \Theta(Q^3\lambda^2 \log\log\lambda),\ \gamma_Q = \Theta(Q^6\lambda^4 \log^2\lambda),\ \text{and } L_Q = \lceil \log_Q \lambda \rceil + 2.$$

4.2   Efficiency of $\mathsf{Convert\text{-}NK}_2$ Measured Against NK_Q

Since ciphertexts in the scheme NK_Q are defined modulo $N_Q \in [1, 2^{\gamma_Q}) \cap \mathbb{Z}$, they are of size γ_Q. A ciphertext of $\mathsf{Convert\text{-}NK}_2$, on the other hand, is an n-tuple of ciphertexts of NK_2, so its size will be $n \cdot \gamma_2 \sim \gamma_2 \log Q$. Proposition 2 tells us that ciphertext size of $\mathsf{Convert\text{-}NK}_2$ is asymptotically smaller than that of NK_Q.

Proposition 2. *For a given security parameter λ and any prime Q, let $\gamma'_2 = \gamma_2 \cdot \log Q$. Then we have*

$$\frac{\gamma'_2}{\gamma_Q} \sim 64 \cdot \frac{\log Q}{Q^6}.$$

Proof. By the argument in the previous section, we have $\gamma_Q = \Theta(Q^6 \lambda^4 \log^2 \lambda)$ where the implied constant does not depend on Q. Therefore (note that γ_2 is γ_Q with $Q = 2$)

$$\frac{\gamma'_2}{\gamma_Q} \sim \frac{\gamma_2 \cdot \log Q}{\gamma_Q} \sim \frac{2^6 \lambda^4 \log^2 \lambda \cdot \log Q}{Q^6 \lambda^4 \log^2 \lambda} \sim \frac{64 \log Q}{Q^6}.$$

□

Then, we would like to compare the speed, in a suitable sense, of homomorphic operations in NK_Q on the one hand and $\mathsf{Convert\text{-}NK}_2$ on the other. That speed is essentially determined by the cost of homomorphic multiplications modulo Q. Now, in NK_Q, a homomorphic multiplication consists of an integer multiplication modulo N_Q followed by a bootstrapping operation, and that latter operation will dominate the cost of the computation[1]. On the other hand, in $\mathsf{Convert\text{-}NK}_2$, a homomorphic multiplication is carried out by homomorphically evaluating the Boolean circuit for multiplication modulo Q using NK_2, which in turns costs as many NK_2 ciphertext refresh operations as there are AND gates in that Boolean circuit BMult_Q. Therefore, we compare precisely those two quantities in the following proposition.

Proposition 3. *For a given security parameter λ and any prime Q, let T_Q be the time complexity of a single ciphertext refresh operation in NK_Q, and T'_2 be the time complexity of carrying out a multiplication mod Q in $\mathsf{Convert\text{-}NK}_2$ (by homomorphically evaluating the Boolean circuit for modular multiplication, with a refresh operation after each AND gate). Then we have*

$$\frac{T'_2}{T_Q} \leq 2176 \cdot \frac{\log^4 Q}{Q^7}.$$

To prove Proposition 3, we need to count a more precise number of operations needed to carry out the Nuida–Kurosawa mod-Q bootstrapping. This is done in the next two lemmas: Lemma 2 gives the number of AND gates used in the half adder HA_Q, and Lemma 3 gives the number of calls to HA_Q in squashed decryption circuit. By combining the two lemmas, we can estimate the number of used homomorphic AND gates in bootstrapping procedure of $\mathsf{Convert\text{-}NK}_2$.

---

[1] One can ask whether it could be beneficial to choose parameters in such a way that refreshed ciphertexts support not just one but *several* levels of multiplication before another bootstrapping is required. The answer is no: to support d additional levels of multiplications, one needs to increase the size η of the secret prime p by a factor 2^d, and hence overall ciphertext size γ by a factor $\Omega(2^{2d})$. This makes all operations on ciphertexts at least $\Omega(2^{2d})$ slower, while one gains a factor at most $O(2^d)$ on the number of required bootstrapping operations, so there is a net efficiency loss overall.

Lemma 2. *One can evaluate $f_{carry,Q}(x,y) = \sum_{i=1}^{Q-1} \binom{x}{i}_Q \binom{y}{Q-i}_Q \bmod Q$ using $4Q - 7$ mod-Q multiplications. In particular, when $Q = 2$, we need only 1 mod-2 multiplication, i.e., 1 AND operation, as we expect.*

Proof. By the definition of $\binom{a}{b}_Q = a(a-1)\cdots(a-b+1)\cdot \mathrm{Inv}_Q(b!)$, we have $f_{carry,Q}(x,y) = \sum_{i=1}^{Q-1}\binom{x}{i}_Q\binom{y}{Q-i}_Q = \sum_{i=1}^{Q-1} x(x-1)\cdots(x-i+1)\cdot y(y-1)\cdots(y-Q+i+1)\mathrm{Inv}_Q(i!(Q-i)!)$. First we compute $Y_1 = (y-1), Y_2 = (y-1)(y-2)$, $\cdots, Y_{Q-2} = (y-1)(y-2)\cdots(y-Q+2)$ which requires $Q-3$ multiplications. And compute $X_0 = yx, X_1 = yx(x-1), \cdots, X_{Q-2} = yx(x-1)\cdots(x-Q+2)$ which is done by $Q-2$ multiplications. Then i-th term in $f_{carry,Q}$ is $X_i \cdot Y_{Q-i-1} \cdot \mathrm{Inv}_Q(i!(Q-i)!)$ that requires 2 more multiplications, and in total $2(Q-1)$ multiplications since we iterate this for $i = 1, \cdots, Q-1$. To sum up, we need $(Q-3) + (Q-2) + 2(Q-1) = 4Q - 7$ mod-Q multiplications to compute $f_{carry,Q}(x,y)$. $\qquad\square$

Lemma 3. *In $\mathsf{NK}_Q.\mathsf{Decrypt}$, one can compute the iterated addition $\sum_{i=1}^{\Theta} s_i z_i$ using HA_Q at most ΘL^2 times.*

Proof. Here we concentrate on counting the number of call to HA_Q only, and full algorithm is described in [NK15, Sect. 4].

Let $a_i = s_i z_i$ and $a_{i;j} = s_i z_{i;j}$ for $1 \le i \le \Theta, 0 \le j \le L$. Then $\sum_{i=1}^{\Theta} s_i z_i = \sum_{i=1}^{\Theta} a_i$ is computed by

$$
\begin{aligned}
a_1 &= a_{1;0} \cdot a_{1;1} \cdots a_{1;L} \\
a_2 &= a_{2;0} \cdot a_{2;1} \cdots a_{2;L} \\
&\qquad\qquad \vdots \\
+)\ a_{\Theta} &= a_{\Theta;0} \cdot a_{\Theta;1} \cdots a_{\Theta;L}
\end{aligned}
$$

(First iteration) For j-th column $(a_{1;j}, a_{2;j}, \cdots, a_{\Theta;j})^\top$, apply HA_Q Θ times sequentially to obtain $(\alpha_j, (\beta_{2;j}, \cdots, \beta_{\Theta;j})^\top)$ such that $\sum_{i=1}^{\Theta} a_{i;j} = \alpha_j + Q \cdot \sum_{i=2}^{\Theta} \beta_{i;j}$. Since we do this for $0 \le j \le L$, we need to apply HA_Q about $\Theta \cdot L$ times.

(Next iteration) Each column has different weight; for j-th column we have the weight of Q^{-j}, and so

$$
\sum_{i=1}^{\Theta} a_{i;j} Q^{-j} = \alpha_j \cdot Q^{-j} + \left(\sum_{i=2}^{\Theta} \beta_{i;j} \right) \cdot Q^{-(j-1)}.
$$

Therefore it suffices to add the following:

$$
\begin{aligned}
\alpha_0 &\cdot \ \alpha_1 \ \cdots \alpha_{L-1} \\
\beta_{2;1} &\cdot \ \beta_{2;2} \cdots \beta_{2;L} \\
&\qquad \vdots \\
+)\ \beta_{\Theta;1} &\cdot \ \beta_{\Theta;2} \cdots \beta_{\Theta;L}
\end{aligned}
$$

Note that α_L is the last digit of the result, and $\beta_{2;0}, \cdots, \beta_{\Theta;0}$ are canceled by modulo Q reduction. Repeat a similar process with the first iteration. To obtain all the digits of the result, we have to iterate these processes about L more times. One can do this by applying HA_Q about ΘL^2 times altogether.   □

Now we present the proof of Proposition 3:

Proof (Proof of Proposition 3). For any constant prime Q, let us denote by t_Q the time complexity of mod-N_Q multiplication. Then T_Q is t_Q multiplied by the number of multiplications in $\mathsf{NK}_Q.\mathsf{Decrypt}$, and T_2' is T_2 multiplied by the number of AND gates in BMult_Q circuit.

As far as we know, the best time complexity for k-bit multiplication is $k \log k 2^{O(\log^* k)}$ where $\log^* k$ represents the iterated logarithm [Für09]. In our case, k is γ_Q and $\log \gamma_Q = \log \Theta(Q^6 \lambda^4 \log^2 \lambda) = 6 \log Q + 4 \log \lambda + 2 \log \log \lambda +$ constant. Here the effect of $\log Q$ is dominated by that of $\log \lambda$, so we can estimate t_2/t_Q by γ_2/γ_Q since we can ignore effect of Q in the part $\log \gamma_Q 2^{O(\log^* \gamma_Q)}$. Furthermore, $\gamma_2/\gamma_Q = 2^6 \lambda^4 \log^2 \lambda / Q^6 \lambda^4 \log^2 \lambda = 64/Q^6$.

By Lemma 3, we call HA_Q in $\mathsf{NK}_Q.\mathsf{Decrypt}$ about ΘL_Q^2 times. Since each half adder HA_Q consists of exactly one evaluation of the polynomial $f_{carry,Q}$, the number of multiplications in $\mathsf{NK}_Q.\mathsf{Decrypt}$ is about $4Q\Theta L_Q^2$ by Lemma 2. On the other hand, we need $17 \log^2 Q$ AND gates for the Boolean circuit BMult_Q as in Proposition 1.

$$\frac{T_2'}{T_Q} \leq \frac{17 \log^2 Q \cdot 8\Theta L_2^2}{4Q\Theta L_Q^2} \cdot \frac{t_2}{t_Q} \sim \frac{34 \log^2 Q \log^2 \lambda}{Q \log^2 \lambda / \log^2 Q} \cdot \frac{64}{Q^6} \sim \frac{2176 \log^4 Q}{Q^7}.$$

□

Remark 1. The value $\frac{64 \log Q}{Q^6}$ is 0.139146 if $Q = 3$ and 0.009511 if $Q = 5$, and becomes much smaller as Q grows. Similarly, the value $\frac{2176 \log^4 Q}{Q^7}$ is 0.809588 for $Q = 5$ and 0.164120 for $Q = 7$. Thus, as shown in Table 1, even for small Q, $\mathsf{Convert\text{-}NK}_2$ is more advantageous than NK_Q in all practical respects.

Table 1. The values $64 \log Q/Q^6$ and $2176 \log^4 Q/Q^7$ for the first five odd primes

Q	$64 \log Q/Q^6$	$2176 \log^4 Q/Q^7$
3	0.139146	6.278936
5	0.009511	0.809588
7	0.001527	0.164120
11	0.000125	0.015993
13	0.000049	0.006502

5   Conclusion

In this work, we have compared the two schemes NK_Q and $Convert-NK_2$, and have seen that the latter is preferable in almost every measure, even for very small values of Q. That conclusion follows from a detailed analysis quantifying the precise dependence of the parameters of the underlying scheme with respect to the modulus Q. It is also based on a particularly simple choice of the Boolean circuits for modular arithmetic; more careful choices may result in an even greater performance advantage in favor of the naive bitwise approach.

Based on our concrete estimates, we conclude that the Nuida–Kurosawa approach is not competitive for any $Q > 3$ (and possibly not even $Q = 3$) as soon as one needs to carry out ciphertext refresh operations—and if one does not need bootstrapping, other somewhat homomorphic schemes with large message space are certainly preferable.

References

[CCK+13]   Cheon, J.H., Coron, J.-S., Kim, J., Lee, M.S., Lepoint, T., Tibouchi, M., Yun, A.: Batch Fully Homomorphic Encryption over the Integers. In: Johansson, T., Nguyen, P.Q. (eds.) EUROCRYPT 2013. LNCS, vol. 7881, pp. 315–335. Springer, Heidelberg (2013). doi:10.1007/978-3-642-38348-9_20

[CLT14]   Coron, J.-S., Lepoint, T., Tibouchi, M.: Scale-invariant fully homomorphic encryption over the integers. In: Krawczyk, H. (ed.) PKC 2014. LNCS, vol. 8383, pp. 311–328. Springer, Heidelberg (2014). doi:10.1007/978-3-642-54631-0_18

[CMNT11]   Coron, J.-S., Mandal, A., Naccache, D., Tibouchi, M.: Fully homomorphic encryption over the integers with shorter public keys. In: Rogaway, P. (ed.) CRYPTO 2011. LNCS, vol. 6841, pp. 487–504. Springer, Heidelberg (2011). doi:10.1007/978-3-642-22792-9_28

[CNT12]   Coron, J.-S., Naccache, D., Tibouchi, M.: Public key compression and modulus switching for fully homomorphic encryption over the integers. In: Pointcheval, D., Johansson, T. (eds.) EUROCRYPT 2012. LNCS, vol. 7237, pp. 446–464. Springer, Heidelberg (2012). doi:10.1007/978-3-642-29011-4_27

[CS15]   Cheon, J.H., Stehlé, D.: Fully homomophic encryption over the integers revisited. In: Oswald, E., Fischlin, M. (eds.) EUROCRYPT 2015. LNCS, vol. 9056, pp. 513–536. Springer, Heidelberg (2015). doi:10.1007/978-3-662-46800-5_20

[DGHV10]   Dijk, M., Gentry, C., Halevi, S., Vaikuntanathan, V.: Fully homomorphic encryption over the integers. In: Gilbert, H. (ed.) EUROCRYPT 2010. LNCS, vol. 6110, pp. 24–43. Springer, Heidelberg (2010). doi:10.1007/978-3-642-13190-5_2

[Für09]   Fürer, M.: Faster integer multiplication. SIAM J. Comput. **39**(3), 979–1005 (2009). doi:10.1137/070711761

[Gen09a]   Gentry. C.: A fully homomorphic encryption scheme. Ph.D. thesis, Stanford University (2009). crypto.stanford.edu/craig

[Gen09b] Gentry, C.: Fully homomorphic encryption using ideal lattices. In: Mitzen-macher, M. (ed.) STOC 2009, pp. 169–178. ACM (2009). doi:10.1145/1536414.1536440

[NK15] Nuida, K., Kurosawa, K.: (Batch) fully homomorphic encryption over inte-gers for non-binary message spaces. In: Oswald, E., Fischlin, M. (eds.) Advances in Cryptology–EUROCRYPT 2015. LNCS, vol. 9056, pp. 537–555. Springer, Heidelberg (2015). doi:10.1007/978-3-662-46800-5_21

[PAD12] Pisa, P.S., Abdalla, M., Duarte, O.C.M.B.: Somewhat homomorphic encryption scheme for arithmetic operations on large integers. In: GIIS 2012, pp. 1–8. IEEE (2012). doi:10.1109/GIIS.2012.6466769

[RAD78] Rivest, R.L., Adleman, L.M., Dertouzos, M.L.: On data banks and privacy homomorphisms. In: DeMillo, R.A. (ed.) Foundations of Secure Computa-tion, pp. 169–180. Academic Press (1978)

[vzGS91] von zur Gathen, J., Seroussi, G.: Boolean circuits versus arithmetic circuits. Inf. Comput. **91**(1), 142–154 (1991). doi:10.1016/0890-5401(91)90078-G

An Efficient Somewhat Homomorphic Encryption Scheme Based on Factorization

Gérald Gavin[✉]

ERIC - Université de Lyon, 5 av. Mendés France, 69676 Bron, France
gavin@univ-lyon1.fr

Abstract. Surprisingly, most of existing provably secure FHE or SWHE schemes are lattice-based constructions. It is legitimate to question whether there is a mysterious link between homomorphic encryptions and lattices. This paper can be seen as a first (partial) negative answer to this question. We propose a very simple private-key (partially) homomorphic encryption scheme whose security relies on factorization. This encryption scheme deals with a secret multivariate rational function ϕ_D defined over $\mathbb{Z}_n$, n being an RSA-modulus. An encryption of x is simply a vector c such that $\phi_D(c) = x + \mathsf{noise}$. To get homomorphic properties, nonlinear operators are specifically developed. We first prove IND-CPA security in the generic ring model assuming the hardness of factoring. We then extend this model in order to integrate lattice-based cryptanalysis and we reduce the security of our scheme (in this extended model) to an algebraic condition. This condition is extensively discussed for several choices of parameters. Some of these choices lead to competitive performance with respect to other existing homomorphic encryptions. While quantum computers are not only dreams anymore, designing factorization-based cryptographic schemes might appear as irrelevant. But, it is important to notice that, in our scheme, the factorization of n is not required to decrypt. The factoring assumption simply ensures that solving nonlinear equations or finding non-null polynomials with many roots is difficult. Consequently, the ideas behind our construction could be re-used in rings satisfying these properties.

1 Introduction

The prospect of outsourcing an increasing amount of data storage and management to cloud services raises many new privacy concerns for individuals and businesses alike. The privacy concerns can be satisfactorily addressed if users encrypt the data they send to the cloud. If the encryption scheme is homomorphic, the cloud can still perform meaningful computations on the data, even though it is encrypted.

The theoretical problem of constructing a fully homomorphic encryption scheme (FHE) supporting arbitrary functions f, was only recently solved by the breakthrough work of Gentry [6]. More recently, further fully homomorphic schemes were presented [4,7,16,17] following Gentry's framework. The underlying tool behind all these schemes is the use of Euclidean lattices, which have

© Springer International Publishing AG 2016
S. Foresti and G. Persiano (Eds.): CANS 2016, LNCS 10052, pp. 451–464, 2016.
DOI: 10.1007/978-3-319-48965-0_27

previously proved powerful for devising many cryptographic primitives. A central aspect of Gentry's fully homomorphic scheme (and the subsequent schemes) is the ciphertext refreshing Recrypt operation. Even if many improvements have been made, this operation remains very costly [8,12].

In many real-world applications, in the medical, financial, and the advertising domains, which require only that the encryption scheme is *somewhat* homomorphic. Somewhat homomorphic encryption schemes (SWHE), which support a limited number of homomorphic operations, can be much faster, and more compact than fully homomorphic encryption schemes. Even if several quite efficient lattice-based SWHE exist in the literature, significant efficiency improvements should be done for most real-world applications. This paper aims at elaborating an efficient SWHE whose security relies on factorization.

Many cryptographic constructions are based on the famous problem LWE [14]. In particular, this cryptographic problem is currently the most relevant to build FHE [2,9]. Typically, the secret key is a vector $s \in \mathbb{Z}_n^\kappa$ and an encryption c of a value $x \ll n$ is a randomly chosen vector satisfying[1] $s \cdot c = x + \mathsf{noise}$. This scheme is born (partially) additively homomorphic making it vulnerable against lattice-based attacks. We propose a slight modification to remove this homomorphic property. In our scheme, the secret key becomes a pair of vectors (s_1, s_2) and c is a randomly chosen vector satisfying $s_1 \cdot c / s_2 \cdot c = x + \mathsf{noise} \pmod{n}$. Clearly, the vector sum is not a homomorphic operator anymore. This is a *sine qua non* condition for overcoming lattice-based attacks. Indeed, as a ciphertext c is a vector, it is always possible to write it as a linear combination of other known ciphertexts. Thus, if the vector sum were a homomorphic operator, the cryptosystem would not be secure at all. This simple remark suffices to prove the weakness of the homomorphic cryptosystems presented in [11,18]. In order to use the vector sum as a homomorphic operator, noise should be injected into the encryptions as done in all existing FHE [3,4,6,7,16,17] and lattice-based attacks can be mount to recover linear combinations with small coefficients. To resist against such attacks, the dimension of c should be chosen sufficiently large which dramatically degrades performance.

To obtain homomorphic properties, nonlinear homomorphic operators Add and Mult should be developed and published. Quadratic homomorphic operators can be naturally defined. However, it should be ensured that these operators do not leak information about the secret key. We get results in this sense under the factoring assumption where n is a product of large secret primes. In particular, we prove the IND-CPA security of our scheme in the generic ring model [1,10] for any $\kappa \geq 2$. In this model, the CPA attacker is assumed to only perform arithmetic operations $+, -, \times, /$. A security proof in the generic model indicates that the idea of basing the security on factorization is not totally flawed. This leads us more or less to the situation of RSA where it was recently shown that breaking the security of RSA in the generic ring model is as difficult as factoring [1]. A classical objection against security analysis in the generic ring model deals with the Jacobi symbol J_n. For concreteness, it was shown in [10] that computing

---

[1] $s \cdot c$ denoting the scalar product between s and c.

J_n is difficult in the generic ring model while it is not in general. However, this result is neither surprising nor relevant because J_n is not a rational function[2]. Indeed, we can even show that $\phi(x) = J_n(x)$ with probability smaller than $1/2$ provided ϕ is a rational function and x uniform over $\mathbb{Z}_n^*$. In our scheme, the function ϕ defined by $\phi(c) = x + \mathsf{noise}$ is rational suggesting that a security analysis in the generic ring model is meaningful.

However, the security analysis in the generic ring model is not sufficient because lattice-based cryptanalysis exploiting the fact that $x + \mathsf{noise}$ is small is not considered in this model. In Sect. 5, we propose a general characterization of lattice-based attacks which naturally extends the generic ring model. We reduce the non-existence of such attacks to an algebraic condition. This condition is discussed in Sect. 5.3 for several choices of κ. We prove that this condition is satisfied for $\kappa = \Theta(\lambda)$ proving the non-existence of lattice-based attacks. Moreover, the simplest and most natural lattice-based attack is shown inefficient provided $\kappa = \Omega(\log \lambda)$. By assuming that this attack is also the most efficient, choosing $\kappa = \Theta(\log \lambda)$ could hopefully ensure the non-existence of efficient lattice-based attacks.

Notation. *We use standard Landau notations. Throughout this paper, we let λ denote the security parameter: all known attacks against the cryptographic scheme under scope should require $2^{\Omega(\lambda)}$ bit operations to mount.*

– *$\delta \geq 2$ is a positive integer independent of λ.*
– *The inner product of two vectors v and v' is denoted by $v \cdot v'$*
– *The set of all square $2\kappa - by - 2\kappa$ matrices over $\mathbb{Z}_n$ is denoted by $\mathbb{Z}_n^{2\kappa \times 2\kappa}$. The ith row of $S \in \mathbb{Z}_n^{2\kappa \times 2\kappa}$ is denoted by s_i and $\mathcal{L}_i$ denotes the linear function defined by $\mathcal{L}_i(v) = s_i \cdot v$.*
– *A δ-RSA modulus n is a product of δ η-bit primes $p_1 \cdots p_\delta$ where η is chosen sufficiently large to ensure that the factorization of n requires $\Omega(2^\lambda)$ bit operations provided $p_1, \ldots, p_\delta$ are randomly chosen.*
– *The set of the positive integer strictly smaller than ξ is denotes by $I_\xi = \{0, \ldots, \xi - 1\}$.*

Remark 1. The number $M(m,d)$ of m-variate monomials of degree d is equal to $\binom{d + m - 1}{d}$. In particular, $M(2\kappa, \kappa) > 3^\kappa$ for any $\kappa \geq 2$.

Because of the lack of space, most of the proofs were omitted. They can be found in [5].

2   Preliminary Definitions and Results

Let $\delta \geq 2$ be a positive integer (independent of the security parameter) and let $n = p_1 \cdots p_\delta$ be a randomly chosen δ-RSA modulus. Given a r-variate function ϕ and a subset $I \subseteq \mathbb{Z}_n^r$, $z_{\phi,I}$ denotes the probability over I that $\phi(x) = 0$,

---

[2] It comes from the fact that $J_n(x) \mod p$ (resp. $J_n(x) \mod q$) is not a function of $x \mod p$ (resp. $x \mod q$).

$$z_{\phi,I} \stackrel{\text{def}}{=} \frac{|\{x \in I | \phi(x) = 0\}|}{|I|}$$

$z_{\phi,\mathbb{Z}_n^r}$ will be simply denoted by z_ϕ.

2.1 Roots of Polynomials

The following result proved in [1] establishes that it is difficult to output a polynomial ϕ such that z_ϕ is non-negligible without knowing the factorization of n. The security of RSA in the generic ring model can be quite straightforwardly derived from this result (see [1]).

Theorem 1 *(Lemma 4 of [1]). Assuming factoring is hard, there is no p.p.t-algorithm $\mathcal{A}$ which inputs n and which outputs[3] a $\{+, -, \times\}$-circuit computing a non-null polynomial $\phi \in \mathbb{Z}_n[X]$ such that z_ϕ is non-negligible.*

Thanks to this lemma, showing that two polynomials[4] are equal with non-negligible probability becomes an algebraic problem: it suffices to prove that they are identically equal. This lemma is a very powerful tool which is the heart of the security proofs proposed in this paper. We extend this result to the multivariate case.

Proposition 1. *Assuming factoring is hard, there is no p.p.t algorithm $\mathcal{A}$ which inputs n and which outputs (see Footnote 3) a $\{+, -, \times\}$-circuit computing a non-null polynomial $\phi \in \mathbb{Z}_n[X_1, \ldots, X_r]$ such that z_ϕ is non-negligible.*

The following proposition yields links between $z_{\phi,I}$ and z_ϕ for particular subsets $I \subseteq \mathbb{Z}_n^r$.

Proposition 2. *Let $\phi \in \mathbb{Z}_n[X_1, \ldots, X_r]$ and let $I = I_{\xi_1} \times \cdots \times I_{\xi_r}$ with $\xi_j \geq \max(p_1, \ldots, p_\delta)$ for any $j = 1, \ldots, r$. If z_ϕ is negligible then $z_{\phi,I}$ is negligible.*

By considering the notation of the two previous propositions, if $\phi \leftarrow \mathcal{A}(n)$ and $z_{\phi,I}$ is non-negligible then ϕ is null[5] assuming factoring is hard. This is the heart of our security proofs.

2.2 κ-symmetry

The following definition naturally extends the classical definition of symmetric polynomials.

Definition 1. A polynomial $\phi \in \mathbb{Z}_n[X_{11}, \ldots, X_{1t}, \ldots, X_{\kappa 1} \ldots, X_{\kappa t}]$ is said to be κ-symmetric if for any permutation σ of $\{1, \ldots, \kappa\}$,

$$\phi(X_{11}, \ldots, X_{1t}, \ldots, X_{\kappa 1}, \ldots, X_{\kappa t})$$
$$= \phi(X_{\sigma(1)1}, \ldots, X_{\sigma(1)t}, \ldots, X_{\sigma(\kappa)1}, \ldots, X_{\sigma(\kappa)t})$$

---

[3] with non-negligible probability (the coin toss being the choice of n and the internal randomness of $\mathcal{A}$).

[4] built without knowing the factorization of n.

[5] with overwhelming probability.

This property is at the heart of our construction. Informally, all the values known by the CPA attacker are evaluations of κ-symmetry polynomials while the decryption function[6] does not satisfy this property. Our security proofs are all based on this fact.

2.3   Rational Functions

Throughout this paper, we will consider the class of rational functions useful in our security proof in the generic ring model.

Definition 2. A function $\phi : \mathbb{Z}_n^r \to \mathbb{Z}_n$ is said to be rational if there exists a $\{+, -, \times, /\}$-circuit computing this function.

Throughout this paper, recovering a rational function means recovering a $\{+, -, \times, /\}$-circuit computing this function. The following result states that a rational function can be represented by a $\{+, -, \times, /\}$-circuit or equivalently by two $\{+, -, \times\}$-circuits.

Lemma 1. *Given $\mathcal{C}$ be a polynomial-size $\{+, -, \times, /\}$-circuit, we denote by $\phi_\mathcal{C}$ the (rational) function computing by $\mathcal{C}$. There exists a p.p.t. algorithm $\mathcal{A}$ such that $\mathcal{A}(\mathcal{C})$ outputs two polynomial-size $\{+, -, \times\}$-circuits $\mathcal{C}', \mathcal{C}''$ satisfying $\phi_\mathcal{C} = \phi_{\mathcal{C}'} / \phi_{\mathcal{C}''}$.*

3   A Somewhat Homomorphic Encryption (SWHE)

3.1   A Private-Key Encryption

Let $\delta > 2$ be a constant and let λ be a security parameter and let η denote the bit size of the prime factors of δ-RSA moduli.

Definition 3. The functions KeyGen, Encrypt, Decrypt are defined as follows:

- KeyGen(λ, δ). Let κ be a parameter indexed by λ. Let ξ be an arbitrary $(\eta{+}1)$-bit integer, let n be a δ-RSA modulus chosen at random and let S be an invertible matrix of $\mathbb{Z}_n^{2\kappa \times 2\kappa}$ chosen at random. The ith row of S is denoted by s_i and $\mathcal{L}_i$ denotes the linear function defined by $\mathcal{L}_i(\boldsymbol{v}) = s_i \cdot \boldsymbol{v}$. Output

$$K = \{S\} \; ; \; pp = \{n, \xi\}$$

- Encrypt$(K, pp, x \in I_\xi)$. Choose at random $r_1, r_2, r_2', \ldots, r_\kappa, r_\kappa' \in \mathbb{Z}_n^*$, $k \in I_\xi$ and output

$$c = S^{-1} \begin{pmatrix} r_1 \overline{x} \\ r_1 \\ r_2 \\ r_2' \\ \cdots \\ r_\kappa \\ r_\kappa' \end{pmatrix}$$

where $\overline{x} = x + k\xi$.

---

[6] which is not a polynomial but a rational function.

– Decrypt$(K, pp, \boldsymbol{c} \in \mathbb{Z}_n^{2\kappa})$. Output $x = \mathcal{L}_1(\boldsymbol{c})/\mathcal{L}_2(\boldsymbol{c}) \mod n \mod \xi$

In the rest of the paper, it will be assumed that $pp = \{n, \xi\}$ is public. Correctness can be straightforwardly shown by noticing that $\mathcal{L}_1(\boldsymbol{c}) = r_1\overline{x}$ and $\mathcal{L}_2(\boldsymbol{c}) = r_1$. As claimed in the introduction, $\boldsymbol{c}$ is a randomly chosen vector satisfying $\mathcal{L}_1(\boldsymbol{c})/\mathcal{L}_2(\boldsymbol{c}) = \overline{x}$. However, we have adopted a slightly more complex definition in order to introduce material useful when defining the homomorphic operators.

3.2   The Multiplicative Operator

Let $S \leftarrow \mathsf{KeyGen}(\lambda, \delta)$.

Proposition 3. *There exists a (unique) tuple of quadratic 4κ-variate polynomials $(q_1, \ldots, q_{2\kappa})$ such that for any $\boldsymbol{u}, \boldsymbol{v} \in \mathbb{Z}_n^{2\kappa}$ it is ensured that*

$$S(q_1(\boldsymbol{u}, \boldsymbol{v}), \ldots, q_{2\kappa}(\boldsymbol{u}, \boldsymbol{v})) = (a_1 b_1, \ldots, a_{2\kappa} b_{2\kappa})$$

where $a = S\boldsymbol{u}$, $b = S\boldsymbol{v}$.

Proof. (Sketch.) It suffices to define the polynomials q_i by

$$\begin{pmatrix} q_1(\boldsymbol{u}, \boldsymbol{v}) \\ \vdots \\ q_{2\kappa}(\boldsymbol{u}, \boldsymbol{v}) \end{pmatrix} = S^{-1} \begin{pmatrix} \mathcal{L}_1(\boldsymbol{u})\mathcal{L}_1(\boldsymbol{v}) \\ \vdots \\ \mathcal{L}_{2\kappa}(\boldsymbol{u})\mathcal{L}_{2\kappa}(\boldsymbol{v}) \end{pmatrix} \qquad \square$$

We consider the function MultGen which inputs S and outputs the **expanded representation** of the polynomials $q_1, \ldots, q_{2\kappa}$ defined in Proposition 3. By using the fact that each quadratic polynomial q_i has $O(\kappa^2)$ monomial, it is not hard to show that the running time of MultGen is $O(\kappa^4)$. The operator Mult $\leftarrow$ MultGen(S) consists of evaluating these polynomials, i.e. Mult$(\boldsymbol{u}, \boldsymbol{v}) = (q_1(\boldsymbol{u}, \boldsymbol{v}), \ldots, q_{2\kappa}(\boldsymbol{u}, \boldsymbol{v}))$, leading to a running time in $O(\kappa^3)$.

Proposition 4. *Mult $\leftarrow$ MultGen(S) is a valid multiplicative homomorphic operator.*

$$\mathsf{Mult}\left(S^{-1}\begin{pmatrix} r_1\overline{x} \\ r_1 \\ \vdots \\ r_\kappa \\ r'_\kappa \end{pmatrix}, S^{-1}\begin{pmatrix} t_1\overline{y} \\ t_1 \\ \vdots \\ t_\kappa \\ t'_\kappa \end{pmatrix}\right) = S^{-1}\begin{pmatrix} r_1 t_1 \overline{xy} \\ r_1 t_1 \\ \vdots \\ r_\kappa t_\kappa \\ r'_\kappa t'_\kappa \end{pmatrix}$$

Fig. 1. Description of the operator Mult $\leftarrow$ MultGen(S)

3.3   The Additive Operator

Let $S \leftarrow \mathsf{KeyGen}(\lambda, \delta)$.

Proposition 5. *There exists a (unique) tuple of quadratic 4κ-variate polynomials $(q_1, \ldots, q_{2\kappa})$ such that for any $\boldsymbol{u}, \boldsymbol{v} \in \mathbb{Z}_n^{2\kappa}$ it is ensured that*

$$S(q_1(\boldsymbol{u}, \boldsymbol{v}), \ldots, q_{2\kappa}(\boldsymbol{u}, \boldsymbol{v})) = (a_1 b_2 + a_2 b_1, a_2 b_2, \ldots, a_{2\kappa-1} b_{2\kappa} + a_{2\kappa} b_{2\kappa-1}, a_{2\kappa} b_{2\kappa})$$

where $a = S\boldsymbol{u}, \ b = S\boldsymbol{v}$.

Proof. (Sketch.) It suffices to define the polynomials q_i by

$$\begin{pmatrix} q_1(\boldsymbol{u}, \boldsymbol{v}) \\ \vdots \\ q_{2\kappa}(\boldsymbol{u}, \boldsymbol{v}) \end{pmatrix} = S^{-1} \begin{pmatrix} \mathcal{L}_1(\boldsymbol{u})\mathcal{L}_2(\boldsymbol{v}) + \mathcal{L}_2(\boldsymbol{u})\mathcal{L}_1(\boldsymbol{v}) \\ \mathcal{L}_2(\boldsymbol{u})\mathcal{L}_2(\boldsymbol{v}) \\ \vdots \\ \mathcal{L}_{2\kappa-1}(\boldsymbol{u})\mathcal{L}_{2\kappa}(\boldsymbol{v}) + \mathcal{L}_{2\kappa}(\boldsymbol{u})\mathcal{L}_{2\kappa-1}(\boldsymbol{v}) \\ \mathcal{L}_{2\kappa}(\boldsymbol{u})\mathcal{L}_{2\kappa}(\boldsymbol{v}) \end{pmatrix}$$

$\square$

We consider the function AddGen which inputs S and outputs the **expanded representation** of the polynomials $q_1, \ldots, q_{2\kappa}$ defined in Proposition 5. By using the fact that each quadratic polynomial q_i has $O(\kappa^2)$ monomial, it is not hard to show that the running time of AddGen is $O(\kappa^4)$. The operator $\mathsf{Add} \leftarrow \mathsf{AddGen}(S)$ consists of evaluating these polynomials, i.e. $\mathsf{Add}(\boldsymbol{u}, \boldsymbol{v}) = (q_1(\boldsymbol{u}, \boldsymbol{v}), \ldots, q_{2\kappa}(\boldsymbol{u}, \boldsymbol{v}))$, leading to a running time in $O(\kappa^3)$.

Proposition 6. *$\mathsf{Add} \leftarrow \mathsf{AddGen}(S)$ is a valid additive homomorphic operator.*

3.4   Discussion

Clearly the operators Add and Mult are valid homomorphic operators provided $\delta \geq 4$. Note that these operators are commutative. By publishing these homomorphic operators, we get a somewhat homomorphic private-key encryption scheme. Arithmetic circuits of depth $\delta/2 \approx \log n / 2 \log \xi$ can be evaluated. For instance, if n is a 10-RSA Modulus, circuits of depth 5 can be evaluated.

$$\mathsf{Add}\left(S^{-1}\begin{pmatrix} r_1\overline{x} \\ r_1 \\ \vdots \\ r_\kappa \\ r'_\kappa \end{pmatrix}, S^{-1}\begin{pmatrix} t_1\overline{y} \\ t_1 \\ \vdots \\ t_\kappa \\ t'_\kappa \end{pmatrix}\right) = S^{-1}\begin{pmatrix} r_1 t_1(\overline{x} + \overline{y}) \\ r_1 t_1 \\ \vdots \\ r_\kappa t'_\kappa + r'_\kappa t_\kappa \\ r'_\kappa t'_\kappa \end{pmatrix}$$

Fig. 2. Description of the operator $\mathsf{Add} \leftarrow \mathsf{AddGen}(S)$

The classic way (see [15]) to transform a private-key cryptosystem into a public-key cryptosystem consists of publicizing encryptions c_i of known values x_i and using the homomorphic operators to encrypt x. Let Encrypt1 denote this new encryption function. Assuming the IND-CPA security of the private-key cryptosystem, it suffices that $\mathsf{Encrypt1}(pk,x)$ and $\mathsf{Encrypt}(K,pp,x)$ are computationally indistinguishable to ensure the IND-CPA security of the public-key cryptosystem.

4 Security Analysis

All the security results of this section are true for any $\kappa \geq 2$. Thus, to simplify notation, we set $\kappa = 2$ throughout this section. Let $K = \{S\} \leftarrow \mathsf{KeyGen}(\lambda, \delta)$. To break semantic security, an attacker is required to find a function φ satisfying

$$\mathsf{Adv}^\varphi \overset{\text{def}}{=} |\Pr(\varphi \circ \mathsf{Encrypt}(K, pp, 1) = 1) - \Pr(\varphi \circ \mathsf{Encrypt}(K, pp, 0) = 1)|$$

is non-negligible.

Externalizing the generation of n. To clearly understand the role of the factoring assumption in our security proof, it is important to notice that the factorization of n is not used by KeyGen. Consequently, the generation of n could be externalized[7] (for instance generated by an oracle). In other words, n could be a public input of KeyGen. This means that all the polynomials considered in this section are built without using the factorization of n implying that they are equal to 0 with negligible probability provided they are not null (according to Proposition 1).

Randomness θ_n. After n is publicized, the CPA attacker receives the public operators Add and Mult and it has access to an encryption oracle. For any $1 \leq i \leq t$, it chooses $x_i \in I_\xi$ and receives encryptions $c_i = S^{-1}(r_i \overline{x}_i, r_i, r'_i, r''_i)$ of x_i from the encryption oracle. The randomness of its knowledge comes from the internal randomness of KeyGen and the one of the encryption oracle. This randomness is encapsulated in the tuple θ_n of elements belonging to $\mathbb{Z}_n$ defined by

$$\theta_n = (s_1, s_2, r_1 \overline{x}_1, r_1 \ldots, r_t \overline{x}_t, r_t, s_3, s_4, r'_1, r''_1 \ldots, r'_t, r''_t)$$

Knowledge of the CPA attacker. We first assume that $\Delta = \det S$ is revealed to the CPA attacker. By doing this, it can be assumed that $(\Delta \cdot c_i)_{i=1,\ldots,t}$, $\Delta \cdot$Add and $\Delta \cdot$Mult are revealed to the CPA attacker instead of $(c_i)_{i=1,\ldots,t}$, Add and Mult. It follows that the CPA attacker receives a tuple $\alpha_n \in \mathbb{Z}_n^m$ where each component is the evaluation over θ_n of a polynomial[8] α_i, i.e. $\alpha_n = (\alpha_1(\theta_n), \ldots, \alpha_m(\theta_n))$. All our security analysis is based on the fact that the polynomials α_i are κ-symmetric[9] (see Definition 1). Throughout this section, we consider the function

---

[7] ensuring that its factorization was forgotten just after its generation.

[8] α_i can be seen as a $\{+, -, \times\}$-circuit C (independent of n) with $|\theta_n|$ inputs.

[9] it   means   that $\alpha_i(s_1, s_2, r_1 \overline{x}_1, r_1 \ldots, r_t \overline{x}_t, r_t, s_3, s_4, r'_1, r''_1 \ldots, r'_t, r''_t)$ $=$ $\alpha_i(s_3, s_4, r'_1, r''_1 \ldots, r'_t, r''_t, s_1, s_2, r_1 \overline{x}_1, r_1 \ldots, r_t \overline{x}_t, r_t)$. It should be noticed that $\det S$ is a κ-symmetric polynomial defined over θ_n.

$\widehat{\alpha}$ defined by $\widehat{\alpha}(\theta_n, \boldsymbol{z}) = (\alpha_1(\theta_n), \dots, \alpha_m(\theta_n), \boldsymbol{z})$ for any $\boldsymbol{z} \in \mathbb{Z}_n^4$. By construction, we have

$$(\alpha_n, \boldsymbol{c}) = \widehat{\alpha}(\theta_n, \boldsymbol{c})$$

4.1 Generic Ring Model

A Generic Ring Algorithm (GRA) (see [1]) defined over a ring $\mathcal{R}$ (here $\mathcal{R} = \mathbb{Z}_n$) is an algorithm where only arithmetic operations $+, -, \times, /$ and equality tests are allowed. In the special case $\mathcal{R} = \mathbb{Z}_n$, equality tests are not needed. This is implicitly shown in [1] as a straightforward consequence of Proposition 1. Indeed, this proposition ensures that two rational functions[10] are either equal with negligible probability or equal with overwhelming probability. It follows that a GRA is simply a $\{+, -, \times, /\}$-circuit computing a rational function φ. We say that our scheme is IND-CPA secure in the classical generic model if there does not exist any p.p.t algorithm $\mathcal{A}$ such that $\mathcal{A}(n)$ outputs a $\{+, -, \times, /\}$-circuit of a rational function φ satisfying

$$|\mathrm{Pr}(\varphi \circ \widehat{\alpha}(\theta_n, \mathsf{Encrypt}(K, pp, 1)) = 1) - \mathrm{Pr}(\varphi \circ \widehat{\alpha}(\theta_n, \mathsf{Encrypt}(K, pp, 0)) = 1)| \tag{1}$$

is non-negligible.

Lemma 2. *SWHE is IND-CPA secure in the classical generic ring model assuming the hardness of factoring.*

However, this result is not surprising because the decryption function is not rational[11]. We propose to extend this model by enhancing the power of the attacker: informally, we let it use the function $\mod \xi$. By doing this, the CPA attacker only needs to recover the evaluation $p(\overline{x})$ of a polynomial p in order to recover x or at least to break IND-CPA security in this model. Indeed, if the degree of p and its coefficients are small enough[12] then $p(\overline{x}) \mod n \mod \xi = p(x) \mod \xi$. This extension is encapsulated in the next definition.

Definition 4 (Generic IND-CPA security). Our scheme is generically IND-CPA secure if there does not exist any p.p.t algorithm $\mathcal{A}$ such that $\mathcal{A}(n)$ outputs[13] a $\{+, -, \times, /\}$-circuit computing a rational function φ, $x \in I_\xi$ and a non-constant polynomial p satisfying

$$\varphi \circ \widehat{\alpha}(\theta_n, \boldsymbol{c})[= \varphi(\alpha_n, \boldsymbol{c})] = p(\overline{x}) \tag{2}$$

with non-negligible probability over $\theta_n, \boldsymbol{c} \leftarrow \mathsf{Encrypt}(K, pp, x)$.

---

[10] built in polynomial-time under the factoring assumption.

[11] as explained for J_n in the introduction, there does not exist a rational function equal to the decryption function with non-negligible probability.

[12] Ideally $p(\overline{x}) = \overline{x}$..

[13] with non-negligible probability, the coin toss being the internal randomness of $\mathcal{A}$ and the choice of n.

4.2   Hardness of Factoring $\Rightarrow$ Generic IND-CPA Security

In this section, we prove the generic IND-CPA security of our scheme. The proof exploits intrinsic symmetry properties of our construction. Informally, only functions (indexed by S) which are stable by permuting the two first rows of S with the two last ones can be generically recovered. In particular, the decryption function $\mathcal{L}_1/\mathcal{L}_2$ cannot be generically recovered.

Theorem 2. *SWHE is generically IND-CPA secure assuming the hardness of factoring.*

5   Lattice-Based Cryptanalysis

Throughout this section, we adopt the notation of the previous section. In particular, α_n denotes the knowledge of the CPA attacker and θ_n denotes the internal randomness coming from KeyGen and the encryption oracle used to produce α_n. In the previous section, we prove the generic IND-CPA security of our encryption scheme under the factoring assumption for any $\kappa \geq 2$. This indicates that the idea of basing the security on factorization is not totally flawed. However, this is not sufficient because lattice-based cryptanalysis is excluded from this analysis: indeed lattice-based algorithms *work outside* $\mathbb{Z}_n$ and they compute functions which may be not rational.

Throughout this section, we will consider the polynomial $\Phi_R = \mathcal{L}_2 \cdots \mathcal{L}_{2\kappa}$. This polynomial is indexed by S (and thus θ_n) and it can be seen as a degree-κ homogeneous polynomial ϕ_R defined over $\theta_n, \boldsymbol{c}$, i.e.

$$\phi_R(\theta_n, \boldsymbol{c}) = \Phi_R(\boldsymbol{c}) = \prod_{\ell=1,\ldots,\kappa} s_{2\ell} \cdot \boldsymbol{c} = \prod_{\ell=1,\ldots,\kappa} \left(\sum_{i=1}^{2\kappa} s_{2\ell,i} \cdot c_i \right)$$

5.1   A Basic Example

Let $x \in I_\xi$, let $\boldsymbol{c} \leftarrow \mathsf{Encrypt}(K, pp, x)$ and let Φ_X be the polynomial defined by $\Phi_X = \Phi_R \cdot \mathcal{L}_1/\mathcal{L}_2$. By construction,

$$\Phi_X(\boldsymbol{c})/\Phi_R(\boldsymbol{c}) = \overline{x}$$

Φ_X (also Φ_R) is a homogeneous degree-κ polynomial, i.e.

$$\Phi_X(\boldsymbol{c}) = \sum_{e_1+\cdots+e_{2\kappa}=\kappa} a_{e_1,\ldots,e_{2\kappa}} c_1^{e_1} \cdots c_{2\kappa}^{e_{2\kappa}}$$

According to Theorem 2, the CPA attacker cannot generically recover both Φ_R and Φ_X. Nevertheless, let us assume that it can generically derive Φ_R from its knowledge α_n. It follows that

$$\sum_{e_1+\cdots+e_{2\kappa}=\kappa} a_{e_1,\ldots,e_{2\kappa}} \cdot \frac{c_1^{e_1} \cdots c_{2\kappa}^{e_{2\kappa}}}{\Phi_R(\boldsymbol{c})} = \overline{x} \ll n \tag{3}$$

By exploiting the fact that $\overline{x}$ is small relatively to n and by considering sufficiently many encryptions, the monomial coefficients $a_{e_1,\ldots,e_{2\kappa}}$ of Φ_X could be classically recovered by using a lattice basis reduction algorithm, e.g. LLL or BKZ. However, this attack requires first to recover Φ_R. In the next section, we propose a characterization of lattice-based attacks and we show that recovering Φ_R or a multiple of Φ_R is a necessary condition to mount a lattice-based attack. This condition will be discussed in Sect. 5.3.

5.2 Characterization of Lattice-Based Attacks

In this section, we propose a general characterization of lattice-based attacks which naturally extends the generic ring model.

Given $x \in I_\xi$, let us imagine that the CPA attacker is able to recover functions $\varphi_1, \ldots, \varphi_t$ such that there are coefficients $a_1, \ldots, a_t \in \mathbb{Z}_n$ and a function ε satisfying

$$a_1 \cdot \varphi_1(c) + \cdots + a_t \cdot \varphi_t(c) = \varepsilon(c)$$

where $c \leftarrow \mathsf{Encrypt}(K, pp, x)$ and $\varepsilon(c) \ll n$. By sampling sufficiently many encryptions c, the coefficients $a_1, \ldots, a_t$ and thus ε can be recovered by solving an approximate-SVP. This is a relevant attack if the knowledge of ε can be used to break IND-CPA security. This attack can be identified to the tuple $(\varphi_1, \ldots, \varphi_t)$. This is formally encapsulated in the following definition where the quantities $\varphi_1(c), \ldots, \varphi_t(c)$ are generically derived and where $\varepsilon(c) = p(\overline{x})$, p being a polynomial.

Definition 5 (Lattice-based attacks). A lattice-based attack is an efficient algorithm $\mathcal{A}$ such that $\mathcal{A}(n)$ outputs[14] a tuple of rational functions $(\varphi_1, \ldots, \varphi_t)$, $x \in I_\xi$ and a non-constant polynomial p such that there exist[15] functions $a_1, \ldots, a_t$ satisfying

$$a_1(\theta_n) \cdot \varphi_1 \circ \widehat{\alpha}(\theta_n, c) + \ldots + a_t(\theta_n) \cdot \varphi_t \circ \widehat{\alpha}(\theta_n, c) = p(\overline{x}) \qquad (4)$$

with non-negligible probability the choice of θ_n, $c \leftarrow \mathsf{Encrypt}(K, pp, x)$.

If there exists a lattice-based attack $\mathcal{A}$ then the CPA attacker can obviously use it to recover rational functions $\varphi_1, \ldots, \varphi_t$ satisfying (4) then it can hope to recover $a_1(\theta_n), \ldots, a_t(\theta_n)$ and thus to break IND-CPA security by using lattice basis reduction algorithms exploiting the fact that $\overline{x} \ll n$.

Theorem 3. Let $\mathcal{A}$ be a lattice-based attack and assume that $(\phi_i'/\phi_i)_{i=1,\ldots,t}$, $x, p \leftarrow \mathcal{A}(n)$ satisfies (4). Assuming the hardness of factoring, there exists[16] $i \in \{1, \ldots, t\}$ such that $\gcd(\phi_i \circ \widehat{\alpha}, \phi_R) = \phi_R$.

---

[14] with non-negligible, the toss coin being the internal randomness of $\mathcal{A}$ and the choice of n.

[15] Theorem 2 ensures that $a_1(\theta_n), \ldots, a_t(\theta_n)$ cannot be generically derived from α_n.

[16] with overwhelming probability.

Corollary 1. *There does not exist*[17] *any polynomial-size* $\{+, -, \times\}$*-circuit computing a polynomial* ϕ *satisfying* $\gcd(\phi \circ \widehat{\alpha}, \phi_R) = \phi_R \Rightarrow$ *There does not exist any lattice-based attack assuming the hardness of factoring,*

This corollary provides a sufficient algebraic condition ensuring the existence of lattice-based attacks. This condition is discussed in the next section.

5.3   Analysis

We discuss Theorem 3 and Corollary 1 for several choices of κ.

- $\kappa = \Theta(\lambda)$. As mentioned at the beginning of this section, each value known by the CPA attacker is an evaluation over θ_n of a κ-symmetric polynomial. We enhance the power of the CPA attacker by allowing it to recover evaluations $\alpha_i(\theta_n)$ of arbitrarily chosen κ-symmetric polynomials $(\alpha_i)_{i=1,\dots,t}$. Each monomial coefficient of Φ_R is a κ-symmetric polynomial defined over S. However, its expanded representation is exponential-size provided $\kappa = \Theta(\lambda)$. The question arising here consists of wondering whether Φ_R can be efficiently and generically written using only $(\alpha_i(\theta_n))_{i=1,\dots,t}$. We provide a negative answer to this question.

Proposition 7. *Assuming the hardness of factoring, there does not exist any lattice-based attack provided* $\kappa = \Theta(\lambda)$.

This result is fundamental in the sense that it formally proves the non-existence of lattice-based attacks for some choices of κ.

- $\kappa \geq t \log_3 \lambda$. In this case, we do not have any formal result excluding the possibility to generically recover Φ_R. However, the attack described in Sect. 5.1 is not efficient. Indeed, Φ_X has a number of monomials larger than λ^t (see Remark 1) implying that the dimension of the lattice considered in this attack is also larger than λ^t, e.g. Φ_X has more than 2×10^7 monomials for $\kappa \geq 10$. As the approximation obtained in polynomial-time with the best known lattice basis reduction algorithm is exponential, it suffices to adjust t in order that this approximation is not good enough. This choice of κ would be relevant by assuming that this attack is the most efficient. We are convinced that this assumption is true legitimating this choice of κ.

6   Efficiency

Our scheme can evaluate arithmetic circuit of depth smaller than $\delta/2$. A ciphertext is a 2κ-vector in $\mathbb{Z}_n$, implying that the ratio of ciphertext size to plaintext size is approximately equal to $4\kappa\delta$. By assuming that the size of a δ-RSA modulus is $O(\delta)$, the running time of Encrypt/ Decrypt/ Add/ Mult is $O(\delta^2\kappa)$, $O(\delta^2\kappa)$, $O(\delta^2\kappa^3)$, $O(\delta^2\kappa^3)$. The security analysis proposed in the previous section is not

---

[17] with overwhelming probability over the choice of n.

sufficient to determine κ. The performance of our scheme is very competitive with respect to classic schemes with $\kappa = \Theta(\log \lambda)$ but poor with $\kappa = \Theta(\lambda)$. For instance, if we choose $\kappa = 10$ (a choice potentially relevant according to the previous section), applying the homomorphic operators requires around 2000 modular multiplications. Our security analysis should be refined to optimize the choice of κ.

7   Future Work

Our security proof is not complete and the main challenge is to completely reduce the security of our scheme to the factorization.

Another interesting question consists of wondering whether this SWHE can be boostrapped in order to obtain an FHE scheme. We did not think about this and we do not have any idea about the way to achieve it.

Randomizing the homomorphic operators (see [5]) gives hope for another motivating perspective. The factoring assumption defeats the whole "post-quantum" purpose of multivariate cryptography [13]. In our opinion, this assumption could be removed by introducing randomness into homomorphic operators in order to maintain the truth of the formal results proved under the factoring assumption.

It is important to notice that the factorization of n is not used by the decryption function of our scheme. The factoring assumption simply ensures that solving nonlinear equations or finding non-null polynomials with many roots is difficult. Consequently, the ideas behind our construction can be straightforwardly re-used in rings satisfying these properties.

Acknowledgment. The authors thank the reviewers for their helpful remarks.

References

1. Aggarwal, D., Maurer, U.: Breaking RSA generically is equivalent to factoring. In: Joux, A. (ed.) EUROCRYPT 2009. LNCS, vol. 5479, pp. 36–53. Springer, Heidelberg (2009)
2. Brakerski, Z., Vaikuntanathan, V.: Efficient fully homomorphic encryption from (standard) LWE. In: Proceedings of the 2011 IEEE 52nd Annual Symposium on Foundations of Computer Science, FOCS 2011, pp. 97–106. IEEE Computer Society, Washington, DC (2011)
3. Brakerski, Z., Vaikuntanathan, V.: Efficient fully homomorphic encryption from (standard) LWE. Cryptology ePrint Archive, Report 2011/344 (2011). http://eprint.iacr.org/
4. Coron, J.-S., Naccache, D., Tibouchi, M.: Public key compression and modulus switching for fully homomorphic encryption over the integers. In: Pointcheval, D., Johansson, T. (eds.) EUROCRYPT 2012. LNCS, vol. 7237, pp. 446–464. Springer, Heidelberg (2012)
5. Gavin, G.: An efficient somewhat homomorphic encryption scheme based on factorization. Cryptology ePrint Archive, Report 2016/897 (2016). http://eprint.iacr.org/2016/897

6. Gentry, C.: Fully homomorphic encryption using ideal lattices. In: STOC, pp. 169–178 (2009)

7. Gentry, C., Halevi, S., Smart, N.P.: Fully homomorphic encryption with polylog overhead. In: Pointcheval, D., Johansson, T. (eds.) EUROCRYPT 2012. LNCS, vol. 7237, pp. 465–482. Springer, Heidelberg (2012)

8. Gentry, C., Halevi, S., Smart, N.P.: Homomorphic evaluation of the AES circuit. In: Safavi-Naini, R., Canetti, R. (eds.) CRYPTO 2012. LNCS, vol. 7417, pp. 850–867. Springer, Heidelberg (2012)

9. Gentry, C., Sahai, A., Waters, B.: Homomorphic encryption from learning with errors: conceptually-simpler, asymptotically-faster, attribute-based. In: Canetti, R., Garay, J.A. (eds.) CRYPTO 2013, Part I. LNCS, vol. 8042, pp. 75–92. Springer, Heidelberg (2013)

10. Jager, T., Schwenk, J.: On the analysis of cryptographic assumptions in the generic ring model. In: Matsui, M. (ed.) ASIACRYPT 2009. LNCS, vol. 5912, pp. 399–416. Springer, Heidelberg (2009)

11. Kipnis, A., Hibshoosh, E.: Efficient methods for practical fully homomorphic symmetric-key encrypton, randomization and verification. Cryptology ePrint Archive, Report 2012/637 (2012). http://eprint.iacr.org/

12. Lauter, K., Naehrig, M., Vaikuntanathan, V.: Can homomorphic encryption be practical? IACR Cryptology ePrint Archive 2011, p. 405 (2011)

13. Patarin, J.: Hidden fields equations (HFE) and isomorphisms of polynomials (IP): two new families of asymmetric algorithms. In: Maurer, U. (ed.) EUROCRYPT 1996. LNCS, vol. 1070, pp. 33–48. Springer, Heidelberg (1996). doi:10.1007/3-540-68339-9_4

14. Regev, O.: On lattices, learning with errors, random linear codes, and cryptography. In: Proceedings of the 37th Annual ACM Symposium on Theory of Computing, Baltimore, MD, USA, pp. 84–93, 22–24 May 2005

15. Rothblum, R.: Homomorphic encryption: from private-key to public-key. In: Ishai, Y. (ed.) TCC 2011. LNCS, vol. 6597, pp. 219–234. Springer, Heidelberg (2011). doi:10.1007/978-3-642-19571-6_14

16. Stehlé, D., Steinfeld, R.: Faster Fully Homomorphic Encryption. In: Abe, M. (ed.) ASIACRYPT 2010. LNCS, vol. 6477, pp. 377–394. Springer, Heidelberg (2010)

17. van Dijk, M., Gentry, C., Halevi, S., Vaikuntanathan, V.: Fully Homomorphic Encryption over the Integers. In: Gilbert, H. (ed.) EUROCRYPT 2010. LNCS, vol. 6110, pp. 24–43. Springer, Heidelberg (2010)

18. Xiao, L., Bastani, O., Yen, I-L.: An efficient homomorphic encryption protocol for multi-user systems. IACR Cryptology ePrint Archive 2012, p. 193 (2012)

Information Theoretic Security

Efficient, XOR-Based, Ideal (t, n)−threshold Schemes

Liqun Chen[1,2], Thalia M. Laing[3(✉)], and Keith M. Martin[3]

[1] Hewlett-Packard Enterprise, Bristol, UK
liqun.chen@hpe.com
[2] University of Surrey, Guildford, UK
liqun.chen@surrey.ac.uk
[3] Information Security Group, Royal Holloway, University of London, Egham, UK
{thalia.laing,keith.martin}@rhul.ac.uk

Abstract. We propose a new, lightweight (t, n)−threshold secret sharing scheme that can be implemented using only XOR operations. Our scheme is based on an idea extracted from a patent application by Hewlett Packard that utilises error correction codes. Our scheme improves on the patent by requiring fewer randomly generated bits and by reducing the size of shares given to each player, thereby making the scheme ideal. We provide a security proof and efficiency analysis. We compare our scheme to existing schemes in the literature and show that our scheme is more efficient than other schemes, especially when t is large.

Keywords: Threshold · Secret sharing · Perfect · Efficient · Ideal · Error correction

1 Introduction

A (t, n)−threshold secret sharing scheme provides a method for distributing a secret k amongst n players in such a way that any t players can uniquely reconstruct the secret and $t - 1$ players learn no information about the secret.

Secret sharing can be utilised in distributed systems to store information, such as a decryption key, across n servers. A user wishing to access the encrypted data could retrieve shares from any t servers and combine them to recover the key and decrypt the data. A system such as this would enable greater availability, as there is no single point of failure, and add redundancy, thereby improving reliability in case of failures. Furthermore, secret sharing offers security without the reliance on cryptographic keys. In an encryption system, the decryption key must be stored securely and an adversary that gains access to the key would render the encrypted data insecure. If the key were dispersed via a (t, n)−threshold scheme, the adversary would need to extract the shares from t of the n servers in order to recover it. Learning shares from up to $t - 1$ servers would reveal no information. A system with these benefits is of particular interest given the growth of constrained devices in potentially insecure locations, such as devices

© Springer International Publishing AG 2016
S. Foresti and G. Persiano (Eds.): CANS 2016, LNCS 10052, pp. 467–483, 2016.
DOI: 10.1007/978-3-319-48965-0_28

in the Internet of Things. An adversary may find it easy to extract the information stored on a constrained device, but no information would be learnt if the information extracted were a share of a key rather than the key itself.

Blakley and Shamir first introduced (t, n)−threshold schemes in 1979 [2,3]. Shamir's scheme achieves minimal share sizes and requires generating minimal randomness. The scheme is elegant but, despite improvements in implementation, has a fairly heavy computational cost because the recovery procedure relies on Lagrange interpolation. Given the increase in constrained devices, there have been efforts to create schemes that achieve the properties of Shamir's scheme but can be implemented using only XOR operations. These schemes claim to be lighter than Shamir's and therefore more applicable to limited devices.

A novel (t, n)−threshold scheme that achieves the properties of Shamir's scheme and can be implemented using only XOR operations is presented here. Our scheme is based on a computationally secure scheme by Hewlett Packard (HP) [1], from which we extracted a (t, n)−threshold scheme. We have improved their scheme by requiring fewer randomly generated bits and achieving smaller share sizes for each player. We present a proof of security and provide an efficiency analysis. We then compare our scheme with other threshold schemes that have the same properties (minimal share size and XOR based implementation).

Kurihara et al. presented the first XOR based, ideal (t, n)−threshold in [5] as a generalisation of the work in [4], which considered $(3, n)$−threshold schemes. Kurihara et al.'s scheme constructs shares by XORing pieces of the secret with multiple random numbers and distributing these amongst the players. Recovery is possible by multiplying a vector consisting of the shares by a matrix generated via Gaussian elimination, which is computationally heavy. Kurihara et al. analysed the efficiency of their scheme and compared it to Shamir's scheme.

Since Kurihara et al.'s scheme, few schemes achieving the same properties have been proposed. Lv et al. proposed one such scheme in [6] and a multisecret analogue in [7], but Wang and Desmedt [8] show that in [6] the size of the shares are smaller than the size of the secret and therefore cannot be correct. Their criticism is, however, only true when more than one secret is being dispersed. Nonetheless, Lv et al.'s scheme does have a number of flaws, such as incompatible matrix-vector multiplications and an incorrect analysis of the number of randomly generated values and will therefore not be further considered.

Wang and Desmedt proposed their own (t, n)−threshold scheme that is equivalent to an error correcting code [8]. They proved their scheme to be secure and claimed it could be implemented using only XOR and cyclic shift operations. However, they do not provide an exact distribution algorithm, an efficiency analysis or compare their scheme to the current literature.

1.1 Contributions

Our contribution can be summarised as follows:

- We present a new, ideal (t, n)−threshold secret sharing scheme based on an idea from a patent application by HP [1]. The scheme is defined in the Galois

Field $GF(2^\ell)$ and requires only XORs and shift operations for both distribution and recovery. The scheme could be generalised to any Galois Field; we have specified $q = 2$ as this is likely to be the case when implemented.

− We provide a proof of security for our scheme and show it is ideal. No proof of security was presented for IIP's scheme.
− We analyse the complexity of our proposed scheme with respect to the number of bitwise XOR operations required.
− We compare our scheme to existing XOR based, ideal (t,n)−threshold schemes in the literature. In order to conduct this analysis, we have provided the first efficiency analysis of the scheme presented by Wang and Desmedt [8].

1.2 Organisation

This paper is organised as follows. In Sect. 2 we present notation and provide definitions. In Sect. 3 we define our scheme and in Sect. 4 we prove our scheme is an ideal, (t,n)−threshold scheme. An efficiency analysis of the distribution and recovery algorithms of the scheme is given in Sect. 5. In Sect. 6, we analyse the efficiency of Wang and Desmedt's scheme [8] and compare this with Kurihara et al.'s scheme [5], Shamir's scheme [3] and our scheme.

2 Preliminaries

In this section, the definitions and notation used will be introduced.

2.1 Secret Sharing Schemes

Let $n, t \in \mathbb{N}, t \le n$. A (t,n)−*threshold scheme* is a method of distributing a *secret k* amongst a set of n *players* in such a way that any subset of t players can uniquely recover the secret and any subset of fewer than t players cannot learn any information about the secret.

A (t,n)−threshold scheme can be defined using information theoretic notation [9]. Let K denote the discrete random variable corresponding to the choice of secret and let A denote the discrete random variable corresponding to the set of share given to the players in the set $A \subseteq \mathcal{P}$.

Definition 1. *A dealer distributes a secret k amongst a set $\mathcal{P} = \{P_0, \ldots, P_{n-1}\}$ of n players. Let $t \le n$ be the threshold and let Γ be a set containing all sets of at least t players. A (t,n)−threshold scheme consists of two algorithms: Share and Recover. Share is a probabilistic algorithm that takes as input the secret k and outputs an $n-$vector S. Each player P_i receives a share $S[i]$. Players then input their shares to the Recover algorithm, which satisfies the following properties:*

(1) Any set B of fewer than t players learns no information about the secret: $\forall B \notin \Gamma, H(K|B) = H(K)$, and
(2) any set A of at least t players can uniquely recover the secret. Information theoretically: $\forall A \in \Gamma, H(K|A) = 0$.

These two conditions will be referred to as (1) privacy and (2) recoverability.

Note that schemes achieving the privacy requirement are said to have *perfect security*. Shamir proposed the first (t, n)−threshold scheme in 1979 [3].

Definition 2 (Shamir's (t, n)−threshold scheme). *Let $\mathcal{P}$ be a set of n players $\mathcal{P} = \{P_0, P_1, \ldots, P_{n-1}\}$ and let $p > n$ be some prime. Let $r_1, r_2, \ldots, r_{t-1}$ be $t - 1$ values generated uniformly at random from $\mathbb{Z}_p$. For a given secret $k \in \mathbb{Z}_p$, let $f \in \mathbb{Z}_p[x]$ be the polynomial defined by*

$$f(x) = k + r_1 x + r_2 x^2 + \cdots + r_{t-1} x^{t-1}.$$

Allocate to each player P_i the share $\boldsymbol{S}[i] = f(i + 1)$.

Any set of t or more players can use polynomial interpolation on their shares to recover the polynomial $f(x)$ and thus calculate $k = f(0)$. However, given fewer than t shares there exists a polynomial in $\mathbb{Z}_p[x]$ of degree $t - 1$ for any $k \in \mathbb{Z}_p$. Thus $t - 1$ shares reveals no information about k.

In any (t, n)−threshold scheme distributing a key of λ bits requires the generation of a minimum of $\lambda(t - 1)$ bits of randomness for distribution [19].

The *information rate* ρ of a scheme is the ratio of the size of the secret to the size of the largest share. In any (t, n)−threshold scheme the share given to each player must be at least the size of the secret [9], so $\rho \geq 1$. Schemes that meet this bound have every share equal to the size of the secret and are called *ideal*. Shamir's scheme is an ideal scheme.

Schemes with smaller share sizes can be constructed by relaxing the requirement for the scheme to achieve perfect security, meaning that sets of fewer than t players learn some information about the secret. Ramp schemes achieve this.

Definition 3. *A $(t_0, t_1; n)$−ramp scheme is a method of distributing a secret k such that any set of at least t_1 players can pool their shares to uniquely recover the secret. A set of t_0 or fewer players reveals no information about the secret.*

Observe that a (t, n)−threshold scheme is a $(t - 1, t; n)$−ramp scheme. There is no bound on the amount of information a set of between t_0 and t_1 players can learn about k. In a $(0, t, n)$−threshold scheme, there are no security constraints; only recoverability for t players must be satisfied. In Sect. 2.3 it is shown that a $(0, t; n)$−ramp scheme is equivalent to an information dispersal algorithm.

If we wish the security of the ramp scheme to be maximised with respect to the limit on the size of each share then the information theoretic knowledge about the secret is likely to increase linearly with respect to the number of participants pooling their shares. This motivates the following definition [10].

Definition 4. *A $(t_0, t_1; n)$−ramp scheme is said to be* linear *if, for any set of players $A \subseteq \mathcal{P}$ such that $|A| = r$, where $t_0 \leq r \leq t_1$,*

$$H(\boldsymbol{K}|\boldsymbol{A}) = \frac{t_1 - r}{t_1 - t_0} H(\boldsymbol{K}). \tag{1}$$

Intuitively, a linear $(t_0, t_1; n)$-ramp scheme reveals no information about the secret k to a set containing up to t_0 players. Then, for every further player contributing a share, a fixed amount of information is learnt about k. This continues in a linear fashion until t_1 players have pooled their shares and k is learnt completely. In fact, after t_0 shares are pooled, every further share reveals $\frac{1}{t_1 - t_0}$ bits of information about k.

2.2 Error Correcting Codes

An error correcting code (ECC) is a method of encoding data with some redundant information to ensure the original data can be recovered, even if a number of errors occur during either data transmission or storage [11].

Definition 5. *An* error correcting code *(ECC) C of* length n *over a finite alphabet F is a subset of F^n. The elements of C are called* codewords. *The* size *of C is $|C| = m$. The* minimum distance *of C is the minimum Hamming distance between any two distinct codewords in C and is denoted by d.*

ECCs are able to detect and correct a number of errors. A code C is e_1-*error detecting* if, whenever a codeword $u \in C$ is sent and between 1 and e_1 errors occur, the received word v is not a codeword, so the receiver will know something has gone wrong in the channel and the error will be detected. A code C is e_2-*error correcting* if, whenever $u \in C$ is a codeword, and v is a word of length n over F such that $v \neq u$ and the Hamming distance between u and v is at most e_2, then v is decoded to u using nearest neighbour decoding.

Let C be a code of length n. We say that C is *linear* if for all $u, w \in C$, we have $u + w \in C$, where addition is done modulo q with $|F| = q$. Intuitively, a linear code is a code in which linear combinations of the codewords are also codewords. If $u_1, \ldots, u_t$ is a basis for a linear code C, then we say C has *dimension t*. Each codeword in C is of length n and there are q^t possible codewords in C. Let d be the minimum distance of C. We say that C is an $[n, t, d]$-*code*.

One important type of ECC is a maximum distance separable code [11].

Definition 6. *A* maximum distance separable *(MDS) code is a linear code that meets the Singleton bound: $d = n - t + 1$.*

MDS codes have the maximum possible Hamming distance between codewords and each can be separated into message symbols and check symbols. A code in which the message string appears in the codeword is called *systematic*. In an MDS code, recovery of a codeword is possible from any t of the n symbols. MDS codes are e error correcting and $2e = n - t$ error detecting. For a received word with a errors and b erasures, the codeword will be uniquely recovered if $2a + b < 2e$. One example of an MDS code is a Reed Solomon (RS) code [12].

The notions of (t, n)-threshold schemes and MDS codes are closely related. In 1983, Karnin et al. observed that every ideal (t, n)-threshold scheme determines a unique MDS code and vice versa [13]. Furthermore, a $[n, t, n-t+1]$-MDS code is equivalent to a linear $(0, t; n)$−ramp scheme [14]. An RS code is a type of MDS code, and thus is also equivalent to a linear ramp scheme.

A (t, n)−*optimal erasure code* is an ECC that transforms a message of t symbols into a codeword of length n such that any t received symbols from the codeword allow reconstruction of the message. An erasure code cannot necessarily correct errors, but can correct up to $n - t$ erasures [15]. A (t, n)−erasure code is equivalent to a (t, n)−information dispersal algorithm.

2.3   Information Dispersal Algorithms

Information dispersal was first introduced by Rabin in 1989 [16].

Definition 7. *Let $t, n \in \mathbb{N}, t \leq n$. A (t, n)−information dispersal algorithm (IDA) consists of a message space $\mathcal{M}$ and two algorithms Share and Recover. Share takes as input a message $m \in \mathcal{M}$ and outputs an n−vector S. Recover takes as input elements of the vector S. If at least t elements are submitted correctly to Recover, the algorithm will output the original message m.*

Intuitively, a (t, n)−IDA shares data between n players such that any set of at least t players can recover the data. This is equivalent to the recoverability property of a (t, n)−threshold scheme, but there are no privacy requirements on an IDA. Any (t, n)−threshold scheme is an IDA, but it is possible to achieve smaller share sizes in a (t, n)−IDA than in a (t, n)−threshold scheme.

Systematic IDA. Using systematic erasure codes, Plank and Resch [17] present a systematic (t, n)−IDA consisting of two algorithms: $Share^{\text{IDA}}$ and $Recover^{\text{IDA}}$.

$Share^{\text{IDA}}$ is a probabilistic algorithm that takes as input a message M to be distributed between n players. M is parsed into a t−vector M where each element is in the Galois Field $F = GF(2^\lambda)$. Let G be a publically known $n \times t$ binary matrix such that the first t rows form the $t \times t$ identity matrix I_t and the final $n - t$ rows are filled with bits such that any t of the n rows of G are linearly independent. Multiply G and M to calculate an n−vector C, where multiplication of elements $b \in \{0, 1\}$ and $d \in F$ is defined as follows: $\{0, 1\} \times F \to F$, where $0 \times d = 0 \in F$ and $1 \times d = d \in F$.

Each player P_i is then given the element $C[i]$ as their share. Note that, because the first t rows of G form the identity matrix, the first t elements of C will be identical to elements in M. This matrix-multiplication is shown in (2).

$$\begin{pmatrix} 1 & 0 & \cdots & 0 \\ 0 & 1 & \cdots & 0 \\ \vdots & \vdots & \ddots & \vdots \\ 0 & 0 & \cdots & 1 \\ G[t][0] & G[t][1] & \cdots & G[t][t-1] \\ \vdots & \vdots & \ddots & \vdots \\ G[n-1][0] & G[n-1][1] & \cdots & G[n-1][t-1] \end{pmatrix} \begin{pmatrix} M[0] \\ M[1] \\ \cdots \\ M[t-1] \end{pmatrix} = \begin{pmatrix} M[0] \\ M[1] \\ \cdots \\ M[t-1] \\ C[t] \\ \cdots \\ C[n-1] \end{pmatrix} \quad (2)$$

In order to recover M, t shares are submitted to $Recover^{\text{IDA}}$. A new t-vector C' is created consisting of the t pooled shares. A $t \times t$ matrix G' is then formed, which consists of the t rows of G corresponding to the shares pooled. This matrix is then inverted and multiplied by the vector C' to return $M = (G')^{-1} \cdot C'$.

Plank and Resch's systematic IDA is a systematic variant of Rabin's IDA [16], which uses a matrix G consisting entirely of random bits. The systematic version is more efficient because only the final $n - t$ elements of C are encoded; the first t elements can be directly copied from the vector M.

As mentioned in Sect. 2.1, an IDA is equivalent to a $(0, t; n)$-ramp scheme. In particular, Plank and Resch's systematic IDA is a linear $(0, t; n)$-ramp scheme if $M \in \{0, 1\}^{\ell}$ has *maximal entropy*, meaning that $H(M) = 2^{\ell}$.

Theorem 1. *Plank and Resch's systematic IDA is a linear $(0, t; n)$-ramp scheme if the message $M \in \{0, 1\}^{\ell}$ has maximal entropy $H(M) = 2^{\ell}$.*

Proof. A set of t players are able to recover M by constructing the vector C', creating the corresponding G' and then calculating $(G')^{-1} \cdot C'$. Therefore the systematic IDA satisfies the recoverability property of a ramp scheme.

Now we must show that the IDA is linear. Recall from Sect. 2.2 that a $(t_0, t_1; n)$-ramp scheme is linear if (1) is satisfied. So, we must show that, for any set of players A, such that $|A| = r$ for $0 \le r \le t$,

$$H(M|A) = \frac{t - r}{t} H(M).$$

As $H(M) = 2^{\ell}$, when M is parsed into t equal sized elements to form the t-vector M, each element has entropy $M[i] = \frac{2^{\ell}}{t}$. So each element of M learnt reduces the entropy of M by exactly $\frac{2^{\ell}}{t}$. Thus,

$$H(M|A) = 2^{\ell} - \left(r \frac{2^{\ell}}{t} \right) = \frac{2^{\ell}(t - r)}{t} = \frac{t - r}{t} \times 2^{\ell} = \frac{t - r}{t} H(M),$$

as required. Therefore the systematic IDA is a linear $(0, t; n)$-ramp scheme. $\square$

3   An Efficient (t, n)-threshold Scheme

In this section, we present our (t, n)-threshold scheme, based on an idea extracted from HP's scheme [1]. Our scheme improves HP's by requiring the generation of fewer random bits, by decreasing the size of each player's share thereby making the scheme ideal, and by using the systematic IDA described in Sect. 2.3 to minimise encoding. Our scheme is defined in the Galois Field $F = GF(2^{\ell})$, as this is likely the chosen field for implementation. The scheme could, however, be generalised to any Galois field $GF(q^{\ell})$.

3.1   Share

Our scheme constitutes two algorithms, *Share* and *Recover*. Both algorithms are presented in Figs. 1 and 2 respectively.

Share(k) is a probabilistic algorithm that takes as input a secret $k \in \{0,1\}^{\lambda}$. The secret k is considered as a string of t words, with each word consisting of $\lceil \frac{\lambda}{t} \rceil$ bits, by parsing k into t elements. Let $GF(2^{\lceil \frac{\lambda}{t} \rceil})$, then $k \in F^t$. If λ is divisible by t, k will parse exactly into t words. If not, k must be padded with exactly $(-\lambda) \mod t$ elements to ensure each word is an element in F and $k \in F^t$. For ease of notation, it will be assumed that λ is divisible by t throughout.

Step 1 of the algorithm randomly generates $t - 1$ *dummy keys*, labelled $r_1, \ldots, r_{t-1} \in GF(2^{\lambda})$. As was done with k, these are parsed into t words, so each $r_i \in F^t$. In Step 2, k and the dummy keys are XORed to produce $k' \in F^t$.

All the dummy keys $r_1, \ldots, r_{t-1}$ and k' are then treated as $t-$vectors over F and independently dispersed via the $Share^{\text{IDA}}$ algorithm described in Sect. 2.3. This results in t vectors of length n: $\boldsymbol{R_1}, \ldots, \boldsymbol{R_{t-1}}$ and $\boldsymbol{K'} \in F^n$. The first t elements of the output from the IDA are equal to the t elements from the input vector. The final $n - t$ elements are check symbols.

Elements of each of these $n-$vectors are then given to the n players in Step 5 in such a way that every player receives t elements: each element will be from a distinct vector and will be from a different position in each vector. Let $\boldsymbol{R_i}[j]$ denote the jth element in the vector $\boldsymbol{R_i}$. One possible distribution process can be illustrated by constructing a $t \times n$ matrix M, where each $n-$vector output by the systematic IDA defines a row of M, where

$$M = \begin{pmatrix} \boldsymbol{K'}[0] & \boldsymbol{K'}[1] & \ldots & \boldsymbol{K'}[n-2] & \boldsymbol{K'}[n-1] \\ \boldsymbol{R_1}[0] & \boldsymbol{R_1}[1] & \ldots & \boldsymbol{R_1}[n-2] & \boldsymbol{R_1}[n-1] \\ \ldots & \ldots & \ldots\ldots & & \ldots \\ \boldsymbol{R_{t-1}}[0] & \boldsymbol{R_{t-1}}[1] & \ldots & \boldsymbol{R_{t-1}}[n-2] & \boldsymbol{R_{t-1}}[n-1] \end{pmatrix}. \tag{3}$$

A new matrix can then be constructed from M by shifting elements in row i, for $0 \le i \le t$, i places to the left, resulting in the matrix

$$M' = \begin{pmatrix} \boldsymbol{K'}[0] & \boldsymbol{K'}[1] & \ldots \boldsymbol{K'}[n-2] & \boldsymbol{K'}[n-1] \\ \boldsymbol{R_1}[1] & \boldsymbol{R_1}[2] & \ldots \boldsymbol{R_1}[n-1] & \boldsymbol{R_1}[0] \\ \ldots & \ldots & \ldots\ldots & \ldots \\ \boldsymbol{R_{t-1}}[t] & \boldsymbol{R_{t-1}}[t+1] & \ldots \boldsymbol{R_{t-1}}[t-2] & \boldsymbol{R_{t-1}}[t-1] \end{pmatrix}. \tag{4}$$

The elements in column i of M' are then concatenated and given to P_i as their share. Label the share given to player P_i for $0 \le i \le n - 1$ as $\boldsymbol{S}[i] \in F^t$.

3.2   Recover

The *Recover(S)* algorithm requires the input of shares from at least t players. Steps 1, 2 and 3 check that a sufficient number of shares are contributed. If $\boldsymbol{S}[i] = \Diamond$, player i has not contributed their share to the *Recover* algorithm. If fewer than t shares are submitted, the algorithm will fail and output $\bot$. Otherwise,

Procedure *Share(k)*

1. For $i \leftarrow 1$ to $t - 1$ do
   $r_i \overset{\$}{\leftarrow} \{0,1\}^\lambda$
2. $k' = k \oplus r_1 \oplus \cdots \oplus r_{t-1}$
3. $K' \leftarrow Share^{\text{IDA}}(k')$
4. For $i \leftarrow 1$ to $t - 1$ do
   $R_i \leftarrow Share^{\text{IDA}}(r_i)$
5. For $i \leftarrow 0$ to $n - 1$ do
   $S[i] \leftarrow K'[(i)]R_1[i + 1 \mod n]$
   $\ldots R_j[i + j \mod n]$
   $\ldots R_{t-1}[i + (t - 1) \mod n]$
6. Return S

Fig. 1. Our (t,n)-threshold *Share* algorithm

Procedure *Recover(S)*

1. $j = 0$
2. For $i \leftarrow 0$ to $n - 1$ do
   If $S[i] \neq \Diamond$, then $j = j + 1$
3. If $j < t$, return $\perp$
4. For $i \leftarrow 0$ to $n - 1$ do
   $K'[(i)]R_1[i + 1 \mod n]$
   $\ldots R_j[i + j \mod n] \ldots$
   $R_{t-1}[i + (t - 1) \mod n] \leftarrow S[i]$
5. $k' \leftarrow Recover^{\text{IDA}}(K')$
6. For $i \leftarrow 1$ to $t - 1$ do
   $r_i \leftarrow Recover^{\text{IDA}}(R_i)$
7. $k = k' \oplus r_1 \oplus r_2 \oplus \cdots \oplus r_{t-1}$
8. Return k

Fig. 2. Our (t,n)-threshold *Recover* algorithm

Step 4 parses each player's share $S[i]$ into its t elements and, in Steps 5 and 6, t-vectors are constructed from the available shares. These are used to recover k' and $r_1, r_2, \ldots, r_{t-1}$ via the $Recover^{\text{IDA}}$ algorithm, as in Sect. 2.3. These recovered values are then XORed in Step 7 to retrieve the key, k.

In our scheme, $t - 1$ dummy keys are generated. This is an improvement on HP's scheme where t are generated [1]. The generation of fewer dummy keys results in smaller dimensions for the matrices M and M', thereby decreasing the size of the shares given to each player. Therefore, in our scheme, each player receives t elements in F, rather than $t + 1$ elements. Finally, we specify a systematic IDA, rather than using a general RS code, to distribute k' and the dummy keys. The systematic IDA requires the encoding of only the final $n - t$ words, thereby making the scheme more efficient.

It will be shown in the next section that generating only $t - 1$ dummy keys and using a systematic IDA is sufficient to ensure the (t,n)-threshold scheme achieves the recoverability and privacy properties required, as in Definition 1.

4 Security Analysis

It will now be proved that the (t,n)-threshold scheme presented in Sect. 3 satisfies the recoverability and privacy requirements, as in Definition 1. The original HP scheme has no such analysis [1]. The proof given here can easily be adapted to prove the security of the key distribution in the HP scheme.

The structure of the proof is as follows. In Lemma 1, it is shown that any distribution of elements from the matrix M to the n players that allows any t players to learn at least t shares in every row of M will allow recovery of the secret. Theorem 2 then shows that the distribution of elements from M via M' satisfies this condition, thus the scheme achieves recoverability. Lemma 2 shows that any distribution of elements from the matrix M to the players that allows no more than $t-1$ players to learn at most $t-1$ elements in each column of M achieves privacy. Theorem 3 shows that the distribution of elements from M via M' satisfies this property, thus achieving privacy. Together, Theorems 2 and 3 show that our scheme satisfies the requirements to be a (t,n)−threshold scheme, as in Definition 1. It will then be shown that our scheme is ideal.

4.1   Recoverability

Lemma 1. *Let n players be allocated elements from the matrix M. If any set of at least t players learns at least t elements in every row of M, k can be recovered.*

Proof. Assume fragments from the $t \times n$ matrix M are allocated such that any t players learn at least t shares in every row. We wish to show that a set of (at least) t players can pool their shares and learn $k', r_1, \ldots, r_{t-1}$, then recover k. Each row $M[i]$ of M, when transposed and considered as an n−vector, is the output of the systematic (t,n)−IDA. In particular, $M[0]^T \leftarrow Share^{\mathrm{IDA}}(k')$ and $M[i]^T \leftarrow Share^{\mathrm{IDA}}(r_i)$ for $1 \leq i \leq t-1$. For any row $M[i]$ of M, t players can form a t−vector $M'[i]$ and use this vector as input to $Recover^{\mathrm{IDA}}$. This will return the dispersed value: k' if $i = 0$, or r_i if $1 \leq i \leq t-1$. The players can repeat this procedure for every row of M and reconstruct all the values $k', r_1, \ldots, r_{t-1}$. Once these values are obtained, they are able to add them and output k.   □

Theorem 2. *The (t,n)−threshold scheme satisfies the property that any set of t players learn at least t elements in every row of M.*

Proof. Each player is given a column of the matrix M', where M' is formed by shifting row i of M, for $0 \leq i \leq t-1$, i places to the left. As each player is allocated a distinct column of M', each player is necessarily given a distinct element from every row. Therefore, when any t players pool their shares, there will be t distinct elements in every row.   □

Theorem 2 shows that the scheme meets the requirements in Lemma 1 and hence meets the recoverability requirements of a (t,n)−threshold scheme.

4.2   Privacy

Now we must prove that the privacy requirement is also satisfied. Intuitively, the following lemma shows that an unauthorised set of players must be prevented from learning all elements in a given column of M, otherwise the players could calculate the corresponding part of k by XORing all elements in that column.

Lemma 2. *If elements from M are allocated such that any set A of at most $t-1$ players learn no information about at least one element from every column, then no information is learnt about k. In information theoretic terms, $H(\boldsymbol{K}) = H(\boldsymbol{K}|S)$, where S is the set of shares given to the players in A.*

Proof. Let k be a string of λ bits. Assume a set A of at most $t-1$ players collectively knows a set S of elements from the matrix M. Assume that players in A can learn no information about at least one element from every column in M. We must first note that the IDA used in the $(t,n)-$threshold scheme is systematic, therefore the result of XORing any of the first t columns of the matrix M will give the corresponding fragment of the key k. Similarly, if we add any of the final $n-t$ columns of M, the output will be the corresponding entry of the codeword vector for $k \Rightarrow Share^{\mathrm{IDA}}(K)$.

For any given column j, for $0 \leq j \leq n-1$, S can contain any number of elements (but not every element) of $M[j]$, the jth column of M. So S will contain at most $t-1$ of the t elements in each column. Without loss of generality, choose a column j; we will prove that no information is learnt about k from this individual column. This argument can then be applied to every other column of M.

Denote the set of elements in column j and not in S as S'_j. Note that $|S'_j| \geq 1$. Let s_j be the XOR of all the elements in S. Let b_j be the XOR of all elements in S'_j, so b_j is the XOR of all elements in column j that are unknown to A.

Assume the key k is also distributed via the IDA, resulting in the vector K. Denote the jth element of K as $K[j]$. Note that $s_j \oplus b_j = K[j]$. As the dummy keys are all randomly generated, each value r_i has entropy 2^λ. Thus each element of R_i has entropy $\frac{2^\lambda}{t}$, and so $H(b_j) = \frac{2^\lambda}{t}$.

Now, we can equate this to a one-time pad. The value s_j is equivalent to a known ciphertext and b_j is equivalent to a key. The XOR of these would reveal the plaintext message $K[j]$. As b_j has entropy $H(b_j) = 2^\lambda$, the value $K[j]$ also has entropy 2^λ. Thus no information is learnt about $K[j]$. $\square$

Theorem 3. *The $(t,n)-$threshold scheme satisfies the condition that any set of $t-1$ players learns no information about at least one element in every column.*

Proof. In the scheme, each player is given a column of the matrix M', so each player will receive exactly one element from each row of M. Therefore any set of $t-1$ players will learn exactly $t-1$ elements of each row. As the IDA is a linear $(0, t; n)-$ramp scheme and because each of the dummy keys and k are generated uniformly at random, players with only $t-1$ elements are unable to learn any further elements from each row. Each player will also be given elements that come from $n-t$ distinct columns of M. Therefore a set of up to $t-1$ players can pool their shares and learn at most $t-1$ shares in each column. $\square$

Theorem 3 proves that the scheme meets the requirements of Lemma 2 and thus satisfies the privacy requirement. Therefore the scheme presented in Sect. 3 satisfies both the recoverability and privacy requirements to be a $(t,n)-$threshold scheme. Note that this security analysis is not specific to the systematic IDA and any general $(0, t; n)-$ramp scheme could be used.

4.3 Information Rate

Finally, we will comment on the information rate of the scheme, which is an improvement of HP's original scheme [1] by a factor of $\frac{t}{t+1}$.

Theorem 4. *Let $k \in \{0,1\}^\lambda$. The $(t,n)-$threshold scheme has an information rate of 1 if λ is divisible by t and is therefore ideal. If λ is not divisible by t, each share has $\lambda \mod t$ more elements than the secret.*

Proof. In general, $(-\lambda) \mod t$ bits of padding will be added to k, so that each element in the matrix M will consist of $\lceil \frac{\lambda}{t} \rceil$ bits. Each player will receive t elements from M, and thus the size of each player's share will be $\lceil \frac{\lambda}{t} \rceil t$ bits. Therefore, the information rate is calculated as

$$\rho = \lambda \div \left(\left\lceil \frac{\lambda}{t} \right\rceil t \right).$$

If λ is divisible by t, then $\rho = 1$ and the scheme is ideal.   □

5   Efficiency Analysis

Our $(t,n)-$threshold scheme can be implemented using only XORs and cyclic shifts. In this section, the complexity of both *Share* and *Recover* with respect to the number of bitwise XORs is computed. We also consider what computations can be pre-computed, before the dealer has knowledge of the key k.

5.1   Complexity of *Share*

The *Share* protocol requires the generation of $t-1$ random strings (dummy keys r_i for $1 \le i \le t-1$) of λ bits. These dummy keys are XORed with the secret k to output k'. In total, this requires $t-1$ XORs of λ bit strings. However, $t-2$ of these XORs can be pre-computed (XORing the dummy keys).

The dummy keys and k' are then dispersed via the systematic IDA. This is computationally the most expensive operation. Each value is treated as a $t-$vector (where element in $F = \{0,1\}^{\frac{\lambda}{t}}$) and multiplied by an $n \times t$ binary matrix G to output an $n-$vector. As the first t rows of the matrix G form the $t \times t$ identity matrix, the first $t-$elements of the $n-$vector will be identical as those in the input $t-$vector. Therefore, only the final $n-t$ elements of the $n-$vector need to be computed, which is done by multiplying the final $n-t$ rows of G with the input $t-$vector. This computation requires $(n-t)(t-1)$ XORs of $\frac{\lambda}{t}$ bit strings. No multiplications are required as G is a binary matrix and so multiplication can be implemented as a lookup table. Each of the $t-1$ dummy keys $r_i, 1 \le i \le t-1$ and k' must be dispersed via the IDA, resulting in $t(n-t)(t-1)$ XORs of $\frac{\lambda}{t}$ bit strings.

Of these XORs, the distribution of the random values via the systematic IDA can be pre-computed. There are $t-1$ random values to be dispersed, meaning that $\mathcal{O}(nt) \cdot \lambda$ bitwise XORs can be pre-computed. The dispersal of k' cannot be pre-computed, which requires $\mathcal{O}(n) \cdot \lambda$ bitwise XORs.

Therefore, without pre-computation, a total of

$$\frac{t(n-t)(t-1)\lambda}{t} + (t-1) \cdot \lambda = \mathcal{O}(nt) \cdot \lambda$$

bitwise XORs are required. Of these, $\mathcal{O}(tn) \cdot \lambda$ can be pre-computed and $\mathcal{O}(n) \cdot \lambda$ require knowledge of k.

We do not consider the computation costs of constructing the matrix G, as it is easy to construct and is a public matrix that can be pre-computed and reused.

5.2   Complexity of *Recover*

Recovering the dummy keys and k' is achieved by multiplying the t contributed shares with a $t \times t$ matrix M constructed from the relevant rows of G. The complexity of the *Recover* algorithm can vary dependent on which rows of M are used. The best case is that all t shares submitted to *Recover* will correspond to the t rows of M that form the identity matrix I_t. In this case, no XORs will be required to recover the dummy keys and k'. Therefore recovery requires only $t - 1$ XORs of strings of length λ to calculate k, totalling $\mathcal{O}(t) \cdot \lambda$ bitwise XORs.

In the worst case scenario, the $n - t$ corresponding rows of M that are not a part of the identity matrix I_t will be used to reconstruct the dummy keys and k'. This would require $\mathcal{O}(n - t)(t - 1)$ XORs of $\frac{\lambda}{t}$ bit strings. This must be repeated for each of the t values, totalling $\mathcal{O}(nt) \cdot \lambda$ bitwise XORs.

If each player contributes a share to *Recover* with equal probability, the best-case scenario happens with probability $1 \div \binom{n}{t}$, as exactly one t−set of players out of a possible $\binom{n}{t}$ sets will yield the best case. If players do not contribute shares with equal probability, it may be possible to give players more likely to contribute a share that corresponds to a row of the identity matrix to minimise computations. If $t = n$, the best case scenario will always occur.

6   Comparison to Other Schemes

In this section, we discuss the efficiency of other (t, n)−threshold schemes, then compare the current schemes to our proposed scheme.

6.1   Other Schemes

Kurihara et al. [5] present a complexity analysis on the number of bitwise XORs required in their scheme. For some prime $p \geq n$, their scheme requires the generation of $(t - 1)(p - 1)\lceil\frac{\lambda}{p-1}\rceil$ bits. Their *Share* algorithm requires $\mathcal{O}(nt) \cdot \lambda$ bitwise XORs. Of these XORs, $\mathcal{O}(nt) \cdot \lambda$ require knowledge of only the random strings and can be pre-computed, whereas $\mathcal{O}(n) \cdot \lambda$ cannot. Each player's share is $\lceil\frac{\lambda}{p-1}\rceil(p - 1)$ bits. If λ is divisible by $p - 1$, the scheme is ideal.

To recover the secret, a matrix M is computed using Gaussian elimination, which has complexity $\mathcal{O}(t^3 p^3)$. As M can be pre-computed and reused, we include the computation of M in Fig. 3 as optional. Recovery then requires $\mathcal{O}(tp) \cdot \lambda$ bitwise XORs. As p is close to n, we let $p = n$ in Fig. 3.

Wang and Desmedt. [8] present an efficient, ideal (t, n)−threshold scheme for $\lambda \geq n$, equivalent to an $[q, t, q - t + 1]$−MDS code, for some prime $q \geq \lambda + 1$.

A specific distribution algorithm is not defined. Instead, they define the scheme to be a collection of $(q - 1) \times q$ matrices that satisfy $q(q - t)$ linear constraints, with each column of the matrix forming a share for a player, excluding the first which defines the secret. Two ways of calculating the matrices are suggested and either requires only XORs and bit shifts.

One of their suggestions is as follows. Choose a prime $q \geq \lambda + 1$. Randomly generate t elements $f_0, \ldots, f_{t-1} \in \{0, 1\}^q$ and create a $q \times t$ matrix F of these values, where each column corresponds to a random string. A $t \times n$ binary matrix G is then constructed where elements are coefficients of the generator polynomial of the Galois Field $GF(2^\lambda)$. Generating the elements of G is done by choosing a primitive element α of $GF(2^\lambda)$ and calculating

$$g(x) = (x - 1)(x - \alpha) \ldots (x - \alpha^{n-t-1}) = g_0 + g_1 x + \cdots + g_{n-t} x^{n-t}.$$

This requires $(n - t)^2 - 1$ XORs, while multiplication can be implemented via a lookup table, as before. So the pre-computation required is $\mathcal{O}(n^2)$ bitwise XORs.

The two matrices F and G are then multiplied together. As G is a binary matrix, multiplication can be implemented as a lookup table and so only $q(t-1)n$ bitwise XORs are required. As q is near to λ, we note this as $\mathcal{O}(nt) \cdot \lambda$ bitwise XORs in Fig. 3. Each player is given a column from the output matrix n−vector, which is a string of q bits. If $q = \lambda + 1$, the scheme is ideal.

The recovery procedure for the scheme is equivalent to a decoding procedure presented by Blaum and Roth [18] that decodes an array code with at most r erasures and no errors. The procedure requires $\mathcal{O}(r(q^2 + r))$ XOR operations. The number of erasures Wang and Desmedt's scheme can correct is $n - t$, thus the decoding algorithm requires $\mathcal{O}((n - t)(q^2 + n - n)) = \mathcal{O}(nq^2)$ XORs. The elements in F each have λ bits, and thus there are $\mathcal{O}(nq^2) \cdot \lambda$ bitwise XOR operations. The value q is of the same magnitude as λ, and so the recovery algorithm requires $\mathcal{O}(nq^2) \cdot \lambda = \mathcal{O}(n) \cdot \lambda^3$ bitwise XOR operations.

6.2 Discussion

Figure 3 presents a summary of the number of bitwise XORs required in our scheme, the two schemes considered and Shamir's scheme. The second and third columns consider the complexities of the distribution algorithms if as much pre-computation is done as possible. The fourth column considers the distribution complexities if no pre-computation is possible and the fifth considers recovery.

The table does not consider the share size and the randomness required for each scheme. This is because all schemes are essentially ideal and all schemes (apart from Wang and Desmedt's) require the generation of a minimum amount of randomness $((t - 1)\lambda$ bits [19]). Wang and Desmedt's scheme requires the random generation of $t \times m$ bits, where $m \geq \lambda + 1$.

Note that much of the computation for the distribution in Shamir's scheme can be pre-computed. This is because the dealer possesses all coefficients of the

Scheme	Pre-computation	Share complexity	Share without pre-computation	Recover complexity
Our Scheme	$\mathcal{O}(nt)\cdot\lambda$	$\mathcal{O}(n)\cdot\lambda$	$\mathcal{O}(nt)\cdot\lambda$	$\mathcal{O}(t)\cdot\lambda \le x \le \mathcal{O}(nt)\cdot\lambda$
Kurihara et al. [5]	$\mathcal{O}(n^3t^3)$ or $\mathcal{O}(nt)\,\lambda$	$\mathcal{O}(n)\cdot\lambda$	$\mathcal{O}(n^3t^3)$ or $\mathcal{O}(nt)\cdot\lambda$	$\mathcal{O}(nt)\cdot\lambda$
Shamir [3]	$\mathcal{O}(nt)\cdot\lambda$	$\mathcal{O}(n)\cdot\lambda$	$\mathcal{O}(nt)\cdot\lambda$	$\mathcal{O}(t\log^2 t)\cdot\lambda$
Wang and Desmedt [8]	$\mathcal{O}(n^2)$	$\mathcal{O}(nt)\cdot\lambda$	$\mathcal{O}(nt)\cdot\lambda$	$\mathcal{O}(n)\cdot\lambda^3$

Fig. 3. Comparing bitwise XORs in $(t, n)-$threshold schemes with λ bit secrets

polynomial f and most of the inputs to f are fixed. Therefore sharing the secret would require only adding the secret to each pre-computed value.

If pre-computation is impossible and the construction of M in Kurihara et al.'s scheme is ignored, all four schemes have the same distribution complexity. However, if pre-computation is possible, our scheme has an equivalent complexity to Shamir's scheme and Kurihara et al.'s scheme (again, assuming we ignore the construction of M). Wang and Desmedt's scheme has a heavier complexity and allowing for pre-computation does not decrease the distribution complexity. If the complexity of computing M in Kurihara et al.'s scheme is taken into account, their scheme has by far the heaviest distribution algorithm.

In the best case scenario for our scheme, the recovery complexity is dependent only on t. This is the same as Shamir's scheme but with a lower complexity.

Kurihara et al. discuss how their recovery procedure is dependent on both t and n. This is in contrast to Shamir's scheme, which is dependent only on t. Kurihara et al. say their scheme is more efficient than Shamir's when t is close to n. However, when n is large and t is small, Shamir's is faster. In the worst case scenario for our *Recover* algorithm, the number of bitwise XORs is equivalent to Kurihara et al.'s. Therefore, their argument holds true for our scheme also.

In contrast, Wang and Desmedt's scheme has a complexity dependent only on n, but a factor of λ^3. Being dependent only on n means the scheme will not be able to take advantage of a low threshold value. Also, in many applications, λ may be considerably larger than both n and t, meaning that Wang and Desmedt's scheme may be considerably slower than Kurihara et al.'s scheme and ours.

One other aspect to consider is that of implementation. Our scheme uses a linear $(0, t; n)-$ramp scheme, which is equivalent to a $[n, t, n-t+1]-$MDS code. Rather than using the systematic IDA in our scheme, any MDS code for which there already exists an implementation could be used; as the two are equivalent, the security proof from Sect. 4 would still hold true. This is also true for Wang and Desmedt's scheme, as their scheme is equivalent to an array code.

6.3 Conclusion

We presented an XOR based $(t, n)-$threshold scheme. We presented a security proof and efficiency analysis and compared our scheme to other schemes with equivalent properties. Our scheme has an equivalent, or more efficient, *Share* complexity to the other schemes considered, especially when pre-computation is possible. The complexity of *Recover* is, in the worst case scenario, equivalent to Kurihara et al.'s scheme, which is faster than Shamir's when t is large. In the best case scenario, our *Recover* complexity is independent of n and faster than all other proposed schemes. Furthermore, our scheme is ideal and, unlike Wang and Desmedt's scheme, requires minimal randomness.

Further work will consider non-ideal (t, n)−threshold schemes and whether compromises can be met (with respect to the share size, the number of random bits generated or specifying values for t) that would allow fewer bitwise XORs.

References

1. Chen, L., Camble, P.T., Watkins, M.R., Henry, I.J.: Utilizing error correction (ECC) for secure secret sharing. Hewlett Packard Enterprise Development LP, World Intellectual Property Organisation. Patent Number WO2016048297 (2016). https://www.google.com/patents/WO2016048297A1?cl=en
2. Blakely, G.: Safeguarding cryptographic keys. In: Proceedings of the National Computer Conference, vol. 48, pp. 313–317 (1979)
3. Shamir, A.: How to share a secret. Commun. ACM **22**(11), 612–613 (1979). ACM
4. Kurihara, J., Kiyomoto, S., Fukushima, K., Tanaka, T.: A fast (3, n)-threshold secret sharing scheme using exclusive-or operations. IEICE Trans. Fundam. Electron. Commun. Comput. Sci. **91**(1), 127–138 (2008). IEICE
5. Kurihara, J., Kiyomoto, S., Fukushima, K., Tanaka, T.: A new (k,n)-threshold secret sharing scheme and its extension. In: Wu, T.-C., Lei, C.-L., Rijmen, V., Lee, D.-T. (eds.) ISC 2008. LNCS, vol. 5222, pp. 455–470. Springer, Heidelberg (2008). doi:10.1007/978-3-540-85886-7_31
6. Lv, C., Jia, X., Tian, L., Jing, J., Sun, M.: Efficient ideal threshold secret sharing schemes based on exclusive-or operations. In: 4th International Conference on Network and System Security (NSS), pp. 136–143. IEEE (2010)
7. Lv, C., Jia, X., Lin, J., Jing, J., Tian, L., Sun, M.: Efficient secret sharing schemes. In: Park, J.J., Lopez, J., Yeo, S.-S., Shon, T., Taniar, D. (eds.) Secure and Trust Computing, Data Management, and Application. Communications in Computer and Information Science, vol. 186, pp. 114–121. Springer, Heidelberg (2011)
8. Wang, Y., Desmedt, Y.: Efficient secret sharing schemes achieving optimal information rate. In: Information Theory Workshop (ITW), pp. 516–520. IEEE (2014)
9. Beimel, A.: Secret-sharing schemes: a survey. In: Chee, Y.M., Guo, Z., Ling, S., Shao, F., Tang, Y., Wang, H., Xing, C. (eds.) IWCC 2011. LNCS, vol. 6639, pp. 11–46. Springer, Heidelberg (2011)
10. Jackson, W., Martin, K.M.: A combinatorial interpretation of ramp schemes. Australas. J. Comb. **14**, 52–60 (1996). Centre for Combinatorics
11. MacWilliams, F., Sloane, N.: The Theory of Error Correcting Codes. Elsevier, Amsterdam (1977)
12. Reed, I., Solomon, G.: Polynomial codes over certain finite fields. J. Soc. Ind. Appl. Math. **8**(2), 300–304 (1960)
13. Karnin, E.D., Greene, J.W., Hellman, M.E.: On secret sharing systems. IEEE Trans. Inf. Theor. **29**(1), 35–41 (1983). IEEE

14. Chen, H., Cramer, R.: Algebraic geometric secret sharing schemes and secure multi-party computations over small fields. In: Dwork, C. (ed.) CRYPTO 2006. LNCS, vol. 4117, pp. 521–536. Springer, Heidelberg (2006). doi:10.1007/11818175_31

15. Krawczyk, H.: Distributed fingerprints and secure information dispersal. In: Proceedings of the Twelfth Annual ACM Symposium on Principles of Distributed Computing, pp. 207–218. ACM (1993)

16. Rabin, M.: Efficient dispersal of information for security, load balancing, and fault tolerance. J. ACM (JACM) 36(2), 335–348 (1989). ACM

17. Resch, J.K., Plank, J.S.: AONT-RS: blending security and performance in dispersed storage systems. In: FAST-2011: 9th USENIX Conference on File and Storage Technologie, pp. 191–202. USENIX Association (2011)

18. Blaum, M., Roth, R.: New array codes for multiple phased burst correction. IEEE Trans. Inf. Theor. 39(1), 66–77 (1993). IEEE

19. Blundo, C., De Santis, A., Vaccaro, U.: Randomness in distribution protocols. Inf. Comput. 131(2), 111–139 (1996). Elsevier

Efficient and Secure Multiparty Computations Using a Standard Deck of Playing Cards

Takaaki Mizuki[✉]

Cyberscience Center, Tohoku University,
6–3 Aramaki-Aza-Aoba, Aoba, Sendai 980–8578, Japan
tm-paper+cardstd@g-mail.tohoku-university.jp

Abstract. It is known that secure multiparty computation can be performed using physical cards with identical backs, and numerous card-based cryptographic protocols have been proposed. Almost all existing protocols require multiple cards that have the same pattern on their face sides; thus, a standard deck of playing cards cannot be used for executing these protocols. However, there is one exception: Niemi and Renvall's protocols, proposed in 1999, can be used with standard playing cards. In this paper, we continue their efforts to improve secure multiparty computation using a standard deck of playing cards, and propose efficient AND, XOR, and copy protocols that require significantly fewer shuffles compared to previous protocols.

1 Introduction

Secure multiparty computation enables a group of players to learn only the value of a predetermined function of their private inputs (without revealing more information than necessary). Although such a cryptographic task is usually implemented digitally on computers and/or network systems, there is another research direction in which cryptographic protocols are implemented physically (e.g. [4,6]). In this paper, we consider the use of a deck of physical cards. In fact, it is known that secure multiparty computation can be conducted using physical cards with identical backs (such as $\boxed{?}$), and numerous card-based cryptographic protocols have been designed. Almost all existing protocols use cards whose face sides have a pattern such as black $\boxed{♣}$ or red $\boxed{♡}$; further, multiple cards having the same pattern are necessary (e.g., [1,2,7,8,11,12,14–16]). This paper begins with a brief introduction to such protocols.

1.1 Mainstream Card-Based Protocols

Most card-based protocols manipulate Boolean values based on the following encoding:

$$\boxed{♣}\boxed{♡} = 0, \quad \boxed{♡}\boxed{♣} = 1. \tag{1}$$

That is, considering a pair of black and red cards, postulate that bit value 0 represents the left card being black, and bit value 1 represents the left card being

© Springer International Publishing AG 2016
S. Foresti and G. Persiano (Eds.): CANS 2016, LNCS 10052, pp. 484–499, 2016.
DOI: 10.1007/978-3-319-48965-0_29

red. Based on this encoding rule (1), input is given to a card-based protocol. For example, the secure NOT computation, which is the simplest protocol, receives a pair of face-down cards equaling the value of input bit $a \in \{0, 1\}$ (which is called a *commitment* to a), and reverses their order to obtain a commitment to negation $\bar{a}$:

$$\underset{a}{\boxed{?}\,\boxed{?}} \;\rightarrow\; \overset{\rightleftharpoons}{\boxed{?}\,\boxed{?}} \;\rightarrow\; \underset{\bar{a}}{\boxed{?}\,\boxed{?}}.$$

Another example: given commitments to input bits a and b

$$\underset{a}{\underbrace{\boxed{?}\,\boxed{?}}}\,\underset{b}{\underbrace{\boxed{?}\,\boxed{?}}},$$

a protocol for secure AND computation outputs a commitment to $a \wedge b$

$$\underset{a \wedge b}{\boxed{?}\,\boxed{?}}$$

without revealing any information about the values of a and b after applying a predetermined series of operations such as shuffling, rearranging, and turning over cards [2, 7, 11, 12, 16].

One of the efficient AND protocols works with two additional cards [11]:

$$\underset{a}{\underbrace{\boxed{?}\,\boxed{?}}}\,\underset{b}{\underbrace{\boxed{?}\,\boxed{?}}}\,\boxed{\clubsuit}\,\boxed{\heartsuit} \;\rightarrow \cdots \rightarrow\; \underset{a \wedge b}{\underbrace{\boxed{?}\,\boxed{?}}}\,\boxed{\clubsuit}\,\boxed{\heartsuit}\,\boxed{\clubsuit}\,\boxed{\heartsuit};$$

during the protocol's execution, several operations are performed, among them a shuffling operation called a *random bisection cut* (the details of which will be introduced in Sect. 3.1) is applied once. In regard to XOR computation, it is known that one random bisection cut enables a secure XOR to be performed without any additional cards [11]:

$$\underset{a}{\underbrace{\boxed{?}\,\boxed{?}}}\,\underset{b}{\underbrace{\boxed{?}\,\boxed{?}}} \;\rightarrow \cdots \rightarrow\; \underset{a \oplus b}{\underbrace{\boxed{?}\,\boxed{?}}}\,\boxed{\clubsuit}\,\boxed{\heartsuit}.$$

Furthermore, making two copied commitments can be achieved with four additional cards and one random bisection cut [11]:

$$\underset{a}{\underbrace{\boxed{?}\,\boxed{?}}}\,\boxed{\clubsuit}\,\boxed{\heartsuit}\,\boxed{\clubsuit}\,\boxed{\heartsuit} \;\rightarrow \cdots \rightarrow\; \underset{a}{\underbrace{\boxed{?}\,\boxed{?}}}\,\underset{a}{\underbrace{\boxed{?}\,\boxed{?}}}\,\boxed{\clubsuit}\,\boxed{\heartsuit}.$$

There are also other protocols designed for specific functions such as the adder [14] and 3-variable Boolean functions [15].

Because the above-mentioned protocols require multiple cards having the same pattern (such as $\boxed{\clubsuit}$ and $\boxed{\heartsuit}$), a standard deck of playing cards, unfortunately, cannot be utilized to execute these protocols. (Note that each card in a standard deck has a unique pattern on its face side, namely its suit and number.)

1.2   Use of a Standard Deck of Playing Cards

As seen thus far, almost all existing protocols do not work with a standard deck of playing cards. However, there is one exception: Niemi and Renvall's protocols [13] proposed in 1999 can be executed with the use of a normal deck of playing cards.

A standard, commercially available deck of playing cards consists of 52 cards (excluding jokers). Each card's face has a unique pattern (its suit and number), and hence we can easily create a total order on the set of these 52 cards. Therefore, hereafter we assume the following deck of 52 cards:

$$\boxed{1}\boxed{2}\boxed{3}\boxed{4}\boxed{5}\boxed{6} \cdots \boxed{52},$$

where, of course, the backs of all cards are identical $\boxed{?}$.

Similar to encoding rule (1) mentioned before, Niemi and Renvall [13] considered an encoding rule based on which of two cards is smaller or larger. That is, for any two cards $\boxed{i}\boxed{j}$ with $1 \le i < j \le 52$, they define the encoding rule as:

$$\boxed{i}\boxed{j} = 0, \quad \boxed{j}\boxed{i} = 1. \tag{2}$$

Thus, 0 represents the left card being smaller, and 1 represents the left card being larger. We can naturally consider a commitment as well, and throughout this paper, a commitment to bit x using two cards $\boxed{i}\boxed{j}$ is written as

$$\underbrace{\boxed{?}\boxed{?}}_{[x]^{\{i,j\}}},$$

where we call such a set $\{i, j\}$ a *base* of the commitment. For example,

$$\underbrace{\boxed{?}\boxed{?}}_{[x]^{\{1,2\}}}$$

is a commitment of base $\{1, 2\}$; when we turn over these two cards, the order $\boxed{1}\boxed{2}$ implies $x = 0$, and $\boxed{2}\boxed{1}$ implies $x = 1$. Under this encoding rule, reversing the order of two cards constituting a commitment also corresponds to the NOT computation.

Based on encoding rule (2), Niemi and Renvall designed a protocol for realizing the following as a secure AND computation with five cards [13]:

$$\boxed{5}\underbrace{\boxed{?}\boxed{?}}_{[a]^{\{1,2\}}}\underbrace{\boxed{?}\boxed{?}}_{[b]^{\{3,4\}}} \to \cdots \to \boxed{5}\underbrace{\boxed{?}\boxed{?}}_{[a \wedge b]^{\{1,4\}}}\boxed{2}\boxed{3}.$$

During the protocol's execution, a random cut, which represents a cyclic shuffle, is applied an average of 9.5 times.

Regarding XOR computation, they showed that, on average, seven random cuts would provide the following result with four cards [13]:

$$\boxed{?}\boxed{?}\boxed{?}\boxed{?} \rightarrow \cdots \rightarrow \boxed{4}\ \boxed{?}\boxed{?}\ \boxed{3}.$$
$$\underbrace{\quad}_{[a]\{1,2\}}\underbrace{\quad}_{[b]\{3,4\}} \qquad\qquad \underbrace{\quad}_{[a\oplus b]\{1,2\}}$$

Furthermore, as for copying a commitment, 5.5 random cuts suffice to realize the following with six cards [13]:

$$\boxed{5}\boxed{?}\boxed{?}\boxed{6}\boxed{3}\boxed{4} \rightarrow \cdots \rightarrow \boxed{5}\boxed{?}\boxed{?}\boxed{6}\boxed{?}\boxed{?}.$$
$$\underbrace{\quad\ \ }_{[a]\{1,2\}} \qquad\qquad\qquad \underbrace{\quad\ \ }_{[a]\{1,2\}}\ \ \underbrace{\quad\ \ }_{[a]\{3,4\}}$$

The details of these three existing protocols will be introduced in Sect. 2.

1.3 Our Results

In this paper, we focus on secure multiparty computation using a standard deck of playing cards (as introduced in Sect. 1.2), and enhance the efficiency. That is, we propose efficient AND, XOR, and copy protocols. As seen later, our three protocols will be constructed partially based on the ideas behind the mainstream card-based protocols [11] that use custom-made cards $\boxed{\clubsuit}\boxed{\heartsuit}$ and random bisection cuts.

Table 1 indicates the performance of our three protocols. As shown by the table data, our protocols require significantly fewer shuffles. Specifically, whereas the existing protocol requires an average of 9.5 shuffles for AND computation, our protocol terminates after applying exactly 4 shuffles. As for both XOR computation and secure copy, our protocols require only one shuffle. Because the "cost" of a card-based protocol comes mainly from shuffling operations in general, reducing the number of required shuffles is very important. (Note that the "cost" would be directly linked to human motivation to execute a protocol practically.) Further, whereas the existing protocols are so-called Las Vegas algorithms that require an average number of trials to be conducted, our protocols always terminate after applying a fixed number of shuffles.

Furthermore, our protocols utilize random bisection cuts, whereas existing protocols use random cuts. The details will be discussed in the succeeding sections. Although the random bisection cut may be an unfamiliar shuffling operation, humans can easily implement a random bisection cut that is similar to a random cut (as will be seen in Sect. 3.1).

When considering the number of required cards, our protocols work with the same number of cards as the existing protocols for both XOR computation and secure copy; however, for AND computation, our protocol requires three more cards than the existing protocol. This might be perceived as a disadvantage; however, we believe that such a three-card increase would not be an issue, because card players can use the 52 cards as they like after they buy a standard deck of playing cards at a toy store.

Table 1. Performance comparison between existing protocols and our protocols

	# of cards	# of shuffles		
		avg.	fixed	total
○ AND computation				
Niemi-Renvall [13] (Sect. 2.2)	5	9.5	0	9.5
Ours (Sect. 3)	8	0	4	4
○ XOR computation				
Niemi-Renvall [13] (Sect. 2.3)	4	7	0	7
Ours (Sect. 4)	4	0	1	1
○ Secure copy				
Niemi-Renvall [13] (Sect. 2.4)	6	4.5	1	5.5
Ours (Sect. 5)	6	0	1	1

The remainder of this paper is organized as follows. First, in Sect. 2, we introduce the details of the existing protocols. Then, in Sect. 3, we propose an efficient AND protocol. Next, we describe an efficient XOR protocol in Sect. 4, and an efficient copy protocol in Sect. 5. Finally, the paper is concluded in Sect. 6.

2   Niemi-Renvall Protocols

In this section, we introduce the details of the three protocols provided by Niemi and Renvall [13]. As preliminary information, we first introduce the random cut and its application to card searching in Sect. 2.1. Then, we explain the AND protocol in Sect. 2.2, the XOR protocol in Sect. 2.3, and the copy protocol in Sect. 2.4.

2.1   Random Cuts and Search for Cards

As mentioned previously, a random cut represents a cyclic shuffle; given a sequence of cards, it shifts their positions randomly without changing the order apart from cyclic rotation. For instance, consider five cards $\boxed{1}\boxed{2}\boxed{3}\boxed{4}\boxed{5}$ placed with their faces down (on a table) in this order:

$$\boxed{?}\boxed{?}\boxed{?}\boxed{?}\boxed{?};$$

then, applying a random cut results in one of the following five sequences (if the table had eyes):

$$\boxed{1}\boxed{2}\boxed{3}\boxed{4}\boxed{5} \quad \boxed{5}\boxed{1}\boxed{2}\boxed{3}\boxed{4} \quad \boxed{4}\boxed{5}\boxed{1}\boxed{2}\boxed{3} \quad \boxed{3}\boxed{4}\boxed{5}\boxed{1}\boxed{2} \quad \boxed{2}\boxed{3}\boxed{4}\boxed{5}\boxed{1},$$

where each case occurs with a probability of exactly 1/5.

It is known that Humans are able to implement a random cut easily [18].

Next, as an application of the random cut, we explain a technique to search for designated cards. For example, assume that five cards from $\{1, 2, 3, 4, 5\}$ are placed with their faces down:

$$\boxed{?}\,\boxed{?}\,\boxed{?}\,\boxed{?}\,\boxed{?},$$

and that their order is unknown, i.e., we do not know which one of 5! possible orders the sequence represents. Now, suppose that we want to search for card $\boxed{2}$. To this end, we apply a random cut to the sequence of five cards, and then reveal the first card (counting from the left). Unless the face-up card is $\boxed{2}$, turn over the card, apply a random cut, and reveal the first card again. Repeating this, we obtain the following after an average of five trials:

$$\boxed{2}\,\boxed{?}\,\boxed{?}\,\boxed{?}\,\boxed{?}.$$

Note that the order of the sequence following $\boxed{2}$ has not changed, apart from the cyclic rotation, and that no information has leaked other than the fact that $\boxed{2}$ is the first card.

Generalizing this, given a sequence of face-down cards from a set $C \subseteq \{1, 2, \ldots, 52\}$ together with target cards $S \subseteq C$, we can find a card contained in S after applying an average of $|C|/|S|$ random cuts. As we soon show, Niemi and Renvall's protocols frequently use this random-cut-based search as their sub-protocol.

2.2 And Computation

Here, we elaborate Niemi and Renvall's AND protocol. The protocol uses five cards $\boxed{1}\,\boxed{2}\,\boxed{3}\,\boxed{4}\,\boxed{5}$. The first four cards are utilized for commitments to bit a and b, and the remaining $\boxed{5}$ is an additional card; thus, input to the protocol is:

$$\boxed{5}\,\boxed{?}\,\boxed{?}\,\boxed{?}\,\boxed{?}.$$
$$\underbrace{}_{[a]\{1,2\}}\ \underbrace{}_{[b]\{3,4\}}$$

Now, consider the following rearrangement of the sequence of input cards:

$$\boxed{5}\,\boxed{?}\,\boxed{?}\,\boxed{?}\,\boxed{?}$$
$$\times$$
$$\boxed{5}\,\boxed{?}\,\boxed{?}\,\boxed{?}\,\boxed{?}.$$

The four face-down cards would be in one of these four possible sequences depending on values (a, b):

(a,b)	seq. of cards				
$(0,0)$	5	1	3	2	4
$(0,1)$	5	1	4	2	3
$(1,0)$	5	2	3	1	4
$(1,1)$	5	2	4	1	3

Suppose here that we could somehow delete both cards ⊡2 and ⊡3 :

(a,b)	seq. of cards
$(0,0)$	5 1 ⋮⋮⋮⋮ 4
$(0,1)$	5 1 4 ⋮⋮⋮⋮
$(1,0)$	5 ⋮⋮⋮⋮ 1 4
$(1,1)$	5 ⋮⋮⋮⋮ 4 1

then, one can easily notice that only when $(a,b) = (1,1)$, i.e., $a \wedge b = 1$, the order would be 5 4 1 ; when $a \wedge b = 0$, it would be 5 1 4 . Therefore, this implies that we could obtain

$$5 \quad \underbrace{?\ ?}_{[a \wedge b]^{\{1,4\}}} .$$

Based on this idea, an AND protocol is constructed immediately.

1. For input sequence

$$5 \quad \underbrace{?\ ?}_{[a]^{\{1,2\}}} \underbrace{?\ ?}_{[b]^{\{3,4\}}},$$

turn over card 5 and rearrange the sequence as:

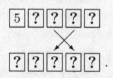

2. Using the random-cut-based search (explained in Sect. 2.1), find card ⊡2 or ⊡3 , and then discard it. This step requires an average of $5/2 = 2.5$ trials.
3. For the sequence of the remaining four cards, find the card, ⊡2 or ⊡3 , that has not been found at the previous step, and then discard it. This step requires an average of $4/1 = 4$ trials.
4. For the sequence of the remaining three cards, using the random-cut-based search, find card 5 to obtain a commitment to $a \wedge b$:

$$5 \quad \underbrace{?\ ?}_{[a \wedge b]^{\{1,4\}}} .$$

This step requires an average of $3/1 = 3$ trials.

This is Niemi and Renvall's AND protocol, which requires $2.5 + 4 + 3 = 9.5$ random cuts on average.

2.3   XOR Computation

Here, we explain Niemi and Renvall's XOR protocol, which requires no additional cards, and performs an XOR computation using only input commitments.

1. For input sequence

$$[a]^{\{1,2\}} \ [b]^{\{3,4\}}$$

rearrange it as:

Now, similar to the case of the AND protocol above, the sequence of these four cards is the same as the left below; if we could somehow delete card 3, then it would be the same as the right:

(a,b)	seq. of cards					seq. of cards			
$(0,0)$	1	3	2	4	$\Rightarrow$	1		2	4
$(0,1)$	1	4	2	3		1	4	2	
$(1,0)$	2	3	1	4		2		1	4
$(1,1)$	2	4	1	3		2	4	1	

Note that if we cyclically shift the three cards so that 4 is the first card, then the two cards following 4 would be a commitment to $a \oplus b$ of base $\{1,2\}$.

2. Using the random-cut-based search, find card 3, and then discard it. This step requires an average of four trials.

3. Using the random-cut-based search, find card 4, and obtain a commitment to $a \oplus b$:

$$4 \quad [?][?]$$

$$[a \oplus b]^{\{1,2\}}$$

This step requires an average of three trials.

This is Niemi and Renvall's XOR protocol, which requires $4 + 3 = 7$ random cuts on average.

2.4   Secure Copy

Here, we explain Niemi and Renvall's copy protocol. The protocol makes two copied commitments to input bit a with four additional cards.

1. For input sequence

$$\boxed{5}\;\underbrace{\boxed{?}\,\boxed{?}}_{[a]^{\{1,2\}}}\;\boxed{6}\;\boxed{3}\;\boxed{4},$$

turn over cards $\boxed{3}\,\boxed{4}$, and apply a random cut[1] to the two face-down cards to create a commitment to a uniformly distributed random bit r:

$$\boxed{5}\;\underbrace{\boxed{?}\,\boxed{?}}_{[a]^{\{1,2\}}}\;\boxed{6}\;\underbrace{\boxed{?}\,\boxed{?}}_{[r]^{\{3,4\}}}.$$

Turn over cards $\boxed{5}$ and $\boxed{6}$ as well:

$$\boxed{?}\;\underbrace{\boxed{?}\,\boxed{?}}_{[a]^{\{1,2\}}}\;\boxed{?}\;\underbrace{\boxed{?}\,\boxed{?}}_{[r]^{\{3,4\}}}.$$

2. Using the random-cut-based search, find a card in $\{1,2,3,4\}$, and reveal the fourth card. (This requires $6/4 = 1.5$ trials on average.) For instance, if we found $\boxed{1}$, we have either

$$\boxed{1}\,\boxed{?}\,\boxed{?}\,\boxed{3}\,\boxed{?}\,\boxed{?}\quad\text{or}\quad\boxed{1}\,\boxed{?}\,\boxed{?}\,\boxed{4}\,\boxed{?}\,\boxed{?}.$$

If the two face-up cards are from either $\{1,3\}$ or $\{2,4\}$, then $r = a$. Otherwise, i.e., they are from either $\{1,4\}$ or $\{2,3\}$, $\bar{r} = a$.

3. Turn over the two face-up cards, and find a card in $\{5,6\}$ using the random-cut-based search. (This requires $6/2 = 3$ trials on average.) In this case, we have

$$\boxed{5}\;\underbrace{\boxed{?}\,\boxed{?}}_{[a]^{\{1,2\}}}\;\underbrace{\boxed{?}\,\boxed{?}}_{[r]^{\{3,4\}}}\quad\text{or}\quad\boxed{6}\;\underbrace{\boxed{?}\,\boxed{?}}_{[r]^{\{3,4\}}}\;\underbrace{\boxed{?}\,\boxed{?}}_{[a]^{\{1,2\}}}.$$

Apply the NOT computation to the commitment to r in the case of $\bar{r} = a$. Thus, in either case, we obtain

$$\boxed{5}\;\underbrace{\boxed{?}\,\boxed{?}}_{[a]^{\{1,2\}}}\;\boxed{6}\;\underbrace{\boxed{?}\,\boxed{?}}_{[a]^{\{3,4\}}}.$$

This is Niemi and Renvall's copy protocol, which requires one fixed number of a random cut together with $1.5 + 3 = 4.5$ random cuts on average.

3   Our AND Protocol

In this section, we propose an efficient AND protocol. Whereas Niemi and Renvall's AND protocol requires an average of 9.5 random cuts (as seen in Sect. 2.2), our protocol requires exactly four random bisection cuts.

---

[1]   Because there are only two cards here, it is just a shuffle.

As preliminary information, we first introduce the random bisection cut [11] in Sect. 3.1. Then, in Sect. 3.2, we propose a method for changing the base of a commitment using a random bisection cut. Next, in Sect. 3.3, we introduce an "opaque commitment pair," which is a new concept. Finally, we present our protocol in Sect. 3.4.

3.1 Random Bisection Cuts

The random bisection cut is a shuffling operation that was proposed in 2009 [11]. Since the random bisection cut appeared, the performance of card-based protocols has increased significantly (e.g., [8, 11, 14, 15]). As described later, this paper applies random bisection cuts to a standard deck of playing cards to provide efficient protocols.

In a random bisection cut, a given sequence of cards is bisected, and then the two portions are switched (or not) with a probability of $1/2$. For example, consider four cards $\boxed{1}\,\boxed{2}\,\boxed{3}\,\boxed{4}$ placed with their faces down in this order:

$$\underbrace{\boxed{?}\,\boxed{?}}_{[0]\{1,2\}}\,\underbrace{\boxed{?}\,\boxed{?}}_{[0]\{3,4\}}.$$

Apply a random bisection cut (denoted by $[\,\cdot\,|\,\cdot\,]$) to the sequence:

$$\left[\,\boxed{?}\,\boxed{?}\,\middle\|\,\boxed{?}\,\boxed{?}\,\right].$$

Then, the sequence of these four cards will be either

$$\underbrace{\boxed{?}\,\boxed{?}}_{[0]\{1,2\}}\,\underbrace{\boxed{?}\,\boxed{?}}_{[0]\{3,4\}}\quad\text{or}\quad\underbrace{\boxed{?}\,\boxed{?}}_{[0]\{3,4\}}\,\underbrace{\boxed{?}\,\boxed{?}}_{[0]\{1,2\}},$$

where each case occurs with a probability of exactly $1/2$.

Similar to the random cut, it is known that the random bisection cut can be easily performed by humans [18].

3.2 Change of Base

Here, we propose a method for changing the base of a commitment using a random bisection cut.

Take a commitment of base $\{1, 2\}$

$$\underbrace{\boxed{?}\,\boxed{?}}_{[a]\{1,2\}}.$$

as an example, and assume that we have other cards $\boxed{3}\,\boxed{4}$. We want to convert the base into $\{3, 4\}$; of course, we do not want to reveal the value of bit a. The following procedure achieves this.

1. Turn over $\boxed{3}\,\boxed{4}$ so that they become a commitment to 0:

$$\underbrace{\boxed{?}\,\boxed{?}}_{[a]^{\{1,2\}}}\underbrace{\boxed{?}\,\boxed{?}}_{[0]^{\{3,4\}}}.$$

2. Rearrange the sequence, apply a random bisection cut, and rearrange it again:

Then, we have

$$\underbrace{\boxed{?}\,\boxed{?}}_{[a\oplus r]^{\{1,2\}}}\;\underbrace{\boxed{?}\,\boxed{?}}_{[r]^{\{3,4\}}}$$

where r is a uniformly distributed random bit.

3. Reveal the first two cards; then, we know whether $r = a$ or $r = \bar{a}$, and hence we have

$$\underbrace{\boxed{1}\,\boxed{2}\,\boxed{?}\,\boxed{?}}_{[a]^{\{3,4\}}}\;\text{or}\;\underbrace{\boxed{2}\,\boxed{1}\,\boxed{?}\,\boxed{?}}_{[\bar{a}]^{\{3,4\}}}.$$

(In the latter case, apply the NOT computation to the commitment to transform it into a commitment to a.)

Note that, because r is random, the information about a does not leak even if the commitment to $a \oplus r$ is revealed.

Thus, the base of a given commitment can be easily changed.

Our AND protocol utilizes this change-of-base method. The method seems quite useful because any base can be assigned to a given commitment whose base is unknown. In addition, the method can be used for detecting irregular cards such as jokers among two face-down cards placed as an input commitment. (This is a similar idea to that behind the checking-input method designed for custom-made cards $\boxed{\clubsuit}\,\boxed{\heartsuit}$ [10].)

3.3   Opaque Commitment Pair

Here, we consider a situation in which the base of a commitment is opaque. Now, assume that there are two commitments under $\{1, 2, 3, 4\}$:

$$\underbrace{\boxed{?}\,\boxed{?}}_{[a]^{B_1}}\underbrace{\boxed{?}\,\boxed{?}}_{[b]^{B_2}}$$

where we do not know which base is $\{1, 2\}$. That is, we cannot determine whether (i) $B_1 = \{1, 2\}$ and $B_2 = \{3, 4\}$, or (ii) $B_1 = \{3, 4\}$ and $B_2 = \{1, 2\}$

(the probabilities of events (i) and (ii) are both $1/2$, and these events are independent of any input values). We call two such commitments an *opaque commitment pair*, and write it as

$$\underbrace{\fbox{?}\,\fbox{?}}_{[a]\{1,2\},\{3,4\}}\quad\underbrace{\fbox{?}\,\fbox{?}}_{[b]\{1,2\},\{3,4\}}.$$

Given an opaque commitment pair, if the base of one of the two commitments is found, then the base of the other commitment is also determined. For instance, for the above opaque commitment pair, if we turn over the first commitment (to a) and know that its base was $\{1,2\}$, then the base of the commitment to b is determined, and hence we have

$$\underbrace{\fbox{?}\,\fbox{?}}_{[b]\{3,4\}}.$$

Furthermore, assume that there are a commitment to b and an opaque commitment pair

$$\underbrace{\fbox{?}\,\fbox{?}}_{[b]\{3,4\}}\quad\underbrace{\fbox{?}\,\fbox{?}}_{[0]\{5,6\},\{7,8\}}\quad\underbrace{\fbox{?}\,\fbox{?}}_{[0]\{5,6\},\{7,8\}}.$$

Then, we can make the base of the commitment to b opaque. That is, applying the change-of-base method shown in Sect. 3.2 to the first and third commitments results in

$$\underbrace{\fbox{?}\,\fbox{?}}_{[0]\{5,6\},\{7,8\}}\quad\underbrace{\fbox{?}\,\fbox{?}}_{[b]\{5,6\},\{7,8\}}.$$

3.4 Description of Our Protocol

Now, we are ready to present our AND protocol. The protocol performs a secure AND computation using eight cards, as follows.

1. Arrange input commitments and two commitments to 0:

$$\underbrace{\fbox{?}\,\fbox{?}}_{[a]\{1,2\}}\underbrace{\fbox{?}\,\fbox{?}}_{[b]\{3,4\}}\fbox{5}\,\fbox{6}\,\fbox{7}\,\fbox{8}\;\rightarrow\;\underbrace{\fbox{?}\,\fbox{?}}_{[a]\{1,2\}}\underbrace{\fbox{?}\,\fbox{?}}_{[b]\{3,4\}}\underbrace{\fbox{?}\,\fbox{?}}_{[0]\{5,6\}}\underbrace{\fbox{?}\,\fbox{?}}_{[0]\{7,8\}}.$$

2. Apply a random bisection cut to the third and fourth commitments:

$$\underbrace{\fbox{?}\,\fbox{?}}_{[a]\{1,2\}}\underbrace{\fbox{?}\,\fbox{?}}_{[b]\{3,4\}}\left[\fbox{?}\,\fbox{?}\,\big|\,\fbox{?}\,\fbox{?}\right];$$

then, we have an opaque commitment pair:

$$\underbrace{\fbox{?}\,\fbox{?}}_{[a]\{1,2\}}\underbrace{\fbox{?}\,\fbox{?}}_{[b]\{3,4\}}\underbrace{\fbox{?}\,\fbox{?}}_{[0]\{5,6\},\{7,8\}}\underbrace{\fbox{?}\,\fbox{?}}_{[0]\{5,6\},\{7,8\}}.$$

3. Apply the change-of-base method presented in Sect. 3.2 to the second and fourth commitments:

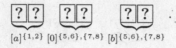

$[a]^{\{1,2\}}$ $[0]^{\{5,6\},\{7,8\}}$ $[b]^{\{5,6\},\{7,8\}}$

(From here up through step 5, simulate the AND protocol [11] that is based on custom-made cards ♣♡.)

4. For the sequence of these six cards, apply rearrangements and a random bisection cut as:

Then, we have either

(i) [?][?] [?][?] [?][?]   or   (ii) [?][?] [?][?] [?][?] ,

$[a]^{\{1,2\}}$ $[0]^{\{5,6\},\{7,8\}}$ $[b]^{\{5,6\},\{7,8\}}$ $[\bar{a}]^{\{1,2\}}$ $[b]^{\{5,6\},\{7,8\}}$ $[0]^{\{5,6\},\{7,8\}}$

where each case occurs with a probability of exactly 1/2.

5. Reveal the first two cards.

(a) Assume that the two face-up cards are [1][2]. Then, in the case of (i) above, we have $a = 0$, and hence $a \wedge b = 0$ and $\bar{a} \wedge b = b$. In the case of (ii), we have $a = 1$, and hence $a \wedge b = b$ and $\bar{a} \wedge b = 0$. Therefore, in either case, we have

[1][2]   [?][?]   [?][?] .

$[a \wedge b]^{\{5,6\},\{7,8\}}$ $[\bar{a} \wedge b]^{\{5,6\},\{7,8\}}$

(b) Assume that the two face-up cards are [2][1]. Similarly, we have

[2][1]   [?][?]   [?][?] .

$[\bar{a} \wedge b]^{\{5,6\},\{7,8\}}$ $[a \wedge b]^{\{5,6\},\{7,8\}}$

6. After applying a random bisection cut (namely, a shuffle) to the commitment to $\bar{a} \wedge b$, reveal it to find the base of the commitment to $a \wedge b$; then, we obtain

[?][?]   or   [?][?] .

$[a \wedge b]^{\{5,6\}}$ $[a \wedge b]^{\{7,8\}}$

This is our AND protocol, which uses four random bisection cuts in total. At step 5, although we reveal the first commitment, no information about bit a leaks because both (i) and (ii) occur with a probability of 1/2.

We can easily give a more formal proof of the security by using the "Koch-Walzer-Härtel diagram [7]" although we omit it due to the page limitation.

4   Our XOR Protocol

In this section, we propose an efficient XOR protocol. Whereas Niemi and Renvall's XOR protocol requires an average of seven random cuts (as seen in Sect. 2.3), our protocol terminates after only one random bisection cut. The protocol is obtained by simulating the XOR protocol [11] (which is based on custom-made cards ♣ ♡).

1. Arrange two commitments:

$$\boxed{?}\,\boxed{?}\;\boxed{?}\,\boxed{?}.$$

$$[a]^{\{1,2\}}\;[b]^{\{3,4\}}$$

2. Rearrange the sequence, apply a random bisection cut, and rearrange it again:

$$\boxed{?}\boxed{?}\boxed{?}\boxed{?}\;\times\;\boxed{?}\boxed{?}\boxed{?}\boxed{?}\;\rightarrow\;\Big[\,\boxed{?}\boxed{?}\,\big\|\,\boxed{?}\boxed{?}\,\Big]\;\rightarrow\;\boxed{?}\boxed{?}\boxed{?}\boxed{?}\;\times\;\boxed{?}\boxed{?}\boxed{?}\boxed{?}.$$

Then, we have

$$\boxed{?}\,\boxed{?}\qquad\boxed{?}\,\boxed{?}$$

$$[a\oplus r]^{\{1,2\}}\;[b\oplus r]^{\{3,4\}}$$

where r is a uniformly distributed random bit.

3. Reveal the first commitment; then, we have

$$\boxed{1}\,\boxed{2}\;\boxed{?}\,\boxed{?}\quad\text{or}\quad\boxed{2}\,\boxed{1}\;\boxed{?}\,\boxed{?}\;.$$

$$[a\oplus b]^{\{3,4\}}\qquad\qquad [a\oplus b]^{\{3,4\}}$$

5   Our Copy Protocol

In this section, we propose an efficient copy protocol. Whereas Niemi and Renvall's copy protocol requires an average of 5.5 random cuts (as seen in Sect. 2.4), our protocol terminates after only one random bisection cut. The protocol is obtained by simulating the copy protocol [11] as well.

1. Arrange an input commitment and two commitments to 0:

$$\boxed{?}\boxed{?}\,\boxed{3}\,\boxed{4}\,\boxed{5}\,\boxed{6}\;\rightarrow\;\boxed{?}\boxed{?}\,\boxed{?}\boxed{?}\,\boxed{?}\boxed{?}.$$

$$[a]^{\{1,2\}}\qquad\qquad\qquad [a]^{\{1,2\}}\;[0]^{\{3,4\}}\;[0]^{\{5,6\}}$$

2. Apply rearrangements and a random bisection cut as:

Then, we have

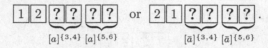

$$[a \oplus r]^{\{1,2\}} \; [r]^{\{3,4\}} \; [r]^{\{5,6\}}$$

where r is a uniformly distributed random bit.

3. Reveal the first commitment; then, we have

$$\boxed{1}\,\boxed{2}\,\boxed{?}\boxed{?}\,\boxed{?}\boxed{?} \quad \text{or} \quad \boxed{2}\,\boxed{1}\,\boxed{?}\boxed{?}\,\boxed{?}\boxed{?}\,.$$

$$[a]^{\{3,4\}} \; [a]^{\{5,6\}} \qquad\qquad [\bar{a}]^{\{3,4\}} \; [\bar{a}]^{\{5,6\}}$$

6   Conclusion

Although almost all existing card-based protocols cannot be executed with a standard deck of playing cards, there is one exception: Niemi and Renvall's protocols [13] achieve secure AND, XOR, and copy computations using normal playing cards. In this paper, we continued their efforts to improve card-based protocols that use a standard deck of playing cards, and proposed efficient AND, XOR, and copy protocols. Our protocols were constructed by applying random bisection cuts [11] to a standard deck of playing cards; as a result, we succeeded in significantly reducing the number of required shuffles. Specifically, for AND computation, whereas the existing protocol requires an average of 9.5 random cuts, our protocol terminates after applying exactly four random cuts. Regarding XOR computation and copy, the existing protocols require an average of seven and 5.5 random cuts, respectively; in contrast, our protocols require only one random bisection cut.

An intriguing future work might involve finding lower bounds on the number of required cards and shuffles. It should be noted that there is a formalization for the card-based computation model [9]; a standard deck of playing cards is within the model. Therefore, to obtain lower bounds, the existing formalization could be useful.

The card-based protocol is easy to understand. By combining our AND, XOR, and copy protocols, any function can be securely computed using a commercially available deck of cards. We hope that people all over the world would perform secure multiparty computation in their daily activities by utilizing our protocols that require only a standard deck of cards. For example, to avoid an awkward situation, a group of friends can determine whether or not they go out for a drink by securely computing the conjunction $x_1 \wedge x_2 \wedge \cdots \wedge x_n$ of their NO/YES input bits $x_1, x_2, \ldots, x_n$. All they need is a deck of playing cards. Furthermore, in the literature, playing cards related to cryptography have been studied (e.g., [3, 5, 17]). These can reveal the underlying concepts of cryptography to non-specialists.

Acknowledgments. We thank the anonymous referees, whose comments have helped us to improve the presentation of the paper. This work was supported by JSPS KAK-ENHI Grant Number 26330001.

References

1. den Boer, B.: More efficient match-making and satisfiability. In: Quisquater, J.-J., Vandewalle, J. (eds.) EUROCRYPT 1989. LNCS, vol. 434, pp. 208–217. Springer, Heidelberg (1990)
2. Crépeau, C., Kilian, J.: Discreet solitary games. In: Stinson, D.R. (ed.) CRYPTO 1993. LNCS, vol. 773, pp. 319–330. Springer, Heidelberg (1994)
3. Duan, Z., Yang, C.: Unconditional secure communication: a Russian cards protocol. J. Comb. Optim. **19**(4), 501–530 (2010)
4. Fisch, B., Freund, D., Naor, M.: Physical zero-knowledge proofs of physical properties. In: Garay, J.A., Gennaro, R. (eds.) CRYPTO 2014, Part II. LNCS, vol. 8617, pp. 313–336. Springer, Heidelberg (2014)
5. Fischer, M.J., Wright, R.N.: Bounds on secret key exchange using a random deal of cards. J. Cryptol. **9**(2), 71–99 (1996)
6. Glaser, A., Barak, B., Goldston, R.J.: A zero-knowledge protocol for nuclear warhead verification. Nature **510**(7506), 497–502 (2014)
7. Koch, A., Walzer, S., Härtel, K.: Card-based cryptographic protocols using a minimal number of cards. In: Iwata, T., Cheon, J.H. (eds.) ASIACRYPT 2015. LNCS, vol. 9452, pp. 783–807. Springer, Heidelberg (2015). doi:10.1007/978-3-662-48797-6_32
8. Mizuki, T., Kumamoto, M., Sone, H.: The five-card trick can be done with four cards. In: Wang, X., Sako, K. (eds.) ASIACRYPT 2012. LNCS, vol. 7658, pp. 598–606. Springer, Heidelberg (2012)
9. Mizuki, T., Shizuya, H.: A formalization of card-based cryptographic protocols via abstract machine. Int. J. Inf. Secur. **13**(1), 15–23 (2014)
10. Mizuki, T., Shizuya, H.: Practical card-based cryptography. In: Ferro, A., Luccio, F., Widmayer, P. (eds.) FUN 2014. LNCS, vol. 8496, pp. 313–324. Springer, Heidelberg (2014)
11. Mizuki, T., Sone, H.: Six-Card secure AND and four-card secure XOR. In: Deng, X., Hopcroft, J.E., Xue, J. (eds.) FAW 2009. LNCS, vol. 5598, pp. 358–369. Springer, Heidelberg (2009)
12. Niemi, V., Renvall, A.: Secure multiparty computations without computers. Theor. Comput. Sci. **191**(1–2), 173–183 (1998)
13. Niemi, V., Renvall, A.: Solitaire zero-knowledge. Fundam. Inf. **38**(1,2), 181–188 (1999)
14. Nishida, T., Hayashi, Y., Mizuki, T., Sone, H.: Card-based protocols for any boolean function. In: Jain, R., Jain, S., Stephan, F. (eds.) TAMC 2015. LNCS, vol. 9076, pp. 110–121. Springer, Heidelberg (2015)
15. Nishida, T., Hayashi, Y., Mizuki, T., Sone, H.: Securely computing three-input functions with eight cards. IEICE Trans. Fundam. Electron. Commun. Comput. Sci. **E98.A**(6), 1145–1152 (2015)
16. Stiglic, A.: Computations with a deck of cards. Theor. Comput. Sci. **259**(1–2), 671–678 (2001)
17. Swanson, C.M., Stinson, D.R.: Combinatorial solutions providing improved security for the generalized Russian cards problem. Des. Codes Crypt. **72**(2), 345–367 (2014)
18. Ueda, I., Nishimura, A., Hayashi, Y., Mizuki, T., Sone, H.: How to implement a random bisection cut. In: Theory and Practice of Natural Computing. LNCS. Springer, Heidelberg (2016, to appear)

Efficient Card-Based Cryptographic Protocols for Millionaires' Problem Utilizing Private Permutations

Takeshi Nakai[1]([✉]), Yuuki Tokushige[1], Yuto Misawa[2], Mitsugu Iwamoto[1], and Kazuo Ohta[1]

[1] Department of Informatics, The University of Electro-Communications, 1-5-1 Chofugaoka, Chofu, Tokyo 182-8585, Japan
{t-nakai,yuuki.tokushige,mitsugu,kazuo.ohta}@uec.ac.jp
[2] Smart Card Systems Department, Toshiba Corporation, 1, Komukai, Toshiba-cho, Saiwai-ku, Kawasaki 212-8583, Japan
yuto1.misawa@toshiba.co.jp

Abstract. We propose several efficient card-based cryptographic protocols for the millionaires' problem by introducing a new operation called *Private Permutation* (PP) instead of the *shuffle* used in existing card-based cryptographic protocols. Shuffles are useful randomization techniques for designing card-based cryptographic protocols for logical gates, and this approach seems to be almost optimal. This fact, however, implies that there is room for improvements if we do not use logical gates as building blocks for secure computing, and we show that such an improvement is actually possible for the millionaires' problem. Our key technique, PP, is a natural randomization operation for permuting a set of cards behind the player's back, and hence, a shuffle can be decomposed into two PPs with one communication between them. Thus PP not only allows us to transform Yao's seminal protocol into a card-based cryptographic protocol, but also enables us to propose entirely novel and efficient protocols by securely updating bitwise comparisons between two numbers. Furthermore, it is interesting to remark that one of the proposed protocols has a remarkably deep connection to the well-known logical puzzle known as *"The fork in the road"*.

1 Introduction

Background. Multiparty computation (MPC) can be realized by using several cards, and such a special implementation of MPC is known as a *card-based cryptographic protocol* [2,5]. Much of the research related to card-based cryptographic protocols has been devoted to secure computation of logical gates such as AND and XOR[1], since any computation can be implemented by their combinations.

Y. Misawa—This work was carried out when he was affiliated to the University of Electro-Communications.

[1] In card-based cryptographic protocols, NOT is easy to implement, and an OR operation is easily derived from an AND operation.

© Springer International Publishing AG 2016
S. Foresti and G. Persiano (Eds.): CANS 2016, LNCS 10052, pp. 500–517, 2016.
DOI: 10.1007/978-3-319-48965-0_30

The central issue when designing efficient card-based cryptographic protocols for logical gates is to minimize the number of cards required in the protocol. For instance, Mizuki–Sone [9] realized AND and XOR operations on two binary inputs with six and four cards, respectively, and recently, Koch–Walzer–Härtel [7] reduced the number of cards to five in AND[2]. On the other hand, randomization is also important in order to realize secure card-based cryptographic protocols. In this regard, an operation known as *shuffle* is considered to be useful for implementing logical gates securely with a smaller number of cards, and the usage of this operation has been extensively studied thus far.

We note that shuffles in card-based cryptographic protocols are different from those in ordinary card games in terms of two points: The first difference is that a shuffle in a card-based cryptographic protocol specifies a certain permutation, whereas a shuffle in ordinary card games permutes the set of cards in a completely random manner. The second difference is that the result of a permutation *must not* be known to *any* players (including the player performing the shuffle). For instance, a *random bisection cut* [9] is a useful type of shuffles in the following manner: an even number of cards are divided into two sets consisting of the same number of cards, and these two sets are permuted (in this case, exchanged) many times until *none* of the players can recognize how many times the two sets of cards are permuted.

Motivation and Our Idea. We observe here that the following two problems exist in card-based cryptographic protocols based on logical gates and shuffles:

(1) Constructing a protocol by using logical gates is a general technique, but it can be less efficient than protocols specially developed to perform a certain function.
(2) From the viewpoint of MPC, a shuffle is not a single operation since it requires at least two players to communicate with each other[3], and hence, a card-based cryptographic protocol is not efficient if it uses a shuffle as a building block.

We discuss (1) and (2) in detail before we propose our idea:

(1) In the secure computing of logical gates by card-based cryptographic protocols, it is known that one bisection cut is necessary and sufficient in state-of-the-art card-based cryptographic protocols [9]. This fact implies that, when we compute a certain function, random bisection cuts are necessary at least with the number of logical gates so as to represent the function. For instance, consider the case of the *millionaires' problem* initiated by Yao's seminal work [1], which is a secure two-party computation involving a comparison of two numbers without making each millionaire's wealth public. Comparing two numbers less than $m \in$

---

[2] We assume in this paper that the results are correctly computed with a probability 1. If a computation error is allowed with small probability, it is shown in [7] that four cards are sufficient.

[3] Although this fact is mentioned in [7], the efficiency of the protocol based on this fact is not discussed by these authors, and hence, they use shuffles as building blocks.

$\mathbb{N}$ by logical gates can be realized as in Fig. 1, in which logical AND and OR operations are necessary $2\lceil \log m \rceil - 1$ and $2\lceil \log m \rceil - 2$ times, respectively[4]. When executing these logical operations, the COPY operation [9] is also necessary for $\neg a_i$ and b_i in each comparison of bits, and hence, $6\lceil \log m \rceil - 5$ random bisection cuts are necessary in total in order to implement the millionaires' problem as shown in Fig. 1. Noticing that a random bisection cut is necessary for randomization, it seems difficult to reduce this number as long as we implement the millionaires' problem based on logical operations as shown in Fig. 1.

We can expect this inefficiency to be resolved if we design a card-based cryptographic protocol specialized for the function computed in the protocol, although an improvement such as this has not been studied intensively to date. Proceeding with this idea, it is natural to recall Yao's solution to the *millionaires' problem* ([1], see Sect. 3.1) since it does not depend on logical gates but specializes in comparing two numbers privately. As we will see in Sect. 3.1, for instance, Yao's protocol involves public key encryption, which is difficult to implement by logical gates, but is easy to realize by using face-down cards *without* public/private keys! As a result, it is easy to implement Yao's protocol by cards if we do *not* restrict ourselves to using card-based cryptographic protocols for *logical gates*.

When implementing Yao's protocol by using cards that do not depend on logical gates, it should become clear that his protocol uses *private computation* since it is an MPC protocol. On the other hand, every operation is assumed to be *public* in existing card-based cryptographic protocols. Hence, in this paper, we explicitly allow such a private operation if it is possible to implement by cards.

---

input: $a = (a_n...a_2\,a_1)_2$, $b = (b_n...b_2\,b_1)_2$;
$f_1 = \bar{a}_1 \wedge b_1$;
for(i : 2 to n) {
     $f_i = \bar{a}_i \wedge b_i \vee (\bar{a}_i \vee b_i) \wedge f_{i-1}$;
}
output: f_n ;
   if $f_n = 0$ then $a \geq b$
   if $f_n = 1$ then $a < b$

Fig. 1. Comparing protocol constructed by logical gates

(2) In previous work, a shuffle is considered as a building block for randomization, but actually, it is not a single operation from the viewpoint of MPC. For instance, a random bisection cut by Alice can be realized as follows: Alice first generates a random number r_A and permutes bisected cards r_A times behind her back, and sends the permuted cards to the other player, say Bob. Bob privately generates a random number r_B and permutes bisected cards r_B times behind

---

[4] Throughout this paper, logarithmic base is 2.

his back. If r_A and r_B are kept private by Alice and Bob, respectively, this protocol shuffles bisected cards $r_A + r_B$ times, and no one can know the number of permutations.

Note that such private randomness and private operations ((r_A, r_B) and permutation in this example, respectively) are often used in MPC. Hence, we call such a permutation behind someone's back *Private Permutation* (PP). The introduction of PPs makes it easy to see that shuffles, including a random bisection cut, generally consist of at least two PPs and one communication among these PPs. Note that the number of PPs and communications is considered as computational cost, and the number of cards is considered as memory cost.

Table 1. Comparison of Proposed Card-based Cryptographic Protocols

Protocols	# of Comm.	# of PP	# of cards
Logical gates (Fig. 1)	$6\lceil \log m \rceil - 5$	$12\lceil \log m \rceil - 10$	$4\lceil \log m \rceil + 2$
Proposed protocol I (Yao)	1	2	$2m$
Proposed protocol II (storage)	$2\lceil \log m \rceil$	$2\lceil \log m \rceil$	$4\lceil \log m \rceil + 2$

Our Contributions. As shown above, the concept of a PP is motivated by (1) and (2). We propose two protocols corresponding to (1) and (2), denoted as proposed protocols I and II, respectively. The evaluations of our results presented in this paper are summarized in Table 1, where we use the number of communications, PPs, and cards as efficiency measures.

We resolve problem (1) by constructing a card-based cryptographic protocol for the millionaires' problem based on Yao's protocol for two numbers less than or equal to m (proposed protocol I). Even though this protocol is naïve, *only one communication and two PPs* are sufficient, which is a considerable improvement of card-based cryptographic protocols based on logical gates ($6\lceil \log m \rceil - 5$ and $12\lceil \log m \rceil - 10$, respectively). On the other hand, the number of cards required by the protocol is $2m$, which is much worse than the card-based millionaires' problem based on logical gates ($4\lceil \log m \rceil + 2$).

Regarding problem (2), we expect that a more efficient card-based protocol can be proposed in terms of the number of communications, PPs, and cards. Actually, we propose an entirely new and efficient card-based cryptographic protocol specially developed to solve the millionaires' problem. This protocol succeeds in reducing the number of communications and PPs to almost 1/3 and 1/6, respectively, compared to the protocol for logical gates, whereas the number of cards remains the same (see Proposed protocol II in Table 1). The new protocol compares two numbers bit by bit, starting from the less significant bit, and the compared results are recorded on cards, called *storage*. The results recorded in storage need to be kept secret from both Alice and Bob, to solve the millionaires' problem securely. Hence, we show how to manipulate the storage privately by using PPs. It is very interesting to note that the technique on which this manipulation is based proved to be the same as that of the well-known logical puzzle *"The Fork in the Road⁵"* [6, p. 25]. This observation will be introduced when explaining the idea of the proposed protocol II in Sect. 4.1.

Organization. The remaining part of this paper is organized as follows: We introduce several notations, basic operations of cards including PP, and the security notion for card-based cryptographic protocols in Sect. 2. In Sect. 3, the card-based cryptographic protocol for the millionaires' problem based on Yao's protocol is presented. Section 4 is devoted to the proposal of a new card-based cryptographic protocol *with storage*, which is efficient from the viewpoint of the number of communications and PPs. We summarize our results in Sect. 5 and discuss the improvements of the protocol proposed in Sect. 4.

2   Preliminaries

2.1   Notations and Basic Operations

In card-based cryptographic protocols, we normally use two types of cards such as ♣ and ♡, which are represented in the following sentences by ♣ and ♡, respectively. We assume that two cards with the same mark are indistinguishable. We also assume that all cards have the same design on their reverse sides, and that they are indistinguishable and represented as ?. The Boolean values 0 and 1 are encoded as ♣♡ and ♡♣, respectively. Note that we regard the sequence of cards as a vector. In this paper, we use the following fundamental card operations [8]. Note that these operations are executed *publicly*.

- Face up: ? ↦ ♣, ? ↦ ♡
- Face down: ♣ ↦ ?, ♡ ↦ ?
- Swap: ?? (represents $x \in \{0,1\}$) ↦ ?? (represents $\neg x \in \{0,1\}$)

If a pair of face-down cards for the Boolean value $x \in \{0,1\}$, it is called *commitment*. The term Swap indicates reversal of the left and the right of the commitment.

---

⁵ This problem is summarized as follows: An logician finds himself on an island inhabited by two tribes: liars and truth-tellers. Members of the one tribe always tell the truth, whereas members of the other tribe always tell lies. The logician reaches a fork in a road and has to ask a native bystander which branch he should take to reach the village. He has no way of telling whether the native is a truth-teller or a liar. The logician only asks *one* question. From the reply he knows which road to take. What question does he ask?.

2.2   Random Bisection Cut and Private Permutation

Random Bisection Cut. This is a key technique to realize efficient card-based cryptographic protocols for logical gates, e.g., 6-card AND protocol [9], which is described as follows:

For a positive integer v, suppose that there is a sequence of $2v$ face-down cards. Denote the left and right halves by u_1 and u_2, respectively.

$$
\overbrace{\boxed{?}\boxed{?}\cdots\boxed{?}}^{v \text{ cards}}\overbrace{\boxed{?}\boxed{?}\cdots\boxed{?}}^{v \text{ cards}} \tag{1}
$$
$$
\underbrace{}_{=:u_1}\underbrace{}_{=:u_2}
$$

Then, u_1 and u_2 are interchanged or left unchanged with probability $1/2$. Depicting this by using figures, one of either

$$
\underbrace{\boxed{?}\boxed{?}\cdots\boxed{?}}_{u_1}\underbrace{\boxed{?}\boxed{?}\cdots\boxed{?}}_{u_2} \quad \text{or} \quad \underbrace{\boxed{?}\boxed{?}\cdots\boxed{?}}_{u_2}\underbrace{\boxed{?}\boxed{?}\cdots\boxed{?}}_{u_1} \tag{2}
$$

is selected with a probability $1/2$. If *no player knows* whether one of the above is selected, such a shuffle is known as a *random bisection cut*.

A random bisection cut is known to be a convenient randomization technique for implementing card-based protocols for logical gates securely. However, it has two drawbacks.

The first drawback is that it is not known how to use this technique other than in the card-based cryptographic protocols for logical gates. In other words, this technique is not useful for implementing Yao's protocol, for instance, as a card-based cryptographic protocol because it does not use logical gates.

The second drawback is that it is not possible for one player to realize this technique. That is, a random bisection cut by Alice can be realized as follows: Alice first generates a random number r_A and permutes the bisected cards r_A times behind her back, and sends the permuted cards to the other player, say Bob. Bob privately generates a random number r_B and permutes the bisected cards r_B times behind his back. If r_A and r_B are kept private by Alice and Bob, respectively, this protocol permutes the bisected cards $r_A + r_B$ times, and no one can know the number of permutations. As long as we implement card-based cryptographic protocols based on logical gates, at least one shuffle such as a random bisection cut is necessary for *every* logical gate, which would have a highly adverse impact on the efficiency of the protocols.

Private Permutation. We resolve the above-mentioned drawbacks by decomposing the shuffle operation into the private permutations behind the player's back and the communication between them. Hence, we introduce a new randomization operation called *Private Permutation* (PP), which can be formalized as follows:

For a positive integer t, let $c \in \{\clubsuit, \heartsuit\}^t$ be a vector consisting of t face-down cards. For a set $\mathcal{P}_t$ of all permutations over[6] $[t] := \{1, 2, \ldots, t\}$, let $\mathcal{R}_t \subset \mathcal{P}_t$

---

[6] In this paper, we define $[n] := \{1, 2, \ldots, n\}$ for an integer $n \in \mathbb{N}$.

be a set of possible permutations. We also define $\mathcal{R}_t = \{\pi_0, \pi_1, \ldots, \pi_{|\mathcal{R}_t|-1}\}$. Then, for a positive integer t and a set of possible permutations $\mathcal{R}_t$, the private permutation is formalized as follows:

$$\mathsf{PP}^{[t]}_{\mathcal{R}_t}(c, s) := \pi_s(c), \quad s = 0, 1, \ldots, |\mathcal{R}_t| - 1.$$

Note that the same function was introduced by others [7,8] although we impose an additional assumption on this function. Namely, we assume that *the player executing* $\mathsf{PP}^{[t]}_{\mathcal{R}_t}$ *keeps s secret, whereas he/she makes the other parameters public*, which is easy to realize by permuting the cards behind the player's back. This requirement is firstly introduced in this paper explicitly by considering that shuffle implicitly assumes the necessity of PPs. Note that, in the existing card-based cryptographic protocols, every operation other than shuffle is assumed to be executed in public. Note that, not only the random bisection cut, but also several different types of *shuffles*, e.g., [10] can be realized by PPs in a similar manner by specifying $\mathcal{R}_t$ appropriately.

For instance, consider the set of permutations capable of randomly *interchanging* the first and the latter halves of a vector as follows: For a positive integer v, $\mathcal{R}^{\mathrm{ic}}_{2v} := \{\pi_0, \pi_1\} \subset \mathcal{P}_{2v}$ where

$$\pi_0 := (1, \ldots, v, v+1, \ldots, 2v), \text{ and } \pi_1 := (v+1, \ldots, 2v, 1, \ldots, v), \qquad (3)$$

which means that $\pi_0(c) = (u_1, u_2)$ and $\pi_1(c) = (u_2, u_1)$ for $c := (u_1, u_2)$ given by (1). Then, the random bisection cut for $2v$ cards is represented as $\mathsf{PP}^{[2v]}_{\mathcal{R}^{\mathrm{ic}}_{2v}}(c, s) = \pi_s(c)$ where s is chosen from $\{0, 1\}$ uniformly at random and it is known only by the player executing this operation. In executing the random bisection cut, for the sequence of cards c, Alice executes $\mathsf{PP}^{[2v]}_{\mathcal{R}^{\mathrm{ic}}_{2v}}(c, r_A) =: c'$ by using her private randomness $r_A \in \{0, 1\}$, and c' is sent to Bob. Bob also executes $\mathsf{PP}^{[2v]}_{\mathcal{R}^{\mathrm{ic}}_{2v}}(c', r_B)$ by using his private randomness $r_B \in \{0, 1\}$.

Efficiency Measures. Most of the previous work, e.g., [8,11], considers the number of shuffles as the *computational complexity* since shuffle is the most time-consuming operation. On the other hand, in this paper we consider that the computational complexity is evaluated by the number of PPs and communications since such measures are suitable for MPC. In this paper, successive PPs executed by one player without communication and/or face up is counted as *one* PP since the composition of permutations is also regarded as a permutation and the subsequent private permutation can be executed at once behind the player's back.

2.3 Security Notion

Throughout this paper, we assume that both Alice and Bob are semi-honest players. Following [4], we introduce the security notion (perfect secrecy) of card-based cryptographic protocols for the millionaires' problem.

In defining the security of card-based cryptographic protocols, *view* plays a key role. View is roughly defined to be *a vector of random variables*[7] *corresponding to the data that each player can obtain in the protocol.* More precisely, view is a vector which consists of random variables corresponding to the input of the player, the output of the protocol, public information all players can gain, and random values which are used when the player makes a random choice.

For a fixed integer $m \in \mathbb{N}$, let $a \in [m]$ and $b \in [m]$ be positive integers representing the wealth of Alice and Bob respectively. In this case, the inputs by Alice and Bob for the protocol are a and b, respectively. The common output of the millionaires' problem for Alice and Bob is represented as $\chi^{\mathrm{ge}}(a, b)$ where

$$\chi^{\mathrm{ge}}(u, v) := \begin{cases} 1 & \text{if } u \geq v \\ 0 & \text{otherwise,} \end{cases} \tag{4}$$

for positive integers $u, v \in [m]$.

The information obtained by Alice and Bob in the protocol can be classified into *private information* denoted by r_A and r_B, and *public information* denoted by λ. Hence, Alice's (resp. Bob's) view can be described as the sequence of random variables corresponding to her (resp. his) input a (resp. b), output of the protocol, private information r_A (resp., r_B) and public information λ. The private information r_A (resp., r_B) is the random number generated by Alice (resp., Bob) and used in PPs. The public information is the cards that Alice and Bob made public by turning them face up. Note that, in ordinary MPC, view includes information that each player receives via private channel, but in card-based cryptographic protocols, there is no private channel. Only face-up cards can reveal information, and hence, we can define the face-up cards are included in the view as public information. Let R_A, R_B, and Λ be random variables corresponding to the values r_A, r_B, and λ, respectively. Then, the views of Alice and Bob are represented as $(A, \chi^{\mathrm{ge}}(A, B), R_A, \Lambda)$ and $(B, \chi^{\mathrm{ge}}(A, B), R_B, \Lambda)$, respectively.

Intuitively, if all Alice's (resp., Bob's) private and public information can be simulated from Alice's (resp., Bob's) input and output, we can say that no information is contained in the private and public information other than Alice's (resp., Bob's) input and output. Hence, we can formulate perfect secrecy of card-based cryptographic protocols for the millionaires' problem as follows:

Definition 1 (Perfect secrecy). *Consider the millionaires' problem for Alice and Bob. We say that the card-based cryptographic protocol for the millionaires' problem is perfectly secure if there exist polynomial-time simulators S_A and S_B such that for all possible inputs a and b, it holds that*

$$\mathsf{S}_A(a, c_{a,b}) \overset{\mathrm{perf}}{\equiv} (a, \chi^{\mathrm{ge}}(a, b), R_A, \Lambda) \quad \text{and} \quad \mathsf{S}_B(b, c_{a,b}) \overset{\mathrm{perf}}{\equiv} (b, \chi^{\mathrm{ge}}(a, b), R_B, \Lambda) \tag{5}$$

---

[7] Throughout the paper, random variables are represented by capital letters. The probability that a random variable X takes a value x is represented by $\Pr\{X = x\}$ which is also written as $P_X(x)$ for short. Mathematically, random variable is defined to be a map from probability space to the set of real numbers. However, for simplicity, we allow the cards $\clubsuit, \heartsuit$ to be treated as the values of random variables in each view.

where $U \overset{\text{perf}}{\equiv} V$ means that the (joint) probability distributions P_U and P_V corresponding to the random variables U and V, respectively, are perfectly the same.

3   Proposed Protocol I: Card-Based Cryptographic Protocol for Millionaires' Problem Based on Yao's Solution

3.1   Yao's Solution and Our Idea Behind the Proposed Protocol I

We propose a card-based cryptographic protocol that resolves the millionaires' problem by cards based on Yao's original solution. Before providing our protocol, we explain Yao's public key based solution [1] with the following:

Yao's Solution to the Millionaires' Problem. For a fixed integer $m \in \mathbb{N}$, assume that Alice and Bob have wealth represented by positive integers a and b, respectively, where $a, b \in [m]$. Let $\mathcal{X} := [2^N - 1]$ be a set of N-bit integers. $(\mathsf{Enc}_A, \mathsf{Dec}_A)$ is a public-key encryption of Alice. Hence, $\mathsf{Enc}_A : \mathcal{X} \to \mathcal{X}$ is an encryption under Alice's public key, and Dec_A is a decryption under Alice's private key.

⟨1⟩ Bob selects a random N-bit integer $x \in \mathcal{X}$, and computes $c := \mathsf{Enc}_A(x)$ privately.

⟨2⟩ Bob sends Alice the number $c - b + 1$

⟨3⟩ For $i = 1, 2, \ldots, m$, Alice computes privately the values of $y_i = \mathsf{Dec}_A(c - b + i)$.

⟨4⟩ Alice generates a random prime p of $N/2$ bits, and computes the values $z_i := y_i \bmod p$ for $i = 1, 2, \ldots, m$. If $|z_u - z_v| \geq 2$ for all distinct $u, v \in [m]$, then go to next step; otherwise generates another random prime and repeat the process until all z_u differ by at least 2;

⟨5⟩ Alice makes $z' = (z_1, z_2, \ldots, z_a, z_{a+1} + 1, z_{a+2} + 1, \ldots, z_m + 1)$; each value is in the mod p sense.

⟨6⟩ Alice sends Bob p and the vector z'.

⟨7⟩ Bob looks at the b-th number in z'. If it is equal to $x \bmod p$, then $a \geq b$, otherwise $a < b$.

⟨8⟩ Bob sends Alice the result.

Our Idea Behind Proposed Protocol I. We first point out that the key steps of Yao's protocol are ⟨5⟩–⟨7⟩, where Alice *privately* adds 1 to z_{a+1} to z_m in the m-dimensional vector, and sends the vector to Bob. He *privately* checks the b-th value in the vector, and outputs the result. These private operation can be implemented by PP, which corresponds to the step ⟨3⟩ in the following proposed protocol I.

Note that, in Yao's solution, ⟨1⟩–⟨4⟩ are necessary for realizing the key steps ⟨5⟩–⟨7⟩ securely, since they prevent the vector z' in ⟨5⟩ from leaking Alice's wealth a to Bob. However, in a card-based cryptographic protocol, these steps can be replaced with *single step* since face down play the role of encryption. Furthermore, the communication in ⟨8⟩ can be removed in the card-based protocol since face-up cards on the tabletop can immediately be recognized by both Alice and Bob.

3.2 Proposed Protocol I

Based on the ideas discussed in the previous section, we propose a card-based cryptographic protocol for the millionaires' problem based on Yao's solution. We refer to this protocol *proposed protocol I*. The definitions of a, b, m are same in the previous section.

Proposed Protocol I (Card-based Yao's Solution)

(1) Alice prepares m pairs of ♣♡ and turn them all face down. This preparation is represented in a vector form as $(\boldsymbol{x}_1, \boldsymbol{x}_2, \ldots, \boldsymbol{x}_m)$ where $\boldsymbol{x}_1 = \boldsymbol{x}_2 = \cdots = \boldsymbol{x}_m = ♣♡$.

(2) For $i = 1, 2, \ldots, m$, repeat the operation in which Alice swaps $\boldsymbol{x}_i$ if $i > a$; otherwise do not. Each swap operation must be executed *privately*, and it is described as the following PP with respect to $\mathcal{R}_2^{\mathrm{ic}} := \{\pi_0, \pi_1\}$ which is given by (3) with $v = 1$:

$$\mathsf{PP}_{\mathcal{R}_2^{\mathrm{ic}}}^{[2]}(\boldsymbol{x}_i, \chi^{\mathrm{ge}}(i-1, a)), \ i = 1, 2, \ldots, m, \tag{6}$$

where $\chi^{\mathrm{ge}}(\cdot, \cdot)$ is defined in (4), i.e., $\chi^{\mathrm{ge}}(i-1, a) = 1$ iff $i > a$. As a result, Alice *privately* generates the sequence of cards $\boldsymbol{x}' := (\boldsymbol{x}_1', \boldsymbol{x}_2', \ldots, \boldsymbol{x}_m')$ where $\boldsymbol{x}_i' := \mathsf{PP}_{\mathcal{R}_2^{\mathrm{ic}}}^{[2]}(\boldsymbol{x}_i, \chi^{\mathrm{ge}}(i-1, a))$.

(3) Alice sends Bob $\boldsymbol{x}'$.

(4) Bob *privately* moves $\boldsymbol{x}_b'$ to the first element of $\boldsymbol{x}'$, which is described as the following PP:

$$\mathsf{PP}_{\mathcal{R}_{2m}^{\mathrm{mf}}}^{[2m]}(\boldsymbol{x}', b-1) = \pi_{b-1}(\boldsymbol{x}') \tag{7}$$

where $\mathcal{R}_{2m}^{\mathrm{mf}} := \{\pi_i\}_{i=0}^{m-1}$ such that $\pi_i : \boldsymbol{x}' \mapsto (\boldsymbol{x}_{i+1}, \boldsymbol{x}_1, \ldots, \boldsymbol{x}_i, \boldsymbol{x}_{i+2}, \ldots, \boldsymbol{x}_m)$.

(5) Bob reveals the left most commitment of $\mathsf{PP}_{\mathcal{R}_{2m}^{\mathrm{mf}}}^{[2m]}(\boldsymbol{x}', b-1)$, i.e., $\boldsymbol{x}_b'$. If the value represented by $\boldsymbol{x}_b'$ is 0, then $a \geq b$, otherwise $a < b$.

The remaining cards are completely randomized by Alice or Bob in public in order to discard the information of $\boldsymbol{x}'$ except for $\boldsymbol{x}_b'$. We call this operation "the remaining cards are *discarded*," hereafter.

Note that steps (1) and (2) in the proposed protocol correspond to step ⟨1⟩–⟨5⟩, and the steps (3) and (4) correspond to steps ⟨6⟩ and ⟨7⟩, respectively, which shows that the step (2) considerably simplifies Yao's protocol. We omit the proof of correctness of the proposed protocol since it is almost obvious from Yao's protocol.

Note that $(\mathsf{Enc}_A, \mathsf{Dec}_A)$ in Yao's millionaires' protocol must be public-key encryption since a is obtained by Bob in step ⟨5⟩ if $(\mathsf{Enc}_A, \mathsf{Dec}_A)$ is a private key encryption. On the other hand, in the proposed protocol I, such leakage of a to Bob is prevented by requiring that all cards except x_b' are completely randomized by Alice or Bob publicly at the end of the protocol.

Efficiency of the proposed protocol I. In the proposed protocol, note that the constant numbers for PP and communication are sufficient. We use two PPs in steps (2) and (4), and one communication in step (3), and this outperforms the protocol based on logical gates (see Fig. 1). We note that the steps (4) and (5) are necessary so that Bob turns x_b' face up publicly without making b public[8].

We can show the perfect secrecy of the proposed protocol in the following theorem, but we omit the proof since it is almost obvious.

Theorem 1. *The proposed protocol I is perfectly secure; it satisfies* (5) *in Definition 1.*

Remark. Thanks to the special operations of card, e.g., face up, face down, and swap, etc., the proposed protocol I is not only a direct transformation of Yao's, but also is superior to the original protocol. For instance, the proposed protocol I does not use any randomness, whereas randomness is necessary for generating public/private keys in the original solution by Yao. Furthermore, it is worth observing that both Alice and Bob can know the output result simultaneously in the proposed protocol I, whereas Yao's original protocol, Bob is required to announce his result to Alice (see step ⟨8⟩).

4   Proposed Protocol II: Card-Based Cryptographic Protocol for Millionaires' Problem with Storage

4.1   Ideas Behind Proposed Protocol II

In order to reduce the number of cards to below $2m$, it is natural to represent the wealth of Alice and Bob as binary numbers with $\lceil \log m \rceil$ bits (i.e., $2\lceil \log m \rceil$ cards). This approach enables us to consider the strategy by comparing the Alice's and Bob's wealth bit-by-bit starting from their least significant bit although our strategy is not based on the use of logical gates.

Let $(a_n, \ldots, a_1)$ and $(b_n, \ldots, b_1)$ be the binary representation of the positive integers a and b, respectively, where $n := \lceil \log m \rceil$ and $a_i, b_i \in \{0, 1\}$, $i = 1, 2, \ldots, n$. For each $i \in [n]$, assume that a_i and b_i are represented by pairs of cards $\alpha_{i,l}\alpha_{i,r}$ and $\beta_{i,l}\beta_{i,r}$, respectively, where $\alpha_{i,l}\alpha_{i,r}, \beta_{i,l}\beta_{i,r} \in \{\clubsuit\heartsuit, \heartsuit\clubsuit\}$. For instance, $a_i = 1$ is represented by cards as $\alpha_{i,l}\alpha_{i,r} = \heartsuit\clubsuit$.

Note that, however, such a two-card representation of binary numbers is redundant in a bit-by-bit comparison since we can represent 0 and 1 by $\clubsuit$ and $\heartsuit$, respectively[9]. In this one-card representation, $\alpha_{i,l}$ and $\beta_{i,l}$ suffice to represent

---

[8] Private selection of x_b' and making it public are formally realized in this manner.

[9] However, we note that a one-card representation cannot express arbitrary binary numbers. Hence, $4\lceil \log m \rceil$ (i.e., $2\lceil \log m \rceil$ cards for Alice and Bob) cards are at least necessary when comparing two binary numbers less than m.

a_i and b_i, respectively. Further, their negations, $\neg a_i$ and $\neg b_i$, are also represented by $\alpha_{i,r}$ and $\beta_{i,r}$, respectively. In the following, we consider a scenario in which Alice prepares $(a_n, \ldots, a_i)$ by using a two-card representation, and then, Alice and Bob use a one-card representation for comparison.

We compare the bits of Alice and Bob by preparing a device (equipped by a card) called *comparison storage*, denoted by $cs \in \{\clubsuit, \heartsuit\}$, that records the bit-by-bit comparison results. Our idea is roughly as follows: We assume that Bob compares $\beta_{i,l}$ (i.e., b_i) with Alice's card $\alpha_{i,l}$ (i.e., a_i) from $i = 1$ to n, and he overwrites cs with $\beta_{i,l}$ (i.e., b_i) if $\beta_{i,l} \neq \alpha_{i,l}$ (i.e., $b_i \neq a_i$) while cs remains *untouched* if this is not the case (i.e., $b_i = a_i$). Recalling that Bob overwrites the comparison storage with *his* bit, Bob is shown to be *richer* if the comparison storage is $\heartsuit$ (i.e., 1) at the end of the protocol. Similarly, Alice is shown to be *richer* if the comparison storage is $\clubsuit$ (i.e., 0) at the end of the protocol. As is easily understood, however, this rough idea presents two problems:

(P1) If Bob were to directly compare his bits with those of Alice, such a comparison strategy would easily leaks Alice's bits to Bob.

(P2) The fact of overwriting the comparison result or not leaks Bob's bits to Alice.

(P1) can be avoided by considering the following modified randomized strategy: Since Alice prepares $(a_n, \ldots, a_i)$ by two-card representations, she sends Bob $\alpha_{i,l}$ (i.e., a_i) or $\alpha_{i,r}$ (i.e., $\neg a_i$) with probability $1/2$. Such a randomization is effective for concealing the value of Alice's bit from Bob, but we encounter another problem:

(P3) Since Alice sends $\alpha_{i,w}$ to Bob $w \in \{l, r\}$ with a probability of $1/2$, he cannot tell whether $a_i \neq b_i$ or not.

Problems **(P2)** and **(P3)** are simultaneously resolved by introducing another storage called *dummy storage*, denoted by $ds \in \{\clubsuit, \heartsuit\}$, and communicating the pair of cs and ds between Alice and Bob. Hereafter, we refer to the pair consisting of cs and ds as *storage*.

In order to resolve problem **(P2)**, it suffices for Bob to overwrite cs and ds corresponding to the results of $a_i \neq b_i$ and $a_i = b_i$, respectively, which enables him to hide his bit from Alice. However, due to **(P3)**, Bob cannot determine which one of cs and ds should be overwritten. Hence, we focus on how to resolve problem **(P3)** hereafter.

Problem **(P3)** can be rephrased using binary numbers as follows: Let $a_i' \in \{0, 1\}$ be a binary number that Bob receives, but he does not know whether $a_i' = a_i$ (in the case of $w = l$) or $a_i' = \neg a_i$ (in the case of $w = r$). Our main object is to find $a_i \neq b_i$ or $a_i = b_i$ even if either one of $a_i' = a_i$ or $a_i' = \neg a_i$ is sent[10].

Our basic idea for resolving **(P3)** is that Bob uses the fact that what he knows is either $\alpha_{i,w} \neq \beta_{i,l}$ or $\alpha_{i,w} = \beta_{i,l}$. Making use of this fact, Alice and Bob

---

[10] This problem is very similar to the well-known logical problem *"The Fork in the Road,"* that is remarked upon later.

treat cs and ds as an *ordered pair* of face-down cards, and assume that either (cs, ds) or (ds, cs) is determined by *Alice's private random choice* $w \in \{l, r\}$ as follows:

- If Alice selects $w = l$ and sends Bob $\alpha_{i,l} \in \{\clubsuit, \heartsuit\}$ (i.e., a_i), then she sends him (cs, ds) with $\alpha_{i,l}$.
- If Alice selects $w = r$ and sends Bob $\alpha_{i,r} \in \{\clubsuit, \heartsuit\}$ (i.e., $\neg a_i$), then she sends him (ds, cs) with $\alpha_{i,r}$.

We can see that the order of cs and ds is synchronized with $w \in \{l, r\}$ (i.e., a_i and $\neg a_i$) in *Alice*. Owing to this synchronization, Bob can correctly overwrite cs only when $a_i \neq b_i$ by implementing the following strategy, even if he does not know which one of cs and ds should be overwritten. Let (σ_l, σ_r) be the storage Bob receives from Alice.

- If $\alpha_{i,w} \neq \beta_{i,l}$ (i.e., $a_i' \neq b_i$) holds, Bob overwrites *the left* element σ_l of the storage (σ_l, σ_r) with $\beta_{i,l}$ (i.e., b_i).
- If $\alpha_{i,w} = \beta_{i,l}$ (i.e., $a_i' = b_i$) holds, Bob overwrites *the right* element σ_r of the storage (σ_l, σ_r) with $\beta_{i,l}$ (i.e., b_i).

Let (σ_l', σ_r') be the storage overwritten by Bob, and he returns (σ_l', σ_r') to Alice. Then, by using $w \in \{l, r\}$ that Alice generated, she *privately* rearranges (σ_l', σ_r') so as to place cs and ds on the left and the right, respectively. After repeating these procedures from $i = 1$ to n, Bob is shown to be richer if $cs = \heartsuit$ (i.e., 1) whereas the contrary is true if $cs = \clubsuit$ (i.e., 0).

Table 2. Synchronization mechanism in the proposed protocol with storage

a_i ($\alpha_{i,l}$)	b_i ($\beta_{i,l}$)	$(cs, ds), w = l$			$(ds, cs), w = r$		
		a_i' ($\alpha_{i,l}$)	$a_i' \neq b_i$	Overwrite	a_i' ($\alpha_{i,r}$)	$a_i' \neq b_i$	Overwrite
0 ($\clubsuit$)	1 ($\heartsuit$)	0 ($\clubsuit$)	True	left $= cs$	1 ($\heartsuit$)	False	right $= cs$
1 ($\heartsuit$)	0 ($\clubsuit$)	1 ($\heartsuit$)	True	left $= cs$	0 ($\clubsuit$)	False	right $= cs$
0 ($\clubsuit$)	0 ($\clubsuit$)	0 ($\clubsuit$)	False	right $= ds$	1 ($\heartsuit$)	True	left $= ds$
1 ($\heartsuit$)	1 ($\heartsuit$)	1 ($\heartsuit$)	False	right $= ds$	0 ($\clubsuit$)	True	left $= ds$

It is easy to see from Table 2 that our synchronization strategy for storage works well. This is best clarified by discussing the proposed protocol by using binary numbers rather than cards. For instance, consider the case where Alice compares her bit $a_i = 1$ with Bob's bit $b_i = 0$ (the second line in Table 2). If Alice selects $w = l$, Bob receives a bit $a_i = 1$ and compares it with Bob's bit $b_i = 0$. Since $a_i' \neq b_i$, the left-hand side element of the storage, i.e., cs, is overwritten by $b_i = 0$. On the other hand, if Alice selects $w = r$, Bob receives a bit $a_i' = \neg a_i = 0$ and compares it with his bit $b_i = 0$. Since $a_i' = b_i = 0$, the right-hand side element of the storage, i.e., cs, is overwritten by $b_i = 0$. Anyway, cs is correctly overwritten by $b_i = 1$ ($> a_i = 0$) as expected.

Remark. It is interesting to note that the logic of the above synchronization strategy is the same as that of the well-known logical puzzle "*The Fork in the Road,*" [6, p. 25] (see footnote 7). Note that the point of the "The Fork in the Road" is that we need to obtain the correct answer (correct branch) from "*yes-no-questions,*" regardless of whether the native bystander tells the truth. Similarly, in our synchronization strategy, we require the correct compared result ($a_i \neq b_i$ or $a_i = b_i$) from "*same-or-different-questions,*" regardless of whether Bob receives $\alpha_{i,l}$ (i.e., a_i) or $\alpha_{i,r}$ (i.e., $\neg a_i$).

4.2 Proposed Protocol II

Based on the discussion in the previous section, we propose the card-based cryptographic protocol which uses storage and synchronization between the random selection $w \in \{l, r\}$ and the order of cs and ds, for the Millionaires' problem. For the upper bound $m \in \mathbb{N}$ of the wealth of Alice and Bob, let $n := \lceil \log m \rceil$.

Proposed Protocol II (Protocol for Millionaires' Problem with Storage)

(1) Alice prepares a face-down ♣ and a face-down ♡ (This card can be arbitrary since it is a dummy card.) as the output storage cs and the dummy storage ds, respectively. We call the pair consisting of cs and ds *storage*. She also prepares a sequence of $2n$ cards $(\alpha_{1,l}\alpha_{1,r}, \alpha_{2,l}\alpha_{2,r}, \ldots, \alpha_{n,l}\alpha_{n,r})$, which is a binary representation of her wealth $a \in [m]$. Bob also prepares the sequence of $2n$ cards $(\beta_{1,l}\beta_{1,r}, \beta_{2,l}\beta_{2,r}, \ldots, \beta_{n,l}\beta_{n,r})$, which is the binary representation of his wealth $b \in [m]$.

(2) For $i = 1, 2, \ldots, n$, repeat the following operations (2-i)–(2-v):

   (2-i) Alice *privately* chooses $w \in \{l, r\}$ uniformly at random. Then, execute the following PP with respect to $\mathcal{R}_2^{ic}$ which is defined in (3) with $v = 1$:

$$(\sigma_l, \sigma_r) := \mathsf{PP}_{\mathcal{R}_2^{ic}}^{[2]}((cs, ds), \chi^{eq}(w, r)) \tag{8}$$

   where $\chi^{eq}(w, r) = 1$ if $w = r$, and $\chi^{eq}(w, r) = 0$ otherwise.

  (2-ii) Alice sends Bob (σ_l, σ_r) in addition to $\alpha_{i,w}$.

 (2-iii) Bob turns $\alpha_{i,w}$ face up, and he compares $\beta_{i,l}$ with $\alpha_{i,w}$ in *his mind.* If they are *different,* he *privately* overwrites σ_l with $\beta_{i,l}$, otherwise he *privately* overwrites σ_r with $\beta_{i,r}$. This operation can be described as the following PP with respect to $\mathcal{R}_2^{ow1} := \{\pi_0, \pi_1\}$ where $\pi_0 := (\sigma_l, \beta_{i,l}, \sigma_r)$ and $\pi_1 = (\beta_{i,l}, \sigma_r, \sigma_l)$. :

$$(\sigma_l', \sigma_r', \eta) := \mathsf{PP}_{\mathcal{R}_2^{ow1}}^{[3]}((\sigma_l, \sigma_r, \beta_{i,l}), \overline{\chi^{eq}}(\beta_{i,l}, \alpha_{i,w})) \tag{9}$$

   where $\overline{\chi^{eq}}(\cdot, \cdot) := 1 - \chi^{eq}(\cdot, \cdot)$. The extra card η is discarded without turning it face up.

> (2-iv) Bob sends Alice (σ'_l, σ'_r).
>
> (2-v) Alice rearranges the storage cards *privately* depending on the random value w chosen in (2-i), i.e., execute the PP such that
>
> $$\mathsf{PP}^{[2]}_{\mathcal{R}^{\mathrm{ic}}_2}((\sigma'_l, \sigma'_r), \chi^{\mathsf{eq}}(w, l)), \tag{10}$$
>
> which is used for the new storage cards (cs, ds).
>
> (3) Alice turns cs face up to output. If the card is ♣, then $a \geq b$. Otherwise, $a < b$. After completing the protocol, ds is discarded without revealing.

Example of proposed protocol II. We show a simple example for understanding how the proposed protocol II works correctly. Consider the case where we compare $a = 0$ of Alice and $b = 2$ of Bob, which are represented by $(\alpha_{1,l}\alpha_{1,r}, \alpha_{2,l}\alpha_{2,r}) := (♣♡, ♣♡)$ and $(\beta_{1,l}\beta_{1,r}, \beta_{2,l}\beta_{2,r}) := (♡♣, ♣♡)$, respectively, since $(a_1, a_0) = (0, 0)$ and $(b_1, b_0) = (1, 0)$. We also set $(cs, ds) = (♣, ♡)$.

We first consider the case of $i = 1$. If Alice chooses $w = l$ in step (2-i), (8) becomes $(\sigma_l, \sigma_r) = (cs, ds) = (♣, ♡)$ since $\chi^{\mathsf{eq}}(w, r) = \chi^{\mathsf{eq}}(l, r) = 0$. Then, she sends Bob $(\sigma_l, \sigma_r) = (♣, ♡)$ and $\alpha_{1,l} = ♣$ in step (2-ii). In step (2-iii), Bob compares $\beta_{1,l} = ♣$ with $\alpha_{1,l} = ♣$, which results in $\overline{\chi^{\mathsf{eq}}}(\beta_{1,l}, \alpha_{1,l}) = 0$. Then, he outputs $(\sigma'_l, \sigma'_r) = (\sigma_l, \beta_{1,l}) = (♣, ♣)$ by overwriting the *right* element of $(\sigma_l, \sigma_r) = (♣, ♡)$ with $\beta_{1,l} = ♣$ *privately*, since (9) becomes $(\sigma'_l, \sigma'_r, \eta) = (\sigma_l, \beta_{1,l}, \sigma_r)$ due to $\overline{\chi^{\mathsf{eq}}}(\beta_{1,l}, \alpha_{1,l}) = 0$. Bob discards $\sigma_r = ♡$.

On the other hand, consider the case where Alice chooses $w = r$ in step (2-i); Then, (8) in step (2-i) becomes $(\sigma_l, \sigma_r) = (ds, cs) = (♡, ♣)$ since $\chi^{\mathsf{eq}}(w, r) = \chi^{\mathsf{eq}}(r, r) = 1$. She sends Bob $(\sigma_l, \sigma_r) = (♡, ♣)$ and $\alpha_{1,r} = ♡$ in step (2-ii). Bob compares $\beta_{1,l} = ♣$ and $\alpha_{1,r} = ♡$, and outputs $(\sigma'_l, \sigma'_r) = (♣, ♣)$ by overwriting the *left* element of $(\sigma_l, \sigma_r) = (♡, ♣)$ with $\beta_{1,l} = ♣$ *privately* as a result of (9).

As a result, regardless of the selection of $w \in \{l, r\}$, storage becomes $(cs, ds) = (♣, ♣)$, which means that the dummy storage is overwritten by the Bob's bit since $a_0 = b_0$. Then, Bob send it to Alice in step in (2-iv). In step (2-v), Alice sets $(cs, ds) := (♣, ♣)$ due to (10) for the storage sent from Bob.

Next, consider the case of $i = 2$: If Alice selects $w = l$ in step (2-i), she generates $(\sigma_l, \sigma_r) = (cs, ds) = (♣, ♣)$ from (8), and sends it with $\alpha_{2,l} = ♣$ to Bob in step (2-ii). Then, Bob compares $\beta_{2,l} = ♡$ with $\alpha_{2,l} = ♣$ in step (2-iii). Since $\beta_{2,l} \neq \alpha_{2,l}$, he generates $(\sigma'_l, \sigma'_r) = (\beta_{2,l}, \sigma_r) = (♡, ♣)$ by overwriting the *left* element of $(\sigma_l, \sigma_r) = (♣, ♣)$ with $\beta_{2,l} = ♡$ *privately* according to (9). Bob sends $(\sigma'_l, \sigma'_r) = (♡, ♣)$ to Alice, and she obtains $(cs, ds) := (♡, ♣)$ due to (10). Similar argument holds when Alice selects $w = r$, which is omitted here.

Finally, the output value correctly becomes $cs = ♡$ as $a < b$ regardless of random choices of Alice.

Efficiency of the proposed protocol II. This protocol requires two communications for every bit therefore it requires $2\lceil \log m \rceil$ communications. We note that the sequence of PPs executed in steps (2-iii) and (2-iv) can be regarded as one PP. Similarly, steps (2-v) and (2-i), when i is incremented, can also be regarded as one PP. Hence, this protocol requires $2\lceil \log m \rceil$ PPs. The number of cards is $4\lceil \log m \rceil + 2$.

Theorem 2. *The proposed protocol II is perfectly secure; it satisfies* (5) *in Definition 1.*

Proof. First, consider the randomness used by Alice and Bob denoted by R_A and R_B, respectively. From step (2-i), the value of R_A is the choice of w which is randomly selected from $\{l, r\}$ with a probability of $1/2$. Hence, R_A can obviously be simulated by S_A by using n independent uniform binary numbers. Similar to proposed protocol I, Bob does not use any randomness, and hence, S_A does not have to simulate R_B.

Then, considering the simulation of public information Λ which corresponds the face-up cards in step (2-iii), it is easy to see that Alice can generate λ by using a, i.e., her $2n$ cards, and the selection w. Hence, Λ is easily simulated by S_A. For Bob, $\alpha_{i,w}$ seems to be uniform over $\{\heartsuit, \clubsuit\}$ since he does not know the value of w selected randomly by Alice.

Therefore, simulators S_A and S_B exist, which completes the proof. $\square$

5   Concluding Remarks

In this paper, we proposed two efficient card-based cryptographic protocols (called proposed protocols I and II) for the millionaires' problem by introducing a new operation called *private permutation* (PP). Proposed protocol I is constructed based on Yao's solution. This solution was realized by using public key encryption instead of logical gates, and hence, it could not be straightforwardly implemented to card-based cryptographic protocols based on logical gates. However, we show that Yao's solution can be easily implemented by using cards if we do not restrict ourselves by logical gates and use PPs instead. This protocol could be realized with one communication and two PPs, and is therefore much more effective than the existing protocol (see Table 1). However, the number of cards increases. It is worth mentioning that proposed protocol I is not only a direct transformation of Yao's protocol, but is also superior to the original protocol in the sense that randomness and the announcement of the result are not required as opposed to Yao's original protocol.

Proposed protocol II is entirely novel. It constitutes the communication of two types of storage for recording the compared result between two players. This proposed protocol is superior to the existing protocol based on logical gates with respect to the number of communications and PPs, whereas the number of cards is the same as the existing protocol. Furthermore, it is interesting to remark that proposed protocol II and the well-known logical puzzle known as "The Fork in the Road," are deeply related.

In the following, we briefly mention that proposed protocol II can be improved in two directions. Due to space limitations, the detailed explanation will appear at in the full version of the paper.

The first direction of improvement is the following: According to Table 1, proposed protocol II has not improved in terms of the number of cards. Hence, the first improvement is that proposed protocol II can be realized with only six cards. Our idea is that we do not need to represent the input as binary numbers by using $2\lceil \log m \rceil$ cards, but that it is sufficient to remember the input *in the player's mind*. Then, two cards are sufficient to represent the player's input since these two cards can be *reused*.

The second improvement is as follows: Proposed protocol II cannot be used for composing the other protocol[11] since each player is required to know his/her inputs. In order to resolve this, we can use an improved technique called *selection and substitution protocols* inspired by 6-card AND protocol [9]. Introducing this idea enables us to propose the card-based millionaires' problem while concealing the input and the output where the number of communications and PPs are almost 1/2 compared to the card-based cryptographic protocol for the millionaires' problem based on logical gates.

Acknowledgement. We are grateful to the anonymous reviewers for their careful reading of our manuscript and their insightful comments, which greatly improved the paper. This work was supported by JSPS KAKENHI Grant Numbers JP15H02710 and JP26420345.

References

1. Yao, A.: Protocols for secure computations. In: IEEE Symposium on FOCS, vol. 23, pp. 160–164. IEEE (1982)
2. Boer, B.: More efficient match-making and satisfiability The Five Card Trick. In: Quisquater, J.-J., Vandewalle, J. (eds.) EUROCRYPT 1989. LNCS, vol. 434, pp. 208–217. Springer, Heidelberg (1990). doi:10.1007/3-540-46885-4_23
3. Canetti, R.: Security and composition of multiparty cryptographic protocols. J. of Cryptology **13**, 143–202 (2000)
4. Cramer, R., Dåmgard, I., Nielsen, J.B.: Secure Multiparty Computation and Secret Sharing. Cambridge University Press, Cambridge (2015)
5. Crépeau, C., Kilian, J.: Discreet solitary games. In: Stinson, D.R. (ed.) CRYPTO 1993. LNCS, vol. 773, pp. 319–330. Springer, Heidelberg (1994). doi:10.1007/3-540-48329-2_27
6. Gardner, M.: Hexaflexagons and Other Mathematical Diversions: The First Scientific American Book of Puzzles and Games. University of Chicago Press, Chicago (1956)
7. Koch, A., Walzer, S., Härtel, K.: Card-based cryptographic protocols using a minimal number of cards. In: Iwata, T., Cheon, J.H. (eds.) ASIACRYPT 2015. LNCS, vol. 9452, pp. 783–807. Springer, Heidelberg (2015). doi:10.1007/978-3-662-48797-6_32
8. Mizuki, T., Shizuya, H.: A formalization of card-based cryptographic protocols via abstract machine. Int. J. Inf. Secur. **13**(1), 15–23 (2014)
9. Mizuki, T., Sone, H.: Six-card secure AND and four-card secure XOR. In: Deng, X., Hopcroft, J.E., Xue, J. (eds.) FAW 2009. LNCS, vol. 5598, pp. 358–369. Springer, Heidelberg (2009). doi:10.1007/978-3-642-02270-8_36

---

[11] Note that the term "composing" used here does not imply *composable security* [3].

10. Niemi, V., Renvall, A.: Secure multiparty computations without computer. Theoret. Comput. Sci. **191**(1, 2), 173–183 (1998)
11. Shinagawa, K., Mizuki, T., Schuldt, J.C.N., Nuida, K., Kanayama, N., Nishide, T., Hanaoka, G., Okamoto, E.: Multi-party computation with small shuffle complexity using regular polygon cards. In: Au, M.-H., Miyaji, A. (eds.) ProvSec 2015. LNCS, vol. 9451, pp. 127–146. Springer, Heidelberg (2015). doi:10.1007/978-3-319-26059-4_7

Malware and Attacks

Evaluation on Malware Classification by Session Sequence of Common Protocols

Shohei Hiruta[1]([⊠]), Yukiko Yamaguchi[2], Hajime Shimada[2], Hiroki Takakura[3], Takeshi Yagi[4], and Mitsuaki Akiyama[4]

[1] Graduate School of Information Science, Nagoya University, Nagoya, Aichi, Japan
hiruta@net.itc.nagoya-u.ac.jp
[2] Information Technology Center, Nagoya University, Nagoya, Aichi, Japan
{yamaguchi,shimada}@itc.nagoya-u.ac.jp
[3] National Institute of Informatics, Chiyoda-ku, Tokyo, Japan
takakura@nii.ac.jp
[4] NTT Secure Platform Laboratories, Musashino, Tokyo, Japan
{yagi.takeshi,akiyama.mitsuaki}@lab.ntt.co.jp

Abstract. Recent malware is becoming sophisticated year by year. It often uses common protocols like HTTP to imitate normal communications. So, we have to consider activities in common protocols when we analyze malware. Meanwhile, the number of malware analysts is insufficient compared to new malware generation speed. To solve this problem, there is expectation to a malware classification method which classifies huge number malware with quickness and accurate. With this method, malware analysts can dedicate to the investigation of new types of malware. In this paper, we propose a malware classification method using Session Sequence of common protocols which classifies malware into new or existing one. Furthermore, if the malware is classified as existing malware, the proposed method also classifies it into existing malware families. We evaluated our proposed method with traffics of 502 malware samples. The experimental results shows that our method can correctly judge and classify in 84.5 % accuracy.

Keywords: Malware classification · Traffic analysis · Similarity calculation

1 Introduction

Recently, increasing of cyber attacks has been a serious social problem. Typical cyber attacks effectively use various malware because the expansion of the black market makes attackers get the source code of the malware. Therefore, to evade the detection by antivirus software, attackers can easily generate various malware by modifying a part of the code or combining multiple malware codes. In addition, the infection technique has been sophisticated year by year (e.g. targeted email attacks, watering holing, and so on) so that it is difficult to completely prevent the malware infection. So, we have to consider an effective countermeasures under an assumption that the malware has already intruded [1,2].

© Springer International Publishing AG 2016
S. Foresti and G. Persiano (Eds.): CANS 2016, LNCS 10052, pp. 521–531, 2016.
DOI: 10.1007/978-3-319-48965-0_31

To consider the malware analysis as countermeasures, it is important to estimate the behavior, purpose, and impact of malware activity. First, current malware commonly applies obfuscation and encryption. Second, current malware changes its activities based on infected terminal environment. As an alternative malware detection approach, there is a method which analyzes malware specific communication traffics such as IRC based C&C (Command and Control) communications. But the latest malware widely utilizes well used protocols. For example, one malware performs C&C communications with DNS queries. On the other hand, the number of malware analysts is insufficient absolutely and it is hard to deal with current large number of various malware with manual analysis. To solve this problem, we have to prepare a system to classify a large number of malware with quickness and accuracy.

In this paper, we propose a malware classification method using Session Sequence of common protocols such as HTTP, HTTPS, DNS, and so on. The procedure of the proposed method is as follows. First, we extract different features from individual protocols from malware traffics. Second, we represent malware traffics as a series of string named Session Sequence. Third, we calculate similarities of Session Sequence to make it possible to judge whether a malware is new malware or existing malware. Finally, we classify malware that is judged existing into proper malware families.

2   Related Works

As a malware classification method, dynamic analysis is often used. Dynamic analysis is divided into system behavior based one and network behavior based one. Recently, classification methods using network behavior of malware are receiving a lot of attention. Perdisci et al. proposed malware clustering system by extracting HTTP traffic traces and analyzing their similarity [3]. This system detects malware using signature by the result of clusters generated from HTTP payload. However, this system cannot detect malware that uses HTTPS. Morales et al. analyzed network behavior of malware [4]. They focused on behavior of DNS, NetBIOS, TCP, UDP, and ICMP protocols. Rafique et al. proposed algorithms which classifies malware families by modeling their different network behaviors on HTTP, SMTP, UDP, and TCP [5]. Both of them extract different features from different protocols. However, they did not consider the time sequences of malware traffics.

Lim et al. proposed a malware classification method based on traffic flow of malware [6]. They extracted features from not only from protocols ARP, RARP, IGMP, TCP, and UDP but also the other network layer such as IP address, port number, and so on. They used traffic flows with arranging these features in time sequences for classification of malware. As a method which combines dynamic and static analysis, we proposed a malware classification method based on cluster sequences and fuzzy hashing result of malware binaries [7]. We extracted per-packet features from malware traffics, service port number, packet length and communication protocol. Both of them classified malware by arranging features in time sequences. However, they used the same features from different protocols. It is causing a decrease in accuracy rate.

To achieve high classification accuracy, we utilize information of different features for individual protocols and features of time sequences, and proposed a method to classify new malware to new malware class.

3   Proposed Method

3.1   Overview

We propose a method which uses Session Sequence of common protocols to classify sophisticated malware. To achieve high classification accuracy, we add new features which is described in Sect. 3.2.

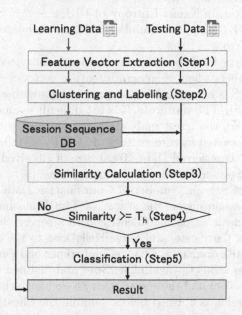

Fig. 1. Overview of proposed method

Figure 1 shows a flow of the proposed method. We apply feature vector extraction, clustering and labeling to learning data, and stores result to Session Sequence DB. We also apply feature vector extraction, clustering, labeling to testing data. The detail of procedure in the figure is described in the following sections.

3.2   Feature Vector Extraction (Step 1)

We excepted that network traffic features contain beneficial information for malware classification. We estimated that similar malware generates partially similar traffics because malware with same purpose is usually generated by same tool. It is also important to extract different feature vectors for individual protocols because the latest malware communicates with multiple protocols. In addition to ICMP, TCP, and UDP which is used in previous researches, we extracted independent feature vectors from HTTP(80/TCP), HTTPS(443/TCP), SMTP(25/TCP), DNS(53/UDP), and SSDP(1900/UDP) because they are communication protocols which are largely related to malware activities.

HTTP. Recent malware often communicates with HTTP to camouflage as normal communication. Thus, we generated feature vectors of HTTP as follows:

Total Size of Transferred Data, Total Size of Received Data,
Duration of Session, Type of Traffic Data,
Entropy of Domain Name, Entropy of URI,
Number of GET Requests, Number of POST Requests,
Number of Errors

We used MIME type for Type of Traffic Data. We converted individual MIME types to the numbers when we generate feature vectors.

HTTPS. HTTPS is a protocol for communicating with encrypted messages of HTTP using SSL/TLS protocols. It is too difficult to analyze the encrypted communication. So, the latest malware communicates with HTTPS instead of HTTP. We generated feature vectors of HTTPS as follows:

Total Size of Transferred Data, Total Size of Received Data,
Duration of Session, Entropy of Domain Name,
Exit Status of Session, Number of Continuation Data

Exit Status of Session means the status of TLS Handshake. In TLS Handshake, firstly, a client sends the ClientHello to a server. Secondly, the server sends ServerHello, Certificate, and ServerHelloDone to the client. Thirdly, the client sends ClientKeyExchange, ChangeChipherSpec and Finished to the server. Finally, the server sends ChangeChipherSpec and Finished to the client. After this process, the client and the server start to exchange their data. In feature vectors, if the session is finished before sending the ClientHello, we gave 0 to Exit Status of Session. If the session is completed all of this process, we gave 5 to Exit Status of Session.

SMTP. SMTP is often used by malware which sends spam mails. We generated feature vectors of SMTP as follows:

Total Size of Mails, Number of Mails, Number of Errors

TCP. Malware also uses other TCP protocols excluding listed in above ones. We treat them as TCP. We generated feature vectors of TCP as follows:

Total Size of Transferred Data, Total Size of Received Data,
Number of Transferred Data, Number of Received Data,
Duration of Session, Entropy of Domain Name

DNS. Recent attackers generate a large number of domain names using domain generation algorithm in order to avoid detection by the black lists. Thus, domain name which recent malware uses varies with time because they are generated with pseudorandom number. Also, malware performing C&C communication emerges DNS query to resolve FQDN. So, we thought that we can get specific features from DNS. We used three states by name resolution result, Successful Name Resolution, Unsuccessful Name Resolution, and Error.

SSDP. SSDP is a protocol which is used for searching and responding to UPnP devices on network. This protocol is often misused in DDoS attack. For SSDP, we assigned a single traffic label in Session Sequence.

UDP. Malware also uses other UDP protocols excluding listed in above ones. We treat them as UDP. We generated feature vectors of UDP, Total Size of Data, Traffic Direction.

ICMP. From [4], malware often communicates with ICMP. For ICMP, we assigned three states, Echo Message, Echo Reply Message, and Destination Unreachable Message.

3.3 Clustering and Labeling (Step 2)

First, feature vectors of learning data obtained by feature extraction are classified by k-means++ [8] for individual protocols, HTTP, HTTPS, SMTP, TCP, and UDP. k-means++ is a non-hierarchical clustering algorithm and it classifies given data into k clusters. After the cluster generation, we assign labels to each of them, convert learning data to Session Sequences and register them into Session Sequence DB. Other protocols, DNS, SSDP, and ICMP, are not clustered. We allocated label to individual states of them.

After Session Sequence generation from learning data, we can apply labeling to testing data. Firstly, feature vectors of testing data are assigned to the nearest clusters generated by learning data for individual protocols. After the assignment, we convert testing data to Session Sequences based on cluster labels. For DNS, SSDP, and ICMP, we apply the same processes as learning data.

Table 1. Examples of generated session sequence

Malware Family	Session Sequence
Win32/FiseriaInstaller 1	!*AI;;=^^^!f!2=f
Win32/FiseriaInstaller 2	!*A7;;=^^!f^=!3f
Win32/TrojanDownloader.Agent 1	!X!;X;X;X;
Win32/TrojanDownloader.Agent 2	!X!;X;X;X;

Table 1 shows Session Sequence of 4 malware traffics as examples. We assigned DNS to {!, ", #} and HTTP to {), *, ..., Z} in this example. From this example, it seems that malware can be classified based on them.

3.4   Similarity Calculation (Step 3)

We calculate similarities between Session Sequences of individual learning data and testing data obtained in Sect. 3.3. Similarity R of Session Sequence s_1 and s_2 is calculated as follows:

$$R = \frac{c}{(t_1 + t_2) - c} \tag{1}$$

$$t_i = |s_i| + (n - 1) \tag{2}$$

Where t_i is the number of tokens given by n-gram of Session Sequence s_i. Tokens are $\{|\,|\text{h}, |\text{hi}, \text{hir}, \ldots, \text{al}|\}$ when a string "hiruta" is converted to tokens by 3-gram. c is the number of common tokens between s_1 and s_2. R becomes a value from 0.0 to 1.0.

3.5   New Malware Judgement (Step 4)

We expected that the malware may contain some characteristic seen in Session Sequences of past malware even if it is quite new one. However, several new functions that is adopted by the new malware affect the similarity calculation with the past one. So, from the results of the similarity calculation, we judge whether the malware is new malware or existing malware based on the threshold T_h. If the similarity R is smaller than T_h, the malware is judged as new malware. If the R is lager than T_h, the malware is judged as existing malware and go to the next step.

3.6   Classification (Step 5)

If the malware that is judged as existing malware in Sect. 3.5, it is classified into proper malware families in this step. We classify the malware into families that the malware shows the highest similarity. If there are multiple malware families that the malware shows the highest similarity, all of them becomes the classification results.

4   Evaluation

4.1   Experimental Data

We used 502 malware samples as experimental data which are collected from November 2013 to October 2014. The traffic data is obtained by executing the malware samples with the sandbox [9]. We sorted the 502 malware samples in date order. Then, we divided them into 238 learning data (older ones in timeline) and 264 testing data (latter ones in timeline). The learning data were classified into 28 families and the testing data were classified into 23 families by ESET-NOD32. 10 families are included in both learning and testing data.

If several samples have the same feature values, the clustering assigns them to one cluster. From the point of performance view, our method threats them as one sample. Then we generated clusters by k-means++ for individual protocols, HTTP, HTTPS, SMTP, TCP, and UDP. Table 2 shows the determined k and the number of features. We determined the k value by varying k value from 3 to 100 and obtained k value which shows the best result.

Table 2. Number of generated clusters

Protocol	HTTP	HTTPS	SMTP	TCP	UDP
k	50	3	3	5	5
Number of features	3879	144	44	444	251

We also determined the parameters same way. We obtained 3 for n of n-gram and 0.75 for threshold T_h. We used five criteria for performance evaluation, such as $Accuracy$, $Precision_{new}$, $Recall_{new}$, $Precision_{existing}$ and $Recall_{existing}$. These values are calculated by $TruePositive(TP)$, $FalsePositive(FP)$, $FalseNegative(FN)$ and $TrueNegative(TN)$ which defined as shown in Table 3.

Table 3. Definition of TP, FP, FN and TN

Result Correct	New ($R < T_h$)	Existing ($R >= T_h$)	
New	TP	FN	
Existing	FP	TN	
		Correct	Incorrect

The formulas for the five values are as follows:

$$Accuracy = \frac{TP + TN}{TP + FP + FN + TN} \tag{3}$$

$$Precision_{new} = \frac{TP}{TP + FP} \tag{4}$$

$$Recall_{new} = \frac{TP}{TP + FN} \tag{5}$$

$$Precision_{existing} = \frac{TN}{FN + TN} \tag{6}$$

$$Recall_{existing} = \frac{TN}{FP + TN} \tag{7}$$

We also use $Classification Accuracy$ (CA) for criterion. CA represents the classification accuracy of existing malware to existing malware class. The formula is as follows:

$$CA = \frac{Correct}{FP + TN} \tag{8}$$

We determined new malware and existing malware as follows. As denoted above, we sorted all malware in date order of collected day. If the malware detection name on ESET-NOD32 did not exist when we collected the malware, we regarded the malware as a new malware because we have to determine it with information in that day in practical operation. If the malware detection name existed when we collected, we regarded it as a existing malware. As a result, 149 malware samples were rated as new and 115 malware samples were rated as existing in 264 testing data.

4.2   Results

Table 4 shows the detailed classification results by the proposed method. As calculated from Table 4, the proposed method achieves 72.7 % $Accuracy$, 71.5 % $Precision_{new}$, and 86.0 % $Recall_{new}$, 75.3 % $Precision_{existing}$, and 55.7 % $Recall_{existing}$, respectively. From above the result, to reduce FN result, our proposed method has to sacrifice some FP result even if we tuned parameter so that $Recall_{existing}$ result becomes slightly worse. Also, the 60 malware samples are classified correctly and achieves 52.2 % CA. This result also comes from poor FP result.

Table 4. Detailed classification results using malware family names granularity

Result	New ($R < T_h$)	Existing ($R >= T_h$)		Total
Correct				
New	128		21	149
Existing	51		64	115
		60	4	
Total	179		85	264

Table 5 shows the execution times of individual steps when we examined 238 learning and 264 testing. The execution times are the average of 10 executions. Table 6 shows the data amount of learning and testing data. Execution environment is as follows:

- OS: Ubuntu 14.04
- CPU: Intel(R) Core(TM) i7-4770 CPU @ 3.40 GHz
- Memory: 2.0 GB

As shown from Tables 5 and 6, the total time to judge and classify the 264 testing data is about 39.9 s. So, the proposed method can judge and classify malware in real-time.

Table 5. Average execution time of each step

Time [sec] Step	Learning	Testing
Step 1	12.2	31.8
Step 2	0.3	0.13
Step 3	-	8.0

Table 6. PCAP size and the number of sessions and features

	Learning	Testing
PCAP Size [GB]	0.14	0.61
Number of Sessions	35,494	20,001
Number of Features	4,762	5,183

4.3 Consideration

In Sect. 4.2, we used only malware family names and did not consider variant names. However, there is a possibility that the proposed method regards the new variant malware as a new malware if it changes its characteristic drastically. In this case, the proposed method classifies those type of variant malware to a new malware so that it increases FP rate. For example, there are Win32/FiseriaInstaller.L in learning data and Win32/FiseriaInstaller.H in testing data. The similarity between them is low so that Win32/FiseriaInstaller.H is judged as a new malware in testing and the result is treated as FP. Therefore, we also experimented based variant names of malware. Under this condition, Win32/FiseriaInstaller.H is treated as a new malware so that the result in above example is treated as TP.

The malware used in the experiment was the same in Sect. 4.1. On the other hand, the 238 learning data were classified into 35 types of variants and the 264 testing data were classified into 31 types of variants. 8 types of variants are included in both learning and testing data. Also, 188 malware samples were treated as new and 76 malware samples were treated as existing in testing data.

Table 7 shows the detailed classification results based variant names of malware. The notation of the table is identical to Table 4.

Table 7. Detailed classification results using malware variant names

Result Correct	New ($R < T_h$)	Existing ($R >= T_h$)		Total
New	163	25		188
Existing	16	60		76
		60	0	
Total	179	85		264

As shown in Table 7, the proposed method achieved 84.5 % $Accuracy$, 91.1 % $Precision_{new}$, 86.7 % $Recall_{new}$, 70.6 % $Precision_{existing}$, and 78.9 % $Recall_{existing}$, respectively. Also, the number of the malware classified correctly was 60 so that CA becomes 78.9 %. Almost of them have improved from the value in Table 4 excluding $Presicion_{existing}$. Especially, $Precision_{new}$ and $Recall_{new}$ are improved dramatically. As a result, 91.1 % of malware which is rated as new malware is really new malware and 86.7 % of new malware could be correctly judged. In Table 4, 128 malware samples were correctly judged as new malware by using malware family names but 163 malware samples were correctly judged as new malware using malware variant names. So, we can find that 35 malware samples were new variant malware in testing data. From above results, the proposed method is further useful under fine grained malware classification because it can classify the malware into not only new malware family but also new variant in a family.

5   Conclusion and Future Works

In this paper, we proposed malware classification method using Session Sequence of common protocols because current malware widely utilize common protocols to imitate normal traffic. As a common protocol, we used HTTP, HTTPS, SMTP, TCP, DNS, SSDP, UDP, and ICMP for feature extraction.

We evaluated our method with traffics of 502 malware samples which are separated into 238 learning data and 264 testing data. The results show that we achieved 84.5 % $Accuracy$. Also, this method can judge and classify 264 malware about 39.9 sec which is enough speed for real-time classification. However, this method could not classify malware that has exactly the same Session Sequences. We consider that we have to use the other feature to classify such malware, but it sometimes requires additional costs.

As our future works, first, we will apply the our proposed method to much more malware and evaluate the performances. Second, we will refine the extracting feature vectors, especially HTTP, because feature vectors of HTTP often belonged same clusters even though they were different values. Finally, we will improve clustering algorithm such as x-means or DBSCAN which are determine by automatic the optimal number of clusters because it takes some time to determine them by manually.

References

1. Information-technology Promotion Agency: Design and operational guide to protect against advanced persistent threats, 2nd edn. (2011). https://www.ipa.go.jp/files/000017299.pdf
2. Cichonski, P., Millar, T., Grance, T., Scarfone, K.: Computer security incident handling guide. Technical report, SP 800-61 Rev. 2, Gaithersburg (2012)
3. Perdisci, R., Lee, W., Feamster, N.: Behavioral clustering of HTTP-based malware and signature generation using malicious network traces. In: USENIX Symposium on Networked Systems Design and Implementation, NSDI, San Jose (2010)
4. Morales, J.A., Al-Bataineh, A., Xu, S., Sandhu, R.: Analyzing and exploiting network behaviors of malware. In: Jajodia, S., Zhou, J. (eds.) SecureComm 2010. LNICST, vol. 50, pp. 20–34. Springer, Heidelberg (2010)

5. Rafique, Z.M., Chen, P., Hyugens, C., Joosen, W.: Evolutionary algorithms for classification of malware families through different network behaviors. In: Proceedings of the 2014 Conference on Genetic and Evolutionary Computation, pp. 1167–1174. ACM, Vancouver (2014)

6. Lim, H., Yamaguchi, Y., Shimada, H , Takakura, H,: Malware classification method based on sequence of traffic flow. In: Proceedings of 1st International Conference on Information Systems Security and Privacy, Angers, pp. 230–237 (2015)

7. Hiruta, S., Yamaguchi, Y., Shimada, H., Takakura, H.: Evaluation on malware classification by combining traffic analysis and fuzzy hashing of malware binary. In: Proceedings of the 2015 International Conference on Security and Management, Las Vegas, pp. 89–95 (2015)

8. Arthur, D., Vassilvitskii, S.: k-means++: the Advantages of careful seeding. In: SODA 2007 Proceeding of the Eigtheenth Annual ACM-SIAM Symposium on Discrete Algorithms, New Orleans, pp. 1027–1035 (2007)

9. Aoki, K., Yagi, T., Iwamura, M., Itoh, M.: Controlling malware HTTP communications in dynamic analysis system using search engine. In: The 3rd International Workshop on Cyberspace Safety and Security, Milan (2011)

An Efficient Approach to Detect TorrentLocker Ransomware in Computer Systems

Faustin Mbol, Jean-Marc Robert[(⊠)], and Alireza Sadighian

École de technologie supérieure (ETS), Montréal, Canada
jean-marc.robert@etsmtl.ca

Abstract. TorrentLocker is a ransomware that encrypts sensitive data located on infected computer systems. Its creators aim to ransom the victims, if they want to retrieve their data. Unfortunately, antiviruses have difficulties to detect such polymorphic malware. In this paper, we propose a novel approach to detect online suspicious processes accessing a large number of files and encrypting them. Such a behavior corresponds to the classical scenario of a malicious ransomware. We show that the *Kullback-Liebler divergence* can be used to detect with high effectiveness whether a process transforms structured input files (such as JPEG files) into unstructured encrypted files, or not. We focus mainly on JPEG files since irreplaceable pictures represent in many cases the most valuable data on personal computers or smartphones.

1 Introduction

Scareware are designed to frighten users and force them to quickly purchase software to protect their private data or prevent irreversible hardware damages [9]. A particular class of scareware encrypts the data of infected systems, and asks their user to pay a ransom (usually, in Bitcoins) to re-gain access to their data. These malware, known as *ransomware*, follow usually three phases [8]: (1) Seek a new target; (2) Prevent legitimate access to local information; and (3) Display ransom message and try to extort some money.

Even if cryptoviruses encrypting the data of infected systems have been conceptualized twenty years ago [21], the number of ransomware attacks has only dramatically increased in the recent years. Around four million ransomware samples have been identified in 2015 indicating an upward trend, since fewer than 1.5 millions were analyzed two years before [7]. For example, *Cryptolocker* has supposedly infected approximately 250 thousands computer systems around the world [10]. Some analysts have estimated that may have brought in millions to its creators. Naturally, such an assertion is hard to verify. *TorrentLocker* [14] is another example that currently gains in popularity. Once TorrentLocker has infected a system, it encrypts the first two megabytes of all the existing files found on that system. Encrypting partially the files is sufficient to conceal the information and is more efficient for the malware.

Considering the increasing number of ransomware attacks, proposing novel detection mechanisms is more crucial than ever. Traditionally, malware detection

© Springer International Publishing AG 2016
S. Foresti and G. Persiano (Eds.): CANS 2016, LNCS 10052, pp. 532–541, 2016.
DOI: 10.1007/978-3-319-48965-0_32

solutions are either based on static analyses such as classical signature databases, or based on dynamic anomaly-based approaches [4]. The latter solutions are the only ones that can cope with polymorphic malware as TorrentLocker or *zero-day* malware.

Many recent security reports (e.g., [1,12]) focus on the advancements of ransomware attacks and their level of sophistication instead of providing some insights about effective defense solutions. Our work proposes a novel approach to detect an abnormal behavior which is typically attributed to ransomware. This solution is relatively simple to implement and requires only few resources.

Our main contribution presents a solution to identify processes encrypting large numbers of structured files with high entropy (such as JPEG files). We propose to use the *Kullback-Liebler divergence* measure to detect processes which read structured files with high entropy and overwrite them with unstructured encrypted files. Detecting the encryption of low entropy files is relatively simple, since the encryption process would increase the entropy of the resulting files drastically.

In this paper, we mainly focus on JPEG files, since they represent in many cases the most valuable data that a user has on his/her personal computer or smartphone. People may have tens of thousands of pictures on their systems. They represent usually priceless souvenirs, which cannot be retrieved otherwise (if proper back-ups have not been done). Therefore, the goal is to detect the effect of file-encrypting ransomware as soon as possible to prevent that too many files are *lost*. On the other hand, detecting the transformation of JPEG files is relatively challenging due to their internal structure. They are composed of large compressed blocks, which have high entropy (as if they were encrypted).

2 File Differentiation Measures

Two differentiation measures can be naturally used to distinguish between different types of files. The first one is the classical *Shannon entropy* of the probability distribution of a random variable, which measures the uncertainty or variability associated with the variable [6].

Definition 1. *The entropy of a discrete random variable X from a sample space $\Omega = \{x_1, x_2, \cdots, x_n\}$, with its probability distribution p is defined as:*

$$H(X) = - \sum_{i=1}^{n} \mathsf{p}(x_i) \log \mathsf{p}(x_i) \tag{1}$$

The larger $H(X)$ is, the more unpredictable the outcome of X is. The maximal value of the entropy is $\log n$. This corresponds to the case where values are uniformly distributed over the sample space. Shannon entropy has been employed in the past to detect various types of malware [2,16,20].

The second one is the *Kullback-Leibler (KBL) divergence* [6], also known as the *relative entropy*, which determines the distance between two probability distributions on a random variable.

Definition 2. *Given two probability distributions* p *and* q *over a discrete random variable* X *from a sample space* $\Omega = \{x_1, x_2, \cdots, x_n\}$, *the KBL divergence or relative entropy* $D(p \parallel q)$ *is defined as follows:*

$$D(p \parallel q) = \sum_{i=1}^{n} \log \left(\frac{p(x_i)}{q(x_i)} \right) * p(x_i) \tag{2}$$

This value is null if and only if both probability distributions are equal. This criterion has been also used in the past to detect various types of malware [5,11].

In order to define the sample spaces of the selected criteria, the files can be simply seen as streams of N-grams. For $N = 1$, the files are interpreted as 8-bit characters. Similarly, for $N = 2$, the files are interpreted as 16-bit characters. In this latter case, the 2-grams can either overlap or not. The former one has been chosen to avoid any alignment issue. Notice that it is not useful to consider higher values of N. For example, if $N = 3$, the sample space would be composed of 2^{24} elements. Since JPEG files are usually composed of about 2^{24} bytes, the probability distribution p would be defined by few elements for each value of x_i.

3   Related Work

Nowadays, ransomware protection is a security challenge attracting many researchers. A summary of recent work is presented in this section.

Gazet [8] proposed an analysis of three ransomware families based on their code quality, functionality, and cryptographic primitives. They showed that these ransomware succeeded for massive propagation but not for mass extortion. In a similar way, Kharraz *et al.* [12] analyzed 1,359 ransomware samples categorized into fifteen different ransomware families. They showed that a large number of existing ransomware are not as complex as reported. They mostly use superficial techniques to lock the victim systems or encrypt their files. Cabaj *et al.* [3] analyzed the network behavior of CryptoWall using an honeypot and an automatic malware analysis system. Kim *et al.* [13] proposed a model based on social engineering techniques to detect Cryptolocker ransomware. Finally, Léveillé [14] analyzed in detail the functionality and characteristics of TorrentLocker.

Mobile phones ransomware is another area investigated by researchers. Mercaldo *et al.* [15] proposed a model checking approach to detect Android ransomware. In this work, they have mainly used formal models to detect ransomware with high efficiency. Andronio *et al.* [1] developed a proactive ransomware detection approach based on machine learning techniques. It includes a text classifier to identify the threatening messages, an emulator to detect locking strategies, and the application tracking to detect encryption flows. Finally, Song *et al.* [19] proposed to monitor processes and file directories using statistical methods based on processor and memory usage, and I/O rates.

Differentiation criteria, such as Shannon entropy [6] and Kullback-Liebler divergence [6] have been used to detect various malware. Perdisci *et al.* [16] presented an efficient approach to detect packed executables used by virus developers. They used Shannon entropy to identify these malicious codes.

Cooper *et al.* [5] employed the Kullback-Liebler divergence to differentiate between legitimate and malicious application behaviors at the source code level in Android systems. They showed that the divergence between malicious and legitimate applications can be significantly high even if they have similar behavior.

Very recently, Scaife *et al.* [18] presented CryptoLock, which has the same goal as our solution. In fact, this is the most relevant work to be compared with. They proposed to identify ransomware by detecting processes that (1) read large number of files and (2) overwrite them with altered files (most likely, encrypted). Their solution is mainly based on file fingerprinting [17] that represents a significant burden on the solution. It selects statistically improbable features (with respect to the Shannon entropy) of a file and hashes them into a Bloom filter. Each insertion into the table requires the computation of a hashing function (e.g., SHA-1). Two given files are similar if and only if the two corresponding Bloom filters are similar (i.e., have almost the same bits set to one). Hence, CryptoLock identifies a ransomware according to three primary criteria (file special number, file fingerprinting, and Shannon entropy) and two secondary criteria (file deletion, and file funnelling – reading a large number of unrelated files). Notice that the three primary criteria have to be present to declare that a process is a ransomware. This means that the process under surveillance should transform the resulting output files significantly with respect to the input files, *and* these output files should have high entropy.

In summary, no definite solution to detect or react to file-encrypting ransomware exists yet. Motivated by this fact, we propose a novel approach to detect file-encrypting ransomware such as TorrentLocker based on their inherent behavior, which transforms large numbers of files in a short period of time.

4   The Proposed Approach to Detect TorrentLocker

When a system is infected, TorrentLocker launches a large number of processes to encrypt the files in parallel. A naïve approach to reveal this infection would simply be to detect processes showing some *abnormal behavior* such as (1) opening a large number of files or, more specifically, (2) opening a large number of JPEG files (which leaves the other files unprotected). Unfortunately, such a behavior can be observed for legitimate applications such as *iPhoto* or *PhotoFinder*.

We therefore propose to diagnose a potential TorrentLocker (or, in fact, any file-encrypting ransomware) infection by detecting the following behavior:

Abnormal Behavior. *A process has an* abnormal behavior *if (1) it opens a large number of files and (2) the structure of the input stream is different from the structure of the output stream.*

The latter criterion of the behavior is rather vague. The objective is to find a simple criterion to distinguish between JPEG files and encrypted files. Notice that most parts of the JPEG files are close to encrypted/compressed data. If we can differentiate between these two cases, it should be simpler to differentiate between highly structured text files or Word files, and encrypted files. In the next sections, two such criteria are considered: *Shannon entropy* and *Kullback-Lieber divergence.*

4.1 Shannon Entropy to Distinguish Files

To evaluate the usefulness of the Shannon entropy to distinguish between raw JPEG files and encrypted JPEG files, an experiment has been done on a data set composed of 150 JPEG files. These files were independently encrypted using the AES-256 encryption algorithm in CBC mode.

Table 1. Comparing entropy values of JPEG files and encrypted files for N-grams

Block size	$N = 1$	$N = 2$
Encrypted files	7.9998	15.9545
JPEG files	7.9684	15.7201

Table 1 compares the average values of the Shannon entropy of the JPEG files and the encrypted JPEG files. Analyzing these results, we have to conclude that it would be difficult (almost impossible) to distinguish JPEG files from encrypted files using the Shannon entropy as differentiation criterion. The values are too close to each other. This may lead to a high rate of false positive detection (blocking a legitimate process) or a high rate of false negative detection (allowing a malicious ransomware to encrypt as many files as possible). Obviously, this latter option has the worst impact.

We should notice that this observation on the inappropriateness of Shannon entropy does not contradict the results presented by Scaife *et al.* [18]. CryptoLock uses the Shannon entropy simply to determine if the overwritten files have a high probability of being encrypted. If a legitimate process reads and overwrites JPEG files, CryptoLock would not flag this process as a potential ransomware even though the output files look like encrypted files due to their high entropy. The similarity function (*sdhash*) would represent the main criterion in this case. The input files and the corresponding output files should have a perfect similarity score, since the legitimate process does not alter the files.

Our objective is to replace the costly similarity function and find a criterion capturing the transformation made by malicious ransomware. In the following, we introduce another differentiation criteria, called Kulback-Liebler divergence.

4.2 Kullback-Liebler Divergence to Distinguish Files

The Kullback-Liebler divergence notion is the next obvious choice to distinguish between encrypted files and other types of files. An ideal encryption algorithm should produce encrypted files which look liked random files. Hence, the distributions of their N-grams should be close to the uniform distribution.

For our second experiment, we used a data set of 2000 JPEG files split into twelve categories, such as sport, animal, landscape, residential, space, etc. These files have been subsequently encrypted using the AES-256 encryption algorithm in CBC mode. Table 2 summarizes the results. For both sizes of the N-grams, the Kullback-Lieber divergence $D(\mathsf{p} \parallel \mathsf{q})$ can distinguish between JPEG files and encrypted files. The distribution of the N-grams q has been compared to the uniform distribution p.

Table 2. KBL divergence values of JPEG files for $N = 1$ and 2

File types	Block size	Minimum	Average	Maximum	Variance
JPEG	$N = 1$	0.007	0.0189	0.1456	1.0044e-04
	$N = 2$	0.0428	0.1737	0.2535	Negligible
Encrypted	$N = 1$	3.4939e-04	0.0013	0.0149	5.4710e-07
	$N = 2$	0.0078	0.1105	0.1497	0.0018

To analyze further the case of 1-grams, Fig. 1 presents the distribution of all the 2000 Kullback-Lieber divergence values for both the encrypted files and the JPEG files. It shows clearly that most of the values for the JPEG files are around 0.01 and for the encrypted files are around 0.001. It is important to develop an approach to differentiate these two types of files as accurate as possible, if we want to deploy it in some mass market products.

5   Evaluation

5.1   Choosing KBL Threshold Based on the Accuracy Rate

In order to efficiently distinguish JPEG files from encrypted files using Kullback-Liebler divergence, an appropriate threshold value τ should be determined. Thus, if the Kullback-Leiber divergence of a input stream is below the threshold τ, the corresponding file would be assumed to be an encrypted file. Unfortunately, some files would be misclassified by this detection mechanism. The effectiveness of this approach can be evaluated with the *accuracy* equation:

$$\mathcal{A} = \frac{TP + TN}{TP + TN + FP + FN} \tag{3}$$

where a True Positive (TP) is an image detected as an image, a False Negative (FN) is an image detected as an encrypted file, a True Negative (TN) is an encrypted file detected as an encrypted file, and, finally, a False Positive (FP) is an encrypted file detected as an image.

Table 3 lists some threshold values and corresponding results of our tests. From the results, we can conclude that it is sufficient to analyse the 1-grams of the input/output streams of any process to detect whether or not the process

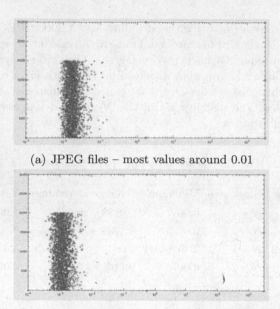

(a) JPEG files – most values around 0.01

(b) Encrypted JPEG files – most values around 0.001

Fig. 1. Clouds of points of the KBL divergence values for the 1-grams.

Table 3. Summary of the results obtained for different KBL thresholds

N = 1				N = 2			
Threshold	JPEG FN	Encrypted FP	$\mathcal{A}$	Threshold	JPEG FN	Encrypted FP	$\mathcal{A}$
0.005	0	5	99.88 %	0.14	24	68	90.1 %
0.007	0	1	99.98 %	0.15	32	0	96.4 %
0.009	27	1	99.3 %	0.16	41	0	95.4 %

encrypts its input files. The fact that 1-grams are sufficient would have a major impact on the performance of the detection mechanism. It would simply has to maintain a 256-position table to compute the divergence value for a given process.

5.2 Improving Effectiveness by Calculating KBL Values for First Kilobytes

TorrentLocker only encrypts the first two megabytes of the files. To provide a more efficient solution to detect TorrentLocker, we have calculated the Kullback-Liebler divergence values for the first 128, 256 and 512 KB of the files. Only 1000 files satisfy this size limit. Thus, we did the experiments with 1000 JPEG files and the corresponding encrypted files. Table 4 summarizes the results.

Considering a number of different thresholds, we obtained the results listed in Table 5 for the first 128, 256 and 512 KB. The results confirm that even by analyzing the first kilobytes of the files, we are able to differentiate JPEG files

Table 4. KBL divergence values of truncated JPEG files for $N = 1$ and 2

File types	Block size	Minimum	Average	Maximum	Variance
JPEG	$N = 1$	0.007	0.0189	0.1456	1.0044e-04
	$N = 2$	0.0428	0.1737	0.2535	Negligible
Encrypted	$N = 1$	3.4939e-04	0.0013	0.0149	5.4710e-07
	$N = 2$	0.0078	0.1105	0.1497	0.0018

from encrypted files. In fact, considering a threshold of 0.002, Kullback-Liebler divergence can distinguish JPEG files from encrypted files based only on the first 128, 256 and 512 KB with a detection rate 99.95 %.

Table 5. Detection rate considering only partial files

	128 Kb			256 Kb			512 Kb		
Threshold	JPEG FN	Encrypted FP	$\mathcal{A}$	JPEG FN	Encrypted FP	$\mathcal{A}$	JPEG FN	Encrypted FP	$\mathcal{A}$
0.0005	-	-	-	1	467	76 %	1	0	99.95 %
0.0010	1	474	76 %	1	0	99.95 %	1	0	99.95 %
0.0020	1	0	99.95 %	1	0	99.95 %	1	0	99.95 %
0.0060	3	0	99.85 %	3	0	99.85 %	2	0	99.85 %

6   Conclusions

In this paper, we propose an anomaly-based approach to detect file-encrypting ransomware such as TorrentLocker in computer systems.

As TorrentLocker encrypts all the files on the infected systems, one solution to detect its presence is to find processes encrypting a large number of files quickly. In order to detect encrypted files, we analyzed a number of criteria to differentiate normal files from encrypted files. We have focused on the JPEG files since they represent quite often the most valuable files on personal systems. On the other hand, since JPEG files are already compressed files and have high entropy, they represent a critical use case for any ransomware detection mechanism.

In our experiments, we used the Kullback-Liebler divergence to analyze a data set composed of 4000 files: 2000 JPEG and 2000 encrypted files using AES-256 algorithm in CBC mode. We have accomplished a series of tests to find the appropriate thresholds giving efficient detection rates. Our experiments show clearly that we can distinguish JPEG files form encrypted files with a high accuracy rate. This can be achieved efficiently by the analysis of the 1-grams of incoming and outgoing flows of a process with the Kullback-Liebler divergence.

Our proof-of-concept has been done offline. The next step is to implement this approach on a computer system monitoring online the processes running on a computer system. One way to do this is to develop a file system driver monitoring the behavior of the processes. As soon as a process seems to transform inappropriately its files, the system may chose to slow down the file interaction while asking to the user whether or not the process is legitimate. Some legitimate processes may present real challenges. For example, file compression tools may be particularly at risk. Thus, it may be important that the randomware detection solution includes a white-list for these legitimate processes.

Malware detection is an arms race between the malware designers and the anti-malware developers. One way to evade the solution proposed in this paper is to use an encryption algorithm preserving the distribution function p. Such an algorithm can be easily found. Any mono-alphabetic substitution would simply permute the values of incoming files. Such an encryption algorithm may be easily reversed. We leave this challenge for future works.

Acknowledgments. The authors would like to thank the anonymous referees who have pointed out the very recent and relevant paper on CryptoLock. The authors would like also to thank Marc-Étienne M. Léveillé, a malware researcher of ESET, who has provided an execution trace of TorrentLocker. This work is partially supported by Canada NSERC Discovery Grants.

References

1. Andronio, N., Zanero, S., Maggi, F.: HELDROID: dissecting and detecting mobile ransomware. In: Bos, H., Monrose, F., Blanc, G. (eds.) RAID 2015. LNCS, vol. 9404, pp. 382–404. Springer, Heidelberg (2015). doi:10.1007/978-3-319-26362-5_18
2. Arora, R., Singh, A., Pareek, H., Edara, U.R.: A heuristics-based static analysis approach for detecting packed PE binaries. Int. J. Secur. Appl. **7**(5), 257–268 (2013)
3. Cabaj, K., Gawkowski, P., Grochowski, K., Osojca, D.: Network activity analysis of cryptowall ransomware. Przeglad Elektrotechniczny **91**(11), 201–204 (2015)
4. Chandola, V., Banerjee, A., Kumar, V.: Anomaly detection: a survey. ACM Comput. Surv. **41**(3), 1–58 (2009)
5. Cooper, V.: Android malware detection based on kullback-leibler divergence. In: Proceedings of the 29th Annual ACM Symposium on Applied Computing - Student Research Abstract, pp. 1695–1696. ACM (2014)
6. Cover, T.M., Thomas, J.A.: Elements of Information Theory, 2nd edn. John Wiley & Sons, New York (2006)
7. Gamer, N.: Trend micro (2016). http://blog.trendmicro.com/ransomware-one-of-the-biggest-threats-in-2016/
8. Gazet, A.: Comparative analysis of various ransomware virii. J. Comput. Virol. **6**(1), 77–90 (2010)
9. Giles, J.: Scareware: the inside story. New Sci. **205**(2753), 38–41 (2010)
10. Jarvis, K.: Cryptolocker ransomware (2014). http://www.secureworks.com/cyber-threat-intelligence/threats/cryptolocker-ransomware/
11. Khan, H., Mirza, F., Khayam, S.A.: Determining malicious executable distinguishing attributes and low-complexity detection. J. Comput. Virol. **7**(2), 95–105 (2011)
12. Kharraz, A., Robertson, W., Balzarotti, D., Bilge, L., Kirda, E.: Cutting the gordian knot: a look under the hood of ransomware attacks. In: Almgren, M., Gulisano, V., Maggi, F. (eds.) DIMVA 2015. LNCS, vol. 9148, pp. 3–24. Springer, Heidelberg (2015). doi:10.1007/978-3-319-20550-2_1

13. Kim, D., Soh, W., Kim, S.: Design of quantification model for prevent of cryptolocker. Indian J. Sci. Technol. **8**, 19 (2015)

14. M. Léveillé, M.-E.: Torrentlocker ransomware in a country near you (2014). http://www.welivesecurity.com/2014/12/16/torrentlocker-ransomware-in-a-country-near-you/

15. Mercaldo, F., Nardone, V., Santone, A., Visaggio, C.A.: Ransomware steals your phone. Formal methods rescue it. In: Albert, E., Lanese, I. (eds.) FORTE 2016. LNCS, vol. 9688, pp. 212–221. Springer, Heidelberg (2016). doi:10.1007/978-3-319-39570-8_14

16. Perdisci, R., Lanzi, A., Lee, W.: Classification of packed executables for accurate computer virus detection. Pattern Recogn. Lett. **29**(14), 1941–1946 (2008)

17. Roussev, V.: Data fingerprinting with similarity digests. In: Chow, K.-P., Shenoi, S. (eds.) DigitalForensics 2010. IAICT, vol. 337, pp. 207–226. Springer, Heidelberg (2010). doi:10.1007/978-3-642-15506-2_15

18. Scaife, N., Carter, H., Traynor, P., Butler, K.R.: Cryptolock (and drop it): stopping ransomware attacks on user data. In: Proceedings of the IEEE International Conference on Distributed Computing Systems (ICDCS), pp. 303–312. IEEE (2016)

19. Song, S., Kim, B., Lee, S.: The effective ransomware prevention technique using process monitoring on android platform. Mob. Inf. Syst., 1–8 (2016)

20. Ugarte-Pedrero, X., Santos, I., Sanz, B., Laorden, C., Bringas, P.G.: Countering entropy measure attacks on packed software detection. In: Proceedings of the IEEE Consumer Communications and Networking Conference (CCNC), pp. 164–168. IEEE (2012)

21. Young, A., Yung, M.: Cryptovirology: extortion-based security threats and countermeasures. In: Proceedings of the IEEE Symposium on Security and Privacy, pp. 129–140. IEEE (1996)

Detecting Malware Through Anti-analysis Signals - A Preliminary Study

Joash W.J. Tan[1] and Roland H.C. Yap[2(✉)]

[1] Centre for Strategic Infocomm Technologies, Singapore, Singapore
tan.wj@csit.gov.sg
[2] School of Computing, National University of Singapore, Singapore, Singapore
ryap@comp.nus.edu.sg

Abstract. Malware is often designed to make analysis difficult – behaving differently if it detects that it is in an analysis environment. We propose that such *anti-analysis malware* can be detected by their anti-analysis behavior in terms of certain signals. Signals form semantic features of potential anti-analysis techniques and are characterized as: weak, strong, or composite. We prototype a system to show the viability of detection. Experiments on malware and also non-malware show that both malware and non-malware can exhibit signals, however, anti-analysis malware tends to have more and stronger signals. We present the malware with an environment which behaves either like an analysis environment or not – we find anti-analysis malware behave differently in both cases. Normal programs, however, do not exhibit such behavior even when they have some weak signals. Signal detection is shown to have potential of distinguishing anti-analysis malware from non-malware.

1 Introduction

Understanding or reverse engineering of malware through dynamic analysis is aided by tools such as sandboxes, debuggers, emulators and virtual machines (VM). In response, malware authors make it difficult for their malware to be analysed using measures to hinder such analysis, e.g. the Simda malware detects various sandbox environments, security tools, VMs, etc. Furthermore, when the malware detects an analysis environment, it may behave differently such as terminating or executing a benign payload. A 2014 study selected 200 K malware samples, running each on a real system and VMware [2]. They found that 20 % of the malware detected the presence of the VM – aborting execution. Thus, anti-analysis malware makes malware analysis more difficult or renders tools ineffective [1]. We call malware which detects dynamic analysis environments, security tools, VMs, etc., as *anti-analysis malware*.

In this paper, we propose that the use of anti-analysis techniques gives a good indication that an unknown binary is malware or not. We also want to distinguish anti-analysis malware from non-malware. We propose to discover anti-analysis malware by: (i) its use of anti-analysis techniques; and (ii) behavioral differences when its anti-analysis tests succeed. We differ from other behavioral approaches

S. Foresti and G. Persiano (Eds.): CANS 2016, LNCS 10052, pp. 542–551, 2016.
DOI: 10.1007/978-3-319-48965-0_33

as we characterize and differentiate the behavior of malware and non-malware in terms of potential anti-analysis techniques. Note that as shown in the experiments, non-malware may use similar features (weak signals) as malware.

We implement a prototype in PIN [9] for Windows, *AADetect*, to detect the use of anti-analysis techniques during execution as signals. We apply run-time counter-measures to change the perception of the program under test as to whether a signal usable by anti-analysis is present or not. Contrary to expectations, experiments show that both malware and non-malware to exhibit signals. However, malware have stronger signals than normal programs. When anti-analysis counter-measures are applied, malware can have significant behavior deviation from when counter-measures are not used. We found that non-malware do not behave in this way. This suggests our techniques are promising to detect anti-analysis malware from non-malware. Our techniques can be combined with existing analysis environments and sandboxes [3–8,10].

1.1 Related Works

Fine-grained instrumentation [6,7] has been used to detect anti-analysis behaviors in malware but large-scale deployment of fine-grained instrumentation is problematic, e.g. a slow emulated environment can have server-side timeouts [10].

The malware can be run in multiple analysis systems to detect differences in behavior [3–8,10]. Many works focus on malware but not on non-malware, e.g. Balzarotti et al. [3], show that the malware system call execution trace can be different under an emulated environment. An important difference with our work is that although there is a behavioral comparison of differences, we compare signals which are semantically related to potential anti-analysis techniques. Most of the other works compare behavior in terms of differences at the system resource, system call or network traffic level, i.e. at the level of the operating system. Our signals are semantically different since they measure certain kinds of anti-analysis checks and techniques. We are not restricted by limitations such as system calls, e.g. `IsDebuggerPresent` is not a system call. We do not require deterministic execution requirements [3,8], and the anti-analysis malware can in-principle behave non-deterministically.

We investigate not only the anti-analysis behavior of malware but also differentiate with non-malware (under different execution environments). Our environments however differ in that we turn on and off the signals deliberately. This is subtly different from running with different execution environments. Rather having an execution profile which is compared, we focus on comparing the signal behavioral profile under different environments as a way to differentiate between anti-analysis malware and normal programs.

We have focused our implementation and experiments on Windows. Malware can be in other operating systems. Petsas et al. [11] show anti-analysis techniques can evade dynamic analysis in Android emulated environments. Many of their anti-analysis heuristics can be treated as signals.

2   Detecting Anti-analysis Techniques

We believe that most anti-analysis techniques, by their very nature, can be detected in some fashion if it occurs at runtime. We call a *signal* an indicator of whether a certain runtime behavior, which may be associated with a certain anti-analysis technique, occurs during execution, e.g. the IsDebuggerPresent API in Windows indicates if a process is being debugged. A call to IsDebuggerPresent() is a signal, but it might not mean that the process is anti-analysis malware.

We categorize signals as: *strong signals* or *weak signals*. Intuitively, a strong signal is a feature which is more likely to occur in anti-analysis malware. A weak signal, however, is a feature which may be used in anti-analysis techniques but also has legitimate purposes. Thus, it can occur in malware and also normal programs. We also consider signals which can be considered together as *composite signals*. Table 1 gives a possible list of signals – the signals are either Windows APIs[1] or x86 instructions. This list is by no means exhaustive – one can easily add more. Our preliminary experiments show that this small set already gives promising results.

Weak Signals. A *weak signal* is a signal which may be associated with anti-analysis techniques but also used in normal programs, e.g. our experiments show that the IsDebuggerPresent API is used in non-malware. Thus, by itself, a weak signal may not give much evidence that a program is anti-analysis malware. However, we also consider the accumulated evidence of all detected signals. (See also the strong form of the IsDebuggerPresent signal).

Another weak signal which occurs in normal programs is FindFirstFileEx which is used to search through a directory for a file matching a filename or file attributes. It is typically used to enumerate the files which occurs in normal programs but malware may combine this with searching for particular filenames. Thus, a weak signal can be used in combination with other signals, see below.

Some weak signals are requests for information which may appear legitimate, i.e. the API may be used in normal programs. However, there is also a clear rationale for malware to also want this information. Some examples are: RegEnumKeyEx (used to enumerate through the registry keys), GetUserNameEx (gets user name), and RDSTC (reading the processor time stamp counter).

Strong Signals. A *strong signal* is meant for signals which give a greater likelihood that an anti-analysis technique has been used. Some examples of strong signals follow. VMware provides a specific communication port (it is a side channel for a program to communicate with VMware). As this is not really a communication port but a backdoor channel, in normal Windows without VMware, the runtime behavior is different. Detecting I/O to such a port (using the IN instruction) suggests that the program is trying to perform a VMware backdoor

---

[1] A system call is also a Windows API but not all APIs lead to system calls.

Table 1. Detection signals

API/Instruction	Strong	Weak	Composite
Registry Checks:			
RegOpenKeyEx, RegQueryValueEx	*		
RegEnumKeyEx		*	*
Process Checks:			
GetProcessImageFileName, GetModuleBaseName		*	*
Filesystem Checks:			
PathFileExist, GetModuleHandleEx, GetFileAttributes, LdrGetDllHandle, CreateFile	*		
LdrGetProcedureAddress		*	
FindFirstFileEx		*	*
User Check: GetUserNameEx		*	*
Debugger Check			
IsDebuggerPresent		*	
IsDebuggerPresent (PEB)	*		
CheckRemoteDebuggerPresent	*		
Special Instructions			
SLDT, SIDT, SGDT, CPUID, IN	*		
Timing Checks:			
RDTSC, NtDelayExecution		*	
Comparison Checks			
wcsstr, wcscmp, wcsicmp, strstr, strcmp, stricmp, mbsstr, mbscmp, mbsicmp			*

command which suggests: (i) it is anti-analysis malware; or (ii) the program is a special program having VMware features, e.g. a VMware utility. Some strong signals are simply whether the API/instruction has been used but in others, the values of the parameters are used to determine between a strong signal or no signal at all, e.g. the port parameter in the x86 IN instruction.

A weak signal may also have a strong version, for example, the IsDebuggerPresent (PEB) signal in Table 1. In its weak version, it is a call to the IsDebuggerPresent API. However, in Windows, this information is also stored as a flag in the PEB (Process Environment Block). The PEB is an opaque data structure in memory used internally by Windows. We consider IsDebuggerPresent (PEB) a strong signal as it means that the flag is read directly, bypassing the recommended IsDebuggerPresent API.[2]

---

[2] The API implementation reads the flag, so is not a system call.

Composite Signals. A *composite signal* consists of two or more other signals. It is intended to be stronger than its original signals which may be weak. We do not differentiate between the signal strength of strong and composite signals other than they are both stronger than weak signals. For example, the GetUserNameEx API returns the user name associated with the thread which may be used by normal programs (a weak signal). However, if the data is then used in a string comparison function to compare special string values associated with anti-analysis, e.g. "sandbox" or "vmware", this would appear more likely to be an anti-analysis behavior. Thus, we consider a weak GetUserNameEx signal together with checks for specific strings to be a composite signal. In a similar way, the weak FindFirstFileEx signal combines with specific checks for certain filenames which exist in a VM, e.g. a driver like vmmouse.sys.

The use of the RegOpenKeyEx API only means that the program is accessing a registry key - a common operation in Windows, hence, by default a weak signal. However, specific key values containing VMware as a sub-string, would be a strong signal of attempting to detect or some interaction with VMware. For example, if the lpSubKey parameter contains the value "SOFTWARE/VMware, Inc./VMware Tools", then we consider it to be a composite signal.

We also treat the number of signals or a program time metric such as instruction count when we compare the result of two runs, one with anti-analysis countermeasures and one without, to be a composite signal. This is mainly just to make the treatment more uniform.

3   Implementation

We aim to detect malware which are Windows binaries by executing them. Packed malware are also handled. We implemented a prototype, AADetect, to execute binaries using the Intel PIN dynamic binary instrumentation tool [9] which supports binary files without modification and allows for dynamically generated or self-modifying code (e.g. unpackers).

Detecting Anti-analysis Signals. The implementation of AADetect in PIN is mostly straightforward, detecting the signals in Table 1 which are either Windows APIs or particular x86 instructions. It is easy to add to this list. PIN is used to instrument the code so that our routines are called whenever the particular instruction is executed or the API is called. Depending on the signal, the parameters or values for that signal also need to be checked, e.g. the value of the registry key or sub-keys. In order to detecting the IsDebuggerPresent (PEB) signal, we additionally instrument memory references to the PEB. We also count the number of basic blocks which have been JIT-ted by PIN to measure execution code coverage and the total number of instructions executed.

Anti-analysis Countermeasures. Suppose the anti-analysis malware behaves differently if its tests detect the presence of some analysis environment or tool.

Simply monitoring its execution for anti-analysis signals is not enough, rather, we need to change the semantics of the API or instruction so that its anti-analysis code gives a certain result.

We employ two different execution modes to expose the malware anti-analysis behaviors. In *countermeasure mode*, we want to behave as if the analysis environment or tool associated with the signals is not present. For example, regardless of whether the code is running in VMware or not, we will report for the tests associated with signals for VMware as if we are not running in VMware. We do this by modifying the API or instruction results appropriately. We assume that the implementation of the countermeasures succeed in evading the anti-analysis tests in the malware. As a result, the malware is fooled into expressing its malicious behavior.

Non-countermeasure mode is the opposite of countermeasure mode, we pretend that the malware succeeds in its anti-analysis tests. Namely, the results of the API or instruction is similar to when the malware is being run within a VM, sandbox or debugger, for the implemented signals, regardless of whether this is the case. Being the opposite of countermeasure mode, we expect that the malware will execute its (benign) anti-analysis behavior rather than its real (malicious) payload, i.e. terminate execution.

Once we have signals from runs in countermeasure and non-countermeasure mode, any difference in behavior can be another composite signal. We count the number of different basic blocks and instructions executed, and threads created.

Table 2. Non-malware tested & signals found

Non-malware	Weak signals detected
CMD shell, Process Explorer, Chrome, Internet Explorer	RDTSC
SSH Secure Shell Client, Realterm	IsDebuggerPresent
Task Manager, Notepad, Calculator, MSPaint, uTorrent, Visual Studio, Word, Excel, Daemon Tools Lite	RDTSC, IsDebuggerPresent
Firefox, Avira, Skype, Windows Photo Viewer, NVIDIA GeForce Experience	RDTSC, IsDebuggerPresent, NtDelayExecution
Windows Media Player	RDTSC, IsDebuggerPresent, GetUserNameEx
Notepad++	RDTSC, IsDebuggerPresent, GetUserNameEx, NtDelayExecution

4 Experiments

We present preliminary experiments with AADetect to test our hypothesis that evaluating anti-analysis behavior of a program can identify anti-analysis malware from non-malware. We tested with 69 Windows malware from 39 families

Table 3. Summary of Detection Results for Malware and Normal Programs Stg: Strong, Cpx: Complex, Wk: Weak, BB: #Basic Blocks (unit 10^6), Inst: #Instructions in M (unit 10^6), Thr: #Threads

#	Program	Countermeasures						Non-Countermeasures					
		Stg	Cpx	Wk	BB	Inst	Thr	Stg	Cpx	Wk	Δ BB	Δ Inst	Δ Thr
	Malware												
2	Agent	4	0	6	0.0001	0.51	10	0	0	1	-0.0001	-0.305	-9
5	AutoIt	7	0	3	77.17	1012.62	5	0	0	2	-74.85	-987.60	-3
7	Badur	0	0	19	0.047	1.106	10	0	0	5	-0.047	-0.917	-9
12	Carberp.C	8	0	2	6.928	357.01	1	0	0	2	0	-0.00008	0
18	Gaertob.A	7	4	5	0.0004	0.135	1	1	1	5	-0.00003	-0.00009	0
26	Injector	2	0	5	0.00001	0.215	6	0	0	1	-0.000000	-0.149	0
29	Keygen	1	0	1	72.51	1601.8	11	1	0	1	-65.56	-1504.7	-10
31	Kryptik	15	0	2	2.450	78.901	2	0	0	1	-0.026	-0.362	0
32	Llac	6	0	8	39.96	488.74	5	0	0	3	-37.97	-467.33	-3
34	MalwareF	15	8	4	0.093	1.127	1	0	0	1	-0.031	-0.418	0
35	Nakuru.A	0	0	25	0.006	0.384	6	0	0	12	-0.0003	-0.034	0
41	Rebhip	0	0	2	54.425	694.29	2	0	0	2	-54.394	-693.75	0
48	Rebhip.A	7	0	3	7.466	22.823	2	0	0	2	-7.466	-22.758	+6
52	Simda	13	0	3	0.101	1.431	1	1	0	3	-0.004	-0.053	0
56	Simda.B	23	0	2	2.44	78.747	2	0	0	1	-2.196	-78.707	-1
58	SoftPulse	14	0	6	266.36	3281.60	7	2	0	2	-266.34	-3281.38	-6
61	VBInject	3	0	7	0.00016	0.521	9	0	0	3	-0.00011	-0.332	-8
68	Vobfus	3	0	8	0.00014	0.428	10	0	0	8	0	-0.001	-2
69	Yuner.A	1	0	1	49.497	477.20	5	0	0	2	-47.310	-461.34	-4
	Non-Malware												
	Chrome	0		1				0		1			
	CMD	0		1				0		1			
	IE	0		1				0		1			
	Proc. Exp.	0		1				0		1			
	RealTerm	0		1				0		1			
	SSH Client	0		1				0		1			
	Calculator	0		2				0		2			
	Excel	0		2				0		2			
	Visual Studio	0		2				0		2			
	Word	0		2				0		2			
	MSPaint	0		2				0		2			
	Notepad	0		2				0		2			
	Task Manager	0		2				0		2			
	uTorrent	0		2				0		2			
	Avira	0		3				0		3			
	Daemon Tools	0		3				0		3			
	Firefox	0		3				0		3			
	GeForce Exp.	0		3				0		3			
	Skype	0		3				0		3			
	Media Player	0		3				0		3			
	Photo Viewer	0		3				0		3			
	Notepad++	0		4				0		4			

including the well known Simda family. These malware are from Offensive Computing, VirusShare, Malwr and some other sources which are already known to be anti-analysis malware or ones we checked through manual analysis. For non-malware programs, we tested with 22 common Windows software in Table 2 which also lists the signals found. We execute all the malware and normal executables with AADetect in countermeasure and non-countermeasure mode. AADetect produces signals which can be compared including runtime measures.

The results of signals found by AADetect on the sample malware and the normal programs tested are summarized in Table 3 – giving the number of strong, weak and composite signals detected. We have tested all malware samples but have only listed some of them (mainly one per family). We also found the samples not listed to give similar behavior. The first column (#) gives the malware instance number. Columns 3–8 are the results in countermeasure mode while columns 9–14 give the corresponding results in non-countermeasure mode. The signal count is the number of times a strong, complex or weak signal is detected. Δ gives the difference in number of basic blocks, instructions and threads executed between the two modes. Although we present signal and execution statistics, we can also show detailed signal execution trace information (not presented due to lack of space). The non-malware programs are interactive, so the number of basic blocks and threads depends on the GUI interaction, hence, statistics are not given as they are incomparable between modes.

We found anti-analysis malware gives many signals. Many malware have many strong signals in addition to weak signals. We only detected weak signals with some malware (Keygen, Nakuru.A, Rebhip, Yuner.A). Complex signals are fewer but it may be due to the small set of signals used. What is unexpected is that normal software also exhibit signals. However, we only found only weak signals, see Tables 2 and 3. In particular, the weak IsDebuggerPresent signal occurs frequently. Many malware exhibit more and stronger signals than normal programs but some of them may appear to have similar signals to normal programs, i.e. Rebhip (2 x IsDebuggerPresent) versus Calculator both with 2 weak signals. However, we will see below there are other and more signal differences.

We see that anti-analysis malware behave differently depending on whether they detect the analysis environment or not. In countermeasure mode, where the signals to measure the analysis environment are masked, the malware usually executed more basic blocks and instructions with possibly more threads. We expect this happens when the malware is executing its true behavior. In non-countermeasure mode, the effect of the signals is to always detect that there is an analysis environment present, thus, we expect that the malware will hide its behavior. As expected, there are less basic blocks, instructions and threads. In one case, Rebhip.A, there are more threads, perhaps this is intended to confuse malware analysis. We see that in most cases, the number of signals decreases, which suggests that these malware are all taking evasive action depending on the results of the anti-analysis techniques.

Normal software (non-malware) have a very different signal and execution profile from the anti-analysis malware. There are only a few weak signals and we found signals are unaffected by the execution mode.

Overall we can see that the results show that simply at an overall signal statistics level, anti-analysis malware already has a clear difference in its signal profile compared with normal programs. We believe that this shows that our signal detection under a two mode approach can be effective in giving good evidence that a program is anti-analysis malware simply because normal programs behave quite differently. For each executable tested, we have the full execution trace signal profile with signal parameters. This gives further insights and results but is not presented due to lack of space.

5   Discussion

Our prototype is only meant to show the viability of anti-analysis detection through signals and execution modes. We have only implemented some signals, mainly the well known ones. There are also many different ways to detect the signals. However, even with the limited signals and prototype implementation, there is a clear differentiation between the anti-analysis malware and normal programs evaluated.

A question is whether AADetect PIN can itself be detected. In principle, multiple implementations using different ways of detecting signals and possibly different instrumentation systems can be employed. This can also be combined with different sandboxes or analysis environments as well (e.g. as in [3–8,10]), giving even more and diverse signals for comparison.

Our focus is malware with anti-analysis features. If the malware is not anti-analysis, we may not be able to get any good signal differentiation. However, this can then be regarded a good situation for malware analysts: (a) anti-analysis malware is detected by its anti-analysis behavior; or (b) if the malware does not employ anti-analysis, it is likely to be easier to analyse. In either case, it increases the likelihood of finding the malware.

We now discuss some potential applications of AADetect. AADetect may be used during malware analysis in order to obtain evidence of anti-analysis behaviors in known malware. As AADetect uses dynamic binary instrumentation in the execution of samples, the identification of anti-analysis techniques are done dynamically instead of statically. This means that we can identify the anti-analysis techniques which are actually executed during runtime. It may be useful for the configuration of emulators in order for it to avoid detection by anti-analysis malware. Additionally, this may also aid malware analysts in understanding the anti-analysis techniques being employed. In particular, the signal execution profile shows the sequencing and timing of the signals used by the program, malware or non-malware.

AADetect may be useful in the discovery of new and unknown malware. Apart from exhibiting malicious behavior, new malware may also exhibit anti-analysis behavior. Identification of anti-analysis techniques used in a sample may give malware analysts an indication of the sample's possible malicious contents. In other words, we can filter samples which are suspicious from those that are benign using anti-analysis detection. In contrast, most legitimate software applications probably do not attempt to exploit the presence of an analysis environment.

6   Conclusion

Our initial work shows that analysing malware in terms of signals with underlying semantics in how they can be used for anti-analysis has promise to detect anti-analysis malware without the need of signatures. It is also useful in differentiating anti-analysis malware from non-malware. We present a practical and lightweight approach which can be easily extended with more kinds of signals. It may also be useful to incorporate into antivirus systems. Finally, we remark that as it is not possible for any analysis, lightweight or heavyweight, to detect all malware. Thus, our analysis using signals can complement existing techniques based on operating system behaviors.

References

1. https://www.fireeye.com/blog/threat-research/2011/01/the-dead-giveaways-of-vm-aware-malware.html
2. http://www.symantec.com/connect/blogs/does-malware-still-detect-virtual-machines
3. Balzarotti, D., Cova, M., Karlberger, C., Kruegel, C., Kirda, E., Vigna, G.: Efficient detection of split personalities in malware. In: NDSS (2010)
4. Chen, X., Andersen, J., Mao, Z.M., Bailey, M., Nazario, J.: Towards an understanding of anti-virtualization and anti-debugging behavior in modern malware. In: DSN (2008)
5. Deng, Z., Zhang, X., Xu, D.: SPIDER: stealthy binary program instrumentation and debugging via hardware virtualization. In: ACSAC (2013)
6. Johnson, N.M., Caballero, J., Chen, K.Z., McCamant, S., Poosankam, P., Reynaud, D., Song, D.: Differential slicing: identifying causal execution differences for security applications. In: S&P (2011)
7. Kang, M.G., Yin, H., Hanna, S., McCamant, S., Song, D.: Emulating emulation resistant malware. In: VMSec (2009)
8. Kirat, D., Vigna, G., Kruegel, C.: BareCloud: Bare-metal analysis-based evasive malware detection. In: USENIX Security (2014)
9. Luk, C.K., Cohn, R., Muth, R., Patil, H., Klauser, A., Lowney, G., Wallace, S., Reddi, V.J., Hazelwood, K.: Pin: building customized program analysis tools with dynamic instrumentation. In: PLDI (2005)
10. Lindorfer, M., Kolbitsch, C., Milani Comparetti, P.: Detecting environment-sensitive malware. In: Sommer, R., Balzarotti, D., Maier, G. (eds.) RAID 2011. LNCS, vol. 6961, pp. 338–357. Springer, Heidelberg (2011). doi:10.1007/978-3-642-23644-0_18
11. Petsas, T., Voyatzis, G., Athanasopoulos, E., Polychronakis, M., Ioannidis, S.: Rage against the virtual machine: hindering dynamic analysis of android malware. In: EUROSEC (2014)
12. Vishnani, K., Pais, A.R., Mohandas, R.: Detecting and defeating split personality malware. In: Secureware (2011)

Attackers in Wireless Sensor Networks Will Be Neither Random Nor Jumping – Secrecy Amplification Case

Radim Ošťádal[✉], Petr Švenda, and Vashek Matyáš

Masaryk University, Brno, Czech Republic
ostadal@mail.muni.cz, {svenda,matyas}@fi.muni.cz

Abstract. Partially compromised network is a pragmatic assumption in many real-life scenarios. Secrecy amplification protocols provide a significant increase in the number of secure communication links by re-establishing new keys via different communication paths. Our paper shows that research in the area of secrecy amplification protocols for ad-hoc networks has been based on rather simplified foundations w. r. t. attacker models. The attacker does not behave randomly and different attacker capabilities and behaviour have to be considered. We provide means to experimental work with parametrisable attacker capabilities and behaviour in realistic simulations, and evaluate the impact of the realistic attacker properties on the performance of major amplification protocols (Full details, paper supplementary material and source codes can be found at http://crcs.cz/papers/cans2016.).

We also show which secrecy amplification protocols perform best in different attacker settings and help to select a protocol that exhibits good results in a prevalent number of inspected scenarios.

1 Introduction

Ad-hoc networks of nodes with varying capabilities (including quite limited ones) often handle sensitive information and security of such networks is a typical baseline requirement. Such networks consist of numerous interacting devices, price of which should often be as low as possible – limiting computational and storage resources, also avoiding expensive tamper resistance. Lightweight security solutions are preferable, providing a low computational and communication overhead. When considering key management, symmetric cryptography is the preferred approach, yet with a low number of pre-distributed keys. While all results we present can be applied to general ad-hoc networks, we present them directly on wireless sensor networks (WSNs) as typical representatives.

Attackers in such an environment can be categorised into different classes with respect to link key management. The most prevalent node-compromise model [5] assumes that the attacker is able to capture a fraction of deployed

V. Matyáš—Partly supported by the Czech Science Foundation project GBP202/12/G061.

S. Foresti and G. Persiano (Eds.): CANS 2016, LNCS 10052, pp. 552–561, 2016.
DOI: 10.1007/978-3-319-48965-0_34

nodes and to extract keying material from captured nodes. No tamper resistance of nodes is assumed because of their low production cost. A real world attacker model (also called weakened attacker model) was defined in [1]. In this model, an attacker is able to monitor only a small proportion of communications within a network during the deployment phase when the link keys are being established.

Substantial improvements in resilience against node capture or key exchange eavesdropping can be achieved when a group of neighbouring nodes cooperates in an additional secrecy amplification (referred to as amplification protocols hereafter) after the initial key establishment protocol. Amplification protocols were shown to be very effective, yet for the price of a significant communication overhead. The overall aim is to provide amplification protocols that can secure a high number of links yet require only a small number of messages and are easy to execute and synchronize in parallel executions in the real network. Different types of amplification protocols were studied – node-oriented protocols, group-oriented protocols, and hybrid-design protocols.

Previous work on amplification protocols considered the close connection between the attacker model and a key establishment scheme used [1,5,13]. Partially compromised networks with only two different compromise patterns were inspected throughout literature – *random compromise* and *key infection* patterns. Random compromise pattern is the result of the node compromise attacker model together with a probabilistic pre-distribution key establishment scheme [5]. The key infection pattern assumes the weakened attacker model together with the key establishment where link keys are being exchanged in plaintext. After an initial compromise, a global passive attacker that is able to monitor all communication on the entire network was expected in both cases.

We argue that those scenarios are not sufficient and here we provide a more realistic setting for the attacker. Firstly, we question the initial compromise patterns inspected so far, as the attacker presence in the network during the deployment and a relatively short initial key establishment phase is a strong assumption. We focus on a network where all neighbours already share unique link keys, so the key establishment protocol is not important. The attacker is able to initially compromise several nodes and extract all keys shared with its neighbours. We inspect multiple compromise patterns resulting from different attacker strategies, not only the random compromise pattern. Secondly, we do not expect the global attacker during the amplification phase as this would not be the case in real life (e.g., wireless receiver sensitivity limiting the attacker eavesdropping range). A realistic attacker has to be present in the network and will need to keep her stronghold in the network during the amplification phase. She has to eavesdrop as many random nonces used during the amplification process as possible. The attacker is parametrised by her capabilities and behaviour (e.g., initial compromise pattern, eavesdropping range, attacker movement and her speed etc.).

Apart from the attacker characteristics, we want to move the amplification protocol simulation to a more realistic setting. A significant part of recent work is based on results from SensorSim, a dedicated simulator developed specifically for security analysis of key distribution protocols and message routing by the authors of [17]. We extend the KMSforWSN framework that was introduced in [6]. Our extension is available as open source[1]. The advantages and disadvantages of both simulators are further discussed in the next section.

Our goals are:

1. To evaluate the impact of the realistic attacker properties on the performance of major amplification protocols.
2. To move the evaluation of amplification protocols to a more realistic environment (suitable and realistic simulator).
3. To select one (or two) amplification protocols that exhibit good results in a prevalent number of inspected scenarios for further implementation and deeper analysis. Those are left for a future work.

The paper roadmap is as follows: the next section provides an overview of related work on different attacker models, the current state of amplification protocols research and advantages and disadvantages of different simulators. Section 3 describes parametrisable attacker capabilities and behaviour together with experiment settings and network lifetime from deployment up to evaluation. Section 4 evaluates the impact of attacker parameters on the success rate of 7 major amplification protocols. The best performing amplification protocol is selected and conclusions are provided in Sect. 5.

2   Related Work

Attacker models: Several different attacker models were defined in the literature. We differentiate two basic categories based on a level of attacker interaction with the network. The global passive attacker is able to monitor all communication around the entire sensor network without influencing it. The global active attacker is the classic attacker from the Needham-Schroeder model [12]. She is able to alter and copy any message, replay messages or inject any false material. She might drop part of the communication at her will. Those attacker models define the attacker capabilities during the amplification process.

Another two attacker classes were introduced in literature with respect to initial network compromise – a node compromise model [5] and a real world attacker model [1]. The node-compromise model is an extension of the Needham-Schroeder model. The attacker is able to capture a fraction of deployed nodes and extract their keying material as no physical control over deployed nodes is assumed. Real world attacker model is defined in [1] and assumes that the attacker does not have physical access to the deployment site and is able to monitor only a small proportion on the communications of the sensor network during the deployment phase. Once the key exchange is complete, she is able to monitor all communication and execute any active attack at will.

Compromise patterns: A compromise pattern provides us with a conditional probability that link Y is compromised when another link X is compromised

---

[1] Available (with other supplementary materials) at http://crcs.cz/papers/cans2016.

after an attack. The characteristics of a particular compromise pattern may significantly influence the success rate of an amplification protocols executed later. The random compromise pattern arises when a probabilistic key pre-distribution scheme of [5] and many later variants of [2,4,10,11] are used and an attacker extracts keys from several randomly captured nodes. The random compromise pattern exhibits an almost uncorrelated pattern. To the contrary, the key infection compromise pattern forms a significantly correlated pattern due to an eavesdropper locality. During the key establishment, link keys are being exchanged in plaintext. The original idea of key infection was presented in [1] and later extended by [3,8,17].

Secrecy amplification: The secrecy amplification (SA) concept was originally introduced in [1] for the key infection plaintext key exchange, but can be used for any partially compromised network. An SA protocol can be executed to secure (again) some of the compromised links, resulting in a less compromised network. During the amplification protocol, a group of neighbours cooperates together to exchange random nonces that will be later used to update original link keys. Nonces have to be securely transported to both nodes to update the mutual key. A particular amplification protocol specifies the exact way the generated nonces are transported.

A network owner usually does not know which concrete link key was compromised by an attacker and which was not. SA can be executed as a response to a (presumed) partial compromise already happened or as a preventive measure for potential future compromise. SA can be also executed as another layer of protection even if a particular link key might not be compromised at all.

Amplification protocols can try all possible paths, yet for the price of a huge communication overhead. Proposed amplification protocols, therefore, aim to find a good tradeoff between the number of paths tried and the probability of finding at least one secure path for nonce delivery.

Different classes of amplification protocols use different means to improve a security throughout the network. Although all amplification protocols aim to setup new (possibly secure) link key, three main distinct classes of amplification protocols exist. Details of all inspected protocols are provided in [14].

A node-oriented protocol sends key updates via every possible neighbour or neighbours by a simple protocol. Note that node-oriented protocol is executed for all possible k-tuples of neighbours in the network. A number of such k-tuples can be high, especially for dense networks. We further inspect five selected node oriented protocols: Pull [3], Push [1], Multi-hop Pull (M-Pull) [3], Multi-hop Push (M-Push) [1] and NO Best [17].

A group-oriented protocol shares new key values inside a bigger group of cooperating nodes identified by their geographical areas in a form of relative distance to selected nodes [17]. Group-oriented protocols have some crucial disadvantages – problematic synchronisation of parallel executions and complicated security analysis due to a high number of nodes involved. We omit group-oriented protocols from further analysis.

A hybrid-design protocol uses sub-protocols (similarly to node-oriented), rel- ative distances (similarly to group-oriented) and additionally utilise several repetitions of the whole process to achieve required success rate. We further inspect two hybrid designed protocols: HD Final and HD Best [13].

Simulation environment: An essential part of amplification protocol evaluation usually is a simulation environment. The evaluation on a real sensor network is usually impossible due to cost and time requirements. We provide a brief comparison of the SensorSim simulator used during the SA protocol design in previous work and the KMSforWSN framework used to conduct our research.

The SensorSim simulator is a tool for very fast evaluation of existing amplification protocols [17]. New amplification protocols can be also generated using evolutionary algorithms [17]. The main advantage of SensorSim is the speed of simulation. However, it lacks many essential components for a realistic simulation, like radio signal propagation or MAC layer collisions. All protocols in SensorSim are evaluated based only on a set of properties, such as a number of nodes, node positions or defined communication range.

KMSforWSN framework is a tool for an automated evaluation of KMS properties in WSNs, built on top of MiXiM [9], a WSN framework for the OMNeT++ simulator [16]. We extend it with two new modules to reflect different attacker models and also to implement an SA capability. The definition of channel and physical layer settings is based on previous research on real parameters of TelosB sensors for outdoor environment [15]. In our work, we simulate the network execution not only as a graph discovery problem (as in SensorSim), but full emulation of code running on virtual nodes is provided, with an application logic executed and messages passed to the communication stack.

3   Parameterized Attacker

Our aim is to define the attacker with fully parametrisable capabilities and behaviour. Attacker parameters can be divided into two separate groups – *behaviour* parameters and *resource* parameters. The *behaviour* parameters characterise attacker strategy and behaviour during the attacker activity (e.g., different movement pattern or starting position). The *resource* parameters define available resources and attacker capabilities, both initial and extended (e.g., the number of cooperating attackers or eavesdropping range).

We summarise particular phases of the entire simulation and provide a definition of all inspected attacker parameters, followed by baseline values.

Network lifetime: The entire attacker simulation for amplification protocols and its evaluation consist of 5 phases. Firstly, a network consisting of 100 legitimate nodes is deployed randomly over the plane of 115×115 m. The size was chosen purposefully to have a network with a density of 7.5 neighbours on average. After the deployment, an attacker conducts the initial compromise. This initial compromise is done before the actual amplification protocol is executed.

We evaluate all compromise patterns defined in [7] and the total number of compromised links is 50 %. Secondly, the nonce distribution phase of amplification protocols and attacker eavesdropping take place simultaneously. The nonce distribution phase should influence network operations just shortly, so we limit the length to only 100 s. Such length is enough to exchange most messages without collisions. The attacker is present in the network during the whole nonce distribution phase and she tries to eavesdrop on as much communication as possible. Her success depends on particular values assigned to examined attacker parameters. Lastly, nonces are mutually confirmed among neighbouring nodes and the simulation is concluded with a protocol evaluation.

Attacker parameters: Every parameter from both defined groups can be assigned a value from a specific set of possible values described in this section. Possible values for attacker *behaviour* parameters follow.

(I) Initial compromise pattern: We are inspecting four different patterns: (1) Random nodes are selected and compromised in the *random* attacker pattern. (2) The attacker walking around the network and picking outermost nodes presents the *outermost* attacker pattern. (3) The attacker moving directly to a centre of the network from a random location on an edge of the network, picking up nodes in a close vicinity of his trajectory, presents a *direct centre* attacker pattern. (4) The *centre drop* attacker pattern simulates the possibility of parachute drop or digging under the network. The closest nodes to the centre of the network are compromised up to a selected threshold.

(II) Movement pattern of the attacker: During the nonce distribution phase, attackers move within the WSN deployment area according to an assigned pattern. We evaluate several different patterns to see how they influence the attacker success in eavesdropping nonce messages: (1) The *stationary pattern* is characterised by attackers staying in their initial positions and not moving at all. (2) Attackers move on a straight line with a constant speed in the *linear* movement pattern. When the attacker approaches an area border, she reflects at the same angle. (3) The *random* pattern is described by attackers choosing the point within the deployment area randomly (distributed uniformly over the area) and moving directly to it with constant speed. After reaching the point, attacker selects the next point, again in a random manner. (4) Attackers move in a circle of a particular diameter in the *circle* pattern. We inspect three different diameters of 10, 20 and 40 m. (5) The square *patrol* pattern is characterised by the attacker systematically patrolling a square area with a side of different length – particularly 10, 20 and 30 m.

(III) Initial location of the attackers: We inspect three different settings for the initial location of attackers when the nonce distribution phase starts: (1) All the attackers start from the same place in a *corner* of the deployment area. (2) Attackers are at *random* positions within the area. (3) Attackers cooperate and choose the *suitable* places to capture as much communication as possible (selected coordinates are [57.5, 57.5], [30, 30], [85, 30], [85, 85] and [30, 85] within the deployment area).

(IV) Movement speed of attackers: Attackers move at a constant speed. We inspect a range of speeds from a very slow walk up to the movement speed of a car or a flying drone.

The success of the attacker is closely connected with invested resources. The hypothesis to be verified is whether the more resources available, the more successful attacker is. We are also interested in a determination of a limit of attacker capabilities, where amplification protocols still represent a meaningful strategy.

We inspect three different *resource* parameters. A number of attackers (parameter V) determines the number of cooperating attackers and level of their collaboration. Eavesdropping range (parameter VI) defines the radius where attackers are able to intercept the communication. A number of malware infected nodes (parameter VII) denotes the number of nodes under attacker's passive control. More information and respective details are provided in [14], Sect. 3.2.

Experiment setting: Evaluating the impact of particular attacker parameters on the overall success rate of amplification protocols, we successively inspect different values for selected parameter, while the rest of parameters are fixed to baseline values. As so, baseline values should be as little influencing as possible to have a clear result on the inspected parameter. The following baseline values are used: *random* initial compromise pattern, *random* movement pattern, *random* initial location of attackers, movement speed of 1.5 m/s ($\sim$ normal walk), 5 cooperating attackers, eavesdropping range of 30 m, and no malware infected nodes.

All provided experimental results are an average of one hundred repetitions with different seeds for a random number generator. The evaluation was conducted on a dedicated machine with 96 cores at 2.00 GHz. The total computation time was more than 6 core years.

4   Experimental Results

We have determined a ranking of amplification protocols based on their performance in a prevalent number of inspected cases. *The highest number of secured link keys is provided by the HD Best protocol, closely followed by the HD Final protocol.* Hybrid designed protocols provide better results than node-oriented protocols during the evaluation of all parameters. The NO Best protocol outperforms the rest of node-oriented protocols. Multi-hop Pull and Multi-hop Push protocols provide us with similar success rates and both outperform the Push protocol. The Pull protocol exhibits the worst results. Please note that the Pull protocol sends only a half of nonces compared to the Push protocol.

Impact of compromise patterns: We have inspected four different initial compromise patterns (parameter I). In all cases, a compromised portion of link keys is 50 %. This results in a different number of compromised nodes for every pattern. Full comparison and exact values are provided in [14], Sect. 4.1. Significantly worse results are provided by all amplification protocols on *direct centre* and *centre drop* compromise patterns due to the high concentration of compromised nodes in one area. *However, hybrid designed protocols are able to achieve nearly 95 % of secured links from initial 50 % even with those unsuitable settings.* The initial compromise pattern is the only parameter where we can observe a significant difference in performance of HD Final and HD Best protocols

Impact of movement patterns: Different movement patterns (parameter II) were examined and results are shown in Fig. 1. *The most successful strategy for the attacker is to stay in the same place (stationary pattern) as she is able to eavesdrop all communication within a particular area.* Comparable results are achieved by the *circle* pattern with a small radius of 5 m and by the systematic patrolling over a small square area. The reason for the attacker's success is the same as in the *stationary* case. The worst movement pattern for the attacker is *linear* as the attacker spends a lot of time in a border area where eavesdrops less communication. Altogether, amplification protocols are able to achieve 75 % of secured link keys from the initial 50 % even in the worst case of the *stationary* pattern.

Impact of position and speed: Evaluating results of different initial starting positions (parameter III) of attackers, all amplification protocols exhibit the highest success rate for attackers starting in the *corner* of the deployment area. Attackers are able to monitor only a small part of the network from the beginning. We observe a constant drop in the success rate of 2 % between *random* and *suitable* attacker's starting positions for all amplification protocols. Comparing the *corner* and *random* starting positions, the hybrid designed protocols exhibit the least drop in the success rate whereas the single hop node-oriented protocols show the highest drop.

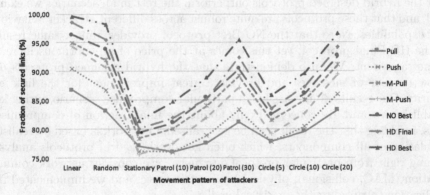

Fig. 1. Success rate of amplification protocols for different movement patterns of attackers. The number in brackets after *Patrol* and *Circle* patterns denotes the length of square area side and the circle diameter respectively. The initial compromise rate is 50 % of all link keys

Following observation holds for comparison of different movement speeds of attackers (parameter IV). *The slower movement speed of attackers, the worse results achieved by amplification protocols in general.* The reason is that the attacker is able to eavesdrop most of the messages in a particular area and amplification protocols are not able to secure additional link keys in that region. This result is in line with the observation of the case of *stationary* movement pattern. Hybrid design protocols are able to face the challenge much better than node-oriented protocols and provide significantly better results for slow attackers up to a speed $1.5\,\text{m/s}$. For a higher attacker speed, which means decreased attacker success, hybrid designed protocols provide still better success ratios, however, the differences are not so eminent as the overall success rate is already high.

Impact of *resource* parameters: The evaluation of parameters from the *resource* group supports the hypothesis stated at the beginning. The more resources available to the attacker, the more successful the attacker is. This holds for the increasing number of attackers, larger eavesdropping range and the increasing number of malware infected nodes. Hybrid designed protocols are able to provide reasonable improvement (85 % of secured links from original 50 %) for up to 10 cooperating attackers, 40 m of attacker eavesdropping range, or up to 7 malware infected nodes out of 29 compromised. Detailed results are provided in [14], Appendix A.

5   Conclusions

Our work shows how narrow the view of attackers in ad hoc networks has been so far. We provide a more realistic view of that attacker, with a definition of her capabilities and behaviour. With respect to the protocols examined, we show that the hybrid designed protocols outperform the rest in all scenarios we examined, and that these protocols are quite robust across different attacker behaviour and capabilities. Note that the NO Best protocol provides almost same results as the HD Final protocol, yet this comes at the price of an enormous increase of messages sent. We also demonstrate that the hybrid designed protocols use a low number of messages and provide a great improvement for the link key security. Our results do not assume a particular compromise scenario during key establishment and are concerned only about the final fraction of compromised links, implying that the results can be generalised. Our work is based on realistic simulation of all components, which often get overlooked in protocols analyses coming right from particular protocol designers – we consider network communication (MAC, collisions), physical layer setting, etc. and we implemented the application to run directly on virtual nodes.

We found that one of the most significant parameters influencing the final performance of SA protocols is the initial compromise pattern. This is the first work with analysis of additional initial compromise patterns apart from the random one.

Last but not least, we point out that often the most favorable strategy for an attacker is to stay in one place during the whole secrecy amplification process.

References

1. Anderson, R., Chan, H., Perrig, A.: Key infection: smart trust for smart dust. In: 12th IEEE International Conference on Network Protocols, pp. 206–215. IEEE (2004)
2. Chan, H., Perrig, A., Song, D.: Random key predistribution schemes for sensor networks. In: IEEE Symposium on Security and Privacy, pp. 197–213 (2003)
3. Cvrček, D., Švenda, P.: Smart dust security-key infection revisited. Electron. Notes Theoret. Comput. Sci. **157**, 11–25 (2006). Elsevier
4. Pietro, R.D., Mancini, L.V., Mei, A.: Random key-assignment for secure wireless sensor networks. In: 1st ACM Workshop on Security of Ad Hoc and Sensor Networks, pp. 62–71 (2003)
5. Eschenauer, L., Gligor, V. D.: A key-management scheme for distributed sensor networks. In: 9th ACM Conference on Computer and Communications Security, Washington, DC, USA, pp. 41–47. ACM (2002)
6. Jurnečka, F., Stehlík, M., Matyáš, V.: Evaluation of key management schemes in wireless sensor networks. In: Mauw, S., Jensen, C.D. (eds.) STM 2014. LNCS, vol. 8743, pp. 198–203. Springer, Heidelberg (2014). doi:10.1007/978-3-319-11851-2_16
7. Jurnečka, F., Stehlík, M., Matyáš, V.: On node capturing attacker strategies. In: Christianson, B., Malcolm, J., Matyáš, V., Švenda, P., Stajano, F., Anderson, J. (eds.) Security Protocols 2014. LNCS, vol. 8809, pp. 300–315. Springer, Heidelberg (2014)
8. Kim, Y.-H., Kim, M.H., Lee, D.-H., Kim, C.: A key management scheme for commodity sensor networks. In: Syrotiuk, V.R., Chávez, E. (eds.) ADHOC-NOW 2005. LNCS, vol. 3738, pp. 113–126. Springer, Heidelberg (2005)
9. Köpke, A., et al.: Simulating wireless and mobile networks in OMNeT++ the MiXiM vision. In: Proceedings of the 1st International Conference on Simulation Tools and Techniques for Communications, Networks and Systems & Workshops, p. 71. ICST (2008)
10. Liu, D., Ning, P.: Establishing pairwise keys in distributed sensor networks. In: 10th ACM Conference on Computer and Communications Security, pp. 52–61. ACM Press (2003)
11. Liu, D., Ning, P., Li, R.: Establishing pairwise keys in distributed sensor networks. ACM Trans. Inf. Syst. Secur. **8**(1), 41–77 (2005)
12. Needham, R.M., Schroeder, M.D.: Using encryption for authentication in large networks of computers. Commun. ACM **21**(12), 993–999 (1978)
13. Ošťádal, R., Švenda, P., Matyáš, V.: A new approach to secrecy amplification in partially compromised networks (invited paper). In: Chakraborty, R.S., Matyas, V., Schaumont, P. (eds.) SPACE 2014. LNCS, vol. 8804, pp. 92–109. Springer, Heidelberg (2014)
14. Ošťádal, R., Švenda, P., Matyáš, V.: Attackers in Wireless Sensor Networks Will Be Neither Random nor Jumping - Secrecy Amplification Case, Extended Version, Technical report FIMU-RS-2016-04. Masaryk University, Czech Republic (2016)
15. Stetsko, A., Stehlik, M., Matyas, V.: Calibrating and comparing simulators for wireless sensor networks. In: 2011 IEEE 8th International Conference on Mobile Adhoc and Sensor Systems (MASS), pp. 733–738. IEEE (2011)
16. Varga, A.: Using the OMNeT++ discrete event simulation system in education. IEEE Trans. Educ. **42**(4), 11 (1999)
17. Švenda, P., Sekanina, L. , Matyáš, V.: Evolutionary design of secrecy amplification protocols for wireless sensor networks. In: Second ACM Conference on Wireless Network Security, pp. 225–236 (2009)

Improved Attacks on Extended Generalized Feistel Networks

Valérie Nachef[(⊠)], Nicolas Marrière, and Emmanuel Volte

Department of Mathematics, University of Cergy-Pontoise, CNRS UMR 8088,
2 Avenue Adolphe Chauvin, 95011 Cergy-Pontoise Cedex, France
{valerie.nachef,nicolas.marriere,emmanuel.volte}@u-cergy.fr

Abstract. In SAC 2013, Berger et al. defined Extended Generalized
Feistel Networks (EGFN) and analyzed their security. They proposed
designs with 8 or 16 branches. This class of schemes is well-suited for
cryptographic applications. Using the minimal number of active S-boxes,
the authors showed that for 64-bits messages divided into 8 branches,
at least seven rounds are needed for security against differential and
linear cyptanalysis. They proved that 10 rounds are required against
integral attacks and 9 rounds against impossible differential attacks. In
this paper, we propose a method that allows to attack up to 18 rounds
the design with 8 branches. We also mention the results for the 16-branch
design.

Keywords: Generic attacks on feistel type schemes · Pseudo-random
permutations · Differential cryptanalysis on block ciphers

1 Introduction

Many block ciphers are based on Feistel-type constructions. Some of them use
balanced Feistel constructions that divide a $2n$-bit plaintext into 2 n-bit branches
and apply a round function from n bits to n bits. DES [3,4], Camellia [1],
Simon [6] are such networks. Generalized Feistel Network divides the plaintext
into k branches of n bits and in that case, there are many more possibilities for
the choice of round functions. There are Unbalanced Feistel Networks with contracting functions where the round functions is from $(k-1)n$ bits to n bits. These
networks are also called Source-Heavy and are used for example in RC2 [17]
or SHA-1 [2]. When the round functions are from n bits to $(k-1)n$ bits, we
have an unbalanced Feistel Network with expanding functions also known as
Target-Heavy. This design is used in REDOC III [21] for example. Other possibilities for the round functions lead to other generalized Feistel networks as
Type-1 (CAST 256 [5], Lesamnta [10]), Type-2 (RC6 [16], CLEFIA [18]), Type-
3 (MARS [8]). All these ciphers have been extensively studied on different points
of view: security, diffusion and different kinds of attacks as linear, differential,
impossible differential or even boomerang attacks. A way to evaluate security
against differential or linear cryptanalysis is to count the minimal number of

© Springer International Publishing AG 2016
S. Foresti and G. Persiano (Eds.): CANS 2016, LNCS 10052, pp. 562–572, 2016.
DOI: 10.1007/978-3-319-48965-0_35

active S-boxes crossed along the cipher by differential and linear characteristics.
In [7], the authors proposed a new class of schemes, called Extended Generalized
Feistel Networks (EGFN) well suited for cryptographic applications. They first
represented Feistel Networks using matrix representation and then they optimized parameters such as diffusion delay, number of round functions per round,
cost of full diffusion to define this new class of schemes. Two examples are given,
with 8 or 16 branches. For EGFN, with 8 branches of 8-bit length, the number
of active S-boxes shows that to prevent differential or linear cryptanalysis, at
least 7 rounds are needed. In order to avoid integral attacks, it is necessary to
perform at least 10 rounds and against impossible differential attacks, one needs
at least 9 rounds. In this paper, using the variance method described in [19], we
show that it is possible to attack up to 18 rounds using differential attacks for
any word length. We provide the numbers of messages needed for NCPA (Non
Adaptive Chosen Plaintext Attack) and KPA (Known Plaintext Attack) up to
18 rounds. The paper is organized as follows. In Sect. 2, we give the notation and
present an overview of the attacks and describe the variance method. In Sect. 3,
we provide examples of computations of expectations and standard deviations
when we have some conditions on the inputs and the outputs and we are testing a random permutation. Section 4 is dedicated to the definition of EGFN and
attacks on these schemes. We prove that looking at the number of active S-boxes
is not enough for security since we can attack more rounds than expected. We
also provide simulation results.

2   Notations - Overview of the Attacks

2.1   Notation

The input is denoted by $[I_1, I_2, \ldots, I_8]$ the output by $[S_1, S_2, \ldots, S_8]$. Each I_s,
S_s is an element of $\{0,1\}^n$. When we have m messages, $I_s(i)$ represents part s
of the input of message number i. The same notation is used for the outputs as
well. We use differential attacks, i.e. attacks where we study how differences on
pairs of input variables will propagate following a differential characteristic, and
give relations between pairs of input/output variables. The number of rounds is
denoted by r.

We use plaintext/ciphertext pairs. On the input variables, the notation
$[\mathbf{0}, \mathbf{0}, \Delta_k^3, \ldots, \Delta_k^0]$ means that the pair of messages (i, j) satisfies $I_1(i) = I_1(j)$,
$I_2(i) = I_2(j)$, and $I_s(i) \oplus I_s(j) = \Delta_s^0$, $3 \leq s \leq 8$. The differential of the outputs
i and j after round t is denoted by $[\Delta_1^t, \Delta_2^t, \Delta_3^t, \ldots, \Delta_k^t]$. At each round, internal
variables are defined by the structure of the scheme. In our attacks, we deter-
mine equalities that have to be satisfied by the inputs and the outputs. With a
scheme, some equalities on the internal variables on some rounds will allow the
differential path to propagates. On an intermediate round, when equalities on
the internal variables are needed in order to get a differential characteristic, we
use the notation $\mathbf{0}$ to mean that the corresponding internal variables are equal
in messages i and j. When we write 0, this means that the differential path
propagates without any constraint on the internal functions.

2.2   Overview of the Attacks

Generic attacks that we will consider on EGFN are distinguishers that allow to determine the maximal number of rounds needed to distinguish a permutation computed by the EGNF from a random permutation. Depending on the number of rounds, it is possible to find some relations between the input and output variables. These relations hold conditionally to equalities on some internal variables due to the cipher structure. The attacks consist in using m plaintext/ciphertexts pairs and counting the number of couples of these pairs that satisfy the relations between the input and output variables. Then, it is possible to compare $\mathcal{N}_{perm}$, the number of such couples obtained with a random permutation, with $\mathcal{N}_{EGFN}$, the corresponding number for the studied EGFN. The attacks are successful, i.e. we are able to distinguish a permutation generated by an EGFN from a random permutation, in three cases. The first case occurs when $\mathcal{N}_{EGFN}$ is significantly greater than $\mathcal{N}_{perm}$. For example, attacks on unbalanced Feistel cipher with expanding functions used the fact that $\mathcal{N}_{EGFN}$ is significantly greater than $\mathcal{N}_{perm}$ [13,15,20]. The second case happens when $\mathcal{N}_{EGFN}$ is significantly smaller than $\mathcal{N}_{perm}$, this is the case for impossible attacks for example. For the third case, $\mathcal{N}_{perm}$ and $\mathcal{N}_{EGFN}$ have the same order, but the difference $|\mathbb{E}(\mathcal{N}_{EGFN}) - \mathbb{E}(\mathcal{N}_{perm})|$ is larger than both standard deviations $\sigma(\mathcal{N}_{perm})$ and $\sigma(\mathcal{N}_{EGFN})$, where $\mathbb{E}$ denotes the expectation function. In that case, the attacks work thanks to the Chebychev formula, which states that for any random variable X, and any $\alpha > 0$, we have $\mathbb{P}(|X - \mathbb{E}(X)| \geq \alpha\sigma(x)) \leq \frac{1}{\alpha^2}$. Using this formula, it is then possible to construct a prediction interval for $\mathcal{N}_{EGFN}$ for example, in which future computations will fall, with a good probability. It is important to notice that for our attacks, it is enough to compute $\mathbb{E}(\mathcal{N}_{perm})$, $\mathbb{E}(\mathcal{N}_{EGFN})$ and $\sigma(\mathcal{N}_{perm})$. In order to compute $\sigma(\mathcal{N}_{perm})$, we need to take into account the fact that the structures obtained from the m plaintext/ciphertext tuples are not independent. However, their mutual dependence is very small. To compute $\sigma(\mathcal{N}_{perm})$, we will use this well-known formula, see [9], p. 97, that we will call the "Covariance Formula": if $x_1, \ldots x_n$, are random variables, then if V represents the variance, we have $V(\sum_{i=1}^{n} x_i) = \sum_{i=1}^{n} V(x_i) + 2\sum_{i=1}^{n-1}\sum_{j=i+1}^{n}[\mathbb{E}(x_i\, x_j) - \mathbb{E}(x_i)\mathbb{E}(x_j)]$. The computation of standard deviation and the use of the covariance formula usually allow to attacks more rounds than other attacks. This technique has been used for classical Feistel schemes in [12], for contracting Feistel schemes in [14] and for generalized Feistel schemes in [11].

3   Expectations and Standard Deviation for KPA on Random Permutations

Even number of rounds. In KPA, when attacking an even number of rounds, we count the number of (i, j) such that $I_4(i) = I_4(j)$ and $S_5(i) \oplus S_5(j) = I_5(i) \oplus I_5(j)$. Then the exact values for the expectation and standard deviation obtained thanks the tool developed in [19] are:

$$\mathbb{E}(\mathcal{N}_{perm}) = \frac{m(m-1)}{2} \frac{2^{30n} - 2^{23n} - 2^{22n} + 2^{16n}}{(2^{8n}(2^{8n}-1))^2}$$

$$\mathbb{E}(\mathcal{N}_{perm}) \simeq \frac{m^2}{2} \left(\frac{1}{2^{2n}} - \frac{1}{2^{9n}} - \frac{1}{2^{10n}} + O(\frac{1}{2^{10n}}) \right)$$

and

$$V(\mathcal{N}_{perm}) = -\mathbb{E}(\mathcal{N}_{perm})^2 + \frac{m(m-1)}{(2^{8n}(2^{8n}-1)(2^{8n}-2)(2^{8n}-3))^2} P(n,m)$$

with $P(n,m)$ is a polynomial in m and n obtained by the computer program and whose expression is quite long. Then we obtain: $V(\mathcal{N}_{perm}) \simeq \mathbb{E}(\mathcal{N}_{perm})$.

Odd number of rounds. In KPA, when the number on rounds is odd, we count the number of (i,j) such that $I_4(i) = I_4(j)$, $S_8(i) = S_8(j)$ and $S_1(i) \oplus S_1(j) = I_5(i) \oplus I_5(j)$.

Then the exact values for the expectation and standard deviation obtained thanks the tool developed in [19] are:

$$\mathbb{E}(\mathcal{N}_{perm}) = \frac{m(m-1)}{2} \frac{2^{29n} - 2 \cdot 2^{22n} + 2^{16n}}{(2^{8n}(2^{8n}-1))^2}$$

$$\mathbb{E}(\mathcal{N}_{perm}) \simeq \frac{m^2}{2} \left(\frac{1}{2^{3n}} - 2\frac{1}{2^{10n}} + 2\frac{1}{2^{11n}} + O(\frac{1}{2^{16n}}) \right)$$

and where, as previously, $P(n,m)$ is given by the computer program and we get that $V(\mathcal{N}_{perm}) \simeq \mathbb{E}(\mathcal{N}_{perm})$ as well.

4   Extended Generalized Feistel Networks

4.1 ·Description

The input is denoted by $[I_1, I_2, \ldots, I_8]$. At each round 4 internal functions from n bits to n bits are used. For round r, we denote these rounds functions by $f_{t,r}$, $t = 1, 2, 3, 4$. For example, after one round, the output is $[S_1, S_2, \ldots, S_8]$ with

$$\begin{cases} S_1 = I_5 \oplus f_{4,1}(I_4) \\ S_2 = I_6 \oplus I_4 \oplus f_{3,1}(I_3) \\ S_3 = I_7 \oplus I_4 \oplus f_{2,1}(I_2) \\ S_4 = I_8 \oplus I_2 \oplus I_3 \oplus I_4 \oplus f_{1,1}(I_1) \end{cases} \qquad \begin{cases} S_5 = I_1 \\ S_6 = I_2 \\ S_7 = I_3 \\ S_8 = I_4 \end{cases}$$

At round ℓ, four internal variables are introduced on the first four branches. Let us call them $X^\ell, Y^\ell, Z^\ell, T^\ell$.

After one round, the output is $[X^1, Y^1, Z^1, T^1, I_1, I_2, I_3, I_4]$. More generally, after round ℓ, the output is $[X^\ell, Y^\ell, Z^\ell, T^\ell, X^{\ell-1}, Y^{\ell-1}, Z^{\ell-1}, T^{\ell-1}]$. One round of EGFN with 8 branches is represented in Fig. 1.

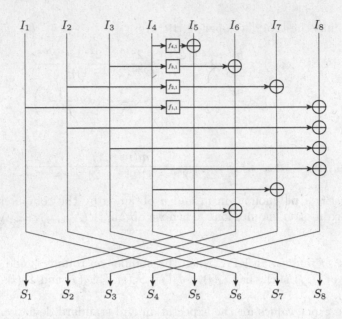

Fig. 1. One round of EGFN

4.2   Generic Attacks on EGFN with 8 Branches

We will detail the attacks on EGFN with 8 branches and just state the results for EGFN with 16 branches.

Simple Attacks on the First Rounds.

Attack one round. After one round, with one message, we get an attack since we just have to check whether for example $S_5 = I_1$. With a random permutation, this happens with probability $\frac{1}{2^n}$ whereas this is satisfied with probability 1 with an EGFN.

Attack on two rounds. Here we have a NCPA with 2 messages and a KPA with $2^{n/2}$ messages. The attacks proceed as follows. We first choose 2 messages such that $I_4(1) = I_4(2)$ and we check if $S_1(1) \oplus S_1(2) = I_5(1) \oplus I_5(2)$. This is satisfied with probability 1 for an EGFN and with probability $\frac{1}{2^n}$ for a random permutation. This NCPA can be transformed into a KPA as follows. If we generate $2^{n/2}$ messages, then by the birthday paradox, we will obtain with a good probability 2 indices i, j with $i \neq j$ and such that $I_4(i) = I_4(j)$. Then we just have to check if $S_1(i) \oplus S_1(j) = I_5(i) \oplus I_5(j)$.

Attack on three rounds. After the third round, it is easy to check that $S_5 = I_1 \oplus f_{1,2}(I_8 \oplus I_2 \oplus I_3 \oplus I_4 \oplus f_{4,1}(I_1))$. This allows to mount a NCPA with only 2 messages. We choose them such that $I_1(1) = I_1(2), I_2(1) = I_2(2), I_3(1) = I_3(2)$, $I_4(1) = I_4(2)$ and $I_8(1) = I_8(2)$. The, we check if $S_5(1) = S_5(2)$. The probability is 1 for an EGFN and $\frac{1}{2^n}$ for a random permutation. As previously, the NCPA can be transformed into a KPA needing $2^{5n/2}$ messages. But there is a better attack that needs only 2^n messages as we will see. We count the number of (i,j) such that we have: $I_4(i) = I_4(j)$, $S_8(i) = S_8(j)$ and $S_1(i) \oplus S_1(j) = I_5(i) \oplus I_5(j)$. Here, we have $\mathcal{N}_{perm} \simeq \frac{m(m-1)}{2 \cdot 2^{3n}}$. With an EFGN, it is easy to see that $S_8(i) = S_8(j) \Rightarrow S_1(i) \oplus S_1(j) = I_5(i) \oplus I_5(j)$. This show that $\mathcal{N}_{EGFN} \simeq \frac{m(m-1)}{2 \cdot 2^{2n}}$. Thus with about 2^n messages, it is possible to distinguish an EGFN from a random permutation.

Attack on four rounds. There is a NCPA with about $2^{\frac{n}{2}}$ messages. We choose m messages such that $I_4 = 0$. Then we count the number of (i,j), such that $i \neq j$ and $I_5(i) \oplus I_5(j) = S_5(i) \oplus S_5(j)$. With a random permutation, we have that $\mathcal{N}_{perm} \simeq \frac{m(m-1)}{2 \cdot 2^n}$. With an EGFN, the equality $I_5(i) \oplus I_5(j) = S_5(i) \oplus S_5(j)$ is satisfied either at random or due to the following equality $T^2(i) = T^2(j)$. $\mathbb{E}(\mathcal{N}_{EGFN}) \simeq 2\mathbb{E}(\mathcal{N}_{perm})$. With about $2^{n/2}$ messages, it is possible to distinguish a random permutation from an EGFN in NCPA. We can transform this attack into a KPA with 2^n messages.

Attack on five rounds. For the NCPA, we choose m messages such that $\forall i, 1 \leq i \leq m$, $I_1(i) = I_2(i) = I_3(i) = I_4(i) = I_8(i) = 0$. The conditions on the input imply that for all i, we have $T^1(i) = 0$. Moreover, we have: $S_5 = X^4 = I_1 \oplus f_{4,2}(T^1) \oplus f_{4,4}(T^3)$. Then we count the number of (i,j), such that $i \neq j$ and $S_5(i) = S_5(j)$. With a random permutation, we obtain that $\mathcal{N}_{perm} \simeq \frac{m(m-1)}{2 \cdot 2^n}$. With an EGFN, the equality $S_5(i) = S_5(j)$ is satisfied either at random or due to the following equality $T^3(i) = T^3(j)$. $\mathbb{E}(\mathcal{N}_{EGFN}) \simeq 2\mathbb{E}(\mathcal{N}_{perm})$. With about $2^{n/2}$ messages, it is possible to distinguish a random permutation from an EGFN in NCPA. This attack can be transformed into a KPA with $2^{5n/2}$ messages but there is a better KPA that we describe now. We will make use of the differential characteristics described in Table 1. Since these characteristics will be used up to 18 rounds, we provide the differential path up to 18 rounds.

We count the number of indices (i,j), such that $i \neq j$, $I_4(i) = I_4(j)$, $I_5(i) \oplus I_5(j) = S_1(i) \oplus S_1(j)$ and $S_8(i) = S_8(j)$. With a random permutation, we have $\mathcal{N}_{perm} \simeq \frac{m(m-1)}{2 \cdot 2^{3n}}$. With an EGFN, the conditions can be satisfied at random or because we have: $T^2(i) = T^2(j)$ and $T^4(i) = T^4(j)$. This shows that $\mathbb{E}(\mathcal{N}_{EGFN}) \simeq 2\mathbb{E}(\mathcal{N}_{perm})$ and that with about $2^{3n/2}$ messages, it is possible to distinguish an EGFN from a random permutation.

Attacks Using the Computation of Standard deviation When $r \geq 6$. After 6 rounds, we need to compute the standard deviation in order to perform

Table 1. Characteristics for attacks on EGFN with 8 branches

round	Δ_1^0	Δ_2^0	Δ_3^0	0	Δ_5^0	Δ_6^0	Δ_7^0	Δ_8^0
1	Δ_5^0						0	
2				0	Δ_5^0			
3	Δ_5^0						0	
4				0	Δ_5^0			
5	Δ_5^0						0	
6				0	Δ_5^0			
7	Δ_5^0						0	
8				0	Δ_5^0			
9	Δ_5^0						0	
10				0	Δ_5^0			
11	Δ_5^0						0	
12				0	Δ_5^0			
13	Δ_5^0						0	
14				0	Δ_5^0			
15	Δ_5^0						0	
16				0	Δ_5^0			
17	Δ_5^0						0	
18				0	Δ_5^0			

our attacks. We use the differential characteristics of Table 1, except for 5 and 7 rounds.

NCPA. For NCPA, when the number of rounds is even, we choose m messages such that $\forall i$, $1 \leq i \leq m$ $I_4(i) = 0$. The attacks are shown in Table 2. In order to determine the number of messages needed for the attack, we use the fact that the difference of the expectations has to be greater than the standard deviation as explained in Sect. 2.2. The expectation for EGFN is also computed thanks to the computer program from [19].

We now give attacks when the number of rounds is odd. For $r = 7, 9$, we choose m messages such that $\forall i$, $1 \leq i \leq m$, $I_1(i) = I_2(i) = I_3(i) = I_4(i) = I_5(i) = 0$. Notice that with these conditions, there are only 2^{3n} available messages. The conditions on the input imply that for all i, we have $T^1(i) = 0$. After 7 rounds,

Table 2. NCPA on $2r$ rounds, $r \geq 3$

Differential	$E(\mathcal{N}_{perm})$	$E(\mathcal{N}_{EGFN_8})$		$\sigma(\mathcal{N}_{perm})$	m
$\Delta_5^0 = \Delta_5^{2r}$	$\frac{m^2}{2 \cdot 2^n}$	$\frac{m^2}{2 \cdot 2^n} + \frac{m^2}{2 \cdot 2^{(r-1)n}} + O(\frac{m^2}{2^{rn}})$		$\frac{m}{\sqrt{2} \cdot 2^n}$	$2^{(r-3/2)n}$

we have $S_5 = X^6 = I_1 \oplus f_{1,2}(T^1) \oplus f_{1,4}(T^3) \oplus f_{1,6}(T^5)$ and after 9 rounds, we have $S_5 = X^8 = I_1 \oplus f_{1,2}(T^1) \oplus f_{1,4}(T^3) \oplus f_{1,6}(T^5) \oplus f_{1,8}(T^7)$. When the number of rounds is odd and greater than or equal to 11, the previous attack does not work anymore, since we will need more than 2^{3n} messages. Thus we perform the attacks described in Table 3.

Table 3. NCPA on $2r + 1$ rounds, $r \geq 5$

r	Differential	$E(\mathcal{N}_{perm})$	$E(\mathcal{N}_{EGFN_8})$	$\sigma(\mathcal{N}_{perm})$	m
7	$\Delta_1^0 = \Delta_5^7$	$\frac{m^2}{2 \cdot 2^n}$	$\frac{m^2}{2 \cdot 2^n} + \frac{m^2}{2 \cdot 2^{2n}} + +O(\frac{m^2}{2^{3n}})$	$\frac{m}{\sqrt{2} \cdot 2^{n/2}}$	$2^{3n/2}$
9	$\Delta_1^0 = \Delta_5^9$	$\frac{m^2}{2 \cdot 2^n}$	$\frac{m^2}{2 \cdot 2^n} + \frac{m^2}{2 \cdot 2^{3n}} + O(\frac{m^2}{2^{4n}})$	$\frac{m}{\sqrt{2} \cdot 2^{n/2}}$	$2^{5n/2}$
$2r+1, r \geq 5$	$\Delta_8^{2r+1} = 0$ $\Delta_5^0 = \Delta_1^{2r+1}$	$\frac{m^2}{2 \cdot 2^{2n}}$	$\frac{m^2}{2 \cdot 2^{2n}} + \frac{m^2}{2 \cdot 2^{rn}} + O(\frac{m^2}{2^{(r+1)n}})$	$\frac{m}{\sqrt{2} \cdot 2^n}$	$2^{(r-1)n}$

KPA. Again, we have two kinds of attacks according to the parity of the number of rounds. The attacks follows the differential characteristics given in Table 1 and are explained in Table 4. For example, for 6 rounds, the computer program from [19] gives:

$$E(\mathcal{N}_{EGFN_8}) = \frac{m(m-1)}{2 \cdot 2^{2n}} \frac{(1 + \frac{1}{2^n} - \frac{1}{2^{2n}} + \frac{1}{2^{4n}} - \frac{3}{2^{5n}} + \frac{2}{2^{6n}} - \frac{1}{2^{7n}})}{(1 - \frac{1}{2^{8n}})}$$

Table 4. KPA for more than 6 rounds

Rounds	Differential	$E(\mathcal{N}_{perm})$	$E(\mathcal{N}_{EGFN_8})$	$\sigma(\mathcal{N}_{perm})$	m
$2r$	$\Delta_4^0 = 0$ $\Delta_5^0 = \Delta_5^{2r}$	$\frac{m^2}{2 \cdot 2^{2n}}$	$\frac{m^2}{2 \cdot 2^{2n}} + \frac{m^2}{2 \cdot 2^{rn}} + O(\frac{m^2}{2^{(r+1)n}})$	$\frac{m}{\sqrt{2} \cdot 2^n}$	$2^{(r-1)n}$
$2r+1$	$\Delta_4^0 = 0$ $\Delta_8^{2r+1} = 0$ $\Delta_5^0 = \Delta_1^{2r+1}$	$\frac{m^2}{2 \cdot 2^{3n}}$	$\frac{m^2}{2 \cdot 2^{3n}} + \frac{m^2}{2 \cdot 2^{(r+1)n}} + O(\frac{m^2}{2^{(r+2)n}})$	$\frac{m}{\sqrt{2} \cdot 2^{3n/2}}$	$2^{(r-\frac{1}{2})n}$

4.3   Simulations

We have made simulations of several attacks for small values of n. The results are consistent with the theoretical study and are provided in Table 5. The process of the simulations is as follow: we choose a random instance of EGFN and a random permutation (generated by a classical Feisel scheme with 20 rounds). Then we start the attack for m messages and we count the number of plaintext/ciphertext pairs that verify the relations involved for the EGFN and for the permutation. Finally, we repeat the process 200 times in order to compute the mean value for EGFN and for the permutation and the standard deviation for the permutation.

Table 5. Experimental results with 200 tries

r	n	m	$\mathbb{E}(N_{perm})$	$\mathbb{E}(N_{EGFN})$	Difference	$\sigma(N_{perm})$	% success
10	3	2^{13}	524 254	525 376	1 122	752	72
10	4	2^{17}	33 554 466	33 562 415	7 949	5 586	73
11	3	2^{15}	1 048 469	1 049 971	1 502	991	74
11	4	2^{20}	134 218 546	134 261 461	42 915	12 460	82
12	3	2^{16}	33 553 817	33 565 842	12 025	5 638	65

4.4   Summary of the Results

As long as the difference of the expectations is smaller than the standard deviations with a number of messages smaller than 2^{8n}, we can mount the attacks provided in Tables 2, 3 and 4. We stop when we reach the whole codebook and this gives the maximal number of rounds that we can attack with this method. The results are summarized in Table 6. We provide the number of messages needed for each attack.

Table 6. Complexity of the attacks on EGFN with 8 branches

Rounds	NCPA	KPA	Rounds	NCPA	KPA
1	1	1	10	$2^{7n/2}$	2^{4n}
2	2	$2^{n/2}$	11	2^{4n}	$2^{9n/2}$
3	2	2^{n}	12	$2^{9n/2}$	2^{5n}
4	$2^{n/2}$	2^{n}	13	2^{5n}	$2^{11n/2}$
5	$2^{n/2}$	$2^{3n/2}$	14	$2^{11n/2}$	2^{6n}
6	$2^{3n/2}$	2^{2n}	15	2^{6n}	$2^{13n/2}$
7	$2^{3n/2}$	$2^{5n/2}$	16	$2^{13n/2}$	2^{7n}
8	$2^{5n/2}$	2^{3n}	17	2^{7n}	$2^{15n/2}$
9	$2^{5n/2}$	$2^{7n/2}$	18	2^{8n}	2^{8n}

Remark 1. EGFN with 16 branches is described in [7]. The attacks are quite similar and it is possible to show that there exists attacks up to 34 rounds.

5.   Conclusion

In this paper, we described several generic attacks on EGFN. Simulations confirm the theoretical analysis of this scheme. We were able to attack more rounds than stated in paper where the EGFN were designed.

References

1. Camellia home page. https://info.isl.ntt.co.jp/crypt/eng/camellia/
2. Secure Hash Standard. Federal Information Processing Standard Publication 180–4. US Department of Commerce, National Institute of Standard and Technology, Technical report (2012)
3. Encryption Algorithm for Computer Data Protection. Technical Report Federal Register 40(52) 12134, National Bureau of Standards, March 1975
4. Notice of a Proposed Federal Information Processing Data Encryption. Technical Report Federal Register 40(149) 12607, National Bureau of Standards, August 1975
5. Adams, C., Heys, H., Tavares, S., Wiener, M.: The CAST-256 Encryption Algorithm. Technical report, AES Submission (1998)
6. Beaulieu, R., Shors, D., Smith, J., Treatman-Clarck, S., Weeks, B., Wingers, L.: The Simon and Speck Families of Lightweight Block Ciphers. Cryptology ePrint archive: 2013/404: Listing for 2013
7. Berger, T.P., Minier, M., Thomas, G.: Extended generalized feistel networks using matrix representation. In: Lange, T., Lauter, K., Lisoněk, P. (eds.) SAC 2013. LNCS, vol. 8282, pp. 289–305. Springer, Heidelberg (2014)
8. Burwick, C., Coppersmith, D., DÁvignon, E., Gennaro, R., Halevi, S., Jutla, C., Matyas Jr., S.M., OĆonnor, L., Peyravian, M., Safford, D., Zunic, N.: MARS - a candidate cipher for AES. Technical report, AES Submission (1998)
9. Hoel, P.G., Port, S.C., Stone, C.J.: Introduction to Probability Theory. Houghton Mifflin Company, Boston (1971)
10. Hirose, S., Kuwakado, H., Yoshida, H.: SHA-3 Proposal: Lesamnta (2009)
11. Nachef, V., Volte, E., Patarin, J.: Differential attacks on generalized feistel schemes. In: Abdalla, M., Nita-Rotaru, C., Dahab, R. (eds.) CANS 2013. LNCS, vol. 8257, pp. 1–19. Springer, Heidelberg (2013)
12. Patarin, J.: Generic attacks on feistel schemes. In: Boyd, C. (ed.) ASIACRYPT 2001. LNCS, vol. 2248, pp. 222–238. Springer, Heidelberg (2001)
13. Patarin, J., Nachef, V., Berbain, C.: Generic Attacks on Unbalanced Feistel Schemes with Expanding Functions - Extended version. Cryptology ePrint archive: 2007/449: Listing for 2007
14. Patarin, J., Nachef, V., Berbain, C.: Generic attacks on unbalanced feistel schemes with contracting functions. In: Lai, X., Chen, K. (eds.) ASIACRYPT 2006. LNCS, vol. 4284, pp. 396–411. Springer, Heidelberg (2006)
15. Patarin, J., Nachef, V., Berbain, C.: Generic attacks on unbalanced feistel schemes with expanding functions. In: Kurosawa, K. (ed.) ASIACRYPT 2007. LNCS, vol. 4833, pp. 325–341. Springer, Heidelberg (2007)
16. Rivest, R.L., Robshaw, M., Sidney, R., Yin, Y.L.: The RC6 Block Cipher. Technical report, AES Submission (1998)
17. Rivest, R.L.: A Description of the RC2 Encryption Algorithm. File draft-rivest-rc2desc-00.txt. ftp://ftp.ietf.org/internet-drafts/
18. Shirai, T., Shibutani, K., Akishita, T., Moriai, S., Iwata, T.: The 128-Bit blockcipher CLEFIA (extended abstract). In: Biryukov, A. (ed.) FSE 2007. LNCS, vol. 4593, pp. 181–195. Springer, Heidelberg (2007)
19. Volte, E., Nachef, V., Marrière, N.: Automatic Expectation and Variance Computing for Attacks on Feistel Schemes. Cryptology ePrint archive: 2016/136: Listing for 2016

20. Volte, E., Nachef, V., Patarin, J.: Improved generic attacks on unbalanced feistel schemes with expanding functions. In: Abe, M. (ed.) ASIACRYPT 2010. LNCS, vol. 6477, pp. 94–111. Springer, Heidelberg (2010)
21. Wood. Method of Cryptographically Transforming Electronic Digital Data from One Form to Another (1991)

When Constant-Time Source Yields Variable-Time Binary: Exploiting Curve25519-donna Built with MSVC 2015

Thierry Kaufmann[1(✉)], Hervé Pelletier[1], Serge Vaudenay[2], and Karine Villegas[3]

[1] Kudelski Security, Cheseaux, Switzerland
{thierry.kaufmann,herve.pelletier}@kudelskisecurity.com
[2] EPFL, Lausanne, Switzerland
serge.vaudenay@epfl.ch
[3] Nagravision, Cheseaux, Switzerland
karine.villegas@nagra.com

Abstract. The elliptic curve *Curve25519* has been presented as protected against state-of-the-art timing attacks [2]. This paper shows that a timing attack is still achievable against a particular *X25519* implementation which follows the RFC 7748 requirements [10]. The attack allows the retrieval of the complete private key used in the ECDH protocol. This is achieved due to timing leakage during Montgomery ladder execution and relies on a conditional branch in the Windows runtime library 2015. The attack can be applied remotely.

Keywords: Side-channel · Timing attack · ECC · RFC 7748 · X25519

1 Introduction

Side-channel attacks are a proven practical means of attack against cryptographic implementations [5]. They make use of physical quantities, e.g., electromagnetic emanations, power consumption, photon emissions, timing variations, etc., to retrieve some sensitive information such as a secret key. Timing attacks were first presented in 1996 by Kocher [8]. They have been shown to be very effective while easily performed. In particular side-channel timing attacks are not intrusive and do not require high-end equipment nor necessarily physical access to the targeted system. Thus they can be applied remotely.

Elliptic curves are increasingly used in cryptography. The asymmetric keys of an ECC implementation are smaller than those required for an RSA implementation with the same cryptographic security. RFC 7748 [10] presents an ECC design that uses regular operations and is thus supposed to be resistant to side-channel timing attacks. The RFC is intended to prevent use of curves which have inherent side-channel leakage weaknesses. Classical side-channel attacks against such poor ECC implementations are published regularly, e.g., [1,6].

© Springer International Publishing AG 2016
S. Foresti and G. Persiano (Eds.): CANS 2016, LNCS 10052, pp. 573–582, 2016.
DOI: 10.1007/978-3-319-48965-0_36

In this paper we show that having regular operations is necessary but not sufficient. It is not possible to ensure a side-channel attack proof system in a high level environment. Indeed, we do not have real control over a high performance ecosystem like a server (high-level programming language, compiler/linker, pre-processor options, etc.). In the following sections we present a timing attack capable of retrieving the private key used in the ECDH protocol remotely.

2   State of the Art

In his paper [8], Kocher pointed out that it is common for a cryptosystem to take different amounts of time to execute the same calculation for different inputs. This is due to many factors including code architecture, compiler, processor optimizations, and cache. He showed that rather simple timing attacks could be perpetrated on implementations of Diffie-Hellman, RSA, and DSS. He particularly targeted modular exponentiation, which has a secret or sensitive input-dependent execution.

Later, Brumley and Boneh showed that it was possible to mount remote timing attacks by implementing an attack against OpenSSL [3]. By measuring the time between sending a decryption request to a server and the reception of the response they were able to extract the private key of the server. They exploited the fact that the *sliding window* exponentiation (an optimization of *square and multiply*) uses Montgomery reduction in order to reduce modulo q. This reduction uses an extra step ("extra reduction") in some specific cases and this creates a difference in timing which can be exploited. They showed that the noise due to network communication overhead could be eliminated by sampling several times. Their attacks required however the network to have less than 1ms of variance.

In 2011, Brumley and Tuveri [4] showed that remote timing attacks were still feasible on ECC implementations that were meant to be more resistant to this kind of attack. They showed that the fixed-sequence Montgomery ladder used in the computation of the scalar multiplication was not sufficient to fully protect against their attack. They were able to recover the private key remotely, using a lattice attack [7].

3   Curve25519

The *Curve25519* was first presented by Bernstein in 2006 [2]. It is an elliptic curve of the form $y^2 = x^3 + 486662x^2 + x$, which is birationally equivalent to the Edwards curve: $1 \cdot x^2 + y^2 = 1 + (121665/121666)x^2y^2$. It exists over the field $\mathbb{F}_p$, with $p = 2^{255} - 19$. The order of the base point is the prime $p_1 = 2^{252} + 27742317777372353535851937790883648493$. By design, there is no need for special processing for $\mathcal{O}$ (infinite) or points outside the curve and any 32-byte sequence can be used as public key. Only the x-coordinate of the points is used in the computations.

The implementation of this curve for ECDH (called $X25519$) makes use of a 32-byte secret key and a 32-byte public key. The secret key begins with the bits 01 and the last three bits are set to 0.

The value of the x-coordinate of the base point is 9 with prime order p_1 (written above) over the field $\mathbb{F}_p$.

The exchange works in the following way:

- Each user takes the public string 9 (x-coordinate of the base point on the curve) and multiplies it by their secret key key_i. The result is in fact the public key K_i (only the x-coordinate of the point) of each user.
- The public keys are exchanged and both users then compute $key_i * K_j$, with K_j a point on the curve and key_i the scalar.
- Each user ends up with the point $key_i * key_j * 9$ (respectively $key_j * key_i * 9$), which is the shared secret.

$Curve25519$ was presented in 2006 by Bernstein with security in mind. This curve naturally provides state-of-the-art timing-attack protection. Particularly the implementation avoids input-dependent branches, input-dependent array indices, and other instructions with input-dependent timings. Moreover, by nature, this curve offers high speed computation and free key compression. In order to speed up the computation the integers are loaded into the floating-point registers. Some parts of the code are directly written in assembly language.

3.1 Curve25519-donna

Adam Langley implemented this curve (in C) in order to compute ECDH. This version, called $Donna$ [9], follows the RFC recommendations.

It is based on Bernstein's implementation and makes use of a modified version of the Montgomery ladder to compute the point multiplications (for projective coordinates). This Montgomery ladder allows computation of the addition and doubling in an interleaved way and is intended to do this in a constant time regardless of input. It makes use of an accessory swap function whose execution is also expected to run with constant time. These functions are described in RFC 7748 [10].

The coordinates of the points of the elliptic curve are represented by a reduced-degree reduced-coefficient polynomial and each polynomial coefficient is represented over 64 bits.

Representation of the Integers Modulo $2^{255} - 19$. Elements of $\mathbb{Z}/(2^{255} - 19)$ can be seen as elements of R (for $x = 1$), the ring of polynomials $\sum_i u_i x^i$ where u_i is an integer multiple of $2^{\lceil 25.5i \rceil}$.

The coordinates of the points on the curve (integers modulo $2^{255} - 19$) are represented by such a polynomial with the requirement of being reduced-degree and reduced-coefficient.

Reduced-degree means that the degree of the polynomial is small. In this case the maximum degree of the polynomial is 9. Limiting the degree of the polynomial allows reduction of the number of coefficient multiplications when multiplying the integer.

Reduced-coefficient means restricting the highest possible value of a coefficient. For this implementation, the value of the coefficient $u_i/2^{\lceil 25.5i \rceil}$ is limited from 2^{-25} to 2^{25}.

In summary, the coordinates are represented by the 10 coefficients u_0, $u_1/2^{26}$, $u_2/2^{51}$, $u_3/2^{77}$, $u_4/2^{102}$, $u_5/2^{128}$, $u_6/2^{153}$, $u_7/2^{179}$, $u_8/2^{204}$, $u_9/2^{230}$ from the polynomial $u_0 + u_1 x + ... + u_9 x^9$. The value of a coordinate is given by $X = u_0 + u_1 + ... + u_9$. Note that this representation is not unique, but is faster to compute than the *smallest* representation [2].

4   Attack

4.1   Environment

The attack was performed on two computers running 64-bit Windows 7 OS. The first computer was equipped with the Intel processor *i5-2400* (3.1 GHz, 4 cores, 4 threads, *Sandy Bridge* architecture), while the processor of the second PC was a dual Intel Xeon E5-2630v2 (2.6 GHz, 12 cores, 24 threads, *Ivy Bridge*). The code was compiled for 32-bit architectures using Visual Studio 2015 (MSVC). It makes use of the Windows runtime libraries 2015. The program was written in C.

In order to be as close as possible to a real case we did not change the default enabled options in the BIOS: *Hardware Prefetcher*, *Adjacent Cache Line Prefetcher*, *DCU Streamer Prefetcher*, and *DCU IP Prefetcher*.

Counter. In order to measure timings we made use of the assembly instruction for Intel processors called *rdtsc* (for *Read Time-Stamp Counter*) which allows reading of the time stamp counter of the processor. The time-stamp counter is contained in a 64-bit MSR (Model-Specific Register). Using this command before and after the processing, it was possible to determine the elapsed number of clock cycles. This instruction is not portable as it can only be applied to Intel processors.

4.2   Timing Leakage Observation

Although the computation of the scalar multiplication should be time-constant, we spotted some timing differences depending on the value of the key. When comparing the mean value (over 10,000 measurements) of the execution times of the multiplication of the base point 9 with either the same key or different keys, we observed some differences (Fig. 1). We made three observations from the results shown on Fig. 1.

First, the counter induces some timing differences. Two identical executions do not take the same number of cycles.

Second, the variance of the timing executions is different for the execution of the same computation and the computation with different values of key. This implies some input-dependent instructions.

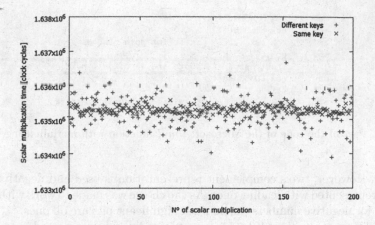

Fig. 1. Computation times depending on the key.

Third, the timing difference seen is small. For 256 bits the difference is at most 4000 clock cycles while the overall computation takes about 1.6 million clock cycles.

4.3   Timing Leakage Origin

After a careful analysis of the binary code, the observed timing leakage appeared to be coming from the assembly function *llmul.asm* found in the Windows runtime library[1]. The function *llmul.asm* is called to compute the multiplication of two 64-bit integers. It contains a branch condition which causes differences in execution time (see Fig. 2, line 65). If both operands of the multiplication have their 32 most significant bits equal to 0 then the multiplication of these words is avoided as the computation is correctly judged to be 0.

This runtime function is called by the program when executing the multiplication with a constant in the function *fscalar_product* (Listing 1.1) in the Montgomery ladder algorithm described in [10]. There was no way to see that this ordinary multiplication could cause a difference of timing, especially as a carry is never needed with coefficients being smaller than 2^{25}.

Listing 1.1. Code in *fscalar_product function*

```
for (i = 0; i < 10; ++i) {
        output[i] = in[i] * scalar;
}
```

We saw in Sect. 3.1 that the coefficients representing the coordinates are bounded between -2^{25} and 2^{25}, thus smaller than 2^{32} and representable over 32

---

[1] A runtime library is a library for a specific environment. It contains pieces of code that can be called by a program executed in this environment.

```
61          mov     eax,HIWORD(A)
62          mov     ecx,HIWORD(B)
63          or      ecx,eax         ;test for both hiwords zero.
64          mov     ecx,LOWORD(B)
65          jnz     short hard      ;both are zero, just mult ALO and BLO
66          mov     eax,LOWORD(A)
67          mul     ecx
68          ret     16              ; callee restores the stack
```

Fig. 2. Part of the code of the Microsoft *llmul* function with incriminating line

bits only. However, two's complement representation is used and negative numbers are represented with leading ones. As the choice was made to work with 64-bit integers, for negative numbers the 32 most significant bits are all ones.

In addition, the *scalar* (121665) is a positive integer represented over 32 bits and the 32 most significant bits are therefore all 0. Thus the execution of the second part of the code of *llmul* only depends on the sign of the coefficient. We can say that the computation time of a key bit (k_i) in the Montgomery ladder is dependent on the number of negative coefficients representing the coordinates of the point being processed.

4.4   Timing Attack

In the Montgomery ladder, the value of the key bit k_i only decides which coordinates will be doubled and which ones will be added. Let's call c_{ij} the jth coefficient of the polynomial representing the intermediate value of the new Z-coordinate of the point which is multiplied by the scalar for the bit k_i in the Montgomery ladder.

The values of the coefficients c_{ij}'s depend on several parameters: the base point, the values of the previously processed bits of the key, and k_i. For a given base point and fixing the previous bits (more significant) it is possible to count the number of negative coefficients among the c_{ij}'s, by executing the code until k_i. Depending on the base point and the key there can be a different number of negative coefficients when $k_i = 0$ or $k_i = 1$. This difference can go from 0 to 10 which is still a very small difference in terms of clock cycles.

Attack Core Idea. We can see the overall computation time (called F below) as the time required to process all the previous bits, the attacked bit and the next bits. For a key $k = k_{l-1}k_{l-2}...k_1k_0$ and a base point P, we have:

$$
\begin{aligned}
F(k, P) = &\sum_{j>i} f(k_j|k_{l-1}, k_{l-2}, ..., k_{j+1}, P) \\
&+ f(k_i|k_{l-1}, k_{l-2}, ..., k_{i+1}, P) \\
&+ \sum_{j<i} f(k_j|k_{l-1}, k_{l-2}, ..., k_i, ..., k_{j+1}, P)
\end{aligned}
\tag{1}
$$

where f is the time of the processing of 1 bit in the Montgomery ladder.

Keeping this in mind, if we choose base points so that there is the same number of negative coefficients for the ith bit k_i, the time due to the processing of the other bits (before and after) can be assumed to be random from one execution to another.

Thus taking the mean over n executions with different base points P_j's, we have:

$$F_\mu(k, P_j\text{'s}) = \frac{1}{n} \sum_{j=1}^{n} \left(f(k_i | k_{l-1}, k_{l-2}, ..., k_{i+1}, P_j) + N(\mu_N, \sigma^2) \right) \qquad (2)$$

where N is some Gaussian noise of mean μ_N and standard deviation σ. We know that the average of Gaussian noises tends to the mean:

$$F_\mu(k, P_j\text{'s}) \cong \frac{1}{n} \sum_{j=1}^{n} f(k_i | k_{l-1}, k_{l-2}, ..., k_{i+1}, P_j) + \mu_N \qquad (3)$$

Then, for different sets of base points A and B:

$$F_\mu(k, P_j\text{'s} \in A) > F_\mu(k, P_j\text{'s} \in B) \Rightarrow$$

$$\frac{1}{n} \sum_{j=1}^{n} f(k_i | k_{l-1}, ..., k_{i+1}, P_j\text{'s} \in A) > \frac{1}{n} \sum_{j=1}^{n} f(k_i | k_{l-1}, ..., k_{i+1}, P_j\text{'s} \in B) \qquad (4)$$

If we select base points causing more negative coefficients when the bit k_i is 0 or 1 respectively (let's call the sets $high_0$ and $high_1$ respectively) and compare the overall computation times, we are able to find the value of k_i:

$$k_i = \begin{cases} 0, & \text{if } F_\mu(k, Pi_j\text{'s} \in high_0) > F_\mu(k, Pi_j\text{'s} \in high_1) \\ 1, & \text{otherwise} \end{cases} \qquad (5)$$

Timing Measurements. The attack procedure is described in Algorithm 1. We maintain a *constructed* key (key_c) with the bits we found from the *unknown* key (key_u). The base points are chosen by picking a point value at random, executing the scalar multiplication routing and simply counting the number of negative coefficients for the cases when $k_i = 0$ and $k_i = 1$. We want the difference between those two values to be at least 8. If we compare the average of the times to compute the scalar multiplication for base points of $high_0$ with the mean of the times for base points of $high_1$ then the difference does not depend on the rest of the bits.

It can be noted that the difference in the number of negative coefficients between base points of $high_0$ and the ones of the base points of $high_1$ is at least 6 (a high value is at least 8 and a low value can be at most 2, thus the minimum is $8 - 2 = 6$).

Algorithm 1. Attack Procedure

1: Knowing the i first bits of key_u, set the first bits of key_c to these values
2: Executing the code separately with key_c and a random base point, we count the number of negative coefficients in the polynomial representation of the point when multiplying by the bit $i + 1$, for $k_{i+1} = 0$ and $k_{i+1} = 1$. We call them $coeff_0$ and $coeff_1$ respectively.
3: **if** $coeff_0 - coeff_1 > 7$ **then**
4:     Add base point to the set $high_0$
5: **else**
6:     **if** $coeff_0 - coeff_1 < -7$ **then**
7:         Add base point to the set $high_1$
8: Repeat steps 2 to 7 until we have 200 points in each set.
9: For each base point $high_0$ and $high_1$, compute 25,000 times the scalar multiplication with key_u and measure the overall time of execution.
10: For each base point, take the mean value over the 15 minimum values of timing measured. We call these means μ_i's.
11: Compute the mean (μ_{high_0}) of the μ_i's for base points in $high_0$
12: Compute the mean (μ_{high_1}) of the μ_i's for base points in $high_1$
13: If $\mu_{high_0} > \mu_{high_1}$, then $k_{i+1} = 0$, otherwise $k_{i+1} = 1$
14: Repeat steps 2 to 13 until the same value for k_{i+1} was found twice.
15: Set k_{i+1} to the value found twice and go to 1 for the next bit

---

5   Results

Although the distribution of the μ_i's is not a clean Gaussian distribution it is possible to get some coherent results when taking the minimum values. When comparing the average values of the $high_0$ and $high_1$ base points computation times, we observe a difference as expected (Fig. 3). In order to obtain some more accurate timing measurements, each ECC execution was associated to a specific core (affinity selection) on the server. It seems that, contrary to Linux systems, Windows has an aggressive management of power consumption of cores, which induces bigger variations in the timing measurements.

5.1   Evaluation of the Attack

This attack works but it takes some time to recover all the bits of the key. The time required to compute one ECC computation is around 1.6 million clock cycles. 25,000 measurements per base point are needed. There are 400 base points per bit and this is performed 2 to 3 times per bit. On the Intel Xeon processor, at 2.6 GHz, this represents about 15 s for the 25,000 measurements. As 5 bits are fixed, we need to recover 251 bits. Hence, we need about 1 month to recover the whole key with this method.

The measurements need to be repeated many times because the execution times can vary significantly and we are looking for a very small difference in timing. Taking the mean over the 15 minimum values appears to be a good compromise as the minimum value is more stable than the mean of the measures

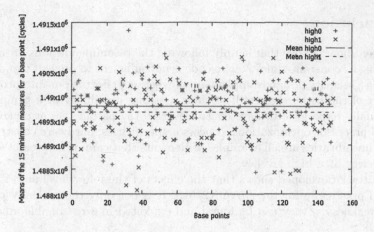

Fig. 3. Comparison of the means of $high_0$ and $high_1$ for $k_i = 0$

but, if this minimum value is rare (e.g., because of what is running on the same processor), it can lead to errors. This is certainly not the most efficient way. It is however robust and allows targeting of all sorts of systems which may have very different behaviors. Creating a precise model of the distribution of the measurements would take time and would remain specific to a given system.

As the attack requires knowledge of the bits preceding the bit being attacked, it is not possible to target a specific bit of the key without processing all the previous bits. Furthermore, once a mistake is made in the presumed value of a bit, the chance of correctly recovering the subsequent bits is negligible (the attack makes no sense as we choose the base points $high_0$ and $high_1$ for another key).

Fine tuning the number of measurements and base points could be performed in order to decrease the time of the attack. Furthermore, when there are only a few bits left to recover, a brute-force attack might be faster than continuing the attack until the very last bit of the key.

Other analyses based on the "profiled attack" approach with a parametric template (on a multi-dimensional Gaussian model) or a machine learning system could be interesting to investigate.

5.2 Extension to Remote Attacks

As the overall times of computation are measured, the attack was expected to also be feasible remotely. In order to test this hypothesis we measured response times of network communications on a local server (ping requests). When we added the network delays to the timings of the overall computations and applied the attack, we were still able to retrieve the correct values of the bits.

6   Conclusion

It has been shown above that simply following the recommendations of the RFC and having a "constant-time" source code is not sufficient to prevent timing leakage. Once a security design is implemented, whatever effort is put into protecting each part of the code, there still remains a strong possibility of a timing leak. It is virtually *impossible* to have control over all the parameters at stake. Compiler and processor optimizations, processor specificities, hardware construction, and runtime libraries are all examples of elements that cannot be predicted when implementing at a high level.

The attack developed shows that the effects of these low-level actors can be exploited practically for the curve X25519. It is not only theoretically possible to find weaknesses, they can be found and exploited in a reasonable amount of time.

Nevertheless, the idea of ensuring that the design itself is secure by using a formalized approach such as RFC is however an important step in minimizing the side-channel leakage of any final system.

This paper also highlights one particular aspect: the potential weakness of other codes implemented using the Windows runtime library.

References

1. Belgarric, P., Fouque, P.-A., Macario-Rat, G., Tibouchi, M.: Side-Channel Analysis of Weierstrass and Koblitz Curve ECDSA on Android Smartphones. Cryptology ePrint Archive, Report 2016/231 (2016)
2. Bernstein, D.J.: Curve25519: new Diffie-Hellman speed records. In: Yung, M., Dodis, Y., Kiayias, A., Malkin, T. (eds.) PKC 2006. LNCS, vol. 3958, pp. 207–228. Springer, Heidelberg (2006). doi:10.1007/11745853_14
3. Brumley, D., Boneh, D.: Remote timing attacks are practical. Computer Networks, pp. 701–716 (2005)
4. Brumley, B.B., Tuveri, N.: Remote timing attacks are still practical. In: Atluri, V., Diaz, C. (eds.) ESORICS 2011. LNCS, vol. 6879, pp. 355–371. Springer, Heidelberg (2011)
5. Chari, S., Rao, J.R., Rohatgi, P.: Template Attacks. In: Kaliski, B.S., Koç, K., Paar, C. (eds.) CHES 2002. LNCS, vol. 2523, pp. 13–28. Springer, Heidelberg (2003). doi:10.1007/3-540-36400-5_3
6. Genkin, D., Pachmanov, L., Pipman, I., Tromer, E., Yarom, Y.: ECDSA key extraction from mobile devices via nonintrusive physical side channels. Cryptology ePrint Archive, Report 2016/230 (2016)
7. Howgrave-Graham, N., Smart, N.P.: Lattice attacks on digital signature schemes. Des. Codes Crypt. 23(3), 283–290 (2001)
8. Kocher, P.C.: Timing Attacks on implementations of Diffie-Hellman, RSA, DSS, and other systems. In: Koblitz, N. (ed.) CRYPTO 1996. LNCS, vol. 1109, pp. 104–113. Springer, Heidelberg (1996). doi:10.1007/3-540-68697-5_9
9. Langley, A.: Implementation of curve25519-donna. http://code.google.com/p/curve25519-donna. Accessed 16 Sep 2015
10. Turner, S., Langley, A., Hamburg, M.: Elliptic Curves for Security. IETF RFC 7748, January 2016

MultiParty Computation and Functional Encryption

On the Power of Public-key Function-Private Functional Encryption

Vincenzo Iovino[1]([⊠]), Qiang Tang[1], and Karol Żebrowski[2]

[1] University of Luxembourg, Luxembourg City, Luxembourg
{vincenzo.iovino,qiang.tang}@uni.lu
[2] University of Warsaw, Warsaw, Poland
kz277580@students.mimuw.edu.pl

Abstract. In the public-key setting, known constructions of *function-private* functional encryption (FPFE) were limited to very restricted classes of functionalities like inner-product [Agrawal *et al.* - PKC 2015]. Moreover, its power has not been well investigated. In this paper, we construct FPFE for general functions and explore its powerful applications, both for general and specific functionalities.

As warmup, we construct from FPFE a natural generalization of a signature scheme endowed with functional properties, that we call *functional anonymous signature* (FAS) scheme. In a FAS, Alice can sign a circuit C chosen from some distribution D to get a signature σ and can publish a verification key that allows anybody holding a message m to verify that (1) σ is a valid signature of Alice for *some* (possibly unknown to him) circuit C and (2) $C(m) = 1$. Beyond unforgeability the security of FAS guarantees that the signature σ hide as much information as possible about C except what can be inferred from knowledge of D.

Then, we show that FPFE can be used to construct in a black-box way functional encryption schemes for randomized functionalities (RFE).

As further application, we show that specific instantiations of FPFE can be used to achieve adaptively-secure CNF/DNF encryption for bounded degree formulae (BoolEnc). Though it was known how to implement BoolEnc from inner-product encryption (IPE) [Katz *et al.* - EURO-CRYPT 2008], as already observed by Katz *et al.* this reduction only works for selective security and completely breaks down for adaptive security; however, we show that the reduction works if the IPE scheme is function-private.

Finally, we present a general picture of the relations among all these related primitives. One key observation is that Attribute-based Encryption with function privacy implies FE, a notable fact that sheds light on the importance of the function privacy property for FE.

Keywords: Functional Encryption · Function privacy · Inner-Product Encryption · Obfuscation · Digital signatures

© Springer International Publishing AG 2016
S. Foresti and G. Persiano (Eds.): CANS 2016, LNCS 10052, pp. 585–593, 2016.
DOI: 10.1007/978-3-319-48965-0_37

1   Introduction

Functional Encryption (FE) [1] is a sophisticated type of encryption that allows to finely control the amount of information that can be revealed by a decryption operation. Progressively, more expressive forms of FE were constructed in a series of works (see, e.g., [2–6]) culminating in the breakthrough of Garg *et al.* [7].

The security notion in these works only take in account the privacy of the message but nothing is guaranteed for the privacy of the *function*. In the symmetric-key setting, a preliminary study of FE with function privacy was initiated by Shen *et al.* [8] for the inner-product functionality [4], subsequently followed by constructions for general functionalities [9]. Boneh *et al.* [10] put forward the study of function privacy for FE providing constructions for the Identity-Based Encryption (IBE) functionality, then followed by works that considered the subspace membership [11] and the inner-product [12,13] functionalities.

In the public-key setting, the function can not be hidden completely since the adversary can always try to infer partial information about it using the public key. For this reason, Boneh *et al.* [10] consider functions chosen from high min-entropy distributions. Precisely, in the context of IBE they propose an IND style real-or-random definition of function privacy, that stipulates that as long as the identity id was chosen from a sufficiently high min-entropy distribution, the adversary should not be able to distinguish the token for id from a token for a uniformly random identity. Agrawal *et al.* [13] consider stronger simulation-based definitions for function privacy but with non-standard simulators (a necessity motivated by broad impossibility results in the area).

It seems that a meaningful simulation-based security notion of public-key function-private functional encryption (FPFE) for some expressive enough class of Boolean circuits would imply virtual black box (VBB) obfuscation for the same class of circuits and thus it seems unachievable even for NC^1 circuits. For such reasons, we stick with the indistinguishability-based (IND-based) definition and defer to future works the study of stronger security notions. Specifically, in the case of Boolean circuits, we consider what we call *pairs of ensembles of efficiently samplable feasible entropy distributions*, a strengthening of a notion defined by Agrawal *et al.* [13] which abstracts the unpredictability property of Boneh *et al.* [10]. Formal definition is given in the full version. Note that we put the constraint that the distributions be efficiently samplable. This is because, in the context of function privacy, as well as for functional anonymous signatures that we will introduce later, users sample the cryptographic objects from efficiently samplable distributions. This subtle difference turns out to be very important; indeed it is the key to make such primitives *composable*.

To our knowledge no previous work in literature considered public-key FPFE for more general functionalities, like poly-sized circuits or even NC^1 circuits. This leads to the main questions that we study in this work:

Can we achieve public-key FPFE for more general functionalities, like at least NC^1 or even all poly-sized circuits, from reasonable assumptions? And what applications and other primitives can we build from FPFE (not necessarily for general functionalities)?

Based on the existence of *quasi-siO* proposed by Bitansky, Canetti, Kalai and Paneth [14],[1] we answer *affirmatively* to the first question. The solution we propose is conceptually simple and elegant but we believe that the key is in having discovered and identified quasi-siO as the main building block, a relation that was not known before in the literature.

Note that quasi-siO is a weakened version of strong iO (siO), which guarantees that no efficient adversary can distinguish two feasible entropy distributions D_0 or D_1. The weakening lies in the fact that quasi-siO requires the distributions to be efficiently samplable.

We answer the second question by mainly demonstrating the implication with respect to functional anonymous signatures, FE for randomized functionalities, and adaptive security for efficient Boolean formulae encryption (for this application we do not require FPFE for general functionalities). Though some of our results can seem basic, this is a due to our recognition of the power of these primitives not studied so far, and some applications we derive from them improve the state of the art in the field or solve known problems. Thus, we deem the simplicity of our approach a positive feature not a shortcoming.

Our results are not only an example of the power and of the applications of FPFE but also and mainly of the power siO/quasi-siO, and in the full version we show equivalences between them.

Public-key FPFE based on Quasi-siO. To the aim of having conceptually simple and general constructions, we construct a FPFE scheme by nesting a generic FE scheme (without function privacy) with a siO.

Specifically our FPFE scheme FPFE will use the underlying FE scheme FE as a black box and will have identical procedures except that a token for a circuit C will consist of a token of FE for the circuit $qsi\mathcal{O}(C)$, where $qsi\mathcal{O}$ is a quasi-siO: that is, setting $C' = qsi\mathcal{O}(C)$, a token of FPFE for C will be a token of FE for C'. Intuitively, even though this token is computed with a non function-private scheme, as it is built on the top of circuit obfuscated with quasi-siO, it should leak as little information as possible. In fact, we confirm this intuition providing formal reductions. Note here that the underlying FE scheme guarantees the privacy of the encrypted messages and quasi-siO is only used to add the extra layer of function privacy.

The modularity of our approach allows to instantiate a FPFE for a class of circuits C assuming only a quasi-siO for the same class of circuits until the class $\mathcal{C}$ is enough expressive, specifically includes at least all NC^1 circuits. Furthermore, it generalizes easily to multi-inputs FE (MIFE, in short) [15] allowing to construct the first MIFE scheme with function privacy (FPMIFE, in short).

---

[1] The name quasi-siO is ours. The authors define a weakening of the their notion of siO (see the following) without explicitly naming it.

The definition of a FPFE scheme and its security and construction from quasi-siO is presented in the full version. We observe that the reverse direction also holds. In fact, a quasi-siO $qsi\mathcal{O}$ for class of circuits $\mathcal{C}$ can be constructed from a FPFE scheme FPFE for the same class in the following way. For any input C the algorithm $qsi\mathcal{O}(C)$ outputs the public-key of the FPFE scheme and a token Tok for C of FPFE. To evaluate such obfuscated circuit on an input x, the evaluation algorithm associated with $qsi\mathcal{O}$ takes as input the public-key and Tok and encrypts[2] x to get Ct and evaluates Tok on Ct to get $C(m)$. The correctness of FPFE and its INDFP-Security (given in the full version) imply that such obfuscator is a quasi-siO. This construction also reaffirms that a meaningful simulation-based security notion for FPFE for a class $\mathcal{C}$ would imply VBB obfuscation for $\mathcal{C}$, and thus is unachievable in general. For such reason we stick with an IND-based definition of function privacy.

Functional Anonymous Signatures. As warmup we construct from FPFE a new primitive called *Functional Anonymous Signature* (FAS, in short). Recall that the Naor's transformation[3] allows to transform an identity-based encryption (IBE) scheme [16] in a signature scheme. The idea is that the token for an identity id acts as a signature for it. Such signature can be verified by encrypting the pair (r, id) for a random string r and testing whether the token (i.e., the signature) evaluated on such ciphertext returns r. By the security property of IBE, such signature is unforgeable. We generalize this concept to FE and propose what we call FAS. With FAS, a user Alice can sign a Boolean circuit C allowing Bob holding an input m to verify (1) that the signature was issued by Alice and that (2) $C(m) = 1$.

We envision a scenario where the signature of Alice of a circuit C hides C if it is drawn from a feasible entropy distribution. In this case, the intent of Bob is to verify (1) that Alice signed some circuit C, that is not known to him, and (2) verify that his input m satisfies the circuit, e.g., $C(m) = 1$.

We foresee FAS to be a very useful primitive in practice, e.g. in the following authenticated policy verification mechanism. Alice, the head of a company, can publish her verification key and with the corresponding secret key can sign an hidden policy P chosen from some known distribution D and send the signature σ of P to the server of her company. The secretary of the company, who is assumed to be honest but curious, can grant Bob access to some private document iff the access pattern m held by Bob verifies the signature of Alice, and in particular her hidden policy, i.e., $P(m) = 1$. If the signature is verified by the access pattern of Bob, then the secretary has the guarantee that (1) the policy was signed by Alice and (2) the access pattern of Bob satisfies such policy.

Both Bob and the secretary have no information about the policy except what can be inferred from the distribution D. Due to the possibility of using

---

[2] Actually, for this implication to hold we only need "data privacy", i.e., security of the encryptions. In fact, we could assume that the messages be encrypted in clear. Precisely, according to the definitions (given in the full version), we only need INDFP-Security and not also IND-Security.

[3] Such transformation was first reported in Boneh and Franklin [16].

universal circuits in FAS, the role of access pattern and policy can be inverted, that is Alice can sign an access pattern and Bob holding a policy can verify whether his policy satisfies her access pattern. It is easy to see that FAS implies traditional signature schemes.

We define FAS with a notion of unforgeability that we call *functional unforgeability*, that suits for most applications of FAS. The notion does not consider as valid the forgery of a circuit more restricted than a circuit for which a signature was seen.[4]

To see why such condition is not too restrictive, consider the above application. In that case, the security of FAS should prevent some unauthorized user to claim that Alice signed a document who authorizes him. This is exactly what the condition states. Note also that being Alice semi-trusted we do not consider a breach of security if she is able to forge a signature for a circuit C' more restricted than the circuit C of which she received a signature from Alice (a circuit C' is said to be more restricted than C if $C'(x) = 1$ implies $C(x) = 1$). Only malicious users have the interest to forge new signatures and in this case their scope is to forge signatures for circuits that authorize them, so a forgery for a more restricted circuit (or a functionally equivalent one) must not be considered a successful attack.

However, for other applications such security could not suffice but we show that it is possible to make FAS unforgeable according to the classical notion of unforgeability (i.e., requiring that any PPT adversary can not forge a signature for a circuit C' different (as bit string) from any circuit C for which it saw a signature) just adding a traditional unforgeable scheme on the top of it. Beyond unforgeability, we require *anonymity*, namely that a signature σ hide as much information as possible about C except what can be inferred from knowledge of the distribution from which C is drawn.

FPFE fits perfectly in the picture, and in fact we show that it implies FAS in a black-box way. Specifically, we show how to extend the Naor's transformation to construct FAS for a class of circuits $\mathcal{C}$ from Attribute-based Encryption (ABE, in short) with function privacy, a weaker notion of FPFE, for the same class $\mathcal{C}$. Related primitives are content-concealing signatures and confidential signatures ([17,18]) that can be viewed as a weak form of FAS schemes without functional capabilities (or alternatively for the class of equality predicates). The definition of FAS, its security and construction from ABE with function privacy (FPABE, in short) are presented in the full version.

We mention that it is possible to construct FAS in a more direct way from quasi-siO, but our aim is also to show equivalences among FAS, quasi-siO and FPFE (see Sect. 1).

Functional Encryption for Randomized Functionalities. Goyal *et al.* [19] put forward the first construction of FE supporting *randomized* circuits. In this setting, the challenge is to guarantee that the circuit be evaluated on fresh

---

[4] That is, it is not considered as a valid forgery if an adversary given a signature of circuit C can sign another circuit C' that computes the same function as C or is more restricted than C.

randomness that can not be maliciously chosen. A tentative solution to the problem would be to include the seed of a pseudo-random function in the token. Unfortunately, this approach fails since the token is not guaranteed to hide the function that the circuit is supposed to compute.

This leaves open the possibility that this basic idea could work assuming a FE whose token hides the function (i.e., with function privacy), and in fact we are able to confirm this intuition by showing a black-box construction of FE for randomized circuits (RFE, in short) from FPFE for (deterministic) circuits. We adopt an indistinguishability-based security for RFE, but unlike Goyal *et al.* we do not take in account the problem of dishonest encryptors that goes beyond the scope of our work (and concerns not only RFE but FE and FPE as well). Our construction of RFE also preserves the function privacy of the underlying FPFE and thus satisfies the standard notion of function privacy where the adversary can ask distributions of deterministic circuits. We call this notion FPRFE.

The definition of RFE, its security and its construction from FPFE are presented in the full version.

Adaptively-secure FE for CNF/DNF formulae of bounded degree. Here we assume that the reader is familiar with inner-product encryption (IPE) introduced by Katz *et al.* [4].

Katz *et al.* show how to implement polynomial evaluation from IPE and how to build FE for a subclass of Boolean formulae with a bounded number (at most logarithmic in the security parameter) of variables (BoolEnc). Hereafter, for simplicity we focus on DNF formulae (of bounded degree) and thus we will call such FE scheme DNFEnc. Analogous considerations hold for other classes of Boolean formulae that can be derived from IPE, e.g., CNF formulae.

For instance conjunctions can be handled in the following way. Consider the predicate AND_{I_1,I_2} where $\mathsf{AND}_{I_1,I_2}(x_1,x_2) \overset{\triangle}{=} 1$ if both $x_1 = I_1$ and $x_2 = I_2$. Then, we can choose a random $r \leftarrow \mathbb{Z}_p$ (here we assume that the coefficient of the polynomial are over $\mathbb{Z}_p$) and letting the token correspond to the polynomial $p(x_1,x_2) \overset{\triangle}{=} r \cdot (x_1 - I_1) + (x_2 - I_2)$. If $\mathsf{AND}_{I_1,I_2}(x_1,x_2) = 1$ then $p(x_1,x_2) = 0$, whereas if $\mathsf{AND}_{I_1,I_2}(x_1,x_2) = 0$ then, with all but negligible probability over the choices of r, it will hold that $p(x_1,x_2) \neq 0$. Disjunctions can be implemented by defining a polynomial $p'(x_1,x_2) \overset{\triangle}{=} (x_1 - I_1) \cdot (x_2 - I_2)$. It is straightforward that conjunctions and disjunctions can be combined to get DNF formulae but, as the Katz *et al.*'s transform from DNF formulae to polynomials grows super-polynomially in the number of variables, we have to put a bound on it.

As Katz *et al.* observe, in general the token may leak the value of r in which case the adversary will be able to find x_1, x_2 such that $\mathsf{AND}_{I_1,I_2}(x_1,x_2) = 0$ yet $p(x_1,x_2) = 0$. Since, however, they consider the "selective" notion of security (where the adversary must commit to x_1, x_2 at the outset of the experiment), this is not a problem in their setting. On the other hand, disjunctions can be handled without issues.

Anyhow, this implies that even adaptively-secure IPE schemes [6] can not be directly employed in this transformation and thus to construct an adaptively-secure DNFEnc. FPFE turns out to be useful in this context: assuming that the underlying IPE satisfies our notion of function privacy, we show that an adaptively-secure IPE with function privacy implies an adaptively-secure DNFEnc. The idea is that, being the token function-private, it hides the value r so that the adversary cannot make the reduction to fail. In the full version [20], we prove this fact.

It is out of the scope of this work to provide concrete instantiations of function-private schemes that suit for our scopes but our result emphasizes the importance of function-privacy even for practical matters. For instance, the IPE scheme of Agrawal et al. [21] is clearly subject to function-privacy attacks and thus cannot be employed in the Katz et al.'s transformation whereas, though not backed by any security proof, the IPE schemes of Katz et al. does not seem subject to any of such attacks. Thus, our result suggests that care has to be taken when instantiating the transformation.

Relation Between Primitives. It is easy to see that quasi-siO implies iO that in turn is known to imply (along with one-way functions) FE [22]. Thus, quasi-siO implies FPFE. Moreover, FAS can be used to construct a quasi-siO as follows. An obfuscation of circuit C will consist of a signature for C and the verification key of the FAS scheme, and to evaluate the obfuscated circuit on an input x, just run the verification algorithm of FAS with input the verification key, the signature and the message m. From the anonymity of FAS, such obfuscator is easily seen to be a quasi-siO. Note that this implication does not assume FAS with any kind of unforgeability. Since FPFE implies FPABE, that in turn implies FAS, we have that FAS, FPFE and quasi-siO are *equivalent* primitives (i.e., they imply each other). One of the key points highlighted by our results is that FPABE implies quasi-siO and thus iO that in turn (assuming in addition one-way functions) implies FE [22], a notable fact that sheds light on the importance and power of function privacy for FE. Indeed, even though ABE is not known to imply FE, our results show that the additional property of function privacy suffices for it.

Acknowledgements. Vincenzo Iovino is supported by the Luxembourg National Research Fund (FNR grant no. 7884937) and Qiang Tang is supported by a CORE (junior track) grant from the Luxembourg National Research Fund.

References

1. Boneh, D., Sahai, A., Waters, B.: Functional encryption: definitions and challenges. In: Ishai, Y. (ed.) TCC 2011. LNCS, vol. 6597, pp. 253–273. Springer, Heidelberg (2011)
2. Boneh, D., Di Crescenzo, G., Ostrovsky, R., Persiano, G.: Public key encryption with keyword search. In: Cachin, C., Camenisch, J.L. (eds.) EUROCRYPT 2004. LNCS, vol. 3027, pp. 506–522. Springer, Heidelberg (2004)

3. Boneh, D., Waters, B.: Conjunctive, subset, and range queries on encrypted data. In: Vadhan, S.P. (ed.) TCC 2007. LNCS, vol. 4392, pp. 535–554. Springer, Heidelberg (2007). doi:10.1007/978-3-540-70936-7_29

4. Katz, J., Sahai, A., Waters, B.: Predicate encryption supporting disjunctions, polynomial equations, and inner products. In: Smart, N.P. (ed.) EUROCRYPT 2008. LNCS, vol. 4965, pp. 146–162. Springer, Heidelberg (2008)

5. Lewko, A., Okamoto, T., Sahai, A., Takashima, K., Waters, B.: Fully secure functional encryption: attribute-based encryption and (hierarchical) inner product encryption. In: Gilbert, H. (ed.) EUROCRYPT 2010. LNCS, vol. 6110, pp. 62–91. Springer, Heidelberg (2010)

6. Okamoto, T., Takashima, K.: Adaptively attribute-hiding (hierarchical) inner product encryption. In: Pointcheval, D., Johansson, T. (eds.) EUROCRYPT 2012. LNCS, vol. 7237, pp. 591–608. Springer, Heidelberg (2012)

7. Garg, S., Gentry, C., Halevi, S., Raykova, M., Sahai, A., Waters, B.: Candidate indistinguishability obfuscation and functional encryption for all circuits. In: 54th Annual IEEE Symposium on Foundations of Computer Science, FOCS 2013, Berkeley, CA, USA, pp. 40–49. IEEE Computer Society, 26–29 October 2013

8. Shen, E., Shi, E., Waters, B.: Predicate privacy in encryption systems. In: Reingold, O. (ed.) TCC 2009. LNCS, vol. 5444, pp. 457–473. Springer, Heidelberg (2009). doi:10.1007/978-3-642-00457-5_27

9. Brakerski, Z., Segev, G.: Function-private functional encryption in the private-key setting. In: Dodis, Y., Nielsen, J.B. (eds.) TCC 2015, Part II. LNCS, vol. 9015, pp. 306–324. Springer, Heidelberg (2015)

10. Boneh, D., Raghunathan, A., Segev, G.: Function-private identity-based encryption: hiding the function in functional encryption. In: Canetti, R., Garay, J.A. (eds.) CRYPTO 2013, Part II. LNCS, vol. 8043, pp. 461–478. Springer, Heidelberg (2013)

11. Boneh, D., Raghunathan, A., Segev, G.: Function-private subspace-membership encryption and its applications. In: Sako, K., Sarkar, P. (eds.) ASIACRYPT 2013, Part I. LNCS, vol. 8269, pp. 255–275. Springer, Heidelberg (2013)

12. Agrawal, S., Agrawal, S., Badrinarayanan, S., Kumarasubramanian, A., Prabhakaran, M., Amit S.: Function private functional encryption and property preserving encryption: New definitions and positive results. Cryptology ePrint Archive, (2013). http://eprint.iacr.org/2013/744

13. Agrawal, S., Agrawal, S., Badrinarayanan, S., Kumarasubramanian, A., Prabhakaran, M., Sahai, A.: On the practical security of inner product functional encryption. In: Katz, J. (ed.) Public-Key Cryptography - PKC 2015. LNCS, vol. 9020, pp. 777–798. Springer, Heidelberg (2015)

14. Bitansky, N., Canetti, R., Kalai, Y.T., Paneth, O.: On virtual grey box obfuscation for general circuits. In: Garay, J.A., Gennaro, R. (eds.) CRYPTO 2014, Part II. LNCS, vol. 8617, pp. 108–125. Springer, Heidelberg (2014)

15. Goldwasser, S., Gordon, S.D., Goyal, V., Jain, A., Katz, J., Liu, F.-H., Sahai, A., Shi, E., Zhou, H.-S.: Multi-input functional encryption. In: Nguyen, P.Q., Oswald, E. (eds.) EUROCRYPT 2014. LNCS, vol. 8441, pp. 578–602. Springer, Heidelberg (2014)

16. Boneh, D., Franklin, M.: Identity-based encryption from the weil pairing. In: Kilian, J. (ed.) CRYPTO 2001. LNCS, vol. 2139, pp. 213–229. Springer, Heidelberg (2001)

17. Canetti, R.: Towards realizing random oracles: hash functions that hide all partial information. In: Kaliski Jr., B.S. (ed.) CRYPTO 1997. LNCS, vol. 1294, pp. 455–469. Springer, Heidelberg (1997)

18. Dent, A.W., Fischlin, M., Manulis, M., Stam, M., Schröder, D.: Confidential signatures and deterministic signcryption. In: Nguyen, P.Q., Pointcheval, D. (eds.) PKC 2010. LNCS, vol. 6056, pp. 462–479. Springer, Heidelberg (2010)
19. Goyal, V., Jain, A., Koppula, V., Sahai, A.: Functional encryption for randomized functionalities. In: Dodis, Y., Nielsen, J.B. (eds.) TCC 2015, Part II. LNCS, vol. 9015, pp. 325–351. Springer, Heidelberg (2015)
20. Iovino, V., Tang, Q., Żebrowski, K.: On the power of public-key functional encryption with function privacy. Cryptology ePrint Archive, Report 2015/470 (2015). http://eprint.iacr.org/2015/470
21. Agrawal, S., Freeman, D.M., Vaikuntanathan, V.: Functional encryption for inner product predicates from learning with errors. In: Lee, D.H., Wang, X. (eds.) ASIACRYPT 2011. LNCS, vol. 7073, pp. 21–40. Springer, Heidelberg (2011)
22. Waters, B.: A punctured programming approach to adaptively secure functional encryption. In: Gennaro, R., Robshaw, M. (eds.) CRYPTO 2015. LNCS, vol. 9216, pp. 678–697. Springer, Heidelberg (2015)

A New Technique for Compacting Secret Key in Attribute-Based Broadcast Encryption

Sébastien Canard[1], Duong Hieu Phan[2], and Viet Cuong Trinh[3,4(✉)]

[1] Orange Labs - Applied Crypto Group, Lannion, France
[2] XLIM - CNRS - University of Limoges, Limoges, France
[3] KINDI Lab, Qatar University, Doha, Qatar
[4] Hong Duc University, Thanh Hóa, Vietnam
cuongtrinhviet@gmail.com

Abstract. Public-key encryption has been generalized to adapt to more and more practical applications. Broadcast encryption, introduced by Fiat and Naor in 1993, aims for applications in pay-TV or satellite transmission and allows a sender to securely send private messages to any subset of users, the target set. Sahai and Waters introduced Attribute-based Encryption (ABE) to define the target set in a more structural way via access policies on attributes. Attribute-based Broadcast Encryption (ABBE) combines the functionalities of both in an efficient way. In the relevant applications such as pay-TV, the users are given a relatively small device with very limited secure memory in a smartcard. Therefore, it is of high interest to construct schemes with compact secret key of users. Even though extensively studied in the recent years, it is still an open question of constructing an efficient ABBE with constant-size private keys for general forms of access policy such as CNF or DNF forms. This question was partially solved at ESORICS '15 where Phuong et al. introduced a constant secret-key size ABBE. But they manage restrictive access policies only supporting AND-gates and wildcards. In this paper, we solve this open question and propose an efficient constant-size private key ciphertext-policy attribute-based broadcast encryption scheme for DNF form. In particular, we also present the optimization in implementing our proposed scheme.

Keywords: Attribute-based broadcast encryption · Ciphertext-policy · DNF

1 Introduction

We are actually in a very active period of development of cryptography. Modern technologies, namely cloud computing and big data, require the design of advanced cryptographic schemes supporting new functionalities. In many applications that involve a large set of users, one needs to have stronger and more flexible capabilities to encrypt data than the traditional public key encryption: the encryption should take into account specific policies in such a way that only receivers with suitable rights can decrypt the encrypted messages.

© Springer International Publishing AG 2016
S. Foresti and G. Persiano (Eds.): CANS 2016, LNCS 10052, pp. 594–603, 2016.
DOI: 10.1007/978-3-319-48965-0_38

Attribute-Based Encryption. Sahai and Waters [14] introduced the concept of *attribute-based encryption* (ABE) in which the encryption and decryption can be based on the user's attributes. Since then, there are a lot of development in this area with many interesting results [7,11,13,14,16], to name a few. Actually, there are two categories of ABE. *ciphertext-policy* attribute-based encryption (CP-ABE) and *key-policy* attribute-based encryption (KP-ABE). In a CP-ABE scheme, the secret key is associated with a set of attributes and the ciphertext is associated with an access policy (structure) over the universe of attributes: a user can then decrypt a given ciphertext if the set of attributes related to his/her secret key satisfies the access policy underlying the ciphertext. In contrast, in a KP-ABE scheme, each secret key corresponds to an access policy and a set of attributes is associated with the ciphertext. Concerning the access structure, fine-grained access control is the most desired and also well formalized as boolean formula in disjunctive normal form (DNF) or in conjunctive normal form (CNF).

Attribute-Based Broadcast Encryption. In some practical cases, one may want to remove the right to decrypt to some specific users. The notion of attribute-based broadcast encryption (ABBE) has then been introduced in [10] to address the problem of user revocation. More precisely, in such a system, the broadcaster is capable of revoking any receiver and the collusion of revoked users cannot decrypt any ciphertext even if they possess sufficient attributes to satisfy the access policy. In traditional attribute-based encryption schemes, the revocation can be performed based on attributes (resp., negative attributes as some non-monotonic schemes [11,16]), by adding the AND of a clause containing the attributes corresponding to non-revoked users (resp., negative attributes corresponding to revoked users). However, this will give an inefficient solution as the ciphertext grows linearly to the number of non–revoked users (resp., revoked users), which is large. An attribute-based broadcast encryption (ABBE) scheme should allow individual receivers to be directly revoked in an efficient way.

Several ABBE schemes have been proposed in [3,7–10]. As in a broadcast encryption, it is of great importance to construct a scheme with compact secret key. Such a scheme can have practical applications such as in pay-TV or satellite transmission where the user's device are relatively small and the secure memory is often implemented in a smartcard. While broadcast encryption with constant-size secret key has been solved by Boneh, Gentry and Waters in [2], the extension of BGW technique to ABBE setting make the secret key longer, due to the obligation of combining different attributes in the decryption, as shown in [7]. The problem of designing constant-size private key ABBE schemes supporting fine-grained access control was partially solved in ESORICS '15 [12]. But the problem is still open since the proposed non-monotonic scheme only manages restrictive access policies supporting AND-gates and wildcards: they do not treat the case of CNF or DNF forms. More precisely, if the access policy is $A_1 \wedge * \wedge A_2$, where $*$ is a wildcard, then any user whose attribute set contains exactly three attributes (no more no less) and two of them are A_1, A_2 can decrypt the ciphertext. This obliviously can reduce the ciphertext size, however in exchange, the secret key size now is $3 + 2(N_1 + 1)$ elements, where N_1 is the maximal number of wildcards can appear in an access policy, N_1 is fixed at the setup phase.

Our Contributions. Even though extensively studied in the recent years, it is still an open question of constructing an efficient ABBE with constant-size private keys for general forms of access policy such as CNF or DNF. We here solve this open question for the DNF form by providing several new techniques in this field.

Our initial new idea is to extend the Delerablée's technique (for constructing an IBBE scheme [5]) to our context of CP-ABBE. More precisely, each attribute in our ABBE corresponds to an identity in Delerablée's IBBE scheme. To obtain the "broadcast" property, we also add an additional identity for each user. The resulting scheme then contains two kinds of "IBBE identities": one user's identity and the additional identities that represent the attributes the user possesses. We then succeed in combining all these information into a compact secret key. More intuition behind our construction as well as the security proof of our scheme will be given further in the paper.

We give in Table 1 a detailed comparison among our scheme and several other CP-ABE and CP-ABBE schemes supporting fine-grained access control. It shows that, regarding the efficiency, our CP-ABBE scheme enjoys the following properties:

- it is the first efficient CP-ABBE scheme which simultaneously achieves constant-size private key and supports fine-grained access control;
- regarding the decryption, a user in our scheme only needs to compute two parings, in contrast to almost existing CP-ABE and CP-ABBE schemes supporting fine-grained access control where each user needs to perform at least $|I|$ pairings computations in the decryption, where $|I|$ is the number of attributes needed to satisfy a ciphertext policy. Moreover, as we will see, one of the two pairing can be delegated to a third party.

We show at the full version of the paper that our scheme can be truly implemented in a prototype for a smartphone based cloud storage use case. In particular, we show how to alleviate some parts of our scheme so as to obtain a very practical system, and we give some concrete benchmarks.

Organization of the Paper. The paper is now organized as follows. The next section presents the security definitions and the assumptions we need to prove the security. In Sect. 3, we present our new construction. Section 4 is devoted to the security proof of the scheme. Finally, in Sect. 5, we talk about our real implementation.

2   Preliminaries

We give here our main scenario, several preliminaries regarding definition and security model for a CP-ABBE scheme and the security assumptions we will need.

Table 1. n is the maximal number of users, N is the maximal number of attributes, m is the number of clauses in a CNF/DNF access policy, (in some systems from linear secret sharing matrix framework, ℓ denotes the number of rows of the LSSS matrix (the number of attributes in an access formula, counting the reused attributes), ℓ^* denotes the maximal of ℓ which is equal to the size of the attribute universe, $|S_u|$ denotes the number of attributes of a private key, $|I|$ is the number of attributes of a private key to satisfy a ciphertext policy, $|p|$ denotes element in $\mathbb{Z}_p$, P denotes pairing computation, ex denotes the exponentiation, mex[v] the multi-exponentiation with v terms, mul denotes the multiplication, k_{max} denotes the maximal number of times where one attribute can be reused in an access formula. Note that [8,9] support fully collusion-resistant blackbox traceability

	$|ciphertext|$	$|sk|$	$|pk|$	Enc time	Dec time	Assump	Revoc
[15]	$2\ell + 1$	$|S_u| + 2$	$N + 3$	$(3\ell + 2)$ex	$(2|I| + 1)P$	q-type	No
[6]	$(\ell + 1)$	$k_{max}|S_u| + 2$	$N + 3$	$(2\ell + 2)$ex	$2P$	BDHE	No
[7]	$O(m)$	$O(N)$	$O(N)$	$(\ell + 2m)$ex	$O(|I|)P$	GDDHE	Yes
[13]	$3\ell + 2$	$2|S_u| + 2$	$6 + N|p|$	$(5\ell + 2)$ex	$(3|I| + 1)P$	q-type	No
[4]	$2\ell^* + 2$	$2\ell^* + 4$	$2\ell^* + 3$	$O(\ell^2)$mul	$4P$	SXDH	No
[8]	$17\sqrt{n} + 2\ell$	$4 + |S_u|$	$4\sqrt{n} + N$	$(O(\sqrt{n}) + 3\ell)$ex	$(10 + 2|I|)P$	q-type	Yes
[9]	$16\sqrt{n} + 3\ell$	$2 + \sqrt{n} + 2|S_u|$	$5 + 5\sqrt{n}$	$(O(\sqrt{n}) + 3\ell)$ex	$(9 + 3|I|)P$	q-type	Yes
Ours	$m + 1$	1	$O(N.n)$	2ex + $m\cdot$ mex[$n + m + N$]	$2P$	GDDHE	Yes

2.1 Practical Scenario

All along the paper, we will consider the following scenario. A company wishes to put in place a CP-ABBE scheme for its staff, so that they can store and share sensitive documents, using a non-trusted cloud platform for storage (such as e.g., Dropbox or GoogleDrive). More precisely, we consider three kinds of attributes in the studied system.

- The role of the user in the company: boss, manager, developer, expert.
- The team in which the user is: team$_1$, $\cdots$, team$_k$.
- The project on which the user can work: project$_1$, $\cdots$, project$_\ell$.

Based on that attributes, and a unique specific identity, anyone can encrypt and upload documents, using the CP-ABBE scheme and a chosen DNF access control policy of the form

$$\beta = \text{boss} \vee (\text{manager} \wedge \text{team}_4) \vee (\text{developer} \wedge \text{project}_5) \vee (\text{expert} \wedge \text{project}_2).$$

Finally, anyone with the correct attributes will be able to obtain the document in clear.

2.2 Ciphertext-Policy Attribute-Based Broadcast Encryption

In this paper, we will consider the similar definition and security model for a CP-ABBE scheme as in [7]. Formally, a CP-ABBE scheme consists of three probabilistic algorithms as follows.

Setup$(1^\lambda, n, \{S_u\}_{u \in [n]})$: Takes as input the security parameter λ, the maximal number of users n, and the attribute repartition S_u (the user's attribute set) for each user u. It returns the public parameters param of the system, and n private keys sk_u which will be distributed to each respective user. The set $\mathcal{K}$ corresponds to the key space for session keys.

Encrypt$(\mathsf{param}, \mathbb{A}, S)$: Takes as input an access policy $\mathbb{A}$, the target set S, and public parameter param. It outputs the session key $K \in \mathcal{K}$, and the header Hdr which includes the access policy $\mathbb{A}$ and the target set S.

Decrypt$(sk_u, \mathsf{Hdr}, \mathsf{param})$: Takes as input the header Hdr, the private key sk_u of a user u, together with the parameters param. It outputs the session key K if and only if S_u satisfies $\mathbb{A}$ and $u \in S$. Otherwise, it outputs $\bot$.

Security Model. This security model is called *semantic security with full static collusions*. In fact, a CP-ABBE scheme is said to be secure in this model if given a challenge header and all private keys of revoked users to an adversary. It is impossible for the adversary to infer any information about the session key. Formally, we now recall the security model for a CP-ABBE scheme by the following probabilistic game between an attacker $\mathcal{A}$ and a challenger $\mathcal{C}$.

1. The challenger $\mathcal{C}$ and the adversary $\mathcal{A}$ are given a system consisting of N attributes.
2. $\mathcal{A}$ outputs a target access policy $\mathbb{A}$, target set S as well as a repartition $\{S_u\}_{u \in [n]}$ which he intends to attack.
3. $\mathcal{C}$ runs the algorithm **Setup**$(1^\lambda, n, \{S_u\}_{u \in [n]})$ and gives to $\mathcal{A}$ the public parameters param and the private keys sk_u corresponding to the users u that $\mathcal{A}$ may control, i.e., S_u doesn't satisfy $\mathbb{A}$ or S_u satisfies $\mathbb{A}$ but $u \notin S$.
4. $\mathcal{C}$ runs the algorithm **Encrypt**$(\mathsf{param}, \mathbb{A}, S)$ and obtains a header Hdr and a session key $K \in \mathcal{K}$. Next, $\mathcal{C}$ draws a bit b uniformly at random, sets $K' = K$ if bit $b = 0$, $K' \xleftarrow{\$} \mathcal{K}$ if bit $b = 1$ and finally gives (K', Hdr) to $\mathcal{A}$.
5. The adversary $\mathcal{A}$ outputs a guess bit b'.

As usual, $\mathcal{A}$ wins the game if $b = b'$, and its advantage is defined as

$$Adv^{ind}(\lambda, n, \{S_u\}_{u \in [n]}, \mathcal{A}) = |2Pr[b = b'] - 1|$$

where the probability is taken over the random bit b and all the bits used in the simulation of the algorithms **Setup**$(.)$, and **Encrypt**$(.)$. The semantic security against full static collusions is defined as follows.

Definition 1. *A CP-ABBE scheme is semantically secure against full static collusions if for all randomized polynomial-time adversaries $\mathcal{A}$ and for all access policies involving at most N attributes defined by $\{S_u\}_{\in [n]}$,*

$$Adv^{ind}(1^\lambda, n, \{S_u\}_{u \in [n]}, \mathcal{A})$$

is a negligible function of λ when N, n are at most polynomial in λ.

2.3   Access Structures

Definition 2 (Access Structures). *Let $\{P_1, P_2, \ldots, P_n\}$ be a set of parties. A collection $\mathbb{A} \subseteq 2^{\{P_1, P_2, \ldots, P_n\}}$ is monotone if $\forall B, C$: if $B \in \mathbb{A}$ and $B \subset C$ then $C \in \mathbb{A}$. An access structure (respectively, monotone access structure) is a collection (respectively, monotone collection) $\mathbb{A}$ of non-empty subsets of $\{P_1, P_2, \ldots, P_n\}$, i.e, $\mathbb{A} \subseteq 2^{\{P_1, P_2, \ldots, P_n\}} \setminus \{\emptyset\}$. The sets in $\mathbb{A}$ are called the authorized sets, and the sets not in $\mathbb{A}$ are called the unauthorized sets.*

In this paper, we consider the monotone access structures. However, as shown in [15], it is also possible to extend such case to the general access structures, at the cost of a doubled number of attributes in the system.

2.4   Bilinear Maps and (P, Q, f) − GDDHE Assumptions

Let $\mathbb{G}, \widetilde{\mathbb{G}}$ and $\mathbb{G}_T$ denote three finite multiplicative abelian groups of large prime order $p > 2^\lambda$ where λ is the security parameter. Let g be a generator of $\mathbb{G}$ and $\tilde{g}$ be a generator of $\widetilde{\mathbb{G}}$. We assume that there exists an admissible asymmetric bilinear map $e : \mathbb{G} \times \widetilde{\mathbb{G}} \to \mathbb{G}_T$, meaning that for all $a, b \in \mathbb{Z}_p$, (i) $e(g^a, \tilde{g}^b) = e(g, \tilde{g})^{ab}$, (ii) $e(g^a, \tilde{g}^b) = 1$ iff $a = 0$ or $b = 0$, and (iii) $e(g^a, \tilde{g}^b)$ is efficiently computable. In the sequel, the set $(p, \mathbb{G}, \widetilde{\mathbb{G}}, \mathbb{G}_T, e)$ is called a bilinear map group system.

Let $(p, \mathbb{G}, \widetilde{\mathbb{G}}, \mathbb{G}_T, e)$ be a bilinear map group system and $g \in \mathbb{G}$ (resp. $\tilde{g} \in \widetilde{\mathbb{G}}$) be a generator of $\mathbb{G}$ (resp. $\widetilde{\mathbb{G}}$). We set $g_T = e(g, \tilde{g}) \in \mathbb{G}_T$. Let s, n be positive integers and $P, Q, R \in \mathbb{F}_p[X_1, \ldots, X_n]^s$ be three s-tuples of n-variate polynomials over $\mathbb{F}_p$. Thus, P, Q and R are just three lists containing s multivariate polynomials each. We write $P = (p_1, p_2, \ldots, p_s)$, $Q = (q_1, q_2, \ldots, q_s)$, $R = (r_1, r_2, \ldots, r_s)$ and impose that $p_1 = q_1 = r_1 = 1$. For any function $h : \mathbb{F}_p \to \Omega$ and any vector $(x_1, \ldots, x_n) \in \mathbb{F}_p^n$, $h(P(x_1, \ldots, x_n))$ stands for $\big(h(p_1(x_1, \ldots, x_n)), \ldots, h(p_s(x_1, \ldots, x_n))\big) \in \Omega^s$. We use a similar notation for the s-tuples Q and R. Let $f \in \mathbb{F}_p[X_1, \ldots, X_n]$. It is said that f depends on (P, Q, R), which denotes $f \in \langle P, Q, R \rangle$, when there exists a linear decomposition (with an efficient isomorphism between $\mathbb{G}$ and $\widetilde{\mathbb{G}}$):

$$f = \sum_{1 \leq i,j \leq s} a_{i,j} \cdot p_i \cdot q_j + \sum_{1 \leq i,j \leq s} b_{i,j} \cdot p_i \cdot p_j + \sum_{1 \leq i \leq s} c_i \cdot r_i,$$

where $a_{i,j}, b_{i,j}, c_i \in \mathbb{Z}_p$.

We moreover have $b_{i,j} = 0$ when there is no efficiently computable homomorphism between $\mathbb{G}$ and $\widetilde{\mathbb{G}}$. Let P, Q, R be as above and $f \in \mathbb{F}_p[X_1, \ldots, X_n]$. The (P, Q, R, f) − GDDHE problem is defined as follows.

Definition 3 $((P, Q, R, f)$ − GDDHE) [1].
Given the vector $H(x_1, \ldots, x_n) = (g^{P(x_1, \ldots, x_n)}, \tilde{g}^{Q(x_1, \ldots, x_n)}, g_T^{R(x_1, \ldots, x_n)}) \in \mathbb{G}^s \times \widetilde{\mathbb{G}}^s \times \mathbb{G}_T^s$ as above and $T \in \mathbb{G}_T$ decide whether $T = g_T^{f(x_1, \ldots, x_n)}$.

The (P, Q, R, f) − GDDHE assumption says that it is hard to solve the (P, Q, R, f) − GDDHE problem if f is linearly independent of (P, Q, R). In this paper, we will prove that our scheme is semantically secure under this assumption.

3   Construction

3.1   Intuition Behind Our Construction

Delerablée's technique. In this paper, we extend the Delerablée's technique of constructing an IBBE scheme [5] into our CP-ABBE context. In [5], the user's private key is of the form $g^{\frac{1}{\alpha+\mathsf{ID}_u}}$, the ciphertext is constructed corresponding to a target set of identities $S = (\mathsf{ID}_{i_1}, \ldots, \mathsf{ID}_{i_k})$ is of the form

$$g^{\prod_{j=i_1}^{j=i_k}(\alpha+\mathsf{ID}_j)}$$

and as long as user's identity is "divided" by S (it means $\mathsf{ID}_u \in S$), she can decrypt. In our scheme, each user u possesses a set of attributes S_u and each clause in the DNF access policy is a set of attributes β_i: as long as there is at least a set β_i which is "divided" by S_u then the user u can decrypt.

Our adaptation. When applying the above technique in ABE's context, the result is in the reversed form in which a user can decrypt if S_u is "divided" by β_i. To deal with this problem, we employ a reversed technique to generate the user's private key by using the user's "reversed" attribute set $\mathcal{U} \setminus S_u$, where $\mathcal{U}$ is the attribute universe. Now, if β_i is "divided" by S_u then $\mathcal{U} \setminus S_u$ is "divided" by $\mathcal{U} \setminus \beta_i$. We then produce the ciphertext in the same way as in [5] (by using $\mathcal{U} \setminus \beta_i$ instead of β_i).

Re-use randomness vs. collusion. In our ABBE scheme, the access policy contains many clauses, each clause β_i corresponds to a target set in the Delerablée's IBBE scheme, and it is related to a ciphertext component C_i. In order to make the decryption work, all the components C_i are required to use the same randomness and the collusion can take some advantage in exploiting this point. In order to neutralize the advantage of the adversary, we will make use of the "dummy technique" by choosing a random dummy attribute set in creating each C_i. Consequently, each C_i is randomized since the random dummy attribute set now plays the role of a fresh randomness.

3.2   Our Scheme

We now describe our scheme which uses the type 3 paring.

Setup$(1^\lambda, n, \{S_u\}_{\in[n]})$: Assume that the maximum number of attributes is N, the maximum number of clauses in an access policy is N'.

Assume that the attribute universe is $\mathcal{U} = \{A_1, \ldots, A_N\} \in \mathbb{Z}_p^N$, the dummy attribute universe is $\mathcal{U}' = \{B_{i,j}\}_{\substack{i \in [N'] \\ j \in [N']}} \in \mathbb{Z}_p^{N' \times N'}$, suppose that the set of identities of users in the system is $\mathcal{ID} = \{\mathsf{ID}_1, \ldots, \mathsf{ID}_n\} \in \mathbb{Z}_p^n$. The algorithm generates a bilinear map group system $D = (p, \mathbb{G}, \widetilde{\mathbb{G}}, \mathbb{G}_T, e)$, then chooses $h \xleftarrow{\$} \widetilde{\mathbb{G}}, g \xleftarrow{\$} \mathbb{G}$ and $\alpha, \gamma \xleftarrow{\$} \mathbb{Z}_p$. Finally, it outputs:

$$\mathsf{param} = (\mathcal{U}, \mathcal{U}', \mathcal{ID}, D, \{h^{\alpha^r \cdot \gamma^t}\}_{\substack{r=0,\ldots,N \\ t=0,\ldots,n+N'}}, h^{\frac{\gamma}{\alpha}}, \ldots, h^{\frac{\gamma^{n+N'}}{\alpha}}, g^\alpha, e(g,h))$$

and

$$sk_u = g^{\frac{1}{(\gamma+\mathsf{ID}_u)\cdot\Pi_{i\in\mathcal{U}\setminus S_u}(\alpha+A_i)}}.$$

Encrypt(param, $\beta = (\beta_1 \vee \beta_2 \vee \cdots \vee \beta_m), S$): the algorithm first checks that $\beta_i \neq \beta_j$ for all $i, j \in [m], i \neq j$, then picks a random $k \in \mathbb{Z}_p$ then computes:

$$C_0 = g^{-k.\alpha}, K = e(g,h)^k$$
$$C_1 = h^{k.\,\Pi_{j\in[m]}(\gamma+B_{1,j})\cdot\,\Pi_{i\in\mathcal{U}\setminus\beta_1}(\alpha+A_i)\cdot\,\Pi_{i\in S}(\gamma+\mathsf{ID}_i)}, \ldots,$$
$$C_m = h^{k.\,\Pi_{j\in[m]}(\gamma+B_{m,j})\cdot\,\Pi_{i\in\mathcal{U}\setminus\beta_m}(\alpha+A_i)\cdot\,\Pi_{i\in S}(\gamma+\mathsf{ID}_i)}$$

Finally, it outputs K and $\mathsf{Hdr} = (C_0, C_1, \ldots, C_m)$ which includes β and S.

Decrypt(sk_u, Hdr, param): the algorithm first finds the set β_j such that $\beta_j \subset S_u$ and checks that $u \in S$, then computes $K' =$

$$h^{\frac{1}{\alpha}(\Pi_{i\in[m]}(\gamma+B_{j,i})\cdot\,\Pi_{i\in S_u\setminus\beta_j}(\alpha+A_i)\cdot\,\Pi_{i\in S,i\neq u}(\gamma+\mathsf{ID}_i)-\Pi_{i\in[m]}B_{j,i}\cdot\,\Pi_{i\in S_u\setminus\beta_j}A_i\cdot\,\Pi_{i\in S,i\neq u}\mathsf{ID}_i)}$$

Note that it is able to compute K' from the param. It finally computes

$$K = (e(C_0, K') \cdot e(sk_u, C_j))^{\frac{1}{\Pi_{i\in[m]}B_{j,i}\cdot\,\Pi_{i\in S_u\setminus\beta_j}A_i\cdot\,\Pi_{i\in S,i\neq u}\mathsf{ID}_i}}.$$

4   Security

Intuitively, following the security model in the Sect. 2.2 we need to prove that given all elements corresponding to the public global parameters, the private decryption keys of corrupted users, and the challenge header, the adversary $\mathcal{A}$ cannot distinguish between a real session key K and a random element in $\mathbb{G}_T$. Therefore, if we define P, Q, R to be the list of polynomials consisting of all elements corresponding to the public global parameters, the private decryption keys of corrupted users, and the challenge header, we need to prove that the following $(P, Q, R, f) - \mathsf{GDDHE}$ assumption holds (that means f is independent to (P, Q, R)), where f corresponds to the real session key. The definition of P, Q, R and f for our $(P, Q, R, f) - \mathsf{GDDHE}$ instance is given by Fig. 1.

Lemma 1. *In the* $(P, Q, R, f) - \mathsf{GDDHE}$ *assumption above,* (P, Q, R) *and* f *are linearly independent.*

The semantic security of our scheme now is stated as follows.

Theorem 1. *If there exists an adversary* $\mathcal{A}$ *that solves the semantic security of our scheme with advantage* $Adv^{ind}(.)$, *then we can construct a simulator to solve an instance of the* $(P, Q, R, f) - \mathsf{GDDHE}$ *problem above with the same advantage* $Adv^{ind}(.)$.

We refer the proofs of the above lemma and theorem to the full version of the paper.

$$P = \left\{ \alpha, -k\alpha, \left(\frac{1}{(\gamma + \mathsf{ID}_u) \prod_{i \in \mathcal{U} \setminus S_u} (\alpha + A_i)} \right)_{u \in [n']} \right\}$$

$$Q = \left\{ \left(\alpha^r \cdot \gamma^t \right)_{\substack{r=0,\dots,N \\ t=0,\dots,n+N'}}, \left(\frac{\gamma^i}{\alpha} \right)_{i \in [n+N']}, \right.$$

$$\left. \left(k \cdot \prod_{j \in [m]} (\gamma + B_{i,j}) \prod_{j \in \mathcal{U} \setminus \beta_i} (\alpha + A_j) \cdot \prod_{j \in S} (\gamma + \mathsf{ID}_j) \right)_{i=1,\dots,m} \right\}$$

$$R = \{1\}, \qquad\qquad f = k$$

for all n' corrupted user u, $1 \le n' < n$.

Fig. 1. (P, Q, R, f) – GDDHE instance

5   Implementation and Optimization

We have implemented our CP-ABBE in the scenario given in Sect. 2.1. We have tested several values for the number n of users and the maximum number of attributes N, we also give some tricks when implementing to optimize the encryption phase and decryption phase. We refer the optimization and benchmarks of our implementation to the full version of the paper.

Acknowledgments. This work was partially supported by the French ANR Project ANR-12-INSE-0014 SIMPATIC and partially conducted within the context of the Vietnamese Project Pervasive and Secure Information Service Infrastructure for Internet of Things based on Cloud Computing.

References

1. Boneh, D., Boyen, X., Goh, E.-J.: Hierarchical identity based encryption with constant size ciphertext. In: Cramer, R. (ed.) EUROCRYPT 2005. LNCS, vol. 3494, pp. 440–456. Springer, Heidelberg (2005). doi:10.1007/11426639_26
2. Boneh, D., Gentry, C., Waters, B.: Collusion resistant broadcast encryption with short ciphertexts and private keys. In: Shoup, V. (ed.) CRYPTO 2005. LNCS, vol. 3621, pp. 258–275. Springer, Heidelberg (2005). doi:10.1007/11535218_16
3. Canard, S., Trinh, V.C.: Private ciphertext-policy attribute-based encryption schemes with constant-size ciphertext supporting CNF access policy (2015). http://eprint.iacr.org/2015/891
4. Chen, J., Gay, R., Wee, H.: Improved dual system ABE in prime-order groups via predicate encodings. In: Oswald, E., Fischlin, M. (eds.) EUROCRYPT 2015. LNCS, vol. 9057, pp. 595–624. Springer, Heidelberg (2015). doi:10.1007/978-3-662-46803-6_20
5. Delerablée, C.: Identity-based broadcast encryption with constant size ciphertexts and private keys. In: Kurosawa, K. (ed.) ASIACRYPT 2007. LNCS, vol. 4833, pp. 200–215. Springer, Heidelberg (2007). doi:10.1007/978-3-540-76900-2_12
6. Hohenberger, S., Waters, B.: Attribute-based encryption with fast decryption. In: Kurosawa, K., Hanaoka, G. (eds.) PKC 2013. LNCS, vol. 7778, pp. 162–179. Springer, Heidelberg (2013). doi:10.1007/978-3-642-36362-7_11

7. Junod, P., Karlov, A.: An efficient public-key attribute-based broadcast encryption scheme allowing arbitrary access policies. In: ACM Workshop on Digital Rights Management, pp. 13–24. ACM Press (2010)

8. Liu, Z., Cao, Z., Wong, D.S.: Blackbox traceable CP-ABE: how to catch people leaking their keys by selling decryption devices on eBay. In: Sadeghi, A.-R., Gligor, V.D., Yung, M. (eds.) ACM CCS 2013, Berlin, Germany, pp. 475–486. ACM Press, 4–8 November 2013

9. Liu, Z., Wong, D.S.: Practical attribute-based encryption: traitor tracing, revocation, and large universe. In: ACNS 15 (2015)

10. Lubicz, D., Sirvent, T.: Attribute-based broadcast encryption scheme made efficient. In: Vaudenay, S. (ed.) AFRICACRYPT 2008. LNCS, vol. 5023, pp. 325–342. Springer, Heidelberg (2008). doi:10.1007/978-3-540-68164-9_22

11. Ostrovsky, R., Sahai, A., Waters, B.: Attribute-based encryption with non-monotonic access structures. In: Ning, P., di Vimercati, S.D.C., Syverson, P.F. (eds.) ACM CCS 2007, Alexandria, Virginia, USA, pp. 195–203. ACM Press, 28–31 October 2007

12. Phuong, T.V.X., Yang, G., Susilo, W., Chen, X.: Attribute based broadcast encryption with short ciphertext and decryption key. In: Pernul, G., Ryan, P.Y.A., Weippl, E. (eds.) ESORICS 2015. LNCS, vol. 9327, pp. 252–269. Springer, Heidelberg (2015). doi:10.1007/978-3-319-24177-7_13

13. Rouselakis, Y., Waters, B.: Practical constructions and new proof methods for large universe attribute-based encryption. In: Sadeghi, A.-R., Gligor, V.D., Yung, M. (eds.) ACM CCS 2013, Berlin, Germany, pp. 463–474. ACM Press, 4–8 November 2013

14. Sahai, A., Waters, B.: Fuzzy identity-based encryption. In: Cramer, R. (ed.) EUROCRYPT 2005. LNCS, vol. 3494, pp. 457–473. Springer, Heidelberg (2005). doi:10.1007/11426639_27

15. Waters, B.: Ciphertext-policy attribute-based encryption: an expressive, efficient, and provably secure realization. In: Catalano, D., Fazio, N., Gennaro, R., Nicolosi, A. (eds.) PKC 2011. LNCS, vol. 6571, pp. 53–70. Springer, Heidelberg (2011). doi:10.1007/978-3-642-19379-8_4

16. Yamada, S., Attrapadung, N., Hanaoka, G., Kunihiro, N.: A framework and compact constructions for non-monotonic attribute-based encryption. In: Krawczyk, H. (ed.) PKC 2014. LNCS, vol. 8383, pp. 275–292. Springer, Heidelberg (2014). doi:10.1007/978-3-642-54631-0_16

An Efficient Construction of Non-Interactive Secure Multiparty Computation

Satoshi Obana[1(✉)] and Maki Yoshida[2]

[1] Hosei University, Tokyo, Japan
obana@hosei.ac.jp
[2] NICT, Tokyo, Japan
maki-yos@nict.go.jp

Abstract. An important issue of secure multi-party computation (MPC) is to improve the efficiency of communication. Non-interactive MPC (NIMPC) introduced by Beimel et al. in Crypto 2014 completely avoids interaction in the information theoretical setting by allowing a correlated randomness setup where the parties get *correlated* random strings beforehand and *locally* compute their messages sent to an external output server. The goal of this paper is to reduce the communication complexity in terms of the size of random strings and messages. In this paper, we present an efficient construction of NIMPC, which is designed for arbitrary functions. In contrast to the previous NIMPC protocols, which separately compute each output bit, the proposed protocol simultaneously computes all output bits. As a result, the communication complexity of the proposed protocol is $\frac{\lceil \log d \rceil \cdot L}{\lceil \log d \rceil + L}$ times smaller than that of the best known protocol where d and L denote the size of input domain and the output length. Thus, the proposed protocol is the most efficient if both input and output lengths are larger than two.

1 Introduction

Secure multiparty computation (MPC for short) is a cryptographic protocol that enables multiple party P_i $(i = 1, \ldots, n)$ to jointly compute various functions without revealing their inputs. The problem is first raised by Yao [11], and further developed by Goldreich, Micali, Wigderson in the computational setting [6], and by Ben-Or, Goldwasser, Wigderson in the information theoretical setting [2]. Their seminal works are followed by a large number of literature (e.g., [3–5,7–10]), and MPC is still one of the hottest topics in the area of cryptography. In CRYPTO 2014 [1], Beimel et al. have introduced a novel type of MPC called non-interactive multiparty computation (NIMPC for short). In NIMPC for a function f, given correlated randomness $(r_1, \ldots, r_n)$, each party P_i who possess a private input x_i computes a message m_i from x_i and r_i so that the output $f(x_1, \ldots, x_n)$ is computed from $m_1, m_2, \ldots, m_n$. NIMPC completely gets rid of interaction among parties since the message m_i is locally computed by P_i. Beimel et al. have presented the security model of NIMPC against honest-but-curious adversaries in the information-theoretical setting. One of the main

© Springer International Publishing AG 2016
S. Foresti and G. Persiano (Eds.): CANS 2016, LNCS 10052, pp. 604–614, 2016.
DOI: 10.1007/978-3-319-48965-0_39

positive results in [1] is to show the possibility of fully robust NIMPC for various classes of functions including the class of *arbitrary* functions. The fully robustness here means that any set of corrupted parties learn nothing about inputs of uncorrupted parties and the function they aim to evaluate other than the information inferred from their inputs and output. On the negative side in [1], the communication complexity of the proposed protocols are very large (exponential in the input length) except for special classes of functions. The approach taken in [1] to realize NIMPC for *arbitrary* functions $h : \mathcal{X} \to \{0,1\}^L$ is as follows.

1. Construct an NIMPC protocol for the set of arbitrary *indicator* functions where index function $h_a(x)$ outputs 1 if $x = a$ holds, and otherwise 0. Let δ_{ind} be the communication complexity of the NIMPC protocol.
2. Express any *boolean* function as a sum of indicator functions and construct an NIMPC protocol for the boolean function by using the NIMPC protocols for each indicator function. The communication complexity of this NIMPC protocol for boolean functions is $\delta_{\text{ind}} \cdot |\mathcal{X}|$.
3. For any function *outputting more than one bit*, compute each output bit separately with the NIMPC protocols for the corresponding boolean functions. The communication complexity of the resulting protocol is $\delta_{\text{ind}} \cdot L \cdot |\mathcal{X}|$.

The second step in this approach implies an exponential communication complexity in the input length.

Unfortunately, the inefficiency of NIMPC for arbitrary functions is provably unavoidable. In [12], Yoshida and Obana derived a lower bound on the communication complexity that is linear in the number of target functions. Thus, for the case of NIMPC for arbitrary functions, the communication complexity is $L \cdot |\mathcal{X}|$, i.e., linear both in the output length and size of input domain, or exponential in the input length. Although they significantly reduces the communication complexity much closer to the lower bound by presenting a more efficient NIMPC protocol for indicator functions in the above first step, a quadratic gap still remains (see Table 1). That is, there is a room to reduce the communication complexity.

Our contribution: We presents an efficient NIMPC protocol for arbitrary functions $h : \mathcal{X} \to \{0,1\}^L$. Table 1 compares the proposed protocol with the previous results. The communication complexity of the proposed protocol is $\lceil \log_2 d \rceil \cdot (\lceil \log_2 d \rceil + L) \cdot n^2 \cdot |\mathcal{X}|$, which offers the smallest communication complexity known so far.

To improve the efficiency, we modify the three-step approach employed in [1, 12] to compute all output bits simultaneously. The key idea is to introduce *generalized* indicator functions $h_{a,v}(x)$ outputting $v \in \{0,1\}^L$ if $x = a$ holds, and otherwise 0^L. More concretely, our approach to realize NIMPC for arbitrary functions $h : \mathcal{X} \to \{0,1\}^L$ is as follows:

1. Construct an NIMPC protocol for the set of arbitrary *generalized* indicator functions outputting multiple-bit which are freely defined. Let δ_{gind} be the communication complexity of the NIMPC protocol.

Table 1. The communication complexity of n-player NIMPC protocols for arbitrary functions $h : \mathcal{X} \to \{0,1\}^L$ where $\mathcal{X} = \mathcal{X}_1 \times \cdots \times \mathcal{X}_n$ and $|\mathcal{X}_i| \leq d$ for all $1 \leq i \leq n$

	The communication complexity
Lower bound in [12]	$L \cdot |\mathcal{X}|$
Protocol in [1]	$d^2 \cdot L \cdot n^2 \cdot |\mathcal{X}|$
Protocol in [12]	$\lceil \log_2 d \rceil^2 \cdot L \cdot n^2 \cdot |\mathcal{X}|$
Our protocol (Sect. 3)	$\lceil \log_2 d \rceil \cdot (\lceil \log_2 d \rceil + L) \cdot n^2 \cdot |\mathcal{X}|$

2. Express any function outputting multiple-bit as a sum of generalized indicator functions and construct an NIMPC protocol for the function by using the NIMPC protocols for each generalized indicator function. The communication complexity of the resulting protocol is $\delta_{\text{gind}} \cdot |\mathcal{X}|$.

This approach works fine if δ_{gind} is smaller than $\delta_{\text{ind}} \cdot L$. In the previous protocols for indicator functions in [1,12], the messages $m_1, m_2, \ldots, m_n$ are vectors whose summation is zero if and only if the output is one. Thus, the vectors have one-bit information. To achieve $\delta_{\text{gind}} < \delta_{\text{ind}} \cdot L$, we embed the L-bit output information into the vectors while keeping the linear (in)dependency of vectors. As a result, we have $\delta_{\text{gind}} = \lceil \log_2 d \rceil \cdot (\lceil \log_2 d \rceil + L) \cdot n^2$, which is smaller than the best known $\delta_{\text{ind}} \cdot L = \lceil \log_2 d \rceil^2 \cdot L \cdot n^2$, if both input length $\lceil \log_2 d \rceil$ and output length L are larger than two. Thus, the proposed protocol becomes more efficient than the previous protocols as we have larger input and output domains.

The rest of this paper is organized as follows. In Sect. 2, we recall the notations and definitions of NIMPC. In Sect. 3, we present a construction of an NIMPC protocol for arbitrary functions based on an NIMPC protocol for the generalized indicator functions. Section 4 concludes the paper.

2 Preliminaries

For an integer n, let $[n]$ be the set $\{1, 2, \ldots, n\}$. For a set $\mathcal{X} = \mathcal{X}_1 \times \cdots \times \mathcal{X}_n$ and $T \subseteq [n]$, we denote $\mathcal{X}_T \triangleq \prod_{i \in T} \mathcal{X}_i$. For $x \in \mathcal{X}$, we denote by x_T the restriction of x to $\mathcal{X}_T$, and for a function $h : \mathcal{X} \to \Omega$, a subset $T \subseteq [n]$, its complement $\overline{T} \subseteq [n]$, and $x_{\overline{T}} \in \mathcal{X}_{\overline{T}}$, we denote by $h|_{\overline{T}, x_{\overline{T}}} : \mathcal{X} \to \Omega$ the function h where the inputs of $\overline{T}$ are fixed to $x_{\overline{T}}$. For a set S, let $|S|$ denote its size (i.e., cardinality of S).

An NIMPC protocol for a family of functions $\mathcal{H}$ is defined by three algorithms: (1) a randomness generation function GEN, which given a description of a function $h \in \mathcal{H}$ generates n correlated random inputs $R_1, \ldots, R_n$, (2) a local encoding function ENC_i ($1 \leq i \leq n$), which takes an input x_i and a random input R_i and outputs a message, and (3) a decoding algorithm DEC that reconstructs $h(x_1, \ldots, x_n)$ from the n messages. The formal definition is given as follows:

Definition 1 (NIMPC: Syntax and Correctness [1]). *Let $\mathcal{X}_1, \ldots, \mathcal{X}_n$, $\mathcal{R}_1$, $\ldots$, $\mathcal{R}_n$, $\mathcal{M}_1, \ldots, \mathcal{M}_n$ and Ω be finite domains. Let $\mathcal{X} \triangleq \mathcal{X}_1 \times \cdots \times \mathcal{X}_n$ and let $\mathcal{H}$ be a family of functions $h : \mathcal{X} \to \Omega$. A non-interactive secure multi-party computation (NIMPC) protocol for $\mathcal{H}$ is a triplet $\Pi = (\mathsf{GEN}, \mathsf{ENC}, \mathsf{DEC})$ where*

- *$\mathsf{GEN} : \mathcal{H} \to \mathcal{R}_1 \times \cdots \times \mathcal{R}_n$ is a random function,*
- *ENC is an n-tuple deterministic functions $(\mathsf{ENC}_1, \ldots, \mathsf{ENC}_n)$, where $\mathsf{ENC}_i : \mathcal{X}_i \times \mathcal{R}_i \to \mathcal{M}_i$,*
- *$\mathsf{DEC} : \mathcal{M}_1 \times \cdots \times \mathcal{M}_n \to \Omega$ is is a deterministic function satisfying the following correctness requirement: for any $x = (x_1, \ldots, x_n) \in \mathcal{X}$ and $h \in \mathcal{H}$,*

$$\Pr[R = (R_1, \ldots, R_n) \leftarrow \mathsf{GEN}(h) : \mathsf{DEC}(\mathsf{ENC}(x, R)) = h(x)] = 1, \qquad (1)$$

where $\mathsf{ENC}(x, R) \triangleq (\mathsf{ENC}_1(x_1, R_1), \ldots, \mathsf{ENC}_n(x_n, R_n))$.

The communication complexity of Π is the summation of $\log |\mathcal{R}_1|, \ldots, \log |\mathcal{R}_n|$, $\log |\mathcal{M}_1|, \ldots, \log |\mathcal{M}_n|$. The individual communication complexity of Π is the maximum of $\log |\mathcal{R}_1|, \ldots, \log |\mathcal{R}_n|, \log |\mathcal{M}_1|, \ldots, \log |\mathcal{M}_n|$.

We next show the definition of robustness for NIMPC, which states that a coalition can only learn the information they should. In the above setting, a coalition T can repeatedly encode any inputs for T and decode h with the new encoded inputs and the original encoded inputs of $\overline{T}$. Thus, the following robustness requires that they learn no other information than the information obtained from oracle access to $h|_{\overline{T}, x_{\overline{T}}}$.

Definition 2 (NIMPC: Robustness [1]). *For a subset $T \subseteq [n]$, we say that an NIMPC protocol Π for $\mathcal{H}$ is T-robust if there exists a randomized function Sim_T (a "simulator") such that, for every $h \in \mathcal{H}$ and $x_{\overline{T}} \in \mathcal{X}_{\overline{T}}$, we have $Sim_T(h|_{\overline{T}, x_{\overline{T}}}) \equiv (M_{\overline{T}}, R_T)$, where R and M are the joint randomness and messages defined by $R \leftarrow \mathsf{GEN}(h)$ and $M_i \leftarrow \mathsf{ENC}_i(x_i, R_i)$.*

For an integer $0 \le t \le n$, we say that Π is t-robust if it is T-robust for every $T \subseteq [n]$ of size $|T| \le t$. We say that Π is fully robust (or simply refer to Π as an NIMPC for $\mathcal{H}$) if Π is n-robust. Finally, given a concrete function $h : \mathcal{X} \to \Omega$, we say that Π is a (t-robust) NIMPC protocol for h if it is a (t-robust) NIMPC for $\mathcal{H} = \{h\}$.

As the same simulator Sim_T is used for every $h \in \mathcal{H}$ and the simulator has only access to $h|_{\overline{T}, x_{\overline{T}}}$, NIMPC hides both h and the inputs of $\overline{T}$. An NIMPC protocol is 0-robust if it is $\emptyset$-robust. In this case, the only requirement is that the messages $(M_1, \ldots, M_n)$ reveal $h(x)$ and nothing else.

An NIMPC protocol is also described in the language of protocols in [1]. Such a protocol involves n players $P_1, \ldots, P_n$, each holding an input $x_i \in \mathcal{X}_i$, and an external "output server," a player P_0 with no input. The protocol may have an additional input, a function $h \in \mathcal{H}$.

Definition 3 (NIMPC: Protocol Description [1]). *For an NIMPC protocol Π for $\mathcal{H}$, let $P(\Pi)$ denote the protocol that may have an additional input, a function $h \in \mathcal{H}$, and proceeds as follows.*

Protocol $P(\Pi)(h)$

- **Offline preprocessing:** *Each player P_i, $1 \leq i \leq n$, receives the random input $R_i \triangleq \mathsf{GEN}(h)_i \in \mathcal{R}_i$.*
- **Online messages:** *On input R_i, each player P_i, $1 \leq i \leq n$, sends the message $M_i \triangleq \mathsf{ENC}_i(x_i, R_i) \in \mathcal{M}_i$ to P_0.*
- **Output:** *P_0 computes and outputs $\mathsf{DEC}(M_1, \ldots, M_n)$.*

Informally, the relevant properties of protocol $P(\Pi)$ are given as follows:

- For any $h \in \mathcal{H}$ and $x \in \mathcal{X}$, the output server P_0 outputs, with probability 1, the value $h(x_1, \ldots, x_n)$.
- Fix $T \subseteq [n]$. Then, Π is T-robust if in $P(\Pi)$ the set of players $\{P_i\}_{i \in T} \cup \{P_0\}$ can simulate their view of the protocol (i.e., the random inputs $\{R_i\}_{i \in T}$ and the messages $\{M_i\}_{i \in \overline{T}}$) given oracle access to the function h restricted by the other inputs (i.e., $h|_{\overline{T}, x_{\overline{T}}}$).
- Π is 0-robust if and only if in $P(\Pi)$ the output server P_0 learns nothing but $h(x_1, \ldots, x_n)$.

A lower bound on the communication complexity for any finite set of functions $\mathcal{H}$ was derived in [12]. In addition, a lower bound for the set of arbitrary functions was derived as a corollary. These results state that the communication complexity cannot be smaller than the logarithm of the size of the target class, and thus for the set of arbitrary functions, reducing the communication complexity to polynomial in the input length is impossible.

Proposition 1 (Lower bound for Any Finite Set of Functions, Theorem 1 in [12]). *Fix finite domains $\mathcal{X}_1, \ldots, \mathcal{X}_n$ and Ω. Let $\mathcal{X} \triangleq \mathcal{X}_1, \ldots, \mathcal{X}_n$ and $\mathcal{H}$ a set of functions $h : \mathcal{X} \rightarrow \Omega$. Then, any fully robust NIMPC protocol Π for $\mathcal{H}$ satisfies $\sum_{i=1}^{n} \log |\mathcal{R}_i| \geq \log |\mathcal{H}|$, and $\sum_{i=1}^{n} \log |\mathcal{M}_i| \geq \log |\Omega|$.*

Proposition 2 (Lower Bound for Arbitrary Functions, Corollary 1 in [12]). *Fix finite domains $\mathcal{X}_1, \ldots, \mathcal{X}_n$ such that $|\mathcal{X}_i| \geq d$ for all $1 \leq i \leq n$. Let $\mathcal{X} \triangleq \mathcal{X}_1 \times \cdots \times \mathcal{X}_n$ and $\mathcal{H}_{\mathrm{all}}^L$ the set of all functions $h : \mathcal{X} \rightarrow \{0, 1\}^L$. Any NIMPC protocol Π for $\mathcal{H}_{\mathrm{all}}^L$ satisfies $\sum_{i=1}^{n} \log |\mathcal{R}_i| \geq L \cdot |\mathcal{X}| \geq d^n \cdot L$, and $\sum_{i=1}^{n} \log |\mathcal{M}_i| \geq L$.*

We show the definition of indicator functions.

Definition 4 (Indicator Functions [1]). *Let $\mathcal{X}$ be a finite domain. For n-tuple $a = (a_1, \ldots, a_n) \in \mathcal{X}$, let $h_a : \mathcal{X} \rightarrow \{0, 1\}$ be the function defined by $h_a(a) = 1$, and $h_a(x) = 0$ for all $a \neq x \in \mathcal{X}$. Let $h_0 : \mathcal{X} \rightarrow \{0, 1\}$ be the function that is identically zero on $\mathcal{X}$. Let $\mathcal{H}_{\mathrm{ind}} \triangleq \{h_a\}_{a \in \mathcal{X}} \cup \{h_0\}$ be the set of all indicator functions together with h_0.*

We define a function family $\mathcal{H}_{\text{ind}}^L$ where $\mathcal{H}_{\text{ind}}^L$ is a generalization of $\mathcal{H}_{\text{ind}}$.

Definition 5 (Generalized Indicator Functions). *For $v \in \{0,1\}^L \setminus \{0^L\}$ and $a = (a_1, \ldots, a_n) \in \mathcal{X}$, we define a function $h_{a,v}$ as follows.*

$$h_{a,v}(x) = \begin{cases} v & if x = a \\ 0^L & otherwise \end{cases}$$

Let $h_0^L : \mathcal{X} \to \{0,1\}^L$ be the function that is identically 0^L on $\mathcal{X}$ then we define the family of function $\mathcal{H}_{ind}^L = \{h_{a,v}\}_{a \in \mathcal{X}, v \in \{0,1\}^L} \cup \{h_0\}$.

In [1,12], using the fact that every function $h : \mathcal{X} \to \{0,1\}$ can be expressed as the sum of indicator functions $h = \sum_{a \in \mathcal{X}, h(a)=1} h_a$, NIMPC for arbitrary function $h : \mathcal{X} \to \{0,1\}$ is realized by $|\mathcal{X}|$ independent invocation of NIMPC for H_{ind}. In contrast, we express arbitrary function $h : \mathcal{X} \to \{0,1\}^L$ as the sum of $h_{a,v} \in \mathcal{H}_{\text{ind}}^L$, that is, $h = \sum_{a \in \mathcal{X}, h(a) \neq 0^L} h_{a,h(a)}$, and will use NIMPC for $\mathcal{H}_{\text{ind}}^L$ to construct NIMPC for $\mathcal{H}_{\text{all}}^L$.

3 Proposed Construction

In this section, we presents NIMPC for $\mathcal{H}_{\text{all}}^L$, arbitrary functions with L-bit output. The communication complexity of the proposed protocol is $\lceil \log_2 d \rceil \cdot (\lceil \log_2 d \rceil + L) \cdot n^2 \cdot |\mathcal{X}|$, which is the most efficient NIMPC for $\mathcal{H}_{\text{all}}^L$ known so far.

3.1 A Fully Robust NIMPC for $\mathcal{H}_{\text{ind}}^L$

We are going to construct an NIMPC for the function family $\mathcal{H}_{\text{ind}}^L$. The protocol is constructed by slightly modifying NIMPC for $\mathcal{H}_{\text{ind}}$ given in [12]. More precisely, we introduce additional L-bit vectors $v_{i,j} \in \mathbb{F}_2^L$ to the protocol in [12], which makes it possible to support L-bit output in NIMPC. Vectors $v_{i,j}$ (for $i \in [n], j \in [\lceil \log_2 d_i \rceil]$) are chosen in such a way that linear combination of $v_{i,j}$s associate with input $x = (x_1, \ldots, x_n)$ will yield output value v if and only if input x is identical to a. The concrete description of the proposed protocol is given as follows.

For $i \in [n]$, let $d_i = |\mathcal{X}_i|$ and ϕ_i a one-to-one mapping from $\mathcal{X}_i$ to $[d_i]$. Let $l_i = \lceil \log_2 d_i \rceil$ and $s = \sum_{i=1}^n l_i$. Fix a function $h \in \mathcal{H}_{\text{ind}}^L$ that we want to compute.

- **Offline preprocessing:** If $h = h_0$ then choose s linearly independent random vectors $\{m_{i,j}\}_{i \in [n], j \in [l_i]} \in \mathbb{F}_2^s$ and s random vectors $\{v_{i,j}\}_{i \in [n], j \in [l_i]} \in \mathbb{F}_2^L$. If $h = h_{a,v}$ for some $a = (a_1, \ldots, a_n) \in \mathcal{X}$ and $v \in \{0,1\}^L$, denote the binary representation of $\phi_i(a_i)$ by $b_i = (b_{i,1}, \ldots, b_{i,l_i})$ and define a set of indices I_i by $I_i = \{j \in [l_i] \mid b_{i,j} = 1\}$. Choose s random vectors $\{m_{i,j}\}_{i \in [n], j \in [l_i]} \in \mathbb{F}_2^s$ under the constraint that $\sum_{i=1}^n \sum_{j \in I_i} m_{i,j} = \mathbf{0}$ and there are no other linear relations between them. Then choose s random vectors $\{v_{i,j}\}_{i \in [n], j \in [l_i]} \in \mathbb{F}_2^L$ under the constraint that $\sum_{i=1}^n \sum_{j \in I_i} v_{i,j} = v$. Define $\mathsf{GEN}(h) \triangleq R = (R_1, \ldots, R_n)$, where $R_i = \{m_{i,j}, v_{i,j}\}_{j \in [l_i]}$.

- **Online messages:** For an input x_i, let $\hat{b}_i = (\hat{b}_{i,1}, \ldots, \hat{b}_{i,l_i})$ be the binary representation of $\phi_i(x_i)$. Let $\hat{I}_i$ be the set of indices defined by $\hat{I}_i = \{j \in [l_i] \mid \hat{b}_{i,j} = 1\}$.
  $\mathsf{ENC}(x, R) \triangleq (M_1, \ldots, M_n)$ where $M_i = (m_i, v_i)$ such that $m_i = \sum_{j \in \hat{I}_i} m_{i,j}$, and $v_i = \sum_{j \in \hat{I}_i} v_{i,j}$.
- **Output** $h(x_1, \ldots, x_n)$: $\mathsf{DEC}(M_1, \ldots, M_n) = \sum_{i=1}^n v_i$ if $\sum_{i=1}^n M_i = \mathbf{0}$ holds. Otherwise $\mathsf{DEC}(M_1, \ldots, M_n) = 0^L$.

Theorem 1. *Fix finite domains $\mathcal{X}_1, \ldots, \mathcal{X}_n$ such that $|\mathcal{X}_i| \leq d$ for all $1 \leq i \leq n$ and let $\mathcal{X} \triangleq \mathcal{X}_1 \times \cdots \times \mathcal{X}_n$. Then, there is an NIMPC protocol for $\mathcal{H}_{ind}^L$ with the communication complexity $\lceil \log_2 d \rceil \cdot (\lceil \log_2 d \rceil + L) \cdot n^2$.*

Proof. First, we will show the correctness. Let $M_i = (m_i, v_i)$, then $\sum_{i=1}^n m_i = \sum_{i=1}^n \sum_{j \in \hat{I}_i} m_{i,j}$ and $\sum_{i=1}^n v_i = \sum_{i=1}^n \sum_{j \in \hat{I}_i} v_{i,j}$ hold. If $h = h_{a,v}$ for some $a \in \mathcal{X}$, then $\sum_{i=1}^n m_i$ equals $\mathbf{0}$ if and only if $I_i = \hat{I}_i$ for all $i \in [n]$, i.e., $a = x$. In this case $\sum_{i=1}^n \sum_{j \in \hat{I}_i} v_{i,j} = \sum_{i=1}^n \sum_{j \in I_i} v_{i,j} = v$ holds. This means $\mathsf{DEC}(M_1, \ldots, M_n) = v$ if and only if $x = a$. If $h = h_0$, then $\sum_{i=1}^n m_i$ never be zero since all vectors $m_{i,j}$ were chosen to be linearly independent in this case. This means $\mathsf{DEC}(M_1, \ldots, M_n) = 0^L$ holds for any $x \in \mathcal{X}$.

To prove robustness, fix a subset $T \subseteq [n]$ and $x_{\overline{T}} \in \mathcal{X}_{\overline{T}}$. The encodings $M_{\overline{T}}$ of $\overline{T}$ consist of the vectors $\{m_i, v_i\}_{i \in \overline{T}}$. The randomness R_T consists of the vectors $\{m_{i,j}, v_{i,j}\}_{i \in T, j \in [l_i]}$. If $h|_{\overline{T}, x_{\overline{T}}} \equiv 0$, there are two possible cases. The first case is $h = h_0$. In this case all $m_{i,j}$ (for $i \in [n], j \in [l_i]$) are uniformly distributed under the constraint that they are linearly independent, and all $v_{i,j}$ are uniformly distributed over $\mathbb{F}_2^L$. Therefore, vectors $m_i = \sum_{j \in I_i} m_{i,j}$ (for $i \in \overline{T}$) and $m_{i,j}$ (for $i \in T, j \in [l_i]$) are also uniformly distributed in $\mathbb{F}_2^s$ under the constraint that they are linearly independent. Further, vectors v_i (for $i \in \overline{T}$) and $v_{i,j}$ (for $i \in T, j \in [l_i]$) are uniformly distributed over $\mathbb{F}_2^L$. The second case to consider is $h = h_{a,v}$ for some a, v and $a_{\overline{T}} \neq x_{\overline{T}}$. In this case, $m_{i,j}$ (for $i \in [n], j \in [l_i]$) are uniformly distributed under the constraint that they are linearly independent and $\sum_{i=1}^n \sum_{j \in I_i} m_{i,j} = \mathbf{0}$. Likewise, $v_{i,j}$ (for $i \in [n], j \in [l_i]$) are uniformly distributed under the constraint $\sum_{i=1}^n \sum_{j \in I_i} v_{i,j} = v$. Since $a_{\overline{T}} \neq x_{\overline{T}}$ holds, $I_i \neq \hat{I}_i$ for some i. This means all $m_{i,j}$ (for $i \in T, j \in [l_i]$) and all $m_i = \sum_{j \in \hat{I}_i} m_{i,j}$ (for $i \in \overline{T}$) are uniformly distributed under the constraint that they are linearly independent since $\sum_{i=1}^n \sum_{j \in I_i} m_{i,j} = \mathbf{0}$ is a only relation holding among $m_{i,j}$. Likewise, all $v_{i,j}$ (for $i \in T, j \in [l_i]$) and all $v_i = \sum_{j \in \hat{I}_i} v_{i,j}$ (for $i \in \overline{T}$) are uniformly distributed since $\sum_{i=1}^n \sum_{j \in I_i} m_{i,j} = v$ is a only relation holding among $v_{i,j}$. From the above argument, we conclude that the $m_{i,j}$ (for $i \in T, j \in [l_i]$) and m_i (for $i \in \overline{T}$) are uniformly distributed under the constraint that are linearly independent, and $v_{i,j}$ (for $i \in T, j \in [l_i]$) and v_i (for $i \in \overline{T}$) are uniformly distributed in both cases. If $h|_{\overline{T}, x_{\overline{T}}}(x_T) = 1$ for some $x_T \in \mathcal{X}_T$, then $\sum_{i \in \overline{T}} m_i + \sum_{i \in T} \sum_{j \in \hat{I}_i} m_{i,j} = \mathbf{0}$ and there are no other linear relations among them. Further, $\sum_{i \in \overline{T}} v_i + \sum_{i \in T} \sum_{j \in \hat{I}_i} v_{i,j} = v$ holds and there are no other relations among them.

Formally, to prove the robustness, we describe a simulator Sim_T: the simulator queries $h|_{\overline{T},x_{\overline{T}}}$ on all possible inputs in $\mathcal{X}_T$. If all answers are zero, this simulator generates random independent vectors $\{m_i, v_i\}_{i \in \overline{T}}$ and $\{m_{i,j}, v_{i,j}\}_{i \in T, j \in [l_i]}$. Otherwise, there is an $x_T \in \mathcal{X}_T$ such that $h|_{\overline{T},x_{\overline{T}}}(x_T) = 1$, and the simulator outputs random vectors $\{m_i, v_i\}_{i \in \overline{T}}, \{m_{i,j}, v_{i,j}\}_{i \in T, j \in [l_i]}$ under the constrains described above, that is, all vectors are independent with the exception that $\sum_{i \in \overline{T}} m_i + \sum_{i \in T} \sum_{j \in \hat{I}_i} m_{i,j} = \mathbf{0}$, and $\sum_{i \in \overline{T}} v_i + \sum_{i \in T} \sum_{j \in \hat{I}_i} v_{i,j} = v$,

The correlated randomness R_i is composed of $l_i \leq \lceil \log_2 d \rceil$ binary vectors of length $s \leq \lceil \log_2 d \rceil \cdot n$ and l_i binary vectors of length L whereas the encoding is the summation of some of them. Therefore, the communication complexity is at most $\lceil \log_2 d \rceil \cdot (\lceil \log_2 d \rceil + L) \cdot n^2$. $\qquad \square$

The following lemmas that are used to prove Theorem 2 are derived from the discussion in the proof of Theorem 1.

Lemma 1. *Fix a subset $T \subseteq [n]$ and let $x \neq a$. Then the distribution of $(R_T, M_{\overline{T}})$ for $h = h_{a,v}$ and that for $h = h_0$, are identical in the above construction.*

Proof. When $x \neq a$ and $h = h_{a,v}$, all vectors in $\{m_{i,j}, v_{i,j}\}_{j \in [l_j]}$ for $i \in T$ and $m_i = \sum_{j \in \hat{I}_i} m_{i,j}$, $v_i = \sum_{j \in \hat{I}_i} v_{i,j}$ for $i \in \overline{T}$ are independently and uniformly distributed since $\sum_{i \in [n]} \sum_{j \in I_i} m_{i,j} = \mathbf{0}$ and $\sum_{i \in [n]} \sum_{j \in I_i} v_{i,j} = v$ are only relations held among $m_{i,j}$ and $v_{i,j}$ and $I_i \neq \hat{I}_i$ holds. Therefore, the distribution is identical to that for $h = h_0$. $\qquad \square$

Lemma 2. *Fix a subset $T \subseteq [n]$ and let $a = (a_T, a_{\overline{T}})$, $a' = (a_T, a'_{\overline{T}})$. Then the distribution of $(R_T, M_{\overline{T}})$ for $h = h_{a,v}, x_{\overline{T}} = a_{\overline{T}}$ and that for $h = h_{a',v}, x_{\overline{T}} = a'_{\overline{T}}$ are identical in the above construction.*

Proof. In both cases, all vectors $\{m_{i,j}, v_{i,j}\}_{j \in [l_j]}$ for $i \in T$ and m_i for $i \in \overline{T}$ are independently and uniformly distributed with the exception that $\sum_{i \in \overline{T}} m_i + \sum_{i \in T} \sum_{j \in I_i} m_{i,j} = \mathbf{0}$, and $\sum_{i \in \overline{T}} v_i + \sum_{i \in T} \sum_{j \in I_i} v_{i,j} = v$ where I_i for $i \in T$ denotes a set of indices such that the binary representation of $\phi_i(a_i)$ is equal to 1. Since $a = (a_T, a_{\overline{T}})$ and $a' = (a_T, a'_{\overline{T}})$, I_i for a and a' are identical for any $i \in T$, which means $(R_T, M_{\overline{T}})$ for $h = h_{a,v}, x = a$ and that for $h = h_{a',v}, x = a'$ are identically distributed. $\qquad \square$

3.2 A Fully Robust NIMPC for $\mathcal{H}_{\mathrm{all}}^L$

In this section, we present an NIMPC for all boolean functions $\mathcal{H}_{\mathrm{all}}^L$ with input domain $\mathcal{X} = \mathcal{X}_1 \times \cdots \times \mathcal{X}_n$ and L-bit output. The idea is to express any $h : \mathcal{X} \to \{0,1\}^L$ as a sum of indicator function $\mathcal{H}_{\mathrm{ind}}^L$ with L-bit output. The idea is similar to the previous constructions. Though, in contrast to existing constructions that realize NIMPC for $\mathcal{H}_{\mathrm{all}}$ by $|\mathcal{X}| \cdot L$ invocation of NIMPC for $\mathcal{H}_{\mathrm{all}}^1$, the proposed construction realize NIMPC for $\mathcal{H}_{\mathrm{all}}$ in more direct manner, that is, $|\mathcal{X}|$ invocation of $\mathcal{H}_{\mathrm{ind}}^L$ to construct $\mathcal{H}_{\mathrm{all}}$. The communication complexity of the resulting construction is much smaller than the existing constructions since a single invocation of the proposed NIMPC for $\mathcal{H}_{\mathrm{ind}}^L$ is much more efficient than L invocation of the existing NIMPC for $\mathcal{H}_{\mathrm{ind}}$. The following theorem presents a compiler to construct $\mathcal{H}_{\mathrm{all}}$ from $\mathcal{H}_{\mathrm{ind}}^L$.

Theorem 2. *Fix finite domains $\mathcal{X}_1, \ldots, \mathcal{X}_n$ such that $|\mathcal{X}_i| \leq d$ for all $1 \leq i \leq n$ and let $\mathcal{X} \triangleq \mathcal{X}_1 \times \cdots \times \mathcal{X}_n$. Let $\mathcal{H}_{\mathrm{all}}$ be the set of all functions $h : \mathcal{X} \to \{0,1\}^L$. Then, there exists an NIMPC protocol for $\mathcal{H}_{\mathrm{all}}$ with the communication complexity $\lceil \log_2 d \rceil \cdot (\lceil \log_2 d \rceil + L) \cdot n^2 \cdot |\mathcal{X}|$.*

Proof. Let $\Pi_{\mathrm{ind}}^L = (\mathsf{GEN}', \mathsf{ENC}', \mathsf{DEC}')$ be NIMPC for $\mathcal{H}_{\mathrm{ind}}^L$ described in Sect. 3.1 and let $h : \mathcal{X} \to \{0,1\}^L$ that we want to compute. We construct a protocol $\mathsf{P}(\Pi)(h)$ for $\mathcal{H}_{\mathrm{all}}$ as follows.

- **Offline preprocessing:** Let $I \subseteq \mathcal{X}$ be the set of inputs $x \in \mathcal{X}$ such that $h(x) = v$ for some $v \neq 0^L$. For each $a \in I$, let $R^a = (R_1^a, \ldots, R_n^a) \leftarrow \mathsf{GEN}'(h_{a,v})$. For $a \in \mathcal{X} \setminus I$, let $R^a \leftarrow \mathsf{GEN}'(h_0)$. Then, choose random permutation π of $\mathcal{X}$ and let $R_{i,b} = R_i^{\pi(b)}$ for $i \in [n], b \in \mathcal{X}$. Define $GEN(h) \triangleq R = (R_1, \ldots, R_n)$, where $R_i = \{R_{i,b}\}_{b \in \mathcal{X}}$.
- **Online messages:** For an input x_i, P_i computes $M_{i,b} \triangleq \mathsf{ENC}_i'(x_i, R_{i,b})$ for every $b \in \mathcal{X}$. Define $\mathsf{ENC}(x, R) \triangleq (M_1, \ldots, M_n)$ where $M_i = \{M_{i,b}\}_{b \in \mathcal{X}}$.
- **Output $h(x_1, \ldots, x_n)$:** $\mathsf{DEC}(M_1, \ldots, M_n) = v$ if and only if there exists $b \in \mathcal{X}$ such that $\mathsf{DEC}'(M_{1,b}, \ldots, M_{n,b}) = v$. Otherwise $\mathsf{DEC}(M_1, \ldots, M_n) = 0^L$.

First we will show the correctness of the above protocol. Fix $x = (x_1, \ldots, x_n) \in \mathcal{X}$. $\mathsf{DEC}(M_1, \ldots, M_n) = v (\neq 0^L)$ holds if and only if $\mathsf{DEC}'(M_{1,b}', \ldots, M_{n,b}') = v$ holds for some $b \in \mathcal{X}$, that is, $\mathsf{DEC}'(\mathsf{ENC}'(x_1, R_1^a), \ldots, \mathsf{ENC}'(x_n, R_n^a)) = v$ holds for $a = \pi(b)$. Since underlying $\Pi_{\mathrm{ind}}^L = (\mathsf{GEN}', \mathsf{ENC}', \mathsf{DEC}')$ satisfies correctness, this happens if and only if $h_{a,v}(x) = v$ holds for some $a \in I$, that is, $h(x_1, \ldots, x_n) = v$.

Next we will show the robustness of the protocol. We construct a simulator Sim_T based on the simulator $\mathsf{Sim}_T^{\Pi_{\mathrm{ind}}^L}$ (the simulator for Π_{ind}^L). The simulator Sim_T first queries $h|_{\overline{T}, x_{\overline{T}}}(x_T)$ for every $x_T \in \mathcal{X}_T$. Let $I' \subseteq \mathcal{X}_T$ be the set of $x_T \in \mathcal{X}_T$ such that $h|_{\overline{T}, x_{\overline{T}}}(x_T) = v$ for some $v \neq 0^L$. For every $a_T \in I'$, Sim_T computes $(R_T^{a_T}, M_{\overline{T}}^{a_T}) = \mathsf{Sim}_T^{\Pi_{\mathrm{ind}}^L}(h_{a,v})$ where $a = (a_T, a_{\overline{T}})$ for arbitrarily chosen $a_{\overline{T}} \in \mathcal{X}_{\overline{T}}$. Here $(R_T^{a_T}, M_{\overline{T}}^{a_T})$ completely simulates the distribution of $(R_T, M_{\overline{T}})$ for $h = h_{\hat{a},v}$, $x = \hat{a}$ where $\hat{a} = (a_T, \hat{a}_{\overline{T}})$ and $\hat{a}_{\overline{T}}$ are inputs possessed by $\overline{T}$ since Lemma 2 proves that $(R_T, M_{\overline{T}})$ for $h = h_{\hat{a},v}$, $x_{\overline{T}} = a_{\overline{T}}$ and $(R_T, M_{\overline{T}})$ for $h = h_{\hat{a},v}$, $x_{\overline{T}} = \hat{a}_{\overline{T}}$ are identically distributed, and $\mathsf{Sim}_T^{\Pi_{\mathrm{ind}}^L}$ completely simulates the distribution (since Π_{ind^L} is fully robust). Then simulator Sim_T samples $(R_T, M_{\overline{T}}) = \mathsf{Sim}_T^{\Pi_{\mathrm{ind}}^L}(h_0)$ for $|\mathcal{X}| - |I'|$ times. As a result, we obtains $|\mathcal{X}|$ output of the simulator $\mathsf{Sim}_T^{\Pi_{\mathrm{ind}}^L}$. Here, distributions of these $|\mathcal{X}| - |I'|$ simulation results for $h = h_0$ are identical to those for $h = h_{a,v}$ ($a \in \mathcal{X} \setminus I'$) since Lemma 1 proves that when $x \neq a$ holds, $(R_T, M_{\overline{T}})$ for $h = h_0$ and $(R_T, M_{\overline{T}})$ for $h = h_{a,v}$ (for any $a \in \mathcal{X}$ and $v \in \mathbb{F}_2^L$) are identically distributed, and $\mathsf{Sim}_T^{\Pi_{\mathrm{ind}}^L}$ completely simulates the distribution (since Π_{ind^L} is fully robust). The simulator Sim_T then randomly permutes the order of these outputs, and returns the permuted outputs as its simulation result. The above discussion shows that distribution of the simulation result is identical to the distribution of $(R_T, M_{\overline{T}})$.

The communication complexity of the resulting protocol is $\lceil \log_2 d \rceil \cdot (\lceil \log_2 d \rceil + L) \cdot n^2 \cdot |\mathcal{X}|$ since the protocol is obtained by $|\mathcal{X}|$ invocation of Π_{ind}^L with the communication complexity $\lceil \log_2 d \rceil \cdot (\lceil \log_2 d \rceil + L) \cdot n^2$. $\qquad\square$

4 Conclusion

We have presented a more efficient protocol of n-player NIMPC for the set of arbitrary functions $\mathcal{H}_{\text{all}}^L$, by which the communication complexity is $\frac{\lceil \log d \rceil \cdot L}{\lceil \log d \rceil + L}$ times smaller than the best known one in [12].

Though the proposed construction is the most efficient with respect to the communication complexity, there still remains a gap between the lower bound in [12] and our upper bound. Therefore, reducing the gap will be a challenging future work.

References

1. Beimel, A., Gabizon, A., Ishai, Y., Kushilevitz, E., Meldgaard, S., Paskin-Cherniavsky, A.: Non-interactive secure multiparty computation. In: Garay, J.A., Gennaro, R. (eds.) CRYPTO 2014, Part II. LNCS, vol. 8617, pp. 387–404. Springer, Heidelberg (2014)
2. Ben-Or, M., Goldwasser, S., Wigderson, A.: Completeness theorems for non-cryptographic fault-tolerant distributed computation. In: The 20th Annual ACM Symposium on Theory of Computing (STOC 1988), pp. 1–10 (1988)
3. Chaum, D., Crépeau, C., Damgård, I.: Multiparty unconditionally secure protocols. In: The 20th Annual ACM Symposium on Theory of Computing (STOC 1988), pp. 11–19 (1988)
4. Cramer, R., Damgård, I.B., Maurer, U.M.: General secure multi-party computation from any linear secret-sharing scheme. In: Preneel, B. (ed.) EUROCRYPT 2000. LNCS, vol. 1807, pp. 316–335. Springer, Heidelberg (2000)
5. Data, D., Prabhakaran, M.M., Prabhakaran, V.M.: On the communication complexity of secure computation. In: Garay, J.A., Gennaro, R. (eds.) CRYPTO 2014, Part II. LNCS, vol. 8617, pp. 199–216. Springer, Heidelberg (2014)
6. Goldreich, O., Micali, S., Wigderson, A.: How to play any mental game, or a completeness theorem for protocols with an honest majority. In: The 19th Annual ACM Symposium on Theory of Computing (STOC 1987), pp. 218–229 (1987)
7. Hirt, M., Maurer, U.: Player simulation and general adversary structures in perfect multiparty computation. J. Cryptology 13(1), 31–60 (2000)
8. Maurer, U.M.: Secure multi-party computation made simple. In: Cimato, S., Galdi, C., Persiano, G. (eds.) SCN 2002. LNCS, vol. 2576, pp. 14–28. Springer, Heidelberg (2003)
9. Hirt, M., Tschudi, D.: Efficient general-adversary multi-party computation. In: Sako, K., Sarkar, P. (eds.) ASIACRYPT 2013. LNCS, vol. 8270, pp. 181–200. Springer, Heidelberg (2013). doi:10.1007/978-3-642-42045-0_10

10. Rabin, T., Ben-Or, M.: Verifiable secret sharing and multiparty protocols with honest majority. In: The 21st Annual ACM Symposium on Theory of Computing (STOC 1989), pp. 73–85 (1989)
11. Yao, A.C.: Protocols for secure computations. In: The 23rd Annual Symposium on Foundations of Computer Science (FOCS 1982), pp. 160–164 (1982)
12. Yoshida, M., Obana, S.: On the (in)efficiency of non-interactive secure multiparty computation. In: Kwon, S., Yun, A. (eds.) ICISC 2015. LNCS, vol. 9558, pp. 185–193. Springer, Heidelberg (2016). doi:10.1007/978-3-319-30840-1_12

An MPC-Based Privacy-Preserving Protocol for a Local Electricity Trading Market

Aysajan Abidin, Abdelrahaman Aly$^{(\boxtimes)}$, Sara Cleemput,
and Mustafa A. Mustafa

KU Leuven, ESAT-COSIC and iMinds, Kasteelpark Arenberg 10,
3001 Leuven, Heverlee, Belgium
{aysajan.abidin,abdelrahaman.aly,
sara.cleemput,mustafa.mustafa}@esat.kuleuven.be

Abstract. This paper proposes a decentralised and privacy-preserving local electricity trading market. The market employs a bidding protocol based on secure multiparty computation and allows users to trade their excess electricity among themselves. The bid selection and trading price calculation are performed in a decentralised and privacy-preserving manner. We implemented the market in C++ and tested its performance with realistic data sets. Our simulation results show that the market tasks can be performed for 2500 bids in less than four minutes in the "online" phase, showing its feasibility for a typical electricity trading period.

Keywords: Secure multiparty computation · Local electricity trading market · Smart grid · Renewable energy source · Security and Privacy

1 Introduction

The Smart Grid (SG) is an electricity grid supporting bidirectional communication between components in the grid. An important component of SG is Smart Meters (SMs) which allow real-time grid management [1]. Potential benefits of SG include improved grid efficiency and reliability, and seamless integration of Renewable Energy Sources (RESs), e.g., solar panels, into the grid. When these RESs generate more electricity than their owners need, the excess electricity is fed back to the grid. Currently, users get some compensation from their suppliers for such excess electricity at a regulated (low) price. However, users with such excess electricity may be interested in selling directly to other users at a competitive price for monetary gains. Enabling that would also incentivise more users to own RESs. To address this, a local electricity market that allows RES owners to trade their excess electricity with other households in their neighbourhood has been proposed in [2]. However, such a market has user privacy risks, since users' bids/offers reveal private information about their lifestyle [3].

There are various proposals for an electricity trading market that allows users to trade with each other or suppliers [4,5]. However, none of these addresses the privacy concerns. The security and privacy concerns in such a local market have

© Springer International Publishing AG 2016
S. Foresti and G. Persiano (Eds.): CANS 2016, LNCS 10052, pp. 615–625, 2016.
DOI: 10.1007/978-3-319-48965-0_40

been analysed in [2], and initial ideas (without a concrete solution) for designing one has been proposed in [6]. In this work, we not only propose a concrete secure and privacy-preserving solution for such a local market for trading electricity, but also test it in realistic scenarios.

Contributions. Our contributions are: (i) a concrete decentralised and privacy-preserving protocol for a local electricity trading market using MPC, (ii) a security and complexity analysis of our protocol, and (iii) an implementation, evaluation and analysis of the protocol using realistic bidding data sets.

2   Preliminaries

System Model and Market Overview. As shown in Fig. 1, a local electricity market comprises the following entities: RESs, SMs, users, suppliers and computational servers. The market operation, as proposed in [2], consists of:

- **Bid Submission:** Prior to each trading period, users submit their bids to the market to inform the market how much electricity they are willing to sell or buy during the trading period and for what price per unit.
- **Trading Price Computation:** The local market performs a double auction trading and generates the supply and demand curve. The intersection of these two curves is used to determine the trading price, amount of electricity traded, as well as which users will trade on the market.
- **Informing Users/Suppliers:** The market informs (i) the users about the amount of electricity they traded and the trading price, and (ii) the suppliers about the amount of electricity agreed to be traded by their respective users.

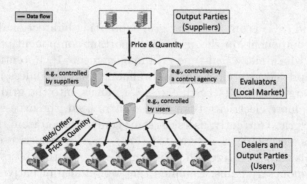

Fig. 1. A local MPC-based market for trading electricity from RESs

Threat Model and Assumptions. Users and suppliers are malicious. They may try to modify data sent by SMs in an attempt to gain financial advantage or influence the trading price on the market. Computational servers are honest-but-curious. They follow the protocol specifications, but they may attempt to learn individual users' bids. External entities are malicious. They may eavesdrop data in transit and/or modify the data in an attempt to disrupt the market. In addition, we make the following assumptions: (i) each entity has a unique identity, (ii) SMs are tamper-evident, (iii) all entities are time synchronized, (iv) the communication channels between entities are secure and authentic, and (v) users are rational, i.e., they try to buy/sell electricity for the best possible price.

Functional and Privacy Requirements. Our protocol should meet the following functional requirements: (i) the local market should receive users' bids, calculate the trading price, and inform the users and suppliers of the market outcome, (ii) each user should learn if their bid was accepted and the vol. of electricity they traded, as well as the trading price, and (iii) each supplier should learn the amount of electricity traded by their customers on the market in each trading period. It should also satisfy the following privacy requirements [2,6]: (i) confidentiality of users' bids and amount of electricity traded, (ii) users' privacy preservation, i.e., RES and/or trading user identity and location privacy, and trading session unlinkability, and (iii) minimum data disclosure.

Security Definition Under MPC. MPC allows any set of mutually distrustful parties to compute any function such that no party learns more than their original input and the computed output, i.e., parties $p_1, ..., p_n$ can compute $y = f(x_1, ..., x_n)$, where x_i is the secret input of p_i, in a distributed fashion with guaranteed correctness such that p_i learns only y. MPC can be achieved using secret sharing schemes [7,8], garbled circuits [9] and homomorphic encryption [10].

On the security notion: a secure protocol over MPC discloses to an adversary the same information as if the computations were carried out by a trusted (non-corruptible) third party. This definition allows a variety of adversarial and communication models offering various security levels: perfect, statistical or computational. Seminal results prove that any functionality can be calculated with perfect security against active and passive adversaries [7,8] under the arithmetic circuit paradigm. Other relevant recent contributions in the area include [11,12]. Note that any oblivious functionality built in this way would be as secure as the underlying MPC protocols used for its execution. Finally, note that under this scenario, functionality, also referred to as sub-protocols, like the ones used in this work, can be used for modular composition under the hybrid model introduced by Canetti [13]. We make use of the following existing functionality:

- **Secure Comparison:** Methods for secure comparison using MPC offer either perfect or statistical security and are constructed under the same assumptions [14]. Moreover, mechanisms as [15] by Catrina and de Hoogh introduced inequality tests at constant complexity.
- **Secure Sorting:** Secure Sorting using MPC can be achieved by sorting networks and other data-oblivious mechanisms, including the randomize shell-sort from Goodrich [16]. Moreover, Hamada et al. [17] introduced a technique to facilitate the use of comparison sorting algorithms. This technique consists of

Table 1. Notation

Symbol	Meaning
t_i	i-th time slot
$[q]_j$	Electricity volume in absolute terms from the j-th bid
$[p]_j$	Unit price enclosed in the j-th bid
$[d]_j$	Binary value corresponding to the j-th bid: 1 indicates a demand bid and 0 a supply bid
$[s]_j$	Unique supplier identifier $s \in \{1, .., |S|\}$ where S is the set of all suppliers. Moreover, s is encoded in a $\{0,1\}$ vector, i.e., $[s]_{jk} \leftarrow 1$ on the k-th position corresponds to the suppliers unique identifier, and $[s]_{jk} \leftarrow 0$ otherwise, for all $j \in B$.
$[b]_j$	Bid's unique identifier from the j-th bid
$[\phi]$	Volume of electricity traded on the market for period t_i
$[\sigma]$	Market's trading price (price of the lowest supply bid) for t_i
$[a]_i$	Binary value: 1 indicates the bid i was accepted, 0 otherwise
$[S]^\phi$	Set of the volume of electricity traded by supplier affiliation where $[s]_i^\phi$ stands for the summation of all the accepted bids from users affiliated to the supplier i, for all $i \in S$

randomly permuting the vector before sorting, so that the results of some of the intermediate secure comparisons can be made public.

– **Secure Permutation:** Leur et al. [18] analysed various permutation mechanisms, like the use of vector multiplication by a permutation matrix and sorting networks. Czumaj et al. [19] proposed alternatives for obliviously permuting a vector in (almost) $\mathcal{O}(n \times log(n))$, when n is the vector size.

Notation. Square brackets denote encrypted or secretly shared values. Assignments that are a result of any securely implemented operation are represented by the infix operator: $[z] \leftarrow [x] + [y]$. This extends to any operation over securely distributed data since its result would be of a secret nature too. Vectors are denoted by capital letters. For a vector, say B, B_i represents its i-th element and $|B|$ its size. The bids originated by SMs are considered as the initial input data. Each bid is a tuple $([q], [p], [d], [s], [b])$ and B is the vector of all bids. We assume that (i) all bid elements belong to $\mathbb{Z}_M$, where M is a sufficiently large number so no overflow occurs, and (ii) the number of bids (or at least their upper bound) is publicly known. Any other data related to the bid is kept secret. If the protocol admits a single supply and demand bid per SM, the computation of this upper bound is trivial. Markets could opt for enforcing all SMs to submit a bid regardless of whether they participate or not in the market. Let $\top$ be a sufficiently big number such that it is greater than any input value from the users but $\top << M$. In this scenario, non-participating SMs would have to replace their input values by $[0]$ and $[\top]$ accordingly. Table 1 lists the notations.

3   Privacy-Preserving Protocol for Electricity Trading

In our protocol, users submit their private inputs to a virtualized entity consisting of multiple computational servers that function as evaluators. The number of evaluators depend on the application, and it could be as many as the number of parties involved in the computation. However, this is costly in terms of performance. In our setting, we assume three computational parties: one comes from the RES owners, another from the suppliers and a third one from a local control agency. Depending on the underlying MPC protocol, some randomizations might be precomputed in an "offline" phase by a trusted dealer who is not directly involved at any level of the computations [11]. The amount and purpose of the randomly generated numbers depend on such MPC primitives and the security model used by the market. Our protocol consists of five steps:

Preprocessing for trading period t_i

1. **Bidders:** Before the start of t_{i-2}, each user prepares and sends his bid to the computational parties. If a linear secure secret sharing scheme (e.g., [20]) is used, each user generates as many shares as the number of computational parties, and sends each of the shares to a different computational party.
2. **Evaluators:** To randomly permute the bidders' input, upon reception, each share is multiplied with a column of a randomized permutation matrix which was precomputed "offline". This is still performed before the start of t_{i-2}.

Evaluation for trading period t_i

3. **Evaluation:** The evaluation is performed at t_{i-2}. In this phase, the trading price and traded volume are computed, and accepted and rejected bids are identified, in a data-oblivious fashion. Algorithm 1 gives a detailed overview of our secure auction evaluation. It calculates the trading price $[\sigma]$, the volume of electricity traded $[\phi]$ and the vector of adjudicated demand and supply bids $[A]$. It does it by obliviously calculating the aggregation of the demand bids $[\delta]$, and then iterating over the set of all bids in B using their volume to match $[\delta]$. To access the vector of accepted supply bids, it is enough to compute $[A]_j \times (1 - [d]_j) \times [b]_j$. To find the vector of accepted demand bids, it is sufficient to calculate $(1 - [A]_j) \times ([d]_j) \times [b]_j$.

Inform Bidders and Suppliers (before the end of period t_{i-2})

4. **Bidders:** To hide the order of the bids, the vector of all bids $[B]$, together with the associated vector $[A]$, are shuffled again. Then, the evaluators use the **open** operation of the underlying MPC primitive on $[\sigma]$ (for t_i) and $[b]_j$, for all $j \in B$. Each evaluator sends the shares corresponding to the tuple B_{b_j} to the bidder that originated the bid identified by b_j. The bidder then reconstructs the shares and learns if his bid was accepted or rejected.
5. **Suppliers:** Evaluators send the shares of the volume aggregation S_j^ϕ, for all $j \in S$, to the corresponding supplier. Suppliers also learn the market trading price. Both, bidders and suppliers are informed of the results at t_{i-2}.

Algorithm 1. Smart Market Clearance.

Input: Vector of n bid tuples $B = ([q], [p], [d], [s], [b])$
Output: Clearance price $[\sigma]$, volume of traded electricity $[\phi]$, vector of accepted bids $[A]$ of
      size $|B|$, vector of aggregated volume traded by supplier S^ϕ of size $|S|$

1 **for** $i \leftarrow 1$ **to** n **do**
2 | $[\delta] \leftarrow [\delta] + [q]_j \times [d]_j$;
3 **end**
4 $[\nu] \leftarrow [0]$;
5 $[S^\phi] \leftarrow \{0_1, ..., 0_{|S|}\}$;
6 $[A] \leftarrow \{0_1, ..., 0_{|B|}\}$;
7 **for** $k \leftarrow 1$ **to** n **do**
8     $[c] \leftarrow [\nu] < [\delta]$;
9     $[\sigma] \leftarrow ((1 - [d]_j) \times [c]) \times ([p]_j - [\sigma]) + [\sigma]$;
10    $[\phi] \leftarrow ((1 - [d]_j) \times [c]) \times [q]_j + [\phi]$;
11   **for** $k \leftarrow 1$ **to** $|S|$ **do**
12 | $[s]_k^\phi \leftarrow ([s]_{jk} \times ((1 - [d]_j) \times [c]) \times [q]_j + [s]_k^\phi$;
13   **end**
14    $[a]_j \leftarrow [c]$;
15    $[\nu] \leftarrow [\nu] + [c] \times [q]_j$;
16 **end**

Correctness and Complexity. The general goal of the protocol is to find the trading price and to identify the accepted and rejected bids. Any supply bid below the trading price, and any demand bid above this price is automatically accepted and vice versa. The market equilibrium can be identified when the price of a given supply allocation surpasses the price of the next cheapest available demand allocation. In other words, when supply equals demand, the market equilibrium can be identified if the price of supply is at least the price of demand.

In our protocol, we proceed to sort all bids regardless of whether they are demand or supply bids. Following Algorithm 1, we then proceed to identify and select bids until the aggregated demand ($[\delta] \leftarrow \sum_i^{|B|} [q]_i \times [d]_i$) is matched (note that to maintain secrecy we iterate over the set of all bids), choosing the bids in ascending order of price. If a supply bid is selected, this implies that there is no supply bid that could be allocated to reduce $[\delta]$, and hence is not part of the market clearance. Using $[d]_i$ cancels the supply bid's effect over $[\delta]$, and provides us with sufficient tools to identify it. The opposite occurs when a demand bid is selected. At the end of Algorithm 1, the bids used to reduce $[\delta]$ can be identified, which correspond to all the supply and demand bids with prices below and above the trading price, respectively. From this, the set of accepted and rejected bids follows. The trading price is set to the price of the last selected supply bid. The protocol complexity grows linearly with the number of bids, which is the main factor influencing the performance. The number of suppliers rarely varies over time, and is of limited size. The complexity of Algorithm 1 is $\mathcal{O}(|B| \times |S|)$. Note that secure vector permutation can be achieved in $\mathcal{O}(n \times log(n))$, where n is the size of the vector (the vector of the Bids $[B]$, in our case). Moreover, the sorting methods used by our secure market can achieve $\mathcal{O}(n \times log(n))$.

Security Analysis. The MPC mechanisms used in protocol steps 1-5 constitute a unique arithmetic circuit (addition and multiplication) with no leakage, making privacy straight forward. Moreover, the protocol can be computed with perfect security on the information theoretic model against passive and active adversaries under Canetti's hybrid model [13] by using available MPC protocols such as BGW [7]. We refer the reader to [21] for a complete set of proofs of security and composability for BGW. Indeed, results in BGW [7] and CDN [8] showed that any function can be computed using MPC with the aforementioned security levels by providing secure addition and multiplication under an arithmetic circuit paradigm. There are also promising results on more restricted models, e.g., dishonest majority [11] with computational security. Moreover, there exist privacy-preserving sub-protocols (arithmetic circuits) for sorting, comparison and vector permutation over MPC that can be used, and that provide the same security guarantees with no leakage. These are integrated into a single arithmetic circuit in a modular fashion, i.e., our protocol. Thus, the security of our protocol readily follows. In other words, the order of the operations (multiplications and additions) is predetermined beforehand by the publicly available circuit, i.e., our protocol simulation can be achieved by invoking the corresponding simulators of the sub-protocols used, and/or atomic operations in its predefined order.

4 Experimentation and Discussion

We executed our experimentation using the BGW-based MPC Toolkit [22] which includes all the underlying crypto primitives and sub-protocols we report, together with our own introduced code. The library was compiled with NTL (Number Theory Library) [23] that itself was compiled using GMP (GNU Multiple Precision Library). These two libraries are used for the modulo arithmetic that is used by the underlying MPC protocols. Each instance of the prototype comprises two CPU threads: one manages message exchanges and the other executes the protocol. Moreover, each instance required little more than 1 MB of allocated memory during our most memory demanding test.

Data Generation. We generated the data using a realistic data from Belgium. First we picked a time slot and date, i.e., between 13:00 h and 13:30 h on 5-th of May 2016, during which 2382 MW solar electricity was generated in Belgium by Solar Panels (SPs) with total capacity 2953 MW [24], i.e., on average each SP produced electricity approximately equal to 81.66 % of its capacity. The average electricity consumption data of a Belgian household for the same time slot was 0.637 kW [25], so for each user we generated a random consumption data for this slot with mean equal to 0.637 kW, standard deviation equal to 0.20 and variance equal to 0.04. Then, we randomly chose 30 % of the users to have installed SPs at their homes, and to each of the SPs we randomly assigned 2.3, 3.6 or 4, 7 kW electricity generation capacity. After that, we randomly generated the electricity output of each SP during this time slot with a mean equal to the SP's capacity multiplied with the efficiency factor for the time slot, i.e., 81.66 %, standard deviation equal to 0.20 and variance equal to 0.04. Once we generated the electricity consumption and generation data for each user with a SP, we simply subtracted the latter from the first value to find the amount of each user's excess electricity.

We assumed that there are 10 suppliers in the market and randomly assigned one to each user. We set the retail electricity sell price of the suppliers to 0.20 €/kWh and the retail buy price to 0.04 €/kWh. For the bid price selection, we divided the retail electricity sell and buy price difference into nine ranges each including several (overlapping) prices, e.g., range 2 includes three prices: 0.04, 0.05 and 0.06 €/kWh, whereas range 7 includes four prices: 0.17, 0.18, 0.19 and 0.20 €/kWh. Then, for each user, depending on how much excess electricity she has for sell (or wants to buy), we picked randomly one of the prices from the appropriate price range. For selecting the appropriate price range we assumed that if users have a lot of excess electricity, they would choose a lower asking price, but if they have a little, they would ask for a higher price. In summary, for each user we generated: unique user ID, amount of electricity for the bid, bid price, supply or demand bid indicator, and ID of the user's contracted supplier.

Security. Our security target was to build a prototype for the classic scenario of semi-honest adversaries under the information theoretic model (private authenticated channels) and threshold corruption. This is achieved by the underlying BGW primitives and Shamir Secret Sharing (honest majority). This is a necessary configuration to achieve perfect security as long as the adversary does not corrupt more than halve of the parties. However, the prototype offers statistical security on the size of its input given that it uses the same comparison method as in [15]. The security of such method depends on input parameters l and k, l is the bit-size of the numbers and k a security parameter. Under the assumption that the channel is perfect, this task is decoupled from the prototype operation.

Table 2. List of primitives used by secure prototype

Primitive	Protocol
Sharing	Shamir Secret Sharing [20]
Multiplication	Gennaro et al. [26]
Inequality Test	Catrina and Hoogh [15]
Random Bit Generation	Damgård et al. [14]
Sorting: QuickSort	Hamada et al. [17]
Permutation: Sorting Network	Lai et al. [18]

Characteristics, Environment and Setting. Our prototype was built in C++ following an object oriented approach, with modularity and composability in mind. It has an engine that separates communication and cryptographic tasks. Table 2 shows the list of the sub-protocols we used. We executed our tests on a single 64-bit Linux server with $2 * 2 * 10$-cores with Intel Xeon E5-2687W microprocessors at 3.1 GHz and 25 MB of cache available, and with memory of

Table 3. Overall results

Bids	Com. rounds	Comparisons	CPU time (s)	On-line phase (s)
100	$\approx 1.40 \cdot 10^5$	965	2.96	1.01
500	$\approx 1.96 \cdot 10^6$	14628	40.40	11.35
1000	$\approx 7.03 \cdot 10^6$	53508	147.76	39.80
1500	$\approx 15.61 \cdot 10^6$	118956	320.79	86.14
2000	$\approx 26.97 \cdot 10^6$	208132	562.50	145.78
2500	$\approx 43.15 \cdot 10^6$	330912	894.01	235.82

256 GB. All our tests were performed under a 3-party setting, with two available cores for each instance. We ran our tests starting with a baseline of a realistic scenario with 100 bids and then monotonically increased the number of bids to 2500. Each test scenario was repeated 10 times to reduce the impact of the noise.

Results. Our prototype requires bit randomization for the comparison methods. The task of generating such values could be executed beforehand, in an "offline" phase. The "online" phase would execute the remaining tasks and utilize the randomization values generated during the "offline" phase. For a case with 2500 bids, the prototype took 678.50 s for either sending or waiting for other parties' messages (as our prototype is synchronous) and 215.52 s for other computational tasks (crypto primitives). Hence, ca. 75 % of the computational time was for transmission related tasks. We have also measured the computational cost at every test instance. Table 3 shows a more complete break down of our results. From these results we can conclude the following.

- The 2500-bids instance total time on the "online" phase is less than 4 min, and less than 15 min with the "offline" phase included, which is still less than a typical trading period of 30 min.
- The asymptotic behaviour on the growth of the computational time seems to adjust to the behaviour included in the complexity analysis.
- The performance of the prototype could be improved by the use of techniques such as, PRSS [27], to reduce the cost of generating random bits. Moreover, other optimizations can be put in place based on the experimental setting.
- During our tests ca. 95 % of the computational time was spent on sorting the bids. As suppliers are not involved in this, their influence on the computational costs is limited, i.e., our prototype can be adjusted to scenarios with larger supplier sets without much overhead.

5 Conclusions

We proposed a privacy-preserving protocol for a local market that allows users to trade their excess electricity among themselves. Our protocol employs a bidding scheme based on MPC, and the bid selection and the trading price calculation are performed in a decentralised and privacy-preserving manner. We also implemented the protocol in C++ and tested its performance with realistic data. Our simulation results show its feasibility for a typical electricity trading period of 30 min as the market tasks are performed (for 2500 bids) in less than 4 min in the "online" phase. Future work will include balancing suppliers' accounts based on the electricity traded by users without violating users' privacy.

Acknowledgments. This work was supported by KIC InnoEnergy SE via KIC "SAGA" project, European Commission FP7 project "EKSISTENZ" grant number: 607049, and the European Commission through the ICT programme under contract FP7-ICT-2013-10-SEP-210076296 (PRACTICE).

References

1. Farhangi, H.: The path of the smart grid. IEEE Power Energ. Mag. **8**(1), 18–28 (2010)
2. Mustafa, M.A., Cleemput, S., Abidin, A.: A local electricity trading market: security analysis. In: IEEE PES ISGT-Europe, pp. 1–6 (2016)
3. Hart, G.W.: Nonintrusive appliance load monitoring. Proc. IEEE **80**(12), 1870–1891 (1992)
4. Lee, W., Xiang, L., Schober, R., Wong, V.W.S.: Direct electricity trading in smart grid: a coalitional game analysis. IEEE J. Sel. Areas Commun. **32**(7), 1398–1411 (2014)
5. Tushar, W., Yuen, C., Smith, D.B., Poor, H.V.: Price discrimination for energy trading in smart grid: a game theoretic approach. IEEE Trans. Smart Grid **PP**(99), 1–12 (2016)
6. Abidin, A., Aly, A., Cleemput, S., Mustafa, M.A.: Towards a local electricity trading market based on secure multiparty computation (2016). http://securewww.esat.kuleuven.be/cosic/publications/article-2664.pdf
7. Ben-Or, M., Goldwasser, S., Wigderson, A.: Completeness theorems for non-cryptographic fault-tolerant distributed computation. In: STOC, pp. 1–10. ACM (1988)
8. Chaum, D., Crépeau, C., Damgård, I.: Multiparty unconditionally secure protocols. In: STOC, pp. 11–19. ACM (1988)
9. Goldreich, O., Micali, S., Wigderson, A.: How to play any mental game or a completeness theorem for protocols with honest majority. In: STOC, pp. 218–229. ACM (1987)
10. Paillier, P.: Public-key cryptosystems based on composite degree residuosity classes. In: Stern, J. (ed.) EUROCRYPT 1999. LNCS, vol. 1592, pp. 223–238. Springer, Heidelberg (1999). doi:10.1007/3-540-48910-X_16
11. Damgård, I., Pastro, V., Smart, N., Zakarias, S.: Multiparty computation from somewhat homomorphic encryption. In: Safavi-Naini, R., Canetti, R. (eds.) CRYPTO 2012. LNCS, vol. 7417, pp. 643–662. Springer, Heidelberg (2012). doi:10.1007/978-3-642-32009-5_38
12. Bendlin, R., Damgård, I., Orlandi, C., Zakarias, S.: Semi-homomorphic encryption and multiparty computation. In: Paterson, K.G. (ed.) EUROCRYPT 2011. LNCS, vol. 6632, pp. 169–188. Springer, Heidelberg (2011). doi:10.1007/978-3-642-20465-4_11

13. Canetti, R.: Security and composition of multiparty cryptographic protocols. J. Cryptol. **13**(1), 143–202 (2000)
14. Damgård, I.B., Fitzi, M., Kiltz, E., Nielsen, J.B., Toft, T.: Unconditionally secure constant-rounds multi-party computation for equality, comparison, bits and exponentiation. In: Halevi, S., Rabin, T. (eds.) TCC 2006. LNCS, vol. 3876, pp. 285–304. Springer, Heidelberg (2006). doi:10.1007/11681878_15
15. Catrina, O., de Hoogh, S.: Secure multiparty linear programming using fixed-point arithmetic. In: Gritzalis, D., Preneel, B., Theoharidou, M. (eds.) ESORICS 2010. LNCS, vol. 6345, pp. 134–150. Springer, Heidelberg (2010). doi:10.1007/978-3-642-15497-3_9
16. Goodrich, M.T.: Randomized shellsort: a simple data-oblivious sorting algorithm. J. ACM **58**(6), 27:1–27:26 (2011)
17. Hamada, K., Kikuchi, R., Ikarashi, D., Chida, K., Takahashi, K.: Practically efficient multi-party sorting protocols from comparison sort algorithms. In: Kwon, T., Lee, M.-K., Kwon, D. (eds.) ICISC 2012. LNCS, vol. 7839, pp. 202–216. Springer, Heidelberg (2013). doi:10.1007/978-3-642-37682-5_15
18. Laur, S., Willemson, J., Zhang, B.: Round-efficient oblivious database manipulation. In: Lai, X., Zhou, J., Li, H. (eds.) ISC 2011. LNCS, vol. 7001, pp. 262–277. Springer, Heidelberg (2011). doi:10.1007/978-3-642-24861-0_18
19. Czumaj, A., Kanarek, P., Kutylowski, M., Lorys, K.: Delayed path coupling and generating random permutations via distributed stochastic processes. In: SODA 1999, pp. 271–280. SIAM (1999)
20. Shamir, A.: How to share a secret. Commun. ACM **22**(11), 612–613 (1979)
21. Asharov, G., Lindell, Y.: A full proof of the BGW protocol for perfectly secure multiparty computation. J. Cryptol. 1–94 (2011)
22. Aly, A.: Network flow problems with secure multiparty computation. Ph.D. thesis, Universté catholique de Louvain, IMMAQ (2015)
23. Shoup, V.: NTL: a library for doing number theory (2001). http://www.shoup.net/ntl/
24. www.elia.be/en/grid-data/power-generation/Solar-power-generation-data
25. http://vreg.be/nl/verbruiksprofielen-elektriciteit
26. Gennaro, R., Rabin, M.O., Rabin, T.: Simplified VSS and fast-track multiparty computations with applications to threshold cryptography. In: PODC 1998, pp. 101–111. ACM (1998)
27. Cramer, R., Damgård, I.B., Ishai, Y.: Share conversion, pseudorandom secret-sharing and applications to secure computation. In: Kilian, J. (ed.) TCC 2005. LNCS, vol. 3378, pp. 342–362. Springer, Heidelberg (2005). doi:10.1007/978-3-540-30576-7_19

Implementation of Verified Set Operation Protocols Based on Bilinear Accumulators

Luca Ferretti[✉], Michele Colajanni, and Mirco Marchetti

Department of Engineering "Enzo Ferrari",
University of Modena and Reggio Emilia, Modena, Italy
{luca.ferretti,michele.colajanni,mirco.marchetti}@unimore.it

Abstract. This paper proposes an efficient protocol for verifiable delegation of computation over outsourced set collections. It improves state of the art protocols by using asymmetric bilinear pairing settings for improved performance with respect to previous proposals based on symmetric settings. Moreover, it extends update operations by supporting efficient modifications over multiple sets. With respect to previous work the proposed protocol has a modular design, that clearly identifies its main building blocks and well-defined interfaces among them. This novel conceptualization allows easier auditing of the protocol security properties and serves as the blueprint of a novel implementation that is released publicly (https://weblab.ing.unimore.it/people/ferretti/versop/). To the best of our knowledge, this is the first public implementation of a protocol for verifiable sets operations.

1 Introduction

Many approaches for securing distributed systems focus on controlling network and system activities [2,3,9,15], and do not rely on cryptography. Moreover, most applications of cryptography to data outsourcing scenarios focus on confidentiality [11,12]. On the other hand, the proposed protocol guarantees the correctness of results in scenarios where data and computation are delegated to an untrusted server. With respect to previous protocols proposed in literature [7,19], this paper proposes three main contributions.

This is the first protocol for verifiable set operations that relies on asymmetric bilinear pairings, while all previous proposals leverage symmetric parings. Asymmetric settings are preferable, since they are characterized by lower computational costs, thus resulting in performance optimization for the whole protocol. Moreover, this is the first protocol for verifiable sets operations that provides efficient support for insertions, deletions and updates over multiple sets at once. This is achieved by designing a variant update protocol for accumulation trees that allows the owner to provide an aggregate proof for multiple update operations. Finally, while previous works describe a *monolithic* protocol, with no high-level components and interfaces among them, in this paper we model the proposed protocol as a combination of three modular components, each exposing well-defined interfaces.

© Springer International Publishing AG 2016
S. Foresti and G. Persiano (Eds.): CANS 2016, LNCS 10052, pp. 626–636, 2016.
DOI: 10.1007/978-3-319-48965-0_41

We release a public implementation of the protocol described in this paper based on open-source cryptographic libraries [1,16,22], that we extend and wrap to obtain modular components with higher-level interfaces. To the best of our knowledge, this is the first public implementation of a protocol for verifiable operations over a collection of sets.

The remainder of this paper proceeds as follows. Section 2 provides a short description of the main cryptographic primitives that form the basis for our protocol. Section 3 describes the reference scenario, introduces its main actors and gives an overview of the proposed protocol and of its main modules. Sections 4 and 5 describe the details of the protocol modules. Finally, Sect. 6 outlines concluding remarks and propose future work.

2   Cryptographic Building Blocks

Polynomial Representations of Sets. A set X can be represent through a characteristic polynomial $C_X(s) = \prod_{x \in X}(x + s)$, where s is a formal variable that is used as secret information in cryptographic protocols, and the elements of the set $x \in X$ are the addition opposite of the polynomial solutions [13,18]. The polynomial is defined over Z_p, where p is a large prime number. We denote as $h_z(\cdot)$ and $\phi_z(\cdot)$ hash functions that accept as inputs arbitrary binary strings and elliptic curve elements, and that produce elements in $Z_p - \{0\}$. We assume that those functions are automatically applied when the elements of the input set X of $C_X(s)$ are not in Z_p. The polynomial $C_X(s)$ can be also represented and computed through its coefficient form. By denoting the coefficients as $\{a_i\}_{i=[\|X\|]}$, the characteristic polynomial of set X is computed as $C_X(s) = \sum_{i=1}^{|X|} a_i \cdot s^i$. Coefficients can be computed efficiently from its roots by using FFT interpolation algorithms [21]. Our implementation wraps algorithms of the NTL library [22] and integrates them with hash functions of the Charm framework [1] to provide high-level interfaces to compute characteristic polynomials of sets defined over the most common data domains.

Bilinear Pairings. In this paper we focus on asymmetric pairing settings (either Type 2 or Type 3 pairings [8,14]) that are usually faster than symmetric pairings adopted by previous work [7]. We denote as $(p, \mathbb{G}_1, \mathbb{G}_2, \mathbb{G}_T, g_1, g_2, \hat{e})$ the public parameters that define an asymmetric bilinear pairing setting. Let g_1, g_2 be generators of cyclic groups $\mathbb{G}_1, \mathbb{G}_2$ of prime order p (that we represent as multiplicative), $\mathbb{G}_T$ a multiplicative cyclic group of the same order and $\hat{e} : \mathbb{G}_1 \times \mathbb{G}_2 \to \mathbb{G}_T$ be the pairing function that satisfies the following properties: bilinearity: $\hat{e}(m^a, n^b) = \hat{e}(m, n)^{ab} \, \forall m, n \in \mathbb{G}_1 \times \mathbb{G}_2, \forall a, b \in \mathbb{Z}_p^* \times \mathbb{Z}_p^*$; non-degeneracy: $\hat{e}(g_1, g_2) \neq 1$; computability: there exists an efficient one-way algorithm to compute $\hat{e}(m, n)$, $\forall m, n \in \mathbb{G}_1 \times \mathbb{G}_2$. Our implementation is based on the Charm cryptographic framework [1], that wraps the *PBC* library [16]. We plan to extend our implementation with faster open source backend libraries, such as [5,17].

Bilinear Accumulators. Informally, a cryptographic accumulator is a small constant size data structure (a *digest*) that can authenticate an arbitrary number of values [4]. In this paper we are interested in bilinear (map) accumulators (BMA) [18] (also *set accumulators*), that implement valid cryptographic accumulators based on bilinear pairings and characteristic polynomial representations of sets. Let $(p, \mathbb{G}_1, \mathbb{G}_2, \mathbb{G}_T, g_1, g_2, \hat{e})$ be the parameters of the asymmetric bilinear pairing setting, $s \in \mathbb{Z}_p^*$ be the secret key and $[g_1^s, \ldots, g_1^{s^q}, g_2^s, \ldots, g_2^{s^q}]$ be the public key, where q is the maximum number of values that can be stored in the accumulator. The BMA of a set X, that we denote as f_X, can be computed by using two algorithms: $f_{sk}(X)$, that uses the secret key s, and $f_{pk}(X)$, that only uses the public key, as following: $f_{sk}(X) = g_1^{C_X(s)} = g_1^{\prod_{i=1}^{|X|}(x_i+s)}$, $f_{pk}(X) = \prod_{i=1}^{|X|} \left(g_1^{s^i}\right)^{a_i}$. To prove that a value $x \in X$ is stored in the BMA, a party (that knows the whole set X) must produce a *witness* $w_Y \in \mathbb{G}_2$ such that $\hat{e}(f_{pk}(x), w_Y) \stackrel{?}{=} \hat{e}(f_X, g_2)$, where w_Y is the BMA of the set $Y = X \backslash \{x\}$ computed over $\mathbb{G}_2$. The equation to compute w_Y, that we denote as $w_{pk}(Y)$, is: $w_{pk}(Y) = \prod_{i=1}^{|Y|} \left(g_2^{s^i}\right)^{a_i}$, where $\{a_i\}_{i \in [|Y|]}$ is the set of the coefficients of the characteristic polynomial $C_Y(s)$. Both $f_{pk}(\cdot)$ and $w_{pk}(\cdot)$ are BMA functions that are usually represented by the same notation in symmetric pairing settings. We denote as f_X and w_X elements of $\mathbb{G}_1$ and $\mathbb{G}_2$, respectively. Our implementation of BMAs protocols extends those of characteristic polynomials and bilinear pairings.

Extractable Collision-Resistant Hash Functions. An *extractable collision resistant hash* (ECRH) function is a cryptographic function that can produce a *succinct non-interactive argument-of-knowledge* (SNARK) to demonstrate the correctness of some simple computation [6]. In this paper we are interested in ECRH functions that prove the correct computation of BMAs. Let $(p, \mathbb{G}_1, \mathbb{G}_2, \mathbb{G}_T, g_1, g_2, \hat{e})$ be the parameters of the asymmetric bilinear pairing setting, $(s, \alpha) \in \mathbb{Z}_p^* \times \mathbb{Z}_p^*$ be the secret key and $[g_1^s, \ldots, g_1^{s^q}, g_2^s, \ldots, g_2^{s^q}, g_1^\alpha, g_1^{\alpha s}, \ldots, g_1^{\alpha s^q}, g_2^\alpha, g_2^{\alpha s}, \ldots, g_2^{\alpha s^q}]$ be the public key. We denote as F_X the ECRH of set X. It is computed as $F_X = (f_X, f_X')$ [6], where f_X is the BMA of set X and f_X' is the BMA of set X computed with public key $[g_1^{\alpha s}, \ldots, g_1^{\alpha s^q}]$, as $f_{pk}'(X) = \prod_{i=1}^{|X|} \left(g_1^{\alpha s^i}\right)^{a_i}$. As discussed in [6], function f_X' represents a proof of correct computation for the BMA f_X based on security assumptions that extend the *knowledge of exponent* assumption [10], first described to guarantee chosen-ciphertext security of asymmetric encryption. We denote as F_X, f_X' the black-box output of the functions $(f_{pk}(X), f_{pk}'(X))$ and $f_{pk}'(X)$. ECRH functions can be verified publicly through a pairing operation: $\hat{e}(f_X, g_2^\alpha) \stackrel{?}{=} \hat{e}(f_X', g_2)$. Note that the public key of our protocol does not uses the array of elements $[g_2^\alpha, g_2^{\alpha s}, \ldots, g_2^{\alpha s^q}]$. From an implementation perspective, ECRH functions are bilinear accumulators. Thus, our implementation adds an additional higher-level interface to that of BMAs.

3   Scenario and Protocol Overview

We assume that an organization that owns data (*owner*) outsources data and computations to an external *server*. Outsourced data are in the form of a collection of sets. Each set is associated to a label and can include one or more elements. Outsourced data can be queried by one or more *users*, that interact directly with the *server*. A query is an arbitrary combination of set operations expressed over the input sets. Any composition of set operations can be modeled by an abstract syntax tree (AST), where leaves are input sets and intermediate nodes are set operations. The AST corresponding to an example query "$(A \cup B \cup C) \cup (D \cap E)$" issued by the *user* is shown in Fig. 1. The leaves represent the sets involved in the query, referred by their labels, while intermediate nodes are the three set operations. Each output edge of an intermediate node represents the intermediate result of the corresponding set operation and the input of another set operation. The output of the root node represents the plaintext data returned to the *user*. The *server* proves the correctness of the inputs (π'_{leaf}) and of the operations ($\pi'_\cap, \pi'_\cup$) through different specialized routines that use bilinear accumulators to represent input and output sets. The proposed protocol builds a chain of such proofs along the vertexes of the AST, thus proving correctness of the whole computation. We distinguish three main categories of proofs.

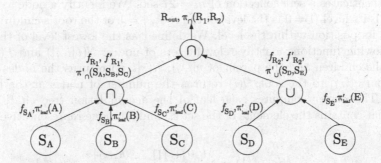

Fig. 1. AST and proofs for a verified hierarchical set operation

Proofs of correctness for the input sets. A *user* does not know any content stored in the sets collection, except the set of the available labels used to issue queries. Given a query by a *user*, the *server* returns BMAs for all input sets involved in the query and proofs of correctness that demonstrate that each BMA represents the set associated to the requested label. The proposed protocol produces these proofs by using an *accumulation tree*, that we describe in Sect. 4.

Proofs of correct computation for single set operations. Given a single set operation, the *server* is able to produce proofs of correct computation based on the BMAs of the input sets. A *user* can verify the correctness of the output by knowing the authenticated BMAs that represent the input sets and the proof for the set operation. We describe single set operation protocols in Sect. 5.

Proofs of knowledge for all intermediate results. To bind the output of a set operation as the input of another set operation, the proposed protocol produces proofs of knowledge for all intermediate results. Sections 4 and 5, describe how the *server* produces proof of correctness for intermediate results.

4   Accumulation Tree Protocols

An accumulation trees is an authenticated data structure based on constant size N-ary trees that allow efficient authentication of data by building many levels of hierarchical authentication structures, each authenticating the lower one by using cryptographic accumulators as intermediate nodes [20]. The proposed protocol leverages accumulation tree based on bilinear accumulators to authenticate all the input sets involved in a query issued by a *user*. Accumulation trees support three operations: *setup, update* and *leaf queries*. Setup and update operations are used to initialize and modify the accumulation tree accordingly with the content of the sets collection. Leaf queries allow to prove correctness of the inputs used in queries issued by *users*. **Notation.** We refer to an accumulation tree as A_k, where k is the *version* of the tree (the number of update operations). The tree has $m = |D|$ leaves, each representing a set of the sets collection and identified by a label $\ell \in \mathcal{L}$. Figure 2 shows an example accumulation tree based an an N-ary tree that authenticates a sets collection of $m = 27$ sets. We identify a node as $v[i, j]$, where i is its level ($i = 0$ is the level of the root, $i = 1$ of the root's children, ...) and j is its position within the level. We define t as the lowest level of the tree. The following functions identify relevant sets of nodes: $N(v[i, j])$ and $P(v[i, j])$ return the children and the parent of $v[i, j]$; $R(v[i, j])$ returns the nodes in the path from $v[i, j]$ to the root; $J(i)$ returns the number of nodes at the level i. **Setup.** The *owner* computes each leaf of the accumulation tree $v[t, \ell]$ as the BMA that contains the elements of the set S_ℓ and a unique representative of the label ℓ:

$$v[t, \ell] = f_{sk}(S_\ell \cup \{\ell\}) = g_1^{(h_z(\ell)+s)\prod_{x \in S_\ell}(h_z(x)+s)}, \ \forall \ell \in L \tag{1}$$

The *owner* then computes each non-leaf node as the BMA of its children $N(v[i, j])$:

$$v[i, j] = f_{sk}(N(v[i, j])) = g_1^{\prod_{x \in N(v[i,j])}(\phi_z(x)+s)}, \forall i = t - 1, \ldots, 0, \forall j = 1, \ldots, J(i) \tag{2}$$

The *owner* sends the accumulation tree to the *server* as the authentication structure A_0, and its root $v[0, 0]$ to the *users* as the digest d_0. The *owner* maintains the accumulation tree locally to execute updates on the *server*.

Update. The implemented update protocol improves the one described and used in [7, 19, 20] by allowing insertion and deletion of multiple elements on many sets through a single operation, and producing a single proof demonstrating the correctness of all updates at once. Since the updated version of the accumulation

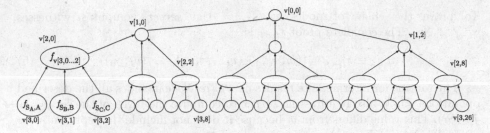

Fig. 2. Example of accumulation tree for $m = 27$ sets and degree equal to 3 ($\varepsilon = 1/3$)

tree generated by the proposed protocol is equal to that the original protocol, the security proofs proposed for the original protocol still hold.

We model the update operation $\mathcal{U}$ as an associative array $\{\ell : (add_\ell, del_\ell)\}$, where add_ℓ is the set of values inserted in S_ℓ and del_ℓ is the set of values deleted from S_ℓ. To update the leaves of the accumulation tree, the *source* computes the characteristic polynomials of inserted ($C_{add_\ell}(s)$) and deleted values ($C_{del_\ell}(s)$) for each set. These polynomials are used to update each leaf $v[t, \ell]$ as following:

$$v'[t, \ell] = v[t, \ell]^{C_{add_\ell}(s) \cdot C_{del_\ell}(s)^{-1}}, \ \forall \ell \in \mathcal{U} \tag{3}$$

Then the *owner* updates the intermediate nodes of the accumulation tree in the path from an updated leaf to the root. All the updated leaves and intermediate nodes are stored in the *upd* data structure. The *owner* maintains locally the new version of the accumulation tree A_{k+1} and sends only *upd* to the *server*. After the *server* confirms the update, the *owner* can delete the old version A_k and distribute its root as the new digest d_{k+1} to the *users*.

Leaf query. We distinguish two variants of leaf queries: those used to guarantee correctness of plaintext sets returned to *users*, and those used to guarantee correctness of input sets used in hierarchical queries. We denote the routines that implement the protocols for plaintext results as *queryTreePlaintext* and *verifyTreePlaintext*, and those for intermediate results as *queryTreeNode* and *verifyTreeNode*. Given a label ℓ, the *server* uses the *queryTreePlaintext* (*queryTreeNode*) protocol to return the set S_ℓ (the BMA f_{S_ℓ}) and the proof π_{leaf} (π'_{leaf}) that authenticates the set (the BMA) with respect to the accumulation tree A_k. A *user* that knows the digest d_k can execute a protocol *verifyTreePlaintext* (*verifyTreeNode*) to verify the correctness of S_ℓ (f_{S_ℓ}).

The *server* builds π_{leaf} by including all nodes in the path from the requested leaf to the root, and witnesses that authenticate the chain of nodes. We denote as v_t the leaf corresponding to ℓ ($v[t, \ell]$), and $v_{t-1}, \dots, v_1$ the nodes in the path from the leaf to the root (excluded). We denote as γ_i the witness that binds v_i to v_{i+1}, computed as the BMA of the children of node v_i except the node whose correctness we must prove, that is v_{i-1}:

$$\gamma_i = f_{pk}(N(v_i) \backslash \{v_{i-1}\}) \tag{4}$$

To prove the chain of nodes $v_t, \ldots, v_1$, the *server* computes witnesses $\gamma_{t-1}, \ldots, \gamma_0$. The complete proof π_{leaf} is:

$$\pi_{leaf} \equiv \pi'_{leaf} = ((v_t, \gamma_{t-1}), (v_{t-1}, \gamma_{t-2}), \ldots, (v_1, \gamma_0)) \tag{5}$$

The routine for intermediate results *queryTreeNode* includes all the described operations, but it also requires the *server* to compute the BMA of the set f_{S_ℓ} as $f_{pk}(S_\ell)$. This value differs from v_t because it does not include the representative of the label ℓ (see Eq. (1)).

The verification routines involve three phases: *(a)* results verification (plaintext or their BMA) by using the leaf node v_t; *(b)* verification of $v_t, \ldots, v_1$ by using the witnesses $\gamma_{t-1}, \ldots, \gamma_1$; *(c)* verification of v_1 by using the witness γ_0 and the digest d_k (that is v_0) trustfully obtained by the *owner*.

$$(a) \qquad \hat{e}(f_{pk}(S_\ell), g_2^{h_z(\ell)} \cdot g_2^s) \stackrel{?}{=} \hat{e}(v_t, g_2)$$

$$(b) \qquad \hat{e}(\gamma_i, g_2^{\phi_z(v_{i+1})} \cdot g_2^s) \stackrel{?}{=} \hat{e}(v_i, g_2), \forall i = t-1, \ldots, 1$$

$$(c) \qquad \hat{e}(\gamma_0, g_2^{\phi_z(v_1)} \cdot g_2^s) \stackrel{?}{=} \hat{e}(d_k, g_2) \tag{6}$$

If any of the previous conditions is not verified, the *user* rejects the results returned by the *server*.

5   Verified Set Operations

The proposed protocol supports *union* and *intersection* set operations. To demonstrate the correctness of these operations through BMAs, it is necessary to express them in terms of operations among their characteristic polynomials. To solve this issue, we reduce unions and intersections to a combination of primitive operations that we can prove through characteristic polynomials: *subset*, *multiset union* and *disjointness*.

Subset and multiset union. Let us consider sets A and X such that $A \subset X$. By construction, C_X (the characteristic polynomial of X) is divisible by C_A, thus there exists a witness polynomial W such that $C_X = C_A \cdot W$. The proof of a subset relation is the witness W, computed as the characteristic polynomial of the set $B = X \backslash A$. Verification is computed through the bilinear pairing function.

Another operation that we can prove by using a single witness is multiset union. Let us consider two input sets A and B and their multiset union $X = A + B$ (informally referred to as *multiset concatenation* in [7]). The output set X includes duplicate elements if A and B are not disjoint. Multiset union can be mapped to a multiplication operation between the characteristic polynomials of A and B, as $C_X = C_A \cdot C_B$. Given X, (or its BMA f_X), the proof of multiset union only includes the BMAs of the input sets A and B computed in the correct bilinear group ($\mathbb{G}_1$ or $\mathbb{G}_2$). Verification can be computed as $\hat{e}(f_A, w_B) \stackrel{?}{=} \hat{e}(f_X, g_2)$ or $\hat{e}(f_B, w_A) \stackrel{?}{=} \hat{e}(f_X, g_2)$. Subset and multiset union operations only support two input sets due to the nature of the pairing function $\hat{e}$.

Set disjointness. The proof for sets disjointness can be reduced to a proof of divisibility between polynomials: if and only if the intersection between the sets is the empty set, then the *gcd* of the characteristic polynomials of the sets is equal to 1. Consider sets $S_1, \ldots, S_n$. If $\cap_{i \in [n]} S_i = \emptyset$, then the *gcd* of the characteristic polynomials $C_{S_i}, \forall i \in [n]$ is equal to 1. Hence, there exists unique polynomials $\dot{q}_i$ such that $\sum_{i \in [n]} (C_{S_i} \cdot \dot{q}_i) = 1$. Polynomials $\{\dot{q}_i\}$ can be computed by executing iteratively the extended euclidean algorithm for finite field couples of polynomials [19]. Our implementation is based on the extended euclidean algorithms provided by the NTL library [22]. The proof for sets disjointness $\pi_\emptyset(S_1, \ldots, S_n)$ and its verification are as following:

$$\pi_\emptyset(S_1, \ldots, S_n) = (w_{\dot{q}_1}, \ldots, w_{\dot{q}_n}) \tag{7}$$

$$verifyDisjoint(\pi_\emptyset, f_{S_1}, \ldots, f_{S_n}) : \prod_{i \in [n]} \hat{e}(f_{S_i}, w_{\dot{q}_i}) \stackrel{?}{=} \hat{e}(g_1, g_2) \tag{8}$$

Set intersection. We consider input sets $S_1, \ldots, S_n$ and a set I that is the output of set intersection $I = \bigcap_{i \in [n]} S_i$. If I is empty or equal to one of the input sets, the operation can be reduced to a disjointness or a subset proof. Otherwise, the proof relies on two properties: I is a subset of all sets: $I \subset S_i, \forall i \in [n]$; the set complements of each set S_i are disjoint to I: $\bigcap(S_i \backslash I) = \emptyset$. In the following we distinguish proofs computed for plaintext results $(\pi_\cap)$, from those computed for intermediate results $(\pi'_\cap)$.

Proof $\pi_\cap$ includes the proof of disjointness $\pi_\emptyset$ for all the set complements, plus the BMAs of all the set complements:

$$\pi_\cap = (f_{S_1 \backslash I}, \ldots f_{S_n \backslash I}, \pi_\emptyset(S_1 \backslash I, \ldots, S_n \backslash I)) \tag{9}$$

Proof $\pi'_\cap$ includes the proof of disjointness $\pi_\emptyset$ for all the set complements, plus the ECRH functions of all the set complements. Due to the construction of ECRH functions we can denote $\pi'_\cap$ through two equivalent notations:

$$\pi'_\cap(I, S_1, \ldots, S_n) = (w_I, F_{S_1 \backslash I}, \ldots F_{S_n \backslash I}, \pi_\emptyset) \equiv (w_I, f'_{S_1 \backslash I}, \ldots f'_{S_n \backslash I}, \pi_\cap) \tag{10}$$

Verifying $\pi_\cap$ requires verifying the subset and disjunction properties:

$$verifyIntersectionPlaintext(\pi_\cap, I, f_{S_1}, \ldots, f_{S_n}) :$$

$$\forall i \in [n], \hat{e}(f_{S_i \backslash I}, w_{pk}(I)) \stackrel{?}{=} \hat{e}(f_{S_i}, g_2), \quad \prod_{i \in [n]} \hat{e}(f_{S_i}, w_{\dot{q}_i}) \stackrel{?}{=} \hat{e}(g_1, g_2) \tag{11}$$

Verifying $\pi'_\cap$ requires to verify the ECRH functions, the witness of the intersection and the plaintext intersection proof $\pi_\cap$ (with the small variant of already having the witness $w_I = w_{pk}(I)$ available):

$$verifyIntersectionNode(\pi'_\cap, f_I, f_{S_1}, \ldots, f_{S_n}) :$$

$$\hat{e}(f_I, g_2) \stackrel{?}{=} \hat{e}(g_1, w_I), \qquad \forall i \in [n], \hat{e}(f_{S_i \backslash I}, g_2^\alpha) \stackrel{?}{=} \hat{e}(f'_{S_i \backslash I}, g_2),$$

$$verifyIntersectionPlaintext(\pi_\cap, w_I, f_{S_1}, \ldots, f_{S_n}) \tag{12}$$

Set union. We consider two input sets A and B and the set $U = A \cup B$. It is possible to prove set union by using the set inclusion-exclusion principle [7]: $A \cup B = (A + B) \backslash (A \cap B)$. Since $(A \cap B) \subseteq (A + B)$ by construction, the set difference operation can also be proved as the multiset union $A + B = (A \cup B) + (A \cap B)$. Thus, set union proof must include an intermediate intersection proof $(A \cap B)$, knowledge proofs for the intermediate result $A \cap B$) and witnesses for multiset union.

$$\pi'_\cup(A, B) = (\pi'_\cap, F_{A \cap B}, w_{A \cap B}, w_B), \qquad \pi_\cup(A, B) = (\pi'_\cap, F_{A \cap B}, w_B) \qquad (13)$$

Plaintext and intermediate proofs are verified in similar ways, where verification of intermediate results require a pairing operation to test the correctness of element $w_{A \cap B}$:

$$verifyUnionPlaintext(\pi_\cup, U, f_A, f_B):$$

$$\hat{e}(f_{A \cap B}, g_2^\alpha) \overset{?}{=} \hat{e}(f'_{A \cap B}, g_2), \qquad \hat{e}(f_B, g_2) \overset{?}{=} \hat{e}(g_1, w_B),$$

$$\hat{e}(f_A, w_B) \overset{?}{=} \hat{e}(f_{A \cap B}, \hat{w}_{pk}(U)),$$

$$verifyIntersectionNode(\pi'_\cap, f_{A \cap B}, f_A, f_B) \qquad (14)$$

$$verifyUnionNode(\pi'_\cup, f_U, f_A, f_B):$$

$$\hat{e}(f_{A \cap B}, g_2^\alpha) \overset{?}{=} \hat{e}(f'_{A \cap B}, g_2), \qquad \hat{e}(f_{A \cap B}, g_2) \overset{?}{=} \hat{e}(g_1, w_{A \cap B}),$$

$$\hat{e}(f_B, g_2) \overset{?}{=} \hat{e}(g_1, w_B), \qquad \hat{e}(f_A, w_B) \overset{?}{=} \hat{e}(f_U, w_{A \cap B}),$$

$$verifyIntersectionNode(\pi'_\cap, f_{A \cap B}, f_A, f_B) \qquad (15)$$

Note that set union natively supports only two inputs: in the case of union operations among multiple sets, the query must be handled as a hierarchical query composed by multiple binary operations.

6   Conclusions

This paper describes the implementation of a protocol for efficient verifiable delegation of set operations based on bilinear accumulators. We extended literature by detailing a modular implementation that identifies the main building blocks of the protocol and defines standard interfaces. We extend the original protocols by proposing a variant for asymmetric bilinear pairings and an improved update protocol for multiple sets. We implemented the protocol and released it publicly. This is the first public implementation of a protocol for verifiable sets operations.

Acknowledgments. This work was supported by MAECI-CyberLab-2015/2016.

References

1. Akinyele, J.A., Garman, C., Miers, I., Pagano, M.W., Rushanan, M., Green, M., Rubin, A.D.: Charm: a framework for rapidly prototyping cryptosystems. J. Crypt. Eng. **3**(2), 111–128 (2016). http://charm-crypto.com/

2. Andreolini, M., Colajanni, M., Marchetti, M.: A collaborative framework for intrusion detection in mobile networks. Inf. Sci. **321**(C), 179–192 (2015)
3. Andreolini, M., Colajanni, M., Pietri, M., Tosi, S.: Adaptive, scalable and reliable monitoring of big data on clouds. J. Parallel Distrib. Comput. **79**(C), 67–79 May 2015
4. Benaloh, J., De Mare, M.: One-way accumulators: a decentralized alternative to digital signatures. In: Proceedings of IACR CRYPTO (1993)
5. Beuchat, J.-L., González-Díaz, J.E., Mitsunari, S., Okamoto, E., Rodríguez-Henríquez, F., Teruya, T.: High-speed software implementation of the optimal ate pairing over barreto–naehrig curves. In: International Conference on Pairing-Based Cryptography, 20 July 2016. https://github.com/herumi/ate-pairing
6. Bitansky, N., Canetti, R., Chiesa, A., Tromer, E.: From extractable collision resistance to succinct non-interactive arguments of knowledge, and back again. In: Proceedings of 2012 ACM Third International Conference on Innovations in Theoretical Computer Science (2012)
7. Canetti, R., Paneth, O., Papadopoulos, D., Triandopoulos, N.: Verifiable set operations over outsourced databases. In: Proceedings of 2014 IACR International Conference on Public-Key Cryptography (2014)
8. Chatterjee, S., Hankerson, D., Menezes, A.: On the efficiency and security of pairing-based protocols in the type 1 and type 4 settings. In: Hasan, M.A., Helleseth, T. (eds.) WAIFI 2010. LNCS, vol. 6087, pp. 114–134. Springer, Heidelberg (2010). doi:10.1007/978-3-642-13797-6_9
9. Colajanni, M., Gozzi, D., Marchetti, M.: Enhancing interoperability and stateful analysis of cooperative network intrusion detection systems. In: Proceedings of ACM Symposium on Architecture for Networking and Communications (2007)
10. Damgård, I.B.: Towards practical public key systems secure against chosen ciphertext attacks. In: Feigenbaum, J. (ed.) CRYPTO 1991. LNCS, vol. 576, pp. 445–456. Springer, Heidelberg (1992). doi:10.1007/3-540-46766-1_36
11. Ferretti, L., Colajanni, M., Marchetti, M.: Distributed, concurrent, and independent access to encrypted cloud databases. IEEE Trans. Parallel Distrib. Syst. **25**(2), 437–446 (2014)
12. Ferretti, L., Pierazzi, F., Colajanni, M., Marchetti, M.: Scalable architecture for multi-user encrypted sql operations on cloud database services. IEEE Trans. Cloud Comput. **2**(4), 448–458 (2014)
13. Freedman, M.J., Nissim, K., Pinkas, B.: Efficient private matching and set intersection. In: Proceedings of IACR CRYPTO (2004)
14. Galbraith, S.D., Paterson, K.G., Smart, N.P.: Pairings for cryptographers. Discrete Appl. Math. **156**(16), 3113–3121 (2008)
15. Lodi, G., Querzoni, L., Baldoni, R., Marchetti, M., Colajanni, M., Bortnikov, V., Chockler, G., Dekel, E., Laventman, G., Roytman, A.: Defending financial infrastructures through early warning systems: the intelligence cloud approach. In: Proceedings of 5th ACM Workshop CSIIRW (2009)
16. Lynn, B.: On the implementation of pairing-based cryptosystems. Ph.D. thesis, Stanford University, 20 July 2016. https://crypto.stanford.edu/pbc/
17. Naehrig, M., Niederhagen, R., Schwabe, P.: New software speed records for cryptographic pairings. In: Abdalla, M., Barreto, P.S.L.M. (eds.) LATINCRYPT 2010. LNCS, vol. 6212, pp. 109–123. Springer, Heidelberg (2010). doi:10.1007/978-3-642-14712-8_7
18. Nguyen, L.: Accumulators from bilinear pairings and applications. In: Menezes, A. (ed.) CT-RSA 2005. LNCS, vol. 3376, pp. 275–292. Springer, Heidelberg (2005). doi:10.1007/978-3-540-30574-3_19

19. Papamanthou, C., Tamassia, R., Triandopoulos, N.: Optimal verification of operations on dynamic sets. In: Rogaway, P. (ed.) CRYPTO 2011. LNCS, vol. 6841, pp. 91–110. Springer, Heidelberg (2011). doi:10.1007/978-3-642-22792-9_6

20. Papamanthou, C., Tamassia, R., Triandopoulos, N.: Authenticated hash tables. In: Proceedings of 15th ACM Conference on Computer and Communications Security (2008)

21. Preparata, F.P., Sarwate, D.V.: Computational complexity of fourier transforms over finite fields. Math. Comput. **31**(139), 740–751 (1977)

22. Shoup, V.: NTL: a library for doing number theory, 20 July 2016. http://www.shoup.net/ntl/

Multi-core FPGA Implementation of ECC with Homogeneous Co-Z Coordinate Representation

Bo-Yuan Peng[1(✉)], Yuan-Che Hsu[2], Yu-Jia Chen[2], Di-Chia Chueh[2],
Chen-Mou Cheng[3], and Bo-Yin Yang[1]

[1] Academia Sinica, Taipei, Taiwan
{bypeng,by}@crypto.tw
[2] National Taiwan University, Taipei, Taiwan
{b01901138,b01901017,b01901020}@ntu.edu.tw
[3] Osaka University, Suita, Japan
chenmou.cheng@gmail.com

Abstract. Elliptic Curve Cryptography is gaining popularity, and optimization opportunities exist on several different levels: algorithm, architecture, and/or implementation. To support a wide variety of curves and at the same time resist timing/power-based side-channel attacks, our scalar multiplication is implemented using the Co-Z ladder due to Hutter, Joye, and Sierra. We analyze the parallelism of the Co-Z ladder and show that a 12-core (though inefficient) system can complete a ladder step with the fastest speed. We also combine optimizations at every level in an efficient multi-core FPGA implementation. The size of the prime modulus can also be changed easily, for which we have implemented and tested up to 528-bits used in the NIST P-521 curve. Based on this building block, we have developed a multi-core architecture that supports multiple parallel modular additions, multiplications, and inverses.

Keywords: ECC · Co-Z · Multi-core · FPGA · Montgomery reduction

1 Introduction

Elliptic Curve Cryptography (ECC), invented independently by Koblitz and Miller [1,2], has seen use for information security in the last decade. The most important operations in ECC are scalar multiplication and point (group) addition. Most ECC implementations require many arithmetic operations modulo a prime (of 256–521 bits, as per security level). These are complex, resource-intensive operations. Efficient network security solutions become necessaries with many possible trade-offs among cost, power consumption, security level, and flexibility.

Flexibility in a security solution can be achieved via FPGAs, a practice that recently became more fashionable [6]. For networking applications, a functional unit may be cloned dozens of times on the FPGA such that, properly scheduled, many similar operations can run simultaneously. We do can the same with big

© Springer International Publishing AG 2016
S. Foresti and G. Persiano (Eds.): CANS 2016, LNCS 10052, pp. 637–647, 2016.
DOI: 10.1007/978-3-319-48965-0_42

integer modular multiplications in ECC. Of course, n copies of the key unit usually yield less than n times speed-up, due to bottlenecks in the algorithm.

We have developed an architecture with multiple Montgomery Reduction cores. Each Montgomery Reduction core includes two multipliers and completes one Montgomery multiplication in 66 cycles. The frequency can be more than 30 MHz at the maximum 528 bits, using the Xilinx® Zynq-7000™ All Programmable SoC. We use this architecture to implement a general high-security ECC engine compatible with all short Weierstrass curves and prime moduli up to 521 bits. These include the 256-bit secure NIST [13] curves. Without the comfort afforded by Montgomery or Edwards curves, we use the Co-Z ladder by Hutter et al. [8] for scalar multiplications to gain some side-channel resilience.

Our design is modular and scalable (in numbers of cores and also bitlength down to 256); we also describe, to the best of our knowledge, for the first time how the Co-Z ladder can be flexibly implemented with Montgomery reduction units. The main ladderstep can be performed in as few as 3 rounds of big integer multiplications (plus extra modular additions) with 12 Montgomery cores.

The full version (link cf. Sect. 5) has more details and the remainder of the paper is structured as follows:

- Section 2 surveys the history and related works, including the formulas that evaluates the scalar multiplications and designs related to what we used.
- Section 3 analyzes the degree of parallelism of the Co-Z ladderstep and describe the requirements an optimal scheduling of this step.
- Section 4 describes our hardware architecture with modular and flexible Montgomery multipliers, our implementation and test results in detail.
- Section 5 concludes after discussing possible follow-ups.

2   History and Related Work

ECC and Notations. Koblitz and Miller [1,2] independently suggested using discrete logarithms on the rational points of an elliptic curve group over a finite field for cryptosystems. In this paper we stick to nonsingular (a, $b \in \mathbb{F}_p$ with $4a^3 + 27b^2 \neq 0$) elliptic curves in short Weierstrass form over prime fields,

$$\mathcal{E}(\mathbb{F}_p) := \{(x, y) \in \mathbb{F}_p \times \mathbb{F}_p \,|\, y^2 = x^3 + ax + b\} \cup \{\mathcal{O}\} \qquad (1)$$

$\mathcal{E}(\mathbb{F}_p)$ comprises points satisfying the curve equation $\mathcal{E} : y^2 = x^3 + ax + b$ plus a "point at infinity" $\mathcal{O}$. We can define an abelian group on $\mathcal{E}(\mathbb{F}_p)$ such that $\mathcal{O}$ is the unit element, and any three co-linear points add up to $\mathcal{O}$.

The *scalar multiplication* $\mathbf{Q} = \langle k \rangle \mathbf{P}$, is defined as repeated addition on k copies of a point $\mathbf{P}$. On good curves, it is difficult given $\mathbf{P}$ and $\mathbf{Q}$ to find k such that $\mathbf{Q} = \langle k \rangle \mathbf{P}$ (takes time $\Theta(\sqrt{q})$ with the best methods we know). This is the elliptic curve discrete logarithm problem (ECDLP). A scalar multiplication $\mathbf{Q} = \langle k \rangle \mathbf{P}$ in contrast takes time polylog(p) given k and $\mathbf{P}$.

Computing Scalar Multiplication and Coordinates. In the early days of cryptography, exponentiations use the double-and-add approach. However, Kocher noted that we can break such implementations using *side-channel attacks* (SCA) [10], by observing timing or power usage patterns.

An approach to scalar multiplication more resilient to simple SCA is *differential addition chains.* The original example, where we can compute $\langle 2 \rangle \mathbf{Q}$ and $\mathbf{P} + \mathbf{Q}$ from $\mathbf{P}, \mathbf{Q}, \mathbf{P} - \mathbf{Q}$, is the *Montgomery ladder* [4].

Point Representations and Co-Z ladder for NIST Curves. The representation of (X, Y, Z) denoting the point $(X/Z, Y/Z)$, a *homogeneous projective coordinate*, is a *scaling factor* to avoid computing inverses in $\mathbb{F}_p$. Similarly, in *Jacobian* coordinates on short Weierstrass curves $(X; Y; Z)$ denotes the point $(X/Z^2, Y/Z^3)$.

Usually twisted Edwards curves [3] (birationally equivalent to Montgomery curves) offers the best all-around performance. The Montgomery curve/ladder combination is one of the best methods to implement ECC for security and speed today, illustrating the importance of a good set of choices of algorithm, curve and representation (cf. [12]). In some cases compatibility for short Weierstrass curves not equivalent to Montgomery curves (e.g., NIST [13] curves) is required.

In 2011, Hutter *et al.* described a very good general differential chain implementation for scalar multiplications on a general short Weierstrass curve [8], which somehow remained obscure (e.g., omitted by [12]). Like the original Montgomery chain, only the X-parts of homogeneous projective coordinates are tracked. A main feature of the new method is that the two points $\mathbf{R_0}$ and $\mathbf{R_1}$ shares Z coordinates during each ladderstep. The y coordinates can be reconstructed at the end, enabling compressed public keys and signatures. We call this the *Co-Z ladder.*

Co-Z Ladder Formulas. Let $\mathbf{P_1} = (X_1, Y_1, Z)$, $\mathbf{P_2} = (X_2, Y_2, Z)$ and $\mathbf{P_1} - \mathbf{P_2} = \pm \mathbf{P}$ where $\mathbf{P} = (x_P, y_P)$. Further let $\mathbf{P_1} + \mathbf{P_2} = (X_1', Y_1', Z')$ and $\langle 2 \rangle \mathbf{P_2} = (X_2', Y_2', Z')$. Given (X_1, X_2, Z) and x_P we can compute $U = (X_1 - X_2)^2$ and $V = 4X_2(X_2^2 + aZ^2) + 4bZ^3$ first, and then (X_1', X_2', Z') via

$$\begin{cases} X_1' = V[(X_1 + X_2)(X_1^2 + X_2^2 - U + 2aZ^2) + 4bZ^3 - x_P ZU], \\ X_2' = U[(X_2^2 - aZ^2)^2 - 8bZ^3 X_2], \quad Z' = UVZ. \end{cases} \tag{2}$$

Algorithm 1 (cf. [8]) evaluates formulas (2). Most of the computation is in 11 big-integer multiplications (denoted as $\mathfrak{M}$) and 5 big-integer squarings (denoted as $\mathfrak{S}$), or $11\mathfrak{M} + 5\mathfrak{S}$. Note that multiplications by either a or $4b$ may be faster. Hutter *et al.* also noted we can forget Z and instead track (T_P, T_a, T_b) where $T_P = x_P Z$, $T_a = aZ^2$ and $T_b = 4bZ^3$, with $10\mathfrak{M} + 5\mathfrak{S}$ per ladderstep.

Components of the Co-Z Ladder. A scalar multiplication in the NIST P-521 curve takes about 8000 modular multiplications (treating squaring and multiplication as the same), and we are yet to build the requisite multiplier. The multi-staged Montgomery reduction method [5] is presently the de facto standard approach for generic modular multiplications. This is well-studied and we

Algorithm 1. Montgomery Ladderstep in homogeneous Co-Z coordinate.

Input: X_1, X_2, Z, x_P, a, $4b$
Output: X_1', X_2', Z'

1 $R_1 \leftarrow Z^2$	9 $R_9 \leftarrow X_2 \times R_8$	17 $R_{17} \leftarrow X_2 + X_2$	25 $R_{25} \leftarrow Z \times R_{20}$
2 $R_2 \leftarrow a \times R_1$	10 $R_{10} \leftarrow R_9 + R_9$	18 $R_{18} \leftarrow R_{17} \times R_4$	26 $R_{26} \leftarrow x_P \times R_{25}$
3 $R_3 \leftarrow Z \times R_1$	11 $R_{11} \leftarrow R_{10} + R_{10}$	19 $R_{19} \leftarrow R_7 - R_{18}$	27 $R_{27} \leftarrow R_{24} - R_{26}$
4 $R_4 \leftarrow 4b \times R_3$	12 $R_{12} \leftarrow R_{11} + R_4$	20 $R_{20} \leftarrow R_{16}^2$	28 $X_1' \leftarrow R_{27} \times R_{12}$
5 $R_5 \leftarrow X_2^2$	13 $R_{13} \leftarrow R_8 + R_2$	21 $R_{21} \leftarrow R_{15} - R_{20}$	29 $X_2' \leftarrow R_{20} \times R_{19}$
6 $R_6 \leftarrow R_5 - R_2$	14 $R_{14} \leftarrow X_1^2$	22 $R_{22} \leftarrow R_{16} + R_{17}$	30 $Z' \leftarrow R_{25} \times R_{12}$
7 $R_7 \leftarrow R_6^2$	15 $R_{15} \leftarrow R_{13} + R_{14}$	23 $R_{23} \leftarrow R_{22} \times R_{21}$	
8 $R_8 \leftarrow R_5 + R_2$	16 $R_{16} \leftarrow X_1 - X_2$	24 $R_{24} \leftarrow R_{23} + R_4$	

omit details about Montgomery modular multiplier unit. In practice our implementation need to fit the FPGA platform and the practical requirement.

3 Task Scheduling in the Co-Z Ladder

Whenever multipliers are being added, two questions are inevitably raised. One question is that if n Montgomery cores can used efficiently. Can formula (2) be completed within $\lceil 16/n \rceil$ of big-integer multiplications? And the other is the least number of rounds of big-integer multiplications for formula (2).

These are classical problems in parallel computing, that becomes practical to those seeking to speed up ECC. To solve this problem, the targeted algorithm will be transformed into a *task schedule graph*, which is a directed acyclic graph (DAG) in which each directed edge implies the causality between the steps (vertices in the graph) in the algorithm. Solving the famous DAG scheduling problem then gives the answers to the above two questions [16].

Here we analyze the degrees of parallelism of Algorithm 1. Compared with multiplication, the big-integer addition/subtraction is much faster, so we will focus on the scheduling of former. Preferably, we would like to have all our Montgomery cores to run and stop (almost) at the same time to ease our scheduling task. The relationship between the number of Montgomery cores and the number of rounds of big-integer multiplications required is shown in Table 1.

Table 1. # rounds of big-number multiplications required to perform Co-Z ladderstep in [8]. In '†' cases, small and fixed a and b may improve the performance by one round. Also, tracking (T_P, T_a, T_b) instead of Z only takes 5 round in the 3-core case

# cores	2	3	4	5	enough
# rounds	$8^\dagger$	$6^\dagger$	5	4	3 (12 cores)

When using 2 or 3 cores, tracking (T_P, T_a, T_b) instead of Z has a different task schedule graph with the critical path of length 5. One can easily construct a 8-round schedule for the 2-core case and 5-round schedule for 3-core case, which will be found in the full version (cf. Sect. 5).

3.1   4 and 5 Cores: Critical Paths Evaluating (X_1, X_2, Z)

The task schedule graph of Algorithm 1 with ADD/SUB blocks omitted is shown in Fig. 1(a). See the full version to get the full task schedule graphs. Each edge indicates the causality between the connected blocks (indicating the big-integer multiplications), where the left block is performed earlier than the right one.

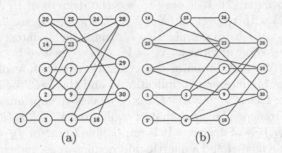

(a)   (b)

Fig. 1. The task schedule graph of Algorithm 1, where the ADD/SUB blocks are omitted. Figure (a) is the original and Fig. (b) is the modified one for the multi-core purpose

The critical path is $\langle 1, 3, 4, 18, 28 \rangle$, which can be reduced. We can see $4bZ^3$ which is evaluated at step 4 is originally evaluated as the product of $4b$ and Z^3, but actually it can be evaluated from the product of $4bZ$ and Z^2, both of which are of degree 2. Since Z^3 is referenced only in step 4, we can modify step 3 and 4 in Algorithm 1, resulting in the modified task schedule graph shown in Fig. 1(b). Now the critical path length is 4 with respect to rounds of big-integer multiplications.

This observation may be generalized to more cases. To evaluate the value of a monomial $x = x_0^{r_0}, ..., x_{n-1}^{r_{n-1}}$ with total degree $r = \sum r_i$, it is the best to generate the divisor $x_a = x_0^{a_0}, ..., x_{n-1}^{a_{n-1}}$ and $x_b = x_0^{b_0}, ..., x_{n-1}^{a_{n-1}}$, where $x = x_a x_b$, $\lceil r/2 \rceil - 1 \leq a = \sum a_i \leq \lceil r/2 \rceil$ and $\lceil r/2 \rceil - 1 \leq b = \sum b_i \leq \lceil r/2 \rceil$ if we want to shrink the critical path generating x. This will be important in Sect. 3.2.

A 5-Montgomery-core schedule with 4 rounds can be created directly from Fig. 1(b). Observing that $11\mathfrak{M} + 5\mathfrak{S}$ are required in the algorithm, as well as that only step 28, 29, and 30 (3 in total) can be performed in the last round, there will be 13 big-integer multiplications yet to be performed *before* the last round. Therefore, there exists a 4-Montgomery-core system that can perform Algorithm 1 in 5 rounds of big-integer multiplications. An additional note is that when it is the case that a and $4b$ are constants, both 2-Montgomery-core and 3-Montgomery-core systems can perform Algorithm 1 with one round fewer than original cases. This fact makes it more competitive than evaluating $(X_1, X_2, T_P, T_a, T_b)$.

3.2 How Many Cores Are Required for the Fastest Performance?

The next problem in implementing the Co-Z approach is the resource requirement if we want to speed up to the extreme. How many rounds of big-integer multiplications are required at least and thus how many cores are required?

By induction, we can see that to evaluate a monomial of degree n, the best approach will take $\lceil \lg n \rceil$ rounds of multiplications. To estimate the requirement, let us analyze formula (2). It is easy to see the degrees of U, V, X_1', X_2' and Z' in formula (2) with respect to $(X_1, X_2, Z, x_P, a, 4b)$ are 2, 4, 8, 8 and 7, respectively. It is obvious that evaluating U using one big-integer multiplication is optimal. It is a good news that $X_1' = V \times f_{X_1'}(\cdot)$ where both V and $f_{X_1'}(\cdot)$ are of degree 4. We may optimize the evaluation procedure of V and $f_{X_1'}(\cdot)$ (with 2 rounds of big-integer multiplications) and then get the optimal flow to evaluate X_1'. The fact $Z' = UVZ = UZ \times V$ makes the optimization procedure of evaluating Z' to depend also on that of evaluating V. $X_2' = U \times f_{X_2'}(\cdot)$ brings a problem, as $f_{X_2'}(\cdot)$ is of degree 6. It is impossible to factor $f_{X_2'}(\cdot)$ as a product of a quadratic polynomial and a quartic polynomial. A second choice is given by

$$f_{X_2'} = X_2^2(X_2^2 - 2aZ \times Z) + Z^2[(aZ)^2 - 8bX_2Z] \tag{3}$$

We can then evalaute X_2' in 3 rounds. To evaluate V and $f_{X_1'}(\cdot)$, we observe that

$$V = 4X_2 \times X_2^2 + 4X_2Z \times aZ + 4bZ \times Z^2 \tag{4}$$

$$f_{X_1'} = 2X_1X_2(X_1 + X_2) + aZ \times 2Z(X_1 + X_2) + 4bZZ^2 - x_PZU \tag{5}$$

Now we can build a 12-Montgomery-core system to perform Algorithm 1, and the key schedule how to use the Montgomery cores is given as Table 2.

Table 2. Scheduling for Algorithm 1 with 12 cores

R#	List of multiplication
1	U, X_2^2, aZ, Z^2, X_2Z, $4bZ$, x_PZ, $(X_1 + X_2)Z$, X_1X_2
2	$M_1 = U \cdot X_2^2$, $M_2 = aZ \cdot Z$, $M_3 = U \cdot Z^2$, $M_4 = (aZ)^2$, $M_5 = 4b \cdot X_2Z$, $M_6 = X_2 \cdot X_2^2$, $M_7 = aZ \cdot X_2Z$, $M_8 = 4bZ \cdot Z^2$, $M_9 = U \cdot Z$, $M_{10} = (X_1 + X_2)Z \cdot aZ$, $M_{11} = (X_1 + X_2)X_1X_2$, $M_{12} = U \cdot x_PZ$ $f_{X_1'} = 2M_{11} + 2M_{10} + M_8 - M_{12}$, $V = 4M_6 + 4M_7 + M_8$
3	$X_1' = V \cdot f_{X_1'}$, $Z' = M_9 \cdot V$, $X_2' = M_1 \cdot (X_2^2 - 2M_2) + M_3 \cdot (M_4 - 2M_5)$

4   Implementation and Results

We show our result with 5- and 12-Montgomery-core systems. For the 5-core system, the maximum bit sizes are scalable and we provide the results for 264-bit (for 256-bit fields) and for 528-bit (for 521-bit or 512-bit fields) operations in ECC. The Montgomery reduction cores, standing for the big integer multipliers, are of base $d = 2^8$. The detailed design for the Montgomery reduction cores is shown in the full version. A remark is given here that additional BRAM blocks (named as $xP^{-1}P$ pools) are allocated in order to restore pre-evaluated values that are often used in the Montgomery cores.

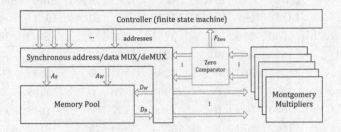

Fig. 2. The proposed block diagram

Figure 2 illustrates the hardware architecture of a multi-multiplication-core system. Each Montgomery multiplier will get two inputs (A, B) and generate one output R. When there are 2 or more Montgomery multipliers, a typical choice to use a MUX/deMUX to collect the outputs of the Montgomery multipliers, and to dispatch the value in the memory to the specified inputs of the multipliers. This approach will cost more cycles on the MUX/deMUX. A finite state machine or a controller handles the addresses for the memory pool. There are paths from the input of the whole system to the write-data buses, and the controller can assign some pre-defined direct values to the write-data buses. The data buses do not bother the controller directly, but there are some cases in which we need to check if the outputs of the large number arithmetic units become 0. One comparator to zero, whose comparison result is a flag for the controller, is installed from the output bus of each large number arithmetic unit.

In this work, Xilinx® Zynq-7000™ All Programmable SoC (APSoC) on Xilinx® ZC706 Evaluation Kit is adopted for the 5-core system and the 12-core system. We also show our result about the resource requirement for multiple 3-core and 5-core ECC engines in one system on ZC706 board, which implies that to build multiple 3-core engines in one system is better if there are sufficient resources to build a 12-core system. The DSP slices are *not* needed — they were going to be used for multimedia purpose specified by the original client.

In our system, the functions of ECC operations that are often used include:

1. Re-configurable parameters of a, b, p, $q = |\mathcal{E}|$, and the base point G.
2. Scalar multiplication with the scalar k and the element $\mathbf{P}$ in $\mathcal{E}$.
3. Group point addition of elements $\mathbf{P}$ and $\mathbf{Q}$ in the elliptic group $\mathcal{E}$. The classical approach by Cohen *et al.* [9] is applied.
4. Big-number MUL/ADD/SUB operations modulo the group order $q = |\mathcal{E}|$.
5. find the big-number inverse modulo $q = |\mathcal{E}|$. Montgomery inversion [4] is not in our hardware. Due to its simple state machine, add it should be easy.

Table 3. Resource used for 5- and 12-Montgomery-core systems on ZC706 Kit. n in $\mathcal{S}_{m,n}$ implies the maximum n-bit compatibility m-core design. No DSP slices are used

Module	$\mathcal{S}_{5,264}$ $f_{max} = 83.33\,\text{MHz}$			$\mathcal{S}_{5,528}$ $f_{max} = 62.50\,\text{MHz}$			$\mathcal{S}_{12,264}$ $f_{max} = 45\,\text{MHz}$		
	Slice LUT6	Slice Reg	18 Kb BRAM	Slice LUT6	Slice Reg	18 Kb BRAM	Slice LUT6	Slice Reg	18 Kb BRAM
Mont. mul. (each)	2080	280	0	3455	545	0	2052	280	0
$xP^{-1}P$ pool	1635	559	40	3226	1096	75	1339	559	96
Diff. adder	247	103	0	1288	103	0	5132	165	0
(X, Y, Z) recovery	1395	76	0	1968	76	0	1109	74	0
Other FSM	1630	932	0	2306	1727	0	1613	932	0
Memory pool	7662	2673	8	19554	5324	15	18162	6366	8
Misc. modules	3973	1786	0	656	3412	0	2362	1987	0
Total	26941	7529	48	46269	14458	90	54337	1344	104

4.1   5-Montgomery-Core System

The 5-Montgomery-core system is implemented on ZC706 Evaluation Kit, on which a Z-7045 APSoC equivalent to a Kintex®-7 FPGA is used. There are 218600 LUTs and a Dual ARM® Cortex™-A9 MPCore™ processor on this APSoC [7], where the protocols (such as ECDH or ECDSA) is implemented on the ARM processor. A parameter setting the maximum compatible bit-size is configured in the 5-core system in our design. Here a 264-bit version and a 528-bit version are synthesized and tested with NIST curves, Brainpool curve P_{512} r1 [14], and SEC P_{256} k1 curve [15] (a.k.a. the Bitcoin curve) are tested in both of the systems. The resource requirements and time performances of the 264-bit version and the 528-bit version are given as Tables 3 and 4.

Table 4. Performance of $\mathbf{Q} = \langle k \rangle \mathbf{P}$ in various $\{5, 12\}$-core systems on ZC706 Kit

Elliptic curve	$\mathcal{S}_{5,264}$ @ 83.33 MHz		$\mathcal{S}_{5,528}$ @ 62.50 MHz		$\mathcal{S}_{12,264}$ @ 45 MHz	
	Cycles	Time (ms)	Cycles	Time (ms)	Cycles	Time (ms)
NIST P_{224}	95657	1.148	133085	2.129	130513	2.900
NIST P_{256}	109001	1.308	152429	2.439	148721	3.305
SEC P_{256} k1 (BitCoin)	109001	1.308	152429	2.439	148721	3.305
NIST P_{384}	-	-	226432	3.623	-	-
Brainpool P_{512} r1	-	-	301421	4.823	-	-
NIST P_{521}	-	-	306659	4.907	-	-

It should be noticed that there are two similar but different sorts of LUTs, so the LUT count of each module only implies the size scale of the module, and varies a little if the module is placed with different floor plans.

4.2   12-Montgomery-Core System

A 12-Montgomery-core system is implemented in our design to show the scalability of customized number of cores. However, we found that we can only implement a 12-core system with a maximum 264-bit size. 528-bit version can be synthesized, but will face a routing procedure failure due to routes too congested. Tables 3 and 4 show the test results.

MUX/deMUX problem on the memory pool will be more severe in the 12-core system, and many Montgomery cores will be frequently useless during the computation. It is not practical to use a 12-core system as one ECC engine.

4.3   3-Core Vs 5-Core

Our ECC engine is designed as a custom IP to provide the hardware support of the ARM processor in Zynq-7000. A reasonable idea for the hardware/software co-design is to provide multiple ECC engines in the embedded system. We have run the implementation process to test how many ECC engines with our design can be put in the same system in ZC706 kit. The resource requirement of the multi-ECC-engine system is shown in Table 5.

Table 5. Resource usage and effectiveness of scalar multiplication for multi-ECC-engine systems on ZC706 Kit. $f = 40\,\text{MHz}$ and NIST P_{521} curve applied for $S_{n,528}$ and NIST P_{256} curve applied for $S_{n,264}$. Complete results can be found in the full version

ECC engine	Count	Average LUT count	System LUT count	blocks/(s × kLUT)
$S_{3,528}$	4	38585	159788	3.163
7.913 ms	5	Fail (routes too congested)		
$S_{5,528}$	3	51797	165830	2.360
7.666 ms	4	Fail (more than 218600)		
$S_{3,264}$	10	19596	210083	18.085
2.632 ms	11	Fail (more than 218600)		
$S_{5,264}$	6	26930	190417	11.563
2.725 ms	7	Fail (more than 218600)		
$S_{12,264}$	2	54332	112070	4.7999
3.718 ms	3	Fail (partial conflict)		

We may use the throughput-resource ratio blocks/(s × kLUT) to evaluate the effectiveness of the system we have built. The bigger the ratio is, the more effective the system is. In a 5-core ECC engine there are sometimes some multipliers running dummy operations, so we can see the throughput-resource ratio is much lower. It is more effective to build 3-core engines in the system. Also we can see that a 12-core engine system is not effective.

5   Conclusion and Future Work

We have shown the power and the limitation of multiple big-integer multiplication cores on the implementation of the Co-Z ladders for ECC. The numbers suggest that a 3-Montgomery-core system achieve the best throughput-resource ratio. We have also shown that it is possible to build a fast Montgomery ladder using the Co-Z approach with a 12-Montgomery-core system.

The system in our design can be improved in several ways. For the design of the block memory restoring the large numbers, the MUX/deMUX approach may be changed. LaForest *et al.* [18–20] provide the solution in saving the clock cycles reading and writing data from or into the memory, with the cost being duplicated block memory modules used. Also the design of the controller can be improved. The total finite state machine which constructs the controller is huge. The controller controls the input and the output flows for all of the multipliers. It is possible to re-design the controller as several controllers, each of which controls only one multiplier.

Full version http://precision.moscito.org/by-publ/recent/CoZ-long.pdf.

References

1. Koblitz, N.: Ellptic curve cryptosystems. Math. Comput. **48**(177), 203–209 (1987)
2. Miller, V.S.: Use of elliptic curves in cryptography. In: Williams, H.C. (ed.) CRYPTO 1985. LNCS, vol. 218, pp. 417–426. Springer, Heidelberg (1986). doi:10. 1007/3-540-39799-X_31
3. Bernstein, D.J., Birkner, P., Joye, M., Lange, T., Peters, C.: Twisted edwards curves. In: Vaudenay, S. (ed.) AFRICACRYPT 2008. LNCS, vol. 5023, pp. 389–405. Springer, Heidelberg (2008). doi:10.1007/978-3-540-68164-9_26
4. Peter, L.: Montgomery: speeding the pollard and elliptic curve methods of factorization. Math. Comput. **48**(177), 243–264 (1987)
5. Peter, L.: Montgomery: modular multiplication without trial division. Math. Comput. **44**(170), 519–521 (1985)
6. Land, I., Kenny, R., Brown, L., Pelt, R.: Shifting from software to hardware for network security, White Paper. Altera, February 2016. https://www.altera.com/content/dam/altera-www/global/en_US/pdfs/literature/wp/wp-01261-shifting-from-software-to-hardware-for-network-security.pdf
7. Zynq-7000 All Programmable SoCs Product Tables and Product Selection Guide. Xilinx (2015). http://www.xilinx.com/support/documentation/selection-guides/zynq-7000-product-selection-guide.pdf
8. Hutter, M., Joye, M., Sierra, Y.: Memory-constrained implementations of elliptic curve cryptography in Co-Z coordinate representation. In: Nitaj, A., Pointcheval, D. (eds.) AFRICACRYPT 2011. LNCS, vol. 6737, pp. 170–187. Springer, Heidelberg (2011). doi:10.1007/978-3-642-21969-6_11

9. Cohen, H., Miyaji, A., Ono, T.: Efficient elliptic curve exponentiation using mixed coordinates. In: Ohta, K., Pei, D. (eds.) ASIACRYPT 1998. LNCS, vol. 1514, pp. 51–65. Springer, Heidelberg (1998). doi:10.1007/3-540-49649-1_6

10. Kocher, P.C.: Timing attacks on implementations of Diffie-Hellman, RSA, DSS, and other systems. In: Koblitz, N. (ed.) CRYPTO 1996. LNCS, vol. 1109, pp. 104–113. Springer, Heidelberg (1996). doi:10.1007/3-540-68697-5_9

11. Coron, J.-S.: Resistance against differential power analysis for elliptic curve cryptosystems. In: Koç, Ç.K., Paar, C. (eds.) CHES 1999. LNCS, vol. 1717, pp. 292–302. Springer, Heidelberg (1999)

12. Bernstein, D.J., Lange, T.: Explicit-Formulas Database. https://hyperelliptic.org/EFD/

13. National Institute of Standards and Technology: Digital Signature Standard. FIPS Publication 186-2, February 2000

14. Brainpool, E.C.C.: ECC brainpool standard curves and curve generation. http://www.ecc-brainpool.org/download/Domain-parameters.pdf

15. Research, C.: SEC 2: Recommended Elliptic Curve Domain Parameters (2000)

16. Kwok, Y.-K., Ahmad, I.: Static scheduling algorithms for allocating directed task graphs to multiprocessors. J. ACM CSUR $31(4)$, 406–471 (1999)

17. Pedro, M.C., Massolino, L.B., Chaves, R., Mentens, N.: Low Power Montgomery Modular Multiplication on Reconfigurable Systems, Crypto ePrint 2016/280

18. LaForest, C.E., Gregory Steffan, J.: Efficient multi-ported memories for FPGAs. In: Proceedings of the ACM(SIGDA) FPGA, pp. 41–50 (2010)

19. Laforest, C.E., Liu, M.G., Rapati, E.R., Steffan, J.G.: Multi-ported memories for FPGAs via XOR. In: Proceedings of the ACM FPGA, pp. 209–218 (2012)

20. Laforest, C.E., Li, Z., O'rourke, T., Liu, M.G., Steffan, J.G.: Composing multi-ported memories on FPGAs. J. ACM Trans. Reconfig. Technol. Syst. $7(3)$ (2014). Article 16

Network Security, Privacy, and Authentication

DNSSEC Misconfigurations in Popular Domains

Tianxiang Dai[✉], Haya Shulman, and Michael Waidner

Fraunhofer Institute for Secure Information Technology SIT, Darmstadt, Germany
{tianxiang.dai,haya.shulman,michael.waidner}@sit.fraunhofer.de

Abstract. DNSSEC was designed to protect the Domain Name System (DNS) against DNS cache poisoning and domain hijacking. When widely adopted, DNSSEC is expected to facilitate a multitude of future applications and systems, as well as security mechanisms, that would use the DNS for distribution of security tokens, such as, certificates, IP prefix authentication for routing security, anti-spam mechanisms. Multiple efforts are invested in adopting DNSSEC and in evaluating challenges towards its deployment.

In this work we perform a study of errors and misconfigurations in signed domains. To that end, we develop a DNSSEC framework and a webpage for reporting the most up to date statistics and provide reports with vulnerabilities and misconfigurations. Our tool also supports retrieval of historical data and enables to perform long-term studies and observations of changes in the security landscape of DNS. We make our tool and the collected data available via an online webservice.

1 Introduction

Domain Name System (DNS), [RFC1034, RFC1035], has a key role in the Internet. The correctness and availability of DNS are critical to the security and functionality of the Internet. Initially designed to translate domain names to IP addresses, the DNS infrastructure has evolved into a complex ecosystem, and the complexity of the DNS infrastructure is continuously growing with the increasing range of purposes and client base. DNS is increasingly utilised to facilitate a wide range of applications and constitutes an important building block in the design of scalable network infrastructures.

There is a long history of attacks against DNS, most notably, DNS cache poisoning, [5–7,12,14,17]. DNS cache poisoning attacks are known to be practiced by governments, e.g., for censorship [1] or for surveillance [11], as well as by cyber criminals. In the course of a DNS cache poisoning attack, the attacker provides spoofed records in DNS responses, in order to redirect the victims to incorrect hosts for credential theft, malware distribution, censorship and more.

To mitigate the threat from the DNS cache poisoning attacks, the IETF designed and standardised Domain Name System Security Extensions (DNSSEC) [RFC4033-RFC4035]. Unfortunately DNSSEC requires significant changes to the DNS infrastructure as well as to the protocol, and although proposed and standardised already in 1997, it is still not widely deployed. Studies show that less than 1 % of the domains are signed with DNSSEC, [9,19] and

© Springer International Publishing AG 2016
S. Foresti and G. Persiano (Eds.): CANS 2016, LNCS 10052, pp. 651–660, 2016.
DOI: 10.1007/978-3-319-48965-0_43

about 3 % of the DNS resolvers validate DNSSEC records, [3,13]. However, the situation is improving and following the recent ICANN regulation, [15], the registrars are turning domain signing into an automated task, as the procedures for automated domain signing by the registrars and hosting providers are becoming widely supported. Now that the DNSSEC is taking off, tools for evaluating problems with signed domains are critical, since they can alert the domain owners as well as clients of the potential pitfalls. Although tools for studying DNSSEC exist, and we compare them with our tool in Related Work, Sect. 2, our tool detects and reports misconfigurations and cryptographic vulnerabilities which were not performed prior to our work.

In this work we perform a study of miconfigurations among DNSSEC-signed domains. We first collect a list of popular signed domains, and then measure the different misconfigurations and problems among them. We provide access to our tool through a webpage, which can be accessed at: https://dnssec.cad.sit.fraunhofer.de.

Contributions. We designed and implemented a framework, *DNSSEC misconfiguration validation engine*, which collects signed domains from multiple sources, analyses the misconifgurations among them, and processes them into reports. Our reports quantify two types of vulnerabilities in signed domains: *cryptographic failures* (those preventing a DNS resolver from establishing a chain of trust or domains using vulnerable DNSSEC keys) and *transport failures* (e.g., lack of support of TCP or EDNS). We use our engine to perform Internet-wide collection of 1349 Top-Level Domains (TLDs) and top-1M Alexa (www.alexa.com) domains.

We collected statistics between March and September 2016 with our tool, and report on the current status as well as improvements that we detected over time. Our study indicates that 90 % of TLDs and 1.66 % of Alexa domains are signed. Among signed domains, 0.89 % TLDs and 19.46 % Alexa domains cannot establish a chain of trust to the root zone; among those Alexa domains, 85.5 % are Second-Level Domains (SLDs). We also checked for the presence of DNSSEC keys in domains with a broken chain of trust, in other repositories for DNSSEC keys distribution. Of the 19.46 % of the Alexa domains, only 51 have a DLV resource record in dlv.isc.org. Namely, majority of the signed domains do not provide any benefit by signing their records, since the clients anyway cannot validate the signatures. We find domains with vulnerable DNSSEC keys, using even RSA modulus. In contrast to February 2016, where 3 % of TLDs did not have support for TCP, all TLDs currently support TCP. However, 12.88 % of Alexa domains have nameservers which still cannot serve DNS responses over TCP.

The reports and statistics can be accessed at https://dnssec.cad.sit.fraunhofer.de.

Organisation. In Sect. 2 we compare our research to related work. In Sect. 3 we describe our DNSSEC configuration validation engine, its components and the data collection that we performed with. In Sect. 4 we perform a measurement of signed domains and characterise causes for the misconfigured signed domains. We conclude this work in Sect. 5.

2   Related Work

The research and operational communities invested significant efforts in generating online services for studying DNS. We review some of the central services.

OARC's DNS Reply Size Test Server is an online service for testing responses size of DNS. The clients can use the tool to evaluate the maximum response size that their network can support. This test is especially critical for adoption of DNSSEC, since DNSSEC enabled responses typically exceed the standard size of 512 bytes.

Multiple online services were designed for evaluating the security of port selection algorithms, most notably porttest.dns-oarc.net; see survey and analysis in [6]. The tools study the randomness in ports selected by the DNS resolver.

Recently multiple tools were proposed for checking DNSSEC adoption on zones. For instance, DNSViz, given a domain name, visualises all the keys the domain has and signatures over DNS records. It also checks that it is possible to establish a chain of trust from the root to the target domain. SecSpider provides overall statistics for DNSSEC deployment on zones, by collecting signed DNS records and keys from the zones.

Our tool complements the existing tools by allowing to study insecurity or misconfigurations on a given domain, as well as analysing statistics of the misconfigurations over a given time period, and for a set of domains. In contrast to existing tools which provide an analysis for a given domain that they receive in an input, our tool is invoked periodically over the datasets that it uses, analyses the data and produces reports with statistics. The reports contain misconfigurations on the transport layer, such as support of TCP, as well as on the cryptographic aspects, such as vulnerable keys and lack of chain of trust. Our tool provides important insights to clients accessing domains as well as for domain owners, and allows researchers to study changes in security and configurations of domains over time.

Prior studies measuring adoption of DNSSEC, investigated validation on the DNS resolvers' side, [13], showing that a large fraction of DNS resolvers do not perform correct validation of DNSSEC signatures. Other works investigated obstacles towards adoption of DNSSEC, suggesting mitigations and alternative mechanisms, [8–10].

Our tool provides insights on the status of adoption of DNSSEC among zones and on misconfigurations within signed domains in DNS hierarchy, as well as on the failures on nameservers, such as failures to serve responses over TCP.

3   DNSSEC Adoption/Configuration Framework

In this section we present our framework for collecting and processing domains, illustrated in Fig. 1. In the rest of this section we explain the components of our

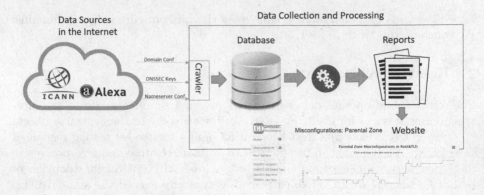

Fig. 1. DNSSEC adoption and configuration evaluation framework.

DNSSEC validation engine, including data sources and data collection, and the analysis of the data and processing into reports and online web page.

Domains Crawler. We developed a crawler to collect and store DNSSEC-signed domains.

Data Sources. We collected sources of DNSSEC signed zones that we feed to the database as 'crawling seeds':

(1) the root and Top Level Domain (TLD) zone files – we obtained the root and TLD zone files (e.g., for `com`, `net`, `org`, `info`) from the Internet Corporation for Assigned Names and Numbers (ICANN). In total we study 1301 TLDs.
(2) we scanned the top-1M popular domains according to Alexa www.alexa.com.

4 Evaluating Vulnerabilities in DNSSEC Adoption

In this section we provide our measurement of adoption of DNSSEC among the domains in our dataset, i.e., the Top Level Domains (TLDs) and Second Level Domains (SLDs) (based on the data sources in Sect. 3), and report on misconfigurations and vulnerabilities.

Quantifying Signed Domains. We define DNSSEC-signed domains as those with `DNSKEY` and `RRSIG` records. To check for the fraction of signed domains, we checked for existence of `DNSKEY` and `RRSIG` records in our dataset. Our results show that 90 % of the TLDs and 1.66 % of the SLDs are signed.

In Fig. 2 we plot the results we collected between March and September 2016. The upper line indicates the total number of TLDs/SLDs, while the lower line indicates the number of DNSSEC-signed TLDs/SLDs. In that time interval the number of new TLDs increased by 250 and we observe roughly the same increase in the number of signed TLDs. The graph also shows a growth in a number of new

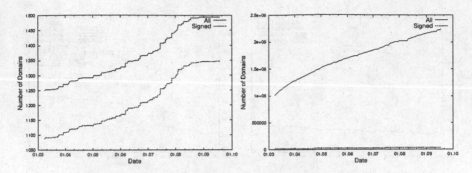

Fig. 2. All TLDs vs. signed TLDs (left). All SLDs vs. signed SLDs (right).

SLDs. However, in contrast to the steady increase in signed TLDs, the results indicate a negligible increase in newly signed SLDs. The significant and constant growth in the number of signed TLDs indicates that there is an increased awareness to DNSSEC adoption. One of the main reason for lack of increase in SLDs is that many registrars still do not support automated procedures for DNSSEC.

Crypto-Algorithms in Signed Domains. The signed zones can use an arbitrary number of DNSSEC-standardised algorithms[1]. In addition, [RFC4641,RFC6781] list mandatory support for RSA and recommend avoiding large keys (specifying a range of 512–2048 bits for (ZSK) key size and recommending a default value of 1024 bits); in order to avoid fragmentation, communication and computation overhead and other problems with large keys and signatures. In particular, [RFC6781] states "it is estimated that most zones can safely use 1024-bit keys for at least the next ten years".

We analysed our dataset of signed domains, and plot the results in Fig. 3. For TLDs, the upper two lines are RSA-SHA256 and RSA-SHA1-NSEC3 correspondingly. The two lines in the bottom are RSA-SHA512 and RSA-SHA1. For SLDs, the upper four lines correspond to RSA-SHA256, RSA-SHA1-NSEC3, RSA-SHA1 and ECDSA-P256-SHA256. DSA, RSA-SHA512 and ECDSA-P384-SHA384 are in the bottom.

Our measurement shows that there is hardly any support for other cryptographic algorithms, e.g., those that produce short signatures, such as ECC, since the motivation to add more overhead to the transmitted data is low. Indeed, most domains adopt different versions of RSA, which produces larger keys and signatures.

RSA, with different digest implementations (SHA1, SHA256, SHA512), dominates among the signed TLDs, and there is no support for other algorithms among the TLDs, Fig. 4. In contrast, there is some, albeit still limited, attempt to adopt also other cryptographic algorithms, such as DSA and EC in SLDs, see Fig. 3. Indeed, ECDSA-P256 is ranked third among the cryptographic

---

[1] http://www.iana.org/assignments/dns-sec-alg-numbers/dns-sec-alg-numbers.
xhtml.

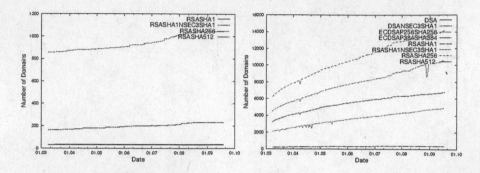

Fig. 3. DNSSEC algorithms adoption between March-September 2016 in signed TLDs (left) and signed SLDs (right).

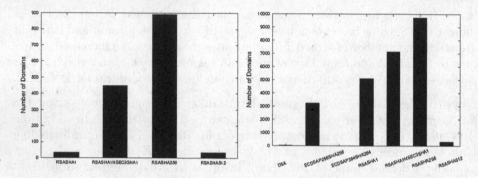

Fig. 4. DNSSEC algorithms in signed TLDs (left), in signed SLDs (right).

algorithms, just behind RSA-SHA1 (including RSA-SHA1 and RSA-SHA1-NSEC3) and RSA-SHA256. ECDSA-P256 is gaining more popularity and grows steadily. This also shows that more and more admins are adopting new algorithms to improve DNSSEC performance.

We measured the key sizes in use by the different variations of RSA algorithms, we plot our results in Fig. 5 on the right. It's a CDF of key size in signed domains. We can see about 34 % of TLDs and 52 % of SLDs are still using keys shorter than or equal to 1024 bits. As for keys only, almost 1.4M keys are below 1024 bits, and 10 K keys are 512 bits long. These are really vulnerable. [18] showed that factoring 512 bit keys on a cloud is a practical task. For updated statistics on keys and DNSSEC algorithms see our webpage.

We also checked the digest algorithms used in DNSSEC. There are mainly three digest algorithms employed by DNSSEC, SHA1, SHA256 and SHA512. SHA1 has been known to be considerably weak. [16] showed a collision attack against SHA1. Google also announced that they would completely block SHA1 certificates in 2017 [2]. Digests are used in three ways in DNSSEC. First, in digital signature RRSIG along with RSA or ECC. Second, for authenticated proof of the non-existence, in NSEC3. Third, as anchor for Key Signing Key, in DS.

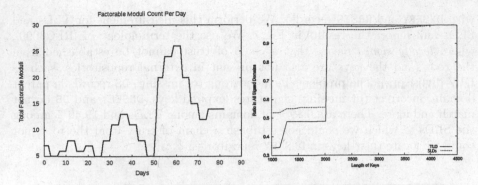

Fig. 5. Keys with even RSA moduli (left) and key sizes in TLDs and SLDs (right).

For digests in signature `RRSIG` as can be seen in Fig. 3 on the left for TLDs, SHA256 is still the most popular and grows faster than the others. The growth in adoption of SHA1 slows down. And there's almost no increase in SHA512. This indicates that there is an increased awareness to sunset SHA1 and promote SHA256, while SHA512 is still not essential. When we look at the SLDs on the right, SHA1 (including RSA-SHA1 and RSA-SHA1-NSEC3, 2nd and 3rd lines) has almost the same share as SHA256 (including RSA-SHA256 and ECDSA-P256, 1st and 4th lines). The good point is that SHA256 is growing faster than SHA1. But it still needs time to move from SHA1 to SHA256.

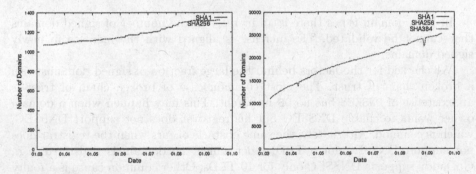

Fig. 6. DNSSEC DS digest algorithms between March-September 2016 in signed TLDs (left), in signed SLDs (right).

For digests in `DS` this is even more important, since a `DS` RR is the entry point of a zone. As can be seen in Fig. 6, SHA256 overwhelms SHA1 in TLDs. Among SLDs, number of domains using `DS` with SHA256 grows much faster than that using SHA1 only. This indicates the increased awareness of vulnerability of SHA1.

Broken Chain of Trust. Finally we evaluate whether the DNS resolvers can establish a chain of trust from the root to the signed domains (i.e., those with `DNSKEY` and `RRSIG` records). We perform this measurement for TLDs and SLDs and report the results in Fig. 7. We use the terminology of [RFC3090], where *locally signed* means that a chain of trust cannot be established from the root (and the keys are also not present in external repositories, such as DLV dlv.isc.org). The problems include wrong (or missing) `DS` records in parent domain, incorrect (or missing) signatures, expired keys, `DNSKEY` and `DS` do not match and more. There are 0.89 % of domains among TLDs and 19.46 % among the SLDs to which we could not establish a chain of trust from the root, nor could we locate their keys in `DNSKEY` repositories.

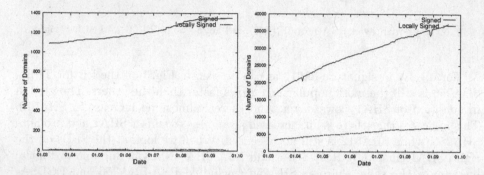

Fig. 7. TLDs with broken chain of trust vs. secure (left). SLDs with broken chain of trust vs. secure (right).

In both domain types there is an increase in the number of signed domains that cannot be validated. The increase is aligned with the increase in newly signed domains.

We checked for the factors behind the large fraction of signed domains with a broken chain of trust. The most common case of broken chain of trust is an existence of `DNSKEY` but no `DS` in parent. This may happen when a domain owner wants to enable DNSSEC but his registrar does not support DNSSEC, which is common. Alternately, the same obstacle occurs when the registrar does not support DNSSEC for a TLD under which the domain is registered, e.g., GoDaddy supports DNSSEC only for 10 TLDs. Other common cause is a faulty `DS` record. This may happen when the domain operator transfers/updates the domain/key or changes the name servers.

To fix these problems, it is recommended to move domains to the registrars that support DNSSEC. If the TLD is not supported by the registrar, the DLV service should be utilised. To track for misconfigurations, we provide our tool for a public use, which can be accessed at: https://dnssec.cad.sit.fraunhofer.de.

RSA Keys with Even Moduli. Distinct moduli that share a prime factor will result in public keys that appear different but whose private keys are efficiently computable by calculating the greatest common divisor (GCD). For calculation of GCD of every pair of keys we followed the approach in [4] and used the *fast* *pairwise GCD* quasilinear-time algorithm for factoring a collection of integers into coprimes; we compiled and used the source code (https://factorable.net/resources.html) provided by [4].

After calculating group-GCD on all the DNSKEY records, we found 16 even RSA moduli.

The keys with even RSA moduli belonged to domains hosted or registered by known registrars, such as Network Solutions, GoDaddy, OnlineNic. In Fig. 5 we plot our measurements of factorable RSA keys, collected over a period of March-September 2016.

5   Conclusion

In this work we measured adoption of DNSSEC among TLDs and SLDs, and then studied the security of the signed domains. To that end, we designed and developed a tool that periodically collects data from signed domains, analyses it and produces reports with statistics. Our data collection indicates that a large fraction of signed domains have cryptographic misconfigurations, leading to insecurity. The misconfigurations are either due to a broken chain of trust, preventing the DNS resolver from validating the supplied DNS records, or due to vulnerable cryptographic keys.

We developed an online service for providing updated reports and statistics on adoption of DNSSEC, vulnerabilities and misconfigurations: https://dnssec.cad.sit.fraunhofer.de.

Acknowledgments. The research reported in this paper has been supported by the German Federal Ministry of Education and Research (BMBF) and by the Hessian Ministry of Science and the Arts within CRISP www.crisp-da.de/.

References

1. Anderson, D.: Splinternet behind the great firewall of china. Queue **10**(11), 40 (2012)
2. Google Online Security Blog: An Update on SHA-1 Certificates in Chrome (2015). https://security.googleblog.com/2015/12/an-update-on-sha-1-certificates-in.html
3. Fukuda, K., Sato, S., Mitamura, T.: A technique for counting DNSSEC validators. In: 2013 Proceedings IEEE INFOCOM, pp. 80–84. IEEE (2013)
4. Heninger, N., Durumeric, Z., Wustrow, E., Halderman, J.A.: Mining your PS, QS: detection of widespread weak keys in network devices. In: Presented as part of the 21st USENIX Security Symposium (USENIX Security 12), pp. 205–220 (2012)
5. Herzberg, A., Shulman, H.: Fragmentation Considered Poisonous: or one-domain-to-rule-them-all.org. In: The Conference on Communications and Network Security IEEE CNS 2013, Washington, D.C., U.S. IEEE (2013)
6. Herzberg, A., Shulman, H.: Socket overloading for fun and cache poisoning. In: C.N.P. Jr. (ed.) ACM Annual Computer Security Applications Conference (ACM ACSAC), New Orleans, Louisiana, U.S, December 2013

7. Herzberg, A., Shulman, H.: Vulnerable delegation of DNS resolution. In: Crampton, J., Jajodia, S., Mayes, K. (eds.) ESORICS 2013. LNCS, vol. 8134, pp. 219–236. Springer, Heidelberg (2013). doi:10.1007/978-3-642-40203-6_13

8. Herzberg, A., Shulman, H.: Negotiating DNSSEC algorithms over legacy proxies. In: Gritzalis, D., Kiayias, A., Askoxylakis, I. (eds.) CANS 2014. LNCS, vol. 8813, pp. 111–126. Springer, Heidelberg (2014). doi:10.1007/978-3-319-12280-9_8

9. Herzberg, A., Shulman, H.: Retrofitting security into network protocols: the case of DNSSEC. Internet Comput. **18**(1), 66–71 (2014). IEEE

10. Herzberg, A., Shulman, H., Crispo, B.: Less is more: cipher-suite negotiation for DNSSEC. In: Computer Security Applications Conference, ACSAC 2014. Annual. IEEE (2014)

11. Hu, M.: Taxonomy of the snowden disclosures. Wash Lee L. Rev. **72**, 1679–1989 (2015)

12. Kaminsky, D.: It's the End of the Cache As We Know It. In Black Hat conference, August 2008. http://www.blackhat.com/presentations/bh-jp-08/bh-jp-08-Kaminsky/BlackHat-Japan-08-Kaminsky-DNS08-BlackOps.pdf

13. Lian, W., Rescorla, E., Shacham, H., Savage, S.: Measuring the practical impact of DNSSEC deployment. In: Proceedings of USENIX Security (2013)

14. Shulman, H., Waidner, M.: Fragmentation considered leaking: port inference for DNS poisoning. In: Boureanu, I., Owesarski, P., Vaudenay, S. (eds.) ACNS 2014. LNCS, vol. 8479, pp. 531–548. Springer, Heidelberg (2014). doi:10.1007/978-3-319-07536-5_31

15. Internet Society: ICANNs 2013 RAA Requires Domain Name Registrars To Support DNSSEC (2013)

16. Stevens, M., Karpman, P., Peyrin, T.: Freestart collision for full sha-1. Cryptology ePrint Archive, Report 2015/967 (2015). http://eprint.iacr.org/2015/967

17. Stewart, J.: DNS cache poisoning-the next generation (2003)

18. Valenta, L., Cohney, S., Liao, A., Fried, J., Bodduluri, S., Heninger, N.: Factoring as a service

19. Yang, H., Osterweil, E., Massey, D., Lu, S., Zhang, L.: Deploying cryptography in internet-scale systems: a case study on DNSSEC. IEEE Trans. Dependable Secur. Comput. **8**(5), 656–669 (2011)

Integral Privacy

Vicenç Torra[1](✉) and Guillermo Navarro-Arribas[2]

[1] School of Informatics, University of Skövde, Skövde, Sweden
vtorra@his.se
[2] Department of Information and Communication Engineering,
Universitat Autònoma de Barcelona, Catalonia, Spain
guillermo.navarro@uab.cat

Abstract. When considering data provenance some problems arise from the need to safely handle provenance related functionality. If some modifications have to be performed in a data set due to provenance related requirements, e.g. remove data from a given user or source, this will affect not only the data itself but also all related models and aggregated information obtained from the data. This is specially aggravated when the data are protected using a privacy method (e.g. masking method), since modification in the data and the model can leak information originally protected by the privacy method. To be able to evaluate privacy related problems in data provenance we introduce the notion of integral privacy as compared to the well known definition of differential privacy.

1 Introduction

Data provenance permits to track where data come from and how these data have been combined in order to produce new data elements. Data provenance is used to improve data quality, and have been used in a quite number of different areas including scientific data, e-science, accounting (financial data), and medical data [1,3,9].

Data privacy is the area that studies methods and techniques to avoid the involuntary release of sensitive data [5,10,11]. Methods are used because of companies own interest to keep their information private, but also because of existing regulations. In 2016 the new EU General Data Protection Regulation was entered into force, a regulation that shall apply from 25 May 2018. This regulation consolidates two rights: the right to be forgotten and the right to amend.

Companies need appropriate software so that they can guarantee these two rights to their customers. Note that the right to be forgotten does not only imply that customers can force the deletion of records with their data, but also that aggregated data and inferences extracted from their data need to be reconsidered and eventually modified or also deleted.

Data provenance has a tight relation with data privacy. On the one hand, data provenance is essential to implement these two rights. We need to keep track of how data is processed and aggregated in order to know what needs to be deleted, amended or reconsidered when records are deleted or amended.

S. Foresti and G. Persiano (Eds.): CANS 2016, LNCS 10052, pp. 661–669, 2016.
DOI: 10.1007/978-3-319-48965-0_44

Otherwise, we will need to delete all what follows from a record once there is a requirement to delete such record.

On the other hand, data provenance poses specific questions to data privacy. Note that provenance information may be confidential, provenance information cannot be modified at will, etc. See e.g. [2,7], for a review of problems and solutions related to data provenance and data privacy.

In this paper we discuss privacy models. We present a new privacy model insipired on data provenance, on the two mentioned rights, and how all these aspects relate to data privacy.

We call this model integral privacy, to compare it with differential privacy [6]. As we will see later, while differential privacy focus on the *output* of a function from the data (a computation), this model focus on the *input*. While differential privacy computes differences between outputs, here we consider a set of modifications of the input.

The structure of the paper is as follows. In Sect. 2 we review the notation we use in the paper. In Sect. 3 we present our definition and in Sect. 4 we compare integral privacy with differential privacy. The paper finishes with a summary and a discussion of future work.

2   Notation and Problem Set up

We will consider a set X (a file or a database) to which we have applied some modifications μ to reach a data set X'. We will denote the fact that X' is constructed from X with some modifications μ by the expression $X' = X + \mu$.

Then, using algorithm A we extract knowledge G and G' from X and X', respectively. If we apply a masking method ρ to X and X' we get χ and χ' from which we obtain knowledge Γ and Γ' using algorithm A. Figure 1 represents these data sets, methods and algorithms. This conforms the full picture of our scenario. Provenance data are included in all the data sets and the figure shows all possible cases one can find in processing the original data set X.

3   Integral Privacy

In this section we propose our definition for privacy. It focuses on the modification μ that apply to the original dataset X following the notation introduced in Sect. 2. We make explicit our assumptions on what an intruder may know. We then state the intruders goal. We consider that the intruder can be a person that is working outside the data holder (the company with the database X) or an insider with partial access to the data and the knowledge extracted (either from the database or possibly also using some information obtained from other sources).

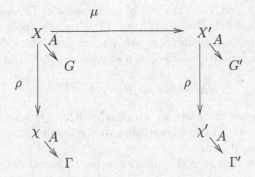

Fig. 1. Original file X with protected file χ and knowledge/models G and Γ extracted from X and χ, respectively. Updated file X' and protected file χ' with knowledge/models G' and Γ' extracted from X and χ', respectively. Protection method ρ and knowledge discovery algorithm A.

3.1 Specific Scenario #1

To introduce the notion of integral privacy we first consider an scenario where the intruder knows: $S \subset X$, G, G'. That is, the intruder has partial knowledge of the data in the database (the worst case scenario is when $S = X$, the best case scenario is when $S = \emptyset$).

The privacy requirements are that intruders cannot be able to determine μ and $S' \subseteq X \setminus S$ with certainty. That is, that the intruder cannot find neither records from the file, nor information about the modifications.

3.2 Intruder's Goal

The main goal of the intruder can be summarized as follows. Given $S \subset X$, G, G', find the set of possible modifications μ that are consistent with data $S \subseteq X$ and knowledge G and G', and find elements in $X \setminus S$. Under the transparency principle, we may assume that the intruder knows the algorithm A used to generate G.

We illustrate this problem with an example. The example uses ID3, one of the simplest decision tree learning algorithms for categorical data and with no pruning. In the worst case scenario (i.e., when $S = X$), and assuming that G is obtained by means of the application of the ID3 algorithm to X, this problem is to find the modifications μ such that $G = ID3(X)$ and $G' = ID3(X + \mu)$. In the general setting, the problem is to find the following set of modifications, for a given algorithm A

$$\mathcal{M} = \{\mu | G = A(X) \text{ and } G' = A(X + \mu)\}.$$

On the Set of Modifications. For a large number of machine learning algorithms, the set of modifications $\mathcal{M}$ is not a singleton. To support this statement, let us consider *Gen* and *Gen'* the set of generators of G and G', respectively. That is, the set of data that lead to G and G' when we apply to them the algorithm A. Then, note that when there are several generators *Gen* and *Gen'*, the set of possible transformations μ is not a singleton. Note that

$$\cup_{g\in Gen,g\in Gen'}\{g'-g\}\subseteq \mathcal{M}.$$

Now we consider a few cases in which algorithms ensure that a model has different generators. In all these cases, due to the result above, we will have sets $\mathcal{M}$ that are not a singleton.

We first consider that A is the algorithm for 1-nearest neighbor. It is known that the model built can be represented with a Voronoi tesselation. Let X be defined in a domain D. When all regions are open (i.e., as in Fig. 2 (left)), then we can construct sets $\hat{X}$ with $\hat{X}\cap X=\emptyset$ and such that generate the same map. They consist of displacing the points in X out of the map. See Fig. 2 (center). When there are closed regions (i.e., as in Fig. 2 (right)), the points of closed regions cannot be changed. So, in case that another set $\hat{X}$ can generate the same map, there will be points that cannot be changed $\hat{X}\cap X\neq\emptyset$.

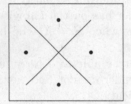 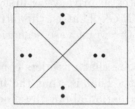 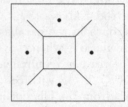

Fig. 2. Three Voronoi maps. The first one (left) containing only open regions, the second one (center) with the same regions but with the original generators and a new set of generators. The third one (right) with a closed region.

In these constructions, we were considering that X and $\hat{X}$ had the same number of points (records). We will consider a more general case now in which X and $\hat{X}$ have a different number of records. This causes that the model from X and the model from $\hat{X}$ have a different number of regions.

In a classification problem, what is rellevant for our model is the class associated to each element. In the case of Voronoi tesselations for a 1-nearest neighbor this can be modeled with colors (or assignments) to each region. Let $G_c(p)$ be the color assigned to position p in the map. We say that two Voronoi tesselations G and G' are color-equivalent if $G_c(p)=G'_c(p)$ for all p even in the case that the number of regions is different.

Let us consider the case of a Voronoi tesselation in which the color of adjacent regions is all different. Then, the question is whether there exist a set $\hat{X}$ (with more records than X) such that the Voronoi tesselation generated from $\hat{X}$ is color-equivalent to the one in X.

Let x be the points in X. Let a, c be two points of X such that they generate a border in G. Let z be the point, $z = (a+c)/2$. Then, the points $a_c = (a+z)/2$ and the point $c_a = (c+z)/2$ are included in $\hat{X}$.

We can prove that all p that are at the same distance from a and c, they are also at the same distance from a_c and c_a. This can be proven as the two right triangles defined by the points (a_c, z, p) and (c_a, z, p) have two sides with the same length. So, the third should also have the same length. This implies that, at least for some examples, the border of the regions we have in X are also border of regions in $\hat{X}$. In such cases the procedure results into another set $\hat{X}$ (with a different number of elements) that represents the same map. That is, the model built from X and $\hat{X}$ is the same: $G = A(X) = \hat{G} = A(\hat{X})$.

Decision tree learning returns a decision tree from a data set. In the case of ID3, the tree is built for categorical data recursively selecting at each point the attribute that maximizes the information gain (or minimizes the entropy). Data sets that lead to the same entropy will produce the same trees. Nevertheless, even in the case of different entropies, the trees will be the same if the set of attributes that maximize the entropy are the same.

For any linear regression model, the number of sets that can generate the model is infinite. However, when constraints exist for the generators (e.g. integer data in a given domain) this may not be the case.

We have shown that when different datasets can generate the same knowledge, $\mathcal{M}$ is not a singleton. In addition to that, for some algorithms, when μ is a set of valid modifications, then there is another set $\mu \subseteq \mu'$ that is also a valid set of modifications. The following example illustrates this case.

Example 1. Let X be a set of n records where $n-1$ of them are of class $+$ and 1 is of class $-$. Then, let $G = A(X)$ be a decision tree with two branches and one question. Let $G' = A(X')$ be a decision tree with a single node and no question assigning always the class $+$. Then, it is clear that all modifications in $\mathcal{M}$ include the deletion of the record in class $-$.

Therefore, if μ corresponds to the deletion of the record in class $-$ and μ' are all other possible modifications, then μ' includes μ. In this framework, we can consider the set (or sets) of possible transformations, and the lattice defined from this set of transformations and the subset inclusion. Note that it is also rellevant to consider the intersection of all $m \in \mathcal{M}$. In the example, this intersection corresponds to the deletion of the record of class $-$. Similarly, it is relevant to consider the minimal elements of the lattice. That is, the modifications that are minimal with respect to the set inclusion. The minimal modifications are rellevant for an intruder.

We finish this discussion with the following remarks.

- When we only allow deletions, the number of modifications is finite (for a finite database). Therefore, the set of minimal modifications is also finite.
- The set of generators of a real data set is smaller than the set of possible generators. In real applications, not all modifications are possible, and not all possible modifications are equally plausible.

3.3   Privacy Problem

In order to take into account the intruder goal described in Sect. 3.2 we consider the following privacy problem.

Find algorithms A that maximize the uncertainty of the intruder (with respect to the set of possible modifications). That is, we are interested in machine learning methods A such that the set

$$\mathcal{M} = \{\mu | G = A(X) \text{ and } G' = A(X + \mu)\}. \tag{1}$$

is large, and such that

$$\cap_{m \in \mathcal{M}} m = \emptyset. \tag{2}$$

The rational of this definition is that intruders cannot use their knowledge on the set of possible modifications to infer that a particular modification has taken place. The larger the set of modifications, the larger the uncertainty of the intruder. In addition, we do not want that even in the case of a large set, all modifications agree on a small set. This is to avoid situations as the one in Example 1.

3.4   Integral Privacy Definitions

On the basis of the previous discussion we introduce some definitions for privacy.

We define i-integral privacy when $\mathcal{M}$ defined according to Eq. 1 is *large* and such that the intersection in Eq. 2 is empty.

We define integral privacy à la k-anonymity, when the set $\mathcal{M}$ contains at least k alternatives.

We define k-anonymous integral privacy when the set $\mathcal{M}$ has at least k minimal elements.

With these definitions, we can consider solving the privacy problem above (for integral privacy) combining machine learning algorithms with data privacy algorithms. In this case, we define $\hat{A}(X) = A(\rho(X))$. Then, the scenario is similar to the one above but permits us to find good masking methods for a given algorithm A. The formulation is as follows.

Given X, G, G', and an algorithm A, a good masking method ρ is the one that makes the set

$$\mathcal{M} = \{\mu | G = A(\rho(X)) and G' = A(\rho(X + \mu))\}$$

large and such that $\cap_{m \in \mathcal{M}} m = \emptyset$.

We can consider additional restrictions for the set $\mathcal{M}$ as above.

3.5   Other Specific Scenarios

Section 3.1 introduced the main scenario that motivates the definition of integral privacy, but one can find other cases and possible scenarios. Here we provide a brief description of 4 more cases that can arise from the main problem description from Sect. 2.

- **Scenario #2.** Known by the intruder: χ, χ'. Intruders should not determine neither $S \subseteq X$ nor μ with certainty. That is, the intruder cannot find neither records from the file, nor information about the modifications.
- **Scenario #3.** Known by the intruder: X', G, G'. Similar to the first scenario from Sect. 3.1 but with X' instead of X.
- **Scenario #4 and #5.** Similar to cases #1 and #3 but knowledge is generated from $\rho(X)$. That is, we are considering Γ and Γ'. Under the transparency principle, we can also presume that the intruder is aware of methods ρ and A.

These three scenarios complement the one introduced previously and can contribute with more examples of the utility of our definition of integral privacy. It is important to note that some of these scenarios are equivalent to already existing problems in data privacy. For instance, scenario #2 can be considered as the problem of publishing protected dynamic data. Note also that when in scenario #1 we have that the algorithm A is a masking method ρ, it can be seen as equivalent to the second scenario.

4   Integral Privacy and Differential Privacy

Our model can be considered as related to differential privacy. Nevertheless, the focus of our model differs to the focus in differential privacy.

In differential privacy, the main issue is to compute a query in a way that the output is insensitive to addition (or removal) of a single element of the database. This is achieved considering this computation as randomized and requiring that the distributions of the two outputs (the output of the computation on the original data set and the one of adding an element to it) are approximately the same. That is, for all X and x,

$$Distr(G(X)) \sim Distr(G(X + x)).$$

Note that this is for all databases X and for all possible elements that can be added into a database. Algorithms exist for achieving this goal, although for some type of data the noise required to ensure enough similarity may be very large. See e.g. [8].

Let us consider this problem from a different perspective. Let us assume that we know $G(X)$ and $G(X + x)$ (or their distribution) and that we know X. Consider for example the case of applying a decision tree learning algorithm to a data set. So $G(X)$ is a decision tree obtained from X using the algorithm. Then, $G(X + x)$ is also a decision tree. It can be the case that this other decision tree is quite different to $G(X)$ but that the set of possible records x that have generated $G(X + x)$ is very large.

For example, let X be a set with all records in the same class $+$ and then any record in class $-$ expands the tree. Alternatively, let $X + \mu$ be a set of records with classes + and − but with most of the records in + and only a few in − (so few that the deletion of one by a decision tree learning with pruning removes the − class). For this example, we can consider that privacy is guaranteed at an appropriate level. Note that, in general, differential privacy (on $G(X)$ vs. $G(X + x)$) would not consider the process safe.

If we are interested in both types of privacy, we can define the concept of differintegral privacy that forces the data to satisfy differential privacy and integral privacy at appropriate levels. The term differintegral is borrowed from fractional calculus [4].

5   Conclusions

In this paper we have introduced the definition of integral privacy. The main goal is to provide tools for researchers to study data privacy when provenance data is present. We have provided a motivating scenario that yields the concept of integral privacy. This definition can be further developed in future works to comprise a framework for evaluating privacy in data provenance. Further work is needed to compute the set of modifications in different scenarios. This will permit us to evaluate methods with respect to disclosure risk and utility. Another line of future research corresponds to the case when instead of a single method A for extracting knowledge, we apply several of them $A_1, A_2, \ldots, A_n$ and thus we need to consider G_1 and G'_1, G_2 and G'_2, $\ldots$, G_n and G'_n.

Acknowledgments. Partial support by the Spanish MINECO (project TIN2014-55243-P) and Catalan AGAUR (2014-SGR-691) is acknowledged.

References

1. Barbier, G., Feng, Z., Gundecha, P., Liu, H.: Provenance Data in Social Media. Morgan & Claypool Publishers, San Rafael (2013)
2. Bertino, E., Ghinita, G., Kantarcioglu, M., Nguyen, D., Park, J., Sandhu, R., Sultana, S., Thuraisingham, B., Xu, S.: A roadmap for privacy-enhanced secure data provenance. J. Intell. Inf. Syst. **43**, 481–501 (2014)
3. Buneman, P., Khanna, S., Wang-Chiew, T.: A characterization of data provenance. In: International Conference on Database Theory, pp. 316–330. Springer
4. Das, S.: Functional Fractional Calculus. Springer, Dordrecht (2008)
5. Domingo-Ferrer, J., Torra, V.: A quantitative comparison of disclosure control methods for microdata. In: Doyle, P., Lane, J.I., Theeuwes, J.J.M., Zayatz, L., (eds.) Confidentiality, Disclosure, Data Access: Theory and Practical Applications for Statistical Agencies, North-Holland, pp. 111–134 (2001)
6. Dwork, C.: Differential privacy. In: Bugliesi, M., Preneel, B., Sassone, V., Wegener, I. (eds.) ICALP 2006. LNCS, vol. 4052, pp. 1–12. Springer, Heidelberg (2006)
7. Hasan, R., Sion, R., Winslett, M.: (2007) Introducing secure provenance: problems and challenges. In: Proceedings StorageSST. ACM, New York (2007)
8. Muralidhar, K., Sarathy, R.: Generating sufficiency-based non-synthetic perturbed data. Trans. Data Priv. **1**(1), 17–33 (2008)

9. Simmhan, Y.L., Plale, B., Gannon, D.: A survey of data provenance in e-science. ACM Sigmod Rec. **34**(3), 31–36 (2005)
10. Torra, V., Navarro-Arribas, G.: Data Privacy, WIREs Data Mining and Knowledge Discovery, 4(4), 269–280 (2014)
11. Winkler, W.E.: Re-identification methods for masked microdata. In: Domingo-Ferrer, J., Torra, V. (eds.) PSD 2004. LNCS, vol. 3050, pp. 216–230. Springer, Heidelberg (2004)

Sharing Is Caring, or Callous?

Yu Pu[✉] and Jens Grossklags

College of Information Sciences and Technology,
The Pennsylvania State University, University Park, USA
{yxp134,jensg}@ist.psu.edu

Abstract. The practice of third-party applications (social apps) on social networks sites (SNSs) to collect information about users' friends has raised awareness of the problem known as *interdependent privacy*. Although studies have quantified the value which app users place on their friends' personal information, i.e., interdependent privacy value, few have investigated factors that affect the valuation of interdependent privacy. In particular, research indicates that social capital, which is an immaterial resource that can yield positive social outcomes, plays an important role in individuals' decision-making. Motivated by these works, we study the complex and yet undetermined relationship between interdependent privacy value and social capital. In addition, in order to gain a thorough understanding of interdependent privacy valuation, our study also examines its relationships with factors such as app data collection context (i.e., whether or not data collection is relevant to app performance), individuals' number of friends within SNSs, and demographics.

Keywords: Interdependent privacy · Social app adoption · Social capital · Social network sites · App data collection context

1 Introduction

Privacy risks associated with third-party applications (apps) on social network sites (SNSs) are increasing commensurate with apps' popularity. In addition, the growing relevance of interdependent privacy issues has introduced a new dimension of privacy concerns in the context of social apps. In a nutshell, interdependency of privacy refers to the phenomenon that within a networked system, privacy of individuals not only depends on their own behaviors, but is also influenced by decisions of others [1]. In particular, in the interconnected setting of SNSs we can observe that sharing decisions of users allow apps to easily collect personal information about their friends, thereby emphasizing the problem of interdependent privacy [13].

In our previous work, we have investigated the monetary value app users place on information about their friends within SNSs [14,15], which we referred to as the *value of interdependent privacy*. We further conducted an exploratory study to build a model about the formation process of interdependent privacy valuation [14]. However, several questions remained about factors serving as

© Springer International Publishing AG 2016
S. Foresti and G. Persiano (Eds.): CANS 2016, LNCS 10052, pp. 670–680, 2016.
DOI: 10.1007/978-3-319-48965-0_45

antecedents of interdependent privacy value, and the impact of some factors was only partially examined [14]. The current study reports the results from a secondary data analysis of our previously collected data (from [14]) capturing additional in-depth analysis of several explanatory factors of the valuation of interdependent privacy in the context of social app adoption.

A particular key motivator for our study is the complex and yet still empirically undetermined relationship between social capital and interdependent privacy [8]. Broadly speaking, social capital is a resource accumulated through individuals' interactions with others [5]. In particular, there are two kinds of social capital: bridging social capital and bonding social capital [16]. Bridging social capital, which is linked to loose connections between acquaintances, helps individuals to broaden world views and opens up opportunities for information gathering [22]. Bonding social capital, which derives from close-knit relationships between family members and close friends, is associated with trust and reciprocity, and provides strong emotional or substantive support for one another [16,22].

In this study, we aim to empirically investigate how social capital, both bridging social capital and bonding social capital, influences the value of interdependent privacy in the context of social app adoption. In addition, in order to gain a thorough understanding of interdependent privacy valuation, we also want to explore how it is affected by other factors such as app data collection context, number of friends, concern for friends' privacy, and demographics. We conduct a series of regression analyses on data obtained from our previous work to address these research goals.

Although we fail to find a significant association between bridging social capital and interdependent privacy value, our analysis suggests that the value app users place on their friends' information is reversely related to their perceived level of bonding social capital. In addition, we find the impact of bonding social capital on interdependent privacy value varies with app data collection context. We further detect a cross-over interaction between number of friends and data collection context on interdependent privacy valuation. In particular, we find when app users notice data collection about friends is useful for app performance, the more friends they have, the less value they place on their friends' information.

2 Related Work

The emergence of SNSs provides individuals with many new ways to interact with a wide variety of others, ranging from close contacts to strangers [22], which raises the question how engaging with SNSs influences one's ability to form and maintain social capital. A stream of research provides empirical support for the positive relationship between the use of SNSs and accumulation of social capital [6,18]. In contrast to these studies which treat SNS use as a monolithic activity, other works address how social capital is affected by different types of SNS use [2,3,7], finding that not all usage of SNSs results in social capital growth.

Only a few academic works explore how privacy is related to social capital. Particularly, Ellison et al. [8] argue that in order to accumulate social capital from interactions within SNSs, one must be willing to disclose information about the self. Stutzman et al. [19] demonstrate that the relationship between privacy concern and social capital is mediated by one's willingness to disclose on SNSs.

These studies investigate how disclosure behaviors and privacy concerns influence social capital outcomes, but not the other way around. Our study examines whether and how social capital can be used to predict privacy valuation. Applied to our context of interest, we aim to uncover the impact of social capital on the value app users place on their friends' information.

3   Development of Research Question

Social capital and privacy have a complex relationship [8]. Considering also interdependent privacy, its relationship with social capital adds an additional layer of complexity. On the one hand, previous research indicates disclosure behaviors are positively related to social capital perceptions [8,19]. In other words, the more information one releases online, the more likely one is going to accumulate social capital. In our study's context, app users who have a higher level of social capital might be more open to disclose information *about themselves*. However, it remains unknown as to which degree such individuals are also more willing to share *others' information*. In fact, we may posit the existence of a spill-over effect such that when individuals are more open to share their own information, they are also more likely to engage in disclosure behaviors about their friends' information. Applying this reasoning to the valuation of interdependent privacy, app users with a higher level of social capital may be more likely to value their friends' privacy less.

On the other hand, social capital, which is accumulated through interactions within communities, is an immaterial resource from which individuals gain benefits such as emotional support [16], exposure to diverse ideas [22], and chances of accessing non-redundant information [12]. In order to maintain such immaterial resources and continue to enjoy their benefits, individuals, including app users in our context, would likely think twice before taking actions that are harmful to other community members. In this manner, the higher the level of social capital app users have, the less likely they are going to reveal their friends' information to apps, i.e., they place a higher monetary value on their friends privacy. These two contradictory perspectives motivate us to investigate what role social capital plays in the valuation process of interdependent privacy.

In addition, prior research reveals that individuals' privacy concerns are influenced by whether or not information requests are context-relevant [10]. For example, Wang et al. [21] find users are typically unconcerned about giving away their friends' birthday information to a birthday app, but become uncomfortable when that app also tries to get access to information unrelated to its stated purpose. Therefore, in our study, we also examine how *app data collection context* impacts the value social app users place on their friends' information.

When we refer to the interdependent privacy *value*, we mean the monetary value an app user places on the profile information of all his/her friends within

SNSs. As different app users have a different number of friends on SNSs, we are interested in investigating the impact of the self-reported *number of friends* on interdependent privacy valuation. Further, our previous research reveals individuals' privacy concerns are significantly associated with privacy values [14]. Our secondary analysis aims to confirm this relationship. In addition, we study whether interdependent privacy values vary with demographic information such as app users' gender, age, education level, and income level.

To sum up, in order to better explain the valuation process of interdependent privacy in app adoption contexts, our study empirically addresses the following two-part research question:

RQ a: *What roles do bridging and bonding social capital play in individuals' valuation of interdependent privacy in the scenario of social app adoption?*
RQ b: *What roles do app data collection context, number of friends within SNSs, concern for friends' privacy, and demographics play in individuals' valuation of interdependent privacy in the scenario of social app adoption?*

4 Method

To address our two-part research question, we are conducting a secondary analysis of our collected data from an online survey with a population of social app users [14]. The survey included three parts.

In the first part, we collected participants' demographic information such as gender, age, education level, as well as income level. In addition, we also asked participants to report the number of friends they have on their primary SNS.

The second part implemented a conjoint analysis study to elicit the value participants place on their friends' information. In addition, in order to explore how app users' valuation of their *friends' privacy* is affected by different app data collection contexts, we introduced the following two treatment scenarios which were part of the conjoint study instructions:

T1: *The information the app collects about user's friends is not useful for app's functionality.*
T2: *The information the app collects about user's friends is useful for app's functionality.*

In the second part of our survey, we first randomly placed participants in one of the two treatment scenarios. Following the methodology of conjoint analysis (see details in [14]), we then asked participants to rank 9 different versions of an app which differed in the levels of four app attributes. Through analyzing participants' rankings of these app versions, we were able to quantify the value participants place on their friends' information (see details in [14]).

The last part of the survey included items that measure participants' perceptions of social capital, as well as concerns for interdependent privacy. To the extent possible, these items were based upon or motivated by previously validated instruments in order to increase reliability. With respect to social capital, both bridging social capital and bonding social capital were measured by five questions based on scales proposed by Williams [22]. Adapting from 4 items in Smith et al. [17] that measure own privacy concern, a similar set of questions was developed to assess individuals' concerns for friends' privacy. All items were measured on a Likert-type scale with $1 =$ strongly disagree to $5 =$ strongly agree.

5   Data Description

Data collection was conducted in June 2015. Our final sample includes responses of 295 participants for data analysis. Of the participants, 50.2 % are male and 49.8 % are female. Our sample covers a wide range of age categories, from 18 to over 50, as well as education levels, ranging from less than high school to higher education degrees such as PhD. In terms of income level, our participants have yearly incomes that range from less than \$25,000 to more than \$100,000. A majority of participants reported to have 201–500 friends on their primary SNS.

In the sample, 144 participants were assigned to T1 (app-irrelevant data collection context), and 151 were assigned to T2 (app-relevant data collection context). Following the methodology of conjoint analysis (see details in [14]), we calculated the interdependent privacy value for each treatment. On average, participants in T1 value their friends' information at \$1.01 ($SD = 2.00$), which is slightly larger than the monetary value, \$0.68 ($SD = 1.56$), that their counterparts in T2 place on friends' privacy.

We established three instruments to measure bridging social capital ($Mean = 3.57, SD = 0.66$), bonding social capital ($Mean = 3.07, SD = 0.87$), and interdependent privacy concern ($Mean = 4.37, SD = 0.72$). Each of these three instruments demonstrates a high value of Cronbach's alpha (0.78 for bridging social capital, 0.82 for bonding social capital, and 0.92 for interdependent privacy concern), indicating high reliability of these survey instruments.

6   Results

To investigate the two-part research question as to how the measured factors affect the value of interdependent privacy in social app adoption scenarios, we conduct a series of regression analyses. Specifically, we treat the value of interdependent privacy as the dependent variable, gender and treatment as categorical independent variables, and age, income level, education level, number of friends, privacy concern, bridging and bonding social capital as continuous independent variables.

Besides studying main effects of each independent variable, we also explore the possible interactions between these variables. Following the methodology used by Steinfield et al. [18], we analyze each new interaction term with a different regression model, i.e., Model 1 & 2. Specifically, besides independent variables, Model 1 explores how number of friends interacts with treatment. By including another interaction term, Model 2 considers both the interaction between number of friends and treatment, and the interaction between bonding social capital and treatment. We show results of both regression models in Table 1.

6.1 Model 1

Regarding the effects of demographic factors in Model 1, female participants value friends' information higher than male ($p < 0.05$); and older individuals are more likely to express a higher interdependent privacy valuation than younger participants ($p < 0.01$). However, neither education level nor income level are significantly related to the value of friends' information.

When it comes to main effects of social capital, we find both bridging and bonding social capital have negative effects on privacy valuation. However, only the impact of bonding social capital is significant ($p < 0.1$). The influence of bridging social capital on interdependent privacy valuation is not only small, i.e., $\beta = -0.02$, but also insignificant.

In addition, interdependent privacy concern is positively and significantly associated with the value of interdependent privacy ($p < 0.05$), which is in line with our previous findings [14].

For treatment and number of friends, we not only observe significant main effects ($p < 0.1$ and $p < 0.05$, respectively), but we also notice a significant interaction between them ($p < 0.05$). We plot the interaction effect in Fig. 1, where a larger value on the horizontal line indicates a higher self-reported number of friends. We notice that for individuals in T1, where friends' data is irrelevant for apps' functionality, the more friends participants have, the higher the value they place on interdependent privacy. However, in the case of relevant data collection, social app users with a larger number of friends on their primary SNS tend to value the privacy of all their friends less.

6.2 Model 2

Model 2 extends the previous model by also exploring the interaction between bonding social capital and treatment. Compared with the results in Model 1, significances of all variables (except treatment) remain the same or improve when the new interaction term is added. Since the newly introduced interaction term involves treatment, we are not surprised at the change of the significance level associated with the treatment main effect. In terms of the direction of impact, only that of bridging social capital changes from negative to positive. Since the influence of bridging social capital on interdependent privacy value is very small and not significant, we believe its direction to be influenced by chance.

As expected, the interaction between bonding social capital and treatment is significant ($p < 0.1$), indicating the relationship between bonding social capital and interdependent privacy value varies with app data collection context. We visualize the interaction effect in Fig. 2. The horizontal line marks a Likert-type scale of bonding social capital, where a larger scale value indicates a higher level of bonding social capital. We observe that although in both treatments

Table 1. Regressions explaining value of interdependent privacy

Independent variables	Coefficients	
	Model 1	Model 2
Intercept	−1.47	−1.00
Gender:		
−Male	−0.50**	−0.48**
−Female	0.50**	0.48**
Age	0.20***	0.20***
Education level	−0.01	−0.01
Income level	0.04	0.06
Number of friends	0.27**	0.30***
Treatment:		
−T1	−1.32*	−0.15
−T2	1.32*	0.15
Bridging social capital	−0.02	0.002
Bonding social capital	−0.24*	−0.47***
Interdependent privacy concern	0.30**	0.30**
Number of friends × Treatment:		
−Number of friends × T1	0.39**	0.42***
−Number of friends × T2	−0.39**	−0.42***
Bonding social capital × Treatment:		
−Bonding social capital × T1	–	−0.42*
−Bonding social capital × T2	–	0.42*
$N = 295$	$R^2 = 0.12$	$R^2 = 0.13$
	$F = 4.03^{***}$	$F = 3.99^{***}$

$^*p < 0.1$, $^{**}p < 0.05$, $^{***}p < 0.01$
$^-$Variable not included in regression model

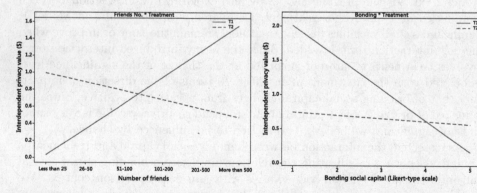

Fig. 1. Interaction of number of friends and treatment

Fig. 2. Interaction of bonding social capital and treatment

interdependent privacy value decreases with an increase of bonding social capital, the value changes more quickly in T1 than in T2.

7   Discussion

Our regression analysis first contributes to uncover the relationship between bonding social capital and interdependent privacy value. Specifically, we find that the value social app users place on friends' personal information is reversely related to their perceptions of bonding social capital. Recall the two contradictory views we have discussed regarding the association between interdependent privacy value and social capital. Our finding partly supports the view that individuals with a high level of social capital (in our case only bonding social capital) express a lower valuation for interdependent privacy; perhaps because they are more used to and are more willing to engage in disclosure behaviors. As to the other view that individuals are reluctant to reveal information about others in order to maintain and protect social capital, we believe such reluctance either does not exist or is outweighed by individuals' eagerness to grow bonding social capital through information disclosure behaviors.

Bonding social capital also significantly interacts with our treatment manipulation, i.e., app data collection context. Specifically, the difference as to the value of interdependent privacy between people with a high level of bonding social capital and others is larger in T1 (irrelevant data collection) than in T2 (relevant data collection). One possible explanation is that compared with app users with a high level of bonding social capital, the willingness to disclose friends' data by those with low bonding social capital perceptions is more sensitive to app data collection context. In particular, although individuals with a low level of bonding social capital are reluctant to disclose friends' data in the situation where such information is not useful to apps' functionality, they nevertheless become willing to reveal friends' data to apps when they believe such disclosure behaviors improve app performance. In contrast, individuals with a perceived high level of bonding social capital may assume that bonding social capital can consistently be gained through disclosure behaviors and may therefore be more used to and more prone to reveal information to others even if such information sharing is not useful to an app's functionality.

Although bonding social capital significantly impacts the valuation of interdependent privacy, our work suggests that bridging social capital does not. A possible explanation might be that bridging social capital is valued less or can be much more easily gained than bonding social capital [6]. As such, individuals are less likely to disclose information or to sacrifice privacy for gaining weak ties that correspond to bridging social capital.

We further find that the impact of number of friends on how much individuals value friends' information depends on app data collection context. Specifically, we detect a significant cross-over interaction between number of friends and treatment. As anticipated, when data collection is not useful for an app's functionality (T1), the more friends individuals have, the more value they place on information of all their friends. However, we observe an opposite association in T2, i.e., individuals with more friends actually value their friends' information less. One possible explanation of this seemingly counter-intuitive finding is that in the case where shared data is relevant for an app's functionality, individuals might believe that sharing information about *more* friends results in even better app performance. As such, under this particular data collection context, individuals with more friends would be more willing to share all their friends' information, thereby reducing the value they place on such information. This further indicates that people might trade off friends' privacy for benefits they gain from apps, suggesting individuals can be considered as "privacy egoists" [15].

8   Conclusions

By conducting a secondary data analysis on data collected from a comprehensive online survey, our paper contributes to a better understanding of the valuation of interdependent privacy in social app adoption contexts, which in turn benefits the policy discussion on app privacy. Our results suggest that app users are "privacy egoists" [15] not only because they appear to trade off their friends' information for accruing social capital, but also due to the fact that they seem eager to reveal friends' data when they believe such disclosure behaviors result in better app performance. Given that, it seems to be unwise to rely on individuals themselves to protect *their friends'* privacy. Rather, interventions need to be considered for the problem space of interdependent privacy in social app adoption scenarios. For example, it is important that baseline policies are introduced to rigorously limit apps' unfettered access to friends' personal information [20].

Several limitations should be considered. Although our paper empirically detects the negative association between interdependent privacy value and bonding social capital, additional work is needed to further examine the relationship between social capital and the valuation of other types of personal information. Further, we restrict our investigation of interdependent privacy valuation to app adoption scenarios. To contribute to the generalizability of our findings, it is prudent to also study the valuation process of interdependent privacy in other settings (e.g., genetic privacy [9], location privacy [11] or data analytics [4]).

Acknowledgments. We thank the anonymous reviewers for their valuable comments. All remaining errors are our own.

References

1. Biczók, G., Chia, P.H.: Interdependent privacy: let me share your data. In: Sadeghi, A.-R. (ed.) FC 2013. LNCS, vol. 7859, pp. 338–353. Springer, Heidelberg (2013). doi:10.1007/978-3-642-39884-1_29
2. Burke, M., Kraut, R., Marlow, C.: Social capital on Facebook: differentiating uses and users. In: Proceedings of the SIGCHI Conference on Human Factors in Computing Systems, pp. 571–580. ACM (2011)

3. Burke, M., Marlow, C., Lento, T.: Social network activity and social well-being. In: Proceedings of the SIGCHI Conference on Human Factors in Computing Systems, pp. 1909–1912. ACM (2010)
4. Chessa, M., Grossklags, J., Loiseau, P.: A game-theoretic study on non-monetary incentives in data analytics projects with privacy implications. In: Proceedings of the 28th Computer Security Foundations Symposium (CSF), pp. 90–104 (2015)
5. Coleman, J.: Social capital in the creation of human capital. Am. J. Sociol. **94**, S95–S120 (1988)
6. Ellison, N., Steinfield, C., Lampe, C.: The benefits of Facebook friends: social capital and college students use of online social network sites. J. Comput. Mediated Commun. **12**(4), 1143–1168 (2007)
7. Ellison, N., Steinfield, C., Lampe, C.: Connection strategies: social capital implications of Facebook-enabled communication practices. New Media Soc. **13**(6), 873–892 (2011)
8. Ellison, N., Vitak, J., Steinfield, C., Gray, R., Lampe, C.: Negotiating privacy concerns and social capital needs in a social media environment. In: Privacy Online: Perspectives on Privacy and Self-disclosure in the Social Web, pp. 19–32 (2011)
9. Humbert, M., Ayday, E., Hubaux, J.-P., Telenti, A.: On non-cooperative genomic privacy. In: Böhme, R., Okamoto, T. (eds.) FC 2015. LNCS, vol. 8975, pp. 407–426. Springer, Heidelberg (2015). doi:10.1007/978-3-662-47854-7_24
10. Nissenbaum, H.: Privacy as contextual integrity. Washington Law Rev. **79**(1), 119–157 (2004)
11. Olteanu, A.M., Huguenin, K., Shokri, R., Humbert, M., Hubaux, J.P.: Quantifying interdependent privacy risks with location data. Rapport LAAS n16018 (2016)
12. Paxton, P.: Is social capital declining in the United States? A multiple indicator assessment. Am. J. Sociol. **105**(1), 88–127 (1999)
13. Pu, Y., Grossklags, J.: An economic model and simulation results of app adoption decisions on networks with interdependent privacy consequences. In: Poovendran, R., Saad, W. (eds.) GameSec 2014. LNCS, vol. 8840, pp. 246–265. Springer, Heidelberg (2014). doi:10.1007/978-3-319-12601-2_14
14. Pu, Y., Grossklags, J.: Towards a model on the factors influencing social app users valuation of interdependent privacy. Proc. Priv. Enhancing Technol. **2016**(2), 61–81 (2015)
15. Pu, Y., Grossklags, J.: Using conjoint analysis to investigate the value of interdependent privacy in social app adoption scenarios. In: Proceedings of the International Conference on Information Systems (ICIS) (2015)
16. Putnam, R.: Bowling Alone: The Collapse and Revival of American Community. Simon and Schuster, New York (2001)
17. Smith, J., Milberg, S., Burke, S.: Information privacy: measuring individuals' concerns about organizational practices. MIS Q. **20**(2), 167–196 (1996)
18. Steinfield, C., DiMicco, J., Ellison, N., Lampe, C.: Bowling online: social networking and social capital within the organization. In: Proceedings of the International Conference on Communities and Technologies (C & T), pp. 245–254 (2009)
19. Stutzman, F., Vitak, J., Ellison, N., Gray, R., Lampe, C.: Privacy in interaction: exploring disclosure and social capital in Facebook. In: Proceedings of the Annual International Conference on Weblogs and Social Media (ICWSM) (2012)
20. Turow, J., Hoofnagle, C., Mulligan, D., Good, N., Grossklags, J.: The Federal Trade Commission and consumer privacy in the coming decade. I/S J. Law Policy Inf. Soc. **3**(3), 723–749 (2007)

21. Wang, N., Wisniewski, P., Xu, H., Grossklags, J.: Designing the default privacy settings for Facebook applications. In: Companion Publication of the ACM Conference on Computer Supported Cooperative Work and Social Computing (CSCW), pp. 249–252 (2014)
22. Williams, D.: On and off the 'net: scales for social capital in an online era. J. Comput. Mediated Commun. **11**(2), 593–628 (2006)

Improving the Sphinx Mix Network

Filipe Beato[1], Kimmo Halunen[2(✉)], and Bart Mennink[1]

[1] Department Electrical Engineering, ESAT/COSIC, KU Leuven, and iMinds,
Leuven, Belgium
{filipe.beato,bart.mennink}@esat.kuleuven.be
[2] VTT Technical Research Center of Finland, Oulu, Finland
kimmo.halunen@vtt.fi

Abstract. Secure mix networks consider the presence of multiple nodes that relay encrypted messages from one node to another in such a way that anonymous communication can be achieved. We consider the Sphinx mix formatting protocol by Danezis and Goldberg (IEEE Security and Privacy 2009), and analyze its use of symmetric-key cryptographic primitives. We scrutinize the reliance on multiple distinct primitives, as well as the use of the ancient LIONESS cipher, and suggest various paths towards improving the security and efficiency of the protocol.

Keywords: Sphinx · Mix network · Authenticated encryption · Sponge

1 Introduction

With the large growth of Internet services, modern users rely more on digital and ubiquitous communications. In this digital domain, privacy needs to be protected against the very nature of the communications, which tend to be easily traceable and produce massive amounts of metadata. Hiding the metadata of communications is hard, but there are systems, called mix networks, that provide such capabilities. One example is the Sphinx [15] mix network, that is used in privacy protecting applications. The Sphinx mix network format provides security against powerful adversaries and good communications possibilities such as replies, which are not easily available in other such systems.

The Sphinx protocol (see Sect. 2) uses internally many symmetric-key primitives. At first, there is the SHA-2 hash function for hashing. It also includes a HMAC mode [6] to support message authentication. Then, Sphinx uses the LIONESS blockcipher [1], an encryption functionality that is made out of the SEAL stream cipher [28] and a keyed version of the SHA-1 hash function, and evaluates these functions on the message via a Feistel structure. In addition, Sphinx uses a pseudorandom generator to generate entropy for the key. All of these are used in a strongly intertwined manner.

LIONESS is proven to be secure, assuming that SEAL and SHA-1 are sufficiently secure [1], making it particularly useful for Sphinx because of its goal to achieve provable security. However, LIONESS has been outpaced by reality. Attacks on SEAL [17] and SHA-1 [29], the most recent result being a free-start collision attack on the full SHA-1, show weaknesses in the security of LIONESS.

© Springer International Publishing AG 2016
S. Foresti and G. Persiano (Eds.): CANS 2016, LNCS 10052, pp. 681–691, 2016.
DOI: 10.1007/978-3-319-48965-0_46

Contribution. We suggest to replace the encryption and authentication functionalities by one *authenticated encryption* (AE) functionality. This optimization allows for improved security as the payload now gets authenticated without any efficiency cost. There are existing solutions to AE (see Sect. 1.1), but not all schemes are suitable. We suggest two approaches for AE suited for Sphinx that allow for an elimination of many symmetric-key primitive calls, or more formally, for merging these calls into one, contributing for simplicity and efficiency of the design.

First proposal (Sect. 4) is based on the keyed version of the sponge as an adaption of the full-state SpongeWrap [10,11,25]. It internally uses a large unkeyed permutation, the state of which is separated into a capacity and a rate. The capacity determines the security bound, and the rate determines the speed at which data is processed. By using a large permutation, one can make a proper balance between the capacity and the rate, and achieve a high level of security. Second proposal (Sect. 5) is blockcipher based, and is resistant to nonce reuse with an unconventional nonce reuse resistant AE schemes such as [3,20]: while other designs consist of a mode built on top of AES, we follow a "tweakable tweakable blockcipher" approach. We give a powerful construction of a tweakable blockcipher mode on top of a tweakable blockcipher, in such a way that the scheme allows for sufficiently large message and associated data, while still being simple and nonce reuse resistant. For a specific instantiation of the construction, we suggest Threefish, a tweakable blockcipher with 1024-bit state by Ferguson et al. used for the Skein hash function family [16]. (Less suitable alternatives are discussed in the full version of the paper.) Threefish has withstood a wide variety of cryptanalysis [5,22,23].

In Sect. 6, we apply our schemes of Sect. 4 and Sect. 5 to the Sphinx format. The new Sphinx format of Fig. 4 improves over the earlier one in terms of simplicity, efficiency and security.

1.1 Related Work on Authenticated Encryption

AE enjoys a long and steady line of research, which is continued in the ongoing CAESAR competition [13]. The classical approach to design AE schemes is to build the generic mode of operation on top of a blockcipher in order to process data blocks iteratively [3,8,20]. A more novel approach is to design AE based on permutations. The most well-known approach is SpongeWrap by Bertoni et al. [10] which got recently generalized by Jovanovic et al. [21] and Mennink et al. [25], and many CAESAR submissions follow this idea. Different permutation based approaches include APE [2] and PAEQ [12].

The sponge based proposal in this work follows the literature. Regarding our blockcipher based approach, we have deviated from the state of the art. The reason is that conventional modes often entail overhead and the security level is then dominated by what the underlying primitive offers. For blockcipher based modes, using AES internally delivers at most 128-bit security, and often there exist already distinguishability attacks in complexity of about 2^{64} (cf. Bellare et al. [7]). Note that for messages of, say, 1024 bits, a classical AES based mode still requires at least 8 AES evaluations. We remark that also AEZ [20], or more detailed the latest version v4 in the CAESAR competition [19], is also inherently a mode based on 4 and 10 rounds of AES, and has 64-bit security as well. Recent cryptanalysis on AEZ [14,18] has moreover shined a negative light on its security.

2   Sphinx Mix Format

Mix networks rely on mix message formats that provide efficiency and security properties. Sphinx [15] is the most compact mix message format, which is provably secure and efficient. Sphinx relies on the *Sphinx blinding logic* technique for generating a session key with nested MAC computations over the public pseudonyms of each predecessor mix. The private key associated to the public key (i.e., pseudonym) is only known by the user, while the session key is used for the encryption of the message. Figure 1 is a high-level depiction of Sphinx.

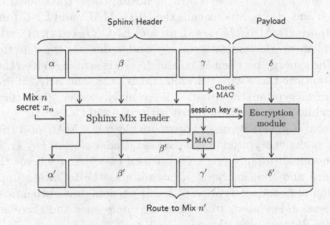

Fig. 1. High-level description of Sphinx [15]

Internally, Sphinx uses many cryptographic primitives. First, there are five hash functions, which are used to hash group elements to key bit strings. Then, it uses a pseudorandom generator PRG and a MAC function for the computation of the nested MAC. Finally, an encryption scheme ENC encrypts the payload at every mix. The hash functions are instantiated using appropriately truncated SHA256 hash functions, and SHA256-HMAC-128 is used as the MAC function. For the encryption, Sphinx relies on the LIONESS blockcipher by Anderson and Biham [1]. This blockcipher is made out of the SEAL stream cipher and a keyed version of the SHA-1 hash function, and evaluates these functions on the message via a Feistel structure. In more detail, denote the stream cipher by S_k and the keyed hash function by H_k. Consider a LIONESS key $k = (k_1, k_2, k_3, k_4)$, where k_1, k_3 will be used to key the stream cipher and k_2, k_4 to key the hash function. To encrypt a message m, LIONESS first splits it into two blocks $m_l \| m_r \leftarrow m$.

These blocks are then transformed using a 4-round Feistel structure: $m_r \leftarrow m_r \oplus S_{k_1}(m_l)$, $m_l \leftarrow m_l \oplus H_{k_2}(m_r)$, $m_r \leftarrow m_r \oplus S_{k_3}(m_l)$, $m_l \leftarrow m_l \oplus H_{k_4}(m_r)$. The updated $m_l \| m_r$ constitutes the ciphertext c.

Due to the security parameter choices, the Sphinx construction needs an encryption scheme with a state of at least 1408 bits plus the message length. Based on this, LIONESS appears to be a good option as it has the potential to have a large state and thus act as the permutation required by the Sphinx system. In addition, LIONESS enjoys a security proof if the underlying hash function SHA-1 and stream cipher SEAL are secure [1]. However, the security of LIONESS is undermined by the results mentioned in the introduction.

Besides the doubtful use of LIONESS in the first place, it is noteworthy that Sphinx uses different symmetric-key primitives for various purposes: i.e., SHA-1 is used in LIONESS and SHA-2 for hashing and MACing. These functions are often intertwined, and particularly, three of the cryptographic hash functions are used to transform a secret non-identity group element s to secret keys to the PRG, MAC, and ENC. In other words, denoting these three hash functions as H_{PRG}, H_{MAC}, and H_{ENC}, Sphinx calls the PRG, MAC, and ENC functionalities with $\text{PRG}(H_{\text{PRG}}(s))$, $\text{MAC}(H_{\text{MAC}}(s), m)$ and $\text{ENC}(H_{\text{ENC}}(s), m)$, where s is the secret group element, the secret session key, and m denotes the data to be MACed or ENCed. The synergy between MAC and H_{MAC} is striking, given the designers' choice to instantiate those with SHA256-HMAC-128, and SHA256, respectively. For the case of encryption, the situation is not much clearer, given that LIONESS uses SHA-1 while H_{ENC} is instantiated with SHA256.

Finally, from Fig. 1, it becomes apparent that γ is a MAC of β (using session key s), and δ is the encryption of the payload (under session key s). By merging these two functionalities into one *authenticated encryption* scheme that authenticates β and δ and that encrypts δ, one obtains the following improvements: Authentication of β and encryption of δ still persists, but authentication of δ is *for free*, the session key needs to be processed *only once* and there is no need to implement two distinct algorithms.

As such, our main goal in this work is to introduce an AE scheme that suits Sphinx, which will be done in Sects. 3, 4 and 5. The potential employment of the new schemes in Sphinx will be considered in Sect. 6 in such a way that the remaining above-mentioned issues (such as the redundant usage of cryptographic primitives) are resolved on the fly.

3   Authenticated Encryption

For $n \in \mathbb{N}$, $\{0,1\}^n$ is the set of n-bit strings, and $\{0,1\}^{\leq n} = \bigcup_{i=0}^{n} \{0,1\}^i$. For two bit strings M, N, their concatenation is denoted by $M \| N$ and $M \oplus N$ denotes their bitwise XOR. Furthermore, if $M \in \{0,1\}^{\leq n-1}$, then $\text{pad}_n(M) = M \| 10^{n-1-|M|}$. For a string $N \in \{0,1\}^n$, we define by $\text{unpad}_n(N)$ the unique string $M \in \{0,1\}^{\leq n-1}$ such that $\text{pad}_n(M) = N$. For $m \leq n$ and $N \in \{0,1\}^n$, we denote by $\lceil N \rceil_m$ the leftmost m bits and by $\lfloor N \rfloor_{n-m}$ the rightmost $n-m$ bits of N, in such a way that $N = \lceil N \rceil_m \| \lfloor N \rfloor_{n-m}$.

Authenticated Encryption (AE). Let $\mu, \nu, \alpha, \tau, \sigma \in \mathbb{N}$ be size values that satisfy $\mu \le \nu$. Here, μ denotes the size of the message, ν the size of the ciphertext, τ the size of the associated data, and σ the size of the nonce. The value α determines the size of the authentication tag. If no authentication is needed, we have $\alpha = 0$.

An authenticated encryption scheme AE is composed of three algorithms: KeyGen, Enc, and Dec. KeyGen is a randomized algorithm that gets as input $\kappa \in \mathbb{N}$ and outputs a random key $key \leftarrow \{0,1\}^\kappa$. The Enc and Dec algorithms are defined as follows:

$$\text{Enc}: \{0,1\}^\kappa \times \{0,1\}^{\le \mu} \times \{0,1\}^{\le \tau} \times \{0,1\}^\sigma \to \{0,1\}^{\le \nu} \times \{0,1\}^\alpha,$$
$$(key, msg, meta, nonce) \mapsto (ctxt, auth),$$

$$\text{Dec}: \{0,1\}^\kappa \times \{0,1\}^{\le \nu} \times \{0,1\}^\alpha \times \{0,1\}^{\le \tau} \times \{0,1\}^\sigma \to \{0,1\}^{\le \mu} \cup \{\bot\},$$
$$(key, ctxt, auth, meta, nonce) \mapsto msg/\bot.$$

Dec outputs the unique msg satisfying $\text{Enc}(key, msg, meta, nonce) = (ctxt, auth)$, or it returns $\bot$ if no such message exists. Enc also outputs $meta$ and $nonce$. We allow for a small amount of ciphertext expansion (from μ to ν bits), as long as the encrypted ciphertext $(ctxt, auth, meta, nonce)$ is of size at most $\lambda_{\max}$.

Threat Model. We consider an adversary $\mathcal{A}$ to be any entity attempting to passively access the shared information by monitoring the communication channel, with no incentive to tamper with the content. $\mathcal{A}$ is allowed to generate encryptions under a secret and unknown key. In this case, $\mathcal{A}$ should not learn the encrypted content, beyond that revealed in the associated data.

More technically, adversary $\mathcal{A}$ has query access to Enc under a secret key key, and it tries to find irregularities among the queries, i.e., some relation that is not likely to hold for a random function. For a function F, let $\text{Func}(F)$ be the set of all functions f with the same interface as F. The advantage $\mathbf{Adv}_{\text{AE}}^{\text{cpa}}(\mathcal{A})$ of an adversary $\mathcal{A}$ in breaking the secrecy of an authenticated encryption scheme AE is defined as

$$\left| \Pr\left(key \xleftarrow{\$} \text{KeyGen}(\kappa) \ : \ \mathcal{A}^{\text{Enc}_{key}} = 1 \right) - \Pr\left(\$ \xleftarrow{\$} \text{Func}(\text{Enc}_{key}) \ : \ \mathcal{A}^\$ = 1 \right) \right|$$

We denote by $\mathbf{Adv}_{\text{AE}}^{\text{cpa}}(Q, T)$ the maximum advantage over all adversaries that make at most Q encryption queries and operate in time T. Depending on the scheme, the adversary $\mathcal{A}$ may be limited to being nonce respecting, so that every query must be made under a different nonce.

For the authenticity of AE, we consider $\mathcal{A}$ to have access to the encryption functionality Enc under a secret key key, and say that $\mathcal{A}$ *forges* an authentication tag if it manages to output a tuple $(ctxt, auth, meta, nonce) \in \{0,1\}^{\le \nu} \times \{0,1\}^\alpha \times \{0,1\}^{\le \tau} \times \{0,1\}^\sigma$ such that $\text{Dec}(key, ctxt, auth, meta, nonce) = msg \ne \bot$ and $(msg, meta, nonce)$ was never queried to Enc before. The forgery attempt may be made under a nonce $nonce$ that has appeared before. The advantage of $\mathcal{A}$ in breaking the authenticity of authenticated encryption scheme AE is defined as $\mathbf{Adv}_{\text{AE}}^{\text{auth}}(\mathcal{A}) = \Pr\left(key \xleftarrow{\$} \text{KeyGen}(\kappa) \ : \ \mathcal{A}^{\text{Enc}_{key}} \text{ forges} \right)$. We denote by $\mathbf{Adv}_{AE}^{auth}(Q, R, T)$ the maximum advantage over all adversaries that make at most Q encryption queries, R forgery attempts, and operate in time T.

4   Solution 1: Sponge

The Sponge functions introduced by Bertoni et al. [11] specifically for cryptographic hashing can also be used in a broad spectrum of keyed applications, including message authentication [4,9,26,27] and stream encryption [10,25]. We will use the keyed sponge in the full-state duplex mode [25], to describe an AE scheme that is suited for the use in Sphinx. As keyed Sponges are merely stream based encryption, a unique nonce is required for every encryption.

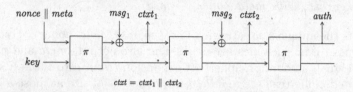

$$ctxt = ctxt_1 \parallel ctxt_2$$

Fig. 2. AE based on a Sponge. Padding of data is excluded from the figure

The realization of our AE scheme using the sponge is dubbed $AE^{\pi,\ell,n}$ and indexed by a permutation π of width b and parameters ℓ and $n \leq b$ which specify the parsing of the message blocks: it considers at most ℓ message blocks of n bits. The parameter ℓ can be arbitrarily large, but it is used to show how the length affects the security bound. $AE^{\pi,\ell,n}$ operates on keys of size $\kappa \leq b - n$ bits, messages and ciphertexts can be of length at most $\mu = \ell \cdot n - 1$ (the scheme does not use ciphertext expansion, hence $\mu = \nu$), and the sizes of the associated data and nonce should satisfy $\sigma + \tau \leq n - 1$. The size of the authentication tag is $\alpha \leq n$ (this is for simplicity, the scheme generalizes to $\alpha > n$). $AE^{\pi,\ell,n}$ is depicted in Fig. 2. The algorithms are in the full version of this paper.

Security. $AE^{\pi,\ell,n}$ is a full-state duplex construction [25]. In the full version of this paper, we prove that if π is an ideal permutation, we have security against *nonce-respecting* adversaries up to bounds $\mathbf{Adv}_{AE^{\pi,\ell,n}}^{cpa}(Q, T) \leq \frac{(\ell_\alpha Q)^2}{2^{b-n}} + \frac{\ell_\alpha QS}{2^\kappa}$ and $\mathbf{Adv}_{AE^{\pi,\ell,n}}^{auth}(Q, R, T) \leq \frac{(\ell_\alpha Q)^2}{2^{b-n}} + \frac{\ell_\alpha QS}{2^\kappa} + \frac{R}{2^\alpha}$, where ℓ_α as ℓ, if $\alpha = 0$, and $\ell + 1$ otherwise, S is the maximal number of evaluations of π that can be made in time T.

5   Solution 2: Tweakable Blockcipher Based

The second approach is to apply a large tweakable blockcipher. A tweakable blockcipher $\widetilde{E} : \mathcal{K} \times \mathcal{T} \times \mathcal{M} \to \mathcal{M}$ takes as input a key $k \in \mathcal{K}$, a tweak $t \in \mathcal{T}$, and a message $m \in \mathcal{M}$, and outputs a ciphertext $c \in \mathcal{M}$. It is a permutation for every choice of (k, t).

For our AE functionality AE, we need a tweakable blockcipher with a large state $\mathcal{M}$. We suggest *Threefish*, a tweakable blockcipher by Ferguson et al. used for the Skein hash function family [16]. Threefish supports block sizes of 256, 512, and 1024 bits. The key size equals the block size, and the tweak size is 128 bits. We focus on the largest variant, Threefish-1024, which for readability we simply denote 3fish:

$$\text{3fish}: \{0,1\}^{1024} \times \{0,1\}^{128} \times \{0,1\}^{1024} \to \{0,1\}^{1024},$$
$$(k, t, m) \mapsto c.$$

3fish can be used for AE directly by placing the associated data and nonce into the tweak and encrypting based on the key and this tweak. While the state size of 3fish is large enough, the tag size is not. One way to resolve this is to employ a random oracle that maps the associated data and nonce to a string of size 128 bits, but this would degrade the security of the construction as forgeries can be found in a complexity 2^{64}. Another way to enlarge the tweak space without adjusting the cipher itself is by using it in a tweakable mode of operation.

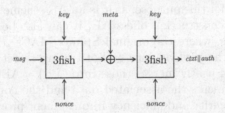

Fig. 3. AE based on LRW[3fish]. Padding of data is excluded from the figure

Liskov et al. [24] introduced two tweakable modes of operation: while these constructions are originally designed to add a tweak input to a blockcipher, they can equally well be applied to tweakable blockciphers themselves to enlarge the tweak space. We will consider one of these constructions, which makes two evaluations of the underlying cipher:

$$\text{LRW[3fish]}: \{0,1\}^{1024} \times \{0,1\}^{1024} \times \{0,1\}^{128} \times \{0,1\}^{1024} \to \{0,1\}^{1024},$$
$$(k, t, t', m) \mapsto \text{3fish}(k, t', \text{3fish}(k, t', m) \oplus t).$$

This construction can be used to realize $\text{AE}^{\text{LRW[3fish]}}$ as illustrated in Fig. 3 and a formal description is given in the full version of the paper. It operates on keys of size $\kappa = 1024$ bits, messages can be of arbitrary length but of size at most $\mu = 1023 - \alpha$, the nonce should be of size $\sigma \le 127$, and the associated data should be of size at most $\tau \le 1023$. The ciphertexts are of size *exactly* $\nu = 1024 - \alpha$ bits, where α is the size of the authentication tag. The latter is required to make decryption possible.

Security. In the full version of this paper, we prove that $\text{AE}^{\text{LRW}[3\text{fish}]}$ is secure against *nonce reusing* adversaries under the assumption that 3fish is a secure tweakable blockcipher. Formally, we prove that

$$\mathbf{Adv}^{\text{cpa}}_{\text{AE}^{\text{LRW}[3\text{fish}]}}(Q,T) \leq \Theta\left(\frac{Q^2}{2^n}\right) + \mathbf{Adv}^{\widetilde{\text{sprp}}}_{3\text{fish}}(2Q,T') \text{ and}$$

$$\mathbf{Adv}^{\text{auth}}_{\text{AE}^{\text{LRW}[3\text{fish}]}}(Q,R,T) \leq \Theta\left(\frac{(Q+R)^2}{2^n}\right) + \mathbf{Adv}^{\widetilde{\text{sprp}}}_{3\text{fish}}(2(Q+R),T') + \frac{R2^{n-\alpha}}{2^n - Q}$$

where $\mathbf{Adv}^{\widetilde{\text{sprp}}}_{\widetilde{E}}(Q,T)$ denotes the maximum security advantage of any tweakable blockcipher adversary that makes Q queries, runs in time T and $T' \approx T$.

6   Improving the Sphinx

A naive solution to the state of affairs for Sphinx (Sect. 2) would be to replace SEAL by a more modern stream cipher and to replace SHA-1 by SHA-3, but there is little point in doing so: versatility of Sponges in general and SHA-3 in particular enables encryption using SHA-3 on the fly; putting a four-round Feistel construction on top of it is overkill. Instead, it makes more sense to simply *replace* LIONESS by a keyed version of the SHA-3. The construction of Sect. 4 is particularly suited for this purpose, as it is an AE scheme based on the SHA-3 permutation. As the construction offers AE, it can also be used to replace the MAC. In other words, where the original Sphinx MACs β into authentication tag γ and encrypts the payload into δ (both using secret session key s), the construction of Sect. 4 neatly merges those into $(\delta, \gamma) = \text{AE}(s, \text{payload}, \beta)$

where β now represents the associated data and the nonce. We have henceforth obtained the security and efficiency improvement promised in Sect. 2.

It seems logical to also replace the remaining cryptographic functionalities in Sphinx by SHA-3. However, a second thought reveals that there is little point in doing so: first hashing a key through SHA-3 and then considering the keyed version of the SHA-3 based on this key is less efficient *and* less secure than considering the keyed version of the SHA-3 based on the original key. Therefore, it suffices to have a mapping transforming the secret session key into a bit string.

The downside of the SHA-3 based approach is that the AE scheme of Sect. 4 does not offer security against nonce reusing adversaries, and in the solution above, β represents the associated data as well as the nonce. In Sphinx, the β values are generated using the PRG, and thus random, but collisions may appear. One can also use the Threefish based mode of Sect. 5, and use the Skein hash function family [16] to serve for hashing, as it uses Threefish natively.

Either approach makes the encryption functionality of Sphinx more secure and more efficient. Figure 4 depicts our proposal of using AE in Sphinx. Our AE solutions support associated data as input which could be used for the processing of the header, it natively allows for authentication, and could potentially be used as MAC function. These advantages could be used to integrate part of the nested MAC functionality of Sphinx within the AE. Using our AE schemes in Sphinx *additionally* authenticates the payload for free.

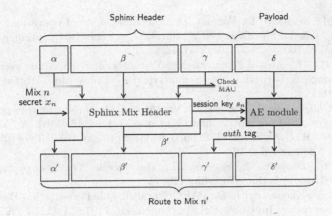

Fig. 4. Using the AE scheme of Sects. 4 or 5 in Sphinx

Acknowledgments. This work was supported in part by the Research Council KU Leuven: GOA TENSE (GOA/11/007). Bart Mennink is a Postdoctoral Fellow of the Research Foundation – Flanders (FWO).

References

1. Anderson, R., Biham, E.: Two practical and provably secure block ciphers: BEAR and LION. In: Gollmann, D. (ed.) FSE 1996. LNCS, vol. 1039, pp. 113–120. Springer, Heidelberg (1996). doi:10.1007/3-540-60865-6_48

2. Andreeva, E., Bilgin, B., Bogdanov, A., Luykx, A., Mennink, B., Mouha, N., Yasuda, K.: APE: authenticated permutation-based encryption for lightweight cryptography. In: Cid, C., Rechberger, C. (eds.) FSE 2014. LNCS, vol. 8540, pp. 168–186. Springer, Heidelberg (2015). doi:10.1007/978-3-662-46706-0_9

3. Andreeva, E., Bogdanov, A., Luykx, A., Mennink, B., Tischhauser, E., Yasuda, K.: Parallelizable and authenticated online ciphers. In: Sako, K., Sarkar, P. (eds.) ASIACRYPT 2013, Part I. LNCS, vol. 8269, pp. 424–443. Springer, Heidelberg (2013). doi:10.1007/978-3-642-42033-7_22

4. Andreeva, E., Daemen, J., Mennink, B., Van Assche, G.: Security of keyed sponge constructions using a modular proof approach. In: Leander, G. (ed.) FSE 2015. LNCS, vol. 9054, pp. 364–384. Springer, Heidelberg (2015). doi:10.1007/978-3-662-48116-5_18

5. Aumasson, J.-P., Çalık, Ç., Meier, W., Özen, O., Phan, R.C.-W., Varıcı, K.: Improved cryptanalysis of skein. In: Matsui, M. (ed.) ASIACRYPT 2009. LNCS, vol. 5912, pp. 542–559. Springer, Heidelberg (2009). doi:10.1007/978-3-642-10366-7_32

6. Bellare, M., Canetti, R., Krawczyk, H.: Keying hash functions for message authentication. In: Koblitz, N. (ed.) CRYPTO 1996. LNCS, vol. 1109, pp. 1–15. Springer, Heidelberg (1996). doi:10.1007/3-540-68697-5_1

7. Bellare, M., Desai, A., Jokipii, E., Rogaway, P.: A concrete security treatment of symmetric encryption. In: FOCS 1997, pp. 394–403. IEEE Computer Society (1997)

8. Bellare, M., Rogaway, P., Wagner, D.: The EAX mode of operation. In: Roy, B., Meier, W. (eds.) FSE 2004. LNCS, vol. 3017, pp. 389–407. Springer, Heidelberg (2004). doi:10.1007/978-3-540-25937-4_25

9. Bertoni, G., Daemen, J., Peeters, M., Van Assche, G.: On the security of the keyed sponge construction. In: Symmetric Key Encryption Workshop (SKEW 2011) (2011)

10. Bertoni, G., Daemen, J., Peeters, M., Van Assche, G.: Duplexing the sponge: single-pass authenticated encryption and other applications. In: Miri, A., Vaudenay, S. (eds.) SAC 2011. LNCS, vol. 7118, pp. 320–337. Springer, Heidelberg (2012). doi:10.1007/978-3-642-28496-0_19

11. Bertoni, G., Daemen, J., Peeters, M., Van Assche, G.: Sponge functions. In: ECRYPT Hash Function Workshop (2007)

12. Biryukov, A., Khovratovich, D.: PAEQ: Parallelizable Permutation-Based Authenticated Encryption. In: Chow, S.S.M., Camenisch, J., Hui, L.C.K., Yiu, S.M. (eds.) ISC 2014. LNCS, vol. 8783, pp. 72–89. Springer, Heidelberg (2014). doi:10.1007/978-3-319-13257-0_5

13. CAESAR: Competition for Authenticated Encryption: Security, Applicability, and Robustness, March 2014

14. Chaigneau, C., Gilbert, H.: Is AEZ v4.1 sufficiently resilient against key-recovery attacks? IACR Trans. Symmetric Cryptol. 1(1) (2017, to appear)

15. Danezis, G., Goldberg, I.: Sphinx: a compact and provably secure mix format. In: IEEE S 2009, pp. 269–282. IEEE Computer Society (2009)

16. Ferguson, N., Lucks, S., Schneier, B., Whiting, D., Bellare, M., Kohno, T., Callas, J., Walker, J.: The Skein hash function family. Submission to NIST's SHA-3 Competition (2010)

17. Fluhrer, S.R.: Cryptanalysis of the SEAL 3.0 pseudorandom function family. In: Matsui, M. (ed.) FSE 2001. LNCS, vol. 2355, p. 135. Springer, Heidelberg (2002). doi:10.1007/3-540-45473-X_11

18. Fuhr, T., Leurent, G., Suder, V.: Collision attacks against CAESAR candidates. In: Iwata, T., Cheon, J.H. (eds.) ASIACRYPT 2015. LNCS, vol. 9453, pp. 510–532. Springer, Heidelberg (2015). doi:10.1007/978-3-662-48800-3_21

19. Hoang, V.T., Krovetz, T., Rogaway, P.: AEZ v4: authenticated encryption by enciphering. Submission to CAESAR Competition (2015)

20. Hoang, V.T., Krovetz, T., Rogaway, P.: Robust authenticated-encryption AEZ and the problem that it solves. In: Oswald, E., Fischlin, M. (eds.) EUROCRYPT 2015. LNCS, vol. 9056, pp. 15–44. Springer, Heidelberg (2015). doi:10.1007/978-3-662-46800-5_2

21. Jovanovic, P., Luykx, A., Mennink, B.: Beyond $2^{c/2}$ security in sponge-based authenticated encryption modes. In: Sarkar, P., Iwata, T. (eds.) ASIACRYPT 2014. LNCS, vol. 8873, pp. 85–104. Springer, Heidelberg (2014). doi:10.1007/978-3-662-45611-8_5

22. Khovratovich, D., Nikolić, I.: Rotational cryptanalysis of ARX. In: Hong, S., Iwata, T. (eds.) FSE 2010. LNCS, vol. 6147, pp. 333–346. Springer, Heidelberg (2010). doi:10.1007/978-3-642-13858-4_19

23. Khovratovich, D., Nikolić, I., Rechberger, C.: Rotational rebound attacks on reduced skein. In: Abe, M. (ed.) ASIACRYPT 2010. LNCS, vol. 6477, pp. 1–19. Springer, Heidelberg (2010). doi:10.1007/978-3-642-17373-8_1

24. Liskov, M., Rivest, R.L., Wagner, D.: Tweakable block ciphers. In: Yung, M. (ed.) CRYPTO 2002. LNCS, vol. 2442, p. 31. Springer, Heidelberg (2002). doi:10.1007/3-540-45708-9_3

25. Mennink, B., Reyhanitabar, R., Vizár, D.: Security of full-state keyed sponge and duplex: applications to authenticated encryption. In: Iwata, T., Cheon, J.H. (eds.) ASIACRYPT 2015. LNCS, vol. 9453, pp. 465–489. Springer, Heidelberg (2015). doi:10.1007/978-3-662-48800-3_19

26. Naito, Y., Yasuda, K.: New bounds for keyed sponges with extendable output: independence between capacity and message length. In: Peyrin, T. (ed.) FSE 2016. LNCS, vol. 9783, pp. 3–22. Springer, Heidelberg (2016). doi:10.1007/978-3-662-52993-5_1

27. Gaži, P., Pietrzak, K., Tessaro, S.: The exact PRF security of truncation: tight bounds for keyed sponges and truncated CBC. In: Gennaro, R., Robshaw, M. (eds.) CRYPTO 2015. LNCS, vol. 9215, pp. 368–387. Springer, Heidelberg (2015). doi:10.1007/978-3-662-47989-6_18

28. Rogaway, P., Coppersmith, D.: A software-optimized encryption algorithm. In: Anderson, R. (ed.) FSE 1993. LNCS, vol. 809, pp. 56–63. Springer, Heidelberg (1994). doi:10.1007/3-540-58108-1_8

29. Stevens, M., Karpman, P., Peyrin, T.: Freestart collision for full SHA-1. In: Fischlin, M., Coron, J.-S. (eds.) EUROCRYPT 2016. LNCS, vol. 9665, pp. 459–483. Springer, Heidelberg (2016). doi:10.1007/978-3-662-49890-3_18

User Authentication from Mouse Movement Data Using SVM Classifier

Bashira Akter Anima[1], Mahmood Jasim[1],
Khandaker Abir Rahman[2(✉)], Adam Rulapaugh[2],
and Md Hasanuzzaman[1]

[1] University of Dhaka, Dhaka, Bangladesh
anima_csedu@yahoo.com, mahmood.jasim.0@gmail.com,
hzamancsdu@yahoo.com
[2] Saginaw Valley State University, University Center, MI, USA
{krahman, ajrulapa}@svsu.edu

Abstract. This paper presents a robust user authentication system by gleaning raw mouse movement data. The data was collected using a publicly available tool called Recording User Input (RUI) from 23 subjects analyzed for three types of mouse actions - Mouse Move, Point-and-Click on Left or Right mouse button, and Drag-and-Drop. Samples are broken down to unit blocks comprising a certain number of actions and from each block seventy-four features are extracted to construct feature vectors. The proposed system was rigorously tested against public benchmark data. Experiment results generated by using the Support Vector Machine (SVM) classifier shows a False Rejection Rate (FRR) of 1.1594 % and a False Acceptance Rate (FAR) of 1.9053 % when the block size was set for 600 actions. After reducing dimensions using Principle Component Analysis (PCA), SVM classifier shows FRR of 1.2081 % and FAR of 2.3604 %. Compared with the existing methods based on mouse movements, our method shows significantly lower error rates, which we opine are viable enough to become an alternate to conventional authentication systems.

Keywords: Biometric · Cyber behavioral biometrics · Mouse dynamics · Person identification · SVM

1 Introduction

One of the preliminary tasks in the field of information security is to make sure that the person who is accessing the system which may contain sensitive and confidential information, is the right person. To ensure so, a person can be classified genuine or intruder by the method of user authentication which in general falls into two categories - (1) to authenticate a person by something he/she possesses such as tokens, ID and (2) to authenticate by something he/she knows, for example, by knowing a password or PIN number. However, there are limitations in these traditional approaches. For instance, tokens or IDs can be lost, stolen or misplaced and a person may forget his PIN number or password. Alternatively, it is possible that an intruder may acquire one's password using automated password cracking tools. To deal with these issues,

© Springer International Publishing AG 2016
S. Foresti and G. Persiano (Eds.): CANS 2016, LNCS 10052, pp. 692–700, 2016.
DOI: 10.1007/978-3-319-48965-0_47

biometrics [1] are introduced to identifies a person by using unique physical or behavioral characteristics that the person possesses.

Although a physical biometric system such as fingerprint, retina, and iris scan provide stronger security, it also requires expensive hardware to record user's biometric data. On the other hand, cyber behavioral biometric such as keystroke or mouse dynamics which are generated naturally when a user interacts in cyberspace; (1) do not require specialized hardware and therefore, is inexpensive and (2) unobtrusive. For these reasons research in these fields has been gaining momentum in recent days.

In this research work, we focused on mouse dynamics that means the characteristics of a user which are collected by analyzing the inputs performed by a pointing device such as mouse. In this system, only the availability of a mouse is required. Based on a user's mouse actions, some features are extracted and stored for every user profile. When the user uses the system again, the system matches his actions with his profile and determines whether it is a genuine user or an intruder.

Contribution of the paper follows:

- 48 new features are proposed and 74 total features has been defined and processed for the experiments. This rich feature set, combined with the data processing and classification methods we adopted, was the key to achieving impressively low FRR of 1.1594 % and FAR of 1.9053 %.
- Performances comparison (see in Sect. 3) between our method and other existing methods has been compiled. The comparison clearly indicates the merits of our system.

The rest of the paper is organized as follows: Sect. 2 describes the proposed system. Section 3 presents experimental results with performances of the proposed system and Sect. 4 describes the contributions, limitations and future plan for improvement.

2 Proposed System Description

The proposed system is divided into three major components. The components are (I) Data Acquisition, Processing, and Segmentation, (II) Feature Extraction and Normalization, and (III) Training and Classification.

2.1 Data Acquisition, Processing, and Segmentation

Mouse data are collected by using a publicly available logging tool named Recording User Input (RUI) [2] where different mouse actions are observed and recorded for 23 volunteers. The dataset contains 284 h of raw mouse data with an average of 45 sessions per user. Users are given with an individual choice of operating environments and applications. Users were asked to use their computer and mouse in a normal, everyday fashion.

For each action (listed below), data are formatted as Elapsed Time (in milliseconds), Action Type, X-Coordinate, and Y-Coordinate. Elapsed time means the time difference in milliseconds between the start time of monitoring the system and the time after the specific action has occurred. Action types are:

(I) Mouse Move, (II) Press Left Button, (III) Release Left Button, (IV) Press Right Button and (V) Release Right Button. X-Coordinate and Y-Coordinate are pixel location values of x and y coordinates of the mouse on the screen respectively. Table 1 shows four sample actions recorded by the tool RUI. Raw mouse data are then processed into three upper level mouse actions: Mouse Move, Point-and-Click on left or right mouse button and Drag-and-Drop.

Table 1. Example of four mouse action instances recorded by the mouse logging tool RUI.

Elapsed time (in ms)	Action	X-coordinate (in pixels)	Y-coordinate (in pixels)
0.33	Moved	204	492
0.338	Moved	206	479
0.354	Pressed Left	206	479
0.394	Released Left	206	479

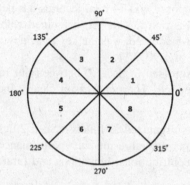

Fig. 1. Direction of mouse movement divided by octants of 45° intervals.

In segmentation step, the processed data is divided into different block sizes based on the number of mouse actions. A block consists of a set of aforementioned mouse actions. Block sizes of 350, 400, 450, 500, 550, and 600 are used. From each block, a set of features are extracted.

2.2 Feature Extraction and Normalization

In this step, features are extracted from the preprocessed dataset. Features are selected in a way that makes the system compact, efficient and at the same time consist of some unique characteristics of an individual.

For each action type, twenty-two features are calculated from each block. These are; Mean and Standard Deviation of time (in milliseconds) to perform a specific type of action in a block, Mean and Standard Deviation of travel distance (in pixels) to perform a specific type of action in a block, Number of a specific type of mouse action (N) in a block, Ratio of number of mouse actions (N) and total number of actions in

Table 2. List of features extracted from each block.

Features	Number of features
Mean of Time	3
Standard Deviation of Time	3
Mean of Travel Distance	3
Standard Deviation of Travel Distance	3
Number of Mouse Actions	3
Ratio of Mouse Action and Total Number of Actions	3
Direction Specific Mean Time	24
Direction Specific Mean Mouse Movement Distance	24
Total Mouse Movement Distance in each direction	8
Total Features	74

block (NB), proposed direction specific mean time ($\bar{X}_{tj}^K$) and proposed direction specific mean mouse movement distance ($\bar{X}_{dj}^K$). Here, direction of the mouse movement is described by octant of $45°$ intervals with $0°$ to $360°$ spans [see in Fig. 1] for every mouse action. Thus, there are 66 features for three mouse action type. The newly proposed features are described below.

Proposed direction specific mean time to perform a specific type of action in a block ($\bar{X}_{tj}^K$) is a ratio between total time to perform a type of action in K direction and total time to perform the same type of action throughout the block.

$$\bar{X}_{tj}^K = \frac{\sum_{j=1}^M X_{tj}^K}{\sum_{i=1}^N X_{ti}} \tag{1}$$

X_{tj}^K is the time to perform an action of $J(1, 2, \ldots, M)$ samples in $K(1, 2, \ldots, 8)$ directions, X_{ti} is the time to perform an action of $I(1, 2, \ldots, N)$ samples.

Proposed direction specific mean mouse movement distance to perform a specific type of action in a block ($\bar{X}_{dj}^K$) is a ratio between total travel distance to perform a type of action in K direction and total travel distance to perform the same type of action throughout the block.

$$\bar{X}_{dj}^K = \frac{\sum_{j=1}^M X_{dj}^K}{\sum_{i=1}^N X_{di}} \tag{2}$$

Where X_{dj}^K is the mouse movement distance of $J(1, 2, \ldots, M)$ samples in $K(1, 2, \ldots, 8)$ directions, X_{di} is the mouse movement distance of $I(1, 2, \ldots, N)$ samples.

Eight more features are also calculated which are the total mouse movement distance in each direction, $\sum_{j=1}^M X_{dj}^K$ where X_{dj}^K is the mouse movement distance of $J(1, 2, \ldots, M)$ samples in $K(1, 2, \ldots, 8)$ directions. Therefore, the total number of features is 74 where the total number of proposed features is 48 for three mouse action type. See Table 2 for the full list of features. These features are used to construct a feature vector for each user. The dimension of each feature vector is the number of selected features which is 74. Before classifying, data of the feature vector are normalized in a scale. This helps to avoid attributes in greater numeric ranges overshadowing those in smaller numeric ranges. By doing this, training and testing data will be in the same scale. In this proposed system, data is normalized into the scale of zero to one by using Min-Max Normalization.

2.3 Training and Classification

To analyze how the classifier is checking a genuine user, at first the classifier is trained with a set of randomly selected data for a selected user from the dataset. The training data pattern contains patterns of the legitimate user. The classifier is also trained with imposter patterns labeled with the legitimate patterns. Then the other portions of the dataset which are treated as testing patterns are applied to the classifier. After testing, it is analyzed that how the system is classifying genuine data by examining the predicted label.

In this proposed system, Support Vector Machine (SVM) [3] classifier is used for training and testing purposes. We adopted the classifier SVM since it has been widely used in the field of object recognition, speech recognition, biometrics, image retrieval, image regression etc. It is highly accepted classifiers since it offers a result with good performances. Sometimes it outperformed other classifiers, such as neural network.

In case of SVM, two techniques are applied. One is using original feature vector (with 74 features) and the other is using dimensionally reduced feature vector by applying Principal Component Analysis (PCA) [4]. PCA is a mathematical technique of matching patterns in high dimensions of data. It helps to reduce the dimension of the data, so when the dataset is larger, PCA plays an important role by reducing the dimensions and selecting a subset.

To implement the system using SVM classifier, an open source package LIBSVM [5] is used. The popular choice of Kernel function is Gaussian Radial Basis Function (RBF). Kernel parameters are obtained by applying fivefold cross validation technique. The system applies SVM on original feature space as well as SVM on dimensionally reduced feature space using PCA.

3 Experimental Results and Discussion

The proposed system is implemented in a Windows 7 system with 1.70 GHz Intel Core i3 4005U CPU with 4.00 GB of RAM. Other remaining part of the system such as processing, segmentation, scaling, and classification were performed with MATLAB R2013a.

The proposed system is tested by using a public benchmark data [6, 7]. In the public benchmark dataset, four types of actions are defined which are; (1) Mouse Movement (MM) which means normal mouse movement, (2) Silence which means the time when the mouse does not move, (3) Point and Click (PC) which defines mouse movement which is followed by mouse button press and release, and (4) Drag and Drop (DD) which relates with the combination of mouse actions such as mouse movement, mouse button press and then release sequentially. Before experimenting data for silence action are deducted from the benchmark dataset. Note that from these four actions, three upper level actions are derived as mentioned in Sect. 2.1.

Performance is measured by computing False Acceptance Rate (FAR) and False Rejection Rate (FRR).

3.1   Results of Classification

Experiments are performed on different sizes of blocks (350, 400, 450, 500, 550, and 600 actions) each with 74 features derived from the public dataset. Table 3 shows that among different block sizes of actions, block size of 600 actions provides better result. In case of block size of 600 actions, SVM and SVM (+PCA) show FRR of 1.1594 % and 1.2081 % respectively. Again, for block size of 600 actions, SVM and SVM (+PCA) show FAR of 1.9053 % and 2.3604 % respectively.

Table 3. Performance for different block sizes using SVM and SVM (+PCA).

Block size (number of action)	SVM		SVM (+PCA)	
	FRR (%)	FAR (%)	FRR (%)	FAR (%)
350	1.4631	2.3358	1.5291	2.6496
400	1.3685	2.2234	1.4616	2.5512
450	1.2917	2.2114	1.3746	2.4789
500	1.1902	2.0379	1.3030	2.3574
550	1.1619	2.0020	1.2327	2.3941
600	1.1594	1.9053	1.2081	2.3604

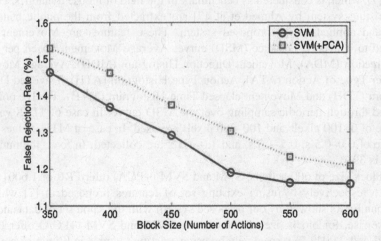

Fig. 2. Comparison of SVM and SVM (+PCA) Classifiers based on FRR.

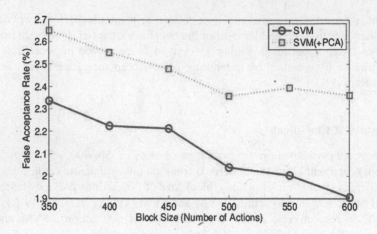

Fig. 3. Comparison of SVM and SVM (+PCA) Classifiers based on FAR.

After studying the performance result for different classification techniques, it is observed that the performance rate of the SVM with original feature space offers better result.

The comparison based on the performance rate of FRR and FAR shown in Figs. 2 and 3 respectively.

3.2 Comparison with Related Works

The results found in our experiments are compared with the results found by Ahmed et al. in [7], which is considered as benchmark in the field of mouse dynamics. Features of an existing system by Ahmed et al. [7] are extracted from the public benchmark dataset and applied to the proposed system. These features are Movement Speed compared to Travelled Distance (MSD) curve, Average Movement Speed per Movement Direction (MDA), Movement Direction Histogram (MDH), Average Movement Speed per Type of Action (ATA), Action Type Histogram (ATH), Travelled Distance Histogram (TDH) and Movement elapsed Time Histogram (MTH). Twelve points are computed through periodic sampling over the MSD curve. In case of TDH, values in the range of 0–100 pixels and 100–200 pixels are used. In case of MTH, values within the range of 0.0–0.5 s, 0.5–1.0 s, and 1.0–1.5 s are collected. In total, the number of features is 39.

For block size of 600 actions, SVM and SVM (+PCA) offer FRR of 1.6001 % and 1.7851 % respectively by using existing set of features proposed in [7] which are higher than FRRs showed by our proposed system with the same set of data and block size. Likewise, for block size of 600 actions, SVM and SVM (+PCA) offer FAR of 2.9798 % and 2.9042 % respectively by using existing features in [7] which are higher than ours. This clearly indicates the merits of our newly proposed features.

Several other researches showed impressive results in recent times. Below we mention the notable works and compare their outcomes with ours.

(1) In the work of Ahmed et al. [7], they offer FRR of 2.4614 % and FAR of 2.4649 %. To gain this performance the number of required actions is 2000 where the actions include point and click, drag and drop, mouse move and silence.

(2) Nakkabi et al. [6] also show FRR of 0.36 % and FAR of 0 for same number of mouse actions. However, the number of mouse action is large and not always practical to play a tile game to use the system.

(3) Pusara and Bordley [8] offered a web based authentication system where decision tree is used as a classifier. It shows good result where false negative rate is 1.75 % and false positive rate is 0.43 %. However, it only consists of eleven users' involvement.

(4) In the works of Muthumari et al. [9] they proposed 6.25 % FRR and 7.25 % FAR using Learning Vector Quantization (LVQ) method.

(5) In their other work [10], Kernel Principle Component Analysis (KPCA) method is used to reduce the dimension of the feature vector and one class support vector machine is used as a classifier which offered 8.25 % FRR and 8.98 % FAR.

(6) In the method of Lakshmipriya et al. [11], holistic and procedural features are used and Nearest Neighbor Algorithm is applied to extract the features. It offers FRR of 7.70 % and FAR of 8.75 %.

(7) In the method of Rahman et al. [12], similarity score method has been used which is based on statistical normal distribution. They found equal error rate (EER) to be 6.7 %.

Compared with the above existing methods, our method shows significantly lower error rates by processing even fewer number of actions (maximum 600 for instance). The works which show lower error rates than ours, suffers from either inadequate population size (such as in [8]) or impractical due to restricted testing environment (see in [6]).

4 Conclusion

In this system, three types of mouse actions: Mouse Move, Point-and-Click on left or right mouse buttons and Drag-and-Drop are obtained. The processed data is divided into blocks where block means a set of specific number of mouse actions. Seventy-four features are extracted from each block to form a feature vector where the number of new features is forty-eight. For each type of mouse action, the features are calculated from mean and standard deviation of travel distance, mean and standard deviation of elapsed time to perform an action, mean number of mouse actions, proposed direction specific mean time of an action and direction specific mean travel distance. The direction of the mouse movement action is described by an octant of 45° intervals. Using these features a person's mouse movement distance and total time to perform an action are described with eight values instead of one direction. The data of the feature vector is normalized into the scale of zero to one. After normalizing the feature vector is applied to classifiers. Support Vector Machine (SVM) with original feature space and Support Vector Machine (SVM) with dimensionally reduced feature space by Principal Component Analysis (PCA) are used in the system. To test the system, public benchmark dataset is used. Performances are measured and analyzed for six different block sizes. After experimenting it is observed that the system provides better performance of the block size of 600. Experiment result shows that, in case of original feature space SVM offers 1.1594 % FRR and 1.9053 % FAR. In case of dimensionally reduced feature space by PCA, SVM classifier offers 1.2081 % FRR and 2.3604 % FAR.

This system did not consider some actions due to inadequacy of benchmark dataset. In future, more types of actions such as Double Click, Mouse Wheel etc., will be considered. A larger dataset is expected to be gathered and tested against our system. With some impressive initial results, we believe this system could be used with other conventional authentication systems to build a multi-modal authentication system.

Acknowledgements. This work was done under the assistance of Ministry of Posts, Telecommunications and Information Technology Fellowship given by the Information and Communication Technology division of Ministry of Posts, Telecommunications and Information Technology, Government of the People's Republic of Bangladesh.

References

1. Jain, A.K., Pankanti, S.: Biometric identification. Commun. ACM **43**, 91–98 (2000)
2. Kukreja, U., Stevenson, W.E., Ritter, F.E.: RUI: recording user input from interfaces under Windows and Mac OS X. Behav. Res. Methods **38**(4), 656–659 (2011)
3. Cristianini, N., Shawe-Taylor, J.: An Introduction to Support Vector Machines: And Other Kernel-based Learning Methods. Cambridge University Press, New York (2000)
4. Jolliffe, I.: Principal Component Analysis. Springer, New York (1986)
5. Chang, C.C., Lin, C.J.: LIBSVM: a library for support vector machines. ACM Trans. Intell. Syst. Technol. **2**, 1–27 (2011). Article No. 27
6. Nakkabi, Y., Traoré, I., Ahmed, A.A.E.: Improving mouse dynamics biometric performance using variance reduction via extractors with separate features. Trans. Sys. Man Cyber. Part A **40**(6), 1345–1353 (2010)
7. Ahmed, A.A.E., Traoré, I.: A new biometric technology based on mouse dynamics. IEEE Trans. Dependable Sec. Comput. **4**(3), 165–179 (2007)
8. Pusara, M., Brodley, C.E.: User re-authentication via mouse movements. In: ACM Workshop on Visualization and Data Mining for Computer Security. ACM Press (2004)
9. Muthumari, R.S., Pepsi, M.B.B.: Mouse gesture based authentication using machine learning algorithm. In: International Conference on Advanced Communication Control and Computing Technologies (2014)
10. Muthumari, G., Shenbagaraj, R., Pepsi, M.B.B.: Authentication of user based on mouse-behavior data using classification. In: IEEE International Conference on Innovations in Engineering and Technology (ICIETŠ) (2014)
11. Lakshmipriya, D., Balakrishnan, J.R.: Holistic and procedural features for authenticating users **16**, 98–101 (2014)
12. Rahman, K.A., Moormann, R., Dierich, D., Hossain, M.: Continuous user verification via mouse activities. In: Dziech, A., et al. (eds.) MCSS 2015. CCIS, vol. 566, pp. 170–181. Springer, Heidelberg (2015). doi:10.1007/978-3-319-26404-2_14

Distance Bounding Based on PUF

Mathilde Igier and Serge Vaudenay[✉]

EPFL, 1015 Lausanne, Switzerland
serge.vaudenay@epfl.ch
http://lasec.epfl.ch

Abstract. Distance Bounding (DB) is designed to mitigate relay attacks. This paper provides a complete study of the DB protocol of Kleber et al. based on Physical Unclonable Functions (PUFs). We contradict the claim that it resists to Terrorist Fraud (TF). We propose some slight modifications to increase the security of the protocol and formally prove TF-resistance, as well as resistance to Distance Fraud (DF), and Man-In-the-Middle attacks (MiM) which include relay attacks.

1 Introduction

Wireless devices are subject to relay attacks. It is problematic because these devices are at the basis for authentication in many domains like payment with credit cards, building access control, or biometric passports [15,16]. To ensure the security of wireless devices against relay attacks, Brands and Chaum [8] introduced the notion of *Distance Bounding* (DB) protocols in 1993. The idea is that a prover P must prove that he is close to a verifier V. Several attack models exist to make the verifier accept with a prover too far away from the verifier. The attacks described in the literature are: 1. *Distance Fraud attacks (DF)* [8]: A far away prover P tries to make V accept. No participant is close to V. 2. *Mafia Fraud attacks (MF)* [10]: A malicious actor A who does not hold the secret tries to make V accept using an honest but far away prover P. 3. *Terrorist Fraud (TF)* [10]: A malicious actor A who does not hold the secret tries to make V accept by colluding with a malicious far away prover P who holds the secret.

Avoine et al. [1] proposed the complete but rather informal ABKLM model. Dürholz et al. [11] provided a formal model to prove the security of the protocols. However, this model is too strong as admitted by the authors [12], and it is difficult to prove TF security in this model. Another model was proposed by Boureanu et al. [4].

Most of the proposed protocols are vulnerable to TF attacks but a few protocols provide security against all types of threats: the protocol of Fischlin and Onete [13], the SKI protocol [5,6], DBopt protocols [7], the public-key DB protocols ProProx [26] and eProProx [25], and the anonymous DB protocol SPADE [9]. However, all these proofs are made on the assumption that in TF, the prover does not want to give his credential to the adversary for further application. This assumption is weak and does not correspond to reality. None of the DB protocols in the plain model can provide TF security without this assumption, so,

© Springer International Publishing AG 2016
S. Foresti and G. Persiano (Eds.): CANS 2016, LNCS 10052, pp. 701–710, 2016.
DOI: 10.1007/978-3-319-48965-0_48

we should consider alternate models. DF and TF security are easier to provide using tamper resistant hardware on the prover side because the prover cannot access his secret. Kılınç and Vaudenay [19] provide a new model for distance bounding protocols with secure hardware. In this model, the game consists of several verifier instances including a distinguished one V, hardware with their instances, instances of provers and actors. There is one distinguished hardware h with instances far away from V. The winning condition of this game is that V accepts.

- The DB protocol is DF-secure if the winning probability is negligible whenever there is no instance close to V.
- The DB protocol is MiM-secure if the winning probability is negligible whenever an honest prover is holding h (i.e. it can only be accessed by an honest and far away prover).
- The DB protocol is TF-secure if the winning probability is negligible.

PUFs are tamper resistant hardware used in counterfeiting detection [22,23] and authentication protocols [3,14]. A PUF is a physical component which maps a challenge to a response. By definition, a PUF, as it is described in [21], has the following properties: non clonable, non emulable, a response R_i gives negligible information on a response R_j with $R_i \neq R_j$ and a PUF cannot be distinguished from a random oracle (as discussed in [2]). For simplicity reasons, we will treat PUFs as random oracles with access limited to their holder. The aim of our work is to provide a provably secure protocol using PUF in DB protocols. A TF-secure DB protocol based on PUF was proposed in [18]. Nevertheless, this protocol assumes that provers implement their protocol while using a PUF. In the model of Kleber et al. [20], the prover can implement any malicious protocol while accessing to the PUF, the protocol in [18] is trivially TF-insecure in this stronger model.[1] Kleber et al. design a protocol in [20] which is claimed to be secure in their model. However we contradict that fact in this paper and propose to modify it in order to improve the security.

Our contribution in this paper is as follows: 1. We show that the protocol proposed by Kleber et al. [20] is not secure against *Terrorist Fraud* which contradicts the claims from their authors; 2. We provide some slight modifications of this protocol which we call pufDB to improve its security; 3. We provide proofs of security for this pufDB protocol for the following attacks: *Distance Fraud* and *Mafia Fraud*; 4. We prove the security of pufDB protocol against *Terrorist Fraud* when the prover is limited in the amount of bits per round he can send. The security strengthens when the distance from the prover to the verifier increases. To the best of our knowledge, pufDB is the first protocol which provides TF security even when the prover is allowed to leak his secret.

Due to limited space, proofs of our results are deferred to the full version of this paper [17]. The full version includes the analysis for two other threat models: impersonation fraud and distance hijacking. It also describes some attacks to lower bound the necessary number of rounds for security.

---

[1] In this protocol, the PUF is not used during the fast phase, so the malicious prover can give whatever is needed to complete the protocol to a close-by adversary.

2   The Kleber et al. Protocol

2.1   Details of the Protocol

The verifier is called V and the prover P. The main idea of the protocol proposed by Kleber et al. [20] is to replace the PRF in P of conventional Distance Bounding protocols by a PUF. In this protocol, it is possible to use both Challenge-response PUF and a public PUF.[2] The protocol is made of two distinct phases: the preparation phase and the time critical phase.

Prior to the protocol, it is assumed that V can query the PUF and store a number of challenge-response pairs (CRP), at a round i such that $r_i = PUF(C_i)$. A CRP is defined as $(C_i, r_i), 0 \leq i < n$ with n the number of rounds. There is always a set of CRPs corresponding to PC to complete the run. A set of CRPs shall not be used in protocols more than once.

In the time critical phase, only one bit can be sent from V to P in a round. However the PUF needs a big space of challenges to be secure. Therefore V transmits a pre-challenge PC to P during the preparation phase. Then, in the time critical phase, the pre-challenge is combined with the challenges c_i received by P to generate a challenge $C_i = \mathrm{PC}_0...PC_{n-2-i}||c_0c_1...c_i$ for the PUF. It is assumed that the hardware is such that the PUF can precompute C_i and when the prover receives the last bit of C_i he can return the response r_i in almost no time. The time critical phase consists of n transmission rounds. The verifier V starts the clock when he sends a challenge c_i and stops the clock when he receives the response r_i. In the paper, T_{max} and E_{max} are defined. T_{max} is the maximal number of responses which can arrive too late. E_{max} is the maximal number of errors admitted in the responses. (A late response is not checked.)

We note that if one c_i is incorrectly received by P, then all subsequent PUF computations will produce random outputs, independently from the expected r_i. So, this protocol is not tolerant to reception errors by P.

The protocol is claimed to be provably secure for all types of Fraud by Kleber et al. [20]. They prove the security of their protocol using the model of Dürholz et al. [11]. They only give a proof of security against Terrorist Fraud attacks. In fact, in the model defined by Kılınç et al. [19], when the protocol uses hardware, the proof that the protocol is secure against Terrorist Fraud attacks gives a proof of security against all the other types of attacks. However, when there is no additional restriction in the protocol, this protocol is insecure against Terrorist Fraud attack as we show in the Sect. 2.2. To prove the security against Terrorist Fraud, Kleber et al. assume that the probability for the adversary to win the game is equal to $\left(\frac{1}{2}\right)^{n-E_{max}-T_{max}}$. We contradict this assumption.

---

[2] Normally, a PUF is non emulable so the verifier should first borrow the PUF to get input-output pairs. To avoid it, we can use Public-PUF also called SIMPL system (SIMulation Possible but Laborious). SIMPL systems guarantee that the response to a challenge cannot be computed faster with a simulator of the PUF than with the real PUF. Anyone can compute the right response but it takes much more time with the simulator of the PUF.

2.2 A Terrorist Fraud Attack

Notations. d_{VP} is the distance between V and the far away prover P, t_{VP} is the signal propagation time between V and P (it is assume that $\frac{d_{VP}}{t_{VP}}$ is a constant such as the speed of light); Similarly, d_{AP} is the distance between A and the far away prover P, t_{AP} is the signal propagation time between A and P; B is the maximal distance allowed by the protocol, t_B is the maximal signal propagation time over the distance B; Finally, T is the time between sending two consecutive challenges c_i and c_{i+1}.

In this scenario a malicious far away prover colludes with an adversary close to the verifier. In the protocol of Kleber et al. the adversary receives PC from the verifier. He can send it to the malicious prover who holds the PUF. There is no information concerning the distance d_{AP} between P and A nor about the time T in between rounds. A forwards every message from V to P. To answer a challenge c_i on time, P is missing m bits. He computes 2^m PUF values and sends them to A so that A will always be able to respond on time. For instance, if t_m denotes the time it takes for P to compute the 2^m values and to transmit them to A (without time of flight), the attack works if

$$t_{AP} + t_{VA} \leq t_B + \frac{(mT - t_m)}{2} \tag{1}$$

As an example, with $m = 1$, P has two PUF values to compute and to send and the condition is $t_{AP} + t_{VA} \leq t_B + \frac{T - t_1}{2}$. Since there is no information on d_{AP}, d_{VA} and T, we can have $d_{AP} = B$, $d_{VA} = B$ and $T \geq t_1 + 2t_B$, in that configuration Eq. (1) is true. Then A can pass the round if he is in the previous configuration. He can pass all rounds with high probability, so the protocol is not secure against Terrorist Fraud.

More concretely, we assume $m = 1$, $B = 3\,\text{m}$ and $t_B = 10\,\text{ns}$. We consider V running at $1\,\text{GHz}$ and have one clock cycle between rounds, so $T = 1\,\mu\text{s}$. We consider a faster malicious prover P running at $10\,\text{GHz}$ so that he can evaluate two challenges with the PUF (corresponding to the possible challenges for $m = 1$) in $t_m = 200\,\text{ns}$. With $d_{VA} = B$, the attack succeeds for $t_{AP} = 400\,\text{ns}$ i.e. $d_{VP} = 120\,\text{m}$. The attack is possible because there is a huge amount of time between the reception of r_i and the emission of c_{i+1}, but these figures clearly show it is a quite realistic scenario.

2.3 Slight Modifications of the Protocol

We choose to slightly modify the protocol of Kleber et al. [20] to improve its security. We call pufDB the new protocol. pufDB is presented on Fig. 1. First, we impose a regular rhythm for sending the challenges, second, the $(n - 1)$ bits of PC are sent with the same rhythm as if there were challenges in the time critical phase but expecting no answer. The prover begins to send responses when he receives the first bit of challenge c_0. With this slight change, we make sure there is no more time left for attacks in between the transmission of PC and c_0 than there is in between the transmission of each c_i and this time is bounded.

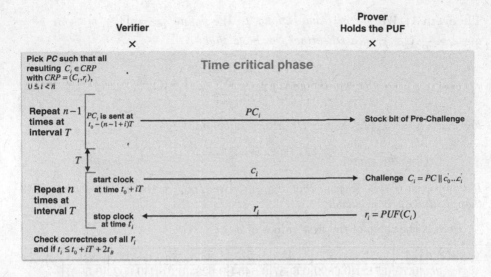

Fig. 1. The pufDB protocol

Moreover, we assume that P cannot accept consecutive challenges separated by time lower than $\frac{T}{2}$, so, we cannot speed up P by sending challenges too fast.[3] Finally, another modification is that we concatenate PC with the challenges without dropping any bit. So, $C_i = PC||c_0...c_i$ is of $n + i$ bits. This guarantees domain separation for the functions computing the responses. So, to summarize, we use the three following requirements: 1. The elapsed time between sending each bit of $PC||c_0...c_{n-1}$ by V is exactly T; 2. The elapsed time in between receiving two consecutive bits by P is at least $\frac{T}{2}$; 3. PC is concatenated to $c_0...c_i$ without dropping any bit.

We denote by t_0 the time when the verifier sends c_0 to the prover. So c_i is sent at time $t_0 + iT$ and PC_i is sent at time $t_0 + (i - n + 1)T$.

Lemma 1 (Number of missing bits). *For each round i, the number of challenges which did not arrive yet to the far away prover P when it becomes critical to send the response r_i is $m = \lceil 2(\frac{t_{VP} - t_B}{T}) \rceil$. The number of possible C_i is 2^m.*

3 Distance Fraud Analysis of PufDB

To prove resistance against Distance Fraud attacks, it is necessary to prove that a far away prover P who holds the PUF has a negligible probability to win the game presented in Sect. 2. The idea of a Distance Fraud attack is to find a way for the far away prover P to send r_i such that it arrives on time to V. To arrive on time, the response r_i should be sent before receiving the challenge c_i. So, there are chances for the response to be wrong.

---

[3] We allow challenges to arrive faster than a period T to capture the Doppler effect when P moves towards V. With $\frac{T}{2}$ as a limit, P can move at 20 % of the light speed!.

Theorem 1. *We use m from Lemma 1. We define $q_m = \prod_{l=1}^{m} p_l^{\frac{1}{m}}$ for $p_l = \frac{1}{2} + \frac{1}{2} \times \frac{1}{2^{2^l}} \binom{2^l}{2^l-1}$, in a DF-attack, we have that*

$$\Pr(win\ the\ game) \leq \sum_{i=0}^{E_{max}+T_{max}} \binom{n}{i} q_m{}^n$$

For $2(E_{max} + T_{max}) \leq n$ any DF-attack is bounded by

$$\Pr(win\ the\ game) \leq e^{-n \times \left(2\left(\frac{1}{2} - \frac{E_{max}+T_{max}}{n}\right)^2 - \ln(2q_m)\right)} = bound_{DF}$$

If there exist $\alpha, \beta \in \mathbb{R}$ such that $E_{max} \leq \alpha n$, $T_{max} \leq \beta n$ and $\alpha + \beta < 0.049$ then, $bound_{DF}$ is negligible.

Here is the table of the first values of q_m:

m	1	2	3	4	5	6	7	8	9
q_m	0.75	0.7181	0.6899	0.6657	0.6454	0.6283	0.6141	0.6022	0.5921

So depending on m, q_m smoothly goes from $\frac{3}{4}$ to $\frac{1}{2}$ as m grows. p_l decreases and tends towards $\frac{1}{2}$, so q_m decreases and tends towards $\frac{1}{2}$ as well.

For $m \geq 2n - 1$, we can have a better bound. The adversary has no bit to compute the PUF (not even the bits of PC), so we can redo the analysis and obtain

$$\Pr(\text{win the game}) \leq \sum_{i=0}^{E_{max}+T_{max}} \binom{n}{i} p_n{}^n \leq e^{-n \times \left(2\left(\frac{1}{2} - \frac{E_{max}+T_{max}}{n}\right)^2 - \ln(2p_n)\right)}$$

These results are unchanged when using a public PUF.

4   Mafia Fraud Analysis of PufDB

To prove resistance against Mafia Fraud attacks it is necessary to prove that if an honest far away prover P holds the PUF, an adversary close to V has a negligible probability to win the game presented in Sect. 2.

We prove security against Man-in-the-Middle (MiM) attacks. We first informally describe what is the best possible attack. A is a malicious actor. Before receiving a challenge c_i from the verifier V, he sends a guessed challenge c_i' to a far away prover P. He receives r_i' from the prover. If $c_i' = c_i$ then the adversary sends r_i' to the verifier. In this case, the adversary wins the round with probability 1.

Pre-asking gives an extra chance to pass a round. But if one c_i is incorrectly guessed, any subsequent pre-asking request will return some useless random bits. So the best strategy is to start pre-asking until there exists a round i such that $c_i' \neq c_i$, then to continue with the impersonation attack strategy.

We have not considered replay attacks because A has no time to begin any other instance of the protocol if P does not answer at frequency larger than $\frac{T}{2}$.

Actually, let V be the distinguisher verifier in a MiM attack and PC the value that he sends. As the PUF is held by a single participant, there are no concurrent sessions for P. Sending c_i to P takes at least $\frac{(n+1)T}{2}$ time but during this time, the session for V terminates. So, only one session of P receives c_i, for each i.

Theorem 2. *In any MiM attack, we have*

$$\Pr(\text{win the game}) \leq \left(\frac{1}{2}\right)^{n+1-T_{max}} \times \sum_{i=0}^{E_{max}+1} \binom{n+1-T_{max}}{i}$$

This is bounded by $e^{-2(n+1-T_{max})\times\left(\frac{1}{2}-\frac{E_{max}+1}{n+1-T_{max}}\right)^2}$ *when* $2E_{max} + T_{max} \leq n+1$. *For* $E_{max} \leq \alpha n$, $T_{max} \leq \beta n$, *and* $2\alpha + \beta < 1$, *this is negligible.*

Using a public PUF just adds a negligible term in the bound.

5   Terrorist Fraud Analysis of PufDB

In Terrorist Fraud attacks, an adversary A colludes with a far away malicious prover P to make V accept. Without any limitation on the power of the verifier the protocol is insecure against TF. In our model, the prover is limited on the communication complexity. With this limitation, the prover can compute all the challenges but he has a limitation on the amount of bits he can send to A. He can compress the 2^m bits of the table of responses for each round into s bits and send to A the compressed version. From the s bits received and the challenge sent by V, A can try to recover the response.

Lemma 2. *Let s and l be two positive integers and $N = 2^l$. We define $p_{l,s} = 1 - \frac{1}{N}E(\min_C d(f,C))$ where f is a random boolean function of l-bit input and the minimum is over sets C of up to 2^s elements. We define*

$$p_{l,s}^* = 1 - \frac{1}{2^N}\sum_{i=0}^{R+1}\frac{i}{N}N_i' \quad , \quad \bar{p}_{l,s} = \frac{1}{2} + \frac{1}{\sqrt{N}} \times \left(\sqrt{\frac{s\ln 2}{2}} + \sqrt{\frac{2}{2^s} + \frac{1}{N}}\right) + \frac{1}{N}$$

where R is the maximum value such that $\sum_{i=0}^{R} 2^s \binom{N}{i} \leq 2^N$ and $N_i' = 2^s \binom{N}{i}$ for $0 \leq i \leq R$, $N_i' = 0$ for $i > R+1$, and $N_{R+1}' = 2^N - 2^s \sum_{i=0}^{R}\binom{N}{i}$. We have $p_{l,s} \leq p_{l,s}^*$. For $s \leq \frac{2^l}{2}$, we also have $p_{l,s}^* \leq \bar{p}_{l,s}$.

Theorem 3. *We use m as defined in Lemma 1. We assume that the malicious prover is limited to s bits of transmission per round to the adversary in a TF-attack. We use $q_{m,s} = \prod_{l=1}^{m} p_{l,s}^{\frac{1}{m}}$ and we have*

$$\Pr(\text{win the game}) \leq \sum_{i=0}^{E_{max}+T_{max}} \binom{n}{i} q_{m,s}^{n}$$

where $p_{l,s}$ is defined in Lemma 2. For $2(E_{max} + T_{max}) \leq n$ a TF-attack has a success probability bounded by

$$\Pr(win\ the\ game) \leq e^{-n \times \left(2\left(\frac{1}{2} - \frac{E_{max}+T_{max}}{n}\right)^2 - \ln(2q_{m,s})\right)} = bound_{TF}$$

If there exist $\alpha, \beta \in \mathbb{R}$ such that $E_{max} \leq \alpha n$, $T_{max} \leq \beta n$ then the protocol is secure when $\alpha + \beta < \frac{1}{2} - \sqrt{\frac{\ln(2q_m)}{2}}$.

Using a public PUF just adds a negligible term in the bound.

We have the following relation:

$$\text{Packet transmission time} = \frac{\text{Packet size}}{\text{Bit rate}}$$

The adversary succeeds to send s bits when $\frac{d_{AP}}{c} + \frac{s}{\text{Bit rate}} \leq T$ with $\frac{d_{AP}}{c}$ the packet traveling time is in ns, this is negligible compared to T in µs. So, we get the relation $s \leq \text{Bit rate} \times T$. For wireless communication, the maximal bit rate is of order $1\,\text{Gbps}$ and we define $T = 1\,µs$. So the prover can send maximum $s = 1000$ bits to the adversary. So the maximal s is $s = 2^{10}$.

For a noisy communication such that $E_{max} = 5\%n$ and $T_{max} = 0$ with $s = 2^{10}$, if the prover is close to the verifier ($m \leq 18$), pufDB cannot be proven secure against TF-attacks.

If the prover is close to the verifier then he can help the adversary in doing the authentication himself or in giving directly the device to the adversary. So, we can assume that the prover is quite far from the adversary proportionally to the distance allowed. For instance, if we consider that $d_{VP} = 3000\,\text{m}$, $B = 3\,\text{m}$, $T = 1\,µs$ and the speed of the light $c = 3.10^8\,\text{m.s}^{-1}$ we get $t_B = 10\,\text{ns}$ and $m = 20$. For $s = 2^{10}$, we obtain $q_{m,s} = 0.7917$ so the protocol achieves a security level of 2^{-10} in 110 rounds, and 2^{-20} in 307 rounds.

If we can lower T to $T = 100\,\text{ns}$ and $t_B = 10\,\text{ns}$ then the prover can send at most $s = 2^7$ bits to the adversary and we have security for a noisy communication with $E_{max} = 5\%n$ and $T_{max} = 0$ for $m \geq 15$ which corresponds to $t_{VP} > 71t_B$.

Table 1. Efficiency of the protocols against DF and MF for completeness 99% under noise 5% ($T_{max} = 0$)

Protocol	n (security level of 2^{-10})	n (security level of 2^{-20})
SKI	48	91
FO	84	151
DBopt (DB2,DB3)	24	43
pufDB ($m = 1$)	345	474
pufDB ($m > 2n - 1$)	26	45

6   Conclusion

Until pufDB, none of the existing protocol has provided Terrorist Fraud resistance in the plain model without assuming that the adversary would not share his secret, which is not a realistic assumption. The protocol of Kleber et al. is not secure against Terrorist Fraud attacks. pufDB is an improvement of this protocol. We prove security against Distance Fraud and Mafia Fraud. We further prove the security against TF using a reasonable limitations on the number of transmission per round.

We compare with other distance bounding protocols. The parameters in pufDB, SKI [5,6], FO [13,24] and DBopt [7] are taken such that the protocols achieve 99 % completeness with a noise of 5 % as it is described in [7]. If we take the worst case for pufDB (i.e. $m = 1$), pufDB needs more rounds than the previous protocols to achieve the same security level. However, for m large, pufBD is more efficient than SKI and FO to achieve security against DF and MF and it almost reaches the optimal bounds of DBopt (Table 1).

Acknowledgments. The authors thank Negar Kiyvash and Daniel Cullina for their valuable help in the proof of Lemma 2.

References

1. Avoine, G., Bingöl, M.A., Kardaş, S., Lauradoux, C., Martin, B.: A framework for analyzing RFID distance bounding protocols. J. Comput. Secur. **19**(2), 289–317 (2001)
2. Bolotnyy, L., Robins, G.: Physically unclonable function-based security and privacy in RFID systems. In: IEEE International Conference on Pervasive Computing and Communications (2007)
3. Bolotnyy, L.B., Robins, G.: Physically unclonable function-based security and privacy in RFID systems. In: IEEE International Conference on Pervasive Computing and Communications (PerCom 2007), pp. 211–220 (2007)
4. Boureanu, I., Mitrokotsa, A., Vaudenay, S.: Practical and provably secure distance-bounding. In: The 16th Information Security Conference, Dallas, Texas, USA, pp. 13–15, November 2013
5. Boureanu, I., Mitrokotsa, A., Vaudenay, S.: Secure and lightweight distance-bounding. In: Avoine, G., Kara, O. (eds.) LightSec 2013. LNCS, vol. 8162, pp. 97–113. Springer, Heidelberg (2013). doi:10.1007/978-3-642-40392-7_8
6. Boureanu, I., Mitrokotsa, A., Vaudenay, S.: Towards secure distance bounding. In: Moriai, S. (ed.) FSE 2013. LNCS, vol. 8424, pp. 55–68. Springer, Heidelberg (2014). doi:10.1007/978-3-662-43933-3_4
7. Boureanu, I., Vaudenay, S.: Optimal proximity proofs. In: 10th International Conference on Information Security and Cryptology (INSCRYPT 2014), pp. 13–15, December 2014
8. Brands, S., Chaum, D.: Distance bounding protocols. In: Helleseth, T. (ed.) EUROCRYPT 1993. LNCS, vol. 765, pp. 344–359. Springer, Heidelberg (1994). doi:10.1007/3-540-48285-7_30
9. Bultel, X., Gambs, S., Gérault, D., Lafourcade, P., Onete, C., Robert, J-M.: A prover-anonymous and terrorist-fraud resistant distance bounding protocol. In: Wisec, Spade (2016)

10. Desmedt, Y.: Major security problems with the 'unforgeable' (Feige)-Fiat- Shamir proofs of identity and how to overcome them. In: Proceedings of the 6th Worldwide Congress on Computer and Communications Security and Protection (SecuriCom), pp. 147–159, March 1988
11. Dürholz, U., Fischlin, M., Kasper, M., Onete, C.: A formal approach to distance-bounding RFID protocols. In: Lai, X., Zhou, J., Li, H. (eds.) ISC 2011. LNCS, vol. 7001, pp. 47–62. Springer, Heidelberg (2011). doi:10.1007/978-3-642-24861-0_4
12. Fischlin, M., Onete, C.: Subtle kinks in distance-bounding: an analysis of prominent protocols. In: Proceedings of WISEC, pp. 195–206 (2013)
13. Fischlin, M., Onete, C.: Terrorism in distance bounding: modeling terrorist-fraud resistance. In: Jacobson, M., Locasto, M., Mohassel, P., Safavi-Naini, R. (eds.) ACNS 2013. LNCS, vol. 7954, pp. 414–431. Springer, Heidelberg (2013). doi:10. 1007/978-3-642-38980-1_26
14. Frikken, K.B., Blanton, M., Atallah, M.J.: Robust authentication using physically unclonable functions. In: Samarati, P., Yung, M., Martinelli, F., Ardagna, C.A. (eds.) ISC 2009. LNCS, vol. 5735, pp. 262–277. Springer, Heidelberg (2009). doi:10. 1007/978-3-642-04474-8_22
15. Hancke, G.: A Practical Relay Attack on ISO14443 Proximity Cards (2005). http:// www.cl.cam.ac.uk/gh275/relay.pdf
16. Hlaváč, M., Rosa, T.: A Note on the Relay Attacks on e-passports. The case of Czech e-passports. Cryptology ePrint Archive, Report 2007/244 (2007)
17. Igier, M., Vaudenay, S.: Distance bounding based on PUF. Cryptology ePrint Archive, Report 2016/901 (2016)
18. Kardaş, S., Kiraz, M.S., Bingöl, M.A., Demirci, H.: A novel RFID distance bounding protocol based on physically unclonable functions. In: Juels, A., Paar, C. (eds.) RFIDSec 2011. LNCS, vol. 7055, pp. 78–93. Springer, Heidelberg (2012). doi:10. 1007/978-3-642-25286-0_6
19. Kılınç, H., Vaudenay, S.: Optimal Distance Bounding with Secure Harware (under submission)
20. Kleber, S., Van Der Heijden, R.W., Kopp, H., Kargl, F.: Terrorist fraud resistance of distance bounding protocols employing physical unclonable functions. In: IEEE International Conference and Workshops on Networked Systems (NetSys) 2015
21. Rührmair, U., Sölter. J., Sehnke, F.: On the Foundations of Physical Unclonable Functions. Cryptology ePrint Archive, Report 2009/277 (2009)
22. Shariati, S., Koeune, F., Standaert, F.-X.: Security analysis of image-based PUFs for anti-counterfeiting. In: De Decker, B., Chadwick, D.W. (eds.) CMS 2012. LNCS, vol. 7394, pp. 26–38. Springer, Heidelberg (2012). doi:10.1007/978-3-642-32805-3_3
23. Tuyls, P., Batina, L.: RFID-tags for anti-counterfeiting. In: Pointcheval, D. (ed.) CT-RSA 2006. LNCS, vol. 3860, pp. 115–131. Springer, Heidelberg (2006). doi:10. 1007/11605805_8
24. Vaudenay, S.: On modeling terrorist frauds. In: Susilo, W., Reyhanitabar, R. (eds.) ProvSec 2013. LNCS, vol. 8209, pp. 1–20. Springer, Heidelberg (2013). doi:10.1007/ 978-3-642-41227-1_1
25. Vaudenay, S.: On privacy models for RFID. In: Kurosawa, K. (ed.) ASIACRYPT 2007. LNCS, vol. 4833, pp. 68–87. Springer, Heidelberg (2015). doi:10.1007/ 978-3-540-76900-2_5
26. Vaudenay, S.: Sound proof of proximity of knowledge. In: Au, M.-H., et al. (eds.) ProvSec 2015. LNCS, vol. 9451, pp. 105–126. Springer, Heidelberg (2015). doi:10. 1007/978-3-319-26059-4_6

Posters

Denying Your Whereabouts:
A Secure and Deniable Scheme
for Location-Based Services

Tassos Dimitriou[1,2](✉) and Naser Al-Ibrahim[1]

[1] Computer Engineering Department, Kuwait University, Kuwait City, Kuwait
{tassos.dimitriou,naser.a.kw}@ieee.org
[2] Research Academic Computer Technology Institute, Patras, Greece

Abstract. Location Based Services (LBS) is often used in applications that allow users to interact with the environment and query for the location of persons, objects and services. However, such systems may undermine user privacy since the frequent collection of location data may reveal considerable information about an individual's daily habits and profile. In this work, we present our Deniable-LBS scheme which gives users the ability to deny being in a particular location even if this location has been monitored by an internal or external party.

1 Introduction

The rapid progression of mobile computing technologies, wireless communication, and location-sensing in recent years have inspired the development of applications that involve Location Based Services (LBS). Examples of such applications include navigation, finding places of interest, locating your friends, keeping track of your pet or children, and so on. However, while these applications help users with their day-to-day activities, they also raise serious privacy concerns due to continuous tracking of a user's location [1,2].

Typical LBS systems work by having clients log in to some server which then pushes location updates to registered users. However, from a privacy point of view such centralized solutions are unacceptable, as they give complete access to user sensitive location information. Although decentralized solutions exist [3], here we argue that a new level of privacy is needed to secure social interactions offered by LBS systems. Consider for example the scenario where Eve, a friend of Bob, records and subsequently distributes the complete location traces received from Bob (who he met, where, when, etc.) to his wife Alice. Or the case where a government agency, after collecting all (encrypted) transcripts of communication, obtain access to user's cryptographic keys, thus being able to tie a person to a particular location [4].

As existing solutions (see [5] for a more general survey) focus on securing the interactions between a user and the service provider and/or between the

T. Dimitriou—Research supported by Kuwait University, Research Grant No. QE 02/15.

users themselves, they implicitly consider a person's communication partners as trusted. While such interactions need remain personal, the use of cryptographic mechanisms that lack repudiation may lead to privacy breaches as explained above. Hence our main focus is towards providing *deniability* in LBS services. Our contributions can be summarized as follows:

- We developed a protocol "Deniable-LBS" that allows users to share live location data without the privacy implications mentioned above.
- Our protocol does not rely on Trusted Third Parties (TTPs). This is achieved by using a P2P network topology. Members of our LBS System, connect with each other by using online users as a reference instead of a central server.
- We guarantee privacy against internal and external threats.
- We ensure that when communication between parties is over, no one (not even the parties involved) can (re)produce a transcript of this interaction.
- We optimize the protocol by allowing users to join and leave an existing session without the need to re-run the protocol from scratch.

The rest of this paper is organized as follows: Our proposed scheme is introduced in Sect. 2. We evaluate its properties from both a security and efficiency point of view in Sect. 3. Finally, Sect. 4 concludes this work.

2   Deniable-LBS Scheme

We start by modeling our system by denoting P the set of protocol participants $\{U_1, U_2, U_3, ...U_n\}$, where at anytime, a subset of P may decide to create a group in order to exchange location information. We assume the existence of a broadcast channel that can be used to exchange protocol messages among users. Once a message is broadcasted, anybody can read it. Thus, this public channel acts like a bulletin board where messages can be read by protocol participants. Alternatively, arbitrary point-to-point connections among participants can be assumed. However, in both cases, the network is considered to be non-private and asynchronous. In the sequel, we assume that each user $U_i \in P$ has a set of public-private keys (PK_i, SK_i), where the public key PK_i is available to other protocol participants in a trustworthy manner. To obtain our Deniable-LBS system, the following key properties need to be ensured:

- Only users participating in a particular session should be able to see each other's location data. After executing our protocol, a shared *group key* will be derived, which can be used to ensure confidentiality.
- Authentication is required in order for participants to have a consistent view of entities taking part in a protocol run. Group members should be authenticated *directly* and not with the help of any third party.
- *Ephemeral* public/private keys will be used to authenticate a user to others, help distinguish messages coming from different participants and successfully authenticate location data.

– Most importantly, in the context of Deniable-LBS users should have the ability to *repudiate* being in a particular location even if everyone in the system is saying otherwise.

Our proposed scheme functions in a straightforward manner. Any user that would like to share his/her location with other users would have to create a group. We provide confidentiality and authentication among different groups by using a shared group key and ephemeral private/public keys which will be derived by group members using the Deniable-AKE protocol. This protocol is based on a protocol originally proposed by Bohli and Steinwandt [6] along with improvements from Van Gundy [7]. Our protocol extends these results by allowing users to leave and join the group *dynamically* without having to re-run the whole protocol again. Each location sent by a user will be signed with his/her ephemeral key and encrypted using the session group key. Finally upon dispersing of the group, members will publish their ephemeral keys to create plausible deniability. The protocol is structured in four main phases.

Deniable-AKE [6]: In the first stage (Deniable Authenticated Key Exchange), users will agree and authenticate all parameters that will be used in the protocol. Additionally, a shared group key Sk_i for a subset of participants P_i will be derived along with the generation, exchange, and authentication of ephemeral keys. A snapshot of the protocol is shown in Algorithm 1.

Location Sharing: The majority of communications takes place in the second phase. The main objective in this stage is to ensure that current group members can share confidential information (location, messages, etc.) with the assurance of origin authentication. Any member who wants to share his/her location L would have to do the following: encrypt the location using the group key Sk_i, sign the encrypted location using his/her ephemeral signing key s_i, and finally broadcast the resulting message to the group. Any member who receives a message from a group participant would have to check first if the location received has been tampered with, then proceeds to decrypt the location.

Joins and Leaves: The objectives of this stage are to allow members to join and leave existing groups dynamically. In both cases, the session key for the group must be *updated* in order to protect previous transcripts from the users who are about to join and future transcripts from the users who are about to leave.

The *Join* procedure starts by selecting two neighboring members p and q from the old session group to act as *representatives* in order to establish a new session group key. The representatives and the new members will form a new group by structuring themselves on a ring topology, requiring that the representatives also remain as immediate neighbors in the new group.

More formally, we consider a group of $m+2$ users $\{\hat{U}_1, \hat{U}_2, \ldots, \hat{U}_{m+2}\}$, where $(\hat{U}_1, \hat{U}_2) = (p, q)$ and $\hat{U}_{i+2} = U_{i+n}$, for $i = 1, \ldots, m$. This new set of users will invoke *Deniable Key Agreement* previously mentioned to establish a new intermediate group NG. Thus, each user $\hat{U}_i$ will generate a new key share $\hat{k}_i$, an ephemeral private-public keypair $(\hat{s}_i, \hat{S}_i)$, and a Diffie-Hellman key for the circular key agreement $(\hat{x}_i, \hat{y}_i = g^{\hat{x}_i})$ as per the requirements of the algorithm.

Algorithm 1. Deniable-AKE(P)

Input: Group of participants P, Participant identities pid, generator g, secure hash function $H(x)$
Output: Session Key Sk, Session Identifier S_{id} and Ephemeral Public Keys S_i.

1: **for all** $U_i \in P$ **do**
2:     $(S_i, s_i) = Sig.GEN()$ ▷ Ephemeral public-private key pair
3:     $k_i \xleftarrow{R} \{0,1\}^k$ ▷ k-bit random number
4:     $x_i \xleftarrow{R} Z_q, y_i = g^{x_i}$
5:     **Send:** $M_i^1 = (H(k_i), y_i, S_i, U_i)$ ▷ To all participants
6: **for all** $U_i \in P$ **do**
7:     $S_{id_i} = H(pid_i \| H(k_1) \| H(k_2) \| H(k_3) \| \cdots \| H(k_n))$
8:     $r_i \xleftarrow{R} Z_q, z_i = g^{r_i}$
9:     **Send:** $M_i^2 = (S_{id_i}, U_i, z_i)$ ▷ To all participants
10: **for all** $U_i \in P$ **do**
11:     $t_i^l = H(y_{i-1}^{x_i}) = H(g^{x_i x_{i-1}})$
12:     $t_i^r = H(y_{i+1}^{x_i}) = H(g^{x_i x_{i+1}})$
13:     $T_i = t_i^l \oplus t_i^r$
14:     **Send:** $M_i^3 = (k_i \oplus t_i^r, T_i, U_i)$ ▷ To all participants
15: **for all** $U_i \in P$ **do**
16:     Compute $Q = T_1 \oplus T_2 \oplus ... \oplus T_n$. If $Q \neq 0$ **then abort**
17:     EXTRACT( )   ▷ Extract k_i from all members
18:     **if** not $(S_1 \neq S_j ... \neq S_n$ for all $j \in \{2, ... n-1\})$ **then**
19:         **abort**   ▷ Ephemeral public keys not different
20:     $Sk_i = H(pid_i \| k_1 \| k_2 \| \cdots \| k_n)$
21:     $Sconf_i = H((y_1, S_1, k_1) \| \cdots \| (y_n, S_n, k_n))$
22:     $c_i = H(Sk_i \| Sconf_i) \mod q$
23:     $\sigma_i = Sig.Sign(s_i, c_i)$ ▷ Proving knowledge of ephemeral signing key s_i
24:     $d_i = r_i - c_i \cdot \alpha_i$ ▷ Schnorr signature of challenge c_i
25:     **Send:** $M_i^4 = (d_i, U_i, \sigma_i)$ ▷ To all participants
26: **Verify:** $z_j = g^{d_j}(PK_j)^{c_i}, \forall j \in \{1, 2, 3, \ldots, n\} \backslash \{i\}$
27: **Verify:** $Sig.Verify(S_j, c_i, \sigma_j), \forall j \in \{1, 2, 3, \ldots, n\} \backslash \{i\}$

However, one of the representatives (the one who is the *right* neighbor of the other representative in the old group – in this case $\hat{U}_1$), will use the hash of the previous session key sk_{old} for its Diffie-Hellman key: $\hat{x}_1 = H(sk_{old}), \hat{y}_1 = g^{\hat{x}_1}$. Users $\{\hat{U}_1, \hat{U}_2, \ldots, \hat{U}_{m+2}\}$ will then follow the steps dictated by *Deniable-AKE* to create a new deniable session with a new group key sk_{new}. The only requirement needed in order to allow old members $U_2, \ldots, U_{n-1}$ to recover sk_{new} is that when a broadcast takes place, we consider this information to be available to the old members as well. Hence old members can verify proper execution of the steps, check the signatures and obtain the ephemeral keys of the new members. Additionally, from the values transmitted they now have: the Diffie-Hellman public key $\hat{y}_i = g^{\hat{x}_i}$, $\hat{T}_i = \hat{t}_{l_i} \oplus \hat{t}_{r_i}$ and $\hat{k}_i \oplus \hat{t}_{r_i}$, for all users $\hat{U}_i$.

The *Leave* procedure starts by first updating the ring topology to reflect the new neighborhood structure of nodes. The intuition behind this procedure is that existing members only have to agree on a new group key to ensure privacy of future interactions. Hence, they don't have to run the deniable agreement protocol again since they already possess deniable but authenticated credentials (e.g. their ephemeral keys – details omitted due to space restrictions).

Closure: Finally, an implicit fourth phase takes care of group dispersing when all members decide to leave the group or when there is a time limit for keeping a session alive. In that case all members will just have to publish their ephemeral private keys, thus ensuring plausible deniability of their whereabouts.

3   Analysis and Evaluation

We start by analyzing the complexity of the different procedures in terms of messages transmitted, exponentiations computed and hash operations performed.

Deniable-AKE: Assuming a total of n users, Algorithm 1 exerts a total of $7n$ hash operations, $6n$ exponentiations and $4n$ message broadcasts.

Join: The Join algorithm requires only $n-1$ hash operations and $n-1$ exponentiations, where n is the number of participants in the old group. Assuming m new members and n old members calling the Join procedure, the total cost, including the execution of Deniable-AKE on $m+2$ users, amounts to $7m+n-13$ hash operations, $6m+n+11$ exponentiations and $4(m+2)$ message broadcasts.

Leave: Since the Leave procedure only requires remaining group members to generate a new group key, it can be shown that Leave will require at most $8m$ hash operations, $8m$ exponentiations and $5m$ message broadcasts.

Finally, Table 1 illustrates a comparison of our proposed protocol with mpOTR, showing the number of operations *each* participant must perform.

Table 1. Comparison with mpOTR [8]

Protocol	Messages	Hash	Symmetric generation	Symmetric encryption	Signature	Scalability
Deniable-LBS	$O(n)$	$O(1)$	$O(1)$	$O(1)$	$O(1)$	Yes
mpOTR	$O(n)$	$O(n)$	$O(n)$	$O(n)$	$O(n)$	No

We implemented a prototype of our proposed Deniable-LBS scheme in Java. We relied on SHA256, the Java built-in secure random number generator, and we set $|q| = 224$ bits, i.e. the order of the cyclic group and the size of the random numbers used throughout. For exchanging authenticated information during the actual communication of location data, we relied on ephemeral keys based on RSA with a modulus of size 1024 bits. Figure 1 shows the latency in seconds of our Join procedure over different group sizes. We measure latency as the time required by Join so that all group members agree on the common key. The figure demonstrates the savings obtained over re-running Deniable-AKE from scratch.

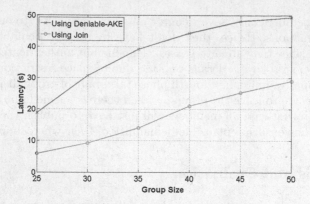

Fig. 1. Performance evaluation of our Join protocol. Each data point in the plots is averaged over 500 independent runs

4   Conclusions

In this work we presented Deniable-LBS, a proposal that offers privacy and deniability in Location-Based Services against external entities, system providers and also between communicating parties themselves. Our system complements the usual privacy guarantees of typical LBS systems by ensuring that when communication is over nobody can (re)produce a transcript of this interaction. Thus, no group member can be linked to information that has been leaked or illegally obtained. Hence, our protocol provides plausible deniability.

Acknowledgments. The authors would like to thank the reviewers for their useful comments.

References

1. Krumm, J.: A survey of computational location privacy. Pers. Ubiq. Comput. **13**(6), 391–399 (2009)
2. Krontiris, I., Freiling, F.C., Dimitriou, T.: Location privacy in urban sensing networks: research challenges and directions. Wirel. Comm. **17**(5), 30–35 (2010). IEEE
3. Solanas, A., Domingo-Ferrer, J., Martínez-Ballesté, A.: Location privacy in location-based services: beyond ttp-based schemes. In: The 1st International Workshop on Privacy in Location-Based Applications, pp. 12–23 (2008)
4. Murphy, J., Fontecilla, A.: Social media evidence in criminal proceedings: an uncertain frontier. In: Bloomberg BNA (2013)
5. Bettini, C., Jajodia, S., Samarati, P., Wang, S.X.: Privacy in Location-Based Applications: Research Issues and Emerging Trends, vol. 5599. Springer, Heidelberg (2009)
6. Bohli, J.-M., Steinwandt, R.: Deniable group key agreement. In: Nguyên, P.Q. (ed.) VIETCRYPT 2006. LNCS, vol. 4341, pp. 298–311. Springer, Heidelberg (2006)
7. Van Gundy, M.: Improved deniable signature key exchange for mpOTR (2013)
8. Goldberg, I., Ustaoğlu, B., Van Gundy, M.D., Chen, H.: Multi-party off-the-record messaging. In: The 16th ACM CCS, pp. 358–368. ACM (2009)

Range Query Integrity in Cloud Data Streams with Efficient Insertion

Francesco Buccafurri[(✉)], Gianluca Lax, Serena Nicolazzo,
and Antonino Nocera

DIIES, University Mediterranea of Reggio Calabria, Via Graziella,
Località Feo di Vito, 89122 Reggio Calabria, Italy
{bucca,lax,s.nicolazzo,a.nocera}@unirc.it

Abstract. Cloud computing provides users with the possibility to store their data in third-party servers. These data centers may be untrusted or susceptible to attacks, hence they could return compromised query results once interrogated. Query integrity has been widely investigated in the literature, and a number of methods have been proposed to allow users to verify that query results are *complete* (i.e., no qualifying tuples are omitted), *fresh* (i.e., the newest version of the results are returned), and *correct* (i.e., the result values are not corrupted). In this paper, we identify a specific scenario in which classical techniques for query integrity appear little suitable and we propose a new solution to overcome these drawbacks. The scenario considered, instantiated in a realistic video surveillance setting, is that of data streams in which append operations and range queries are dominant, and the efficiency is a critical factor.

Keywords: Cloud computing · Range queries · Integrity

1 Introduction

Cloud computing has recently emerged as an innovative paradigm leading towards the availability of ubiquitous access to resources and computation capabilities to everyone. This raises significant drawbacks in terms of data security and privacy [1,3,10]. Indeed, users cannot have any assurance about the integrity of query results on data saved in the cloud, because servers can be malicious, hacked or lazy [6,7,11].

The term integrity means that results has to be *(i)* complete, i.e., no record satisfying the query conditions is omitted in the response, *(ii)* fresh, i.e., the results refer to the latest version of the database, and *(iii)* correct, i.e., the result records are not corrupted.

In the literature, all the existing solutions for query integrity mainly belong to two kinds of families: probabilistic and deterministic [10]. The first family is composed of techniques providing probabilistic models to detect integrity violations [2,4,12]. As for the deterministic approaches, which our proposal belongs to, they detect integrity violations with certainty relying on some additional data that the server should add to the response [5,8,9,13].

© Springer International Publishing AG 2016
S. Foresti and G. Persiano (Eds.): CANS 2016, LNCS 10052, pp. 719–724, 2016.
DOI: 10.1007/978-3-319-48965-0_50

In this work, we propose a new approach for the verification of query result integrity in cloud. In our work, we make explicit reference to a scenario with a network of *battery-powered cameras* (such as drones, micro-drones, insect spy drones) that monitor a high size area and store images into a cloud server. Besides allowing data storage, this server provides an interface to access data and to perform query processing on behalf of the data owner, who administrates and analyzes query results in accordance to specific application-related requirements. Due to the *battery-powered* nature of the cameras, the recording is enabled only on request to allow battery saving. As battery saving assumes a very important aspect, excessive computation on recording sensors should be avoided. Our proposal reduces from logarithmic to constant the space and time complexity of insertion operations, yet maintaining the same complexity as the approaches of the state of the art for verifying the integrity of query results.

In the next section, we briefly present the core of the approach. Due to space limitations, we do not include in this paper the security analysis showing that query completeness, freshness, and correctness are guaranteed.

2   Description of the Approach

Our approach to verify query-result integrity can be classified as a deterministic technique [10]. This type of approach makes use of authenticated data structure and allows the verification of a query result through verification objects that should be included in the results. In the following of this section, we will present our scheme in detail. We start by introducing some basic definitions.

Definition 1. *Given a camera device s_i, we define the image sequence generated by s_i as: $F^i = \{f^i_{t_1}, f^i_{t_2}, \ldots, f^i_{t_n}\}$, where: (i) $f^i_{t_j}$ is the image captured at the instant t_j for each $1 \leq j \leq n$ and (ii) $t_j < t_{j+1}$ (i.e., the instant t_j comes before t_{j+1} in time) for each $1 \leq j < n$. $f^i_{t_j}$ is a tuple $\langle a_1, \ldots, a_p \rangle$, where $a_1 = t_j$ is the tuple timestamp, and $a_2, \ldots, a_p$ are further attributes*[1]. In words, an image sequence represents a track associated with a camera device and independent sequences for different devices are maintained. Each image together with all support attribute is stored as a new tuple in the database. Therefore, throughout the paper, we will refer to a tuple as an element of an image sequence.

Definition 2. *Given two instants t_l and t_u with $t_1 \leq t_l \leq t_u \leq t_n$, a range query $Q^i(t_l, t_u)$ on F^i asks for all the images $f^i_{t_x}$ such that $t_l \leq t_x \leq t_u$.*

Basically, a range query is defined as a request to obtain all the images recorded by a given device s_i during the interval $[t_l, t_u]$, where t_l and t_u, with $t_l \leq t_u$, are valid timestamps during the device recording lifecycle, i.e., its total recording interval $[t_1, t_n]$.

Given a device image sequence F^i, our approach works by organizing tuples associated with F^i in a chain. The link between two elements is built so that

---

[1] Examples of such attributes are geographic coordinates, coding, and resolution (their exact definition is out of the scope of this paper).

the owner can always verify the chain validity. Specifically, given an image $f_{t_j}^i = \langle a_1, \ldots, a_p \rangle$, our approach modifies it by adding an attribute encoding a link towards the next tuple in our database according to the timestamp value. Therefore, the modified tuple has now the following structure $\hat{f}_{t_j}^i = \langle t_j, attr_2, \ldots, attr_p, MAC \rangle$, where the attribute MAC is a message authentication code and is computed by means of the function $HMAC(v, K_i)$ implementing the $HMAC$ protocol with SHA-256 as cryptographic hash function, $v = (f_{t_j}^i \| e)$, K_i is a secret shared by the s_i camera and the data owner, and e can be either the next tuple $f_{t_{j+1}}^i$ of s_i, or a special element defined hereafter. Indeed, the chain is completed with the insertion of dummy entries representing *markers* that are used to both validate the head of the chain and to reduce the integrity verification costs by splitting F^i in time buckets. These elements are pre-added in the database and are known to all the actors involved in our scenario (i.e., they are part of the public scheme of our protocol). Figure 1 shows the structure of the chain where dashed elements $d_{T_w} \ldots d_{T_{w+1}}$ represent *markers*, whereas the grey ones are normal tuples.

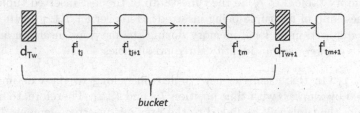

Fig. 1. An example of the chain of a single device image sequence

Concerning the *markers*, they have the following basic structure: $d_{T_w} = \langle T_w, ID_b \rangle$, where T_w is the *marker* pre-fixed time (i.e., T_w is chosen by the owner during the system initialization phase), and ID_b is the bucket identifier. Clearly, each *marker* has also to maintain different attributes, namely $MAC_1, \ldots, MAC_n$, representing links to devices $s_1, \ldots, s_n$, to complete the integrity chain described above. Therefore, the complete structure of *markers* will be: $\hat{d}_{T_w} = \langle T_w, ID_b, MAC_1, \ldots, MAC_n \rangle$, where MAC_i is a message authentication code associated with the device s_i and is computed by means of the function $HMAC(v^i, K_i)$ implementing the $HMAC$ protocol with SHA-256 as cryptographic hash function, $v^i = T_w \| ID_b \| e$, K_i is a secret shared by the s_i camera and the data owner, and e can be either the next s_i tuple $f_{t_{j+1}}^i$ (the first tuple in the corresponding bucket) or the next *marker* $d_{T_{w+1}}$.

According to our scheme, the number of *markers* and their time position (T_w) are established on the basis of the database life period: the *marker* time positions can be simply uniformly distributed in the whole database life period or can follow specific patterns decided by the owner. For instance, he may decide to intensify the number of *markers* during specific time intervals, such as rush hours or critical daily moments. Initial *marker* values are stored in m_tab.

During this phase, all system entities are informed of the exact position of each *marker*. Observe that, in this initialization phase, the values of each attribute MAC_i is set to *null*.

Now, if the camera s_i wants to insert a new tuple, the procedure is as follows. In the initial phase, no previous tuples have been inserted so the table associated with the camera sequence F^i, say s_i_tab, is empty. In this case, s_i has to link the new tuple to the *marker* with the higher time position T_w such that $t_j \geq T_w$, where t_j is the tuple timestamp. Therefore, once the right *marker* has been found, s_i will perform an update on m_tab to set the attribute $MAC_i = HMAC(d_{T_w}||f^i_{t_j}, K_i)$ of the *marker* $\hat{d}_{T_w}$. After this, it inserts the new tuple in s_i_tab with its MAC attribute set to *null* and also stores it altogether with the time position T_{w+1} of the next *marker* in its local memory. The memorization of these parameters is useful for future insertions as will be clearer in the following. Observe that, we assume that the data owner can always read the device on-board memory, thus at every moment he can know the timestamp of the last tuple inserted by each device.

Consider now the case in which a device, say s_i, has to insert a new tuple in a non-empty table. Let t_j be the timestamp of the last inserted tuple and t_z be the timestamp of the tuple being inserted. Moreover let T_{w+1} be the *marker* time that s_i stored in its local memory during the previous insertion and T_{w+2} be the next *marker*, we can identify three possibilities:

1. $\mathbf{t_z} < \mathbf{T_{w+1}}$. In this case, the new tuple will belong to the existing bucket delimited by *markers* with time position T_w and T_{w+1}. Therefore, to maintain the chain, the tuple will be linked to the previous inserted element. To do so, the device performs an update on s_i_tab to change the MAC attribute of the previous inserted tuple from $MAC = null$ to $MAC = HMAC(f^i_{t_j}||f^i_{t_z}, K_i)$ and insert the new tuple in the database. Finally, it update the last inserted tuple in its local memory.

2. $\mathbf{T_{w+1}} \leq \mathbf{t_z} < \mathbf{T_{w+2}}$. The tuple will belong to a new bucket right next the current one; then, s_i will perform an update on s_i_tab to change the MAC attribute of the previous inserted tuple from *null* to $HMAC(f^i_{t_j}||d_{T_{w+1}}, K_i)$, an update on m_tab to set $MAC_i = HMAC(d_{T_{w+1}}||f^i_{t_z}, K_i)$ for the row corresponding to the *marker* with time position T_{w+1}. Finally, it inserts the new tuple in s_i_tab with the MAC attribute set to *null* and also stores it altogether with the time position T_{w+2} of the next *marker* in its local memory.

3. $\mathbf{t_z} \geq \mathbf{T_{w+2}}$. In this case, the tuple will belong to a new non-adjacent bucket; therefore, starting from the *marker* with time T_{w+1}, s_i has to find the *marker* with the higher time position T_{w+q} (with $q > 1$) such that $t_z \geq T_{w+q}$. Then, s_i will perform an update on s_i_tab to change the MAC attribute of the previous inserted tuple from *null* to $HMAC(f^i_{t_j}||d_{T_{w+1}}, K_i)$, two updates on m_tab, the first to set the attribute $MAC_i = HMAC(d_{T_{w+1}}||d_{T_{w+q}}, K_i)$ for the row corresponding to the *marker* $\hat{d}_{T_{w+1}}$ and the second to set the attribute $MAC_i = HMAC(d_{T_{w+q}}||f^i_{t_z}, K_i)$ for the row corresponding to the *marker* $\hat{d}_{T_{w+q}}$. Finally, it inserts the new tuple in s_i_tab with the MAC

attribute set to *null* and also stores it altogether with the time position T_{w+q+1} of the next *marker* in its local memory.

Our approach implements also an aging mechanism for automatically deleting older tuples to limit the database size. Deletion is carried out only on discrete time intervals, i.e., only the removal of an entire non-empty bucket at a time is allowed. In this mechanism, the *markers* play a key role. Indeed, as only discrete deletion is allowed, each *marker* represents a milestone maintaining device chains when previous elements are removed. Data owner can always compute the first *marker* in the database still valid.

Suppose the data owner submits the range query $Q^i(t_l, t_u)$, meaning that all snapshots recorded by the device s_i in the time interval $[t_l, t_u]$ should be returned intact as result. Our protocol enforces that the query processor module, cloud-side located, returns the tuples belonging to all the buckets involved in the interval $[t_l, t_u]$ along with all the *markers* linked to elements of such buckets. Moreover, as additional information, the data owner knows the time position of each *marker* and, for each device, knows the last tuple inserted in the database. Observe that, this requirement is easy to satisfy because all devices have an internal memory in which this information is stored and we assume that the data owner can access it at every moment. To verify the integrity of the result obtained, the data owner performs the following steps.

(1) First, he verifies the head and tail of the chain. Specifically, as for the head he verifies if the time value of the first *marker*, say T_f, is lower than or equal to t_l. Concerning the tail, instead, we can identify two cases: *(i)* t_u is lower than or equal to the time value of the last *marker* of the query result. In this case the tail is verified and no further checks are required. *(ii)* t_u is greater than the time value of the last *marker* of the query result. In this case the owner has also to verify if the last tuple stored by s_i is present in the query result.

(2) Then, starting from the first *marker*, he verifies each chain link by iteratively computing the MAC attribute of each element and comparing it with the value returned by the cloud.

3   Conclusion

In this paper, we presented a scheme for the verification of range queries done on untrusted servers of a cloud computing scenario. Our scheme enables users to have proof of the integrity of query results in terms of completeness, correctness and freshness. In the referred scenario, typical solutions, which are based on digital signature schemes or Merkle Hash Tree, have drawbacks related to the cost of data insertions, which our proposal overcomes. As a future development, we plan to extend our work considering a more general case in which the insertion and deletion of tuples in the database is not sequential w.r.t. the chosen attribute. This enhancement will introduce further security issues to investigate.

Acknowledgment. This work has been partially supported by the Program "Programma Operativo Nazionale Ricerca e Competitività" 2007–2013, Distretto Tecnologico CyberSecurity funded by the Italian Ministry of Education, University and Research.

References

1. Buccafurri, F., Lax, G., Nicolazzo, S., Nocera, A.: A privacy-preserving solution for tracking people in critical environments. In: Proceedings of the International Workshop on Computers, Software & Applications (COMPSAC 2014), pp. 146–151, Västerås, Sweden. IEEE Computer Society (2014)
2. Buccafurri, F., Lax, G., Nicolazzo, S., Nocera, A.: Generating k-anonymous logs of people tracing systems in surveilled environments. In: SEBD, pp. 37–44 (2014)
3. Buccafurri, F., Lax, G., Nicolazzo, S., Nocera, A.: Accountability-preserving anonymous delivery of cloud services. In: Fischer-Hübner, S., Lambrinoudakis, C., López, J. (eds.) TrustBus 2015. LNCS, vol. 9264, pp. 124–135. Springer, Heidelberg (2015)
4. De Capitani, S., di Vimercati, S., Foresti, S., Jajodia, S.P., Samarati, P.: Integrity for join queries in the cloud. IEEE Trans. Cloud Comput. **1**(2), 187–200 (2013)
5. Hong, J., Wen, T., Gu, Q., Sheng, G.: Query integrity verification based-on mac chain in cloud storage. In: 2014 IEEE/ACIS 13th International Conference on Computer and Information Science (ICIS), pp. 125–129. IEEE (2014)
6. Jensen, M., Schwenk, J., Gruschka, N., Iacono, L.L.: On technical security issues in cloud computing. In: IEEE International Conference on Cloud Computing, CLOUD 2009, pp. 109–116. IEEE (2009)
7. Kaufman, L.M.: Data security in the world of cloud computing. IEEE Secur. Priv. **7**(4), 61–64 (2009)
8. Li, F., Hadjieleftheriou, M., Kollios, G., Reyzin, L.: Authenticated index structures for aggregation queries. ACM Trans. Inf. Syst. Secur. (TISSEC) **13**(4), 32 (2010)
9. Pang, H., Jain, A., Ramamritham, K., Tan, K.-L.: Verifying completeness of relational query results in data publishing. In: Proceedings of the 2005 ACM SIGMOD International Conference on Management of Data, pp. 407–418. ACM (2005)
10. Samarati, P.: Data security and privacy in the cloud. In: Huang, X., Zhou, J. (eds.) ISPEC 2014. LNCS, vol. 8434, pp. 28–41. Springer, Heidelberg (2014)
11. Subashini, S., Kavitha, V.: A survey on security issues in service delivery models of cloud computing. J. Netw. Comput. Appl. **34**(1), 1–11 (2011)
12. Xie, M., Wang, H., Yin, J., Meng, X.: Integrity auditing of outsourced data. In: Proceedings of the 33rd International Conference on Very Large Databases, pp. 782–793. VLDB Endowment (2007)
13. Yang, Z., Gao, S., Xu, J., Choi, B.: Authentication of range query results in mapreduce environments. In: Proceedings of the Third International Workshop on Cloud Data Management, pp. 25–32. ACM (2011)

Vulnerability Analysis Using Google and Shodan

Kai Simon(✉)

Kai Simon – Consulting, 67663 Kaiserslautern, Germany
kai.simon@kaisimon-consulting.de

Abstract. There is a continuously increasing number of attacks on publicly available systems in the internet. This requires an intensified consideration of security issues and vulnerabilities of IT systems by security responsibles and service providers. Beside classical methods and tools for penetration testing, there exist additional approaches using publicly available search engines. In this paper we present an alternative approach for vulnerability analysis with both classical as well as subject-specific engines. Based on an extension and combination of their functionality, this approach provides a method for obtaining promising results for audits of IT systems, both quantitatively and qualitatively.

1 Introduction

There is an continuously increasing number of attacks on publicly available systems throughout the last years.[1] This results in a growing demand for security audits of IT systems, both corporate internal as well as by external service contractors. For this purpose, primarily classical tools such as Nmap or Nessus are used. These tools share the common technique of directly contacting the target system. Depending on the test configuration, the tests passively scan for existing vulnerabilities or actively try to exploit them. Information on potential vulnerabilities are provided in terms of plugins.

The beforehand mentioned tools and services directly contact target systems to scan for vulnerabilities. These days, there exists also indirect test techniques. In preparation for eventual user (i.e., any internet user) search queries, existing internet websites are accessed in advance and the obtained information is processed and indexed. Furthermore, beside classical search engines (e.g. Google or Bing) there also exist so called subject-specific alternatives. Instead of indexing the main content of the websites, they specifically process the retrieved meta information about systems, involved software and their versions. Hence, they provide an interesting opportunity for collecting data for security auditors as well as attackers, without revealing their identity.

In the following, classical search engines as well as subject area focused alternatives are presented and evaluated for the purpose of vulnerability analysis. On one side, they are evaluated separately and on the other hand in combination to each other. Finally the results are measured with respect to quality and quantity and potential optimization opportunities are presented.

---

[1] http://www.pwc.com/gsiss

© Springer International Publishing AG 2016
S. Foresti and G. Persiano (Eds.): CANS 2016, LNCS 10052, pp. 725–730, 2016.
DOI: 10.1007/978-3-319-48965-0_51

2   Related Work

The usage of specially crafted queries for classic search engines with the intention to collect vulnerability information, so called "Dorks", was presented by Johnny Long in [2] as dork-analysis. Zhang et al. describe in [7] their work on the quantitative evaluation of Google dorks. The evaluation carried out is primarily concerned with the identifiable vulnerability types, their distribution and potential countermeasures. The method used is not reproducible because raw data used are no longer available. Several authors discovered the widespread and daily usage of these dork analysis techniques predominately by botnets in the underground.[2]

Shodan, a subject-specific search engine, was used by Radvanovsky und Brodsky in the SHINE project (SHodan INtelligence Extraction). The purpose of SHINE was the investigation of vulnerabilities in industrial control systems (ICS) systems. We optimized the detection rate of vulnerabilities based on Shodan raw data. Here, an approach is used, that extracts identification information from Shodan banner information and matches this information to existing vulnerability databases. This approach is also used by ShoVAT (Shodan-based vulnerability assessment tool), which was developed by Genge und Enăchescu [1]. However, their primary focus is on runtime performance optimization and less on qualitative aspects. For qualitative verification, only 40 university addresses have been used as reference set. In addition, only an incomprehensible amount of Nessus results were used for their comparison. Finally, banner information retrieved from their test servers and routers, seem to be beyond the default configuration of those devices with respect to vulnerability information.

Further related work in this area such as [3–6] was done by students under our supervision.

3   Classical Search Engines

Information on the internet consists of more than 45 billion webpages[3]. Finding relevant web pages and information is often not that trivial. For improving the traceability of information and usability for users, the contents of individual websites are systematically and automatically structured. This task is performed by classical search engines such as Google or Bing. The world-wide dominance of the search engine Google is more than 90 %[4].

This section describes our approach and tool for evaluating vulnerability tests with google dorks using the Google search engine. Beside the base search request to the search engine, this comprises further post-processing of the retrieved results for both improving the quality of detected vulnerabilities as well as a reduction of *false positives*.

---

[2] http://www.imperva.com/docs/HII_The_Convergence_of_Google_and_Bots_Searching_for_Security_Vulnerabilities_using_Automated_Botnets.pdf.

[3] http://www.worldwidewebsize.com.

[4] http://gs.statcounter.com.

Figure 1 shows the schematic structure of the implementation. The implementation requires as input the name of the domain to check. In the following the individual stages of our tool are described in detail:

- Stage 1 requests the results from Google for a given dork list and the specified domain as input. Basically, the list of dorks used for testing was created from scratch, as existing Dork databases turned out to be outdated.
- Stage 2 processes the results obtained by Google. For this purpose, we developed filters using regular expressions to reduce the number of *false positives*. As search engines ignore particular characters and returns also many findings belonging to just one host, that only vary in the concerned subpath.
- Stage 3 finally reviews obtained results. Only for verification purposes, the server is automatically contacted directly and the banner is retrieved. Subsequently, the corresponding dork filter is reapplied to the banner data. This provides confirmed vulnerability results.

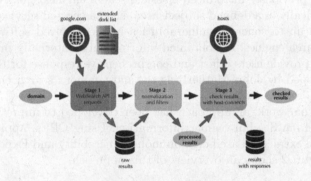

Fig. 1. Google-based tool

We evaluated *Precision* and *Recall* of our results to provide a measurable assessment of the approach. For evaluating the *Precision*, no domain filter was used to limit the observation scope. This yielded 1,070 result entries from Google. With the post-processing in stage 2 an amount of 686 entries could be eliminated by the extended regular expression filter and 24 entries were identified as duplicates. Ultimately, 360 vulnerabilities could be extracted, that were automatically examined in stage 3. In this step, 200 results were confirmed as *true positive* and 160 results as *false positive*, resulting in a *Precision* of the Google-based tool of 55.6 %, as shown in Eq. 1.

$$Precision = \frac{true\ positives}{true\ positives + false\ positives} = \frac{200}{200 + 160} = 0.556 \quad (1)$$

For evaluating the *Recall* of our approach, a second verification run with the Google-based tool was executed. As described, this test was limited to the mentioned German domain scope, because here the vulnerabilities could be verified manually.

$$Recall = \frac{true\ positives}{true\ positives + false\ negatives} = \frac{34}{605 + 419} = 0.033 \qquad (2)$$

In summary, our optimized test approach archived a *Precision* of 55.6 %. However, the *Recall* of only 3.3 % is rather small. According to our observations, we assume that a more comprehensive dork list will slightly increase the *Recall* of the method. Another negative impact is indepted to counter-measures of the Google search engine. Basically, this testing approach for vulnerabilities is not promising as comprehensive penetration testing tool due to the insufficient accuracy rate. Nevertheless, as complement to traditional penetration testing or for the purpose of a fast detection of zero-day vulnerabilities, this methods is still of interest.

4   Subject-Specific Search Engines

In contrast to previously introduced classical search engines, this type scan the internet specifically in a defined subject area, such as hosted services, SSL/TLS vulnerabilities up to concrete vulnerabilities in the involved software. Similar to classical search engines, the obtained information is internally processed and aggregated to provide users a fast and comprehensive response for their queries. Shodan developed by John Matherly is the most famous search engine in this area.

As part of our work, an approach has been developed to improve the detection of CPEs from Shodan banner information. Using CPEs, appropriate vulnerabilities are extracted based on Common Vulnerability and Exposure (CVE) databases. Figure 2 shows an overview of this approach.

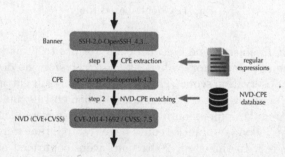

Fig. 2. Shodan-based approach

Figure 3 illustrates the schematic structure of the developed tool for detecting and classifying vulnerabilities. Based on the input of the target domain, the final result will be prepared containing vulnerabilities and their criticality level with reference to IP address and port. Following, the tool are explained in more detail:

- Stages 1 requests all information stored in Shodan for a particular domain. This search query is called "host-search" request. The response is grouped by IP address and port.
- Stage 2 extracts the IP address from the responses of stage 1 and perform a "host" request at Shodan for each address. Tests have shown that these requests contain further information about the IP address, such as vulnerabilities (based on CVEs).
- Stage 3 determines CPEs from raw data retrieved in stage 2, based on our own self prepared data base. Compared to Shodan about 50 % more CPEs could be retrieved. Additionally, more Level 4 CPEs could be determined; containing not only product identifier but also its version information.
- Stage 4 loades available CVE information from NIST and processed for future usages. This enables a mapping from CPE to CVE/CVSS in stage 5.
- Stage 5 links the obtained CPE information of stage 3 with information about vulnerabilities (CVE/CVSS) from stage 4.
- Stage 6 is involved in the quality evaluation and prepares the comparison results of an appropriate Nessus test run.
- Stage 7 finally automatically performs a quality evaluation based on the inputs from stage 5 and 6, i.e., the information of the manually improved Shodan results and the Nessus vulnerabilities.

For evaluating the *Precision*, a subdomain with 768 IP addresses was used. The restriction resulted in 137 potential CVE findings, which were validated manually against a targeted penetration test using Tenable Nessus. This confirmed all 137 results (*true positives*) and no refuted results (*false positives*),

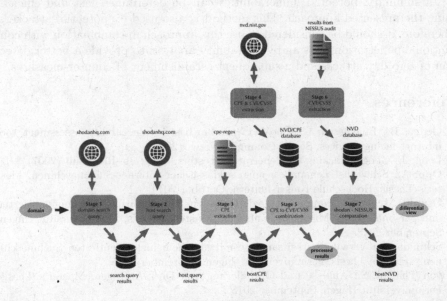

Fig. 3. Shodan-based tool

eventuating in a accuracy of 100 % for the observed test range, shown in Eq. 3:

$$Precision = \frac{true\ positives}{true\ positives + false\ positives} = \frac{137}{137 + 0} = 1 \tag{3}$$

The determination of the *Recall* is challenging as the actual number of existing vulnerabilities of the target systems is unknown and cannot be determined with certainty. In addition, the findings of the Shodan-based tool are difficult to quantitatively compare directly with Nessus. Therefore, several estimations have to be considered for the following evaluation:

$$Recall = \frac{true\ positives}{relevant\ elements} = \frac{79}{401} = 0.197 \tag{4}$$

The method revealed a maximum *Precision* of 100 %. The *Recall* rate of 19.7 % is acceptable, however, currently represents only an estimation and is yet to be verified. In summary, the results are encouraging and better than expected. Overall, with our Shodan-based tool a fast and inexpensive test for vulnerabilities can be performed.

5   Conclusion

In this work, an alternative approach for vulnerability analysis using publicly available classical as well as subject-specific search engines was presented. A quality model and the consequent evaluation of the search engines enables the categorization of these data sources with respect to result quality as well as coverage. This provides a rating scale and an opportunity for future analysis.

In summary, potential vulnerabilities can be determined fast and efficient using the presented approach. This method is also used by potential attackers. Therefore, it should be considered to use this approach in combination with conventional penetration tests and vulnerability analysis to provide a better detection of zero day attacks and a subsequent establishment of counter-measures.

References

1. Genge, B., Enăchescu, C.: ShoVAT: shodan-based vulnerability assessment tool internet-facing services. Secur. Commun. Netw. (2015)
2. Long, J.: Google Hacking for Penetration Testers. Syngress, Rockland (2007)
3. Opp, A.: Schwachstellenanalyse mittels klassischer Internet-Suchmaschinen. Master's Thesis, Hochschule Kaiserslautern, October 2014
4. Oswald, M.: Verwendung von Google Dorks zur Durchführung von anonymisierten und personalisierten Massensuchanfragen. Master's Thesis, Fernuniversität Hagen, September 2015
5. Schmidt, O.: Verwundbarkeitsanalyse mittels themenfeldorientierten Suchmaschinen. Master's Thesis, Fernuniversität Hagen, September 2015
6. von Thaden, S.: Analyse und Optimierung von Dork-Anfragen. Master's Thesis, Fernuniversität Hagen, September 2015
7. Zhang, J., Notani, J., Gu, G.: Characterizing google hacking: a first large-scale quantitative study, November 2015

Language-Based Hypervisors

Enrico Budianto[1], Richard Chow[1(✉)], Jonathan Ding[2], and Michael McCool[3]

[1] Intel Corporation, Santa Clara, USA
[2] Intel Corporation, Shanghai, China
[3] Intel Corporation, Tokyo, Japan
{richard.chow,jonathan.ding,michael.mccool}@intel.com

Abstract. We describe how to build a Language-Based Hypervisor (LBH) that can run untrusted applications (or modules) inside secure containers within a single language runtime instance. The LBH allows execution of untrusted code at a fine-grained level while controlling access to APIs, data, and resources. The LBH and untrusted applications are written in the same language and run together as one process on top of a single language interpreter or runtime. We use JavaScript as an example and describe how LBH can be implemented at the language level without modification to the runtime itself.

Keywords: JavaScript · Security · Containers · Isolation

1 Introduction

While JavaScript has long been used to build popular web applications and browser extensions, JavaScript now has expanded to HTML5 mobile applications (e.g., WebView, Windows 8 Metro Apps), server-side applications (built with Node.js, an extension of Chrome's V8 JavaScript engine), and emerging Internet-of-Things applications. The universality of JavaScript has accelerated its popularity as JavaScript developers can now code everything from small IoT devices on the front end to giant server farms on the back end.

The traditional client-side web has isolated web applications with mechanisms provided by the browser (for instance, iframes). These mechanisms, however, do not exist in server and IoT JavaScript platforms like Node.js.

Furthermore, as JavaScript development is modular in nature it is common to rely on third-party components and libraries. For instance, at the time of this writing the npm registry (for the Node.js platform) hosts over a quarter million packages. External modules run with the same privilege as the JavaScript interpreter as there is no good way to sandbox these modules within an application. Needless to say, these modules may be malicious or vulnerable. Script injection also is a problem on these newer platforms. Finally, applications running on these JavaScript platforms run with same privileges as the platforms themselves.

In memoriam of Enrico, who passed away after this work, done as an intern at Intel.

© Springer International Publishing AG 2016
S. Foresti and G. Persiano (Eds.): CANS 2016, LNCS 10052, pp. 731–736, 2016.
DOI: 10.1007/978-3-319-48965-0_52

In some use cases, a single device may need to run JavaScript applications from different, mutually untrusting sources. Running these applications on separate interpreters (or OS-level containers) is possible but would be resource-intensive, and may be infeasible on smaller devices. However, running such applications on a single interpreter instance exposes them to attack. These issues are not unique to JavaScript – other scripting languages such as Python also lack mechanisms for application confinement and isolation, let alone confinement of modules within an application.

In this paper, we propose a mechanism to isolate modules running inside a single interpreter. We describe how to build a Language-Based Hypervisor (LBH) entirely from the features provided in an interpreted or scripted language. In terms of JavaScript, an LBH is a JavaScript application that can transparently run multiple "worker" JavaScript applications and can securely isolate them from each other and from the system, and can also monitor their resource consumption. LBH also enables privileged code to run safely, according to user-defined policy.

2   Background and Related Work

One way to achieve isolation is to run JavaScript applications or modules in different processes and let the operating system provide the secure isolation. There are two difficulties here. The first is the performance overhead of supporting multiple JavaScript interpreters. The second is that the initial attraction of the JavaScript programming model lies in its program-once-runs-anywhere nature. Relying on operating system constructs breaks this model as JavaScript calls have to be replaced by inter-process communication mechanisms. Similar solutions, but even more heavyweight, are running JavaScript applications in different virtual machines, containers (e.g., Docker), or TEEs.

The Caja compiler is a tool by Google to securely embed third-party HTML, CSS, and JavaScript in a website. To achieve application isolation, they build containers similar to our containers. However, there are two differences. First, Caja uses a web component called an *iframe* to securely load its code. An iframe is an isolation component specific to web browsers and does not exist as a built-in JavaScript feature. Second, the concept of a "hypervisor" that manages communication between multiple embedded scripts does not exist in Caja. Typically, embedded third-party web pages run individually with minimum communication to the main web page or each other. In contrast, our LBH is designed to control – but not eliminate – the interfaces between connected applications and modules. Inter-component communication is essential.

In the academic literature, previous work has also concentrated on JavaScript isolation in the web browser context. Akhawe et al. [1] describe JavaScript containers; similar to Caja, however, their work relies on HTML5 primitives, such as iframe and windows.postMessage. These features do not exist in most JavaScript device platforms. Bhargavan et al. [2] also describe some features of a secure JavaScript container, but the containers described are limited in usefulness, for instance, the code cannot communicate with the other parties. Similarly, Maffeis et al. [4] applies fully only to the web environment and can be implemented only partially on most JavaScript platforms. Their work also does not discuss how to securely communicate between two pieces of code without using an existing HTML5 framework.

3   Design and Approach

Here we explain the conceptual design of LBH and its implementation for one scripting language, JavaScript. LBH is designed as a container-based solution. Each container confines a piece of worker code and isolates itself from being accessed by any other worker code, much like an `iframe` for HTML5-based web applications. In our design, we introduce a privileged container, code that is responsible for carrying out privileged instructions (e.g., secure updates, secure outgoing communication) on behalf of worker applications, as well as code to store and protect sensitive information. We design the LBH to have one privileged container with one-way access to the non-privileged containers. Applications running within a non-privileged container do not have access outside their own container aside from certain, publicly defined APIs (see Sect. 3.1).

LBH is a framework that, given a set of JavaScript applications S running on the same device, will transform S into a packaged application P that consists of S and additional JavaScript logic to isolate applications in S from each other. During the pre-deployment phase, LBH statically analyzes applications in S to (1) detect and remove any global instances in the applications and (2) determines privileged JavaScript APIs that are being used. This analysis is important to build an API policy that controls which APIs are being used by the application. During deployment the policy ensures that only those APIs are allowed to be accessed and no others.

After statically analyzing the applications, LBH rewrites the applications in S to perform certain operations. First, LBH generates shim code to redefine functions that perform external module inclusion (e.g., `require` function). This guarantees that access to resources via JavaScript APIs is always obtained via downcall to the trusted container – hence enforcing the notion of least privilege. Second, LBH rewrites the application to redefine certain JavaScript functions used to carry out sensitive operations, such as creating outgoing HTTP requests such as `XMLHttpRequest()`. By redefining such functions, any outgoing request will now be equipped with a token to guarantee integrity and authority of the request – the code added through rewriting will make sure the privileged container intercepts each outgoing request and attaches a token to each request.

Once the application rewriting for S is done, LBH auto-generates the logic for the privileged container. LBH also generates the code for the worker containers: function wrappers with empty content. As a final step, LBH copies the rewritten application code in S into corresponding containers. The execution order of the applications can be specified, if desired. At this point, the whole process results in a packaged application P and is ready to be deployed into a device.

3.1 Design Details

As a proof-of-concept, we show an approach for how LBH might be built with the JavaScript language. The specific techniques used are highly specialized to JavaScript, but we expect analogous techniques could be used with other languages. However, the main challenge is that this is a tricky area (see [3]), and more analysis and testing is needed to build confidence that our specific techniques block all possible ways to "break out" of a container. In this section, we discuss container design for JavaScript, some of the possible ways of escaping containers, and technical mitigations. Our discussion in this section is related to, but different from, work by Bhargavan et al. [2] or Maffeis et al. [3].

One of the key challenges of building a logical container for these applications is to ensure memory safety. The JavaScript engine runs entire scripts in the same execution environment, and therefore there is no in-built notion of memory or process separation between two pieces of code. However, we can isolate by leveraging existing JavaScript language features. The first step is to provide separate namespaces by putting two pieces of code in two different function wrappers. Figure 1a shows how two pieces of code can be transformed to protect their local namespaces from each other. The function wrapper acts as a container for the application which automatically offers separate namespacing for *non-global* objects in the code. However, this technique is not sufficient to protect JavaScript code running in a container from being accessed by applications running in other containers. For example, malicious code could access all the properties of the object using the keyword `this`, see Fig. 1b. This is harmful because code in other containers can enumerate all the functions, get the source code, or even execute targeted functions.

```
var obj = {
   containerApp1 : function(){
      // Application logic for App1
   },

   containerApp2 : function(){
      // Application logic for App2
   },
};

obj.containerApp1();
obj.containerApp2();
```

(a) Memory safety of code through functions

```
var obj = {
   containerApp1 : function(){
      // Application logic for App1
   },

   containerApp2 : function(){
      // list functions within obj
      for(var x in this){
      ...
      }

      // Access App1
      this.containerApp1();
   },
};

obj.containerApp1();
obj.containerApp2();
```

(b) App2 accesses App1 using keyword `this`

Fig. 1. Code examples

To mitigate this problem, we first randomize the name of the function wrapper associated to each application. This way, the attacker cannot learn the function names of other applications. Second, we prevent all JavaScript code inside the container from accessing the properties of variable `obj` in Fig. 1a using an ECMAScript feature called `Object.defineProperty`. This feature defines accessibility of a property in an object. For example, if a flag value of `enumerable` is set to `false` for a property p, the property p will not be visible to the other scripts during the enumeration process (e.g., enumerate properties using `for-in`).

Finally, we address global variables in workers. Global variables can be used by the attacker as a channel to influence the value of non-global objects being used in an application container or in the privileged container, breaking the isolation between containers. To handle this problem, we randomize the variable names used in applications before deployment. In addition, we can "monkey-patch" every function call so that all calls are tied to the local `this` context, using `Function.prototype.apply` instead of a direct function call. For non-dynamically-generated code this can be done statically during a pre-deployment phase and therefore will not affect the overall performance of the applications.

An application running in a non-privileged container should not have access to JavaScript objects outside its container. Having an external reference could potentially lead to an attack on the entire codebase through control of certain critical JavaScript objects. The first line of defense against external references is by restricting access to global variables, which we discussed previously. Next, our bootstrap code executes a piece of JavaScript logic that performs an *external reference cleanup* process in order to prevent confined applications from obtaining illegal external references.

Scoping rules in JavaScript by default let variables in the global context and functions that wrap the container be accessible from the confined application. Therefore, we need to place container variables and functions in a different function scope, not in the global context. However, there are certain objects that need to be put in global context, such as an object `message` used as a messaging interface for containers. For these kinds of objects, we make sure that properties of those objects are not enumerable and writable using `Object.defineProperty`.

Another way of bypassing the external reference restriction is by making use of the `arguments.callee.caller` property. This property gives access to all the functions preceding an attacker's function – and in particular, this includes functions located in the privileged LBH container. We solve this issue by inserting one line at the top of each worker function. This line assigns `null` to `arguments.callee` so that the container code cannot access external references, see Fig. 2.

```
// rewritten code to hide arguments.callee
function f_in_worker(){
        arguments.callee = null; // inserted during rewriting

        // rest of the code
};
```

Fig. 2. Prevent recursive caller access from within a container

JavaScript can dynamically create code at runtime through `eval` and `new Function()`, and such code cannot be re-written in a pre-deployment analysis. In particular, dynamically created global variables will not be handled by our randomization and global variable removal process, which is done statically on the source code. Global variables in general are not a recommended practice, but dynamically creating variables can occur with obfuscated JavaScript code. JavaScript obfuscation can use functions to dynamically create objects.

To address dynamically created global variables, one option is for the LBH, during the re-writing process, to replace calls to `eval` and `new Function()` with versions that would perform the re-writing process recursively at runtime on strings passed into `eval` and `new Function()`. This would convert the global objects to local objects and re-write invocations of `arguments.callee.caller`. Of course, the simplest option would be to simply block dynamically created code, although this breaks full compatibility.

4   Summary and Future Work

We have introduced the concept of Language-based Hypervisors (LBH), a privileged program for runtimes such as Node.js that can run multiple applications and modules and securely isolate them from each other based on policy. Our approach is rooted on concepts of language-based security, where language features are used to add security to applications.

We see several areas for future study. Performance analysis of LBH is a key concern, both for memory and execution time. Also, JavaScript containers are very difficult to build (see [3] for examples of subtle problems in client-side web JavaScript containers), and our proposed LBH would benefit from community analysis and testing. We also plan to address the problem of denial-of-service by a worker application "using up" the finite resources on the platform, such as CPU time or memory. One idea is that LBH can insert code in loops and function headers to instrument and control resource consumption. Finally, we plan to extend the LBH concept to other languages such as Python.

References

1. Akhawe, D., Saxena, P., Song, D.: Privilege separation in HTML5 applications. In: Proceedings of the 21st USENIX Conference on Security Symposium, Security 2012, USENIX Association, Berkeley, CA, USA, pp. 23–23 (2012)
2. Bhargavan, K., Delignat-Lavaud, A., Maffeis, S.: Language-based defenses against untrusted browser origins. In: Proceedings of the 22Nd USENIX Conference on Security, SEC 2013, USENIX Association, Berkeley, CA, USA, pp. 653–670 (2013)
3. Maffeis, S., Mitchell, J.C., Taly, A.: Object capabilities and isolation of untrusted web applications. In: 2010 IEEE Symposium on Security and Privacy (SP), pp. 125–140. IEEE (2010)
4. Maffeis, S., Taly, A.: Language-based isolation of untrusted JavaScript. In: Proceedings of the 2009 22nd IEEE Computer Security Foundations Symposium, CSF 2009, pp. 77–91. IEEE Computer Society, Washington, DC (2009)

Internet Censorship in Italy: A First Look at 3G/4G Networks

Giuseppe Aceto[1,2], Antonio Montieri[2(✉)], and Antonio Pescapè[1,2]

[1] University of Napoli Federico II, Naples, Italy
{giuseppe.aceto,pescape}@unina.it
[2] NM2 srl, Naples, Italy
montieri@nm-2.com

Abstract. The techniques used to enforce Internet Censorship vary, and as a consequence the users can experience different results while accessing the same censored content in different contexts. While the corpus of Internet censorship studies is growing, to the best of our knowledge we are the first to focus on censorship detection on 3G/4G (hereafter *mobile*) network operators. After an introduction on the censorship detection platform and tests we adopted, we report the preliminary results of an experimental campaign we performed in Italy using the five major mobile operators. Our analysis shows that there is no homogeneity of treatment for a censored resource across different mobile operators, with 99.5 % of resources showing at least two different treatments, and the pairs of operators differing in the treatment of 32.5 % up to 99.5 % of censored resources. These results have significance regarding the transparency and precision of censorship, and the possibilities for circumvention and detection strategies.

Keywords: Internet censorship · Censorship detection · Active measurements · Mobile networks · Italy

1 Introduction

The regulatory action of governments over the access to online information has fostered the practice of Internet Censorship, i.e. the intentional impairing of a client application in reaching a requested resource or service, enforced by a third party (neither the user, nor the server operator) [5]. Such action can produce different effects, depending on the censoring technique, and often directly or indirectly causes a communication error, giving the user the false impression that an outage of some kind is the cause of inaccessibility. Moreover, the effectiveness, the side effects, and the means for circumventing the censorship are all dependent on the specific censoring technique that is applied. Finally, Internet Censorship

This work is partially funded by art. 11 DM 593/2000 for NM2 srl (Italy). This work has been also carried out thanks to a *Google Faculty Research Award* for the project UBICA (User-Based Internet Censorship Analysis).

© Springer International Publishing AG 2016
S. Foresti and G. Persiano (Eds.): CANS 2016, LNCS 10052, pp. 737–742, 2016.
DOI: 10.1007/978-3-319-48965-0_53

varies over time, national borders, and network infrastructure (access provider, backbone networks). We have researched Internet Censorship in previous measurement campaigns [3,4], and a corpus of experimental studies on this topic is growing [6–10], often including detection methods and tools, but to the best of our knowledge none has focused on censorship detection from mobile phones, before this work. We refer to [5] for the definitions and an in-depth analysis of the state-of-art of Internet Censorship detection. In this poster we present the platform used, our methodology, and the preliminary results of our analysis of censorship as enacted by five major 3G/4G *Mobile Network Operators (MNOs)* in Italy, during a measurement campaign. More specifically, we characterize the results of the tests according to four different parameters, whose combination (or *aggregated behavior*) affects both the final outcome that a mobile user would experience, and the circumvention method that is effective in that case. In the preliminary results we report how variably a censored resource is managed, varying the operator, and a pairwise comparison of MNOs in terms of targets with the same aggregated. The results clearly show how there is a significant variation across different MNOs. We are performing further analyses on the dataset (not shown in this abstract), namely:

- detailing the most common aggregated behavior;
- reporting the distribution of behaviors per operator;
- deriving the circumvention techniques that are most likely to succeed with each MNO;
- evaluating the stability over time of the observed behaviors.

2   UBICA

UBICA (User-Based Internet Censorship Analysis) is a platform that provides users with a *censorship monitoring* system. Figure 1 shows the main components of UBICA architecture. The platform leverages a globally distributed deployment of *probes* belonging to different kinds (router-based, headless client, GUI-client) that are orchestrated by a central *Management Server*. The platform provides: (i) dynamically updated censorship tests; (ii) dynamically updated targets to be verified; (iii) support for different types of probing clients; (iv) automatic censorship detection and censorship technique identification. The client has been designed to be highly portable, composed of a core measurement-related part and leverages standard UNIX utilities and mature network diagnostic tools.

The probes perform *active measurements* to collect evidences of censorship, periodically retrieving a list of test requirements (i.e. target lists and code) from the Management Server. After the evidence collection, each probe packs all the results in a report file and uploads it back to the Management Server. The reports are asynchronously parsed by such server and the significant information is stored in a SQL database. The *Analysis Engine* periodically processes data in the database, performing the censorship detection analyses through the following measurements.

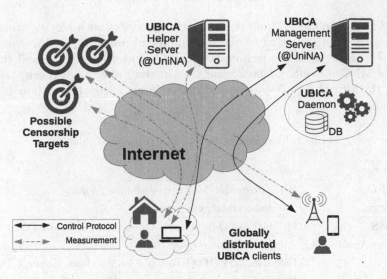

Fig. 1. UBICA architecture diagram.

DNS resolution. Given a fully qualified domain name, a DNS request of `type`
`A` is issued from the probe towards its default resolver. The tool used to issue
the request is `nslookup`. To distinguish among different DNS tampering techniques [5], the same request is issued also towards one or more open resolvers,
used as control resolvers from inside the censored network.

TCP reachability. This test tries to set up a TCP connection to verify a possible filtering triggered by *IP:port*, starting a three-way handshake with a given
timeout. The input parameters are *targetIP:port* and a timeout value in seconds.

HTTP reachability. An HTTP GET request is issued by this test: the response—
or lack of it—and additional application level values are collected from the server.
The HTTP header field *User-Agent (UA)* is conveniently set choosing it from
a list previously defined (see Table 1). The tool used to issue the request and
collect application level information is `curl`. The report from this test includes
several values, such as content type, HTTP response code, number of redirects,
etc., not reported for the sake of brevity.

3   Methodology

Experimental campaigns conducted in this work by mean of UBICA leverages
headless clients equipped with Kubuntu 14.04 and connected to Internet through
smartphones—tethering USB—acting as gateways. In Table 1 a summary of the
factors taken into account is provided. Notably, selected MNOs account for the
96.6 % of the Italian market, and PosteMobile owns the 52.1 % of the Mobile Virtual Network Operators' market share [1]. An up-to-date list of possibly censored

targets has been obtained from [2], containing websites both blocked from judicial authority and suggested by the community of users. Since *DNS-tampering* is a widely used censorship technique, name resolutions are performed through both the MNO-provided (*default*) and the Google Public DNS (*open*) resolver. Finally, the list of UAs has been conveniently chosen for testing both mobile and desktop agents.

Table 1. Summary of factors and considered values.

Factor	Values
MNO	H3G, PosteMobile, TIM, Vodafone, Wind
Target	200 censored targets from [2]
DNS	Default (MNO-provided), Open (Google Public DNS)
User-Agent (UA)	Safari 5.1 (iPhone - iOS 5.0),
	IEMobile 7.11 (HTC Touch 3G - Windows Mobile 6.1),
	Google Chrome 41.0 (Desktop - Windows 7)

When a user requests a resource from a target, he experiences a number of different behaviors depending on the specific combination of the factors reported in Table 1. In order to facilitate their description, the possible outcomes a user can experience have been clustered into *aggregated behaviors*. In more detail, for each combination of MNOs and targets taken into account: (i) default and open DNS resolutions can be equal or different, (ii) the redirections a request is possibly subjected to, can be dependent on the UA or not, (iii) default and (iv) open DNS resolutions can return various outcomes.

Indeed, when the default resolver is leveraged, the DNS server could reply with a *forged response* not corresponding to the legitimate DNS database entry (i.e. *DNS hijacking*). More specifically, a forged response is a Resource Record of `type A` containing an IP address that does not correspond to the actual IP address obtained from the legit resolution of the requested resource [5].

Since in this case the DNS resolver acts as the *censoring device*, changing the default resolver with an open resolver will bypass the censoring device and thus allow open access to the Internet. Even though a user can correctly obtain the requested content leveraging the Google Public DNS, he could also experience a number of erroneous outcomes. Instead of the expected Resource Record, the open resolver might return an error response `NXDOMAIN` of type "no such domain". Moreover the request could incur a *connection timeout*, a connection termination by *TCP reset*, or an *HTTP error* response (i.e. 4xx and 5xx status codes).

4   Preliminary Results

In this section we provide an overview of the factors that mostly influence the browsing experience of a general user requesting a resource from a censored target. The dataset introduced in this work has been collected through preliminary

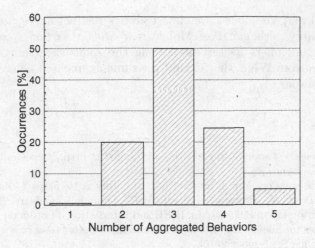

Fig. 2. Percentage of targets exhibiting a different number of aggregated behaviors when MNO is changed.

experimentations conducted in February 2016. An interesting result stemming out from these experimentations is the relationship existing between the MNO leveraged to access to the Internet and the aggregated behaviors observed. More in details, given a target, the number of different behaviors experienced by a user when he changes the MNO used to connect to the network, is an index of how differently each MNO treats various targets possibly censored. As shown in Fig. 2, 0.5 % of the targets (i.e. only 1 target) have the same aggregated behavior for all the MNOs, whilst the majority of them (100 out of 200 targets) exhibits 3 different behaviors. These results confirm that varying the MNO that offers connectivity, a user might experience distinct outcomes even in the case he wanted to retrieve the same content. However, 95 % of the targets exhibit at most 4 aggregated behaviors, showing at least 1 behavior in common between 2 MNOs.

Table 2. Pair-wise variation in censorship application between MNOs. A 100 % variation means that all targets have different behaviors between considered MNOs.

MNO	PosteMobile	TIM	Vodafone	Wind
H3G	92.5 %	32.5 %	94 %	75 %
PosteMobile		99 %	60 %	95 %
TIM			99.5 %	65.5 %
Vodafone				65 %

Table 2 summarizes the variation in the aggregated behaviors obtained between analyzed MNOs. Lowest pair-wise variation has been observed for H3G and TIM, that show different behaviors only for 32.5 % of the targets. On the contrary, TIM and Vodafone have almost always distinct aggregated behaviors (99.5 %). Notably, although PosteMobile is a *Mobile Virtual Network Operator (MVNO)* and offers its services leasing the radio spectrum and network infrastructures from Wind, they exhibit the same aggregated behaviors for only 10 out of 200 targets.

References

1. MVNO News - Osservatorio MVNO, July 2016. http://www.mvnonews.com/osservatorio-mvno/
2. Osservatorio sulla censura di Internet in Italia, July 2016. https://censura.bofh.it/
3. Aceto, G., Botta, A., Pescapé, A., Awan, M.F., Ahmad, T., Qaisar, S.B.: Analyzing internet censorship in Pakistan. In: IEEE 2nd International Forum on Research and Technologies for Society and Industry Leveraging a better tomorrow (IEEE RTSI), Bologna, Italy, September 2016
4. Aceto, G., Botta, A., Pescapè, A., Feamster, N., Faheem Awan, M., Ahmad, T., Qaisar, S.: Monitoring internet censorship with UBICA. In: Steiner, M., Barlet-Ros, P., Bonaventure, O. (eds.) TMA 2015. LNCS, vol. 9053, pp. 143–157. Springer, Heidelberg (2015)
5. Aceto, G., Pescapé, A.: Internet censorship detection: a survey. Comput. Netw. **83**, 381–421 (2015)
6. Burnett, S., Feamster, N.: Encore: lightweight measurement of web censorship with cross-origin requests. SIGCOMM Comput. Commun. Rev. **45**(4), 653–667 (2015)
7. Chaabane, A., Chen, T., Cunche, M., De Cristofaro, E., Friedman, A., Kaafar, M.A.: Censorship in the wild: analyzing internet filtering in Syria. In: Proceedings of the 2014 Conference on Internet Measurement Conference, IMC 2014, pp. 285–298. ACM, New York (2014)
8. Di Florio, A., Verde, N.V., Villani, A., Vitali, D., Mancini, L.V.: Bypassing censorship: a proven tool against the recent internet censorship in Turkey. In: 2014 IEEE International Symposium on Software Reliability Engineering Workshops (ISSREW), pp. 389–394. IEEE (2014)
9. Ensafi, R., Knockel, J., Alexander, G., Crandall, J.R.: Detecting intentional packet drops on the internet via TCP/IP side channels. In: Faloutsos, M., Kuzmanovic, A. (eds.) PAM 2014. LNCS, vol. 8362, pp. 109–118. Springer, Heidelberg (2014). doi:10.1007/978-3-319-04918-2_11
10. Jones, B., Lee, T.-W., Feamster, N., Gill, P.: Automated detection and fingerprinting of censorship block pages. In: Proceedings of the 2014 Conference on Internet Measurement Conference, IMC 2014, pp. 299–304. ACM, New York (2014)

A Privacy-Preserving Model
for Biometric Fusion

Christina-Angeliki Toli[✉], Abdelrahaman Aly, and Bart Preneel

Department of Electrical Engineering, KU Leuven-ESAT/COSIC & iMinds,
Kasteelpark Arenberg 10, Bus 2452, 3001 Leuven-Heverlee, Belgium
{christina-angeliki.toli,abdelrahaman.aly,bart.preneel}@esat.kuleuven.be
http://www.esat.kuleuven.be/cosic

Abstract. Biometric designs have attracted attention in practical technological schemes with high requirements in terms of accuracy, security
and privacy. Nevertheless, multimodalities have been approached with
skepticism, as fusion deployments are affected by performance metrics.
In this paper, we introduce a basic fusion model blueprint for a privacy-
preserving cloud-based user verification/authentication. We consider the
case of three modalities, permanently "located" in different databases of
semi-honest providers, being combined according to their strength performance parameters, in a user-specific weighted score level fusion. Secure
multiparty computation techniques are utilized for protecting confidentiality and privacy among the parties.

Keywords: Biometrics · Multimodalities · Fusion · Performance metrics · Identity authentication · Reliability · Cloud computing · Secure
multiparty computation · Applied cryptography · Privacy

1 Introduction

Over the last decade, biometric-based systems have been part of the daily routine for identity verification. This is specially true for online services. Moving the
existing technology to cloud-based platforms could be proven effective for many
access control or surveillance applications with millions of users. Nevertheless,
with all eyes on security, privacy challenges encountered in the transmission of
personal data across the parties could be characterized as extremely serious. The
reader could take into account the following attacking scenarios [1,2]. Additionally, to store several biometric templates under the same user's identity in one
database could not only be a difficult feat, considering the restricted access on
templates from competing biometric suppliers, but also discouraged or illegal [3].
Multibiometrics were originally introduced to alleviate the inherent limitations
of single biometric modalities that render them unable to correspond at the high
security requirements. Furthermore, the confidence on the functionality of a biometric scheme is determined by some specific metrics: False Acceptance Rate
(FAR) shows if a system incorrectly recognizes an intruder while False Rejection Rate (FRR), the percentage of valid inputs which are incorrectly rejected

© Springer International Publishing AG 2016
S. Foresti and G. Persiano (Eds.): CANS 2016, LNCS 10052, pp. 743–748, 2016.
DOI: 10.1007/978-3-319-48965-0_54

for an authorized person. Being inspired by biometric applications on cloud we introduce a model for a verification protocol based on fusion and designed to operate in a cloud environment for privacy-preserving biometric recognition and identification purposes.

To reduce privacy threats, we employ Secure Multiparty Computation (MPC), thus avoiding any centralized repository and using the stored templates by the service providers in a decentralized manner. That way we can authenticate an individual based on his/her biometric characteristics, searching, matching and combining the results, and return a reliable decision guaranteeing the secrecy of the new (fresh/raw) and old (stored) biometric templates. Applications include a cloud-based border control system that integrates stored unimodal biometrics by a set of different recognition services, evaluating them accordingly to their FAR to prevent access to unauthorized individuals. Contrary, a cloud-based surveillance solution, operating to automatically screen the crowd in order to identify a person sets up a FRR respective fusion mechanism. We refer the reader to [4–7] for a more detailed treatment on MPC.

Contribution: We provide a view of a decentralized cloud based mechanism for multimodal user verification, using distrustful database providers. The service is provided under strong privacy-preserving constraints, where the only thing the involved entity learns is the final output.

Our main contribution includes the following:

- Design uses previously stored unimodals, providing the advantage of handling information without extra unnecessarily storage of fused data.
- We incorporate FAR and FRR rates of uncorrelated biometrics in a user-specific transformation-based score level fusion. Weights are assigned to each trait according to its strength performance.
- Since biometric data transmitted across the network and design involves various distrustful service providers, MPC is considered to be a suitable mechanism for the execution of our protocols. In this way, no information related to the raw, stored traits or the final output is revealed to the cloud parties.

Motivation: Even though several proposals on multimodal fusion, performance rates and secure cloud-based biometric applications can be found in the literature, the combination of these results seems to be a challenging task. Given that utilizing more than two biometrics offers improved identification efficiency [8], we make use of the three most popular and robust biometric body traits (face, iris and fingerprint) for our model. However, the concept of integration is considered as an open problem [9], and it is an undeniable admission since that we assume a cloud-based setting, many privacy risks arise. Thus, it is necessary to enhance security between the non-trust parties, protecting intermediate computations and user's information. The novelty of our model lies on bridging the gaps of cloud-based biometric identification, ensuring the privacy between the involved entities and the user, whenever data transmitted across the network.

2 Environment and Settings

The scenario is as follows: an involved entity provides the fresh biometric templates to three unimodal cloud biometric service providers that store old templates of faces, irides and fingerprints, separately. The involved entity needs to verify/authenticate a user's identity with better accuracy than when operating with single modal module. The verification process takes place in the cloud and has to guarantee the privacy of the user's data (fresh and old templates). Figure 1 illustrates the generic form of the proposed biometric authentication access control system.

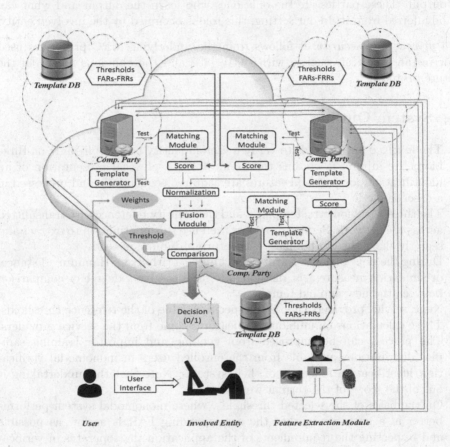

Fig. 1. Proposed model for multimodal verification.

Parties and Roles: Parties involved in our protocol fulfill at least one or more of the following roles during the verification process:

- **Dealers:** Any subset of parties that provide the private inputs for the computation in shared/encrypted to the parties responsible of the computation (computational parties). In our case, an involved entity delivers the fresh extracted templates, and the service providers are the owners of the stored templates. Both have also to provide other metrics, the proportions, thresholds and rates in shared form as well.

- **Computational Parties:** Any subset of parties in charge of the computation. They are also in charge of communicating the necessary results of the computation to the output parties in shared form. Typically, the computational parties are distrustful parties with competing interests, in this case, for instance, they could be represented by the service providers (3) or any coalition composed by control agencies, service providers and civil entities.
- **Output Parties:** Any subset of parties in charge of the reconstruction the output. These parties are the only ones who learn the output and what can be inferred from it. In our setting, this role is occupied by the involved entity.

On privacy and security: it follows from the underlying MPC primitives used (for instance perfect security with BGW [4]), and the oblivious nature of the future protocol.

3   System Outline

1. The involved entity needs to verify a user's identity based obligingly on three biometric inputs. It obtains the user's data (a physical presentation of an identification document). Features are acquired sequentially and processed in a cascade mode.
2. The three new biometric templates and the identity references are transmitted across the network. Service providers then use this information to extract and secretly share the old templates, or return a dummy instead.
3. During the next phase, a feature matching algorithm i.e., Hamming distance, or similarity measurement methods are used to give a degree of comparison between the new and old templates.
4. Next, service providers choose the specified value of the reference thresholds. These calculations on unibiometric features come from the service providers. The process can be improved from genuine and impostor training samples distributions available from the enrolled users in monomodal verification/identification functions of their systems. Note that this undertaking is out of the scope of the current work.
5. On the basis of the selected thresholds, where monomodal system performs better in a such a way that the corresponding FAR is as low as possible and respecting the requirements of the application that operates in verification/authentication mode, the matching score that mostly reflects the similarity between the new and one of the old stored template set is selected from the generated vector for each modality, respectively.
6. The matching module output by three non-homogeneous biometrics and consequently scores have to be transformed into a common domain, before combination. The application has to normalize the results in the cloud by placing the three obtained matching scores in the same numerical range varied over $\{0, .., 1\}$. Fractional representation can be utilized for its MPC adaptation.

7. Weights are selected by the involved entity (according to the FAR, FRR that each service provider considers to be permissible). These weights, assigned to the three modalities, are in the range of $\{0, ..., 1\}$ for the user u as $w_{face,u}$, $w_{iris,u}$ and $w_{fingerprint,u}$, such that the constraint $w_{face,u} + w_{iris,u} + w_{fingerprint,u} = 1$ is satisfied. As before, fractional representation can be used during our MPC adaptation.

8. Normalized matching scores are fused in ideally to output one from three. A user-specific weighted sum rule is then applied in order to determine the final result of the score level fusion for multimodal identity verification.

9. Finally, the involved entity determines a threshold $\perp$ and communicates it to the computational parties. The final acceptance happens in case of an individual has been authenticated as a previously successfully enrolled user. Regarding rejection, this simply means that the system failed to surpass the threshold $\perp$, not leaking whether the user is enrolled or not on any or all the databases.

4   Usability and Limitations

Usability: The generic verification model introduced by this paper incorporates three popular and well studied modalities into a fusion method, operating in cloud. Note that the system could operate in *identification mode*, without requesting the presence of an ID by the user, where the biometric templates are contrasted against the hole database. Thus, the proposal could be used in identity management applications and surveillance oriented models. The authentication accuracy is based on utilizing physically uncorrelated biometrics that can present significant improvements at performance, even when the quality of the samples is sub-optimal.

Limitations: One clear limitation of our model is related to interoperability issues, regarding the matching sensors of the involved service providers. This is due to the fact that biometric data is usually matched by sensors produced by different manufactures, this proposal is restricted in its ability to fuse templates originating from disparate sensors. For that reason, one of the major challenges in the biometrics recognition domain is the use of similar types of sensors, establishing a common technological behavior, something that reflects effort and cost ineffectiveness. Moreover, the system might be affected by the restrictions put in place by the use of MPC, for instance, a viable protocol might prefer the use of Hamming distance for simplicity and avoid the use of floating point arithmetic.

5   Conclusion and Discussion

We present a model for privacy-preserving fusion in a non-traditional, but reality representative distrustful environment. We incorporate multiple biometric traits, for cloud-based identity authentication, and make use of MPC techniques to offer privacy. Moreover, multimodal fusion gives better results than using a single matching module in the context of security and reliability. In general, it is indisputable that biometrics fusion has a critical role to play in identification systems and different fusion mechanisms work differently for every combination of data, rules and tools, while optimality is conflicting with regard to the retrieval performance rates. Furthermore, identity-purposed databases for online authentication mechanisms, seriously enhance risks from different perspectives and for each assessment separately. MPC restricts the misuses of private biometric information at the levels required by realistic applications. Future solutions for these major issues can support the feasibility of large-scale privacy enhancing biometric identity management technologies.

Acknowledgements. This work was supported in part by the Research Council KU Leuven: C16/15/058. In addition, it will contribute to ICT programme under contract FP7-ICT-2013-10-SEP-210076296 PRACTICE of the European Commission through the Horizon 2020 research and innovation programme.

References

1. Bhattasali, T., Saeed, K., Chaki, N., Chaki, R.: A survey of security and privacy issues for biometrics based remote authentication in cloud. In: Saeed, K., Snášel, V. (eds.) CISIM 2014. LNCS, vol. 8838, pp. 112–121. Springer, Heidelberg (2014)
2. di Vimercati, S.D.C., Foresti, S., Samarati, P.: Data security issues in cloud scenarios. In: Jajodia, S., Mazumdar, C. (eds.) ICISS 2015. LNCS, vol. 9478, pp. 3–10. Springer, Heidelberg (2015). doi:10.1007/978-3-319-26961-0_1
3. Kindt, E.J.: Privacy and Data Protection Issues of Biometric Applications - A Comparative Legal Analysis. Springer, Netherlands (2013)
4. Ben-Or, M., Goldwasser, S., Wigderson, A.: Completeness theorems for non-cryptographic fault-tolerant distributed computation. In: STOC, pp. 1–10. ACM (1988)
5. Chaum, D., Crépeau, C., Damgård, I.: Multiparty unconditionally secure protocols. In: STOC, pp. 11–19. ACM (1988)
6. Maurer, U.: Secure multi-party computation made simple. Discrete Appl. Math. **154**(2), 370–381 (2006). Coding and Cryptography
7. Damgård, I., Pastro, V., Smart, N., Zakarias, S.: Multiparty computation from somewhat homomorphic encryption. In: Safavi-Naini, R., Canetti, R. (eds.) CRYPTO 2012. LNCS, vol. 7417, pp. 643–662. Springer, Heidelberg (2012)
8. Ross, A., Jain, A.K.: Information fusion in biometrics. Pat. Recogn. Lett. **24**(13), 2115–2125 (2003)
9. Ross, A., Nandakumar, K., Jain, A.K.: Handbook of Multibiometrics. International Series on Biometrics. Springer, Secaucus (2006)

Hybrid WBC: Secure and Efficient White-Box Encryption Schemes

Jihoon Cho[1], Kyu Young Choi[1], Orr Dunkelman[2(✉)], Nathan Keller[3],
Dukjae Moon[1], and Aviya Vaidberg[3]

[1] Security Research Group, Samsung SDS, Inc., Seoul, Republic of Korea
{jihoon1.cho,ky12.choi,dukjae.moon}@samsung.com
[2] Computer Science Department, University of Haifa, Haifa, Israel
orrd@cs.haifa.ac.il
[3] Department of Mathematics, Bar-Ilan University, Ramat-Gan, Israel
nkeller@math.biu.ac.il, aviya.v5@gmail.com

Abstract. White-box cryptography aims at providing security against
an adversary that has access to the encryption process. Numerous white-
box encryption schemes were proposed since the introduction of white-
box cryptography by Chow et al. in 2002. However, most of them are
slow, and thus, can be used in practice only to protect very small amounts
of information, such as encryption keys.

In this extended abstract we present a new threat model for white-
box cryptography which corresponds to the practical abilities of the
adversary in a wide range of applications. Furthermore, we study design
criteria for white-box primitives that are important from the industry
point of view. Finally, we propose a class of new primitives that combine
a white-box algorithm with a standard block cipher to obtain white-box
protection for encrypting long messages, with high security and reasonable performance.

1 Introduction

The *white-box* threat model in secret-key cryptography, introduced by Chow et
al. [4] in 2002, considers an adversary that is accessible to the entire information on the encryption process, and can even change parts of it at will. The
range of applications in which the white-box threat model is relevant is already
extensive and continues to grow rapidly. One example is the Digital Rights Management (DRM) realm, where the legitimate user (who, of course, has full access
to the encryption process), may be adversarial. Another example is resource-
constrained Internet-of-Things (IoT) devices applied in an insecure environment
(like RFID tags on the products in a supermarket). Yet another example is
smartphones and public cloud services. While certain security-critical services
in such devices are provided with support of hardware security features, such as
'secure element' or TrustZone in mobile devices or 'hardware security modules'
in the cloud, most services are implemented as software operating within Rich

© Springer International Publishing AG 2016
S. Foresti and G. Persiano (Eds.): CANS 2016, LNCS 10052, pp. 749–754, 2016.
DOI: 10.1007/978-3-319-48965-0_55

OS. The main reasons for that are low cost, development efficiency and complicated ecosystems. As a result, the cryptographic implementations are vulnerable to a wide variety of attacks in which the adversary has 'white-box' capabilities.

The ever-growing range of applications where the white-box threat model is relevant necessitates devising secure and efficient solutions for white-box cryptography. And indeed, numerous white-box primitives were proposed since the introduction of white-box cryptography in 2002. These primitives can be roughly divided into two classes.

The first class includes algorithms which take an existing block cipher (usually AES or DES), and use various methods to 'obfuscate' the encryption process, so that a white-box adversary will not be able to extract the secret key. Pioneered by Chow et al. [4], this approach was followed by quite a few designers. An advantage of these designs is their relation to the original ciphers, which makes transition to the white-box primitive and compatibility with other systems much easier. Unfortunately, most of these designs were broken by practical attacks a short time after their presentation. In addition, all designs of this class are orders of magnitude slower than the 'black-box' primitives they are based upon.

The second class includes new block ciphers designed especially with white-box protection in mind, like the ASASA and SPACE families [1,2]. An important advantage of these designs is their better performance and higher security (though, some of them were also broken, see [5]). On the other hand, transition from existing designs to the entirely new ciphers is not an easy task, and so, quite often commercial users will be reluctant to make such a major change in the design.

In this extended abstract we propose a class of new primitives which provide strong security with respect to a 'real-life' white-box adversary, and on the other hand, are convenient for practical use – meaning that the performance is reasonable and that transition from currently used primitives to the new primitives is relatively easy. To this end, in Sect. 2 we present a new threat model for white-box cryptography which corresponds to the practical abilities of the adversary in a wide range of applications. Once the security model is set, we study design criteria for white-box primitives that are important from the industry point of view. In Sect. 3 we propose a class of new primitives that combine a white-box algorithm with a standard block cipher to obtain white-box protection for encrypting long messages, with high security and reasonable performance. Preliminary security analysis of the new primitives, along with a comparison with previous works, can be found in the full version of this paper [3].

2   Practical Requirements and Design Strategy

2.1   Security Requirements – A New Threat Model

Unlike the classical black-box model, in white-box cryptography the abilities of the adversary are not clearly defined, and different threat models are implicitly used by different authors.

The works of Chow et al. [4] and their successors implicitly assume that there is a part of the encryption process, called *external encoding*, which is performed outside of the encryption device and cannot be accessed by the white-box adversary. Such an assumption is not realistic in scenarios where the entire encryption process is implemented in software.

Instead, we propose the following threat model, which is relevant in a wide variety in realistic scenarios. Assume that the same white-box encryption scheme is used in many devices, with at most a small difference between them (e.g., a unique identification number that is used in the encryption process). Further, assume that the adversary can mount an 'expensive' white-box attack on at most a few devices (e.g., by purchasing them and then analyzing in depth), and he is willing to break the encryption of *all other devices*. Formally, we assume that the adversary has a white-box access to several devices from the family and only black-box access to all devices in the family. Using the white-box access, the adversary can obtain full information on the devices he took control of. His goal is to break the encryption schemes of all other devices. Thus, the security goal in this model can be thought of as *minimizing the damage from one-time compromise*.

Our threat model is well suited for IoT environment. IoT devices are usually manufactured in a production line simply assembling flash memories with the same binary programmed including cryptographic keys, i.e. the same cryptographic keys are shared across multiple devices. This is because it would be quite expensive to embed separate keys into each device either in production lines or by consumers; additional key-embedding process and related key management, as well as adding UX layers to IoT devices, generally require considerable cost. In such an IoT environment, an adversary may implement the white-box attack for a single device, and try to compromise the whole system using the obtained key or any critical information, along with capabilities from the conventional black-box model.

We note that this threat model does not fit for *all* applications of white-box cryptography. However, it seems relevant in sufficiently many scenarios for being considered specifically.

2.2 Performance and Cost Requirements

While industry accepts the need in strong security of the algorithms, it is often the case that practical efficiency considerations are prioritized by commercial users over security considerations. Hence, if we want to design a primitive that will be employed in practice, we should take into account the main practical requirements from the industry point of view.

The main two design criteria we concentrate on are the following:

Reasonable performance. Previously suggested white-box algorithms except the SPACE family are 12 to 55 times slower than AES. White-box primitives have thus been used to protect relatively small sizes of data. We aim at using the white-box primitive to protect large amounts of data, and so, the encryption speed must be reasonably fast – ideally, almost as fast as the AES.

Low transition cost. The new architecture should be designed so as to minimize the modification of the existing development or manufacturing process related to cryptographic implementations. Interestingly, this may be the most important factor for commercial adoption in reality.

2.3   Design Strategies

The practical requirements listed above lead to the following design considerations.

First, if we use a white-box algorithm to encrypt each block of the message then the performance of the resulting encryption scheme is the same as that of the white-box algorithm. For most of the currently existing white-box algorithms, this means that the scheme is very slow. Moreover, even for the SPACE family whose members are not so slow, standard 'software obfuscation techniques' aimed at protecting the security of the running code, make the encryption process much slower, and thus too slow for our purposes. As a result, it is desirable to use the white-box algorithm to encrypt only part of the message blocks, and encrypt most blocks with a 'classical' algorithm.

Second, almost all existing solutions for data protection in data communication such as SSL, TLS and SSH are based on a shared secret (e.g. session key). Designers of some solutions for data communication want to apply this session key in white-box encryption with minimum modification of their cryptographic implementation. However, they cannot use this key directly in a white-box scheme since the initiation of a white-box algorithm is slow and in general is separate from running environment. In addition, in many cases users request a certificate algorithm to be used in their implementation. Hence, we aim at applying a session key directly in the components of our scheme, except the white-box algorithm.

Third, the most effective way to minimize the damage from one-time compromise is to encrypt each message by a one-time key which is protected by white-box algorithms. However, managing these one-time keys is a big burden and existing key exchange protocols do not provide a one-time session key. Thus, we will encrypt the nonce by a white-box algorithm and use it in the encryption process as a replacement for a one-time key.

3   The New Primitives

3.1   General Structure and Security Goals

Our primitives use two separate keys – one for a white-box primitive and another for a 'classical' encryption algorithm (e.g., AES), where the white-box algorithm is only used for encryption of a nonce (e.g. initial vector (IV) or a counter) while the classical algorithm is used for encryption of plaintexts. The keys K_1 and K_2 are assumed to be permanent and may be shared by many devices, while the nonce in changed in every encryption session.

We restrict the use of our scheme to encrypting messages of length at most 2^{64} blocks in a single session (i.e. without rekeying). Furthermore, as common in nonce-based algorithms, we do not allow re-use of the nonce.

The security level we aim at is data complexity of 2^{64} and memory and time complexities of 2^{80}. That is, any white-box attack that can recover the secret key K_1, or distinguish our scheme from random, or recover part of the plaintext in a non-compromised session, should require either more than 2^{64} messages, or more than 2^{80} time or more than 2^{80} memory.

3.2   The New Hybrid White-Box Schemes

In this subsection we present two new hybrid white-box schemes, which – according to our preliminary analysis – are secure in the white-box model.

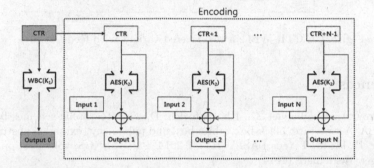

Fig. 1. F-CTR-WBC: a white-box variant of AES-CTR with a 256-bit block and a feed-forward operation

The first scheme, called F-CTR-WBC and presented in Fig. 1, is similar to the standard CTR mode of operation using the AES block cipher, but with three differences. First, a counter CTR is encrypted using a white-box primitive (e.g., white-box-AES or a member of the SPACE family). Second, the scheme contains a feed-forward operation (in order to thwart a trivial attack in the white-box model presented in [3]). Third, the block length is increased to 256 bits (e.g., by using Rijndael-256 instead of AES), in order to make a time-memory tradeoff attack presented in [3] infeasible. Our experiments show that this scheme is only 1.3 times slower than AES-CTR.

The second scheme we propose, presented in Fig. 2, is a bit more complex, using AES with feed-forward also in the counter update function. If the full AES is used in both layers of the scheme, it is almost two times slower than F-CTR-WBC with Rijndael-256. However, as the upper layer is used mainly to reduce the relation between consecutive inputs to the second-layer AES and their relation to the initial CTR, it is actually sufficient to use 3-round AES-128 in the upper layer. As a result, this scheme has roughly the same performance like F-CTR-WBC presented above.

Initial security analysis of both schemes is presented in [3].

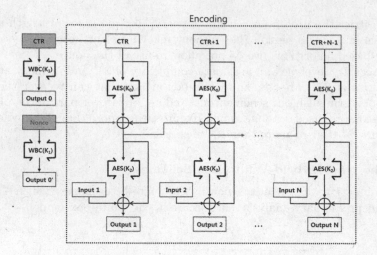

Fig. 2. UF-CTR-WBC: a two-layered variant with feed-forwards

References

1. Biryukov, A., Bouillaguet, C., Khovratovich, D.: Cryptographic schemes based on the ASASA structure: black-box, white-box, and public-key (extended abstract). In: Sarkar, P., Iwata, T. (eds.) ASIACRYPT 2014, Part I. LNCS, vol. 8873, pp. 63–84. Springer, Heidelberg (2014)
2. Bogdanov, A., Isobe, T.: White-box cryptography revisited: space-hard ciphers. In: Proceedings of Computer and Communications Security (CCS 2015), pp. 1058–1069. ACM (2015)
3. Cho, J., Choi, K.Y., Dunkelman, O., Keller, N., Moon, D., Vaidberg, A.: Hybrid WBC: Secure and Efficient White-Box Encryption Schemes, IACR eprint report 2016:679 (2016)
4. Chow, S., Eisen, P., Johnson, H., Van Oorschot, P.C.: White-box cryptography and an AES implementation. In: Nyberg, K., Heys, H. (eds.) SAC 2002. LNCS, vol. 2595, pp. 250–270. Springer, Heidelberg (2003). doi:10.1007/3-540-36492-7_17
5. Gilbert, H., Plût, J., Treger, J.: Key-recovery attack on the ASASA cryptosystem with expanding S-boxes. In: Gennaro, R., Robshaw, M. (eds.) CRYPTO 2015, Part I. LNCS, vol. 9215, pp. 475–490. Springer, Heidelberg (2015). doi:10.1007/978-3-662-47989-6_23

Moving in Next Door: Network Flooding as a Side Channel in Cloud Environments

Yatharth Agarwal[1], Vishnu Murale[2], Jason Hennessey[3(✉)], Kyle Hogan[3], and Mayank Varia[3]

[1] Phillips Academy, Andover, USA
yagarwal@andover.edu
[2] Buckingham Browne & Nichols School, Cambridge, USA
vmurale@bbns.org
[3] Boston University, Boston, USA
{henn,klhogan,varia}@bu.edu

Abstract. Co-locating multiple tenants' virtual machines (VMs) on the same host underpins public clouds' affordability, but sharing physical hardware also exposes consumer VMs to side channel attacks from adversarial co-residents. We demonstrate passive bandwidth measurement to perform traffic analysis attacks on co-located VMs. Our attacks do not assume a privileged position in the network or require any communication between adversarial and victim VMs. Using a single feature in the observed bandwidth data, our algorithm can identify which of 3 potential YouTube videos a co-resident VM streamed with 66 % accuracy. We discuss defense from both a cloud provider's and a consumer's perspective, showing that effective defense is difficult to achieve without costly under-utilization on the part of the cloud provider or over-utilization on the part of the consumer.

Keywords: Cloud privacy · Encrypted communication analysis · Network virtualization · Side channel · Traffic analysis

1 Introduction

In response to an increasingly digital age, researchers have developed cryptographic protocols to protect cyber-privacy. However, the gap between protocols' physical implementations and the theoretical context in which they are usually considered introduces the potential for side channel attacks. Side channels are flows of information exposed by the physical implementation of a system and typically not included in any proofs of security [8]. For example, despite the encryption SSH performs on each keystroke, Song et al. extracted about 1 bit of information per pair of keystrokes from timing information on when the keystrokes were sent [9].

Y. Agarwal and V. Murale are equally contributed.

© Springer International Publishing AG 2016
S. Foresti and G. Persiano (Eds.): CANS 2016, LNCS 10052, pp. 755–760, 2016.
DOI: 10.1007/978-3-319-48965-0_56

The rise of cloud computing exacerbates the threat that side channels pose. Cloud providers issue customers virtual machines (VMs), often *co-locating* different customers' VMs to increase resource utilization and amortize costs. Thus, a customer's VM may be placed on the same host as a different, potentially adversarial VM. Ristenpart et al. and others have shown that a co-resident adversary can leverage this sharing of a physical platform, particularly the shared caches, to compromise the isolation of a victim's VM [5,7].

Our contributions. This paper examines the network interface side channel. We empirically demonstrate load measurement and behavior profiling on two commercial cloud environments: DigitalOcean and the Massachusetts Open Cloud. Our raw data collection component is available in an open-source repository.[1]

Our experimental setup involves a malicious VM, denoted FLOODER, that saturates the network interface to put its bandwidth in contention with that of the targeted co-resident customer's VM, VICTIM. Data from test trials helped calibrate FLOODER's observations to estimate VICTIM's load over time. Such data can be used to determine when a competitor's traffic spikes or learn statistics about a cloud environment that doesn't publish its utilization.

The raw data becomes more valuable when paired with encrypted communications analyses to determine, for example, which website VICTIM is visiting. After test trials had trained a classification algorithm, we showed the algorithm could identify which YouTube video VICTIM was streaming with 66 % accuracy compared to 33 % for random guessing. This result represents a macro-approach relying on estimating bandwidth instead of the usual micro-approach of collecting individual packets. Thus, we do not require FLOODER to have a privileged position on the network or any kind of affiliation with the cloud provider.

By contrast, previous work was conducted on local testbeds and furthermore required a malicious client to remain connected to VICTIM on the order of seconds to reliably measure throughput [1]. This limited potential targets to web or media servers that offered large downloads publicly. The single long connection cannot be substituted simply with short, repeated ones if VICTIM uses DDoS protection. Our threat model imposes no such restriction.

2   Environments

We consider two cloud tenants: an honest VICTIM and a malicious FLOODER. As the name suggests, FLOODER sends as many packets as the network can process; various choices for packet sizes, sleep times, and internet protocols are described in Sect. 3.

We assume that the cloud provider is a trusted entity whose switch usage data isn't directly published. Additionally, we assume that the cloud provider is unaffiliated with adversaries, so FLOODER cannot directly request co-residency with VICTIM. However, researchers have demonstrated indirect achievement of co-residency with specific victims on commercial clouds [1,4,7]. Therefore, we

---

[1] https://github.com/YatharthROCK/primes-data-collection.

presume here that co-residency is achievable and build from there. We consider 4 scenarios.

Environment A. VICTIM and FLOODER occupied different MacBook Pros connected via ethernet to the same LAN network. Both VICTIM and FLOODER connected to clients over the internet via a 10 MB/s downlink.

Environment B. VICTIM and FLOODER occupied different physical Sun v20z servers running Ubuntu 16.04 x64, and both connected to clients on the same LAN via a dedicated switch capable of a throughput of 12 MB/s.

Environment C. VICTIM and FLOODER ran as different processes on a $10/mo VM running Ubuntu 14.04 x64 on DigitalOcean, a production cloud. Both connected to clients on different VMs in the same data center, NYC-2.

Environment D. VICTIM and FLOODER occupied co-located m1.medium VMs running Ubuntu 14.04 x64 on the Massachusetts Open Cloud (MOC), a production cloud environment. Both connected to different clients with a throughput on the order of 40 MB/s.

3 Load Measurement

With an increase in VICTIM's network activity, we observed a corresponding decrease in FLOODER's throughput in all four environments described above, including two production clouds. We confirmed an inversely linear relationship and, on the basis of test runs, calibrated a tool to output an estimate for VICTIM's load based on FLOODER's observations (see Fig. 1).

Data collection used TCP instead of UDP. UDP sent packets fast enough to congest the network and thus achieved very low goodput. Having FLOODER sleep between transmissions of UDP packets improved goodput until a point,

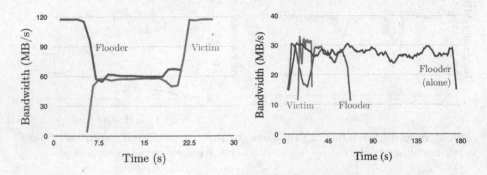

Fig. 1. Inverse linear relationship between VICTIM's and FLOODER's throughput (in green and blue respectively). Left shows data collected in Environment C; Right shows data collected in Environment D. Right additionally overlays (in red) FLOODER throughput in a follow-up trial without VICTIM activity. Note that the fluctuations in FLOODER's throughput due to VICTIM's activity are distinguishably larger than those caused by unrelated environmental factors. (Color figure online)

after which goodput decreased again. We were not able to saturate the network interface enough with UDP for VICTIM's and FLOODER's bandwidth to be in contention.

Data was collected using 4000-byte packets as we determined this packet size resulted in the most consistent bandwidth across trials. Consistency in the bandwidth aids in distinguishing fluctuations in FLOODER's bandwidth caused by VICTIM's activity from those caused by unrelated environmental factors. Even then, environmental noise was significantly higher in Environment D than in Environments A, B, and C.

4   Profiling

Correlating data gathered from side channels with known behaviors makes the data much more meaningful. We demonstrate that the continuous estimate of VICTIM's load from our tool in the previous section can serve as a foundation for encrypted communication analysis.

We considered the case of streaming 4K YouTube videos and observed 'bandwidth fingerprints' unique to the video being streamed (see Fig. 2(a)). Variable bitrate (VBR) technology, which lets a higher bitrate be allocated to more complex segments of media files, contributes to this phenomenon [2].

We trained our classification algorithm on 60 trials of 3 different videos using the feature of delays between bandwidth dips. After recursively weighing the importance of the dips, we fit the learning data with 75 % accuracy. On a new set of 60 trials, the trained algorithm achieved an accuracy of 66 % compared to the 33 % accuracy of random guessing (see Fig. 2(b)).

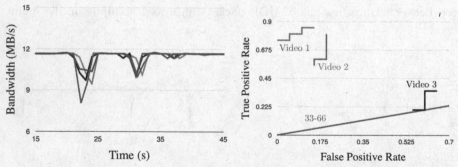

(a) VICTIM load while streaming the same video in multiple trials.

(b) ROC curves for our algorithm ("33-66" curve represents random classification).

Fig. 2. Classification of YouTube video in environment A.

This result attests to the feasibility of determining which YouTube video VICTIM streamed with passive load measurement in the cloud as well as of applying other encrypted communication analysis attacks like those demonstrated by Dyer, Miller and others [3,6,9,10].

5   Counter-Measures and Future Vision

Each of the three agents that participate in this paper's threat model (the cloud provider, the victim, and the adversary) face trade-offs in defending or executing the presented attack.

A Cloud Provider's Perspective. A provider has incentive to protect the privacy of customers' information as loss of trust translates into loss of business. However, this can be at odds with overall utilization and thus the economies of scale offered by the cloud. Perfect co-resident isolation could be achieved, for example, by dedicating a network port to each VM, but this would be prohibitively expensive, especially for VMs that are relatively small compared to the host. Future work exploring this tradeoff would seek to identify what level of network isolation is required (such as switch- or hypervisor-based methods) to render network flooding attacks ineffective in specific scenarios.

A second approach would be to automatically detect flooding activity within the cloud. Cloud providers could then thwart the attack by terminating suspicious VMs, migrating them to another host, or rate limiting their traffic. Each option comes with its own tradeoffs: terminating a VM without notice could violate service level agreements, migrating VMs could be prohibitively costly and would not prevent the VM from attacking any tenants on its new host, and rate limiting would need to balance network utilization with privacy protection.

A Customer's Perspective. A tenant on a cloud can thwart attackers' attempts by preventing them from becoming co-located with his or her VMs [7]. To achieve this, he or she can provision VMs so as to consume the resources of an entire physical host or take advantage of host isolation options like Amazon EC2's Dedicated Hosts. Many clouds including the MOC allow customers to create affinity groups which preferentially co-locate their own machines. Alternatively, customers can try to mask their signal by adding bandwidth noise, though this can be difficult to do efficiently and might incur additional costs [3].

An Adversary's Perspective. Improving the presented attack encompasses increasing the accuracy and precision of the data gathered via the flooding technique as well as improving the analysis of that data. Using UDP instead of TCP to flood VICTIM promises improvements due to UDP's statelessness, allowing increased control over packet timing and size. Additionally, having a malicious client connect directly to VICTIM, as done in [1], would help to control for environmental fluctuation in FLOODER's client's throughput. To work around provider rate limits, a promising avenue of research includes micro-bursts, flooding for brief periods of time, as well as using multiple FLOODERs working together. In terms of analysis, a more intelligent classifier trained on a greater number of features would allow for more accurate YouTube video identification, especially as the number of videos VICTIM could potentially have streamed increases.

Acknowledgements. We would like to acknowledge the MIT PRIMES program and thank in particular Dr. Slava Gerovitch and Dr. Srini Devadas for their support. We are also grateful to Boston University, the Hariri Institute, and the Massachusetts Open Cloud. This paper is based upon work supported by the National Science Foundation under Grants No. 1414119 and 1413920.

References

1. Bates, A.M., Mood, B., Pletcher, J., Pruse, H., Valafar, M., Butler, K.R.B.: Detecting co-residency with active traffic analysis techniques. In: Proceedings of the 2012 ACM Workshop on Cloud Computing Security, pp. 1–12. ACM (2012)
2. Chen, S., Wang, R., Wang, X., Zhang, K.: Side-channel leaks in web applications: a reality today, a challenge tomorrow. In: Proceedings of the 2010 IEEE Symposium on Security and Privacy, SP 2010, pp. 191–206. IEEE Computer Society, Washington (2010)
3. Dyer, K.P., Coull, S.E., Ristenpart, T., Shrimpton, T.: Peek-a-boo, i still see you: why efficient traffic analysis countermeasures fail. In: Proceedings of the 2012 IEEE Symposium on Security and Privacy, SP 2012, pp. 332–346. IEEE Computer Society, Washington (2012)
4. Herzberg, A., Shulman, H., Ullrich, J., Weippl, E.R.: Cloudoscopy: services discovery and topology mapping. In: Proceedings of the 2013 ACM Cloud Computing Security Workshop, CCSW 2013, pp. 113–122. ACM (2013)
5. Liu, F., Yarom, Y., Ge, Q., Heiser, G., Lee, R.B.: Last-level cache side-channel attacks are practical. In: 2015 IEEE Symposium on Security and Privacy, pp. 605–622, May 2015
6. Miller, B., Huang, L., Joseph, A.D., Tygar, J.D.: I know why you went to the clinic: risks and realization of HTTPS traffic analysis. CoRR abs/1403.0297 (2014)
7. Ristenpart, T., Tromer, E., Shacham, H., Savage, S.: Hey, you, get off of my cloud: exploring information leakage in third-party compute clouds. In: Proceedings of the 2009 ACM Conference on Computer and Communications Security, pp. 199–212. ACM (2009)
8. Rohatgi, P.: Side-channel attacks. In: Handbook of Information Security, Threats, Vulnerabilities, Prevention, Detection, and Management, vol. 3. Wiley (2006)
9. Song, D.X., Wagner, D., Tian, X.: Timing analysis of keystrokes and timing attacks on SSH. In: 10th USENIX Security Symposium. USENIX (2001)
10. Wright, C.V., Ballard, L., Monrose, F., Masson, G.M.: Language identification of encrypted voip traffic: Alejandra y roberto or alice and bob? In: Proceedings of 16th USENIX Security Symposium, SS 2007, pp. 4:1–4:12. USENIX Association, Berkeley (2007)

Author Index

Printed in the United States
By Bookmasters